Benner's Mechanical Translation of the Torah

Jeff A. Benner

"Benner's Mechanical Translation of the Torah," by Jeff A. Benner. ISBN 978-1-63868-208-0 (softcover); 978-1-63868-207-3 (eBook).

Published 2025 by Virtualbookworm.com Publishing Inc., P.O. Box 9949, College Station, TX 77842, US. ©2025, Jeff A. Benner. All rights reserved. Any part of this book may be copied for educational purposes only, without prior permission.

Contents

ABOUT THE MECHANICAL TRANSLATION 1
    The Need for a Mechanical Translation 1
    The Inadiquecies of a translation 2
    Is a Mechanical Translation Possible? 3
    What is a Mechanical Translation? 4
    The Mechanics of this Translation 7
    Hebrew Names in the Mechanical Translation 10
    Hebrew Nouns in the Mechanical Translation 12
    Hebrew numbers in the Mechanical Translation 13
    Verse Numbers 13

THE BOOK OF GENESIS 15
    Chapter 1 15
    Chapter 2 16
    Chapter 3 18
    Chapter 4 20
    Chapter 5 21
    Chapter 6 23
    Chapter 7 24
    Chapter 8 25
    Chapter 9 27
    Chapter 10 28
    Chapter 11 29
    Chapter 12 31
    Chapter 13 32
    Chapter 14 33
    Chapter 15 35
    Chapter 16 36
    Chapter 17 37
    Chapter 18 39
    Chapter 19 41
    Chapter 20 43
    Chapter 21 44
    Chapter 22 46
    Chapter 23 48
    Chapter 24 49
    Chapter 25 53

- CHAPTER 26 55
- CHAPTER 27 57
- CHAPTER 28 60
- CHAPTER 29 61
- CHAPTER 30 63
- CHAPTER 31 66
- CHAPTER 32 69
- CHAPTER 33 71
- CHAPTER 34 73
- CHAPTER 35 74
- CHAPTER 36 76
- CHAPTER 37 78
- CHAPTER 38 80
- CHAPTER 39 82
- CHAPTER 40 84
- CHAPTER 41 85
- CHAPTER 42 88
- CHAPTER 43 91
- CHAPTER 44 93
- CHAPTER 45 95
- CHAPTER 46 97
- CHAPTER 47 99
- CHAPTER 48 101
- CHAPTER 49 103
- CHAPTER 50 104

THE BOOK OF EXODUS **107**
- CHAPTER 1 107
- CHAPTER 2 108
- CHAPTER 3 110
- CHAPTER 4 111
- CHAPTER 5 113
- CHAPTER 6 115
- CHAPTER 7 116
- CHAPTER 8 118
- CHAPTER 9 120
- CHAPTER 10 122
- CHAPTER 11 125
- CHAPTER 12 125
- CHAPTER 13 129

- Chapter 14 130
- Chapter 15 132
- Chapter 16 134
- Chapter 17 136
- Chapter 18 137
- Chapter 19 139
- Chapter 20 141
- Chapter 21 142
- Chapter 22 144
- Chapter 23 146
- Chapter 24 148
- Chapter 25 149
- Chapter 26 151
- Chapter 27 153
- Chapter 28 155
- Chapter 29 157
- Chapter 30 160
- Chapter 31 162
- Chapter 32 163
- Chapter 33 166
- Chapter 34 167
- Chapter 35 170
- Chapter 36 172
- Chapter 37 174
- Chapter 38 175
- Chapter 39 177
- Chapter 40 179

THE BOOK OF LEVITICUS 183
- Chapter 1 183
- Chapter 2 184
- Chapter 3 185
- Chapter 4 186
- Chapter 5 188
- Chapter 6 190
- Chapter 7 192
- Chapter 8 194
- Chapter 9 197
- Chapter 10 198
- Chapter 11 200

- Chapter 12 202
- Chapter 13 203
- Chapter 14 207
- Chapter 15 210
- Chapter 16 212
- Chapter 17 215
- Chapter 18 216
- Chapter 19 218
- Chapter 20 220
- Chapter 21 222
- Chapter 22 223
- Chapter 23 225
- Chapter 24 228
- Chapter 25 229
- Chapter 26 232
- Chapter 27 235

THE BOOK OF NUMBERS **239**
- Chapter 1 239
- Chapter 2 241
- Chapter 3 243
- Chapter 4 245
- Chapter 5 248
- Chapter 6 250
- Chapter 7 252
- Chapter 8 255
- Chapter 9 257
- Chapter 10 258
- Chapter 11 260
- Chapter 12 263
- Chapter 13 264
- Chapter 14 265
- Chapter 15 268
- Chapter 16 270
- Chapter 17 272
- Chapter 18 274
- Chapter 19 276
- Chapter 20 278
- Chapter 21 280
- Chapter 22 282

Chapter 23 285
Chapter 24 286
Chapter 25 288
Chapter 26 289
Chapter 27 292
Chapter 28 293
Chapter 29 295
Chapter 30 297
Chapter 31 298
Chapter 32 301
Chapter 33 303
Chapter 34 305
Chapter 35 307
Chapter 36 309

THE BOOK OF DEUTERONOMY 311

Chapter 1 311
Chapter 2 314
Chapter 3 316
Chapter 4 318
Chapter 5 321
Chapter 6 324
Chapter 7 325
Chapter 8 327
Chapter 9 329
Chapter 10 331
Chapter 11 332
Chapter 12 335
Chapter 13 337
Chapter 14 339
Chapter 15 340
Chapter 16 342
Chapter 17 344
Chapter 18 345
Chapter 19 347
Chapter 20 348
Chapter 21 350
Chapter 22 352
Chapter 23 354
Chapter 24 355

CHAPTER 25	357
CHAPTER 26	358
CHAPTER 27	360
CHAPTER 28	361
CHAPTER 29	366
CHAPTER 30	368
CHAPTER 31	370
CHAPTER 32	372
CHAPTER 33	375
CHAPTER 34	377

DICTIONARY **379**
   PREFIXES AND SUFFIXES 379
   CONJUGATIONS 381
   HEBREW NAMES 383

LEXICON CROSS REFERENCES **397**

Benner's Mechanical Translation of the Torah

About the Mechanical Translation

The Need for a Mechanical Translation

Many theological discussions, teachings and debates use phrases like "The Bible says" or "God says." From a technical point of view, the problem with these statements is the assumption the Bible was written in English, which, of course, is not true.

The Bible does not say, "*In the beginning God created the heavens and the earth.*" A more accurate statement would be, "The Bible says, בראשית ברא אלהים את השמים ואת הארץ (*bereshiyt bara elohiym et hashamayim v'et ha'arets*), which is often translated and interpreted as, 'In the beginning God created the heavens and the earth.'"

While this may sound trivial, it is, in fact, a very important issue. Many theological differences, divisions and arguments are based on faulty interpretations of the text that could easily be resolved by examining the original language of the Bible. Once the Hebrew text is recognized, its meanings and interpretations can be discussed properly.

As one example, the Hebrew word ראשית (*reshiyt*) is translated as "beginning" in Genesis 1:1 in the King James Version. But the King James Version also translates this same Hebrew word as "chief" (1 Samuel 15:21) and "principle thing" (Proverbs 4:7). The Hebrew word ראשית (*reshiyt*) may be interpreted as "beginning," but its more literal meaning is related to the idea of "height," as in the height, origin or beginning of an event, the height of someone in rank or the height of importance.

Rather than attempting an interpretation from the English, at the least, one should attempt to understand the text from its Hebraic origin. This can be achieved through the use of an English Bible and a concordance, where the student is able to find the Hebrew word used in the text that lies behind the English translation. When using this tool, it quickly becomes evident that the English translators of the text were not very consistent in how they translated Hebrew words.

For instance, the Hebrew word נפש (*nephesh*) is usually translated in the KJV as soul, but also as: *appetite, beast, body, breath, creature, dead, desire, ghost, heart, life, lust, man, mind, person, pleasure, self, thing* and *will.*

While it is true that one English word cannot translate one Hebrew word perfectly and some translational liberties are necessary, this should be done only out of necessity, and the change should be noted in a footnote to aid the student with proper understanding and interpretation.

The Inadiquecies of a translation

The English vocabulary and its definitions are very inadequate in conveying the meanings of Hebrew words. In the following passages from the KJV, we find the word "teach," an English word meaning "to impart knowledge or skill through instruction:"

> Exodus 18:20; *And thou shalt <u>teach</u> them ordinances and laws, and shalt shew them the way wherein they must walk, and the work that they must do.*
>
> Exodus 24:12; *And the LORD said unto Moses, Come up to me into the mount, and be there: and I will give thee tables of stone, and a law, and commandments which I have written; that thou mayest <u>teach</u> them.*
>
> Deuteronomy 4:1; *Now therefore hearken, O Israel, unto the statutes and unto the judgments, which I <u>teach</u> you, for to do them, that ye may live, and go in and possess the land which the LORD God of your fathers giveth you.*
>
> Deuteronomy 4:9; *Only take heed to thyself, and keep thy soul diligently, lest thou forget the things which thine eyes have seen, and lest they depart from thy heart all the days of thy life: but <u>teach</u> them thy sons, and thy sons' sons;*
>
> Deuteronomy 6:7; *And thou shalt <u>teach</u> them diligently unto thy children, and shalt talk of them when thou sittest in thine house, and when thou walkest by the*

way, and when thou liest down, and when thou risest up.

Job 33:33; *If not, hearken unto me: hold thy peace, and I shall teach thee wisdom.*

Each use of the word "teach" in these six passages is the English translation of six different Hebrew words, each with its own unique meaning:

Exodus 18:20; זהר (*zahar*) – To advise caution

Exodus 24:12; ירה (*yarah*) – To point out the direction to go

Deuteronomy 4:1; למד (*lamad*) – To urge to go in a specific direction

Deuteronomy 4:9; ידע (*yada*) – To provide experience

Deuteronomy 6:7; שמן (*shaman*) – To sharpen

Job 33:33; אלף (*alaph*) – To show through example

The original meaning of these six Hebrew words are completely erased and lost when they are simply translated as "teach," demonstrating the need of going beyond the simple translations.

Is a Mechanical Translation Possible?

It has been said that a word-for-word translation is not possible, as each word can have several meanings and the context determines how each word is to be translated. This is not exactly true, and it is possible to translate each word the same way each time it occurs. However, the problem is that we need to understand the Hebrew vocabulary from an Hebraic perspective. To demonstrate this philosophy, let's use the English word "branch" as an example:

What is a branch? Most people would think of the "branch" of a tree such as in the sentence below:

The bird landed on the branch.

Now examine the word "branch." in the following sentence:

The bank said there is a branch on 1st Street.

Notice that the same word is used, but the context shows a different application for this word. The word "branch" can also be used for the "branch" of a river, a family line or a "branch" of science.

The literal meaning of the word "branch" is a division or section.

The Hebrew word for a "branch" is מטה (*mateh*) and is used in the following passages:

> Exodus 4:17 - *and you will take this branch [staff] in your hand*
>
> Exodus 31:2 - *The son of Hur, from the branch [tribe] of Judah*
>
> Isaiah 9:3(4) - *For you have broken the yoke of his burden, and the branch [yoke] of his shoulder*

Now let's look at a Hebrew word where the connections may not be as obvious. Each of the following passages has the Hebrew word איל (*ayil*) meaning, "someone or something that is strong and large in stature, a 'buck:'"

> Exodus 15:15 - *the bucks [chiefs] of Moab*
>
> Exodus 29:16 - *and you will slaughter the buck [a male from the sheep or goats]*
>
> Ezekiel 40:16 - *and their bucks [posts] within the gate*
>
> Isaiah 61:3 - *they will be called bucks [trees] of righteousness, a planting of YHWH*

As demonstrated, a "Mechanical," word-for-word, translation is possible, but it will require the reader to learn the vocabulary of that translation from an Hebraic rather than from an English perspective.

What is a Mechanical Translation?

This translation is the work of Jeff A. Benner, founder of the Ancient Hebrew Research Center (www.ancient-hebrew.org), Excavating the Bible (www.excavatingthebible.com) and author of over a dozen books related to the Biblical Hebrew alphabet, language and culture.

When Mr. Benner first started studying the Bible with a *Strong's Dictionary and Concordance* in hand, he found that the translators were not very consistent in how they translated various Hebrew words. For instance, the Hebrew verb נתן (N.T.N), which literally means "to give," is translated in the King James Version of the Bible as; *add, aloud, apply, appoint, ascribe, assign, avenge, bestow, bring, cast, cause, charge, come, commit, consider, count, cry, deliver, direct, distribute, do, fasten, forth, frame, get, grant, hang, have, heal, heed, lay, leave, left, lend, let, lift, make, occupy, offer, ordain, over, oversight, pay, perform, place, plant, pour, present, print, pull, put, recompense, requite, restore, send, set, shoot, show, sing, sit, slander, strike, submit, suffer, take, thrust, tie, trade, turn, utter, weep, willingly, withdrew, would, yell,* and *yield.*

These inconsistencies in translation launched Mr. Benner's desire to learn Biblical Hebrew. Once he was able to read the Bible in Hebrew, he believed that there was a better way to translate the Bible, which could be understood by those who did not Hebrew, but still remain true to the vocabulary, grammar and style of the Hebrew text. Mr. Benner spent fifteen years writing his translation of the Torah using the Mechanical Translation method that he developod, where each word would be translated faithfully according to its original linguistic and cultural perspective. Mr. Benner's vision of this translation included a translation that;

1. eliminates personal and religious bias on the part of the translator,
2. translates each Hebrew word, prefix and suffix, exactly the same way, every time it occurs in the text,
3. can be read and understood by the average person who does not have any prior knowledge of the Hebrew language,
4. includes a dictionary of each word used in the translation as well as a concordance, and
5. can be used as a tool by those who are learning to read Biblical Hebrew.

To better understand the philosophies and methodologies of this translational project, let's take a closer look at each of the points above.

Personal and Religious Bias

It has been argued that it is impossible to eliminate bias into any translation, especially one of a religious nature. However, Mr. Benner has developed a method that almost completely removes the possibility of any personal or religious bias within the translation. This is achieved through a two-fold process.

The first process is through the Lexicon. Each translation and definition of each word in the lexicon is chosen based primarily on its etymology (what the word's meaning is based on its relationship to other words and roots), context (how the word is used throughout the Bible) and culture (what the word meant to those who lived within that culture).

The second part of the process simply involves replacing the Hebrew word, prefix or suffix with its corresponding English word from the Lexicon. This method of translation also has the unique quality of allowing the reader who disagrees with the translation of a Hebrew word, to simply replace that word with his own; and, as the translation is accompanied with a concordance, to find the location of each occurrence of that word quite simply.

A word for word translation

Every translation to date, including interlinear Bibles and literal translations, translates the Hebrew text according to context. The problem with this is that the context can be interpreted differently based upon the translator's personal opinions of what that context is. In contrast, a word-for-word, prefix-for-prefix and suffix-for-suffix translation is very mechanical and prevents the translator from "fixing" the text.

One advantage to this method of translation is that the reader is able to see the text in its pure and original Hebrew format. However, there is one major drawback to this method of translation. Hebrew syntax (sentence structure and style) is very different from English syntax, and a reader that has no background in Hebrew syntax would be completely lost in the translation. To alleviate this problem, the "mechanical" translation is accompanied with a "revised mechanical" translation.

Easily read and understood

The "revised mechanical" translation re-arranges the words of the "mechanical" translation into more readable and understandable English syntax. This method of translation is common among other translations, but the changes are invisible to the reader. With the "mechanical" and "revised mechanical" translations side by side, the reader is able to see the changes that are made.

There are times when the "revised mechanical" translation is difficult to read and may not make perfect sense, but this is due to the fact that the Hebrew structure of a given sentence itself is sometimes difficult to read. While most other translations "fix" the text so that it will always be read easily, this translation preserves the difficulties. It is the opinion of Mr. Benner that those who will be interested in this translation will be willing to put in the extra effort to understand a difficult passage.

The Mechanics of this Translation

The Masoretic Hebrew Text Used in this translation

The Hebrew text of the MT of the *Torah* is the *Biblia Hebraica Stuttgartensia*, which is based on the *Leningrad Codex*. When there is a spelling difference between this Hebrew text and the *Leningrad Codex*, the spelling variation will be noted in the footnotes.

Hebrew Words in the Mechanical Translation

Hebrew words, including nouns, adjectives, prepositions, etc., are written in all upper-case letters. If two English words are used to translate a single Hebrew word, a dot (.) will be placed between the two words. Hebrew words will frequently include one or two prefixes. Prefixes are written in all lower-case letters and are followed by the tilde (~). Some words will include a suffix, which is also written in all lower-case letters, and is preceded by the tilde (~). The lexicon also includes a list of all the prefixes and suffixes found in the MT. Below are examples of words with prefixes and suffixes, which appear in the MT.

Table 1 – Example of Hebrew Words in the MT

Hebrew	Prefix	Word	Suffix	Mech. Trans.
היבשה	the~	DRY.GROUND		the~DRY.GROUND

About the Mechanical Translation

כאשר	like~	WHICH		like~WHICH
ידך		HAND	~you(ms)	HAND~you(ms)
ובנים	and~	SON	~s	and~SON~s

Hebrew Verbs in the Mechanical Translation

Hebrew Verbs are written in all upper-case letters and have a (V) after them. Hebrew verb conjugations identify such aspects as the gender and number of the subject (*I, we, you, he, she* and *they*), the tense (*did* and *will*) and the verb form (*make, be, self, much* and *>*). Participle and Imperative verb conjugations will also be identified (*!*, *ed* and *ing*). The translations of these words identifying verb conjugations are written in all lower case and in italics and the Lexicon includes a list of all the conjugations and their meanings. Some verbs will also identify the gender and number of the object (such as; him, her, you, etc.) and some may also include a prefix and/or a suffix (such as; and, the, to, etc.).

Hebrew verbs have two tenses, perfect (a completed action, identified in the MT with the prefix "*did~*") and imperfect (an incomplete action, identified in the MT with the prefix "*will~*"). In addition, most Hebrew verbs will identify the number and gender of the subject of the verb. As an example, the Hebrew verb אמר (*amar*) is a verb meaning "to say" and is in the perfect tense and identifies the subject of the verb as third person, masculine singular. The MT will translate this verb as "*he~did~*SAY(V)" and the *Revised Mechanical Translation* (RMT) will translate it as "he said." The Hebrew verb תאמר (*tomer*) is again the verb meaning "to say" but is in the imperfect tense and identifies the subject of the verb as second person, masculine singular. The MT will translate this verb as "*you~will~*SAY(V)" and the RMT will translate it as "you will say."

When being translated, Hebrew verbs whose tenses are related to action (completed and incomplete), must be converted to English verbs related to time (past, present and future). In most cases the perfect tense (completed action) is translated into the English past tense verbs and imperfect tense (incomplete action) is translated into present or future tense English verbs. However, in some cases this style of translating will not accurately convey the meaning of the

Hebrew. For instance, in Genesis 22:2 the word *"you(ms)~did~LOVE(V)"* is written in the perfect tense meaning a completed action but, if translated into English as "you loved" (past tense), it would imply that he was no longer loved. Therefore, in this instance, the verb will be translated as "you love" (present tense).

When the prefix "and~" is added to a verb, the tense is usually reversed. For instance, the verb *"he~will~SAY(V)"* would be translated in the RMT as "he will say" but the verb *"and~he~will~SAY(V)"* will be translated in the RMT as "and he said."

The subject of the verb will usually follow the verb. For instance, אמר אב (*amar av*) will be written in the MT as *"he~did~SAY(V) Father"* and translated as "father said" in the RMT. In some instances the subject of the verb will precede the verb instead. This is the past perfect tense of the verb (see Genesis 3:13). When this occurs, the RMT will use the word "had."

Emphasis is often placed on a Hebrew verb by writing it twice. The RMT will translate this verb once and add an adverb such as 'quickly,' 'greatly,' 'completely' or 'surely' before it.

The *Piel* form of verbs, identified in the MT with the prefix *"much~,"* is an intensive form of the verb and is usually translated in the RMT with an adverb.

Verb participles, identified by "~ing" in the MT, identify an action or one of action. As an example, the participle "Feed-ing" may be translated in the RMT as "feeding" (see Genesis 37:2) or "feeder" (one who feeds, a shepherd or herdsman, see Genesis 13:7).

Hebrew verbs can be easily identified by their prefixes or suffixes attached to the verb. Many verbs will be preceded by *did~*, *will~*, *had~*, !~ or >~ or followed by~*ing* or~*ed*.

Below are examples of verbs with prefixes, suffixes and conjugations, which appear in the MT.

Table 2 – Example of Hebrew Verbs in the MT

Hebrew	Prefix	Conjugation	Verb	Suffix	Mech. Trans.
יאמר		*he~will~*	SAY(V)		*he~will~*SAY(V)

About the Mechanical Translation

Hebrew					
ושמרת	and~	you$^{(ms)}$~did~	SAFE-GUARD$^{(V)}$		and~you$^{(ms)}$~did~SAFE-GUARD$^{(V)}$
דברך		>~much~	SPEAK$^{(V)}$	~you$^{(ms)}$	>~much~SPEAK$^{(V)}$~you$^{(ms)}$

Hebrew Names in the Mechanical Translation

In our western culture we are comfortable using names, such as Noah or Adam, as simple identifiers with no actual meaning attached to the name. But, this is not the case with Hebrew names where each name is a word or a combination of words with a meaning. For instance, the name עבר (*ever* - see Genesis 10:21) is usually transliterated as 'Ever' or 'Eber,' but is a Hebrew word meaning "cross over." The MT and the RMT will represent this name as "Ever," and the lexicon will provide the translation of all names.

An individual descended from Ever is identified as עברי (*eevriy* - see Genesis 14:13) where the suffix י (*iy*) means "one of." The MT will translate this name as "Ever~of" and the RMT as "one of Ever." A people descended from Ever is identified as עברים (*eevriym* - see 40:15) where the suffix ים (*iym*) identifies the name as a plural meaning "ones of." The MT will translate this name as "Ever~s" and the RMT as "ones of Ever."

The common pronunciation of the word 'Pharoah' comes from the Greek translation called the *Septuagint*. In the Hebrew text this is pronounced *Paroh* (*pah-roh*), unless it follows a vowel, in which case it will be pronounced Pha'roh (*phah-roh*)

Each name in the MT is a transliteration of the Hebrew and begins with an upper-case letter. Names may also include prefixes and suffixes such as the examples below:

Table 3 – Example of Hebrew Names in the MT

Hebrew	Prefix	Name	Meaning	Suffix	Mech. Trans.
במצרים	in~	Mits'rayim	STRAIT~s2		in~Mits'rayim

| סכתה | | Sukhot | BOOTH~s | ~unto | Sukhot~unto |

The Names of God

The name Jehovah/Yahweh is written in Hebrew with four letters - יהוה (*YHWH*). These four letters, as a Hebrew word, is the third person, masculine, singular, imperfect tense of the verb הוה (*hawah*) and literally means "he exists." In this translation this name is transliterated as "YHWH."

The Hebrew word אלהים (*elohiym*), commonly translated as "God" in most modern translations, is a masculine plural noun literally meaning "powers." This word is used in Genesis 1:1 as the subject of the verb ברא (*bara*) meaning "he shaped," where the "he" identifies the subject of the verb as a masculine singular. Because of this conflict in number, where the verb identifies the subject as being a singular (he), but the subject is a plural word (*elohiym*), it is apparent that the word אלהים (*elohiym*) is a proper name, not a noun, and is therefore transliterated as "Elohiym" in the Mechanical Translation. However, *Elohiym* is often translated as "gods" when it is used in a plural sense, such as we see in Exodus 15:11, where it mentions all the "Elohiym" of Mitsrayim (Egypt). But in other places, such as in Genesis 3:5 where we read, "you will be like Elohiym," it is not clear if the word "*Elohiym*" is being used for YHWH or for other *elohiym*. Some scholars translate this as "you will be like God," whereas other versions translate it as "you will be like gods." In order to remain true to the mechanical nature of this translation, this translation will always treat the Hebrew word אלהים (*elohiym*) as a proper name (Elohiym) and leave the interpretation of this word to the preference of the reader.

The Hebrew words אדני (*adonai* - meaning "my lords", see Genesis 15:2) and שדי (*shaddai* - meaning "my breasts", see Genesis 17:1) are frequently used for God and will also be treated as proper names.

Hebrew Nouns in the Mechanical Translation

Some words have various nuances of meaning. In most cases the context will help define the nuance, but in some cases the nuance cannot be determined. For instance, in Genesis 4:26 the word "DRILL" can be interpreted as "begin" or "profane;" but, the context does not make clear which nuance is intended.

In the MT, words written with a period between them represent one Hebrew word. For instance, the Hebrew word תהום (*tehom* – see Genesis 1:2) means a deep sea and will be represented by "DEEP.SEA" in the MT but will be written as "deep sea" in the RMT.

The English translation chosen for each Hebrew word was chosen based on two criteria. First the translation had to be close in meaning to the Hebrew (although, keep in mind the lexicon more precisely defines this word) and, secondly, it was to be a unique word that was not used for any other word. As an example, the Hebrew words קום (*qum*) and רום (*rum*) both mean to "raise" so the meaning of "RISE" has been assigned to קום (*qum*) and "RAISE.UP" to רום (*rum*).

Most Hebrew words can be used in a literal or figurative application which will usually be defined by the context where it is used. For instance, the word 'hand' can literally refer to the hand, as in Genesis 22:6. But this same word is used in Genesis 9:2 figuratively to mean "at hand" or "in possession."

While the RMT strives to translate each Hebrew word exactly the same way each time it appears, there will be times where the context of the passage or English sentence structure will require the word to be translated differently. For instance, in Genesis 4:25 the MT has the phrase "SEED OTHER UNDER." The word "OTHER" can also be translated as "another" and the word "UNDER" can also be translated as "in place of." Therefore, this phrase is translated in the RMT as "another seed in place of."

Intensity of a word can be expressed by repeating a word in the Hebrew text. For instance, in Genesis 7:19 the word "many" is repeated to express a "great many." In these cases, the RMT will translate the two words only once and add the word "great" or another adjective to express this intensity.

Questions are usually formed in the text by using such words as "what," "where," "if," etc. But the Hebrew language can also form the text into a question by using the "interrogative *'hey'*" (in the Hebrew this is represented by the letter ה (*h*) as a prefix and will be translated in the MT as "?~"). For instance, the phrase "NOT HE *he~did*~SAY^(V)" would be translated in the RMT as "he did not say," but in Genesis 20:5 this phrase is written as "?~NOT HE *he~did~* SAY^(V)" and is translated as "did he not say" in the RMT.

A noun followed by a pronoun, such as "HAND~him," which is found in Genesis 3:22, would literally be translated as "hand of him," but the RMT will translate this as "his hand."

Some Hebrew words are always written in the plural, such as פנים (*paniym* - faces) and מים (*mayim* – waters). This idiomatic form does not always imply that the word is plural and will usually be translated in the singular in the RMT.

Hebrew numbers in the Mechanical Translation

There are two different types of plurals in Hebrew, simple plural and double plural. The word "HUNDRED" is a singular word and refers to "one hundred." The simple plural "HUNDRED~s" refers to a number of hundreds such as in the phrase "THREE HUNDRED~s" (this would be translated as "three hundred" in the RMT). When the same word is written in the double plural "HUNDRED~s2," its translation would be "two hundred."

When a Hebrew number is written in the simple plural form, it is multiplied by ten. For instance, the word "THREE~s" would mean thirty. The only exception is the plural form of ten ("TEN~s") which means twenty.

Verse Numbers

The verse numbers in the Hebrew Bible differ from Christian Bibles. The MT will use the verse numbers found in the Hebrew Bible, but where a verse number is different from the Christian Bibles, the Christian Bible number will follow the Hebrew Bible number in parenthesis.

About the Mechanical Translation

Benner's Mechanical Translation of the Torah

The Book of Genesis

Chapter 1

1:1 in~SUMMIT *he~did*~SHAPE⁽ⱽ⁾ Elohiym AT the~SKY~s2 and~AT the~LAND **1:2** and~the~LAND *she~did*~EXIST⁽ⱽ⁾ CONFUSION and~UNFILLED and~DARKNESS UPON FACE~s DEEP.WATER and~WIND Elohiym *much~*FLUTTER⁽ⱽ⁾*~ing*⁽ᶠˢ⁾ UPON FACE~s the~WATER~s2 **1:3** and~*he~will*~SAY⁽ⱽ⁾ Elohiym *he~will*~EXIST⁽ⱽ⁾ LIGHT and~*he~will*~EXIST⁽ⱽ⁾ LIGHT **1:4** and~*he~will*~SEE⁽ⱽ⁾ Elohiym AT the~LIGHT GIVEN.THAT FUNCTIONAL and~*he~will~make*~SEPARATE⁽ⱽ⁾ Elohiym BETWEEN the~LIGHT and~BETWEEN the~DARKNESS **1:5** and~*he~will*~CALL.OUT⁽ⱽ⁾ Elohiym to~LIGHT DAY and~to~DARKNESS *he~did*~CALL.OUT⁽ⱽ⁾ NIGHT and~*he~will*~EXIST⁽ⱽ⁾ EVENING and~*he~will*~EXIST⁽ⱽ⁾ MORNING DAY UNIT **1:6** and~*he~will*~SAY⁽ⱽ⁾ Elohiym *he~will*~EXIST⁽ⱽ⁾ SHEET in~MIDST the~WATER~s2 and~*he~will*~EXIST⁽ⱽ⁾ *make~*SEPARATE⁽ⱽ⁾*~ing*⁽ᵐˢ⁾ BETWEEN WATER~s2 to~WATER~s2 **1:7** and~*he~will*~DO⁽ⱽ⁾ Elohiym AT the~SHEET and~*he~will~make*~SEPARATE⁽ⱽ⁾ BETWEEN the~WATER~s2 WHICH from~UNDER to~SHEET and~BETWEEN the~WATER~s2 WHICH from~UPON to~SHEET and~*he~will*~EXIST⁽ⱽ⁾ SO **1:8** and~*he~will*~CALL.OUT⁽ⱽ⁾ Elohiym to~SHEET SKY~s2 and~*he~will*~EXIST⁽ⱽ⁾ EVENING and~*he~will*~EXIST⁽ⱽ⁾ MORNING DAY SECOND **1:9** and~*he~will*~SAY⁽ⱽ⁾ Elohiym *he~will~be*~BOUND.UP⁽ⱽ⁾ the~WATER~s2 from~UNDER the~SKY~s2 TO AREA UNIT and~*she~be*~SEE⁽ⱽ⁾ the~DRY.GROUND and~*he~will*~EXIST⁽ⱽ⁾ SO **1:10** and~*he~will*~CALL.OUT⁽ⱽ⁾ Elohiym to~DRY.GROUND LAND and~to~COLLECTION the~WATER~s2 *he~did*~CALL.OUT⁽ⱽ⁾ SEA~s and~*he~will*~SEE⁽ⱽ⁾ Elohiym GIVEN.THAT FUNCTIONAL **1:11** and~*he~will*~SAY⁽ⱽ⁾ Elohiym *she~will~make*~SPROUT⁽ⱽ⁾ the~LAND GRASS HERB *make~*SOW⁽ⱽ⁾*~ing*⁽ᵐˢ⁾ SEED TREE PRODUCE DO⁽ⱽ⁾*~ing*⁽ᵐˢ⁾ PRODUCE to~KIND~him WHICH SEED~him in~him UPON the~LAND and~*he~will*~EXIST⁽ⱽ⁾ SO **1:12** and~*she~will~make*~GO.OUT⁽ⱽ⁾ the~LAND GRASS HERB *make~*SOW⁽ⱽ⁾*~ing*⁽ᵐˢ⁾ SEED to~KIND~him and~TREE DO⁽ⱽ⁾*~ing*⁽ᵐˢ⁾ PRODUCE WHICH SEED~him in~him to~KIND~him and~*he~will*~SEE⁽ⱽ⁾ Elohiym GIVEN.THAT FUNCTIONAL **1:13** and~*he~will*~EXIST⁽ⱽ⁾ EVENING and~*he~will*~EXIST⁽ⱽ⁾ MORNING DAY THIRD **1:14** and~*he~will*~SAY⁽ⱽ⁾ Elohiym *he~will*~EXIST⁽ⱽ⁾ LUMINARY~s in~SHEET the~SKY~s2 to~>~*make~*SEPARATE⁽ⱽ⁾ BETWEEN the~DAY and~BETWEEN the~NIGHT and~*they~did*~EXIST⁽ⱽ⁾ to~SIGN~s and~to~APPOINTED~s and~to~DAY~s and~YEAR~s **1:15** and~*they~did*~EXIST⁽ⱽ⁾ to~LUMINARY~s in~SHEET the~SKY~s2 to~>~*make~*LIGHT⁽ⱽ⁾ UPON the~LAND and~*he~will*~EXIST⁽ⱽ⁾ SO **1:16** and~*he~will*~DO⁽ⱽ⁾ Elohiym AT TWO the~LUMINARY~s the~GREAT~s AT the~LUMINARY the~GREAT to~REGULATION the~DAY and~AT the~LUMINARY the~SMALL to~REGULATION the~NIGHT and~AT the~STAR~s **1:17** and~*he~will*~GIVE⁽ⱽ⁾ AT~them⁽ᵐ⁾ Elohiym in~SHEET the~SKY~s2 to~>~*make~*LIGHT⁽ⱽ⁾

UPON the~LAND **1:18** and~to~>~REGULATE$^{(v)}$ in~the~DAY and~in~NIGHT and~to~>~*make*~SEPARATE$^{(v)}$ BETWEEN the~LIGHT and~BETWEEN the~ DARKNESS and~*he~will*~SEE$^{(v)}$ Elohiym GIVEN.THAT FUNCTIONAL **1:19** and~ *he~will*~EXIST$^{(v)}$ EVENING and~*he~will*~EXIST$^{(v)}$ MORNING DAY FOURTH **1:20** and~*he~will*~SAY$^{(v)}$ Elohiym *they$^{(m)}~will*~SWARM$^{(v)}$ the~ WATER~s2 SWARMER SOUL LIVING and~FLYER *he~will*~much~FLY$^{(v)}$ UPON the~LAND UPON FACE~s SHEET the~SKY~s2 **1:21** and~*he~will*~SHAPE$^{(v)}$ Elohiym AT the~CROCODILE~s the~GREAT~s and~AT ALL SOUL the~LIVING the~TREAD$^{(v)}$~*ing$^{(fs)}$* WHICH *they$^{(m)}~did*~SWARM$^{(v)}$ the~WATER~s2 to~KIND~ them$^{(m)}$ and~AT ALL FLYER WING to~KIND~him and~*he~will*~SEE$^{(v)}$ Elohiym GIVEN.THAT FUNCTIONAL **1:22** and~*he~will*~much~KNEEL$^{(v)}$ AT~them$^{(m)}$ Elohiym to~>~SAY$^{(v)}$ *!$^{(mp)}$*~REPRODUCE$^{(v)}$ and~ *!$^{(mp)}$*~INCREASE$^{(v)}$ and~ *!$^{(mp)}$*~ FILL$^{(v)}$ AT the~WATER~s2 in~the~SEA~s and~the~FLYER *he~did*~INCREASE$^{(v)}$ in~the~LAND **1:23** and~*he~will*~EXIST$^{(v)}$ EVENING and~*he~will*~EXIST$^{(v)}$ MORNING DAY FIFTH **1:24** and~*he~will*~SAY$^{(v)}$ Elohiym *she~will~make~* GO.OUT$^{(v)}$ the~LAND SOUL LIVING to~KIND~her BEAST and~TREADER and~ LIVING~him LAND to~KIND~her and~*he~will*~EXIST$^{(v)}$ SO **1:25** and~*he~will*~ DO$^{(v)}$ Elohiym AT LIVING the~LAND to~KIND~her and~AT the~BEAST to~ KIND~her and~AT ALL TREADER the~GROUND to~KIND~him and~*he~will*~ SEE$^{(v)}$ Elohiym GIVEN.THAT FUNCTIONAL **1:26** and~*he~will*~SAY$^{(v)}$ Elohiym *we~will*~DO$^{(v)}$ HUMAN in~IMAGE~us like~LIKENESS~us and~*he~did*~RULE$^{(v)}$ in~FISH the~SEA and~in~FLYER the~SKY~s2 and~in~the~BEAST and~in~ALL the~LAND and~in~ALL the~TREADER the~TREAD$^{(v)}$~*ing$^{(ms)}$* UPON the~ LAND **1:27** and~*he~will*~SHAPE$^{(v)}$ Elohiym AT the~HUMAN in~IMAGE~him in~IMAGE Elohiym *he~did*~SHAPE$^{(v)}$ AT~him MALE and~FEMALE *he~did*~ SHAPE$^{(v)}$ AT~them$^{(m)}$ **1:28** and~*he~will*~much~KNEEL$^{(v)}$ AT~them$^{(m)}$ Elohiym and~*he~will*~SAY$^{(v)}$ to~them$^{(m)}$ Elohiym *!$^{(mp)}$*~REPRODUCE$^{(v)}$ and~ *!$^{(mp)}$*~ INCREASE$^{(v)}$ and~ *!$^{(mp)}$*~FILL$^{(v)}$ AT the~LAND and~ *!$^{(mp)}$*~SUBDUE$^{(v)}$~her and~ *!$^{(mp)}$*~RULE$^{(v)}$ in~FISH the~SEA and~in~FLYER the~SKY~s2 and~in~ALL LIVING the~TREAD$^{(v)}$~*ing$^{(fs)}$* UPON the~LAND **1:29** and~*he~will*~SAY$^{(v)}$ Elohiym LOOK *I~did*~GIVE$^{(v)}$ to~you$^{(mp)}$ AT ALL HERB SOW$^{(v)}$~*ing$^{(ms)}$* SEED WHICH UPON FACE~s ALL the~LAND and~AT ALL the~TREE WHICH in~him PRODUCE TREE SOW$^{(v)}$~*ing$^{(ms)}$* SEED to~you$^{(mp)}$ *he~will*~EXIST$^{(v)}$ to~FOOD **1:30** and~ to~ALL LIVING the~LAND and~to~ALL FLYER the~SKY~s2 and~to~ALL the~ TREAD$^{(v)}$~*ing$^{(ms)}$* UPON the~LAND WHICH in~him SOUL LIVING AT ALL GREEN HERB to~FOOD and~*he~will*~EXIST$^{(v)}$ SO **1:31** and~*he~will*~SEE$^{(v)}$ Elohiym AT ALL WHICH *he~did*~DO$^{(v)}$ and~LOOK FUNCTIONAL MANY and~*he~will*~ EXIST$^{(v)}$ EVENING and~*he~will*~EXIST$^{(v)}$ MORNING DAY the~SIXTH

Chapter 2

2:1 and~*they$^{(m)}~will~be*~FINISH$^{(v)}$ the~SKY~s2 and~the~LAND and~ALL ARMY~them$^{(m)}$ **2:2** and~*he~will*~much~FINISH$^{(v)}$ Elohiym in~the~DAY the~

SEVENTH BUSINESS~him WHICH *he~did*~DO^(V) and~*he~will*~CEASE^(V) in~the~ DAY the~SEVENTH from~ALL BUSINESS~him WHICH *he~did*~DO^(V) **2:3** and~*he~will~much*~KNEEL^(V) Elohiym AT DAY the~SEVENTH and~*he~will~much*~SET.APART^(V) AT~him GIVEN.THAT in~him *he~did*~CEASE^(V) from~ALL BUSINESS~him WHICH *he~did*~SHAPE^(V) Elohiym to~>~DO^(V) **2:4** THESE BIRTHING~s the~SKY~s2 and~the~LAND in~>~*be*~SHAPE^(V)~them^(m) in~DAY >~DO^(V) **YHWH** Elohiym LAND and~SKY~s2 **2:5** and~ALL SHRUB the~FIELD BEFORE *he~will*~EXIST^(V) in~the~LAND and~ALL HERB the~FIELD BEFORE *he~will*~SPRING.UP^(V) GIVEN.THAT NOT *he~did~make*~PRECIPITATE^(V) **YHWH** Elohiym UPON the~LAND and~HUMAN WITHOUT to~>~SERVE^(V) AT the~GROUND **2:6** and~MIST *he~will*~GO.UP^(V) FROM the~LAND and~*he~did~make*~DRINK^(V) AT ALL FACE~s the~GROUND **2:7** and~*he~will*~MOLD^(V) **YHWH** Elohiym AT the~HUMAN DIRT FROM the~GROUND and~*he~will*~EXHALE^(V) in~NOSE~s2~him BREATH LIVING~s and~*he~will*~EXIST^(V) the~HUMAN to~SOUL LIVING **2:8** and~*he~will*~PLANT^(V) **YHWH** Elohiym GARDEN in~Eden from~EAST and~*he~will*~PLACE^(V) THERE AT the~HUMAN WHICH *he~did*~MOLD^(V) **2:9** and~*he~will~make*~SPRING.UP^(V) **YHWH** Elohiym FROM the~GROUND ALL TREE *be*~CRAVE^(V)~*ing*^(ms) to~APPEARANCE and~FUNCTIONAL to~NOURISHMENT and~TREE the~LIVING~s in~MIDST the~GARDEN and~TREE the~DISCERNMENT FUNCTIONAL and~DYSFUNCTIONAL **2:10** and~RIVER GO.OUT^(V)~*ing*^(ms) from~Eden to~>~*make*~DRINK^(V) AT the~GARDEN and~from~THERE *he~will~be*~DIVIDE.APART^(V) and~*he~did*~EXIST^(V) to~FOUR HEAD~s **2:11** TITLE the~UNIT Pishon HE the~GO.AROUND^(V)~*ing*^(ms) AT ALL LAND the~Hhawilah WHICH THERE the~GOLD **2:12** and~GOLD the~LAND the~SHE FUNCTIONAL THERE the~AMBER and~STONE the~ONYX **2:13** and~TITLE the~RIVER the~SECOND Giyhhon HE the~GO.AROUND^(V)~*ing*^(ms) AT ALL LAND Kush **2:14** and~TITLE the~RIVER the~THIRD Hhideqel HE the~WALK^(V)~*ing*^(ms) EASTWARD Ashur and~the~RIVER the~FOURTH HE Perat **2:15** and~*he~will*~TAKE^(V) **YHWH** Elohiym AT the~HUMAN and~*he~will~make*~DEPOSIT^(V)~him in~GARDEN Eden to~>~SERVE^(V)~her and~to~>~SAFEGUARD^(V)~her **2:16** and~*he~will~much*~DIRECT^(V) **YHWH** Elohiym UPON the~HUMAN to~>~SAY^(V) from~ALL TREE the~GARDEN >~EAT^(V) *you*^(ms)~*will*~EAT^(V) **2:17** and~from~TREE the~DISCERNMENT FUNCTIONAL and~DYSFUNCTIONAL NOT *you*^(ms)~*will*~EAT^(V) FROM~him GIVEN.THAT in~DAY *you*^(ms)~>~EAT^(V) FROM~him >~DIE^(V) *you*^(ms)~*will*~DIE^(V) **2:18** and~*he~will*~SAY^(V) **YHWH** Elohiym NOT FUNCTIONAL >~EXIST^(V) the~HUMAN to~STRAND~him *I~will*~DO^(V) to~him HELP like~OPPOSITE~him **2:19** and~*he~will*~MOLD^(V) **YHWH** Elohiym FROM the~GROUND ALL LIVING the~FIELD and~AT ALL FLYER the~SKY~s2 and~*he~will~make*~COME^(V) TO the~HUMAN to~>~SEE^(V) WHAT *he~will*~CALL.OUT^(V) to~him and~ALL WHICH *he~will*~CALL.OUT^(V) to~him the~HUMAN SOUL LIVING HE TITLE~him **2:20** and~*he~will*~CALL.OUT^(V) the~HUMAN TITLE~s to~ALL the~BEAST and~to~FLYER the~SKY~s2 and~to~ALL LIVING the~FIELD and~to~HUMAN NOT *he~did*~FIND^(V) HELP like~OPPOSITE~him **2:21** and~*he~will~make*~FALL^(V) **YHWH** Elohiym TRANCE UPON the~HUMAN and~*he~*

will~SLEEP(V) and~*he*~*will*~TAKE(V) UNIT from~RIB~s~him and~*he*~*will*~SHUT(V) FLESH UNDER~her **2:22** and~*he*~*will*~BUILD(V) **YHWH** Elohiym AT the~RIB WHICH *he*~*did*~TAKE(V) FROM the~HUMAN to~WOMAN and~*he*~*will*~make~COME(V)~her TO the~HUMAN **2:23** and~*he*~*will*~SAY(V) the~HUMAN THIS the~FOOTSTEP BONE from~BONE~s~me and~FLESH from~FLESH~me to~THIS *he*~*will*~be~CALL.OUT(V) WOMAN GIVEN.THAT from~MAN *be*~TAKE(V)~*ed*(fs) THIS **2:24** UPON SO *he*~*will*~LEAVE(V) MAN AT FATHER~him and~AT MOTHER~him and~*he*~*did*~ADHERE(V) in~WOMAN~him and~*they*~*did*~EXIST(V) to~FLESH UNIT **2:25** and~*they*(m)~*will*~EXIST(V) TWO~them(m) NUDE~s the~HUMAN and~WOMAN~him and~NOT *they*(m)~*will*~self~BE.ASHAMED(V)

Chapter 3

3:1 and~the~SERPENT *he*~*did*~EXIST(V) SUBTLE from~ALL LIVING the~FIELD WHICH *he*~*did*~DO(V) **YHWH** Elohiym and~*he*~*will*~SAY(V) TO the~WOMAN MOREOVER GIVEN.THAT *he*~*did*~SAY(V) Elohiym NOT *you*(mp)~*will*~EAT(V) from~ALL TREE the~GARDEN **3:2** and~*she*~*will*~SAY(V) the~WOMAN TO the~SERPENT from~PRODUCE TREE the~GARDEN *we*~*will*~EAT(V) **3:3** and~from~PRODUCE the~TREE WHICH in~MIDST the~GARDEN *he*~*did*~SAY(V) Elohiym NOT *you*(mp)~*will*~EAT(V) FROM~him and~NOT *you*(mp)~*will*~TOUCH(V) in~him OTHERWISE *you*(mp)~*will*~DIE(V)~must **3:4** and~*he*~*will*~SAY(V) the~SERPENT TO the~WOMAN NOT >~DIE(V) *you*(mp)~*will*~DIE(V)~must **3:5** GIVEN.THAT KNOW(V)~*ing*(ms) Elohiym GIVEN.THAT in~DAY >~EAT(V)~*you*(mp) FROM~him and~*they*(f)~*did*~be~OPEN.UP(V) EYE~s2~*you*(mp) and~*you*(mp)~*did*~EXIST(V) like~Elohiym KNOW(V)~*ing*(mp) FUNCTIONAL and~DYSFUNCTIONAL **3:6** and~*she*~*will*~SEE(V) the~WOMAN GIVEN.THAT FUNCTIONAL the~TREE to~NOURISHMENT and~GIVEN.THAT YEARNING HE to~the~EYE~s2 and~*be*~CRAVE(V)~*ing*(ms) the~TREE to~>~make~CALCULATE(V) and~*she*~*will*~TAKE(V) from~PRODUCE~him and~*she*~*will*~EAT(V) and~*she*~*will*~GIVE(V) ALSO to~MAN~her WITH~her and~*he*~*will*~EAT(V) **3:7** and~*they*(f)~*will*~be~OPEN.UP(V) EYE~s2 TWO~them(m) and~*they*(m)~*will*~KNOW(V) GIVEN.THAT NAKED~s THEY(m) and~*they*(m)~*will*~SEW.TOGETHER(V) LEAF FIG and~*they*(m)~*will*~DO(V) to~them(m) LOIN.WRAP~s **3:8** and~*they*(m)~*will*~HEAR(V) AT VOICE **YHWH** Elohiym *self*~WALK(V)~*ing*(ms) in~GARDEN to~WIND the~DAY and~*he*~*will*~*self*~WITHDRAW(V) the~HUMAN and~WOMAN~him from~FACE~s **YHWH** Elohiym in~MIDST TREE the~GARDEN **3:9** and~*he*~*will*~CALL.OUT(V) **YHWH** Elohiym TO the~HUMAN and~*he*~*will*~SAY(V) to~him WHERE~*you*(ms) **3:10** and~*he*~*will*~SAY(V) AT VOICE~*you*(ms) *I*~*did*~HEAR(V) in~GARDEN and~*I*~*will*~FEAR(V) GIVEN.THAT NAKED I and~*I*~*will*~WITHDRAW(V) **3:11** and~*he*~*will*~SAY(V) WHO *he*~*did*~make~BE.FACE.TO.FACE(V) to~*you*(ms) GIVEN.THAT NAKED YOU(ms) ?~FROM the~TREE WHICH *I*~*did*~much~DIRECT(V)~*you*(ms) to~EXCEPT >~EAT(V) FROM~him *you*(ms)~will~EAT(V) **3:12** and~he~will~SAY(V) the~HUMAN the~WOMAN WHICH *you*(ms)~*did*~GIVE(V) BY~me SHE *she*~*did*~GIVE(V) to~me FROM the~TREE and~*I*~will~EAT(V) **3:13** and~*he*~will~EAT(V) **YHWH** Elohiym to~WOMAN WHAT THIS *you*(fs)~*did*~DO(V) and~*she*~will~SAY(V) the~WOMAN the~SERPENT *he*~*did*~make~DECEIVE(V)~me and~*I*~will~EAT(V) **3:14** and~*he*~will~SAY(V) **YHWH** Elohiym TO the~SERPENT GIVEN.THAT *you*(ms)~*did*~DO(V) THIS SPIT.UPON(V)~*ed*(ms) YOU(ms) from~ALL the~BEAST and~from~ALL LIVING the~FIELD UPON BELLY~you(ms) *you*(ms)~will~WALK(V) and~DIRT *you*(ms)~will~EAT(V) ALL DAY~s LIVING~s~you(ms) **3:15** and~HOSTILITY *I*~will~SET.DOWN(V) BETWEEN~you(ms) and~BETWEEN the~WOMAN and~BETWEEN SEED~you(ms) and~BETWEEN SEED~her HE *he*~will~FALL.UPON(V)~you(ms) HEAD and~YOU(ms) *you*(ms)~will~FALL.UPON(V)~him HEEL **3:16** TO the~WOMAN *he*~*did*~SAY(V) >~make~INCREASE(V) *I*~will~make~INCREASE(V) HARDSHIP~you(fs) and~PREGNANCY~you(fs) in~DISTRESSING.PAIN *you*(fs)~will~BRING.FORTH(V) SON~s and~TO MAN~you(fs) FOLLOWING~you(fs) and~HE *he*~will~REGULATE(V) in~you(fs) **3:17** and~to~HUMAN *he*~*did*~SAY(V) GIVEN.THAT *you*(ms)~*did*~HEAR(V) to~VOICE WOMAN~you(ms) and~*you*(ms)~will~EAT(V) FROM the~TREE WHICH *I*~*did*~much~DIRECT(V)~you(ms) to~>~SAY(V) NOT *you*(ms)~will~EAT(V) FROM~him SPIT.UPON(V)~*ed*(ms) the~GROUND in~the~CROSS.OVER(V)~*ed*(ms)~you(ms) in~HARDSHIP~you(ms) *you*(ms)~will~EAT(V)~her ALL DAY~s LIVING~s~you(ms) **3:18** and~BRAMBLE and~THISTLE *she*~will~make~SPRING.UP(V) to~you(fs) and~*you*(ms)~*did*~EAT(V) AT HERB the~FIELD **3:19** in~SWEAT NOSE~s~you(ms) *you*(ms)~will~EAT(V) BREAD UNTIL >~TURN.BACK(V)~you(ms) TO the~GROUND GIVEN.THAT FROM~her *you*(ms)~*did*~be~TAKE(V) GIVEN.THAT DIRT YOU(ms) and~TO DIRT *you*(ms)~will~TURN.BACK(V) **3:20** and~*he*~will~CALL.OUT(V) the~HUMAN TITLE WOMAN~him Hhawah GIVEN.THAT SHE *she*~*did*~EXIST(V) MOTHER ALL LIVING **3:21** and~*he*~will~DO(V) **YHWH** Elohiym to~HUMAN and~to~WOMAN~him TUNIC~s SKIN and~*he*~will~make~WEAR(V)~them(m) **3:22** and~*he*~will~SAY(V) **YHWH** Elohiym THOUGH the~HUMAN *he*~*did*~EXIST(V) like~UNIT FROM~us to~>~KNOW(V) FUNCTIONAL and~DYSFUNCTIONAL and~NOW OTHERWISE *he*~will~SEND(V) HAND~him and~*he*~*did*~TAKE(V) ALSO from~TREE the~LIVING~s and~*he*~*did*~EAT(V) and~*he*~*did*~LIVE(V) to~DISTANT **3:23** and~*he*~will~SEND(V)~him **YHWH** Elohiym from~GARDEN Eden to~>~SERVE(V) AT the~GROUND WHICH *he*~*did*~be~TAKE(V) from~THERE **3:24** and~*he*~will~much~CAST.OUT(V) AT the~HUMAN and~*he*~will~DWELL(V) from~EAST to~GARDEN Eden AT the~KERUV~s and~AT BLAZING the~SWORD the~*self*~OVERTURN(V)~*ing*(fs) to~>~SAFEGUARD(V) AT ROAD TREE the~LIVING~s

Chapter 4

4:1 and~the~HUMAN *he~did~*KNOW[V] AT Hhawah WOMAN~him and~*she~will~*CONCEIVE[V] and~*she~will~*BRING.FORTH[V] AT Qayin and~*she~will~*SAY[V] *I~did~*PURCHASE[V] MAN AT **YHWH** **4:2** and~*she~will~make~*ADD[V] to~>~BRING.FORTH[V] AT BROTHER~him AT Hevel and~*he~will~*EXIST[V] Hevel FEED[V]~*ing*[ms] FLOCKS and~Qayin *he~did~*EXIST[V] SERVE[V]~*ing*[ms] GROUND **4:3** and~*he~will~*EXIST[V] from~CONCLUSION DAY~s and~*he~will~make~*COME[V] Qayin from~PRODUCE the~GROUND DEPOSIT to~ **YHWH** **4:4** and~Hevel *he~did~make~*COME[V] ALSO HE from~ FIRSTBORN.FEMALE~s FLOCKS~him and~from~FAT~them[f] and~*he~will~*LOOK.WITH.RESPECT[V] **YHWH** TO Hevel and~TO DEPOSIT~him **4:5** and~TO Qayin and~TO DEPOSIT~him NOT *he~did~*LOOK.WITH.RESPECT[V] and~*he~will~*FLARE.UP[V] to~Qayin MANY and~*they*[m]~*will~*FALL[V] FACE~s~him **4:6** and~*he~will~*SAY[V] **YHWH** TO Qayin to~WHAT *he~did~*FLARE.UP[V] to~you[fs] and~to~WHAT *they~did~*FALL[V] FACE~s~you[ms] **4:7** ?~NOT IF *you*[ms]~*will~make~*DO.WELL[V] >~LIFT.UP[V] and~IF NOT *you*[ms]~*will~make~*DO.WELL[V] to~OPENING FAILURE STRETCH.OUT[V]~*ing*[ms] and~TO~you[ms] FOLLOWING~him and~YOU[ms] *you*[ms]~*will~*REGULATE[V] in~him **4:8** and~*he~will~*SAY[V] Qayin TO Hevel BROTHER~him and~*he~will~*EXIST[V] in~>~ EXIST[V]~them[m] in~the~FIELD and~*he~will~*RISE[V] Qayin TO Hevel BROTHER~him and~*he~will~*KILL[V]~him **4:9** and~*he~will~*SAY[V] **YHWH** TO Qayin WHERE Hevel BROTHER~you[ms] and~*he~will~*SAY[V] NOT *I~did~*KNOW[V] ?~SAFEGUARD[V]~*ing*[ms] BROTHER~me I **4:10** and~*he~will~*SAY[V] WHAT *you*[ms]~*did~*DO[V] VOICE BLOOD~s BROTHER~you[ms] CRY.OUT[V]~*ing*[mp] TO~me FROM the~GROUND **4:11** and~NOW SPIT.UPON[V]~*ed*[ms] YOU[ms] FROM the~GROUND WHICH *she~did~*PART[V] AT MOUTH~her to~>~ TAKE[V] AT BLOOD~s BROTHER~you[ms] from~HAND~ you[ms] **4:12** GIVEN.THAT *you*[ms]~*will~*SERVE[V] AT the~GROUND NOT *she~will~make~*ADD[V] >~GIVE[V] STRENGTH~her to~you[fs] STAGGER[V]~*ing*[ms] and~NOD[V]~*ing*[ms] *you*[ms]~*will~*EXIST[V] in~the~LAND **4:13** and~*he~will~*SAY[V] Qayin TO **YHWH** GREAT TWISTEDNESS~me from~>~ LIFT.UP[V] **4:14** THOUGH *you*[ms]~*did~much~*CAST.OUT[V] AT~me the~DAY from~UPON FACE~s the~GROUND and~from~FACE~s~you[ms] *I~will~be~* HIDE[V] and~*I~did~*EXIST[V] STAGGER[V]~*ing*[ms] and~NOD[V]~*ing*[ms] in~the~ LAND and~*he~did~*EXIST[V] ALL FIND[V]~*ing*[ms]~me *he~will~*KILL[V]~ me **4:15** and~*he~will~*SAY[V] to~him **YHWH** to~SO ALL KILL[V]~*ing*[ms] Qayin SEVENTH.TIME~s2 *he~will~be~make~*AVENGE[V] and~*he~will~*PLACE[V] **YHWH** to~Qayin SIGN to~EXCEPT >~*make~*HIT[V] AT~him ALL FIND[V]~*ing*[ms]~ him **4:16** and~*he~will~*GO.OUT[V] Qayin from~to~FACE~s **YHWH** and~*he~will~*SETTLE[V] in~LAND Nod EASTWARD Eden **4:17** and~*he~will~*KNOW[V] Qayin AT WOMAN~him and~*she~will~*CONCEIVE[V] and~*she~will~*BRING.FORTH[V] AT Hhanokh and~*he~will~*EXIST[V] BUILD[V]~*ing*[ms] CITY and~ *he~will~*CALL.OUT[V] TITLE the~CITY like~TITLE SON~him

Hhanokh **4:18** and~*he*~*will*~*be*~BRING.FORTH⁽ᵛ⁾ to~Hhanokh AT Irad and~
Irad *he*~*did*~BRING.FORTH⁽ᵛ⁾ AT Mehhuya'el and~Mehhuya'el *he*~*did*~
BRING.FORTH⁽ᵛ⁾ AT Metusha'el and~Metusha'el *he*~*did*~BRING.FORTH⁽ᵛ⁾ AT
Lamekh **4:19** and~*he*~*will*~TAKE⁽ᵛ⁾ to~him Lamekh TWO WOMAN~s TITLE
the~UNIT Adah and~TITLE the~SECOND Tsilah **4:20** and~*she*~*will*~
BRING.FORTH⁽ᵛ⁾ Adah AT Yaval HE *he*~*did*~EXIST⁽ᵛ⁾ FATHER~of SETTLE⁽ᵛ⁾~
ing⁽ᵐˢ⁾ TENT and~LIVESTOCK **4:21** and~TITLE BROTHER~him Yuval HE *he*~
did~EXIST⁽ᵛ⁾ FATHER~of ALL SEIZE.HOLD⁽ᵛ⁾~*ing*⁽ᵐˢ⁾ HARP and~
REED.PIPE **4:22** and~Tsilah ALSO SHE *she*~*did*~BRING.FORTH⁽ᵛ⁾ AT Tuval-
Qayin SHARPEN⁽ᵛ⁾~*ing*⁽ᵐˢ⁾ ALL CRAFTSMAN COPPER and~IRON and~SISTER
Tuval-Qayin Na'amah **4:23** and~*he*~*will*~SAY⁽ᵛ⁾ Lamekh to~WOMAN~s~him
Adah and~Tsilah !⁽ᶠᵖ⁾~HEAR⁽ᵛ⁾ VOICE~me WOMAN~s Lamekh !⁽ᶠᵖ⁾~*make*~
WEIGH.OUT⁽ᵛ⁾ SPEECH~me GIVEN.THAT MAN I~*did*~KILL⁽ᵛ⁾ to~WOUND~me
and~BOY to~STRIPED.BRUISE~me **4:24** GIVEN.THAT SEVENTH.TIME~s2 *he*~
will~*be*~*make*~AVENGE⁽ᵛ⁾ Qayin and~Lamekh SEVEN~s and~
SEVEN **4:25** and~*he*~*will*~KNOW⁽ᵛ⁾ HUMAN YET.AGAIN AT WOMAN~him
and~*she*~*will*~BRING.FORTH⁽ᵛ⁾ SON and~*she*~*will*~CALL.OUT⁽ᵛ⁾ AT TITLE~him
Shet GIVEN.THAT *he*~*did*~SET.DOWN⁽ᵛ⁾ to~me Elohiym SEED OTHER UNDER
Hevel GIVEN.THAT *he*~*did*~KILL⁽ᵛ⁾~him Qayin **4:26** and~to~Shet ALSO HE
BRING.FORTH⁽ᵛ⁾~*ed*⁽ᵐˢ⁾ SON and~*he*~*will*~CALL.OUT⁽ᵛ⁾ AT TITLE~him Enosh
AT.THAT.TIME *he*~*did*~*be*~*make*~DRILL⁽ᵛ⁾ to~>~CALL.OUT⁽ᵛ⁾ in~TITLE **YHWH**

Chapter 5

5:1 THIS SCROLL BIRTHING~s HUMAN in~DAY >~SHAPE⁽ᵛ⁾ Elohiym HUMAN
in~LIKENESS Elohiym *he*~*did*~DO⁽ᵛ⁾ AT~him **5:2** MALE and~FEMALE *he*~*did*~
SHAPE⁽ᵛ⁾~them⁽ᵐ⁾ and~*he*~*will*~much~KNEEL⁽ᵛ⁾ AT~them⁽ᵐ⁾ and~*he*~*will*~
CALL.OUT⁽ᵛ⁾ AT TITLE~them⁽ᵐ⁾ HUMAN in~DAY >~*be*~SHAPE⁽ᵛ⁾~
them⁽ᵐ⁾ **5:3** and~*he*~*will*~LIVE⁽ᵛ⁾ HUMAN THREE~s and~HUNDRED YEAR
and~*he*~*will*~*make*~BRING.FORTH⁽ᵛ⁾ in~LIKENESS~him like~IMAGE~him
and~*he*~*will*~CALL.OUT⁽ᵛ⁾ AT TITLE~him Shet **5:4** and~*they*⁽ᵐ⁾~*will*~EXIST⁽ᵛ⁾
DAY~s HUMAN AFTER >~*make*~BRING.FORTH⁽ᵛ⁾~him AT Shet EIGHT
HUNDRED~s YEAR and~*he*~*will*~*make*~BRING.FORTH⁽ᵛ⁾ SON~s and~
DAUGHTER~s **5:5** and~*they*⁽ᵐ⁾~*will*~EXIST⁽ᵛ⁾ ALL DAY~s HUMAN WHICH *he*~
did~LIVE⁽ᵛ⁾ NINE HUNDRED~s YEAR and~THREE~s YEAR and~*he*~*will*~
DIE⁽ᵛ⁾ **5:6** and~*he*~*will*~LIVE⁽ᵛ⁾ Shet FIVE YEAR~s and~HUNDRED YEAR and~
he~*will*~*make*~BRING.FORTH⁽ᵛ⁾ AT Enosh **5:7** and~*he*~*will*~LIVE⁽ᵛ⁾ Shet
AFTER >~*make*~BRING.FORTH⁽ᵛ⁾~him AT Enosh SEVEN YEAR~s and~EIGHT
HUNDRED~s YEAR and~*he*~*will*~*make*~BRING.FORTH⁽ᵛ⁾ SON~s and~
DAUGHTER~s **5:8** and~*they*⁽ᵐ⁾~*will*~EXIST⁽ᵛ⁾ ALL DAY~s Shet TWO TEN YEAR
and~NINE HUNDRED~s YEAR and~*he*~*will*~DIE⁽ᵛ⁾ **5:9** and~*he*~*will*~LIVE⁽ᵛ⁾
Enosh NINE~s YEAR and~*he*~*will*~*make*~BRING.FORTH⁽ᵛ⁾ AT
Qeynan **5:10** and~*he*~*will*~LIVE⁽ᵛ⁾ Enosh AFTER >~*make*~BRING.FORTH⁽ᵛ⁾~

him AT Qeynan FIVE TEN YEAR and~EIGHT HUNDRED~s YEAR and~he~will~make~BRING.FORTH$^{(V)}$ SON~s and~DAUGHTER~s **5:11** and~they$^{(m)}$~will~EXIST$^{(V)}$ ALL DAY~s Enosh FIVE YEAR~s and~NINE HUNDRED~s YEAR and~he~will~DIE$^{(V)}$ **5:12** and~he~will~LIVE$^{(V)}$ Qeynan SEVEN~s YEAR and~he~will~make~BRING.FORTH$^{(V)}$ AT Mahalalel **5:13** and~he~will~LIVE$^{(V)}$ Qeynan AFTER >~make~BRING.FORTH$^{(V)}$~him AT Mahalalel FOUR~s YEAR and~EIGHT HUNDRED~s YEAR and~he~will~make~BRING.FORTH$^{(V)}$ SON~s and~DAUGHTER~s **5:14** and~they$^{(m)}$~will~EXIST$^{(V)}$ ALL DAY~s Qeynan TEN YEAR~s and~NINE HUNDRED~s YEAR and~he~will~DIE$^{(V)}$ **5:15** and~he~will~LIVE$^{(V)}$ Mahalalel FIVE YEAR~s and~SIX~s YEAR and~he~will~make~BRING.FORTH$^{(V)}$ AT Yared **5:16** and~he~will~LIVE$^{(V)}$ Mahalalel AFTER >~make~BRING.FORTH$^{(V)}$~him AT Yared THREE~s YEAR and~EIGHT HUNDRED~s YEAR and~he~will~make~BRING.FORTH$^{(V)}$ SON~s and~DAUGHTER~s **5:17** and~they$^{(m)}$~will~EXIST$^{(V)}$ ALL DAY~s Mahalalel FIVE and~NINE~s YEAR and~EIGHT HUNDRED~s YEAR and~he~will~DIE$^{(V)}$ **5:18** and~he~will~LIVE$^{(V)}$ Yared TWO and~SIX~s YEAR and~HUNDRED YEAR and~he~will~make~BRING.FORTH$^{(V)}$ AT Hhanokh **5:19** and~he~will~LIVE$^{(V)}$ Yared AFTER >~make~BRING.FORTH$^{(V)}$~him AT Hhanokh EIGHT HUNDRED~s YEAR and~he~will~make~BRING.FORTH$^{(V)}$ SON~s and~DAUGHTER~s **5:20** and~they$^{(m)}$~will~EXIST$^{(V)}$ ALL DAY~s Yared TWO and~SIX~s YEAR and~NINE HUNDRED~s YEAR and~he~will~DIE$^{(V)}$ **5:21** and~he~will~LIVE$^{(V)}$ Hhanokh FIVE and~SIX~s YEAR and~he~will~make~BRING.FORTH$^{(V)}$ AT Metushelahh **5:22** and~he~will~self~WALK$^{(V)}$ Hhanokh AT the~Elohiym AFTER >~make~BRING.FORTH$^{(V)}$~him AT Metushelahh THREE HUNDRED~s YEAR and~he~will~make~BRING.FORTH$^{(V)}$ SON~s and~DAUGHTER~s **5:23** and~he~will~EXIST$^{(V)}$ ALL DAY~s Hhanokh FIVE and~SIX~s YEAR and~THREE HUNDRED~s YEAR **5:24** and~he~will~self~WALK$^{(V)}$ Hhanokh AT the~Elohiym and~WITHOUT~him GIVEN.THAT he~did~TAKE$^{(V)}$ AT~him Elohiym **5:25** and~he~will~LIVE$^{(V)}$ Metushelahh SEVEN and~EIGHT~s YEAR and~HUNDRED YEAR and~he~will~make~BRING.FORTH$^{(V)}$ AT Lamekh **5:26** and~he~will~LIVE$^{(V)}$ Metushelahh AFTER >~make~BRING.FORTH$^{(V)}$~him AT Lamekh TWO and~EIGHT~s YEAR and~SEVEN HUNDRED~s YEAR and~he~will~make~BRING.FORTH$^{(V)}$ SON~s and~DAUGHTER~s **5:27** and~they$^{(m)}$~will~EXIST$^{(V)}$ ALL DAY~s Metushelahh NINE and~SIX~s YEAR and~NINE HUNDRED~s YEAR and~he~will~DIE$^{(V)}$ **5:28** and~he~will~LIVE$^{(V)}$ Lamekh TWO and~EIGHT~s YEAR and~HUNDRED YEAR and~he~will~make~BRING.FORTH$^{(V)}$ SON **5:29** and~he~will~CALL.OUT$^{(V)}$ AT TITLE~him No'ahh to~>~SAY$^{(V)}$ THIS he~will~much~COMFORT$^{(V)}$~us from~WORK~us and~from~HARDSHIP HAND~s2~us FROM the~GROUND WHICH he~did~much~SPIT.UPON$^{(V)}$~her **YHWH 5:30** and~he~will~LIVE$^{(V)}$ Lamekh AFTER >~make~BRING.FORTH$^{(V)}$~him AT No'ahh FIVE and~NINE~s YEAR and~FIVE HUNDRED~s YEAR and~he~will~make~BRING.FORTH$^{(V)}$ SON~s and~DAUGHTER~s **5:31** and~he~will~EXIST$^{(V)}$ ALL DAY~s Lamekh SEVEN and~SEVEN~s YEAR and~SEVEN HUNDRED~s YEAR and~he~will~DIE$^{(V)}$ **5:32** and~he~will~EXIST$^{(V)}$ No'ahh

SON FIVE HUNDRED~s YEAR and~he~will~make~BRING.FORTH⁽ⱽ⁾ No'ahh AT Shem AT Hham and~AT Yaphet

Chapter 6

6:1 and~he~will~EXIST⁽ⱽ⁾ GIVEN.THAT he~did~make~DRILL⁽ⱽ⁾ the~HUMAN to~>~INCREASE.IN.NUMBER⁽ⱽ⁾ UPON FACE~s the~GROUND and~DAUGHTER~s BRING.FORTH⁽ⱽ⁾~ed⁽ᵐᵖ⁾ to~them⁽ᵐ⁾ **6:2** and~they⁽ᵐ⁾~will~SEE⁽ⱽ⁾ SON~s the~Elohiym AT DAUGHTER~s the~HUMAN GIVEN.THAT FUNCTIONAL~s THEY⁽ᶠ⁾ and~they⁽ᵐ⁾~will~TAKE⁽ⱽ⁾ to~them⁽ᵐ⁾ WOMAN~s from~ALL WHICH they~did~CHOOSE⁽ⱽ⁾ **6:3** and~he~will~SAY⁽ⱽ⁾ **YHWH** NOT he~will~MODERATE⁽ⱽ⁾ WIND~me in~the~HUMAN to~DISTANT in~which~ALSO HE FLESH and~they~did~EXIST⁽ⱽ⁾ DAY~s~him HUNDRED and~TEN~s YEAR **6:4** the~Nephilim~s they~did~EXIST⁽ⱽ⁾ in~the~LAND in~the~DAY~s the~THEY⁽ᵐ⁾ and~ALSO AFTER SO WHICH they⁽ᵐ⁾~will~COME⁽ⱽ⁾ SON~s the~Elohiym TO DAUGHTER~s the~HUMAN and~they⁽ᵐ⁾~will~BRING.FORTH⁽ⱽ⁾ to~them⁽ᵐ⁾ THEY⁽ᵐ⁾ the~COURAGEOUS~s WHICH from~DISTANT MAN~s the~TITLE **6:5** and~he~will~SEE⁽ⱽ⁾ **YHWH** GIVEN.THAT ABUNDANT DYSFUNCTIONAL the~HUMAN in~the~LAND and~ALL THOUGHT INVENTION~s HEART~him ONLY DYSFUNCTIONAL ALL the~DAY **6:6** and~he~will~be~COMFORT⁽ⱽ⁾ **YHWH** GIVEN.THAT he~did~DO⁽ⱽ⁾ AT the~HUMAN in~the~LAND and~he~will~self~DISTRESS⁽ⱽ⁾ TO HEART~him **6:7** and~he~will~SAY⁽ⱽ⁾ **YHWH** I~will~WIPE.AWAY⁽ⱽ⁾ AT the~HUMAN WHICH I~did~SHAPE⁽ⱽ⁾ from~UPON FACE~s the~GROUND from~HUMAN UNTIL BEAST UNTIL TREADER and~UNTIL FLYER the~SKY~s2 GIVEN.THAT I~did~be~COMFORT⁽ⱽ⁾ GIVEN.THAT I~did~DO⁽ⱽ⁾~them⁽ᵐ⁾ **6:8** and~No'ahh he~did~FIND⁽ⱽ⁾ BEAUTY in~EYE~s2 **YHWH** **6:9** THESE BIRTHING~s No'ahh No'ahh MAN STEADFAST.ONE WHOLE he~did~EXIST⁽ⱽ⁾ in~GENERATION~s~him AT the~Elohiym he~did~self~WALK⁽ⱽ⁾ No'ahh **6:10** and~he~will~make~BRING.FORTH⁽ⱽ⁾ No'ahh THREE SON~s AT Shem AT Hham and~AT Yaphet **6:11** and~she~will~be~DAMAGE⁽ⱽ⁾ the~LAND to~FACE~s the~Elohiym and~she~will~be~FILL⁽ⱽ⁾ the~LAND VIOLENCE **6:12** and~he~will~SEE⁽ⱽ⁾ Elohiym AT the~LAND and~LOOK she~did~be~DAMAGE⁽ⱽ⁾ GIVEN.THAT he~did~make~DAMAGE⁽ⱽ⁾ ALL FLESH AT ROAD~him UPON the~LAND **6:13** and~he~will~SAY⁽ⱽ⁾ Elohiym to~No'ahh CONCLUSION ALL FLESH he~did~COME⁽ⱽ⁾ to~FACE~s~me GIVEN.THAT she~did~FILL⁽ⱽ⁾ the~LAND VIOLENCE from~FACE~s~them⁽ᵐ⁾ and~LOOK~me make~DAMAGE⁽ⱽ⁾~ing⁽ᵐˢ⁾~them⁽ᵐ⁾ AT the~LAND **6:14** !⁽ᵐˢ⁾~DO⁽ⱽ⁾ to~you⁽ᵐˢ⁾ VESSEL TREE~s GOPHER NEST~s you⁽ᵐˢ⁾~will~DO⁽ⱽ⁾ AT the~VESSEL and~you⁽ᵐˢ⁾~did~COVER⁽ⱽ⁾ AT~her from~HOUSE and~from~OUTSIDE in~the~COVERING **6:15** and~THIS WHICH you⁽ᵐˢ⁾~will~DO⁽ⱽ⁾ AT~her THREE HUNDRED~s AMMAH LENGTH the~VESSEL FIVE~s AMMAH WIDTH~her and~THREE~s AMMAH HEIGHT~her **6:16** GLISTENING you⁽ᵐˢ⁾~will~DO⁽ⱽ⁾ to~the~VESSEL and~TO AMMAH you⁽ᵐˢ⁾~will~much~FINISH⁽ⱽ⁾~her from~to~UPWARD~her and~OPENING the~VESSEL in~SIDE~her you⁽ᵐˢ⁾~will~PLACE⁽ⱽ⁾ LOWER.PART~s SECOND~s and~THIRD~s you⁽ᵐˢ⁾~will~DO⁽ⱽ⁾~her **6:17** and~I LOOK~me *make~COME⁽ⱽ⁾~ing⁽ᵐˢ⁾* AT the~FLOOD WATER~s2 UPON the~LAND to~>~much~DAMAGE⁽ⱽ⁾ ALL FLESH WHICH in~him WIND LIVING~s from~UNDER the~SKY~s2 ALL WHICH in~the~LAND *he~will~*EXPIRE⁽ⱽ⁾ **6:18** and~*I~did~make~*RISE⁽ⱽ⁾ AT COVENANT~me AT~you⁽ᶠˢ⁾ and~*you⁽ᵐˢ⁾~did~*COME⁽ⱽ⁾ TO the~VESSEL YOU⁽ᵐˢ⁾ and~SON~s~you⁽ᵐˢ⁾ and~WOMAN~you⁽ᵐˢ⁾ and~WOMAN~s SON~s~you⁽ᵐˢ⁾ AT~you⁽ᶠˢ⁾ **6:19** and~from~ALL the~LIVING from~ALL FLESH TWO from~ALL you⁽ᵐˢ⁾~*will~make~*COME⁽ⱽ⁾ TO the~VESSEL to~>~*make~*LIVE⁽ⱽ⁾ AT~you⁽ᶠˢ⁾ MALE and~FEMALE *they⁽ᵐ⁾~will~*EXIST⁽ⱽ⁾ **6:20** from~the~FLYER to~KIND~him and~FROM the~BEAST to~KIND~her from~ALL TREADER the~GROUND to~KIND~him TWO from~ALL *they⁽ᵐ⁾~will~*COME⁽ⱽ⁾ TO~you⁽ᵐˢ⁾ to~>~*make~*LIVE⁽ⱽ⁾ **6:21** and~YOU⁽ᵐˢ⁾ *!⁽ᵐˢ⁾~*TAKE⁽ⱽ⁾ to~you⁽ᵐˢ⁾ from~ALL NOURISHMENT WHICH *he~will~be~*EAT⁽ⱽ⁾ and~*you⁽ᵐˢ⁾~did~*GATHER⁽ⱽ⁾ TO~you⁽ᵐˢ⁾ and~*he~did~*EXIST⁽ⱽ⁾ to~you⁽ᵐˢ⁾ and~to~them⁽ᵐ⁾ to~FOOD **6:22** and~*he~will~*DO⁽ⱽ⁾ No'ahh like~ALL WHICH *he~did~much~*DIRECT⁽ⱽ⁾ AT~him Elohiym SO *he~did~*DO⁽ⱽ⁾

Chapter 7

7:1 and~*he~will~*SAY⁽ⱽ⁾ **YHWH** to~No'ahh *!⁽ᵐˢ⁾~*COME⁽ⱽ⁾ YOU⁽ᵐˢ⁾ and~ALL HOUSE~you⁽ᵐˢ⁾ TO the~VESSEL GIVEN.THAT AT~you⁽ᵐˢ⁾ *I~did~*SEE⁽ⱽ⁾ STEADFAST.ONE to~FACE~s~me in~the~GENERATION the~THIS **7:2** from~ALL the~BEAST the~CLEAN *you⁽ᵐˢ⁾~will~*TAKE⁽ⱽ⁾ to~you⁽ᵐˢ⁾ SEVEN SEVEN MAN and~WOMAN~him and~FROM the~BEAST WHICH NOT CLEAN SHE TWO MAN and~WOMAN~him **7:3** ALSO from~FLYER the~SKY~s2 SEVEN SEVEN MALE and~FEMALE to~>~*much~*LIVE⁽ⱽ⁾ SEED UPON FACE~s ALL the~LAND **7:4** GIVEN.THAT to~DAY~s YET.AGAIN SEVEN I *make~*PRECIPITATE⁽ⱽ⁾~*ing⁽ᵐˢ⁾* UPON the~LAND FOUR~s DAY and~FOUR~s NIGHT and~*I~did~*WIPE.AWAY⁽ⱽ⁾ AT ALL the~SUBSTANCE WHICH *I~did~*DO⁽ⱽ⁾ from~UPON FACE~s the~GROUND **7:5** and~*he~will~*DO⁽ⱽ⁾ No'ahh like~ALL WHICH *he~did~much~*DIRECT⁽ⱽ⁾~him **YHWH** **7:6** and~No'ahh SON SIX HUNDRED~s YEAR and~the~FLOOD *he~did~*EXIST⁽ⱽ⁾ WATER~s2 UPON the~LAND **7:7** and~*he~will~*COME⁽ⱽ⁾ No'ahh and~SON~s~him and~WOMAN~him and~WOMAN~s SON~s~him AT~him TO the~VESSEL from~FACE~s WATER~s2 the~FLOOD **7:8** FROM the~BEAST the~CLEAN and~FROM the~BEAST WHICH WITHOUT~her CLEAN and~FROM the~FLYER and~ALL WHICH TREAD⁽ⱽ⁾~*ing⁽ᵐˢ⁾* UPON the~GROUND **7:9** TWO TWO *they~did~*COME⁽ⱽ⁾ TO No'ahh TO the~VESSEL MALE and~FEMALE like~WHICH *he~did~much~*DIRECT⁽ⱽ⁾ Elohiym AT No'ahh **7:10** and~*he~will~*EXIST⁽ⱽ⁾ to~SEVEN the~DAY~s and~WATER~s2 the~FLOOD *they~did~*EXIST⁽ⱽ⁾ UPON the~LAND **7:11** in~YEAR SIX HUNDRED~s YEAR to~LIVING~s No'ahh in~the~

NEW.MOON the~SECOND in~SEVEN TEN DAY to~the~NEW.MOON in~the~ DAY the~THIS *they~did~be*~CLEAVE.OPEN⁽ᵛ⁾ ALL SPRING~s DEEP.WATER ABUNDANT and~CHIMNEY~s the~SKY~s2 *they~did~be*~OPEN⁽ᵛ⁾ **7:12** and~ *he~will*~EXIST⁽ᵛ⁾ the~RAIN.SHOWER UPON the~LAND FOUR~s DAY and~ FOUR~s NIGHT **7:13** in~BONE the~DAY the~THIS *he~did*~COME⁽ᵛ⁾ No'ahh and~Shem and~Hham and~Yaphet SON~s No'ahh and~WOMAN No'ahh and~THREE WOMAN~s SON~s~him AT~them⁽ᵐ⁾ TO the~VESSEL **7:14** THEY⁽ᵐ⁾ and~ALL the~LIVING to~KIND~her and~ALL the~BEAST to~KIND~her and~ ALL the~TREADER the~TREAD⁽ᵛ⁾~*ing*⁽ᵐˢ⁾ UPON the~LAND to~KIND~him and~ ALL the~FLYER to~KIND~him ALL BIRD ALL WING **7:15** and~*they*⁽ᵐ⁾*~will*~ COME⁽ᵛ⁾ TO No'ahh TO the~VESSEL TWO TWO from~ALL the~FLESH WHICH in~him WIND LIVING~s **7:16** and~the~COME⁽ᵛ⁾~*ing*⁽ᵐᵖ⁾ MALE and~FEMALE from~ALL FLESH *they~did*~COME⁽ᵛ⁾ like~WHICH *he~did~much*~DIRECT⁽ᵛ⁾ AT~ him Elohiym and~*he~will*~SHUT⁽ᵛ⁾ **YHWH** in~UNTIL~him **7:17** and~*he~will*~ EXIST⁽ᵛ⁾ the~FLOOD FOUR~s DAY UPON the~LAND and~*they*⁽ᵐ⁾*~will*~ INCREASE⁽ᵛ⁾ the~WATER~s2 and~*they*⁽ᵐ⁾*~will*~LIFT.UP⁽ᵛ⁾ AT the~VESSEL and~ *she~will*~RAISE.UP⁽ᵛ⁾ from~UPON the~LAND **7:18** and~*they*⁽ᵐ⁾*~will*~ OVERCOME⁽ᵛ⁾ the~WATER~s2 and~*they*⁽ᵐ⁾*~will*~INCREASE⁽ᵛ⁾ MANY UPON the~LAND and~*she~will*~WALK⁽ᵛ⁾ the~VESSEL UPON FACE~s the~WATER~ s2 **7:19** and~the~WATER~s2 *they~did*~OVERCOME⁽ᵛ⁾ MANY MANY UPON the~LAND and~*they*⁽ᵐ⁾*~will~much*~COVER.OVER⁽ᵛ⁾ ALL the~HILL~s the~ HIGH~s WHICH UNDER ALL the~SKY~s2 **7:20** FIVE TEN AMMAH from~to~ UPWARD~her *they~did*~OVERCOME⁽ᵛ⁾ the~WATER~s2 and~*they*⁽ᵐ⁾*~will*~ *much*~COVER.OVER⁽ᵛ⁾ the~HILL~s **7:21** and~*he~will*~EXPIRE⁽ᵛ⁾ ALL FLESH the~TREAD⁽ᵛ⁾~*ing*⁽ᵐˢ⁾ UPON the~LAND in~the~FLYER and~in~the~BEAST and~in~the~LIVING and~in~ALL the~SWARMER the~SWARM⁽ᵛ⁾~*ing*⁽ᵐˢ⁾ UPON the~LAND and~ALL the~HUMAN **7:22** ALL WHICH BREATH WIND LIVING~s in~NOSE~s2~him from~ALL WHICH in~the~DRIED.OUT *they~did*~ DIE⁽ᵛ⁾ **7:23** and~*he~will*~WIPE.AWAY⁽ᵛ⁾ AT ALL the~SUBSTANCE WHICH UPON FACE~s the~GROUND from~HUMAN UNTIL BEAST UNTIL TREADER and~UNTIL FLYER the~SKY~s2 and~*they*⁽ᵐ⁾*~will~be*~WIPE.AWAY⁽ᵛ⁾ FROM the~LAND and~*he~will~be*~REMAIN⁽ᵛ⁾ SURELY No'ahh and~WHICH AT~him in~the~VESSEL **7:24** and~*they*⁽ᵐ⁾*~will*~OVERCOME⁽ᵛ⁾ the~WATER~s2 UPON the~LAND FIVE~s and~HUNDRED DAY

Chapter 8

8:1 and~*he~will*~REMEMBER⁽ᵛ⁾ Elohiym AT No'ahh and~AT ALL the~LIVING and~AT ALL the~BEAST WHICH AT~him in~the~VESSEL and~*he~will~make*~ CROSS.OVER⁽ᵛ⁾ Elohiym WIND UPON the~LAND and~*they*⁽ᵐ⁾*~will*~SUBSIDE⁽ᵛ⁾ the~WATER~s2 **8:2** and~*they*⁽ᵐ⁾*~will~be*~SHUT⁽ᵛ⁾ SPRING~s DEEP.WATER and~CHIMNEY~s the~SKY~s2 and~*he~will~be*~RESTRICT⁽ᵛ⁾ the~ RAIN.SHOWER FROM the~SKY~s2 **8:3** and~*they*⁽ᵐ⁾*~will*~TURN.BACK⁽ᵛ⁾ the~

WATER~s2 from~UPON the~LAND >~WALK⁽ᵛ⁾ and~>~TURN.BACK⁽ᵛ⁾ and~
they⁽ᵐ⁾~will~DIMINISH⁽ᵛ⁾ the~WATER~s2 from~EXTREMITY FIVE~s and~
HUNDRED DAY **8:4** and~she~will~REST⁽ᵛ⁾ the~VESSEL in~the~NEW.MOON
the~SEVENTH in~SEVEN TEN DAY to~the~NEW.MOON UPON HILL~s
Ararat **8:5** and~the~WATER~s2 they~did~EXIST⁽ᵛ⁾ >~WALK⁽ᵛ⁾ and~>~
DIMINISH⁽ᵛ⁾ UNTIL the~NEW.MOON the~TENTH in~the~TENTH in~UNIT to~
the~NEW.MOON they~did~be~SEE⁽ᵛ⁾ HEAD~s the~HILL~s **8:6** and~he~will~
EXIST⁽ᵛ⁾ from~CONCLUSION FOUR~s DAY and~he~will~OPEN⁽ᵛ⁾ No'ahh AT
WINDOW the~VESSEL WHICH he~did~DO⁽ᵛ⁾ **8:7** and~he~will~much~SEND⁽ᵛ⁾
AT the~RAVEN and~he~will~GO.OUT⁽ᵛ⁾ >~GO.OUT⁽ᵛ⁾ and~>~TURN.BACK⁽ᵛ⁾
UNTIL >~DRY.OUT⁽ᵛ⁾ the~WATER~s2 from~UPON the~LAND **8:8** and~he~
will~much~SEND⁽ᵛ⁾ AT the~DOVE from~AT~him to~>~SEE⁽ᵛ⁾ ?~they~did~
BELITTLE⁽ᵛ⁾ the~WATER~s2 from~UPON FACE~s the~GROUND **8:9** and~NOT
she~did~FIND⁽ᵛ⁾ the~DOVE OASIS to~PALM FOOT~her and~she~will~
TURN.BACK⁽ᵛ⁾ TO~him TO the~VESSEL GIVEN.THAT WATER~s2 UPON FACE~s
ALL the~LAND and~he~will~SEND⁽ᵛ⁾ HAND~him and~he~will~TAKE⁽ᵛ⁾~her
and~he~will~make~COME⁽ᵛ⁾ AT~her TO~him TO the~VESSEL **8:10** and~he~
will~TWIST⁽ᵛ⁾ YET.AGAIN SEVEN DAY~s OTHER~s and~he~will~make~ADD⁽ᵛ⁾
!⁽ᵐˢ⁾~much~SEND⁽ᵛ⁾ AT the~DOVE FROM the~VESSEL **8:11** and~she~will~
COME⁽ᵛ⁾ TO~him the~DOVE to~APPOINTED.TIME EVENING and~LOOK LEAF
OLIVE PREY in~MOUTH~her and~he~will~KNOW⁽ᵛ⁾ No'ahh GIVEN.THAT
they~did~BELITTLE⁽ᵛ⁾ the~WATER~s2 from~UPON the~LAND **8:12** and~he~
will~TWIST⁽ᵛ⁾ YET.AGAIN SEVEN DAY~s OTHER~s and~he~will~much~SEND⁽ᵛ⁾
AT the~DOVE and~NOT she~did~ADD⁽ᵛ⁾ >~TURN.BACK⁽ᵛ⁾ TO~him
YET.AGAIN **8:13** and~he~will~EXIST⁽ᵛ⁾ in~UNIT and~SIX HUNDRED~s YEAR
in~the~FIRST in~UNIT to~the~NEW.MOON they~did~DRY.UP⁽ᵛ⁾ the~
WATER~s2 from~UPON the~LAND and~he~will~make~TURN.ASIDE⁽ᵛ⁾
No'ahh AT ROOF.COVERING the~VESSEL and~he~will~SEE⁽ᵛ⁾ and~LOOK
they~did~DRY.UP⁽ᵛ⁾ FACE~s the~GROUND **8:14** and~in~the~NEW.MOON
the~SECOND in~SEVEN and~TEN~s DAY to~the~NEW.MOON she~did~
DRY.OUT⁽ᵛ⁾ the~LAND **8:15** and~he~will~much~SPEAK⁽ᵛ⁾ Elohiym TO No'ahh
to~>~SAY⁽ᵛ⁾ **8:16** !⁽ᵐˢ⁾~GO.OUT⁽ᵛ⁾ FROM the~VESSEL YOU⁽ᵐˢ⁾ and~WOMAN~
you⁽ᵐˢ⁾ and~SON~s~you⁽ᵐˢ⁾ and~WOMAN~s SON~s~you⁽ᵐˢ⁾ AT~
you⁽ᶠˢ⁾ **8:17** ALL the~LIVING WHICH AT~you⁽ᵐˢ⁾ from~ALL FLESH in~the~
FLYER and~in~the~BEAST and~in~ALL the~TREADER the~TREAD⁽ᵛ⁾~ing⁽ᵐˢ⁾
UPON the~LAND !⁽ᵐᵖ⁾~make~GO.OUT⁽ᵛ⁾ AT~you⁽ᶠˢ⁾ and~they~did~SWARM⁽ᵛ⁾
in~the~LAND and~they~did~REPRODUCE⁽ᵛ⁾ and~they~did~INCREASE⁽ᵛ⁾
UPON the~LAND **8:18** and~he~will~GO.OUT⁽ᵛ⁾ No'ahh and~SON~s~him
and~WOMAN~him and~WOMAN~s SON~s~him AT~him **8:19** ALL the~
LIVING ALL the~TREADER and~ALL the~FLYER ALL TREAD⁽ᵛ⁾~ing⁽ᵐˢ⁾ UPON
the~LAND to~CLAN~s~them⁽ᵐ⁾ they~did~GO.OUT⁽ᵛ⁾ FROM the~
VESSEL **8:20** and~he~will~BUILD⁽ᵛ⁾ No'ahh ALTAR to~**YHWH** and~he~will~
TAKE⁽ᵛ⁾ from~ALL the~BEAST the~CLEAN and~from~ALL the~FLYER the~
CLEAN and~he~will~make~GO.UP⁽ᵛ⁾ ASCENSION.OFFERING~s in~the~
ALTAR **8:21** and~he~will~make~SMELL⁽ᵛ⁾ **YHWH** AT AROMA the~SWEET

and~*he~will~*SAY⁽ᵛ⁾ **YHWH** TO HEART~him NOT *I~will~make~*ADD⁽ᵛ⁾ to~>~ *much~*BELITTLE⁽ᵛ⁾ YET.AGAIN AT the~GROUND in~the~CROSS.OVER⁽ᵛ⁾*~ed*⁽ᵐˢ⁾ the~HUMAN GIVEN.THAT THOUGHT HEART the~HUMAN DYSFUNCTIONAL from~YOUNG.AGE~s*~him* and~NOT *I~will~make~*ADD⁽ᵛ⁾ YET.AGAIN to~>~ *make~*HIT⁽ᵛ⁾ AT ALL LIVING like~WHICH *I~did~*DO⁽ᵛ⁾ **8:22** YET.AGAIN ALL DAY~s the~LAND SEED and~HARVEST and~COLD and~HOT and~SUMMER and~WINTER and~DAY and~NIGHT NOT *they*⁽ᵐ⁾*~will~*CEASE⁽ᵛ⁾

Chapter 9

9:1 and~*he~will~much~*KNEEL⁽ᵛ⁾ Elohiym AT No'ahh and~AT SON~s~him and~*he~will~*SAY⁽ᵛ⁾ to~them⁽ᵐ⁾ *!*⁽ᵐᵖ⁾*~*REPRODUCE⁽ᵛ⁾ and~ *!*⁽ᵐᵖ⁾*~*INCREASE⁽ᵛ⁾ and~ *!*⁽ᵐᵖ⁾*~*FILL⁽ᵛ⁾ AT the~LAND **9:2** and~FEARING~you⁽ᵐᵖ⁾ and~ TREMBLING.IN.FEAR~you⁽ᵐᵖ⁾ *he~will~*EXIST⁽ᵛ⁾ UPON ALL LIVING the~LAND and~UPON ALL FLYER the~SKY~s2 in~ALL WHICH *she~will~*TREAD⁽ᵛ⁾ the~ GROUND and~in~ALL FISH~s the~SEA in~HAND~you⁽ᵐᵖ⁾ *they~did~be~* GIVE⁽ᵛ⁾ **9:3** ALL TREADER WHICH HE LIVING to~you⁽ᵐᵖ⁾ *he~will~*EXIST⁽ᵛ⁾ to~ FOOD like~GREEN HERB *I~did~*GIVE⁽ᵛ⁾ to~you⁽ᵐᵖ⁾ AT ALL **9:4** SURELY FLESH in~SOUL~him BLOOD~him NOT *you*⁽ᵐᵖ⁾*~will~*EAT⁽ᵛ⁾ **9:5** and~SURELY AT BLOOD~you⁽ᵐᵖ⁾ to~SOUL~s~you⁽ᵐᵖ⁾ *I~will~*SEEK⁽ᵛ⁾ from~HAND ALL LIVING *I~ will~*SEEK⁽ᵛ⁾*~him* and~from~HAND the~HUMAN from~HAND MAN BROTHER~him *I~will~*SEEK⁽ᵛ⁾ AT SOUL the~HUMAN **9:6** POUR.OUT⁽ᵛ⁾*~ing*⁽ᵐˢ⁾ BLOOD the~HUMAN in~the~HUMAN BLOOD~him *he~will~be~*POUR.OUT⁽ᵛ⁾ GIVEN.THAT in~IMAGE Elohiym *he~did~*DO⁽ᵛ⁾ AT the~HUMAN **9:7** and~ YOU⁽ᵐᵖ⁾ *!*⁽ᵐᵖ⁾*~*REPRODUCE⁽ᵛ⁾ and~ *!*⁽ᵐᵖ⁾*~*INCREASE⁽ᵛ⁾ *!*⁽ᵐᵖ⁾*~*SWARM⁽ᵛ⁾ in~the~ LAND and~ *!*⁽ᵐᵖ⁾*~*INCREASE⁽ᵛ⁾ in~her **9:8** and~*he~will~*SAY⁽ᵛ⁾ Elohiym TO No'ahh and~TO SON~s~him AT~him to~>~*SAY*⁽ᵛ⁾ **9:9** and~I LOOK~me *make~* RISE⁽ᵛ⁾*~ing*⁽ᵐˢ⁾ AT COVENANT~me AT~you⁽ᵐᵖ⁾ and~AT SEED~you⁽ᵐᵖ⁾ AFTER~ you⁽ᵐᵖ⁾ **9:10** and~AT ALL SOUL the~LIVING WHICH AT~you⁽ᵐᵖ⁾ in~the~FLYER in~the~BEAST and~in~ALL LIVING the~LAND AT~you⁽ᵐᵖ⁾ from~ALL GO.OUT⁽ᵛ⁾*~ing*⁽ᵐᵖ⁾ the~VESSEL to~ALL LIVING the~LAND **9:11** and~*I~did~ make~*RISE⁽ᵛ⁾ AT COVENANT~me AT~you⁽ᵐᵖ⁾ and~NOT *he~will~be~*CUT⁽ᵛ⁾ ALL FLESH YET.AGAIN from~WATER~s2 the~FLOOD and~NOT *he~will~*EXIST⁽ᵛ⁾ YET.AGAIN FLOOD to~>~*much~*DAMAGE⁽ᵛ⁾ the~LAND **9:12** and~*he~will~* SAY⁽ᵛ⁾ Elohiym THIS SIGN the~COVENANT WHICH I GIVE⁽ᵛ⁾*~ing*⁽ᵐˢ⁾ BETWEEN~ me and~BETWEEN~you⁽ᵐᵖ⁾ and~BETWEEN ALL SOUL LIVING WHICH AT~ you⁽ᵐᵖ⁾ to~GENERATION~s DISTANT **9:13** AT BOW~me *I~did~*GIVE⁽ᵛ⁾ in~ CLOUD and~*she~did~*EXIST⁽ᵛ⁾ to~SIGN COVENANT BETWEEN~me and~ BETWEEN the~LAND **9:14** and~*he~did~*EXIST⁽ᵛ⁾ in~>~*much~*CONJURE⁽ᵛ⁾*~*me CLOUD UPON the~LAND and~*she~did~be~*SEE⁽ᵛ⁾ the~BOW in~ CLOUD **9:15** and~*I~did~*REMEMBER⁽ᵛ⁾ AT COVENANT~me WHICH BETWEEN~me and~BETWEEN~you⁽ᵐᵖ⁾ and~BETWEEN ALL SOUL LIVING in~ ALL FLESH and~NOT *he~will~*EXIST⁽ᵛ⁾ YET.AGAIN the~WATER~s2 to~FLOOD

The Book of Genesis

to~>~much~DAMAGE⁽ᵛ⁾ ALL FLESH **9:16** and~she~did~EXIST⁽ᵛ⁾ the~BOW in~ CLOUD and~I~did~SEE⁽ᵛ⁾~her to~>~REMEMBER⁽ᵛ⁾ COVENANT DISTANT BETWEEN Elohiym and~BETWEEN ALL SOUL LIVING in~ALL FLESH WHICH UPON the~LAND **9:17** and~he~will~SAY⁽ᵛ⁾ Elohiym TO No'ahh THIS SIGN the~COVENANT WHICH I~did~make~RISE⁽ᵛ⁾ BETWEEN~me and~BETWEEN ALL FLESH WHICH UPON the~LAND **9:18** and~they⁽ᵐ⁾~will~EXIST⁽ᵛ⁾ SON~s No'ahh the~GO.OUT⁽ᵛ⁾~ing⁽ᵐᵖ⁾ FROM the~VESSEL Shem and~Hham and~ Yaphet and~Hham HE FATHER~of Kena'an **9:19** THREE THESE SON~s No'ahh and~from~THESE she~did~SCATTER⁽ᵛ⁾ ALL the~LAND **9:20** and~he~will~ make~DRILL⁽ᵛ⁾ No'ahh MAN the~GROUND and~he~will~PLANT⁽ᵛ⁾ VINEYARD **9:21** and~he~will~GULP⁽ᵛ⁾ FROM the~WINE and~he~will~ BE.DRUNK⁽ᵛ⁾ and~he~will~make~self~REMOVE.THE.COVER⁽ᵛ⁾ in~MIDST TENT~her **9:22** and~he~will~SEE⁽ᵛ⁾ Hham FATHER~of Kena'an AT NAKEDNESS FATHER~him and~he~will~make~BE.FACE.TO.FACE⁽ᵛ⁾ to~TWO BROTHER~s~him in~the~OUTSIDE **9:23** and~he~will~TAKE⁽ᵛ⁾ Shem and~ Yaphet AT the~APPAREL and~they⁽ᵐ⁾~will~PLACE⁽ᵛ⁾ UPON SHOULDER TWO~ them⁽ᵐ⁾ and~they⁽ᵐ⁾~will~WALK⁽ᵛ⁾ BACKWARD and~they⁽ᵐ⁾~will~much~ COVER.OVER⁽ᵛ⁾ AT NAKEDNESS FATHER~them⁽ᵐ⁾ and~FACE~s~them⁽ᵐ⁾ BACKWARD and~NAKEDNESS FATHER~them⁽ᵐ⁾ NOT they~did~ SEE⁽ᵛ⁾ **9:24** and~he~will~AWAKE⁽ᵛ⁾ No'ahh from~WINE~him and~he~will~ KNOW⁽ᵛ⁾ AT WHICH he~did~DO⁽ᵛ⁾ to~him SON~him the~SMALL **9:25** and~ he~will~SAY⁽ᵛ⁾ SPIT.UPON⁽ᵛ⁾~ed⁽ᵐˢ⁾ Kena'an SERVANT SERVANT~s he~will~ EXIST⁽ᵛ⁾ to~BROTHER~s~him **9:26** and~he~will~SAY⁽ᵛ⁾ KNEEL⁽ᵛ⁾~ed⁽ᵐˢ⁾ **YHWH** Elohiym Shem and~he~will~EXIST⁽ᵛ⁾ Kena'an SERVANT to~them⁽ᵐ⁾ **9:27** he~ will~make~SPREAD.WIDE⁽ᵛ⁾ Elohiym to~Yaphet and~he~will~DWELL⁽ᵛ⁾ in~ TENT~s Shem and~he~will~EXIST⁽ᵛ⁾ Kena'an SERVANT to~them⁽ᵐ⁾ **9:28** and~ he~will~LIVE⁽ᵛ⁾ No'ahh AFTER the~FLOOD THREE HUNDRED~s YEAR and~ FIVE~s YEAR **9:29** and~they⁽ᵐ⁾~will~EXIST⁽ᵛ⁾ ALL DAY~s No'ahh NINE HUNDRED~s YEAR and~FIVE~s YEAR and~he~will~DIE⁽ᵛ⁾

Chapter 10

10:1 and~THESE BIRTHING~s SON~s No'ahh Shem Hham and~Yaphet and~ they⁽ᵐ⁾~will~be~BRING.FORTH⁽ᵛ⁾ to~them⁽ᵐ⁾ SON~s AFTER the~ FLOOD **10:2** SON~s Yaphet Gomer and~Magog and~Madai and~Yawan and~Tuval and~Meshek and~Tiras **10:3** and~SON~s Gomer Ashkanaz and~ Riphat and~Togarmah **10:4** and~SON~s Yawan Elishah and~Tarshish Kit~s and~Dodan~s **10:5** from~THESE they~did~be~DIVIDE.APART⁽ᵛ⁾ ISLAND~s the~NATION~s in~LAND~s~them⁽ᵐ⁾ MAN to~TONGUE~him to~CLAN~s~ them⁽ᵐ⁾ in~NATION~s~them⁽ᵐ⁾ **10:6** and~SON~s Hham Kush and~Mits'rayim and~Put and~Kena'an **10:7** and~SON~s Kush Seva and~Hhawilah and~ Savtah and~Ramah and~Savtekha and~SON~s Ramah Sheva and~ Dedan **10:8** and~Kush he~did~BRING.FORTH⁽ᵛ⁾ AT Nimrod HE he~did~

make~DRILL(V) to~>~EXIST(V) COURAGEOUS in~the~LAND **10:9** HE *he~did~*EXIST(V) COURAGEOUS HUNTER to~FACE~s **YHWH** UPON SO *he~will~be~*SAY(V) like~Nimrod COURAGEOUS HUNTER to~FACE~s **YHWH** **10:10** and~*she~will~*EXIST(V) SUMMIT KINGDOM~him Bavel and~Erekh and~Akad and~Kalneh in~LAND Shinar **10:11** FROM the~LAND the~SHE *he~did~*GO.OUT(V) Ashur and~*he~will~*BUILD(V) AT Ninweh and~AT Rehhovot-Ghir and~AT Kalahh **10:12** and~AT Resen BETWEEN Ninweh and~BETWEEN Kalahh SHE the~CITY the~GREAT **10:13** and~Mits'rayim *he~did~*BRING.FORTH(V) AT Lud~s and~AT Anam and~AT Lehav~s and~AT Naphtuhh~s **10:14** and~AT Patros~s and~AT Kasluhh~s WHICH *they~did~*GO.OUT(V) from~THERE Peleshet~s and~AT Kaphtor~s **10:15** and~Kena'an *he~did~*BRING.FORTH(V) AT Tsidon FIRSTBORN~him and~AT Hhet **10:16** and~AT the~Yevus~of and~AT the~Emor~of and~AT the~Girgash~of **10:17** and~AT the~Hhiw~of and~AT the~Araq~of and~AT the~Sin~of **10:18** and~AT the~Arwad~of and~AT the~Tsemar~of and~AT the~Hhamat~of and~AFTER *they~did~be~*SCATTER.ABROAD(V) CLAN~s the~Kena'an~of **10:19** and~*he~will~*EXIST(V) BORDER the~Kena'an~of from~Tsidon >~COME(V)~*you*(ms)~& Gerar~unto UNTIL Ghaza >~COME(V)~*you*(ms)~& Sedom~unto and~Ghamorah and~Admah and~Tseviim UNTIL Lesha **10:20** THESE SON~s Hham to~CLAN~s~them(m) to~TONGUE~s~them(m) in~LAND~s~them(m) in~NATION~s~them(m) **10:21** and~to~Shem BRING.FORTH(V)~*ed*(ms) ALSO HE FATHER~of ALL SON~s Ever BROTHER~of Yaphet the~GREAT **10:22** SON~s Shem Elam and~Ashur and~Arpakhshad and~Lud and~Aram **10:23** and~SON~s Aram Uts and~Hhul and~Getar and~Mash **10:24** and~Arpakhshad *he~did~*BRING.FORTH(V) AT *he~did~*SEND(V) and~Shelahh *he~did~*BRING.FORTH(V) AT Ever **10:25** and~to~Ever BRING.FORTH(V)~*ed*(ms) TWO SON~s TITLE the~UNIT Peleg GIVEN.THAT in~DAY~s~him *she~did~be~*SPLIT(V) the~LAND and~TITLE BROTHER~him Yaqtan **10:26** and~Yaqtan *he~did~*BRING.FORTH(V) AT Almodad and~AT Sheleph and~AT Hhatsarmawet and~AT Yerahh **10:27** and~AT Hadoram and~AT Uzal and~AT Diqlah **10:28** and~AT Uval and~AT Aviyma'el and~AT Sheva **10:29** and~AT Ophir and~AT Hhawilah and~AT Yovav ALL THESE SON~s Yaqtan **10:30** and~*he~will~*EXIST(V) SETTLING~them(m) from~Mesha >~COME(V)~*you*(ms)~& Sephar~unto HILL the~EAST **10:31** THESE SON~s Shem to~CLAN~s~them(m) to~TONGUE~s~them(m) in~LAND~s~them(m) to~NATION~s~them(m) **10:32** THESE CLAN~s SON~s No'ahh to~BIRTHING~s~them(m) in~NATION~s~them(m) and~from~THESE *they~did~be~*DIVIDE.APART(V) the~NATION~s in~the~LAND AFTER the~FLOOD

Chapter 11

11:1 and~*he~will~*EXIST(V) ALL the~LAND LIP UNIT and~WORD~s UNIT~s **11:2** and~*he~will~*EXIST(V) in~>~JOURNEY(V)~them(m) from~EAST

The Book of Genesis

and~they⁽ᵐ⁾~will~FIND⁽ⱽ⁾ LEVEL.VALLEY in~LAND Shinar and~they⁽ᵐ⁾~will~SETTLE⁽ⱽ⁾ THERE **11:3** and~they⁽ᵐ⁾~will~SAY⁽ⱽ⁾ MAN TO COMPANION~him !⁽ᵐˢ⁾~PROVIDE⁽ⱽ⁾~& we~will~MAKE.BRICKS⁽ⱽ⁾ BRICK~s and~we~will~CREMATE⁽ⱽ⁾~& to~CREMATING and~she~will~EXIST⁽ⱽ⁾ to~them⁽ᵐ⁾ the~BRICK to~STONE and~the~SLIME he~did~EXIST⁽ⱽ⁾ to~them⁽ᵐ⁾ to~MORTAR **11:4** and~they⁽ᵐ⁾~will~SAY⁽ⱽ⁾ !⁽ᵐˢ⁾~PROVIDE⁽ⱽ⁾~& we~will~BUILD⁽ⱽ⁾ to~us CITY and~TOWER and~HEAD~him in~the~SKY~s2 and~we~will~DO⁽ⱽ⁾ to~us TITLE OTHERWISE we~will~SCATTER.ABROAD⁽ⱽ⁾ UPON FACE~s ALL the~LAND **11:5** and~he~will~GO.DOWN⁽ⱽ⁾ YHWH to~>~SEE⁽ⱽ⁾ AT the~CITY and~AT the~TOWER WHICH they~did~BUILD⁽ⱽ⁾ SON~s the~HUMAN **11:6** and~he~will~SAY⁽ⱽ⁾ YHWH THOUGH PEOPLE UNIT and~LIP UNIT to~ALL~them⁽ᵐ⁾ and~THIS >~make~DRILL⁽ⱽ⁾~them⁽ᵐ⁾ to~>~DO⁽ⱽ⁾ and~NOW NOT he~will~be~FENCE.IN⁽ⱽ⁾ from~them⁽ᵐ⁾ ALL WHICH they⁽ᵐ⁾~will~PLOT⁽ⱽ⁾ to~>~DO⁽ⱽ⁾ **11:7** !⁽ᵐˢ⁾~PROVIDE⁽ⱽ⁾~& we~will~GO.DOWN⁽ⱽ⁾~& and~we~will~MIX⁽ⱽ⁾~& THERE LIP~them⁽ᵐ⁾ WHICH NOT they⁽ᵐ⁾~will~HEAR⁽ⱽ⁾ MAN LIP COMPANION~him **11:8** and~he~will~make~SCATTER.ABROAD⁽ⱽ⁾ YHWH AT~them⁽ᵐ⁾ from~THERE UPON FACE~s ALL the~LAND and~they⁽ᵐ⁾~will~TERMINATE⁽ⱽ⁾ to~>~BUILD⁽ⱽ⁾ the~CITY **11:9** UPON SO he~did~CALL.OUT⁽ⱽ⁾ TITLE~her Bavel GIVEN.THAT THERE he~did~MIX⁽ⱽ⁾ YHWH LIP ALL the~LAND and~from~THERE he~did~make~SCATTER.ABROAD⁽ⱽ⁾~them⁽ᵐ⁾ YHWH UPON FACE~s ALL the~LAND **11:10** THESE BIRTHING~s Shem Shem SON HUNDRED YEAR and~he~will~make~BRING.FORTH⁽ⱽ⁾ AT Arpakhshad YEAR~s2 AFTER the~FLOOD **11:11** and~he~will~LIVE⁽ⱽ⁾ Shem AFTER >~make~BRING.FORTH⁽ⱽ⁾~him AT Arpakhshad FIVE HUNDRED~s YEAR and~he~will~make~BRING.FORTH⁽ⱽ⁾ SON~s and~DAUGHTER~s **11:12** and~Arpakhshad he~did~LIVE⁽ⱽ⁾ FIVE and~THREE~s YEAR and~he~will~make~BRING.FORTH⁽ⱽ⁾ AT he~did~SEND⁽ⱽ⁾ **11:13** and~he~will~LIVE⁽ⱽ⁾ Arpakhshad AFTER >~make~BRING.FORTH⁽ⱽ⁾~him AT Shelahh THREE YEAR~s and~FOUR HUNDRED~s YEAR and~he~will~make~BRING.FORTH⁽ⱽ⁾ SON~s and~DAUGHTER~s **11:14** and~Shelahh he~did~LIVE⁽ⱽ⁾ THREE~s YEAR and~he~will~make~BRING.FORTH⁽ⱽ⁾ AT Ever **11:15** and~he~will~LIVE⁽ⱽ⁾ Shelahh AFTER >~make~BRING.FORTH⁽ⱽ⁾~him AT Ever THREE YEAR~s and~FOUR HUNDRED~s YEAR and~he~will~make~BRING.FORTH⁽ⱽ⁾ SON~s and~DAUGHTER~s **11:16** and~he~will~LIVE⁽ⱽ⁾ Ever FOUR and~THREE~s YEAR and~he~will~make~BRING.FORTH⁽ⱽ⁾ AT Peleg **11:17** and~he~will~LIVE⁽ⱽ⁾ Ever AFTER >~make~BRING.FORTH⁽ⱽ⁾~him AT Peleg THREE~s YEAR and~FOUR HUNDRED~s YEAR and~he~will~make~BRING.FORTH⁽ⱽ⁾ SON~s and~DAUGHTER~s **11:18** and~he~will~LIVE⁽ⱽ⁾ Peleg THREE~s YEAR and~he~will~make~BRING.FORTH⁽ⱽ⁾ AT !⁽ᵐᵖ⁾~FEED⁽ⱽ⁾ **11:19** and~he~will~LIVE⁽ⱽ⁾ Peleg AFTER >~make~BRING.FORTH⁽ⱽ⁾~him AT !⁽ᵐᵖ⁾~FEED⁽ⱽ⁾ NINE YEAR~s and~HUNDRED~s2 YEAR and~he~will~make~BRING.FORTH⁽ⱽ⁾ SON~s and~DAUGHTER~s **11:20** and~he~will~LIVE⁽ⱽ⁾ !⁽ᵐᵖ⁾~FEED⁽ⱽ⁾ TWO and~THREE~s YEAR and~he~will~make~BRING.FORTH⁽ⱽ⁾ AT Serug **11:21** and~he~will~LIVE⁽ⱽ⁾ !⁽ᵐᵖ⁾~FEED⁽ⱽ⁾ AFTER >~make~BRING.FORTH⁽ⱽ⁾~him AT Serug SEVEN YEAR~s and~HUNDRED~s2 YEAR and~he~will~make~BRING.FORTH⁽ⱽ⁾ SON~s and~DAUGHTER~s **11:22** and~he~will~LIVE^(V) Serug THREE~s YEAR and~he~will~make~BRING.FORTH^(V) AT Nahhor **11:23** and~he~will~LIVE^(V) Serug AFTER >~make~BRING.FORTH^(V)~him AT Nahhor HUNDRED~s2 YEAR and~he~will~make~BRING.FORTH^(V) SON~s and~DAUGHTER~s **11:24** and~he~will~LIVE^(V) Nahhor NINE and~TEN~s YEAR and~he~will~make~BRING.FORTH^(V) AT Terahh **11:25** and~he~will~LIVE^(V) Nahhor AFTER >~make~BRING.FORTH^(V)~him AT Terahh NINE TEN YEAR and~HUNDRED YEAR and~he~will~make~BRING.FORTH^(V) SON~s and~DAUGHTER~s **11:26** and~he~will~LIVE^(V) Terahh SEVEN~s YEAR and~he~will~make~BRING.FORTH^(V) AT Avram AT Nahhor and~AT Haran **11:27** and~THESE BIRTHING~s Terahh Terahh he~did~make~BRING.FORTH^(V) AT Avram AT Nahhor and~AT Haran and~Haran he~did~make~BRING.FORTH^(V) AT Lot **11:28** and~he~will~DIE^(V) Haran UPON FACE~s Terahh FATHER~him in~LAND KINDRED~him in~Ur Kesed~s **11:29** and~he~will~TAKE^(V) Avram and~Nahhor to~them^(m) WOMAN~s TITLE WOMAN Avram Sarai and~TITLE WOMAN Nahhor Milkah DAUGHTER Haran FATHER~of Milkah and~FATHER~of Yiskah **11:30** and~she~will~EXIST^(V) Sarai STERILE WITHOUT to~her CHILD **11:31** and~he~will~TAKE^(V) Terahh AT Avram SON~him and~AT Lot SON Haran SON SON~him and~AT Sarai DAUGHTER-IN-LAW~him WOMAN Avram SON~him and~they^(m)~will~GO.OUT^(V) AT~them^(m) from~Ur Kesed~s to~>~WALK^(V) LAND~unto Kena'an and~they^(m)~will~COME^(V) UNTIL Hharan and~they^(m)~will~SETTLE^(V) THERE **11:32** and~they^(m)~will~EXIST^(V) DAY~s Terahh FIVE YEAR~s and~HUNDRED~s2 YEAR and~he~will~DIE^(V) Terahh in~Hharan

Chapter 12

12:1 and~he~will~SAY^(V) **YHWH** TO Avram !^(ms)~WALK^(V) to~you^(ms) from~LAND~you^(ms) and~from~KINDRED~you^(ms) and~from~HOUSE FATHER~you^(ms) TO the~LAND WHICH I~will~make~SEE^(V)~you^(ms) **12:2** and~I~will~DO^(V)~you^(ms) to~NATION GREAT and~I~will~much~KNEEL^(V)~you^(ms) and~I~will~MAGNIFY^(V) TITLE~you^(ms) and~!^(ms)~EXIST^(V) PRESENT **12:3** and~I~will~much~KNEEL^(V) & much~KNEEL^(V)~ing^(mp)~you^(ms) and~much~BELITTLE^(V)~ing^(mp)~you^(ms) I~will~SPIT.UPON^(V) and~they~did~be~KNEEL^(V) in~you^(ms) ALL CLAN~s the~GROUND **12:4** and~he~will~WALK^(V) Avram like~WHICH he~did~much~SPEAK^(V) TO~him **YHWH** and~he~will~WALK^(V) AT~him Lot and~Avram SON FIVE YEAR~s and~SEVEN~s YEAR in~>~GO.OUT^(V)~him from~Hharan **12:5** and~he~will~TAKE^(V) Avram AT Sarai WOMAN~him and~AT Lot SON BROTHER~him and~AT ALL GOODS~them^(m) WHICH they~did~ACCUMULATE^(V) and~AT the~SOUL WHICH they~did~DO^(V) in~Hharan and~they^(m)~will~GO.OUT^(V) to~>~WALK^(V) LAND~unto Kena'an and~they^(m)~will~COME^(V) LAND~unto Kena'an **12:6** and~he~will~CROSS.OVER^(V) Avram in~the~LAND UNTIL AREA Shekhem UNTIL GREAT.TREE Moreh and~the~Kena'an~of AT.THAT.TIME in~the~LAND **12:7** and~he~will~be~SEE^(V) **YHWH**

TO Avram and~*he~will~*SAY$^{(V)}$ to~SEED~you$^{(ms)}$ *I~will~*GIVE$^{(V)}$ AT the~LAND the~THIS and~*he~will~*BUILD$^{(V)}$ THERE ALTAR to~**YHWH** the~*be~*SEE$^{(V)}$~ *ing*$^{(ms)}$ TO~him **12:8** and~*he~will~make~*ADVANCE$^{(V)}$ from~THERE the~HILL~ unto from~EAST to~Beyt-El and~*he~will~*EXTEND$^{(V)}$ TENT~her Beyt-El from~ SEA and~the~Ay from~EAST and~*he~will~*BUILD$^{(V)}$ THERE ALTAR to~**YHWH** and~*he~will~*CALL.OUT$^{(V)}$ in~TITLE **YHWH 12:9** and~*he~will~*JOURNEY$^{(V)}$ Avram >~WALK$^{(V)}$ and~>~JOURNEY$^{(V)}$ the~SOUTH~unto **12:10** and~*he~will~* EXIST$^{(V)}$ HUNGER in~the~LAND and~*he~will~*GO.DOWN$^{(V)}$ Avram Mits'rayim~unto to~>~IMMIGRATE$^{(V)}$ THERE GIVEN.THAT HEAVY the~ HUNGER in~the~LAND **12:11** and~*he~will~*EXIST$^{(V)}$ like~WHICH *he~did~ make~*COME.NEAR$^{(V)}$ to~>~COME$^{(V)}$ Mits'rayim~unto and~*he~will~*SAY$^{(V)}$ TO Sarai WOMAN~him LOOK PLEASE *I~did~*KNOW$^{(V)}$ GIVEN.THAT WOMAN BEAUTIFUL APPEARANCE YOU$^{(fs)}$ **12:12** and~*he~did~*EXIST$^{(V)}$ GIVEN.THAT *they*$^{(m)}$*~will~*SEE$^{(V)}$ AT~you$^{(fs)}$ the~Mits'rayim~s and~*they~did~*SAY$^{(V)}$ WOMAN~him THIS and~*they~did~*KILL$^{(V)}$ AT~me and~AT~you$^{(fs)}$ *they*$^{(m)}$*~ will~much~*LIVE$^{(V)}$ **12:13** *!*$^{(fs)}$~SAY$^{(V)}$ PLEASE SISTER~me YOU$^{(fs)}$ to~THAT *he~ will~*DO.WELL$^{(V)}$ to~me in~the~CROSS.OVER$^{(V)}$~*ed*$^{(ms)}$~you$^{(fs)}$ and~*she~did~* LIVE$^{(V)}$ SOUL~me in~ON.ACCOUNT.OF~you$^{(fs)}$ **12:14** and~*he~will~*EXIST$^{(V)}$ like~>~COME$^{(V)}$ Avram Mits'rayim~unto and~*they*$^{(m)}$*~will~*SEE$^{(V)}$ the~ Mits'rayim~s AT the~WOMAN GIVEN.THAT BEAUTIFUL SHE MANY **12:15** and~*they*$^{(m)}$*~will~*SEE$^{(V)}$ AT~her NOBLE~s Paroh and~*they*$^{(m)}$*~ will~much~*SHINE$^{(V)}$ AT~her TO Paroh and~TAKE$^{(V)}$~*ed*$^{(fs)}$ the~WOMAN HOUSE Paroh **12:16** and~to~Avram *he~did~make~*DO.WELL$^{(V)}$ in~the~ CROSS.OVER$^{(V)}$~*ed*$^{(ms)}$~her and~*he~will~*EXIST$^{(V)}$ to~him FLOCKS and~CATTLE and~DONKEY~s and~SERVANT~s and~MAID~s and~SHE-DONKEY~s and~ CAMEL~s **12:17** and~*he~will~*TOUCH$^{(V)}$ **YHWH** AT Paroh TOUCH~s GREAT~s and~AT HOUSE~him UPON WORD Sarai WOMAN Avram **12:18** and~*he~ will~*CALL.OUT$^{(V)}$ Paroh to~Avram and~*he~will~*SAY$^{(V)}$ WHAT THIS *you*$^{(ms)}$*~ did~*DO$^{(V)}$ to~me to~WHAT NOT *you*$^{(ms)}$*~did~make~*BE.FACE.TO.FACE$^{(V)}$ to~ me GIVEN.THAT WOMAN~you$^{(ms)}$ SHE **12:19** to~WHAT *you*$^{(ms)}$*~did~*SAY$^{(V)}$ SISTER~me SHE and~*I~will~*TAKE$^{(V)}$ AT~her to~me to~WOMAN and~NOW LOOK WOMAN~you$^{(ms)}$ *!*$^{(ms)}$*~*TAKE$^{(V)}$ and~*!*$^{(ms)}$~WALK$^{(V)}$ **12:20** and~*he~will~ much~*DIRECT$^{(V)}$ UPON~him Paroh MAN~s and~*they*$^{(m)}$*~will~much~*SEND$^{(V)}$ AT~him and~AT WOMAN~him and~AT ALL WHICH to~him

Chapter 13

13:1 and~*he~will~make~*GO.UP$^{(V)}$ Avram from~Mits'rayim HE and~ WOMAN~him and~ALL WHICH to~him and~Lot WITH~him the~SOUTH~ unto **13:2** and~Avram HEAVY MANY in~LIVESTOCK in~SILVER and~in~ GOLD **13:3** and~*he~will~*WALK$^{(V)}$ to~JOURNEY~s~him from~SOUTH and~ UNTIL Beyt-El UNTIL the~AREA WHICH *he~did~*EXIST$^{(V)}$ THERE TENT~her in~ the~FIRST.TIME BETWEEN Beyt-El and~BETWEEN the~Ay **13:4** TO AREA the~ALTAR WHICH *he~did*~DO^(V) THERE in~the~FIRST and~*he~will*~CALL.OUT^(V) THERE Avram in~TITLE **YHWH** **13:5** and~ALSO to~Lot the~WALK^(V)~*ing*^(ms) AT Avram *he~did*~EXIST^(V) FLOCKS and~CATTLE and~TENT~s **13:6** and~NOT *he~did*~LIFT.UP^(V) AT~them^(m) the~LAND to~>~SETTLE^(V) TOGETHER GIVEN.THAT *he~did*~EXIST^(V) GOODS~them^(m) ABUNDANT and~NOT *they~did*~BE.ABLE^(V) to~>~SETTLE^(V) TOGETHER **13:7** and~*he~will*~EXIST^(V) DISPUTE BETWEEN FEED^(V)~*ing*^(mp) LIVESTOCK Avram and~BETWEEN FEED^(V)~*ing*^(mp) LIVESTOCK Lot and~the~Kena'an~of and~the~Perez~of AT.THAT.TIME SETTLE^(V)~*ing*^(ms) in~the~LAND **13:8** and~*he~will*~SAY^(V) Avram TO Lot DO.NOT PLEASE *she~will*~EXIST^(V) CONTENTION BETWEEN~me and~BETWEEN~you^(ms) and~BETWEEN FEED^(V)~*ing*^(mp)~me and~BETWEEN FEED^(V)~*ing*^(mp)~you^(ms) GIVEN.THAT MAN~s BROTHER~s WE **13:9** ?~NOT ALL the~LAND to~FACE~s~you^(ms) *!*^(ms)~*be*~DIVIDE.APART^(V) PLEASE from~UPON~me IF the~LEFT.HAND and~*I~will*~make~GO.RIGHT^(V)~& and~IF the~RIGHT.HAND and~*I~will*~make~LEFT.HAND~& **13:10** and~*he~will*~LIFT.UP^(V) Lot AT EYE~s2~him and~*he~will*~SEE^(V) AT ALL ROUNDNESS the~Yarden GIVEN.THAT ALL~her DRINKING to~FACE~s >~*much*~DAMAGE^(V) **YHWH** AT Sedom and~AT Ghamorah like~GARDEN **YHWH** like~LAND Mits'rayim >~COME^(V)~*you*^(ms)~& Tso'ar **13:11** and~*he~will*~CHOOSE^(V) to~him Lot AT ALL ROUNDNESS the~Yarden and~*he~will*~JOURNEY^(V) Lot from~EAST and~*they*^(m)~*will*~DIVIDE.APART^(V) MAN from~UPON BROTHER~him **13:12** Avram *he~did*~SETTLE^(V) in~LAND Kena'an and~Lot *he~did*~SETTLE^(V) in~CITY~s the~ROUNDNESS and~*he~will*~PITCH.TENT^(V) UNTIL Sedom **13:13** and~MAN~s Sedom DYSFUNCTIONAL~s and~FAILURE~s to~**YHWH** MANY **13:14** and~**YHWH** *he~did*~SAY^(V) TO Avram AFTER *!*^(ms)~*be*~DIVIDE.APART^(V) Lot from~WITH~him *!*^(ms)~LIFT.UP^(V) PLEASE EYE~s2~you^(ms) and~*!*^(ms)~SEE^(V) FROM the~AREA WHICH YOU^(ms) THERE NORTH~unto and~SOUTH~unto and~EAST~unto and~SEA~unto **13:15** GIVEN.THAT AT ALL the~LAND WHICH YOU^(ms) SEE^(V)~*ing*^(ms) to~you^(ms) *I~will*~GIVE^(V)~her and~to~SEED~you^(ms) UNTIL DISTANT **13:16** and~*I~did*~PLACE^(V) AT SEED~you^(ms) like~DIRT the~LAND WHICH IF *he~will*~BE.ABLE^(V) MAN to~>~RECKON^(V) AT DIRT the~LAND ALSO SEED~you^(ms) *he~will*~*be*~RECKON^(V) **13:17** *!*^(ms)~RISE^(V) *!*^(ms)~*self*~WALK^(V) in~the~LAND to~LENGTH~her and~to~WIDTH~her GIVEN.THAT to~you^(ms) *I~will*~GIVE^(V)~her **13:18** and~*he~will*~PITCH.TENT^(V) Avram and~*he~will*~COME^(V) and~*he~will*~SETTLE^(V) in~GREAT.TREE~s Mamre WHICH in~Hhevron and~*he~will*~BUILD^(V) THERE ALTAR to~**YHWH**

Chapter 14

14:1 and~*he~will*~EXIST^(V) in~DAY~s Amraphel KING Shinar Aryokh KING Elasar Kedarla'omer KING Elam and~Tidal KING Goyim **14:2** *they~did*~DO^(V) BATTLE AT Bera KING Sedom and~AT Birsha KING Ghamorah Shinav KING

Admah and~Shemever KING Tseviim and~KING Bela SHE Tso'ar **14:3** ALL
THESE *they~did*~COUPLE$^{(V)}$ TO VALLEY the~Sidim HE SEA the~
SALT **14:4** TWO TEN YEAR *they~did*~SERVE$^{(V)}$ AT Kedarla'omer and~THREE
TEN YEAR *they~did*~REBEL$^{(V)}$ **14:5** and~in~FOUR TEN YEAR *he~did*~COME$^{(V)}$
Kedarla'omer and~the~KING~s WHICH AT~him and~*they$^{(m)}$~will~make*~
HIT$^{(V)}$ AT Rapha~s in~Ashterot-Qar'nayim and~AT the~Zuz~s in~Ham and~AT
the~Eym~s in~Shaweh-Qiryatayim **14:6** and~AT the~Hhor~of in~MOUNT~
them$^{(m)}$ Se'iyr UNTIL Eyl-Paran WHICH UPON the~WILDERNESS **14:7** and~
they$^{(m)}$~will~TURN.BACK$^{(V)}$ and~*they$^{(m)}$~will*~COME$^{(V)}$ TO Eyn-Mishpat SHE
Qadesh and~*they$^{(m)}$~will~make*~HIT$^{(V)}$ AT ALL FIELD the~Amaleq~of and~
ALSO AT the~Emor~of the~SETTLE$^{(V)}$~*ing$^{(ms)}$* in~Hhats'tson-Tamar **14:8** and~
he~will~GO.OUT$^{(V)}$ KING Sedom and~KING Ghamorah and~KING Admah
and~KING Tseviim and~KING Bela SHE Tso'ar and~*they$^{(m)}$~will*~ARRANGE$^{(V)}$
AT~them$^{(m)}$ BATTLE in~VALLEY the~Sidim **14:9** AT Kedarla'omer KING Elam
and~Tidal KING Goyim and~Amraphel KING Shinar and~Aryokh KING Elasar
FOUR KING~s AT the~FIVE **14:10** and~VALLEY the~Sidim WELL~s WELL~s
SLIME and~*they$^{(m)}$~will*~FLEE$^{(V)}$ KING Sedom and~Ghamorah and~*they$^{(m)}$~
will*~FALL$^{(V)}$ THERE~unto and~the~*be*~REMAIN$^{(V)}$~*ing$^{(mp)}$* HILL~unto *they~
did*~FLEE$^{(V)}$ **14:11** and~*they$^{(m)}$~will*~TAKE$^{(V)}$ AT ALL GOODS Sedom and~
Ghamorah and~AT ALL FOODSTUFF~them$^{(m)}$ and~*they$^{(m)}$~will*~
WALK$^{(V)}$ **14:12** and~*they$^{(m)}$~will*~TAKE$^{(V)}$ AT Lot and~AT GOODS~him SON
BROTHER~of Avram and~*they$^{(m)}$~will*~WALK$^{(V)}$ and~HE SETTLE$^{(V)}$~*ing$^{(ms)}$* in~
Sedom **14:13** and~*he~will*~COME$^{(V)}$ the~ESCAPED and~*he~will~make*~
BE.FACE.TO.FACE$^{(V)}$ to~Avram the~Ever~of and~HE DWELL$^{(V)}$~*ing$^{(ms)}$* in~
GREAT.TREE~s Mamre the~Emor~of BROTHER~of Eshkol and~BROTHER~of
Aner and~THEY$^{(m)}$ MASTER~s COVENANT Avram **14:14** and~*he~will*~HEAR$^{(V)}$
Avram GIVEN.THAT *he~did~be*~CAPTURE$^{(V)}$ BROTHER~him and~*he~will*~
EMPTY AT EXPERIENCED~s~him BORN~s HOUSE~him EIGHT TEN and~THREE
HUNDRED~s and~*he~will*~PURSUE$^{(V)}$ UNTIL Dan **14:15** and~*he~will~be*~
DISTRIBUTE$^{(V)}$ UPON~them$^{(m)}$ NIGHT HE and~SERVANT~s~him and~*he~will*~
make~them$^{(m)}$HIT$^{(V)}$~them$^{(m)}$ and~*he~will*~PURSUE$^{(V)}$~them$^{(m)}$ UNTIL Hhovah
WHICH from~LEFT.HAND to~Dameseq **14:16** and~*he~will~make*~
TURN.BACK$^{(V)}$ AT ALL the~GOODS and~ALSO AT Lot BROTHER~him and~
GOODS~him *he~did~make*~TURN.BACK$^{(V)}$ and~ALSO AT the~WOMAN~s
and~AT the~PEOPLE **14:17** and~*he~will*~GO.OUT$^{(V)}$ KING Sedom to~>~
MEET$^{(V)}$~him AFTER >~TURN.BACK$^{(V)}$~him from~>~*make*~HIT$^{(V)}$ AT
Kedarla'omer and~AT the~KING~s WHICH AT~him TO VALLEY Shaweh HE
VALLEY the~KING **14:18** and~Malkiy-Tsedeq KING Shalem *he~did~make*~
GO.OUT$^{(V)}$ BREAD and~WINE and~HE ADMINISTRATOR to~MIGHTY.ONE
Elyon **14:19** and~*he~will~much*~KNEEL$^{(V)}$~him and~*he~will*~SAY$^{(V)}$ KNEEL$^{(V)}$~
ed$^{(ms)}$ Avram to~MIGHTY.ONE Elyon PURCHASE$^{(V)}$~*ing$^{(ms)}$* SKY~s2 and~
LAND **14:20** and~KNEEL$^{(V)}$~*ed$^{(ms)}$* MIGHTY.ONE Elyon WHICH *he~did~much*~
DELIVER.UP$^{(V)}$ NARROW~s~you$^{(ms)}$ in~HAND~you$^{(ms)}$ and~*he~will*~GIVE$^{(V)}$ to~
him TENTH.PART from~ALL **14:21** and~*he~will*~SAY$^{(V)}$ KING Sedom TO
Avram !$^{(ms)}$~GIVE$^{(V)}$ to~me the~SOUL and~the~GOODS !$^{(ms)}$~TAKE$^{(V)}$ to~

you⁽ᶠˢ⁾ **14:22** and~*he*~*will*~SAY⁽ⱽ⁾ Avram TO KING Sedom *I*~*did*~*make*~ RAISE.UP⁽ⱽ⁾ HAND~me TO **YHWH** MIGHTY.ONE Elyon PURCHASE⁽ⱽ⁾~*ing*⁽ᵐˢ⁾ SKY~s2 and~LAND **14:23** IF from~THREAD and~UNTIL LACE SANDAL and~IF *I*~*will*~TAKE⁽ⱽ⁾ from~ALL WHICH to~you⁽ᶠˢ⁾ and~NOT you⁽ᵐˢ⁾~*will*~SAY⁽ⱽ⁾ I *I*~*did*~*make*~BE.RICH⁽ⱽ⁾ AT Avram **14:24** APART.FROM ONLY WHICH *they*~ *did*~EAT⁽ⱽ⁾ the~YOUNG.MAN~s and~DISTRIBUTION the~MAN~s WHICH *they*~*did*~WALK⁽ⱽ⁾ AT~me Aner Eshkol and~Mamre THEY⁽ᵐ⁾ *they*⁽ᵐ⁾~*will*~ TAKE⁽ⱽ⁾ DISTRIBUTION~them⁽ᵐ⁾

Chapter 15

15:1 AFTER the~WORD~s the~THESE *he*~*did*~EXIST⁽ⱽ⁾ WORD **YHWH** TO Avram in~the~VISION to~>~SAY⁽ⱽ⁾ DO.NOT you⁽ᵐˢ⁾~*will*~FEAR⁽ⱽ⁾ Avram I SHIELD to~you⁽ᶠˢ⁾ WAGE~you⁽ᵐˢ⁾ >~*make*~INCREASE⁽ⱽ⁾ MANY **15:2** and~*he*~ *will*~SAY⁽ⱽ⁾ Avram Adonai **YHWH** WHAT you⁽ᵐˢ⁾~*will*~GIVE⁽ⱽ⁾ to~me and~I WALK⁽ⱽ⁾~*ing*⁽ᵐˢ⁾ BARREN and~SON ACQUISITION HOUSE~me HE Dameseq Eli'ezer **15:3** and~*he*~*will*~SAY⁽ⱽ⁾ Avram THOUGH to~me NOT you⁽ᵐˢ⁾~*did*~ GIVE⁽ⱽ⁾ SEED and~LOOK SON HOUSE~me POSSESS⁽ⱽ⁾~*ing*⁽ᵐˢ⁾ AT~ me **15:4** and~LOOK WORD **YHWH** TO~him to~>~SAY⁽ⱽ⁾ NOT *he*~*will*~ POSSESS⁽ⱽ⁾~you⁽ᵐˢ⁾ THIS GIVEN.THAT IF WHICH *he*~*will*~GO.OUT⁽ⱽ⁾ from~ ABDOMEN~s~you⁽ᵐˢ⁾ HE *he*~*will*~POSSESS⁽ⱽ⁾~you⁽ᵐˢ⁾ **15:5** and~*he*~*will*~ *make*~GO.OUT⁽ⱽ⁾ AT~him the~OUTSIDE~unto and~*he*~*will*~SAY⁽ⱽ⁾ *!*⁽ᵐˢ⁾~ *make*~STARE⁽ⱽ⁾ PLEASE the~SKY~s2 unto and~*!*⁽ᵐˢ⁾~COUNT⁽ⱽ⁾ the~STAR~s IF you⁽ᵐˢ⁾~*will*~BE.ABLE⁽ⱽ⁾ to~>~COUNT⁽ⱽ⁾ AT~them⁽ᵐ⁾ and~*he*~*will*~SAY⁽ⱽ⁾ to~ him IN.THIS.WAY *he*~*will*~EXIST⁽ⱽ⁾ SEED~you⁽ᵐˢ⁾ **15:6** and~*he*~*will*~*make*~ SECURE⁽ⱽ⁾ in~**YHWH** and~*he*~*will*~THINK⁽ⱽ⁾~her to~him STEADFASTNESS **15:7** and~*he*~*will*~SAY⁽ⱽ⁾ TO~him I **YHWH** WHICH *I*~*did*~ *make*~GO.OUT⁽ⱽ⁾~you⁽ᵐˢ⁾ from~Ur Kesed~s to~>~GIVE⁽ⱽ⁾ to~you⁽ᵐˢ⁾ AT the~ LAND the~THIS to~>~POSSESS⁽ⱽ⁾~her **15:8** and~*he*~*will*~SAY⁽ⱽ⁾ Adonai **YHWH** in~WHAT *I*~*will*~KNOW⁽ⱽ⁾ GIVEN.THAT *I*~*will*~POSSESS⁽ⱽ⁾~ her **15:9** and~*he*~*will*~SAY⁽ⱽ⁾ TO~him *!*⁽ᵐˢ⁾~TAKE⁽ⱽ⁾~& to~me HEIFER *much*~ BE.THREEFOLD⁽ⱽ⁾~*ing*⁽ᶠˢ⁾ and~SHE-GOAT *much*~BE.THREEFOLD⁽ⱽ⁾~*ing*⁽ᶠˢ⁾ and~ BUCK *much*~BE.THREEFOLD⁽ⱽ⁾~*ing*⁽ᵐˢ⁾ and~TURTLEDOVE and~ YOUNG.PIGEON **15:10** and~*he*~*will*~TAKE⁽ⱽ⁾ to~him AT ALL THESE and~*he*~ *will*~CUT.IN.TWO⁽ⱽ⁾ AT~them⁽ᵐ⁾ in~the~MIDST and~*he*~*will*~GIVE⁽ⱽ⁾ MAN CUT.PIECE~him to~>~MEET⁽ⱽ⁾ COMPANION~him and~AT the~BIRD NOT *he*~ *did*~CUT.IN.TWO⁽ⱽ⁾ **15:11** and~*he*~*will*~GO.DOWN⁽ⱽ⁾ the~BIRD.OF.PREY UPON the~CORPSE~s and~*he*~*will*~*make*~GUST⁽ⱽ⁾ AT~them⁽ᵐ⁾ Avram **15:12** and~*he*~*will*~EXIST⁽ⱽ⁾ the~SUN to~>~COME⁽ⱽ⁾ and~TRANCE *she*~*did*~FALL⁽ⱽ⁾ UPON Avram and~LOOK TERROR DARK GREAT FALL⁽ⱽ⁾~*ing*⁽ᶠˢ⁾ UPON~him **15:13** and~*he*~*will*~SAY⁽ⱽ⁾ to~Avram >~KNOW⁽ⱽ⁾ you⁽ᵐˢ⁾~*will*~ KNOW⁽ⱽ⁾ GIVEN.THAT IMMIGRANT *he*~*will*~EXIST⁽ⱽ⁾ SEED~you⁽ᵐˢ⁾ in~LAND NOT to~them⁽ᵐ⁾ and~*they*~*did*~SERVE⁽ⱽ⁾~them⁽ᵐ⁾ and~*they*~*did*~*much*~

AFFLICT⁽ⱽ⁾ AT~them⁽ᵐ⁾ FOUR HUNDRED~s YEAR **15:14** and~ALSO AT the~
NATION WHICH *they*⁽ᵐ⁾~*will*~SERVE⁽ⱽ⁾ MODERATE⁽ⱽ⁾~*ing*⁽ᵐˢ⁾ I and~AFTER SO
they⁽ᵐ⁾~*will*~GO.OUT⁽ⱽ⁾ in~GOODS GREAT **15:15** and~YOU⁽ᵐˢ⁾ *you*⁽ᵐˢ⁾~*will*~
COME⁽ⱽ⁾ TO FATHER~s~you⁽ᵐˢ⁾ in~COMPLETENESS *you*⁽ᵐˢ⁾~*will*~*be*~BURY⁽ⱽ⁾
in~GRAY-HEADED FUNCTIONAL **15:16** and~GENERATION FOURTH *they*⁽ᵐ⁾~
will~TURN.BACK⁽ⱽ⁾ TO.THIS.POINT GIVEN.THAT NOT COMPLETENESS
TWISTEDNESS the~Emor~of UNTIL TO.THIS.POINT **15:17** and~*he*~*will*~
EXIST⁽ⱽ⁾ the~SUN *she*~*did*~COME⁽ⱽ⁾ and~TWILIGHT *he*~*did*~EXIST⁽ⱽ⁾ and~
LOOK OVEN SMOKE and~TORCH FIRE WHICH *he*~*did*~CROSS.OVER⁽ⱽ⁾
BETWEEN the~DIVIDED.PART~s the~THESE **15:18** in~the~DAY the~HE *he*~
did~CUT⁽ⱽ⁾ **YHWH** AT Avram COVENANT to~>~SAY⁽ⱽ⁾ to~SEED~you⁽ᵐˢ⁾ *I*~*did*~
GIVE⁽ⱽ⁾ AT the~LAND the~THIS from~RIVER Mits'rayim UNTIL the~RIVER
the~GREAT RIVER Perat **15:19** AT the~Qayin~of and~AT the~Qenaz~of and~
AT the~Qadmon~of **15:20** and~AT the~Hhet~of and~AT the~Perez~of and~
AT the~Rapha~s **15:21** and~AT the~Emor~of and~AT the~Kena'an~of and~
AT the~Girgash~of and~AT the~Yevus~of

Chapter 16

16:1 and~Sarai WOMAN Avram NOT *she*~*did*~BRING.FORTH⁽ⱽ⁾ to~him and~
to~her MAID Mits'rayim~s and~TITLE~her Hagar **16:2** and~*she*~*will*~SAY⁽ⱽ⁾
Sarai TO Avram LOOK PLEASE *he*~*did*~STOP⁽ⱽ⁾~me **YHWH** from~>~
BRING.FORTH⁽ⱽ⁾ *!*⁽ᵐˢ⁾~COME⁽ⱽ⁾ PLEASE TO MAID~me POSSIBLY *I*~*will*~BUILD⁽ⱽ⁾
FROM~her and~*he*~*will*~HEAR⁽ⱽ⁾ Avram to~VOICE Sarai **16:3** and~*she*~*will*~
TAKE⁽ⱽ⁾ Sarai WOMAN Avram AT Hagar the~Mits'rayim~of MAID~her from~
CONCLUSION TEN YEAR~s to~>~SETTLE⁽ⱽ⁾ Avram in~LAND Kena'an and~*she*~
will~GIVE⁽ⱽ⁾ AT~her to~Avram MAN~her to~him to~WOMAN **16:4** and~*he*~
will~COME⁽ⱽ⁾ TO Hagar and~*she*~*will*~CONCEIVE⁽ⱽ⁾ and~*she*~*will*~SEE⁽ⱽ⁾
GIVEN.THAT *she*~*did*~CONCEIVE⁽ⱽ⁾ and~*she*~*will*~BELITTLE⁽ⱽ⁾
FEMALE.OWNER~her in~EYE~s2~her **16:5** and~*she*~*will*~SAY⁽ⱽ⁾ Sarai TO
Avram VIOLENCE~me UPON~you⁽ᵐˢ⁾ I *I*~*did*~GIVE⁽ⱽ⁾ MAID~me in~BOSOM~
you⁽ᵐˢ⁾ and~*she*~*will*~SEE⁽ⱽ⁾ GIVEN.THAT *she*~*did*~CONCEIVE⁽ⱽ⁾ and~*I*~*will*~
BELITTLE⁽ⱽ⁾ in~EYE~s2~her *he*~*will*~DECIDE⁽ⱽ⁾ **YHWH** BETWEEN~me and~
BETWEEN~you⁽ᵐˢ⁾ **16:6** and~*he*~*will*~SAY⁽ⱽ⁾ Avram TO Sarai LOOK MAID~
you⁽ᶠˢ⁾ in~HAND~you⁽ᶠˢ⁾ *!*⁽ᶠˢ⁾~DO⁽ⱽ⁾ to~her the~FUNCTIONAL in~EYE~s2~you⁽ᶠˢ⁾
and~*she*~*will*~AFFLICT⁽ⱽ⁾~her Sarai and~*she*~*will*~FLEE.AWAY⁽ⱽ⁾ from~
FACE~s~her **16:7** and~*he*~*will*~FIND⁽ⱽ⁾~her MESSENGER **YHWH** UPON EYE
the~WATER~s2 in~the~WILDERNESS UPON the~EYE in~ROAD
Shur **16:8** and~*he*~*will*~SAY⁽ⱽ⁾ Hagar MAID Sarai WHERE from~THIS *you*⁽ᶠˢ⁾~
did~COME⁽ⱽ⁾ and~WHEREVER *you*⁽ᶠˢ⁾~*will*~WALK⁽ⱽ⁾ and~*she*~*will*~SAY⁽ⱽ⁾
from~FACE~s Sarai FEMALE.OWNER~me I FLEE.AWAY⁽ⱽ⁾~*ing*⁽ᶠˢ⁾ **16:9** and~
he~*will*~SAY⁽ⱽ⁾ to~her MESSENGER **YHWH** *!*⁽ᶠˢ⁾~TURN.BACK⁽ⱽ⁾ TO
FEMALE.OWNER~you⁽ᶠˢ⁾ and~*!*⁽ᶠˢ⁾~*self*~AFFLICT⁽ⱽ⁾ UNDER HAND~s2~

her **16:10** and~*he*~*will*~SAY(V) to~her MESSENGER **YHWH** >~*make*~INCREASE(V) *I*~*will*~*make*~INCREASE(V) AT SEED~*you*(fs) and~NOT *he*~*will*~*be*~COUNT(V) from~ABUNDANCE **16:11** and~*he*~*will*~SAY(V) to~her MESSENGER **YHWH** LOOK~*you*(fs) PREGNANT and~*you*(fs)~*did*~BRING.FORTH(V) SON and~*you*(fs)~*did*~CALL.OUT(V) TITLE~him Yishma'el GIVEN.THAT *he*~*did*~HEAR(V) **YHWH** TO AFFLICTION~*you*(fs) **16:12** and~HE *he*~*will*~EXIST(V) WILD.ASS HUMAN HAND~him in~the~ALL and~HAND ALL in~him and~UPON FACE~s ALL BROTHER~s~him *he*~*will*~DWELL(V) **16:13** and~*she*~*will*~CALL.OUT(V) TITLE **YHWH** the~SPEAK(V)~*ing*(ms) TO~her YOU(ms) El-Ra'iy GIVEN.THAT *she*~*did*~SAY(V) ?~ALSO AT.THIS.POINT *I*~*did*~SEE(V) AFTER SEE(V)~*ing*(ms)~me **16:14** UPON SO *he*~*did*~CALL.OUT(V) to~the~WELL Be'er-Lahhiy-Ro'iy LOOK BETWEEN Qadesh and~BETWEEN Bered **16:15** and~*she*~*will*~BRING.FORTH(V) Hagar to~Avram SON and~*he*~*will*~CALL.OUT(V) Avram TITLE SON~him WHICH *she*~*did*~BRING.FORTH(V) Hagar Yishma'el **16:16** and~Avram SON EIGHT~s YEAR and~SIX YEAR~s in~>~BRING.FORTH(V) Hagar AT Yishma'el to~Avram

Chapter 17

17:1 and~*he*~*will*~EXIST(V) Avram SON NINE~s YEAR and~NINE YEAR~s and~*he*~*will*~*be*~SEE(V) **YHWH** TO Avram and~*he*~*will*~SAY(V) TO~him I MIGHTY.ONE Shaddai *!*(ms)~*self*~WALK(V) to~FACE~s~me and~*!*(ms)~EXIST(V) WHOLE **17:2** and~*I*~*will*~GIVE(V)~& COVENANT~me BETWEEN~me and~BETWEEN~*you*(ms) and~*I*~*will*~*make*~INCREASE(V) AT~*you*(ms) in~MANY MANY **17:3** and~*he*~*will*~FALL(V) Avram UPON FACE~s~him and~*he*~*will*~much~SPEAK(V) AT~him Elohiym to~>~SAY(V) **17:4** I LOOK COVENANT~me AT~*you*(fs) and~*you*(ms)~*did*~EXIST(V) to~FATHER MULTITUDE NATION~s **17:5** and~NOT *he*~*will*~*be*~CALL.OUT(V) YET.AGAIN AT TITLE~*you*(ms) Avram and~*he*~*did*~EXIST(V) TITLE~*you*(ms) Avraham GIVEN.THAT FATHER MULTITUDE NATION~s *I*~*did*~GIVE(V)~*you*(ms) **17:6** and~*I*~*did*~*make*~REPRODUCE(V) AT~*you*(ms) in~MANY MANY and~*I*~*did*~GIVE(V)~*you*(ms) to~NATION~s and~KING~s FROM~*you*(ms) *they*(m)~*will*~GO.OUT(V) **17:7** and~*I*~*did*~*make*~RISE(V) AT COVENANT~me BETWEEN~me and~BETWEEN~*you*(ms) and~BETWEEN SEED~*you*(ms) AFTER~*you*(ms) to~GENERATION~s~*them*(m) to~COVENANT DISTANT to~>~EXIST(V) to~*you*(ms) to~Elohiym and~to~SEED~*you*(ms) AFTER~*you*(ms) **17:8** and~*I*~*did*~GIVE(V) to~*you*(ms) and~to~SEED~*you*(ms) AFTER~*you*(ms) AT LAND IMMIGRATION~s~*you*(ms) AT ALL LAND Kena'an to~HOLDINGS DISTANT and~*I*~*did*~EXIST(V) to~*them*(m) to~Elohiym **17:9** and~*he*~*will*~SAY(V) Elohiym TO Avraham and~YOU(ms) AT COVENANT~me *you*(ms)~*will*~SAFEGUARD(V) YOU(ms) and~SEED~*you*(ms) AFTER~*you*(ms) to~GENERATION~s~*them*(m) **17:10** THIS COVENANT~me WHICH *you*(mp)~*will*~SAFEGUARD(V) BETWEEN~me and~BETWEEN~*you*(mp) and~BETWEEN SEED~*you*(ms) AFTER~*you*(ms) >~*be*~SNIP.OFF(V) to~*you*(mp) ALL

MALE **17:11** and~*you*$^{(mp)}$~*did*~CUT.OFF$^{(V)}$ AT FLESH FORESKIN~you$^{(mp)}$ and~ *he*~*did*~EXIST$^{(V)}$ to~SIGN COVENANT BETWEEN~me and~BETWEEN~ you$^{(mp)}$ **17:12** and~SON EIGHT DAY~s *he*~*will*~*be*~SNIP.OFF$^{(V)}$ to~you$^{(mp)}$ ALL MALE to~GENERATION~s~you$^{(mp)}$ BORN HOUSE and~ACQUIRED SILVER from~ALL SON FOREIGNER WHICH NOT from~SEED~you$^{(ms)}$ HE **17:13** >~*be*~ SNIP.OFF$^{(V)}$ *he*~*will*~*be*~SNIP.OFF$^{(V)}$ BORN HOUSE~you$^{(ms)}$ and~ACQUIRED SILVER~you$^{(ms)}$ and~*she*~*did*~EXIST$^{(V)}$ COVENANT~me in~FLESH~you$^{(mp)}$ to~ COVENANT DISTANT **17:14** and~UNCIRCUMCISED MALE WHICH NOT *he*~ *will*~*be*~SNIP.OFF$^{(V)}$ AT FLESH FORESKIN~him and~*she*~*did*~*be*~CUT$^{(V)}$ the~ SOUL the~SHE from~PEOPLE~s~her AT COVENANT~me *he*~*did*~*make*~ BREAK$^{(V)}$ **17:15** and~*he*~*will*~SAY$^{(V)}$ Elohiym TO Avraham Sarai WOMAN~ you$^{(ms)}$ NOT *you*$^{(ms)}$~*will*~CALL.OUT$^{(V)}$ AT TITLE~her Sarai GIVEN.THAT Sarah TITLE~her **17:16** and~*I*~*did*~*much*~KNEEL$^{(V)}$ AT~her and~ALSO *I*~*did*~GIVE$^{(V)}$ FROM~her to~you$^{(ms)}$ SON and~*I*~*did*~*much*~KNEEL$^{(V)}$~her and~*she*~*did*~ EXIST$^{(V)}$ to~NATION~s KING~s PEOPLE~s FROM~her they$^{(m)}$~*will*~ EXIST$^{(V)}$ **17:17** and~*he*~*will*~FALL$^{(V)}$ Avraham UPON FACE~s~him and~*he*~ *will*~LAUGH$^{(V)}$ and~*he*~*will*~SAY$^{(V)}$ in~HEART~him ?~to~SON HUNDRED YEAR *he*~*will*~*be*~BRING.FORTH$^{(V)}$ and~IF Sarah ?~DAUGHTER NINE~s YEAR *she*~ *will*~BRING.FORTH$^{(V)}$ **17:18** and~*he*~*will*~SAY$^{(V)}$ Avraham TO the~Elohiym WOULD.THAT Yishma'el *he*~*will*~LIVE$^{(V)}$ to~FACE~s~you$^{(ms)}$ **17:19** and~*he*~ *will*~SAY$^{(V)}$ Elohiym NEVERTHELESS Sarah WOMAN~you$^{(ms)}$ BRING.FORTH$^{(V)}$~ *ing*$^{(fs)}$ to~you$^{(ms)}$ SON and~*you*$^{(ms)}$~*did*~CALL.OUT$^{(V)}$ AT TITLE~him Yits'hhaq and~*I*~*did*~*make*~RISE$^{(V)}$ AT COVENANT~me AT~him to~COVENANT DISTANT to~SEED~him AFTER~him **17:20** and~to~Yishma'el *I*~*did*~HEAR$^{(V)}$~you$^{(ms)}$ LOOK *I*~*did*~*much*~KNEEL$^{(V)}$ AT~him and~*I*~*did*~*make*~REPRODUCE$^{(V)}$ AT~ him and~*I*~*did*~*make*~INCREASE$^{(V)}$ AT~him in~MANY MANY TWO TEN CAPTAIN~s *he*~*will*~*make*~BRING.FORTH$^{(V)}$ and~*I*~*did*~GIVE$^{(V)}$~him to~ NATION GREAT **17:21** and~AT COVENANT~me *I*~*will*~*make*~RISE$^{(V)}$ AT Yits'hhaq WHICH *she*~*will*~BRING.FORTH$^{(V)}$ to~you$^{(ms)}$ Sarah to~the~ APPOINTED the~THIS in~the~YEAR the~OTHER **17:22** and~*he*~*will*~*much*~ FINISH$^{(V)}$ to~>~*much*~SPEAK$^{(V)}$ AT~him and~*he*~*will*~*make*~GO.UP$^{(V)}$ Elohiym from~UPON Avraham **17:23** and~*he*~*will*~TAKE$^{(V)}$ Avraham AT Yishma'el SON~him and~AT ALL BORN~s HOUSE~him and~AT ALL ACQUIRED SILVER~ him ALL MALE in~MAN~s HOUSE Avraham and~*he*~*will*~SNIP.OFF$^{(V)}$ AT FLESH FORESKIN~them$^{(m)}$ in~BONE the~DAY the~THIS like~WHICH *he*~*did*~ *much*~SPEAK$^{(V)}$ AT~him Elohiym **17:24** and~Avraham SON NINE~s and~NINE YEAR in~>~*be*~*make*~SNIP.OFF$^{(V)}$~him FLESH FORESKIN~him **17:25** and~ Yishma'el SON~him SON THREE TEN YEAR in~>~*be*~*make*~SNIP.OFF$^{(V)}$~him AT FLESH FORESKIN~him **17:26** in~BONE the~DAY the~THIS *he*~*did*~*be*~ SNIP.OFF$^{(V)}$ Avraham and~Yishma'el SON~him **17:27** and~ALL MAN~s HOUSE~him BORN HOUSE and~ACQUIRED SILVER from~AT SON FOREIGNER *they*~*did*~*be*~SNIP.OFF$^{(V)}$ AT~him

Chapter 18

18:1 and~*he~will~be*~SEE$^{(V)}$ TO~him **YHWH** in~GREAT.TREE~s Mamre and~ HE SETTLE$^{(V)}$~*ing*$^{(ms)}$ OPENING the~TENT like~HOT the~DAY **18:2** and~*he~ will~*LIFT.UP$^{(V)}$ EYE~s2~him and~*he~will~*SEE$^{(V)}$ and~LOOK THREE MAN~s *be~* STAND.UP$^{(V)}$~*ing*$^{(mp)}$ UPON~him and~*he~will~*SEE$^{(V)}$ and~*he~will~*RUN$^{(V)}$ to~ >~MEET$^{(V)}$~them$^{(m)}$ from~OPENING the~TENT and~*he~will~self~* BEND.DOWN$^{(V)}$ LAND~unto **18:3** and~*he~will~*SAY$^{(V)}$ Adonai IF PLEASE *I~ did~*FIND$^{(V)}$ BEAUTY in~EYE~s2~you$^{(ms)}$ DO.NOT PLEASE *you*$^{(ms)}$~*will~* CROSS.OVER$^{(V)}$ from~UPON SERVANT~you$^{(ms)}$ **18:4** *he~will~be~much~* TAKE$^{(V)}$ PLEASE SMALL.AMOUNT WATER~s2 and~ *!*$^{(mp)}$~BATHE$^{(V)}$ FOOT~s2~ you$^{(mp)}$ and~ *!*$^{(ms)}$~*be~*LEAN$^{(V)}$ UNDER the~TREE **18:5** and~*I~will~*TAKE$^{(V)}$~her FRAGMENT BREAD and~ *!*$^{(mp)}$~HOLD.UP$^{(V)}$ HEART~you$^{(mp)}$ AFTER *you*$^{(mp)}$~*will~* CROSS.OVER$^{(V)}$ GIVEN.THAT UPON SO *you*$^{(mp)}$~*did~*CROSS.OVER$^{(V)}$ UPON SERVANT~you$^{(mp)}$ and~*they*$^{(m)}$~*will~*SAY$^{(V)}$ SO *you*$^{(ms)}$~*will~*DO$^{(V)}$ like~WHICH *you*$^{(ms)}$~*did~much~*SPEAK$^{(V)}$ **18:6** and~*he~will~much~*HURRY$^{(V)}$ Avraham the~TENT~unto TO Sarah and~*he~will~*SAY$^{(V)}$ *!*$^{(fs)}$~*much~*HURRY$^{(V)}$ THREE SE'AH~s GRAIN.FLOUR FLOUR *!*$^{(fs)}$~KNEAD$^{(V)}$ and~ *!*$^{(fs)}$~DO$^{(V)}$ BAKED.BREAD~s **18:7** and~TO the~CATTLE *he~did~*RUN$^{(V)}$ Avraham and~ *he~will~*TAKE$^{(V)}$ SON CATTLE TENDER and~FUNCTIONAL and~*he~will~*GIVE$^{(V)}$ TO the~YOUNG.MAN and~*he~will~much~*HURRY$^{(V)}$ to~>~DO$^{(V)}$ AT~ him **18:8** and~*he~will~*TAKE$^{(V)}$ CHEESE and~FAT and~SON the~CATTLE WHICH *he~did~*DO$^{(V)}$ and~*he~will~*GIVE$^{(V)}$ to~FACE~s~them$^{(m)}$ and~HE STAND$^{(V)}$~*ing*$^{(ms)}$ UPON~them$^{(m)}$ UNDER the~TREE and~*they*$^{(m)}$~*will~* EAT$^{(V)}$ **18:9** and~*they*$^{(m)}$~*will~*SAY$^{(V)}$ TO~him WHERE Sarah WOMAN~you$^{(ms)}$ and~*he~will~*SAY$^{(V)}$ LOOK in~the~TENT **18:10** and~*he~will~*SAY$^{(V)}$ >~ TURN.BACK$^{(V)}$ *I~will~*TURN.BACK$^{(V)}$ TO~you$^{(ms)}$ like~the~APPOINTED.TIME LIVING and~LOOK SON to~Sarah WOMAN~you$^{(ms)}$ and~Sarah HEAR$^{(V)}$~*ing*$^{(fs)}$ OPENING the~TENT and~HE AFTER~him **18:11** and~Avraham and~Sarah BEARD~s COME$^{(V)}$~*ing*$^{(mp)}$ in~the~DAY~s *he~did~*TERMINATE$^{(V)}$ to~>~EXIST$^{(V)}$ to~Sarah PATH like~the~WOMAN~s **18:12** and~*she~will~*LAUGH$^{(V)}$ Sarah in~INSIDE~her to~>~SAY$^{(V)}$ AFTER *I~*>~WEAR.OUT$^{(V)}$ *she~did~*EXIST$^{(V)}$ to~me PLEASURE and~LORD~me *he~did~*BE.OLD$^{(V)}$ **18:13** and~*he~will~*SAY$^{(V)}$ **YHWH** TO Avraham to~WHAT THIS *she~did~*LAUGH$^{(V)}$ Sarah to~>~SAY$^{(V)}$?~ MOREOVER INDEED *I~will~*BRING.FORTH$^{(V)}$ and~I *I~did~*BE.OLD$^{(V)}$ **18:14** ?~ *he~did~be~*PERFORM$^{(V)}$ from~**YHWH** WORD to~the~APPOINTED *I~will~* TURN.BACK$^{(V)}$ TO~you$^{(ms)}$ like~the~APPOINTED.TIME LIVING and~to~Sarah SON **18:15** and~*she~will~much~*DENY$^{(V)}$ Sarah to~>~SAY$^{(V)}$ NOT *I~did~* LAUGH$^{(V)}$ GIVEN.THAT *she~did~*FEAR$^{(V)}$ and~*he~will~*SAY$^{(V)}$ NOT GIVEN.THAT *you*$^{(fs)}$~*did~*LAUGH$^{(V)}$ **18:16** and~*they*$^{(m)}$~*will~*RISE$^{(V)}$ from~THERE the~ MAN~s and~*they*$^{(m)}$~*will~*make~LOOK.DOWN$^{(V)}$ UPON FACE~s Sedom and~ Avraham WALK$^{(V)}$~*ing*$^{(ms)}$ WITH~them$^{(m)}$ to~>~*much~*SEND$^{(V)}$~ them$^{(m)}$ **18:17** and~**YHWH** *he~did~*SAY$^{(V)}$ the~*much~*COVER.OVER$^{(V)}$~*ing*$^{(ms)}$ I from~Avraham WHICH I DO$^{(V)}$~*ing*$^{(ms)}$ **18:18** and~Avraham >~EXIST$^{(V)}$ *he~*

The Book of Genesis

will~EXIST⁽ᵛ⁾ to~NATION GREAT and~NUMEROUS and~*they*~*did*~*be*~KNEEL⁽ᵛ⁾ in~him ALL NATION~s the~LAND **18:19** GIVEN.THAT *I*~*did*~KNOW⁽ᵛ⁾~him to~ THAT WHICH *he*~*will*~*much*~DIRECT⁽ᵛ⁾ AT SON~s~him and~AT HOUSE~him AFTER~him and~*they*~*did*~SAFEGUARD⁽ᵛ⁾ ROAD **YHWH** to~>~DO⁽ᵛ⁾ STEADFASTNESS and~DECISION to~THAT >~*make*~COME⁽ᵛ⁾ **YHWH** UPON Avraham AT WHICH *he*~*did*~*much*~SPEAK⁽ᵛ⁾ UPON~him **18:20** and~*he*~*will*~ SAY⁽ᵛ⁾ **YHWH** YELL Sedom and~Ghamorah GIVEN.THAT *she*~*did*~ INCREASE.IN.NUMBER⁽ᵛ⁾ and~FAILURE~them⁽ᵐ⁾ GIVEN.THAT *she*~*did*~ BE.HEAVY⁽ᵛ⁾ MANY **18:21** *I*~*will*~GO.DOWN⁽ᵛ⁾~her PLEASE and~*I*~*will*~SEE⁽ᵛ⁾ the~like~YELL~her the~COME⁽ᵛ⁾~*ing*⁽ᶠˢ⁾ TO~me *they*~*did*~DO⁽ᵛ⁾ COMPLETION and~IF NOT *I*~*will*~KNOW⁽ᵛ⁾~& **18:22** and~*they*⁽ᵐ⁾~*will*~TURN⁽ᵛ⁾ from~THERE the~MAN~s and~*they*⁽ᵐ⁾~*will*~WALK⁽ᵛ⁾ Sedom~unto and~Avraham YET.AGAIN~him STAND⁽ᵛ⁾~*ing*⁽ᵐˢ⁾ to~FACE~s **YHWH** **18:23** and~*he*~*will*~ DRAW.NEAR⁽ᵛ⁾ Avraham and~*he*~*will*~SAY⁽ᵛ⁾ ?~MOREOVER *you*⁽ᵐˢ⁾~*will*~ CONSUME⁽ᵛ⁾ STEADFAST.ONE WITH LOST **18:24** POSSIBLY THERE.IS FIVE~s STEADFAST.ONE~s in~MIDST the~CITY ?~MOREOVER *you*⁽ᵐˢ⁾~*will*~ CONSUME⁽ᵛ⁾ and~NOT *you*⁽ᵐˢ⁾~*will*~LIFT.UP⁽ᵛ⁾ to~the~AREA to~THAT FIVE~s the~STEADFAST.ONE~s WHICH in~INSIDE~her **18:25** FAR.BE.IT to~*you*⁽ᵐˢ⁾ from~>~DO⁽ᵛ⁾ like~the~WORD the~THIS to~>~*make*~DIE⁽ᵛ⁾ STEADFAST.ONE WITH LOST and~*he*~*did*~EXIST⁽ᵛ⁾ like~the~STEADFAST.ONE like~the~LOST FAR.BE.IT to~*you*⁽ᶠˢ⁾ ?~DECIDE⁽ᵛ⁾~*ing*⁽ᵐˢ⁾ ALL the~LAND NOT *he*~*will*~DO⁽ᵛ⁾ DECISION **18:26** and~*he*~*will*~SAY⁽ᵛ⁾ **YHWH** IF *I*~*will*~FIND⁽ᵛ⁾ in~Sedom FIVE~s STEADFAST.ONE~s in~MIDST the~CITY and~*I*~*did*~LIFT.UP⁽ᵛ⁾ to~ALL the~AREA in~the~CROSS.OVER⁽ᵛ⁾~*ed*⁽ᵐˢ⁾~them⁽ᵐ⁾ **18:27** and~*he*~*will*~ ANSWER⁽ᵛ⁾ Avraham and~*he*~*will*~SAY⁽ᵛ⁾ LOOK PLEASE *I*~*will*~*make*~ TAKE.UPON⁽ᵛ⁾ to~>~*much*~SPEAK⁽ᵛ⁾ TO Adonai and~I DIRT and~ ASH **18:28** POSSIBLY *they*⁽ᵐ⁾~*will*~DIMINISH⁽ᵛ⁾ FIVE~s the~STEADFAST.ONE~s FIVE ?~*you*⁽ᵐˢ⁾~*will*~*make*~DAMAGE⁽ᵛ⁾ in~the~FIVE AT ALL the~CITY and~*he*~ *will*~SAY⁽ᵛ⁾ NOT *I*~*will*~*make*~DAMAGE⁽ᵛ⁾ IF *I*~*will*~FIND⁽ᵛ⁾ THERE FOUR~s and~FIVE **18:29** and~*he*~*will*~*make*~ADD⁽ᵛ⁾ YET.AGAIN to~>~*much*~SPEAK⁽ᵛ⁾ TO~him and~*he*~*will*~SAY⁽ᵛ⁾ POSSIBLY *they*⁽ᵐ⁾~*will*~*be*~FIND⁽ᵛ⁾ THERE FOUR~s and~*he*~*will*~SAY⁽ᵛ⁾ NOT *I*~*will*~DO⁽ᵛ⁾ in~the~CROSS.OVER⁽ᵛ⁾~*ed*⁽ᵐˢ⁾ the~FOUR~s **18:30** and~*he*~*will*~SAY⁽ᵛ⁾ DO.NOT PLEASE *he*~*will*~FLARE.UP⁽ᵛ⁾ to~Adonai and~*I*~*will*~*much*~SPEAK⁽ᵛ⁾~& POSSIBLY *they*⁽ᵐ⁾~*will*~*be*~FIND⁽ᵛ⁾ THERE THREE~s and~*he*~*will*~SAY⁽ᵛ⁾ NOT *I*~*will*~DO⁽ᵛ⁾ IF *I*~*will*~FIND⁽ᵛ⁾ THERE THREE~s **18:31** and~*he*~*will*~SAY⁽ᵛ⁾ LOOK PLEASE *I*~*will*~*make*~ TAKE.UPON⁽ᵛ⁾ to~>~*much*~SPEAK⁽ᵛ⁾ TO Adonai POSSIBLY *they*⁽ᵐ⁾~*will*~*bè*~ FIND⁽ᵛ⁾ THERE TEN~s and~*he*~*will*~SAY⁽ᵛ⁾ NOT *I*~*will*~*make*~DAMAGE⁽ᵛ⁾ in~ the~CROSS.OVER⁽ᵛ⁾~*ed*⁽ᵐˢ⁾ the~TEN~s **18:32** and~*he*~*will*~SAY⁽ᵛ⁾ DO.NOT PLEASE *he*~*will*~FLARE.UP⁽ᵛ⁾ to~Adonai and~*I*~*will*~*much*~SPEAK⁽ᵛ⁾ SURELY the~FOOTSTEP POSSIBLY *they*⁽ᵐ⁾~*will*~*bè*~ FIND⁽ᵛ⁾ THERE TEN and~*he*~*will*~ SAY⁽ᵛ⁾ NOT *I*~*will*~*make*~DAMAGE⁽ᵛ⁾ in~the~CROSS.OVER⁽ᵛ⁾~*ed*⁽ᵐˢ⁾ the~ TEN **18:33** and~*he*~*will*~WALK⁽ᵛ⁾ **YHWH** like~WHICH *he*~*did*~*much*~FINISH⁽ᵛ⁾ to~>~*much*~SPEAK⁽ᵛ⁾ TO Avraham and~Avraham *he*~*did*~TURN.BACK⁽ᵛ⁾ to~ AREA~him

Chapter 19

19:1 and~*they*^(m)~*will*~COME^(v) TWO the~MESSENGER~s Sedom~unto in~the~EVENING and~Lot SETTLE^(v)~*ing*^(ms) in~GATE Sedom and~*he*~*will*~SEE^(v) Lot and~*he*~*will*~RISE^(v) to~>~MEET^(v)~them^(m) and~*he*~*will*~*self*~BEND.DOWN^(v) NOSE~s2 LAND~unto **19:2** and~*he*~*will*~SAY^(v) LOOK PLEASE LORD~s~me *!*^(mp)~TURN.ASIDE^(v) PLEASE TO HOUSE SERVANT~you^(mp) and~*!*^(mp)~STAY.THE.NIGHT^(v) and~*!*^(mp)~BATHE^(v) FOOT~s2~you^(mp) and~*you*^(mp)~*did*~*make*~DEPART.EARLY^(v) and~*you*^(mp)~*did*~WALK^(v) to~ROAD~you^(mp) and~*they*^(m)~*will*~SAY^(v) NOT GIVEN.THAT in~the~STREET *we*~*will*~STAY.THE.NIGHT^(v) **19:3** and~*he*~*will*~PRESS.HARD^(v) in~them^(m) MANY and~*they*^(m)~*will*~TURN.ASIDE^(v) TO~him and~*they*^(m)~*will*~COME^(v) TO HOUSE~him and~*he*~*will*~DO^(v) to~them^(m) BANQUET and~UNLEAVENED.BREAD~s *he*~*did*~BAKE^(v) and~*they*^(m)~*will*~EAT^(v) **19:4** BEFORE *they*^(m)~*will*~LIE.DOWN^(v) and~MAN~s the~CITY MAN~s Sedom *they*~*did*~*be*~GO.AROUND^(v) UPON the~HOUSE from~YOUNG.MAN and~UNTIL BEARD ALL the~PEOPLE from~EXTREMITY **19:5** and~*they*^(m)~*will*~CALL.OUT^(v) TO Lot and~*they*^(m)~*will*~SAY^(v) to~him WHERE the~MAN~s WHICH *they*~*did*~COME^(v) TO~you^(ms) the~NIGHT *!*^(mp)~*make*~GO.OUT^(v)~them^(m) TO~us and~*we*~*did*~KNOW^(v) AT~them^(m) **19:6** and~*he*~*will*~GO.OUT^(v) TO~them^(m) Lot the~OPENING~unto and~the~DOOR *he*~*did*~SHUT^(v) AFTER~him **19:7** and~*he*~*will*~SAY^(v) DO.NOT PLEASE BROTHER~s~me *you*^(mp)~*will*~*make*~BE.DYSFUNCTIONAL^(v) **19:8** LOOK PLEASE to~me TWO DAUGHTER~s WHICH NOT *they*~*did*~KNOW^(v) MAN *I*~*will*~*make*~GO.OUT^(v)~& PLEASE AT~them^(f) TO~you^(mp) and~*!*^(mp)~DO^(v) to~them^(f) like~the~FUNCTIONAL in~EYE~s2~you^(mp) ONLY to~the~MAN~s the~THESE DO.NOT *you*^(mp)~*will*~DO^(v) WORD GIVEN.THAT UPON SO *they*~*did*~COME^(v) in~SHADOW RAFTER~me **19:9** and~*they*^(m)~*will*~SAY^(v) *!*^(ms)~DRAW.NEAR^(v) FURTHER and~*they*^(m)~*will*~SAY^(v) the~UNIT *he*~*did*~COME^(v) to~>~IMMIGRATE^(v) and~*he*~*will*~DECIDE^(v) >~DECIDE^(v) NOW *we*~*will*~*make*~BE.DYSFUNCTIONAL^(v) to~you^(ms) from~them^(m) and~*they*^(m)~*will*~PRESS.HARD^(v) in~the~MAN in~Lot MANY and~*they*^(m)~*will*~DRAW.NEAR^(v) to~>~CRACK^(v) the~DOOR **19:10** and~*they*^(m)~*will*~SEND^(v) the~MAN~s AT HAND~them^(m) and~*they*^(m)~*will*~*make*~COME^(v) AT Lot TO~them^(m) the~HOUSE~unto and~AT the~DOOR *they*~*did*~SHUT^(v) **19:11** and~AT the~MAN~s WHICH OPENING the~HOUSE *they*~*did*~*make*~HIT^(v) in~the~SIGHTLESSNESS from~SMALL and~UNTIL GREAT and~*they*^(m)~*will*~BE.IMPATIENT^(v) to~>~FIND^(v) the~OPENING **19:12** and~*they*^(m)~*will*~SAY^(v) the~MAN~s TO Lot YET.AGAIN WHO to~you^(ms) HERE IN.LAW and~SON~s~you^(ms) and~DAUGHTER~s~you^(ms) and~ALL WHICH to~you^(ms) in~the~CITY *!*^(mp)~*make*~GO.OUT^(v) FROM the~AREA **19:13** GIVEN.THAT *make*~DAMAGE^(v)~*ing*^(mp) WE AT the~AREA the~THIS GIVEN.THAT *she*~*will*~MAGNIFY^(v) CRY~them^(m) AT FACE~s **YHWH** and~*he*~*will*~SEND^(v)~us **YHWH** to~>~DAMAGE^(v)~her **19:14** and~*he*~*will*~GO.OUT^(v) Lot and~*he*~*will*~*much*~SPEAK^(v) TO IN.LAW~s~him TAKE^(v)~*ing*^(mp)

The Book of Genesis

DAUGHTER~s~him and~*he~will*~SAY$^{(V)}$ *!$^{(mp)}$*~RISE$^{(V)}$ *!$^{(mp)}$*~GO.OUT$^{(V)}$ FROM the~AREA the~THIS GIVEN.THAT *make*~DAMAGE$^{(V)}$~*ing$^{(ms)}$* **YHWH** AT the~ CITY and~*he~will*~EXIST$^{(V)}$ like~*much*~LAUGH$^{(V)}$~*ing$^{(ms)}$* in~EYE~s2 IN.LAW~s~ him **19:15** and~like~THAT.ONE the~DAWN *he~did*~GO.UP$^{(V)}$ and~*they$^{(m)}$~ will~make*~COMPEL$^{(V)}$ the~MESSENGER~s in~Lot to~>~SAY$^{(V)}$ *!$^{(ms)}$*~RISE$^{(V)}$ *!$^{(ms)}$*~TAKE$^{(V)}$ AT WOMAN~*you$^{(ms)}$* and~AT TWO DAUGHTER~s~*you$^{(ms)}$* the~ *be*~FIND$^{(V)}$~*ing$^{(fp)}$* OTHERWISE *you$^{(ms)}$~will~be*~CONSUME$^{(V)}$ in~ TWISTEDNESS the~CITY **19:16** and~*he~will~self*~LINGER$^{(V)}$ and~*they$^{(m)}$~will~ make*~SEIZE$^{(V)}$ the~MAN~s in~HAND~him and~in~HAND WOMAN~him and~ in~HAND TWO DAUGHTER~s~him in~PITY **YHWH** UPON~him and~*they$^{(m)}$~ will~make*~GO.OUT$^{(V)}$~him and~*they$^{(m)}$~will~make*~REST$^{(V)}$~him from~ OUTSIDE to~the~CITY **19:17** and~*he~will*~EXIST$^{(V)}$ like~>~*make*~GO.OUT$^{(V)}$~ them$^{(m)}$ AT~them$^{(m)}$ the~OUTSIDE~unto and~*he~will*~SAY$^{(V)}$ *!$^{(ms)}$~be*~ SLIP.AWAY$^{(V)}$ UPON SOUL~*you$^{(ms)}$* DO.NOT *you$^{(ms)}$~will~make*~STARE$^{(V)}$ AFTER~*you$^{(ms)}$* and~DO.NOT *you$^{(ms)}$~will*~STAND$^{(V)}$ in~ALL the~ROUNDNESS the~HILL~unto *!$^{(ms)}$~be*~SLIP.AWAY$^{(V)}$ OTHERWISE *you$^{(ms)}$~will~be*~ CONSUME$^{(V)}$ **19:18** and~*he~will*~SAY$^{(V)}$ Lot TO~them$^{(m)}$ DO.NOT PLEASE Adonai **19:19** LOOK PLEASE *he~did*~FIND$^{(V)}$ SERVANT~*you$^{(ms)}$* BEAUTY in~ EYE~s2~*you$^{(ms)}$* and~*you$^{(ms)}$~will~make*~MAGNIFY$^{(V)}$ KINDNESS~*you$^{(ms)}$* WHICH *you$^{(ms)}$~did*~DO$^{(V)}$ BY~me to~>~*make*~LIVE$^{(V)}$ AT SOUL~me and~I NOT *I~will*~BE.ABLE$^{(V)}$ to~>~*make*~SLIP.AWAY$^{(V)}$ the~HILL~unto OTHERWISE *she~will*~ADHERE$^{(V)}$~me the~DYSFUNCTIONAL and~*I~did*~DIE$^{(V)}$ **19:20** LOOK PLEASE the~CITY the~THIS NEAR to~>~FLEE$^{(V)}$ THERE~unto and~SHE FEW *I~ will~be*~SLIP.AWAY$^{(V)}$ PLEASE THERE~unto ?~NOT FEW SHE and~*she~will*~ LIVE$^{(V)}$ SOUL~me **19:21** and~*he~will*~SAY$^{(V)}$ TO~him LOOK *I~did*~LIFT.UP$^{(V)}$ FACE~s~*you$^{(ms)}$* ALSO to~the~WORD the~THIS to~EXCEPT >~OVERTURN$^{(V)}$~ me AT the~CITY WHICH *you$^{(ms)}$~did~much*~SPEAK$^{(V)}$ **19:22** *!$^{(ms)}$~much*~ HURRY$^{(V)}$ *!$^{(ms)}$~be*~SLIP.AWAY$^{(V)}$ THERE~unto GIVEN.THAT NOT *I~will*~ BE.ABLE$^{(V)}$ to~>~DO$^{(V)}$ WORD UNTIL >~COME$^{(V)}$~*you$^{(ms)}$* THERE~unto UPON SO *he~did*~CALL.OUT$^{(V)}$ TITLE the~CITY Tso'ar **19:23** the~SUN *he~did*~ GO.OUT$^{(V)}$ UPON the~LAND and~Lot *he~did*~COME$^{(V)}$ Tso'ar~ unto **19:24** and~**YHWH** *he~did~make*~PRECIPITATE$^{(V)}$ UPON Sedom and~ UPON Ghamorah BRIMSTONE and~FIRE from~AT **YHWH** FROM the~SKY~ s2 **19:25** and~*he~will*~OVERTURN$^{(V)}$ AT the~CITY~s the~THESE and~AT ALL the~ROUNDNESS and~AT ALL SETTLE$^{(V)}$~*ing$^{(mp)}$* the~CITY~s and~ SPRING.UP$^{(V)}$ the~GROUND **19:26** and~*she~will~make*~STARE$^{(V)}$ WOMAN~ him from~AFTER~him and~*she~will*~EXIST$^{(V)}$ POST SALT **19:27** and~*he~will~ make*~DEPART.EARLY$^{(V)}$ Avraham in~the~MORNING TO the~AREA WHICH *he~did*~STAND$^{(V)}$ THERE AT FACE~s **YHWH** **19:28** and~*he~will~make*~ LOOK.DOWN$^{(V)}$ UPON FACE~s Sedom and~Ghamorah and~UPON ALL FACE~s LAND the~ROUNDNESS and~*he~will*~SEE$^{(V)}$ and~LOOK *he~did*~GO.UP$^{(V)}$ SMOKING the~LAND like~SMOKING the~FURNACE **19:29** and~*he~will*~ EXIST$^{(V)}$ in~>~*much*~DAMAGE$^{(V)}$ Elohiym AT CITY~s the~ROUNDNESS and~ *he~will*~REMEMBER$^{(V)}$ Elohiym AT Avraham and~*he~will~much*~SEND$^{(V)}$ AT Lot from~MIDST the~OVERTURNING in~>~OVERTURN$^{(V)}$ AT the~CITY~s

WHICH *he~did*~SETTLE[(V)] in~them[(f)] Lot **19:30** and~*he~will*~make~GO.UP[(V)] Lot from~Tso'ar and~*he~will*~SETTLE[(V)] in~the~HILL and~TWO DAUGHTER~s~him WITH~him GIVEN.THAT *he~did*~FEAR[(V)] to~>~SETTLE[(V)] in~Tso'ar and~*he~will*~SETTLE[(V)] in~the~CAVE HE and~TWO DAUGHTER~s~him **19:31** and~*she~will*~SAY[(V)] the~FIRSTBORN.FEMALE TO the~LITTLE.ONE FATHER~us *he~did*~BE.OLD[(V)] and~MAN WITHOUT in~the~LAND to~>~COME[(V)] UPON~us like~ROAD ALL the~LAND **19:32** *!*[(ms)]~WALK[(V)]~& *we~will*~make~DRINK[(V)] AT FATHER~us WINE and~*we~will*~LIE.DOWN[(V)] WITH~him and~*we~will*~LIVE[(V)] from~FATHER~us SEED **19:33** and~*they*[(f)]~*will*~make~DRINK[(V)] AT FATHER~them[(f)] WINE in~the~NIGHT HE and~*she~will*~COME[(V)] the~FIRSTBORN.FEMALE and~*she~will*~LIE.DOWN[(V)] AT FATHER~her and~NOT *he~did*~KNOW[(V)] in~>~LIE.DOWN[(V)]~her and~in~>~RISE[(V)]~her **19:34** and~*he~will*~EXIST[(V)] from~MORROW and~*she~will*~SAY[(V)] the~FIRSTBORN.FEMALE TO the~LITTLE.ONE THOUGH *I~did*~LIE.DOWN[(V)] LAST.NIGHT AT FATHER~me *we~will*~make~DRINK[(V)]~him WINE ALSO the~NIGHT and~*!*[(fs)]~COME[(V)] *!*[(fs)]~LIE.DOWN[(V)] WITH~him and~*we~will*~LIVE[(V)] from~FATHER~us SEED **19:35** and~*they*[(f)]~*will*~make~DRINK[(V)] ALSO in~the~NIGHT the~HE AT FATHER~them[(f)] WINE and~*she~will*~RISE[(V)] the~LITTLE.ONE and~*she~will*~LIE.DOWN[(V)] WITH~him and~NOT *he~did*~KNOW[(V)] in~>~LIE.DOWN[(V)]~her and~in~>~RISE[(V)]~her **19:36** and~*they*[(f)]~*will*~CONCEIVE[(V)] TWO DAUGHTER~s Lot from~FATHER~them[(f)] **19:37** and~*she~will*~BRING.FORTH[(V)] the~FIRSTBORN.FEMALE SON and~*she~will*~CALL.OUT[(V)] TITLE~him Mo'av HE FATHER~of Mo'av UNTIL the~DAY **19:38** and~the~LITTLE.ONE ALSO SHE *she~did*~BRING.FORTH[(V)] SON and~*she~will*~CALL.OUT[(V)] TITLE~him Ben-Amiy HE FATHER~of SON~s Amon UNTIL the~DAY

Chapter 20

20:1 and~*he~will*~JOURNEY[(V)] from~THERE Avraham LAND~unto the~SOUTH and~*he~will*~SETTLE[(V)] BETWEEN Qadesh and~BETWEEN Shur and~*he~will*~IMMIGRATE[(V)] in~Gerar **20:2** and~*he~will*~SAY[(V)] Avraham TO Sarah WOMAN~him SISTER~me SHE and~*he~will*~SEND[(V)] Aviymelekh KING Gerar and~*he~will*~TAKE[(V)] AT Sarah **20:3** and~*he~will*~COME[(V)] Elohiym TO Aviymelekh in~the~DREAM the~NIGHT and~*he~will*~SAY[(V)] to~him LOOK~you[(ms)] DIE[(V)]~*ing*[(ms)] UPON the~WOMAN WHICH *you*[(ms)]~*did*~TAKE[(V)] and~SHE MARRY[(V)]~*ed*[(fs)] MASTER **20:4** and~Aviymelekh NOT *he~did*~COME.NEAR[(V)] TO~her and~*he~will*~SAY[(V)] Adonai ?~NATION ALSO STEADFAST.ONE *you*[(ms)]~*will*~KILL[(V)] **20:5** ?~NOT HE *he~did*~SAY[(V)] to~me SISTER~me SHE and~SHE ALSO SHE *she~did*~SAY[(V)] BROTHER~me HE in~MATURE HEART~me and~in~INNOCENCE PALM~s2~me *I~did*~DO[(V)] THIS **20:6** and~*he~will*~SAY[(V)] TO~him the~Elohiym in~the~DREAM ALSO I *I~did*~KNOW[(V)] GIVEN.THAT in~MATURE HEART~you[(ms)] *you*[(ms)]~*did*~DO[(V)] THIS and~I~will~KEEP.BACK⁽ⱽ⁾ ALSO I AT~you⁽ᵐˢ⁾ from~FAILURE~him to~me UPON SO NOT I~did~GIVE⁽ⱽ⁾~you⁽ᵐˢ⁾ to~>~TOUCH⁽ⱽ⁾ TO~her **20:7** and~NOW !⁽ᵐˢ⁾~ *make*~TURN.BACK⁽ⱽ⁾ WOMAN the~MAN GIVEN.THAT ANNOUNCER HE and~ *he~will~self*~PLEAD⁽ⱽ⁾ in~UNTIL~you⁽ᵐˢ⁾ and~ !⁽ᵐˢ⁾~LIVE⁽ⱽ⁾ and~IF WITHOUT~ you⁽ᵐˢ⁾ *make*~TURN.BACK⁽ⱽ⁾~*ing*⁽ᵐˢ⁾ !⁽ᵐˢ⁾~KNOW⁽ⱽ⁾ GIVEN.THAT >~DIE⁽ⱽ⁾ *you*⁽ᵐˢ⁾~*will*~DIE⁽ⱽ⁾ YOU⁽ᵐˢ⁾ and~ALL WHICH to~you⁽ᶠˢ⁾ **20:8** and~*he~will~ make*~DEPART.EARLY⁽ⱽ⁾ Aviymelekh in~the~MORNING and~*he~will~* CALL.OUT⁽ⱽ⁾ to~ALL SERVANT~s~him and~*he~will~much*~SPEAK⁽ⱽ⁾ AT ALL the~WORD~s the~THESE in~EAR~s2~them⁽ᵐ⁾ and~*they*⁽ᵐ⁾~*will*~FEAR⁽ⱽ⁾ the~ MAN~s MANY **20:9** and~*he~will*~CALL.OUT⁽ⱽ⁾ Aviymelekh to~Avraham and~ *he~will~*SAY⁽ⱽ⁾ to~him WHAT *you*⁽ᵐˢ⁾~*did*~DO⁽ⱽ⁾ to~us and~WHAT I~did~ FAIL⁽ⱽ⁾ to~you⁽ᶠˢ⁾ GIVEN.THAT *you*⁽ᵐˢ⁾~*did~make*~COME⁽ⱽ⁾ UPON~me and~ UPON KINGDOM~me FAILURE GREAT WORK~s WHICH NOT *they~did~be*~ DO⁽ⱽ⁾ *you*⁽ᵐˢ⁾~*did*~DO⁽ⱽ⁾ BY~me **20:10** and~*he~will~*SAY⁽ⱽ⁾ Aviymelekh TO Avraham WHAT *you*⁽ᵐˢ⁾~*did*~SEE⁽ⱽ⁾ GIVEN.THAT *you*⁽ᵐˢ⁾~*did*~DO⁽ⱽ⁾ AT the~ WORD the~THIS **20:11** and~*he~will~*SAY⁽ⱽ⁾ Avraham GIVEN.THAT I~*did~* SAY⁽ⱽ⁾ ONLY WITHOUT FEARFULNESS Elohiym in~the~AREA the~THIS and~ *they~did~*KILL⁽ⱽ⁾~me UPON WORD WOMAN~me **20:12** and~ALSO SURE SISTER~me DAUGHTER FATHER~me SHE SURELY NOT DAUGHTER MOTHER~ me and~*she~will~*EXIST⁽ⱽ⁾ to~me to~WOMAN **20:13** and~*he~will~*EXIST⁽ⱽ⁾ like~WHICH *they~did~make*~WANDER⁽ⱽ⁾ AT~me Elohiym from~HOUSE FATHER~me and~I~*will~*SAY⁽ⱽ⁾ to~her THIS KINDNESS~you⁽ᶠˢ⁾ WHICH *you*⁽ᶠˢ⁾~ *will*~DO⁽ⱽ⁾ BY~me TO ALL the~AREA WHICH *we~will~*COME⁽ⱽ⁾ THERE~unto !⁽ᶠˢ⁾~SAY⁽ⱽ⁾ to~me BROTHER~me HE **20:14** and~*he~will~*TAKE⁽ⱽ⁾ Aviymelekh FLOCKS and~CATTLE and~SERVANT~s and~MAID~s and~*he~will~*GIVE⁽ⱽ⁾ to~ Avraham and~*he~will~make*~TURN.BACK⁽ⱽ⁾ to~him AT Sarah WOMAN~ him **20:15** and~*he~will~*SAY⁽ⱽ⁾ Aviymelekh LOOK LAND~me to~FACE~s~ you⁽ᵐˢ⁾ in~the~FUNCTIONAL in~EYE~s2~you⁽ᵐˢ⁾ !⁽ᵐˢ⁾~SETTLE⁽ⱽ⁾ **20:16** and~ to~Sarah *he~did~*SAY⁽ⱽ⁾ LOOK I~*did~*GIVE⁽ⱽ⁾ THOUSAND SILVER to~ BROTHER~you⁽ᶠˢ⁾ LOOK HE to~you⁽ᶠˢ⁾ RAIMENT EYE~s2 to~ALL WHICH AT~ you⁽ᶠˢ⁾ and~AT ALL and~*be~*REBUKE⁽ⱽ⁾~*ing*⁽ᶠˢ⁾ **20:17** and~*he~will~self~* PLEAD⁽ⱽ⁾ Avraham TO the~Elohiym and~*he~will~*HEAL⁽ⱽ⁾ Elohiym AT Aviymelekh and~AT WOMAN~him and~BONDWOMAN~s~him and~*they*⁽ᵐ⁾~ *will~*BRING.FORTH⁽ⱽ⁾ **20:18** GIVEN.THAT >~STOP⁽ⱽ⁾ *he~did~*STOP⁽ⱽ⁾ **YHWH** in~UNTIL ALL BOWELS to~HOUSE Aviymelekh UPON WORD Sarah WOMAN Avraham

Chapter 21

21:1 and~**YHWH** *he~did~*REGISTER⁽ⱽ⁾ AT Sarah like~WHICH *he~did~*SAY⁽ⱽ⁾ and~*he~will~*DO⁽ⱽ⁾ **YHWH** to~Sarah like~WHICH *he~did~much~* SPEAK⁽ⱽ⁾ **21:2** and~*she~will~*CONCEIVE⁽ⱽ⁾ and~*she~will~*BRING.FORTH⁽ⱽ⁾ Sarah to~Avraham SON to~EXTREME.OLD.AGE~s~him to~the~APPOINTED

WHICH *he~did~much~*SPEAK[(V)] AT~him Elohiym **21:3** and~*he~will~*
CALL.OUT[(V)] Avraham AT TITLE SON~him the~*be~*BRING.FORTH[(V)]~*ing*[(ms)] to~
him WHICH *she~did~*BRING.FORTH[(V)] to~him Sarah Yits'hhaq **21:4** and~*he~
will~*SNIP.OFF[(V)] Avraham AT Yits'hhaq SON~him SON EIGHT DAY~s like~
WHICH *he~did~much~*DIRECT[(V)] AT~him Elohiym **21:5** and~Avraham SON
HUNDRED YEAR in~>~*be~*BRING.FORTH[(V)] to~him AT Yits'hhaq SON~
him **21:6** and~*she~will~*SAY[(V)] Sarah LAUGHTER *he~did~*DO[(V)] to~me
Elohiym ALL the~HEAR[(V)]~*ing*[(ms)] *he~will~*LAUGH[(V)] to~me **21:7** and~*she~
will~*SAY[(V)] WHO *he~did~much~*TALK[(V)] to~Avraham *she~did~*make~
SUCKLE[(V)] SON~s Sarah GIVEN.THAT *I~did~*BRING.FORTH[(V)] SON to~
EXTREME.OLD.AGE~s~him **21:8** and~*he~will~*MAGNIFY[(V)] the~BOY and~*he~
will~be~*YIELD[(V)] and~*he~will~*DO[(V)] Avraham BANQUET GREAT in~DAY >~
*be~*YIELD[(V)] AT Yits'hhaq **21:9** and~*she~will~*SEE[(V)] Sarah AT SON Hagar the~
Mits'rayim~of WHICH *she~did~*BRING.FORTH[(V)] to~Avraham *much~*
LAUGH[(V)]~*ing*[(ms)] **21:10** and~*she~will~*SAY[(V)] to~Avraham >~*much~*
CAST.OUT[(V)] the~BONDWOMAN the~THIS and~AT SON~her GIVEN.THAT
NOT *he~will~*POSSESS[(V)] SON the~BONDWOMAN the~THIS WITH SON~me
WITH Yits'hhaq **21:11** and~*he~will~*BE.DYSFUNCTIONAL[(V)] the~WORD
MANY in~EYE~s2 Avraham UPON CONCERNING~s SON~him **21:12** and~*he~
will~*SAY[(V)] Elohiym TO Avraham DO.NOT *he~will~*BE.DYSFUNCTIONAL[(V)] in~
EYE~s2~you[(ms)] UPON the~YOUNG.MAN and~UPON BONDWOMAN~you[(ms)]
ALL WHICH *she~will~*SAY[(V)] TO~you[(ms)] Sarah ![(ms)]~HEAR[(V)] in~VOICE~her
GIVEN.THAT in~Yits'hhaq *he~will~be~*CALL.OUT[(V)] to~you[(ms)]
SEED **21:13** and~ALSO AT SON the~BONDWOMAN to~NATION *I~will~*
PLACE[(V)]~him GIVEN.THAT SEED~you[(ms)] HE **21:14** and~*he~will~*make~
DEPART.EARLY[(V)] Avraham in~the~MORNING and~*he~will~*TAKE[(V)] BREAD
and~SKIN.BAG WATER~s2 and~*he~will~*GIVE[(V)] TO Hagar PLACE[(V)]~*ing*[(ms)]
UPON SHOULDER~her and~AT the~BOY and~*he~will~*SEND[(V)]~her and~*she~
will~*WALK[(V)] and~*she~will~*WANDER[(V)] in~WILDERNESS B'er-
Sheva **21:15** and~*they*[(m)]~*will~*FINISH[(V)] the~WATER~s2 FROM the~
SKIN.BAG and~*she~will~*THROW.OUT[(V)] AT the~BOY UNDER UNIT the~
SHRUB **21:16** and~*she~will~*WALK[(V)] and~*she~will~*SETTLE[(V)] to~her from~
OPPOSITE >~*make~*BE.FAR[(V)] like~*much~*HURL[(V)]~*ing*[(mp)] BOW GIVEN.THAT
*she~did~*SAY[(V)] DO.NOT *I~will~*SEE[(V)] in~DEATH the~BOY and~*she~will~*
SETTLE[(V)] from~OPPOSITE and~*she~will~*LIFT.UP[(V)] AT VOICE~her and~*she~
will~*WEEP[(V)] **21:17** and~*he~will~*HEAR[(V)] Elohiym AT VOICE the~
YOUNG.MAN and~*he~will~*CALL.OUT[(V)] MESSENGER Elohiym TO Hagar
FROM the~SKY~s2 and~*he~will~*SAY[(V)] to~her WHAT to~you[(fs)] Hagar
DO.NOT you[(fs)]~*will~*FEAR[(V)] GIVEN.THAT *he~did~*HEAR[(V)] Elohiym TO VOICE
the~YOUNG.MAN in~WHICH HE THERE **21:18** ![(fs)]~RISE[(V)] ![(fs)]~LIFT.UP[(V)] AT
the~YOUNG.MAN and~![(ms)]~*make~*SEIZE[(V)] AT HAND~you[(fs)] in~him
GIVEN.THAT to~NATION GREAT *I~will~*PLACE[(V)]~him **21:19** and~*he~will~*
OPEN.UP[(V)] Elohiym AT EYE~s2~her and~*she~will~*SEE[(V)] WELL WATER~s2
and~*she~will~*WALK[(V)] and~*she~will~*FILL[(V)] AT the~SKIN.BAG WATER~s2
and~*she~will~*make~DRINK[(V)] AT the~YOUNG.MAN **21:20** and~*he~will~*

EXIST$^{(V)}$ Elohiym AT the~YOUNG.MAN and~he~will~MAGNIFY$^{(V)}$ and~he~will~SETTLE$^{(V)}$ in~the~WILDERNESS and~he~will~EXIST$^{(V)}$ INCREASE$^{(V)}$~ing$^{(ms)}$ BOW **21:21** and~he~will~SETTLE$^{(V)}$ in~WILDERNESS Paran and~she~will~TAKE$^{(V)}$ to~him MOTHER~him WOMAN from~LAND Mits'rayim **21:22** and~he~will~EXIST$^{(V)}$ in~the~APPOINTED.TIME the~SHE and~he~will~SAY$^{(V)}$ Aviymelekh and~Pikhol NOBLE ARMY~him TO Avraham to~>~SAY$^{(V)}$ Elohiym WITH~you$^{(ms)}$ in~ALL WHICH YOU$^{(ms)}$ DO$^{(V)}$~ing$^{(ms)}$ **21:23** and~NOW !$^{(ms)}$~be~SWEAR$^{(V)}$~& to~me in~Elohiym TO.THIS.POINT IF you$^{(ms)}$~will~DEAL.FALSELY$^{(V)}$ to~me and~to~HEIR~me and~to~POSTERITY~me like~the~KINDNESS WHICH I~did~DO$^{(V)}$ WITH~you$^{(ms)}$ you$^{(ms)}$~will~DO$^{(V)}$ BY~me and~WITH the~LAND WHICH you$^{(ms)}$~did~IMMIGRATE$^{(V)}$ in~her **21:24** and~he~will~SAY$^{(V)}$ Avraham I I~will~be~SWEAR$^{(V)}$ **21:25** and~he~will~make~REBUKE$^{(V)}$ Avraham AT Aviymelekh UPON CONCERNING WELL the~WATER~s2 WHICH they~did~PLUCK.AWAY$^{(V)}$ SERVANT~s Aviymelekh **21:26** and~he~will~SAY$^{(V)}$ Aviymelekh NOT I~did~KNOW$^{(V)}$ WHO he~did~DO$^{(V)}$ AT the~WORD the~THIS and~ALSO YOU$^{(ms)}$ NOT you$^{(ms)}$~did~make~BE.FACE.TO.FACE$^{(V)}$ to~me and~ALSO I NOT I~did~HEAR$^{(V)}$ EXCEPT the~DAY **21:27** and~he~will~TAKE$^{(V)}$ Avraham FLOCKS and~CATTLE and~he~will~GIVE$^{(V)}$ to~Aviymelekh and~they$^{(m)}$~will~CUT$^{(V)}$ TWO~them$^{(m)}$ COVENANT **21:28** and~he~will~make~STAND.UP$^{(V)}$ Avraham AT SEVEN SHEEP the~FLOCKS to~STRAND~them$^{(f)}$ **21:29** and~he~will~SAY$^{(V)}$ Aviymelekh TO Avraham WHAT TO.THIS.POINT SEVEN SHEEP the~THESE WHICH you$^{(ms)}$~did~make~STAND.UP$^{(V)}$ to~STRAND~them$^{(f)}$ **21:30** and~he~will~SAY$^{(V)}$ GIVEN.THAT AT SEVEN SHEEP you$^{(ms)}$~will~TAKE$^{(V)}$ from~HAND~me in~the~CROSS.OVER$^{(V)}$~ed$^{(ms)}$ she~will~EXIST$^{(V)}$ to~me to~WITNESS GIVEN.THAT I~did~DIG.OUT$^{(V)}$ AT the~WELL the~THIS **21:31** UPON SO he~did~CALL.OUT$^{(V)}$ to~the~AREA the~HE B'er-Sheva GIVEN.THAT THERE they~did~be~SWEAR$^{(V)}$ TWO~them$^{(m)}$ **21:32** and~they$^{(m)}$~will~CUT$^{(V)}$ COVENANT in~B'er-Sheva and~he~will~RISE$^{(V)}$ Aviymelekh and~Pikhol NOBLE ARMY~him and~they$^{(m)}$~will~TURN.BACK$^{(V)}$ TO LAND Peleshet~s **21:33** and~he~will~PLANT$^{(V)}$ TAMARISK in~B'er-Sheva and~he~will~CALL.OUT$^{(V)}$ THERE in~TITLE **YHWH** MIGHTY.ONE DISTANT **21:34** and~he~will~IMMIGRATE$^{(V)}$ Avraham in~LAND Peleshet~s DAY~s ABUNDANT~s

Chapter 22

22:1 and~he~will~EXIST$^{(V)}$ AFTER the~WORD~s the~THESE and~the~Elohiym he~did~much~TEST$^{(V)}$ AT Avraham and~he~will~SAY$^{(V)}$ TO~him Avraham and~he~will~SAY$^{(V)}$ LOOK~me **22:2** and~he~will~SAY$^{(V)}$!$^{(ms)}$~TAKE$^{(V)}$ PLEASE AT SON~you$^{(ms)}$ AT SOLITARY~you$^{(ms)}$ WHICH you$^{(ms)}$~did~LOVE$^{(V)}$ AT Yits'hhaq and~ !$^{(ms)}$~WALK$^{(V)}$ to~you$^{(ms)}$ TO LAND the~Moriyah and~ !$^{(ms)}$~make~GO.UP$^{(V)}$~him THERE to~ASCENSION.OFFERING UPON UNIT the~HILL~s WHICH I~will~SAY$^{(V)}$ TO~you$^{(ms)}$ **22:3** and~he~will~make~

DEPART.EARLY$^{(V)}$ Avraham in~the~MORNING and~he~will~SADDLE$^{(V)}$ AT DONKEY~him and~he~will~TAKE$^{(V)}$ AT TWO YOUNG.MAN~s~him AT~him and~AT Yits'hhaq SON~him and~he~will~CLEAVE.OPEN$^{(V)}$ TREE~s ASCENSION.OFFERING and~he~will~RISE$^{(V)}$ and~he~will~WALK$^{(V)}$ TO the~ AREA WHICH he~did~SAY$^{(V)}$ to~him the~Elohiym **22:4** in~the~DAY the~ THIRD and~he~will~LIFT.UP$^{(V)}$ Avraham AT EYE~s2~him and~he~will~SEE$^{(V)}$ AT the~AREA from~DISTANCE **22:5** and~he~will~SAY$^{(V)}$ Avraham TO YOUNG.MAN~s~him I$^{(mp)}$~SETTLE$^{(V)}$ to~you$^{(mp)}$ HERE WITH the~DONKEY and~I and~the~YOUNG.MAN we~will~WALK$^{(V)}$~& UNTIL IN.THIS.WAY and~ we~did~self~BEND.DOWN$^{(V)}$ and~we~did~TURN.BACK$^{(V)}$ TO~ you$^{(mp)}$ **22:6** and~he~will~TAKE$^{(V)}$ Avraham AT TREE~s the~ ASCENSION.OFFERING and~he~will~PLACE$^{(V)}$ UPON Yits'hhaq SON~him and~ he~will~TAKE$^{(V)}$ in~HAND~him AT the~FIRE and~AT the~KNIFE and~they$^{(m)}$~ will~WALK$^{(V)}$ TWO~them$^{(m)}$ TOGETHER **22:7** and~he~will~SAY$^{(V)}$ Yits'hhaq TO Avraham FATHER~him and~he~will~SAY$^{(V)}$ FATHER~me and~he~will~ SAY$^{(V)}$ LOOK~me SON~me and~he~will~SAY$^{(V)}$ LOOK the~FIRE and~the~ TREE~s and~WHERE the~RAM to~ASCENSION.OFFERING **22:8** and~he~will~ SAY$^{(V)}$ Avraham Elohiym he~will~SEE$^{(V)}$ to~him the~RAM to~ ASCENSION.OFFERING SON~me and~they$^{(m)}$~will~WALK$^{(V)}$ TWO~them$^{(m)}$ TOGETHER **22:9** and~they$^{(m)}$~will~COME$^{(V)}$ TO the~AREA WHICH he~did~ SAY$^{(V)}$ to~him the~Elohiym and~he~will~BUILD$^{(V)}$ THERE Avraham AT the~ ALTAR and~he~will~ARRANGE$^{(V)}$ AT the~TREE~s and~he~will~BIND$^{(V)}$ AT Yits'hhaq SON~him and~he~will~PLACE$^{(V)}$ AT~him UPON the~ALTAR from~ UPWARD to~the~TREE~s **22:10** and~he~will~SEND$^{(V)}$ Avraham AT HAND~ him and~he~will~TAKE$^{(V)}$ AT the~KNIFE to~>~SLAY$^{(V)}$ AT SON~ him **22:11** and~he~will~CALL.OUT$^{(V)}$ TO~him MESSENGER **YHWH** FROM the~SKY~s2 and~he~will~SAY$^{(V)}$ Avraham Avraham and~he~will~SAY$^{(V)}$ LOOK~me **22:12** and~he~will~SAY$^{(V)}$ DO.NOT you$^{(ms)}$~will~SEND$^{(V)}$ HAND~ you$^{(ms)}$ TO the~YOUNG.MAN and~DO.NOT you$^{(ms)}$~will~DO$^{(V)}$ to~him ANYTHING GIVEN.THAT NOW I~did~KNOW$^{(V)}$ GIVEN.THAT FEARFUL Elohiym YOU$^{(ms)}$ and~NOT you$^{(ms)}$~did~KEEP.BACK$^{(V)}$ AT SON~you$^{(ms)}$ AT SOLITARY~ you$^{(ms)}$ FROM~me **22:13** and~he~will~LIFT.UP$^{(V)}$ Avraham AT EYE~s2~him and~he~will~SEE$^{(V)}$ and~LOOK BUCK AFTER he~did~be~TAKE.HOLD$^{(V)}$ in~NET in~HORN~s~him and~he~will~WALK$^{(V)}$ Avraham and~he~will~TAKE$^{(V)}$ AT the~BUCK and~he~will~make~GO.UP$^{(V)}$~him to~ASCENSION.OFFERING UNDER SON~him **22:14** and~he~will~CALL.OUT$^{(V)}$ Avraham TITLE the~AREA the~HE **YHWH**-Yireh WHICH he~will~be~SAY$^{(V)}$ the~DAY in~HILL **YHWH** he~ will~be~SEE$^{(V)}$ **22:15** and~he~will~CALL.OUT$^{(V)}$ MESSENGER **YHWH** TO Avraham SECOND FROM the~SKY~s2 **22:16** and~he~will~SAY$^{(V)}$ in~me I~ did~be~SWEAR$^{(V)}$ DECLARE$^{(V)}$~ed$^{(ms)}$ **YHWH** GIVEN.THAT SEEING.AS WHICH you$^{(ms)}$~did~DO$^{(V)}$ AT the~WORD the~THIS and~NOT you$^{(ms)}$~did~ KEEP.BACK$^{(V)}$ AT SON~you$^{(ms)}$ AT SOLITARY~you$^{(ms)}$ **22:17** GIVEN.THAT >~ much~KNEEL$^{(V)}$ I~will~much~KNEEL$^{(V)}$~you$^{(ms)}$ and~>~make~INCREASE$^{(V)}$ I~ will~make~INCREASE$^{(V)}$ AT SEED~you$^{(ms)}$ like~STAR~s the~SKY~s2 and~like~ the~SAND WHICH UPON LIP the~SEA and~he~will~POSSESS$^{(V)}$ SEED~you$^{(ms)}$

The Book of Genesis

AT GATE ATTACK$^{(V)}$~*ing$^{(ms)}$*~s~him **22:18** and~*they~did~self*~KNEEL$^{(V)}$ in~ SEED~you$^{(ms)}$ ALL NATION~s the~LAND CONSEQUENCE WHICH *you$^{(ms)}$~did*~ HEAR$^{(V)}$ in~VOICE~me **22:19** and~*he~will*~TURN.BACK$^{(V)}$ Avraham TO YOUNG.MAN~s~him and~*they$^{(m)}$~will*~RISE$^{(V)}$ and~*they$^{(m)}$~will*~WALK$^{(V)}$ TOGETHER TO B'er-Sheva and~*he~will*~SETTLE$^{(V)}$ Avraham B'er-Sheva **22:20** and~*he~will*~EXIST$^{(V)}$ AFTER the~WORD~s the~THESE and~*he~ will~be~make~*BE.FACE.TO.FACE$^{(V)}$ to~Avraham to~>~SAY$^{(V)}$ LOOK *she~did*~ BRING.FORTH$^{(V)}$ Milkah ALSO SHE SON~s to~Nahhor BROTHER~ you$^{(ms)}$ **22:21** AT Uts FIRSTBORN~him and~AT Buz BROTHER~him and~AT Qemu'el FATHER~of Aram **22:22** and~AT Kesed and~AT Hhazo and~AT Pildash and~AT Yidlap and~AT Betu'el **22:23** and~Betu'el *he~did*~ BRING.FORTH$^{(V)}$ AT Rivqah EIGHT THESE *she~did*~BRING.FORTH$^{(V)}$ Milkah to~ Nahhor BROTHER~of Avraham **22:24** and~CONCUBINE~him and~TITLE~her Re'umah and~*she~will*~BRING.FORTH$^{(V)}$ ALSO SHE AT Tevahh and~AT Gahham and~AT Tahhash and~AT Ma'akhah

Chapter 23

23:1 and~*they$^{(m)}$~will*~EXIST$^{(V)}$ LIVING~s Sarah HUNDRED YEAR and~TEN~s YEAR and~SEVEN YEAR~s YEAR~s LIVING~s Sarah **23:2** and~*she~will*~DIE$^{(V)}$ Sarah in~Qiryat-Arba SHE Hhevron in~LAND Kena'an and~*he~will*~COME$^{(V)}$ Avraham to~>~LAMENT$^{(V)}$ to~Sarah and~to~>~WEEP$^{(V)}$~her **23:3** and~*he~ will*~RISE$^{(V)}$ Avraham from~UPON FACE~s DIE$^{(V)}$~*ing$^{(ms)}$*~him and~*he~will*~ much~SPEAK$^{(V)}$ TO SON~s Hhet to~>~SAY$^{(V)}$ **23:4** IMMIGRANT and~SETTLER I WITH~you$^{(mp)}$ *!$^{(mp)}$*~GIVE$^{(V)}$ to~me HOLDINGS GRAVE WITH~you$^{(mp)}$ and~*I~ will*~BURY$^{(V)}$ & DIE$^{(V)}$~*ing$^{(ms)}$*~me from~to~FACE~s~me **23:5** and~*they$^{(m)}$~ will*~ANSWER$^{(V)}$ SON~s Hhet AT Avraham to~>~SAY$^{(V)}$ to~him **23:6** *!$^{(ms)}$*~ HEAR$^{(V)}$~us LORD~me CAPTAIN Elohiym YOU$^{(ms)}$ in~MIDST~us in~CHOSEN GRAVE~s~us *!$^{(ms)}$*~BURY$^{(V)}$ AT DIE$^{(V)}$~*ing$^{(ms)}$*~you$^{(ms)}$ MAN FROM~us AT GRAVE~him NOT *he~will*~RESTRICT$^{(V)}$ FROM~you$^{(ms)}$ from~>~BURY$^{(V)}$ DIE$^{(V)}$~ *ing$^{(ms)}$*~you$^{(ms)}$ **23:7** and~*he~will*~RISE$^{(V)}$ Avraham and~*he~will~self*~ BEND.DOWN$^{(V)}$ to~PEOPLE the~LAND to~SON~s Hhet **23:8** and~*he~will*~ much~SPEAK$^{(V)}$ AT~them$^{(m)}$ to~>~SAY$^{(V)}$ IF THERE.IS AT SOUL~you$^{(ms)}$ to~>~ BURY$^{(V)}$ AT DIE$^{(V)}$~*ing$^{(ms)}$*~me from~to~FACE~s~me *!$^{(mp)}$*~HEAR$^{(V)}$~me and~ *!$^{(mp)}$*~REACH$^{(V)}$ to~me in~Ephron SON Tsohhar **23:9** and~*he~will*~GIVE$^{(V)}$ to~ me AT CAVE the~Makhpelah WHICH to~him WHICH in~EXTREMITY FIELD~ him in~SILVER FULL *he~will*~GIVE$^{(V)}$~her to~me in~MIDST~you$^{(mp)}$ to~ HOLDINGS GRAVE **23:10** and~Ephron SETTLE$^{(V)}$~*ing$^{(ms)}$* in~MIDST SON~s Hhet and~*he~will*~ANSWER$^{(V)}$ Ephron the~Hhet~of AT Avraham in~EAR~s2 SON~s Hhet to~ALL COME$^{(V)}$~*ing$^{(mp)}$* GATE CITY~him to~>~SAY$^{(V)}$ **23:11** NOT LORD~me *!$^{(ms)}$*~HEAR$^{(V)}$~me the~FIELD *I~did*~GIVE$^{(V)}$ to~you$^{(fs)}$ and~the~ CAVE WHICH in~him to~you$^{(ms)}$ *I~did*~GIVE$^{(V)}$~her to~EYE~s2 SON~s PEOPLE~me *I~did*~GIVE$^{(V)}$~her to~you$^{(fs)}$ *!$^{(ms)}$*~BURY$^{(V)}$ DIE$^{(V)}$~*ing$^{(ms)}$*~

you⁽ᵐˢ⁾ **23:12** and~*he~will~self*~BEND.DOWN⁽ⱽ⁾ Avraham to~FACE~s PEOPLE the~LAND **23:13** and~*he~will~much*~SPEAK⁽ⱽ⁾ TO Ephron in~EAR~s2 PEOPLE the~LAND to~>~SAY⁽ⱽ⁾ SURELY IF YOU⁽ᵐˢ⁾ WOULD.THAT *!⁽ᵐˢ⁾~*HEAR⁽ⱽ⁾~me *I~ did~*GIVE⁽ⱽ⁾ SILVER the~FIELD *!⁽ᵐˢ⁾~*TAKE⁽ⱽ⁾ FROM~me and~*I~will~*BURY⁽ⱽ⁾~& AT DIE⁽ⱽ⁾~*ing⁽ᵐˢ⁾~*me THERE~unto **23:14** and~*he~will~*ANSWER⁽ⱽ⁾ Ephron AT Avraham to~>~SAY⁽ⱽ⁾ to~him **23:15** LORD~me *!⁽ᵐˢ⁾~*HEAR⁽ⱽ⁾~me LAND FOUR HUNDRED~s SHEQEL SILVER BETWEEN~me and~BETWEEN~you⁽ᵐˢ⁾ WHAT SHE and~AT DIE⁽ⱽ⁾~*ing⁽ᵐˢ⁾~*you⁽ᵐˢ⁾ *!⁽ᵐˢ⁾~*BURY⁽ⱽ⁾ **23:16** and~*he~will~*HEAR⁽ⱽ⁾ Avraham TO Ephron and~*he~will~*WEIGH⁽ⱽ⁾ Avraham to~Ephron AT the~ SILVER WHICH *he~did~much~*SPEAK⁽ⱽ⁾ in~EAR~s2 SON~s Hhet FOUR HUNDRED~s SHEQEL SILVER CROSS.OVER⁽ⱽ⁾~*ing⁽ᵐˢ⁾* to~the~TRADE⁽ⱽ⁾~ *ing⁽ᵐˢ⁾* **23:17** and~*he~will~*RISE⁽ⱽ⁾ FIELD Ephron WHICH in~Makhpelah WHICH to~FACE~s Mamre the~FIELD and~the~CAVE WHICH in~him and~ ALL the~TREE WHICH in~the~FIELD WHICH in~ALL BORDER~him ALL.AROUND **23:18** to~Avraham to~ACQUIRED to~EYE~s2 SON~s Hhet in~ ALL COME⁽ⱽ⁾~*ing⁽ᵐᵖ⁾* GATE CITY~him **23:19** and~AFTER SO *he~did~*BURY⁽ⱽ⁾ Avraham AT Sarah WOMAN~him TO CAVE FIELD the~Makhpelah UPON FACE~s Mamre SHE Hhevron in~LAND Kena'an **23:20** and~*he~will~*RISE⁽ⱽ⁾ the~FIELD and~the~CAVE WHICH in~him to~Avraham to~HOLDINGS GRAVE from~AT SON~s Hhet

Chapter 24

24:1 and~Avraham *he~did~*BE.OLD⁽ⱽ⁾ *he~did~*COME⁽ⱽ⁾ in~the~DAY~s and~ **YHWH** *he~did~much~*KNEEL⁽ⱽ⁾ AT Avraham in~the~ALL **24:2** and~*he~will~* SAY⁽ⱽ⁾ Avraham TO SERVANT~him BEARD HOUSE~him the~REGULATE⁽ⱽ⁾~ *ing⁽ᵐˢ⁾* in~ALL WHICH to~him *!⁽ᵐˢ⁾~*PLACE⁽ⱽ⁾ PLEASE HAND~you⁽ᵐˢ⁾ UNDER MIDSECTION~me **24:3** and~*I~will~make~*SWEAR⁽ⱽ⁾~you⁽ᵐˢ⁾ in~**YHWH** Elohiym the~SKY~s2 and~Elohiym the~LAND WHICH NOT *you⁽ᵐˢ⁾~will~* TAKE⁽ⱽ⁾ WOMAN to~SON~me from~DAUGHTER~s the~Kena'an~of WHICH I SETTLE⁽ⱽ⁾~*ing⁽ᵐˢ⁾* in~INSIDE~him **24:4** GIVEN.THAT TO LAND~me and~TO KINDRED~me *you⁽ᵐˢ⁾~will~*WALK⁽ⱽ⁾ and~*you⁽ᵐˢ⁾~did~*TAKE⁽ⱽ⁾ WOMAN to~ SON~me to~Yits'hhaq **24:5** and~*he~will~*SAY⁽ⱽ⁾ TO~him the~SERVANT POSSIBLY NOT *she~will~*CONSENT⁽ⱽ⁾ the~WOMAN to~>~WALK⁽ⱽ⁾ AFTER~me TO the~LAND the~THIS ?~>~*make~*TURN.BACK⁽ⱽ⁾ *I~will~make~*TURN.BACK⁽ⱽ⁾ AT SON~you⁽ᵐˢ⁾ TO the~LAND WHICH *you⁽ᵐˢ⁾~did~*GO.OUT⁽ⱽ⁾ from~ THERE **24:6** and~*he~will~*SAY⁽ⱽ⁾ TO~him Avraham *!⁽ᵐˢ⁾~be~*SAFEGUARD⁽ⱽ⁾ to~you⁽ᵐˢ⁾ OTHERWISE *you⁽ᵐˢ⁾~will~*TURN.BACK⁽ⱽ⁾ AT SON~me THERE~ unto **24:7 YHWH** Elohiym the~SKY~s2 WHICH *he~did~*TAKE⁽ⱽ⁾~me from~ HOUSE FATHER~me and~from~LAND KINDRED~me and~WHICH *he~did~ much~*SPEAK⁽ⱽ⁾ to~me and~WHICH *he~did~be~*SWEAR⁽ⱽ⁾ to~me to~>~SAY⁽ⱽ⁾ to~SEED~you⁽ᵐˢ⁾ *I~will~*GIVE⁽ⱽ⁾ AT the~LAND the~THIS HE *he~will~*SEND⁽ⱽ⁾ MESSENGER~him to~FACE~s~you⁽ᵐˢ⁾ and~*you⁽ᵐˢ⁾~did~*TAKE⁽ⱽ⁾ WOMAN to~

The Book of Genesis

SON~me from~THERE **24:8** and~IF NOT *she~will*~CONSENT^(V) the~WOMAN to~>~WALK^(V) AFTER~*you*^(ms) and~*you*^(ms)~*will*~be~ACQUIT^(V) from~SWEARING~me THIS ONLY AT SON~me NOT *you*^(ms)~*will*~TURN.BACK^(V) THERE~unto **24:9** and~*he*~*will*~PLACE^(V) the~SERVANT AT HAND~him UNDER MIDSECTION Avraham LORD~s~him and~*he*~*will*~be~SWEAR^(V) to~him UPON the~WORD the~THIS **24:10** and~*he*~*will*~TAKE^(V) the~SERVANT TEN CAMEL~s from~CAMEL~s LORD~s~him and~*he*~*will*~WALK^(V) and~ALL FUNCTIONAL LORD~s~him in~HAND~him and~*he*~*will*~RISE^(V) and~*he*~*will*~WALK^(V) TO Aram-Nahara'im TO CITY Nahhor **24:11** and~*he*~*will*~*make*~KNEEL^(V) the~CAMEL~s from~OUTSIDE to~the~CITY TO WELL the~WATER~s2 to~APPOINTED.TIME EVENING to~APPOINTED.TIME >~GO.OUT^(V) the~DRAW.WATER^(V)~*ing*^(fp) **24:12** and~*he*~*will*~SAY^(V) **YHWH** Elohiym LORD~me Avraham *!*^(ms)~*make*~MEET^(V) PLEASE to~FACE~s~me the~DAY and~*!*^(ms)~DO^(V) KINDNESS WITH LORD~me Avraham **24:13** LOOK I *be*~STAND.UP^(V)~*ing*^(ms) UPON EYE the~WATER~s2 and~DAUGHTER~s MAN~s the~CITY GO.OUT^(V)~*ing*^(fp) to~>~DRAW.WATER^(V) WATER~s2 **24:14** and~*he*~*did*~EXIST^(V) the~YOUNG.WOMAN WHICH *I*~*will*~SAY^(V) TO~her *!*^(fs)~*make*~EXTEND^(V) PLEASE JAR~*you*^(fs) and~*I*~*will*~GULP^(V) and~*she*~*did*~SAY^(V) *!*^(ms)~GULP^(V) and~ALSO CAMEL~s~*you*^(ms) *I*~*will*~*make*~DRINK^(V) AT~her *you*^(ms)~*did*~*make*~REBUKE^(V) to~SERVANT~*you*^(ms) to~Yits'hhaq and~in~her *I*~*will*~KNOW^(V) GIVEN.THAT *you*^(ms)~*did*~DO^(V) KINDNESS WITH LORD~me **24:15** and~*he*~*will*~EXIST^(V) HE BEFORE *he*~*did*~much~FINISH^(V) to~>~much~SPEAK^(V) and~LOOK Rivqah GO.OUT^(V)~*ing*^(fs) WHICH BRING.FORTH^(V)~ed^(fs) to~Betu'el SON Milkah WOMAN Nahhor BROTHER~of Avraham and~JAR~her UPON SHOULDER~her **24:16** and~the~YOUNG.WOMAN FUNCTIONAL APPEARANCE MANY VIRGIN and~MAN NOT *he*~*did*~KNOW^(V)~her and~*she*~*will*~GO.DOWN^(V) the~EYE~unto and~*she*~*will*~FILL^(V) JAR~her and~*she*~*will*~GO.UP^(V) **24:17** and~*he*~*will*~RUN^(V) the~SERVANT to~>~MEET^(V)~her and~*he*~*will*~SAY^(V) *!*^(fs)~*make*~GUZZLE^(V)~me PLEASE SMALL.AMOUNT WATER~s2 from~JAR~*you*^(fs) **24:18** and~*she*~*will*~SAY^(V) *!*^(ms)~GULP^(V) LORD~me and~*she*~*will*~much~HURRY^(V) and~*she*~*will*~*make*~GO.DOWN^(V) JAR~her UPON HAND~her and~*she*~*will*~*make*~DRINK^(V)~him **24:19** and~*she*~*will*~much~FINISH^(V) to~>~*make*~DRINK^(V)~him and~*she*~*will*~SAY^(V) ALSO to~CAMEL~s~*you*^(ms) *I*~*will*~DRAW.WATER^(V) UNTIL IF *they*~*did*~much~FINISH^(V) to~>~GULP^(V) **24:20** and~*she*~*will*~much~HURRY^(V) and~*she*~*will*~much~UNCOVER^(V) JAR~her TO the~WATERING.TROUGH and~*she*~*will*~RUN^(V) YET.AGAIN TO the~WELL to~>~DRAW.WATER^(V) and~*she*~*will*~DRAW.WATER^(V) to~ALL CAMEL~s~him **24:21** and~the~MAN *self*~CRASH^(V)~*ing*^(ms) to~her *make*~KEEP.SILENT^(V)~*ing*^(ms) to~>~KNOW^(V) ?~*he*~*did*~*make*~PROSPER^(V) **YHWH** ROAD~him IF NOT **24:22** and~*he*~*will*~EXIST^(V) like~WHICH *they*~*did*~much~FINISH^(V) the~CAMEL~s to~>~GULP^(V) and~*he*~*will*~TAKE^(V) the~MAN ORNAMENTAL.RING GOLD BEQA WEIGHT~him and~TWO BRACELET~s UPON HAND~s2~her TEN GOLD WEIGHT~them^(m) **24:23** and~*he*~*will*~SAY^(V) DAUGHTER WHO YOU^(fs) *!*^(fs)~*make*~BE.FACE.TO.FACE^(V) PLEASE to~me ?~THERE.IS HOUSE FATHER~*you*^(fs) AREA to~us to~>~STAY.THE.NIGHT^(V) **24:24** and~*she*~*will*~SAY^(V) TO~him DAUGHTER Betu'el I SON Milkah WHICH *she*~*did*~BRING.FORTH^(V) to~ Nahhor **24:25** and~*she*~*will*~SAY^(V) TO~him ALSO STRAW ALSO PROVENDER ABUNDANT WITH~us ALSO AREA to~>~STAY.THE.NIGHT^(V) **24:26** and~*he*~*will*~BOW.THE.HEAD^(V) the~MAN and~*he*~*will*~*self*~BEND.DOWN^(V) to~ **YHWH 24:27** and~*he*~*will*~SAY^(V) KNEEL^(V)~*ed*^(ms) **YHWH** Elohiym LORD~me Avraham WHICH NOT *he*~*did*~LEAVE^(V) KINDNESS~him and~TRUTH~him from~WITH LORD~me I in~the~ROAD *he*~*did*~GUIDE^(V)~me **YHWH** HOUSE BROTHER~s LORD~me **24:28** and~*she*~*will*~RUN^(V) the~YOUNG.WOMAN and~*she*~*will*~make~BE.FACE.TO.FACE^(V) to~HOUSE MOTHER~her like~the~ WORD~s the~THESE **24:29** and~to~Rivqah BROTHER and~TITLE~him Lavan and~*he*~*will*~RUN^(V) Lavan TO the~MAN the~OUTSIDE~unto TO the~ EYE **24:30** and~*he*~*will*~EXIST^(V) like~>~SEE^(V) AT the~ORNAMENTAL.RING and~AT the~BRACELET~s UPON HAND~s2 SISTER~him and~like~>~HEAR^(V)~ him AT WORD~s Rivqah SISTER~him to~>~SAY^(V) IN.THIS.WAY *he*~*did*~ much~SPEAK^(V) TO~me the~MAN and~*he*~*will*~COME^(V) TO the~MAN and~ LOOK STAND^(V)~*ing*^(ms) UPON the~CAMEL~s UPON the~EYE **24:31** and~*he*~ *will*~SAY^(V) !^(ms)~COME^(V) KNEEL^(V)~*ed*^(ms) **YHWH** to~WHAT *you*^(ms)~*will*~ STAND^(V) in~the~OUTSIDE and~I I~*did*~TURN^(V) the~HOUSE and~AREA to~ the~CAMEL~s **24:32** and~*he*~*will*~COME^(V) the~MAN the~HOUSE~unto and~*he*~*will*~OPEN^(V) the~CAMEL~s and~*he*~*will*~GIVE^(V) STRAW and~ PROVENDER to~the~CAMEL~s and~WATER~s2 to~>~BATHE^(V) FOOT~s2~him and~FOOT~s the~MAN~s WHICH AT~him **24:33** and~*he*~*will*~PLACE^(V) to~ FACE~s~him to~>~EAT^(V) and~*he*~*will*~SAY^(V) NOT *I*~*will*~EAT^(V) UNTIL IF *I*~ *did*~much~SPEAK^(V) WORD~s~me and~*he*~*will*~SAY^(V) !^(ms)~much~ SPEAK^(V) **24:34** and~*he*~*will*~SAY^(V) SERVANT Avraham I **24:35** and~**YHWH** *he*~*did*~much~KNEEL^(V) AT LORD~me MANY and~*he*~*will*~MAGNIFY^(V) and~ *he*~*will*~GIVE^(V) to~him FLOCKS and~CATTLE and~SILVER and~GOLD and~ SERVANT~s and~MAID~s and~CAMEL~s and~DONKEY~s **24:36** and~*she*~ *will*~BRING.FORTH^(V) Sarah WOMAN LORD~me SON to~LORD~me AFTER OLD.AGE~her and~*he*~*will*~GIVE^(V) to~him AT ALL WHICH to~ him **24:37** and~*he*~*will*~make~SWEAR^(V)~me LORD~me to~>~SAY^(V) NOT *you*^(ms)~*will*~TAKE^(V) WOMAN to~SON~me from~DAUGHTER~s the~ Kena'an~of WHICH I SETTLE^(V)~*ing*^(ms) in~LAND~him **24:38** IF NOT TO HOUSE FATHER~me *you*^(ms)~*will*~WALK^(V) and~TO CLAN~me and~*you*^(ms)~*did*~ TAKE^(V) WOMAN to~SON~me **24:39** and~*I*~*will*~SAY^(V) TO LORD~me POSSIBLY NOT *she*~*will*~WALK^(V) the~WOMAN AFTER~me **24:40** and~*he*~ *will*~SAY^(V) TO~me **YHWH** WHICH *I*~*did*~*self*~WALK^(V) to~FACE~s~him *he*~ *will*~SEND^(V) MESSENGER~him AT~*you*^(fs) and~*he*~*did*~make~PROSPER^(V) ROAD~*you*^(ms) and~*you*^(ms)~*did*~TAKE^(V) WOMAN to~SON~me from~CLAN~ me and~from~HOUSE FATHER~me **24:41** AT.THAT.TIME *you*^(ms)~*will*~be~ ACQUIT^(V) from~OATH~me GIVEN.THAT *you*^(ms)~*will*~COME^(V) TO CLAN~me and~IF NOT *they*^(m)~*will*~GIVE^(V) to~*you*^(fs) and~*you*^(ms)~*did*~EXIST^(V) INNOCENT from~OATH~me **24:42** and~*I*~*will*~COME^(V) the~DAY TO the~EYE and~*I*~*will*~SAY^(V) **YHWH** Elohiym LORD~me Avraham IF THERE.IS~*you*^(ms)

The Book of Genesis

PLEASE *make*~PROSPER^(V)~*ing*^(ms) ROAD~me WHICH I WALK^(V)~*ing*^(ms) UPON~her **24:43** LOOK I *be*~STAND.UP^(V)~*ing*^(ms) UPON EYE the~WATER~s2 and~*he*~*did*~EXIST^(V) the~YOUNG.MAIDEN the~GO.OUT^(V)~*ing*^(fs) to~>~DRAW.WATER^(V) and~*I*~*did*~SAY^(V) TO~her *!*^(fs)~*make*~DRINK^(V)~me PLEASE SMALL.AMOUNT WATER~s2 from~JAR~you^(fs) **24:44** and~*she*~*did*~SAY^(V) TO~me ALSO YOU^(ms) *!*^(ms)~GULP^(V) and~ALSO to~CAMEL~s~you^(ms) *I*~*will*~DRAW.WATER^(V) SHE the~WOMAN WHICH *he*~*did*~*make*~REBUKE^(V) **YHWH** to~SON LORD~me **24:45** I BEFORE *I*~*will*~*much*~FINISH^(V) to~>~*much*~SPEAK^(V) TO HEART~me and~LOOK Rivqah GO.OUT^(V)~*ing*^(fs) and~JAR~her UPON SHOULDER~her and~*she*~*will*~GO.DOWN^(V) the~EYE~unto and~*she*~*will*~DRAW.WATER^(V) and~*I*~*will*~SAY^(V) TO~her *!*^(fs)~*make*~DRINK^(V)~me PLEASE **24:46** and~*she*~*will*~*much*~HURRY^(V) and~*she*~*will*~*make*~GO.DOWN^(V) JAR~her from~UPON~her and~*she*~*will*~SAY^(V) *!*^(ms)~GULP^(V) and~ALSO CAMEL~s~you^(ms) *I*~*will*~*make*~DRINK^(V) and~*I*~*will*~GULP^(V) and~ALSO the~CAMEL~s *she*~*did*~*make*~DRINK^(V) **24:47** and~*I*~*will*~INQUIRE^(V) AT~her and~*I*~*will*~SAY^(V) DAUGHTER WHO YOU^(fs) and~*she*~*will*~SAY^(V) DAUGHTER Betu'el SON Nahhor WHICH *she*~*did*~BRING.FORTH^(V) to~him Milkah and~*I*~*will*~PLACE^(V) the~ORNAMENTAL.RING UPON NOSE~her and~the~BRACELET~s UPON HAND~s2~her **24:48** and~*I*~*will*~BOW.THE.HEAD^(V) and~*I*~*will*~*self*~BEND.DOWN^(V) to~**YHWH** and~*I*~*will*~*much*~KNEEL^(V) AT **YHWH** Elohiym LORD~me Avraham WHICH *he*~*did*~*make*~GUIDE^(V)~me in~ROAD TRUTH to~>~TAKE^(V) AT DAUGHTER BROTHER~of LORD~me to~SON~him **24:49** and~NOW IF THERE.IS~you^(mp) DO^(V)~*ing*^(mp) KINDNESS and~TRUTH AT LORD~me *!*^(mp)~*make*~BE.FACE.TO.FACE^(V) to~me and~IF NOT *!*^(mp)~*make*~BE.FACE.TO.FACE^(V) to~me and~*I*~*did*~TURN^(V) UPON RIGHT.HAND OR UPON LEFT.HAND **24:50** and~*he*~*will*~ANSWER^(V) Lavan and~Betu'el and~*they*^(m)~*will*~SAY^(V) from~**YHWH** *he*~*did*~GO.OUT^(V) the~WORD NOT we~*will*~BE.ABLE^(V) *!*^(ms)~*much*~SPEAK^(V) TO~you^(ms) DYSFUNCTIONAL OR FUNCTIONAL **24:51** LOOK Rivqah to~FACE~s~you^(ms) *!*^(ms)~TAKE^(V) and~*!*^(ms)~WALK^(V) and~*she*~*will*~EXIST^(V) WOMAN to~SON LORD~s~you^(ms) like~WHICH *he*~*did*~*much*~SPEAK^(V) **YHWH 24:52** and~*he*~*will*~EXIST^(V) like~WHICH *he*~*did*~HEAR^(V) SERVANT Avraham AT WORD~s~them^(m) and~*he*~*will*~*self*~BEND.DOWN^(V) LAND~unto to~**YHWH 24:53** and~*he*~*will*~*make*~GO.OUT^(V) the~SERVANT UTENSIL~s SILVER and~UTENSIL~s GOLD and~GARMENT~s and~*he*~*will*~GIVE^(V) to~Rivqah and~ORNAMENT~s *he*~*did*~GIVE^(V) to~BROTHER~her and~to~MOTHER~her **24:54** and~*they*^(m)~*will*~EAT^(V) and~*they*^(m)~*will*~GULP^(V) HE and~the~MAN~s WHICH WITH~him and~*they*^(m)~*will*~STAY.THE.NIGHT^(V) and~*they*^(m)~*will*~RISE^(V) in~the~MORNING and~*he*~*will*~SAY^(V) *!*^(mp)~SEND^(V)~me to~LORD~me **24:55** and~*he*~*will*~SAY^(V) BROTHER~her and~MOTHER~her *she*~*will*~SETTLE^(V) the~YOUNG.WOMAN AT~us DAY~s OR TENTH.ONE AFTER you^(ms)~*will*~WALK^(V) **24:56** and~*he*~*will*~SAY^(V) TO~them^(m) DO.NOT you^(mp)~*will*~DELAY^(V) AT~me and~**YHWH** *he*~*did*~*make*~PROSPER^(V) ROAD~me *!*^(mp)~SEND^(V)~me and~*I*~*will*~WALK^(V)~& to~LORD~me **24:57** and~*they*^(m)~*will*~SAY^(V) *he*~*did*~*be*~MEET^(V) to~YOUNG.WOMAN and~we~*will*~INQUIRE^(V) AT

MOUTH~her **24:58** and~*they*⁽ᵐ⁾~*will*~CALL.OUT⁽ⱽ⁾ to~Rivqah and~*they*⁽ᵐ⁾~*will*~SAY⁽ⱽ⁾ TO~her ?~*you*⁽ᶠˢ⁾~*will*~WALK⁽ⱽ⁾ WITH the~MAN the~THIS and~she~*will*~SAY⁽ⱽ⁾ I~*will*~WALK⁽ⱽ⁾ **24:59** and~*they*⁽ᵐ⁾~*will*~much~SEND⁽ⱽ⁾ AT Rivqah SISTER~them⁽ᵐ⁾ and~AT *make*~SUCKLE⁽ⱽ⁾~*ing*⁽ᶠˢ⁾~her and~AT SERVANT Avraham and~AT MAN~s~him **24:60** and~*they*⁽ᵐ⁾~*will*~much~KNEEL⁽ⱽ⁾ AT Rivqah and~*they*⁽ᵐ⁾~*will*~SAY⁽ⱽ⁾ to~her SISTER~us YOU⁽ᶠˢ⁾ !⁽ᶠˢ⁾~EXIST⁽ⱽ⁾ to~THOUSAND~s MYRIAD and~*he*~*will*~POSSESS⁽ⱽ⁾ SEED~you⁽ᶠˢ⁾ AT GATE HATE⁽ⱽ⁾~*ing*⁽ᵐᵖ⁾~him **24:61** and~*she*~*will*~RISE⁽ⱽ⁾ Rivqah and~YOUNG.WOMAN~s~her and~*they*⁽ᶠ⁾~*will*~RIDE⁽ⱽ⁾ UPON the~CAMEL~s and~*they*⁽ᶠ⁾~*will*~WALK⁽ⱽ⁾ AFTER the~MAN and~*he*~*will*~TAKE⁽ⱽ⁾ the~SERVANT AT Rivqah and~*he*~*will*~WALK⁽ⱽ⁾ **24:62** and~Yits'hhaq *he*~*did*~COME⁽ⱽ⁾ from~>~COME⁽ⱽ⁾ Be'er-Lahhiy-Ro'iy and~HE SETTLE⁽ⱽ⁾~*ing*⁽ᵐˢ⁾ in~LAND the~SOUTH **24:63** and~*he*~*will*~GO.OUT⁽ⱽ⁾ Yits'hhaq to~MEDITATE⁽ⱽ⁾ in~the~FIELD to~>~TURN⁽ⱽ⁾ EVENING and~*he*~*will*~LIFT.UP⁽ⱽ⁾ EYE~s2~him and~*he*~*will*~SEE⁽ⱽ⁾ and~LOOK CAMEL~s COME⁽ⱽ⁾~*ing*⁽ᵐᵖ⁾ **24:64** and~*she*~*will*~LIFT.UP⁽ⱽ⁾ Rivqah AT EYE~s2~her and~*she*~*will*~SEE⁽ⱽ⁾ AT Yits'hhaq and~*she*~*will*~FALL⁽ⱽ⁾ from~UPON the~CAMEL **24:65** and~*she*~*will*~SAY⁽ⱽ⁾ TO the~SERVANT WHO the~MAN THIS.ONE the~WALK⁽ⱽ⁾~*ing*⁽ᵐˢ⁾ in~the~FIELD to~>~MEET⁽ⱽ⁾~us and~*he*~*will*~SAY⁽ⱽ⁾ the~SERVANT HE LORD~me and~*she*~*will*~TAKE⁽ⱽ⁾ the~VEIL and~*she*~*will*~*self*~COVER.OVER⁽ⱽ⁾ **24:66** and~*he*~*will*~much~COUNT⁽ⱽ⁾ the~SERVANT to~Yits'hhaq AT ALL the~WORD~s WHICH *he*~*did*~DO⁽ⱽ⁾ **24:67** and~*he*~*will*~*make*~COME⁽ⱽ⁾~her Yits'hhaq the~TENT~ unto Sarah MOTHER~him and~*he*~*will*~TAKE⁽ⱽ⁾ AT Rivqah and~*she*~*will*~EXIST⁽ⱽ⁾ to~him to~WOMAN and~*he*~*will*~LOVE⁽ⱽ⁾~her and~*he*~*will*~be~COMFORT⁽ⱽ⁾ Yits'hhaq AFTER MOTHER~him

Chapter 25

25:1 and~*he*~*will*~*make*~ADD⁽ⱽ⁾ Avraham and~*he*~*will*~TAKE⁽ⱽ⁾ WOMAN and~TITLE~her Qeturah **25:2** and~*she*~*will*~BRING.FORTH⁽ⱽ⁾ to~him AT Zimran and~AT Yaq'shan and~AT Medan and~AT Mid'yan and~AT Yish'baq and~AT Shu'ahh **25:3** and~Yaq'shan *he*~*did*~BRING.FORTH⁽ⱽ⁾ AT Sheva and~AT Dedan and~SON~s Dedan *they*~*did*~EXIST⁽ⱽ⁾ Ashur~s and~Letush~s and~Le'um~s **25:4** and~SON~s Mid'yan Eyphah and~Epher and~Hhanokh and~Avida and~Elda'ah ALL THESE SON~s Qeturah **25:5** and~*he*~*will*~GIVE⁽ⱽ⁾ Avraham AT ALL WHICH to~him to~Yits'hhaq **25:6** and~to~SON~s the~CONCUBINE~s WHICH to~Avraham *he*~*did*~GIVE⁽ⱽ⁾ Avraham CONTRIBUTION~s and~*he*~*will*~much~SEND⁽ⱽ⁾~them⁽ᵐ⁾ from~UPON Yits'hhaq SON~him in~YET.AGAIN~him LIVING EAST~unto TO LAND EAST **25:7** and~THESE DAY~s YEAR~s LIVING~s Avraham WHICH LIVING HUNDRED YEAR and~SEVEN~s YEAR and~FIVE YEAR~s **25:8** and~*he*~*will*~EXPIRE⁽ⱽ⁾ and~*he*~*will*~DIE⁽ⱽ⁾ Avraham in~GRAY-HEADED FUNCTIONAL BEARD and~PLENTY and~*he*~*will*~be~GATHER⁽ⱽ⁾ TO PEOPLE~s~

him **25:9** and~*they*⁽ᵐ⁾~*will*~BURY⁽ᵛ⁾ AT~him Yits'hhaq and~Yishma'el SON~s~him TO CAVE the~Makhpelah TO FIELD Ephron SON Tsohhar the~Hhet~of WHICH UPON FACE~s Mamre **25:10** the~FIELD WHICH *he*~*did*~PURCHASE⁽ᵛ⁾ Avraham from~AT SON~s Hhet THERE~unto *he*~*did*~*be*~*much*~BURY⁽ᵛ⁾ Avraham and~Sarah WOMAN~him **25:11** and~*he*~*will*~EXIST⁽ᵛ⁾ AFTER DEATH Avraham and~*he*~*will*~*much*~KNEEL⁽ᵛ⁾ Elohiym AT Yits'hhaq SON~him and~*he*~*will*~SETTLE⁽ᵛ⁾ Yits'hhaq WITH Be'er-Lahhiy-Ro'iy **25:12** and~THESE BIRTHING~s Yishma'el SON Avraham WHICH *she*~*did*~BRING.FORTH⁽ᵛ⁾ Hagar the~Mits'rayim~of MAID Sarah to~Avraham **25:13** and~THESE TITLE~s SON~s Yishma'el in~TITLE~s~them⁽ᵐ⁾ to~BIRTHING~s~them⁽ᵐ⁾ FIRSTBORN Yishma'el Nevayot and~Qedar and~Adbe'el and~Mivsam **25:14** and~Mishma and~Dumah and~Masa **25:15** Hhadad and~Teyma Yetur Naphish Qedmah **25:16** THESE THEY⁽ᵐ⁾ SON~s Yishma'el and~THESE TITLE~s~them⁽ᵐ⁾ in~COURTYARD~s~them⁽ᵐ⁾ and~in~ROW.OF.TENTS~s~them⁽ᵐ⁾ TWO TEN CAPTAIN~s to~TRIBE~s~them⁽ᵐ⁾ **25:17** and~THESE YEAR~s LIVING~s Yishma'el HUNDRED YEAR and~THREE~s YEAR and~SEVEN YEAR~s and~*he*~*will*~EXPIRE⁽ᵛ⁾ and~*he*~*will*~DIE⁽ᵛ⁾ and~*he*~*will*~*be*~GATHER⁽ᵛ⁾ TO PEOPLE~s~him **25:18** and~*they*⁽ᵐ⁾~*will*~DWELL⁽ᵛ⁾ from~Hhawilah UNTIL Shur WHICH UPON FACE~s Mits'rayim >~COME⁽ᵛ⁾~*you*⁽ᵐˢ⁾~& Ashur~unto UPON FACE~s ALL BROTHER~s~him *he*~*did*~FALL⁽ᵛ⁾ **25:19** and~THESE BIRTHING~s Yits'hhaq SON Avraham Avraham *he*~*did*~*make*~BRING.FORTH⁽ᵛ⁾ AT Yits'hhaq **25:20** and~*he*~*will*~EXIST⁽ᵛ⁾ Yits'hhaq SON FOUR~s YEAR in~>~TAKE⁽ᵛ⁾~him AT Rivqah DAUGHTER Betu'el the~Aram~of from~Padan-Aram SISTER Lavan the~Aram~of to~him to~WOMAN **25:21** and~*he*~*will*~INTERCEDE⁽ᵛ⁾ Yits'hhaq to~**YHWH** to~IN.FRONT WOMAN~him GIVEN.THAT STERILE SHE and~*he*~*will*~*be*~INTERCEDE⁽ᵛ⁾ to~him **YHWH** and~*she*~*will*~CONCEIVE⁽ᵛ⁾ Rivqah WOMAN~him **25:22** and~*they*⁽ᵐ⁾~*will*~*self*~CRUSH⁽ᵛ⁾ the~SON~s in~INSIDE~her and~*she*~*will*~SAY⁽ᵛ⁾ IF SO to~WHAT THIS I and~*she*~*will*~WALK⁽ᵛ⁾ to~>~SEEK⁽ᵛ⁾ AT **YHWH** **25:23** and~*he*~*will*~SAY⁽ᵛ⁾ **YHWH** to~her TWO NATION~s in~WOMB~you⁽ᶠˢ⁾ and~TWO COMMUNITY~s from~ABDOMEN~s~you⁽ᶠˢ⁾ *they*~*will*~*be*~DIVIDE.APART⁽ᵛ⁾ and~COMMUNITY from~COMMUNITY *he*~*will*~BE.STRONG⁽ᵛ⁾ and~ABUNDANT *he*~*will*~SERVE⁽ᵛ⁾ LITTLE.ONE **25:24** and~*they*⁽ᵐ⁾~*will*~FILL⁽ᵛ⁾ DAY~s her to~>~BRING.FORTH⁽ᵛ⁾ and~LOOK TWIN~s in~WOMB~her **25:25** and~*he*~*will*~GO.OUT⁽ᵛ⁾ the~FIRST RUDDY ALL~him like~ROBE HAIR and~*they*⁽ᵐ⁾~*will*~CALL.OUT⁽ᵛ⁾ TITLE~him Esaw **25:26** and~AFTER SO *he*~*did*~GO.OUT⁽ᵛ⁾ BROTHER~him and~HAND~him TAKE.HOLD⁽ᵛ⁾~*ing*⁽ᶠˢ⁾ in~HEEL Esaw and~*he*~*will*~CALL.OUT⁽ᵛ⁾ TITLE~him Ya'aqov and~Yits'hhaq SON SIX~s YEAR in~>~BRING.FORTH⁽ᵛ⁾ AT~them⁽ᵐ⁾ **25:27** and~*they*⁽ᵐ⁾~*will*~MAGNIFY⁽ᵛ⁾ the~YOUNG.MAN~s and~*he*~*will*~EXIST⁽ᵛ⁾ Esaw MAN KNOW⁽ᵛ⁾~*ing*⁽ᵐˢ⁾ GAME MAN FIELD and~Ya'aqov MAN MATURE SETTLE⁽ᵛ⁾~*ing*⁽ᵐˢ⁾ TENT~s **25:28** and~*he*~*will*~LOVE⁽ᵛ⁾ Yits'hhaq AT Esaw GIVEN.THAT GAME in~MOUTH~him and~Rivqah LOVE⁽ᵛ⁾~*ing*⁽ᶠˢ⁾ AT Ya'aqov **25:29** and~*he*~*will*~*make*~SIMMER⁽ᵛ⁾ Ya'aqov STEW and~*he*~*will*~COME⁽ᵛ⁾ Esaw FROM the~FIELD and~HE TIRED **25:30** and~*he*~*will*~SAY⁽ᵛ⁾ Esaw TO Ya'aqov !⁽ᵐˢ⁾~*make*~

PROVIDE.FOOD(V)~me PLEASE FROM the~RED the~RED the~THIS GIVEN.THAT TIRED I UPON SO he~did~CALL.OUT(V) TITLE~him Edom **25:31** and~he~will~SAY(V) Ya'aqov !(ms)~SELL(V)~& like~the~DAY AT BIRTHRIGHT~you(ms) to~me **25:32** and~he~will~SAY(V) Esaw LOOK I WALK(V)~ing(ms) to~>~DIE(V) and~to~WHAT THIS to~me BIRTHRIGHT **25:33** and~he~will~SAY(V) Ya'aqov !(ms)~be~SWEAR(V)~& to~me like~the~DAY and~he~will~be~SWEAR(V) to~him and~he~will~SELL(V) AT BIRTHRIGHT~him to~Ya'aqov **25:34** and~Ya'aqov he~did~GIVE(V) to~Esaw BREAD and~STEW LENTIL~s and~he~will~EAT(V) and~he~will~GULP(V) and~he~will~RISE(V) and~he~will~WALK(V) and~he~will~DISDAIN(V) Esaw AT the~BIRTHRIGHT

Chapter 26

26:1 and~he~will~EXIST(V) HUNGER in~the~LAND from~to~STRAND the~HUNGER the~FIRST WHICH he~did~EXIST(V) in~DAY~s Avraham and~he~will~WALK(V) Yits'hhaq TO Aviymelekh KING Peleshet~s Gerar~unto **26:2** and~he~will~be~SEE(V) TO~him YHWH and~he~will~SAY(V) DO.NOT you(ms)~will~GO.DOWN(V) Mits'rayim~unto !(ms)~DWELL(V) in~the~LAND WHICH I~will~SAY(V) TO~you(ms) **26:3** !(ms)~IMMIGRATE(V) in~the~LAND the~THIS and~I~will~EXIST(V) WITH~you(ms) and~I~will~much~KNEEL(V)~you(ms) GIVEN.THAT to~you(ms) and~to~SEED~you(ms) I~will~GIVE(V) AT ALL the~LAND~s the~THESE and~I~did~make~RISE(V) AT the~SWEARING WHICH I~did~be~SWEAR(V) to~Avraham FATHER~you(ms) **26:4** and~I~did~make~INCREASE(V) AT SEED~you(ms) like~STAR~s the~SKY~s2 and~I~did~GIVE(V) to~SEED~you(ms) AT ALL the~LAND~s the~THESE and~they~did~self~KNEEL(V) in~SEED~you(ms) ALL NATION~s the~LAND **26:5** CONSEQUENCE WHICH he~did~HEAR(V) Avraham in~VOICE~me and~he~will~SAFEGUARD(V) CHARGE~me DIRECTIVE~s~me CUSTOM~s~me and~TEACHING~s~me **26:6** and~he~will~SETTLE(V) Yits'hhaq in~Gerar **26:7** and~they(m)~will~INQUIRE(V) MAN~s the~AREA to~WOMAN~him and~he~will~SAY(V) SISTER~me SHE GIVEN.THAT he~did~FEAR(V) to~>~SAY(V) WOMAN~me OTHERWISE they(m)~will~KILL(V)~me MAN~s the~AREA UPON Rivqah GIVEN.THAT FUNCTIONAL APPEARANCE SHE **26:8** and~he~will~EXIST(V) GIVEN.THAT they~did~PROLONG(V) to~him THERE the~DAY~s and~he~will~make~LOOK.DOWN(V) Aviymelekh KING Peleshet~s in~UNTIL the~WINDOW and~he~will~SEE(V) and~LOOK Yits'hhaq much~LAUGH(V)~ing(ms) AT Rivqah WOMAN~him **26:9** and~he~will~CALL.OUT(V) Aviymelekh to~Yits'hhaq and~he~will~SAY(V) SURELY LOOK WOMAN~you(ms) SHE and~HOW you(ms)~did~SAY(V) SISTER~me SHE and~he~will~SAY(V) TO~him Yits'hhaq GIVEN.THAT I~did~SAY(V) OTHERWISE I~will~DIE(V) UPON~her **26:10** and~he~will~SAY(V) Aviymelekh WHAT THIS you(ms)~did~DO(V) to~us like~SMALL.AMOUNT he~did~LIE.DOWN(V) UNIT the~PEOPLE AT WOMAN~you(ms) and~you(ms)~did~make~COME(V) UPON~us GUILT **26:11** and~he~will~much~DIRECT(V) Aviymelekh AT ALL the~PEOPLE

to~>~SAY$^{(v)}$ the~TOUCH$^{(v)}$~ing$^{(ms)}$ in~the~MAN the~THIS and~in~WOMAN~
him >~DIE$^{(v)}$ he~will~be~make~DIE$^{(v)}$ **26:12** and~he~will~SOW$^{(v)}$ Yits'hhaq
in~the~LAND the~SHE and~he~will~FIND$^{(v)}$ in~the~YEAR the~SHE HUNDRED
SHA'AR~s and~he~will~much~KNEEL$^{(v)}$~him **YHWH 26:13** and~he~will~
MAGNIFY$^{(v)}$ the~MAN and~he~will~WALK$^{(v)}$ >~WALK$^{(v)}$ and~MAGNIFIED
UNTIL GIVEN.THAT he~did~MAGNIFY$^{(v)}$ MANY **26:14** and~he~will~EXIST$^{(v)}$
to~him LIVESTOCK FLOCKS and~LIVESTOCK CATTLE and~SERVE$^{(v)}$~ed$^{(fs)}$
ABUNDANT and~they$^{(m)}$~will~much~BE.ZEALOUS$^{(v)}$ AT~him
Peleshet~s **26:15** and~ALL the~WELL~s WHICH they~did~DIG.OUT$^{(v)}$
SERVANT~s FATHER~him in~DAY~s Avraham FATHER~him they~did~much~
SHUT.UP$^{(v)}$~them$^{(m)}$ Peleshet~s and~they$^{(m)}$~will~much~FILL$^{(v)}$~them$^{(m)}$ DIRT
26:16 and~he~will~SAY$^{(v)}$ Aviymelekh TO Yits'hhaq !$^{(ms)}$~WALK$^{(v)}$ from~
WITH~us GIVEN.THAT you$^{(ms)}$~did~BE.ABUNDANT$^{(v)}$ FROM~us
MANY **26:17** and~he~will~WALK$^{(v)}$ from~THERE Yits'hhaq and~he~will~
CAMP$^{(v)}$ in~WADI Gerar and~he~will~SETTLE$^{(v)}$ THERE **26:18** and~he~will~
TURN.BACK$^{(v)}$ Yits'hhaq and~he~will~DIG.OUT$^{(v)}$ AT WELL~s the~WATER~s2
WHICH they~did~DIG.OUT$^{(v)}$ in~DAY~s Avraham FATHER~him and~they~
did~much~SHUT.UP$^{(v)}$~them$^{(m)}$ Peleshet~s AFTER DEATH Avraham and~he~
will~CALL.OUT$^{(v)}$ to~them$^{(f)}$ TITLE~s like~TITLE~s WHICH he~did~CALL.OUT$^{(v)}$
to~them$^{(f)}$ FATHER~him **26:19** and~they$^{(m)}$~will~DIG.OUT$^{(v)}$ SERVANT~s
Yits'hhaq in~the~WADI and~they$^{(m)}$~will~FIND$^{(v)}$ THERE WELL WATER~s2
LIVING~s **26:20** and~they$^{(m)}$~will~DISPUTE$^{(v)}$ FEED$^{(v)}$~ing$^{(mp)}$ Gerar WITH
FEED$^{(v)}$~ing$^{(mp)}$ Yits'hhaq to~>~SAY$^{(v)}$ to~us the~WATER~s2 and~he~will~
CALL.OUT$^{(v)}$ TITLE the~WELL Eseq GIVEN.THAT they~did~self~STRIVE$^{(v)}$
WITH~him **26:21** and~they$^{(m)}$~will~DIG.OUT$^{(v)}$ WELL OTHER and~they$^{(m)}$~
will~DISPUTE$^{(v)}$ ALSO UPON~her and~he~will~CALL.OUT$^{(v)}$ TITLE~her
Sitnah **26:22** and~he~will~make~ADVANCE$^{(v)}$ from~THERE and~he~will~
DIG.OUT$^{(v)}$ WELL OTHER and~NOT they~did~DISPUTE$^{(v)}$ UPON~her and~he~
will~CALL.OUT$^{(v)}$ TITLE~her Rehhovot and~he~will~SAY$^{(v)}$ GIVEN.THAT NOW
he~did~make~WIDEN$^{(v)}$ **YHWH** to~us and~we~will~REPRODUCE$^{(v)}$ in~the~
LAND **26:23** and~he~will~make~GO.UP$^{(v)}$ from~THERE B'er-
Sheva **26:24** and~he~will~be~SEE$^{(v)}$ TO~him **YHWH** in~the~NIGHT the~HE
and~he~will~SAY$^{(v)}$ I Elohiym Avraham FATHER~you$^{(ms)}$ DO.NOT you$^{(ms)}$~will~
FEAR$^{(v)}$ GIVEN.THAT AT~you$^{(ms)}$ I and~I~did~much~KNEEL$^{(v)}$~you$^{(ms)}$ and~I~
did~make~INCREASE$^{(v)}$ AT SEED~you$^{(ms)}$ in~the~CROSS.OVER$^{(v)}$~ed$^{(ms)}$
Avraham SERVANT~me **26:25** and~he~will~BUILD$^{(v)}$ THERE ALTAR and~he~
will~CALL.OUT$^{(v)}$ in~TITLE **YHWH** and~he~will~EXTEND$^{(v)}$ THERE TENT~him
and~they$^{(m)}$~will~DIG$^{(v)}$ THERE SERVANT~s Yits'hhaq WELL **26:26** and~
Aviymelekh he~did~WALK$^{(v)}$ TO~him from~Gerar and~Ahhuzat PARTNER~
him and~Pikhol NOBLE ARMY~him **26:27** and~he~will~SAY$^{(v)}$ TO~them$^{(m)}$
Yits'hhaq WHY you$^{(mp)}$~did~COME$^{(v)}$ TO~me and~YOU$^{(mp)}$ you$^{(mp)}$~did~
HATE$^{(v)}$ AT~me and~you$^{(mp)}$~will~SEND$^{(v)}$~me from~AT~you$^{(mp)}$ **26:28** and~
they$^{(m)}$~will~SAY$^{(v)}$ >~SEE$^{(v)}$ we~did~SEE$^{(v)}$ GIVEN.THAT he~did~EXIST$^{(v)}$
YHWH WITH~you$^{(fs)}$ and~we~will~SAY$^{(v)}$ she~will~EXIST$^{(v)}$ PLEASE OATH
BETWEEN~s~us BETWEEN~s~us and~BETWEEN~you$^{(ms)}$ and~she~did~be~

CUT$^{(V)}$ COVENANT WITH~you$^{(fs)}$ **26:29** IF you$^{(ms)}$~will~DO$^{(V)}$ WITH~us DYSFUNCTIONAL like~WHICH NOT we~did~TOUCH$^{(V)}$ and~like~WHICH we~ did~DO$^{(V)}$ WITH~you$^{(ms)}$ ONLY FUNCTIONAL and~we~will~much~SEND$^{(V)}$~ you$^{(ms)}$ in~COMPLETENESS YOU$^{(ms)}$ NOW KNEEL$^{(V)}$~ed$^{(ms)}$ YHWH **26:30** and~ he~will~DO$^{(V)}$ to~them$^{(m)}$ BANQUET and~they$^{(m)}$~will~EAT$^{(V)}$ and~they$^{(m)}$~ will~GULP$^{(V)}$ **26:31** and~they$^{(m)}$~will~make~DEPART.EARLY$^{(V)}$ in~the~ MORNING and~they$^{(m)}$~will~be~SWEAR$^{(V)}$ MAN to~BROTHER~him and~he~ will~much~SEND$^{(V)}$~them$^{(m)}$ Yits'hhaq and~they$^{(m)}$~will~WALK$^{(V)}$ from~AT~ him in~COMPLETENESS **26:32** and~he~will~EXIST$^{(V)}$ in~the~DAY the~HE and~they$^{(m)}$~will~COME$^{(V)}$ SERVANT~s Yits'hhaq and~they$^{(m)}$~will~make~ BE.FACE.TO.FACE$^{(V)}$ to~him UPON CONCERNING the~WELL WHICH they~ did~DIG.OUT$^{(V)}$ and~they$^{(m)}$~will~SAY$^{(V)}$ to~him we~did~FIND$^{(V)}$ WATER~ s2 **26:33** and~he~will~CALL.OUT$^{(V)}$ AT~her Shivah UPON SO TITLE the~CITY B'er-Sheva UNTIL the~DAY the~THIS **26:34** and~he~will~EXIST$^{(V)}$ Esaw SON FOUR~s YEAR and~he~will~TAKE$^{(V)}$ WOMAN AT Yehudit DAUGHTER Be'eri the~Hhet~of and~AT Basmat DAUGHTER Eylon the~Hhet~of **26:35** and~ they$^{(f)}$~will~EXIST$^{(V)}$ GRIEF WIND to~Yits'hhaq and~to~Rivqah

Chapter 27

27:1 and~he~will~EXIST$^{(V)}$ GIVEN.THAT he~did~BE.OLD$^{(V)}$ Yits'hhaq and~ they$^{(f)}$~will~DIM$^{(V)}$ EYE~s2~him from~>~SEE$^{(V)}$ and~he~will~CALL.OUT$^{(V)}$ AT Esaw SON~him the~GREAT and~he~will~SAY$^{(V)}$ TO~him SON~me and~he~ will~SAY$^{(V)}$ TO~him LOOK~me **27:2** and~he~will~SAY$^{(V)}$ LOOK PLEASE I~did~ BE.OLD$^{(V)}$ NOT I~did~KNOW$^{(V)}$ DAY DEATH~me **27:3** and~NOW !$^{(ms)}$~ LIFT.UP$^{(V)}$ PLEASE UTENSIL~you$^{(ms)}$ QUIVER~you$^{(ms)}$ and~BOW~you$^{(ms)}$ and~ !$^{(ms)}$~GO.OUT$^{(V)}$ the~FIELD and~ !$^{(ms)}$~HUNT$^{(V)}$ to~me PROVISIONS **27:4** and~ !$^{(ms)}$~DO$^{(V)}$ to~me DELICACY~s like~WHICH I~did~LOVE$^{(V)}$ and~ !$^{(ms)}$~make~ COME$^{(V)}$ to~me and~I~will~EAT$^{(V)}$ in~the~CROSS.OVER$^{(V)}$~ed$^{(ms)}$ she~will~ much~KNEEL$^{(V)}$~you$^{(ms)}$ SOUL~me in~BEFORE I~will~DIE$^{(V)}$ **27:5** and~Rivqah HEAR$^{(V)}$~ing$^{(fs)}$ in~>~much~SPEAK$^{(V)}$ Yits'hhaq TO Esaw SON~him and~he~ will~WALK$^{(V)}$ Esaw the~FIELD to~>~HUNT$^{(V)}$ GAME to~>~make~ COME$^{(V)}$ **27:6** and~Rivqah she~did~SAY$^{(V)}$ TO Ya'aqov SON~her to~>~SAY$^{(V)}$ LOOK I~did~HEAR$^{(V)}$ AT FATHER~you$^{(ms)}$ >~much~SPEAK$^{(V)}$~ing$^{(ms)}$ TO Esaw BROTHER~you$^{(ms)}$ to~>~SAY$^{(V)}$ **27:7** !$^{(ms)}$~make~COME$^{(V)}$ to~me GAME and~ !$^{(ms)}$~DO$^{(V)}$ to~me DELICACY~s and~I~will~EAT$^{(V)}$ and~I~will~much~KNEEL$^{(V)}$~ you$^{(ms)}$~& to~FACE~s YHWH to~FACE~s DEATH~me **27:8** and~NOW SON~ me !$^{(ms)}$~HEAR$^{(V)}$ in~VOICE~me to~the~WHICH I much~DIRECT$^{(V)}$~ing$^{(fs)}$ AT~ you$^{(fs)}$ **27:9** !$^{(ms)}$~WALK$^{(V)}$ PLEASE TO the~FLOCKS and~ !$^{(ms)}$~TAKE$^{(V)}$ to~me from~THERE TWO MALE.KID~s SHE-GOAT~s FUNCTIONAL~s and~I~will~ DO$^{(V)}$~& AT~them$^{(m)}$ DELICACY~s to~FATHER~you$^{(ms)}$ like~WHICH he~did~ LOVE$^{(V)}$ **27:10** and~you$^{(ms)}$~did~make~COME$^{(V)}$ to~FATHER~you$^{(ms)}$ and~he~ did~EAT$^{(V)}$ in~CROSS.OVER$^{(V)}$ WHICH he~will~much~KNEEL$^{(V)}$~you$^{(ms)}$ to~

The Book of Genesis

FACE~s DEATH~him **27:11** and~*he~will*~SAY[(V)] Ya'aqov TO Rivqah MOTHER~him THOUGH Esaw BROTHER~me MAN HAIR and~I MAN SLICK **27:12** POSSIBLY *he~will*~FEEL[(V)]~me FATHER~me and~*I~did*~EXIST[(V)] in~EYE~s2~him like~*much*~IMITATE[(V)]~*ing*[(ms)] and~*I~will~make*~COME[(V)] UPON~me ANNOYANCE and~NOT PRESENT **27:13** and~*she~will*~SAY[(V)] to~him MOTHER~him UPON~me ANNOYANCE~you[(ms)] SON~me SURELY *![(ms)]*~HEAR[(V)] in~VOICE~me and~*![(ms)]*~WALK[(V)] *![(ms)]*~TAKE[(V)] to~me **27:14** and~*he~will*~WALK[(V)] and~*he~will*~TAKE[(V)] and~*he~will~make*~COME[(V)] to~MOTHER~him and~*she~will*~DO[(V)] MOTHER~him DELICACY~s like~WHICH *he~did*~LOVE[(V)] FATHER~him **27:15** and~*she~will*~TAKE[(V)] Rivqah AT GARMENT~s Esaw SON~her the~GREAT the~PLEASANT~s WHICH AT~her in~the~HOUSE and~*she~will~make*~WEAR[(V)] AT Ya'aqov SON~her the~SMALL **27:16** and~AT SKIN~s MALE.KID~s the~SHE-GOAT~s *she~did~make*~WEAR[(V)] UPON HAND~s2~him and~UPON SMOOTH BACK.OF.THE.NECK~s~him **27:17** and~*she~will*~GIVE[(V)] AT the~DELICACY~s and~AT the~BREAD WHICH *she~did*~DO[(V)] in~HAND Ya'aqov SON~her **27:18** and~*he~will*~COME[(V)] TO FATHER~him and~*he~will*~SAY[(V)] FATHER~me and~*he~will*~SAY[(V)] LOOK~me WHO YOU[(ms)] SON~me **27:19** and~*he~will*~SAY[(V)] Ya'aqov TO FATHER~him I Esaw FIRSTBORN~you[(ms)] *I~did*~DO[(V)] like~WHICH *you[(ms)]~did~much*~SPEAK[(V)] TO~me *![(ms)]*~RISE[(V)] PLEASE *![(ms)]*~SETTLE[(V)]~& and~*![(ms)]*~EAT[(V)] from~GAME~me in~the~CROSS.OVER[(V)]~*ed*[(ms)] *she~will~much*~KNEEL[(V)]~me SOUL~you[(ms)] **27:20** and~*he~will*~SAY[(V)] Yits'hhaq TO SON~him WHAT THIS *you[(ms)]~did~much*~HURRY[(V)] to~>~FIND[(V)] SON~me and~*he~will*~SAY[(V)] GIVEN.THAT *he~did~make*~MEET[(V)] **YHWH** Elohiym~you[(ms)] to~FACE~s~me **27:21** and~*he~will*~SAY[(V)] Yits'hhaq TO Ya'aqov *![(ms)]*~DRAW.NEAR[(V)]~& PLEASE and~*I~will*~GROPE[(V)] SON~me the~YOU[(ms)] THIS SON~me Esaw IF NOT **27:22** and~*he~will*~DRAW.NEAR[(V)] Ya'aqov TO Yits'hhaq FATHER~him and~*he~will*~GROPE[(V)]~him and~*he~will*~SAY[(V)] the~VOICE VOICE Ya'aqov and~the~HAND~s2 HAND~s2 Esaw **27:23** and~NOT *he~did~make*~RECOGNIZE[(V)]~him GIVEN.THAT *they~did*~EXIST[(V)] HAND~s2~him like~HAND~s2 Esaw BROTHER~him HAIR~s and~*he~will~much*~KNEEL[(V)]~him **27:24** and~*he~will*~SAY[(V)] YOU[(ms)] THIS SON~me Esaw and~*he~will*~SAY[(V)] I **27:25** and~*he~will*~SAY[(V)] *![(ms)]*~make~DRAW.NEAR[(V)]~& to~me and~*I~will*~EAT[(V)]~& from~GAME SON~me to~THAT *she~will~much*~KNEEL[(V)]~you[(ms)] SOUL~me and~*he~will~make*~DRAW.NEAR[(V)] to~him and~*he~will*~EAT[(V)] and~*he~will~make*~COME[(V)] to~him WINE and~*he~will*~GULP[(V)] **27:26** and~*he~will*~SAY[(V)] TO~him Yits'hhaq FATHER~him *![(ms)]*~DRAW.NEAR[(V)]~& PLEASE and~*![(ms)]*~KISS[(V)]~& to~me SON~me **27:27** and~*he~will*~DRAW.NEAR[(V)] and~*he~will*~KISS[(V)] to~him and~*he~will~make*~SMELL[(V)] AT AROMA GARMENT~s~him and~*he~will~much*~KNEEL[(V)]~him and~*he~will*~SAY[(V)] *![(ms)]*~SEE[(V)] AROMA SON~me like~AROMA FIELD WHICH *he~did~much*~KNEEL[(V)]~him **YHWH 27:28** and~*he~will*~GIVE[(V)] to~you[(ms)] the~Elohiym from~DEW the~SKY~s2 and~from~OIL~s the~LAND and~ABUNDANCE CEREAL and~FRESH.WINE **27:29** *they[(m)]~will*~SERVE[(V)]~you[(ms)] PEOPLE~s and~*they[(m)]~will*~BEND.DOWN[(V)] to~you[(ms)] COMMUNITY~s *![(ms)]*~

BE⁽ᵛ⁾ OWNER to~BROTHER~s~you⁽ᵐˢ⁾ and~they⁽ᵐ⁾~will~BEND.DOWN⁽ᵛ⁾ to~you⁽ᵐˢ⁾ SON~s MOTHER~you⁽ᵐˢ⁾ SPIT.UPON⁽ᵛ⁾~ing⁽ᵐᵖ⁾~you⁽ᵐˢ⁾ SPIT.UPON⁽ᵛ⁾~ed⁽ᵐˢ⁾ and~much~KNEEL⁽ᵛ⁾~ing⁽ᵐᵖ⁾~you⁽ᵐˢ⁾ KNEEL⁽ᵛ⁾~ed⁽ᵐˢ⁾ **27:30** and~he~will~EXIST⁽ᵛ⁾ like~WHICH he~did~much~FINISH⁽ᵛ⁾ Yits'hhaq to~>~much~KNEEL⁽ᵛ⁾ AT Ya'aqov and~he~will~EXIST⁽ᵛ⁾ SURELY >~GO.OUT⁽ᵛ⁾ he~did~GO.OUT⁽ᵛ⁾ Ya'aqov from~AT FACE~s Yits'hhaq FATHER~him and~Esaw BROTHER~him he~did~COME⁽ᵛ⁾ from~GAME~him **27:31** and~he~will~DO⁽ᵛ⁾ ALSO HE DELICACY~s and~he~will~make~COME⁽ᵛ⁾ to~FATHER~him and~he~will~SAY⁽ᵛ⁾ to~FATHER~him he~will~RISE⁽ᵛ⁾ FATHER~me and~he~will~EAT⁽ᵛ⁾ from~GAME SON~him in~the~CROSS.OVER⁽ᵛ⁾~ed⁽ᵐˢ⁾ she~will~much~KNEEL⁽ᵛ⁾~me SOUL~you⁽ᵐˢ⁾ **27:32** and~he~will~SAY⁽ᵛ⁾ to~him Yits'hhaq FATHER~him WHO YOU⁽ᵐˢ⁾ and~he~will~SAY⁽ᵛ⁾ I SON~you⁽ᵐˢ⁾ FIRSTBORN~you⁽ᵐˢ⁾ Esaw **27:33** and~he~will~TREMBLE⁽ᵛ⁾ Yits'hhaq TREMBLING GREAT UNTIL MANY and~he~will~SAY⁽ᵛ⁾ WHO THEN HE the~HUNT⁽ᵛ⁾ GAME and~he~will~make~COME⁽ᵛ⁾ to~me and~I~will~EAT⁽ᵛ⁾ from~ALL in~BEFORE you⁽ᵐˢ⁾~will~COME⁽ᵛ⁾ and~I~will~much~KNEEL⁽ᵛ⁾~him ALSO KNEEL⁽ᵛ⁾~ed⁽ᵐˢ⁾ he~will~EXIST⁽ᵛ⁾ **27:34** like~>~HEAR⁽ᵛ⁾ Esaw AT WORD~s FATHER~him and~he~will~CRY.OUT⁽ᵛ⁾ CRY GREAT and~BITTER UNTIL MANY and~he~will~SAY⁽ᵛ⁾ to~FATHER~him !⁽ᵐˢ⁾~much~KNEEL⁽ᵛ⁾~me ALSO I FATHER~me **27:35** and~he~will~SAY⁽ᵛ⁾ he~did~COME⁽ᵛ⁾ BROTHER~you⁽ᵐˢ⁾ in~DECEIT and~he~will~TAKE⁽ᵛ⁾ PRESENT~you⁽ᵐˢ⁾ **27:36** and~he~will~SAY⁽ᵛ⁾ ?~GIVEN.THAT he~did~CALL.OUT⁽ᵛ⁾ TITLE~him Ya'aqov and~he~will~RESTRAIN⁽ᵛ⁾~me THIS FOOTSTEP~s2 AT BIRTHRIGHT~me he~did~TAKE⁽ᵛ⁾ and~LOOK NOW he~did~TAKE⁽ᵛ⁾ PRESENT~me and~he~will~SAY⁽ᵛ⁾ ?~NOT you⁽ᵐˢ⁾~did~SET.ASIDE⁽ᵛ⁾ to~me PRESENT **27:37** and~he~will~ANSWER⁽ᵛ⁾ Yits'hhaq and~he~will~SAY⁽ᵛ⁾ to~Esaw THOUGH OWNER I~did~PLACE⁽ᵛ⁾~him to~you⁽ᶠˢ⁾ and~AT ALL BROTHER~s~him I~did~GIVE⁽ᵛ⁾ to~him to~the~SERVANT~s and~CEREAL and~FRESH.WINE I~did~SUPPORT⁽ᵛ⁾~him and~to~you⁽ᵐˢ⁾ THEN WHAT I~will~DO⁽ᵛ⁾ SON~me **27:38** and~he~will~SAY⁽ᵛ⁾ Esaw TO FATHER~him ?~PRESENT UNIT SHE to~you⁽ᵐˢ⁾ FATHER~me !⁽ᵐˢ⁾~much~KNEEL⁽ᵛ⁾~me ALSO I FATHER~me and~he~will~LIFT.UP⁽ᵛ⁾ Esaw VOICE~him and~he~will~WEEP⁽ᵛ⁾ **27:39** and~he~will~ANSWER⁽ᵛ⁾ Yits'hhaq FATHER~him and~he~will~SAY⁽ᵛ⁾ TO~him LOOK from~OIL~s the~LAND he~will~EXIST⁽ᵛ⁾ SETTLING~you⁽ᵐˢ⁾ and~from~DEW the~SKY~s2 from~UPON **27:40** and~UPON SWORD~you⁽ᵐˢ⁾ you⁽ᵐˢ⁾~will~LIVE⁽ᵛ⁾ and~AT BROTHER~you⁽ᵐˢ⁾ you⁽ᵐˢ⁾~will~SERVE⁽ᵛ⁾ and~he~did~EXIST⁽ᵛ⁾ like~WHICH you⁽ᵐˢ⁾~will~make~ROAM⁽ᵛ⁾ and~you⁽ᵐˢ⁾~did~TEAR.OFF⁽ᵛ⁾ YOKE~him from~UPON BACK.OF.THE.NECK~you⁽ᵐˢ⁾ **27:41** and~he~will~HOLD.A.GRUDGE⁽ᵛ⁾ Esaw AT Ya'aqov UPON the~PRESENT WHICH he~did~much~KNEEL⁽ᵛ⁾~him FATHER~him and~he~will~SAY⁽ᵛ⁾ Esaw in~HEART~him they⁽ᵐ⁾~will~COME.NEAR⁽ᵛ⁾ DAY~s MOURNING FATHER~me and~I~will~KILL⁽ᵛ⁾ AT Ya'aqov BROTHER~me **27:42** and~he~will~be~make~BE.FACE.TO.FACE⁽ᵛ⁾ to~Rivqah AT WORD~s Esaw SON~her the~GREAT and~she~will~SEND⁽ᵛ⁾ and~she~will~CALL.OUT⁽ᵛ⁾ to~Ya'aqov SON~her the~SMALL and~she~will~SAY⁽ᵛ⁾ TO~him LOOK Esaw BROTHER~you⁽ᵐˢ⁾ self~COMFORT⁽ᵛ⁾~ing⁽ᵐˢ⁾ to~you⁽ᵐˢ⁾ to~>~KILL⁽ᵛ⁾~you⁽ᵐˢ⁾ **27:43** and~

NOW SON~me !$^{(ms)}$~HEAR$^{(V)}$ in~VOICE~me and~ !$^{(ms)}$~RISE$^{(V)}$!$^{(ms)}$~ FLEE.AWAY$^{(V)}$ to~you$^{(ms)}$ TO Lavan BROTHER~me Hharan~unto **27:44** and~ you$^{(ms)}$~did~SETTLE$^{(V)}$ WITH~him DAY~s UNIT~s UNTIL WHICH she~will~ TURN.BACK$^{(V)}$ FURY BROTHER~you$^{(ms)}$ **27:45** UNTIL >~TURN.BACK$^{(V)}$ NOSE BROTHER~you$^{(ms)}$ FROM~you$^{(ms)}$ and~he~did~FORGET$^{(V)}$ AT WHICH you$^{(ms)}$~ did~DO$^{(V)}$ to~him and~I~did~SEND$^{(V)}$ and~I~did~TAKE$^{(V)}$~you$^{(ms)}$ from~THERE to~WHAT I~will~BE.CHILDLESS$^{(V)}$ ALSO TWO~you$^{(mp)}$ DAY UNIT **27:46** and~ she~will~SAY$^{(V)}$ Rivqah TO Yits'hhaq I~will~LOATHE$^{(V)}$ in~LIVING~s~me from~ FACE~s DAUGHTER~s Hhet IF TAKE$^{(V)}$~ing$^{(ms)}$ Ya'aqov WOMAN from~ DAUGHTER~s Hhet like~THESE from~DAUGHTER~s the~LAND to~WHAT to~ me LIVING~s

Chapter 28

28:1 and~he~will~CALL.OUT$^{(V)}$ Yits'hhaq TO Ya'aqov and~he~will~much~ KNEEL$^{(V)}$ AT~him and~he~will~much~DIRECT$^{(V)}$~him and~he~will~SAY$^{(V)}$ to~ him NOT you$^{(ms)}$~will~TAKE$^{(V)}$ WOMAN from~DAUGHTER~s Kena'an **28:2** !$^{(ms)}$~RISE$^{(V)}$!$^{(ms)}$~WALK$^{(V)}$ Padan-Aram~unto HOUSE~unto Betu'el FATHER~of MOTHER~you$^{(ms)}$ and~ !$^{(ms)}$~TAKE$^{(V)}$ to~you$^{(ms)}$ from~ THERE WOMAN from~DAUGHTER~s Lavan BROTHER~of MOTHER~ you$^{(ms)}$ **28:3** and~MIGHTY.ONE Shaddai he~will~much~KNEEL$^{(V)}$ AT~you$^{(ms)}$ and~he~will~make~REPRODUCE$^{(V)}$~you$^{(ms)}$ and~he~will~make~INCREASE$^{(V)}$~ you$^{(ms)}$ and~you$^{(ms)}$~did~EXIST$^{(V)}$ to~ASSEMBLY PEOPLE~s **28:4** and~he~will~ GIVE$^{(V)}$ to~you$^{(ms)}$ AT PRESENT Avraham to~you$^{(ms)}$ and~to~SEED~you$^{(ms)}$ AT~ you$^{(fs)}$ to~>~POSSESS$^{(V)}$~you$^{(ms)}$ AT LAND IMMIGRATION~s~you$^{(ms)}$ WHICH he~did~GIVE$^{(V)}$ Elohiym to~Avraham **28:5** and~he~will~SEND$^{(V)}$ Yits'hhaq AT Ya'aqov and~he~will~WALK$^{(V)}$ Padan-Aram~unto TO Lavan SON Betu'el the~ Aram~of BROTHER~of Rivqah MOTHER Ya'aqov and~Esaw **28:6** and~he~ will~SEE$^{(V)}$ Esaw GIVEN.THAT he~will~much~KNEEL$^{(V)}$ Yits'hhaq AT Ya'aqov and~he~did~much~SEND$^{(V)}$ AT~him Padan-Aram~unto to~>~TAKE$^{(V)}$ to~him from~THERE WOMAN in~>~much~KNEEL$^{(V)}$~him AT~him and~he~will~ much~DIRECT$^{(V)}$ UPON~him to~>~SAY$^{(V)}$ NOT you$^{(ms)}$~will~TAKE$^{(V)}$ WOMAN from~DAUGHTER~s Kena'an **28:7** and~he~will~HEAR$^{(V)}$ Ya'aqov TO FATHER~ him and~TO MOTHER~him and~he~will~WALK$^{(V)}$ Padan-Aram~ unto **28:8** and~he~will~SEE$^{(V)}$ Esaw GIVEN.THAT DYSFUNCTIONAL~s DAUGHTER~s Kena'an in~EYE~s2 Yits'hhaq FATHER~him **28:9** and~he~will~ WALK$^{(V)}$ Esaw TO Yishma'el and~he~will~TAKE$^{(V)}$ AT Mahhalat DAUGHTER Yishma'el SON Avraham SISTER Nevayot UPON WOMAN~s~him to~him to~ WOMAN **28:10** and~he~will~GO.OUT$^{(V)}$ Ya'aqov from~B'er-Sheva and~he~ will~WALK$^{(V)}$ Hharan~unto **28:11** and~he~will~REACH$^{(V)}$ in~the~AREA and~ he~will~STAY.THE.NIGHT$^{(V)}$ THERE GIVEN.THAT he~did~COME$^{(V)}$ the~SUN and~he~will~TAKE$^{(V)}$ from~STONE~s the~AREA and~he~will~PLACE$^{(V)}$ HEADREST~s~him and~he~will~LIE.DOWN$^{(V)}$ in~the~AREA the~

HE **28:12** and~*he*~*will*~DREAM⁽ᵛ⁾ and~LOOK LADDER *be*~*make*~STAND.UP⁽ᵛ⁾~*ing*⁽ᵐˢ⁾ LAND~unto and~HEAD~him *make*~TOUCH⁽ᵛ⁾~*ing*⁽ᵐˢ⁾ the~SKY~s2~unto and~LOOK MESSENGER~s Elohiym GO.UP⁽ᵛ⁾~*ing*⁽ᵐᵖ⁾ and~GO.DOWN⁽ᵛ⁾~*ing*⁽ᵐᵖ⁾ in~him **28:13** and~LOOK **YHWH** *be*~STAND.UP⁽ᵛ⁾~*ing*⁽ᵐˢ⁾ UPON~him and~*he*~*will*~SAY⁽ᵛ⁾ I **YHWH** Elohiym Avraham FATHER~you⁽ᵐˢ⁾ and~Elohiym Yits'hhaq the~LAND WHICH YOU⁽ᵐˢ⁾ LIE.DOWN⁽ᵛ⁾~*ing*⁽ᵐˢ⁾ UPON~her to~you⁽ᵐˢ⁾ *I*~*will*~GIVE⁽ᵛ⁾~her and~to~SEED~you⁽ᵐˢ⁾ **28:14** and~*he*~*did*~EXIST⁽ᵛ⁾ SEED~you⁽ᵐˢ⁾ like~DIRT the~LAND and~*you*⁽ᵐˢ⁾~*did*~BREAK.OUT⁽ᵛ⁾ SEA~unto and~EAST~unto and~NORTH~unto and~SOUTH~unto and~*they*~*did*~*be*~KNEEL⁽ᵛ⁾ in~you⁽ᵐˢ⁾ ALL CLAN~s the~GROUND and~in~SEED~you⁽ᵐˢ⁾ **28:15** and~LOOK I WITH~you⁽ᶠˢ⁾ and~*I*~*did*~SAFEGUARD⁽ᵛ⁾~you⁽ᵐˢ⁾ in~ALL WHICH *you*⁽ᵐˢ⁾~*will*~WALK⁽ᵛ⁾ and~*I*~*did*~*make*~TURN.BACK⁽ᵛ⁾~you⁽ᵐˢ⁾ TO the~GROUND the~THIS GIVEN.THAT NOT *I*~*will*~LEAVE⁽ᵛ⁾~you⁽ᵐˢ⁾ UNTIL WHICH IF *I*~*did*~DO⁽ᵛ⁾ AT WHICH *I*~*did*~much~SPEAK⁽ᵛ⁾ to~you⁽ᶠˢ⁾ **28:16** and~*he*~*will*~AWAKE⁽ᵛ⁾ Ya'aqov from~SNOOZE~him and~*he*~*will*~SAY⁽ᵛ⁾ SURELY THERE.IS **YHWH** in~the~AREA the~THIS and~I NOT *I*~*did*~KNOW⁽ᵛ⁾ **28:17** and~*he*~*will*~FEAR⁽ᵛ⁾ and~*he*~*will*~SAY⁽ᵛ⁾ WHAT *be*~FEAR⁽ᵛ⁾~*ing*⁽ᵐˢ⁾ the~AREA the~THIS WITHOUT THIS GIVEN.THAT IF HOUSE Elohiym and~THIS GATE the~SKY~s2 **28:18** and~*he*~*will*~*make*~DEPART.EARLY⁽ᵛ⁾ Ya'aqov in~the~MORNING and~*he*~*will*~TAKE⁽ᵛ⁾ AT the~STONE WHICH *he*~*did*~PLACE⁽ᵛ⁾ HEADREST~s~him and~*he*~*will*~PLACE⁽ᵛ⁾ AT~her MONUMENT and~*he*~*will*~POUR.DOWN⁽ᵛ⁾ OIL UPON HEAD~her **28:19** and~*he*~*will*~CALL.OUT⁽ᵛ⁾ AT TITLE the~AREA the~HE Beyt-El and~BUT Luz TITLE the~CITY to~the~FIRST **28:20** and~*he*~*will*~MAKE.A.VOW⁽ᵛ⁾ Ya'aqov VOW to~>~SAY⁽ᵛ⁾ IF *he*~*will*~EXIST⁽ᵛ⁾ Elohiym BY~me and~*he*~*did*~SAFEGUARD⁽ᵛ⁾~me in~the~ROAD the~THIS WHICH I WALK⁽ᵛ⁾~*ing*⁽ᵐˢ⁾ and~*he*~*did*~GIVE⁽ᵛ⁾ to~me BREAD to~>~EAT⁽ᵛ⁾ and~GARMENT to~>~WEAR⁽ᵛ⁾ **28:21** and~*I*~*did*~TURN.BACK⁽ᵛ⁾ in~COMPLETENESS TO HOUSE FATHER~me and~*he*~*will*~EXIST⁽ᵛ⁾ **YHWH** to~me to~Elohiym **28:22** and~the~STONE the~THIS WHICH *I*~*did*~PLACE⁽ᵛ⁾ MONUMENT *he*~*will*~EXIST⁽ᵛ⁾ HOUSE Elohiym and~ALL WHICH *you*⁽ᵐˢ⁾~*will*~GIVE⁽ᵛ⁾ to~me >~*much*~GIVE.A.TENTH⁽ᵛ⁾ *I*~*will*~*much*~GIVE.A.TENTH⁽ᵛ⁾~him to~you⁽ᶠˢ⁾

Chapter 29

29:1 and~*he*~*will*~LIFT.UP⁽ᵛ⁾ Ya'aqov FOOT~s2~him and~*he*~*will*~WALK⁽ᵛ⁾ LAND~unto SON~s EAST **29:2** and~*he*~*will*~SEE⁽ᵛ⁾ and~LOOK WELL in~the~FIELD and~LOOK THERE THREE DROVE~s FLOCKS STRETCH.OUT⁽ᵛ⁾~*ing*⁽ᵐᵖ⁾ UPON~her GIVEN.THAT FROM the~WELL the~SHE *they*⁽ᵐ⁾~*will*~DRINK⁽ᵛ⁾ the~DROVE~s and~the~STONE GREAT UPON MOUTH the~WELL **29:3** and~*they*~*did*~*be*~GATHER⁽ᵛ⁾ THERE~unto ALL the~DROVE~s and~*they*~*will*~ROLL⁽ᵛ⁾ AT the~STONE from~UPON MOUTH the~WELL and~*they*~*did*~*make*~DRINK⁽ᵛ⁾ AT the~FLOCKS and~*they*~*did*~*make*~TURN.BACK⁽ᵛ⁾ AT the~STONE UPON

MOUTH the~WELL to~AREA~her **29:4** and~*he~will*~SAY^(V) to~them^(m) Ya'aqov BROTHER~s~me from~WITHOUT YOU^(mp) and~*they*^(m)~*will*~SAY^(V) from~Hharan WE **29:5** and~*he~will*~SAY^(V) to~them^(m) ?~*you*^(mp)~*did*~KNOW^(V) AT Lavan SON Nahhor and~*they*^(m)~*will*~SAY^(V) we~did~KNOW^(V) **29:6** and~*he~will*~SAY^(V) to~them^(m) ?~COMPLETENESS to~him and~*they*^(m)~*will*~SAY^(V) COMPLETENESS and~LOOK Rahhel DAUGHTER~him *she~did*~COME^(V) WITH the~FLOCKS **29:7** and~*he~will*~SAY^(V) THOUGH YET.AGAIN the~DAY GREAT NOT APPOINTED.TIME >~*be*~GATHER^(V) the~LIVESTOCK *!*^(mp)~*make*~DRINK^(V) the~FLOCKS and~ *!*^(mp)~WALK^(V) *!*^(mp)~FEED^(V) **29:8** and~*they*^(m)~*will*~SAY^(V) NOT *we~will*~BE.ABLE^(V) UNTIL WHICH *they*^(m)~*will~be*~GATHER^(V) ALL the~DROVE~s and~*they~will*~ROLL^(V) AT the~STONE from~UPON MOUTH the~WELL and~*they~did~make*~DRINK^(V) the~FLOCKS **29:9** YET.AGAIN~him >~*much*~SPEAK^(V)~*ing*^(ms) WITH~them^(m) and~Rahhel *she~did*~COME^(V) WITH the~FLOCKS WHICH to~FATHER~her GIVEN.THAT FEED^(V)~*ing*^(fs) SHE **29:10** and~*he~will*~EXIST^(V) like~WHICH *he~did*~SEE^(V) Ya'aqov AT Rahhel DAUGHTER Lavan BROTHER~of MOTHER~him and~AT FLOCKS Lavan BROTHER~of MOTHER~him and~*he~will*~DRAW.NEAR^(V) Ya'aqov and~*he~will*~ROLL^(V) AT the~STONE from~UPON MOUTH the~WELL and~*he~will~make*~DRINK^(V) AT FLOCKS Lavan BROTHER~of MOTHER~him **29:11** and~*he~will*~KISS^(V) Ya'aqov to~Rahhel and~*he~will*~LIFT.UP^(V) AT VOICE~him and~*he~will*~WEEP^(V) **29:12** and~*he~will~make*~BE.FACE.TO.FACE^(V) Ya'aqov to~Rahhel GIVEN.THAT BROTHER~of FATHER~her HE and~GIVEN.THAT SON Rivqah HE and~*she~will*~RUN^(V) and~*she~will~make*~BE.FACE.TO.FACE^(V) to~FATHER~her **29:13** and~*he~will*~EXIST^(V) like~>~HEAR^(V) Lavan AT REPORT Ya'aqov SON SISTER~him and~*he~will*~RUN^(V) to~>~MEET^(V)~him and~*he~will~much*~EMBRACE^(V) to~him and~*he~will~much*~KISS^(V) to~him and~*he~will~make*~COME^(V)~him TO HOUSE~him and~*he~will~much*~COUNT^(V) to~Lavan AT ALL the~WORD~s the~THESE **29:14** and~*he~will*~SAY^(V) to~him Lavan SURELY BONE~me and~FLESH~me YOU^(ms) and~*he~will*~SETTLE^(V) WITH~him NEW.MOON DAY~s **29:15** and~*he~will*~SAY^(V) Lavan to~Ya'aqov ?~GIVEN.THAT BROTHER~me YOU^(ms) and~*you*^(ms)~*did*~SERVE^(V)~me FREELY *!*^(ms)~*make*~BE.FACE.TO.FACE^(V)~& to~me WHAT PAYMENT~you^(ms) **29:16** and~to~Lavan TWO DAUGHTER~s TITLE the~GREAT Le'ah and~TITLE the~SMALL Rahhel **29:17** and~EYE~s2 Le'ah TENDER~s and~Rahhel *she~did*~EXIST^(V) BEAUTIFUL FORM and~BEAUTIFUL APPEARANCE **29:18** and~*he~will*~LOVE^(V) Ya'aqov AT Rahhel and~*he~will*~SAY^(V) *I~will*~SERVE^(V)~you^(ms) SEVEN YEAR~s in~Rahhel DAUGHTER~you^(ms) the~SMALL **29:19** and~*he~will*~SAY^(V) Lavan FUNCTIONAL >~GIVE^(V)~me AT~her to~you^(fs) from~>~GIVE^(V)~me AT~her to~MAN OTHER *!*^(ms)~SETTLE^(V)~& BY~me **29:20** and~*he~will*~SERVE^(V) Ya'aqov in~Rahhel SEVEN YEAR~s and~*they*^(m)~*will*~EXIST^(V) in~EYE~s2~him like~DAY~s UNIT~s in~AFFECTION AT~her **29:21** and~*he~will*~SAY^(V) Ya'aqov TO Lavan *!*^(ms)~PROVIDE^(V)~& AT WOMAN~me GIVEN.THAT *they~did*~FILL^(V) DAY~s~me and~*I~will*~COME^(V)~& TO~her **29:22** and~*he~will*~GATHER^(V) Lavan AT ALL MAN~s the~AREA and~*he~will*~DO^(V) BANQUET **29:23** and~

he~will~EXIST⁽ᵛ⁾ in~the~EVENING and~*he~will*~TAKE⁽ᵛ⁾ AT Le'ah DAUGHTER~him and~*he~will*~make~COME⁽ᵛ⁾ AT~her TO~him and~*he~will*~COME⁽ᵛ⁾ TO~her **29:24** and~*he~will*~GIVE⁽ᵛ⁾ Lavan to~her AT Zilpah MAID~him to~Le'ah DAUGHTER~him MAID **29:25** and~*he~will*~EXIST⁽ᵛ⁾ in~the~MORNING and~LOOK SHE Le'ah and~*he~will*~SAY⁽ᵛ⁾ TO Lavan WHAT THIS *you*⁽ᵐˢ⁾~*did*~DO⁽ᵛ⁾ to~me ?~NOT in~Rahhel *I~did*~SERVE⁽ᵛ⁾ WITH~*you*⁽ᶠˢ⁾ and~to~WHAT *you*⁽ᵐˢ⁾~*did*~much~THROW.DOWN⁽ᵛ⁾~me **29:26** and~*he~will*~SAY⁽ᵛ⁾ Lavan NOT he~will~be~DO⁽ᵛ⁾ SO in~AREA~us to~>~GIVE⁽ᵛ⁾ the~LITTLE.ONE to~FACE~s the~FIRSTBORN.FEMALE **29:27** *!*⁽ᵐˢ⁾~much~FILL⁽ᵛ⁾ WEEK THIS and~we~will~GIVE⁽ᵛ⁾ to~*you*⁽ᵐˢ⁾ ALSO AT THIS in~the~SERVICE WHICH *you*⁽ᵐˢ⁾~*will*~SERVE⁽ᵛ⁾ BY~me YET.AGAIN SEVEN YEAR~s OTHER~s **29:28** and~*he~will*~DO⁽ᵛ⁾ Ya'aqov SO and~*he~will*~much~FILL⁽ᵛ⁾ WEEK THIS and~*he~will*~GIVE⁽ᵛ⁾ to~him AT Rahhel DAUGHTER~him to~him to~WOMAN **29:29** and~*he~will*~GIVE⁽ᵛ⁾ Lavan to~Rahhel DAUGHTER~him AT Bilhah MAID~him to~her to~MAID **29:30** and~*he~will*~COME⁽ᵛ⁾ ALSO TO Rahhel and~*he~will*~LOVE⁽ᵛ⁾ ALSO AT Rahhel from~Le'ah and~*he~will*~SERVE⁽ᵛ⁾ WITH~him YET.AGAIN SEVEN YEAR~s OTHER~s **29:31** and~*he~will*~SEE⁽ᵛ⁾ **YHWH** GIVEN.THAT HATE⁽ᵛ⁾~*ed*⁽ᶠˢ⁾ Le'ah and~*he~will*~OPEN⁽ᵛ⁾ AT BOWELS~her and~Rahhel STERILE **29:32** and~*she~will*~CONCEIVE⁽ᵛ⁾ Le'ah and~*she~will*~BRING.FORTH⁽ᵛ⁾ SON and~*she~will*~CALL.OUT⁽ᵛ⁾ TITLE~him Re'uven GIVEN.THAT *she~did*~SAY⁽ᵛ⁾ GIVEN.THAT *he~did*~SEE⁽ᵛ⁾ **YHWH** in~AFFLICTION~me GIVEN.THAT NOW *he~will*~LOVE⁽ᵛ⁾~me MAN~me **29:33** and~*she~will*~CONCEIVE⁽ᵛ⁾ YET.AGAIN and~*she~will*~BRING.FORTH⁽ᵛ⁾ SON and~*she~will*~SAY⁽ᵛ⁾ GIVEN.THAT *he~did*~HEAR⁽ᵛ⁾ **YHWH** GIVEN.THAT HATE⁽ᵛ⁾~*ed*⁽ᶠˢ⁾ I and~*he~will*~GIVE⁽ᵛ⁾ to~me ALSO AT THIS and~*she~will*~CALL.OUT⁽ᵛ⁾ TITLE~him Shimon **29:34** and~*she~will*~CONCEIVE⁽ᵛ⁾ YET.AGAIN and~*she~will*~BRING.FORTH⁽ᵛ⁾ SON and~*she~will*~SAY⁽ᵛ⁾ NOW the~FOOTSTEP *he~will~be*~JOIN⁽ᵛ⁾ MAN~me TO~me GIVEN.THAT *I~did*~BRING.FORTH⁽ᵛ⁾ to~him THREE SON~s UPON SO *he~did*~CALL.OUT⁽ᵛ⁾ TITLE~him Lewi **29:35** and~*she~will*~CONCEIVE⁽ᵛ⁾ YET.AGAIN and~*she~will*~BRING.FORTH⁽ᵛ⁾ SON and~*she~will*~SAY⁽ᵛ⁾ the~FOOTSTEP *I~will*~make~THROW.THE.HAND⁽ᵛ⁾ AT **YHWH** UPON SO *she~did*~CALL.OUT⁽ᵛ⁾ TITLE~him Yehudah and~*she~will*~STAND⁽ᵛ⁾ from~>~BRING.FORTH⁽ᵛ⁾

Chapter 30

30:1 and~*she~will*~SEE⁽ᵛ⁾ Rahhel GIVEN.THAT NOT *she~did*~BRING.FORTH⁽ᵛ⁾ to~Ya'aqov and~*she~will*~BE.ZEALOUS⁽ᵛ⁾ Rahhel in~SISTER~her and~*she~will*~SAY⁽ᵛ⁾ TO Ya'aqov *!*⁽ᵐˢ⁾~PROVIDE⁽ᵛ⁾~& to~me SON~s and~IF WITHOUT *she~did*~DIE⁽ᵛ⁾ I **30:2** and~*he~will*~FLARE.UP⁽ᵛ⁾ NOSE Ya'aqov in~Rahhel and~*he~will*~SAY⁽ᵛ⁾ ?~UNDER Elohiym I WHICH *he~did*~WITHHOLD⁽ᵛ⁾ FROM~*you*⁽ᶠˢ⁾ PRODUCE WOMB **30:3** and~*she~will*~SAY⁽ᵛ⁾ LOOK BONDWOMAN~me Bilhah *!*⁽ᵐˢ⁾~COME⁽ᵛ⁾ TO~her and~*she~will*~BRING.FORTH⁽ᵛ⁾ UPON KNEE~me

The Book of Genesis

and~I~will~be~BUILD$^{(V)}$ ALSO I FROM~her **30:4** and~*she~will*~GIVE$^{(V)}$ to~him AT Bilhah MAID~her to~WOMAN and~*he~will*~COME$^{(V)}$ TO~her Ya'aqov **30:5** and~*she~will*~CONCEIVE$^{(V)}$ Bilhah and~*she~will*~BRING.FORTH$^{(V)}$ to~Ya'aqov SON **30:6** and~*she~will*~SAY$^{(V)}$ Rahhel *he~did*~MODERATE$^{(V)}$~me Elohiym and~ALSO *he~did*~HEAR$^{(V)}$ in~VOICE~me and~*he~will*~GIVE$^{(V)}$ to~me SON UPON SO *she~did*~CALL.OUT$^{(V)}$ TITLE~him Dan **30:7** and~*she~will*~CONCEIVE$^{(V)}$ YET.AGAIN and~*she~will*~BRING.FORTH$^{(V)}$ Bilhah MAID Rahhel SON SECOND to~Ya'aqov **30:8** and~*she~will*~SAY$^{(V)}$ Rahhel WRESTLING~s Elohiym *I~did~be*~ENTWINE$^{(V)}$ WITH SISTER~me ALSO *I~did*~BE.ABLE$^{(V)}$ and~*she~will*~CALL.OUT$^{(V)}$ TITLE~him Naphtali **30:9** and~*she~will*~SEE$^{(V)}$ Le'ah GIVEN.THAT *she~did*~STAND$^{(V)}$ from~>~BRING.FORTH$^{(V)}$ and~*she~will*~TAKE$^{(V)}$ AT Zilpah MAID~her and~*she~will*~GIVE$^{(V)}$ AT~her to~Ya'aqov to~WOMAN **30:10** and~*she~will*~BRING.FORTH$^{(V)}$ Zilpah MAID Le'ah to~Ya'aqov SON **30:11** and~*she~will*~SAY$^{(V)}$ Le'ah in~FORTUNE and~*she~will*~CALL.OUT$^{(V)}$ AT TITLE~him Gad **30:12** and~*she~will*~BRING.FORTH$^{(V)}$ Zilpah MAID Le'ah SON SECOND to~Ya'aqov **30:13** and~*she~will*~SAY$^{(V)}$ Le'ah in~HAPPINESS~me GIVEN.THAT *they~did~much*~HAPPY$^{(V)}$~me DAUGHTER~s and~*she~will*~CALL.OUT$^{(V)}$ AT TITLE~him Asher **30:14** and~*he~will*~WALK$^{(V)}$ Re'uven in~DAY~s HARVEST WHEAT~s and~*he~will*~FIND$^{(V)}$ MANDRAKES~s in~the~FIELD and~*he~will*~make~COME$^{(V)}$ AT~them$^{(m)}$ TO Le'ah MOTHER~him and~*she~will*~SAY$^{(V)}$ Rahhel TO Le'ah *!*$^{(fs)}$~GIVE$^{(V)}$ PLEASE to~me from~MANDRAKES~s SON~you$^{(fs)}$ **30:15** and~*she~will*~SAY$^{(V)}$ to~her ?~SMALL.AMOUNT >~TAKE$^{(V)}$~you$^{(fs)}$ AT MAN~me and~to~>~TAKE$^{(V)}$ ALSO AT MANDRAKES~s SON~me and~*she~will*~SAY$^{(V)}$ Rahhel to~SO *he~will*~LIE.DOWN$^{(V)}$ WITH~you$^{(fs)}$ the~NIGHT UNDER MANDRAKES~s SON~you$^{(fs)}$ **30:16** and~*he~will*~COME$^{(V)}$ Ya'aqov FROM the~FIELD in~the~EVENING and~*she~will*~GO.OUT$^{(V)}$ Le'ah to~>~MEET$^{(V)}$~him and~*she~will*~SAY$^{(V)}$ TO~me you$^{(ms)}$~will~COME$^{(V)}$ GIVEN.THAT >~HIRE$^{(V)}$ *I~did*~HIRE$^{(V)}$~you$^{(ms)}$ in~MANDRAKES~s SON~me and~*he~will*~LIE.DOWN$^{(V)}$ WITH~her in~the~NIGHT HE **30:17** and~*he~will*~HEAR$^{(V)}$ Elohiym TO Le'ah and~*she~will*~CONCEIVE$^{(V)}$ and~*she~will*~BRING.FORTH$^{(V)}$ to~Ya'aqov SON FIFTH **30:18** and~*she~will*~SAY$^{(V)}$ Le'ah *he~did*~GIVE$^{(V)}$ Elohiym WAGE~me WHICH *I~did*~GIVE$^{(V)}$ MAID~me to~MAN~me and~*she~will*~CALL.OUT$^{(V)}$ TITLE~him Yis'sas'khar **30:19** and~*she~will*~CONCEIVE$^{(V)}$ YET.AGAIN Le'ah and~*she~will*~BRING.FORTH$^{(V)}$ SON SIXTH to~Ya'aqov **30:20** and~*she~will*~SAY$^{(V)}$ Le'ah *he~did*~ENDOW$^{(V)}$~me Elohiym AT~me DOWRY FUNCTIONAL the~FOOTSTEP *he~will*~RESIDE$^{(V)}$~me MAN~me GIVEN.THAT *I~did*~BRING.FORTH$^{(V)}$ to~him SIX SON~s and~*she~will*~CALL.OUT$^{(V)}$ AT TITLE~him Zevulun **30:21** and~AFTER *she~did*~BRING.FORTH$^{(V)}$ DAUGHTER and~*she~will*~CALL.OUT$^{(V)}$ AT TITLE~her Dinah **30:22** and~*he~will*~REMEMBER$^{(V)}$ Elohiym AT Rahhel and~*he~will*~HEAR$^{(V)}$ TO~her Elohiym and~*he~will*~OPEN$^{(V)}$ AT BOWELS~her **30:23** and~*she~will*~CONCEIVE$^{(V)}$ and~*she~will*~BRING.FORTH$^{(V)}$ SON and~*she~will*~SAY$^{(V)}$ *he~did*~GATHER$^{(V)}$ Elohiym AT DISGRACE~me **30:24** and~*she~will*~CALL.OUT$^{(V)}$ AT TITLE~him Yoseph to~>~SAY$^{(V)}$ *he~will~make*~ADD$^{(V)}$ **YHWH**

Benner's Mechanical Translation of the Torah

to~me SON OTHER **30:25** and~he~will~EXIST$^{(V)}$ like~WHICH *she~did~*BRING.FORTH$^{(V)}$ Rahhel AT Yoseph and~he~will~SAY$^{(V)}$ Ya'aqov TO Lavan *!$^{(ms)}$~much~*SEND$^{(V)}$~me and~*I~will~*WALK$^{(V)}$~& TO AREA~me and~to~LAND~me **30:26** *!$^{(ms)}$~*GIVE$^{(V)}$~& AT WOMAN~s~me and~AT BOY~s~me WHICH *I~did~*SERVE$^{(V)}$ AT~you$^{(ms)}$ in~them$^{(f)}$ and~*I~will~*WALK$^{(V)}$~& GIVEN.THAT YOU$^{(ms)}$ *you$^{(ms)}$~did~*KNOW$^{(V)}$ AT SERVICE~me WHICH *I~did~*SERVE$^{(V)}$~you$^{(ms)}$ **30:27** and~he~will~SAY$^{(V)}$ TO~him Lavan IF PLEASE *I~did~*FIND$^{(V)}$ BEAUTY in~EYE~s2~you$^{(ms)}$ *I~did~much~*PREDICT$^{(V)}$ and~he~will~much~KNEEL$^{(V)}$~me **YHWH** in~ON.ACCOUNT.OF~you$^{(ms)}$ **30:28** and~he~will~SAY$^{(V)}$ *!$^{(ms)}$~*PIERCE.THROUGH$^{(V)}$~& WAGE~you$^{(ms)}$ UPON~me and~*I~will~*GIVE$^{(V)}$~& **30:29** and~he~will~SAY$^{(V)}$ TO~him YOU$^{(ms)}$ *you$^{(ms)}$~did~*KNOW$^{(V)}$ AT WHICH *I~did~*SERVE$^{(V)}$~you$^{(ms)}$ and~AT WHICH *he~did~*EXIST$^{(V)}$ LIVESTOCK~you$^{(ms)}$ AT~me **30:30** GIVEN.THAT SMALL.AMOUNT WHICH *he~did~*EXIST$^{(V)}$ to~you$^{(ms)}$ to~FACE~s~me and~he~will~BREAK.OUT$^{(V)}$ to~ABUNDANCE and~he~will~much~KNEEL$^{(V)}$ **YHWH** AT~you$^{(ms)}$ to~FOOT~me and~NOW HOW.LONG *I~will~*DO$^{(V)}$ ALSO I to~HOUSE~me **30:31** and~he~will~SAY$^{(V)}$ WHAT *I~will~*GIVE$^{(V)}$ to~you$^{(fs)}$ and~he~will~SAY$^{(V)}$ Ya'aqov NOT *you$^{(ms)}$~will~*GIVE$^{(V)}$ to~me ANYTHING IF *you$^{(ms)}$~will~*DO$^{(V)}$ to~me the~WORD the~THIS *I~will~*TURN.BACK$^{(V)}$~& *I~will~*FEED$^{(V)}$ FLOCKS~you$^{(ms)}$ *I~will~*SAFEGUARD$^{(V)}$ **30:32** *I~will~*CROSS.OVER$^{(V)}$ in~ALL FLOCKS~you$^{(ms)}$ the~DAY *>~make~*TURN.ASIDE$^{(V)}$ from~THERE ALL RAM SPECKLED and~SPOT$^{(V)}$~*ed$^{(ms)}$* and~ALL RAM BLACK in~the~SHEEP~s and~SPOT$^{(V)}$~*ed$^{(ms)}$* and~SPECKLED in~the~SHE-GOAT~s and~*he~did~*EXIST$^{(V)}$ WAGE~me **30:33** and~*she~did~*ANSWER$^{(V)}$ in~me STEADFASTNESS~me in~DAY TOMORROW GIVEN.THAT *you$^{(ms)}$~will~*COME$^{(V)}$ UPON WAGE~me to~FACE~s~you$^{(ms)}$ ALL WHICH WITHOUT~him SPECKLED and~SPOT$^{(V)}$~*ed$^{(ms)}$* in~the~SHE-GOAT~s and~BLACK in~the~SHEEP~s STEAL$^{(V)}$~*ed$^{(ms)}$* HE AT~me **30:34** and~he~will~SAY$^{(V)}$ Lavan THOUGH WOULD.THAT *he~will~*EXIST$^{(V)}$ like~WORD~you$^{(ms)}$ **30:35** and~*he~will~make~*TURN.ASIDE$^{(V)}$ in~the~DAY the~HE AT the~HE-GOAT~s the~STRIPED~s and~the~SPOT$^{(V)}$~*ed$^{(ms)}$*~s and~AT ALL the~SHE-GOAT~s the~SPECKLED~s and~the~SPOT$^{(V)}$~*ed$^{(fs)}$*~s ALL WHICH Lavan in~him and~ALL BLACK in~the~SHEEP~s and~he~will~GIVE$^{(V)}$ in~HAND SON~s~him **30:36** and~he~will~PLACE$^{(V)}$ ROAD THREE DAY~s BETWEEN~him and~BETWEEN Ya'aqov and~Ya'aqov FEED$^{(V)}$~*ing$^{(ms)}$* AT FLOCKS Lavan the~*be~*LEAVE.BEHIND$^{(V)}$~*ing$^{(fp)}$* **30:37** and~he~will~TAKE$^{(V)}$ to~him Ya'aqov ROD POPLAR MOIST and~HAZEL and~CHESTNUT and~he~will~much~PEEL$^{(V)}$ in~them$^{(f)}$ STRIP WHITE~s EXPOSE the~WHITE WHICH UPON the~ROD~s **30:38** and~*he~will~make~*LEAVE.IN.PLACE$^{(V)}$ AT the~ROD~s WHICH *he~did~much~*PEEL$^{(V)}$ in~TROUGH~s in~WATERING.TROUGH~s the~WATER~s2 WHICH *they$^{(f)}$~will~*COME$^{(V)}$ the~FLOCKS to~*>~*GULP$^{(V)}$ to~IN.FRONT the~FLOCKS and~*they$^{(m)}$~will~*HEAT$^{(V)}$ in~*>~*COME$^{(V)}$~them$^{(f)}$ to~*>~*GULP$^{(V)}$ **30:39** and~*they$^{(m)}$~will~*HEAT$^{(V)}$ the~FLOCKS TO the~ROD~s and~*they$^{(f)}$~will~*BRING.FORTH$^{(V)}$ the~FLOCKS STRIPED~s SPECKLED~s and~the~SPOT$^{(V)}$~*ed$^{(ms)}$* **30:40** and~the~SHEEP~s *he~did~make~*DIVIDE.APART$^{(V)}$ Ya'aqov and~he~will~GIVE$^{(V)}$ FACE~s the~FLOCKS TO STRIPED and~ALL

BLACK in~FLOCKS Lavan and~*he~will*~SET.DOWN^(V) to~him DROVE~s to~ STRAND~him and~NOT *he~did*~SET.DOWN^(V)~them^(m) UPON FLOCKS Lavan **30:41** and~*he~did*~EXIST^(V) in~ALL >~*much*~HEAT^(V) the~FLOCKS the~ be~much~TIE^(V)~*ing*^(fp) and~*he~did*~PLACE^(V) Ya'aqov AT the~ROD~s to~EYE~ s2 the~FLOCKS in~TROUGH~s to~>~*much*~HEAT^(V)~her in~the~ ROD~s **30:42** and~in~>~*make*~ENVELOP^(V) the~FLOCKS NOT *he~will*~ PLACE^(V) and~*he~did*~EXIST^(V) the~ENVELOP^(V)~*ed*^(mp) to~Lavan and~the~ TIE^(V)~*ed*^(mp) to~Ya'aqov **30:43** and~*he~will*~BREAK.OUT^(V) the~MAN MANY MANY and~*he~will*~EXIST^(V) to~him FLOCKS ABUNDANT and~MAID~s and~ SERVANT~s and~CAMEL~s and~DONKEY~s

Chapter 31

31:1 and~*he~will*~HEAR^(V) AT WORD~s SON~s Lavan to~>~SAY^(V) *he~did*~ TAKE^(V) Ya'aqov AT ALL WHICH to~FATHER~us and~from~WHICH to~ FATHER~us *he~did*~DO^(V) AT ALL the~ARMAMENT the~THIS **31:2** and~*he~ will*~SEE^(V) Ya'aqov AT FACE~s Lavan and~LOOK WITHOUT~him WITH~him like~YESTERDAY THREE.DAYS.AGO **31:3** and~*he~will*~SAY^(V) YHWH TO Ya'aqov *!*^(ms)~TURN.BACK^(V) TO LAND FATHER~s~you^(ms) and~to~KINDRED~ you^(ms) and~*I~will*~EXIST^(V) WITH~you^(fs) **31:4** and~*he~will*~SEND^(V) Ya'aqov and~*he~will*~CALL.OUT^(V) to~Rahhel and~to~Le'ah the~FIELD TO FLOCKS~ him **31:5** and~*he~will*~SAY^(V) to~them^(f) SEE^(V)~*ing*^(ms) I AT FACE~s FATHER~ you^(fp) GIVEN.THAT WITHOUT~him TO~me like~YESTERDAY THREE.DAYS.AGO and~Elohiym FATHER~me *he~did*~EXIST^(V) BY~ me **31:6** and~YOU^(fp) *you*^(fp)~*did*~KNOW^(V) GIVEN.THAT in~ALL STRENGTH~ me *I~did*~SERVE^(V) AT FATHER~you^(fp) **31:7** and~FATHER~you^(fp) *he~did*~ *make*~DEAL.DECEITFULLY^(V) in~me and~*he~did*~*make*~PASS.OVER^(V) AT PAYMENT~me TEN TIME~s and~NOT *he~did*~GIVE^(V)~him Elohiym to~>~ *make*~BE.DYSFUNCTIONAL^(V) BY~me **31:8** IF IN.THIS.WAY *he~will*~SAY^(V) SPECKLED~s *he~will*~EXIST^(V) WAGE~you^(ms) and~*they*^(m)~*will*~ BRING.FORTH^(V) ALL the~FLOCKS SPECKLED~s and~IF IN.THIS.WAY *he~will*~ SAY^(V) STRIPED~s *he~will*~EXIST^(V) WAGE~you^(ms) and~*they*^(m)~*will*~ BRING.FORTH^(V) ALL the~FLOCKS STRIPED~s **31:9** and~*he~will*~*make*~ DELIVER^(V) Elohiym AT LIVESTOCK FATHER~you^(mp) and~*he~will*~GIVE^(V) to~ me **31:10** and~*he~will*~EXIST^(V) in~APPOINTED.TIME >~*much*~HEAT^(V) the~ FLOCKS and~*I~will*~LIFT.UP^(V) EYE~s2~me and~*I~will*~SEE^(V) in~the~DREAM and~LOOK the~MALE.GOAT~s the~GO.UP^(V)~*ing*^(mp) UPON the~FLOCKS STRIPED~s SPECKLED~s and~SPOTTED~s **31:11** and~*he~will*~SAY^(V) TO~me MESSENGER the~Elohiym in~the~DREAM Ya'aqov and~*I~will*~SAY^(V) LOOK~ me **31:12** and~*he~will*~SAY^(V) *!*^(ms)~LIFT.UP^(V) PLEASE EYE~s2~you^(ms) and~ *!*^(ms)~SEE^(V) ALL the~MALE.GOAT~s the~GO.UP^(V)~*ing*^(mp) UPON the~FLOCKS STRIPED~s SPECKLED~s and~SPOTTED~s GIVEN.THAT *I~did*~SEE^(V) AT ALL WHICH Lavan DO^(V)~*ing*^(ms) to~you^(fs) **31:13** I the~MIGHTY.ONE Beyt-El

WHICH *you*⁽ᵐˢ⁾~*did*~SMEAR⁽ⱽ⁾ THERE MONUMENT WHICH *you*⁽ᵐˢ⁾~*did*~MAKE.A.VOW⁽ⱽ⁾ *to*~me THERE VOW NOW *!*⁽ᵐˢ⁾~RISE⁽ⱽ⁾ *!*⁽ᵐˢ⁾~GO.OUT⁽ⱽ⁾ FROM *the*~LAND *the*~THIS *and*~*!*⁽ᵐˢ⁾~TURN.BACK⁽ⱽ⁾ TO LAND KINDRED~*you*⁽ᵐˢ⁾ **31:14** *and*~*she*~*will*~ANSWER⁽ⱽ⁾ Rahhel *and*~Le'ah *and*~*they*⁽ᶠ⁾~*will*~SAY⁽ⱽ⁾ *to*~him ?~YET.AGAIN *to*~us DISTRIBUTION *and*~INHERITANCE *in*~HOUSE FATHER~us **31:15** ?~NOT FOREIGN~s *we*~*did*~*be*~THINK⁽ⱽ⁾ *to*~him GIVEN.THAT *he*~*did*~SELL⁽ⱽ⁾~us *and*~*he*~*will*~EAT⁽ⱽ⁾ ALSO >~EAT⁽ⱽ⁾ AT SILVER~us **31:16** GIVEN.THAT ALL *the*~RICHES WHICH *he*~*did*~*make*~DELIVER⁽ⱽ⁾ Elohiym *from*~FATHER~us *to*~us HE *and*~*to*~SON~s~us *and*~NOW ALL WHICH *he*~*did*~SAY⁽ⱽ⁾ Elohiym TO~*you*⁽ᵐˢ⁾ *!*⁽ᵐˢ⁾~DO⁽ⱽ⁾ **31:17** *and*~*he*~*will*~RISE⁽ⱽ⁾ Ya'aqov *and*~*he*~*will*~LIFT.UP⁽ⱽ⁾ AT SON~s~him *and*~AT WOMAN~s~him UPON *the*~CAMEL~s **31:18** *and*~*he*~*will*~DRIVE⁽ⱽ⁾ AT ALL LIVESTOCK~him *and*~AT ALL GOODS~him WHICH *he*~*did*~ACCUMULATE⁽ⱽ⁾ LIVESTOCK MATERIAL~him WHICH *he*~*did*~ACCUMULATE⁽ⱽ⁾ *in*~Padan-Aram *to*~>~COME⁽ⱽ⁾ TO Yits'hhaq FATHER~him LAND~*unto* Kena'an **31:19** *and*~Lavan *he*~*did*~WALK⁽ⱽ⁾ *to*~>~SHEAR⁽ⱽ⁾ AT FLOCKS~him *and*~*she*~*will*~STEAL⁽ⱽ⁾ Rahhel AT *the*~FAMILY.IDOL~s WHICH *to*~FATHER~her **31:20** *and*~*he*~*will*~STEAL⁽ⱽ⁾ Ya'aqov AT HEART Lavan *the*~Aram~*of* UPON UNAWARE *he*~*did*~*make*~BE.FACE.TO.FACE⁽ⱽ⁾ *to*~him GIVEN.THAT FLEE.AWAY⁽ⱽ⁾~*ing*⁽ᵐˢ⁾ HE **31:21** *and*~*he*~*will*~FLEE.AWAY⁽ⱽ⁾ HE *and*~ALL WHICH *to*~him *and*~*he*~*will*~RISE⁽ⱽ⁾ *and*~*he*~*will*~CROSS.OVER⁽ⱽ⁾ AT *the*~RIVER *and*~*he*~*will*~PLACE⁽ⱽ⁾ AT FACE~s~him HILL *the*~Gil'ad **31:22** *and*~*he*~*will*~*be*~*make*~BE.FACE.TO.FACE⁽ⱽ⁾ *to*~Lavan *in*~*the*~DAY *the*~THIRD GIVEN.THAT *he*~*did*~FLEE.AWAY⁽ⱽ⁾ Ya'aqov **31:23** *and*~*he*~*will*~TAKE⁽ⱽ⁾ AT BROTHER~s~him WITH~him *and*~*he*~*will*~PURSUE⁽ⱽ⁾ AFTER~him ROAD SEVEN DAY~s *and*~*he*~*will*~*make*~ADHERE⁽ⱽ⁾ AT~him *in*~HILL *the*~Gil'ad **31:24** *and*~*he*~*will*~COME⁽ⱽ⁾ Elohiym TO Lavan *the*~Aram~*of* *in*~*the*~DREAM *the*~NIGHT *and*~*he*~*will*~SAY⁽ⱽ⁾ *to*~him *!*⁽ᵐˢ⁾~*be*~SAFEGUARD⁽ⱽ⁾ *to*~*you*⁽ᵐˢ⁾ OTHERWISE *you*⁽ᵐˢ⁾~*will*~*much*~SPEAK⁽ⱽ⁾ WITH Ya'aqov *from*~FUNCTIONAL UNTIL DYSFUNCTIONAL **31:25** *and*~*he*~*will*~*make*~OVERTAKE⁽ⱽ⁾ Lavan AT Ya'aqov *and*~Ya'aqov *he*~*did*~THRUST⁽ⱽ⁾ AT TENT~him *in*~*the*~HILL *and*~Lavan *he*~*did*~THRUST⁽ⱽ⁾ AT BROTHER~s~him *in*~HILL *the*~Gil'ad **31:26** *and*~*he*~*will*~SAY⁽ⱽ⁾ Lavan *to*~Ya'aqov WHAT *you*⁽ᵐˢ⁾~*did*~DO⁽ⱽ⁾ *and*~*you*⁽ᵐˢ⁾~*will*~STEAL⁽ⱽ⁾ AT HEART~me *and*~*you*⁽ᵐˢ⁾~*will*~*much*~DRIVE⁽ⱽ⁾ AT DAUGHTER~s~me *like*~CAPTURE⁽ⱽ⁾~*ed*⁽ᶠᵖ⁾ SWORD **31:27** *to*~WHAT *you*⁽ᵐˢ⁾~*did*~*be*~WITHDRAW⁽ⱽ⁾ *to*~>~FLEE.AWAY⁽ⱽ⁾ *and*~*you*⁽ᵐˢ⁾~*will*~STEAL⁽ⱽ⁾ AT~me *and*~NOT *you*⁽ᵐˢ⁾~*did*~*make*~BE.FACE.TO.FACE⁽ⱽ⁾ *to*~me *and*~*I*~*will*~*much*~SEND⁽ⱽ⁾~*you*⁽ᵐˢ⁾ *in*~REJOICING *and*~*in*~SONG~s *in*~TAMBOURINE *and*~*in*~HARP **31:28** *and*~NOT *you*⁽ᵐˢ⁾~*did*~LEAVE.ALONE⁽ⱽ⁾~me *to*~>~*much*~KISS⁽ⱽ⁾ *to*~SON~s~me *and*~*to*~DAUGHTER~s~me NOW *you*⁽ᵐˢ⁾~*did*~*make*~CONFIDENT⁽ⱽ⁾ >~DO⁽ⱽ⁾~him **31:29** THERE.IS *to*~MIGHTY.ONE HAND~me *to*~>~DO⁽ⱽ⁾ WITH~*you*⁽ᵐᵖ⁾ DYSFUNCTIONAL *and*~Elohiym FATHER~*you*⁽ᵐᵖ⁾ LAST.NIGHT *he*~*did*~SAY⁽ⱽ⁾ TO~me *to*~>~SAY⁽ⱽ⁾ *!*⁽ᵐˢ⁾~*be*~SAFEGUARD⁽ⱽ⁾ *to*~*you*⁽ᵐˢ⁾ >~*much*~SPEAK⁽ⱽ⁾ WITH Ya'aqov *from*~FUNCTIONAL UNTIL DYSFUNCTIONAL **31:30** *and*~NOW >~WALK⁽ⱽ⁾ *you*⁽ᵐˢ⁾~*did*~WALK⁽ⱽ⁾ GIVEN.THAT >~*be*~CRAVING⁽ⱽ⁾ *you*⁽ᵐˢ⁾~*did*~

The Book of Genesis

be~CRAVING$^{(V)}$ to~HOUSE FATHER~*you*$^{(ms)}$ to~WHAT *you*$^{(ms)}$~*did*~STEAL$^{(V)}$ AT Elohiym~me **31:31** and~*he*~*will*~ANSWER$^{(V)}$ Ya'aqov and~*he*~*will*~SAY$^{(V)}$ to~Lavan GIVEN.THAT *I*~*did*~FEAR$^{(V)}$ GIVEN.THAT *I*~*did*~SAY$^{(V)}$ OTHERWISE *you*$^{(ms)}$~*will*~PLUCK.AWAY$^{(V)}$ AT DAUGHTER~s~*you*$^{(ms)}$ from~WITH~me **31:32** WITH WHICH *you*$^{(ms)}$~*will*~FIND$^{(V)}$ AT Elohiym~*you*$^{(ms)}$ NOT *he*~*will*~LIVE$^{(V)}$ OPPOSITE BROTHER~s~us *!*$^{(ms)}$~*make*~RECOGNIZE$^{(V)}$ to~*you*$^{(ms)}$ WHAT BY~me and~*!*$^{(ms)}$~TAKE$^{(V)}$ to~*you*$^{(fs)}$ and~NOT *he*~*did*~KNOW$^{(V)}$ Ya'aqov GIVEN.THAT Rahhel *she*~*did*~STEAL$^{(V)}$~them$^{(m)}$ **31:33** and~*he*~*will*~COME$^{(V)}$ Lavan in~TENT Ya'aqov and~in~TENT Le'ah and~in~TENT TWO the~BONDWOMAN~s and~NOT *he*~*did*~FIND$^{(V)}$ and~*he*~*will*~GO.OUT$^{(V)}$ from~TENT Le'ah and~*he*~*will*~COME$^{(V)}$ in~TENT Rahhel **31:34** and~Rahhel *she*~*did*~TAKE$^{(V)}$ AT the~FAMILY.IDOL~s and~*she*~*will*~PLACE$^{(V)}$~them$^{(m)}$ in~DEPRESSION the~CAMEL and~*she*~*will*~SETTLE$^{(V)}$ UPON~them$^{(m)}$ and~*he*~*will*~much~GROPE$^{(V)}$ Lavan AT ALL the~TENT and~NOT *he*~*did*~FIND$^{(V)}$ **31:35** and~*she*~*will*~SAY$^{(V)}$ TO FATHER~her DO.NOT *he*~*will*~FLARE.UP$^{(V)}$ in~EYE~s2 LORD~me GIVEN.THAT NOT *I*~*will*~BE.ABLE$^{(V)}$ to~>~RISE$^{(V)}$ from~FACE~s~*you*$^{(ms)}$ GIVEN.THAT ROAD WOMAN~s to~me and~*he*~*will*~much~SEARCH$^{(V)}$ and~NOT *he*~*did*~FIND$^{(V)}$ AT the~FAMILY.IDOL~s **31:36** and~*he*~*will*~FLARE.UP$^{(V)}$ to~Ya'aqov and~*he*~*will*~DISPUTE$^{(V)}$ in~Lavan and~*he*~*will*~ANSWER$^{(V)}$ Ya'aqov and~*he*~*will*~SAY$^{(V)}$ to~Lavan WHAT OFFENSE~me WHAT FAILURE~me GIVEN.THAT *you*$^{(ms)}$~*did*~INFLAME$^{(V)}$ AFTER~me **31:37** GIVEN.THAT *you*$^{(ms)}$~*did*~much~GROPE$^{(V)}$ AT ALL UTENSIL~me WHAT *you*$^{(ms)}$~*did*~FIND$^{(V)}$ from~ALL UTENSIL~s HOUSE~*you*$^{(ms)}$ *!*$^{(ms)}$~PLACE$^{(V)}$ IN.THIS.WAY OPPOSITE BROTHER~s~me and~BROTHER~s~*you*$^{(ms)}$ and~*they*$^{(m)}$~*will*~*make*~REBUKE$^{(V)}$ BETWEEN TWO~us **31:38** THIS TEN~s YEAR I WITH~*you*$^{(fs)}$ EWE~s~*you*$^{(ms)}$ and~SHE-GOAT~s~*you*$^{(ms)}$ NOT *they*~*did*~much~BE.CHILDLESS$^{(V)}$ and~BUCK~s FLOCKS~*you*$^{(ms)}$ NOT *I*~*did*~EAT$^{(V)}$ **31:39** TORN NOT *I*~*did*~*make*~COME$^{(V)}$ TO~*you*$^{(ms)}$ I *I*~*will*~much~FAIL$^{(V)}$~her from~HAND~me *you*$^{(ms)}$~*will*~SEARCH.OUT$^{(V)}$~her STEAL$^{(V)}$~*ed*$^{(fs)}$ DAY and~STEAL$^{(V)}$~*ed*$^{(fs)}$ NIGHT **31:40** *I*~*did*~EXIST$^{(V)}$ in~the~DAY *he*~*did*~EAT$^{(V)}$~me PARCHING.HEAT and~ICE in~the~NIGHT and~*she*~*will*~TOSS$^{(V)}$ SNOOZE~me from~EYE~s2~me **31:41** THIS to~me TEN~s YEAR in~HOUSE~*you*$^{(ms)}$ *I*~*did*~SERVE$^{(V)}$~*you*$^{(ms)}$ FOUR TEN YEAR in~TWO DAUGHTER~s~*you*$^{(ms)}$ and~SIX YEAR~s in~FLOCKS~*you*$^{(ms)}$ and~*you*$^{(ms)}$~*will*~*make*~PASS.OVER$^{(V)}$ AT PAYMENT~me TEN TIME~s **31:42** UNLESS Elohiym FATHER~me Elohiym Avraham and~AWE Yits'hhaq *he*~*did*~EXIST$^{(V)}$ to~me GIVEN.THAT NOW EMPTINESS *you*$^{(ms)}$~*did*~much~SEND$^{(V)}$~me AT AFFLICTION~me and~AT TOIL PALM~s2~me *he*~*did*~SEE$^{(V)}$ Elohiym and~*he*~*will*~*make*~REBUKE$^{(V)}$ LAST.NIGHT **31:43** and~*he*~*will*~ANSWER$^{(V)}$ Lavan and~*he*~*will*~SAY$^{(V)}$ TO Ya'aqov the~DAUGHTER~s DAUGHTER~s~me and~the~SON~s SON~s~me and~the~FLOCKS FLOCKS~me and~ALL WHICH YOU$^{(ms)}$ SEE$^{(V)}$~*ing*$^{(ms)}$ to~me HE and~to~DAUGHTER~s~me WHAT *I*~*will*~DO$^{(V)}$ to~THESE the~DAY OR to~SON~s~them$^{(f)}$ WHICH *they*~*did*~BRING.FORTH$^{(V)}$ **31:44** and~NOW *!*$^{(ms)}$~WALK$^{(V)}$~& *we*~*will*~CUT$^{(V)}$~& COVENANT I and~YOU$^{(ms)}$ and~*he*~*did*~EXIST$^{(V)}$ to~WITNESS BETWEEN~me and~BETWEEN~you⁽ᵐˢ⁾ **31:45** and~*he~will*~TAKE⁽ⱽ⁾ Ya'aqov STONE and~*he~will*~RAISE.UP⁽ⱽ⁾~her MONUMENT **31:46** and~*he~will*~SAY⁽ⱽ⁾ Ya'aqov to~BROTHER~s~him *!⁽ᵐᵖ⁾*~PICK.UP⁽ⱽ⁾ STONE~s and~*they⁽ᵐ⁾~will*~TAKE⁽ⱽ⁾ STONE~s and~*they⁽ᵐ⁾~will*~DO⁽ⱽ⁾ MOUND and~*they⁽ᵐ⁾~will*~EAT⁽ⱽ⁾ THERE UPON the~MOUND **31:47** and~*he~will*~CALL.OUT⁽ⱽ⁾ to~him Lavan Yegar-Sa'haduta and~Ya'aqov *he~did*~CALL.OUT⁽ⱽ⁾ to~him Galeyd **31:48** and~*he~will*~SAY⁽ⱽ⁾ Lavan the~MOUND the~THIS WITNESS BETWEEN~me and~BETWEEN~you⁽ᵐˢ⁾ the~DAY UPON SO *he~did*~CALL.OUT⁽ⱽ⁾ TITLE~him Galeyd **31:49** and~the~Mitspah WHICH *he~did*~SAY⁽ⱽ⁾ *he~will*~KEEP.WATCH⁽ⱽ⁾ **YHWH** BETWEEN~me and~BETWEEN~you⁽ᵐˢ⁾ GIVEN.THAT *we~will~be*~HIDE⁽ⱽ⁾ MAN PARTNER~him **31:50** IF *you⁽ᵐˢ⁾~will*~AFFLICT⁽ⱽ⁾ AT DAUGHTER~s~me and~IF *you⁽ᵐˢ⁾~will*~TAKE⁽ⱽ⁾ WOMAN~s UPON DAUGHTER~s~me WITHOUT MAN WITH~us *!⁽ᵐˢ⁾*~SEE⁽ⱽ⁾ Elohiym WITNESS BETWEEN~me and~BETWEEN~you⁽ᵐˢ⁾ **31:51** and~*he~will*~SAY⁽ⱽ⁾ Lavan to~Ya'aqov LOOK the~MOUND the~THIS and~LOOK the~MONUMENT WHICH *I~did*~THROW⁽ⱽ⁾ BETWEEN~me and~BETWEEN~you⁽ᵐˢ⁾ **31:52** WITNESS the~MOUND the~THIS and~WITNESS the~MONUMENT IF NOT *I~will*~CROSS.OVER⁽ⱽ⁾ TO~you⁽ᵐˢ⁾ AT the~MOUND the~THIS and~IF YOU⁽ᵐˢ⁾ NOT *you⁽ᵐˢ⁾~will*~CROSS.OVER⁽ⱽ⁾ TO~me AT the~MOUND the~THIS and~AT the~MONUMENT the~THIS to~DYSFUNCTIONAL **31:53** Elohiym Avraham and~Elohiym Nahhor *they⁽ᵐ⁾~will*~DECIDE⁽ⱽ⁾ BETWEEN~us Elohiym FATHER~them⁽ᵐ⁾ and~*he~will~be*~SWEAR⁽ⱽ⁾ Ya'aqov in~AWE FATHER~him Yits'hhaq **31:54** and~*he~will*~SACRIFICE⁽ⱽ⁾ Ya'aqov SACRIFICE in~the~HILL and~*he~will*~CALL.OUT⁽ⱽ⁾ to~BROTHER~s~him to~>~EAT⁽ⱽ⁾ BREAD and~*they⁽ᵐ⁾~will*~EAT⁽ⱽ⁾ BREAD and~*they⁽ᵐ⁾~will*~STAY.THE.NIGHT⁽ⱽ⁾ in~the~HILL

Chapter 32

32:1 (31:55) and~*he~will~make*~DEPART.EARLY⁽ⱽ⁾ Lavan in~the~MORNING and~*he~will~much*~KISS⁽ⱽ⁾ to~SON~s~him and~to~DAUGHTER~s~him and~*he~will~much*~KNEEL⁽ⱽ⁾ AT~them⁽ᵐ⁾ and~*he~will*~WALK⁽ⱽ⁾ and~*he~will*~TURN.BACK⁽ⱽ⁾ Lavan to~AREA~him **32:2 (32:1)** and~Ya'aqov *he~did*~WALK⁽ⱽ⁾ to~ROAD~him and~*they⁽ᵐ⁾~will*~REACH⁽ⱽ⁾ in~him MESSENGER~s Elohiym **32:3 (32:2)** and~*he~will*~SAY⁽ⱽ⁾ Ya'aqov like~WHICH *he~did*~SEE⁽ⱽ⁾~them⁽ᵐ⁾ CAMP Elohiym THIS and~*he~will*~CALL.OUT⁽ⱽ⁾ TITLE the~AREA the~HE Mahhanayim **32:4 (32:3)** and~*he~will*~SEND⁽ⱽ⁾ Ya'aqov MESSENGER~s to~FACE~s~him TO Esaw BROTHER~him LAND~unto Se'iyr FIELD Edom **32:5 (32:4)** and~*he~will~much*~DIRECT⁽ⱽ⁾ AT~them⁽ᵐ⁾ to~>~SAY⁽ⱽ⁾ IN.THIS.WAY *you⁽ᵐˢ⁾~will*~SAY⁽ⱽ⁾~must to~LORD~me to~Esaw IN.THIS.WAY *he~did*~SAY⁽ⱽ⁾ SERVANT~you⁽ᵐˢ⁾ Ya'aqov WITH Lavan *I~did*~IMMIGRATE⁽ⱽ⁾ and~*I~will*~DELAY⁽ⱽ⁾ UNTIL NOW **32:6 (32:5)** and~*he~will*~EXIST⁽ⱽ⁾ to~me OX and~DONKEY FLOCKS and~SERVANT and~MAID and~*I~will*~SEND⁽ⱽ⁾~& to~>~*make*~BE.FACE.TO.FACE⁽ⱽ⁾ to~LORD~me to~>~FIND⁽ⱽ⁾ BEAUTY in~EYE~s2~

you⁽ᵐˢ⁾ **32:7 (32:6)** and~they⁽ᵐ⁾~will~TURN.BACK⁽ⱽ⁾ the~MESSENGER~s TO Ya'aqov to~>~SAY⁽ⱽ⁾ we~did~COME⁽ⱽ⁾ TO BROTHER~you⁽ᵐˢ⁾ TO Esaw and~ALSO WALK⁽ⱽ⁾~ing⁽ᵐˢ⁾ to~>~MEET⁽ⱽ⁾~you⁽ᵐˢ⁾ and~FOUR HUNDRED~s MAN WITH~him **32:8 (32:7)** and~he~will~FEAR⁽ⱽ⁾ Ya'aqov MANY and~he~will~MOLD⁽ⱽ⁾ to~him and~he~will~DIVIDE⁽ⱽ⁾ AT the~PEOPLE WHICH AT~him and~AT the~FLOCKS and~AT the~CATTLE and~the~CAMEL~s to~TWO CAMP~s **32:9 (32:8)** and~he~will~SAY⁽ⱽ⁾ IF he~will~COME⁽ⱽ⁾ Esaw TO the~CAMP the~UNIT and~he~did~make~HIT⁽ⱽ⁾~him and~he~did~EXIST⁽ⱽ⁾ the~CAMP the~be~REMAIN⁽ⱽ⁾~ing⁽ᵐˢ⁾ to~ESCAPED **32:10 (32:9)** and~he~will~SAY⁽ⱽ⁾ Ya'aqov Elohiym FATHER~me Avraham and~Elohiym FATHER~me Yits'hhaq **YHWH** the~SAY⁽ⱽ⁾~ing⁽ᵐˢ⁾ TO~me !⁽ᵐˢ⁾~TURN.BACK⁽ⱽ⁾ to~LAND~you⁽ᵐˢ⁾ and~to~KINDRED~you⁽ᵐˢ⁾ and~I~will~make~DO.WELL⁽ⱽ⁾~& WITH~you⁽ᶠˢ⁾ **32:11 (32:10)** I~did~BE.SMALL⁽ⱽ⁾ from~ALL the~KINDNESS~s and~from~ALL the~TRUTH WHICH you⁽ᵐˢ⁾~did~DO⁽ⱽ⁾ AT SERVANT~you⁽ᵐˢ⁾ GIVEN.THAT in~ROD~me I~did~CROSS.OVER⁽ⱽ⁾ AT the~Yarden the~THIS and~NOW I~did~EXIST⁽ⱽ⁾ to~TWO CAMP~s **32:12 (32:11)** !⁽ᵐˢ⁾~make~DELIVER⁽ⱽ⁾~me PLEASE from~HAND BROTHER~me from~HAND Esaw GIVEN.THAT he~did~FEAR⁽ⱽ⁾ I AT~him OTHERWISE he~will~COME⁽ⱽ⁾ and~he~did~make~HIT⁽ⱽ⁾~me MOTHER UPON SON~s **32:13 (32:12)** and~YOU⁽ᵐˢ⁾ you⁽ᵐˢ⁾~did~SAY⁽ⱽ⁾ >~make~DO.WELL⁽ⱽ⁾ I~will~make~DO.WELL⁽ⱽ⁾ WITH~you⁽ᶠˢ⁾ and~I~did~PLACE⁽ⱽ⁾ AT SEED~you⁽ᵐˢ⁾ like~SAND the~SEA WHICH NOT he~will~be~COUNT⁽ⱽ⁾ from~ABUNDANCE **32:14 (32:13)** and~he~will~STAY.THE.NIGHT⁽ⱽ⁾ THERE in~the~NIGHT the~HE and~he~will~TAKE⁽ⱽ⁾ FROM the~COME⁽ⱽ⁾~ing⁽ᵐˢ⁾ in~HAND~him DEPOSIT to~Esaw BROTHER~him **32:15 (32:14)** SHE-GOAT~s HUNDRED~s2 and~HE-GOAT~s TEN~s EWE~s HUNDRED~s2 and~BUCK~s TEN~s **32:16 (32:15)** CAMEL~s make~SUCKLE⁽ⱽ⁾~ing⁽ᶠᵖ⁾ and~SON~s~them⁽ᵐ⁾ THREE~s COW~s FOUR~s and~BULL~s TEN SHE-DONKEY~s TEN~s and~COLT~s TEN **32:17 (32:16)** and~he~will~GIVE⁽ⱽ⁾ in~HAND SERVANT~s~him DROVE DROVE to~STRAND~him and~he~will~SAY⁽ⱽ⁾ TO SERVANT~s~him !⁽ᵐᵖ⁾~CROSS.OVER⁽ⱽ⁾ to~FACE~s~me and~WIND you⁽ᵐᵖ⁾~will~PLACE⁽ⱽ⁾ BETWEEN DROVE and~BETWEEN DROVE **32:18 (32:17)** and~he~will~much~DIRECT⁽ⱽ⁾ AT the~FIRST to~>~SAY⁽ⱽ⁾ GIVEN.THAT he~will~ENCOUNTER⁽ⱽ⁾~you⁽ᵐˢ⁾ Esaw BROTHER~me and~he~did~INQUIRE⁽ⱽ⁾~you⁽ᵐˢ⁾ to~>~SAY⁽ⱽ⁾ to~WHO YOU⁽ᵐˢ⁾ and~WHEREVER you⁽ᵐˢ⁾~will~WALK⁽ⱽ⁾ and~to~WHO THESE to~FACE~s~you⁽ᵐˢ⁾ **32:19 (32:18)** and~you⁽ᵐˢ⁾~did~SAY⁽ⱽ⁾ to~SERVANT~you⁽ᵐˢ⁾ to~Ya'aqov DEPOSIT SHE SEND⁽ⱽ⁾~ing⁽ᶠˢ⁾ to~LORD~me to~Esaw and~LOOK ALSO HE AFTER~us **32:20 (32:19)** and~he~will~much~DIRECT⁽ⱽ⁾ ALSO AT the~SECOND ALSO AT the~THIRD ALSO AT ALL the~WALK⁽ⱽ⁾~ing⁽ᵐᵖ⁾ AFTER the~DROVE~s to~>~SAY⁽ⱽ⁾ like~the~WORD the~THIS you⁽ᵐˢ⁾~will~much~SPEAK⁽ⱽ⁾~must TO Esaw in~>~FIND⁽ⱽ⁾~you⁽ᵐᵖ⁾ AT~him **32:21 (32:20)** and~you⁽ᵐᵖ⁾~did~SAY⁽ⱽ⁾ ALSO LOOK SERVANT~you⁽ᵐˢ⁾ Ya'aqov AFTER~us GIVEN.THAT he~did~SAY⁽ⱽ⁾ I~will~much~COVER⁽ⱽ⁾~& FACE~s~him in~the~DEPOSIT the~WALK⁽ⱽ⁾~ing⁽ᶠˢ⁾ to~FACE~s~me and~AFTER SO I~will~SEE⁽ⱽ⁾ FACE~s~him POSSIBLY he~will~LIFT.UP⁽ⱽ⁾ FACE~s~me **32:22 (32:21)** and~

she~will~CROSS.OVER⁽ᵛ⁾ the~DEPOSIT UPON FACE~s~him and~HE he~did~
STAY.THE.NIGHT⁽ᵛ⁾ in~the~NIGHT the~HE in~the~CAMP **32:23 (32:22)** and~
he~will~RISE⁽ᵛ⁾ in~the~NIGHT HE and~he~will~TAKE⁽ᵛ⁾ AT TWO WOMAN~s~
him and~AT TWO MAID~s~him and~AT UNIT TEN BOY~s~him and~he~will~
CROSS.OVER⁽ᵛ⁾ AT CROSSING Yaboq **32:24 (32:23)** and~he~will~TAKE⁽ᵛ⁾~
them⁽ᵐ⁾ and~he~will~make~CROSS.OVER⁽ᵛ⁾~them⁽ᵐ⁾ AT the~WADI and~he~
will~make~CROSS.OVER⁽ᵛ⁾ AT WHICH to~him **32:25 (32:24)** and~he~will~
be~LEAVE.BEHIND⁽ᵛ⁾ Ya'aqov to~STRAND~him and~he~will~be~GRAPPLE⁽ᵛ⁾
MAN WITH~him UNTIL >~GO.UP⁽ᵛ⁾ the~DAWN **32:26 (32:25)** and~he~will~
SEE⁽ᵛ⁾ GIVEN.THAT NOT he~did~BE.ABLE⁽ᵛ⁾ to~him and~he~will~TOUCH⁽ᵛ⁾ in~
PALM MIDSECTION~him and~she~will~DISLOCATE⁽ᵛ⁾ PALM MIDSECTION
Ya'aqov in~>~be~GRAPPLE⁽ᵛ⁾~him WITH~him **32:27 (32:26)** and~he~will~
SAY⁽ᵛ⁾ I⁽ᵐˢ⁾~much~SEND⁽ᵛ⁾~me GIVEN.THAT he~did~GO.UP⁽ᵛ⁾ the~DAWN
and~he~will~SAY⁽ᵛ⁾ NOT I~will~much~SEND⁽ᵛ⁾~you⁽ᵐˢ⁾ GIVEN.THAT IF
you⁽ᵐˢ⁾~did~much~KNEEL⁽ᵛ⁾~me **32:28 (32:27)** and~he~will~SAY⁽ᵛ⁾ TO~him
WHAT TITLE~you⁽ᵐˢ⁾ and~he~will~SAY⁽ᵛ⁾ Ya'aqov **32:29 (32:28)** and~he~will~
SAY⁽ᵛ⁾ NOT Ya'aqov he~will~be~SAY⁽ᵛ⁾ YET.AGAIN TITLE~you⁽ᵐˢ⁾ GIVEN.THAT
IF Yisra'eyl GIVEN.THAT you⁽ᵐˢ⁾~did~TURN.AWAY⁽ᵛ⁾ WITH Elohiym and~WITH
MAN~s and~you⁽ᵐˢ⁾~BE.ABLE⁽ᵛ⁾ **32:30 (32:29)** and~he~will~INQUIRE⁽ᵛ⁾
Ya'aqov and~he~will~SAY⁽ᵛ⁾ I⁽ᵐˢ⁾~make~BE.FACE.TO.FACE⁽ᵛ⁾~& PLEASE
TITLE~you⁽ᵐˢ⁾ and~he~will~SAY⁽ᵛ⁾ to~WHAT THIS you⁽ᵐˢ⁾~will~INQUIRE⁽ᵛ⁾ to~
TITLE~me and~he~will~much~KNEEL⁽ᵛ⁾ AT~him THERE **32:31 (32:30)** and~
he~will~CALL.OUT⁽ᵛ⁾ Ya'aqov TITLE the~AREA Peni'el GIVEN.THAT I~did~
SEE⁽ᵛ⁾ Elohiym FACE~s TO FACE~s and~she~will~be~DELIVER⁽ᵛ⁾ SOUL~
me **32:32 (32:31)** and~he~will~COME.UP⁽ᵛ⁾ to~him the~SUN like~WHICH
he~did~CROSS.OVER⁽ᵛ⁾ AT Peni'el and~HE LIMP⁽ᵛ⁾~ing⁽ᵐˢ⁾ UPON
MIDSECTION~him **32:33 (32:32)** UPON SO NOT they⁽ᵐ⁾~will~EAT⁽ᵛ⁾ SON~s
Yisra'eyl AT SINEW the~THIGH.MUSCLE WHICH UPON PALM the~
MIDSECTION UNTIL the~DAY the~THIS GIVEN.THAT he~did~TOUCH⁽ᵛ⁾ in~
PALM MIDSECTION Ya'aqov in~SINEW the~THIGH.MUSCLE

Chapter 33

33:1 and~he~will~LIFT.UP⁽ᵛ⁾ Ya'aqov EYE~s2~him and~he~will~SEE⁽ᵛ⁾ and~
LOOK Esaw he~did~COME⁽ᵛ⁾ and~WITH~him FOUR HUNDRED~s MAN and~
he~will~DIVIDE⁽ᵛ⁾ AT the~BOY~s UPON Le'ah and~UPON Rahhel and~UPON
TWO the~MAID~s **33:2** and~he~will~PLACE⁽ᵛ⁾ AT the~MAID~s and~AT
BOY~s~them⁽ᶠ⁾ FIRST and~AT Le'ah and~BOY~s~her LAST~s and~AT Rahhel
and~AT Yoseph LAST~s **33:3** and~HE he~did~CROSS.OVER⁽ᵛ⁾ to~FACE~s~
them⁽ᵐ⁾ and~he~will~self~BEND.DOWN⁽ᵛ⁾ LAND~unto SEVEN FOOTSTEP~s
UNTIL >~DRAW.NEAR⁽ᵛ⁾~him UNTIL BROTHER~him **33:4** and~he~will~RUN⁽ᵛ⁾
Esaw to~>~MEET⁽ᵛ⁾~him and~he~will~much~EMBRACE⁽ᵛ⁾~him and~he~will~
FALL⁽ᵛ⁾ UPON BACK.OF.THE.NECK~him and~he~will~KISS⁽ᵛ⁾~him and~

they⁽ᵐ⁾~will~WEEP⁽ⱽ⁾ **33:5** and~*he*~*will*~LIFT.UP⁽ⱽ⁾ AT EYE~s2~him and~*he*~will~SEE⁽ⱽ⁾ AT the~WOMAN~s and~AT the~BOY~s and~*he*~*will*~SAY⁽ⱽ⁾ WHO THESE to~you⁽ᶠˢ⁾ and~*he*~*will*~SAY⁽ⱽ⁾ the~BOY~s WHICH *he*~*did*~PROVIDE.PROTECTION⁽ⱽ⁾ Elohiym AT SERVANT~you⁽ᵐˢ⁾ **33:6** and~*they*⁽ᶠ⁾~will~DRAW.NEAR⁽ⱽ⁾ the~MAID~s THEY⁽ᶠ⁾ and~the~BOY~s~them⁽ᶠ⁾ and~*they*⁽ᶠ⁾~will~*self*~BEND.DOWN⁽ⱽ⁾ **33:7** and~*she*~*will*~DRAW.NEAR⁽ⱽ⁾ ALSO Le'ah and~BOY~s~her and~*they*⁽ᵐ⁾~will~*self*~BEND.DOWN⁽ⱽ⁾ and~AFTER *he*~*did*~*be*~DRAW.NEAR⁽ⱽ⁾ Yoseph and~Rahhel and~*they*⁽ᵐ⁾~will~*self*~BEND.DOWN⁽ⱽ⁾ **33:8** and~*he*~*will*~SAY⁽ⱽ⁾ WHO to~you⁽ᵐˢ⁾ ALL the~CAMP the~THIS WHICH *I*~*did*~ENCOUNTER⁽ⱽ⁾ and~*he*~*will*~SAY⁽ⱽ⁾ to~>~FIND⁽ⱽ⁾ BEAUTY in~EYE~s2 LORD~me **33:9** and~*he*~*will*~SAY⁽ⱽ⁾ Esaw THERE.IS to~me ABUNDANT BROTHER~me *he*~*will*~EXIST⁽ⱽ⁾ to~you⁽ᵐˢ⁾ WHICH to~you⁽ᶠˢ⁾ **33:10** and~*he*~*will*~SAY⁽ⱽ⁾ Ya'aqov DO.NOT PLEASE IF PLEASE *I*~*did*~FIND⁽ⱽ⁾ BEAUTY in~EYE~s2~you⁽ᵐˢ⁾ and~*you*⁽ᵐˢ⁾~*did*~TAKE⁽ⱽ⁾ DEPOSIT~me from~HAND~me GIVEN.THAT UPON SO *I*~*did*~SEE⁽ⱽ⁾ FACE~s~you⁽ᵐˢ⁾ like~>~SEE⁽ⱽ⁾ FACE~s Elohiym and~*you*⁽ᵐˢ⁾~*will*~ACCEPT⁽ⱽ⁾~me **33:11** !⁽ᵐˢ⁾~TAKE⁽ⱽ⁾ PLEASE AT PRESENT~me WHICH *she*~*did*~*be*~*make*~COME⁽ⱽ⁾ to~you⁽ᶠˢ⁾ GIVEN.THAT *he*~*did*~PROVIDE.PROTECTION⁽ⱽ⁾~me Elohiym and~GIVEN.THAT THERE.IS to~me ALL and~*he*~*will*~PRESS.HARD⁽ⱽ⁾ in~him and~*he*~*will*~TAKE⁽ⱽ⁾ **33:12** and~*he*~*will*~SAY⁽ⱽ⁾ we~will~JOURNEY⁽ⱽ⁾ and~we~will~WALK⁽ⱽ⁾~& and~*I*~*will*~WALK⁽ⱽ⁾~& to~BE.FACE.TO.FACE⁽ⱽ⁾~you⁽ᵐˢ⁾ **33:13** and~*he*~*will*~SAY⁽ⱽ⁾ TO~him LORD~me KNOW⁽ⱽ⁾~*ing*⁽ᵐˢ⁾ GIVEN.THAT the~BOY~s TENDER~s and~the~FLOCKS and~the~CATTLE GIVE.MILK⁽ⱽ⁾~*ing*⁽ᶠᵖ⁾ UPON~me and~we~*did*~BEAT.OUT⁽ⱽ⁾~them⁽ᵐ⁾ DAY UNIT and~*they*~*did*~DIE⁽ⱽ⁾ ALL the~FLOCKS **33:14** *he*~*will*~CROSS.OVER⁽ⱽ⁾ PLEASE LORD~me to~FACE~s SERVANT~him and~*I* *I*~*will*~*self*~LEAD⁽ⱽ⁾~& to~SOFTLY~me to~FOOT the~BUSINESS WHICH to~FACE~s~me and~to~FOOT the~BOY~s UNTIL WHICH *I*~*will*~COME⁽ⱽ⁾ TO LORD~me Se'iyr~unto **33:15** and~*he*~*will*~SAY⁽ⱽ⁾ Esaw *I*~*will*~*make*~LEAVE.IN.PLACE⁽ⱽ⁾~& PLEASE WITH~you⁽ᵐˢ⁾ FROM the~PEOPLE WHICH AT~me and~*he*~*will*~SAY⁽ⱽ⁾ to~WHAT THIS *I*~*will*~FIND⁽ⱽ⁾ BEAUTY in~EYE~s2 LORD~me **33:16** and~*he*~*will*~TURN.BACK⁽ⱽ⁾ in~the~DAY the~HE Esaw to~ROAD~him Se'iyr~unto **33:17** and~Ya'aqov *he*~*did*~JOURNEY⁽ⱽ⁾ Suk'kot~unto and~*he*~*will*~BUILD⁽ⱽ⁾ to~him HOUSE and~to~LIVESTOCK~him *he*~*did*~DO⁽ⱽ⁾ BOOTH~s UPON SO *he*~*did*~CALL.OUT⁽ⱽ⁾ TITLE the~AREA Suk'kot **33:18** and~*he*~*will*~COME⁽ⱽ⁾ Ya'aqov Shalem CITY Shekhem WHICH in~LAND Kena'an in~>~COME⁽ⱽ⁾~him from~Padan-Aram and~*he*~*will*~CAMP⁽ⱽ⁾ AT FACE~s the~CITY **33:19** and~*he*~*will*~PURCHASE⁽ⱽ⁾ AT PARCEL the~FIELD WHICH *he*~*did*~EXTEND⁽ⱽ⁾ THERE TENT~him from~HAND SON~s DONKEY FATHER~of Shekhem in~HUNDRED QESHIYTAH **33:20** and~*he*~*will*~*make*~STAND.UP⁽ⱽ⁾ THERE ALTAR and~*he*~*will*~CALL.OUT⁽ⱽ⁾ to~him El-Elohey-Yisra'eyl

Chapter 34

34:1 and~*she~will*~GO.OUT[(V)] Dinah DAUGHTER Le'ah WHICH *she~did*~BRING.FORTH[(V)] to~Ya'aqov to~>~SEE[(V)] in~DAUGHTER~s the~LAND **34:2** and~*he~will*~SEE[(V)] AT~her Shekhem SON DONKEY the~Hhiw~of CAPTAIN the~LAND and~*he~will*~TAKE[(V)] AT~her and~*he~will*~LIE.DOWN[(V)] AT~her and~*he~will*~much~AFFLICT[(V)]~her **34:3** and~*she~will*~ADHERE[(V)] SOUL~him in~Dinah DAUGHTER Ya'aqov and~*he~will*~LOVE[(V)] AT the~YOUNG.WOMAN and~*he~will*~much~SPEAK[(V)] UPON HEART the~YOUNG.WOMAN **34:4** and~*he~will*~SAY[(V)] Shekhem TO DONKEY FATHER~him to~>~SAY[(V)] *!(ms)*~TAKE[(V)] to~me AT the~GIRL the~THIS to~WOMAN **34:5** and~Ya'aqov *he~did*~HEAR[(V)] GIVEN.THAT *he~did*~much~BE.DIRTY[(V)] AT Dinah DAUGHTER~him and~SON~s~him *they~did*~EXIST[(V)] AT LIVESTOCK~him in~the~FIELD and~*he~did*~make~KEEP.SILENT[(V)] Ya'aqov UNTIL >~COME[(V)]~them[(m)] **34:6** and~*he~will*~GO.OUT[(V)] DONKEY FATHER~of Shekhem TO Ya'aqov to~>~much~SPEAK[(V)] AT~him **34:7** and~SON~s Ya'aqov *they~did*~COME[(V)] FROM the~FIELD like~>~HEAR[(V)]~them[(m)] and~*they(m)~will~self*~DISTRESS[(V)] the~MAN~s and~*he~will*~FLARE.UP[(V)] to~them[(m)] MANY GIVEN.THAT FOLLY *he~did*~DO[(V)] in~Yisra'eyl to~>~LIE.DOWN[(V)] AT DAUGHTER Ya'aqov and~SO NOT *he~will~be*~DO[(V)] **34:8** and~*he~will*~much~SPEAK[(V)] Hhamor AT~them[(m)] to~>~SAY[(V)] Shekhem SON~me *she~did*~ATTACH[(V)] SOUL~him in~DAUGHTER~you[(mp)] *!(mp)*~GIVE[(V)] PLEASE AT~her to~him to~WOMAN **34:9** and~ *!(mp)~self*~BE.AN.IN-LAW[(V)] AT~us DAUGHTER~s~you[(mp)] *you(mp)~will*~GIVE[(V)] to~us and~AT DAUGHTER~s~us *you(mp)~will*~TAKE[(V)] to~you[(mp)] **34:10** and~AT~us *you(mp)~will*~TURN.BACK[(V)] and~the~LAND *she~will*~EXIST[(V)] to~FACE~s~you[(mp)] *!(mp)*~SETTLE[(V)] and~*!(mp)*~TRADE[(V)]~her and~*!(mp)~be*~TAKE.HOLD[(V)] in~her **34:11** and~*he~will*~SAY[(V)] Shekhem TO FATHER~her and~TO BROTHER~s~her *I~will*~FIND[(V)] BEAUTY in~EYE~s2~you[(mp)] and~WHICH *you(mp)~will*~SAY[(V)] TO~me *I~will*~GIVE[(V)] **34:12** *!(mp)~make*~INCREASE[(V)] UPON~me MANY BRIDE.PRICE and~GIFT and~*I~will*~GIVE[(V)]~& like~WHICH *you(mp)~will*~SAY[(V)] TO~me and~*!(mp)*~GIVE[(V)] to~me AT the~YOUNG.WOMAN to~WOMAN **34:13** and~*they(m)~will*~ANSWER[(V)] SON~s Ya'aqov AT Shekhem and~AT DONKEY FATHER~him in~DECEIT and~*they(m)~will~much*~SPEAK[(V)] WHICH *he~did~much*~BE.DIRTY[(V)] AT Dinah SISTER~them[(m)] **34:14** and~*they(m)~will*~SAY[(V)] TO~them[(m)] NOT *we~will*~BE.ABLE[(V)] to~>~DO[(V)] the~WORD the~THIS to~>~GIVE[(V)] AT SISTER~us to~MAN WHICH to~him FORESKIN GIVEN.THAT DISGRACE SHE to~us **34:15** SURELY in~THIS *we~will~be*~AGREE[(V)] to~you[(mp)] IF *you(mp)~will*~EXIST[(V)] like~THAT.ONE~us to~>~be~SNIP.OFF[(V)] to~you[(mp)] ALL MALE **34:16** and~*we~did*~GIVE[(V)] AT DAUGHTER~s~us to~you[(mp)] and~AT DAUGHTER~s~you[(mp)] *we~will*~TAKE[(V)] to~us and~*we~did*~SETTLE[(V)] AT~you[(mp)] and~*we~did*~EXIST[(V)] to~PEOPLE UNIT **34:17** and~IF NOT *you(mp)~will*~HEAR[(V)] TO~us to~>~be~SNIP.OFF[(V)] and~*we~did*~TAKE[(V)] AT DAUGHTER~us and~*we~did*~WALK[(V)] **34:18** and~

they⁽ᵐ⁾~will~DO.WELL⁽ⱽ⁾ WORD~s~them⁽ᵐ⁾ in~EYE~s2 DONKEY and~in~EYE~s2 Shekhem SON DONKEY **34:19** and~NOT he~did~much~DELAY⁽ⱽ⁾ the~YOUNG.MAN to~>~DO⁽ⱽ⁾ the~WORD GIVEN.THAT he~did~DELIGHT⁽ⱽ⁾ in~DAUGHTER Ya'aqov and~HE be~BE.HEAVY⁽ⱽ⁾~ing⁽ᵐˢ⁾ from~ALL HOUSE FATHER~him **34:20** and~he~will~COME⁽ⱽ⁾ DONKEY and~Shekhem SON~him TO GATE CITY~them⁽ᵐ⁾ and~they⁽ᵐ⁾~will~much~SPEAK⁽ⱽ⁾ TO MAN~s CITY~them⁽ᵐ⁾ to~>~SAY⁽ⱽ⁾ **34:21** the~MAN~s the~THESE COMPLETENESS~s THEY⁽ᵐ⁾ AT~us and~they⁽ᵐ⁾~will~SETTLE⁽ⱽ⁾ in~the~LAND and~they⁽ᵐ⁾~will~TRADE⁽ⱽ⁾ AT~her and~the~LAND LOOK WIDE HAND~s2 to~FACE~s~them⁽ᵐ⁾ AT DAUGHTER~s~them⁽ᵐ⁾ we~will~TAKE⁽ⱽ⁾ to~us to~WOMAN~s and~AT DAUGHTER~s~us we~will~GIVE⁽ⱽ⁾ to~them⁽ᵐ⁾ **34:22** SURELY in~THIS they⁽ᵐ⁾~will~AGREE⁽ⱽ⁾ to~us the~MAN~s to~>~SETTLE⁽ⱽ⁾ AT~us to~>~EXIST⁽ⱽ⁾ to~PEOPLE UNIT in~>~be~SNIP.OFF⁽ⱽ⁾ to~us ALL MALE like~WHICH THEY⁽ᵐ⁾ be~SNIP.OFF⁽ⱽ⁾~ing⁽ᵐᵖ⁾ **34:23** LIVESTOCK~them⁽ᵐ⁾ and~MATERIAL~them⁽ᵐ⁾ and~ALL BEAST~them⁽ᵐ⁾ ?~NOT to~us THEY⁽ᵐ⁾ SURELY we~will~be~AGREE⁽ⱽ⁾~& to~them⁽ᵐ⁾ and~they⁽ᵐ⁾~will~SETTLE⁽ⱽ⁾ AT~us **34:24** and~they⁽ᵐ⁾~will~HEAR⁽ⱽ⁾ TO Hhamor and~TO Shekhem SON~him ALL GO.OUT⁽ⱽ⁾~ing⁽ᵐᵖ⁾ GATE CITY~him and~they⁽ᵐ⁾~will~be~SNIP.OFF⁽ⱽ⁾ ALL MALE ALL GO.OUT⁽ⱽ⁾~ing⁽ᵐᵖ⁾ GATE CITY~him **34:25** and~he~will~EXIST⁽ⱽ⁾ in~the~DAY the~THIRD in~>~EXIST⁽ⱽ⁾~them⁽ᵐ⁾ BE.IN.MISERY⁽ⱽ⁾~ing⁽ᵐᵖ⁾ and~they⁽ᵐ⁾~will~TAKE⁽ⱽ⁾ TWO SON~s Ya'aqov Shimon and~Lewi BROTHER~s Dinah MAN SWORD~him and~they⁽ᵐ⁾~will~COME⁽ⱽ⁾ UPON the~CITY SAFELY and~they⁽ᵐ⁾~will~KILL⁽ⱽ⁾ ALL MALE **34:26** and~AT DONKEY and~AT Shekhem SON~him they~did~KILL⁽ⱽ⁾ to~MOUTH SWORD and~they⁽ᵐ⁾~will~TAKE⁽ⱽ⁾ AT Dinah from~HOUSE Shekhem and~they⁽ᵐ⁾~will~GO.OUT⁽ⱽ⁾ **34:27** SON~s Ya'aqov they~did~COME⁽ⱽ⁾ UPON the~DRILLED~s and~they⁽ᵐ⁾~will~PLUNDER⁽ⱽ⁾ the~CITY WHICH they~did~much~BE.DIRTY⁽ⱽ⁾ SISTER~them⁽ᵐ⁾ **34:28** AT FLOCKS~them⁽ᵐ⁾ and~AT CATTLE~them⁽ᵐ⁾ and~AT DONKEY~s~them⁽ᵐ⁾ and~AT WHICH in~the~CITY and~AT WHICH in~the~FIELD they~did~TAKE⁽ⱽ⁾ **34:29** and~AT ALL FORCE~them⁽ᵐ⁾ and~AT ALL BABIES~them⁽ᵐ⁾ and~AT WOMAN~s~them⁽ᵐ⁾ they~did~CAPTURE⁽ⱽ⁾ and~they⁽ᵐ⁾~will~PLUNDER⁽ⱽ⁾ and~AT ALL WHICH in~the~HOUSE **34:30** and~he~will~SAY⁽ⱽ⁾ Ya'aqov TO Shimon and~TO Lewi you⁽ᵐᵖ⁾~did~DISTURB⁽ⱽ⁾ AT~me to~>~make~STINK⁽ⱽ⁾~me in~SETTLE⁽ⱽ⁾~ing⁽ᵐˢ⁾ the~LAND in~Kena'an~of and~in~Perez~of and~I MORTAL.MAN~s NUMBER and~they~did~be~GATHER⁽ⱽ⁾ UPON~me and~they~did~make~HIT⁽ⱽ⁾~me and~I~did~be~DESTROY⁽ⱽ⁾ I and~HOUSE~me **34:31** and~they⁽ᵐ⁾~will~SAY⁽ⱽ⁾ ?~like~BE.A.HARLOT⁽ⱽ⁾~ing⁽ᶠˢ⁾ he~will~DO⁽ⱽ⁾ AT SISTER~us

Chapter 35

35:1 and~he~will~SAY⁽ⱽ⁾ Elohiym TO Ya'aqov !⁽ᵐˢ⁾~RISE⁽ⱽ⁾ !⁽ᵐˢ⁾~GO.UP⁽ⱽ⁾ Beyt-El and~!⁽ᵐˢ⁾~SETTLE⁽ⱽ⁾ THERE and~!⁽ᵐˢ⁾~DO⁽ⱽ⁾ THERE ALTAR to~MIGHTY.ONE the~*be*~SEE⁽ᵛ⁾~*ing*⁽ᵐˢ⁾ TO~you⁽ᵐˢ⁾ in~>~FLEE.AWAY⁽ᵛ⁾~you⁽ᵐˢ⁾ from~FACE~s Esaw BROTHER~you⁽ᵐˢ⁾ **35:2** and~*he*~*will*~SAY⁽ᵛ⁾ Ya'aqov TO HOUSE~him and~TO ALL WHICH WITH~him *!*⁽ᵐᵖ⁾~*make*~TURN.ASIDE⁽ᵛ⁾ AT Elohiym the~FOREIGNER WHICH in~MIDST~you⁽ᵐᵖ⁾ and~*!*⁽ᵐᵖ⁾~*make*~BE.CLEAN⁽ᵛ⁾ and~*!*⁽ᵐᵖ⁾~*make*~PASS.OVER⁽ᵛ⁾ APPAREL~s~you⁽ᵐᵖ⁾ **35:3** and~*we*~*will*~RISE⁽ᵛ⁾~& and~*we*~*will*~GO.UP⁽ᵛ⁾~& Beyt-El and~*I*~*will*~DO⁽ᵛ⁾~& THERE ALTAR to~MIGHTY.ONE the~ANSWER⁽ᵛ⁾~*ing*⁽ᵐˢ⁾ AT~me in~DAY PERSECUTION~me and~*he*~*will*~EXIST⁽ᵛ⁾ BY~me in~the~ROAD WHICH *I*~*did*~WALK⁽ᵛ⁾ **35:4** and~*they*⁽ᵐ⁾~*will*~GIVE⁽ᵛ⁾ TO Ya'aqov AT ALL Elohiym the~FOREIGNER WHICH in~HAND~them⁽ᵐ⁾ and~AT the~ORNAMENTAL.RING~s WHICH in~EAR~s2~them⁽ᵐ⁾ and~*he*~*will*~SUBMERGE⁽ᵛ⁾ AT~them⁽ᵐ⁾ Ya'aqov UNDER the~OAK WHICH WITH Shekhem **35:5** and~*they*⁽ᵐ⁾~*will*~JOURNEY⁽ᵛ⁾ and~*he*~*will*~EXIST⁽ᵛ⁾ DREAD Elohiym UPON the~CITY~s WHICH ALL.AROUND~s~them⁽ᵐ⁾ and~NOT *they*~*did*~PURSUE⁽ᵛ⁾ AFTER SON~s Ya'aqov **35:6** and~*he*~*will*~COME⁽ᵛ⁾ Ya'aqov Luz~unto WHICH in~LAND Kena'an SHE Beyt-El HE and~ALL the~PEOPLE WHICH WITH~him **35:7** and~*he*~*will*~BUILD⁽ᵛ⁾ THERE ALTAR and~*he*~*will*~CALL.OUT⁽ᵛ⁾ to~the~AREA El-Beyt-El GIVEN.THAT THERE *they*~*did*~*be*~REMOVE.THE.COVER⁽ᵛ⁾ TO~him the~Elohiym in~>~FLEE.AWAY⁽ᵛ⁾~him from~FACE~s BROTHER~him **35:8** and~*she*~*will*~DIE⁽ᵛ⁾ Devorah *make*~SUCKLE⁽ᵛ⁾~*ing*⁽ᶠˢ⁾ Rivqah and~*she*~*will*~*be*~BURY⁽ᵛ⁾ from~UNDER to~Beyt-El UNDER the~GREAT.TREE and~*he*~*will*~CALL.OUT⁽ᵛ⁾ TITLE~him Alon-Bakhut **35:9** and~*he*~*will*~*be*~SEE⁽ᵛ⁾ Elohiym TO Ya'aqov YET.AGAIN in~>~COME⁽ᵛ⁾~him from~Padan-Aram and~*he*~*will*~*much*~KNEEL⁽ᵛ⁾ AT~him **35:10** and~*he*~*will*~SAY⁽ᵛ⁾ to~him Elohiym TITLE~you⁽ᵐˢ⁾ Ya'aqov NOT *he*~*will*~*be*~CALL.OUT⁽ᵛ⁾ TITLE~you⁽ᵐˢ⁾ YET.AGAIN Ya'aqov GIVEN.THAT IF Yisra'eyl *he*~*will*~EXIST⁽ᵛ⁾ TITLE~you⁽ᵐˢ⁾ and~*he*~*will*~CALL.OUT⁽ᵛ⁾ AT TITLE~him Yisra'eyl **35:11** and~*he*~*will*~SAY⁽ᵛ⁾ to~him Elohiym I MIGHTY.ONE Shaddai *!*⁽ᵐˢ⁾~REPRODUCE⁽ᵛ⁾ and~*!*⁽ᵐˢ⁾~INCREASE⁽ᵛ⁾ NATION and~ASSEMBLY NATION~s *he*~*will*~EXIST⁽ᵛ⁾ FROM~you⁽ᵐˢ⁾ and~KING~s from~LOINS~you⁽ᵐˢ⁾ *they*⁽ᵐ⁾~*will*~GO.OUT⁽ᵛ⁾ **35:12** and~AT the~LAND WHICH *I*~*did*~GIVE⁽ᵛ⁾ to~Avraham and~to~Yits'hhaq to~you⁽ᵐˢ⁾ *I*~*will*~GIVE⁽ᵛ⁾~her and~to~SEED~you⁽ᵐˢ⁾ AFTER~you⁽ᵐˢ⁾ *I*~*will*~GIVE⁽ᵛ⁾ AT the~LAND **35:13** and~*he*~*will*~*make*~GO.UP⁽ᵛ⁾ from~UPON~him Elohiym in~the~AREA WHICH *he*~*did*~*much*~SPEAK⁽ᵛ⁾ AT~him **35:14** and~*he*~*will*~*make*~STAND.UP⁽ᵛ⁾ Ya'aqov MONUMENT in~the~AREA WHICH *he*~*did*~*much*~SPEAK⁽ᵛ⁾ AT~him MONUMENT STONE and~*he*~*will*~*make*~POUR⁽ᵛ⁾ UPON~her POURING and~*he*~*will*~POUR.DOWN⁽ᵛ⁾ UPON~her OIL **35:15** and~*he*~*will*~CALL.OUT⁽ᵛ⁾ Ya'aqov AT TITLE the~AREA WHICH *he*~*did*~*much*~SPEAK⁽ᵛ⁾ AT~him THERE Elohiym Beyt-El **35:16** and~*they*⁽ᵐ⁾~*will*~JOURNEY⁽ᵛ⁾ from~Beyt-El and~*he*~*will*~EXIST⁽ᵛ⁾ YET.AGAIN SHORT the~LAND to~>~COME⁽ᵛ⁾ Ephrat~unto and~*she*~*will*~BRING.FORTH⁽ᵛ⁾ Rahhel and~*she*~*will*~*much*~BE.HARD⁽ᵛ⁾ in~>~BRING.FORTH⁽ᵛ⁾~her **35:17** and~*he*~*will*~EXIST⁽ᵛ⁾ in~>~*make*~BE.HARD⁽ᵛ⁾~her in~>~BRING.FORTH⁽ᵛ⁾~her and~*she*~*will*~SAY⁽ᵛ⁾ to~her the~*much*~BRING.FORTH⁽ᵛ⁾~*ing*⁽ᶠˢ⁾ DO.NOT you⁽ᶠˢ⁾~*will*~FEAR⁽ᵛ⁾ GIVEN.THAT ALSO THIS to~you⁽ᶠˢ⁾ SON **35:18** and~*he*~*will*~EXIST⁽ᵛ⁾ in~>~GO.OUT⁽ᵛ⁾ SOUL~her

GIVEN.THAT *she~did*~DIE⁽ᵛ⁾ and~*she~will*~CALL.OUT⁽ᵛ⁾ TITLE~him Ben-Oni and~FATHER~him *he~did*~CALL.OUT⁽ᵛ⁾ to~him Binyamin **35:19** and~*she~ will*~DIE⁽ᵛ⁾ Rahhel and~*she~will~be*~BURY⁽ᵛ⁾ in~ROAD Ephrat~unto SHE Beyt-Lehhem **35:20** and~*he~will~make*~STAND.UP⁽ᵛ⁾ Ya'aqov MONUMENT UPON BURIAL.PLACE~her SHE MONUMENT BURIAL.PLACE Rahhel UNTIL the~ DAY **35:21** and~*he~will*~JOURNEY⁽ᵛ⁾ Yisra'eyl and~*he~will*~EXTEND⁽ᵛ⁾ TENT~ her from~FURTHER to~Migdal-Eyder **35:22** and~*he~will*~EXIST⁽ᵛ⁾ in~>~ DWELL⁽ᵛ⁾ Yisra'eyl in~the~LAND the~SHE and~*he~will*~WALK⁽ᵛ⁾ Re'uven and~ *he~will*~LIE.DOWN⁽ᵛ⁾ AT Bilhah CONCUBINE FATHER~him and~*he~will*~ HEAR⁽ᵛ⁾ Yisra'eyl and~*they⁽ᵐ⁾~will*~EXIST⁽ᵛ⁾ SON~s Ya'aqov TWO TEN **35:23** SON~s Le'ah FIRSTBORN Ya'aqov Re'uven and~Shimon and~Lewi and~Yehudah and~Yis'sas'khar and~Zevulun **35:24** SON~s Rahhel Yoseph and~Binyamin **35:25** and~SON~s Bilhah MAID Rahhel Dan and~ Naphtali **35:26** and~SON~s Zilpah MAID Le'ah Gad and~Asher THESE SON~s Ya'aqov WHICH BRING.FORTH⁽ᵛ⁾~*ed*⁽ᵐˢ⁾ to~him in~Padan-Aram **35:27** and~ *he~will*~COME⁽ᵛ⁾ Ya'aqov TO Yits'hhaq FATHER~him Mamre Qiryat-Arba SHE Hhevron WHICH *he~did*~IMMIGRATE⁽ᵛ⁾ THERE Avraham and~ Yits'hhaq **35:28** and~*they⁽ᵐ⁾~will*~EXIST⁽ᵛ⁾ DAY~s Yits'hhaq HUNDRED YEAR and~EIGHT~s YEAR **35:29** and~*he~will*~EXPIRE⁽ᵛ⁾ Yits'hhaq and~*he~will*~ DIE⁽ᵛ⁾ and~*he~will~be*~GATHER⁽ᵛ⁾ TO PEOPLE~s~him BEARD and~PLENTY DAY~s and~*they⁽ᵐ⁾~will*~BURY⁽ᵛ⁾ AT~him Esaw and~Ya'aqov SON~s~him

Chapter 36

36:1 and~THESE BIRTHING~s Esaw HE Edom **36:2** Esaw *he~did*~TAKE⁽ᵛ⁾ AT WOMAN~s~him from~DAUGHTER~s Kena'an AT Adah DAUGHTER Eylon the~Hhet~of and~AT Ahalivamah DAUGHTER Anah DAUGHTER Tsiv'on the~ Hhiw~of **36:3** and~AT Basmat DAUGHTER Yishma'el SISTER Nevayot **36:4** and~*she~will*~BRING.FORTH⁽ᵛ⁾ Adah to~Esaw AT Eliphaz and~ Basmat *she~did*~BRING.FORTH⁽ᵛ⁾ AT Re'u'eyl **36:5** and~Ahalivamah *she~ did*~BRING.FORTH⁽ᵛ⁾ AT Ye'ish and~AT Yalam and~AT Qorahh THESE SON~s Esaw WHICH BRING.FORTH⁽ᵛ⁾~*ed*⁽ᵐᵖ⁾ to~him in~LAND Kena'an **36:6** and~*he~ will*~TAKE⁽ᵛ⁾ Esaw AT WOMAN~s~him and~AT SON~s~him and~AT DAUGHTER~s~him and~AT ALL SOUL~s HOUSE~him and~AT LIVESTOCK~him and~AT ALL BEAST~him and~AT ALL MATERIAL~him WHICH *he~did*~ ACCUMULATE⁽ᵛ⁾ in~LAND Kena'an and~*he~will*~WALK⁽ᵛ⁾ TO LAND from~ FACE~s Ya'aqov BROTHER~him **36:7** GIVEN.THAT *he~did*~EXIST⁽ᵛ⁾ GOODS~ them⁽ᵐ⁾ ABUNDANT from~>~SETTLE⁽ᵛ⁾ TOGETHER and~NOT *she~did*~ BE.ABLE⁽ᵛ⁾ LAND IMMIGRATION~s~them⁽ᵐ⁾ to~>~LIFT.UP⁽ᵛ⁾ AT~them⁽ᵐ⁾ from~FACE~s LIVESTOCK~s~them⁽ᵐ⁾ **36:8** and~*he~will*~SETTLE⁽ᵛ⁾ Esaw in~ HILL Se'iyr Esaw HE Edom **36:9** and~THESE BIRTHING~s Esaw FATHER~of Edom in~HILL Se'iyr **36:10** THESE TITLE~s SON~s Esaw Eliphaz SON Adah WOMAN Esaw Re'u'eyl SON Basmat WOMAN Esaw **36:11** and~*they⁽ᵐ⁾~will*~

EXIST⁽ᵛ⁾ SON~s Eliphaz Teyman Omar Tsepho and~Gatam and~ Qenaz **36:12** and~Timna *she~did*~EXIST⁽ᵛ⁾ CONCUBINE to~Eliphaz SON Esaw and~*she~will*~BRING.FORTH⁽ᵛ⁾ to~Eliphaz AT Amaleq THESE SON~s Adah WOMAN Esaw **36:13** and~THESE SON~s Re'u'eyl Nahhat and~Zerahh Sham'mah and~Miz'zah THESE *they~did*~EXIST⁽ᵛ⁾ SON~s Basmat WOMAN Esaw **36:14** and~THESE *they~did*~EXIST⁽ᵛ⁾ SON~s Ahalivamah DAUGHTER Anah DAUGHTER Tsiv'on WOMAN Esaw and~*she~will*~BRING.FORTH⁽ᵛ⁾ to~ Esaw AT Ye'ish and~AT Yalam and~AT Qorahh **36:15** THESE CHIEF~s SON~s Esaw SON~s Eliphaz FIRSTBORN Esaw CHIEF Teyman CHIEF Omar CHIEF Tsepho CHIEF Qenaz **36:16** CHIEF Qorahh CHIEF Gatam CHIEF Amaleq THESE CHIEF~s Eliphaz in~LAND Edom THESE SON~s Adah **36:17** and~THESE SON~s Re'u'eyl SON Esaw CHIEF Nahhat CHIEF Zerahh CHIEF Sham'mah CHIEF Miz'zah THESE CHIEF~s Re'u'eyl in~LAND Edom THESE SON~s Basmat WOMAN Esaw **36:18** and~THESE SON~s Ahalivamah WOMAN Esaw CHIEF Ye'ish CHIEF Yalam CHIEF Qorahh THESE CHIEF~s Ahalivamah DAUGHTER Anah WOMAN Esaw **36:19** THESE SON~s Esaw and~THESE CHIEF~s~them⁽ᵐ⁾ HE Edom **36:20** THESE SON~s Se'iyr the~Hhor~of SETTLE⁽ᵛ⁾~*ing*⁽ᵐᵖ⁾ the~ LAND Lotan and~Shoval and~Tsiv'on and~Anah **36:21** and~Dishon and~ Eytser and~ANTELOPE THESE CHIEF~s the~Hhor~of SON~s Se'iyr in~LAND Edom **36:22** and~*they*⁽ᵐ⁾~*will*~EXIST⁽ᵛ⁾ SON~s Lotan Hhoriy and~Heymam and~SISTER Lotan Timna **36:23** and~THESE SON~s Shoval Alwan and~ Manahhat and~Eyval Shepho and~Onam **36:24** and~THESE SON~s Tsiv'on and~Ayah and~Anah HE Anah WHICH *he~did*~FIND⁽ᵛ⁾ AT the~YEMIM in~ the~WILDERNESS in~>~FEED⁽ᵛ⁾~him AT the~DONKEY~s to~Tsiv'on FATHER~ him **36:25** and~THESE SON~s Anah Dishon and~Ahalivamah DAUGHTER Anah **36:26** and~THESE SON~s Dishan Hhemdan and~Eshban and~Yitran and~Keran **36:27** THESE SON~s Eytser Bilhan and~Za'awan and~ Aqan **36:28** THESE SON~s Dishan Uts and~Aran **36:29** THESE CHIEF~s the~ Hhor~of CHIEF Lotan CHIEF Shoval CHIEF Tsiv'on CHIEF Anah **36:30** CHIEF Dishon CHIEF Eytser CHIEF Dishan THESE CHIEF~s the~Hhor~of to~CHIEF~s~ them⁽ᵐ⁾ in~LAND Se'iyr **36:31** and~THESE the~KING~s WHICH *they~did*~ REIGN⁽ᵛ⁾ in~LAND Edom to~FACE~s >~REIGN⁽ᵛ⁾ KING to~SON~s Yisra'eyl **36:32** and~*he~will*~REIGN⁽ᵛ⁾ in~Edom Bela SON Be'or and~TITLE CITY~him Dinhavah **36:33** and~*he~will*~DIE⁽ᵛ⁾ Bela and~*he~will*~REIGN⁽ᵛ⁾ UNDER~him Yovav SON Zerahh from~Botsrah **36:34** and~*he~will*~DIE⁽ᵛ⁾ Yovav and~*he~will*~REIGN⁽ᵛ⁾ UNDER~him Hhusham from~LAND the~ Teyman~of **36:35** and~*he~will*~DIE⁽ᵛ⁾ Hhusham and~*he~will*~REIGN⁽ᵛ⁾ UNDER~him Hadad SON Bedad *make*~HIT⁽ᵛ⁾~*ing*⁽ᵐˢ⁾ AT Mid'yan in~FIELD Mo'av and~TITLE CITY~him Awit **36:36** and~*he~will*~DIE⁽ᵛ⁾ Hadad and~*he~ will*~REIGN⁽ᵛ⁾ UNDER~him Samlah from~Masreyqah **36:37** and~*he~will*~ DIE⁽ᵛ⁾ Samlah and~*he~will*~REIGN⁽ᵛ⁾ UNDER~him Sha'ul from~Rehhovot the~ RIVER **36:38** and~*he~will*~DIE⁽ᵛ⁾ Sha'ul and~*he~will*~REIGN⁽ᵛ⁾ UNDER~him Ba'al-Hhanan SON Akhbor **36:39** and~*he~will*~DIE⁽ᵛ⁾ Ba'al-Hhanan SON Akhbor and~*he~will*~REIGN⁽ᵛ⁾ UNDER~him Hadar and~TITLE CITY~him Pa'u and~TITLE WOMAN~him Meheytaveyl DAUGHTER Matreyd DAUGHTER

The Book of Genesis

Mey-Zahav **36:40** and~THESE TITLE~s CHIEF~s Esaw to~CLAN~s~them$^{(m)}$ to~AREA~s~them$^{(m)}$ in~TITLE~s~them$^{(m)}$ CHIEF Timna CHIEF Alwah CHIEF Yetet **36:41** CHIEF Ahalivamah CHIEF Eylah CHIEF Pinon **36:42** CHIEF Qenaz CHIEF Teyman CHIEF Mivtsar **36:43** CHIEF Magdi'eyl CHIEF Iyram THESE CHIEF~s Edom to~SETTLING~s~them$^{(m)}$ in~LAND HOLDINGS~them$^{(m)}$ HE Esaw FATHER~of Edom

Chapter 37

37:1 and~he~will~SETTLE$^{(V)}$ Ya'aqov in~LAND IMMIGRATION~s FATHER~him in~LAND Kena'an **37:2** THESE BIRTHING~s Ya'aqov Yoseph SON SEVEN TEN YEAR he~did~EXIST$^{(V)}$ FEED$^{(V)}$~ing$^{(ms)}$ AT BROTHER~s~him in~the~FLOCKS and~HE YOUNG.MAN AT SON~s Bilhah and~AT SON~s Zilpah WOMAN~s FATHER~him and~he~will~make~COME$^{(V)}$ Yoseph AT SLANDER~them$^{(m)}$ DYSFUNCTIONAL TO FATHER~them$^{(m)}$ **37:3** and~Yisra'eyl he~did~LOVE$^{(V)}$ AT Yoseph from~ALL SON~s~him GIVEN.THAT SON EXTREME.OLD.AGE~s HE to~him and~he~did~DO$^{(V)}$ to~him TUNIC WRIST~s **37:4** and~they$^{(m)}$~will~SEE$^{(V)}$ BROTHER~s~him GIVEN.THAT AT~him he~did~LOVE$^{(V)}$ FATHER~them$^{(m)}$ from~ALL BROTHER~s~him and~they$^{(m)}$~will~HATE$^{(V)}$ AT~him and~NOT they~did~BE.ABLE$^{(V)}$ >~much~SPEAK$^{(V)}$~him to~COMPLETENESS **37:5** and~he~will~DREAM$^{(V)}$ he~will~make~ADD$^{(V)}$ DREAM and~he~will~make~BE.FACE.TO.FACE$^{(V)}$ to~BROTHER~s~him and~they$^{(m)}$~will~make~ADD$^{(V)}$ YET.AGAIN >~HATE$^{(V)}$ AT~him **37:6** and~he~will~SAY$^{(V)}$ TO~them$^{(m)}$ I$^{(mp)}$~HEAR$^{(V)}$ PLEASE the~DREAM the~THIS WHICH I~did~DREAM$^{(V)}$ **37:7** and~LOOK WE much~BIND.UP$^{(V)}$~ing$^{(mp)}$ BOUND.SHEAF~s in~MIDST the~FIELD and~LOOK she~did~RISE$^{(V)}$ BOUND.SHEAF~me and~ALSO she~did~be~STAND.UP$^{(V)}$ and~LOOK they$^{(f)}$~did~GO.AROUND$^{(V)}$ BOUND.SHEAF~s~you$^{(mp)}$ and~they$^{(f)}$~will~self~BEND.DOWN$^{(V)}$ to~BOUND.SHEAF~me **37:8** and~they$^{(m)}$~will~SAY$^{(V)}$ to~him BROTHER~s~him ?>~REIGN$^{(V)}$ you$^{(ms)}$~will~REIGN$^{(V)}$ UPON~us IF >~REGULATE$^{(V)}$ you$^{(ms)}$~will~REGULATE$^{(V)}$ in~us and~they$^{(m)}$~will~make~ADD$^{(V)}$ YET.AGAIN >~HATE$^{(V)}$ AT~him UPON DREAM~s~him and~UPON WORD~s~him **37:9** and~he~will~DREAM$^{(V)}$ YET.AGAIN DREAM OTHER and~he~will~much~COUNT$^{(V)}$ AT~him to~BROTHER~s~him and~he~will~SAY$^{(V)}$ LOOK I~did~DREAM$^{(V)}$ DREAM YET.AGAIN and~LOOK the~SUN and~the~MOON and~UNIT TEN STAR~s self~BEND.DOWN$^{(V)}$~ing$^{(mp)}$ to~me **37:10** and~he~will~much~COUNT$^{(V)}$ TO FATHER~him and~TO BROTHER~s~him and~he~will~REPROVE$^{(V)}$ in~him FATHER~him and~he~will~SAY$^{(V)}$ to~him WHAT the~DREAM the~THIS WHICH you$^{(ms)}$~did~DREAM$^{(V)}$?>~COME$^{(V)}$ we~will~COME$^{(V)}$ I and~MOTHER~you$^{(ms)}$ and~BROTHER~s~you$^{(ms)}$ to~>~self~BEND.DOWN$^{(V)}$ to~you$^{(ms)}$ LAND~unto **37:11** and~they$^{(m)}$~will~much~BE.ZEALOUS$^{(V)}$ in~him BROTHER~s~him and~FATHER~him he~did~SAFEGUARD$^{(V)}$ AT the~WORD **37:12** and~they$^{(m)}$~will~WALK$^{(V)}$ BROTHER~s~him to~>~FEED$^{(V)}$ AT FLOCKS FATHER~them$^{(m)}$ in~

Benner's Mechanical Translation of the Torah

Shekhem **37:13** and~*he*~*will*~SAY⁽ⱽ⁾ Yisra'eyl TO Yoseph ?~NOT BROTHER~s~ you⁽ᵐˢ⁾ FEED⁽ⱽ⁾~*ing*⁽ᵐᵖ⁾ in~Shekhem !⁽ᵐˢ⁾~WALK⁽ⱽ⁾~& and~*I*~*will*~SEND⁽ⱽ⁾~ you⁽ᵐˢ⁾ TO~them⁽ᵐ⁾ and~*he*~*will*~SAY⁽ⱽ⁾ to~him LOOK~me **37:14** and~*he*~ *will*~SAY⁽ⱽ⁾ to~him !⁽ᵐˢ⁾~WALK⁽ⱽ⁾ PLEASE !⁽ᵐˢ⁾~SEE⁽ⱽ⁾ AT COMPLETENESS BROTHER~s~you⁽ᵐˢ⁾ and~AT COMPLETENESS the~FLOCKS and~ !⁽ᵐˢ⁾~*make*~ TURN.BACK⁽ⱽ⁾~me WORD and~*he*~*will*~SEND⁽ⱽ⁾~him from~VALLEY Hhevron and~*he*~*will*~COME⁽ⱽ⁾ Shekhem~unto **37:15** and~*he*~*will*~FIND⁽ⱽ⁾~him MAN and~LOOK WANDER⁽ⱽ⁾~*ing*⁽ᵐˢ⁾ in~the~FIELD and~*he*~*will*~INQUIRE⁽ⱽ⁾~him the~MAN to~>~SAY⁽ⱽ⁾ WHAT *you*⁽ᵐˢ⁾~*will*~much~SEARCH.OUT⁽ⱽ⁾ **37:16** and~ *he*~*will*~SAY⁽ⱽ⁾ AT BROTHER~s~me I *much*~SEARCH.OUT⁽ⱽ⁾~*ing*⁽ᵐˢ⁾ !⁽ᵐˢ⁾~ *make*~BE.FACE.TO.FACE⁽ⱽ⁾~& PLEASE to~me WHERE THEY⁽ᵐ⁾ FEED⁽ⱽ⁾~ *ing*⁽ᵐᵖ⁾ **37:17** and~*he*~*will*~SAY⁽ⱽ⁾ the~MAN *they*⁽ᵐ⁾~*did*~JOURNEY⁽ⱽ⁾ from~THIS GIVEN.THAT *I*~*did*~HEAR⁽ⱽ⁾ SAY⁽ⱽ⁾~*ing*⁽ᵐᵖ⁾ we~*will*~WALK⁽ⱽ⁾~& Dotan~unto and~*he*~*will*~WALK⁽ⱽ⁾ Yoseph AFTER BROTHER~s~him and~*he*~*will*~FIND⁽ⱽ⁾~ them⁽ᵐ⁾ in~Dotan **37:18** and~*they*⁽ᵐ⁾~*will*~SEE⁽ⱽ⁾ AT~him from~DISTANCE and~in~BEFORE *he*~*will*~COME.NEAR⁽ⱽ⁾ TO~them⁽ᵐ⁾ and~*they*⁽ᵐ⁾~*will*~*self*~ BE.CRAFTY⁽ⱽ⁾ AT~him to~>~*make*~DIE⁽ⱽ⁾~him **37:19** and~*they*⁽ᵐ⁾~*will*~SAY⁽ⱽ⁾ MAN TO BROTHER~him LOOK MASTER the~DREAM~s THIS.ONE *he*~*did*~ COME⁽ⱽ⁾ **37:20** and~NOW !⁽ᵐᵖ⁾~WALK⁽ⱽ⁾ and~we~*will*~KILL⁽ⱽ⁾~him and~*we*~ *will*~*make*~THROW.OUT⁽ⱽ⁾~him in~UNIT the~CISTERN~s and~*we*~*did*~SAY⁽ⱽ⁾ LIVING DYSFUNCTIONAL *she*~*did*~EAT⁽ⱽ⁾~him and~*we*~*will*~SEE⁽ⱽ⁾~& WHAT *they*⁽ᵐ⁾~*will*~EXIST⁽ⱽ⁾ DREAM~s~him **37:21** and~*he*~*will*~HEAR⁽ⱽ⁾ Re'uven and~*he*~*will*~*make*~DELIVER⁽ⱽ⁾~him from~HAND~them⁽ᵐ⁾ and~*he*~*will*~ SAY⁽ⱽ⁾ NOT we~*will*~*make*~HIT⁽ⱽ⁾~him SOUL **37:22** and~*he*~*will*~SAY⁽ⱽ⁾ TO~ them⁽ᵐ⁾ Re'uven DO.NOT *you*⁽ᵐᵖ⁾~*will*~POUR.OUT⁽ⱽ⁾ BLOOD !⁽ᵐᵖ⁾~*make*~ THROW.OUT⁽ⱽ⁾ AT~him TO the~CISTERN the~THIS WHICH in~the~ WILDERNESS and~HAND DO.NOT *you*⁽ᵐᵖ⁾~*will*~SEND⁽ⱽ⁾ in~him to~THAT >~ *make*~DELIVER⁽ⱽ⁾ AT~him from~HAND~them⁽ᵐ⁾ to~>~*make*~TURN.BACK⁽ⱽ⁾~ him TO FATHER~him **37:23** and~*he*~*will*~EXIST⁽ⱽ⁾ like~WHICH *he*~*did*~ COME⁽ⱽ⁾ Yoseph TO BROTHER~s~him and~*they*⁽ᵐ⁾~*will*~*make*~STRIP.OFF⁽ⱽ⁾ AT Yoseph AT TUNIC~him AT TUNIC the~WRIST~s WHICH UPON~ him **37:24** and~*they*⁽ᵐ⁾~*will*~TAKE⁽ⱽ⁾~him and~*they*⁽ᵐ⁾~*will*~*make*~ THROW.OUT⁽ⱽ⁾ AT~him the~CISTERN~unto and~the~CISTERN EMPTY WITHOUT in~him WATER~s2 **37:25** and~*they*⁽ᵐ⁾~*will*~SETTLE⁽ⱽ⁾ to~>~EAT⁽ⱽ⁾ BREAD and~*they*⁽ᵐ⁾~*will*~LIFT.UP⁽ⱽ⁾ EYE~s2~them⁽ᵐ⁾ and~*they*⁽ᵐ⁾~*will*~SEE⁽ⱽ⁾ and~LOOK CARAVAN Yishma'el~s *she*~*did*~COME⁽ⱽ⁾ from~Gil'ad and~ CAMEL~s~them⁽ᵐ⁾ LIFT.UP⁽ⱽ⁾~*ing*⁽ᵐᵖ⁾ SPICE and~BALM and~LAUDANUM WALK⁽ⱽ⁾~*ing*⁽ᵐᵖ⁾ to~>~*make*~GO.DOWN⁽ⱽ⁾ Mits'rayim~unto **37:26** and~*he*~ *will*~SAY⁽ⱽ⁾ Yehudah TO BROTHER~s~him WHAT PROFIT GIVEN.THAT we~ *will*~KILL⁽ⱽ⁾ AT BROTHER~us and~*we*~*did*~COVER.OVER⁽ⱽ⁾ AT BLOOD~ him **37:27** !⁽ᵐᵖ⁾~WALK⁽ⱽ⁾ and~we~*will*~SELL⁽ⱽ⁾~him to~Yishma'el~s and~ HAND~us DO.NOT *she*~*will*~EXIST⁽ⱽ⁾ in~him GIVEN.THAT BROTHER~us FLESH~us HE and~*they*⁽ᵐ⁾~*will*~HEAR⁽ⱽ⁾ BROTHER~s~him **37:28** and~*they*⁽ᵐ⁾~ *will*~CROSS.OVER⁽ⱽ⁾ MAN~s Mid'yan~s TRADE⁽ⱽ⁾~*ing*⁽ᵐᵖ⁾ and~*they*⁽ᵐ⁾~*will*~ DRAW⁽ⱽ⁾ and~*they*⁽ᵐ⁾~*will*~*make*~GO.UP⁽ⱽ⁾ AT Yoseph FROM the~CISTERN and~*they*^(m)~*will*~SELL^(V) AT Yoseph to~Yishma'el~s in~TEN~s SILVER and~ *they*^(m)~*will*~*make*~COME^(V) AT Yoseph Mits'rayim~unto **37:29** and~*he*~*will*~ TURN.BACK^(V) Re'uven TO the~CISTERN and~LOOK WITHOUT Yoseph in~ the~CISTERN and~*he*~*will*~TEAR^(V) AT GARMENT~s~him **37:30** and~*he*~*will*~ TURN.BACK^(V) TO BROTHER~s~him and~*he*~*will*~SAY^(V) the~BOY WITHOUT~ him and~I WHEREVER I *he*~*did*~COME^(V) **37:31** and~*they*^(m)~*will*~TAKE^(V) AT TUNIC Yoseph and~*they*^(m)~*will*~SLAY^(V) HAIRY.GOAT SHE-GOAT~s and~ *they*^(m)~*will*~DIP^(V) AT the~TUNIC in~the~BLOOD **37:32** and~*they*^(m)~*will*~ *much*~SEND^(V) AT TUNIC the~WRIST~s and~*they*^(m)~*will*~*make*~COME^(V) TO FATHER~them^(m) and~*they*^(m)~*will*~SAY^(V) THIS *we*~*did*~FIND^(V) !^(ms)~*make*~ RECOGNIZE^(V) PLEASE the~TUNIC SON~you^(ms) SHE IF NOT **37:33** and~*he*~ *will*~*make*~RECOGNIZE^(V)~her and~*he*~*will*~SAY^(V) TUNIC SON~me LIVING DYSFUNCTIONAL *she*~*did*~EAT^(V)~him >~TEAR.INTO.PIECES^(V) TEAR.INTO.PIECES^(V)~*ed*^(ms) Yoseph **37:34** and~*he*~*will*~TEAR^(V) Ya'aqov APPAREL~s~him and~*he*~*will*~PLACE^(V) SACK in~WAIST~him and~*he*~*will*~ *self*~MOURN^(V) UPON SON~him DAY~s ABUNDANT~s **37:35** and~*they*^(m)~ *will*~RISE^(V) ALL SON~s~him and~ALL DAUGHTER~s~him to~>~*much*~ COMFORT^(V)~him and~*he*~*will*~*much*~REFUSE^(V) to~>~*self*~COMFORT^(V) and~ *he*~*will*~SAY^(V) GIVEN.THAT *I*~*will*~GO.DOWN^(V) TO SON~me MOURNING UNDERWORLD~unto and~*he*~*will*~WEEP^(V) AT~him FATHER~ him **37:36** and~the~Mid'yan~s *they*~*did*~SELL^(V) AT~him TO Mits'rayim to~ Potiphar EUNUCH Paroh NOBLE the~SLAUGHTERING~s

---

Chapter 38

38:1 and~*he*~*will*~EXIST^(V) in~the~APPOINTED.TIME the~SHE and~*he*~*will*~ GO.DOWN^(V) Yehudah from~AT BROTHER~s~him and~*he*~*will*~EXTEND^(V) UNTIL MAN Adulam~of and~TITLE~him Hhiyrah **38:2** and~*he*~*will*~SEE^(V) THERE Yehudah DAUGHTER MAN Kena'an~of and~TITLE~him Shu'a and~*he*~ *will*~TAKE^(V)~her and~*he*~*will*~COME^(V) TO~her **38:3** and~*she*~*will*~ CONCEIVE^(V) and~*she*~*will*~BRING.FORTH^(V) SON and~*he*~*will*~CALL.OUT^(V) AT TITLE~him Eyr **38:4** and~*she*~*will*~CONCEIVE^(V) YET.AGAIN and~*she*~*will*~ BRING.FORTH^(V) SON and~*she*~*will*~CALL.OUT^(V) AT TITLE~him Onan **38:5** and~*she*~*will*~*make*~ADD^(V) YET.AGAIN and~*she*~*will*~ BRING.FORTH^(V) SON and~*she*~*will*~CALL.OUT^(V) AT TITLE~him Sheylah and~ *he*~*did*~EXIST^(V) in~Keziv in~>~BRING.FORTH^(V)~her AT~him **38:6** and~*he*~ *will*~TAKE^(V) Yehudah WOMAN to~Eyr FIRSTBORN~him and~TITLE~her Tamar **38:7** and~*he*~*will*~EXIST^(V) Eyr FIRSTBORN Yehudah DYSFUNCTIONAL in~EYE~s2 **YHWH** and~*he*~*will*~*make*~DIE^(V)~him **YHWH** **38:8** and~*he*~*will*~ SAY^(V) Yehudah to~Onan !^(ms)~COME^(V) TO WOMAN BROTHER~you^(ms) and~ !^(ms)~DO.THE.MARRIAGE.DUTY^(V) AT~her and~!^(ms)~*make*~RISE^(V) SEED to~ BROTHER~you^(ms) **38:9** and~*he*~*will*~KNOW^(V) Onan GIVEN.THAT NOT to~ him *he*~*will*~EXIST^(V) the~SEED and~*he*~*did*~EXIST^(V) IF *he*~*did*~COME^(V) TO

Benner's Mechanical Translation of the Torah

WOMAN BROTHER~him and~*he~did~much*~DAMAGE$^{(V)}$ LAND~unto to~ EXCEPT >~GIVE$^{(V)}$ SEED to~BROTHER~him **38:10** and~*he~will*~ BE.DYSFUNCTIONAL$^{(V)}$ in~EYE~s2 **YHWH** WHICH *he~did*~DO$^{(V)}$ and~*he~will*~ make~DIE$^{(V)}$ ALSO AT~him **38:11** and~*he~will*~SAY$^{(V)}$ Yehudah to~Tamar DAUGHTER-IN-LAW~him *!*$^{(fs)}$~SETTLE$^{(V)}$ WIDOW HOUSE FATHER~you$^{(fs)}$ UNTIL *he~will*~MAGNIFY$^{(V)}$ Sheylah SON~me GIVEN.THAT *he~did*~SAY$^{(V)}$ OTHERWISE *he~will*~DIE$^{(V)}$ ALSO HE like~BROTHER~him and~*she~will*~ WALK$^{(V)}$ Tamar and~*she~will*~SETTLE$^{(V)}$ HOUSE FATHER~her **38:12** and~ *they*$^{(m)}$~*will*~INCREASE$^{(V)}$ the~DAY~s and~*she~will*~DIE$^{(V)}$ DAUGHTER Shu'a WOMAN Yehudah and~*he~will*~be~COMFORT$^{(V)}$ Yehudah and~*he~will*~ make~GO.UP$^{(V)}$ UPON SHEAR$^{(V)}$~*ing*$^{(mp)}$ FLOCKS~him HE and~Hhiyrah COMPANION~him the~Adulam~of Timnat~unto **38:13** and~*he~will*~be~ make~BE.FACE.TO.FACE$^{(V)}$ to~Tamar to~>~SAY$^{(V)}$ LOOK FATHER-IN-LAW~ you$^{(fs)}$ GO.UP$^{(V)}$~*ing*$^{(ms)}$ Timnat~unto to~>~SHEAR$^{(V)}$ FLOCKS~him **38:14** and~ *she~will~make*~TURN.ASIDE$^{(V)}$ GARMENT~s WIDOWHOOD~her from~ UPON~her and~*she~will~much*~COVER.OVER$^{(V)}$ in~the~VEIL and~*she~will*~ self~WRAP$^{(V)}$ and~*she~will*~SETTLE$^{(V)}$ in~OPENING EYE~s2 WHICH UPON ROAD Timnat~unto GIVEN.THAT *she~did*~SEE$^{(V)}$ GIVEN.THAT *he~did*~ MAGNIFY$^{(V)}$ Sheylah and~SHE NOT *she~did~be*~GIVE$^{(V)}$ to~him to~ WOMAN **38:15** and~*he~will*~SEE$^{(V)}$~her Yehudah and~*he~will*~THINK$^{(V)}$~her to~BE.A.HARLOT$^{(V)}$~*ing*$^{(fs)}$ GIVEN.THAT *she~did~much*~COVER.OVER$^{(V)}$ FACE~s~her **38:16** and~*he~will*~EXTEND$^{(V)}$ TO~her TO the~ROAD and~*he~ will*~SAY$^{(V)}$ *!*$^{(ms)}$~PROVIDE$^{(V)}$~& PLEASE *I~will*~COME$^{(V)}$ TO~you$^{(fs)}$ GIVEN.THAT NOT *he~did*~KNOW$^{(V)}$ GIVEN.THAT DAUGHTER-IN-LAW~him SHE and~*she~ will*~SAY$^{(V)}$ WHAT *you*$^{(ms)}$~*will*~GIVE$^{(V)}$ to~me GIVEN.THAT *you*$^{(ms)}$~*will*~ COME$^{(V)}$ TO~me **38:17** and~*he~will*~SAY$^{(V)}$ I *I~will~much*~SEND$^{(V)}$ MALE.KID SHE-GOAT~s FROM the~FLOCKS and~*she~will*~SAY$^{(V)}$ IF *you*$^{(ms)}$~*will*~GIVE$^{(V)}$ TOKEN UNTIL >~SEND$^{(V)}$~*you*$^{(ms)}$ **38:18** and~*he~will*~SAY$^{(V)}$ WHAT the~ TOKEN WHICH *I~will*~GIVE$^{(V)}$ to~you$^{(fs)}$ and~*she~will*~SAY$^{(V)}$ SEAL~you$^{(ms)}$ and~CORD~you$^{(ms)}$ and~BRANCH~you$^{(ms)}$ WHICH in~HAND~you$^{(ms)}$ and~*he~ will*~GIVE$^{(V)}$ to~her and~*he~will*~COME$^{(V)}$ TO~her and~*she~will*~CONCEIVE$^{(V)}$ to~him **38:19** and~*she~will*~RISE$^{(V)}$ and~*she~will*~WALK$^{(V)}$ and~*she~will*~ make~TURN.ASIDE$^{(V)}$ VEIL from~UPON~her and~*she~will*~WEAR$^{(V)}$ GARMENT~s WIDOWHOOD~her **38:20** and~*he~will*~SEND$^{(V)}$ Yehudah AT MALE.KID the~SHE-GOAT~s in~HAND COMPANION~him the~Adulam~of to~ >~TAKE$^{(V)}$ the~TOKEN from~HAND the~WOMAN and~NOT *he~did*~FIND$^{(V)}$~ her **38:21** and~*he~will*~INQUIRE$^{(V)}$ AT MAN~s AREA~her to~>~SAY$^{(V)}$ WHERE the~PROSTITUTE SHE in~the~Eynayim UPON the~ROAD and~*they*$^{(m)}$~*will*~ SAY$^{(V)}$ NOT *she~did*~EXIST$^{(V)}$ in~THIS PROSTITUTE **38:22** and~*he~will*~ TURN.BACK$^{(V)}$ TO Yehudah and~*he~will*~SAY$^{(V)}$ NOT *I~did*~FIND$^{(V)}$~her and~ ALSO MAN~s the~AREA *they~did*~SAY$^{(V)}$ NOT *she~did*~EXIST$^{(V)}$ in~THIS PROSTITUTE **38:23** and~*he~will*~SAY$^{(V)}$ Yehudah *she~will*~TAKE$^{(V)}$ to~her OTHERWISE *we~will*~EXIST$^{(V)}$ to~DESPISE$^{(V)}$ LOOK *I~did*~SEND$^{(V)}$ the~ MALE.KID the~THIS and~YOU$^{(ms)}$ NOT *you*$^{(ms)}$~*did*~FIND$^{(V)}$~her **38:24** and~ *he~will*~EXIST$^{(V)}$ like~from~THREE NEW.MOON~s and~*he~will~be~make*~

BE.FACE.TO.FACE$^{(V)}$ to~Yehudah to~>~SAY$^{(V)}$ *she~did*~BE.A.HARLOT$^{(V)}$ Tamar DAUGHTER-IN-LAW~you$^{(ms)}$ and~ALSO LOOK PREGNANT to~ PROSTITUTION~s and~*he~will*~SAY$^{(V)}$ Yehudah *!*$^{(mp)}$~*make*~GO.OUT$^{(V)}$~her and~*she~will~be*~CREMATE$^{(V)}$ **38:25** SHE *be~make*~GO.OUT$^{(V)}$~*ing*$^{(fs)}$ and~ SHE *she~did*~SEND$^{(V)}$ TO FATHER-IN-LAW~her to~>~SAY$^{(V)}$ to~MAN WHICH THESE to~him I PREGNANT and~*she~will*~SAY$^{(V)}$ *!*$^{(ms)}$~*make*~RECOGNIZE$^{(V)}$ PLEASE to~WHO the~SEAL and~the~CORD~s and~the~BRANCH the~ THESE **38:26** and~*he~will~make*~RECOGNIZE$^{(V)}$ Yehudah and~*he~will*~SAY$^{(V)}$ *she~did*~BE.STEADFAST$^{(V)}$ FROM~me GIVEN.THAT UPON SO NOT *I~did*~ GIVE$^{(V)}$~her to~Sheylah SON~me and~NOT *he~did*~ADD$^{(V)}$ YET.AGAIN to~>~ KNOW$^{(V)}$~her **38:27** and~*he~will*~EXIST$^{(V)}$ in~APPOINTED.TIME >~ BRING.FORTH$^{(V)}$~her and~LOOK TWIN~s in~WOMB~her **38:28** and~*he~will*~ EXIST$^{(V)}$ in~>~BRING.FORTH$^{(V)}$~her and~*he~will*~GIVE$^{(V)}$ HAND and~*she~will*~ TAKE$^{(V)}$ the~*much*~BRING.FORTH$^{(V)}$~*ing*$^{(fs)}$ and~*she~will*~TIE$^{(V)}$ UPON HAND~ him SCARLET to~>~SAY$^{(V)}$ THIS *he~did*~GO.OUT$^{(V)}$ FIRST **38:29** and~*he~will*~ EXIST$^{(V)}$ like~*make*~TURN.BACK$^{(V)}$~*ing*$^{(ms)}$ HAND~him and~LOOK *he~did*~ GO.OUT$^{(V)}$ BROTHER~him and~*she~will*~SAY$^{(V)}$ WHAT *you*$^{(ms)}$~*did*~ BREAK.OUT$^{(V)}$ UPON~you$^{(ms)}$ BREACH and~*he~will*~CALL.OUT$^{(V)}$ TITLE~him BREACH **38:30** and~AFTER *he~did*~GO.OUT$^{(V)}$ BROTHER~him WHICH UPON HAND~him the~SCARLET and~*he~will*~CALL.OUT$^{(V)}$ TITLE~him Zerahh

Chapter 39

39:1 and~Yoseph *he~did~be~make*~GO.DOWN$^{(V)}$ Mits'rayim~unto and~*he~ will*~PURCHASE$^{(V)}$~him Potiphar EUNUCH Paroh NOBLE the~ SLAUGHTERING~s MAN Mits'rayim~of from~HAND the~Yishma'el~s WHICH *!*$^{(mp)}$~*make*~GO.DOWN$^{(V)}$~him THERE~unto **39:2** and~*he~will*~EXIST$^{(V)}$ YHWH AT Yoseph and~*he~will*~EXIST$^{(V)}$ MAN *make*~PROSPER$^{(V)}$~*ing*$^{(ms)}$ and~ *he~will*~EXIST$^{(V)}$ in~HOUSE LORD~s~him the~Mits'rayim~of **39:3** and~*he~ will*~SEE$^{(V)}$ LORD~s~him GIVEN.THAT YHWH AT~him and~ALL WHICH HE DO$^{(V)}$~*ing*$^{(ms)}$ YHWH *make*~PROSPER$^{(V)}$~*ing*$^{(ms)}$ in~HAND~him **39:4** and~*he~ will*~FIND$^{(V)}$ Yoseph BEAUTY in~EYE~s2~him and~*he~will~much*~MINISTER$^{(V)}$ AT~him and~*he~will~make*~REGISTER$^{(V)}$~him UPON HOUSE~him and~ALL THERE.IS to~him *he~did*~GIVE$^{(V)}$ in~HAND~him **39:5** and~*he~will*~EXIST$^{(V)}$ from~AT.THAT.TIME *he~did~make*~REGISTER$^{(V)}$ AT~him in~HOUSE~him and~UPON ALL WHICH THERE.IS to~him and~*he~will~much*~KNEEL$^{(V)}$ YHWH AT HOUSE the~Mits'rayim~of in~ON.ACCOUNT.OF Yoseph and~*he~will*~ EXIST$^{(V)}$ PRESENT YHWH in~ALL WHICH THERE.IS to~him in~the~HOUSE and~in~the~FIELD **39:6** and~*he~will*~LEAVE$^{(V)}$ ALL WHICH to~him in~HAND Yoseph and~NOT *he~did*~KNOW$^{(V)}$ AT~him ANYTHING GIVEN.THAT IF the~ BREAD WHICH HE EAT$^{(V)}$~*ing*$^{(ms)}$ and~*he~will*~EXIST$^{(V)}$ Yoseph BEAUTIFUL FORM and~BEAUTIFUL APPEARANCE **39:7** and~*he~will*~EXIST$^{(V)}$ AFTER the~ WORD~s the~THESE and~*she~will*~LIFT.UP$^{(V)}$ WOMAN LORD~s~him AT

EYE~s2~her TO Yoseph and~*she~will*~SAY⁽ᵛ⁾ *!⁽ᵐˢ⁾*~LIE.DOWN⁽ᵛ⁾~& WITH~ me **39:8** and~*he~will~much*~REFUSE⁽ᵛ⁾ and~*he~will*~SAY⁽ᵛ⁾ TO WOMAN LORD~s~him THOUGH LORD~me NOT *he~did*~KNOW⁽ᵛ⁾ AT~me WHAT in~ the~HOUSE and~ALL WHICH THERE.IS to~him *he~did*~GIVE⁽ᵛ⁾ in~HAND~ me **39:9** WITHOUT~him GREAT in~the~HOUSE the~THIS FROM~me and~ NOT *he~did*~KEEP.BACK⁽ᵛ⁾ FROM~me ANYTHING GIVEN.THAT IF AT~you⁽ᶠˢ⁾ in~WHICH YOU⁽ᶠˢ⁾ WOMAN~him and~HOW *I~will*~DO⁽ᵛ⁾ the~ DYSFUNCTIONAL the~GREAT the~THIS and~*I~did*~FAIL⁽ᵛ⁾ to~ Elohiym **39:10** and~*he~will*~EXIST⁽ᵛ⁾ like~>~*much*~SPEAK⁽ᵛ⁾~her TO Yoseph DAY DAY and~NOT *he~did*~HEAR⁽ᵛ⁾ TO~her to~>~LIE.DOWN⁽ᵛ⁾ BESIDE~her to~>~EXIST⁽ᵛ⁾ WITH~her **39:11** and~*he~will*~EXIST⁽ᵛ⁾ like~the~DAY the~THIS and~*he~will*~COME⁽ᵛ⁾ the~HOUSE~unto to~>~DO⁽ᵛ⁾ BUSINESS~him and~ WITHOUT MAN from~MAN~s the~HOUSE THERE in~the~HOUSE **39:12** and~ *she~will*~SEIZE.HOLD⁽ᵛ⁾~him in~GARMENT~him to~>~SAY⁽ᵛ⁾ *!⁽ᵐˢ⁾*~ LIE.DOWN⁽ᵛ⁾~& WITH~me and~*he~will*~LEAVE⁽ᵛ⁾ GARMENT~him in~HAND~ her and~*he~will*~FLEE⁽ᵛ⁾ and~*he~will*~GO.OUT⁽ᵛ⁾ the~OUTSIDE~ unto **39:13** and~*he~will*~EXIST⁽ᵛ⁾ like~>~SEE⁽ᵛ⁾~her GIVEN.THAT *he~did*~ LEAVE⁽ᵛ⁾ GARMENT~him in~HAND~her and~*he~will*~FLEE⁽ᵛ⁾ the~OUTSIDE~ unto **39:14** and~*she~will*~CALL.OUT⁽ᵛ⁾ to~MAN~s HOUSE~her and~*she~ will*~SAY⁽ᵛ⁾ to~them⁽ᵐ⁾ to~>~SAY⁽ᵛ⁾ *!⁽ᵐᵖ⁾*~SEE⁽ᵛ⁾ *he~did~make*~COME⁽ᵛ⁾ to~us MAN Ever~of to~>~*much*~LAUGH⁽ᵛ⁾ in~us *he~did*~COME⁽ᵛ⁾ TO~me to~>~ LIE.DOWN⁽ᵛ⁾ WITH~me and~*I~will*~CALL.OUT⁽ᵛ⁾ in~VOICE GREAT **39:15** and~ *he~will*~EXIST⁽ᵛ⁾ like~>~HEAR⁽ᵛ⁾~him GIVEN.THAT *I~did~make*~RAISE.UP⁽ᵛ⁾ VOICE~me and~*I~will*~CALL.OUT⁽ᵛ⁾ and~*he~will*~LEAVE⁽ᵛ⁾ GARMENT~him BESIDE~me and~*he~will*~FLEE⁽ᵛ⁾ and~*he~will*~GO.OUT⁽ᵛ⁾ the~OUTSIDE~ unto **39:16** and~*she~will~make*~REST⁽ᵛ⁾ GARMENT~him BESIDE~her UNTIL *!⁽ᵐˢ⁾*~COME⁽ᵛ⁾ LORD~s~him TO HOUSE~him **39:17** and~*she~will~much*~ SPEAK⁽ᵛ⁾ TO~him like~the~WORD~s the~THESE to~>~SAY⁽ᵛ⁾ *he~did*~COME⁽ᵛ⁾ TO~me the~SERVANT the~Ever~of WHICH *you⁽ᵐˢ⁾~did~make*~COME⁽ᵛ⁾ to~us to~>~*much*~LAUGH⁽ᵛ⁾ in~me **39:18** and~*he~will*~EXIST⁽ᵛ⁾ like~>~*make*~ RAISE.UP⁽ᵛ⁾~me VOICE~me and~*I~will*~CALL.OUT⁽ᵛ⁾ and~*he~will*~LEAVE⁽ᵛ⁾ GARMENT~him BESIDE~me and~*he~will*~FLEE⁽ᵛ⁾ the~OUTSIDE~ unto **39:19** and~*he~will*~EXIST⁽ᵛ⁾ like~>~HEAR⁽ᵛ⁾ LORD~s~him AT WORD~s WOMAN~him WHICH *she~did~much*~SPEAK⁽ᵛ⁾ TO~him to~>~SAY⁽ᵛ⁾ like~ the~WORD~s the~THESE *he~did*~DO⁽ᵛ⁾ to~me SERVANT~you⁽ᵐˢ⁾ and~*he~ will*~FLARE.UP⁽ᵛ⁾ NOSE~him **39:20** and~*he~will*~TAKE⁽ᵛ⁾ LORD~s Yoseph AT~ him and~*he~will*~GIVE⁽ᵛ⁾~him TO HOUSE the~PRISON AREA WHICH TIE.UP⁽ᵛ⁾~*ed*⁽ᵐᵖ⁾ the~KING TIE.UP⁽ᵛ⁾~*ed*⁽ᵐᵖ⁾ and~*he~will*~EXIST⁽ᵛ⁾ THERE in~ HOUSE the~PRISON **39:21** and~*he~will*~EXIST⁽ᵛ⁾ **YHWH** AT Yoseph and~*he~ will*~EXTEND⁽ᵛ⁾ TO~him KINDNESS and~*he~will*~GIVE⁽ᵛ⁾ BEAUTY~him in~EYE~ s2 NOBLE HOUSE the~PRISON **39:22** and~*he~will*~GIVE⁽ᵛ⁾ NOBLE HOUSE the~PRISON in~HAND Yoseph AT ALL the~PRISONER~s WHICH in~HOUSE the~PRISON and~AT ALL WHICH DO⁽ᵛ⁾~*ing*⁽ᵐᵖ⁾ THERE HE *he~did*~EXIST⁽ᵛ⁾ DO⁽ᵛ⁾~*ing*⁽ᵐˢ⁾ **39:23** WITHOUT NOBLE HOUSE the~PRISON SEE⁽ᵛ⁾~*ing*⁽ᵐˢ⁾ AT

The Book of Genesis

ALL ANYTHING in~HAND~him in~WHICH **YHWH** AT~him and~WHICH HE DO$^{(V)}$~ing$^{(ms)}$ **YHWH** *make*~PROSPER$^{(V)}$~ing$^{(ms)}$

Chapter 40

40:1 and~*he*~*will*~EXIST$^{(V)}$ AFTER the~WORD~s the~THESE *they*~*did*~FAIL$^{(V)}$ *make*~DRINK$^{(V)}$~ing$^{(ms)}$ KING Mits'rayim and~the~BAKE$^{(V)}$~ing$^{(ms)}$ to~ LORD~s~them$^{(m)}$ to~KING Mits'rayim **40:2** and~*he*~*will*~SNAP$^{(V)}$ Paroh UPON TWO EUNUCH~s~him UPON NOBLE the~*make*~DRINK$^{(V)}$~ing$^{(mp)}$ and~ UPON NOBLE the~BAKE$^{(V)}$~ing$^{(mp)}$ **40:3** and~*he*~*will*~GIVE$^{(V)}$ AT~them$^{(m)}$ in~ CUSTODY HOUSE NOBLE the~SLAUGHTERING~s TO HOUSE the~PRISON AREA WHICH Yoseph TIE.UP$^{(V)}$~ed$^{(ms)}$ THERE **40:4** and~*he*~*will*~REGISTER$^{(V)}$ NOBLE the~SLAUGHTERING~s AT Yoseph AT~them$^{(m)}$ and~*he*~*will*~much~ MINISTER$^{(V)}$ AT~them$^{(m)}$ and~*they*$^{(m)}$~*will*~EXIST$^{(V)}$ DAY~s in~ CUSTODY **40:5** and~*they*$^{(m)}$~*will*~DREAM$^{(V)}$ DREAM TWO~them$^{(m)}$ MAN DREAM~him in~NIGHT UNIT MAN like~INTERPRETATION DREAM~him the~ DRINKING and~the~BAKE$^{(V)}$~ing$^{(ms)}$ WHICH to~KING Mits'rayim WHICH TIE.UP$^{(V)}$~ed$^{(mp)}$ in~HOUSE the~PRISON **40:6** and~*he*~*will*~COME$^{(V)}$ TO~ them$^{(m)}$ Yoseph in~the~MORNING and~*he*~*will*~SEE$^{(V)}$ AT~them$^{(m)}$ and~ LOOK~them$^{(m)}$ BE.SAD$^{(V)}$~ing$^{(mp)}$ **40:7** and~*he*~*will*~INQUIRE$^{(V)}$ AT EUNUCH~s Paroh WHICH AT~him in~CUSTODY HOUSE LORD~s~him to~>~SAY$^{(V)}$ WHY FACE~s~you$^{(mp)}$ DYSFUNCTIONAL~s the~DAY **40:8** and~*they*$^{(m)}$~*will*~SAY$^{(V)}$ TO~him DREAM *we*~*did*~DREAM$^{(V)}$ and~INTERPRET$^{(V)}$~ing$^{(ms)}$ WITHOUT AT~ him and~*he*~*will*~SAY$^{(V)}$ TO~them$^{(m)}$ Yoseph ?~NOT to~Elohiym INTERPRETATION~s !$^{(mp)}$~>~much~COUNT$^{(V)}$ PLEASE to~me **40:9** and~*he*~ *will*~much~COUNT$^{(V)}$ NOBLE the~*make*~DRINK$^{(V)}$~ing$^{(mp)}$ AT DREAM~him to~ Yoseph and~*he*~*will*~SAY$^{(V)}$ to~him in~DREAM~me and~LOOK GRAPEVINE to~FACE~s~me **40:10** and~in~the~GRAPEVINE THREE TWIG~s and~SHE like~BURST.OUT$^{(V)}$~ing$^{(fs)}$ *she*~*did*~GO.UP$^{(V)}$ SHOOT~her *they*~*did*~*make*~ BOIL$^{(V)}$ CLUSTER~s~her GRAPE~s **40:11** and~CUP Paroh in~HAND~me and~ *I*~*will*~TAKE$^{(V)}$ AT the~GRAPE~s and~*I*~*will*~PRESS$^{(V)}$ AT~them$^{(m)}$ TO CUP Paroh and~*I*~*will*~GIVE$^{(V)}$ AT the~CUP UPON PALM Paroh **40:12** and~*he*~ *will*~SAY$^{(V)}$ to~him Yoseph THIS INTERPRETATION~him THREE the~TWIG~s THREE DAY~s THEY$^{(m)}$ **40:13** in~YET.AGAIN THREE DAY~s *he*~*will*~LIFT.UP$^{(V)}$ Paroh AT HEAD~you$^{(ms)}$ and~*he*~*did*~*make*~TURN.BACK$^{(V)}$~you$^{(ms)}$ UPON BASE~you$^{(ms)}$ and~*you*$^{(ms)}$~*did*~GIVE$^{(V)}$ CUP Paroh in~HAND~him like~the~ DECISION the~FIRST WHICH *you*$^{(ms)}$~*did*~EXIST$^{(V)}$ DRINKING~ him **40:14** GIVEN.THAT IF *you*$^{(ms)}$~*did*~REMEMBER$^{(V)}$~me AT~you$^{(ms)}$ like~ WHICH *he*~*will*~DO.WELL$^{(V)}$ to~you$^{(fs)}$ and~*you*$^{(ms)}$~*did*~DO$^{(V)}$ PLEASE BY~me KINDNESS and~*you*$^{(ms)}$~*did*~*make*~REMEMBER$^{(V)}$~me TO Paroh and~*you*$^{(ms)}$~ *did*~*make*~GO.OUT$^{(V)}$~me FROM the~HOUSE the~THIS **40:15** GIVEN.THAT >~be~much~STEAL$^{(V)}$ *I*~*did*~be~much~STEAL$^{(V)}$ from~LAND the~Ever~s and~ ALSO HERE NOT *I*~*did*~DO$^{(V)}$ ANYTHING GIVEN.THAT *they*~*did*~PLACE$^{(V)}$ AT~

me in~the~CISTERN **40:16** and~*he~will*~SEE⁽ᵛ⁾ NOBLE the~BAKE⁽ᵛ⁾~*ing*⁽ᵐᵖ⁾ GIVEN.THAT FUNCTIONAL *he~did*~INTERPRET⁽ᵛ⁾ and~*he~will*~SAY⁽ᵛ⁾ TO Yoseph MOREOVER I in~DREAM~me and~LOOK THREE WICKER.BASKET~s PALENESS UPON HEAD~me **40:17** and~in~the~WICKER.BASKET the~UPPER from~ALL NOURISHMENT Paroh WORK BAKE⁽ᵛ⁾~*ing*⁽ᵐˢ⁾ and~the~FLYER EAT⁽ᵛ⁾~*ing*⁽ᵐˢ⁾ AT~them⁽ᵐ⁾ FROM the~WICKER.BASKET from~UPON HEAD~ me **40:18** and~*he~will*~ANSWER⁽ᵛ⁾ Yoseph and~*he~will*~SAY⁽ᵛ⁾ THIS INTERPRETATION~him THREE the~WICKER.BASKET~s THREE DAY~s THEY⁽ᵐ⁾ **40:19** in~YET.AGAIN THREE DAY~s *he~will*~LIFT.UP⁽ᵛ⁾ Paroh AT HEAD~you⁽ᵐˢ⁾ from~UPON~you⁽ᵐˢ⁾ and~*he~did*~HANG⁽ᵛ⁾ AT~you⁽ᵐˢ⁾ UPON TREE and~*he~did*~EAT⁽ᵛ⁾ the~FLYER AT FLESH~you⁽ᵐˢ⁾ from~UPON~ you⁽ᵐˢ⁾ **40:20** and~*he~will*~EXIST⁽ᵛ⁾ in~the~DAY the~THIRD DAY >~*be~ make*~BRING.FORTH⁽ᵛ⁾ AT Paroh and~*he~will*~DO⁽ᵛ⁾ BANQUET to~ALL SERVANT~s~him and~*he~will*~LIFT.UP⁽ᵛ⁾ AT HEAD NOBLE the~*make*~ DRINK⁽ᵛ⁾~*ing*⁽ᵐᵖ⁾ and~AT HEAD NOBLE the~BAKE⁽ᵛ⁾~*ing*⁽ᵐᵖ⁾ in~MIDST SERVANT~s~him **40:21** and~*he~will*~*make*~TURN.BACK⁽ᵛ⁾ AT NOBLE the~ *make*~DRINK⁽ᵛ⁾~*ing*⁽ᵐᵖ⁾ UPON DRINKING~him and~*he~will*~GIVE⁽ᵛ⁾ the~CUP UPON PALM Paroh **40:22** and~AT NOBLE the~BAKE⁽ᵛ⁾~*ing*⁽ᵐᵖ⁾ *he~did*~ HANG⁽ᵛ⁾ like~WHICH *he~did*~INTERPRET⁽ᵛ⁾ to~them⁽ᵐ⁾ Yoseph **40:23** and~ NOT *he~did*~REMEMBER⁽ᵛ⁾ NOBLE the~*make*~DRINK⁽ᵛ⁾~*ing*⁽ᵐᵖ⁾ AT Yoseph and~*he~will*~FORGET⁽ᵛ⁾~him

Chapter 41

41:1 and~*he~will*~EXIST⁽ᵛ⁾ from~CONCLUSION YEAR~s2 DAY~s and~Paroh DREAM⁽ᵛ⁾~*ing*⁽ᵐˢ⁾ and~LOOK STAND⁽ᵛ⁾~*ing*⁽ᵐˢ⁾ UPON the~STREAM **41:2** and~ LOOK FROM the~STREAM GO.UP⁽ᵛ⁾~*ing*⁽ᶠᵖ⁾ SEVEN COW~s BEAUTIFUL~s APPEARANCE and~FED.FAT~s FLESH and~*they*⁽ᶠ⁾~*will*~FEED⁽ᵛ⁾ in~the~ MARSH.GRASS **41:3** and~LOOK SEVEN COW~s OTHER~s GO.UP⁽ᵛ⁾~*ing*⁽ᶠᵖ⁾ AFTER~them⁽ᶠ⁾ FROM the~STREAM DYSFUNCTIONAL~s APPEARANCE and~ SCRAWNY~s FLESH and~*they*⁽ᶠ⁾~*will*~STAND⁽ᵛ⁾ BESIDE the~COW~s UPON LIP the~STREAM **41:4** and~*they*⁽ᶠ⁾~*will*~EAT⁽ᵛ⁾ the~COW~s DYSFUNCTIONAL~s the~APPEARANCE and~SCRAWNY~s the~FLESH AT SEVEN the~COW~s BEAUTIFUL~s the~APPEARANCE and~the~FED.FAT~s and~*he~will*~AWAKE⁽ᵛ⁾ Paroh **41:5** and~*he~will*~SLEEP⁽ᵛ⁾ and~*he~will*~DREAM⁽ᵛ⁾ SECOND and~ LOOK SEVEN EAR.OF.GRAIN~s GO.UP⁽ᵛ⁾~*ing*⁽ᶠᵖ⁾ in~STALK UNIT FED.FAT~s and~FUNCTIONAL~s **41:6** and~LOOK SEVEN EAR.OF.GRAIN~s SCRAWNY~s and~BLAST⁽ᵛ⁾~*ed*⁽ᶠᵖ⁾ EAST.WIND SPRING.UP⁽ᵛ⁾~*ing*⁽ᶠᵖ⁾ AFTER~ them⁽ᶠ⁾ **41:7** and~*they*⁽ᶠ⁾~*will*~SWALLOW⁽ᵛ⁾ the~EAR.OF.GRAIN~s the~ SCRAWNY~s AT SEVEN the~EAR.OF.GRAIN~s the~FED.FAT~s and~the~ FULL~s and~*he~will*~AWAKE⁽ᵛ⁾ Paroh and~LOOK DREAM **41:8** and~*he~will*~ EXIST⁽ᵛ⁾ in~the~MORNING and~*she~will*~*be*~BEAT⁽ᵛ⁾ WIND~him and~*he~ will*~SEND⁽ᵛ⁾ and~*he~will*~CALL.OUT⁽ᵛ⁾ AT ALL MAGICIAN~s Mits'rayim and~

The Book of Genesis

AT ALL SKILLED.ONE~her and~*he*~*will*~*much*~COUNT$^{(v)}$ Paroh to~them$^{(m)}$ AT DREAM~him and~WITHOUT INTERPRET$^{(v)}$~*ing*$^{(ms)}$ AT~them$^{(m)}$ to~ Paroh **41:9** and~*he*~*will*~*much*~SPEAK$^{(v)}$ NOBLE the~*make*~DRINK$^{(v)}$~*ing*$^{(mp)}$ AT Paroh to~>~SAY$^{(v)}$ AT FAILURE~s~me I *make*~REMEMBER$^{(v)}$~*ing*$^{(ms)}$ the~ DAY **41:10** Paroh *he*~*did*~SNAP$^{(v)}$ UPON SERVANT~s~him and~*he*~*will*~ GIVE$^{(v)}$ AT~me in~CUSTODY HOUSE NOBLE the~SLAUGHTERING~s AT~me and~AT NOBLE the~BAKE$^{(v)}$~*ing*$^{(mp)}$ **41:11** and~*we*~*will*~DREAM$^{(v)}$~& DREAM in~NIGHT UNIT I and~HE MAN like~INTERPRETATION DREAM~him *we*~*did*~DREAM$^{(v)}$ **41:12** and~THERE AT~us YOUNG.MAN Ever~of SERVANT to~NOBLE the~SLAUGHTERING~s and~*we*~*will*~*much*~COUNT$^{(v)}$ to~him and~*he*~*will*~INTERPRET$^{(v)}$ to~us AT DREAM~s~us MAN like~DREAM~him *he*~*did*~INTERPRET$^{(v)}$ **41:13** and~*he*~*will*~EXIST$^{(v)}$ like~WHICH *he*~*did*~ INTERPRET$^{(v)}$ to~us SO *he*~*did*~EXIST$^{(v)}$ AT~me *he*~*did*~*make*~TURN.BACK$^{(v)}$ UPON BASE~me and~AT~him *he*~*did*~HANG$^{(v)}$ **41:14** and~*he*~*will*~SEND$^{(v)}$ Paroh and~*he*~*will*~CALL.OUT$^{(v)}$ AT Yoseph and~*they*~*will*~*make*~RUN$^{(v)}$~ him FROM the~CISTERN and~*he*~*will*~*much*~SHAVE$^{(v)}$ and~*he*~*will*~*much*~ PASS.OVER$^{(v)}$ APPAREL~s~him and~*he*~*will*~COME$^{(v)}$ TO Paroh **41:15** and~ *he*~*will*~SAY$^{(v)}$ Paroh TO Yoseph DREAM *I*~*did*~DREAM$^{(v)}$ and~INTERPRET$^{(v)}$~ *ing*$^{(ms)}$ WITHOUT AT~him and~I *I*~*did*~HEAR$^{(v)}$ UPON~you$^{(ms)}$ to~>~SAY$^{(v)}$ you$^{(ms)}$~*will*~HEAR$^{(v)}$ DREAM to~>~INTERPRET$^{(v)}$ AT~him **41:16** and~*he*~*will*~ ANSWER$^{(v)}$ Yoseph AT Paroh to~>~SAY$^{(v)}$ APART.FROM Elohiym *he*~*will*~ ANSWER$^{(v)}$ AT COMPLETENESS Paroh **41:17** and~*he*~*will*~*much*~SPEAK$^{(v)}$ Paroh TO Yoseph in~DREAM~me LOOK~me STAND$^{(v)}$~*ing*$^{(ms)}$ UPON LIP the~ STREAM **41:18** and~LOOK FROM the~STREAM GO.UP$^{(v)}$~*ing*$^{(fp)}$ SEVEN COW~s FED.FAT~s FLESH and~BEAUTIFUL~s FORM and~*they*$^{(f)}$~*will*~FEED$^{(v)}$ in~the~MARSH.GRASS **41:19** and~LOOK SEVEN COW~s OTHER~s GO.UP$^{(v)}$~ *ing*$^{(fp)}$ AFTER~them$^{(f)}$ HELPLESS~s and~DYSFUNCTIONAL~s FORM MANY and~ THIN~s FLESH NOT *I*~*did*~SEE$^{(v)}$ like~THEY$^{(f)}$ in~ALL LAND Mits'rayim to~the~ DYSFUNCTIONAL **41:20** and~*they*$^{(f)}$~*will*~EAT$^{(v)}$ the~COW~s the~THIN~s and~the~DYSFUNCTIONAL~s AT SEVEN the~COW~s the~FIRST~s the~ FED.FAT~s **41:21** and~*they*$^{(f)}$~*will*~COME$^{(v)}$ TO INSIDE~them$^{(f)}$ and~NOT *he*~ *did*~*be*~KNOW$^{(v)}$ GIVEN.THAT *they*~*did*~COME$^{(v)}$ TO INSIDE~them$^{(f)}$ and~ APPEARANCE~s~them$^{(f)}$ DYSFUNCTIONAL like~WHICH in~the~FIRST.TIME and~*I*~*will*~AWAKE$^{(v)}$ **41:22** and~*I*~*will*~SEE$^{(v)}$ in~DREAM~me and~LOOK SEVEN EAR.OF.GRAIN~s GO.UP$^{(v)}$~*ing*$^{(fp)}$ in~STALK UNIT FULL~s and~ FUNCTIONAL~s **41:23** and~LOOK SEVEN EAR.OF.GRAIN~s WITHER$^{(v)}$~*ed*$^{(fp)}$ SCRAWNY~s BLAST$^{(v)}$~*ed*$^{(fp)}$ EAST.WIND SPRING.UP$^{(v)}$~*ing*$^{(fp)}$ AFTER~ them$^{(m)}$ **41:24** and~*they*$^{(f)}$~*will*~SWALLOW$^{(v)}$ the~EAR.OF.GRAIN~s the~ SCRAWNY~s AT SEVEN the~EAR.OF.GRAIN~s the~FUNCTIONAL~s and~*I*~ *will*~SAY$^{(v)}$ TO the~MAGICIAN~s and~WITHOUT *make*~BE.FACE.TO.FACE$^{(v)}$~ *ing*$^{(ms)}$ to~me **41:25** and~*he*~*will*~SAY$^{(v)}$ Yoseph TO Paroh DREAM Paroh UNIT HE AT WHICH the~Elohiym DO$^{(v)}$~*ing*$^{(ms)}$ *he*~*did*~*make*~ BE.FACE.TO.FACE$^{(v)}$ to~Paroh **41:26** SEVEN COW~s the~FUNCTIONAL~s SEVEN YEAR~s THEY$^{(f)}$ and~SEVEN the~EAR.OF.GRAIN~s the~FUNCTIONAL~s SEVEN YEAR~s THEY$^{(f)}$ DREAM UNIT HE **41:27** and~SEVEN the~COW~s the~

THIN~s and~the~DYSFUNCTIONAL~s the~GO.UP$^{(V)}$~ing$^{(fp)}$ AFTER~them$^{(f)}$ SEVEN YEAR~s THEY$^{(f)}$ and~SEVEN the~EAR.OF.GRAIN~s the~EMPTY~s BLAST$^{(V)}$~ed$^{(fp)}$ the~EAST.WIND they$^{(m)}$~will~EXIST$^{(V)}$ SEVEN YEAR~s HUNGER **41:28** HE the~WORD WHICH I~did~much~SPEAK$^{(V)}$ TO Paroh WHICH the~Elohiym DO$^{(V)}$~ing$^{(ms)}$ he~did~make~SEE$^{(V)}$ AT Paroh **41:29** LOOK SEVEN YEAR~s COME$^{(V)}$~ing$^{(fp)}$ PLENTY GREAT in~ALL LAND Mits'rayim **41:30** and~they~did~RISE$^{(V)}$ SEVEN YEAR~s HUNGER AFTER~ them$^{(f)}$ and~he~did~be~FORGET$^{(V)}$ ALL the~PLENTY in~LAND Mits'rayim and~he~did~much~FINISH$^{(V)}$ the~HUNGER AT the~LAND **41:31** and~NOT he~will~be~KNOW$^{(V)}$ the~PLENTY in~the~LAND from~FACE~s the~HUNGER the~HE AFTER SO GIVEN.THAT HEAVY HE MANY **41:32** and~UPON >~be~ CHANGE$^{(V)}$ the~DREAM TO Paroh FOOTSTEP~s2 GIVEN.THAT be~ PREPARE$^{(V)}$~ing$^{(ms)}$ the~WORD from~WITH the~Elohiym and~much~ HURRY$^{(V)}$~ing$^{(ms)}$ the~Elohiym to~>~DO$^{(V)}$~him **41:33** and~NOW he~will~ SEE$^{(V)}$ Paroh MAN be~UNDERSTAND$^{(V)}$~ing$^{(ms)}$ and~SKILLED.ONE and~he~ will~SET.DOWN$^{(V)}$~him UPON LAND Mits'rayim **41:34** he~will~DO$^{(V)}$ Paroh and~he~will~make~REGISTER$^{(V)}$ OVERSEER~s UPON the~LAND and~he~did~ much~TAKE.A.FIFTH$^{(V)}$ AT LAND Mits'rayim in~SEVEN YEAR~s the~ PLENTY **41:35** and~they$^{(m)}$~will~GATHER.TOGETHER$^{(V)}$ AT ALL FOODSTUFF the~YEAR~s the~FUNCTIONAL~s the~COME$^{(V)}$~ing$^{(fp)}$ the~THESE and~ they$^{(m)}$~will~PILE.UP$^{(V)}$ GRAIN UNDER HAND Paroh FOODSTUFF in~CITY~s and~they~did~SAFEGUARD$^{(V)}$ **41:36** and~he~did~EXIST$^{(V)}$ the~FOODSTUFF to~DEPOSITED to~the~LAND to~SEVEN YEAR~s the~HUNGER WHICH they$^{(f)}$~ will~EXIST$^{(V)}$ in~LAND Mits'rayim and~NOT she~will~be~CUT$^{(V)}$ the~LAND in~ the~HUNGER **41:37** and~he~will~DO.WELL$^{(V)}$ the~WORD in~EYE~s2 Paroh and~in~EYE~s2 ALL SERVANT~s~him **41:38** and~he~will~SAY$^{(V)}$ Paroh TO SERVANT~s~him ?~he~did~be~FIND$^{(V)}$ like~THIS MAN WHICH WIND Elohiym in~him **41:39** and~he~will~SAY$^{(V)}$ Paroh TO Yoseph AFTER >~make~KNOW$^{(V)}$ Elohiym AT~you$^{(ms)}$ AT ALL THIS WITHOUT be~UNDERSTAND$^{(V)}$~ing$^{(ms)}$ and~ SKILLED.ONE like~THAT.ONE~you$^{(ms)}$ **41:40** YOU$^{(ms)}$ you$^{(ms)}$~will~EXIST$^{(V)}$ UPON HOUSE~me and~UPON MOUTH~you$^{(ms)}$ he~will~KISS$^{(V)}$ ALL PEOPLE~ me ONLY the~SEAT I~will~MAGNIFY$^{(V)}$ FROM~you$^{(ms)}$ **41:41** and~he~will~ SAY$^{(V)}$ Paroh TO Yoseph !$^{(ms)}$~SEE$^{(V)}$ I~did~GIVE$^{(V)}$ AT~you$^{(ms)}$ UPON ALL LAND Mits'rayim **41:42** and~he~will~make~TURN.ASIDE$^{(V)}$ Paroh AT RING~him from~UPON HAND~him and~he~will~GIVE$^{(V)}$ AT~her UPON HAND Yoseph and~he~will~make~WEAR$^{(V)}$ AT~him GARMENT~s LINEN and~he~will~ PLACE$^{(V)}$ NECKLACE the~GOLD UPON BACK.OF.THE.NECK~him **41:43** and~ he~will~make~RIDE$^{(V)}$ AT~him in~CHARIOT the~DOUBLE WHICH to~him and~they$^{(m)}$~will~CALL.OUT$^{(V)}$ to~FACE~s~him BEND.THE.KNEE and~>~ GIVE$^{(V)}$ AT~him UPON ALL LAND Mits'rayim **41:44** and~he~will~SAY$^{(V)}$ Paroh TO Yoseph I Paroh and~APART.FROM~you$^{(ms)}$ NOT he~will~make~ RAISE.UP$^{(V)}$ MAN AT HAND~him and~AT FOOT~him in~ALL LAND Mits'rayim **41:45** and~he~will~CALL.OUT$^{(V)}$ Paroh TITLE Yoseph Tsaphnat-Paneyahh and~he~will~GIVE$^{(V)}$ to~him AT Asnat DAUGHTER Potee-Phera ADMINISTRATOR On to~WOMAN and~he~will~GO.OUT$^{(V)}$ Yoseph UPON

The Book of Genesis

LAND Mits'rayim **41:46** and~Yoseph SON THREE~s YEAR in~>~STAND$^{(V)}$~him to~FACE~s Paroh KING Mits'rayim and~he~will~GO.OUT$^{(V)}$ Yoseph from~to~FACE~s Paroh and~he~will~CROSS.OVER$^{(V)}$ in~ALL LAND Mits'rayim **41:47** and~she~will~DO$^{(V)}$ the~LAND in~SEVEN YEAR~s the~PLENTY to~HANDFUL~s **41:48** and~he~will~GATHER.TOGETHER$^{(V)}$ AT ALL FOODSTUFF SEVEN YEAR~s WHICH they~did~EXIST$^{(V)}$ in~LAND Mits'rayim and~he~will~GIVE$^{(V)}$ FOODSTUFF in~CITY~s FOODSTUFF FIELD the~CITY WHICH ALL.AROUND~her he~did~GIVE$^{(V)}$ in~MIDST~her **41:49** and~he~will~PILE.UP$^{(V)}$ Yoseph GRAIN like~SAND the~SEA >~make~INCREASE$^{(V)}$ MANY UNTIL GIVEN.THAT he~did~TERMINATE$^{(V)}$ to~>~COUNT$^{(V)}$ GIVEN.THAT WITHOUT NUMBER **41:50** and~to~Yoseph BRING.FORTH$^{(V)}$~ed$^{(ms)}$ TWO SON~s in~BEFORE she~will~COME$^{(V)}$ YEAR the~HUNGER WHICH she~did~BRING.FORTH$^{(V)}$ to~him Asnat DAUGHTER Potee-Phera ADMINISTRATOR On **41:51** and~he~will~CALL.OUT$^{(V)}$ Yoseph AT TITLE the~FIRSTBORN Menasheh GIVEN.THAT he~did~much~OVERLOOK$^{(V)}$ Elohiym AT ALL LABOR~me and~AT ALL HOUSE FATHER~me **41:52** and~AT TITLE the~SECOND he~did~CALL.OUT$^{(V)}$ Ephrayim GIVEN.THAT he~did~make~REPRODUCE$^{(V)}$~me Elohiym in~LAND AFFLICTION~me **41:53** and~they$^{(f)}$~will~FINISH$^{(V)}$ SEVEN YEAR~s the~PLENTY WHICH he~did~EXIST$^{(V)}$ in~LAND Mits'rayim **41:54** and~they$^{(f)}$~will~make~DRILL$^{(V)}$ SEVEN YEAR~s the~HUNGER to~>~COME$^{(V)}$ like~WHICH he~did~SAY$^{(V)}$ Yoseph and~he~will~EXIST$^{(V)}$ HUNGER in~ALL the~LAND~s and~in~ALL LAND Mits'rayim he~did~EXIST$^{(V)}$ BREAD **41:55** and~she~will~BE.HUNGRY$^{(V)}$ ALL LAND Mits'rayim and~he~will~CRY.OUT$^{(V)}$ the~PEOPLE TO Paroh to~BREAD and~he~will~SAY$^{(V)}$ Paroh to~ALL Mits'rayim !$^{(mp)}$~WALK$^{(V)}$ TO Yoseph WHICH he~will~SAY$^{(V)}$ to~you$^{(mp)}$ you$^{(mp)}$~will~DO$^{(V)}$ **41:56** and~the~HUNGER he~did~EXIST$^{(V)}$ UPON ALL FACE~s the~LAND and~he~will~OPEN$^{(V)}$ Yoseph AT ALL WHICH in~them$^{(m)}$ and~he~will~EXCHANGE$^{(V)}$ to~Mits'rayim and~he~will~SEIZE$^{(V)}$ the~HUNGER in~LAND Mits'rayim **41:57** and~ALL the~LAND they~did~COME$^{(V)}$ Mits'rayim~unto to~>~EXCHANGE$^{(V)}$ TO Yoseph GIVEN.THAT he~did~SEIZE$^{(V)}$ the~HUNGER in~ALL the~LAND

Chapter 42

42:1 and~he~will~SEE$^{(V)}$ Ya'aqov GIVEN.THAT THERE.IS GRAIN.SEEDS in~Mits'rayim and~he~will~SAY$^{(V)}$ Ya'aqov to~SON~s~him to~WHAT you$^{(mp)}$~will~self~SEE$^{(V)}$ **42:2** and~he~will~SAY$^{(V)}$ LOOK I~did~HEAR$^{(V)}$ GIVEN.THAT THERE.IS GRAIN.SEEDS in~Mits'rayim !$^{(mp)}$~GO.DOWN$^{(V)}$ THERE~unto and~!$^{(mp)}$~EXCHANGE$^{(V)}$ to~us from~THERE and~we~will~LIVE$^{(V)}$ and~NOT we~will~DIE$^{(V)}$ **42:3** and~they$^{(m)}$~will~GO.DOWN$^{(V)}$ BROTHER~s Yoseph TEN to~>~EXCHANGE$^{(V)}$ GRAIN from~Mits'rayim **42:4** and~AT Binyamin BROTHER~ of Yoseph NOT he~did~SEND$^{(V)}$ Ya'aqov AT BROTHER~s~him GIVEN.THAT he~did~SAY$^{(V)}$ OTHERWISE he~will~MEET$^{(V)}$~us HARM **42:5** and~they$^{(m)}$~

will~COME⁽ᵛ⁾ SON~s Yisra'eyl to~>~EXCHANGE⁽ᵛ⁾ in~MIDST the~COME⁽ᵛ⁾~
ing⁽ᵐᵖ⁾ GIVEN.THAT he~did~EXIST⁽ᵛ⁾ the~HUNGER in~LAND
Kena'an **42:6** and~Yoseph HE the~GOVERNOR UPON the~LAND HE the~
make~EXCHANGE⁽ᵛ⁾~ing⁽ᵐˢ⁾ to~ALL PEOPLE the~LAND and~they⁽ᵐ⁾~will~
COME⁽ᵛ⁾ BROTHER~s Yoseph and~they⁽ᵐ⁾~will~self~BEND.DOWN⁽ᵛ⁾ to~him
NOSE~s2 LAND~unto **42:7** and~he~will~SEE⁽ᵛ⁾ Yoseph AT BROTHER~s~him
and~he~will~make~RECOGNIZE⁽ᵛ⁾~them⁽ᵐ⁾ and~he~will~self~RECOGNIZE⁽ᵛ⁾
TO~them⁽ᵐ⁾ and~he~will~much~SPEAK⁽ᵛ⁾ AT~them⁽ᵐ⁾ HARD~s and~he~will~
SAY⁽ᵛ⁾ TO~them⁽ᵐ⁾ from~WITHOUT you⁽ᵐᵖ⁾~did~COME⁽ᵛ⁾ and~they⁽ᵐ⁾~will~
SAY⁽ᵛ⁾ from~LAND Kena'an to~>~EXCHANGE⁽ᵛ⁾ FOODSTUFF **42:8** and~he~
will~make~RECOGNIZE⁽ᵛ⁾ Yoseph AT BROTHER~s~him and~THEY⁽ᵐ⁾ NOT
they~will~RECOGNIZE⁽ᵛ⁾~him **42:9** and~he~will~REMEMBER⁽ᵛ⁾ Yoseph AT
the~DREAM~s WHICH he~did~DREAM⁽ᵛ⁾ to~them⁽ᵐ⁾ and~he~will~SAY⁽ᵛ⁾ TO~
them⁽ᵐ⁾ much~TREAD.ABOUT⁽ᵛ⁾~ing⁽ᵐᵖ⁾ YOU⁽ᵐᵖ⁾ to~>~SEE⁽ᵛ⁾ AT NAKEDNESS
the~LAND you⁽ᵐᵖ⁾~did~COME⁽ᵛ⁾ **42:10** and~they⁽ᵐ⁾~will~SAY⁽ᵛ⁾ TO~him NOT
LORD~me and~SERVANT~s~you⁽ᵐˢ⁾ they~did~COME⁽ᵛ⁾ to~>~EXCHANGE⁽ᵛ⁾
FOODSTUFF **42:11** ALL~us SON~s MAN UNIT WE BASE~s WE NOT they~did~
EXIST⁽ᵛ⁾ SERVANT~s~you⁽ᵐˢ⁾ much~TREAD.ABOUT⁽ᵛ⁾~ing⁽ᵐᵖ⁾ **42:12** and~he~
will~SAY⁽ᵛ⁾ TO~them⁽ᵐ⁾ NOT GIVEN.THAT NAKEDNESS the~LAND you⁽ᵐᵖ⁾~
did~COME⁽ᵛ⁾ to~>~SEE⁽ᵛ⁾ **42:13** and~they⁽ᵐ⁾~will~SAY⁽ᵛ⁾ TWO TEN
SERVANT~s~you⁽ᵐˢ⁾ BROTHER~s WE SON~s MAN UNIT in~LAND Kena'an
and~LOOK the~SMALL AT FATHER~us the~DAY and~the~UNIT WITHOUT~
him **42:14** and~he~will~SAY⁽ᵛ⁾ TO~them⁽ᵐ⁾ Yoseph HE WHICH I~did~much~
SPEAK⁽ᵛ⁾ TO~you⁽ᵐᵖ⁾ to~>~SAY⁽ᵛ⁾ much~TREAD.ABOUT⁽ᵛ⁾~ing⁽ᵐᵖ⁾
YOU⁽ᵐᵖ⁾ **42:15** in~THIS you⁽ᵐᵖ⁾~will~be~WATCH.OVER⁽ᵛ⁾ LIVING Paroh IF
you⁽ᵐᵖ⁾~will~GO.OUT⁽ᵛ⁾ from~THIS GIVEN.THAT IF >~COME⁽ᵛ⁾ BROTHER~
you⁽ᵐᵖ⁾ the~SMALL TO.THIS.POINT **42:16** !⁽ᵐᵖ⁾~SEND⁽ᵛ⁾ from~you⁽ᵐᵖ⁾ UNIT
and~he~will~TAKE⁽ᵛ⁾ AT BROTHER~you⁽ᵐᵖ⁾ and~YOU⁽ᵐᵖ⁾ !⁽ᵐᵖ⁾~be~TIE.UP⁽ᵛ⁾
and~they⁽ᵐ⁾~will~be~WATCH.OVER⁽ᵛ⁾ WORD~s~you⁽ᵐᵖ⁾ ?~TRUTH AT~you⁽ᵐᵖ⁾
and~IF NOT LIVING Paroh GIVEN.THAT much~TREAD.ABOUT⁽ᵛ⁾~ing⁽ᵐᵖ⁾
YOU⁽ᵐᵖ⁾ **42:17** and~he~will~GATHER⁽ᵛ⁾ AT~them⁽ᵐ⁾ TO CUSTODY THREE
DAY~s **42:18** and~he~will~SAY⁽ᵛ⁾ TO~them⁽ᵐ⁾ Yoseph in~the~DAY the~
THIRD THIS !⁽ᵐᵖ⁾~DO⁽ᵛ⁾ and~ !⁽ᵐᵖ⁾~LIVE⁽ᵛ⁾ AT the~Elohiym I he~did~
FEAR⁽ᵛ⁾ **42:19** IF BASE~s YOU⁽ᵐᵖ⁾ BROTHER~you⁽ᵐᵖ⁾ UNIT he~will~be~
TIE.UP⁽ᵛ⁾ in~HOUSE CUSTODY~you⁽ᵐᵖ⁾ and~YOU⁽ᵐᵖ⁾ !⁽ᵐᵖ⁾~WALK⁽ᵛ⁾ !⁽ᵐᵖ⁾~
make~COME⁽ᵛ⁾ GRAIN.SEEDS FAMINE HOUSE~s~you⁽ᵐᵖ⁾ **42:20** and~AT
BROTHER~you⁽ᵐᵖ⁾ the~SMALL you⁽ᵐᵖ⁾~will~make~COME⁽ᵛ⁾ TO~me and~
they⁽ᵐ⁾~will~be~SECURE⁽ᵛ⁾ WORD~s~you⁽ᵐᵖ⁾ and~NOT you⁽ᵐᵖ⁾~will~DIE⁽ᵛ⁾
and~they⁽ᵐ⁾~will~DO⁽ᵛ⁾ SO **42:21** and~they⁽ᵐ⁾~will~SAY⁽ᵛ⁾ MAN TO
BROTHER~him NEVERTHELESS GUILT~s WE UPON BROTHER~us WHICH we~
did~SEE⁽ᵛ⁾ PERSECUTION SOUL~him in~>~self~PROVIDE.PROTECTION⁽ᵛ⁾~him
TO~us and~NOT we~did~HEAR⁽ᵛ⁾ UPON SO she~did~COME⁽ᵛ⁾ TO~us the~
PERSECUTION the~THIS **42:22** and~he~will~ANSWER⁽ᵛ⁾ Re'uven AT~them⁽ᵐ⁾
to~>~SAY⁽ᵛ⁾ ?~NOT I~did~SAY⁽ᵛ⁾ TO~you⁽ᵐᵖ⁾ to~>~SAY⁽ᵛ⁾ DO.NOT you⁽ᵐᵖ⁾~
will~FAIL⁽ᵛ⁾ in~the~BOY and~NOT you⁽ᵐᵖ⁾~did~HEAR⁽ᵛ⁾ and~ALSO BLOOD~

ns LOOK be~SEEK⁽ᵛ⁾~ing⁽ᵐˢ⁾ **42:23** and~THEY⁽ᵐ⁾ NOT they~did~KNOW⁽ᵛ⁾ GIVEN.THAT HEAR⁽ᵛ⁾~ing⁽ᵐˢ⁾ Yoseph GIVEN.THAT the~make~MIMIC⁽ᵛ⁾~ing⁽ᵐˢ⁾ BETWEEN~them⁽ᵐ⁾ **42:24** and~he~will~GO.AROUND⁽ᵛ⁾ from~UPON~them⁽ᵐ⁾ and~he~will~WEEP⁽ᵛ⁾ and~he~will~TURN.BACK⁽ᵛ⁾ TO~them⁽ᵐ⁾ and~he~will~ much~SPEAK⁽ᵛ⁾ TO~them⁽ᵐ⁾ and~he~will~TAKE⁽ᵛ⁾ from~AT~them⁽ᵐ⁾ AT Shimon and~he~will~TIE.UP⁽ᵛ⁾ AT~him to~EYE~s2~them⁽ᵐ⁾ **42:25** and~he~ will~much~DIRECT⁽ᵛ⁾ Yoseph and~they⁽ᵐ⁾~will~much~FILL⁽ᵛ⁾ AT UTENSIL~ them⁽ᵐ⁾ GRAIN and~to~>~make~TURN.BACK⁽ᵛ⁾ SILVER~s~them⁽ᵐ⁾ MAN TO SACK~him and~to~>~GIVE⁽ᵛ⁾ to~them⁽ᵐ⁾ PROVISIONS to~the~ROAD and~he~ will~DO⁽ᵛ⁾ to~them⁽ᵐ⁾ SO **42:26** and~they⁽ᵐ⁾~will~LIFT.UP⁽ᵛ⁾ AT GRAIN.SEEDS~them⁽ᵐ⁾ UPON DONKEY~s~them⁽ᵐ⁾ and~they⁽ᵐ⁾~will~WALK⁽ᵛ⁾ from~THERE **42:27** and~he~will~OPEN⁽ᵛ⁾ the~UNIT AT SACK~him to~>~ GIVE⁽ᵛ⁾ PROVENDER to~DONKEY~him in~the~PLACE.OF.LODGING and~he~ will~SEE⁽ᵛ⁾ AT SILVER~him and~LOOK HE in~MOUTH GRAIN.SACK~ him **42:28** and~he~will~SAY⁽ᵛ⁾ TO BROTHER~s~him he~did~be~make~ TURN.BACK⁽ᵛ⁾ SILVER~me and~ALSO LOOK in~GRAIN.SACK~me and~he~ will~GO.OUT⁽ᵛ⁾ HEART~them⁽ᵐ⁾ and~they⁽ᵐ⁾~will~TREMBLE⁽ᵛ⁾ MAN TO BROTHER~him to~>~SAY⁽ᵛ⁾ WHAT THIS he~did~DO⁽ᵛ⁾ Elohiym to~ us **42:29** and~they⁽ᵐ⁾~will~COME⁽ᵛ⁾ TO Ya'aqov FATHER~them⁽ᵐ⁾ LAND~unto Kena'an and~they⁽ᵐ⁾~will~make~BE.FACE.TO.FACE⁽ᵛ⁾ to~him AT ALL the~ MEET⁽ᵛ⁾~ing⁽ᶠᵖ⁾ AT~them⁽ᵐ⁾ to~>~SAY⁽ᵛ⁾ **42:30** he~did~much~SPEAK⁽ᵛ⁾ the~ MAN LORD~s the~LAND AT~us HARD~s and~he~will~GIVE⁽ᵛ⁾ AT~us like~ much~TREAD.ABOUT⁽ᵛ⁾~ing⁽ᵐᵖ⁾ AT the~LAND **42:31** and~we~will~SAY⁽ᵛ⁾ TO~ him BASE~s WE NOT we~did~EXIST⁽ᵛ⁾ much~TREAD.ABOUT⁽ᵛ⁾~ ing⁽ᵐᵖ⁾ **42:32** TWO TEN WE BROTHER~s SON~s FATHER~us the~UNIT WITHOUT~him and~the~SMALL the~DAY AT FATHER~us in~LAND Kena'an **42:33** and~he~will~SAY⁽ᵛ⁾ TO~us the~MAN LORD~s the~LAND in~ THIS I~will~KNOW⁽ᵛ⁾ GIVEN.THAT BASE~s YOU⁽ᵐᵖ⁾ BROTHER~you⁽ᵐᵖ⁾ the~ UNIT !⁽ᵐᵖ⁾~make~REST⁽ᵛ⁾ AT~me and~AT FAMINE HOUSE~s~you⁽ᵐᵖ⁾ !⁽ᵐᵖ⁾~ TAKE⁽ᵛ⁾ and~!⁽ᵐᵖ⁾~WALK⁽ᵛ⁾ **42:34** and~!⁽ᵐᵖ⁾~make~COME⁽ᵛ⁾ AT BROTHER~ you⁽ᵐᵖ⁾ the~SMALL TO~me and~I~will~KNOW⁽ᵛ⁾~& GIVEN.THAT NOT much~ TREAD.ABOUT⁽ᵛ⁾~ing⁽ᵐᵖ⁾ YOU⁽ᵐᵖ⁾ GIVEN.THAT BASE~s YOU⁽ᵐᵖ⁾ AT BROTHER~ you⁽ᵐᵖ⁾ I~will~GIVE⁽ᵛ⁾ to~you⁽ᵐᵖ⁾ and~AT the~LAND you⁽ᵐᵖ⁾~will~ TRADE⁽ᵛ⁾ **42:35** and~he~will~EXIST⁽ᵛ⁾ THEY⁽ᵐ⁾ make~DRAW.OUT⁽ᵛ⁾~ing⁽ᵐᵖ⁾ SACK~s~them⁽ᵐ⁾ and~LOOK MAN POUCH SILVER~him in~SACK~him and~ they⁽ᵐ⁾~will~SEE⁽ᵛ⁾ AT POUCH~s SILVER~s~them⁽ᵐ⁾ THEY⁽ᵐ⁾ and~FATHER~ them⁽ᵐ⁾ and~they⁽ᵐ⁾~will~FEAR⁽ᵛ⁾ **42:36** and~he~will~SAY⁽ᵛ⁾ TO~them⁽ᵐ⁾ Ya'aqov FATHER~them⁽ᵐ⁾ AT~me you⁽ᵐᵖ⁾~did~much~BE.CHILDLESS⁽ᵛ⁾ Yoseph WITHOUT~him and~Shimon WITHOUT~him and~AT Binyamin you⁽ᵐᵖ⁾~will~ TAKE⁽ᵛ⁾ UPON~me they~did~EXIST⁽ᵛ⁾ ALL~them⁽ᶠ⁾ **42:37** and~he~will~SAY⁽ᵛ⁾ Re'uven TO FATHER~him to~>~SAY⁽ᵛ⁾ AT TWO SON~s~me you⁽ᵐˢ⁾~will~ make~DIE⁽ᵛ⁾ IF NOT I~will~make~COME⁽ᵛ⁾~him TO~you⁽ᵐˢ⁾ !⁽ᵐˢ⁾~GIVE⁽ᵛ⁾~& AT~him UPON HAND~me and~I I~will~make~TURN.BACK⁽ᵛ⁾~him TO~ you⁽ᵐˢ⁾ **42:38** and~he~will~SAY⁽ᵛ⁾ NOT he~will~GO.DOWN⁽ᵛ⁾ SON~me WITH~ you⁽ᵐᵖ⁾ GIVEN.THAT BROTHER~him he~did~DIE⁽ᵛ⁾ and~HE to~STRAND~him be~REMAIN⁽ᵛ⁾~ing⁽ᵐˢ⁾ and~he~did~MEET⁽ᵛ⁾~him HARM in~the~ROAD WHICH you⁽ᵐᵖ⁾~will~WALK⁽ᵛ⁾ in~her and~you⁽ᵐᵖ⁾~did~make~GO.DOWN⁽ᵛ⁾ AT GRAY-HEADED~me in~SORROW UNDERWORLD~unto

Chapter 43

43:1 and~the~HUNGER HEAVY in~the~LAND **43:2** and~he~will~EXIST$^{(V)}$ like~WHICH they~did~much~FINISH$^{(V)}$ to~>~EAT$^{(V)}$ AT the~GRAIN.SEEDS WHICH they~did~make~COME$^{(V)}$ from~Mits'rayim and~he~will~SAY$^{(V)}$ TO~them$^{(m)}$ FATHER~them$^{(m)}$!$^{(mp)}$~TURN.BACK$^{(V)}$!$^{(mp)}$~EXCHANGE$^{(V)}$ to~us SMALL.AMOUNT FOODSTUFF **43:3** and~he~will~SAY$^{(V)}$ TO~him Yehudah to~>~SAY$^{(V)}$!$^{(ms)}$~make~WRAP.AROUND$^{(V)}$ he~did~make~WRAP.AROUND$^{(V)}$ in~us the~MAN to~>~SAY$^{(V)}$ NOT you$^{(mp)}$~will~SEE$^{(V)}$ FACE~s~me EXCEPT BROTHER~you$^{(mp)}$ AT~you$^{(mp)}$ **43:4** IF THERE.IS~you$^{(ms)}$ much~SEND$^{(V)}$~ing$^{(ms)}$ AT BROTHER~us AT~us we~will~GO.DOWN$^{(V)}$~& and~we~will~EXCHANGE$^{(V)}$~& to~you$^{(ms)}$ FOODSTUFF **43:5** and~IF WITHOUT~you$^{(ms)}$ much~SEND$^{(V)}$~ing$^{(ms)}$ NOT we~will~GO.DOWN$^{(V)}$ GIVEN.THAT the~MAN he~did~SAY$^{(V)}$ TO~us NOT you$^{(mp)}$~will~SEE$^{(V)}$ FACE~s~me EXCEPT BROTHER~you$^{(mp)}$ AT~you$^{(mp)}$ **43:6** and~he~will~SAY$^{(V)}$ Yisra'eyl to~WHAT you$^{(mp)}$~did~make~BE.DYSFUNCTIONAL$^{(V)}$ to~me to~>~make~BE.FACE.TO.FACE$^{(V)}$ to~the~MAN ?~YET.AGAIN to~you$^{(mp)}$ BROTHER **43:7** and~they$^{(m)}$~will~SAY$^{(V)}$ >~INQUIRE$^{(V)}$ he~did~INQUIRE$^{(V)}$ the~MAN to~us and~to~KINDRED~us to~>~SAY$^{(V)}$?~YET.AGAIN FATHER~you$^{(mp)}$ LIVING ?~THERE.IS to~you$^{(mp)}$ BROTHER and~we~will~make~BE.FACE.TO.FACE$^{(V)}$ to~him UPON MOUTH the~WORD~s the~THESE ?~>~KNOW$^{(V)}$ we~will~KNOW$^{(V)}$ GIVEN.THAT he~will~SAY$^{(V)}$!$^{(mp)}$~make~GO.DOWN$^{(V)}$ AT BROTHER~you$^{(mp)}$ **43:8** and~he~will~SAY$^{(V)}$ Yehudah TO Yisra'eyl FATHER~him !$^{(ms)}$~SEND$^{(V)}$~& the~YOUNG.MAN AT~me and~we~will~RISE$^{(V)}$~& and~we~will~WALK$^{(V)}$~& and~we~will~LIVE$^{(V)}$ and~NOT we~will~DIE$^{(V)}$ ALSO WE ALSO YOU$^{(ms)}$ ALSO BABIES~us **43:9** I~will~BARTER$^{(V)}$~him from~HAND~me you$^{(ms)}$~will~much~SEARCH.OUT$^{(V)}$~him IF NOT I~did~make~COME$^{(V)}$~him TO~you$^{(ms)}$ and~I~did~make~LEAVE.IN.PLACE$^{(V)}$~him to~FACE~s~you$^{(ms)}$ and~I~did~FAIL$^{(V)}$ to~you$^{(ms)}$ ALL the~DAY~s **43:10** GIVEN.THAT UNLESS we~did~self~LINGER$^{(V)}$ GIVEN.THAT NOW we~did~TURN.BACK$^{(V)}$ THIS FOOTSTEP~s2 **43:11** and~he~will~SAY$^{(V)}$ TO~them$^{(m)}$ Yisra'eyl FATHER~them$^{(m)}$ IF SO THEN THIS !$^{(mp)}$~DO$^{(V)}$!$^{(mp)}$~TAKE$^{(V)}$ from~CHOICE.FRUIT the~LAND in~UTENSIL~s~you$^{(mp)}$ and~!$^{(mp)}$~make~GO.DOWN$^{(V)}$ to~the~MAN DEPOSIT SMALL.AMOUNT BALM and~SMALL.AMOUNT HONEY SPICE and~LAUDANUM PISTACHIO and~ALMOND **43:12** and~SILVER DOUBLE !$^{(mp)}$~TAKE$^{(V)}$ in~HAND~you$^{(mp)}$ and~AT the~SILVER the~be~make~TURN.BACK$^{(V)}$~ing$^{(ms)}$ in~MOUTH GRAIN.SACK~s~you$^{(mp)}$ you$^{(mp)}$~will~make~TURN.BACK$^{(V)}$ in~HAND~you$^{(mp)}$ POSSIBLY MISTAKE HE **43:13** and~AT BROTHER~you$^{(mp)}$!$^{(mp)}$~TAKE$^{(V)}$ and~!$^{(mp)}$~RISE$^{(V)}$!$^{(mp)}$~TURN.BACK$^{(V)}$ TO the~MAN **43:14** and~MIGHTY.ONE Shaddai he~will~

The Book of Genesis

GIVE$^{(v)}$ to~you$^{(mp)}$ BOWELS~s to~FACE~s the~MAN and~he~did~much~ SEND$^{(v)}$ to~you$^{(mp)}$ AT BROTHER~you$^{(mp)}$ OTHER and~AT Binyamin and~I like~ WHICH I~did~BE.CHILDLESS$^{(v)}$ I~did~BE.CHILDLESS$^{(v)}$ **43:15** and~they$^{(m)}$~ will~TAKE$^{(v)}$ the~MAN~s AT the~DEPOSIT the~THIS and~DOUBLE SILVER they~will~TAKE$^{(v)}$ in~HAND~them$^{(m)}$ and~AT Binyamin and~they$^{(m)}$~will~ RISE$^{(v)}$ and~they$^{(m)}$~will~GO.DOWN$^{(v)}$ Mits'rayim and~they$^{(m)}$~will~STAND$^{(v)}$ to~FACE~s Yoseph **43:16** and~he~will~SEE$^{(v)}$ Yoseph AT~them$^{(m)}$ AT Binyamin and~he~will~SAY$^{(v)}$ to~the~WHICH UPON HOUSE~him !$^{(ms)}$~make~ COME$^{(v)}$ AT the~MAN~s the~HOUSE~unto and~!$^{(ms)}$~BUTCHER$^{(v)}$ SLAUGHTERING and~!$^{(ms)}$~make~PREPARE$^{(v)}$ GIVEN.THAT AT~me they$^{(m)}$~ will~EAT$^{(v)}$ the~MAN~s in~the~GLISTENING~s2 **43:17** and~he~will~DO$^{(v)}$ the~MAN like~WHICH he~did~SAY$^{(v)}$ Yoseph and~he~will~make~COME$^{(v)}$ the~MAN AT the~MAN~s HOUSE~unto Yoseph **43:18** and~they$^{(m)}$~will~ FEAR$^{(v)}$ the~MAN~s GIVEN.THAT they~did~be~make~COME$^{(v)}$ HOUSE Yoseph and~they$^{(m)}$~will~SAY$^{(v)}$ UPON WORD the~SILVER the~ TURN.BACK$^{(v)}$~ing$^{(ms)}$ in~GRAIN.SACK~s~us in~the~FIRST.TIME WE be~ make~COME$^{(v)}$~ing$^{(mp)}$ to~>~self~ROLL$^{(v)}$ UPON~us and~to~>~self~FALL$^{(v)}$ UPON~us and~to~>~TAKE$^{(v)}$ AT~us to~the~SERVANT~s and~AT DONKEY~s~ us **43:19** and~they$^{(m)}$~will~DRAW.NEAR$^{(v)}$ TO the~MAN WHICH UPON HOUSE Yoseph and~they$^{(m)}$~will~much~SPEAK$^{(v)}$ TO~him OPENING the~ HOUSE **43:20** and~they$^{(m)}$~will~SAY$^{(v)}$ in~me LORD~me >~GO.DOWN$^{(v)}$ we~ did~GO.DOWN$^{(v)}$ in~the~FIRST.TIME to~>~EXCHANGE$^{(v)}$ FOODSTUFF **43:21** and~he~will~EXIST$^{(v)}$ GIVEN.THAT we~did~COME$^{(v)}$ TO the~PLACE.OF.LODGING and~we~will~OPEN$^{(v)}$~& AT GRAIN.SACK~s~us and~LOOK SILVER MAN in~MOUTH GRAIN.SACK~him SILVER~us in~ WEIGHT~him and~we~will~make~TURN.BACK$^{(v)}$ AT~him in~HAND~ us **43:22** and~SILVER OTHER we~did~make~GO.DOWN$^{(v)}$ in~HAND~us to~ >~EXCHANGE$^{(v)}$ FOODSTUFF NOT we~did~KNOW$^{(v)}$ WHO he~did~PLACE$^{(v)}$ SILVER~us in~GRAIN.SACK~s~us **43:23** and~he~will~SAY$^{(v)}$ COMPLETENESS to~you$^{(mp)}$ DO.NOT you$^{(mp)}$~will~FEAR$^{(v)}$ Elohiym~you$^{(mp)}$ and~Elohiym FATHER~you$^{(mp)}$ he~did~GIVE$^{(v)}$ to~you$^{(mp)}$ TREASURE in~GRAIN.SACK~s~ you$^{(mp)}$ SILVER~you$^{(mp)}$ he~did~COME$^{(v)}$ TO~me and~he~will~make~ GO.OUT$^{(v)}$ TO~them$^{(m)}$ AT Shimon **43:24** and~he~will~make~COME$^{(v)}$ the~ MAN AT the~MAN~s HOUSE~unto Yoseph and~he~will~GIVE$^{(v)}$ WATER~s2 and~they$^{(m)}$~will~BATHE$^{(v)}$ FOOT~s2~them$^{(m)}$ and~he~will~GIVE$^{(v)}$ PROVENDER to~DONKEY~s~them$^{(m)}$ **43:25** and~they$^{(m)}$~will~make~ PREPARE$^{(v)}$ AT the~DEPOSIT UNTIL !$^{(ms)}$~COME$^{(v)}$ Yoseph in~the~ GLISTENING~s2 GIVEN.THAT they~did~HEAR$^{(v)}$ GIVEN.THAT THERE they$^{(m)}$~ will~EAT$^{(v)}$ BREAD **43:26** and~he~will~COME$^{(v)}$ Yoseph the~HOUSE~unto and~they$^{(m)}$~will~make~COME$^{(v)}$ to~him AT the~DEPOSIT WHICH in~HAND~ them$^{(m)}$ the~HOUSE~unto and~they$^{(m)}$~will~self~BEND.DOWN$^{(v)}$ to~him LAND~unto **43:27** and~he~will~INQUIRE$^{(v)}$ to~them$^{(m)}$ to~COMPLETENESS and~he~will~SAY$^{(v)}$?~COMPLETENESS FATHER~you$^{(mp)}$ the~BEARD WHICH you$^{(mp)}$~did~SAY$^{(v)}$?~YET.AGAIN~him LIVING **43:28** and~they$^{(m)}$~will~SAY$^{(v)}$ COMPLETENESS to~SERVANT~you$^{(ms)}$ to~FATHER~us YET.AGAIN~him LIVING and~*they*⁽ᵐ⁾~*will*~BOW.THE.HEAD⁽ᵛ⁾ and~*he*~*will*~*self*~BEND.DOWN⁽ᵛ⁾ **43:29** and~*he*~*will*~LIFT.UP⁽ᵛ⁾ EYE~s2~him and~*he*~*will*~SEE⁽ᵛ⁾ AT Binyamin BROTHER~him SON MOTHER~him and~*he*~*will*~SAY⁽ᵛ⁾ ?~THIS BROTHER~you⁽ᵐᵖ⁾ the~SMALL WHICH *you*⁽ᵐᵖ⁾~*did*~SAY⁽ᵛ⁾ TO~me and~*he*~*will*~SAY⁽ᵛ⁾ Elohiym *he*~*will*~PROVIDE.PROTECTION⁽ᵛ⁾~*you*⁽ᵐˢ⁾ SON~me **43:30** and~*he*~*will*~*much*~HURRY⁽ᵛ⁾ Yoseph GIVEN.THAT *they*~*will*~*be*~BURN.BLACK⁽ᵛ⁾ BOWELS~s~him TO BROTHER~him and~*he*~*will*~*much*~SEARCH.OUT⁽ᵛ⁾ to~>~WEEP⁽ᵛ⁾ and~*he*~*will*~COME⁽ᵛ⁾ the~CHAMBER~unto and~*he*~*will*~WEEP⁽ᵛ⁾ THERE~unto **43:31** and~*he*~*will*~BATHE⁽ᵛ⁾ FACE~s~him and~*he*~*will*~GO.OUT⁽ᵛ⁾ and~*he*~*will*~*self*~HOLD.BACK⁽ᵛ⁾ and~*he*~*will*~SAY⁽ᵛ⁾ !⁽ᵐᵖ⁾~PLACE⁽ᵛ⁾ BREAD **43:32** and~*they*⁽ᵐ⁾~*will*~PLACE⁽ᵛ⁾ to~him to~STRAND~him and~to~them⁽ᵐ⁾ to~STRAND~them⁽ᵐ⁾ and~to~Mits'rayim~s the~EAT⁽ᵛ⁾~*ing*⁽ᵐᵖ⁾ AT~him to~STRAND~them⁽ᵐ⁾ GIVEN.THAT NOT *they*⁽ᵐ⁾~*will*~BE.ABLE⁽ᵛ⁾~must the~Mits'rayim~s to~>~EAT⁽ᵛ⁾ AT the~Ever~s BREAD GIVEN.THAT DISGUSTING SHE to~Mits'rayim **43:33** and~*they*⁽ᵐ⁾~*will*~SETTLE⁽ᵛ⁾ to~FACE~s~him the~FIRSTBORN like~BIRTHRIGHT~him and~the~LITTLE.ONE like~YOUTHFULNESS~him and~*they*⁽ᵐ⁾~*will*~MARVEL⁽ᵛ⁾ the~MAN~s MAN TO COMPANION~him **43:34** and~*he*~*will*~LIFT.UP⁽ᵛ⁾ UPRISING~s from~AT FACE~s~him TO~them⁽ᵐ⁾ and~*she*~*will*~INCREASE⁽ᵛ⁾ UPRISING Binyamin from~UPRISING ALL~them⁽ᵐ⁾ FIVE HAND~s and~*they*⁽ᵐ⁾~*will*~GULP⁽ᵛ⁾ and~*they*⁽ᵐ⁾~*will*~BE.DRUNK⁽ᵛ⁾ WITH~him

Chapter 44

44:1 and~*he*~*will*~*much*~DIRECT⁽ᵛ⁾ AT WHICH UPON HOUSE~him to~>~SAY⁽ᵛ⁾ !⁽ᵐˢ⁾~*much*~FILL⁽ᵛ⁾ AT GRAIN.SACK~s the~MAN~s FOODSTUFF like~WHICH *they*⁽ᵐ⁾~*will*~BE.ABLE⁽ᵛ⁾~must >~LIFT.UP⁽ᵛ⁾ and~!⁽ᵐˢ⁾~PLACE⁽ᵛ⁾ SILVER MAN in~MOUTH GRAIN.SACK~him **44:2** and~AT BOWL~me BOWL the~SILVER *you*⁽ᵐˢ⁾~*will*~PLACE⁽ᵛ⁾ in~MOUTH GRAIN.SACK the~SMALL and~AT SILVER GRAIN.SEEDS~him and~*he*~*will*~DO⁽ᵛ⁾ like~WORD Yoseph WHICH *he*~*did*~*much*~SPEAK⁽ᵛ⁾ **44:3** the~MORNING LIGHT and~the~MAN~s *they*~*did*~*be*~*much*~SEND⁽ᵛ⁾ THEY⁽ᵐ⁾ and~DONKEY~s~them⁽ᵐ⁾ **44:4** THEY⁽ᵐ⁾ *they*~*did*~GO.OUT⁽ᵛ⁾ AT the~CITY NOT *they*~*did*~*make*~BE.FAR⁽ᵛ⁾ and~Yoseph *he*~*did*~SAY⁽ᵛ⁾ to~the~WHICH UPON HOUSE~him !⁽ᵐˢ⁾~RISE⁽ᵛ⁾ !⁽ᵐˢ⁾~PURSUE⁽ᵛ⁾ AFTER the~MAN~s and~*you*⁽ᵐˢ⁾~*did*~*make*~OVERTAKE⁽ᵛ⁾~them⁽ᵐ⁾ and~*you*⁽ᵐˢ⁾~*did*~SAY⁽ᵛ⁾ TO~them⁽ᵐ⁾ to~WHAT *you*⁽ᵐᵖ⁾~*did*~*much*~MAKE.RESTITUTION⁽ᵛ⁾ DYSFUNCTIONAL UNDER FUNCTIONAL **44:5** ?~NOT THIS WHICH *he*~*will*~GULP⁽ᵛ⁾ LORD~me in~him and~HE >~*much*~PREDICT⁽ᵛ⁾ *he*~*will*~*much*~PREDICT⁽ᵛ⁾ in~him *you*⁽ᵐᵖ⁾~*did*~*make*~BE.DYSFUNCTIONAL⁽ᵛ⁾ WHICH *you*⁽ᵐᵖ⁾~*did*~DO⁽ᵛ⁾ **44:6** and~*he*~*will*~*make*~OVERTAKE⁽ᵛ⁾ and~*he*~*will*~*much*~SPEAK⁽ᵛ⁾ TO~them⁽ᵐ⁾ AT the~WORD~s the~THESE **44:7** and~*they*⁽ᵐ⁾~*will*~SAY⁽ᵛ⁾ TO~him to~WHAT *he*~*will*~*much*~SPEAK⁽ᵛ⁾ LORD~me like~the~WORD~s the~THESE FAR.BE.IT to~SERVANT~s~*you*⁽ᵐˢ⁾ from~>~DO⁽ᵛ⁾ like~

The Book of Genesis

the~WORD the~THIS **44:8** THOUGH SILVER WHICH *we~did*~FIND$^{(V)}$ in~ MOUTH GRAIN.SACK~s~us *we~did~make*~TURN.BACK$^{(V)}$ TO~you$^{(ms)}$ from~ LAND Kena'an and~HOW *we~will*~STEAL$^{(V)}$ from~HOUSE LORD~s~you$^{(ms)}$ SILVER OR GOLD **44:9** WHICH *he~will~be*~FIND$^{(V)}$ AT~him from~ SERVANT~s~you$^{(ms)}$ and~*he~did*~DIE$^{(V)}$ and~ALSO WE *we~will*~EXIST$^{(V)}$ to~ LORD~me to~the~SERVANT~s **44:10** and~*he~will*~SAY$^{(V)}$ ALSO NOW like~ WORD~s~you$^{(mp)}$ SO HE WHICH *he~will~be*~FIND$^{(V)}$ AT~him *he~will*~EXIST$^{(V)}$ to~me SERVANT and~YOU$^{(mp)}$ *you$^{(mp)}$~will*~EXIST$^{(V)}$ INNOCENT~s **44:11** and~ *they$^{(m)}$~will~much*~HURRY$^{(V)}$ and~*they$^{(m)}$~will~make*~GO.DOWN$^{(V)}$ MAN AT GRAIN.SACK~him LAND~unto and~*they$^{(m)}$~will*~OPEN$^{(V)}$ MAN GRAIN.SACK~ him **44:12** and~*he~will~much*~SEARCH$^{(V)}$ in~the~GREAT *he~did~make*~ DRILL$^{(V)}$ and~in~the~SMALL *he~did~much*~FINISH$^{(V)}$ and~*he~will~be*~FIND$^{(V)}$ the~BOWL in~GRAIN.SACK Binyamin **44:13** and~*they$^{(m)}$~will*~TEAR$^{(V)}$ APPAREL~s~them$^{(m)}$ and~*he~will*~LOAD$^{(V)}$ MAN UPON DONKEY~him and~ *they$^{(m)}$~will*~TURN.BACK$^{(V)}$ the~CITY~unto **44:14** and~*he~will*~COME$^{(V)}$ Yehudah and~BROTHER~s~him HOUSE~unto Yoseph and~HE YET.AGAIN~ him THERE and~*they$^{(m)}$~will*~FALL$^{(V)}$ to~FACE~s~him LAND~unto **44:15** and~ *he~will*~SAY$^{(V)}$ to~them$^{(m)}$ Yoseph WHAT the~WORK the~THIS WHICH *you$^{(mp)}$~did*~DO$^{(V)}$?~NOT *you$^{(mp)}$~did*~KNOW$^{(V)}$ GIVEN.THAT >~*much*~ PREDICT$^{(V)}$ *he~will~much*~PREDICT$^{(V)}$ MAN WHICH like~THAT.ONE~ me **44:16** and~*he~will*~SAY$^{(V)}$ Yehudah WHAT *we~will*~SAY$^{(V)}$ to~LORD~me WHAT *we~will~much*~SPEAK$^{(V)}$ and~WHAT *we~will~self*~BE.STEADFAST$^{(V)}$ the~Elohiym *he~did*~FIND$^{(V)}$ AT TWISTEDNESS SERVANT~s~you$^{(ms)}$ LOOK~us SERVANT~s to~LORD~me ALSO WE ALSO WHICH *he~did~be*~FIND$^{(V)}$ the~ BOWL in~HAND~him **44:17** and~*he~will*~SAY$^{(V)}$ FAR.BE.IT to~me from~>~ DO$^{(V)}$ THIS the~MAN WHICH *he~did~be*~FIND$^{(V)}$ the~BOWL in~HAND~him HE *he~will*~EXIST$^{(V)}$ to~me SERVANT and~YOU$^{(mp)}$ *!$^{(mp)}$*~GO.UP$^{(V)}$ to~ COMPLETENESS TO FATHER~you$^{(mp)}$ **44:18** and~*he~will*~DRAW.NEAR$^{(V)}$ TO~ him Yehudah and~*he~will*~SAY$^{(V)}$ in~me LORD~me *he~will~much*~SPEAK$^{(V)}$ PLEASE SERVANT~you$^{(ms)}$ WORD in~EAR~s2 LORD~me and~DO.NOT *he~will*~ FLARE.UP$^{(V)}$ NOSE~you$^{(ms)}$ in~SERVANT~you$^{(ms)}$ GIVEN.THAT like~THAT.ONE~ you$^{(ms)}$ like~Paroh **44:19** LORD~me *he~did*~INQUIRE$^{(V)}$ AT SERVANT~s~him to~>~*SAY$^{(V)}$* ?~THERE.IS to~you$^{(mp)}$ FATHER OR BROTHER **44:20** and~*we~ will*~SAY$^{(V)}$ TO LORD~me THERE.IS to~us FATHER BEARD and~BOY EXTREME.OLD.AGE~s SMALL and~BROTHER~him *he~did*~DIE$^{(V)}$ and~*he~ will~be*~LEAVE.BEHIND$^{(V)}$ HE to~STRAND~him to~MOTHER~him and~ FATHER~him *he~did*~LOVE$^{(V)}$~him **44:21** and~*she~will*~SAY$^{(V)}$ TO SERVANT~s~you$^{(ms)}$ *!$^{(mp)}$~make*~GO.DOWN$^{(V)}$~him TO~me and~*I~will*~ PLACE$^{(V)}$~& EYE~me UPON~him **44:22** and~*we~will*~SAY$^{(V)}$ TO LORD~me NOT *he~will*~BE.ABLE$^{(V)}$ the~YOUNG.MAN to~>~LEAVE$^{(V)}$ AT FATHER~him and~*he~did*~LEAVE$^{(V)}$ AT FATHER~him and~*he~did*~DIE$^{(V)}$ **44:23** and~*she~ will*~SAY$^{(V)}$ TO SERVANT~s~you$^{(ms)}$ IF NOT *he~will*~GO.DOWN$^{(V)}$ BROTHER~ you$^{(mp)}$ the~SMALL AT~you$^{(mp)}$ NOT *you$^{(mp)}$~will~make*~ADD$^{(V)}$~must to~>~ SEE$^{(V)}$ FACE~s~me **44:24** and~*he~will*~EXIST$^{(V)}$ GIVEN.THAT *we~did*~GO.UP$^{(V)}$ TO SERVANT~you$^{(ms)}$ FATHER~me and~*we~will~make*~BE.FACE.TO.FACE$^{(V)}$

to~him AT WORD~s LORD~me **44:25** and~*he~will*~SAY⁽ᵛ⁾ FATHER~us *!*⁽ᵐᵖ⁾~TURN.BACK⁽ᵛ⁾ *!*⁽ᵐᵖ⁾~EXCHANGE⁽ᵛ⁾ to~us SMALL.AMOUNT FOODSTUFF **44:26** and~*we~will*~SAY⁽ᵛ⁾ NOT *we~will*~BE.ABLE⁽ᵛ⁾ to~>~GO.DOWN⁽ᵛ⁾ IF THERE.IS BROTHER~us the~SMALL AT~us and~*we~will*~GO.DOWN⁽ᵛ⁾ GIVEN.THAT NOT *we~will*~BE.ABLE⁽ᵛ⁾ to~>~SEE⁽ᵛ⁾ FACE~s the~MAN and~BROTHER~us the~SMALL WITHOUT~him AT~us **44:27** and~*he~will*~SAY⁽ᵛ⁾ SERVANT~you⁽ᵐˢ⁾ FATHER~me TO~us YOU⁽ᵐᵖ⁾ *you*⁽ᵐᵖ⁾~*did*~KNOW⁽ᵛ⁾ GIVEN.THAT TWO *she~did*~BRING.FORTH⁽ᵛ⁾ to~me WOMAN~me **44:28** and~*he~will*~GO.OUT⁽ᵛ⁾ the~UNIT from~AT~me and~*I~will*~SAY⁽ᵛ⁾ SURELY >~TEAR.INTO.PIECES⁽ᵛ⁾ *he~did~be~much*~TEAR.INTO.PIECES⁽ᵛ⁾ and~NOT *I~did*~SEE⁽ᵛ⁾~him UNTIL TO.THIS.POINT **44:29** and~*you*⁽ᵐᵖ⁾~*did*~TAKE⁽ᵛ⁾ ALSO AT THIS from~WITH FACE~s~me and~*he~did*~MEET⁽ᵛ⁾~him HARM and~*you*⁽ᵐᵖ⁾~*did~make*~GO.DOWN⁽ᵛ⁾ AT GRAY-HEADED~me in~DYSFUNCTIONAL UNDERWORLD~unto **44:30** and~NOW like~>~COME⁽ᵛ⁾~me TO SERVANT~you⁽ᵐˢ⁾ FATHER~me and~the~YOUNG.MAN WITHOUT~him AT~us and~SOUL~him TIE⁽ᵛ⁾~*ed*⁽ᶠˢ⁾ in~SOUL~him **44:31** and~*he~did*~EXIST⁽ᵛ⁾ like~>~SEE⁽ᵛ⁾~him GIVEN.THAT WITHOUT the~YOUNG.MAN and~*he~did*~DIE⁽ᵛ⁾ and~*!*⁽ᵐᵖ⁾~*make*~GO.DOWN⁽ᵛ⁾ SERVANT~s~you⁽ᵐˢ⁾ AT GRAY-HEADED SERVANT~you⁽ᵐˢ⁾ FATHER~us in~SORROW UNDERWORLD~unto **44:32** GIVEN.THAT SERVANT~you⁽ᵐˢ⁾ *he~did*~BARTER⁽ᵛ⁾ AT the~YOUNG.MAN from~WITH FATHER~me to~>~SAY⁽ᵛ⁾ IF NOT *I~will~make*~COME⁽ᵛ⁾~him TO~you⁽ᵐˢ⁾ and~*I~did*~FAIL⁽ᵛ⁾ to~FATHER~me ALL the~DAY~s **44:33** and~NOW *he~will*~SETTLE⁽ᵛ⁾ PLEASE SERVANT~you⁽ᵐˢ⁾ UNDER the~YOUNG.MAN SERVANT to~LORD~me and~the~YOUNG.MAN *he~will*~GO.UP⁽ᵛ⁾ WITH BROTHER~s~him **44:34** GIVEN.THAT HOW *I~will*~GO.UP⁽ᵛ⁾ TO FATHER~me and~the~YOUNG.MAN WITHOUT~him AT~me OTHERWISE *I~will*~SEE⁽ᵛ⁾ in~the~DYSFUNCTIONAL WHICH *he~will*~FIND⁽ᵛ⁾ AT FATHER~me

Chapter 45

45:1 and~NOT *he~did*~BE.ABLE⁽ᵛ⁾ Yoseph to~>~*self*~HOLD.BACK⁽ᵛ⁾ to~ALL the~*be*~STAND.UP⁽ᵛ⁾~*ing*⁽ᵐᵖ⁾ UPON~him and~*he~will*~CALL.OUT⁽ᵛ⁾ *!*⁽ᵐᵖ⁾~*make*~GO.OUT⁽ᵛ⁾ ALL MAN from~UPON~me and~NOT *he~did*~STAND⁽ᵛ⁾ MAN AT~him in~>~*self*~KNOW⁽ᵛ⁾ Yoseph TO BROTHER~s~him **45:2** and~*he~will*~GIVE⁽ᵛ⁾ AT VOICE~him in~WEEPING and~*they*⁽ᵐ⁾~*will*~HEAR⁽ᵛ⁾ Mits'rayim and~*he~will*~HEAR⁽ᵛ⁾ HOUSE Paroh **45:3** and~*he~will*~SAY⁽ᵛ⁾ Yoseph TO BROTHER~s~him I Yoseph ?~YET.AGAIN FATHER~me LIVING and~NOT *they~did*~BE.ABLE⁽ᵛ⁾ BROTHER~s~him to~>~ANSWER⁽ᵛ⁾ AT~him GIVEN.THAT *they~did~be*~STIR⁽ᵛ⁾ from~FACE~s~him **45:4** and~*he~will*~SAY⁽ᵛ⁾ Yoseph TO BROTHER~s~him *!*⁽ᵐᵖ⁾~DRAW.NEAR⁽ᵛ⁾ PLEASE TO~me and~*they*⁽ᵐ⁾~*will*~DRAW.NEAR⁽ᵛ⁾ and~*he~will*~SAY⁽ᵛ⁾ I Yoseph BROTHER~you⁽ᵐᵖ⁾ WHICH *you*⁽ᵐᵖ⁾~*did*~SELL⁽ᵛ⁾ AT~me Mits'rayim~unto **45:5** and~NOW DO.NOT *you*$^{(mp)}$~will~be~DISTRESS$^{(V)}$ and~DO.NOT *he*~will~FLARE.UP$^{(V)}$ in~EYE~s2~ *you*$^{(mp)}$ GIVEN.THAT *you*$^{(mp)}$~did~SELL$^{(V)}$ AT~me TO.THIS.POINT GIVEN.THAT to~REVIVING *he*~did~SEND$^{(V)}$~me Elohiym to~FACE~s~ *you*$^{(mp)}$ **45:6** GIVEN.THAT THIS YEAR~s2 the~HUNGER in~INSIDE the~LAND and~YET.AGAIN FIVE YEAR~s WHICH WITHOUT PLOWING and~ HARVEST **45:7** and~*he*~will~SEND$^{(V)}$~me Elohiym to~FACE~s~*you*$^{(mp)}$ to~>~ PLACE$^{(V)}$ to~*you*$^{(mp)}$ REMNANT in~the~LAND and~to~>~*make*~LIVE$^{(V)}$ to~ *you*$^{(mp)}$ to~ESCAPED GREAT **45:8** and~NOW NOT YOU$^{(mp)}$ *you*$^{(mp)}$~did~ SEND$^{(V)}$ AT~me TO.THIS.POINT GIVEN.THAT the~Elohiym and~*he*~will~ PLACE$^{(V)}$~me to~FATHER to~Paroh and~to~LORD to~ALL HOUSE~him and~ REGULATE$^{(V)}$~*ing*$^{(ms)}$ in~ALL LAND Mits'rayim **45:9** !$^{(mp)}$~*much*~HURRY$^{(V)}$ and~!$^{(mp)}$~GO.UP$^{(V)}$ TO FATHER~me and~*you*$^{(mp)}$~did~SAY$^{(V)}$ TO~him IN.THIS.WAY *he*~did~SAY$^{(V)}$ SON~*you*$^{(ms)}$ Yoseph *he*~did~PLACE$^{(V)}$~me Elohiym to~LORD to~ALL Mits'rayim !$^{(ms)}$~GO.DOWN$^{(V)}$~& TO~me DO.NOT *you*$^{(ms)}$~will~STAND$^{(V)}$ **45:10** and~*you*$^{(ms)}$~did~SETTLE$^{(V)}$ in~LAND Goshen and~*you*$^{(ms)}$~did~EXIST$^{(V)}$ NEAR TO~me YOU$^{(ms)}$ and~SON~s~*you*$^{(ms)}$ and~ SON~s SON~s~*you*$^{(ms)}$ and~FLOCKS~*you*$^{(ms)}$ and~CATTLE~*you*$^{(ms)}$ and~ALL WHICH to~*you*$^{(fs)}$ **45:11** and~*I*~did~*much*~SUSTAIN$^{(V)}$ AT~*you*$^{(ms)}$ THERE GIVEN.THAT YET.AGAIN FIVE YEAR~s HUNGER OTHERWISE *you*$^{(ms)}$~will~be~ POSSESS$^{(V)}$ YOU$^{(ms)}$ and~HOUSE~*you*$^{(ms)}$ and~ALL WHICH to~ *you*$^{(fs)}$ **45:12** and~LOOK EYE~s2~*you*$^{(mp)}$ SEE$^{(V)}$~*ing*$^{(fp)}$ and~EYE~s2 BROTHER~ me Binyamin GIVEN.THAT MOUTH~me the~*much*~SPEAK$^{(V)}$~*ing*$^{(ms)}$ TO~ *you*$^{(mp)}$ **45:13** and~*you*$^{(mp)}$~did~*make*~BE.FACE.TO.FACE$^{(V)}$ to~FATHER~me AT ALL ARMAMENT~me in~Mits'rayim and~AT ALL WHICH *you*$^{(mp)}$~did~ SEE$^{(V)}$ and~*you*$^{(mp)}$~did~*much*~HURRY$^{(V)}$ and~*you*$^{(mp)}$~did~*make*~GO.DOWN$^{(V)}$ AT FATHER~me TO.THIS.POINT **45:14** and~*he*~will~FALL$^{(V)}$ UPON BACK.OF.THE.NECK~s Binyamin BROTHER~him and~*he*~will~WEEP$^{(V)}$ and~ Binyamin *he*~did~WEEP$^{(V)}$ UPON BACK.OF.THE.NECK~s~him **45:15** and~*he*~ will~*much*~KISS$^{(V)}$ to~ALL BROTHER~s~him and~*he*~will~WEEP$^{(V)}$ UPON~ them$^{(m)}$ and~AFTER SO *they*~did~*much*~SPEAK$^{(V)}$ BROTHER~s~him AT~ him **45:16** and~the~VOICE *he*~will~be~HEAR$^{(V)}$ HOUSE Paroh to~>~SAY$^{(V)}$ *they*~did~COME$^{(V)}$ BROTHER~s Yoseph and~*he*~will~DO.WELL$^{(V)}$ in~EYE~s2 Paroh and~in~EYE~s2 SERVANT~s~him **45:17** and~*he*~will~SAY$^{(V)}$ Paroh TO Yoseph !$^{(ms)}$~SAY$^{(V)}$ TO BROTHER~s~*you*$^{(ms)}$ THIS !$^{(mp)}$~DO$^{(V)}$!$^{(mp)}$~PACK$^{(V)}$ AT CATTLE~*you*$^{(mp)}$ and~ !$^{(mp)}$~WALK$^{(V)}$!$^{(mp)}$~COME$^{(V)}$ LAND~unto Kena'an **45:18** and~ !$^{(mp)}$~TAKE$^{(V)}$ AT FATHER~*you*$^{(mp)}$ and~AT HOUSE~s~ *you*$^{(mp)}$ and~ !$^{(mp)}$~COME$^{(V)}$ TO~me and~*I*~will~GIVE$^{(V)}$~& to~*you*$^{(mp)}$ AT FUNCTIONAL LAND Mits'rayim and~ !$^{(mp)}$~EAT$^{(V)}$ AT FAT the~ LAND **45:19** and~YOU$^{(ms)}$ *you*$^{(ms)}$~did~be~*much*~DIRECT$^{(V)}$~& THIS !$^{(mp)}$~DO$^{(V)}$!$^{(mp)}$~TAKE$^{(V)}$ to~*you*$^{(mp)}$ from~LAND Mits'rayim CART~s to~BABIES~*you*$^{(mp)}$ and~to~WOMAN~s~*you*$^{(mp)}$ and~*you*$^{(mp)}$~did~LIFT.UP$^{(V)}$ AT FATHER~*you*$^{(mp)}$ and~*you*$^{(mp)}$~did~COME$^{(V)}$ **45:20** and~EYE~s2~*you*$^{(mp)}$ DO.NOT *you*$^{(ms)}$~will~ SPARE$^{(V)}$ UPON UTENSIL~s~*you*$^{(mp)}$ GIVEN.THAT FUNCTIONAL ALL LAND Mits'rayim to~*you*$^{(mp)}$ HE **45:21** and~*they*$^{(m)}$~will~DO$^{(V)}$ SO SON~s Yisra'eyl and~*he*~will~GIVE$^{(V)}$ to~them$^{(m)}$ Yoseph CART~s UPON MOUTH Paroh and~

he~will~GIVE⁽ⱽ⁾ to~them⁽ᵐ⁾ PROVISIONS to~the~ROAD **45:22** to~ALL~ them⁽ᵐ⁾ *he~did*~GIVE⁽ⱽ⁾ to~the~MAN REPLACEMENT~s APPAREL~s and~to~ Binyamin *he~did*~GIVE⁽ⱽ⁾ THREE HUNDRED~s SILVER and~FIVE REPLACEMENT~s APPAREL~s **45:23** and~to~FATHER~him *he~did*~SEND⁽ⱽ⁾ like~THIS TEN DONKEY~s LIFT.UP⁽ⱽ⁾~*ing*⁽ᵐᵖ⁾ from~FUNCTIONAL Mits'rayim and~TEN SHE-DONKEY~s LIFT.UP⁽ⱽ⁾~*ing*⁽ᶠᵖ⁾ GRAIN and~BREAD and~MEAT to~ FATHER~him to~the~ROAD **45:24** and~*he~will*~much~SEND⁽ⱽ⁾ AT BROTHER~s~him and~*they*⁽ᵐ⁾~*will*~WALK⁽ⱽ⁾ and~*he~will*~SAY⁽ⱽ⁾ TO~them⁽ᵐ⁾ DO.NOT *you*⁽ᵐᵖ⁾*~will*~SHAKE⁽ⱽ⁾ in~the~ROAD **45:25** and~*they*⁽ᵐ⁾*~will*~ GO.UP⁽ⱽ⁾ from~Mits'rayim and~*they*⁽ᵐ⁾*~will*~COME⁽ⱽ⁾ LAND Kena'an TO Ya'aqov FATHER~them⁽ᵐ⁾ **45:26** and~*they*⁽ᵐ⁾*~will*~make~BE.FACE.TO.FACE⁽ⱽ⁾ to~him to~>~SAY⁽ⱽ⁾ YET.AGAIN Yoseph LIVING and~GIVEN.THAT HE REGULATE⁽ⱽ⁾~*ing*⁽ᵐˢ⁾ in~ALL LAND Mits'rayim and~*he~will*~BE.NUMB⁽ⱽ⁾ HEART~him GIVEN.THAT NOT *he~did*~make~SECURE⁽ⱽ⁾ to~ them⁽ᵐ⁾ **45:27** and~*they*⁽ᵐ⁾*~will*~much~SPEAK⁽ⱽ⁾ TO~him AT ALL WORD~s Yoseph WHICH *he~did*~much~SPEAK⁽ⱽ⁾ TO~them⁽ᵐ⁾ and~*he~will*~SEE⁽ⱽ⁾ AT the~CART~s WHICH *he~did*~SEND⁽ⱽ⁾ Yoseph to~>~LIFT.UP⁽ⱽ⁾ AT~him and~ *she~will*~LIVE⁽ⱽ⁾ WIND Ya'aqov FATHER~them⁽ᵐ⁾ **45:28** and~*he~will*~SAY⁽ⱽ⁾ Yisra'eyl ABUNDANT YET.AGAIN Yoseph SON~me LIVING *I~will*~WALK⁽ⱽ⁾~& and~*I~will*~SEE⁽ⱽ⁾~him in~BEFORE *I~will*~DIE⁽ⱽ⁾

Chapter 46

46:1 and~*he~will*~JOURNEY⁽ⱽ⁾ Yisra'eyl and~ALL WHICH to~him and~*he~ will*~COME⁽ⱽ⁾ B'er-Sheva~unto and~*he~will*~SACRIFICE⁽ⱽ⁾ SACRIFICE~s to~ Elohiym FATHER~him Yits'hhaq **46:2** and~*he~will*~SAY⁽ⱽ⁾ Elohiym to~ Yisra'eyl in~REFLECTION~s the~NIGHT and~*he~will*~SAY⁽ⱽ⁾ Ya'aqov Ya'aqov and~*he~will*~SAY⁽ⱽ⁾ LOOK~me **46:3** and~*he~will*~SAY⁽ⱽ⁾ I the~MIGHTY.ONE Elohiym FATHER~you⁽ᵐˢ⁾ DO.NOT *you*⁽ᵐˢ⁾*~will*~FEAR⁽ⱽ⁾ from~>~GO.DOWN⁽ⱽ⁾ Mits'rayim~unto GIVEN.THAT to~NATION GREAT *I~will*~PLACE⁽ⱽ⁾~you⁽ᵐˢ⁾ THERE **46:4** I *I~will*~GO.DOWN⁽ⱽ⁾ WITH~you⁽ᵐˢ⁾ Mits'rayim~unto and~I *I~ will*~make~GO.UP⁽ⱽ⁾~you⁽ᵐˢ⁾ ALSO >~GO.UP⁽ⱽ⁾ and~Yoseph *he~will*~ SET.DOWN⁽ⱽ⁾ HAND~him UPON EYE~s2~you⁽ᵐˢ⁾ **46:5** and~*he~will*~RISE⁽ⱽ⁾ Ya'aqov from~B'er-Sheva and~*they*⁽ᵐ⁾*~will*~LIFT.UP⁽ⱽ⁾ SON~s Yisra'eyl AT Ya'aqov FATHER~them⁽ᵐ⁾ and~AT BABIES~them⁽ᵐ⁾ and~AT WOMAN~s~ them⁽ᵐ⁾ in~the~CART~s WHICH *he~did*~SEND⁽ⱽ⁾ Paroh to~>~LIFT.UP⁽ⱽ⁾ AT~ him **46:6** and~*they*⁽ᵐ⁾*~will*~TAKE⁽ⱽ⁾ AT LIVESTOCK~s~them⁽ᵐ⁾ and~AT GOODS~them⁽ᵐ⁾ WHICH *they~did*~ACCUMULATE⁽ⱽ⁾ in~LAND Kena'an and~ *they*⁽ᵐ⁾*~will*~COME⁽ⱽ⁾ Mits'rayim~unto Ya'aqov and~ALL SEED~him AT~ him **46:7** SON~s~him and~SON~s SON~s~him AT~him DAUGHTER~s~him and~DAUGHTER~s SON~s~him and~ALL SEED~him *he~did*~make~COME⁽ⱽ⁾ AT~him Mits'rayim~unto **46:8** and~THESE TITLE~s SON~s Yisra'eyl the~ COME⁽ⱽ⁾~*ing*⁽ᵐᵖ⁾ Mits'rayim~unto Ya'aqov and~SON~s~him FIRSTBORN

The Book of Genesis

Ya'aqov Re'uven **46:9** and~SON~s Re'uven Hhanokh and~Palu and~
Hhetsron and~Karmi **46:10** and~SON~s Shimon Yemu'el and~Yamin and~
Ohad and~Yakhin and~Tsohhar and~Sha'ul SON the~Kena'an~s **46:11** and~
SON~s Lewi Gershon Qehat and~Merari **46:12** and~SON~s Yehudah Eyr
and~Onan and~Sheylah and~Perets and~Zerahh and~*he~will~*DIE^(V) Eyr
and~Onan in~LAND Kena'an and~*they*^(m)~*will~*EXIST^(V) SON~s Perets and~
Hhetsron and~Hhamul **46:13** and~SON~s Yis'sas'khar Tola and~Pu'a and~
Yov and~Shimron **46:14** and~SON~s Zevulun Sered and~Eylon and~
Yahh'le'el **46:15** THESE SON~s Le'ah WHICH *she~did~*BRING.FORTH^(V) to~
Ya'aqov in~Padan-Aram and~AT Dinah DAUGHTER~him ALL SOUL SON~s~
him and~DAUGHTER~s~him THREE~s and~THREE **46:16** and~SON~s Gad
Tsiphyon and~Hhagi Shuni and~Etsbon Eyriy and~Arodiy and~
Areliy **46:17** and~SON~s Asher Yimnah and~Yishwah and~Yishwiy and~
Beri'ah and~Serahh SISTER~them^(m) and~SON~s Beri'ah Hhever and~
Malki'el **46:18** THESE SON~s Zilpah WHICH *he~did~*GIVE^(V) Lavan to~Le'ah
DAUGHTER~him and~*she~will~*BRING.FORTH^(V) AT THESE to~Ya'aqov SIX
TEN SOUL **46:19** SON~s Rahhel WOMAN Ya'aqov Yoseph and~
Binyamin **46:20** and~*he~will~be~*BRING.FORTH^(V) to~Yoseph in~LAND
Mits'rayim WHICH *she~did~*BRING.FORTH^(V) to~him Asnat DAUGHTER
Potee-Phera ADMINISTRATOR On AT Menasheh and~AT
Ephrayim **46:21** and~SON~s Binyamin Bela and~Bekher and~Ashbeyl Gera
and~Na'aman Eyhhiy and~Rosh Mupim and~Hhupim and~Ard **46:22** THESE
SON~s Rahhel WHICH BRING.FORTH^(V)~*ed*^(ms) to~Ya'aqov ALL SOUL FOUR
TEN **46:23** and~SON~s Dan Hhush~s **46:24** and~SON~s Naphtali Yahhtse'el
and~Guni and~Yetser and~Shilem **46:25** THESE SON~s Bilhah WHICH *he~
did~*GIVE^(V) Lavan to~Rahhel DAUGHTER~him and~*she~will~*BRING.FORTH^(V)
AT THESE to~Ya'aqov ALL SOUL SEVEN **46:26** ALL the~SOUL the~COME^(V)~
ing^(fs) to~Ya'aqov Mits'rayim~unto GO.OUT^(V)~*ing*^(mp) MIDSECTION~him
from~to~STRAND WOMAN~s SON~s Ya'aqov ALL SOUL SIX~s and~
SIX **46:27** and~SON~s Yoseph WHICH BRING.FORTH^(V)~*ed*^(ms) to~him in~
Mits'rayim SOUL TWO ALL the~SOUL to~HOUSE Ya'aqov the~COME^(V)~*ing*^(fs)
Mits'rayim~unto SEVEN~s **46:28** and~AT Yehudah *he~did~*SEND^(V) to~
FACE~s~him TO Yoseph to~>~*make~*THROW^(V) to~FACE~s~him Goshen~
unto and~*they*^(m)~*will~*COME^(V) LAND~unto Goshen **46:29** and~*he~will~*
TIE.UP^(V) Yoseph CHARIOT~him and~*he~will~make~*GO.UP^(V) to~>~MEET^(V)
Yisra'eyl FATHER~him Goshen~unto and~*he~will~be~*SEE^(V) TO~him and~
*he~will~*FALL^(V) UPON BACK.OF.THE.NECK~s~him and~*he~will~*WEEP^(V)
UPON BACK.OF.THE.NECK~s~him YET.AGAIN **46:30** and~*he~will~*SAY^(V)
Yisra'eyl TO Yoseph *I~will~*DIE^(V)~& the~FOOTSTEP AFTER >~SEE^(V)~me AT
FACE~s~you^(ms) GIVEN.THAT YET.AGAIN~you^(ms) LIVING **46:31** and~*he~will~*
SAY^(V) Yoseph TO BROTHER~s~him and~TO HOUSE FATHER~him *I~will~*
GO.UP^(V) and~*I~will~make~*BE.FACE.TO.FACE^(V)~& to~Paroh and~*I~will~*
SAY^(V)~& TO~him BROTHER~s~me and~HOUSE FATHER~me WHICH in~LAND
Kena'an *they~did~*COME^(V) TO~me **46:32** and~the~MAN~s FEED^(V)~*ing*^(mp)
FLOCKS GIVEN.THAT MAN~s LIVESTOCK *they~did~*EXIST^(V) and~FLOCKS~

them⁽ᵐ⁾ and~CATTLE~them⁽ᵐ⁾ and~ALL WHICH to~them⁽ᵐ⁾ *they~did~make~* COME⁽ᵛ⁾ **46:33** and~*he~did~*EXIST⁽ᵛ⁾ GIVEN.THAT *he~will~*CALL.OUT⁽ᵛ⁾ to~ you⁽ᵐᵖ⁾ Paroh and~*he~did~*SAY⁽ᵛ⁾ WHAT WORK~s~you⁽ᵐᵖ⁾ **46:34** and~ *you⁽ᵐᵖ⁾~did~*SAY⁽ᵛ⁾ MAN~s LIVESTOCK *they~did~*EXIST⁽ᵛ⁾ SERVANT~s~you⁽ᵐˢ⁾ from~YOUNG.AGE~s~us and~UNTIL NOW ALSO WE ALSO FATHER~s~us in~ the~CROSS.OVER⁽ᵛ⁾~*ed⁽ᵐˢ⁾ you⁽ᵐᵖ⁾~will~*SETTLE⁽ᵛ⁾ in~LAND Goshen GIVEN.THAT DISGUSTING Mits'rayim ALL FEED⁽ᵛ⁾~*ing⁽ᵐˢ⁾* FLOCKS

Chapter 47

47:1 and~*he~will~*COME⁽ᵛ⁾ Yoseph and~*he~will~make~*BE.FACE.TO.FACE⁽ᵛ⁾ to~Paroh and~*he~will~*SAY⁽ᵛ⁾ FATHER~me and~BROTHER~s~me and~ FLOCKS~them⁽ᵐ⁾ and~CATTLE~them⁽ᵐ⁾ and~ALL WHICH to~them⁽ᵐ⁾ *they~ did~*COME⁽ᵛ⁾ from~LAND Kena'an and~LOOK~them⁽ᵐ⁾ in~LAND Goshen **47:2** and~from~EXTREMITY BROTHER~s~him *he~did~*TAKE⁽ᵛ⁾ FIVE MAN~s and~*he~will~make~*LEAVE.IN.PLACE⁽ᵛ⁾~them⁽ᵐ⁾ to~FACE~s Paroh **47:3** and~*he~will~*SAY⁽ᵛ⁾ Paroh TO BROTHER~s~him WHAT WORK~s~ you⁽ᵐᵖ⁾ and~*they⁽ᵐ⁾~will~*SAY⁽ᵛ⁾ TO Paroh FEED⁽ᵛ⁾~*ing⁽ᵐˢ⁾* FLOCKS SERVANT~s~you⁽ᵐˢ⁾ ALSO WE ALSO FATHER~s~us **47:4** and~*they⁽ᵐ⁾~will~* SAY⁽ᵛ⁾ TO Paroh to~>~IMMIGRATE⁽ᵛ⁾ in~the~LAND *we~did~*COME⁽ᵛ⁾ GIVEN.THAT WITHOUT FEEDING.PLACE to~the~FLOCKS WHICH to~ SERVANT~s~you⁽ᵐˢ⁾ GIVEN.THAT HEAVY the~HUNGER in~LAND Kena'an and~NOW *they⁽ᵐ⁾~will~*SETTLE⁽ᵛ⁾ PLEASE SERVANT~s~you⁽ᵐˢ⁾ in~LAND Goshen **47:5** and~*he~will~*SAY⁽ᵛ⁾ Paroh TO Yoseph to~>~SAY⁽ᵛ⁾ FATHER~ you⁽ᵐˢ⁾ and~BROTHER~s~you⁽ᵐˢ⁾ *they~did~*COME⁽ᵛ⁾ TO~you⁽ᵐˢ⁾ **47:6** LAND Mits'rayim to~FACE~s~you⁽ᵐˢ⁾ SHE in~BEST the~LAND *!⁽ᵐˢ⁾~make~*SETTLE⁽ᵛ⁾ AT FATHER~you⁽ᵐˢ⁾ and~AT BROTHER~s~you⁽ᵐˢ⁾ *they⁽ᵐ⁾~will~*SETTLE⁽ᵛ⁾ in~ LAND Goshen and~IF *you⁽ᵐˢ⁾~did~*KNOW⁽ᵛ⁾ and~THERE.IS in~them⁽ᵐ⁾ MAN~s FORCE and~*you⁽ᵐᵖ⁾~did~*PLACE⁽ᵛ⁾~them⁽ᵐ⁾ NOBLE~s LIVESTOCK UPON WHICH to~me **47:7** and~*he~will~make~*COME⁽ᵛ⁾ Yoseph AT Ya'aqov FATHER~him and~*he~will~make~*STAND⁽ᵛ⁾~him to~FACE~s Paroh and~*he~ will~much~*KNEEL⁽ᵛ⁾ Ya'aqov AT Paroh **47:8** and~*he~will~*SAY⁽ᵛ⁾ Paroh TO Ya'aqov like~WHAT DAY~s YEAR~s LIVING~s~you⁽ᵐˢ⁾ **47:9** and~*he~will~* SAY⁽ᵛ⁾ Ya'aqov TO Paroh DAY~s YEAR~s IMMIGRATION~s~me THREE~s and~ HUNDRED YEAR SMALL.AMOUNT and~DYSFUNCTIONAL~s *they~did~*EXIST⁽ᵛ⁾ DAY~s YEAR~s LIVING~s~me and~NOT *they~did~make~*OVERTAKE⁽ᵛ⁾ AT DAY~s YEAR~s LIVING~s FATHER~s~me in~DAY~s IMMIGRATION~s~ them⁽ᵐ⁾ **47:10** and~*he~will~much~*KNEEL⁽ᵛ⁾ Ya'aqov AT Paroh and~*he~will~* GO.OUT⁽ᵛ⁾ from~to~FACE~s Paroh **47:11** and~*he~will~make~*SETTLE⁽ᵛ⁾ Yoseph AT FATHER~him and~AT BROTHER~s~him and~*he~will~*GIVE⁽ᵛ⁾ to~ them⁽ᵐ⁾ HOLDINGS in~LAND Mits'rayim in~BEST the~LAND in~LAND Ra'meses like~WHICH *he~did~much~*DIRECT⁽ᵛ⁾ Paroh **47:12** and~*he~will~* SUSTAIN⁽ᵛ⁾ Yoseph AT FATHER~him and~AT BROTHER~s~him and~AT ALL

The Book of Genesis

HOUSE FATHER~him BREAD to~MOUTH the~BABIES **47:13** and~BREAD WITHOUT in~ALL the~LAND GIVEN.THAT HEAVY the~HUNGER MANY and~ *she~will*~FAINT$^{(V)}$ LAND Mits'rayim and~LAND Kena'an from~FACE~s the~ HUNGER **47:14** and~*he~will~much*~PICK.UP$^{(V)}$ Yoseph AT ALL the~SILVER the~*be*~FIND$^{(V)}$~*ing*$^{(ms)}$ in~LAND Mits'rayim and~in~LAND Kena'an in~the~ GRAIN.SEEDS WHICH THEY$^{(m)}$ EXCHANGE$^{(V)}$~*ing*$^{(mp)}$ and~*he~will~make*~ COME$^{(V)}$ Yoseph AT the~SILVER HOUSE~unto Paroh **47:15** and~*he~will*~ BE.WHOLE$^{(V)}$ the~SILVER from~LAND Mits'rayim and~from~LAND Kena'an and~*they*$^{(m)}$~*will*~COME$^{(V)}$ ALL Mits'rayim TO Yoseph to~>~SAY$^{(V)}$ *!*$^{(ms)}$~ PROVIDE$^{(V)}$~& to~us BREAD and~to~WHAT *we~will*~DIE$^{(V)}$ OPPOSITE~you$^{(ms)}$ GIVEN.THAT *he~did*~COME.TO.AN.END$^{(V)}$ SILVER **47:16** and~*he~will*~SAY$^{(V)}$ Yoseph *!*$^{(mp)}$~PROVIDE$^{(V)}$ LIVESTOCK~you$^{(mp)}$ and~*I~will*~GIVE$^{(V)}$~& to~you$^{(mp)}$ in~LIVESTOCK~you$^{(mp)}$ IF *he~did*~COME.TO.AN.END$^{(V)}$ SILVER **47:17** and~ *they*$^{(m)}$~*will~make*~COME$^{(V)}$ AT LIVESTOCK~s~them$^{(m)}$ TO Yoseph and~*he~ will*~GIVE$^{(V)}$ to~them$^{(m)}$ Yoseph BREAD in~the~HORSE~s and~in~LIVESTOCK the~FLOCKS and~in~LIVESTOCK the~CATTLE and~in~the~DONKEY~s and~ *he~will~much*~LEAD$^{(V)}$~them$^{(m)}$ in~the~BREAD in~ALL LIVESTOCK~them$^{(m)}$ in~the~YEAR the~SHE **47:18** and~*she~will*~BE.WHOLE$^{(V)}$ the~YEAR the~SHE and~*they*$^{(m)}$~*will*~COME$^{(V)}$ TO~him in~the~YEAR the~SECOND and~*they*$^{(m)}$~ *will*~SAY$^{(V)}$ to~him NOT *we~will~much*~KEEP.SECRET$^{(V)}$ from~LORD~me GIVEN.THAT IF *he~did*~BE.WHOLE$^{(V)}$ the~SILVER and~LIVESTOCK the~BEAST TO LORD~me NOT *he~did~be*~REMAIN$^{(V)}$ to~FACE~s LORD~me EXCEPT IF BODY~us and~GROUND~us **47:19** to~WHAT *we~will*~DIE$^{(V)}$ to~EYE~s2~ you$^{(ms)}$ ALSO WE ALSO GROUND~us *!*$^{(ms)}$~PURCHASE$^{(V)}$ AT~us and~AT GROUND~us in~the~BREAD and~*we~will*~EXIST$^{(V)}$ WE and~GROUND~us SERVANT~s to~Paroh and~*!*$^{(ms)}$~GIVE$^{(V)}$ SEED and~*we~will*~LIVE$^{(V)}$ and~NOT *we~will*~DIE$^{(V)}$ and~the~GROUND NOT *she~will*~DESOLATE$^{(V)}$ **47:20** and~ *he~will*~PURCHASE$^{(V)}$ Yoseph AT ALL GROUND Mits'rayim to~Paroh GIVEN.THAT *they~did*~SELL$^{(V)}$ Mits'rayim MAN FIELD~him GIVEN.THAT *he~ did*~SEIZE$^{(V)}$ UPON~them$^{(m)}$ the~HUNGER and~*she~will*~EXIST$^{(V)}$ the~LAND to~Paroh **47:21** and~AT the~PEOPLE *he~did~make*~CROSS.OVER$^{(V)}$ AT~him to~CITY~s from~EXTREMITY BORDER Mits'rayim and~UNTIL EXTREMITY~ him **47:22** ONLY GROUND the~ADMINISTRATOR~s NOT *he~did*~ PURCHASE$^{(V)}$ GIVEN.THAT CUSTOM to~the~ADMINISTRATOR~s from~AT Paroh and~*they~did*~EAT$^{(V)}$ AT CUSTOM~them$^{(m)}$ WHICH *he~did*~GIVE$^{(V)}$ to~ them$^{(m)}$ Paroh UPON SO NOT *they~did*~SELL$^{(V)}$ AT GROUND~ them$^{(m)}$ **47:23** and~*he~will*~SAY$^{(V)}$ Yoseph TO the~PEOPLE THOUGH *I~did*~ PURCHASE$^{(V)}$ AT~you$^{(mp)}$ the~DAY and~AT GROUND~you$^{(mp)}$ to~Paroh LO to~ you$^{(mp)}$ SEED and~*you*$^{(mp)}$~*did*~SOW$^{(V)}$ AT the~GROUND **47:24** and~*he~did*~ EXIST$^{(V)}$ in~the~PRODUCTION and~*you*$^{(mp)}$~*did*~GIVE$^{(V)}$ FIFTH to~Paroh and~ FOUR the~HAND~s *he~will*~EXIST$^{(V)}$ to~you$^{(mp)}$ to~SEED the~FIELD and~to~ >~EAT$^{(V)}$~you$^{(mp)}$ and~to~the~WHICH in~HOUSE~s~you$^{(mp)}$ and~to~>~EAT$^{(V)}$ to~BABIES~you$^{(mp)}$ **47:25** and~*they*$^{(m)}$~*will*~SAY$^{(V)}$ you$^{(ms)}$~*did~make*~LIVE$^{(V)}$~ us *we~will*~FIND$^{(V)}$ BEAUTY in~EYE~s2 LORD~me and~*we~did*~EXIST$^{(V)}$ SERVANT~s to~Paroh **47:26** and~*he~will*~PLACE$^{(V)}$ AT~her Yoseph to~

CUSTOM UNTIL the~DAY the~THIS UPON GROUND Mits'rayim to~Paroh to~ the~FIFTH.PART ONLY GROUND the~ADMINISTRATOR~s to~STRAND~ them⁽ᵐ⁾ NOT she~did~EXIST⁽ⱽ⁾ to~Paroh **47:27** and~he~will~SETTLE⁽ⱽ⁾ Yisra'eyl in~LAND Mits'rayim in~LAND Goshen and~they⁽ᵐ⁾~will~be~ TAKE.HOLD⁽ⱽ⁾ in~her and~they⁽ᵐ⁾~will~REPRODUCE⁽ⱽ⁾ and~they⁽ᵐ⁾~will~ INCREASE⁽ⱽ⁾ MANY **47:28** and~he~will~LIVE⁽ⱽ⁾ Ya'aqov in~LAND Mits'rayim SEVEN TEN YEAR and~he~will~EXIST⁽ⱽ⁾ DAY~s Ya'aqov YEAR~s LIVING~s~him SEVEN YEAR~s and~FOUR~s and~HUNDRED YEAR **47:29** and~they⁽ᵐ⁾~will~ COME.NEAR⁽ⱽ⁾ DAY~s Yisra'eyl to~>~DIE⁽ⱽ⁾ and~he~will~CALL.OUT⁽ⱽ⁾ to~ SON~him to~Yoseph and~he~will~SAY⁽ⱽ⁾ to~him IF PLEASE I~did~FIND⁽ⱽ⁾ BEAUTY in~EYE~s2~you⁽ᵐˢ⁾ !⁽ᵐˢ⁾~PLACE⁽ⱽ⁾ PLEASE HAND~you⁽ᵐˢ⁾ UNDER MIDSECTION~me and~you⁽ᵐˢ⁾~did~DO⁽ⱽ⁾ BY~me KINDNESS and~TRUTH DO.NOT PLEASE you⁽ᵐˢ⁾~will~BURY⁽ⱽ⁾~me in~Mits'rayim **47:30** and~I~did~ LIE.DOWN⁽ⱽ⁾ WITH FATHER~s~me and~you⁽ᵐˢ⁾~did~LIFT.UP⁽ⱽ⁾~me from~ Mits'rayim and~you⁽ᵐˢ⁾~did~BURY⁽ⱽ⁾~me in~BURIAL.PLACE~them⁽ᵐ⁾ and~he~ will~SAY⁽ⱽ⁾ I I~will~DO⁽ⱽ⁾ like~WORD~you⁽ᵐˢ⁾ **47:31** and~he~will~SAY⁽ⱽ⁾ !⁽ᵐˢ⁾~ be~SWEAR⁽ⱽ⁾~& to~me and~he~will~be~SWEAR⁽ⱽ⁾ to~him and~he~will~self~ BEND.DOWN⁽ⱽ⁾ Yisra'eyl UPON HEAD the~BED

Chapter 48

48:1 and~he~will~EXIST⁽ⱽ⁾ AFTER the~WORD~s the~THESE and~he~will~ SAY⁽ⱽ⁾ to~Yoseph LOOK FATHER~you⁽ᵐˢ⁾ BE.SICK⁽ⱽ⁾~ing⁽ᵐˢ⁾ and~he~will~ TAKE⁽ⱽ⁾ AT TWO SON~s~him WITH~him AT Menasheh and~AT Ephrayim **48:2** and~he~will~make~BE.FACE.TO.FACE⁽ⱽ⁾ to~Ya'aqov and~he~ will~SAY⁽ⱽ⁾ LOOK SON~you⁽ᵐˢ⁾ Yoseph he~did~COME⁽ⱽ⁾ TO~you⁽ᵐˢ⁾ and~he~ will~self~SEIZE⁽ⱽ⁾ Yisra'eyl and~he~will~SETTLE⁽ⱽ⁾ UPON the~BED **48:3** and~ he~will~SAY⁽ⱽ⁾ Ya'aqov TO Yoseph MIGHTY.ONE Shaddai he~did~be~SEE⁽ⱽ⁾ TO~me in~Luz in~LAND Kena'an and~he~will~much~KNEEL⁽ⱽ⁾ AT~ me **48:4** and~he~will~SAY⁽ⱽ⁾ TO~me LOOK~me make~REPRODUCE⁽ⱽ⁾~ ing⁽ᵐˢ⁾~you⁽ᵐˢ⁾ and~I~did~make~INCREASE⁽ⱽ⁾~you⁽ᵐˢ⁾ and~I~did~GIVE⁽ⱽ⁾~ you⁽ᵐˢ⁾ to~ASSEMBLY PEOPLE~s and~I~did~GIVE⁽ⱽ⁾ AT the~LAND the~THIS to~SEED~you⁽ᵐˢ⁾ AFTER~you⁽ᵐˢ⁾ HOLDINGS DISTANT **48:5** and~NOW TWO SON~s~you⁽ᵐˢ⁾ the~be~BRING.FORTH⁽ⱽ⁾~ing⁽ᵐᵖ⁾ to~you⁽ᵐˢ⁾ in~LAND Mits'rayim UNTIL >~COME⁽ⱽ⁾~me TO~you⁽ᵐˢ⁾ Mits'rayim~unto to~me THEY⁽ᵐ⁾ Ephrayim and~Menasheh like~Re'uven and~Shimon they⁽ᵐ⁾~will~EXIST⁽ⱽ⁾ to~ me **48:6** and~KINDRED~you⁽ᵐˢ⁾ WHICH you⁽ᵐˢ⁾~did~make~BRING.FORTH⁽ⱽ⁾ AFTER~them⁽ᵐ⁾ to~you⁽ᵐˢ⁾ they⁽ᵐ⁾~will~EXIST⁽ⱽ⁾ UPON TITLE BROTHER~s~ them⁽ᵐ⁾ they⁽ᵐ⁾~will~be~CALL.OUT⁽ⱽ⁾ in~INHERITANCE~them⁽ᵐ⁾ **48:7** and~I in~>~COME⁽ⱽ⁾~me from~Padan she~did~DIE⁽ⱽ⁾ UPON~me Rahhel in~LAND Kena'an in~the~ROAD in~YET.AGAIN SHORT LAND to~>~COME⁽ⱽ⁾ Ephrat~ unto and~I~will~BURY⁽ⱽ⁾~her THERE in~ROAD Ephrat SHE Beyt-Lehhem **48:8** and~he~will~SEE⁽ⱽ⁾ Yisra'eyl AT SON~s Yoseph and~he~will~

SAY⁽ⱽ⁾ WHO THESE **48:9** and~*he~will*~SAY⁽ⱽ⁾ Yoseph TO FATHER~him SON~s~ me THEY⁽ᵐ⁾ WHICH *he~did*~GIVE⁽ⱽ⁾ to~me Elohiym in~THIS and~*he~will*~ SAY⁽ⱽ⁾ *!⁽ᵐˢ⁾~*TAKE⁽ⱽ⁾~them⁽ᵐ⁾ PLEASE TO~me and~*I~will~much*~KNEEL⁽ⱽ⁾~ them⁽ᵐ⁾ **48:10** and~EYE~s2 Yisra'eyl *they~did*~BE.HEAVY⁽ⱽ⁾ from~AGE NOT *he~will*~BE.ABLE⁽ⱽ⁾ to~>~SEE⁽ⱽ⁾ and~*he~will~make*~DRAW.NEAR⁽ⱽ⁾ AT~ them⁽ᵐ⁾ TO~him and~*he~will*~KISS⁽ⱽ⁾ to~them⁽ᵐ⁾ and~*he~will~much*~ EMBRACE⁽ⱽ⁾ to~them⁽ᵐ⁾ **48:11** and~*he~will*~SAY⁽ⱽ⁾ Yisra'eyl TO Yoseph >~ SEE⁽ⱽ⁾ FACE~s~you⁽ᵐˢ⁾ NOT *I~did~much*~PLEAD⁽ⱽ⁾ and~LOOK *he~did~make*~ SEE⁽ⱽ⁾ AT~me Elohiym ALSO AT SEED~you⁽ᵐˢ⁾ **48:12** and~*he~will~make*~ GO.OUT⁽ⱽ⁾ Yoseph AT~them⁽ᵐ⁾ from~WITH KNEE~s~him and~*he~will~self*~ BEND.DOWN⁽ⱽ⁾ to~NOSE~s~him LAND~unto **48:13** and~*he~will*~TAKE⁽ⱽ⁾ Yoseph AT TWO~them⁽ᵐ⁾ AT Ephrayim in~RIGHT.HAND~him from~ LEFT.HAND Yisra'eyl and~AT Menasheh in~LEFT.HAND from~RIGHT.HAND Yisra'eyl and~*he~will~make*~DRAW.NEAR⁽ⱽ⁾ TO~him **48:14** and~*he~will*~ SEND⁽ⱽ⁾ Yisra'eyl AT RIGHT.HAND~him and~*he~will*~SET.DOWN⁽ⱽ⁾ UPON HEAD Ephrayim and~HE the~LITTLE.ONE and~AT LEFT.HAND~him UPON HEAD Menasheh *he~did~much*~CALCULATE⁽ⱽ⁾ AT HAND~s2~him GIVEN.THAT Menasheh the~FIRSTBORN **48:15** and~*he~will~much*~KNEEL⁽ⱽ⁾ AT Yoseph and~*he~will*~SAY⁽ⱽ⁾ the~Elohiym WHICH *they~did~self*~WALK⁽ⱽ⁾ FATHER~s~me to~FACE~s~him Avraham and~Yits'hhaq the~Elohiym the~ FEED⁽ⱽ⁾~*ing⁽ᵐˢ⁾* AT~me from~YET.AGAIN~me UNTIL the~DAY the~ THIS **48:16** the~MESSENGER the~REDEEM⁽ⱽ⁾~*ing⁽ᵐˢ⁾* AT~me from~ALL DYSFUNCTIONAL *he~will~much*~KNEEL⁽ⱽ⁾ AT the~YOUNG.MAN~s and~*he~ will~be*~CALL.OUT⁽ⱽ⁾ in~them⁽ᵐ⁾ TITLE~me and~TITLE FATHER~s~me Avraham and~Yits'hhaq and~*they⁽ᵐ⁾~will*~AMPLIFY⁽ⱽ⁾ to~ABUNDANCE in~ INSIDE the~LAND **48:17** and~*he~will*~SEE⁽ⱽ⁾ Yoseph GIVEN.THAT *he~will*~ SET.DOWN⁽ⱽ⁾ FATHER~him HAND RIGHT.HAND~him UPON HEAD Ephrayim and~*he~will*~BE.DYSFUNCTIONAL⁽ⱽ⁾ in~EYE~s2~him and~*he~will*~UPHOLD⁽ⱽ⁾ HAND FATHER~him to~>~*make*~TURN.ASIDE⁽ⱽ⁾ AT~her from~UPON HEAD Ephrayim UPON HEAD Menasheh **48:18** and~*he~will*~SAY⁽ⱽ⁾ Yoseph TO FATHER~him NOT SO FATHER~me GIVEN.THAT THIS the~FIRSTBORN *!⁽ᵐˢ⁾~* PLACE⁽ⱽ⁾ RIGHT.HAND~you⁽ᵐˢ⁾ UPON HEAD~him **48:19** and~*he~will~much*~ REFUSE⁽ⱽ⁾ FATHER~him and~*he~will*~SAY⁽ⱽ⁾ *I~did*~KNOW⁽ⱽ⁾ SON~me *I~did*~ KNOW⁽ⱽ⁾ ALSO HE *he~will*~EXIST⁽ⱽ⁾ to~PEOPLE and~ALSO HE *he~will*~ MAGNIFY⁽ⱽ⁾ and~BUT BROTHER~him the~SMALL *he~will*~MAGNIFY⁽ⱽ⁾ FROM~him and~SEED~him *he~will*~EXIST⁽ⱽ⁾ FILLING the~ NATION~s **48:20** and~*he~will~much*~KNEEL⁽ⱽ⁾~them⁽ᵐ⁾ in~the~DAY the~HE to~>~SAY⁽ⱽ⁾ in~you⁽ᵐˢ⁾ *he~will~much*~KNEEL⁽ⱽ⁾ Yisra'eyl to~>~SAY⁽ⱽ⁾ *he~will*~ PLACE⁽ⱽ⁾~you⁽ᵐˢ⁾ Elohiym like~Ephrayim and~like~Menasheh and~*he~will*~ PLACE⁽ⱽ⁾ AT Ephrayim to~FACE~s Menasheh **48:21** and~*he~will*~SAY⁽ⱽ⁾ Yisra'eyl TO Yoseph LOOK I DIE⁽ⱽ⁾~*ing⁽ᵐˢ⁾* and~*he~did*~EXIST⁽ⱽ⁾ Elohiym WITH~you⁽ᵐᵖ⁾ and~*he~did~make*~TURN.BACK⁽ⱽ⁾ AT~you⁽ᵐᵖ⁾ TO LAND FATHER~s~you⁽ᵐᵖ⁾ **48:22** and~I *I~did*~GIVE⁽ⱽ⁾ to~you⁽ᵐˢ⁾ SHOULDER UNIT UPON BROTHER~s~you⁽ᵐˢ⁾ WHICH *I~did*~TAKE⁽ⱽ⁾ from~HAND the~Emor~of in~SWORD~me and~in~BOW~me

Chapter 49

49:1 and~*he~will*~CALL.OUT(V) Ya'aqov TO SON~s~him and~*he~will*~SAY(V) !(mp)~*be*~GATHER(V) and~*I~will~make*~BE.FACE.TO.FACE(V)~& to~you(mp) AT WHICH *he~will*~CALL.OUT(V) AT~you(mp) in~END the~DAY~s **49:2** !(mp)~*be*~GATHER.TOGETHER(V) and~!(mp)~HEAR(V) SON~s Ya'aqov and~!(mp)~HEAR(V) TO Yisra'eyl FATHER~you(mp) **49:3** Re'uven FIRSTBORN~me YOU(ms) STRENGTH~me and~SUMMIT VIGOR~me REMAINDER >~LIFT.UP(V) and~ REMAINDER STRONG **49:4** RECKLESS like~the~WATER~s2 DO.NOT *you(ms)~will~make*~LEAVE.BEHIND(V) GIVEN.THAT *you(ms)~did*~GO.UP(V) LYING.PLACE~s FATHER~you(ms) AT.THAT.TIME *you(ms)~did~much*~DRILL(V) COUCH~me *he~did*~GO.UP(V) **49:5** Shimon and~Lewi BROTHER~s UTENSIL~s VIOLENCE CAVE~s~them(m) **49:6** in~CONFIDENCE~them(m) DO.NOT *you(ms)~will*~COME(V) SOUL~me in~ASSEMBLY~them(m) DO.NOT *she~will*~UNITE(V) ARMAMENT~me GIVEN.THAT in~NOSE~them(m) *they~did*~KILL(V) MAN and~ in~SELF-WILL~them(m) *they~did*~PLUCK.UP(V) OX **49:7** SPIT.UPON(V)~*ed*(ms) NOSE~them(m) GIVEN.THAT STRONG and~WRATH~them(m) GIVEN.THAT *she~did*~BE.HARD(V) *I~will~much*~DISTRIBUTE(V)~them(m) in~Ya'aqov and~*I~will~make*~SCATTER.ABROAD(V)~them(m) in~Yisra'eyl **49:8** Yehudah YOU(ms) *they(m)~will~make*~THROW.THE.HAND(V)~you(ms) BROTHER~s~you(ms) HAND~you(ms) in~NECK ATTACK(V)~*ing*(mp)~s~you(ms) *they(m)~will~self*~BEND.DOWN(V) to~you(ms) SON~s FATHER~you(ms) **49:9** WHELP LION Yehudah from~PREY SON~me *you(ms)~did*~GO.UP(V) *he~did*~STOOP(V) *he~did*~STRETCH.OUT(V) like~LION and~like~LIONESS WHO *he~will~make*~RISE(V)~him **49:10** NOT *he~will*~TURN.ASIDE(V) STAFF from~Yehudah and~ *much*~INSCRIBE(V)~*ing*(ms) from~BETWEEN FOOT~s2~him UNTIL GIVEN.THAT *he~will*~COME(V) TRANQUILITY and~to~him OBEDIENCE PEOPLE~s **49:11** TIE.UP(V)~*ing*(ms)~me to~GRAPEVINE COLT~him and~to~ the~CHOICE.VINE SON~me SHE-DONKEY~him *he~did~much*~WASH(V) in~ the~WINE CLOTHING~him and~in~BLOOD GRAPE~s COAT~her **49:12** DULL.RED EYE~s2 from~WINE and~WHITE TOOTH~s from~ FAT **49:13** Zevulun to~SHORE SEA~s *he~will*~DWELL(V) and~HE to~SHORE SHIP~s and~FLANK~him UPON Tsidon **49:14** Yis'sas'khar DONKEY CARTILAGE STRETCH.OUT(V)~*ing*(ms) BETWEEN the~SADDLEBAG~s **49:15** and~*he~will*~SEE(V) OASIS GIVEN.THAT FUNCTIONAL and~AT the~LAND GIVEN.THAT *she~did*~BE.DELIGHTFUL(V) and~*he~will*~EXTEND(V) SHOULDER~him to~>~ CARRY(V) and~*he~will*~EXIST(V) to~TASK.WORK SERVE(V)~*ing*(ms) **49:16** Dan *he~will*~MODERATE(V) PEOPLE~him like~UNIT STAFF~s Yisra'eyl **49:17** *he~will*~EXIST(V) Dan SERPENT UPON ROAD ADDER UPON PATH the~BITE(V)~ *ing*(ms) HEEL~s HORSE and~*he~will*~FALL(V) RIDE(V)~*ing*(ms)~him BACK **49:18** to~RELIEF~you(ms) *I~did~much*~BOUND.UP(V) **YHWH 49:19** Gad BAND *he~will*~INVADE(V)~us and~HE *he~will*~INVADE(V) HEEL **49:20** from~ Asher OIL BREAD~him and~HE *he~will*~GIVE(V) TASTY.FOOD KING **49:21** Naphtali DOE SEND(V)~*ed*(fs) the~GIVE(V)~*ing*(ms) STATEMENT~s

BRIGHT **49:22** SON BE.FRUITFUL⁽ⱽ⁾~*ing*⁽ᶠˢ⁾ Yoseph SON BE.FRUITFUL⁽ⱽ⁾~*ing*⁽ᶠˢ⁾ UPON EYE DAUGHTER~s *she~did*~MARCH⁽ⱽ⁾ UPON ROCK.WALL **49:23** and~ *they*⁽ᵐ⁾~*will*~BE.BITTER⁽ⱽ⁾~him and~*they*⁽ᵐ⁾~*did*~INCREASE.IN.NUMBER⁽ⱽ⁾ and~ *they*⁽ᵐ⁾~*will*~HOLD.A.GRUDGE⁽ⱽ⁾~him MASTER~s ARROW~s **49:24** and~*she*~ *will*~SETTLE⁽ⱽ⁾ in~CONSISTENCY BOW~him and~*they*⁽ᵐ⁾~*will*~REFINE⁽ⱽ⁾ ARM~s HAND~s2~him from~HAND~s2 VALIANT Ya'aqov from~THERE FEED⁽ⱽ⁾~*ing*⁽ᵐˢ⁾ STONE Yisra'eyl **49:25** from~MIGHTY.ONE FATHER~you⁽ᵐˢ⁾ and~*he*~*will*~HELP⁽ⱽ⁾~you⁽ᵐˢ⁾ and~AT Shaddai and~*he*~*will*~much~KNEEL⁽ⱽ⁾~ you⁽ᵐˢ⁾ PRESENT~s SKY~s2 from~UPON PRESENT~s DEEP.WATER STRETCH.OUT⁽ⱽ⁾~*ing*⁽ᶠˢ⁾ UNDER PRESENT~s BREAST~s2 and~ BOWELS **49:26** PRESENT~s FATHER~you⁽ᵐˢ⁾ *they*~*did*~OVERCOME⁽ⱽ⁾ UPON PRESENT~s CONCEIVE⁽ⱽ⁾~*ing*⁽ᵐᵖ⁾~me UNTIL YEARNING KNOLL~s DISTANT *they*⁽ᶠ⁾~*will*~EXIST⁽ⱽ⁾ to~HEAD Yoseph and~to~TOP.OF.THE.HEAD DEDICATED BROTHER~s~him **49:27** Binyamin WOLF *he*~*will*~TEAR.INTO.PIECES⁽ⱽ⁾ in~ the~MORNING *he*~*will*~EAT⁽ⱽ⁾ UNTIL and~to~the~EVENING *he*~*will*~ DISTRIBUTE⁽ⱽ⁾ SPOIL **49:28** ALL THESE STAFF~s Yisra'eyl TWO TEN and~THIS WHICH *he*~*did*~much~SPEAK⁽ⱽ⁾ to~them⁽ᵐ⁾ FATHER~them⁽ᵐ⁾ and~*he*~*will*~ much~KNEEL⁽ⱽ⁾ AT~them⁽ᵐ⁾ MAN WHICH like~PRESENT~him *he*~*did*~much~ KNEEL⁽ⱽ⁾ AT~them⁽ᵐ⁾ **49:29** and~*he*~*will*~much~DIRECT⁽ⱽ⁾ AT~them⁽ᵐ⁾ and~ *he*~*will*~SAY⁽ⱽ⁾ TO~them⁽ᵐ⁾ I *we*~*will*~GATHER⁽ⱽ⁾ TO PEOPLE~me *!*⁽ᵐᵖ⁾~BURY⁽ⱽ⁾ AT~me TO FATHER~s~me TO the~CAVE WHICH in~FIELD Ephron the~Hhet~ of **49:30** in~the~CAVE WHICH in~FIELD the~Makhpelah WHICH UPON FACE~s Mamre in~LAND Kena'an WHICH *he*~*did*~PURCHASE⁽ⱽ⁾ Avraham AT the~FIELD from~AT Ephron the~Hhet~of to~HOLDINGS GRAVE **49:31** THERE~unto *they*~*did*~BURY⁽ⱽ⁾ AT Avraham and~AT Sarah WOMAN~him THERE~unto *they*~*did*~BURY⁽ⱽ⁾ AT Yits'hhaq and~AT Rivqah WOMAN~him and~THERE~unto *I*~*did*~BURY⁽ⱽ⁾ AT Le'ah **49:32** LIVESTOCK the~FIELD and~the~CAVE WHICH in~him from~AT SON~s Hhet **49:33** and~ *he*~*will*~much~FINISH⁽ⱽ⁾ Ya'aqov to~>~much~DIRECT⁽ⱽ⁾ AT SON~s~him and~ *he*~*will*~GATHER⁽ⱽ⁾ FOOT~s2~him TO the~BED and~*he*~*will*~EXPIRE⁽ⱽ⁾ and~ *he*~*will*~be~GATHER⁽ⱽ⁾ TO PEOPLE~s~him

Chapter 50

50:1 and~*he*~*will*~FALL⁽ⱽ⁾ Yoseph UPON FACE~s FATHER~him and~*he*~*will*~ WEEP⁽ⱽ⁾ UPON~him and~*he*~*will*~KISS⁽ⱽ⁾ to~him **50:2** and~*he*~*will*~much~ DIRECT⁽ⱽ⁾ Yoseph AT SERVANT~s~him AT the~HEAL⁽ⱽ⁾~*ing*⁽ᵐᵖ⁾ to~>~RIPEN⁽ⱽ⁾ AT FATHER~him and~*they*⁽ᵐ⁾~*will*~RIPEN⁽ⱽ⁾ the~HEAL⁽ⱽ⁾~*ing*⁽ᵐᵖ⁾ AT Yisra'eyl **50:3** and~*they*⁽ᵐ⁾~*will*~FILL⁽ⱽ⁾ to~him FOUR~s DAY GIVEN.THAT SO *they*⁽ᵐ⁾~*will*~FILL⁽ⱽ⁾ DAY~s the~RIPEN⁽ⱽ⁾~*ed*⁽ᵐᵖ⁾ and~*they*⁽ᵐ⁾~*will*~WEEP⁽ⱽ⁾ AT~ him Mits'rayim SEVEN~s DAY **50:4** and~*they*⁽ᵐ⁾~*will*~CROSS.OVER⁽ⱽ⁾ DAY~s TIME.OF.WEEPING~him and~*he*~*will*~much~SPEAK⁽ⱽ⁾ Yoseph TO HOUSE Paroh to~>~SAY⁽ⱽ⁾ IF PLEASE *I*~*did*~FIND⁽ⱽ⁾ BEAUTY in~EYE~s2~you⁽ᵐᵖ⁾ *!*⁽ᵐᵖ⁾~

much~SPEAK^(V) PLEASE in~EAR~s2 Paroh to~>~SAY^(V) **50:5** FATHER~me *he~did~make*~SWEAR^(V)~me to~>~SAY^(V) LOOK I DIE^(V)~*ing*^(ms) in~GRAVE~me WHICH *I~did*~DIG^(V) to~me in~LAND Kena'an THERE~unto *you*^(ms)~*will*~BURY^(V)~me and~NOW *I~will*~GO.UP^(V) PLEASE and~*I~will*~BURY^(V)~& AT FATHER~me and~*I~will*~TURN.BACK^(V)~& **50:6** and~*he~will*~SAY^(V) Paroh *!*^(ms)~GO.UP^(V) and~ *!*^(ms)~BURY^(V) AT FATHER~*you*^(ms) like~WHICH *he~did~make*~SWEAR^(V)~*you*^(ms) **50:7** and~*he~will~make*~GO.UP^(V) Yoseph to~>~BURY^(V) AT FATHER~him and~*they*^(m)~*will*~GO.UP^(V) AT~him ALL SERVANT~s Paroh BEARD~s HOUSE~him and~ALL BEARD~s LAND Mits'rayim **50:8** and~ALL HOUSE Yoseph and~BROTHER~s~him and~HOUSE FATHER~him ONLY BABIES~them^(m) and~FLOCKS~them^(m) and~CATTLE~them^(m) *they~did*~LEAVE^(V) in~LAND Goshen **50:9** and~*he~will~make*~GO.UP^(V) WITH~him ALSO VEHICLE ALSO HORSEMAN~s and~*he~will*~EXIST^(V) the~CAMP HEAVY MANY **50:10** and~*they*^(m)~*will*~COME^(V) UNTIL Goren-Ha'atad WHICH in~OTHER.SIDE the~Yarden and~*they*^(m)~*will*~LAMENT^(V) THERE LAMENTING GREAT and~HEAVY MANY and~*he~will*~DO^(V) to~FATHER~him MOURNING SEVEN DAY~s **50:11** and~*he~will*~SEE^(V) SETTLE^(V)~*ing*^(ms) the~LAND the~Kena'an~of AT the~MOURNING in~Goren-Ha'atad and~*they*^(m)~*will*~SAY^(V) MOURNING HEAVY THIS to~Mits'rayim UPON SO *he~did*~CALL.OUT^(V) TITLE~her Aveyl-Mitsrayim WHICH in~OTHER.SIDE the~Yarden **50:12** and~*they*^(m)~*will*~DO^(V) SON~s~him to~him SO like~WHICH *he~did~much*~DIRECT^(V)~them^(m) **50:13** and~*they*^(m)~*will*~LIFT.UP^(V) AT~him SON~s~him LAND~unto Kena'an and~*they*^(m)~*will*~BURY^(V) AT~him in~CAVE FIELD the~Makhpelah WHICH *he~did*~PURCHASE^(V) Avraham AT the~FIELD to~HOLDINGS GRAVE from~AT Ephron the~Hhet~of UPON FACE~s Mamre **50:14** and~*he~will*~TURN.BACK^(V) Yoseph Mits'rayim~unto HE and~BROTHER~s~him and~ALL the~GO.UP^(V)~*ing*^(mp) AT~him to~>~BURY^(V) AT FATHER~him AFTER >~BURY^(V)~him AT FATHER~him **50:15** and~*they*^(m)~*will*~SEE^(V) BROTHER~s Yoseph GIVEN.THAT *he~did*~DIE^(V) FATHER~them^(m) and~*they*^(m)~*will*~SAY^(V) WOULD.THAT *he~will*~HOLD.A.GRUDGE^(V)~us Yoseph and~>~*make*~TURN.BACK^(V) *he~will~make*~TURN.BACK^(V) to~us AT ALL the~DYSFUNCTIONAL WHICH *we~did*~YIELD^(V) AT~him **50:16** and~*they*^(m)~*will~much*~DIRECT^(V) TO Yoseph to~>~SAY^(V) FATHER~*you*^(ms) *he~did~much*~DIRECT^(V) to~FACE~s DEATH~him to~>~SAY^(V) **50:17** IN.THIS.WAY *you*^(mp)~*will*~SAY^(V) to~Yoseph PLEASE *!*^(ms)~LIFT.UP^(V) PLEASE OFFENSE BROTHER~s~*you*^(ms) and~FAILURE~them^(m) GIVEN.THAT DYSFUNCTIONAL *they~did*~YIELD^(V)~*you*^(ms) and~NOW *!*^(ms)~LIFT.UP^(V) PLEASE to~OFFENSE SERVANT~s Elohiym FATHER~*you*^(ms) and~*he~will*~WEEP^(V) Yoseph in~>~*much*~SPEAK^(V)~them^(m) TO~him **50:18** and~*they*^(m)~*will*~WALK^(V) ALSO BROTHER~s~him and~*they*^(m)~*will*~FALL^(V) to~FACE~s~him and~*they*^(m)~*will*~SAY^(V) LOOK~us to~*you*^(ms) to~the~SERVANT~s **50:19** and~*he~will*~SAY^(V) TO~them^(m) Yoseph DO.NOT *you*^(mp)~*will*~FEAR^(V) GIVEN.THAT ?~UNDER Elohiym I **50:20** and~YOU^(mp) *you*^(mp)~*did*~THINK^(V) UPON~me DYSFUNCTIONAL Elohiym *he~did*~THINK^(V)~her to~FUNCTIONAL to~THAT >~DO^(V) like~the~DAY the~THIS to~>~*make*~LIVE^(V) PEOPLE ABUNDANT **50:21** and~NOW DO.NOT *you*^(mp)~*will*~

FEAR⁽ᵛ⁾ I I~will~much~SUSTAIN⁽ᵛ⁾ AT~you⁽ᵐᵖ⁾ and~AT BABIES~you⁽ᵐᵖ⁾ and~*he~will*~COMFORT⁽ᵛ⁾ AT~them⁽ᵐ⁾ and~*he~will*~much~SPEAK⁽ᵛ⁾ UPON HEART~them⁽ᵐ⁾ **50:22** and~*he~will*~SETTLE⁽ᵛ⁾ Yoseph in~Mits'rayim HE and~HOUSE FATHER~him and~*he~will*~LIVE⁽ᵛ⁾ Yoseph HUNDRED and~TEN YEAR~s **50:23** and~*he~will*~SEE⁽ᵛ⁾ Yoseph to~Ephrayim SON~s THIRD.GENERATION~s ALSO SON~s Makhir SON Menasheh BRING.FORTH⁽ᵛ⁾~*ed*⁽ᵐᵖ⁾ UPON KNEE~s Yoseph **50:24** and~*he~will*~SAY⁽ᵛ⁾ Yoseph TO BROTHER~s~him I DIE⁽ᵛ⁾~*ing*⁽ᵐˢ⁾ and~Elohiym >~REGISTER⁽ᵛ⁾ *he~will*~REGISTER⁽ᵛ⁾ AT~you⁽ᵐᵖ⁾ and~*he~did~make*~GO.UP⁽ᵛ⁾ AT~you⁽ᵐᵖ⁾ FROM the~LAND the~THIS TO the~LAND WHICH *he~did~be*~SWEAR⁽ᵛ⁾ to~Avraham to~Yits'hhaq and~to~Ya'aqov **50:25** and~*he~will~make*~SWEAR⁽ᵛ⁾ Yoseph AT SON~s Yisra'eyl to~>~SAY⁽ᵛ⁾ >~REGISTER⁽ᵛ⁾ *he~will*~REGISTER⁽ᵛ⁾ Elohiym AT~you⁽ᵐᵖ⁾ and~*you*⁽ᵐᵖ⁾~*did~make*~GO.UP⁽ᵛ⁾ AT BONE~s~me from~THIS **50:26** and~*he~will*~DIE⁽ᵛ⁾ Yoseph SON HUNDRED and~TEN YEAR~s and~*they*⁽ᵐ⁾~*will*~RIPEN⁽ᵛ⁾ AT~him and~*he~will*~PLACE⁽ᵛ⁾ in~the~BOX in~Mits'rayim

Benner's Mechanical Translation of the Torah

The Book of Exodus

Chapter 1

1:1 and~THESE TITLE~s SON~s Yisra'eyl the~COME$^{(V)}$~*ing*$^{(mp)}$ Mits'rayim~ unto AT Ya'aqov MAN and~HOUSE~him *they~did*~COME$^{(V)}$ **1:2** Re'uven Shimon Lewi and~Yehudah **1:3** Yis'sas'khar Zevulun and~Binyamin **1:4** Dan and~Naphtali Gad and~Asher **1:5** and~*he~will*~EXIST$^{(V)}$ ALL SOUL GO.OUT$^{(V)}$~*ing*$^{(mp)}$ MIDSECTION Ya'aqov SEVEN~s SOUL and~Yoseph *he~did*~ EXIST$^{(V)}$ in~Mits'rayim **1:6** and~*he~will*~DIE$^{(V)}$ Yoseph and~ALL BROTHER~s~ him and~ALL the~GENERATION the~HE **1:7** and~SON~s Yisra'eyl *they~did*~ REPRODUCE$^{(V)}$ and~*they*$^{(m)}$~*will*~SWARM$^{(V)}$ and~*they*$^{(m)}$~*will*~INCREASE$^{(V)}$ and~*they*$^{(m)}$~*will*~BE.ABUNDANT$^{(V)}$ in~MANY MANY and~*she~will~be*~FILL$^{(V)}$ the~LAND AT~them$^{(m)}$ **1:8** and~*he~will*~RISE$^{(V)}$ KING NEW UPON Mits'rayim WHICH NOT *he~did*~KNOW$^{(V)}$ AT Yoseph **1:9** and~*he~will*~SAY$^{(V)}$ TO PEOPLE~him LOOK PEOPLE SON~s Yisra'eyl ABUNDANT and~NUMEROUS FROM~us **1:10** !$^{(ms)}$~PROVIDE$^{(V)}$~& *we~will~self*~BE.SKILLED$^{(V)}$~& to~him OTHERWISE *he~will*~INCREASE$^{(V)}$ and~*he~did*~EXIST$^{(V)}$ GIVEN.THAT *they*$^{(f)}$~ *will*~MEET$^{(V)}$ BATTLE and~*he~did*~ADD$^{(V)}$ ALSO HE UPON HATE$^{(V)}$~*ing*$^{(mp)}$~us and~*he~did~be*~FIGHT$^{(V)}$ in~us and~*he~did*~GO.UP$^{(V)}$ FROM the~ LAND **1:11** and~*they*$^{(m)}$~*will*~PLACE$^{(V)}$ UPON~him NOBLE~s TASK.WORK~s to~THAT >~*much~*AFFLICT$^{(V)}$~him in~BURDEN~s~them$^{(m)}$ and~*he~will*~ BUILD$^{(V)}$ CITY~s STOREHOUSE~s to~Paroh AT Pitom and~AT Ra'meses **1:12** and~like~WHICH *they*$^{(m)}$~*will*~AFFLICT$^{(V)}$ AT~him SO *he~will*~ INCREASE$^{(V)}$ and~SO *he~will*~BREAK.OUT$^{(V)}$ and~*they*$^{(m)}$~*will*~LOATHE$^{(V)}$ from~FACE~s SON~s Yisra'eyl **1:13** and~*they*$^{(m)}$~*will~make*~SERVE$^{(V)}$ Mits'rayim AT SON~s Yisra'eyl in~WHIP **1:14** and~*they*$^{(m)}$~*will~much*~ BE.BITTER$^{(V)}$ AT LIVING~s~them$^{(m)}$ in~the~SERVICE HARD in~MORTAR and~ in~BRICK~s and~in~ALL SERVICE in~the~FIELD AT ALL SERVICE~them$^{(m)}$ WHICH *they~did*~SERVE$^{(V)}$ in~them$^{(m)}$ in~WHIP **1:15** and~*he~will*~SAY$^{(V)}$ KING Mits'rayim to~the~*much*~BRING.FORTH$^{(V)}$~*ing*$^{(fp)}$ the~Ever~s WHICH TITLE the~UNIT Shiphrah and~TITLE the~SECOND Pu'ah **1:16** and~*he~will*~ SAY$^{(V)}$ in~>~*much*~BRING.FORTH$^{(V)}$~them$^{(f)}$ AT the~Ever~s and~*you*$^{(fp)}$~*did*~ SEE$^{(V)}$ UPON the~STONE.STOOL IF SON HE and~*you*$^{(fp)}$~*did~make*~DIE$^{(V)}$ AT~ him and~IF DAUGHTER SHE and~*she~did*~LIVE$^{(V)}$ **1:17** and~*they*$^{(f)}$~*will*~ FEAR$^{(V)}$ the~*much*~BRING.FORTH$^{(V)}$~*ing*$^{(fp)}$ AT the~Elohiym and~NOT *they~ did*~DO$^{(V)}$ like~WHICH *he~did~much*~SPEAK$^{(V)}$ TO~them$^{(f)}$ KING Mits'rayim and~*they*$^{(f)}$~*will~much*~LIVE$^{(V)}$ AT the~BOY~s **1:18** and~*he~will*~CALL.OUT$^{(V)}$ KING Mits'rayim to~the~*much*~BRING.FORTH$^{(V)}$~*ing*$^{(fp)}$ and~*he~will*~SAY$^{(V)}$ to~them$^{(f)}$ WHY *you*$^{(fp)}$~*did*~DO$^{(V)}$ the~WORD the~THIS and~*they*$^{(f)}$~*will*~ *much*~LIVE$^{(V)}$ AT the~BOY~s **1:19** and~*they*$^{(f)}$~*will*~SAY$^{(V)}$ the~*much*~ BRING.FORTH$^{(V)}$~*ing*$^{(fp)}$ TO Paroh GIVEN.THAT NOT like~the~WOMAN~s the~

Mits'rayim~s the~Ever~s GIVEN.THAT LIVELY~s THEY⁽ᶠ⁾ in~BEFORE *she~will~*
COME⁽ᵛ⁾ TO~them⁽ᶠ⁾ the~*much~*BRING.FORTH⁽ᵛ⁾*~ing*⁽ᶠˢ⁾ and~*they~did~*
BRING.FORTH⁽ᵛ⁾ **1:20** and~*he~will~make~*DO.WELL⁽ᵛ⁾ Elohiym to~the~
*much~*BRING.FORTH⁽ᵛ⁾*~ing*⁽ᶠᵖ⁾ and~*he~will~*INCREASE⁽ᵛ⁾ the~PEOPLE and~
they⁽ᵐ⁾*~will~*BE.ABUNDANT⁽ᵛ⁾ MANY **1:21** and~*he~will~*EXIST⁽ᵛ⁾ GIVEN.THAT
*they~did~*FEAR⁽ᵛ⁾ the~*much~*BRING.FORTH⁽ᵛ⁾*~ing*⁽ᶠᵖ⁾ AT the~Elohiym and~
*he~will~*DO⁽ᵛ⁾ to~them⁽ᵐ⁾ HOUSE~s **1:22** and~*he~will~much~*DIRECT⁽ᵛ⁾
Paroh to~ALL PEOPLE~him to~>~SAY⁽ᵛ⁾ ALL the~SON the~BIRTHED the~
STREAM~unto *you*⁽ᵐᵖ⁾*~will~make~*THROW.OUT⁽ᵛ⁾*~*him and~ALL the~
DAUGHTER *you*⁽ᵐᵖ⁾*~will~much~*LIVE⁽ᵛ⁾*~*must

Chapter 2

2:1 and~*he~will~*WALK⁽ᵛ⁾ MAN from~HOUSE Lewi and~*he~will~*TAKE⁽ᵛ⁾ AT DAUGHTER Lewi **2:2** and~*she~will~*CONCEIVE⁽ᵛ⁾ the~WOMAN and~*she~will~*BRING.FORTH⁽ᵛ⁾ SON and~*she~will~*SEE⁽ᵛ⁾ AT~him GIVEN.THAT FUNCTIONAL HE and~*she~will~*CONCEAL⁽ᵛ⁾*~*him THREE MOON~s **2:3** and~ NOT *she~did~*BE.ABLE⁽ᵛ⁾ YET.AGAIN >~*make~*CONCEAL⁽ᵛ⁾*~*him and~*she~will~*TAKE⁽ᵛ⁾ to~him VESSEL BULRUSH and~*she~will~*PASTE⁽ᵛ⁾ in~the~SLIME and~in~the~PITCH and~*she~will~*PLACE⁽ᵛ⁾ in~her AT the~BOY and~*she~will~*PLACE⁽ᵛ⁾ in~the~REEDS UPON LIP the~STREAM **2:4** and~*she~will~self~*STATION⁽ᵛ⁾ SISTER~him from~DISTANCE to~>~KNOW⁽ᵛ⁾ WHAT *he~will~be~*DO⁽ᵛ⁾ to~him **2:5** and~*she~will~*GO.DOWN⁽ᵛ⁾ DAUGHTER Paroh to~>~BATHE⁽ᵛ⁾ UPON the~STREAM and~YOUNG.WOMAN~s~her WALK⁽ᵛ⁾*~ing*⁽ᶠᵖ⁾ UPON HAND the~STREAM and~*she~will~*SEE⁽ᵛ⁾ AT the~VESSEL in~MIDST the~REEDS and~*she~will~*SEND⁽ᵛ⁾ AT BONDWOMAN~her and~*she~will~*TAKE⁽ᵛ⁾*~*her **2:6** and~*she~will~*OPEN⁽ᵛ⁾ and~*she~will~*SEE⁽ᵛ⁾*~*him AT the~BOY and~LOOK YOUNG.MAN WEEP⁽ᵛ⁾*~ing*⁽ᵐˢ⁾ and~*she~will~*SHOW.PITY⁽ᵛ⁾ UPON~him and~*she~will~*SAY⁽ᵛ⁾ from~BOY~s the~Ever~s THIS **2:7** and~*she~will~*SAY⁽ᵛ⁾ SISTER~him TO DAUGHTER Paroh ?~*I~will~*WALK⁽ᵛ⁾ and~*I~did~*CALL.OUT⁽ᵛ⁾ to~*you*⁽ᶠˢ⁾ WOMAN *make~*SUCKLE⁽ᵛ⁾*~ing*⁽ᶠˢ⁾ FROM the~Ever~s and~*she~will~make~*SUCKLE⁽ᵛ⁾ to~*you*⁽ᶠˢ⁾ AT the~BOY **2:8** and~*she~will~*SAY⁽ᵛ⁾ to~her DAUGHTER Paroh *!*⁽ᶠˢ⁾*~*WALK⁽ᵛ⁾ and~*she~will~*WALK⁽ᵛ⁾ the~YOUNG.MAIDEN and~*she~will~*CALL.OUT⁽ᵛ⁾ AT MOTHER the~BOY **2:9** and~*she~will~*SAY⁽ᵛ⁾ to~her DAUGHTER Paroh *make~!*⁽ᶠˢ⁾*~*WALK⁽ᵛ⁾ AT the~BOY the~THIS and~*make~!*⁽ᶠˢ⁾*~*SUCKLE⁽ᵛ⁾*~*him to~me and~I *I~will~*GIVE⁽ᵛ⁾ AT WAGE~*you*⁽ᶠˢ⁾ and~*she~will~*TAKE⁽ᵛ⁾ the~WOMAN the~BOY and~*she~will~make~*SUCKLE⁽ᵛ⁾*~*him **2:10** and~*he~will~*MAGNIFY⁽ᵛ⁾ the~BOY and~*she~will~make~*COME⁽ᵛ⁾*~*him to~DAUGHTER Paroh and~*he~will~*EXIST⁽ᵛ⁾ to~her to~SON and~*she~will~*CALL.OUT⁽ᵛ⁾ TITLE~him Mosheh and~*she~will~*SAY⁽ᵛ⁾ GIVEN.THAT FROM the~WATER~s2 *I~did~*PLUCK.OUT⁽ᵛ⁾*~*him **2:11** and~*he~will~*EXIST⁽ᵛ⁾ in~the~DAY~s the~THEY⁽ᵐ⁾ and~*he~will~*MAGNIFY⁽ᵛ⁾ Mosheh and~*he~will~*GO.OUT⁽ᵛ⁾ TO BROTHER~s~him and~*he~will~*SEE⁽ᵛ⁾ in~

BURDEN~s~them⁽ᵐ⁾ and~*he~will*~SEE⁽ⱽ⁾ MAN Mits'rayim~of *make*~HIT⁽ⱽ⁾~*ing*⁽ᵐˢ⁾ MAN Ever~of from~BROTHER~s~him **2:12** and~*he~will*~TURN⁽ⱽ⁾ IN.THIS.WAY and~IN.THIS.WAY and~*he~will*~SEE⁽ⱽ⁾ GIVEN.THAT WITHOUT MAN and~*he~will~make*~HIT⁽ⱽ⁾ AT the~Mits'rayim~of and~*he~will*~SUBMERGE⁽ⱽ⁾~him in~the~SAND **2:13** and~*he~will*~GO.OUT⁽ⱽ⁾ in~the~DAY the~SECOND and~LOOK TWO MAN~s Ever~s be~STRUGGLE⁽ⱽ⁾~*ing*⁽ᵐᵖ⁾ and~*he~will*~SAY⁽ⱽ⁾ to~the~LOST to~WHAT *you*⁽ᵐˢ⁾~*will~make*~HIT⁽ⱽ⁾ COMPANION~you⁽ᵐˢ⁾ **2:14** and~*he~will*~SAY⁽ⱽ⁾ WHO *he~did*~PLACE⁽ⱽ⁾~you⁽ᵐˢ⁾ to~MAN NOBLE and~DECIDE⁽ⱽ⁾~*ing*⁽ᵐˢ⁾ UPON~us ?~to~>~KILL⁽ⱽ⁾~me YOU⁽ᵐˢ⁾ SAY⁽ⱽ⁾~*ing*⁽ᵐˢ⁾ like~WHICH *you*⁽ᵐˢ⁾~*did*~KILL⁽ⱽ⁾ AT the~Mits'rayim~of and~*he~will*~FEAR⁽ⱽ⁾ Mosheh and~*he~will*~SAY⁽ⱽ⁾ SURELY *he~did~be*~KNOW⁽ⱽ⁾ the~WORD **2:15** and~*he~will*~HEAR⁽ⱽ⁾ Paroh AT the~WORD the~THIS and~*he~will~much*~SEARCH.OUT⁽ⱽ⁾ to~>~KILL⁽ⱽ⁾ AT Mosheh and~*he~will*~FLEE.AWAY⁽ⱽ⁾ Mosheh from~FACE~s Paroh and~*he~will*~SETTLE⁽ⱽ⁾ in~LAND Mid'yan and~*he~will*~SETTLE⁽ⱽ⁾ UPON the~WELL **2:16** and~to~ADMINISTRATOR Mid'yan SEVEN DAUGHTER~s and~*they*⁽ᶠ⁾~*will*~COME⁽ⱽ⁾ and~*they*⁽ᶠ⁾~*will*~DRAW.UP⁽ⱽ⁾ and~*they*⁽ᶠ⁾~*will*~FILL⁽ⱽ⁾ AT the~TROUGH~s to~>~*make*~DRINK⁽ⱽ⁾ FLOCKS FATHER~them⁽ᶠ⁾ **2:17** and~*they*⁽ᵐ⁾~*will*~COME⁽ⱽ⁾ the~FEED⁽ⱽ⁾~*ing*⁽ᵐᵖ⁾ and~*they*⁽ᵐ⁾~*will*~CAST.OUT⁽ⱽ⁾~them⁽ᵐ⁾ and~*he~will*~RISE⁽ⱽ⁾ Mosheh and~*he~will~make*~RESCUE⁽ⱽ⁾~them⁽ᶠ⁾ and~*he~will~make*~DRINK⁽ⱽ⁾ AT FLOCKS~them⁽ᵐ⁾ **2:18** and~*they*⁽ᶠ⁾~*will*~COME⁽ⱽ⁾ TO Re'u'eyl FATHER~them⁽ᶠ⁾ and~*he~will*~SAY⁽ⱽ⁾ WHY *you*⁽ᶠᵖ⁾~*did~much*~HURRY⁽ⱽ⁾ !⁽ᵐˢ⁾~COME⁽ⱽ⁾ the~DAY **2:19** and~*they*⁽ᶠ⁾~*will*~SAY⁽ⱽ⁾ MAN Mits'rayim~of *he~did~make*~DELIVER⁽ⱽ⁾~us from~HAND the~FEED⁽ⱽ⁾~*ing*⁽ᵐᵖ⁾ and~ALSO >~DRAW.UP⁽ⱽ⁾ *he~did*~DRAW.UP⁽ⱽ⁾ to~us and~*he~will~make*~DRINK⁽ⱽ⁾ AT the~FLOCKS **2:20** and~*he~will*~SAY⁽ⱽ⁾ TO DAUGHTER~s~him and~WHERE~him to~WHAT THIS *you*⁽ᶠᵖ⁾~*did*~LEAVE⁽ⱽ⁾ AT the~MAN !⁽ᶠᵖ⁾~CALL.OUT⁽ⱽ⁾ to~him and~*he~will*~EAT⁽ⱽ⁾ BREAD **2:21** and~*he~will~make*~TAKE.UPON⁽ⱽ⁾ Mosheh to~>~SETTLE⁽ⱽ⁾ AT the~MAN and~*he~will*~GIVE⁽ⱽ⁾ AT Tsiporah DAUGHTER~him to~Mosheh **2:22** and~*she~will*~BRING.FORTH⁽ⱽ⁾ SON and~*he~will*~CALL.OUT⁽ⱽ⁾ AT TITLE~him Gershom GIVEN.THAT *he~did*~SAY⁽ⱽ⁾ IMMIGRANT *I~did*~EXIST⁽ⱽ⁾ in~LAND FOREIGN **2:23** and~*he~will*~EXIST⁽ⱽ⁾ in~the~DAY~s the~ABUNDANT~s the~THEY⁽ᵐ⁾ and~*he~will*~DIE⁽ⱽ⁾ KING Mits'rayim and~*they*⁽ᵐ⁾~*will*~SIGH⁽ⱽ⁾ SON~s Yisra'eyl FROM the~SERVICE and~*they*⁽ᵐ⁾~*will*~YELL.OUT⁽ⱽ⁾ and~*she~will*~GO.UP⁽ⱽ⁾ OUTCRY~them⁽ᵐ⁾ TO the~Elohiym FROM the~SERVICE **2:24** and~*he~will*~HEAR⁽ⱽ⁾ Elohiym AT GROANING~them⁽ᵐ⁾ and~*he~will*~REMEMBER⁽ⱽ⁾ Elohiym AT COVENANT~him AT Avraham AT Yits'hhaq and~AT Ya'aqov **2:25** and~*he~will*~SEE⁽ⱽ⁾ Elohiym AT SON~s Yisra'eyl and~*he~will*~KNOW⁽ⱽ⁾ Elohiym

Chapter 3

3:1 and~Mosheh *he~did*~EXIST$^{(V)}$ FEED$^{(V)}$~*ing*$^{(ms)}$ AT FLOCKS Yitro BE.AN.IN-LAW$^{(V)}$~*ing*$^{(ms)}$~him ADMINISTRATOR Mid'yan and~*he~will*~DRIVE$^{(V)}$ AT the~FLOCKS AFTER the~WILDERNESS and~*he~will*~COME$^{(V)}$ TO HILL the~Elohiym Hhorev~unto **3:2** and~*he~will~be*~SEE$^{(V)}$ MESSENGER **YHWH** TO~him in~GLIMMERING FIRE from~MIDST the~THORN.BUSH and~*he~will*~SEE$^{(V)}$ and~LOOK the~THORN.BUSH BURN$^{(V)}$~*ing*$^{(ms)}$ in~the~FIRE and~the~THORN.BUSH WITHOUT~him EAT$^{(V)}$~*ed*$^{(ms)}$ **3:3** and~*he~will*~SAY$^{(V)}$ Mosheh *I~will*~TURN.ASIDE$^{(V)}$~& PLEASE and~*I~will*~SEE$^{(V)}$ AT the~APPEARANCE the~GREAT the~THIS WHY NOT *he~will*~BURN$^{(V)}$ the~THORN.BUSH **3:4** and~*he~will*~SEE$^{(V)}$ **YHWH** GIVEN.THAT *he~did*~TURN.ASIDE$^{(V)}$ to~>~SEE$^{(V)}$ and~*he~will*~CALL.OUT$^{(V)}$ TO~him Elohiym from~MIDST the~THORN.BUSH and~*he~will*~SAY$^{(V)}$ Mosheh Mosheh and~*he~will*~SAY$^{(V)}$ LOOK~me **3:5** and~*he~will*~SAY$^{(V)}$ DO.NOT *you*$^{(ms)}$~will~COME.NEAR$^{(V)}$ AT.THIS.POINT *!*$^{(ms)}$~CAST.OFF$^{(V)}$ SANDAL~s~*you*$^{(ms)}$ from~UPON FOOT~s2~*you*$^{(ms)}$ GIVEN.THAT the~AREA WHICH YOU$^{(ms)}$ STAND$^{(V)}$~*ing*$^{(ms)}$ UPON~him GROUND SPECIAL HE **3:6** and~*he~will*~SAY$^{(V)}$ I Elohiym FATHER~*you*$^{(ms)}$ Elohiym Avraham Elohiym Yits'hhaq and~Elohiym Ya'aqov and~*he~will~make*~HIDE$^{(V)}$ Mosheh FACE~s~him GIVEN.THAT *he~did*~FEAR$^{(V)}$ from~>~*make*~STARE$^{(V)}$ TO the~Elohiym **3:7** and~*he~will*~SAY$^{(V)}$ **YHWH** >~SEE$^{(V)}$ *I~did*~SEE$^{(V)}$ AT AFFLICTION PEOPLE~me WHICH in~Mits'rayim and~AT CRY~them$^{(m)}$ *I~did*~HEAR$^{(V)}$ from~FACE~s PUSH$^{(V)}$~*ing*$^{(mp)}$~him GIVEN.THAT *I~did*~KNOW$^{(V)}$ AT MISERY~s~him **3:8** and~*I~will*~GO.DOWN$^{(V)}$ to~>~*make*~DELIVER$^{(V)}$~him from~HAND Mits'rayim and~to~>~*make*~GO.UP$^{(V)}$~him FROM the~LAND the~SHE TO LAND FUNCTIONAL and~WIDE TO LAND ISSUE$^{(V)}$~*ing*$^{(fs)}$ FAT and~HONEY TO AREA the~Kena'an~of and~the~Hhet~of and~the~Emor~of and~the~Perez~of and~the~Hhiw~of and~the~Yevus~of **3:9** and~NOW LOOK CRY SON~s Yisra'eyl *she~did*~COME$^{(V)}$ TO~me and~ALSO *I~did*~SEE$^{(V)}$ AT the~SQUEEZING WHICH Mits'rayim SQUEEZE$^{(V)}$~*ing*$^{(mp)}$ AT~them$^{(m)}$ **3:10** and~NOW *!*$^{(ms)}$~WALK$^{(V)}$~& and~*I~will*~SEND$^{(V)}$~*you*$^{(ms)}$ TO Paroh and~>~*make*~GO.OUT$^{(V)}$ AT PEOPLE~me SON~s Yisra'eyl from~Mits'rayim **3:11** and~*he~will*~SAY$^{(V)}$ Mosheh TO the~Elohiym WHO I GIVEN.THAT *I~will*~WALK$^{(V)}$ TO Paroh and~GIVEN.THAT *I~will~make*~GO.OUT$^{(V)}$ AT SON~s Yisra'eyl from~Mits'rayim **3:12** and~*he~will*~SAY$^{(V)}$ GIVEN.THAT *I~will*~EXIST$^{(V)}$ WITH~*you*$^{(fs)}$ and~THIS to~*you*$^{(ms)}$ the~SIGN GIVEN.THAT I *I~did*~SEND$^{(V)}$~*you*$^{(ms)}$ in~>~*make*~GO.OUT$^{(V)}$~*you*$^{(ms)}$ AT the~PEOPLE from~Mits'rayim *you*$^{(mp)}$~*will*~SERVE$^{(V)}$~must AT the~Elohiym UPON the~HILL the~THIS **3:13** and~*he~will*~SAY$^{(V)}$ Mosheh TO the~Elohiym LOOK I *he~did*~COME$^{(V)}$ TO SON~s Yisra'eyl and~*I~did*~SAY$^{(V)}$ to~them$^{(m)}$ Elohiym FATHER~s~*you*$^{(mp)}$ *he~did*~SEND$^{(V)}$~me TO~*you*$^{(mp)}$ and~*they~did*~SAY$^{(V)}$ to~me WHAT TITLE~him WHAT *I~will*~SAY$^{(V)}$ TO~them$^{(m)}$ **3:14** and~*he~will*~SAY$^{(V)}$ Elohiym TO Mosheh *I~will*~EXIST$^{(V)}$ WHICH *I~will*~EXIST$^{(V)}$ and~*he~will*~SAY$^{(V)}$ IN.THIS.WAY *you*$^{(ms)}$~*will*~SAY$^{(V)}$ to~SON~s Yisra'eyl Ehyeh *he~did*~SEND$^{(V)}$~me TO~*you*$^{(mp)}$ **3:15** and~

*he~will~*SAY^(v) YET.AGAIN Elohiym TO Mosheh IN.THIS.WAY *you*^(ms)*~will~*
SAY^(v) TO SON~s Yisra'eyl **YHWH** Elohiym FATHER~s~*you*^(mp) Elohiym
Avraham Elohiym Yits'hhaq and~Elohiym Ya'aqov *he~did~*SEND^(v)~me TO~
you^(mp) THIS TITLE~me to~DISTANT and~THIS MEMORY~me to~
GENERATION GENERATION **3:16** *!*^(ms)*~*WALK^(v) and~*you*^(ms)*~did~*GATHER^(v)
AT BEARD~s Yisra'eyl and~*you*^(ms)*~did~*SAY^(v) TO~them^(m) **YHWH** Elohiym
FATHER~s~*you*^(mp) *he~did~be~*SEE^(v) TO~me Elohiym Avraham Yits'hhaq
and~Ya'aqov to~>~SAY^(v) >~REGISTER^(v) *I~did~*REGISTER^(v) AT~*you*^(mp) and~
AT the~DO^(v)~*ed*^(ms) to~*you*^(mp) in~Mits'rayim **3:17** and~*I~will~*SAY^(v) *I~will~*
make~GO.UP^(v) AT~*you*^(mp) from~AFFLICTION Mits'rayim TO LAND the~
Kena'an~of and~the~Hhet~of and~the~Emor~of and~the~Perez~of and~
the~Hhiw~of and~the~Yevus~of TO LAND ISSUE^(v)~*ing*^(fs) FAT and~HONEY
3:18 and~*they~did~*HEAR^(v) to~VOICE~*you*^(ms) and~*you*^(ms)*~did~*COME^(v)
YOU^(ms) and~BEARD~s Yisra'eyl TO KING Mits'rayim and~*you*^(mp)*~did~*SAY^(v)
TO~him **YHWH** Elohiym the~Ever~s *he~did~be~*MEET^(v) UPON~us and~NOW
*we~will~*WALK^(v)~& PLEASE ROAD THREE DAY~s in~the~WILDERNESS and~
*we~will~*SACRIFICE^(v)~& to~**YHWH** Elohiym~us **3:19** and~*I I~did~*KNOW^(v)
GIVEN.THAT NOT *he~will~*GIVE^(v) AT~*you*^(mp) KING Mits'rayim to~>~WALK^(v)
and~NOT in~HAND FORCEFUL **3:20** and~*I~did~*SEND^(v) AT HAND~me and~*I~
did~*make~HIT^(v) AT Mits'rayim in~ALL *be~*PERFORM^(v)~*ing*^(fp)~me WHICH *I~
will~*DO^(v) in~INSIDE~him and~AFTER SO *he~will~*much~SEND^(v) AT~
you^(mp) **3:21** and~*I~did~*GIVE^(v) AT BEAUTY the~PEOPLE the~THIS in~EYE~s2
Mits'rayim and~*he~did~*EXIST^(v) GIVEN.THAT *you*^(mp)*~will~*WALK^(v)~must
NOT *you*^(mp)*~will~*WALK^(v) EMPTINESS **3:22** and~*she~did~*INQUIRE^(v)
WOMAN from~DWELLER~her and~from~IMMIGRATE^(v)~*ing*^(fs) HOUSE~her
UTENSIL~s SILVER and~UTENSIL~s GOLD and~APPAREL~s and~*you*^(mp)*~did~*
PLACE^(v) UPON SON~s~*you*^(mp) and~UPON DAUGHTER~s~*you*^(mp) and~
you^(mp)*~did~*much~DELIVER^(v) AT Mits'rayim

Chapter 4

4:1 and~*he~will~*ANSWER^(v) Mosheh and~*he~will~*SAY^(v) and~THOUGH NOT
they^(m)*~will~*make~SECURE^(v) to~me and~NOT *they*^(m)*~will~*HEAR^(v) in~
VOICE~me GIVEN.THAT *they*^(m)*~will~*SAY^(v) NOT *he~did~be~*SEE^(v) TO~*you*^(ms)
YHWH 4:2 and~*he~will~*SAY^(v) TO~him **YHWH** WHAT + THIS in~HAND~
you^(ms) and~*he~will~*SAY^(v) BRANCH **4:3** and~*he~will~*SAY^(v) *!*^(ms)*~*make~
THROW.OUT^(v)~him LAND~unto and~*he~will~*make~THROW.OUT^(v)~him
LAND~unto and~*he~will~*EXIST^(v) to~SERPENT and~*he~will~*FLEE^(v) Mosheh
from~FACE~s~him **4:4** and~*he~will~*SAY^(v) **YHWH** TO Mosheh *!*^(ms)*~*SEND^(v)
HAND~*you*^(ms) and~*!*^(ms)*~*TAKE.HOLD^(v) in~TAIL~him and~*he~will~*SEND^(v)
HAND~him and~*he~will~*make~SEIZE^(v) in~him and~*he~will~*EXIST^(v) to~
BRANCH in~PALM~him **4:5** to~THAT *they*^(m)*~will~*make~SECURE^(v)
GIVEN.THAT *he~did~be~*SEE^(v) TO~*you*^(ms) **YHWH** Elohiym FATHER~s~them^(m)

The Book of Exodus

Elohiym Avraham Elohiym Yits'hhaq and~Elohiym Ya'aqov **4:6** and~*he*~*will*~SAY$^{(V)}$ **YHWH** to~him YET.AGAIN *!*$^{(ms)}$~*make*~COME$^{(V)}$ PLEASE HAND~you$^{(ms)}$ in~BOSOM~you$^{(ms)}$ and~*he*~*will*~*make*~COME$^{(V)}$ HAND~him in~BOSOM~him and~*he*~*will*~*make*~GO.OUT$^{(V)}$~her and~LOOK HAND~him *be*~*much*~INFECT$^{(V)}$~*ing*$^{(fs)}$ like~the~SNOW **4:7** and~*he*~*will*~SAY$^{(V)}$ *!*$^{(ms)}$~*make*~TURN.BACK$^{(V)}$ HAND~you$^{(ms)}$ TO BOSOM~you$^{(ms)}$ and~*he*~*will*~*make*~TURN.BACK$^{(V)}$ HAND~him TO BOSOM~him and~*he*~*will*~*make*~GO.OUT$^{(V)}$~her from~BOSOM~him and~LOOK *she*~*did*~TURN.BACK$^{(V)}$ like~FLESH~him **4:8** and~*he*~*did*~EXIST$^{(V)}$ IF NOT *they*$^{(m)}$~*will*~*make*~SECURE$^{(V)}$ to~you$^{(fs)}$ and~NOT *they*$^{(m)}$~*will*~HEAR$^{(V)}$ to~VOICE the~SIGN the~FIRST and~*they*~*did*~*make*~SECURE$^{(V)}$ to~VOICE the~SIGN the~LAST **4:9** and~*he*~*did*~EXIST$^{(V)}$ IF NOT *they*$^{(m)}$~*will*~*make*~SECURE$^{(V)}$ ALSO to~TWO the~SIGN~s the~THESE and~NOT *they*$^{(m)}$~*will*~HEAR$^{(V)}$~must to~VOICE~you$^{(ms)}$ and~*you*$^{(ms)}$~*did*~TAKE$^{(V)}$ from~WATER~s2 the~STREAM and~*you*$^{(ms)}$~*did*~POUR.OUT$^{(V)}$ the~DRY.GROUND and~*they*~*did*~EXIST$^{(V)}$ the~WATER~s2 WHICH *you*$^{(ms)}$~*will*~TAKE$^{(V)}$ FROM the~STREAM and~*they*~*did*~EXIST$^{(V)}$ to~BLOOD in~the~DRY.LAND **4:10** and~*he*~*will*~SAY$^{(V)}$ Mosheh TO **YHWH** in~me Adonai NOT MAN WORD~s I ALSO from~YESTERDAY ALSO from~THREE.DAYS.AGO ALSO from~AT.THAT.TIME >~*much*~SPEAK$^{(V)}$~you$^{(ms)}$ TO SERVANT~you$^{(ms)}$ GIVEN.THAT HEAVY MOUTH and~HEAVY TONGUE I **4:11** and~*he*~*will*~SAY$^{(V)}$ **YHWH** TO~him WHO *he*~*did*~PLACE$^{(V)}$ MOUTH to~the~HUMAN OR WHO *he*~*will*~PLACE$^{(V)}$ MUTE OR SILENT OR SEEING OR BLIND ?~NOT I **YHWH 4:12** and~NOW *!*$^{(ms)}$~WALK$^{(V)}$ and~I *I*~*will*~EXIST$^{(V)}$ WITH MOUTH~you$^{(ms)}$ and~*I*~*did*~*make*~THROW$^{(V)}$~you$^{(ms)}$ WHICH *you*$^{(ms)}$~*will*~*much*~SPEAK$^{(V)}$ **4:13** and~*he*~*will*~SAY$^{(V)}$ in~me Adonai *!*$^{(ms)}$~SEND$^{(V)}$ PLEASE in~HAND *you*$^{(ms)}$~*will*~SEND$^{(V)}$ **4:14** and~*he*~*will*~FLARE.UP$^{(V)}$ NOSE **YHWH** in~Mosheh and~*he*~*will*~SAY$^{(V)}$?~NOT Aharon BROTHER~you$^{(ms)}$ the~Lewi *I*~*did*~KNOW$^{(V)}$ GIVEN.THAT *!*$^{(ms)}$~*much*~SPEAK$^{(V)}$ *he*~*will*~*much*~SPEAK$^{(V)}$ HE and~ALSO LOOK HE GO.OUT$^{(V)}$~*ing*$^{(ms)}$ to~>~MEET$^{(V)}$~you$^{(ms)}$ and~*he*~*did*~SEE$^{(V)}$~you$^{(ms)}$ and~*he*~*did*~REJOICE$^{(V)}$ in~HEART~him **4:15** and~*you*$^{(ms)}$~*did*~*much*~SPEAK$^{(V)}$ TO~him and~*you*$^{(ms)}$~*did*~PLACE$^{(V)}$ AT the~WORD~s in~MOUTH~him and~I *I*~*will*~EXIST$^{(V)}$ WITH MOUTH~you$^{(ms)}$ and~WITH MOUTH~him and~*I*~*did*~*make*~THROW$^{(V)}$ AT~you$^{(mp)}$ AT WHICH *you*$^{(ms)}$~*will*~DO$^{(V)}$~must **4:16** and~*he*~*did*~*much*~SPEAK$^{(V)}$ HE to~you$^{(ms)}$ TO the~PEOPLE and~*he*~*did*~EXIST$^{(V)}$ HE *he*~*will*~EXIST$^{(V)}$ to~you$^{(ms)}$ to~MOUTH and~YOU$^{(ms)}$ *you*$^{(ms)}$~*will*~EXIST$^{(V)}$ to~him to~Elohiym **4:17** and~AT the~BRANCH the~THIS *you*$^{(ms)}$~*will*~TAKE$^{(V)}$ in~HAND~you$^{(ms)}$ WHICH *you*$^{(ms)}$~*will*~DO$^{(V)}$ in~him AT the~SIGN~s **4:18** and~*he*~*will*~WALK$^{(V)}$ Mosheh and~*he*~*will*~TURN.BACK$^{(V)}$ TO Yeter BE.AN.IN-LAW$^{(V)}$~*ing*$^{(ms)}$~him and~*he*~*will*~SAY$^{(V)}$ to~him *I*~*will*~WALK$^{(V)}$~& PLEASE and~*I*~*will*~TURN.BACK$^{(V)}$~& TO BROTHER~s~me WHICH in~Mits'rayim and~*I*~*will*~SEE$^{(V)}$?~YET.AGAIN~them$^{(m)}$ LIVING~s and~*he*~*will*~SAY$^{(V)}$ Yitro to~Mosheh *!*$^{(ms)}$~WALK$^{(V)}$ to~COMPLETENESS **4:19** and~*he*~*will*~SAY$^{(V)}$ **YHWH** TO Mosheh in~Mid'yan *!*$^{(ms)}$~WALK$^{(V)}$ *!*$^{(ms)}$~TURN.BACK$^{(V)}$ Mits'rayim GIVEN.THAT *they*~*did*~DIE$^{(V)}$ ALL the~MAN~s the~*much*~SEARCH.OUT$^{(V)}$~*ing*$^{(mp)}$ AT SOUL~you$^{(ms)}$ **4:20** and~

he~will~TAKE⁽ⱽ⁾ Mosheh AT WOMAN~him and~AT SON~s~him and~*he~will~ make*~RIDE⁽ⱽ⁾~them⁽ᵐ⁾ UPON the~DONKEY and~*he~will*~TURN.BACK⁽ⱽ⁾ LAND~unto Mits'rayim and~*he~will*~TAKE⁽ⱽ⁾ Mosheh AT BRANCH the~ Elohiym in~HAND~him **4:21** and~*he~will*~SAY⁽ⱽ⁾ **YHWH** TO Mosheh in~>~ WALK⁽ⱽ⁾~you⁽ᵐˢ⁾ to~>~TURN.BACK⁽ⱽ⁾ Mits'rayim~unto !⁽ᵐˢ⁾~SEE⁽ⱽ⁾ ALL the~ WONDER~s WHICH *I~did*~PLACE⁽ⱽ⁾ in~HAND~you⁽ᵐˢ⁾ and~*you⁽ᵐˢ⁾~will*~DO⁽ⱽ⁾~ them⁽ᵐ⁾ to~FACE~s Paroh and~*I I~will*~SEIZE⁽ⱽ⁾ AT HEART~him and~NOT *he~ will~much*~SEND⁽ⱽ⁾ AT the~PEOPLE **4:22** and~*you⁽ᵐˢ⁾~did*~SAY⁽ⱽ⁾ TO Paroh IN.THIS.WAY *he~did*~SAY⁽ⱽ⁾ **YHWH** SON~me FIRSTBORN~me Yisra'eyl **4:23** and~*I~will*~SAY⁽ⱽ⁾ TO~you⁽ᵐˢ⁾ !⁽ᵐˢ⁾~*much*~SEND⁽ⱽ⁾ AT SON~me and~*he~will*~SERVE⁽ⱽ⁾~me and~*you⁽ᵐˢ⁾~will~much*~REFUSE⁽ⱽ⁾ to~>~*much*~ SEND⁽ⱽ⁾~him LOOK I KILL⁽ⱽ⁾~*ing*⁽ᵐˢ⁾ AT SON~you⁽ᵐˢ⁾ FIRSTBORN~ you⁽ᵐˢ⁾ **4:24** and~*he~will*~EXIST⁽ⱽ⁾ in~the~ROAD in~the~PLACE.OF.LODGING and~*he~will*~ENCOUNTER⁽ⱽ⁾~him **YHWH** and~*he~will~much*~SEARCH.OUT⁽ⱽ⁾ >~*make*~DIE⁽ⱽ⁾~him **4:25** and~*she~will*~TAKE⁽ⱽ⁾ Tsiporah SHARP.STONE and~ *she~will*~CUT⁽ⱽ⁾ AT FORESKIN SON~her and~*she~will~make*~TOUCH⁽ⱽ⁾ to~ FOOT~s2~him and~*she~will*~SAY⁽ⱽ⁾ GIVEN.THAT IN.LAW BLOOD~s YOU⁽ᵐˢ⁾ to~me **4:26** and~*he~will*~SINK.DOWN⁽ⱽ⁾ FROM~him AT.THAT.TIME *she~did*~ SAY⁽ⱽ⁾ IN.LAW BLOOD~s to~the~CIRCUMCISION~s **4:27** and~*he~will*~SAY⁽ⱽ⁾ **YHWH** TO Aharon !⁽ᵐˢ⁾~WALK⁽ⱽ⁾ to~>~MEET⁽ⱽ⁾ Mosheh the~WILDERNESS~ unto and~*he~will*~WALK⁽ⱽ⁾ and~*he~will*~ENCOUNTER⁽ⱽ⁾~him in~HILL the~ Elohiym and~*he~will*~KISS⁽ⱽ⁾ to~him **4:28** and~*he~will~make*~ BE.FACE.TO.FACE⁽ⱽ⁾ Mosheh to~Aharon AT ALL WORD~s **YHWH** WHICH *he~ did*~SEND⁽ⱽ⁾~him and~AT ALL the~SIGN~s WHICH *he~did~much*~DIRECT⁽ⱽ⁾~ him **4:29** and~*he~will*~WALK⁽ⱽ⁾ Mosheh and~Aharon and~*they*⁽ᵐ⁾~*will*~ GATHER⁽ⱽ⁾ AT ALL BEARD~s SON~s Yisra'eyl **4:30** and~*he~will~much*~ SPEAK⁽ⱽ⁾ Aharon AT ALL the~WORD~s WHICH *he~did~much*~SPEAK⁽ⱽ⁾ **YHWH** TO Mosheh and~*he~will*~DO⁽ⱽ⁾ the~SIGN~s to~EYE~s2 the~ PEOPLE **4:31** and~*he~will~make*~SECURE⁽ⱽ⁾ the~PEOPLE and~*they*⁽ᵐ⁾~*will*~ HEAR⁽ⱽ⁾ GIVEN.THAT *he~did*~REGISTER⁽ⱽ⁾ **YHWH** AT SON~s Yisra'eyl and~ GIVEN.THAT *he~did*~SEE⁽ⱽ⁾ AT AFFLICTION~them⁽ᵐ⁾ and~*they*⁽ᵐ⁾~*will*~ BOW.THE.HEAD⁽ⱽ⁾ and~*they*⁽ᵐ⁾~*will~self*~BEND.DOWN⁽ⱽ⁾

Chapter 5

5:1 and~AFTER *they~did*~COME⁽ⱽ⁾ Mosheh and~Aharon and~*they*⁽ᵐ⁾~*will*~ SAY⁽ⱽ⁾ TO Paroh IN.THIS.WAY *he~did*~SAY⁽ⱽ⁾ **YHWH** Elohiym Yisra'eyl !⁽ᵐˢ⁾~ *much*~SEND⁽ⱽ⁾ AT PEOPLE~me and~*they*⁽ᵐ⁾~*will*~HOLD.A.FEAST⁽ⱽ⁾ to~me in~ the~WILDERNESS **5:2** and~*he~will*~SAY⁽ⱽ⁾ Paroh WHO **YHWH** WHICH *I~will*~ HEAR⁽ⱽ⁾ in~VOICE~him to~>~*much*~SEND⁽ⱽ⁾ AT Yisra'eyl NOT *I~did*~KNOW⁽ⱽ⁾ AT **YHWH** and~ALSO AT Yisra'eyl NOT *I~will~much*~SEND⁽ⱽ⁾ **5:3** and~*they*⁽ᵐ⁾~ *will*~SAY⁽ⱽ⁾ Elohiym the~Ever~s *he~did~be*~MEET⁽ⱽ⁾ UPON~us *we~will*~ WALK⁽ⱽ⁾~& PLEASE ROAD THREE DAY~s in~the~WILDERNESS and~*we~will*~

The Book of Exodus

SACRIFICE⁽ⱽ⁾~& to~**YHWH** Elohiym~us OTHERWISE *he~will*~REACH⁽ⱽ⁾~us in~ the~EPIDEMIC OR in~SWORD **5:4** and~*he~will*~SAY⁽ⱽ⁾ TO~them⁽ᵐ⁾ KING Mits'rayim to~WHAT Mosheh and~Aharon *you*⁽ᵐᵖ⁾~*will*~make~LOOSE⁽ⱽ⁾ AT the~PEOPLE from~WORK~s~him !⁽ᵐᵖ⁾~WALK⁽ⱽ⁾ to~BURDEN~s~ you⁽ᵐᵖ⁾ **5:5** and~*he~will*~SAY⁽ⱽ⁾ Paroh THOUGH ABUNDANT~s NOW PEOPLE the~LAND and~*you*⁽ᵐᵖ⁾~*did*~make~CEASE⁽ⱽ⁾ AT~them⁽ᵐ⁾ from~BURDEN~s~ them⁽ᵐ⁾ **5:6** and~*he~will*~much~DIRECT⁽ⱽ⁾ Paroh in~the~DAY the~HE AT the~PUSH⁽ⱽ⁾~*ing*⁽ᵐᵖ⁾ in~the~PEOPLE and~AT OFFICER~s~him to~>~ SAY⁽ⱽ⁾ **5:7** NOT *you*⁽ᵐᵖ⁾~*will*~make~ADD⁽ⱽ⁾~must to~>~GIVE⁽ⱽ⁾ STRAW to~ the~PEOPLE to~>~MAKE.BRICKS⁽ⱽ⁾ the~BRICK~s like~YESTERDAY THREE.DAYS.AGO THEY⁽ᵐ⁾ *they*⁽ᵐ⁾~*will*~WALK⁽ⱽ⁾ and~*they~did*~much~ COLLECT⁽ⱽ⁾ to~them⁽ᵐ⁾ STRAW **5:8** and~AT SUM the~BRICK~s WHICH THEY⁽ᵐ⁾ DO⁽ⱽ⁾~*ing*⁽ᵐᵖ⁾ YESTERDAY THREE.DAYS.AGO *you*⁽ᵐᵖ⁾~*will*~PLACE⁽ⱽ⁾ UPON~them⁽ᵐ⁾ NOT *you*⁽ᵐᵖ⁾~*will*~TAKE.AWAY⁽ⱽ⁾ FROM~him GIVEN.THAT *be*~ SINK.DOWN⁽ⱽ⁾~*ing*⁽ᵐᵖ⁾ THEY⁽ᵐ⁾ UPON SO THEY⁽ᵐ⁾ CRY.OUT⁽ⱽ⁾~*ing*⁽ᵐᵖ⁾ to~>~ SAY⁽ⱽ⁾ *we~will*~WALK⁽ⱽ⁾~& *we~will*~SACRIFICE⁽ⱽ⁾~& to~Elohiym~us **5:9** *she~ will*~BE.HEAVY⁽ⱽ⁾ the~SERVICE UPON the~MAN~s and~*they*⁽ᵐ⁾~*will*~DO⁽ⱽ⁾ in~ her and~DO.NOT *they*⁽ᵐ⁾~*will*~DO⁽ⱽ⁾ in~WORD~s FALSE **5:10** and~*they*⁽ᵐ⁾~ *will*~GO.OUT⁽ⱽ⁾ PUSH⁽ⱽ⁾~*ing*⁽ᵐᵖ⁾ the~PEOPLE and~OFFICER~s~him and~ *they*⁽ᵐ⁾~*will*~SAY⁽ⱽ⁾ TO the~PEOPLE to~>~SAY⁽ⱽ⁾ IN.THIS.WAY *he~did*~SAY⁽ⱽ⁾ Paroh WITHOUT~me GIVE⁽ⱽ⁾~*ing*⁽ᵐˢ⁾ to~you⁽ᵐᵖ⁾ STRAW **5:11** YOU⁽ᵐᵖ⁾ !⁽ᵐᵖ⁾~ WALK⁽ⱽ⁾ !⁽ᵐᵖ⁾~TAKE⁽ⱽ⁾ to~you⁽ᵐᵖ⁾ STRAW from~WHICH *you*⁽ᵐᵖ⁾~*will*~FIND⁽ⱽ⁾ GIVEN.THAT WITHOUT *be*~TAKE.AWAY⁽ⱽ⁾~*ing*⁽ᵐˢ⁾ from~SERVICE~you⁽ᵐᵖ⁾ WORD **5:12** and~*he~will*~make~SCATTER.ABROAD⁽ⱽ⁾ the~PEOPLE in~ALL LAND Mits'rayim to~much~COLLECT⁽ⱽ⁾ STUBBLE to~STRAW **5:13** and~the~ PUSH⁽ⱽ⁾~*ing*⁽ᵐᵖ⁾ COMPEL⁽ⱽ⁾~*ing*⁽ᵐᵖ⁾ to~>~SAY⁽ⱽ⁾ !⁽ᵐᵖ⁾~much~FINISH⁽ⱽ⁾ WORK~s~you⁽ᵐᵖ⁾ WORD DAY in~DAY~him like~WHICH in~>~EXIST⁽ⱽ⁾ the~ STRAW **5:14** and~*they*⁽ᵐ⁾~*will~be*~make~HIT⁽ⱽ⁾ OFFICER~s SON~s Yisra'eyl WHICH *they~did*~PLACE⁽ⱽ⁾ UPON~them⁽ᵐ⁾ PUSH⁽ⱽ⁾~*ing*⁽ᵐᵖ⁾ Paroh to~>~SAY⁽ⱽ⁾ WHY NOT *you*⁽ᵐᵖ⁾~*did*~much~FINISH⁽ⱽ⁾ CUSTOM~you⁽ᵐᵖ⁾ to~>~ MAKE.BRICKS⁽ⱽ⁾ like~YESTERDAY THREE.DAYS.AGO ALSO YESTERDAY ALSO the~DAY **5:15** and~*they*⁽ᵐ⁾~*will*~COME⁽ⱽ⁾ OFFICER~s SON~s Yisra'eyl and~ *they*⁽ᵐ⁾~*will*~CRY.OUT⁽ⱽ⁾ TO Paroh to~>~SAY⁽ⱽ⁾ to~WHAT *you*⁽ᵐˢ⁾~*will*~DO⁽ⱽ⁾ IN.THIS.WAY to~SERVANT~s~you⁽ᵐˢ⁾ **5:16** STRAW WITHOUT *be*~GIVE⁽ⱽ⁾~ *ing*⁽ᵐˢ⁾ to~SERVANT~s~you⁽ᵐˢ⁾ and~BRICK~s SAY⁽ⱽ⁾~*ing*⁽ᵐᵖ⁾ to~us !⁽ᵐᵖ⁾~DO⁽ⱽ⁾ and~LOOK SERVANT~s~you⁽ᵐˢ⁾ *be*~make~HIT⁽ⱽ⁾~*ing*⁽ᵐᵖ⁾ and~FAILURE PEOPLE~you⁽ᵐˢ⁾ **5:17** and~*he~will*~SAY⁽ⱽ⁾ *be*~SINK.DOWN⁽ⱽ⁾~*ing*⁽ᵐᵖ⁾ YOU⁽ᵐᵖ⁾ *be*~SINK.DOWN⁽ⱽ⁾~*ing*⁽ᵐᵖ⁾ UPON SO YOU⁽ᵐᵖ⁾ SAY⁽ⱽ⁾~*ing*⁽ᵐᵖ⁾ *we~will*~WALK⁽ⱽ⁾~ & *we~will*~SACRIFICE⁽ⱽ⁾~& to~**YHWH** **5:18** and~NOW !⁽ᵐᵖ⁾~WALK⁽ⱽ⁾ !⁽ᵐᵖ⁾~ SERVE⁽ⱽ⁾ and~STRAW NOT *he~will~be*~GIVE⁽ⱽ⁾ to~you⁽ᵐᵖ⁾ and~ MEASURED.AMOUNT BRICK~s *you*⁽ᵐᵖ⁾~*will*~GIVE⁽ⱽ⁾ **5:19** and~*they*⁽ᵐ⁾~*will*~ SEE⁽ⱽ⁾ OFFICER~s SON~s Yisra'eyl AT~them⁽ᵐ⁾ in~DYSFUNCTIONAL to~>~ SAY⁽ⱽ⁾ NOT *you*⁽ᵐᵖ⁾~*will*~TAKE.AWAY⁽ⱽ⁾ from~BRICK~s~you⁽ᵐᵖ⁾ WORD DAY in~ DAY~him **5:20** and~*they*⁽ᵐ⁾~*will*~REACH⁽ⱽ⁾ AT Mosheh and~AT Aharon *be*~ STAND.UP⁽ⱽ⁾~*ing*⁽ᵐᵖ⁾ to~>~MEET⁽ⱽ⁾~them⁽ᵐ⁾ in~>~GO.OUT⁽ⱽ⁾~them⁽ᵐ⁾ from~

AT Paroh **5:21** and~*they*⁽ᵐ⁾~*will*~SAY⁽ⱽ⁾ TO~them⁽ᵐ⁾ *he~will*~SEE⁽ⱽ⁾ **YHWH** UPON~you⁽ᵐᵖ⁾ and~*he~will*~DECIDE⁽ⱽ⁾ WHICH *you*⁽ᵐᵖ⁾~*did~make*~STINK⁽ⱽ⁾ AT AROMA~us in~EYE~s2 Paroh and~in~EYE~s2 SERVANT~s~him to~>~GIVE⁽ⱽ⁾ SWORD in~HAND~them⁽ᵐ⁾ to~>~KILL⁽ⱽ⁾~us **5:22** and~*he~will*~TURN.BACK⁽ⱽ⁾ Mosheh TO **YHWH** and~*he~will*~SAY⁽ⱽ⁾ Adonai to~WHAT *you*⁽ᵐˢ⁾~*did~make*~BE.DYSFUNCTIONAL⁽ⱽ⁾~& to~the~PEOPLE the~THIS to~WHAT THIS *you*⁽ᵐˢ⁾~*did*~SEND⁽ⱽ⁾~me **5:23** and~from~AT.THAT.TIME *I~did*~COME⁽ⱽ⁾ TO Paroh to~>~*much*~SPEAK⁽ⱽ⁾ in~TITLE~you⁽ᵐˢ⁾ *he~did~make*~BE.DYSFUNCTIONAL⁽ⱽ⁾ to~the~PEOPLE the~THIS and~>~*make*~DELIVER⁽ⱽ⁾ NOT *you*⁽ᵐˢ⁾~*did~make*~DELIVER⁽ⱽ⁾ AT PEOPLE~you⁽ᵐˢ⁾

Chapter 6

6:1 and~*he~will*~SAY⁽ⱽ⁾ **YHWH** TO Mosheh NOW *you*⁽ᵐˢ⁾~*will*~SEE⁽ⱽ⁾ WHICH *I~will*~DO⁽ⱽ⁾ to~Paroh GIVEN.THAT in~HAND FORCEFUL *he~will~much*~SEND⁽ⱽ⁾~them⁽ᵐ⁾ and~in~HAND FORCEFUL *he~will~much*~CAST.OUT⁽ⱽ⁾~them⁽ᵐ⁾ from~LAND~him **6:2** and~*he~will~much*~SPEAK⁽ⱽ⁾ Elohiym TO Mosheh and~*he~will*~SAY⁽ⱽ⁾ TO~him I **YHWH** **6:3** and~*I~will*~be~SEE⁽ⱽ⁾ TO Avraham TO Yits'hhaq and~TO Ya'aqov in~MIGHTY.ONE Shaddai and~TITLE~me **YHWH** NOT *I~did*~be~KNOW⁽ⱽ⁾ to~them⁽ᵐ⁾ **6:4** and~ALSO *I~did~make*~RISE⁽ⱽ⁾ AT COVENANT~me AT~them⁽ᵐ⁾ to~>~GIVE⁽ⱽ⁾ to~them⁽ᵐ⁾ AT LAND Kena'an AT LAND IMMIGRATION~them⁽ᵐ⁾ WHICH *they~did*~IMMIGRATE⁽ⱽ⁾ in~her **6:5** and~ALSO I *I~did*~HEAR⁽ⱽ⁾ AT GROANING SON~s Yisra'eyl WHICH Mits'rayim *make*~SERVE⁽ⱽ⁾~*ing*⁽ᵐᵖ⁾ AT~them⁽ᵐ⁾ and~*I~will*~REMEMBER⁽ⱽ⁾ AT COVENANT~me **6:6** to~SO !⁽ᵐˢ⁾~SAY⁽ⱽ⁾ to~SON~s Yisra'eyl I **YHWH** and~*I~did~make*~GO.OUT⁽ⱽ⁾ AT~you⁽ᵐᵖ⁾ from~UNDER BURDEN~s Mits'rayim and~*I~did~make*~DELIVER⁽ⱽ⁾ AT~you⁽ᵐᵖ⁾ from~SERVICE~them⁽ᵐ⁾ and~*I~did*~REDEEM⁽ⱽ⁾ AT~you⁽ᵐᵖ⁾ in~ARM EXTEND⁽ⱽ⁾~*ed*⁽ᶠˢ⁾ and~in~JUDGMENT~s GREAT~s **6:7** and~*I~did*~TAKE⁽ⱽ⁾ AT~you⁽ᵐᵖ⁾ to~me to~PEOPLE and~*I~did*~EXIST⁽ⱽ⁾ to~you⁽ᵐᵖ⁾ to~Elohiym and~*you*⁽ᵐᵖ⁾~*did*~KNOW⁽ⱽ⁾ GIVEN.THAT I **YHWH** Elohiym~you⁽ᵐᵖ⁾ the~*make*~GO.OUT⁽ⱽ⁾~*ing*⁽ᵐˢ⁾ AT~you⁽ᵐᵖ⁾ from~UNDER BURDEN~s Mits'rayim **6:8** and~*I~will*~*make*~COME⁽ⱽ⁾ AT~you⁽ᵐᵖ⁾ TO the~LAND WHICH *I~did*~LIFT.UP⁽ⱽ⁾ AT HAND~me to~>~GIVE⁽ⱽ⁾ AT~her to~Avraham to~Yits'hhaq and~to~Ya'aqov and~*I~did*~GIVE⁽ⱽ⁾ AT~her to~you⁽ᵐᵖ⁾ POSSESSION I **YHWH** **6:9** and~*he~will~much*~SPEAK⁽ⱽ⁾ Mosheh SO TO SON~s Yisra'eyl and~NOT *they~did*~HEAR⁽ⱽ⁾ TO Mosheh from~SHORTNESS WIND and~from~SERVICE HARD **6:10** and~*he~will~much*~SPEAK⁽ⱽ⁾ **YHWH** TO Mosheh to~>~SAY⁽ⱽ⁾ **6:11** !⁽ᵐˢ⁾~COME⁽ⱽ⁾ !⁽ᵐˢ⁾~*much*~SPEAK⁽ⱽ⁾ TO Paroh KING Mits'rayim and~*he~will*~SEND⁽ⱽ⁾ AT SON~s Yisra'eyl from~LAND~him **6:12** and~*he~will~much*~SPEAK⁽ⱽ⁾ Mosheh to~FACE~s **YHWH** to~>~SAY⁽ⱽ⁾ THOUGH SON~s Yisra'eyl NOT *they~did*~HEAR⁽ⱽ⁾ TO~me and~HOW *he~will*~HEAR⁽ⱽ⁾~me Paroh and~I UNCIRCUMCISED LIP~s2 **6:13** and~*he~will~much*~SPEAK⁽ⱽ⁾ **YHWH** TO Mosheh and~TO Aharon and~*he~will~much*~

DIRECT$^{(V)}$~them$^{(m)}$ TO SON~s Yisra'eyl and~TO Paroh KING Mits'rayim to~>~ *make*~GO.OUT$^{(V)}$ AT SON~s Yisra'eyl from~LAND Mits'rayim **6:14** THESE HEAD~s HOUSE FATHER~s~them$^{(m)}$ SON~s Re'uven FIRSTBORN Yisra'eyl Hhanokh and~Palu Hhetsron and~Karmi THESE CLAN~s Re'uven **6:15** and~ SON~s Shimon Yemu'el and~Yamin and~Ohad and~Yakhin and~Tsohhar and~Sha'ul SON the~Kena'an~s THESE CLAN~s Shimon **6:16** and~THESE TITLE~s SON~s Lewi to~BIRTHING~s~them$^{(m)}$ Gershon and~Qehat and~ Merari and~TWO LIVING~s Lewi SEVEN and~THREE~s and~HUNDRED YEAR **6:17** SON~s Gershon Liyvniy and~Shiymiy to~CLAN~s~ them$^{(m)}$ **6:18** and~SON~s Qehat Amram and~Yits'har and~Hhevron and~ Uziy'eyl and~TWO LIVING~s Qehat THREE and~THREE~s and~HUNDRED YEAR **6:19** and~SON~s Merari Mahh'liy and~Mushiy THESE CLAN~s the~ Lewi to~BIRTHING~s~them$^{(m)}$ **6:20** and~*he~will*~TAKE$^{(V)}$ Amram AT Yokheved AUNT~him to~him to~WOMAN and~*she~will*~BRING.FORTH$^{(V)}$ to~ him AT Aharon and~AT Mosheh and~TWO LIVING~s Amram SEVEN and~ THREE~s and~HUNDRED YEAR **6:21** and~SON~s Yits'har Qorahh and~ Nepheg and~Zikh'riy **6:22** and~SON~s Uziy'eyl Miysha'eyl and~El'tsaphan and~Sitriy **6:23** and~*he~will*~TAKE$^{(V)}$ Aharon AT Eliysheva DAUGHTER Amiynadav SISTER Nahhshon to~him to~WOMAN and~*she~will*~ BRING.FORTH$^{(V)}$ to~him AT Nadav and~AT Aviyhu AT Elazar and~AT Iytamar **6:24** and~SON~s Qorahh Asiyr and~Elqanah and~Aviyasaph THESE CLAN~s the~Qorahh~of **6:25** and~Elazar SON Aharon *he~did*~TAKE$^{(V)}$ to~ him from~DAUGHTER~s Putiy'eyl to~him to~WOMAN and~*she~will*~ BRING.FORTH$^{(V)}$ to~him AT Piynhhas THESE HEAD~s FATHER~s the~Lewi~s to~CLAN~s~them$^{(m)}$ **6:26** HE Aharon and~Mosheh WHICH *he~did*~SAY$^{(V)}$ **YHWH** to~them$^{(m)}$ *!$^{(mp)}$~make*~GO.OUT$^{(V)}$ AT SON~s Yisra'eyl from~LAND Mits'rayim UPON ARMY~s~them$^{(m)}$ **6:27** THEY$^{(m)}$ the~*much*~SPEAK$^{(V)}$~*ing*$^{(mp)}$ TO Paroh KING Mits'rayim to~>~*make*~GO.OUT$^{(V)}$ AT SON~s Yisra'eyl from~ Mits'rayim HE Mosheh and~Aharon **6:28** and~*he~will*~EXIST$^{(V)}$ in~DAY *he~ did*~*much*~SPEAK$^{(V)}$ **YHWH** TO Mosheh in~LAND Mits'rayim **6:29** and~*he~ will*~*much*~SPEAK$^{(V)}$ **YHWH** TO Mosheh to~>~SAY$^{(V)}$ I **YHWH** *!$^{(ms)}$~much*~ SPEAK$^{(V)}$ TO Paroh KING Mits'rayim AT ALL WHICH I SPEAK$^{(V)}$~*ing*$^{(ms)}$ TO~ you$^{(ms)}$ **6:30** and~*he~will*~SAY$^{(V)}$ Mosheh to~FACE~s **YHWH** THOUGH I UNCIRCUMCISED LIP~s2 and~HOW *he~will*~HEAR$^{(V)}$ TO~me Paroh

Chapter 7

7:1 and~*he~will*~SAY$^{(V)}$ **YHWH** TO Mosheh *!$^{(ms)}$~*SEE$^{(V)}$ *I~did*~GIVE$^{(V)}$~you$^{(ms)}$ Elohiym to~Paroh and~Aharon BROTHER~you$^{(ms)}$ *he~will*~EXIST$^{(V)}$ ANNOUNCER~you$^{(ms)}$ **7:2** YOU$^{(ms)}$ *you$^{(ms)}$~will*~*much*~SPEAK$^{(V)}$ AT ALL WHICH *I~will*~*much*~DIRECT$^{(V)}$~you$^{(ms)}$ and~Aharon BROTHER~you$^{(ms)}$ *he~will*~ *much*~SPEAK$^{(V)}$ TO Paroh and~*he~did*~*much*~SEND$^{(V)}$ AT SON~s Yisra'eyl from~LAND~him **7:3** and~I *I~will*~*make*~BE.HARD$^{(V)}$ AT HEART Paroh and~*I~*

did~make~INCREASE$^{(v)}$ AT SIGN~s~me and~AT WONDER~s~me in~LAND Mits'rayim **7:4** and~NOT he~will~HEAR$^{(v)}$ TO~you$^{(mp)}$ Paroh and~I~did~GIVE$^{(v)}$ AT HAND~me in~Mits'rayim and~I~did~make~GO.OUT$^{(v)}$ AT ARMY~s~me AT PEOPLE~me SON~s Yisra'eyl from~LAND Mits'rayim in~JUDGMENT~s GREAT~s **7:5** and~they~did~KNOW$^{(v)}$ Mits'rayim GIVEN.THAT I **YHWH** in~>~EXTEND$^{(v)}$~me AT HAND~me UPON Mits'rayim and~I~did~make~GO.OUT$^{(v)}$ AT SON~s Yisra'eyl from~MIDST~them$^{(m)}$ **7:6** and~he~will~DO$^{(v)}$ Mosheh and~Aharon like~WHICH he~did~much~DIRECT$^{(v)}$ **YHWH** AT~them$^{(m)}$ SO they~did~DO$^{(v)}$ **7:7** and~Mosheh SON EIGHT~s YEAR and~Aharon SON THREE and~EIGHT~s YEAR in~>~much~SPEAK$^{(v)}$~them$^{(m)}$ TO Paroh **7:8** and~he~will~SAY$^{(v)}$ **YHWH** TO Mosheh and~TO Aharon to~>~SAY$^{(v)}$ **7:9** GIVEN.THAT he~will~much~SPEAK$^{(v)}$ TO~you$^{(mp)}$ Paroh to~>~SAY$^{(v)}$!$^{(mp)}$~GIVE$^{(v)}$ to~you$^{(mp)}$ WONDER and~you$^{(ms)}$~did~SAY$^{(v)}$ TO Aharon !$^{(ms)}$~TAKE$^{(v)}$ AT BRANCH~you$^{(ms)}$ and~ !$^{(ms)}$~make~THROW.OUT$^{(v)}$ to~FACE~s Paroh he~will~EXIST$^{(v)}$ to~CROCODILE **7:10** and~he~will~COME$^{(v)}$ Mosheh and~Aharon TO Paroh and~they$^{(m)}$~will~DO$^{(v)}$ SO like~WHICH he~did~much~DIRECT$^{(v)}$ **YHWH** and~he~will~make~THROW.OUT$^{(v)}$ Aharon AT BRANCH~him to~FACE~s Paroh and~to~FACE~s SERVANT~s~him and~he~will~EXIST$^{(v)}$ to~CROCODILE **7:11** and~he~will~CALL.OUT$^{(v)}$ ALSO Paroh to~SKILLED.ONE~s and~to~much~DO.SORCERY$^{(v)}$~ing$^{(mp)}$ and~they$^{(m)}$~will~DO$^{(v)}$ ALSO THEY$^{(m)}$ MAGICIAN~s Mits'rayim in~BLAZING~s~them$^{(m)}$ SO **7:12** and~they$^{(m)}$~will~make~THROW.OUT$^{(v)}$ MAN BRANCH~him and~they$^{(m)}$~will~EXIST$^{(v)}$ to~CROCODILE~s and~he~will~SWALLOW$^{(v)}$ BRANCH Aharon AT BRANCH~s~them$^{(m)}$ **7:13** and~he~will~SEIZE$^{(v)}$ HEART Paroh and~NOT he~did~HEAR$^{(v)}$ TO~them$^{(m)}$ like~WHICH he~did~much~SPEAK$^{(v)}$ **YHWH** **7:14** and~he~will~SAY$^{(v)}$ **YHWH** TO Mosheh HEAVY HEART Paroh he~did~much~REFUSE$^{(v)}$ to~>~much~SEND$^{(v)}$ the~PEOPLE **7:15** !$^{(ms)}$~WALK$^{(v)}$ TO Paroh in~the~MORNING LOOK GO.OUT$^{(v)}$~ing$^{(ms)}$ the~WATER~s2~unto and~you$^{(ms)}$~did~be~STAND.UP$^{(v)}$ to~>~MEET$^{(v)}$~him UPON LIP the~STREAM and~the~BRANCH WHICH he~did~be~OVERTURN$^{(v)}$ to~SERPENT you$^{(ms)}$~will~TAKE$^{(v)}$ in~HAND~you$^{(ms)}$ **7:16** and~you$^{(ms)}$~did~SAY$^{(v)}$ TO~him **YHWH** Elohiym the~Ever~s he~did~SEND$^{(v)}$~me TO~you$^{(ms)}$ to~>~SAY$^{(v)}$!$^{(ms)}$~much~SEND$^{(v)}$ AT PEOPLE~me and~they$^{(m)}$~will~SERVE$^{(v)}$~me in~the~WILDERNESS and~LOOK NOT you$^{(ms)}$~did~HEAR$^{(v)}$ UNTIL IN.THIS.WAY **7:17** IN.THIS.WAY he~did~SAY$^{(v)}$ **YHWH** in~THIS you$^{(ms)}$~will~KNOW$^{(v)}$ GIVEN.THAT I **YHWH** LOOK I make~HIT$^{(v)}$~ing$^{(ms)}$ in~the~BRANCH WHICH in~HAND~me UPON the~WATER~s2 WHICH in~the~STREAM and~they~did~be~OVERTURN$^{(v)}$ to~BLOOD **7:18** and~the~FISH WHICH in~the~STREAM she~will~DIE$^{(v)}$ and~he~did~STINK$^{(v)}$ the~STREAM and~they~did~be~BE.IMPATIENT$^{(v)}$ Mits'rayim to~>~GULP$^{(v)}$ WATER~s2 FROM the~STREAM **7:19** and~he~will~SAY$^{(v)}$ **YHWH** TO Mosheh !$^{(ms)}$~SAY$^{(v)}$ TO Aharon !$^{(ms)}$~TAKE$^{(v)}$ BRANCH~you$^{(ms)}$ and~ !$^{(ms)}$~EXTEND$^{(v)}$ HAND~you$^{(ms)}$ UPON WATER~s2 Mits'rayim UPON RIVER~s~them$^{(m)}$ UPON STREAM~s~them$^{(m)}$ and~UPON POOL~s~them$^{(m)}$ and~UPON ALL COLLECTION WATER~s2~them$^{(m)}$ and~they$^{(m)}$~will~EXIST$^{(v)}$ BLOOD and~he~did~EXIST$^{(v)}$ BLOOD in~ALL LAND Mits'rayim and~in~the~TREE~s and~

in~the~STONE~s **7:20** and~*they*⁽ᵐ⁾~*will*~DO⁽ⱽ⁾ SO Mosheh and~Aharon like~ WHICH *he*~*did*~*much*~DIRECT⁽ⱽ⁾ **YHWH** and~*he*~*will*~*make*~RAISE.UP⁽ⱽ⁾ in~ the~BRANCH and~*he*~*will*~*make*~HIT⁽ⱽ⁾ AT the~WATER~s2 WHICH in~the~ STREAM to~EYE~s2 Paroh and~to~EYE~s SERVANT~s~him and~*they*⁽ᵐ⁾~*will*~ *be*~OVERTURN⁽ⱽ⁾ ALL the~WATER~s2 WHICH in~the~STREAM to~ BLOOD **7:21** and~the~FISH WHICH in~the~STREAM *she*~*did*~DIE⁽ⱽ⁾ and~*he*~ *will*~STINK⁽ⱽ⁾ the~STREAM and~NOT *they*~*did*~BE.ABLE⁽ⱽ⁾ Mits'rayim to~>~ GULP⁽ⱽ⁾ WATER~s2 FROM the~STREAM and~*he*~*will*~EXIST⁽ⱽ⁾ the~BLOOD in~ ALL LAND Mits'rayim **7:22** and~*they*⁽ᵐ⁾~*will*~DO⁽ⱽ⁾ SO MAGICIAN~s Mits'rayim in~SECRET~s~them⁽ᵐ⁾ and~*he*~*will*~SEIZE⁽ⱽ⁾ HEART Paroh and~ NOT *he*~*did*~HEAR⁽ⱽ⁾ TO~them⁽ᵐ⁾ like~WHICH *he*~*did*~*much*~SPEAK⁽ⱽ⁾ **YHWH 7:23** and~*he*~*will*~TURN⁽ⱽ⁾ Paroh and~*he*~*will*~COME⁽ⱽ⁾ TO HOUSE~ him and~NOT *he*~*did*~SET.DOWN⁽ⱽ⁾ HEART~him ALSO to~THIS **7:24** and~ *they*⁽ᵐ⁾~*will*~DIG.OUT⁽ⱽ⁾ ALL Mits'rayim ALL.AROUND~s the~STREAM WATER~s2 to~>~GULP⁽ⱽ⁾ GIVEN.THAT NOT *they*~*did*~BE.ABLE⁽ⱽ⁾ to~>~ GULP⁽ⱽ⁾ from~WATER~s2 the~STREAM **7:25** and~*he*~*will*~*be*~FILL⁽ⱽ⁾ SEVEN DAY~s AFTER >~*make*~HIT⁽ⱽ⁾ **YHWH** AT the~STREAM **7:26 (8:1)** and~*he*~ *will*~SAY⁽ⱽ⁾ **YHWH** TO Mosheh !⁽ᵐˢ⁾~COME⁽ⱽ⁾ TO Paroh and~*you*⁽ᵐˢ⁾~*did*~ SAY⁽ⱽ⁾ TO~him IN.THIS.WAY *he*~*did*~SAY⁽ⱽ⁾ **YHWH** !⁽ᵐˢ⁾~*much*~SEND⁽ⱽ⁾ AT PEOPLE~me and~*they*⁽ᵐ⁾~*will*~SERVE⁽ⱽ⁾~me **7:27 (8:2)** and~IF REFUSING YOU⁽ᵐˢ⁾ to~>~*much*~SEND⁽ⱽ⁾ LOOK I SMITE⁽ⱽ⁾~*ing*⁽ᵐˢ⁾ AT ALL BORDER~you⁽ᵐˢ⁾ in~the~FROG~s **7:28 (8:3)** and~*he*~*did*~SWARM⁽ⱽ⁾ the~STREAM FROG~s and~*they*~*did*~GO.UP⁽ⱽ⁾ and~*they*~*did*~COME⁽ⱽ⁾ in~HOUSE~you⁽ᵐˢ⁾ and~in~ CHAMBER LYING.PLACE~you⁽ᵐˢ⁾ and~UPON BED~you⁽ᵐˢ⁾ and~in~HOUSE SERVANT~s~you⁽ᵐˢ⁾ and~in~PEOPLE~you⁽ᵐˢ⁾ and~in~OVEN~s~you⁽ᵐˢ⁾ and~ in~KNEADING.BOWL~s~you⁽ᵐˢ⁾ **7:29 (8:4)** and~in~you⁽ᵐˢ⁾ and~in~PEOPLE~ you⁽ᵐˢ⁾ and~in~ALL SERVANT~s~you⁽ᵐˢ⁾ *they*⁽ᵐ⁾~*will*~GO.UP⁽ⱽ⁾ the~FROG~s

Chapter 8

8:1 (8:5) and~*he*~*will*~SAY⁽ⱽ⁾ **YHWH** TO Mosheh !⁽ᵐˢ⁾~SAY⁽ⱽ⁾ TO Aharon !⁽ᵐˢ⁾~ EXTEND⁽ⱽ⁾ AT HAND~you⁽ᵐˢ⁾ in~BRANCH~you⁽ᵐˢ⁾ UPON the~RIVER~s UPON the~STREAM~s and~UPON the~POOL~s and~ !⁽ᵐˢ⁾~*make*~GO.UP⁽ⱽ⁾ AT the~ FROG~s UPON LAND Mits'rayim **8:2 (8:6)** and~*he*~*will*~EXTEND⁽ⱽ⁾ Aharon AT HAND~him UPON WATER~s2 Mits'rayim and~*she*~*will*~GO.UP⁽ⱽ⁾ the~FROG and~*she*~*will*~*much*~COVER.OVER⁽ⱽ⁾ AT LAND Mits'rayim **8:3 (8:7)** and~ *they*⁽ᵐ⁾~*will*~DO⁽ⱽ⁾ SO the~MAGICIAN~s in~SECRET~s~them⁽ᵐ⁾ and~*they*⁽ᵐ⁾~ *will*~GO.UP⁽ⱽ⁾ AT the~FROG~s UPON LAND Mits'rayim **8:4 (8:8)** and~*he*~ *will*~CALL.OUT⁽ⱽ⁾ Paroh to~Mosheh and~to~Aharon and~*he*~*will*~SAY⁽ⱽ⁾ !⁽ᵐᵖ⁾~*make*~INTERCEDE⁽ⱽ⁾ TO **YHWH** and~*he*~*will*~*make*~TURN.ASIDE⁽ⱽ⁾ the~ FROG~s FROM~me and~from~PEOPLE~me and~*I*~*will*~*much*~SEND⁽ⱽ⁾~& AT the~PEOPLE and~*they*⁽ᵐ⁾~*will*~SACRIFICE⁽ⱽ⁾ to~**YHWH 8:5 (8:9)** and~*he*~*will*~ SAY⁽ⱽ⁾ Mosheh to~Paroh !⁽ᵐˢ⁾~*self*~DECORATE⁽ⱽ⁾ UPON~me to~HOW.LONG *I*~

*will~make~*INTERCEDE$^{(V)}$ to~you$^{(ms)}$ and~to~SERVANT~s~you$^{(ms)}$ and~to~PEOPLE~you$^{(ms)}$ to~>~*make~*CUT$^{(V)}$ the~FROG~s FROM~you$^{(ms)}$ and~from~HOUSE~s~you$^{(ms)}$ ONLY in~the~STREAM *they$^{(f)}$~will~be~*REMAIN$^{(V)}$ **8:6 (8:10)** and~*he~will~*SAY$^{(V)}$ to~TOMORROW and~*he~will~*SAY$^{(V)}$ like~WORD~you$^{(ms)}$ to~THAT *you$^{(ms)}$~will~*KNOW$^{(V)}$ GIVEN.THAT WITHOUT like~**YHWH** Elohiym~us **8:7 (8:11)** and~*they~did~*TURN.ASIDE$^{(V)}$ the~FROG~s FROM~you$^{(ms)}$ and~from~HOUSE~s~you$^{(ms)}$ and~from~SERVANT~s~you$^{(ms)}$ and~from~PEOPLE~you$^{(ms)}$ ONLY in~the~STREAM *they$^{(f)}$~will~be~*REMAIN$^{(V)}$ **8:8 (8:12)** and~*he~will~*GO.OUT$^{(V)}$ Mosheh and~Aharon from~WITH Paroh and~*he~will~*CRY.OUT$^{(V)}$ Mosheh TO **YHWH** UPON WORD the~FROG~s WHICH *he~did~*PLACE$^{(V)}$ to~Paroh **8:9 (8:13)** and~*he~will~*DO$^{(V)}$ **YHWH** like~WORD Mosheh and~*they$^{(m)}$~will~*DIE$^{(V)}$ the~FROG~s FROM the~HOUSE~s FROM the~COURTYARD~s and~FROM the~FIELD~s **8:10 (8:14)** and~*they$^{(m)}$~will~*PILE.UP$^{(V)}$ AT~them$^{(m)}$ SLIME~s SLIME~s and~*she~will~*STINK$^{(V)}$ the~LAND **8:11 (8:15)** and~*he~will~*SEE$^{(V)}$ Paroh GIVEN.THAT *she~did~*EXIST$^{(V)}$ the~RESPITE and~>~*make~*BE.HEAVY$^{(V)}$ AT HEART~him and~NOT *he~did~*HEAR$^{(V)}$ TO~them$^{(m)}$ like~WHICH *he~did~much~*SPEAK$^{(V)}$ **YHWH 8:12 (8:16)** and~*he~will~*SAY$^{(V)}$ **YHWH** TO Mosheh *!$^{(ms)}$~*SAY$^{(V)}$ TO Aharon *!$^{(ms)}$~*EXTEND$^{(V)}$ AT BRANCH~you$^{(ms)}$ and~*!$^{(ms)}$~make~*HIT$^{(V)}$ AT DIRT the~LAND and~*he~did~*EXIST$^{(V)}$ to~GNAT~s in~ALL LAND Mits'rayim **8:13 (8:17)** and~*they$^{(m)}$~will~*DO$^{(V)}$ SO and~*he~will~*EXTEND$^{(V)}$ Aharon AT HAND~him in~BRANCH~him and~*he~will~make~*HIT$^{(V)}$ AT DIRT the~LAND and~*she~will~*EXIST$^{(V)}$ the~GNAT~s in~the~HUMAN and~in~the~BEAST ALL DIRT the~LAND *he~did~*EXIST$^{(V)}$ GNAT~s in~ALL LAND Mits'rayim **8:14 (8:18)** and~*they$^{(m)}$~will~*DO$^{(V)}$ SO the~MAGICIAN~s in~SECRET~s~them$^{(m)}$ to~>~*make~*GO.OUT$^{(V)}$ AT the~GNAT~s and~NOT *they~did~*BE.ABLE$^{(V)}$ and~*she~will~*EXIST$^{(V)}$ the~GNAT~s in~the~HUMAN and~in~the~BEAST **8:15 (8:19)** and~*they$^{(m)}$~will~*SAY$^{(V)}$ the~MAGICIAN~s TO Paroh FINGER Elohiym SHE and~*he~will~*SEIZE$^{(V)}$ HEART Paroh and~NOT *he~did~*HEAR$^{(V)}$ TO~them$^{(m)}$ like~WHICH *he~did~much~*SPEAK$^{(V)}$ **YHWH 8:16 (8:20)** and~*he~will~*SAY$^{(V)}$ **YHWH** TO Mosheh *!$^{(mp)}$~make~*DEPART.EARLY$^{(V)}$ in~the~MORNING and~*!$^{(ms)}$~self~*STAND.UP$^{(V)}$ to~FACE~s Paroh LOOK GO.OUT$^{(V)}$~*ing$^{(ms)}$* the~WATER~s2~unto and~*you$^{(ms)}$~did~*SAY$^{(V)}$ TO~him IN.THIS.WAY *he~did~*SAY$^{(V)}$ **YHWH** *!$^{(ms)}$~much~*SEND$^{(V)}$ PEOPLE~me and~*they$^{(m)}$~will~*SERVE$^{(V)}$~me **8:17 (8:21)** GIVEN.THAT IF WITHOUT~you$^{(ms)}$ *much~*SEND$^{(V)}$~*ing$^{(ms)}$* AT PEOPLE~me LOOK~me *make~*SEND$^{(V)}$~*ing$^{(ms)}$* in~you$^{(ms)}$ and~in~SERVANT~s~you$^{(ms)}$ and~in~PEOPLE~you$^{(ms)}$ and~in~HOUSE~s~you$^{(ms)}$ AT the~HORDE and~*they~did~*FILL$^{(V)}$ HOUSE~s Mits'rayim AT the~HORDE and~ALSO the~GROUND WHICH THEY$^{(m)}$ UPON~her **8:18 (8:22)** and~*I~did~make~*BE.DISTINCT$^{(V)}$ in~the~DAY the~HE AT LAND Goshen WHICH PEOPLE~me STAND$^{(V)}$~*ing$^{(ms)}$* UPON~her to~EXCEPT >~EXIST$^{(V)}$ THERE HORDE to~THAT *you$^{(ms)}$~will~*KNOW$^{(V)}$ GIVEN.THAT I **YHWH** in~INSIDE the~LAND **8:19 (8:23)** and~*I~did~*PLACE$^{(V)}$ RANSOM BETWEEN PEOPLE~me and~BETWEEN PEOPLE~you$^{(ms)}$ to~TOMORROW *he~will~*

The Book of Exodus

EXIST$^{(V)}$ the~SIGN the~THIS **8:20 (8:24)** and~*he~will*~DO$^{(V)}$ **YHWH** SO and~*he~will*~COME$^{(V)}$ HORDE HEAVY HOUSE~unto Paroh and~HOUSE SERVANT~s~him and~in~ALL LAND Mits'rayim *she~will~be*~DAMAGE$^{(V)}$ the~LAND from~FACE~s the~HORDE **8:21 (8:25)** and~*he~will*~CALL.OUT$^{(V)}$ Paroh TO Mosheh and~to~Aharon and~*he~will*~SAY$^{(V)}$ *l$^{(mp)}$~*WALK$^{(V)}$ *l$^{(mp)}$~*SACRIFICE$^{(V)}$ to~Elohiym~*you*$^{(mp)}$ in~the~LAND **8:22 (8:26)** and~*he~will*~SAY$^{(V)}$ Mosheh NOT *be~*PREPARE$^{(V)}$~*ing*$^{(ms)}$ to~>~DO$^{(V)}$ SO GIVEN.THAT DISGUSTING Mits'rayim *we~will*~SACRIFICE$^{(V)}$ to~**YHWH** Elohiym~us THOUGH *we~will*~SACRIFICE$^{(V)}$ AT DISGUSTING Mits'rayim to~EYE~s2~*them*$^{(m)}$ and~NOT *they*$^{(m)}$~*will*~STONE$^{(V)}$~us **8:23 (8:27)** ROAD THREE DAY~s *we~will*~WALK$^{(V)}$ in~the~WILDERNESS and~*we~did*~SACRIFICE$^{(V)}$ to~**YHWH** Elohiym~us like~WHICH *he~will*~SAY$^{(V)}$ TO~us **8:24 (8:28)** and~*he~will*~SAY$^{(V)}$ Paroh I *I~will~much*~SEND$^{(V)}$ AT~*you*$^{(mp)}$ and~*you*$^{(mp)}$~*did*~SACRIFICE$^{(V)}$ to~**YHWH** Elohiym~*you*$^{(mp)}$ in~the~WILDERNESS ONLY >~*make*~BE.FAR$^{(V)}$ NOT *you*$^{(mp)}$~*will~make*~BE.FAR$^{(V)}$ to~>~WALK$^{(V)}$ *l$^{(mp)}$~make*~INTERCEDE$^{(V)}$ in~UNTIL~me **8:25 (8:29)** and~*he~will*~SAY$^{(V)}$ Mosheh LOOK I GO.OUT$^{(V)}$~*ing*$^{(ms)}$ from~WITH~*you*$^{(ms)}$ and~*I~did~make*~INTERCEDE$^{(V)}$ TO **YHWH** and~*he~did*~TURN.ASIDE$^{(V)}$ the~HORDE from~Paroh from~SERVANT~s~him and~from~PEOPLE~him TOMORROW ONLY DO.NOT *he~will~make*~ADD$^{(V)}$ Paroh >~*make*~DEAL.DECEITFULLY$^{(V)}$ to~EXCEPT *l$^{(ms)}$~much*~SEND$^{(V)}$ AT the~PEOPLE to~>~SACRIFICE$^{(V)}$ to~**YHWH 8:26 (8:30)** and~*he~will*~GO.OUT$^{(V)}$ Mosheh from~WITH Paroh and~*he~will*~INTERCEDE$^{(V)}$ TO **YHWH 8:27 (8:31)** and~*he~will*~DO$^{(V)}$ **YHWH** like~WORD Mosheh and~*he~will~make*~TURN.ASIDE$^{(V)}$ the~HORDE from~Paroh from~SERVANT~s~him and~from~PEOPLE~him NOT *he~did~be*~REMAIN$^{(V)}$ UNIT **8:28 (8:32)** and~*he~will~make*~BE.HEAVY$^{(V)}$ Paroh AT HEART~him ALSO in~the~FOOTSTEP the~THIS and~NOT *he~did~much*~SEND$^{(V)}$ AT the~PEOPLE

Chapter 9

9:1 and~*he~will*~SAY$^{(V)}$ **YHWH** TO Mosheh *l$^{(ms)}$~*COME$^{(V)}$ TO Paroh and~*you*$^{(ms)}$~*did~much*~SPEAK$^{(V)}$ TO~him IN.THIS.WAY *he~did*~SAY$^{(V)}$ **YHWH** Elohiym the~Ever~s *l$^{(ms)}$~much*~SEND$^{(V)}$ AT PEOPLE~me and~*they*$^{(m)}$~*will*~SERVE$^{(V)}$~me **9:2** GIVEN.THAT IF REFUSING *YOU*$^{(ms)}$ to~>~*much*~SEND$^{(V)}$ and~YET.AGAIN~*you*$^{(ms)}$ *make*~SEIZE$^{(V)}$~*ing*$^{(ms)}$ in~*them*$^{(m)}$ **9:3** LOOK HAND **YHWH** EXIST$^{(V)}$~*ing*$^{(fs)}$ in~LIVESTOCK~*you*$^{(ms)}$ WHICH in~the~FIELD in~the~HORSE~s in~the~DONKEY~s in~the~CAMEL~s in~the~CATTLE and~in~the~FLOCKS EPIDEMIC HEAVY MANY **9:4** and~*he~did~make*~BE.DISTINCT$^{(V)}$ **YHWH** BETWEEN LIVESTOCK Yisra'eyl and~BETWEEN LIVESTOCK Mits'rayim and~NOT *he~will*~DIE$^{(V)}$ from~ALL to~SON~s Yisra'eyl WORD **9:5** and~*he~will*~PLACE$^{(V)}$ **YHWH** APPOINTED to~>~SAY$^{(V)}$ TOMORROW *he~will*~DO$^{(V)}$ **YHWH** the~WORD the~THIS in~the~LAND **9:6** and~*he~will*~DO$^{(V)}$ **YHWH** AT the~WORD the~THIS from~MORROW and~*he~will*~DIE$^{(V)}$ ALL LIVESTOCK

Mits'rayim and~from~LIVESTOCK SON~s Yisra'eyl NOT *he~did*~DIE^(V) UNIT **9:7** and~*he~will*~SEND^(V) Paroh and~LOOK NOT *he~did*~DIE^(V) from~LIVESTOCK Yisra'eyl UNTIL UNIT and~*he~will*~BE.HEAVY^(V) HEART Paroh and~NOT *he~did*~*much*~SEND^(V) AT the~PEOPLE **9:8** and~*he~will*~SAY^(V) **YHWH** TO Mosheh and~TO Aharon *!*^(mp)~TAKE^(V) to~you^(mp) FILLING CUPPED.HAND~s2~you^(mp) SOOT FURNACE and~*he~did*~SPRINKLE^(V)~him Mosheh the~SKY~s2~unto to~EYE~s2 Paroh **9:9** and~*he~did*~EXIST^(V) to~DUST UPON ALL LAND Mits'rayim and~*he~did*~EXIST^(V) UPON the~HUMAN and~UPON the~BEAST to~BOILS BURST.OUT^(V)~*ing*^(ms) PUSTULE~s in~ALL LAND Mits'rayim **9:10** and~*they*^(m)~*will*~TAKE^(V) AT SOOT the~FURNACE and~*they*^(m)~*will*~STAND^(V) to~FACE~s Paroh and~*he~will*~SPRINKLE^(V) AT~him Mosheh the~SKY~s2~unto and~*he~will*~EXIST^(V) BOILS PUSTULE~s BURST.OUT^(V)~*ing*^(ms) in~the~HUMAN and~in~the~BEAST **9:11** and~NOT *they~did*~BE.ABLE^(V) the~MAGICIAN~s to~>~STAND^(V) to~FACE~s Mosheh from~FACE~s the~BOILS GIVEN.THAT *he~did*~EXIST^(V) the~BOILS in~the~MAGICIAN and~in~ALL Mits'rayim **9:12** and~*he~will*~*much*~SEIZE^(V) **YHWH** AT HEART Paroh and~NOT *he~did*~HEAR^(V) TO~them^(m) like~WHICH *he~did*~*much*~SPEAK^(V) **YHWH** TO Mosheh **9:13** and~*he~will*~SAY^(V) **YHWH** TO Mosheh *!*^(mp)~*make*~DEPART.EARLY^(V) in~the~MORNING and~*!*^(ms)~*self*~STAND.UP^(V) to~FACE~s Paroh and~*you*^(ms)~*did*~SAY^(V) TO~him IN.THIS.WAY *he~did*~SAY^(V) **YHWH** Elohiym the~Ever~s *!*^(ms)~*much*~SEND^(V) AT PEOPLE~me and~*they*^(m)~*will*~SERVE^(V)~me **9:14** GIVEN.THAT in~the~FOOTSTEP the~THIS I SEND^(V)~*ing*^(ms) AT ALL PESTILENCE~s~me TO HEART~you^(ms) and~in~SERVANT~s~you^(ms) and~in~PEOPLE~you^(ms) in~the~CROSS.OVER^(V)~*ed*^(ms) *you*^(ms)~*will*~KNOW^(V) GIVEN.THAT WITHOUT like~THAT.ONE~me in~ALL the~LAND **9:15** GIVEN.THAT NOW *I~did*~SEND^(V) AT HAND~me and~*I~will*~*make*~HIT^(V) AT~you^(ms) and~AT PEOPLE~you^(ms) in~the~EPIDEMIC and~*you*^(ms)~*will*~*be*~KEEP.SECRET^(V) FROM the~LAND **9:16** and~BUT in~the~CROSS.OVER^(V)~*ed*^(ms) THIS *I~did*~*make*~STAND^(V)~you^(ms) in~the~CROSS.OVER^(V)~*ed*^(ms) >~*make*~SEE^(V)~you^(ms) AT STRENGTH~me and~to~THAT >~*much*~COUNT^(V) TITLE~me in~ALL the~LAND **9:17** YET.AGAIN~you^(ms) *self*~BUILD.UP^(V)~*ing*^(ms) in~PEOPLE~me to~EXCEPT >~*much*~SEND^(V)~them^(m) **9:18** LOOK~me *make*~PRECIPITATE^(V)~*ing*^(ms) like~the~APPOINTED.TIME TOMORROW HAILSTONES HEAVY MANY WHICH NOT *he~did*~EXIST^(V) like~THAT.ONE~him in~Mits'rayim to~FROM the~DAY >~*be*~FOUNDED^(V)~her and~UNTIL NOW **9:19** and~NOW *!*^(ms)~SEND^(V) *!*^(ms)~*make*~BE.BOLD^(V) AT LIVESTOCK~you^(ms) and~AT ALL WHICH to~you^(ms) in~the~FIELD ALL the~HUMAN and~the~BEAST WHICH *he~will*~*be*~FIND^(V) in~the~FIELD and~NOT *he~will*~*be*~GATHER^(V) the~HOUSE~unto and~*he~did*~GO.DOWN^(V) UPON~them^(m) the~HAILSTONES and~*they~did*~DIE^(V) **9:20** the~FEAR^(V)~*ing*^(ms) AT WORD **YHWH** from~SERVANT~s Paroh *he~did*~*make*~FLEE^(V) AT SERVANT~s~him and~AT LIVESTOCK~him TO the~HOUSE~s **9:21** and~WHICH NOT *he~did*~PLACE^(V) HEART~him TO WORD **YHWH** and~*he~will*~LEAVE^(V) AT SERVANT~s~him and~AT LIVESTOCK~him in~the~FIELD **9:22** and~*he~will*~SAY^(V) **YHWH** TO Mosheh *!*^(ms)~EXTEND^(V) AT

HAND~you⁽ᵐˢ⁾ UPON the~SKY~s2 and~*he~will*~EXIST⁽ⱽ⁾ HAILSTONES in~ALL LAND Mits'rayim UPON the~HUMAN and~UPON the~BEAST and~UPON ALL HERB the~FIELD in~LAND Mits'rayim **9:23** and~*he~will*~EXTEND⁽ⱽ⁾ Mosheh AT BRANCH~him UPON the~SKY~s2 and~**YHWH** *he~did*~GIVE⁽ⱽ⁾ VOICE~s and~HAILSTONES and~*she~will*~WALK⁽ⱽ⁾ FIRE LAND~unto and~*he~will~ make*~PRECIPITATE⁽ⱽ⁾ **YHWH** HAILSTONES UPON LAND Mits'rayim **9:24** and~ *he~will*~EXIST⁽ⱽ⁾ HAILSTONES and~FIRE *self*~TAKE⁽ⱽ⁾~*ing*⁽ᵐˢ⁾ in~MIDST the~ HAILSTONES HEAVY MANY WHICH NOT *he~did*~EXIST⁽ⱽ⁾ like~THAT.ONE~him in~ALL LAND Mits'rayim from~AT.THAT.TIME *she~did*~EXIST⁽ⱽ⁾ to~ NATION **9:25** and~*he~will~make*~HIT⁽ⱽ⁾ the~HAILSTONES in~ALL LAND Mits'rayim AT ALL WHICH in~the~FIELD from~HUMAN and~UNTIL BEAST and~AT ALL HERB the~FIELD *he~did~make*~HIT⁽ⱽ⁾ the~HAILSTONES and~AT ALL TREE the~FIELD *he~did~much*~CRACK⁽ⱽ⁾ **9:26** ONLY in~LAND Goshen WHICH THERE SON~s Yisra'eyl NOT *he~did*~EXIST⁽ⱽ⁾ HAILSTONES **9:27** and~ *he~will*~SEND⁽ⱽ⁾ Paroh and~*he~will*~CALL.OUT⁽ⱽ⁾ to~Mosheh and~to~Aharon and~*he~will*~SAY⁽ⱽ⁾ TO~them⁽ᵐ⁾ *I~did*~FAIL⁽ⱽ⁾ the~FOOTSTEP **YHWH** the~ STEADFAST.ONE and~I and~PEOPLE~me the~LOST~s **9:28** *!*⁽ᵐᵖ⁾~*make*~ INTERCEDE⁽ⱽ⁾ TO **YHWH** and~ABUNDANT from~>~EXIST⁽ⱽ⁾ VOICE~s Elohiym and~HAILSTONES and~*I~will~much*~SEND⁽ⱽ⁾~& AT~you⁽ᵐᵖ⁾ and~NOT *you*⁽ᵐᵖ⁾*~will~make*~ADD⁽ⱽ⁾~must to~>~STAND⁽ⱽ⁾ **9:29** and~*he~will*~SAY⁽ⱽ⁾ TO~him Mosheh like~>~GO.OUT⁽ⱽ⁾~me AT the~CITY *I~will*~SPREAD.OUT⁽ⱽ⁾ AT PALM~s2~me TO **YHWH** the~VOICE~s *they*⁽ᵐ⁾*~will*~TERMINATE⁽ⱽ⁾~must and~the~HAILSTONES NOT *he~will*~EXIST⁽ⱽ⁾ YET.AGAIN to~THAT *you*⁽ᵐˢ⁾*~ will*~KNOW⁽ⱽ⁾ GIVEN.THAT to~**YHWH** the~LAND **9:30** and~YOU⁽ᵐˢ⁾ and~ SERVANT~s~you⁽ᵐˢ⁾ *I~did*~KNOW⁽ⱽ⁾ GIVEN.THAT BEFORE *you*⁽ᵐᵖ⁾*~will*~ FEAR⁽ⱽ⁾~must from~FACE~s **YHWH** Elohiym **9:31** and~the~FLAX and~the~ BARLEY *she~did~be~much*~HIT⁽ⱽ⁾ GIVEN.THAT the~BARLEY GREEN.GRAIN and~the~FLAX BUDDING **9:32** and~the~WHEAT and~the~SPELT NOT *they~ did~be~much*~HIT⁽ⱽ⁾ GIVEN.THAT LATE~s THEY⁽ᶠ⁾ **9:33** and~*he~will*~ GO.OUT⁽ⱽ⁾ Mosheh from~WITH Paroh AT the~CITY and~*he~will*~ SPREAD.OUT⁽ⱽ⁾ PALM~s2~him TO **YHWH** and~*they*⁽ᵐ⁾*~will*~TERMINATE⁽ⱽ⁾ the~VOICE~s and~the~HAILSTONES and~PRECIPITATION NOT *he~did~be*~ DROP.DOWN⁽ⱽ⁾ LAND~unto **9:34** and~*he~will*~SEE⁽ⱽ⁾ Paroh GIVEN.THAT *he~ did*~TERMINATE⁽ⱽ⁾ the~PRECIPITATION and~the~HAILSTONES and~the~ VOICE~s and~*he~will~make*~ADD⁽ⱽ⁾ to~>~FAIL⁽ⱽ⁾ and~*he~will~make*~ BE.HEAVY⁽ⱽ⁾ HEART~him HE and~SERVANT~s~him **9:35** and~*he~will*~SEIZE⁽ⱽ⁾ HEART Paroh and~NOT *he~did~much*~SEND⁽ⱽ⁾ AT SON~s Yisra'eyl like~ WHICH *he~did~much*~SPEAK⁽ⱽ⁾ **YHWH** in~HAND Mosheh

Chapter 10

10:1 and~*he~will*~SAY⁽ⱽ⁾ **YHWH** TO Mosheh *!*⁽ᵐˢ⁾*~*COME⁽ⱽ⁾ TO Paroh GIVEN.THAT I *I~did~make*~BE.HEAVY⁽ⱽ⁾ AT HEART~him and~AT HEART

SERVANT~s~him to~THAT >~SET.DOWN⁽ⱽ⁾~me SIGN~s~me THESE in~
INSIDE~him **10:2** and~to~THAT *you*⁽ᵐˢ⁾~did~much~COUNT⁽ⱽ⁾ in~EAR~s2
SON~*you*⁽ᵐˢ⁾ and~SON SON~*you*⁽ᵐˢ⁾ AT WHICH *I*~*did*~*self*~WORK.OVER⁽ⱽ⁾ in~
Mits'rayim and~AT SIGN~s~me WHICH *I*~*did*~PLACE⁽ⱽ⁾ in~them⁽ᵐ⁾ and~
you⁽ᵐᵖ⁾~*did*~KNOW⁽ⱽ⁾ GIVEN.THAT I **YHWH** **10:3** and~*he*~*will*~COME⁽ⱽ⁾
Mosheh and~Aharon TO Paroh and~*they*⁽ᵐ⁾~*will*~SAY⁽ⱽ⁾ TO~him IN.THIS.WAY
he~*did*~SAY⁽ⱽ⁾ **YHWH** Elohiym the~Ever~s UNTIL HOW.LONG *you*⁽ᵐˢ⁾~*did*~
much~REFUSE⁽ⱽ⁾ to~>~much~AFFLICT⁽ⱽ⁾ from~FACE~s~me !⁽ᵐˢ⁾~much~
SEND⁽ⱽ⁾ PEOPLE~me and~*they*⁽ᵐ⁾~*will*~SERVE⁽ⱽ⁾~me **10:4** GIVEN.THAT IF
REFUSING YOU⁽ᵐˢ⁾ to~>~much~SEND⁽ⱽ⁾ AT PEOPLE~me LOOK~me *make*~
COME⁽ⱽ⁾~*ing*⁽ᵐˢ⁾ TOMORROW SWARMING.LOCUST in~BORDER~
you⁽ᵐˢ⁾ **10:5** and~*he*~*did*~much~COVER.OVER⁽ⱽ⁾ AT EYE the~LAND and~NOT
he~*will*~BE.ABLE⁽ⱽ⁾ to~>~SEE⁽ⱽ⁾ AT the~LAND and~*he*~*did*~EAT⁽ⱽ⁾ AT
REMAINDER the~ESCAPED the~*be*~REMAIN⁽ⱽ⁾~*ing*⁽ᶠˢ⁾ to~*you*⁽ᵐᵖ⁾ FROM the~
HAILSTONES and~*he*~*did*~EAT⁽ⱽ⁾ AT ALL the~TREE the~SPRING.UP⁽ⱽ⁾~*ing*⁽ᵐˢ⁾
to~*you*⁽ᵐᵖ⁾ FROM the~FIELD **10:6** and~*they*~*did*~FILL⁽ⱽ⁾ HOUSE~s~*you*⁽ᵐˢ⁾
and~HOUSE~s ALL SERVANT~s~*you*⁽ᵐˢ⁾ and~HOUSE~s ALL Mits'rayim WHICH
NOT *they*~*did*~SEE⁽ⱽ⁾ FATHER~s~*you*⁽ᵐˢ⁾ and~FATHER~s FATHER~s~*you*⁽ᵐˢ⁾
from~DAY >~EXIST⁽ⱽ⁾~*you*⁽ᵐᵖ⁾ UPON the~GROUND UNTIL the~DAY the~THIS
and~*he*~*will*~TURN⁽ⱽ⁾ and~*he*~*will*~GO.OUT⁽ⱽ⁾ from~WITH Paroh **10:7** and~
they⁽ᵐ⁾~*will*~SAY⁽ⱽ⁾ SERVANT~s Paroh TO~him UNTIL HOW.LONG *he*~*will*~
EXIST⁽ⱽ⁾ THIS to~us to~SNARE !⁽ᵐˢ⁾~much~SEND⁽ⱽ⁾ AT the~MAN~s and~
they⁽ᵐ⁾~*will*~SERVE⁽ⱽ⁾ AT **YHWH** Elohiym~them⁽ᵐ⁾ ?~BEFORE *you*⁽ᵐˢ⁾~*will*~
KNOW⁽ⱽ⁾ GIVEN.THAT *she*~*did*~PERISH⁽ⱽ⁾ Mits'rayim **10:8** and~*he*~*will*~*be*~
make~TURN.BACK⁽ⱽ⁾ AT Mosheh and~AT Aharon TO Paroh and~*he*~*will*~
SAY⁽ⱽ⁾ TO~them⁽ᵐ⁾ !⁽ᵐᵖ⁾~WALK⁽ⱽ⁾ !⁽ᵐᵖ⁾~SERVE⁽ⱽ⁾ AT **YHWH** Elohiym~*you*⁽ᵐᵖ⁾
WHO and~WHO the~WALK⁽ⱽ⁾~*ing*⁽ᵐᵖ⁾ **10:9** and~*he*~*will*~SAY⁽ⱽ⁾ Mosheh in~
YOUNG.MAN~s~us and~in~BEARD~us *we*~*will*~WALK⁽ⱽ⁾ in~SON~s~us and~
in~DAUGHTER~s~us in~FLOCKS~us and~in~CATTLE~us *we*~*will*~WALK⁽ⱽ⁾
GIVEN.THAT FEAST **YHWH** to~us **10:10** and~*he*~*will*~SAY⁽ⱽ⁾ TO~them⁽ᵐ⁾ *he*~
will~EXIST⁽ⱽ⁾ SO **YHWH** WITH~*you*⁽ᵐᵖ⁾ like~WHICH *I*~*will*~much~SEND⁽ⱽ⁾ AT~
you⁽ᵐᵖ⁾ and~AT BABIES~*you*⁽ᵐᵖ⁾ !⁽ᵐᵖ⁾~SEE⁽ⱽ⁾ GIVEN.THAT DYSFUNCTIONAL
OPPOSITE FACE~s~*you*⁽ᵐᵖ⁾ **10:11** NOT SO !⁽ᵐᵖ⁾~WALK⁽ⱽ⁾ PLEASE the~
WARRIOR~s and~ !⁽ᵐᵖ⁾~SERVE⁽ⱽ⁾ AT **YHWH** GIVEN.THAT AT~her YOU⁽ᵐᵖ⁾
much~SEARCH.OUT⁽ⱽ⁾~*ing*⁽ᵐᵖ⁾ and~*he*~*will*~much~CAST.OUT⁽ⱽ⁾ AT~them⁽ᵐ⁾
from~AT FACE~s Paroh **10:12** and~*he*~*will*~SAY⁽ⱽ⁾ **YHWH** TO Mosheh !⁽ᵐˢ⁾~
EXTEND⁽ⱽ⁾ HAND~*you*⁽ᵐˢ⁾ UPON LAND Mits'rayim in~the~
SWARMING.LOCUST and~*he*~*will*~GO.UP⁽ⱽ⁾ UPON LAND Mits'rayim and~*he*~
will~EAT⁽ⱽ⁾ AT ALL HERB the~LAND AT ALL WHICH *he*~*did*~*make*~REMAIN⁽ⱽ⁾
the~HAILSTONES **10:13** and~*he*~*will*~EXTEND⁽ⱽ⁾ Mosheh AT BRANCH~him
UPON LAND Mits'rayim and~**YHWH** *he*~*did*~much~DRIVE⁽ⱽ⁾ WIND
EAST.WIND in~the~LAND ALL the~DAY the~HE and~ALL the~NIGHT the~
MORNING *he*~*did*~EXIST⁽ⱽ⁾ and~WIND the~EAST.WIND *he*~*did*~LIFT.UP⁽ⱽ⁾ AT
the~SWARMING.LOCUST **10:14** and~*he*~*will*~*make*~GO.UP⁽ⱽ⁾ the~
SWARMING.LOCUST UPON ALL LAND Mits'rayim and~*he*~*will*~REST⁽ⱽ⁾ in~ALL

The Book of Exodus

BORDER Mits'rayim HEAVY MANY to~FACE~s~him NOT *he~did*~EXIST$^{(V)}$ SO SWARMING.LOCUST like~THAT.ONE~him and~AFTER~him NOT *he~will~* EXIST$^{(V)}$ SO **10:15** and~*he~will~much*~COVER.OVER$^{(V)}$ AT EYE ALL the~LAND and~*she~will*~DARKEN$^{(V)}$ the~LAND and~*he~will*~EAT$^{(V)}$ AT ALL HERB the~ LAND and~AT ALL PRODUCE the~TREE WHICH *he~did~make~* LEAVE.BEHIND$^{(V)}$ the~HAILSTONES and~NOT *he~did~be~*LEAVE.BEHIND$^{(V)}$ ALL GREEN in~the~TREE and~in~HERB the~FIELD in~ALL LAND Mits'rayim **10:16** and~*he~will~much*~HURRY$^{(V)}$ Paroh to~>~CALL.OUT$^{(V)}$ to~ Mosheh and~to~Aharon and~*he~will*~SAY$^{(V)}$ *I~did*~FAIL$^{(V)}$ to~**YHWH** Elohiym~you$^{(mp)}$ and~to~you$^{(mp)}$ **10:17** and~NOW *!*$^{(ms)}$~LIFT.UP$^{(V)}$ PLEASE FAILURE~me SURELY the~FOOTSTEP and~*!*$^{(mp)}$~INTERCEDE$^{(V)}$ to~**YHWH** Elohiym~you$^{(mp)}$ and~*he~will~make*~TURN.ASIDE$^{(V)}$ from~UPON~me ONLY AT the~DEATH the~THIS **10:18** and~*he~will*~GO.OUT$^{(V)}$ from~WITH Paroh and~*he~will*~INTERCEDE$^{(V)}$ TO **YHWH** **10:19** and~*he~will*~OVERTURN$^{(V)}$ **YHWH** WIND SEA FORCEFUL MANY and~*he~will*~LIFT.UP$^{(V)}$ AT the~ SWARMING.LOCUST and~*he~will*~THRUST$^{(V)}$~him SEA~unto REEDS NOT *he~ did~be*~REMAIN$^{(V)}$ SWARMING.LOCUST UNIT in~ALL BORDER Mits'rayim **10:20** and~*he~will~much*~SEIZE$^{(V)}$ **YHWH** AT HEART Paroh and~ NOT *he~did~much*~SEND$^{(V)}$ AT SON~s Yisra'eyl **10:21** and~*he~will*~SAY$^{(V)}$ **YHWH** TO Mosheh *!*$^{(ms)}$~EXTEND$^{(V)}$ HAND~you$^{(ms)}$ UPON the~SKY~s2 and~ *he~will*~EXIST$^{(V)}$ DARKNESS UPON LAND Mits'rayim and~*he~will~make~* GROPE$^{(V)}$ DARKNESS **10:22** and~*he~will*~EXTEND$^{(V)}$ Mosheh AT HAND~him UPON the~SKY~s2 and~*he~will*~EXIST$^{(V)}$ DARKNESS THICK.GLOOMINESS in~ ALL LAND Mits'rayim THREE DAY~s **10:23** NOT *they~did*~SEE$^{(V)}$ MAN AT BROTHER~him and~NOT *they~did*~RISE$^{(V)}$ MAN from~UNDER~s~him THREE DAY~s and~to~ALL SON~s Yisra'eyl *he~did*~EXIST$^{(V)}$ LIGHT in~SETTLING~ them$^{(m)}$ **10:24** and~*he~will*~CALL.OUT$^{(V)}$ Paroh TO Mosheh and~*he~will~* SAY$^{(V)}$ *!*$^{(mp)}$~WALK$^{(V)}$ *!*$^{(mp)}$~SERVE$^{(V)}$ AT **YHWH** ONLY FLOCKS~you$^{(mp)}$ and~ CATTLE~you$^{(mp)}$ *he~will~be~make*~LEAVE.IN.PLACE$^{(V)}$ ALSO BABIES~you$^{(mp)}$ *he~will*~WALK$^{(V)}$ WITH~you$^{(mp)}$ **10:25** and~*he~will*~SAY$^{(V)}$ Mosheh ALSO YOU$^{(ms)}$ *you*$^{(ms)}$~*will*~GIVE$^{(V)}$ in~HAND~us SACRIFICE~s and~ ASCENSION.OFFERING~s and~*we~did*~DO$^{(V)}$ to~**YHWH** Elohiym~ us **10:26** and~ALSO LIVESTOCK~us *he~will*~WALK$^{(V)}$ WITH~us NOT *she~will~ be*~REMAIN$^{(V)}$ HOOF GIVEN.THAT FROM~him *we~will*~TAKE$^{(V)}$ to~>~SERVE$^{(V)}$ AT **YHWH** Elohiym~us and~WE NOT *we~will*~KNOW$^{(V)}$ WHAT *we~will~* SERVE$^{(V)}$ AT **YHWH** UNTIL >~COME$^{(V)}$~us THERE~unto **10:27** and~*he~will~* much~SEIZE$^{(V)}$ **YHWH** AT HEART Paroh and~NOT *he~did*~CONSENT$^{(V)}$ to~>~ much~SEND$^{(V)}$~them$^{(m)}$ **10:28** and~*he~will*~SAY$^{(V)}$ to~him Paroh *!*$^{(ms)}$~ WALK$^{(V)}$ from~UPON~me *!*$^{(ms)}$~*be*~SAFEGUARD$^{(V)}$ to~you$^{(ms)}$ DO.NOT *you*$^{(ms)}$~ *will~make*~ADD$^{(V)}$ >~SEE$^{(V)}$ FACE~s~me GIVEN.THAT in~DAY >~SEE$^{(V)}$~you$^{(ms)}$ FACE~s~me *you*$^{(ms)}$~*will*~DIE$^{(V)}$ **10:29** and~*he~will*~SAY$^{(V)}$ Mosheh SO *you*$^{(ms)}$~*did~much*~SPEAK$^{(V)}$ NOT *I~will~make*~ADD$^{(V)}$ YET.AGAIN >~SEE$^{(V)}$ FACE~s~you$^{(ms)}$

Chapter 11

11:1 and~*he~will*~SAY$^{(V)}$ **YHWH** TO Mosheh YET.AGAIN TOUCH UNIT *I~will*~*make*~COME$^{(V)}$ UPON Paroh and~UPON Mits'rayim AFTER SO *he~will*~*much*~SEND$^{(V)}$ AT~you$^{(mp)}$ from~THIS like~>~*much*~SEND$^{(V)}$~him COMPLETION >~*much*~CAST.OUT$^{(V)}$ *he~will*~*much*~CAST.OUT$^{(V)}$ AT~you$^{(mp)}$ from~THIS **11:2** >~*much*~SPEAK$^{(V)}$ PLEASE in~EAR~s2 the~PEOPLE and~ *they*$^{(m)}$~*will*~INQUIRE$^{(V)}$ MAN from~AT COMPANION~him and~WOMAN from~AT FRIEND~her UTENSIL~s SILVER and~UTENSIL~s GOLD **11:3** and~ *he~will*~GIVE$^{(V)}$ **YHWH** AT BEAUTY the~PEOPLE in~EYE~s2 Mits'rayim ALSO the~MAN Mosheh GREAT MANY in~LAND Mits'rayim in~EYE~s2 SERVANT~s Paroh and~in~EYE~s2 the~PEOPLE **11:4** and~*he~will*~SAY$^{(V)}$ Mosheh IN.THIS.WAY *he~did*~SAY$^{(V)}$ **YHWH** like~CENTER the~NIGHT I GO.OUT$^{(V)}$~ *ing*$^{(ms)}$ in~MIDST Mits'rayim **11:5** and~*he~did*~DIE$^{(V)}$ ALL FIRSTBORN in~ LAND Mits'rayim from~FIRSTBORN Paroh the~SETTLE$^{(V)}$~*ing*$^{(ms)}$ UPON SEAT~ him UNTIL FIRSTBORN the~MAID WHICH AFTER the~MILLSTONE~s and~ALL FIRSTBORN BEAST **11:6** and~*she~did*~EXIST$^{(V)}$ CRY GREAT in~ALL LAND Mits'rayim WHICH like~THAT.ONE~him NOT *she~did*~be~EXIST$^{(V)}$ and~like~ THAT.ONE~him NOT *she~will*~*make*~ADD$^{(V)}$ **11:7** and~to~ALL SON~s Yisra'eyl NOT *he~will*~CUT.SHARPLY$^{(V)}$ DOG TONGUE~him to~from~MAN and~UNTIL BEAST to~THAT you$^{(mp)}$~*will*~KNOW$^{(V)}$~must WHICH *he~will*~ *make*~BE.DISTINCT$^{(V)}$ **YHWH** BETWEEN Mits'rayim and~BETWEEN Yisra'eyl **11:8** and~*they~will*~GO.DOWN$^{(V)}$ ALL SERVANT~s~you$^{(ms)}$ THESE TO~me and~*they~did~self*~BEND.DOWN$^{(V)}$ to~me to~>~SAY$^{(V)}$ *I*$^{(ms)}$~ GO.OUT$^{(V)}$ YOU$^{(ms)}$ and~ALL the~PEOPLE WHICH in~FOOT~s~you$^{(ms)}$ and~ AFTER SO *I~will*~GO.OUT$^{(V)}$ and~*he~will*~GO.OUT$^{(V)}$ from~WITH Paroh in~ the~FLAMING NOSE **11:9** and~*he~will*~SAY$^{(V)}$ **YHWH** TO Mosheh NOT *he~ will*~HEAR$^{(V)}$ TO~you$^{(mp)}$ Paroh to~THAT >~INCREASE$^{(V)}$ WONDER~s~me in~ LAND Mits'rayim **11:10** and~Mosheh and~Aharon *they~did*~DO$^{(V)}$ AT ALL the~WONDER~s the~THESE to~FACE~s Paroh and~*he~will*~*much*~SEIZE$^{(V)}$ **YHWH** AT HEART Paroh and~NOT *he~did*~*much*~SEND$^{(V)}$ AT SON~s Yisra'eyl from~LAND~him

Chapter 12

12:1 and~*he~will*~SAY$^{(V)}$ **YHWH** TO Mosheh and~TO Aharon in~LAND Mits'rayim to~>~SAY$^{(V)}$ **12:2** the~NEW.MOON the~THIS to~you$^{(mp)}$ HEAD NEW.MOON~s FIRST HE to~you$^{(mp)}$ to~NEW.MOON~s the~YEAR **12:3** *I*$^{(mp)}$~ *much*~SPEAK$^{(V)}$ TO ALL COMPANY Yisra'eyl to~>~SAY$^{(V)}$ in~the~TENTH.ONE to~the~NEW.MOON the~THIS and~*they*$^{(m)}$~*will*~TAKE$^{(V)}$ to~them$^{(m)}$ MAN RAM to~HOUSE FATHER~s RAM to~the~HOUSE **12:4** and~IF *he~will*~ BE.LESS$^{(V)}$ the~HOUSE from~>~EXIST$^{(V)}$ from~RAM and~*he~did*~TAKE$^{(V)}$ HE

The Book of Exodus

and~DWELLER~him the~NEAR TO HOUSE~him in~WORTH SOUL~s MAN to~ MOUTH >~EAT⁽ᵛ⁾~him you⁽ᵐᵖ⁾~will~ESTIMATE⁽ᵛ⁾ UPON the~RAM **12:5** RAM WHOLE MALE SON YEAR he~will~EXIST⁽ᵛ⁾ to~you⁽ᵐᵖ⁾ FROM the~SHEEP~s and~FROM the~SHE-GOAT~s you⁽ᵐᵖ⁾~will~TAKE⁽ᵛ⁾ **12:6** and~he~did~EXIST⁽ᵛ⁾ to~you⁽ᵐᵖ⁾ to~CHARGE UNTIL FOUR TEN DAY to~the~NEW.MOON the~THIS and~they~did~SLAY⁽ᵛ⁾ AT~him ALL ASSEMBLY COMPANY Yisra'eyl BETWEEN the~EVENING~s2 **12:7** and~they~did~TAKE⁽ᵛ⁾ FROM the~BLOOD and~they~ did~GIVE⁽ᵛ⁾ UPON TWO the~DOORPOST~s and~UPON the~LINTEL UPON the~HOUSE~s WHICH they⁽ᵐ⁾~will~EAT⁽ᵛ⁾ AT~him in~them⁽ᵐ⁾ **12:8** and~ they~did~EAT⁽ᵛ⁾ AT the~FLESH in~the~NIGHT the~THIS ROAST FIRE and~ UNLEAVENED.BREAD~s UPON BITTER.HERBS~s they⁽ᵐ⁾~will~EAT⁽ᵛ⁾~ him **12:9** DO.NOT you⁽ᵐᵖ⁾~will~EAT⁽ᵛ⁾ FROM~him RAW and~BOILED from~ be~much~BOIL⁽ᵛ⁾~ing⁽ᵐˢ⁾ in~the~WATER~s2 GIVEN.THAT IF ROAST FIRE HEAD~him UPON LEG~s~him and~UPON INSIDE~him **12:10** and~NOT you⁽ᵐᵖ⁾~will~make~LEAVE.BEHIND⁽ᵛ⁾ FROM~him UNTIL MORNING and~be~ LEAVE.BEHIND⁽ᵛ⁾~ing⁽ᵐˢ⁾ FROM~him UNTIL MORNING in~the~FIRE you⁽ᵐᵖ⁾~ will~CREMATE⁽ᵛ⁾ **12:11** and~like~IN.THIS.WAY you⁽ᵐᵖ⁾~will~EAT⁽ᵛ⁾ AT~him WAIST~s~you⁽ᵐᵖ⁾ GIRD.UP⁽ᵛ⁾~ed⁽ᵐᵖ⁾ SANDAL~s~you⁽ᵐᵖ⁾ in~FOOT~s~you⁽ᵐᵖ⁾ and~ROD~you⁽ᵐᵖ⁾ in~HAND~you⁽ᵐᵖ⁾ and~you⁽ᵐᵖ⁾~did~EAT⁽ᵛ⁾ AT~him in~ HASTE Pesahh HE to~**YHWH** **12:12** and~I~did~CROSS.OVER⁽ᵛ⁾ in~LAND Mits'rayim in~the~NIGHT the~THIS and~I~did~make~HIT⁽ᵛ⁾ ALL FIRSTBORN in~LAND Mits'rayim from~HUMAN and~UNTIL BEAST and~in~ALL Elohiym Mits'rayim I~will~DO⁽ᵛ⁾ JUDGMENT~s I **YHWH** **12:13** and~he~did~EXIST⁽ᵛ⁾ the~BLOOD to~you⁽ᵐᵖ⁾ to~SIGN UPON the~HOUSE~s WHICH YOU⁽ᵐᵖ⁾ THERE and~I~did~SEE⁽ᵛ⁾ AT the~BLOOD and~I~did~HOP⁽ᵛ⁾ UPON~you⁽ᵐᵖ⁾ and~NOT he~will~EXIST⁽ᵛ⁾ in~you⁽ᵐᵖ⁾ STRIKING to~DAMAGING in~>~make~HIT⁽ᵛ⁾~me in~LAND Mits'rayim **12:14** and~he~did~EXIST⁽ᵛ⁾ the~DAY the~THIS to~ you⁽ᵐᵖ⁾ to~REMEMBRANCE and~you⁽ᵐᵖ⁾~did~HOLD.A.FEAST⁽ᵛ⁾ AT~him FEAST to~**YHWH** to~GENERATION~s~you⁽ᵐᵖ⁾ CUSTOM DISTANT you⁽ᵐᵖ⁾~will~ HOLD.A.FEAST⁽ᵛ⁾ **12:15** SEVEN DAY~s UNLEAVENED.BREAD~s you⁽ᵐᵖ⁾~will~ EAT⁽ᵛ⁾ SURELY in~the~DAY the~FIRST you⁽ᵐᵖ⁾~will~make~CEASE⁽ᵛ⁾ LEAVEN from~HOUSE~s~you⁽ᵐᵖ⁾ GIVEN.THAT ALL EAT⁽ᵛ⁾~ing⁽ᵐˢ⁾ LEAVENED.BREAD and~she~did~be~CUT⁽ᵛ⁾ the~SOUL the~SHE from~Yisra'eyl from~DAY the~ FIRST UNTIL DAY the~SEVENTH **12:16** and~in~the~DAY the~FIRST MEETING SPECIAL and~in~the~DAY the~SEVENTH MEETING SPECIAL he~will~EXIST⁽ᵛ⁾ to~you⁽ᵐᵖ⁾ ALL BUSINESS NOT he~will~be~DO⁽ᵛ⁾ in~them⁽ᵐ⁾ SURELY WHICH he~will~be~EAT⁽ᵛ⁾ to~ALL SOUL HE to~STRAND~him he~will~be~DO⁽ᵛ⁾ to~ you⁽ᵐᵖ⁾ **12:17** and~you⁽ᵐᵖ⁾~did~SAFEGUARD⁽ᵛ⁾ AT the~ UNLEAVENED.BREAD~s GIVEN.THAT in~BONE the~DAY the~THIS I~did~ make~GO.OUT⁽ᵛ⁾ AT ARMY~s~you⁽ᵐᵖ⁾ from~LAND Mits'rayim and~you⁽ᵐᵖ⁾~ did~SAFEGUARD⁽ᵛ⁾ AT the~DAY the~THIS to~GENERATION~s~you⁽ᵐᵖ⁾ CUSTOM DISTANT **12:18** in~the~FIRST in~FOUR TEN DAY to~the~ NEW.MOON in~the~EVENING you⁽ᵐᵖ⁾~will~EAT⁽ᵛ⁾ UNLEAVENED.BREAD~s UNTIL DAY the~UNIT and~TEN~s to~the~NEW.MOON in~the~ EVENING **12:19** SEVEN DAY~s LEAVEN NOT he~will~be~FIND⁽ᵛ⁾ in~

HOUSE~s~you(mp) GIVEN.THAT ALL EAT(V)~ing(ms) make~BE.SOUR(V)~ing(fs) and~she~did~be~CUT(V) the~SOUL the~SHE from~COMPANY Yisra'eyl in~ the~IMMIGRANT and~in~NATIVE the~LAND **12:20** ALL make~BE.SOUR(V)~ ing(fs) NOT you(mp)~will~EAT(V) in~ALL SETTLING~s~you(mp) you(mp)~will~EAT(V) UNLEAVENED.BREAD~s **12:21** and~he~will~CALL.OUT(V) Mosheh to~ALL BEARD~s Yisra'eyl and~he~will~SAY(V) TO~them(m) !(mp)~DRAW(V) and~ !(mp)~ TAKE(V) to~you(mp) FLOCKS to~CLAN~s~you(mp) and~ !(mp)~SLAY(V) the~ Pesahh **12:22** and~you(mp)~did~TAKE(V) BUNCH HYSSOP and~you(mp)~did~ DIP(V) in~the~BLOOD WHICH in~the~BASIN and~you(mp)~did~make~ TOUCH(V) TO the~LINTEL and~TO TWO the~DOORPOST~s FROM the~BLOOD WHICH in~the~BASIN and~YOU(mp) NOT you(mp)~will~GO.OUT(V) MAN from~ OPENING HOUSE~him UNTIL MORNING **12:23** and~he~did~CROSS.OVER(V) **YHWH** to~>~SMITE(V) AT Mits'rayim and~he~did~SEE(V) AT the~BLOOD UPON the~LINTEL and~UPON TWO the~DOORPOST~s and~he~did~HOP(V) **YHWH** UPON the~OPENING and~NOT he~will~GIVE(V) the~make~ DAMAGE(V)~ing(ms) to~>~COME(V) TO HOUSE~s~you(mp) to~>~ SMITE(V) **12:24** and~you(mp)~did~SAFEGUARD(V) AT the~WORD the~THIS to~ CUSTOM to~you(ms) and~to~SON~s~you(ms) UNTIL DISTANT **12:25** and~he~ did~EXIST(V) GIVEN.THAT you(mp)~will~COME(V) TO the~LAND WHICH he~ will~GIVE(V) **YHWH** to~you(mp) like~WHICH he~did~much~SPEAK(V) and~ you(mp)~did~SAFEGUARD(V) AT the~SERVICE the~THIS **12:26** and~he~did~ EXIST(V) GIVEN.THAT they(m)~will~SAY(V) TO~you(mp) SON~s~you(mp) WHAT the~SERVICE the~THIS to~you(mp) **12:27** and~you(mp)~did~SAY(V) SACRIFICE Pesahh HE to~**YHWH** WHICH he~did~HOP(V) UPON HOUSE~s SON~s Yisra'eyl in~Mits'rayim in~>~SMITE(V)~him AT Mits'rayim and~AT HOUSE~s~us he~ did~make~DELIVER(V) and~he~will~BOW.THE.HEAD(V) the~PEOPLE and~ they(m)~will~self~BEND.DOWN(V) **12:28** and~they(m)~will~WALK(V) and~ they(m)~will~DO(V) SON~s Yisra'eyl like~WHICH he~did~much~DIRECT(V) **YHWH** AT Mosheh and~Aharon SO they~did~DO(V) **12:29** and~he~will~ EXIST(V) in~HALF the~NIGHT and~**YHWH** he~did~make~HIT(V) ALL FIRSTBORN in~LAND Mits'rayim from~FIRSTBORN Paroh the~SETTLE(V)~ing(ms) UPON SEAT~him UNTIL FIRSTBORN the~CAPTIVE WHICH in~HOUSE the~CISTERN and~ALL FIRSTBORN BEAST **12:30** and~he~will~RISE(V) Paroh NIGHT HE and~ ALL SERVANT~s~him and~ALL Mits'rayim and~she~will~EXIST(V) CRY GREAT in~Mits'rayim GIVEN.THAT WITHOUT HOUSE WHICH WITHOUT THERE DIE(V)~ing(ms) **12:31** and~he~will~CALL.OUT(V) to~Mosheh and~to~Aharon NIGHT and~he~will~SAY(V) !(mp)~RISE(V) !(mp)~GO.OUT(V) from~MIDST PEOPLE~me ALSO YOU(mp) ALSO SON~s Yisra'eyl and~ !(mp)~WALK(V) !(mp)~ SERVE(V) AT **YHWH** like~>~much~SPEAK(V)~you(mp) **12:32** ALSO FLOCKS~ you(mp) ALSO CATTLE~you(mp) !(mp)~TAKE(V) like~WHICH you(mp)~did~much~ SPEAK(V) and~ !(mp)~WALK(V) and~you(mp)~did~much~KNEEL(V) ALSO AT~ me **12:33** and~she~will~SEIZE(V) Mits'rayim UPON the~PEOPLE to~>~much~ HURRY(V) to~>~much~SEND(V)~them(m) FROM the~LAND GIVEN.THAT they~ did~SAY(V) ALL~us DIE(V)~ing(mp) **12:34** and~he~will~LIFT.UP(V) the~PEOPLE AT DOUGH~him BEFORE he~will~BE.SOUR(V) KNEADING.BOWL~s~them(m)

The Book of Exodus

PRESS.IN$^{(V)}$~ed$^{(fp)}$ in~APPAREL~s~them$^{(m)}$ UPON SHOULDER~them$^{(m)}$ **12:35** and~SON~s Yisra'eyl *they~did*~DO$^{(V)}$ like~WORD Mosheh and~*they$^{(m)}$~will*~INQUIRE$^{(V)}$ from~Mits'rayim UTENSIL~s SILVER and~UTENSIL~s GOLD and~APPAREL~s **12:36** and~**YHWH** *he~did*~GIVE$^{(V)}$ AT BEAUTY the~PEOPLE in~EYE~s2 Mits'rayim and~*they$^{(m)}$~will*~make~INQUIRE$^{(V)}$~them$^{(m)}$ and~*they$^{(m)}$~will*~much~DELIVER$^{(V)}$ AT Mits'rayim **12:37** and~*they$^{(m)}$~will*~JOURNEY$^{(V)}$ SON~s Yisra'eyl from~Ra'meses Suk'kot~unto like~SIX HUNDRED~s THOUSAND ON.FOOT the~WARRIOR~s to~STRAND from~BABIES **12:38** and~ALSO MIXTURE ABUNDANT *he~did*~GO.UP$^{(V)}$ AT~them$^{(m)}$ and~FLOCKS and~CATTLE LIVESTOCK HEAVY MANY **12:39** and~*they$^{(m)}$~will*~BAKE$^{(V)}$ AT the~DOUGH WHICH *!$^{(mp)}$~make*~GO.OUT$^{(V)}$ from~Mits'rayim BAKED.BREAD~s UNLEAVENED.BREAD~s GIVEN.THAT NOT *he~did*~BE.SOUR$^{(V)}$ GIVEN.THAT *they~did~be~much*~CAST.OUT$^{(V)}$ from~Mits'rayim and~NOT *they~did*~BE.ABLE$^{(V)}$ to~>~*self*~LINGER$^{(V)}$ and~ALSO PROVISIONS NOT *they~did*~DO$^{(V)}$ to~them$^{(m)}$ **12:40** and~SETTLING SON~s Yisra'eyl WHICH *they~did*~SETTLE$^{(V)}$ in~Mits'rayim THREE~s YEAR and~FOUR HUNDRED~s YEAR **12:41** and~*he~will*~EXIST$^{(V)}$ from~CONCLUSION THREE~s YEAR and~FOUR HUNDRED~s YEAR and~*he~will*~EXIST$^{(V)}$ in~BONE the~DAY the~THIS *they~did*~GO.OUT$^{(V)}$ ALL ARMY~s **YHWH** from~LAND Mits'rayim **12:42** NIGHT SAFEGUARDING~s HE to~**YHWH** to~>~*make*~GO.OUT$^{(V)}$~them$^{(m)}$ from~LAND Mits'rayim HE the~NIGHT the~THIS to~**YHWH** SAFEGUARDING~s to~ALL SON~s Yisra'eyl to~GENERATION~s~them$^{(m)}$ **12:43** and~*he~will*~SAY$^{(V)}$ **YHWH** TO Mosheh and~Aharon THIS CUSTOM the~Pesahh ALL SON FOREIGNER NOT *he~will*~EAT$^{(V)}$ in~him **12:44** and~ALL SERVANT MAN ACQUIRED SILVER and~*you$^{(ms)}$~did*~SNIP.OFF$^{(V)}$ AT~him AT.THAT.TIME *he~will*~EAT$^{(V)}$ in~him **12:45** SETTLER and~HIRELING NOT *he~will*~EAT$^{(V)}$ in~him **12:46** in~HOUSE UNIT *he~will~be*~EAT$^{(V)}$ NOT *you$^{(ms)}$~will~make*~GO.OUT$^{(V)}$ FROM the~HOUSE FROM the~FLESH OUTSIDE~unto and~BONE NOT *you$^{(mp)}$~will*~CRACK$^{(V)}$ in~him **12:47** ALL COMPANY Yisra'eyl *they$^{(m)}$~will*~DO$^{(V)}$ AT~him **12:48** and~GIVEN.THAT *he~will*~IMMIGRATE$^{(V)}$ AT~you$^{(ms)}$ IMMIGRANT and~*he~did*~DO$^{(V)}$ Pesahh to~**YHWH** >~*be*~SNIP.OFF$^{(V)}$ to~him ALL MALE and~AT.THAT.TIME *he~will*~COME.NEAR$^{(V)}$ to~>~DO~him and~*he~did*~EXIST$^{(V)}$ like~NATIVE the~LAND and~ALL UNCIRCUMCISED NOT *he~will*~EAT$^{(V)}$ in~him **12:49** TEACHING UNIT *he~will*~EXIST$^{(V)}$ to~NATIVE and~to~IMMIGRANT the~IMMIGRATE$^{(V)}$~*ing$^{(ms)}$* in~MIDST~you$^{(mp)}$ **12:50** and~*they$^{(m)}$~will*~DO$^{(V)}$ ALL SON~s Yisra'eyl like~WHICH *he~did~much*~DIRECT$^{(V)}$ **YHWH** AT Mosheh and~AT Aharon SO *they~did*~DO$^{(V)}$ **12:51** and~*he~will*~EXIST$^{(V)}$ in~BONE the~DAY the~THIS *he~did~make*~GO.OUT$^{(V)}$ **YHWH** AT SON~s Yisra'eyl from~LAND Mits'rayim UPON ARMY~s~them$^{(m)}$

Chapter 13

13:1 and~*he*~*will*~*much*~SPEAK$^{(v)}$ **YHWH** TO Mosheh to~>~SAY$^{(v)}$ **13:2** *I*$^{(ms)}$~*much*~SET.APART$^{(v)}$ to~me ALL FIRSTBORN BURSTING ALL BOWELS in~SON~s Yisra'eyl in~the~HUMAN and~in~the~BEAST to~me HE **13:3** and~*he*~*will*~SAY$^{(v)}$ Mosheh TO the~PEOPLE >~REMEMBER$^{(v)}$ AT the~DAY the~THIS WHICH *you*$^{(mp)}$~*did*~GO.OUT$^{(v)}$ from~Mits'rayim from~HOUSE SERVANT~s GIVEN.THAT in~GRASP HAND *he*~*did*~*make*~GO.OUT$^{(v)}$ **YHWH** AT~*you*$^{(mp)}$ from~THIS and~NOT *he*~*will*~*be*~EAT$^{(v)}$ LEAVENED.BREAD **13:4** the~DAY YOU$^{(mp)}$ GO.OUT$^{(v)}$~*ing*$^{(mp)}$ in~NEW.MOON the~GREEN.GRAIN **13:5** and~*he*~*did*~EXIST$^{(v)}$ GIVEN.THAT *he*~*will*~*make*~COME$^{(v)}$~*you*$^{(ms)}$ **YHWH** TO LAND the~Kena'an~of and~the~Hhet~of and~the~Emor~of and~the~Hhiw~of and~the~Yevus~of WHICH *he*~*did*~*be*~SWEAR$^{(v)}$ to~FATHER~s~*you*$^{(ms)}$ to~>~GIVE$^{(v)}$ to~*you*$^{(fs)}$ LAND ISSUE$^{(v)}$~*ing*$^{(fs)}$ FAT and~HONEY and~*you*$^{(ms)}$~*did*~SERVE$^{(v)}$ AT the~SERVICE the~THIS in~the~NEW.MOON the~THIS **13:6** SEVEN DAY~s *you*$^{(ms)}$~*will*~EAT$^{(v)}$ UNLEAVENED.BREAD~s and~in~the~DAY the~SEVENTH FEAST to~**YHWH** **13:7** UNLEAVENED.BREAD~s *he*~*will*~*be*~EAT$^{(v)}$ AT SEVEN the~DAY~s and~NOT *he*~*will*~*be*~SEE$^{(v)}$ to~*you*$^{(ms)}$ LEAVENED.BREAD and~NOT *he*~*will*~*be*~SEE$^{(v)}$ to~*you*$^{(ms)}$ LEAVEN in~ALL BORDER~*you*$^{(ms)}$ **13:8** and~*you*$^{(ms)}$~*did*~*make*~BE.FACE.TO.FACE$^{(v)}$ to~SON~*you*$^{(ms)}$ in~the~DAY the~HE to~>~SAY$^{(v)}$ in~the~CROSS.OVER$^{(v)}$~*ed*$^{(ms)}$ THIS *he*~*did*~DO$^{(v)}$ **YHWH** to~me in~>~GO.OUT$^{(v)}$~me from~Mits'rayim **13:9** and~*he*~*did*~EXIST$^{(v)}$ to~*you*$^{(ms)}$ to~SIGN UPON HAND~*you*$^{(ms)}$ and~to~REMEMBRANCE BETWEEN EYE~s2~*you*$^{(ms)}$ to~THAT *she*~*will*~EXIST$^{(v)}$ TEACHING **YHWH** in~MOUTH~*you*$^{(ms)}$ GIVEN.THAT in~HAND FORCEFUL *he*~*did*~*make*~GO.OUT$^{(v)}$~*you*$^{(ms)}$ **YHWH** from~Mits'rayim **13:10** and~*you*$^{(ms)}$~*did*~SAFEGUARD$^{(v)}$ AT the~CUSTOM the~THIS to~APPOINTED~her from~DAY~s DAY~s~unto **13:11** and~*he*~*did*~EXIST$^{(v)}$ GIVEN.THAT *he*~*will*~*make*~COME$^{(v)}$~*you*$^{(ms)}$ **YHWH** TO LAND the~Kena'an~of like~WHICH *he*~*did*~*be*~SWEAR$^{(v)}$ to~*you*$^{(ms)}$ and~to~FATHER~s~*you*$^{(ms)}$ and~*he*~*did*~GIVE$^{(v)}$~her to~*you*$^{(fs)}$ **13:12** and~*you*$^{(ms)}$~*did*~*make*~CROSS.OVER$^{(v)}$ ALL BURSTING BOWELS to~**YHWH** and~ALL BURSTING BIRTH BEAST WHICH *he*~*will*~EXIST$^{(v)}$ to~*you*$^{(ms)}$ the~MALE~s to~**YHWH** **13:13** and~ALL BURSTING DONKEY *you*$^{(ms)}$~*will*~RANSOM$^{(v)}$ in~RAM and~IF NOT *you*$^{(ms)}$~*will*~RANSOM$^{(v)}$ and~*you*$^{(ms)}$~*did*~BEHEAD$^{(v)}$~him and~ALL FIRSTBORN HUMAN in~SON~s~*you*$^{(ms)}$ *you*$^{(ms)}$~*will*~RANSOM$^{(v)}$ **13:14** and~*he*~*did*~EXIST$^{(v)}$ GIVEN.THAT *he*~*will*~INQUIRE$^{(v)}$~*you*$^{(ms)}$ SON~*you*$^{(ms)}$ TOMORROW to~>~SAY$^{(v)}$ WHAT THIS and~*you*$^{(ms)}$~*did*~SAY$^{(v)}$ TO~him in~GRASP HAND *he*~*did*~*make*~GO.OUT$^{(v)}$~us **YHWH** from~Mits'rayim from~HOUSE SERVANT~s **13:15** and~*he*~*will*~EXIST$^{(v)}$ GIVEN.THAT *he*~*did*~*make*~BE.HARD$^{(v)}$ Paroh to~>~*much*~SEND$^{(v)}$~us and~*he*~*will*~KILL$^{(v)}$ **YHWH** ALL FIRSTBORN in~LAND Mits'rayim from~FIRSTBORN HUMAN and~UNTIL FIRSTBORN BEAST UPON SO I SACRIFICE$^{(v)}$~*ing*$^{(ms)}$ to~**YHWH** ALL BURSTING BOWELS the~MALE~s and~ALL FIRSTBORN SON~s~me

*I~will~*RANSOM^(V) **13:16** and~*he~did~*EXIST^(V) to~SIGN UPON HAND~you^(ms) and~to~MARKER~s BETWEEN EYE~s2~you^(ms) GIVEN.THAT in~GRASP HAND *he~did~make~*GO.OUT^(V)~us **YHWH** from~Mits'rayim **13:17** and~*he~will~*EXIST^(V) in~>~*much~*SEND^(V) Paroh AT the~PEOPLE and~NOT *he~did~*GUIDE^(V)~them^(m) Elohiym ROAD LAND Pelesheth~s GIVEN.THAT NEAR HE GIVEN.THAT *he~did~*SAY^(V) Elohiym OTHERWISE *he~will~be~*COMFORT^(V) the~PEOPLE in~>~SEE^(V)~them^(m) BATTLE and~*they~did~*TURN.BACK^(V) Mits'rayim~unto **13:18** and~*he~will~make~*GO.AROUND^(V) Elohiym AT the~ PEOPLE ROAD the~WILDERNESS SEA REEDS and~ARM.FOR.BATTLE^(V)~*ed*^(mp) *they~did~*GO.UP^(V) SON~s Yisra'eyl from~LAND Mits'rayim **13:19** and~*he~will~*TAKE^(V) Mosheh AT BONE~s Yoseph WITH~him GIVEN.THAT >~*make~*SWEAR^(V) *he~did~make~*SWEAR^(V) AT SON~s Yisra'eyl to~>~SAY^(V) >~ REGISTER^(V) *he~will~*REGISTER^(V) Elohiym AT~you^(mp) and~*you*^(mp)~*did~make~*GO.UP^(V) AT BONE~s~me from~THIS AT~you^(mp) **13:20** and~*they*^(m)~*will~*JOURNEY^(V) from~Suk'kot and~*they*^(m)~*will~*CAMP^(V) in~Eytam in~EXTREMITY the~WILDERNESS **13:21** and~**YHWH** WALK^(V)~*ing*^(ms) to~FACE~s~them^(m) DAYTIME in~PILLAR CLOUD to~>~*make~*GUIDE^(V)~them^(m) the~ROAD and~ NIGHT in~PILLAR FIRE to~>~*make~*LIGHT^(V) to~them^(m) to~>~WALK^(V) DAYTIME and~NIGHT **13:22** NOT *he~will~make~*MOVE.AWAY^(V) PILLAR the~ CLOUD DAYTIME and~PILLAR the~FIRE NIGHT to~FACE~s the~PEOPLE

Chapter 14

14:1 and~*he~will~much~*SPEAK^(V) **YHWH** TO Mosheh to~>~SAY^(V) **14:2** *I*^(ms)~*much~*SPEAK^(V) TO SON~s Yisra'eyl and~*they*^(m)~*will~*TURN.BACK^(V) and~ *they*^(m)~*will~*CAMP^(V) to~FACE~s Piy-Hahhiyrot BETWEEN Migdol and~ BETWEEN the~SEA to~FACE~s Ba'al-Tsephon IN.FRONT~him you^(mp)~will~ CAMP^(V) UPON the~SEA **14:3** and~*he~did~*SAY^(V) Paroh to~SON~s Yisra'eyl *be~*ENTANGLED^(V)~*ing*^(mp) THEY^(m) in~the~LAND *he~did~*SHUT^(V) UPON~ them^(m) the~WILDERNESS **14:4** and~*I~did~much~*SEIZE^(V) AT HEART Paroh and~*he~did~*PURSUE^(V) AFTER~them^(m) and~*I~will~be~*BE.HEAVY^(V)~& in~ Paroh and~in~ALL FORCE~him and~*they~did~*KNOW^(V) Mits'rayim GIVEN.THAT I **YHWH** and~*they*^(m)~*will~*DO^(V) SO **14:5** and~*he~will~be~ make~*BE.FACE.TO.FACE^(V) to~KING Mits'rayim GIVEN.THAT *he~did~*FLEE.AWAY^(V) the~PEOPLE and~*he~will~be~*OVERTURN^(V) HEART Paroh and~ SERVANT~s~him TO the~PEOPLE and~*they*^(m)~*will~*SAY^(V) WHAT THIS *we~did~*DO^(V) GIVEN.THAT *we~did~much~*SEND^(V) AT Yisra'eyl from~>~SERVE^(V)~us **14:6** and~*he~will~*TIE.UP^(V) AT VEHICLE~him and~AT PEOPLE~him *he~did~*TAKE^(V) WITH~him **14:7** and~*he~will~*TAKE^(V) SIX HUNDRED~s VEHICLE CHOOSE^(V)~*ed*^(ms) and~ALL VEHICLE Mits'rayim and~LIEUTENANT~s UPON ALL~him **14:8** and~*he~will~much~*SEIZE^(V) **YHWH** AT HEART Paroh KING Mits'rayim and~*he~will~*PURSUE^(V) AFTER SON~s Yisra'eyl and~SON~s Yisra'eyl GO.OUT^(V)~*ing*^(mp) in~HAND RAISED~*ing*^(fs) **14:9** and~*they*^(m)~*will~*

PURSUE(V) Mits'rayim AFTER~them(m) and~*they*(m)~*will*~make~OVERTAKE(V) AT~them(m) CAMP(V)~*ing*(fp) UPON the~SEA ALL HORSE VEHICLE Paroh and~ HORSEMAN~s~him and~FORCE~him UPON Piy-Hahhiyrot to~FACE~s Ba'al-Tsephon **14:10** and~Paroh *he*~*did*~make~COME.NEAR(V) and~*they*(m)~*will*~ LIFT.UP(V) SON~s Yisra'eyl AT EYE~s2~them(m) and~LOOK Mits'rayim JOURNEY(V)~*ing*(ms) AFTER~them(m) and~*they*(m)~*will*~FEAR(V) MANY and~ *they*(m)~*will*~CRY.OUT(V) SON~s Yisra'eyl TO **YHWH 14:11** and~*they*(m)~*will*~ SAY(V) TO Mosheh ?~from~UNAWARE WITHOUT GRAVE~s in~Mits'rayim *you*(ms)~*did*~TAKE(V)~us to~>~DIE(V) in~the~WILDERNESS WHAT THIS *you*(ms)~ *did*~DO(V) to~us to~>~*make*~GO.OUT(V)~us from~Mits'rayim **14:12** ?~NOT THIS the~WORD WHICH *we*~*did*~*much*~SPEAK(V) TO~*you*(ms) in~Mits'rayim to~>~SAY(V) *!*(ms)~TERMINATE(V) FROM~us and~*we*~*will*~SERVE(V)~& AT Mits'rayim GIVEN.THAT FUNCTIONAL to~us >~SERVE(V) AT Mits'rayim from~ >~DIE(V)~us in~the~WILDERNESS **14:13** and~*he*~*will*~SAY(V) Mosheh TO the~ PEOPLE DO.NOT *you*(mp)~*will*~FEAR(V) *!*(mp)~*self*~STATION(V) and~ *!*(mp)~SEE(V) AT RELIEF **YHWH** WHICH *he*~*will*~DO(V) to~*you*(mp) the~DAY GIVEN.THAT WHICH *you*(mp)~*did*~SEE(V) AT Mits'rayim the~DAY NOT *you*(mp)~*will*~*make*~ ADD(V) to~SEE(V)~them(m) YET.AGAIN UNTIL DISTANT **14:14 YHWH** *will*~*be*~ FIGHT(V) to~*you*(mp) and~YOU(mp) *you*(mp)~*will*~*make*~KEEP.SILENT(V)~ must **14:15** and~*he*~*will*~SAY(V) **YHWH** TO Mosheh WHAT *you*(ms)~*will*~ CRY.OUT(V) TO~me *!*(ms)~*much*~SPEAK(V) TO SON~s Yisra'eyl and~*they*(m)~*will*~ JOURNEY(V) **14:16** and~YOU(ms) *!*(ms)~*make*~RAISE.UP(V) AT BRANCH~*you*(ms) and~ *!*(ms)~EXTEND(V) AT HAND~*you*(ms) UPON the~SEA and~ *!*(ms)~ CLEAVE.OPEN(V)~him and~*they*(m)~*will*~COME(V) SON~s Yisra'eyl in~MIDST the~SEA in~the~DRY.GROUND **14:17** and~I LOOK~me *much*~SEIZE(V)~*ing*(ms) AT HEART Mits'rayim and~*they*(m)~*will*~COME(V) AFTER~them(m) and~*I*~*will*~ *be*~BE.HEAVY(V)~& in~Paroh and~in~ALL FORCE~him in~VEHICLE~him and~ in~HORSEMAN~s~him **14:18** and~*they*~*did*~KNOW(V) Mits'rayim GIVEN.THAT I **YHWH** in~>~*be*~BE.HEAVY(V)~me in~Paroh in~VEHICLE~him and~in~HORSEMAN~s~him **14:19** and~*he*~*will*~JOURNEY(V) MESSENGER the~Elohiym the~WALK(V)~*ing*(ms) to~FACE~s CAMP Yisra'eyl and~*he*~*will*~ WALK(V) from~AFTER~them(m) and~*he*~*will*~JOURNEY(V) PILLAR the~CLOUD from~FACE~s~them(m) and~*he*~*will*~STAND(V) from~AFTER~ them(m) **14:20** and~*he*~*will*~COME(V) BETWEEN CAMP Mits'rayim and~ BETWEEN CAMP Yisra'eyl and~*he*~*will*~EXIST(V) the~CLOUD and~the~ DARKNESS and~*he*~*will*~*make*~LIGHT(V) AT the~NIGHT and~NOT *he*~*did*~ COME.NEAR(V) THIS TO THIS ALL the~NIGHT **14:21** and~*he*~*will*~EXTEND(V) Mosheh AT HAND~him UPON the~SEA and~*he*~*will*~*make*~WALK(V) **YHWH** AT the~SEA in~WIND EAST.WIND STRONG ALL the~NIGHT and~*he*~*will*~ PLACE(V) AT the~SEA to~DRIED.OUT and~*they*(m)~*will*~*be*~CLEAVE.OPEN(V) the~WATER~s2 **14:22** and~*they*(m)~*will*~COME(V) SON~s Yisra'eyl in~MIDST the~SEA in~the~DRY.GROUND and~the~WATER~s2 to~them(m) RAMPART from~RIGHT.HAND~them(m) and~from~LEFT.HAND~them(m) **14:23** and~ *they*(m)~*will*~PURSUE(V) Mits'rayim and~*they*(m)~*will*~COME(V) AFTER~them(m) ALL HORSE Paroh VEHICLE~him and~HORSEMAN~s~him TO MIDST the~

SEA **14:24** and~*he*~*will*~EXIST⁽ⱽ⁾ in~NIGHT.WATCH the~MORNING and~*he*~*will*~*make*~LOOK.DOWN⁽ⱽ⁾ **YHWH** TO CAMP Mits'rayim in~PILLAR FIRE and~CLOUD and~*he*~*will*~CONFUSE⁽ⱽ⁾ AT CAMP Mits'rayim **14:25** and~*he*~*will*~*make*~TURN.ASIDE⁽ⱽ⁾ AT WHEEL CHARIOT~s~him and~*he*~*will*~*much*~DRIVE⁽ⱽ⁾~him in~HEAVINESS and~*he*~*will*~SAY⁽ⱽ⁾ Mits'rayim *I*~*will*~FLEE⁽ⱽ⁾ from~FACE~s Yisra'eyl GIVEN.THAT **YHWH** *be*~FIGHT⁽ⱽ⁾~*ing*⁽ᵐˢ⁾ to~them⁽ᵐ⁾ in~Mits'rayim **14:26** and~*he*~*will*~SAY⁽ⱽ⁾ **YHWH** TO Mosheh *!*⁽ᵐˢ⁾~EXTEND⁽ⱽ⁾ AT HAND~you⁽ᵐˢ⁾ UPON the~SEA and~*they*⁽ᵐ⁾~*will*~TURN.BACK⁽ⱽ⁾ the~WATER~s2 UPON Mits'rayim UPON VEHICLE~him and~UPON HORSEMAN~s~him **14:27** and~*he*~*will*~EXTEND⁽ⱽ⁾ Mosheh AT HAND~him UPON the~SEA and~*he*~*will*~TURN.BACK⁽ⱽ⁾ the~SEA to~>~TURN⁽ⱽ⁾ MORNING to~CONSISTENCY~him and~Mits'rayim FLEE⁽ⱽ⁾~*ing*⁽ᵐᵖ⁾ to~>~MEET⁽ⱽ⁾~him and~*he*~*will*~*much*~SHAKE.OFF⁽ⱽ⁾ **YHWH** AT Mits'rayim in~MIDST the~SEA **14:28** and~*they*⁽ᵐ⁾~*will*~TURN.BACK⁽ⱽ⁾ the~WATER~s2 and~*they*⁽ᵐ⁾~*will*~*much*~COVER.OVER⁽ⱽ⁾ AT the~VEHICLE and~AT the~HORSEMAN~s to~ALL FORCE Paroh the~COME⁽ⱽ⁾~*ing*⁽ᵐᵖ⁾ AFTER~them⁽ᵐ⁾ in~the~SEA NOT he~*did*~*be*~REMAIN⁽ⱽ⁾ in~them⁽ᵐ⁾ UNTIL UNIT **14:29** and~SON~s Yisra'eyl *they*~*did*~WALK⁽ⱽ⁾ in~the~DRY.GROUND in~MIDST the~SEA and~the~WATER~s2 to~them⁽ᵐ⁾ RAMPART from~RIGHT.HAND~them⁽ᵐ⁾ and~from~LEFT.HAND~them⁽ᵐ⁾ **14:30** and~*he*~*will*~*make*~RESCUE⁽ⱽ⁾ **YHWH** in~the~DAY the~HE AT Yisra'eyl from~HAND Mits'rayim and~*he*~*will*~SEE⁽ⱽ⁾ Yisra'eyl AT Mits'rayim DIE⁽ⱽ⁾~*ing*⁽ᵐˢ⁾ UPON LIP the~SEA **14:31** and~*he*~*will*~SEE⁽ⱽ⁾ Yisra'eyl AT the~HAND the~GREAT WHICH *he*~*did*~DO⁽ⱽ⁾ **YHWH** in~Mits'rayim and~*they*⁽ᵐ⁾~*will*~FEAR⁽ⱽ⁾ the~PEOPLE AT **YHWH** and~*they*⁽ᵐ⁾~*will*~*make*~SECURE⁽ⱽ⁾ in~**YHWH** and~in~Mosheh SERVANT~him

Chapter 15

15:1 AT.THAT.TIME *he*~*will*~SING⁽ⱽ⁾ Mosheh and~SON~s Yisra'eyl AT the~SONG the~THIS to~**YHWH** and~*they*⁽ᵐ⁾~*will*~SAY⁽ⱽ⁾ to~>~SAY⁽ⱽ⁾ *I*~*will*~SING⁽ⱽ⁾~& to~**YHWH** GIVEN.THAT >~RISE.UP⁽ⱽ⁾ *he*~*did*~RISE.UP⁽ⱽ⁾ HORSE and~RIDE⁽ⱽ⁾~*ing*⁽ᵐˢ⁾~him *he*~*did*~THROW.DOWN⁽ⱽ⁾ in~the~SEA **15:2** BOLDNESS~me and~MUSIC Yah and~*he*~*will*~EXIST⁽ⱽ⁾ to~me to~RELIEF THIS MIGHTY.ONE~me and~*I*~*will*~*make*~ABIDE⁽ⱽ⁾~him Elohiym FATHER~me and~*I*~*will*~*much*~RAISE.UP⁽ⱽ⁾~him **15:3 YHWH** MAN BATTLE **YHWH** TITLE~him **15:4** CHARIOT~s Paroh and~FORCE~him *he*~*did*~THROW⁽ⱽ⁾ in~the~SEA and~CHOSEN LIEUTENANT~s~him *they*~*did*~*be*~*much*~SINK⁽ⱽ⁾ in~the~SEA REEDS **15:5** DEEP.WATER~s *they*⁽ᵐ⁾~*will*~*much*~COVER.OVER⁽ⱽ⁾~them⁽ᵐ⁾ *they*~*will*~GO.DOWN⁽ⱽ⁾ in~DEPTH~s like~THAT.ONE STONE **15:6** RIGHT.HAND~you⁽ᵐˢ⁾ **YHWH** *be*~BE.EMINENT⁽ⱽ⁾~*ing*⁽ᵐˢ⁾ in~the~STRENGTH RIGHT.HAND~you⁽ᵐˢ⁾ **YHWH** *she*~*will*~DASH.TO.PIECES⁽ⱽ⁾ ATTACK⁽ⱽ⁾~*ing*⁽ᵐˢ⁾ **15:7** and~in~ABUNDANCE MAJESTY~you⁽ᵐˢ⁾ *you*⁽ᵐˢ⁾~*will*~CAST.DOWN⁽ⱽ⁾ RISE⁽ⱽ⁾~*ing*⁽ᵐᵖ⁾~you⁽ᵐˢ⁾ *you*⁽ᵐˢ⁾~*will*~*much*~SEND⁽ⱽ⁾

FLAMING.WRATH~you⁽ᵐˢ⁾ he~will~EAT⁽ᵛ⁾~them⁽ᵐ⁾ like~the~ STUBBLE **15:8** and~in~WIND NOSE~s~you⁽ᵐˢ⁾ they~did~be~PILE⁽ᵛ⁾ WATER~s2 they~did~be~STAND.UP⁽ᵛ⁾ like~THAT.ONE HEAP FLOW⁽ᵛ⁾~ing⁽ᵐᵖ⁾ they~did~CURDLE⁽ᵛ⁾ DEEP.WATER~s in~HEART SEA **15:9** he~did~SAY⁽ᵛ⁾ ATTACK⁽ᵛ⁾~ing⁽ᵐˢ⁾ I~will~PURSUE⁽ᵛ⁾ I~will~make~OVERTAKE⁽ᵛ⁾ I~will~much~DISTRIBUTE⁽ᵛ⁾ SPOIL she~will~be~FILL⁽ᵛ⁾~them⁽ᵐ⁾ SOUL~me I~will~make~DRAW.OUT⁽ᵛ⁾ SWORD~me she~will~make~POSSESS⁽ᵛ⁾~them⁽ᵐ⁾ HAND~me **15:10** you⁽ᵐˢ⁾~did~BLOW⁽ᵛ⁾ in~WIND~you⁽ᵐˢ⁾ he~did~much~COVER.OVER⁽ᵛ⁾~them⁽ᵐ⁾ SEA they~did~BE.OVERSHADOWED⁽ᵛ⁾ like~LEAD in~WATER~s2 EMINENT~s **15:11** WHO like~THAT.ONE~you⁽ᵐˢ⁾ in~the~MIGHTY.ONE~s **YHWH** WHO like~THAT.ONE~you⁽ᵐˢ⁾ be~BE.EMINENT⁽ᵛ⁾~ing⁽ᵐˢ⁾ in~the~SPECIAL be~FEAR⁽ᵛ⁾~ing⁽ᵐˢ⁾ ADORATION~s DO⁽ᵛ⁾~ing⁽ᵐˢ⁾ PERFORMANCE **15:12** you⁽ᵐˢ⁾~did~EXTEND⁽ᵛ⁾ RIGHT.HAND~you⁽ᵐˢ⁾ she~will~SWALLOW⁽ᵛ⁾~them⁽ᵐ⁾ LAND **15:13** you⁽ᵐˢ⁾~did~GUIDE⁽ᵛ⁾ in~KINDNESS~you⁽ᵐˢ⁾ PEOPLE WHEREIN you⁽ᵐˢ⁾~did~REDEEM⁽ᵛ⁾ you⁽ᵐˢ⁾~did~much~LEAD⁽ᵛ⁾ in~BOLDNESS~you⁽ᵐˢ⁾ TO ABODE SPECIAL~you⁽ᵐˢ⁾ **15:14** they~did~HEAR⁽ᵛ⁾ PEOPLE~s they⁽ᵐ⁾~will~SHAKE⁽ᵛ⁾~must AGONY he~did~TAKE.HOLD⁽ᵛ⁾ SETTLE⁽ᵛ⁾~ing⁽ᵐᵖ⁾ Peleshet **15:15** AT.THAT.TIME they~did~be~STIR⁽ᵛ⁾ CHIEF~s Edom BUCK~s Mo'av he~will~TAKE.HOLD⁽ᵛ⁾~them⁽ᵐ⁾ SHAKING.IN.FEAR they~did~be~DISSOLVE⁽ᵛ⁾ ALL SETTLE⁽ᵛ⁾~ing⁽ᵐᵖ⁾ Kena'an **15:16** she~will~FALL⁽ᵛ⁾ UPON~them⁽ᵐ⁾ TERROR and~AWE in~GREAT ARM~you⁽ᵐˢ⁾ they⁽ᵐ⁾~will~BE.SILENT⁽ᵛ⁾ like~STONE UNTIL he~will~CROSS.OVER⁽ᵛ⁾ PEOPLE~you⁽ᵐˢ⁾ **YHWH** UNTIL he~will~CROSS.OVER⁽ᵛ⁾ PEOPLE WHEREIN you⁽ᵐˢ⁾~did~PURCHASE⁽ᵛ⁾ **15:17** you⁽ᵐˢ⁾~will~make~COME⁽ᵛ⁾~them⁽ᵐ⁾ and~you⁽ᵐˢ⁾~will~PLANT⁽ᵛ⁾~them⁽ᵐ⁾ in~HILL INHERITANCE~you⁽ᵐˢ⁾ PEDESTAL to~>~SETTLE⁽ᵛ⁾~you⁽ᵐˢ⁾ you⁽ᵐˢ⁾~did~MAKE⁽ᵛ⁾ **YHWH** SANCTUARY Adonai they~did~much~PREPARE⁽ᵛ⁾ HAND~s2~you⁽ᵐˢ⁾ **15:18 YHWH** he~will~REIGN⁽ᵛ⁾ to~DISTANT and~UNTIL **15:19** GIVEN.THAT he~did~COME⁽ᵛ⁾ HORSE Paroh in~VEHICLE~him and~in~HORSEMAN~s~him in~the~SEA and~he~will~make~TURN.BACK⁽ᵛ⁾ **YHWH** UPON~them⁽ᵐ⁾ AT WATER~s2 the~SEA and~SON~s Yisra'eyl they~did~WALK⁽ᵛ⁾ in~the~DRY.GROUND in~MIDST the~SEA **15:20** and~she~will~TAKE⁽ᵛ⁾ Mir'yam the~ANNOUNCER SISTER Aharon AT the~TAMBOURINE in~HAND~her and~they⁽ᶠ⁾~will~GO.OUT⁽ᵛ⁾ ALL the~WOMAN~s AFTER~her in~TAMBOURINE~s and~in~DANCE~s **15:21** and~she~will~ANSWER⁽ᵛ⁾ to~them⁽ᵐ⁾ Mir'yam I⁽ᵐᵖ⁾~SING⁽ᵛ⁾ to~**YHWH** GIVEN.THAT >~RISE.UP⁽ᵛ⁾ he~did~RISE.UP⁽ᵛ⁾ HORSE and~RIDE⁽ᵛ⁾~ing⁽ᵐˢ⁾~him he~did~THROW.DOWN⁽ᵛ⁾ in~the~SEA **15:22** and~he~will~JOURNEY⁽ᵛ⁾ Mosheh AT Yisra'eyl from~SEA REEDS and~they⁽ᵐ⁾~will~GO.OUT⁽ᵛ⁾ TO WILDERNESS Shur and~they⁽ᵐ⁾~will~WALK⁽ᵛ⁾ THREE DAY~s in~the~WILDERNESS and~NOT they~did~FIND⁽ᵛ⁾ WATER~s2 **15:23** and~they⁽ᵐ⁾~will~COME⁽ᵛ⁾ Marah~unto and~NOT they~did~BE.ABLE⁽ᵛ⁾ to~>~GULP⁽ᵛ⁾ WATER~s2 from~Marah GIVEN.THAT BITTER~s THEY⁽ᵐ⁾ UPON SO he~did~CALL.OUT⁽ᵛ⁾ TITLE~her Marah **15:24** and~they⁽ᵐ⁾~will~be~MURMUR⁽ᵛ⁾ the~PEOPLE UPON Mosheh to~>~SAY⁽ᵛ⁾ WHAT we~will~GULP⁽ᵛ⁾ **15:25** and~he~will~CRY.OUT⁽ᵛ⁾ TO **YHWH** and~he~will~make~THROW⁽ᵛ⁾~him **YHWH** TREE and~he~will~make~

THROW.OUT⁽ᵛ⁾ TO the~WATER~s2 and~*they⁽ᵐ⁾~will*~TASTE.SWEET⁽ᵛ⁾ the~ WATER~s2 THERE *he~did*~PLACE⁽ᵛ⁾ to~him CUSTOM and~DECISION and~ THERE *he~did~much*~TEST⁽ᵛ⁾~him **15:26** and~*he~will*~SAY⁽ᵛ⁾ IF >~HEAR⁽ᵛ⁾ *you⁽ᵐˢ⁾~will*~HEAR⁽ᵛ⁾ to~VOICE **YHWH** Elohiym~you⁽ᵐˢ⁾ and~the~STRAIGHT in~EYE~s2~him *you⁽ᵐˢ⁾~will*~DO⁽ᵛ⁾ and~*you⁽ᵐˢ⁾~did~make*~WEIGH.OUT⁽ᵛ⁾ to~ DIRECTIVE~s~him and~*you⁽ᵐˢ⁾~did*~SAFEGUARD⁽ᵛ⁾ ALL CUSTOM~s~him ALL the~SICKNESS WHICH *I~did*~PLACE⁽ᵛ⁾ in~Mits'rayim NOT *I~will*~PLACE⁽ᵛ⁾ UPON~you⁽ᵐˢ⁾ GIVEN.THAT I **YHWH** HEAL⁽ᵛ⁾~*ing⁽ᵐˢ⁾*~you⁽ᵐˢ⁾ **15:27** and~ *they⁽ᵐ⁾~will*~COME⁽ᵛ⁾ Eyliym~unto and~THERE TWO TEN EYE~s WATER~s2 and~SEVEN~s DATE.PALM~s and~*they⁽ᵐ⁾~will*~CAMP⁽ᵛ⁾ THERE UPON the~ WATER~s2

Chapter 16

16:1 and~*they⁽ᵐ⁾~will*~JOURNEY⁽ᵛ⁾ from~Eyliym and~*they⁽ᵐ⁾~will*~COME⁽ᵛ⁾ ALL COMPANY SON~s Yisra'eyl TO WILDERNESS Sin WHICH BETWEEN BUCK~s and~BETWEEN Sinai in~the~FIVE TEN DAY to~the~NEW.MOON the~ SECOND to~>~GO.OUT⁽ᵛ⁾~them⁽ᵐ⁾ from~LAND Mits'rayim **16:2** and~*they⁽ᵐ⁾~ will~be*~MURMUR⁽ᵛ⁾ ALL COMPANY SON~s Yisra'eyl UPON Mosheh and~ UPON Aharon in~the~WILDERNESS **16:3** and~*they⁽ᵐ⁾~will*~SAY⁽ᵛ⁾ TO~ them⁽ᵐ⁾ SON~s Yisra'eyl WHO *he~will*~GIVE⁽ᵛ⁾ >~DIE⁽ᵛ⁾~us in~HAND **YHWH** in~LAND Mits'rayim in~SETTLE⁽ᵛ⁾~us UPON POT the~FLESH in~>~EAT⁽ᵛ⁾~us BREAD to~SATISFACTION GIVEN.THAT *you⁽ᵐᵖ⁾~did~make*~GO.OUT⁽ᵛ⁾ AT~us TO the~WILDERNESS the~THIS to~>~*make*~DIE⁽ᵛ⁾ AT ALL the~ASSEMBLY the~THIS in~the~HUNGER **16:4** and~*he~will*~SAY⁽ᵛ⁾ **YHWH** TO Mosheh LOOK~me *make*~PRECIPITATE⁽ᵛ⁾~*ing⁽ᵐˢ⁾* to~you⁽ᵐᵖ⁾ BREAD FROM the~SKY~s2 and~*he~will*~GO.OUT⁽ᵛ⁾ the~PEOPLE and~*they~did*~PICK.UP⁽ᵛ⁾ WORD DAY in~DAY~him to~THAT *I~will*~TEST⁽ᵛ⁾~him ?~*he~will*~WALK⁽ᵛ⁾ in~TEACHING~ me IF NOT **16:5** and~*he~did*~EXIST⁽ᵛ⁾ in~the~DAY the~SIXTH and~*they~did~ make*~PREPARE⁽ᵛ⁾ AT WHICH *they⁽ᵐ⁾~will~make*~COME⁽ᵛ⁾ and~*he~did*~ EXIST⁽ᵛ⁾ DOUBLE UPON WHICH *they⁽ᵐ⁾~will*~PICK.UP⁽ᵛ⁾ DAY DAY **16:6** and~ *he~will*~SAY⁽ᵛ⁾ Mosheh and~Aharon TO ALL SON~s Yisra'eyl EVENING and~ *you⁽ᵐᵖ⁾~did*~KNOW⁽ᵛ⁾ GIVEN.THAT **YHWH** *he~did~make*~GO.OUT⁽ᵛ⁾ AT~ you⁽ᵐᵖ⁾ from~LAND Mits'rayim **16:7** and~MORNING and~*you⁽ᵐᵖ⁾~did*~SEE⁽ᵛ⁾ AT ARMAMENT **YHWH** in~>~HEAR⁽ᵛ⁾~him AT MURMURING~s~you⁽ᵐᵖ⁾ UPON **YHWH** and~WE WHAT GIVEN.THAT *you⁽ᵐᵖ⁾~will~be*~MURMUR⁽ᵛ⁾ UPON~ us **16:8** and~*he~will*~SAY⁽ᵛ⁾ Mosheh in~>~GIVE⁽ᵛ⁾ **YHWH** to~you⁽ᵐᵖ⁾ in~the~ EVENING FLESH to~>~EAT⁽ᵛ⁾ and~BREAD in~the~MORNING to~>~ BE.SATISFIED⁽ᵛ⁾ in~>~HEAR⁽ᵛ⁾ **YHWH** AT MURMURING~s~you⁽ᵐᵖ⁾ WHICH YOU⁽ᵐᵖ⁾ *make*~MURMUR⁽ᵛ⁾~*ing⁽ᵐᵖ⁾* UPON~him and~WE WHAT NOT UPON~ us MURMURING~s~you⁽ᵐᵖ⁾ GIVEN.THAT UPON **YHWH** **16:9** and~*he~will*~ SAY⁽ᵛ⁾ Mosheh TO Aharon *!⁽ᵐˢ⁾*~SAY⁽ᵛ⁾ TO ALL COMPANY SON~s Yisra'eyl *!⁽ᵐᵖ⁾*~COME.NEAR⁽ᵛ⁾ to~FACE~s **YHWH** GIVEN.THAT *he~did*~HEAR⁽ᵛ⁾ AT

MURMURING~s~you(mp) **16:10** and~*he~will*~EXIST(v) like~>~*much*~SPEAK(v) Aharon TO ALL COMPANY SON~s Yisra'eyl and~*they*(m)~*will*~TURN(v) TO the~ WILDERNESS and~LOOK ARMAMENT **YHWH** *he~did~be*~SEE(v) in~ CLOUD **16:11** and~*he~will~much*~SPEAK(v) **YHWH** TO Mosheh to~>~ SAY(v) **16:12** *I~did*~HEAR(v) AT MURMURING~s SON~s Yisra'eyl !(ms)~*much*~ SPEAK(v) TO~them(m) to~>~SAY(v) BETWEEN the~EVENING~s2 *you*(mp)~*will*~ EAT(v) FLESH and~in~the~MORNING *you*(mp)~*will*~BE.SATISFIED(v) BREAD and~*you*(mp)~*did*~KNOW(v) GIVEN.THAT I **YHWH** Elohiym~you(mp) **16:13** and~ *he~will*~EXIST(v) in~the~EVENING and~*she~will*~GO.UP(v) the~QUAIL and~ *she~will~much*~COVER.OVER(v) AT the~CAMP and~in~the~MORNING *she~ did*~EXIST(v) LYING.DOWN the~DEW ALL.AROUND to~the~CAMP **16:14** and~ *she~will*~GO.UP(v) LYING.DOWN the~DEW and~LOOK UPON FACE~s the~ WILDERNESS SCRAWNY *be~much*~FLAKE.OFF(v)~*ing*(ms) SCRAWNY like~ HOARFROST UPON the~LAND **16:15** and~*they*(m)~*will*~SEE(v) SON~s Yisra'eyl and~*they*(m)~*will*~SAY(v) MAN TO BROTHER~him WHAT HE GIVEN.THAT NOT *they~did*~KNOW(v) WHAT HE and~*he~will*~SAY(v) Mosheh TO~them(m) HE the~BREAD WHICH *he~did*~GIVE(v) **YHWH** to~you(mp) to~FOOD **16:16** THIS the~WORD WHICH *he~did~much*~DIRECT(v) **YHWH** !(mp)~PICK.UP(v) FROM~ him MAN to~MOUTH >~EAT(v)~him OMER to~the~SKULL NUMBER SOUL~s you(mp) MAN to~the~WHICH in~TENT~him *you*(mp)~*will*~TAKE(v) **16:17** and~ *they*(m)~*will*~DO(v) SO SON~s Yisra'eyl and~*they*(m)~*will*~PICK.UP(v) the~ *make*~INCREASE(v)~*ing*(ms) and~the~*make*~BE.LESS(v)~*ing*(ms) **16:18** and~ *they*(m)~*will*~MEASURE(v) in~the~OMER and~NOT *he~did~make*~EXCEED(v) the~*make*~INCREASE(v)~*ing*(ms) and~the~*make*~BE.LESS(v)~*ing*(ms) NOT *he~ did~make*~DIMINISH(v) MAN to~MOUTH >~EAT(v)~him *they~did*~PICK.UP(v) **16:19** and~*he~will*~SAY(v) Mosheh TO~them(m) MAN DO.NOT *he~will~make*~ LEAVE.BEHIND(v) FROM~him UNTIL MORNING **16:20** and~NOT *they~did*~ HEAR(v) TO Mosheh and~*they*(m)~*will~make*~LEAVE.BEHIND(v) MAN~s FROM~him UNTIL MORNING and~*he~will*~RAISE.UP(v) KERMES~s and~*he~ will*~STINK(v) and~*he~will*~SNAP(v) UPON~them(m) Mosheh **16:21** and~ *they*(m)~*will*~PICK.UP(v) AT~him in~the~MORNING in~the~MORNING MAN like~MOUTH >~EAT(v)~him and~*he~did*~BE.WARM(v) the~SUN and~*he~did~ be*~MELT.AWAY(v) **16:22** and~*he~will*~EXIST(v) in~the~DAY the~SIXTH *they~ did*~PICK.UP(v) BREAD DOUBLE TWO the~OMER to~UNIT and~*they*(m)~*will*~ COME(v) ALL CAPTAIN~s the~COMPANY and~*they*(m)~*will~make*~ BE.FACE.TO.FACE(v) to~Mosheh **16:23** and~*he~will*~SAY(v) TO~them(m) HE WHICH *he~did~much*~SPEAK(v) **YHWH** REST.PERIOD CEASING SPECIAL to~ **YHWH** TOMORROW AT WHICH *you*(mp)~*will*~BAKE(v) !(mp)~BAKE(v) and~AT WHICH *you*(mp)~*will~much*~BOIL(v) !(mp)~BOIL(v) and~AT ALL the~EXCEED(v)~ *ing*(ms) !(mp)~*make*~REST(v) to~you(mp) to~CHARGE UNTIL the~ MORNING **16:24** and~*they*(m)~*will~make*~REST(v) AT~him UNTIL the~ MORNING like~WHICH *he~did~much*~DIRECT(v) Mosheh and~NOT *he~did~ make*~STINK(v) and~MAGGOT NOT *she~did*~EXIST(v) in~him **16:25** and~*he~ will*~SAY(v) Mosheh !(mp)~EAT(v)~him the~DAY GIVEN.THAT CEASING the~DAY to~**YHWH** the~DAY NOT *you*(mp)~*will*~FIND(v)~him in~the~FIELD **16:26** SIX

DAY~s you^(mp)~will~PICK.UP^(V)~him and~in~the~DAY the~SEVENTH CEASING NOT he~will~EXIST^(V) in~him **16:27** and~he~will~EXIST^(V) in~the~DAY the~SEVENTH they~did~GO.OUT^(V) FROM the~PEOPLE to~>~PICK.UP^(V) and~NOT they~did~FIND^(V) **16:28** and~he~will~SAY^(V) **YHWH** TO Mosheh UNTIL WHEREVER you^(mp)~did~much~REFUSE^(V) to~>~SAFEGUARD^(V) DIRECTIVE~s me and~TEACHING~s me **16:29** !^(mp)~SEE^(V) GIVEN.THAT **YHWH** he~did~GIVE^(V) to~you^(mp) the~CEASING UPON SO HE GIVE^(V)~ing^(ms) to~you^(mp) in~the~DAY the~SIXTH BREAD DAY~s2 !^(mp)~SETTLE^(V) MAN UNDER~him DO.NOT he~will~GO.OUT^(V) MAN from~AREA~him in~the~DAY the~SEVENTH **16:30** and~they^(m)~will~CEASE^(V) the~PEOPLE in~the~DAY the~SEVENTH **16:31** and~they^(m)~will~CALL.OUT^(V) HOUSE Yisra'eyl AT TITLE~him Mahn and~HE like~SEED CORIANDER Lavan and~FLAVOR~him like~WAFER in~HONEY **16:32** and~he~will~SAY^(V) Mosheh THIS the~WORD WHICH he~did~much~DIRECT^(V) **YHWH** FILLING the~OMER FROM~him to~CHARGE to~GENERATION~s~you^(mp) to~THAT they^(m)~will~SEE^(V) AT the~BREAD WHICH I~did~make~EAT^(V) AT~you^(mp) in~the~WILDERNESS in~>~make~GO.OUT^(V)~me AT~you^(mp) from~LAND Mits'rayim **16:33** and~he~will~SAY^(V) Mosheh TO Aharon !^(ms)~TAKE^(V) WOVEN.BASKET UNIT and~!^(ms)~GIVE^(V) THERE~unto FILLING the~OMER Mahn and~!^(ms)~make~REST^(V) AT~him to~FACE~s **YHWH** to~CHARGE to~GENERATION~s~you^(mp) **16:34** like~WHICH he~did~much~DIRECT^(V) **YHWH** TO Mosheh and~he~will~make~REST^(V)~him Aharon to~FACE~s the~EVIDENCE to~CHARGE **16:35** and~SON~s Yisra'eyl they~did~EAT^(V) AT the~Mahn FOUR~s YEAR UNTIL >~COME^(V)~them^(m) TO LAND be~SETTLE^(V)~ing^(fs) AT the~Mahn they~did~EAT^(V) UNTIL >~COME^(V)~them^(m) TO EXTREMITY LAND Kena'an **16:36** and~the~OMER TENTH the~EYPHAH HE

Chapter 17

17:1 and~they^(m)~will~JOURNEY^(V) ALL COMPANY SON~s Yisra'eyl from~WILDERNESS Sin to~JOURNEY~s~them^(m) UPON MOUTH **YHWH** and~they^(m)~will~CAMP^(V) in~Rephiydiym and~WITHOUT WATER~s2 to~>~GULP^(V) the~PEOPLE **17:2** and~he~will~DISPUTE^(V) the~PEOPLE WITH Mosheh and~they^(m)~will~SAY^(V) !^(mp)~GIVE^(V) to~us WATER~s2 and~we~will~GULP^(V) and~he~will~SAY^(V) to~them^(m) Mosheh WHAT you^(mp)~will~DISPUTE^(V)~must BY~me WHAT you^(mp)~will~TEST^(V)~must AT **YHWH 17:3** and~he~will~THIRST^(V) THERE the~PEOPLE to~WATER~s2 and~he~will~STAY.THE.NIGHT^(V) the~PEOPLE UPON Mosheh and~he~will~SAY^(V) to~WHAT THIS you^(ms)~did~make~GO.UP^(V)~us from~Mits'rayim to~>~make~DIE^(V) AT~me and~AT SON~s~me and~AT ACQUIRED~s~me in~the~THIRST **17:4** and~he~will~CRY.OUT^(V) Mosheh TO **YHWH** to~>~SAY^(V) WHAT I~will~DO^(V) to~the~PEOPLE the~THIS YET.AGAIN SMALL.AMOUNT and~they~did~STONE^(V)~me **17:5** and~he~will~SAY^(V) **YHWH** TO Mosheh !^(ms)~CROSS.OVER^(V) to~FACE~s the~PEOPLE and~!^(ms)~TAKE^(V) AT~you^(ms) from~BEARD~s Yisra'eyl and~BRANCH~you⁽ᵐˢ⁾ WHICH *you⁽ᵐˢ⁾~did~make*~HIT⁽ⱽ⁾ in~him AT the~ STREAM *!⁽ᵐˢ⁾~TAKE*⁽ⱽ⁾ in~HAND~you⁽ᵐˢ⁾ and~*you⁽ᵐˢ⁾~did*~ WALK⁽ⱽ⁾ **17:6** LOOK~me STAND⁽ⱽ⁾~*ing⁽ᵐˢ⁾* to~FACE~s2~you⁽ᵐˢ⁾ THERE UPON the~BOULDER in~Hhorev and~*you⁽ᵐˢ⁾~did~make*~HIT⁽ⱽ⁾ in~the~BOULDER and~*they~did~*GO.OUT⁽ⱽ⁾ FROM~him WATER~s2 and~*he~did~*GULP⁽ⱽ⁾ the~ PEOPLE and~*he~will~*DO⁽ⱽ⁾ SO Mosheh to~EYE~s2 BEARD~s Yisra'eyl **17:7** and~*he~will~*CALL.OUT⁽ⱽ⁾ TITLE the~AREA Mas'sah and~ Meriyvah UPON DISPUTE SON~s Yisra'eyl and~UPON >~*much~*TEST⁽ⱽ⁾~ them⁽ᵐ⁾ AT **YHWH** to~>~SAY⁽ⱽ⁾ ?~THERE.IS **YHWH** in~INSIDE~us IF WITHOUT **17:8** and~*he~will~*COME⁽ⱽ⁾ Amaleq and~*he~will~be~*FIGHT⁽ⱽ⁾ WITH Yisra'eyl in~Rephiydiym **17:9** and~*he~will~*SAY⁽ⱽ⁾ Mosheh TO Yehoshu'a *!⁽ᵐˢ⁾~CHOOSE*⁽ⱽ⁾ to~us MAN~s and~*!⁽ᵐˢ⁾~*GO.OUT⁽ⱽ⁾ *!⁽ᵐˢ⁾~be*~ FIGHT⁽ⱽ⁾ in~the~Amaleq TOMORROW I *be~*STAND.UP⁽ⱽ⁾~*ing⁽ᵐˢ⁾* UPON HEAD the~KNOLL and~BRANCH the~Elohiym in~HAND~me **17:10** and~*he~will~* DO⁽ⱽ⁾ Yehoshu'a like~WHICH *he~did~*SAY⁽ⱽ⁾ to~him Mosheh to~>~*be~* FIGHT⁽ⱽ⁾ in~the~Amaleq and~Mosheh Aharon and~Hhur *they~did~*GO.UP⁽ⱽ⁾ HEAD the~KNOLL **17:11** and~*he~did~*EXIST⁽ⱽ⁾ like~WHICH *he~will~make~* RAISE.UP⁽ⱽ⁾ Mosheh HAND~him and~*he~did~*OVERCOME⁽ⱽ⁾ Yisra'eyl and~ like~WHICH *he~will~make~*REST⁽ⱽ⁾ HAND~him and~*he~did~*OVERCOME⁽ⱽ⁾ Amaleq **17:12** and~HAND~s2 Mosheh HEAVY~s and~*they⁽ᵐ⁾~will~*TAKE⁽ⱽ⁾ STONE and~*they⁽ᵐ⁾~will~*PLACE⁽ⱽ⁾ UNDER~s~him and~*he~will~*SETTLE⁽ⱽ⁾ UPON~her and~Aharon and~Hhur *they~did~*UPHOLD⁽ⱽ⁾ in~HAND~s2~him from~THIS UNIT and~from~THIS UNIT and~*he~will~*EXIST⁽ⱽ⁾ HAND~s2~him SECURE UNTIL *!⁽ᵐˢ⁾~*COME⁽ⱽ⁾ the~SUN **17:13** and~*he~will~*WEAKEN⁽ⱽ⁾ Yehoshu'a AT Amaleq and~AT PEOPLE~him to~MOUTH SWORD **17:14** and~ *he~will~*SAY⁽ⱽ⁾ **YHWH** TO Mosheh *!⁽ᵐˢ⁾~*WRITE⁽ⱽ⁾ THIS REMEMBRANCE in~ the~SCROLL and~*!⁽ᵐˢ⁾~*PLACE⁽ⱽ⁾ in~EAR~s2 Yehoshu'a GIVEN.THAT >~ WIPE.AWAY⁽ⱽ⁾ *I~will~*WIPE.AWAY⁽ⱽ⁾ AT MEMORY Amaleq from~UNDER the~ SKY~s2 **17:15** and~*he~will~*BUILD⁽ⱽ⁾ Mosheh ALTAR and~*he~will~* CALL.OUT⁽ⱽ⁾ TITLE~him **YHWH**-Nisiy **17:16** and~*he~will~*SAY⁽ⱽ⁾ GIVEN.THAT HAND UPON STOOL Yah BATTLE to~**YHWH** in~the~Amaleq from~ GENERATION GENERATION

Chapter 18

18:1 and~*he~will~*HEAR⁽ⱽ⁾ Yitro ADMINISTRATOR Mid'yan BE.AN.IN-LAW⁽ⱽ⁾~ *ing⁽ᵐˢ⁾* Mosheh AT ALL WHICH *he~did~*DO⁽ⱽ⁾ Elohiym to~Mosheh and~to~ Yisra'eyl PEOPLE~him GIVEN.THAT *he~did~make~*GO.OUT⁽ⱽ⁾ **YHWH** AT Yisra'eyl from~Mits'rayim **18:2** and~*he~will~*TAKE⁽ⱽ⁾ Yitro BE.AN.IN-LAW⁽ⱽ⁾~ *ing⁽ᵐˢ⁾* Mosheh AT Tsiporah WOMAN Mosheh AFTER SEND.OFF~s~ her **18:3** and~AT TWO SON~s~her WHICH TITLE the~UNIT Gershom GIVEN.THAT *he~did~*SAY⁽ⱽ⁾ IMMIGRANT *I~did~*EXIST⁽ⱽ⁾ in~LAND FOREIGN **18:4** and~TITLE the~UNIT Eli'ezer GIVEN.THAT Elohiym FATHER~

The Book of Exodus

me in~HELP~me and~*he~will*~DELIVER$^{(V)}$~me from~SWORD
Paroh **18:5** and~*he~will*~COME$^{(V)}$ Yitro BE.AN.IN-LAW$^{(V)}$~*ing*$^{(ms)}$ Mosheh and~SON~s~him and~WOMAN~him TO Mosheh TO the~WILDERNESS WHICH HE CAMP$^{(V)}$~*ing*$^{(ms)}$ THERE HILL the~Elohiym **18:6** and~*he~will*~SAY$^{(V)}$ TO Mosheh I BE.AN.IN-LAW$^{(V)}$~*ing*$^{(ms)}$~you$^{(ms)}$ Yitro *he~did*~COME$^{(V)}$ TO~you$^{(ms)}$ and~WOMAN~you$^{(ms)}$ and~TWO SON~s~her WITH~her **18:7** and~*he~will*~GO.OUT$^{(V)}$ Mosheh to~>~MEET$^{(V)}$ BE.AN.IN-LAW$^{(V)}$~*ing*$^{(ms)}$~him and~*he~will*~self~BEND.DOWN$^{(V)}$ and~*he~will*~KISS$^{(V)}$ to~him and~*they*$^{(m)}$~*will*~INQUIRE$^{(V)}$ MAN to~COMPANION~him to~COMPLETENESS and~*they*$^{(m)}$~*will*~COME$^{(V)}$ the~TENT~unto **18:8** and~*he~will*~much~COUNT$^{(V)}$ Mosheh to~BE.AN.IN-LAW$^{(V)}$~*ing*$^{(ms)}$~him AT ALL WHICH *he~did*~DO$^{(V)}$ **YHWH** to~Paroh and~to~Mits'rayim UPON CONCERNING~s Yisra'eyl AT ALL the~TROUBLE WHICH *she~did*~FIND$^{(V)}$~them$^{(m)}$ in~the~ROAD and~*he~will*~make~DELIVER$^{(V)}$~them$^{(m)}$ **YHWH** **18:9** and~*he~will*~BE.AMAZED$^{(V)}$ Yitro UPON ALL the~FUNCTIONAL WHICH *he~did*~DO$^{(V)}$ **YHWH** to~Yisra'eyl WHICH *he~did*~make~DELIVER$^{(V)}$~them$^{(m)}$ from~HAND Mits'rayim **18:10** and~*he~will*~SAY$^{(V)}$ Yitro KNEEL$^{(V)}$~*ed*$^{(ms)}$ **YHWH** WHICH *he~did*~make~DELIVER$^{(V)}$ AT~you$^{(mp)}$ from~HAND Mits'rayim and~from~HAND Paroh WHICH *he~did*~make~DELIVER$^{(V)}$ AT the~PEOPLE from~UNDER HAND Mits'rayim **18:11** NOW *I~did*~KNOW$^{(V)}$ GIVEN.THAT GREAT **YHWH** from~ALL the~Elohiym GIVEN.THAT in~the~WORD WHICH *they~did*~SIMMER$^{(V)}$ UPON~them$^{(m)}$ **18:12** and~*he~will*~TAKE$^{(V)}$ Yitro BE.AN.IN-LAW$^{(V)}$~*ing*$^{(ms)}$ Mosheh ASCENSION.OFFERING and~SACRIFICE~s to~Elohiym and~*he~will*~COME$^{(V)}$ Aharon and~ALL BEARD~s Yisra'eyl to~>~EAT$^{(V)}$ BREAD WITH BE.AN.IN-LAW$^{(V)}$~*ing*$^{(ms)}$ Mosheh to~FACE~s the~Elohiym **18:13** and~*he~will*~EXIST$^{(V)}$ from~MORROW and~*he~will*~SETTLE$^{(V)}$ Mosheh to~>~DECIDE$^{(V)}$ AT the~PEOPLE and~*he~will*~STAND$^{(V)}$ the~PEOPLE UPON Mosheh FROM the~MORNING UNTIL the~EVENING **18:14** and~*he~will*~SEE$^{(V)}$ BE.AN.IN-LAW$^{(V)}$~*ing*$^{(ms)}$ Mosheh AT ALL WHICH HE DO$^{(V)}$~*ing*$^{(ms)}$ to~the~PEOPLE and~*he~will*~SAY$^{(V)}$ WHAT the~WORD the~THIS WHICH YOU$^{(ms)}$ DO$^{(V)}$~*ing*$^{(ms)}$ to~the~PEOPLE WHY YOU$^{(ms)}$ SETTLE$^{(V)}$~*ing*$^{(ms)}$ to~STRAND~you$^{(ms)}$ and~ALL the~PEOPLE *be*~STAND.UP$^{(V)}$~*ing*$^{(ms)}$ UPON~you$^{(ms)}$ FROM MORNING UNTIL EVENING **18:15** and~*he~will*~SAY$^{(V)}$ Mosheh to~BE.AN.IN-LAW$^{(V)}$~*ing*$^{(ms)}$~him GIVEN.THAT *he~will*~COME$^{(V)}$ TO~me the~PEOPLE to~>~SEEK$^{(V)}$ Elohiym **18:16** GIVEN.THAT *he~will*~EXIST$^{(V)}$ to~them$^{(m)}$ WORD *he~did*~COME$^{(V)}$ TO~me and~*I~did*~DECIDE$^{(V)}$ BETWEEN MAN and~BETWEEN COMPANION~him and~*I~did*~make~KNOW$^{(V)}$ AT CUSTOM~s the~Elohiym and~AT TEACHING~s~him **18:17** and~*he~will*~SAY$^{(V)}$ BE.AN.IN-LAW$^{(V)}$~*ing*$^{(ms)}$ Mosheh TO~him NOT FUNCTIONAL the~WORD WHICH YOU$^{(ms)}$ DO$^{(V)}$~*ing*$^{(ms)}$ **18:18** >~FADE$^{(V)}$ *you*$^{(ms)}$~*will*~FADE$^{(V)}$ ALSO YOU$^{(ms)}$ ALSO the~PEOPLE the~THIS WHICH WITH~you$^{(fs)}$ GIVEN.THAT HEAVY FROM~you$^{(ms)}$ the~WORD NOT *you*$^{(ms)}$~*will*~BE.ABLE$^{(V)}$ >~DO$^{(V)}$~him to~STRAND~you$^{(ms)}$ **18:19** NOW *!*$^{(ms)}$~HEAR$^{(V)}$ in~VOICE~me *I~will*~GIVE.ADVICE$^{(V)}$~you$^{(ms)}$ and~*he~will*~EXIST$^{(V)}$ Elohiym WITH~you$^{(fs)}$ *!*$^{(ms)}$~EXIST$^{(V)}$ YOU$^{(ms)}$ to~the~PEOPLE FOREFRONT the~Elohiym and~*you*$^{(ms)}$~*did*~make~COME$^{(V)}$ YOU$^{(ms)}$ AT the~WORD~s TO the~Elohiym

18:20 and~you(ms)~did~make~ILLUMINATE(V) AT~them(m) AT the~CUSTOM~s and~AT the~TEACHING~s and~you(ms)~did~make~KNOW(V) to~them(m) AT the~ROAD they(m)~will~WALK(V) in~her and~AT the~WORK WHICH they(m)~will~DO(V)~must **18:21** and~YOU(ms) you(ms)~will~PERCEIVE(V) from~ALL the~PEOPLE MAN~s FORCE FEARFUL~s Elohiym MAN~s TRUTH HATE(V)~ing(mp) PROFIT and~you(ms)~did~PLACE(V) UPON~them(m) NOBLE~s THOUSAND~s NOBLE~s HUNDRED~s NOBLE~s FIVE~s and~NOBLE~s TEN~s **18:22** and~they~did~DECIDE(V) AT the~PEOPLE in~ALL APPOINTED.TIME and~he~did~EXIST(V) ALL the~WORD the~GREAT they(m)~will~make~COME(V) TO~you(ms) and~ALL the~WORD the~SMALL they(m)~will~DECIDE(V) THEY(m) and~!(ms)~make~BELITTLE(V) from~UPON~you(ms) and~they~did~LIFT.UP(V) AT~you(fs) **18:23** IF AT the~WORD the~THIS you(ms)~will~DO(V) and~he~did~much~DIRECT(V)~you(ms) Elohiym and~you(ms)~did~BE.ABLE(V) >~STAND(V) and~ALSO ALL the~PEOPLE the~THIS UPON AREA~him he~will~COME(V) in~COMPLETENESS **18:24** and~he~will~HEAR(V) Mosheh to~VOICE BE.AN.IN-LAW(V)~ing(ms)~him and~he~will~DO(V) ALL WHICH he~did~SAY(V) **18:25** and~he~will~CHOOSE(V) Mosheh MAN~s FORCE from~ALL Yisra'eyl and~he~will~GIVE(V) AT~them(m) HEAD~s UPON the~PEOPLE NOBLE~s THOUSAND~s NOBLE~s HUNDRED~s NOBLE~s FIVE~s and~NOBLE~s TEN~s **18:26** and~they~did~DECIDE(V) AT the~PEOPLE in~ALL APPOINTED.TIME AT the~WORD the~HARD they(m)~will~make~COME(V)~must TO Mosheh and~ALL the~WORD the~SMALL they(m)~did~DECIDE(V) THEY(m) **18:27** and~he~will~much~SEND(V) Mosheh AT BE.AN.IN-LAW(V)~ing(ms)~him and~he~will~WALK(V) to~him TO LAND~him

Chapter 19

19:1 in~the~NEW.MOON the~THIRD to~>~GO.OUT(V) SON~s Yisra'eyl from~LAND Mits'rayim in~the~DAY the~THIS they~did~COME(V) WILDERNESS Sinai **19:2** and~they(m)~will~JOURNEY(V) from~Rephiydiym and~they(m)~will~COME(V) WILDERNESS Sinai and~they(m)~will~CAMP(V) in~the~WILDERNESS and~he~will~CAMP(V) THERE Yisra'eyl OPPOSITE the~HILL **19:3** and~Mosheh he~did~GO.UP(V) TO the~Elohiym and~he~will~CALL.OUT(V) TO~him **YHWH** FROM the~HILL to~>~SAY(V) IN.THIS.WAY you(ms)~will~SAY(V) to~HOUSE Ya'aqov and~you(ms)~will~make~BE.FACE.TO.FACE(V) to~SON~s Yisra'eyl **19:4** YOU(mp) you(mp)~did~SEE(V) WHICH I~did~DO(V) to~Mits'rayim and~I~will~LIFT.UP(V) AT~you(mp) UPON WING~s EAGLE~s and~I~will~make~COME(V) AT~you(mp) TO~me **19:5** and~NOW IF >~HEAR(V) you(mp)~will~HEAR(V) in~VOICE~me and~you(mp)~did~SAFEGUARD(V) AT COVENANT~me and~you(mp)~did~EXIST(V) to~me JEWEL from~ALL the~PEOPLE~s GIVEN.THAT to~me ALL the~LAND **19:6** and~YOU(mp) you(mp)~will~EXIST(V) to~me KINGDOM ADMINISTRATOR~s and~NATION UNIQUE THESE the~WORD~s WHICH you(ms)~will~much~SPEAK(V) TO SON~s Yisra'eyl **19:7** and~

The Book of Exodus

he~will~COME$^{(V)}$ Mosheh and~*he~will*~CALL.OUT$^{(V)}$ to~BEARD~s the~PEOPLE and~*he~will*~PLACE$^{(V)}$ to~FACE~s~them$^{(m)}$ AT ALL the~WORD~s the~THESE WHICH *he~did~much*~DIRECT$^{(V)}$~him **YHWH 19:8** and~*they$^{(m)}$~will*~ANSWER$^{(V)}$ ALL the~PEOPLE TOGETHER and~*they$^{(m)}$~will*~SAY$^{(V)}$ ALL WHICH *he~did~much*~SPEAK$^{(V)}$ **YHWH** *we~will*~DO$^{(V)}$ and~*he~will*~make~TURN.BACK$^{(V)}$ Mosheh AT WORD~s the~PEOPLE TO **YHWH 19:9** and~*he~will*~SAY$^{(V)}$ **YHWH** TO Mosheh LOOK I *he~did*~COME$^{(V)}$ TO~you$^{(ms)}$ in~THICK the~CLOUD in~the~CROSS.OVER$^{(V)}$~ed$^{(ms)}$ *he~will*~HEAR$^{(V)}$ the~PEOPLE in~>~*much*~SPEAK$^{(V)}$~me WITH~you$^{(fs)}$ and~ALSO in~you$^{(ms)}$ *they$^{(m)}$~will*~make~SECURE$^{(V)}$ to~DISTANT and~*he~will*~make~BE.FACE.TO.FACE$^{(V)}$ Mosheh AT WORD~s the~PEOPLE TO **YHWH 19:10** and~*he~will*~SAY$^{(V)}$ **YHWH** TO Mosheh !$^{(ms)}$~WALK$^{(V)}$ TO the~PEOPLE and~*you$^{(ms)}$~did~much*~SET.APART$^{(V)}$~them$^{(m)}$ the~DAY and~TOMORROW and~*they~did~much*~WASH$^{(V)}$ APPAREL~s~them$^{(m)}$ **19:11** and~*they~did*~EXIST$^{(V)}$ be~PREPARE$^{(V)}$~*ing*$^{(mp)}$ to~the~DAY the~THIRD GIVEN.THAT in~the~DAY the~THIRD *he~will*~GO.DOWN$^{(V)}$ **YHWH** to~EYE~s2 ALL the~PEOPLE UPON HILL Sinai **19:12** and~*you$^{(ms)}$~did~make*~BOUND$^{(V)}$ AT the~PEOPLE ALL.AROUND to~>~SAY$^{(V)}$!$^{(mp)}$~be~SAFEGUARD$^{(V)}$ to~you$^{(mp)}$ >~GO.UP$^{(V)}$ in~the~HILL and~>~TOUCH$^{(V)}$ in~EXTREMITY~him ALL the~TOUCH$^{(V)}$~*ing*$^{(ms)}$ in~the~HILL >~DIE$^{(V)}$ *he~will*~be~make~DIE$^{(V)}$ **19:13** NOT *she~will*~TOUCH$^{(V)}$ in~him HAND GIVEN.THAT >~STONE$^{(V)}$ *he~will*~be~STONE$^{(V)}$ OR >~THROW$^{(V)}$ *he~will*~be~THROW$^{(V)}$ IF BEAST IF MAN NOT *he~will*~LIVE$^{(V)}$ in~>~DRAW$^{(V)}$ the~JUBILEE THEY$^{(m)}$ *they$^{(m)}$~will*~GO.UP$^{(V)}$ in~the~HILL **19:14** and~*he~will*~GO.DOWN$^{(V)}$ Mosheh FROM the~HILL TO the~PEOPLE and~*he~will~much*~SET.APART$^{(V)}$ AT the~PEOPLE and~*they$^{(m)}$~will~much*~WASH$^{(V)}$ APPAREL~s~them$^{(m)}$ **19:15** and~*he~will*~SAY$^{(V)}$ TO the~PEOPLE !$^{(mp)}$~EXIST$^{(V)}$ be~PREPARE$^{(V)}$~*ing*$^{(mp)}$ to~THREE DAY~s DO.NOT *you$^{(mp)}$~will*~DRAW.NEAR$^{(V)}$ TO WOMAN **19:16** and~*he~will*~EXIST$^{(V)}$ in~the~DAY the~THIRD in~>~EXIST$^{(V)}$ the~MORNING and~*he~will*~EXIST$^{(V)}$ VOICE~s and~FLASH~s and~CLOUD HEAVY UPON the~HILL and~VOICE RAM.HORN FORCEFUL MANY and~*he~will*~TREMBLE$^{(V)}$ ALL the~PEOPLE WHICH in~the~CAMP **19:17** and~*he~will*~make~GO.OUT$^{(V)}$ Mosheh AT the~PEOPLE to~>~MEET$^{(V)}$ the~Elohiym FROM the~CAMP and~*they$^{(m)}$~will~be~make*~STAND.UP$^{(V)}$ in~LOWER.PART the~HILL **19:18** and~HILL Sinai *he~did*~SMOKE$^{(V)}$ ALL~him from~FACE~s WHICH *he~did*~GO.DOWN$^{(V)}$ UPON~him **YHWH** in~the~FIRE and~*he~will*~make~GO.UP$^{(V)}$ SMOKE~him like~SMOKE the~FURNACE and~*he~will*~TREMBLE$^{(V)}$ ALL the~HILL MANY **19:19** and~*he~will*~EXIST$^{(V)}$ VOICE the~RAM.HORN WALK$^{(V)}$~*ing*$^{(ms)}$ and~FORCEFUL MANY Mosheh *he~will~much*~SPEAK$^{(V)}$ and~the~Elohiym *he~will*~ANSWER$^{(V)}$~him in~VOICE **19:20** and~*he~will*~GO.DOWN$^{(V)}$ **YHWH** UPON HILL Sinai TO HEAD the~HILL and~*he~will*~CALL.OUT$^{(V)}$ **YHWH** to~Mosheh TO HEAD the~HILL and~*he~will*~make~GO.UP$^{(V)}$ Mosheh **19:21** and~*he~will*~SAY$^{(V)}$ **YHWH** TO Mosheh !$^{(ms)}$~GO.DOWN$^{(V)}$!$^{(ms)}$~make~WRAP.AROUND$^{(V)}$ in~the~PEOPLE OTHERWISE *they$^{(m)}$~will*~CAST.DOWN$^{(V)}$ TO **YHWH** to~>~SEE$^{(V)}$ and~*he~did*~FALL$^{(V)}$ FROM~him ABUNDANT **19:22** and~ALSO the~ADMINISTRATOR~s the~be~

DRAW.NEAR⁽ᵛ⁾~ing⁽ᵐᵖ⁾ TO **YHWH** they⁽ᵐ⁾~will~be~make~SET.APART⁽ᵛ⁾ OTHERWISE he~will~BREAK.OUT⁽ᵛ⁾ in~them⁽ᵐ⁾ **YHWH 19:23** and~he~will~ SAY⁽ᵛ⁾ Mosheh TO **YHWH** NOT he~will~BE.ABLE⁽ᵛ⁾ the~PEOPLE to~>~ GO.UP⁽ᵛ⁾ TO HILL Sinai GIVEN.THAT YOU⁽ᵐˢ⁾ you⁽ᵐˢ⁾~did~make~ WRAP.AROUND⁽ᵛ⁾~& in~us to~>~SAY⁽ᵛ⁾ *!⁽ᵐˢ⁾~make~*BOUND⁽ᵛ⁾ AT the~HILL and~you⁽ᵐˢ⁾~did~much~SET.APART⁽ᵛ⁾~him **19:24** and~he~will~SAY⁽ᵛ⁾ TO~ him **YHWH** *!⁽ᵐˢ⁾~*WALK⁽ᵛ⁾ *!⁽ᵐˢ⁾~*GO.DOWN⁽ᵛ⁾ and~you⁽ᵐˢ⁾~did~GO.UP⁽ᵛ⁾ YOU⁽ᵐˢ⁾ and~Aharon WITH~you⁽ᶠˢ⁾ and~the~ADMINISTRATOR~s and~the~ PEOPLE DO.NOT they⁽ᵐ⁾~will~CAST.DOWN⁽ᵛ⁾ to~>~GO.UP⁽ᵛ⁾ TO **YHWH** OTHERWISE he~will~BREAK.OUT⁽ᵛ⁾ in~them⁽ᵐ⁾ **19:25** and~he~will~ GO.DOWN⁽ᵛ⁾ Mosheh TO the~PEOPLE and~he~will~SAY⁽ᵛ⁾ TO~them⁽ᵐ⁾

Chapter 20

20:1 and~he~will~much~SPEAK⁽ᵛ⁾ Elohiym AT ALL the~WORD~s the~THESE to~>~SAY⁽ᵛ⁾ **20:2** I **YHWH** Elohiym~you⁽ᵐˢ⁾ WHICH *I~did~make~*GO.OUT⁽ᵛ⁾~ you⁽ᵐˢ⁾ from~LAND Mits'rayim from~HOUSE SERVANT~s **20:3** NOT he~will~ EXIST⁽ᵛ⁾ to~you⁽ᵐˢ⁾ Elohiym OTHER~s UPON FACE~s~me **20:4** NOT you⁽ᵐˢ⁾~ will~DO⁽ᵛ⁾ to~you⁽ᵐˢ⁾ SCULPTURE and~ALL RESEMBLANCE WHICH in~the~ SKY~s2 from~UPWARD and~WHICH in~the~LAND from~UNDER and~WHICH in~the~WATER~s2 from~UNDER to~the~LAND **20:5** NOT you⁽ᵐˢ⁾~will~self~ BEND.DOWN⁽ᵛ⁾ to~them⁽ᵐ⁾ and~NOT you⁽ᵐˢ⁾~will~be~make~SERVE⁽ᵛ⁾~ them⁽ᵐ⁾ GIVEN.THAT I **YHWH** Elohiym~you⁽ᵐˢ⁾ MIGHTY.ONE ZEALOUS REGISTER⁽ᵛ⁾~ing⁽ᵐˢ⁾ TWISTEDNESS FATHER~s UPON SON~s UPON THIRD.GENERATION~s and~UPON FOURTH.GENERATION~s to~HATE⁽ᵛ⁾~ ing⁽ᵐᵖ⁾~me **20:6** and~DO⁽ᵛ⁾~ing⁽ᵐᵖ⁾ KINDNESS to~the~THOUSAND~s to~ LOVE⁽ᵛ⁾~ing⁽ᵐᵖ⁾~me and~to~SAFEGUARD⁽ᵛ⁾~ing⁽ᵐᵖ⁾ DIRECTIVE~s~ me **20:7** NOT you⁽ᵐˢ⁾~will~LIFT.UP⁽ᵛ⁾ AT TITLE **YHWH** Elohiym~you⁽ᵐˢ⁾ to~ the~FALSENESS GIVEN.THAT NOT he~will~much~ACQUIT⁽ᵛ⁾ **YHWH** AT WHICH he~will~LIFT.UP⁽ᵛ⁾ AT TITLE~him to~the~FALSENESS **20:8** >~ REMEMBER⁽ᵛ⁾ AT DAY the~CEASING to~>~much~SET.APART⁽ᵛ⁾~him **20:9** SIX DAY~s you⁽ᵐˢ⁾~will~SERVE⁽ᵛ⁾ and~you⁽ᵐˢ⁾~did~DO⁽ᵛ⁾ ALL BUSINESS~ you⁽ᵐˢ⁾ **20:10** and~DAY the~SEVENTH CEASING to~**YHWH** Elohiym~you⁽ᵐˢ⁾ NOT you⁽ᵐˢ⁾~will~DO⁽ᵛ⁾ ALL BUSINESS YOU⁽ᵐˢ⁾ and~SON~you⁽ᵐˢ⁾ and~ DAUGHTER~you⁽ᵐˢ⁾ SERVANT~you⁽ᵐˢ⁾ and~BONDWOMAN~you⁽ᵐˢ⁾ and~ BEAST~you⁽ᵐˢ⁾ and~IMMIGRANT~you⁽ᵐˢ⁾ WHICH in~GATE~s~ you⁽ᵐˢ⁾ **20:11** GIVEN.THAT SIX DAY~s he~did~DO⁽ᵛ⁾ **YHWH** AT the~SKY~s2 and~AT the~LAND AT the~SEA and~AT ALL WHICH in~them⁽ᵐ⁾ and~he~will~ REST⁽ᵛ⁾ in~the~DAY the~SEVENTH UPON SO he~did~much~KNEEL⁽ᵛ⁾ **YHWH** AT DAY the~CEASING and~he~will~much~SET.APART⁽ᵛ⁾~him **20:12** *!⁽ᵐˢ⁾~ much~*BE.HEAVY⁽ᵛ⁾ AT FATHER~you⁽ᵐˢ⁾ and~AT MOTHER~you⁽ᵐˢ⁾ to~THAT they⁽ᵐ⁾~will~make~PROLONG⁽ᵛ⁾~must DAY~s~you⁽ᵐˢ⁾ UPON the~GROUND WHICH **YHWH** Elohiym~you⁽ᵐˢ⁾ GIVE⁽ᵛ⁾~ing⁽ᵐˢ⁾ to~you⁽ᶠˢ⁾ **20:13** NOT you⁽ᵐˢ⁾~

will~MURDER⁽ⱽ⁾ **20:14** NOT you⁽ᵐˢ⁾~will~COMMIT.ADULTERY⁽ⱽ⁾ **20:15** NOT you⁽ᵐˢ⁾~will~STEAL⁽ⱽ⁾ **20:16** NOT you⁽ᵐˢ⁾~will~AFFLICT⁽ⱽ⁾ in~COMPANION~ you⁽ᵐˢ⁾ WITNESS FALSE **20:17** NOT you⁽ᵐˢ⁾~will~CRAVE⁽ⱽ⁾ HOUSE COMPANION~you⁽ᵐˢ⁾ NOT you⁽ᵐˢ⁾~will~CRAVE⁽ⱽ⁾ WOMAN COMPANION~ you⁽ᵐˢ⁾ and~SERVANT~him and~BONDWOMAN~him and~OX~him and~ DONKEY~him and~ALL WHICH to~COMPANION~you⁽ᵐˢ⁾ **20:18** and~ALL the~ PEOPLE SEE⁽ⱽ⁾~ing⁽ᵐᵖ⁾ AT the~VOICE~s and~AT the~TORCH~s and~AT VOICE the~RAM.HORN and~AT the~HILL SMOKE and~*he*~*will*~SEE⁽ⱽ⁾ the~PEOPLE and~*they*⁽ᵐ⁾~*will*~STAGGER⁽ⱽ⁾ and~*they*⁽ᵐ⁾~*will*~STAND⁽ⱽ⁾ from~ DISTANCE **20:19** and~*they*⁽ᵐ⁾~*will*~SAY⁽ⱽ⁾ TO Mosheh *!*⁽ᵐˢ⁾~*much*~SPEAK⁽ⱽ⁾ YOU⁽ᵐˢ⁾ WITH~us and~*we*~*will*~HEAR⁽ⱽ⁾~& and~DO.NOT *he*~*will*~*much*~ SPEAK⁽ⱽ⁾ WITH~us Elohiym OTHERWISE *we*~*will*~DIE⁽ⱽ⁾ **20:20** and~*he*~*will*~ SAY⁽ⱽ⁾ Mosheh TO the~PEOPLE DO.NOT you⁽ᵐᵖ⁾~will~FEAR⁽ⱽ⁾ GIVEN.THAT to~ in~CROSS.OVER⁽ⱽ⁾ >~much~TEST⁽ⱽ⁾ AT~you⁽ᵐᵖ⁾ *he*~*did*~COME⁽ⱽ⁾ the~Elohiym and~in~the~CROSS.OVER⁽ⱽ⁾~*ed*⁽ᵐˢ⁾ *she*~*will*~EXIST⁽ⱽ⁾ FEARFULNESS~him UPON FACE~s~you⁽ᵐᵖ⁾ to~EXCEPT you⁽ᵐᵖ⁾~will~FAIL⁽ⱽ⁾ **20:21** and~*he*~*will*~ STAND⁽ⱽ⁾ the~PEOPLE from~DISTANCE and~Mosheh *he*~*did*~*be*~ DRAW.NEAR⁽ⱽ⁾ TO the~THICK.DARKNESS WHICH THERE the~ Elohiym **20:22** and~*he*~*will*~SAY⁽ⱽ⁾ **YHWH** TO Mosheh IN.THIS.WAY you⁽ᵐˢ⁾~ will~SAY⁽ⱽ⁾ TO SON~s Yisra'eyl YOU⁽ᵐᵖ⁾ you⁽ᵐᵖ⁾~did~SEE⁽ⱽ⁾ GIVEN.THAT FROM the~SKY~s2 *I*~*did*~*much*~SPEAK⁽ⱽ⁾ WITH~you⁽ᵐᵖ⁾ **20:23** NOT you⁽ᵐˢ⁾~will~ DO⁽ⱽ⁾~must AT~me Elohiym SILVER and~Elohiym GOLD NOT you⁽ᵐᵖ⁾~will~ DO⁽ⱽ⁾ to~you⁽ᵐᵖ⁾ **20:24** ALTAR GROUND you⁽ᵐˢ⁾~will~DO⁽ⱽ⁾ to~me and~ you⁽ᵐˢ⁾~did~SACRIFICE⁽ⱽ⁾ UPON~him AT ASCENSION.OFFERING~s~you⁽ᵐˢ⁾ and~AT OFFERING.OF.RESTITUTION~s~you⁽ᵐˢ⁾ AT FLOCKS~you⁽ᵐˢ⁾ and~AT CATTLE~you⁽ᵐˢ⁾ in~ALL the~AREA WHICH *I*~*will*~*make*~REMEMBER⁽ⱽ⁾ AT TITLE~me *I*~*will*~COME⁽ⱽ⁾ TO~you⁽ᵐˢ⁾ and~*I*~*did*~*much*~KNEEL⁽ⱽ⁾~ you⁽ᵐˢ⁾ **20:25** and~IF ALTAR STONE~s you⁽ᵐˢ⁾~will~DO⁽ⱽ⁾ to~me NOT you⁽ᵐˢ⁾~ will~BUILD⁽ⱽ⁾ AT~them⁽ᶠ⁾ HEWN.STONE GIVEN.THAT SWORD~you⁽ᵐˢ⁾ you⁽ᵐˢ⁾~ did~make~WAVE⁽ⱽ⁾ UPON~her and~you⁽ᵐˢ⁾~will~much~DRILL⁽ⱽ⁾~ her **20:26** and~NOT you⁽ᵐˢ⁾~will~GO.UP⁽ⱽ⁾ in~STAIR.STEP~s UPON ALTAR~ me WHICH NOT you⁽ᵐˢ⁾~will~be~REMOVE.THE.COVER⁽ⱽ⁾ NAKEDNESS~you⁽ᵐˢ⁾ UPON~him

Chapter 21

21:1 and~THESE the~DECISION~s WHICH you⁽ᵐˢ⁾~will~PLACE⁽ⱽ⁾ to~FACE~s~ them⁽ᵐ⁾ **21:2** GIVEN.THAT you⁽ᵐˢ⁾~will~PURCHASE⁽ⱽ⁾ SERVANT Ever~of SIX YEAR~s *he*~*will*~SERVE⁽ⱽ⁾ and~in~the~SEVENTH *he*~*will*~GO.OUT⁽ⱽ⁾ to~FREE FREELY **21:3** IF in~ARCH~him *he*~*will*~COME⁽ⱽ⁾ in~ARCH~him *he*~*will*~ GO.OUT⁽ⱽ⁾ IF MASTER WOMAN HE and~*she*~*did*~GO.OUT⁽ⱽ⁾ WOMAN~him WITH~him **21:4** IF LORD~s~him *he*~*will*~GIVE⁽ⱽ⁾ to~him WOMAN and~*she*~ *did*~BRING.FORTH⁽ⱽ⁾ to~him SON~s OR DAUGHTER~s the~WOMAN and~

BOY~s~her *she*~*will*~EXIST⁽ᵛ⁾ to~LORD~s~her and~HE *he*~*will*~GO.OUT⁽ᵛ⁾ in~ ARCH~him **21:5** and~IF >~SAY⁽ᵛ⁾ *he*~*will*~SAY⁽ᵛ⁾ the~SERVANT *I*~*did*~LOVE⁽ᵛ⁾ AT LORD~me AT WOMAN~me and~AT SON~s~me NOT *I*~*will*~GO.OUT⁽ᵛ⁾ FREE **21:6** and~*he*~*did*~make~DRAW.NEAR⁽ᵛ⁾~him LORD~s~him TO the~ Elohiym and~*he*~*did*~make~DRAW.NEAR⁽ᵛ⁾~him TO the~DOOR OR TO the~ DOORPOST and~*he*~*did*~BORE.THROUGH⁽ᵛ⁾ LORD~s~him AT EAR~him in~ the~AWL and~*he*~*did*~SERVE⁽ᵛ⁾~him to~DISTANT **21:7** and~GIVEN.THAT *he*~ *will*~SELL⁽ᵛ⁾ MAN AT DAUGHTER~him to~BONDWOMAN NOT *she*~*will*~ GO.OUT⁽ᵛ⁾ like~>~GO.OUT⁽ᵛ⁾ the~SERVANT~s **21:8** IF DYSFUNCTIONAL in~ EYE~s2 LORD~s~her WHICH NOT *he*~*did*~APPOINT⁽ᵛ⁾~her and~*he*~*did*~ make~RANSOM⁽ᵛ⁾~her to~PEOPLE FOREIGN NOT *he*~*will*~REGULATE⁽ᵛ⁾ to~>~ SELL⁽ᵛ⁾~her in~GARMENT~him in~her **21:9** and~IF to~SON~him *he*~*will*~ APPOINT⁽ᵛ⁾~her like~DECISION the~DAUGHTER~s *he*~*will*~DO⁽ᵛ⁾ to~ her **21:10** IF OTHER *he*~*will*~TAKE⁽ᵛ⁾ to~him REMAINS~her RAIMENT~her and~COHABITATION~her NOT *he*~*will*~TAKE.AWAY⁽ᵛ⁾ **21:11** and~IF THREE THESE NOT *he*~*will*~DO⁽ᵛ⁾ to~her and~*she*~*did*~GO.OUT⁽ᵛ⁾ FREELY WITHOUT SILVER **21:12** make~HIT⁽ᵛ⁾~*ing*⁽ᵐˢ⁾ MAN and~*he*~*did*~DIE⁽ᵛ⁾ >~DIE⁽ᵛ⁾ *he*~*will*~ be~make~DIE⁽ᵛ⁾ **21:13** and~WHICH NOT *he*~*did*~LAY.IN.WAIT⁽ᵛ⁾ and~the~ Elohiym *he*~*did*~much~APPROACH⁽ᵛ⁾ to~HAND~him and~*I*~*did*~PLACE⁽ᵛ⁾ to~ you⁽ᵐˢ⁾ AREA WHICH *he*~*will*~FLEE⁽ᵛ⁾ THERE~unto **21:14** and~GIVEN.THAT *he*~*will*~make~SIMMER⁽ᵛ⁾ MAN UPON COMPANION~him to~>~KILL⁽ᵛ⁾~him in~SUBTLETY from~WITH ALTAR~me you⁽ᵐˢ⁾~*will*~TAKE⁽ᵛ⁾~him to~>~ DIE⁽ᵛ⁾ **21:15** and~make~HIT⁽ᵛ⁾~*ing*⁽ᵐˢ⁾ FATHER~him and~MOTHER~him >~ DIE⁽ᵛ⁾ *he*~*will*~be~make~DIE⁽ᵛ⁾ **21:16** and~STEAL⁽ᵛ⁾~*ing*⁽ᵐˢ⁾ MAN and~*he*~ *did*~SELL⁽ᵛ⁾~him and~*he*~*did*~be~FIND⁽ᵛ⁾ in~HAND~him >~DIE⁽ᵛ⁾ *he*~*will*~be~ make~DIE⁽ᵛ⁾ **21:17** and~much~BELITTLE⁽ᵛ⁾~*ing*⁽ᵐˢ⁾ FATHER~him and~ MOTHER~him >~DIE⁽ᵛ⁾ *he*~*will*~be~make~DIE⁽ᵛ⁾ **21:18** and~GIVEN.THAT *they*⁽ᵐ⁾~*will*~DISPUTE⁽ᵛ⁾~must MAN~s and~*he*~*did*~make~HIT⁽ᵛ⁾ MAN AT COMPANION~him in~STONE OR in~FIST and~NOT *he*~*will*~DIE⁽ᵛ⁾ and~*he*~ *did*~FALL⁽ᵛ⁾ to~LYING.PLACE **21:19** IF *he*~*will*~RISE⁽ᵛ⁾ and~*he*~*did*~self~ WALK⁽ᵛ⁾ in~the~OUTSIDE UPON STAVE~him and~*he*~*did*~be~ACQUIT⁽ᵛ⁾ make~HIT⁽ᵛ⁾~*ing*⁽ᵐˢ⁾ ONLY CEASING~him *he*~*will*~GIVE⁽ᵛ⁾ and~>~much~ HEAL⁽ᵛ⁾ *he*~*will*~much~HEAL⁽ᵛ⁾ **21:20** and~GIVEN.THAT *he*~*will*~make~HIT⁽ᵛ⁾ MAN AT SERVANT~him OR AT BONDWOMAN~him in~the~STAFF and~*he*~ *did*~DIE⁽ᵛ⁾ UNDER HAND~him >~AVENGE⁽ᵛ⁾ *he*~*will*~be~ AVENGE⁽ᵛ⁾ **21:21** SURELY IF DAY OR DAY~s2 *he*~*will*~STAND⁽ᵛ⁾ NOT *he*~*will*~ be~make~AVENGE⁽ᵛ⁾ GIVEN.THAT SILVER~him HE **21:22** and~GIVEN.THAT *they*⁽ᵐ⁾~*will*~be~STRUGGLE⁽ᵛ⁾ MAN~s and~*they*~*did*~SMITE⁽ᵛ⁾ WOMAN PREGNANT and~*they*~*did*~GO.OUT⁽ᵛ⁾ BOY~s~her and~NOT *he*~*will*~EXIST⁽ᵛ⁾ HARM >~FINE⁽ᵛ⁾ *he*~*will*~be~FINE⁽ᵛ⁾ like~WHICH *he*~*will*~SET.DOWN⁽ᵛ⁾ UPON~him MASTER the~WOMAN and~*he*~*did*~GIVE⁽ᵛ⁾ in~ JUDGE~s **21:23** and~IF HARM *he*~*will*~EXIST⁽ᵛ⁾ and~*you*⁽ᵐˢ⁾~*did*~GIVE⁽ᵛ⁾~& SOUL UNDER SOUL **21:24** EYE UNDER EYE TOOTH UNDER TOOTH HAND UNDER HAND FOOT UNDER FOOT **21:25** SINGEING UNDER SINGEING WOUND UNDER WOUND STRIPED.BRUISE UNDER

The Book of Exodus

STRIPED.BRUISE **21:26** and~GIVEN.THAT *he~will~make~*HIT$^{(V)}$ MAN AT EYE SERVANT~him OR AT EYE BONDWOMAN~him and~*he~did~much~*DAMAGE$^{(V)}$~her to~FREE *he~will~much~*SEND$^{(V)}$~him UNDER EYE~him **21:27** and~IF TOOTH SERVANT~him OR TOOTH BONDWOMAN~him *he~will~make~*FALL$^{(V)}$ to~FREE *he~will~much~*SEND$^{(V)}$~him UNDER TOOTH~him **21:28** and~GIVEN.THAT *he~will~*GORE$^{(V)}$ OX AT MAN OR AT WOMAN and~*he~did~*DIE$^{(V)}$ >~STONE$^{(V)}$ *he~will~be~*STONE$^{(V)}$ the~OX and~NOT *he~will~be~*EAT$^{(V)}$ AT FLESH~him and~MASTER the~OX INNOCENT **21:29** and~IF OX GORER HE from~YESTERDAY THREE.DAYS.AGO and~*he~did~be~make~*WRAP.AROUND$^{(V)}$ in~MASTER~s~him and~NOT *he~will~*SAFEGUARD$^{(V)}$~him and~*he~did~make~*DIE$^{(V)}$ MAN OR WOMAN the~OX *he~will~be~*STONE$^{(V)}$ and~ALSO MASTER~s~him *he~will~be~make~*DIE$^{(V)}$ **21:30** IF COVERING *he~will~*SET.DOWN$^{(V)}$~*ed*$^{(ms)}$ UPON~him and~*he~did~*GIVE$^{(V)}$ RANSOM.PRICE SOUL~him like~ALL WHICH *he~will~*SET.DOWN$^{(V)}$~*ed*$^{(ms)}$ UPON~him **21:31** OR SON *he~will~*GORE$^{(V)}$ OR DAUGHTER *he~will~*GORE$^{(V)}$ like~the~DECISION the~THIS *he~will~be~*DO$^{(V)}$ to~him **21:32** IF SERVANT *he~will~*GORE$^{(V)}$ the~OX OR BONDWOMAN SILVER THREE~s SHEQEL~s *he~will~*GIVE$^{(V)}$ to~the~LORD~s~him and~the~OX *he~will~be~*STONE$^{(V)}$ **21:33** and~GIVEN.THAT *he~will~*OPEN$^{(V)}$ MAN CISTERN OR GIVEN.THAT *he~will~*DIG$^{(V)}$ MAN CISTERN and~NOT *he~will~much~*COVER.OVER$^{(V)}$~him and~*he~did~*FALL$^{(V)}$ THERE~unto OX OR DONKEY **21:34** MASTER the~CISTERN *he~will~much~*MAKE.RESTITUTION$^{(V)}$ SILVER *he~will~make~*TURN.BACK$^{(V)}$ to~MASTER~s~him and~the~DIE$^{(V)}$~*ing*$^{(ms)}$ *he~will~*EXIST$^{(V)}$ to~him **21:35** and~GIVEN.THAT *he~will~*SMITE$^{(V)}$ OX MAN AT OX COMPANION~him and~*he~did~*DIE$^{(V)}$ and~*they~did~*SELL$^{(V)}$ AT the~OX the~LIVING and~*they~did~*DIVIDE$^{(V)}$ AT SILVER~him and~ALSO AT the~DIE$^{(V)}$~*ing*$^{(ms)}$ *they*$^{(m)}$*~will~*DIVIDE$^{(V)}$~must **21:36** OR *he~did~be~*KNOW$^{(V)}$ GIVEN.THAT OX GORER HE from~YESTERDAY THREE.DAYS.AGO and~NOT *he~will~*SAFEGUARD$^{(V)}$~him MASTER~s~him >~*much~*MAKE.RESTITUTION$^{(V)}$ *he~will~much~*MAKE.RESTITUTION$^{(V)}$ OX UNDER the~OX and~the~DIE$^{(V)}$~*ing*$^{(ms)}$ *he~will~*EXIST$^{(V)}$ to~him **21:37 (22:1)** GIVEN.THAT *he~will~*STEAL$^{(V)}$ MAN OX OR RAM and~*he~did~*BUTCHER$^{(V)}$~him OR *he~did~*SELL$^{(V)}$~him FIVE CATTLE *he~will~much~*MAKE.RESTITUTION$^{(V)}$ UNDER the~OX and~FOUR FLOCKS UNDER the~RAM

Chapter 22

22:1 (22:2) IF in~the~SEARCHING *he~will~be~*FIND$^{(V)}$ the~THIEF and~*he~did~be~make~*HIT$^{(V)}$ and~*he~did~*DIE$^{(V)}$ WITHOUT to~him BLOOD~s **22:2 (22:3)** IF *she~did~*COME.UP$^{(V)}$ the~SUN UPON~him BLOOD~s to~him >~*much~*MAKE.RESTITUTION$^{(V)}$ *he~will~much~*MAKE.RESTITUTION$^{(V)}$ IF WITHOUT to~him and~*he~did~be~*SELL$^{(V)}$ in~THEFT~him **22:3 (22:4)** IF >~be~FIND$^{(V)}$ *she~will~be~*FIND$^{(V)}$ in~HAND~him the~THEFT from~OX UNTIL

DONKEY UNTIL RAM LIVING~s TWO *he~will~much~*
MAKE.RESTITUTION^(v) **22:4 (22:5)** GIVEN.THAT *he~will~make~*BURN^(v) MAN
FIELD OR VINEYARD and~*he~did~much~*SEND^(v) AT CATTLE~her and~*he~
did~much~*BURN^(v) in~FIELD OTHER BEST FIELD~him and~BEST VINEYARD~
him *he~will~much~*MAKE.RESTITUTION^(v) **22:5 (22:6)** GIVEN.THAT *she~will~*
GO.OUT^(v) FIRE and~*she~did~*FIND^(v) BRAMBLE~s and~*he~did~be~*EAT^(v)
STACK OR the~GRAIN.STALK OR the~FIELD >~*much~*MAKE.RESTITUTION^(v)
*he~will~much~*MAKE.RESTITUTION^(v) the~*make~*BURN^(v)~*ing*^(ms) AT the~
BURNING **22:6 (22:7)** GIVEN.THAT *he~will~*GIVE^(v) MAN TO COMPANION~
him SILVER OR UTENSIL~s to~>~SAFEGUARD^(v) and~*he~did~be~much~*
STEAL^(v) from~HOUSE the~MAN IF *he~will~be~*FIND^(v) the~THIEF *he~will~
much~*MAKE.RESTITUTION^(v) TWO **22:7 (22:8)** IF NOT *he~will~be~*FIND^(v)
the~THIEF and~*he~did~be~*COME.NEAR^(v) MASTER the~HOUSE TO the~
Elohiym IF NOT *he~did~*SEND^(v) HAND~him in~BUSINESS COMPANION~
him **22:8 (22:9)** UPON ALL WORD OFFENSE UPON OX UPON DONKEY UPON
RAM UPON OUTER.GARMENT UPON ALL LOST.THING WHICH *he~will~*SAY^(v)
GIVEN.THAT HE THIS UNTIL the~Elohiym *he~will~*COME^(v) WORD TWO~
them^(m) WHICH *he~will~make~*DEPART^(v)~must Elohiym *he~will~much~*
MAKE.RESTITUTION^(v) TWO to~COMPANION~him **22:9 (22:10)** GIVEN.THAT
*he~will~*GIVE^(v) MAN TO COMPANION~him DONKEY OR OX OR RAM and~
ALL BEAST to~>~SAFEGUARD^(v) and~*he~did~*DIE^(v) OR *he~did~be~*CRACK^(v)
OR *he~did~be~*CAPTURE^(v) WITHOUT SEE^(v)~*ing*^(ms) **22:10 (22:11)** SWEARING
YHWH *she~will~*EXIST^(v) BETWEEN TWO~them^(m) IF NOT *he~did~*SEND^(v)
HAND~him in~BUSINESS COMPANION~him and~*he~did~*TAKE^(v) MASTER~s~
him and~NOT *he~will~much~*MAKE.RESTITUTION^(v) **22:11 (22:12)** and~IF >~
STEAL^(v) *he~will~be~*STEAL^(v) from~WITH~him *he~will~much~*
MAKE.RESTITUTION^(v) to~MASTER~s~him **22:12 (22:13)** IF >~
TEAR.INTO.PIECES^(v) *he~will~be~*TEAR.INTO.PIECES^(v) *he~will~make~*
COME^(v)~him WITNESS the~TORN NOT *he~will~much~*
MAKE.RESTITUTION^(v) **22:13 (22:14)** and~GIVEN.THAT *he~will~*INQUIRE^(v)
MAN from~WITH COMPANION~him and~*he~did~be~*CRACK^(v) OR *he~did~*
DIE^(v) MASTER~s~him WITHOUT WITH~him >~*much~*MAKE.RESTITUTION^(v)
*he~will~much~*MAKE.RESTITUTION^(v) **22:14 (22:15)** IF MASTER~s~him
WITH~him NOT *he~will~much~*MAKE.RESTITUTION^(v) IF HIRELING HE *he~
did~*COME^(v) in~WAGE~him **22:15 (22:16)** and~GIVEN.THAT *he~will~much~*
SPREAD.WIDE^(v) MAN VIRGIN WHICH NOT *she~did~be~much~*BETROTH^(v)
and~*he~did~*LIE.DOWN^(v) WITH~her >~HURRY^(v) *he~will~*HURRY^(v)~her to~
him to~WOMAN **22:16 (22:17)** IF >~*much~*REFUSE^(v) *he~will~much~*
REFUSE^(v) FATHER~her to~>~GIVE^(v)~her to~him SILVER *he~will~*WEIGH^(v)
like~BRIDE.PRICE the~VIRGIN~s **22:17 (22:18)** *much~*DO.SORCERY^(v)~*ing*^(fs)
NOT *you*^(ms)~*will~much~*LIVE^(v) **22:18 (22:19)** ALL LIE.DOWN^(v)~*ing*^(ms) WITH
BEAST >~DIE^(v) *he~will~be~make~*DIE^(v) **22:19 (22:20)** SACRIFICE^(v)~*ing*^(ms)
to~the~Elohiym *he~will~be~make~*ASSIGN^(v) EXCEPT to~**YHWH** to~
STRAND~him **22:20 (22:21)** and~IMMIGRANT NOT *you*^(ms)~*will~make~*
SUPPRESS^(v) and~NOT *you*^(ms)~*will~*SQUEEZE^(v)~him GIVEN.THAT

IMMIGRANT~s you$^{(mp)}$~did~EXIST$^{(V)}$ in~LAND Mits'rayim **22:21 (22:22)** ALL WIDOW and~ORPHAN NOT you$^{(ms)}$~will~much~AFFLICT$^{(V)}$~ must **22:22 (22:23)** IF >~much~AFFLICT$^{(V)}$ you$^{(ms)}$~will~much~AFFLICT$^{(V)}$ AT~ him GIVEN.THAT IF >~CRY.OUT$^{(V)}$ he~will~CRY.OUT$^{(V)}$ TO~me >~HEAR$^{(V)}$ I~ will~HEAR$^{(V)}$ CRY~him **22:23 (22:24)** and~he~did~FLARE.UP$^{(V)}$ NOSE~me and~I~did~KILL$^{(V)}$ AT~you$^{(mp)}$ in~SWORD and~they~did~EXIST$^{(V)}$ WOMAN~s~ you$^{(mp)}$ WIDOW~s and~SON~s~you$^{(mp)}$ ORPHAN~s **22:24 (22:25)** IF SILVER you$^{(ms)}$~will~make~JOIN$^{(V)}$ AT PEOPLE~me AT the~AFFLICTION WITH~you$^{(fs)}$ NOT you$^{(ms)}$~will~EXIST$^{(V)}$ to~him like~DECEIVE$^{(V)}$~ing$^{(ms)}$ NOT you$^{(ms)}$~will~ PLACE$^{(V)}$~must UPON~him USURY **22:25 (22:26)** IF >~TAKE.AS.A.PLEDGE$^{(V)}$ you$^{(ms)}$~will~TAKE.AS.A.PLEDGE$^{(V)}$ OUTER.GARMENT COMPANION~you$^{(ms)}$ UNTIL !$^{(ms)}$~COME$^{(V)}$ the~SUN you$^{(ms)}$~will~make~TURN.BACK$^{(V)}$~him to~ him **22:26 (22:27)** GIVEN.THAT SHE RAIMENT~her to~STRAND~her SHE APPAREL~him to~SKIN~him in~WHAT he~will~LIE.DOWN$^{(V)}$ and~he~did~ EXIST$^{(V)}$ GIVEN.THAT he~will~CRY.OUT$^{(V)}$ TO~me and~I~did~HEAR$^{(V)}$ GIVEN.THAT PROTECTIVE I **22:27 (22:28)** Elohiym NOT you$^{(ms)}$~will~much~ BELITTLE$^{(V)}$ and~CAPTAIN in~PEOPLE~you$^{(ms)}$ NOT you$^{(ms)}$~will~ SPIT.UPON$^{(V)}$ **22:28 (22:29)** RIPE.FRUIT~you$^{(ms)}$ and~FRUIT.PRESS~you$^{(ms)}$ NOT you$^{(ms)}$~will~much~DELAY$^{(V)}$ FIRSTBORN SON~s~you$^{(ms)}$ you$^{(ms)}$~will~ GIVE$^{(V)}$ to~me **22:29 (22:30)** SO you$^{(ms)}$~will~DO$^{(V)}$ to~OX~you$^{(ms)}$ to~ FLOCKS~you$^{(ms)}$ SEVEN DAY~s he~will~EXIST$^{(V)}$ WITH MOTHER~him in~the~ DAY the~EIGHTH you$^{(ms)}$~will~GIVE$^{(V)}$~him to~me **22:30 (22:31)** and~MAN~s SPECIAL you$^{(mp)}$~will~EXIST$^{(V)}$~must to~me and~FLESH in~the~FIELD TORN NOT you$^{(mp)}$~will~EAT$^{(V)}$ to~the~DOG you$^{(mp)}$~will~make~THROW.OUT$^{(V)}$~ must AT~him

Chapter 23

23:1 NOT you$^{(ms)}$~will~LIFT.UP$^{(V)}$ REPORT FALSENESS DO.NOT you$^{(ms)}$~will~ SET.DOWN$^{(V)}$ HAND~you$^{(ms)}$ WITH LOST to~>~EXIST$^{(V)}$ WITNESS VIOLENCE **23:2** NOT you$^{(ms)}$~will~EXIST$^{(V)}$ AFTER ABUNDANT~s to~ DYSFUNCTIONAL~s and~NOT you$^{(ms)}$~will~AFFLICT$^{(V)}$ UPON DISPUTE to~>~ EXTEND$^{(V)}$ AFTER ABUNDANT~s to~>~make~EXTEND$^{(V)}$ **23:3** and~HELPLESS NOT you$^{(ms)}$~will~GIVE.HONOR$^{(V)}$ in~DISPUTE~him **23:4** GIVEN.THAT you$^{(ms)}$~ will~REACH$^{(V)}$ OX ATTACK$^{(V)}$~ing$^{(ms)}$~you$^{(ms)}$ OR DONKEY~him WANDER$^{(V)}$~ ing$^{(ms)}$!$^{(ms)}$~make~TURN.BACK$^{(V)}$ you$^{(ms)}$~will~make~TURN.BACK$^{(V)}$~him to~ him **23:5** GIVEN.THAT you$^{(ms)}$~will~SEE$^{(V)}$ DONKEY HATE$^{(V)}$~ing$^{(ms)}$~you$^{(ms)}$ STRETCH.OUT$^{(V)}$~ing$^{(ms)}$ UNDER LOAD~him and~you$^{(ms)}$~did~TERMINATE$^{(V)}$ from~>~LEAVE$^{(V)}$ to~him >~LEAVE$^{(V)}$ you$^{(ms)}$~will~LEAVE$^{(V)}$ WITH~him **23:6** NOT you$^{(ms)}$~will~make~EXTEND$^{(V)}$ DECISION NEEDY~you$^{(ms)}$ in~ DISPUTE~him **23:7** from~WORD FALSE you$^{(ms)}$~will~BE.FAR$^{(V)}$ and~ INNOCENT and~STEADFAST.ONE DO.NOT you$^{(ms)}$~will~KILL$^{(V)}$ GIVEN.THAT NOT I~will~make~BE.STEADFAST$^{(V)}$ LOST **23:8** and~BRIBE NOT you$^{(ms)}$~will~

TAKE⁽ᵛ⁾ GIVEN.THAT the~BRIBE *he~will~much~*BLIND⁽ᵛ⁾ SEEING~s and~*he~ will~much~*TWIST.BACKWARDS⁽ᵛ⁾ WORD~s STEADFAST.ONE~s **23:9** and~ IMMIGRANT NOT *you*⁽ᵐˢ⁾*~will~*SQUEEZE⁽ᵛ⁾ and~YOU⁽ᵐᵖ⁾ *you*⁽ᵐᵖ⁾*~did~*KNOW⁽ᵛ⁾ AT SOUL the~IMMIGRANT GIVEN.THAT IMMIGRANT~s *you*⁽ᵐᵖ⁾*~did~*EXIST⁽ᵛ⁾ in~LAND Mits'rayim **23:10** and~SIX YEAR~s *you*⁽ᵐˢ⁾*~will~*SOW⁽ᵛ⁾ AT LAND~ *you*⁽ᵐˢ⁾ and~*you*⁽ᵐˢ⁾*~did~*GATHER⁽ᵛ⁾ AT PRODUCTION~her **23:11** and~the~ SEVENTH *you*⁽ᵐˢ⁾*~will~*RELEASE⁽ᵛ⁾~her and~*you*⁽ᵐˢ⁾*~did~*LEAVE.ALONE⁽ᵛ⁾~her and~*they~did~*EAT⁽ᵛ⁾ NEEDY~s PEOPLE~*you*⁽ᵐˢ⁾ and~REMAINDER~them⁽ᵐ⁾ *she~will~*EAT⁽ᵛ⁾ LIVING the~FIELD SO *you*⁽ᵐˢ⁾*~will~*DO⁽ᵛ⁾ to~VINEYARD~ *you*⁽ᵐˢ⁾ to~OLIVE~*you*⁽ᵐˢ⁾ **23:12** SIX DAY~s *you*⁽ᵐˢ⁾*~will~*DO⁽ᵛ⁾ WORK~s *you*⁽ᵐˢ⁾ and~in~the~DAY the~SEVENTH *you*⁽ᵐˢ⁾*~will~*CEASE⁽ᵛ⁾ to~THAT *he~ will~*REST⁽ᵛ⁾ OX~*you*⁽ᵐˢ⁾ and~DONKEY~*you*⁽ᵐˢ⁾ and~*he~will~* BREATHE.DEEPLY⁽ᵛ⁾ SON BONDWOMAN~*you*⁽ᵐˢ⁾ and~the~ IMMIGRANT **23:13** and~in~ALL WHICH *I~did~*SAY⁽ᵛ⁾ TO~*you*⁽ᵐᵖ⁾ *you*⁽ᵐᵖ⁾*~will~ be~*SAFEGUARD⁽ᵛ⁾ and~TITLE Elohiym OTHER~s NOT *you*⁽ᵐᵖ⁾*~will~make~* REMEMBER⁽ᵛ⁾ NOT *he~will~be~*HEAR⁽ᵛ⁾ UPON MOUTH~*you*⁽ᵐˢ⁾ **23:14** THREE FOOT~s *you*⁽ᵐˢ⁾*~will~*HOLD.A.FEAST⁽ᵛ⁾ to~me in~the~YEAR **23:15** AT FEAST the~UNLEAVENED.BREAD~s *you*⁽ᵐˢ⁾*~will~*SAFEGUARD⁽ᵛ⁾ SEVEN DAY~s *you*⁽ᵐˢ⁾*~will~*EAT⁽ᵛ⁾ UNLEAVENED.BREAD~s like~WHICH *I~did~much~* DIRECT⁽ᵛ⁾~*you*⁽ᵐˢ⁾ to~APPOINTED NEW.MOON the~GREEN.GRAIN GIVEN.THAT in~him *you*⁽ᵐˢ⁾*~did~*GO.OUT⁽ᵛ⁾ from~Mits'rayim and~NOT *they*⁽ᵐ⁾*~will~be~*SEE⁽ᵛ⁾ FACE~s~me EMPTINESS **23:16** and~FEAST the~ HARVEST FIRST-FRUIT~s WORK~s~*you*⁽ᵐˢ⁾ WHICH *you*⁽ᵐˢ⁾*~will~*SOW⁽ᵛ⁾ in~ the~FIELD and~FEAST the~GATHERING in~>~GO.OUT⁽ᵛ⁾ the~YEAR in~>~ GATHER⁽ᵛ⁾~*you*⁽ᵐˢ⁾ AT WORK~s~*you*⁽ᵐˢ⁾ FROM the~FIELD **23:17** THREE FOOTSTEP~s in~the~YEAR *he~will~be~*SEE⁽ᵛ⁾ ALL MEN~*you*⁽ᵐˢ⁾ TO FACE~s the~LORD **YHWH** **23:18** NOT *you*⁽ᵐˢ⁾*~will~*SACRIFICE⁽ᵛ⁾ UPON LEAVENED.BREAD BLOOD SACRIFICE~me and~NOT *he~will~* STAY.THE.NIGHT⁽ᵛ⁾ FAT FEAST~me UNTIL MORNING **23:19** SUMMIT FIRST-FRUIT~s GROUND~*you*⁽ᵐˢ⁾ *you*⁽ᵐˢ⁾*~will~make~*COME⁽ᵛ⁾ HOUSE **YHWH** Elohiym~*you*⁽ᵐˢ⁾ NOT *you*⁽ᵐˢ⁾*~will~much~*BOIL⁽ᵛ⁾ MALE.KID in~the~FAT MOTHER~him **23:20** LOOK I SEND⁽ᵛ⁾~*ing*⁽ᵐˢ⁾ MESSENGER to~FACE~s~*you*⁽ᵐˢ⁾ to~>~SAFEGUARD⁽ᵛ⁾~*you*⁽ᵐˢ⁾ in~the~ROAD and~to~>~*make~*COME⁽ᵛ⁾~*you*⁽ᵐˢ⁾ TO the~AREA WHICH *I~did~make~*PREPARE⁽ᵛ⁾ **23:21** !⁽ᵐˢ⁾~be~SAFEGUARD⁽ᵛ⁾ from~FACE~s~him and~ !⁽ᵐˢ⁾~HEAR⁽ᵛ⁾ in~VOICE~him DO.NOT *you*⁽ᵐˢ⁾*~will~ make~*BE.BITTER⁽ᵛ⁾ in~him GIVEN.THAT NOT *he~will~*LIFT.UP⁽ᵛ⁾ to~OFFENSE~ *you*⁽ᵐᵖ⁾ GIVEN.THAT TITLE~me in~INSIDE~him **23:22** GIVEN.THAT IF >~ HEAR⁽ᵛ⁾ *you*⁽ᵐˢ⁾*~will~*HEAR⁽ᵛ⁾ in~VOICE~him and~*you*⁽ᵐˢ⁾*~did~*DO⁽ᵛ⁾ ALL WHICH *I~will~much~*SPEAK⁽ᵛ⁾ and~*I~did~*ATTACK⁽ᵛ⁾ AT ATTACK⁽ᵛ⁾~*ing*⁽ᵐᵖ⁾~s *you*⁽ᵐˢ⁾ and~*I~did~*SMACK⁽ᵛ⁾ AT PRESS.IN⁽ᵛ⁾~*ing*⁽ᵐᵖ⁾~ *you*⁽ᵐˢ⁾ **23:23** GIVEN.THAT *he~will~*WALK⁽ᵛ⁾ MESSENGER~me to~FACE~s~ *you*⁽ᵐˢ⁾ and~*he~did~make~*COME⁽ᵛ⁾~*you*⁽ᵐˢ⁾ TO the~Emor~of and~the~ Hhet~of and~the~Perez~of and~the~Kena'an~of the~Hhiw~of and~the~ Yevus~of and~*I~did~make~*KEEP.SECRET⁽ᵛ⁾~him **23:24** NOT *you*⁽ᵐˢ⁾*~will~ self~*BEND.DOWN⁽ᵛ⁾ to~Elohiym~them⁽ᵐ⁾ and~NOT *you*⁽ᵐˢ⁾*~will~be~make~*

SERVE⁽ⱽ⁾~them⁽ᵐ⁾ and~NOT *you⁽ᵐˢ⁾~will*~DO⁽ⱽ⁾ like~WORK~s~them⁽ᵐ⁾ GIVEN.THAT >~much~CAST.DOWN⁽ⱽ⁾ *you⁽ᵐˢ⁾~will*~much~CAST.DOWN⁽ⱽ⁾~ them⁽ᵐ⁾ and~>~much~CRACK⁽ⱽ⁾ *you⁽ᵐˢ⁾~will*~much~CRACK⁽ⱽ⁾ MONUMENT~s~ them⁽ᵐ⁾ **23:25** and~*you⁽ᵐᵖ⁾~will*~SERVE⁽ⱽ⁾ AT **YHWH** Elohiym~you⁽ᵐᵖ⁾ and~ *he~did~*much~KNEEL⁽ⱽ⁾ AT BREAD~you⁽ᵐˢ⁾ and~AT WATER~s2~you⁽ᵐˢ⁾ and~*I~ did~make*~TURN.ASIDE⁽ⱽ⁾ SICKNESS from~INSIDE~you⁽ᵐˢ⁾ **23:26** NOT *you⁽ᵐˢ⁾~ will*~EXIST⁽ⱽ⁾ much~BE.CHILDLESS⁽ⱽ⁾*~ing⁽ᶠˢ⁾* and~STERILE in~LAND~you⁽ᵐˢ⁾ AT NUMBER DAY~s~you⁽ᵐˢ⁾ *I~will*~much~FILL⁽ⱽ⁾ **23:27** AT TERROR~me *I~will*~ much~SEND⁽ⱽ⁾ to~FACE~s~you⁽ᵐˢ⁾ and~*I~did*~CONFUSE⁽ⱽ⁾ AT ALL the~PEOPLE WHICH *you⁽ᵐˢ⁾~will*~COME⁽ⱽ⁾ in~them⁽ᵐ⁾ and~*I~did*~GIVE⁽ⱽ⁾ AT ALL ATTACK⁽ⱽ⁾*~ing⁽ᵐᵖ⁾*~s~you⁽ᵐˢ⁾ TO~you⁽ᵐˢ⁾ NECK **23:28** and~*I~did*~SEND⁽ⱽ⁾ AT the~HORNET to~FACE~s~you⁽ᵐˢ⁾ and~*she~did*~much~CAST.OUT⁽ⱽ⁾ AT the~ Hhiw~of AT the~Kena'an~of and~AT the~Hhet~of from~to~FACE~s~you⁽ᵐˢ⁾ **23:29** NOT *I~will*~much~CAST.OUT⁽ⱽ⁾~him from~FACE~s~you⁽ᵐˢ⁾ in~YEAR UNIT OTHERWISE *she~will*~EXIST⁽ⱽ⁾ the~LAND DESOLATE and~*she~did~* INCREASE.IN.NUMBER⁽ⱽ⁾ UPON~you⁽ᵐˢ⁾ LIVING the~FIELD **23:30** SMALL.AMOUNT SMALL.AMOUNT *I~will*~much~CAST.OUT⁽ⱽ⁾~him from~FACE~s~you⁽ᵐˢ⁾ UNTIL WHICH *you⁽ᵐˢ⁾~will*~REPRODUCE⁽ⱽ⁾ and~*you⁽ᵐˢ⁾~ did*~INHERIT⁽ⱽ⁾ AT the~LAND **23:31** and~*I~did*~SET.DOWN⁽ⱽ⁾ AT BORDER~ you⁽ᵐˢ⁾ from~SEA REEDS and~UNTIL SEA Peleshet~s and~from~WILDERNESS UNTIL the~RIVER GIVEN.THAT *I~will*~GIVE⁽ⱽ⁾ in~HAND~you⁽ᵐᵖ⁾ AT SETTLE⁽ⱽ⁾*~ ing⁽ᵐᵖ⁾* the~LAND and~*you⁽ᵐˢ⁾~did*~much~CAST.OUT⁽ⱽ⁾~them⁽ᵐ⁾ from~ FACE~s~you⁽ᵐˢ⁾ **23:32** NOT *you⁽ᵐˢ⁾~will*~CUT⁽ⱽ⁾ to~them⁽ᵐ⁾ and~to~Elohiym~ them⁽ᵐ⁾ COVENANT **23:33** NOT *they⁽ᵐ⁾~will*~SETTLE⁽ⱽ⁾ in~LAND~you⁽ᵐˢ⁾ OTHERWISE *they⁽ᵐ⁾~will*~make~FAIL⁽ⱽ⁾ AT~you⁽ᵐˢ⁾ to~me GIVEN.THAT *you⁽ᵐˢ⁾~will*~SERVE⁽ⱽ⁾ AT Elohiym~them⁽ᵐ⁾ GIVEN.THAT *he~will*~EXIST⁽ⱽ⁾ to~ you⁽ᵐˢ⁾ to~SNARE

Chapter 24

24:1 and~TO Mosheh *he~did~*SAY⁽ⱽ⁾ *I⁽ᵐˢ⁾~*GO.UP⁽ⱽ⁾ TO **YHWH** YOU⁽ᵐˢ⁾ and~ Aharon Nadav and~Aviyhu and~SEVEN~s from~BEARD~s Yisra'eyl and~ *you⁽ᵐᵖ⁾~did~self*~BEND.DOWN⁽ⱽ⁾ from~DISTANCE **24:2** and~*he~did~be~* DRAW.NEAR⁽ⱽ⁾ Mosheh to~STRAND~him TO **YHWH** and~THEY⁽ᵐ⁾ NOT *they⁽ᵐ⁾~will*~DRAW.NEAR⁽ⱽ⁾ and~the~PEOPLE NOT *they⁽ᵐ⁾~will*~GO.UP⁽ⱽ⁾ WITH~him **24:3** and~*he~will*~COME⁽ⱽ⁾ Mosheh and~*he~will*~much~ COUNT⁽ⱽ⁾ to~the~PEOPLE AT ALL WORD~s **YHWH** and~AT ALL the~ DECISION~s and~*he~will*~ANSWER⁽ⱽ⁾ ALL the~PEOPLE VOICE UNIT and~ *they⁽ᵐ⁾~will*~SAY⁽ⱽ⁾ ALL the~WORD~s WHICH *he~did~*much~SPEAK⁽ⱽ⁾ **YHWH** *we~will*~DO⁽ⱽ⁾ **24:4** and~*he~will*~WRITE⁽ⱽ⁾ Mosheh AT ALL WORD~s **YHWH** and~*he~will*~make~DEPART.EARLY⁽ⱽ⁾ in~the~MORNING and~*he~will*~ BUILD⁽ⱽ⁾ ALTAR UNDER the~HILL and~TWO TEN MONUMENT to~TWO TEN STAFF~s Yisra'eyl **24:5** and~*he~will*~SEND⁽ⱽ⁾ AT YOUNG.MAN~s SON~s

Yisra'eyl and~they[(m)]~will~make~GO.UP[(V)] ASCENSION.OFFERING~s and~ they[(m)]~will~SACRIFICE[(V)] SACRIFICE~s OFFERING.OF.RESTITUTION~s to~ **YHWH** BULL~s **24:6** and~he~will~TAKE[(V)] Mosheh HALF the~BLOOD and~ he~will~PLACE[(V)] in~the~GOBLET~s and~HALF the~BLOOD he~did~ SPRINKLE[(V)] UPON the~ALTAR **24:7** and~he~will~TAKE[(V)] SCROLL the~ COVENANT and~he~will~CALL.OUT[(V)] in~EAR~s2 the~PEOPLE and~they[(m)]~ will~SAY[(V)] ALL WHICH he~did~much~SPEAK[(V)] **YHWH** we~will~DO[(V)] and~ we~will~HEAR[(V)] **24:8** and~he~will~TAKE[(V)] Mosheh AT the~BLOOD and~he~ will~SPRINKLE[(V)] UPON the~PEOPLE and~he~will~SAY[(V)] LOOK BLOOD the~ COVENANT WHICH he~did~CUT[(V)] **YHWH** WITH~you[(mp)] UPON ALL the~ WORD~s the~THESE **24:9** and~he~will~make~GO.UP[(V)] Mosheh and~ Aharon Nadav and~Aviyhu and~SEVEN~s from~BEARD~s Yisra'eyl **24:10** and~they[(m)]~will~SEE[(V)] AT Elohiym Yisra'eyl and~UNDER FOOT~s2~him like~WORK BRICK the~LAPIS.LAZULI and~like~BONE the~SKY~ s2 to~CLEANLINESS **24:11** and~TO LEADER~s SON~s Yisra'eyl NOT he~did~ SEND[(V)] HAND~him and~they[(m)]~will~PERCEIVE[(V)] AT the~Elohiym and~ they[(m)]~will~EAT[(V)] and~they[(m)]~will~GULP[(V)] **24:12** and~he~will~SAY[(V)] **YHWH** TO Mosheh ![(ms)]~GO.UP[(V)] TO~me the~HILL~unto and~![(ms)]~EXIST[(V)] THERE and~I~will~GIVE[(V)]~& to~you[(ms)] AT SLAB~s the~STONE and~the~ TEACHING and~the~DIRECTIVE WHICH I~did~WRITE[(V)] to~>~make~ THROW[(V)]~them[(m)] **24:13** and~he~will~RISE[(V)] Mosheh and~Yehoshu'a much~MINISTER[(V)]~ing[(ms)]~him and~he~will~make~GO.UP[(V)] Mosheh TO HILL the~Elohiym **24:14** and~TO the~BEARD~s he~did~SAY[(V)] ![(mp)]~SETTLE[(V)] to~us in~THIS UNTIL WHICH we~will~TURN.BACK[(V)] TO~you[(mp)] and~LOOK Aharon and~Hhur WITH~you[(mp)] WHO MASTER WORD~s he~will~ DRAW.NEAR[(V)] TO~them[(m)] **24:15** and~he~will~make~GO.UP[(V)] Mosheh TO the~HILL and~he~will~much~COVER.OVER[(V)] the~CLOUD AT the~ HILL **24:16** and~he~will~DWELL[(V)] ARMAMENT **YHWH** UPON HILL Sinai and~ he~will~much~COVER.OVER[(V)]~him the~CLOUD SIX DAY~s and~he~will~ CALL.OUT[(V)] TO Mosheh in~the~DAY the~SEVENTH from~MIDST the~ CLOUD **24:17** and~APPEARANCE ARMAMENT **YHWH** like~FIRE EAT[(V)]~ing[(fs)] in~HEAD the~HILL to~EYE~s2 SON~s Yisra'eyl **24:18** and~he~will~COME[(V)] Mosheh in~MIDST the~CLOUD and~he~will~make~GO.UP[(V)] TO the~HILL and~he~will~EXIST[(V)] Mosheh in~the~HILL FOUR~s DAY and~FOUR~s NIGHT

Chapter 25

25:1 and~he~will~much~SPEAK[(V)] **YHWH** TO Mosheh to~>~SAY[(V)] **25:2** ![(ms)]~ much~SPEAK[(V)] TO SON~s Yisra'eyl and~they[(m)]~will~TAKE[(V)] to~me OFFERING from~AT ALL MAN WHICH he~will~OFFER.WILLINGLY[(V)]~him HEART~him you[(mp)]~will~TAKE[(V)] AT OFFERING~me **25:3** and~THIS the~ OFFERING WHICH you[(mp)]~will~TAKE[(V)] from~AT~them[(m)] GOLD and~SILVER

The Book of Exodus

and~COPPER **25:4** and~BLUE and~PURPLE and~KERMES SCARLET and~LINEN and~SHE-GOAT~s **25:5** and~SKIN~s BUCK~s *be~much*~BE.RED^(V)~*ing*^(mp) and~SKIN~s DEER~s and~TREE~s ACACIA~s **25:6** OIL to~the~LUMINARY SWEET.SPICE~s to~OIL the~OINTMENT and~to~INCENSE.SMOKE the~AROMATIC.SPICE~s **25:7** STONE~s ONYX and~STONE~s INSTALLATION~s to~the~EPHOD and~to~the~BREASTPLATE **25:8** and~*they~did*~DO^(V) to~me SANCTUARY and~*I~did*~DWELL^(V) in~MIDST~them^(m) **25:9** like~ALL WHICH I *make*~SEE^(V)~*ing*^(ms) AT~you^(ms) AT PATTERN the~DWELLING and~AT PATTERN ALL UTENSIL~s~him and~SO *you*^(mp)~*will*~DO^(V) **25:10** and~*they~did*~DO^(V) BOX TREE~s ACACIA~s AMMAH~s2 and~HALF LENGTH~him and~AMMAH and~HALF WIDTH~him and~AMMAH and~HALF HEIGHT~him **25:11** and~*you*^(ms)~*did*~much~OVERLAY^(V) AT~him GOLD CLEAN from~HOUSE and~from~OUTSIDE *you*^(ms)~*will*~much~OVERLAY^(V)~him and~*you*^(ms)~*did*~DO^(V) UPON~him MOLDING GOLD ALL.AROUND **25:12** and~*you*^(ms)~*did*~POUR.DOWN^(V) to~him FOUR RING~s GOLD and~*you*^(ms)~*did*~GIVE^(V)~& UPON FOUR FOOTSTEP~s~him and~TWO RING~s UPON RIB~him the~UNIT and~TWO RING~s UPON RIB~him the~SECOND **25:13** and~*you*^(ms)~*did*~DO^(V) STRAND~s TREE~s ACACIA~s and~*you*^(ms)~*did*~much~OVERLAY^(V) AT~them^(m) GOLD **25:14** and~*you*^(ms)~*did*~*make*~COME^(V) AT the~STRAND~s in~the~RING~s UPON RIB~s the~BOX to~>~LIFT.UP^(V) AT the~BOX in~them^(m) **25:15** in~RING~s the~BOX *they*^(m)~*will*~EXIST^(V) the~STRAND~s NOT *they*^(m)~*will*~TURN.ASIDE^(V) FROM~him **25:16** and~*you*^(ms)~*did*~GIVE^(V) TO the~BOX AT the~EVIDENCE WHICH *I*~*will*~GIVE^(V) TO~you^(ms) **25:17** and~*you*^(ms)~*did*~DO^(V) LID GOLD CLEAN AMMAH~s2 and~HALF LENGTH~her and~AMMAH and~HALF WIDTH~her **25:18** and~*you*^(ms)~*did*~DO^(V) TWO KERUV~s GOLD BEATEN.WORK *you*^(ms)~*will*~DO^(V) AT~them^(m) from~TWO EXTREMITY~s the~LID **25:19** and~*!*^(ms)~DO^(V) KERUV UNIT from~EXTREMITY from~THIS and~KERUV UNIT from~EXTREMITY from~THIS FROM the~LID *you*^(mp)~*will*~DO^(V) AT the~KERUV~s UPON TWO EXTREMITY~s~him **25:20** and~*they~did*~EXIST^(V) the~KERUV~s SPREAD.OUT^(V)~*ing*^(mp) WING~s2 to~UPWARD~unto FENCE.AROUND^(V)~*ing*^(mp) in~WING~s~them^(m) UPON the~LID and~FACE~s~them^(m) MAN TO BROTHER~him TO the~LID *they*^(m)~*will*~EXIST^(V) FACE~s the~KERUV~s **25:21** and~*you*^(ms)~*did*~GIVE^(V) AT the~LID UPON the~BOX from~to~UPWARD~unto and~TO the~BOX *you*^(ms)~*will*~GIVE^(V) AT the~EVIDENCE WHICH *I*~*will*~GIVE^(V) TO~you^(ms) **25:22** and~*I~did*~*be*~APPOINT^(V) to~you^(ms) THERE and~*I~did*~much~SPEAK^(V) AT~you^(ms) from~UPON the~LID from~BETWEEN TWO the~KERUV~s WHICH UPON BOX the~EVIDENCE AT ALL WHICH *I*~*will*~much~DIRECT^(V) AT~you^(ms) TO SON~s Yisra'eyl **25:23** and~*you*^(ms)~*did*~DO^(V) TABLE TREE~s ACACIA~s AMMAH~s2 LENGTH~him and~AMMAH WIDTH~him and~AMMAH and~HALF HEIGHT~him **25:24** and~*you*^(ms)~*did*~much~OVERLAY^(V) AT~him GOLD CLEAN and~*you*^(ms)~*did*~DO^(V) to~him MOLDING GOLD ALL.AROUND **25:25** and~*you*^(ms)~*did*~DO^(V) to~him RIM HAND.SPAN ALL.AROUND and~*you*^(ms)~*did*~DO^(V) MOLDING GOLD to~RIM~him ALL.AROUND **25:26** and~*you*^(ms)~*did*~DO^(V) to~him FOUR RING~s GOLD and~you$^{(ms)}$~did~GIVE$^{(V)}$ AT the~RING~s UPON FOUR the~EDGE~s WHICH to~FOUR FOOT~s2~him **25:27** to~ALONGSIDE the~RIM they$^{(f)}$~will~EXIST$^{(V)}$ the~RING~s to~HOUSE~s to~STRAND~s to~>~ LIFT.UP$^{(V)}$ AT the~TABLE **25:28** and~you$^{(ms)}$~did~DO$^{(V)}$ AT the~STRAND~s TREE~s ACACIA~s and~you$^{(ms)}$~did~much~OVERLAY$^{(V)}$ AT~them$^{(m)}$ GOLD and~he~did~be~LIFT.UP$^{(V)}$ in~them$^{(m)}$ AT the~TABLE **25:29** and~you$^{(ms)}$~did~DO$^{(V)}$ PLATTER~s~him and~PALM~s~him and~JUG~s~him and~SACRIFICIAL.BOWL~s~him WHICH he~will~be~make~POUR$^{(V)}$ in~them$^{(f)}$ GOLD CLEAN you$^{(ms)}$~will~DO$^{(V)}$ AT~them$^{(m)}$ **25:30** and~you$^{(ms)}$~did~GIVE$^{(V)}$ UPON the~TABLE BREAD FACE~s to~FACE~s~me CONTINUALLY **25:31** and~you$^{(ms)}$~did~DO$^{(V)}$ LAMPSTAND GOLD CLEAN BEATEN.WORK she~will~be~DO$^{(V)}$ the~LAMPSTAND MIDSECTION~her and~STALK~her BOWL~s~her KNOB~s~her and~BUD~s~her FROM~her they$^{(m)}$~will~EXIST$^{(V)}$ **25:32** and~SIX STALK~s GO.OUT$^{(V)}$~ing$^{(mp)}$ from~SIDE~s~her THREE STALK~s LAMPSTAND from~SIDE~her the~UNIT and~THREE STALK~s LAMPSTAND from~SIDE~her the~SECOND **25:33** THREE BOWL~s be~much~BE.ALMOND.SHAPED$^{(V)}$~ing$^{(mp)}$ in~the~STALK the~UNIT KNOB and~BUD and~THREE BOWL~s be~much~BE.ALMOND.SHAPED$^{(V)}$~ing$^{(mp)}$ in~the~STALK the~UNIT KNOB and~BUD SO to~SIX the~STALK~s the~GO.OUT$^{(V)}$~ing$^{(mp)}$ FROM the~LAMPSTAND **25:34** and~in~the~LAMPSTAND FOUR BOWL~s be~much~BE.ALMOND.SHAPED$^{(V)}$~ing$^{(mp)}$ KNOB~s~her and~BUD~s~her **25:35** and~KNOB UNDER TWO the~STALK~s FROM~her and~KNOB UNDER TWO the~STALK~s FROM~her and~KNOB UNDER TWO the~STALK~s FROM~her to~SIX the~STALK~s the~GO.OUT$^{(V)}$~ing$^{(mp)}$ FROM the~LAMPSTAND **25:36** KNOB~s~them$^{(m)}$ and~STALK~s~them$^{(m)}$ FROM~her they$^{(m)}$~will~EXIST$^{(V)}$ ALL~her BEATEN.WORK UNIT GOLD CLEAN **25:37** and~you$^{(ms)}$~did~DO$^{(V)}$ AT LAMP~s~her SEVEN and~he~did~make~GO.UP$^{(V)}$ AT LAMP~s~her and~he~did~make~LIGHT$^{(V)}$ UPON Ever FACE~s~her **25:38** and~TONG~s~her and~FIRE.PAN~s~her GOLD CLEAN **25:39** KIKAR GOLD CLEAN he~will~DO$^{(V)}$ AT~her AT ALL the~UTENSIL~s the~THESE **25:40** and~!$^{(ms)}$~SEE$^{(V)}$ and~!$^{(ms)}$~DO$^{(V)}$ in~PATTERN~them$^{(m)}$ WHICH YOU$^{(ms)}$ be~make~SEE$^{(V)}$~ing$^{(ms)}$ in~the~HILL

Chapter 26

26:1 and~AT the~DWELLING you$^{(ms)}$~will~DO$^{(V)}$ TEN CURTAIN~s LINEN be~make~TWIST.TOGETHER$^{(V)}$~ing$^{(ms)}$ and~BLUE and~PURPLE and~KERMES SCARLET KERUV~s WORK THINK$^{(V)}$~ing$^{(ms)}$ you$^{(ms)}$~will~DO$^{(V)}$ AT~them$^{(m)}$ **26:2** LENGTH the~CURTAIN the~UNIT EIGHT and~TEN~s in~the~AMMAH and~WIDTH FOUR in~the~AMMAH the~CURTAIN the~UNIT MEASUREMENT UNIT to~ALL the~CURTAIN~s **26:3** FIVE the~CURTAIN~s they$^{(f)}$~will~EXIST$^{(V)}$ COUPLE$^{(V)}$~ing$^{(fp)}$ WOMAN TO SISTER~her and~FIVE CURTAIN~s COUPLE$^{(V)}$~ing$^{(fp)}$ WOMAN TO SISTER~her **26:4** and~you$^{(ms)}$~did~

The Book of Exodus

DO⁽ⱽ⁾ LOOP~s BLUE UPON LIP the~CURTAIN the~UNIT from~EXTREMITY in~the~COUPLING and~SO you⁽ᵐˢ⁾~will~DO⁽ⱽ⁾ in~LIP the~CURTAIN the~OUTER in~the~JOINT the~SECOND **26:5** FIVE~s LOOP~s you⁽ᵐˢ⁾~will~DO⁽ⱽ⁾ in~the~CURTAIN the~UNIT and~FIVE~s LOOP~s you⁽ᵐˢ⁾~will~DO⁽ⱽ⁾ in~EXTREMITY the~CURTAIN WHICH in~the~JOINT the~SECOND make~RECEIVE⁽ⱽ⁾~ing⁽ᶠᵖ⁾ the~LOOP~s WOMAN TO SISTER~her **26:6** and~you⁽ᵐˢ⁾~did~DO⁽ⱽ⁾ FIVE~s HOOK~s GOLD and~you⁽ᵐˢ⁾~did~much~COUPLE⁽ⱽ⁾ AT the~CURTAIN~s WOMAN TO SISTER~her in~the~HOOK~s and~he~did~EXIST⁽ⱽ⁾ the~DWELLING UNIT **26:7** and~you⁽ᵐˢ⁾~did~DO⁽ⱽ⁾ CURTAIN~s SHE-GOAT~s to~TENT UPON the~DWELLING ONE TEN CURTAIN~s you⁽ᵐˢ⁾~will~DO⁽ⱽ⁾ AT~them⁽ᵐ⁾ **26:8** LENGTH the~CURTAIN the~UNIT THREE~s in~the~AMMAH and~WIDTH FOUR in~the~AMMAH the~CURTAIN the~UNIT MEASUREMENT UNIT to~ONE TEN CURTAIN~s **26:9** and~you⁽ᵐˢ⁾~did~much~COUPLE⁽ⱽ⁾ AT FIVE the~CURTAIN~s to~STRAND and~AT SIX the~CURTAIN~s to~STRAND and~you⁽ᵐˢ⁾~did~DOUBLE.OVER⁽ⱽ⁾ AT the~CURTAIN the~SIXTH TO FOREFRONT FACE~s the~TENT **26:10** and~you⁽ᵐˢ⁾~did~DO⁽ⱽ⁾ FIVE~s LOOP~s UPON LIP the~CURTAIN the~UNIT the~OUTER in~the~COUPLING and~FIVE~s LOOP~s UPON LIP the~CURTAIN the~COUPLING the~SECOND **26:11** and~you⁽ᵐˢ⁾~did~DO⁽ⱽ⁾ HOOK~s COPPER FIVE~s and~you⁽ᵐˢ⁾~did~make~COME⁽ⱽ⁾ AT the~HOOK~s in~the~LOOP~s and~you⁽ᵐˢ⁾~did~much~COUPLE⁽ⱽ⁾ AT the~TENT and~he~did~EXIST⁽ⱽ⁾ UNIT **26:12** and~OVERHANG the~EXCEED⁽ⱽ⁾~ing⁽ᵐˢ⁾ in~CURTAIN~s the~TENT HALF the~CURTAIN the~EXCEED⁽ⱽ⁾~ing⁽ᶠˢ⁾ you⁽ᵐˢ⁾~will~OVERHANG⁽ⱽ⁾ UPON BACK~s the~DWELLING **26:13** and~the~AMMAH from~THIS and~the~AMMAH from~THIS in~the~EXCEED⁽ⱽ⁾~ing⁽ᵐˢ⁾ in~LENGTH CURTAIN~s the~TENT he~will~EXIST⁽ⱽ⁾ OVERHANG⁽ⱽ⁾~ed⁽ᵐˢ⁾ UPON SIDE~s the~DWELLING from~THIS and~from~THIS to~>~much~COVER.OVER⁽ⱽ⁾~him **26:14** and~you⁽ᵐˢ⁾~did~DO⁽ⱽ⁾ ROOF.COVERING to~the~TENT SKIN~s BUCK~s be~much~BE.RED⁽ⱽ⁾~ing⁽ᵐᵖ⁾ and~ROOF.COVERING SKIN~s DEER~s from~to~UPWARD~unto **26:15** and~you⁽ᵐˢ⁾~did~DO⁽ⱽ⁾ AT the~BOARD~s to~the~DWELLING TREE~s ACACIA~s STAND⁽ⱽ⁾~ing⁽ᵐᵖ⁾ **26:16** TEN AMMAH~s LENGTH the~BOARD and~AMMAH and~HALF the~AMMAH WIDTH the~BOARD the~UNIT **26:17** TWO HAND~s to~the~BOARD the~UNIT be~much~JOINED.TOGETHER⁽ⱽ⁾~ing⁽ᶠᵖ⁾ WOMAN TO SISTER~her SO you⁽ᵐˢ⁾~will~DO⁽ⱽ⁾ to~ALL BOARD~s the~DWELLING **26:18** and~you⁽ᵐˢ⁾~did~DO⁽ⱽ⁾ AT the~BOARD~s to~the~DWELLING TEN~s BOARD to~EDGE SOUTH~unto SOUTHWARD~unto **26:19** and~FOUR~s FOOTING~s SILVER you⁽ᵐˢ⁾~will~DO⁽ⱽ⁾ UNDER TEN~s the~BOARD TWO FOOTING~s UNDER the~BOARD the~UNIT to~TWO HAND~s him and~TWO FOOTING~s UNDER the~BOARD the~UNIT to~TWO HAND~s him **26:20** and~to~RIB the~DWELLING the~SECOND to~EDGE NORTH TEN~s BOARD **26:21** and~FOUR~s FOOTING~s~them⁽ᵐ⁾ SILVER TWO FOOTING~s UNDER the~BOARD the~UNIT and~TWO FOOTING~s UNDER the~BOARD the~UNIT **26:22** and~to~FLANK~s2 the~DWELLING SEA~unto you⁽ᵐˢ⁾~will~DO⁽ⱽ⁾ SIX BOARD~s **26:23** and~TWO BOARD~s you⁽ᵐˢ⁾~will~DO⁽ⱽ⁾ to~CORNER.POST~s the~DWELLING in~the~FLANK~s2 **26:24** and~

they$^{(m)}$~will~EXIST$^{(V)}$ BE.DOUBLE$^{(V)}$~ing$^{(mp)}$ from~to~BENEATH and~ TOGETHER they$^{(m)}$~will~EXIST$^{(V)}$ WHOLE UPON HEAD~him TO the~RING the~ UNIT SO he~will~EXIST$^{(V)}$ to~TWO~them$^{(m)}$ to~TWO the~BUTTRESS~s they$^{(m)}$~will~EXIST$^{(V)}$ **26:25** and~they~did~EXIST$^{(V)}$ EIGHT BOARD~s and~ FOOTING~s~them$^{(m)}$ SILVER SIX TEN FOOTING~s TWO FOOTING~s UNDER the~BOARD the~UNIT and~TWO FOOTING~s UNDER the~BOARD the~ UNIT **26:26** and~you$^{(ms)}$~did~DO$^{(V)}$ WOOD.BAR~s TREE~s ACACIA~s FIVE to~ BOARD~s RIB the~DWELLING the~UNIT **26:27** and~FIVE WOOD.BAR~s to~ BOARD~s RIB the~DWELLING the~SECOND and~FIVE WOOD.BAR~s to~ BOARD~s RIB the~DWELLING to~the~FLANK~s2 SEA~unto **26:28** and~the~ WOOD.BAR the~MIDDLEMOST in~MIDST the~BOARD~s make~ FLEE.AWAY$^{(V)}$~ing$^{(ms)}$ FROM the~EXTREMITY TO the~EXTREMITY **26:29** and~ AT the~BOARD~s you$^{(ms)}$~will~much~OVERLAY$^{(V)}$ GOLD and~AT RING~s~ them$^{(m)}$ you$^{(ms)}$~will~DO$^{(V)}$ GOLD HOUSE~s to~the~WOOD.BAR~s and~ you$^{(ms)}$~did~much~OVERLAY$^{(V)}$ AT the~WOOD.BAR~s GOLD **26:30** and~ you$^{(ms)}$~did~make~RISE$^{(V)}$ AT the~DWELLING like~DECISION~him WHICH you$^{(ms)}$~did~be~make~SEE$^{(V)}$ in~the~HILL **26:31** and~you$^{(ms)}$~did~DO$^{(V)}$ TENT.CURTAIN BLUE and~PURPLE and~KERMES SCARLET and~LINEN be~ make~TWIST.TOGETHER$^{(V)}$~ing$^{(ms)}$ WORK THINK$^{(V)}$~ing$^{(ms)}$ he~will~DO$^{(V)}$ AT~ her KERUV~s **26:32** and~you$^{(ms)}$~did~GIVE$^{(V)}$~& AT~her UPON FOUR PILLAR~s ACACIA~s be~much~OVERLAY$^{(V)}$~ing$^{(ms)}$ GOLD and~PEG~s~them$^{(m)}$ GOLD UPON FOUR FOOTING~s SILVER **26:33** and~you$^{(ms)}$~did~GIVE$^{(V)}$~& AT the~TENT.CURTAIN UNDER the~HOOK~s and~you$^{(ms)}$~did~make~COME$^{(V)}$ THERE~unto from~HOUSE to~the~TENT.CURTAIN AT BOX the~EVIDENCE and~she~did~make~SEPARATE$^{(V)}$ the~TENT.CURTAIN to~you$^{(mp)}$ BETWEEN the~SPECIAL and~BETWEEN SPECIAL the~SPECIAL~s **26:34** and~you$^{(ms)}$~did~ GIVE$^{(V)}$ AT the~LID UPON BOX the~EVIDENCE in~SPECIAL the~ SPECIAL~s **26:35** and~you$^{(ms)}$~did~PLACE$^{(V)}$ AT the~TABLE from~OUTSIDE to~the~TENT.CURTAIN and~AT the~LAMPSTAND IN.FRONT the~TABLE UPON RIB the~DWELLING SOUTHWARD~unto and~the~TABLE you$^{(ms)}$~will~ GIVE$^{(V)}$ UPON RIB NORTH **26:36** and~you$^{(ms)}$~did~DO$^{(V)}$ SCREEN to~OPENING the~TENT BLUE and~PURPLE and~KERMES SCARLET and~LINEN be~make~ TWIST.TOGETHER$^{(V)}$~ing$^{(ms)}$ WORK EMBROIDER$^{(V)}$~ing$^{(ms)}$ **26:37** and~you$^{(ms)}$~ did~DO$^{(V)}$ to~the~SCREEN FIVE PILLAR~s ACACIA~s and~you$^{(ms)}$~did~much~ OVERLAY$^{(V)}$ AT~them$^{(m)}$ GOLD and~PEG~s~them$^{(m)}$ GOLD and~you$^{(ms)}$~did~ POUR.DOWN$^{(V)}$ to~them$^{(m)}$ FIVE FOOTING~s COPPER

Chapter 27

27:1 and~you$^{(ms)}$~did~DO$^{(V)}$ AT the~ALTAR TREE~s ACACIA~s FIVE AMMAH~s LENGTH and~FIVE AMMAH~s WIDTH BE.SQUARE$^{(V)}$~ed$^{(ms)}$ he~will~EXIST$^{(V)}$ the~ALTAR and~THREE AMMAH~s HEIGHT~him **27:2** and~you$^{(ms)}$~did~DO$^{(V)}$ HORN~s~him UPON FOUR CORNER~s~him FROM~him they$^{(f)}$~will~EXIST$^{(V)}$

HORN~s~him and~*you*$^{(ms)}$~*did*~*much*~OVERLAY$^{(V)}$ AT~him
COPPER **27:3** and~*you*$^{(ms)}$~*did*~DO$^{(V)}$ POT~s~him to~>~*much*~MAKE.FAT$^{(V)}$~
him and~SHOVEL~s~him and~SPRINKLING.BASIN~s~him and~FORK~s~him
and~FIRE.PAN~s~him to~ALL UTENSIL~s~him *you*$^{(ms)}$~*will*~DO$^{(V)}$
COPPER **27:4** and~*you*$^{(ms)}$~*did*~DO$^{(V)}$ to~him GRATE WORK NETTING COPPER
and~*you*$^{(ms)}$~*did*~DO$^{(V)}$ UPON the~NETTING FOUR RING~s COPPER UPON
FOUR EXTREMITY~s~him **27:5** and~*you*$^{(ms)}$~*did*~GIVE$^{(V)}$~& AT~her UNDER
OUTER.RIM the~ALTAR from~to~BENEATH and~*she*~*did*~EXIST$^{(V)}$ the~
NETTING UNTIL HALF the~ALTAR **27:6** and~*you*$^{(ms)}$~*did*~DO$^{(V)}$ STRAND~s to~
the~ALTAR STRAND~s TREE~s ACACIA~s and~*you*$^{(ms)}$~*did*~*much*~OVERLAY$^{(V)}$
AT~them$^{(m)}$ COPPER **27:7** and~*he*~*did*~*be*~*make*~COME$^{(V)}$ AT STRAND~s~
him in~the~RING~s and~*they*~*did*~EXIST$^{(V)}$ the~STRAND~s UPON TWO RIB~s
the~ALTAR in~>~LIFT.UP$^{(V)}$ AT~him **27:8** BORE.OUT$^{(V)}$~*ed*$^{(ms)}$ SLAB~s *you*$^{(ms)}$~
will~DO$^{(V)}$ AT~him like~WHICH *he*~*did*~*make*~SEE$^{(V)}$ AT~you$^{(ms)}$ in~the~HILL
SO *they*$^{(m)}$~*will*~DO$^{(V)}$ **27:9** and~*you*$^{(ms)}$~*did*~DO$^{(V)}$ AT COURTYARD the~
DWELLING to~EDGE SOUTH SOUTHWARD~unto SLING~s to~the~
COURTYARD LINEN *be*~*make*~TWIST.TOGETHER$^{(V)}$~*ing*$^{(ms)}$ HUNDRED in~the~
AMMAH LENGTH to~the~EDGE the~UNIT **27:10** and~PILLAR~s~him TEN~s
and~FOOTING~s~them$^{(m)}$ TEN~s COPPER and~PEG~s the~PILLAR~s and~
BINDER~s~them$^{(m)}$ SILVER **27:11** and~SO to~EDGE NORTH in~the~LENGTH
SLING~s HUNDRED LENGTH and~PILLAR~s~him TEN~s and~FOOTING~s~
them$^{(m)}$ TEN~s COPPER and~PEG~s the~PILLAR~s and~BINDER~s~them$^{(m)}$
SILVER **27:12** and~WIDTH the~COURTYARD to~EDGE SEA SLING~s FIVE~s
AMMAH PILLAR~s~them$^{(m)}$ TEN and~FOOTING~s~them$^{(m)}$ TEN **27:13** and~
WIDTH the~COURTYARD to~EDGE EAST~unto SUNRISE~unto FIVE~s
AMMAH **27:14** and~FIVE TEN AMMAH SLING~s to~the~SHOULDER.PIECE
PILLAR~s~them$^{(m)}$ THREE and~FOOTING~s~them$^{(m)}$ THREE **27:15** and~to~
the~SHOULDER.PIECE the~SECOND FIVE TEN SLING~s PILLAR~s~them$^{(m)}$
THREE and~FOOTING~s~them$^{(m)}$ THREE **27:16** and~to~GATE the~
COURTYARD SCREEN TEN~s AMMAH BLUE and~PURPLE and~KERMES
SCARLET and~LINEN *be*~*make*~TWIST.TOGETHER$^{(V)}$~*ing*$^{(ms)}$ WORK
EMBROIDER$^{(V)}$~*ing*$^{(ms)}$ PILLAR~s~them$^{(m)}$ FOUR and~FOOTING~s~them$^{(m)}$
FOUR **27:17** ALL PILLAR~s the~COURTYARD ALL.AROUND *be*~*much*~
ATTACH$^{(V)}$~*ing*$^{(mp)}$ SILVER and~PEG~s~them$^{(m)}$ SILVER and~FOOTING~s~
them$^{(m)}$ COPPER **27:18** LENGTH the~COURTYARD HUNDRED in~the~
AMMAH and~WIDTH FIVE~s in~the~FIVE~s and~HEIGHT FIVE AMMAH~s
LINEN *be*~*make*~TWIST.TOGETHER$^{(V)}$~*ing*$^{(ms)}$ and~FOOTING~s~them$^{(m)}$
COPPER **27:19** to~ALL UTENSIL~s the~DWELLING in~ALL SERVICE~him and~
ALL TENT.PEG~s~him and~ALL TENT.PEG~s the~COURTYARD
COPPER **27:20** and~YOU$^{(ms)}$ *you*$^{(ms)}$~*will*~*much*~DIRECT$^{(V)}$ AT SON~s Yisra'eyl
and~*they*$^{(m)}$~*will*~TAKE$^{(V)}$ TO~you$^{(ms)}$ OIL OLIVE REFINED SMASHED to~the~
LUMINARY to~>~*make*~GO.UP$^{(V)}$ LAMP CONTINUALLY **27:21** in~TENT
APPOINTED from~OUTSIDE to~the~TENT.CURTAIN WHICH UPON the~
EVIDENCE *he*~*will*~ARRANGE$^{(V)}$ AT~him Aharon and~SON~s~him from~

EVENING UNTIL MORNING to~FACE~s **YHWH** CUSTOM DISTANT to~ GENERATION~s~them⁽ᵐ⁾ from~AT SON~s Yisra'eyl

Chapter 28

28:1 and~YOU⁽ᵐˢ⁾ *I*⁽ᵐˢ⁾~*make*~COME.NEAR⁽ⱽ⁾ TO~you⁽ᵐˢ⁾ AT Aharon BROTHER~you⁽ᵐˢ⁾ and~AT SON~s~him AT~him from~MIDST SON~s Yisra'eyl to~>~*much*~ADORN⁽ⱽ⁾~him to~me Aharon Nadav and~Aviyhu Elazar and~ Iytamar SON~s Aharon **28:2** and~*you*⁽ᵐˢ⁾~*did*~DO⁽ⱽ⁾ GARMENT~s SPECIAL to~ Aharon BROTHER~you⁽ᵐˢ⁾ to~ARMAMENT and~to~DECORATION **28:3** and~ YOU⁽ᵐˢ⁾ *you*⁽ᵐˢ⁾~*will*~*much*~SPEAK⁽ⱽ⁾ TO ALL SKILLED.ONE~s HEART WHICH *I*~ *did*~*much*~FILL⁽ⱽ⁾~him WIND SKILL and~*they*~*did*~DO⁽ⱽ⁾ AT GARMENT~s Aharon to~>~*much*~SET.APART⁽ⱽ⁾~him to~>~*much*~ADORN⁽ⱽ⁾~him to~ me **28:4** and~THESE the~GARMENT~s WHICH *they*⁽ᵐ⁾~*will*~DO⁽ⱽ⁾ BREASTPLATE and~EPHOD and~CLOAK and~TUNIC WOVEN.MATERIAL TURBAN and~SASH and~*they*~*did*~DO⁽ⱽ⁾ GARMENT~s SPECIAL to~Aharon BROTHER~you⁽ᵐˢ⁾ and~to~SON~s~him to~>~*much*~ADORN⁽ⱽ⁾~him to~ me **28:5** and~THEY⁽ᵐ⁾ *they*⁽ᵐ⁾~*will*~TAKE⁽ⱽ⁾ AT the~GOLD and~AT the~BLUE and~AT the~PURPLE and~AT KERMES the~SCARLET and~AT the~ LINEN **28:6** and~*they*~*did*~DO⁽ⱽ⁾ AT the~EPHOD GOLD BLUE and~PURPLE KERMES SCARLET and~LINEN *be*~*make*~TWIST.TOGETHER⁽ⱽ⁾~*ing*⁽ᵐˢ⁾ WORK THINK⁽ⱽ⁾~*ing*⁽ᵐˢ⁾ **28:7** TWO SHOULDER.PIECE~s COUPLE⁽ⱽ⁾~*ing*⁽ᶠᵖ⁾ he~*will*~ EXIST⁽ⱽ⁾ to~him TO TWO EXTREMITY~s~him and~*he*~*did*~*be*~*much*~ COUPLE⁽ⱽ⁾ **28:8** and~DECORATIVE.BAND EPHOD~him WHICH UPON~him like~WORK~him FROM~him *he*~*will*~EXIST⁽ⱽ⁾ GOLD BLUE and~PURPLE and~ KERMES SCARLET and~LINEN *be*~*make*~TWIST.TOGETHER⁽ⱽ⁾~ *ing*⁽ᵐˢ⁾ **28:9** and~*you*⁽ᵐˢ⁾~*did*~TAKE⁽ⱽ⁾ AT TWO STONE~s ONYX and~*you*⁽ᵐˢ⁾~ *did*~*much*~OPEN⁽ⱽ⁾ UPON~them⁽ᵐ⁾ TITLE~s SON~s Yisra'eyl **28:10** SIX from~ TITLE~s~them⁽ᵐ⁾ UPON the~STONE the~UNIT and~AT TITLE~s the~SIX the~ *be*~LEAVE.BEHIND⁽ⱽ⁾~*ing*⁽ᵐᵖ⁾ UPON the~STONE the~SECOND like~ BIRTHING~s~them⁽ᵐ⁾ **28:11** WORK ENGRAVER STONE OPEN⁽ⱽ⁾~*ed*⁽ᵐᵖ⁾ SEAL *you*⁽ᵐˢ⁾~*will*~*much*~OPEN⁽ⱽ⁾ AT TWO the~STONE~s UPON TITLE~s SON~s Yisra'eyl *be*~*make*~GO.AROUND⁽ⱽ⁾~*ing*⁽ᶠᵖ⁾ PLAIT~s GOLD *you*⁽ᵐˢ⁾~*will*~DO⁽ⱽ⁾ AT~them⁽ᵐ⁾ **28:12** and~*you*⁽ᵐˢ⁾~*did*~PLACE⁽ⱽ⁾ AT TWO the~STONE~s UPON SHOULDER.PIECE~s the~EPHOD STONE~s REMEMBRANCE to~SON~s Yisra'eyl and~*he*~*did*~LIFT.UP⁽ⱽ⁾ Aharon AT TITLE~s~them⁽ᵐ⁾ to~FACE~s **YHWH** UPON TWO SHOULDER.PIECE~s~him to~REMEMBRANCE **28:13** and~ *you*⁽ᵐˢ⁾~*did*~DO⁽ⱽ⁾ PLAIT~s GOLD **28:14** and~TWO CHAIN~s GOLD CLEAN BOUNDARY~s *you*⁽ᵐˢ⁾~*will*~DO⁽ⱽ⁾ AT~them⁽ᵐ⁾ WORK THICK.WOVEN and~ *you*⁽ᵐˢ⁾~*did*~GIVE⁽ⱽ⁾~& AT CHAIN~s the~THICK.WOVEN~s UPON the~ PLAIT~s **28:15** and~*you*⁽ᵐˢ⁾~*did*~DO⁽ⱽ⁾ BREASTPLATE DECISION WORK THINK⁽ⱽ⁾~*ing*⁽ᵐˢ⁾ like~WORK EPHOD *you*⁽ᵐˢ⁾~*will*~DO⁽ⱽ⁾~him GOLD BLUE and~ PURPLE and~KERMES SCARLET and~LINEN *be*~*make*~TWIST.TOGETHER⁽ⱽ⁾~

The Book of Exodus

ing$^{(ms)}$ you$^{(ms)}$~will~DO$^{(V)}$ AT~him **28:16** BE.SQUARE$^{(V)}$~ed$^{(ms)}$ he~will~EXIST$^{(V)}$ DOUBLE.OVER$^{(V)}$~ed$^{(ms)}$ FINGER.SPAN LENGTH~him and~FINGER.SPAN WIDTH~him **28:17** and~you$^{(ms)}$~did~much~FILL$^{(V)}$ in~him SETTING STONE FOUR ROW~s STONE ROW CARNELIAN OLIVINE and~EMERALD the~ROW the~UNIT **28:18** and~the~ROW the~SECOND TURQUOISE LAPIS.LAZULI and~FLINT **28:19** and~the~ROW the~THIRD OPAL AGATE and~ AMETHYST **28:20** and~the~ROW the~FOURTH TOPAZ and~ONYX and~ JASPER be~much~WEAVE$^{(V)}$~ing$^{(ms)}$ GOLD they$^{(m)}$~will~EXIST$^{(V)}$ in~ SETTING~s~them$^{(m)}$ **28:21** and~the~STONE~s they$^{(f)}$~will~EXIST$^{(V)}$ UPON TITLE~s SON~s Yisra'eyl TWO TEN UPON TITLE~s~them$^{(m)}$ OPEN$^{(V)}$~ed$^{(mp)}$ SEAL MAN UPON TITLE~him they$^{(f)}$~will~EXIST$^{(V)}$ to~TWO TEN STAFF **28:22** and~you$^{(ms)}$~did~DO$^{(V)}$ UPON the~BREASTPLATE CHAIN~s EDGING WORK THICK.WOVEN GOLD CLEAN **28:23** and~you$^{(ms)}$~did~DO$^{(V)}$ UPON the~ BREASTPLATE TWO RING~s GOLD and~you$^{(ms)}$~did~GIVE$^{(V)}$ AT TWO the~ RING~s UPON TWO EXTREMITY~s the~BREASTPLATE **28:24** and~you$^{(ms)}$~ did~GIVE$^{(V)}$~& AT TWO THICK.WOVEN~s the~GOLD UPON TWO the~RING~s TO EXTREMITY~s the~BREASTPLATE **28:25** and~AT TWO EXTREMITY~s TWO the~THICK.WOVEN~s you$^{(ms)}$~will~GIVE$^{(V)}$ UPON TWO the~PLAIT~s and~ you$^{(ms)}$~did~GIVE$^{(V)}$~& UPON SHOULDER.PIECE~s the~EPHOD TO FOREFRONT FACE~s~him **28:26** and~you$^{(ms)}$~did~DO$^{(V)}$ TWO RING~s GOLD and~you$^{(ms)}$~did~PLACE$^{(V)}$ AT~them$^{(m)}$ UPON TWO EXTREMITY~s the~ BREASTPLATE UPON LIP~him WHICH TO Ever the~EPHOD HOUSE~ unto **28:27** and~you$^{(ms)}$~did~DO$^{(V)}$ TWO RING~s GOLD and~you$^{(ms)}$~did~ GIVE$^{(V)}$~& AT~them$^{(m)}$ UPON TWO SHOULDER.PIECE~s the~EPHOD from~to~ BENEATH from~FOREFRONT FACE~s~him to~ALONGSIDE JOINT~him from~ UPWARD to~DECORATIVE.BAND the~EPHOD **28:28** and~they$^{(m)}$~will~ TIE.ON$^{(V)}$ AT the~BREASTPLATE RING~s~him TO RING~s the~EPHOD in~ CORD BLUE to~>~EXIST$^{(V)}$ UPON DECORATIVE.BAND the~EPHOD and~NOT he~will~be~LOOSEN$^{(V)}$ the~BREASTPLATE from~UPON the~ EPHOD **28:29** and~he~did~LIFT.UP$^{(V)}$ Aharon AT TITLE~s SON~s Yisra'eyl in~ BREASTPLATE the~DECISION UPON HEART~him in~>~COME$^{(V)}$~him TO the~ SPECIAL to~REMEMBRANCE to~FACE~s YHWH CONTINUALLY **28:30** and~ you$^{(ms)}$~did~GIVE$^{(V)}$ TO BREASTPLATE the~DECISION AT the~Uriym and~AT the~Tumiym and~they~did~EXIST$^{(V)}$ UPON HEART Aharon in~>~COME$^{(V)}$~ him to~FACE~s YHWH and~he~did~LIFT.UP$^{(V)}$ Aharon AT DECISION SON~s Yisra'eyl UPON HEART~him to~FACE~s YHWH CONTINUALLY **28:31** and~ you$^{(ms)}$~did~DO$^{(V)}$ AT CLOAK the~EPHOD ENTIRELY BLUE **28:32** and~he~did~ EXIST$^{(V)}$ MOUTH HEAD~him in~MIDST~him LIP he~will~EXIST$^{(V)}$ to~MOUTH~ him ALL.AROUND WORK BRAID$^{(V)}$~ing$^{(ms)}$ like~MOUTH COLLAR he~will~ EXIST$^{(V)}$ to~him NOT he~will~be~TEAR$^{(V)}$ **28:33** and~you$^{(ms)}$~did~DO$^{(V)}$ UPON HEM~s~him POMEGRANATE~s BLUE and~PURPLE and~KERMES SCARLET UPON HEM~s~him ALL.AROUND and~BELL~s GOLD in~MIDST~them$^{(m)}$ ALL.AROUND **28:34** BELL GOLD and~POMEGRANATE BELL GOLD and~ POMEGRANATE UPON HEM~s the~CLOAK ALL.AROUND **28:35** and~he~did~ EXIST$^{(V)}$ UPON Aharon to~>~much~MINISTER$^{(V)}$ and~he~did~be~HEAR$^{(V)}$

VOICE~him in~>~COME⁽ᵛ⁾~him TO the~SPECIAL to~FACE~s **YHWH** and~in~ >~GO.OUT⁽ᵛ⁾~him and~NOT *he~will*~DIE⁽ᵛ⁾ **28:36** and~*you*⁽ᵐˢ⁾~*did*~DO⁽ᵛ⁾ BLOSSOM GOLD CLEAN and~*you*⁽ᵐˢ⁾~*did*~much~OPEN⁽ᵛ⁾ UPON~him OPEN⁽ᵛ⁾~ *ed*⁽ᵐᵖ⁾ SEAL SPECIAL to~**YHWH 28:37** and~*you*⁽ᵐˢ⁾~*did*~PLACE⁽ᵛ⁾ AT~him UPON CORD BLUE and~*he~did*~EXIST⁽ᵛ⁾ UPON the~TURBAN TO FOREFRONT FACE~s the~TURBAN *he~will*~EXIST⁽ᵛ⁾ **28:38** and~*he~did*~EXIST⁽ᵛ⁾ UPON FOREHEAD Aharon and~*he~did*~LIFT.UP⁽ᵛ⁾ Aharon AT TWISTEDNESS the~ SPECIAL~s WHICH *they*⁽ᵐ⁾~*will*~*make*~SET.APART⁽ᵛ⁾ SON~s Yisra'eyl to~ALL CONTRIBUTION SPECIAL~s~them⁽ᵐ⁾ and~*he~did*~EXIST⁽ᵛ⁾ UPON FOREHEAD~ him CONTINUALLY to~SELF-WILL to~them⁽ᵐ⁾ to~FACE~s **YHWH 28:39** and~ *you*⁽ᵐˢ⁾~*did*~much~WEAVE⁽ᵛ⁾ the~TUNIC LINEN and~*you*⁽ᵐˢ⁾~*did*~DO⁽ᵛ⁾ TURBAN LINEN and~SASH *you*⁽ᵐˢ⁾~*will*~DO⁽ᵛ⁾ WORK EMBROIDER⁽ᵛ⁾~*ing*⁽ᵐˢ⁾ **28:40** and~to~SON~s Aharon *you*⁽ᵐˢ⁾~*will*~DO⁽ᵛ⁾ TUNIC~s and~*you*⁽ᵐˢ⁾~*did*~ DO⁽ᵛ⁾ to~them⁽ᵐ⁾ SASH~s and~HEADDRESS~s *you*⁽ᵐˢ⁾~*will*~DO⁽ᵛ⁾ to~them⁽ᵐ⁾ to~ARMAMENT and~to~DECORATION **28:41** and~*you*⁽ᵐˢ⁾~*did*~*make*~ WEAR⁽ᵛ⁾ AT~them⁽ᵐ⁾ AT Aharon BROTHER~*you*⁽ᵐˢ⁾ and~AT SON~s~him AT~ him and~*you*⁽ᵐˢ⁾~*did*~SMEAR⁽ᵛ⁾ AT~them⁽ᵐ⁾ and~*you*⁽ᵐˢ⁾~*did*~much~FILL⁽ᵛ⁾ AT HAND~them⁽ᵐ⁾ and~*you*⁽ᵐˢ⁾~*did*~much~SET.APART⁽ᵛ⁾ AT~them⁽ᵐ⁾ and~*they*~ *did*~much~ADORN⁽ᵛ⁾ to~me **28:42** and~!⁽ᵐˢ⁾~DO⁽ᵛ⁾ to~them⁽ᵐ⁾ UNDERGARMENT~s STRAND to~>~much~COVER.OVER⁽ᵛ⁾ FLESH NAKEDNESS from~WAIST~s and~UNTIL MIDSECTION~s *they*⁽ᵐ⁾~*will*~EXIST⁽ᵛ⁾ **28:43** and~ *they~did*~EXIST⁽ᵛ⁾ UPON Aharon and~UPON SON~s~him in~>~COME⁽ᵛ⁾~ them⁽ᵐ⁾ TO TENT APPOINTED OR in~>~DRAW.NEAR⁽ᵛ⁾~them⁽ᵐ⁾ TO the~ ALTAR to~>~much~MINISTER⁽ᵛ⁾ in~the~SPECIAL and~NOT *they*⁽ᵐ⁾~*will*~ LIFT.UP⁽ᵛ⁾ TWISTEDNESS and~*they~did*~DIE⁽ᵛ⁾ CUSTOM DISTANT to~him and~to~SEED~him AFTER~him

Chapter 29

29:1 and~THIS the~WORD WHICH *you*⁽ᵐˢ⁾~*will*~DO⁽ᵛ⁾ to~them⁽ᵐ⁾ to~>~ much~SET.APART⁽ᵛ⁾ AT~them⁽ᵐ⁾ to~>~much~ADORN⁽ᵛ⁾ to~me !⁽ᵐˢ⁾~TAKE⁽ᵛ⁾ BULL UNIT SON CATTLE and~BUCK~s TWO WHOLE~s **29:2** and~BREAD UNLEAVENED.BREAD~s and~PIERCED.BREAD~s UNLEAVENED.BREAD~s MIX⁽ᵛ⁾~*ed*⁽ᶠᵖ⁾ in~the~OIL and~THIN.BREAD~s UNLEAVENED.BREAD~s SMEAR⁽ᵛ⁾~*ed*⁽ᵐᵖ⁾ in~the~OIL FLOUR WHEAT~s *you*⁽ᵐˢ⁾~*will*~DO⁽ᵛ⁾ AT~ them⁽ᵐ⁾ **29:3** and~*you*⁽ᵐˢ⁾~*did*~GIVE⁽ᵛ⁾ AT~them⁽ᵐ⁾ UPON WICKER.BASKET UNIT and~*you*⁽ᵐˢ⁾~*did*~*make*~COME.NEAR⁽ᵛ⁾ AT~them⁽ᵐ⁾ in~the~ WICKER.BASKET and~AT the~BULL and~AT TWO the~BUCK~s **29:4** and~AT Aharon and~AT SON~s~him *you*⁽ᵐˢ⁾~*will*~*make*~COME.NEAR⁽ᵛ⁾ TO OPENING TENT APPOINTED and~*you*⁽ᵐˢ⁾~*did*~BATHE⁽ᵛ⁾ AT~them⁽ᵐ⁾ in~the~WATER~ s **29:5** and~*you*⁽ᵐˢ⁾~*did*~TAKE⁽ᵛ⁾ AT the~GARMENT~s and~*you*⁽ᵐˢ⁾~*did*~ *make*~WEAR⁽ᵛ⁾ AT Aharon AT the~TUNIC and~AT CLOAK the~EPHOD and~AT the~EPHOD and~AT the~BREASTPLATE and~*you*⁽ᵐˢ⁾~*did*~GIRD⁽ᵛ⁾ to~him in~

The Book of Exodus

DECORATIVE.BAND the~EPHOD **29:6** and~*you*^(ms)~*did*~PLACE^(V) the~TURBAN UPON HEAD~him and~*you*^(ms)~*did*~GIVE^(V) AT DEDICATION the~SPECIAL UPON the~TURBAN **29:7** and~*you*^(ms)~*did*~TAKE^(V) AT OIL the~OINTMENT and~*you*^(ms)~*did*~POUR.DOWN^(V) UPON HEAD~him and~*you*^(ms)~*did*~SMEAR^(V) AT~him **29:8** and~AT SON~s~him *you*^(ms)~*will*~*make*~COME.NEAR^(V) and~*you*^(ms)~*did*~*make*~WEAR^(V)~them^(m) TUNIC~s **29:9** and~*you*^(ms)~*did*~GIRD.UP^(V) AT~them^(m) SASH Aharon and~SON~s~him and~*you*^(ms)~*did*~SADDLE^(V) to~them^(m) HEADDRESS~s and~*she*~*did*~EXIST^(V) to~them^(m) ADMINISTRATION to~CUSTOM DISTANT and~*you*^(ms)~*did*~*much*~FILL^(V) HAND Aharon and~HAND SON~s~him **29:10** and~*you*^(ms)~*did*~*make*~COME.NEAR^(V) AT the~BULL to~FACE~s TENT APPOINTED and~*he*~*did*~SUPPORT^(V) Aharon and~SON~s~him AT HAND~s2~them^(m) UPON HEAD the~BULL **29:11** and~*you*^(ms)~*did*~SLAY^(V) AT the~BULL to~FACE~s **YHWH** OPENING TENT APPOINTED **29:12** and~*you*^(ms)~*did*~TAKE^(V) from~BLOOD the~BULL and~*you*^(ms)~*did*~GIVE^(V)~& UPON HORN~s the~ALTAR in~FINGER~*you*^(ms) and~AT ALL the~BLOOD *you*^(ms)~*will*~POUR.OUT^(V) TO BOTTOM.BASE the~ALTAR **29:13** and~*you*^(ms)~*did*~TAKE^(V) AT ALL the~FAT the~*much*~COVER.OVER^(V)~*ing*^(ms) AT the~INSIDE and~AT the~LOBE UPON the~HEAVY and~AT TWO the~KIDNEY~s and~AT the~FAT WHICH UPON~them^(f) and~*you*^(ms)~*did*~*make*~BURN.INCENSE^(V) the~ALTAR~unto **29:14** and~AT FLESH the~BULL and~AT SKIN~him and~AT DUNG~him *you*^(ms)~*will*~CREMATE^(V) in~the~FIRE from~OUTSIDE to~the~CAMP FAILURE HE **29:15** and~AT the~BUCK the~UNIT *you*^(ms)~*will*~TAKE^(V) and~*they*~*did*~SUPPORT^(V) Aharon and~SON~s~him AT HAND~s2~them^(m) UPON HEAD the~BUCK **29:16** and~*you*^(ms)~*did*~SLAY^(V) AT the~BUCK and~*you*^(ms)~*did*~TAKE^(V) AT BLOOD~him and~*you*^(ms)~*did*~SPRINKLE^(V) UPON the~ALTAR ALL.AROUND **29:17** and~AT the~BUCK *you*^(ms)~*will*~*much*~DIVIDE.INTO.PIECES^(V) to~PIECE~s~him and~*you*^(ms)~*did*~BATHE^(V) INSIDE~him and~LEG~s~him and~*you*^(ms)~*did*~GIVE^(V) UPON PIECE~s~him and~UPON HEAD~him **29:18** and~*you*^(ms)~*did*~*make*~BURN.INCENSE^(V) AT ALL the~BUCK the~ALTAR~unto ASCENSION.OFFERING HE to~**YHWH** AROMA SWEET FIRE.OFFERING to~**YHWH** HE **29:19** and~*you*^(ms)~*did*~TAKE^(V) AT the~BUCK the~SECOND and~*he*~*did*~SUPPORT^(V) Aharon and~SON~s~him AT HAND~s2~them^(m) UPON HEAD the~BUCK **29:20** and~*you*^(ms)~*did*~SLAY^(V) AT the~BUCK and~*you*^(ms)~*did*~TAKE^(V) from~BLOOD~him and~*you*^(ms)~*did*~GIVE^(V)~& UPON TIP EAR Aharon and~UPON TIP EAR SON~s~him the~RIGHT and~UPON THUMB HAND~them^(m) the~RIGHT and~UPON THUMB FOOT~them^(m) the~RIGHT and~*you*^(ms)~*did*~SPRINKLE^(V) AT the~BLOOD UPON the~ALTAR ALL.AROUND **29:21** and~*you*^(ms)~*did*~TAKE^(V) FROM the~BLOOD WHICH UPON the~ALTAR and~from~OIL the~OINTMENT and~*you*^(ms)~*did*~*make*~SPATTER^(V) UPON Aharon and~UPON GARMENT~s~him and~UPON SON~s~him and~UPON GARMENT~s SON~s~him AT~him and~*he*~*did*~SET.APART^(V) HE and~GARMENT~s~him and~SON~s~him and~GARMENT~s SON~s~him AT~him **29:22** and~*you*^(ms)~*did*~TAKE^(V) FROM the~BUCK the~FAT and~the~RUMP and~AT the~FAT the~*much*~COVER.OVER^(V)~*ing*^(ms) AT the~INSIDE and~AT LOBE the~HEAVY and~

AT TWO the~KIDNEY~s and~AT the~FAT WHICH UPON~them[f] and~AT THIGH the~RIGHT.HAND GIVEN.THAT BUCK INSTALLATION~s HE **29:23** and~ ROUNDNESS BREAD UNIT and~PIERCED.BREAD BREAD OIL UNIT and~ THIN.BREAD UNIT from~WICKER.BASKET the~UNLEAVENED.BREAD~s WHICH to~FACE~s **YHWH 29:24** and~*you[ms]~did*~PLACE[V] the~ALL UPON PALM~s2 Aharon and~UPON PALM~s2 SON~s~him and~*you[ms]~did~make*~ WAVE[V] AT~them[m] WAVING to~FACE~s **YHWH 29:25** and~*you[ms]~did*~ TAKE[V] AT~them[m] from~HAND~them[m] and~*you[ms]~did~make*~ BURN.INCENSE[V] the~ALTAR~unto UPON the~ASCENSION.OFFERING to~ AROMA SWEET to~FACE~s **YHWH** FIRE.OFFERING HE to~**YHWH 29:26** and~ *you[ms]~did*~TAKE[V] AT the~CHEST from~BUCK the~INSTALLATION~s WHICH to~Aharon and~*you[ms]~did~make*~WAVE[V] AT~him WAVING to~FACE~s **YHWH** and~*he~did*~EXIST[V] to~you[ms] to~SHARE **29:27** and~*you[ms]~did~ much*~SET.APART[V] AT CHEST the~WAVING and~AT THIGH the~OFFERING WHICH *he~did~be~make*~WAVE[V] and~WHICH *he~did~be~make*~ RAISE.UP[V] from~BUCK the~INSTALLATION~s from~WHICH to~Aharon and~ from~WHICH to~SON~s~him **29:28** and~*he~did*~EXIST[V] to~Aharon and~ to~SON~s~him to~CUSTOM DISTANT from~AT SON~s Yisra'eyl GIVEN.THAT OFFERING HE and~OFFERING *he~will*~EXIST[V] from~AT SON~s Yisra'eyl from~SACRIFICE~s OFFERING.OF.RESTITUTION~s~them[m] OFFERING~ them[m] to~**YHWH 29:29** and~GARMENT~s the~SPECIAL WHICH to~Aharon *they[m]~will*~EXIST[V] to~SON~s~him AFTER~him to~>~SMEAR[V] in~them[m] and~to~>~*much*~FILL[V] in~them[m] AT HAND~them[m] **29:30** SEVEN DAY~s *he~will*~WEAR[V]~them[m] the~ADMINISTRATOR UNDER~him from~SON~s~ him WHICH *he~will*~COME[V] TO TENT APPOINTED to~>~*much*~MINISTER[V] in~the~SPECIAL **29:31** and~AT BUCK the~INSTALLATION~s *you[ms]~will*~ TAKE[V] and~*you[ms]~did~much*~BOIL[V] AT FLESH~him in~AREA UNIQUE **29:32** and~*he~did*~EAT[V] Aharon and~SON~s~him AT FLESH the~ BUCK and~AT the~BREAD WHICH in~the~WICKER.BASKET OPENING TENT APPOINTED **29:33** and~*they~did*~EAT[V] AT~them[m] WHICH *he~did~be~ much*~COVER[V] in~them[m] to~>~*much*~FILL[V] AT HAND~them[m] to~>~ *much*~SET.APART[V] AT~them[m] and~BE.STRANGE[V]~*ing[ms]* NOT *he~will*~ EAT[V] GIVEN.THAT SPECIAL THEY[m] **29:34** and~IF *he~will~be*~ LEAVE.BEHIND[V] from~FLESH the~INSTALLATION~s and~FROM the~BREAD UNTIL the~MORNING and~*you[ms]~did*~CREMATE[V] AT the~*be*~ LEAVE.BEHIND[V]~*ing[ms]* in~the~FIRE NOT *he~will~be*~EAT[V] GIVEN.THAT SPECIAL HE **29:35** and~*you[ms]~did*~DO[V] to~Aharon and~to~SON~s~him like~IN.THIS.WAY like~ALL WHICH *I~did~much*~DIRECT[V] AT~you[mp] SEVEN DAY~s *you[ms]~will~much*~FILL[V] HAND~them[m] **29:36** and~BULL FAILURE *you[ms]~will*~DO[V] to~the~DAY UPON the~ATONEMENT~s and~*you[ms]~did~ much*~FAIL[V] UPON the~ALTAR in~>~*much*~COVER[V]~you[ms] UPON~him and~*you[ms]~did*~SMEAR[V] AT~him to~>~*much*~SET.APART[V]~ him **29:37** SEVEN DAY~s *you[ms]~will~much*~COVER[V] UPON the~ALTAR and~*you[ms]~did~much*~SET.APART[V] AT~him and~*he~did*~EXIST[V] the~ ALTAR SPECIAL SPECIAL~s ALL the~TOUCH[V]~*ing[ms]* in~the~ALTAR *he~will*~

SET.APART⁽ⱽ⁾ **29:38** and~THIS WHICH *you⁽ᵐˢ⁾*~*will*~DO⁽ⱽ⁾ UPON the~ALTAR SHEEP~s SON~s YEAR TWO to~the~DAY CONTINUALLY **29:39** AT the~SHEEP the~UNIT *you⁽ᵐˢ⁾*~*will*~DO⁽ⱽ⁾ in~the~MORNING and~AT the~SHEEP the~SECOND *you⁽ᵐˢ⁾*~*will*~DO⁽ⱽ⁾ BETWEEN the~EVENING~s2 **29:40** and~ONE.TENTH FLOUR MIX⁽ⱽ⁾~*ed⁽ᵐˢ⁾* in~OIL SMASHED QUARTER the~HIYN and~POURING FOURTH the~HIYN WINE to~the~SHEEP the~UNIT **29:41** and~AT the~SHEEP the~SECOND *you⁽ᵐˢ⁾*~*will*~DO⁽ⱽ⁾ BETWEEN the~EVENING~s2 like~DEPOSIT the~MORNING and~like~POURING~her *you⁽ᵐˢ⁾*~*will*~DO⁽ⱽ⁾ to~her to~AROMA SWEET FIRE.OFFERING to~**YHWH** **29:42** ASCENSION.OFFERING CONTINUALLY to~GENERATION~s~*you⁽ᵐᵖ⁾* OPENING TENT APPOINTED to~FACE~s **YHWH** WHICH *I*~*will*~*be*~APPOINT⁽ⱽ⁾ to~*you⁽ᵐᵖ⁾* THERE~unto to~>~much~SPEAK⁽ⱽ⁾ TO~*you⁽ᵐˢ⁾* THERE **29:43** and~*I*~*did*~*be*~APPOINT⁽ⱽ⁾ THERE~unto to~SON~s Yisra'eyl and~*he*~*did*~*be*~SET.APART⁽ⱽ⁾ in~ARMAMENT~me **29:44** and~*I*~*did*~much~SET.APART⁽ⱽ⁾ AT TENT APPOINTED and~AT the~ALTAR and~AT Aharon and~AT SON~s~him *I*~*will*~much~SET.APART⁽ⱽ⁾ to~>~much~ADORN⁽ⱽ⁾ to~me **29:45** and~*I*~*did*~DWELL⁽ⱽ⁾ in~MIDST SON~s Yisra'eyl and~*I*~*did*~EXIST⁽ⱽ⁾ to~them⁽ᵐ⁾ to~Elohiym **29:46** and~*they*~*did*~KNOW⁽ⱽ⁾ GIVEN.THAT I **YHWH** Elohiym~them⁽ᵐ⁾ WHICH *I*~*did*~make~GO.OUT⁽ⱽ⁾ AT~them⁽ᵐ⁾ from~LAND Mits'rayim to~>~DWELL⁽ⱽ⁾~me in~MIDST~them⁽ᵐ⁾ I **YHWH** Elohiym~them⁽ᵐ⁾

Chapter 30

30:1 and~*you⁽ᵐˢ⁾*~*did*~DO⁽ⱽ⁾ ALTAR PLACE.TO.BURN INCENSE.SMOKE TREE~s ACACIA~s *you⁽ᵐˢ⁾*~*will*~DO⁽ⱽ⁾ AT~him **30:2** AMMAH LENGTH~him and~AMMAH WIDTH~him BE.SQUARE⁽ⱽ⁾~*ed⁽ᵐˢ⁾* *he*~*will*~EXIST⁽ⱽ⁾ and~AMMAH~s2 HEIGHT~him FROM~him HORN~s~him **30:3** and~*you⁽ᵐˢ⁾*~*did*~much~OVERLAY⁽ⱽ⁾ AT~him GOLD CLEAN AT ROOF~him and~AT WALL~s~him ALL.AROUND and~AT HORN~s~him and~*you⁽ᵐˢ⁾*~*did*~DO⁽ⱽ⁾ to~him MOLDING GOLD ALL.AROUND **30:4** and~TWO RING~s GOLD *you⁽ᵐˢ⁾*~*will*~DO⁽ⱽ⁾ to~him from~UNDER to~MOLDING~him UPON TWO RIB~s~him *you⁽ᵐˢ⁾*~*will*~DO⁽ⱽ⁾ UPON TWO SIDE~s~him and~*he*~*did*~EXIST⁽ⱽ⁾ to~HOUSE~s to~STRAND~s to~>~LIFT.UP⁽ⱽ⁾ AT~him in~THEY⁽ᵐ⁾ **30:5** and~*you⁽ᵐˢ⁾*~*did*~DO⁽ⱽ⁾ AT the~STRAND~s TREE~s ACACIA~s and~*you⁽ᵐˢ⁾*~*did*~much~OVERLAY⁽ⱽ⁾ AT~them⁽ᵐ⁾ GOLD **30:6** and~*you⁽ᵐˢ⁾*~*did*~GIVE⁽ⱽ⁾~& AT~him to~FACE~s the~TENT.CURTAIN WHICH UPON BOX the~EVIDENCE to~FACE~s the~LID WHICH UPON the~EVIDENCE WHICH *I*~*will*~*be*~APPOINT⁽ⱽ⁾ to~*you⁽ᵐˢ⁾* THERE~unto **30:7** and~*he*~*did*~*make*~BURN.INCENSE⁽ⱽ⁾ UPON~him Aharon INCENSE.SMOKE AROMATIC.SPICE~s in~the~MORNING in~the~MORNING in~>~*make*~DO.WELL⁽ⱽ⁾~him AT the~LAMP~s *he*~*will*~*make*~BURN.INCENSE⁽ⱽ⁾~her **30:8** and~in~>~*make*~GO.UP⁽ⱽ⁾ Aharon AT the~LAMP~s BETWEEN the~EVENING~s2 *he*~*will*~*make*~BURN.INCENSE⁽ⱽ⁾~her INCENSE.SMOKE CONTINUALLY to~FACE~s **YHWH** to~GENERATION~s~

you⁽ᵐᵖ⁾ **30:9** NOT you⁽ᵐᵖ⁾~will~make~GO.UP⁽ⱽ⁾ UPON~him INCENSE.SMOKE BE.STRANGE⁽ⱽ⁾~ing⁽ᶠˢ⁾ and~ASCENSION.OFFERING and~DEPOSIT and~ POURING NOT you⁽ᵐᵖ⁾~will~POUR⁽ⱽ⁾ UPON~him **30:10** and~he~did~much~ COVER⁽ⱽ⁾ Aharon UPON HORN~s~him UNIT in~the~YEAR from~BLOOD FAILURE the~ATONEMENT~s UNIT in~the~YEAR he~will~much~COVER⁽ⱽ⁾ UPON~him to~GENERATION~s~you⁽ᵐᵖ⁾ SPECIAL SPECIAL~s HE to~ **YHWH 30:11** and~he~will~much~SPEAK⁽ⱽ⁾ **YHWH** TO Mosheh to~>~ SAY⁽ⱽ⁾ **30:12** GIVEN.THAT you⁽ᵐˢ⁾~will~LIFT.UP⁽ⱽ⁾ AT HEAD SON~s Yisra'eyl to~REGISTER⁽ⱽ⁾~ed⁽ᵐᵖ⁾~them⁽ᵐ⁾ and~they~did~GIVE⁽ⱽ⁾ MAN COVERING SOUL~him to~**YHWH** in~>~REGISTER⁽ⱽ⁾ AT~them⁽ᵐ⁾ and~NOT he~will~ EXIST⁽ⱽ⁾ in~them⁽ᵐ⁾ STRIKING in~>~REGISTER⁽ⱽ⁾ AT~them⁽ᵐ⁾ **30:13** THIS they⁽ᵐ⁾~will~GIVE⁽ⱽ⁾ ALL the~CROSS.OVER⁽ⱽ⁾~ing⁽ᵐˢ⁾ UPON the~REGISTER⁽ⱽ⁾~ ed⁽ᵐᵖ⁾ ONE.HALF the~SHEQEL in~SHEQEL the~SPECIAL TEN~s GERAH the~ SHEQEL ONE.HALF the~SHEQEL OFFERING to~**YHWH 30:14** ALL the~ CROSS.OVER⁽ⱽ⁾~ing⁽ᵐˢ⁾ UPON the~REGISTER⁽ⱽ⁾~ed⁽ᵐᵖ⁾ from~SON TEN~s YEAR and~UPWARD~unto he~will~GIVE⁽ⱽ⁾ OFFERING **YHWH 30:15** the~RICH NOT he~will~make~INCREASE⁽ⱽ⁾ and~the~HELPLESS NOT he~will~make~ BE.LESS⁽ⱽ⁾ from~ONE.HALF the~SHEQEL to~>~GIVE⁽ⱽ⁾ AT OFFERING **YHWH** to~>~much~COVER⁽ⱽ⁾ UPON SOUL~s~you⁽ᵐᵖ⁾ **30:16** and~you⁽ᵐˢ⁾~did~TAKE⁽ⱽ⁾ AT SILVER the~ATONEMENT~s from~AT SON~s Yisra'eyl and~you⁽ᵐˢ⁾~did~ GIVE⁽ⱽ⁾ AT~him UPON SERVICE TENT APPOINTED and~he~did~EXIST⁽ⱽ⁾ to~ SON~s Yisra'eyl to~REMEMBRANCE to~FACE~s **YHWH** to~>~much~COVER⁽ⱽ⁾ UPON SOUL~s~you⁽ᵐᵖ⁾ **30:17** and~he~will~much~SPEAK⁽ⱽ⁾ **YHWH** TO Mosheh to~>~SAY⁽ⱽ⁾ **30:18** and~you⁽ᵐˢ⁾~did~DO⁽ⱽ⁾ CAULDRON COPPER and~ BASE~him COPPER to~>~BATHE⁽ⱽ⁾ and~you⁽ᵐˢ⁾~did~GIVE⁽ⱽ⁾ AT~him BETWEEN TENT APPOINTED and~BETWEEN the~ALTAR and~you⁽ᵐˢ⁾~did~ GIVE⁽ⱽ⁾ THERE~unto WATER~s2 **30:19** and~they~did~BATHE⁽ⱽ⁾ Aharon and~ SON~s~him FROM~him AT HAND~s2~them⁽ᵐ⁾ and~AT FOOT~s2~ them⁽ᵐ⁾ **30:20** in~>~COME⁽ⱽ⁾~them⁽ᵐ⁾ TO TENT APPOINTED they⁽ᵐ⁾~will~ BATHE⁽ⱽ⁾ WATER~s2 and~NOT they⁽ᵐ⁾~will~DIE⁽ⱽ⁾ OR in~>~DRAW.NEAR⁽ⱽ⁾~ them⁽ᵐ⁾ TO the~ALTAR to~>~much~MINISTER⁽ⱽ⁾ to~>~make~ BURN.INCENSE⁽ⱽ⁾ FIRE.OFFERING to~**YHWH 30:21** and~they~did~BATHE⁽ⱽ⁾ HAND~s2~them⁽ᵐ⁾ and~FOOT~s2~them⁽ᵐ⁾ and~NOT they⁽ᵐ⁾~will~DIE⁽ⱽ⁾ and~ she~did~EXIST⁽ⱽ⁾ to~them⁽ᵐ⁾ CUSTOM DISTANT to~him and~to~SEED~him to~GENERATION~s~them⁽ᵐ⁾ **30:22** and~he~will~much~SPEAK⁽ⱽ⁾ **YHWH** TO Mosheh to~>~SAY⁽ⱽ⁾ **30:23** and~YOU⁽ᵐˢ⁾ !⁽ᵐˢ⁾~TAKE⁽ⱽ⁾ to~you⁽ᵐˢ⁾ SWEET.SPICE~s HEAD MYRRH FREE.FLOWING FIVE HUNDRED~s and~ CINNAMON SWEET.SPICE ONE.HALF~him FIVE~s and~HUNDRED~s2 and~ STALK SWEET.SPICE FIVE~s and~HUNDRED~s2 **30:24** and~CASSIA FIVE HUNDRED~s in~SHEQEL the~SPECIAL and~OIL OLIVE HIYN **30:25** and~ you⁽ᵐˢ⁾~did~DO⁽ⱽ⁾ AT~him OIL OINTMENT SPECIAL SPICE.MIXTURE OINTMENT.MIXTURE WORK COMPOUND⁽ⱽ⁾~ing⁽ᵐˢ⁾ OIL OINTMENT SPECIAL he~will~EXIST⁽ⱽ⁾ **30:26** and~you⁽ᵐˢ⁾~did~SMEAR⁽ⱽ⁾ in~him AT TENT APPOINTED and~AT BOX the~EVIDENCE **30:27** and~AT the~TABLE and~AT ALL UTENSIL~s~him and~AT the~LAMPSTAND and~AT UTENSIL~s~her and~

AT ALTAR the~INCENSE.SMOKE **30:28** and~AT ALTAR the~
ASCENSION.OFFERING and~AT ALL UTENSIL~s~him and~AT the~CAULDRON
and~AT BASE~him **30:29** and~*you*$^{(ms)}$~*did*~*much*~SET.APART$^{(V)}$ AT~them$^{(m)}$
and~*they*~*did*~EXIST$^{(V)}$ SPECIAL SPECIAL~s ALL the~TOUCH$^{(V)}$~*ing*$^{(ms)}$ in~
them$^{(m)}$ he~will~SET.APART$^{(V)}$ **30:30** and~AT Aharon and~AT SON~s~him
you$^{(ms)}$~*will*~SMEAR$^{(V)}$ and~*you*$^{(ms)}$~*did*~*much*~SET.APART$^{(V)}$ AT~them$^{(m)}$ to~
>~*much*~ADORN$^{(V)}$ to~me **30:31** and~TO SON~s Yisra'eyl *you*$^{(ms)}$~*will*~
much~SPEAK$^{(V)}$ to~>~SAY$^{(V)}$ OIL OINTMENT SPECIAL he~will~EXIST$^{(V)}$ THIS to~
me to~GENERATION~s~you$^{(mp)}$ **30:32** UPON FLESH HUMAN NOT he~will~
POUR.DOWN$^{(V)}$ and~in~SUM NOT *you*$^{(mp)}$~*will*~DO$^{(V)}$ like~THAT.ONE~him
SPECIAL HE SPECIAL he~will~EXIST$^{(V)}$ to~you$^{(mp)}$ **30:33** MAN WHICH he~will~
COMPOUND$^{(V)}$ like~THAT.ONE~him and~WHICH he~will~GIVE$^{(V)}$ FROM~him
UPON BE.STRANGE$^{(V)}$~*ing*$^{(ms)}$ and~he~did~be~CUT$^{(V)}$ from~PEOPLE~s~
him **30:34** and~*he*~*will*~SAY$^{(V)}$ YHWH TO Mosheh !$^{(ms)}$~TAKE$^{(V)}$ to~you$^{(ms)}$
AROMATIC.SPICE~s NATAPH and~ONYCHA and~GALBANUM
AROMATIC.SPICE~s and~FRANKINCENSE REFINED STRAND in~STRAND he~
will~EXIST$^{(V)}$ **30:35** and~*you*$^{(ms)}$~*did*~DO$^{(V)}$ AT~her INCENSE.SMOKE
SPICE.MIXTURE WORK COMPOUND$^{(V)}$~*ing*$^{(ms)}$ be~*much*~SEASON$^{(V)}$~*ing*$^{(ms)}$
CLEAN SPECIAL **30:36** and~*you*$^{(ms)}$~*did*~PULVERIZE$^{(V)}$ FROM~her >~*make*~
BEAT.SMALL$^{(V)}$ and~*you*$^{(ms)}$~*did*~GIVE$^{(V)}$~& FROM~her to~FACE~s the~
EVIDENCE in~TENT APPOINTED WHICH I~will~be~APPOINT$^{(V)}$ to~you$^{(ms)}$
THERE~unto SPECIAL SPECIAL~s she~will~EXIST$^{(V)}$ to~you$^{(mp)}$ **30:37** and~
the~INCENSE.SMOKE WHICH *you*$^{(ms)}$~*will*~DO$^{(V)}$ in~SUM~her NOT *you*$^{(mp)}$~
will~DO$^{(V)}$ to~you$^{(mp)}$ SPECIAL she~will~EXIST$^{(V)}$ to~you$^{(ms)}$ to~
YHWH **30:38** MAN WHICH he~will~DO$^{(V)}$ like~THAT.ONE~her to~>~*make*~
SMELL$^{(V)}$ in~her and~he~did~be~CUT$^{(V)}$ from~PEOPLE~s~him

Chapter 31

31:1 and~*he*~*will*~*much*~SPEAK$^{(V)}$ YHWH TO Mosheh to~>~SAY$^{(V)}$ **31:2** !$^{(ms)}$~
SEE$^{(V)}$ I~*did*~CALL.OUT$^{(V)}$ in~TITLE Betsaleyl SON Uriy SON Hhur to~BRANCH
Yehudah **31:3** and~I~will~*much*~FILL$^{(V)}$ AT~him WIND Elohiym in~SKILL and~
in~INTELLIGENCE and~in~DISCERNMENT and~in~ALL BUSINESS **31:4** to~>~
THINK$^{(V)}$ INVENTION~s to~>~DO$^{(V)}$ in~the~GOLD and~in~the~SILVER and~in~
the~COPPER **31:5** and~in~the~ENGRAVING STONE to~>~*much*~FILL$^{(V)}$ and~
in~the~ENGRAVING TREE to~>~DO$^{(V)}$ in~ALL BUSINESS **31:6** and~I LOOK I~
did~GIVE$^{(V)}$ AT~him AT Ahaliyav SON Ahhiysamahh to~BRANCH Dan and~in~
HEART ALL SKILLED.ONE HEART I~*did*~GIVE$^{(V)}$ SKILL and~*they*~*did*~DO$^{(V)}$ AT
ALL WHICH I~*did*~*much*~DIRECT$^{(V)}$~you$^{(ms)}$ **31:7** AT TENT APPOINTED and~
AT the~BOX to~the~EVIDENCE and~AT the~LID WHICH UPON~him and~AT
ALL UTENSIL~s the~TENT **31:8** and~AT the~TABLE and~AT UTENSIL~s~him
and~AT the~LAMPSTAND the~CLEAN and~AT ALL UTENSIL~s~her and~AT
ALTAR the~INCENSE.SMOKE **31:9** and~AT ALTAR the~ASCENSION.OFFERING

and~AT ALL UTENSIL~s~him and~AT the~CAULDRON and~AT BASE~him **31:10** and~AT GARMENT~s the~BRAIDED.WORK and~AT GARMENT~s the~SPECIAL to~Aharon the~ADMINISTRATOR and~AT GARMENT~s SON~s~him to~>~*much*~ADORN$^{(V)}$ **31:11** and~AT OIL the~OINTMENT and~AT INCENSE.SMOKE the~AROMATIC.SPICE~s to~the~SPECIAL like~ALL WHICH *I~did~much~*DIRECT$^{(V)}$~you$^{(ms)}$ *they*$^{(m)}$~*will*~DO$^{(V)}$ **31:12** and~*he~will~*SAY$^{(V)}$ **YHWH** TO Mosheh to~>~SAY$^{(V)}$ **31:13** and~YOU$^{(mp)}$ *!*$^{(ms)}$~*much*~SPEAK$^{(V)}$ TO SON~s Yisra'eyl to~>~SAY$^{(V)}$ SURELY AT CEASING~s~me *you*$^{(mp)}$~*will~*SAFEGUARD$^{(V)}$ GIVEN.THAT SIGN SHE BETWEEN~me and~BETWEEN~you$^{(mp)}$ to~GENERATION~s~you$^{(mp)}$ to~>~KNOW$^{(V)}$ GIVEN.THAT I **YHWH** *much~*SET.APART$^{(V)}$~*ing*$^{(ms)}$~*you*$^{(ms)}$ **31:14** and~*you*$^{(mp)}$~*did~*SAFEGUARD$^{(V)}$ AT the~CEASING GIVEN.THAT SPECIAL SHE to~you$^{(mp)}$ *much~*DRILL$^{(V)}$~*ing*$^{(mp)}$~*her* >~DIE$^{(V)}$ *he~will~be~make~*DIE$^{(V)}$ GIVEN.THAT ALL the~DO$^{(V)}$~*ing*$^{(ms)}$ in~her BUSINESS and~*she~did~be~*CUT$^{(V)}$ the~SOUL the~SHE from~INSIDE PEOPLE~s~her **31:15** SIX DAY~s *he~will~be~*DO$^{(V)}$ BUSINESS and~in~the~DAY the~SEVENTH CEASING REST.PERIOD SPECIAL to~**YHWH** ALL the~DO$^{(V)}$~*ing*$^{(ms)}$ BUSINESS in~DAY the~CEASING >~DIE$^{(V)}$ *he~will~be~make~*DIE$^{(V)}$ **31:16** and~*they~did~*SAFEGUARD$^{(V)}$ SON~s Yisra'eyl AT the~CEASING to~>~DO$^{(V)}$ AT the~CEASING to~GENERATION~s~them$^{(m)}$ COVENANT DISTANT **31:17** BETWEEN~me and~BETWEEN SON~s Yisra'eyl SIGN SHE to~DISTANT GIVEN.THAT SIX DAY~s *he~did~*DO$^{(V)}$ **YHWH** AT the~SKY~s2 and~AT the~LAND and~in~the~DAY the~SEVENTH *he~did~*CEASE$^{(V)}$ and~*he~will~*BREATHE.DEEPLY$^{(V)}$ **31:18** and~*he~will~*GIVE$^{(V)}$ TO Mosheh like~>~*much~*FINISH$^{(V)}$~him to~>~*much~*SPEAK$^{(V)}$ AT~him in~HILL Sinai TWO SLAB~s the~EVIDENCE SLAB~s STONE WRITE$^{(V)}$~*ed*$^{(mp)}$ in~FINGER Elohiym

Chapter 32

32:1 and~*he~will~*SEE$^{(V)}$ the~PEOPLE GIVEN.THAT *he~did~much~*BE.ASHAMED$^{(V)}$ Mosheh to~>~GO.DOWN$^{(V)}$ FROM the~HILL and~*he~will~be~*ASSEMBLE$^{(V)}$ the~PEOPLE UPON Aharon and~*they*$^{(m)}$~*will~*SAY$^{(V)}$ TO~him *!*$^{(ms)}$~RISE$^{(V)}$ *!*$^{(ms)}$~DO$^{(V)}$ to~us Elohiym WHICH *they*$^{(m)}$~*will~*WALK$^{(V)}$ to~FACE~s~us GIVEN.THAT THIS Mosheh the~MAN WHICH *he~did~make~*GO.UP$^{(V)}$~us from~LAND Mits'rayim NOT *we~did~*KNOW$^{(V)}$ WHAT *he~did~*EXIST$^{(V)}$ to~him **32:2** and~*he~will~*SAY$^{(V)}$ TO~them$^{(m)}$ Aharon *!*$^{(mp)}$~*much~*TEAR.OFF$^{(V)}$ ORNAMENTAL.RING~s the~GOLD WHICH in~EAR~s2 WOMAN~s~you$^{(mp)}$ SON~s~you$^{(mp)}$ and~DAUGHTER~s~you$^{(mp)}$ and~ *!*$^{(mp)}$~*make~*COME$^{(V)}$ TO~me **32:3** and~*they*$^{(m)}$~*will~self~*TEAR.OFF$^{(V)}$ ALL the~PEOPLE AT ORNAMENTAL.RING~s the~GOLD WHICH in~EAR~s2~them$^{(m)}$ and~*they*$^{(m)}$~*will~make~*COME$^{(V)}$ TO Aharon **32:4** and~*he~will~*TAKE$^{(V)}$ from~HAND~them$^{(m)}$ and~*he~will~*SMACK$^{(V)}$ AT~him in~the~ENGRAVING.TOOL and~*he~will~*DO$^{(V)}$~him BULLOCK CAST.IMAGE and~*they*$^{(m)}$~*will~*SAY$^{(V)}$ THESE Elohiym~you$^{(ms)}$ Yisra'eyl WHICH *they~did~make~*

The Book of Exodus

GO.UP(v)~you(ms) from~LAND Mits'rayim **32:5** and~*he*~*will*~SEE(v) Aharon and~*he*~*will*~BUILD(v) ALTAR to~FACE~s~him and~*he*~*will*~CALL.OUT(v) Aharon and~*he*~*will*~SAY(v) FEAST to~**YHWH** TOMORROW **32:6** and~*they*(m)~*will*~*make*~DEPART.EARLY(v) from~MORROW and~*they*(m)~*will*~*make*~GO.UP(v) ASCENSION.OFFERING~s and~*they*(m)~*will*~*make*~DRAW.NEAR(v) OFFERING.OF.RESTITUTION~s and~*he*~*will*~SETTLE(v) the~PEOPLE to~>~EAT(v) and~>~GULP(v) and~*they*(m)~*will*~RISE(v) to~>~*much*~LAUGH(v) **32:7** and~*he*~*will*~*much*~SPEAK(v) **YHWH** TO Mosheh *!*(ms)~WALK(v) *!*(ms)~GO.DOWN(v) GIVEN.THAT *he*~*did*~*much*~DAMAGE(v) PEOPLE~you(ms) WHICH *you*(ms)~*did*~*make*~GO.UP(v) from~LAND Mits'rayim **32:8** *they*~*did*~TURN.ASIDE(v) QUICKLY FROM the~ROAD WHICH *I*~*did*~*much*~DIRECT(v)~them(m) *they*~*did*~DO(v) to~them(m) BULLOCK CAST.IMAGE and~*they*(m)~*will*~*self*~BEND.DOWN(v) to~him and~*they*(m)~*will*~SACRIFICE(v) to~him and~*they*(m)~*will*~SAY(v) THESE Elohiym~you(ms) Yisra'eyl WHICH *they*~*did*~*make*~GO.UP(v)~you(ms) from~LAND Mits'rayim **32:9** and~*he*~*will*~SAY(v) **YHWH** TO Mosheh *I*~*did*~SEE(v) AT the~PEOPLE the~THIS and~LOOK PEOPLE HARD NECK HE **32:10** and~NOW *!*(fs)~*make*~REST(v) to~me and~*he*~*will*~FLARE.UP(v) NOSE~me in~them(m) and~*I*~*will*~*much*~FINISH(v)~them(m) and~*I*~*will*~DO(v)~& AT~you(ms) to~NATION GREAT **32:11** and~*he*~*will*~*much*~TWIST(v) Mosheh AT FACE~s **YHWH** Elohiym~him and~*he*~*will*~SAY(v) to~WHAT **YHWH** *he*~*will*~FLARE.UP(v) NOSE~you(ms) in~PEOPLE~you(ms) WHICH *you*(ms)~*did*~*make*~GO.OUT(v) from~LAND Mits'rayim in~STRENGTH GREAT and~in~HAND FORCEFUL **32:12** to~WHAT *they*(m)~*will*~SAY(v) Mits'rayim to~>~SAY(v) in~DYSFUNCTIONAL *he*~*did*~*make*~GO.OUT(v)~them(m) to~>~KILL(v) AT~them(m) in~HILL~s and~to~>~*much*~FINISH(v)~them(m) from~UPON FACE~s the~GROUND *!*(ms)~TURN.BACK(v) from~FLAMING.WRATH NOSE~you(ms) and~*!*(ms)~*be*~COMFORT(v) UPON the~DYSFUNCTIONAL to~PEOPLE~you(ms) **32:13** *!*(ms)~REMEMBER(v) to~Avraham to~Yits'hhaq and~to~Yisra'eyl SERVANT~s~you(ms) WHICH *you*(ms)~*did*~*be*~SWEAR(v) to~them(m) in~you(fs) and~*you*(ms)~*will*~*much*~SPEAK(v) TO~them(m) *I*~*will*~*make*~INCREASE(v) AT SEED~you(mp) like~STAR~s the~SKY~s2 and~ALL the~LAND the~THIS WHICH *I*~*did*~SAY(v) *I*~*will*~GIVE(v) to~SEED~you(mp) and~*they*~*did*~INHERIT(v) to~DISTANT **32:14** and~*he*~*will*~*be*~COMFORT(v) **YHWH** UPON the~DYSFUNCTIONAL WHICH *he*~*did*~*much*~SPEAK(v) to~>~DO(v) to~PEOPLE~him **32:15** and~*he*~*will*~TURN(v) and~*he*~*will*~GO.DOWN(v) Mosheh FROM the~HILL and~TWO SLAB~s the~EVIDENCE in~HAND~him SLAB~s WRITE(v)~ed(mp) from~TWO OTHER.SIDE~them(m) from~THIS and~from~THIS THEY(m) WRITE(v)~ed(mp) **32:16** and~the~SLAB~s WORK Elohiym THEY(m) and~the~THING.WRITTEN THING.WRITTEN Elohiym HE ENGRAVE(v)~ed(ms) UPON the~SLAB~s **32:17** and~*he*~*will*~HEAR(v) Yehoshu'a AT VOICE the~PEOPLE in~LOUD.NOISE and~*he*~*will*~SAY(v) TO Mosheh VOICE BATTLE in~the~CAMP **32:18** and~*he*~*will*~SAY(v) WITHOUT VOICE >~ANSWER(v) BRAVERY and~WITHOUT VOICE >~ANSWER(v) DEFEAT VOICE >~ANSWER(v) I HEAR(v)~ing(ms) **32:19** and~*he*~*will*~EXIST(v) like~WHICH *he*~*did*~COME.NEAR(v) TO the~CAMP and~*he*~*will*~SEE(v) AT the~BULLOCK and~DANCE~s and~*he*~*will*~

FLARE.UP$^{(v)}$ NOSE Mosheh and~*he*~*will*~*make*~THROW.OUT$^{(v)}$ from~HAND~s2~him AT the~SLAB~s and~*he*~*will*~CRACK$^{(v)}$ AT~them$^{(m)}$ UNDER the~HILL **32:20** and~*he*~*will*~TAKE$^{(v)}$ AT the~BULLOCK WHICH *they*~*did*~DO$^{(v)}$ and~*he*~*will*~CREMATE$^{(v)}$ in~the~FIRE and~*he*~*will*~GRIND$^{(v)}$ UNTIL WHICH *he*~*did*~BEAT.SMALL$^{(v)}$ and~*he*~*will*~DISPERSE$^{(v)}$ UPON FACE~s the~WATER~s2 and~*he*~*will*~*make*~DRINK$^{(v)}$ AT SON~s Yisra'eyl **32:21** and~*he*~*will*~SAY$^{(v)}$ Mosheh TO Aharon WHAT *he*~*did*~DO$^{(v)}$ to~you$^{(ms)}$ the~PEOPLE the~THIS GIVEN.THAT *you*$^{(ms)}$~*did*~*make*~COME$^{(v)}$ UPON~him FAILURE GREAT **32:22** and~*he*~*will*~SAY$^{(v)}$ Aharon DO.NOT *he*~*will*~FLARE.UP$^{(v)}$ NOSE LORD~me YOU$^{(ms)}$ *you*$^{(ms)}$~*did*~KNOW$^{(v)}$ AT the~PEOPLE GIVEN.THAT in~DYSFUNCTIONAL HE **32:23** and~*they*$^{(m)}$~*will*~SAY$^{(v)}$ to~me *!*$^{(ms)}$~DO$^{(v)}$ to~us Elohiym WHICH *they*$^{(m)}$~*will*~WALK$^{(v)}$ to~FACE~s~us GIVEN.THAT THIS Mosheh the~MAN WHICH *he*~*did*~*make*~GO.UP$^{(v)}$~us from~LAND Mits'rayim NOT *we*~*did*~KNOW$^{(v)}$ WHAT *he*~*did*~EXIST$^{(v)}$ to~him **32:24** and~*I*~*will*~SAY$^{(v)}$ to~them$^{(m)}$ to~WHO GOLD *!*$^{(mp)}$~*self*~TEAR.OFF$^{(v)}$ and~*they*$^{(m)}$~*will*~GIVE$^{(v)}$ to~me and~*I*~*will*~*make*~THROW.OUT$^{(v)}$~him in~the~FIRE and~*he*~*will*~GO.OUT$^{(v)}$ the~BULLOCK the~THIS **32:25** and~*he*~*will*~SEE$^{(v)}$ Mosheh AT the~PEOPLE GIVEN.THAT LOOSE$^{(v)}$~*ed*$^{(ms)}$ HE GIVEN.THAT *he*~*did*~LOOSE$^{(v)}$~her Aharon to~DERISION in~RISE$^{(v)}$~*ing*$^{(mp)}$~them$^{(m)}$ **32:26** and~*he*~*will*~STAND$^{(v)}$ Mosheh in~GATE the~CAMP and~*he*~*will*~SAY$^{(v)}$ WHO to~**YHWH** TO~me and~*they*$^{(m)}$~*will*~GATHER$^{(v)}$ TO~him ALL SON~s Lewi **32:27** and~*he*~*will*~SAY$^{(v)}$ to~them$^{(m)}$ IN.THIS.WAY *he*~*did*~SAY$^{(v)}$ **YHWH** Elohiym Yisra'eyl *!*$^{(mp)}$~PLACE$^{(v)}$ MAN SWORD~him UPON MIDSECTION~him *!*$^{(mp)}$~CROSS.OVER$^{(v)}$ and~*!*$^{(mp)}$~TURN.BACK$^{(v)}$ from~GATE to~GATE in~the~CAMP and~*!*$^{(mp)}$~KILL$^{(v)}$ MAN AT BROTHER~him and~MAN AT COMPANION~him and~MAN AT NEAR~him **32:28** and~*they*$^{(m)}$~*will*~DO$^{(v)}$ SON~s Lewi like~WORD Mosheh and~*he*~*will*~FALL$^{(v)}$ FROM the~PEOPLE in~the~DAY the~HE like~THREE THOUSAND~s MAN **32:29** and~*he*~*will*~SAY$^{(v)}$ Mosheh *!*$^{(mp)}$~FILL$^{(v)}$ HAND~you$^{(mp)}$ the~DAY to~**YHWH** GIVEN.THAT MAN in~SON~him and~in~BROTHER~him and~to~>~GIVE$^{(v)}$ UPON~you$^{(mp)}$ the~DAY PRESENT **32:30** and~*he*~*will*~EXIST$^{(v)}$ from~MORROW and~*he*~*will*~SAY$^{(v)}$ Mosheh TO the~PEOPLE YOU$^{(mp)}$ *you*$^{(mp)}$~*did*~FAIL$^{(v)}$ FAILURE GREAT and~NOW *I*~*will*~GO.UP$^{(v)}$ TO **YHWH** POSSIBLY *I*~*will*~*much*~COVER$^{(v)}$~& in~UNTIL FAILURE~you$^{(mp)}$ **32:31** and~*he*~*will*~TURN.BACK$^{(v)}$ Mosheh TO **YHWH** and~*he*~*will*~SAY$^{(v)}$ PLEASE *he*~*did*~FAIL$^{(v)}$ the~PEOPLE the~THIS FAILURE GREAT and~*they*$^{(m)}$~*will*~DO$^{(v)}$ to~them$^{(m)}$ Elohiym GOLD **32:32** and~NOW IF *you*$^{(ms)}$~*will*~LIFT.UP$^{(v)}$ FAILURE~them$^{(m)}$ and~IF WITHOUT *!*$^{(ms)}$~WIPE.AWAY$^{(v)}$~me PLEASE from~SCROLL~you$^{(ms)}$ WHICH *you*$^{(ms)}$~*did*~WRITE$^{(v)}$ **32:33** and~*he*~*will*~SAY$^{(v)}$ **YHWH** TO Mosheh WHO WHICH *he*~*did*~FAIL$^{(v)}$ to~me *I*~*will*~WIPE.AWAY$^{(v)}$~him from~SCROLL~me **32:34** and~NOW *!*$^{(ms)}$~WALK$^{(v)}$ *!*$^{(ms)}$~GUIDE$^{(v)}$ AT the~PEOPLE TO WHICH *I*~*did*~*much*~SPEAK$^{(v)}$ to~you$^{(fs)}$ LOOK MESSENGER~me *he*~*will*~WALK$^{(v)}$ to~FACE~s~you$^{(ms)}$ and~in~DAY >~REGISTER$^{(v)}$~me and~*I*~*did*~REGISTER$^{(v)}$ UPON~them$^{(m)}$ FAILURE~them$^{(m)}$ **32:35** and~*he*~*will*~SMITE$^{(v)}$ **YHWH** AT the~PEOPLE UPON WHICH *they~did~*DO⁽ᵛ⁾ AT the~BULLOCK WHICH *he~did~* DO⁽ᵛ⁾ Aharon

Chapter 33

33:1 and~*he~will~much~*SPEAK⁽ᵛ⁾ **YHWH** TO Mosheh *!*⁽ᵐˢ⁾~WALK⁽ᵛ⁾ *!*⁽ᵐˢ⁾~ GO.UP⁽ᵛ⁾ from~THIS YOU⁽ᵐˢ⁾ and~the~PEOPLE WHICH *you*⁽ᵐˢ⁾~*did~make~* GO.UP⁽ᵛ⁾ from~LAND Mits'rayim TO the~LAND WHICH *I~did~be~*SWEAR⁽ᵛ⁾ to~Avraham to~Yits'hhaq and~to~Ya'aqov to~>~SAY⁽ᵛ⁾ to~SEED~you⁽ᵐˢ⁾ *I~ will~*GIVE⁽ᵛ⁾~her **33:2** and~*I~did~*SEND⁽ᵛ⁾ to~FACE~s~you⁽ᵐˢ⁾ MESSENGER and~*I~did~much~*CAST.OUT⁽ᵛ⁾ AT the~Kena'an~of the~Emor~of and~the~ Hhet~of and~the~Perez~of the~Hhiw~of and~the~Yevus~of **33:3** TO LAND ISSUE⁽ᵛ⁾~*ing*⁽ᶠˢ⁾ FAT and~HONEY GIVEN.THAT NOT *I~will~*GO.UP⁽ᵛ⁾ in~INSIDE~ you⁽ᵐˢ⁾ GIVEN.THAT PEOPLE HARD NECK YOU⁽ᵐˢ⁾ OTHERWISE *I~will~much~* FINISH⁽ᵛ⁾~you⁽ᵐˢ⁾ in~the~ROAD **33:4** and~*he~will~*HEAR⁽ᵛ⁾ the~PEOPLE AT the~WORD the~DYSFUNCTIONAL the~THIS and~*they*⁽ᵐ⁾~*will~self~*MOURN⁽ᵛ⁾ and~NOT *they~did~*SET.DOWN⁽ᵛ⁾ MAN TRAPPINGS~him UPON~ him **33:5** and~*he~will~*SAY⁽ᵛ⁾ **YHWH** TO Mosheh *!*⁽ᵐˢ⁾~SAY⁽ᵛ⁾ TO SON~s Yisra'eyl YOU⁽ᵐᵖ⁾ PEOPLE HARD NECK MOMENT UNIT *I~will~*GO.UP⁽ᵛ⁾ in~ INSIDE~you⁽ᵐˢ⁾ and~*I~will~much~*FINISH⁽ᵛ⁾~you⁽ᵐˢ⁾ and~NOW *!*⁽ᵐˢ⁾~*make~* GO.DOWN⁽ᵛ⁾ TRAPPINGS~you⁽ᵐˢ⁾ from~UPON~you⁽ᵐˢ⁾ and~*I~will~*KNOW⁽ᵛ⁾~ & WHAT *I~will~*DO⁽ᵛ⁾ to~you⁽ᶠˢ⁾ **33:6** and~*they*⁽ᵐ⁾~*will~self~*DELIVER⁽ᵛ⁾ SON~s Yisra'eyl AT TRAPPINGS~them⁽ᵐ⁾ from~HILL Hhorev **33:7** and~Mosheh *he~ will~*TAKE⁽ᵛ⁾ AT the~TENT and~*he~did~*EXTEND⁽ᵛ⁾ to~him from~OUTSIDE to~ the~CAMP >~*make~*BE.FAR⁽ᵛ⁾ FROM the~CAMP and~*he~did~*CALL.OUT⁽ᵛ⁾ to~him TENT APPOINTED and~*he~did~*EXIST⁽ᵛ⁾ ALL *much~*SEARCH.OUT⁽ᵛ⁾~ *ing*⁽ᵐˢ⁾ **YHWH** *he~will~*GO.OUT⁽ᵛ⁾ TO TENT APPOINTED WHICH from~ OUTSIDE to~the~CAMP **33:8** and~*he~did~*EXIST⁽ᵛ⁾ like~>~GO.OUT⁽ᵛ⁾ Mosheh TO the~TENT *they*⁽ᵐ⁾~*will~*RISE⁽ᵛ⁾ ALL the~PEOPLE and~*they~did~ be~*STAND.UP⁽ᵛ⁾ MAN OPENING TENT~him and~*they~did~make~*STARE⁽ᵛ⁾ AFTER Mosheh UNTIL >~COME⁽ᵛ⁾~him the~TENT~unto **33:9** and~*he~did~* EXIST⁽ᵛ⁾ like~>~COME⁽ᵛ⁾ Mosheh the~TENT~unto *he~will~*GO.DOWN⁽ᵛ⁾ PILLAR the~CLOUD and~*he~did~*STAND⁽ᵛ⁾ OPENING the~TENT and~*he~did~ much~*SPEAK⁽ᵛ⁾ WITH Mosheh **33:10** and~*he~did~*SEE⁽ᵛ⁾ ALL the~PEOPLE AT PILLAR the~CLOUD STAND⁽ᵛ⁾~*ing*⁽ᵐˢ⁾ OPENING the~TENT and~*he~did~*RISE⁽ᵛ⁾ ALL the~PEOPLE and~*they~did~self~*BEND.DOWN⁽ᵛ⁾ MAN OPENING TENT~ him **33:11** and~*he~did~much~*SPEAK⁽ᵛ⁾ **YHWH** TO Mosheh FACE~s TO FACE~s like~WHICH *he~will~much~*SPEAK⁽ᵛ⁾ MAN TO COMPANION~him and~*he~did~*TURN.BACK⁽ᵛ⁾ TO the~CAMP and~*much~*MINISTER⁽ᵛ⁾~*ing*⁽ᵐˢ⁾~ him Yehoshu'a SON Nun YOUNG.MAN NOT *he~will~make~*MOVE.AWAY⁽ᵛ⁾ from~MIDST the~TENT **33:12** and~*he~will~*SAY⁽ᵛ⁾ Mosheh TO **YHWH** *!*⁽ᵐˢ⁾~ SEE⁽ᵛ⁾ YOU⁽ᵐˢ⁾ SAY⁽ᵛ⁾~*ing*⁽ᵐˢ⁾ TO~me *!*⁽ᵐˢ⁾~*make~*GO.UP⁽ᵛ⁾ AT the~PEOPLE the~THIS and~YOU⁽ᵐˢ⁾ NOT *you*⁽ᵐˢ⁾~*did~make~*KNOW⁽ᵛ⁾~me AT WHICH

you⁽ᵐˢ⁾~will~SEND⁽ⱽ⁾ WITH~me and~YOU⁽ᵐˢ⁾ *you⁽ᵐˢ⁾~did*~SAY⁽ⱽ⁾ *I~did~*
KNOW⁽ⱽ⁾*~you*⁽ᵐˢ⁾ in~TITLE and~ALSO *you⁽ᵐˢ⁾~did~*FIND⁽ⱽ⁾ BEAUTY in~EYE~s2~
me **33:13** and~NOW IF PLEASE *I~did~*FIND⁽ⱽ⁾ BEAUTY in~EYE~s2~you⁽ᵐˢ⁾
*!⁽ᵐˢ⁾~make~*KNOW⁽ⱽ⁾~me PLEASE AT ROAD~you⁽ᵐˢ⁾ and~*I~will~*KNOW⁽ⱽ⁾*~*
you⁽ᵐˢ⁾ to~THAT *I~will~*FIND⁽ⱽ⁾ BEAUTY in~EYE~s2~you⁽ᵐˢ⁾ and~ *!⁽ᵐˢ⁾~*SEE⁽ⱽ⁾
GIVEN.THAT PEOPLE~you⁽ᵐˢ⁾ the~NATION the~THIS **33:14** and~*he~will~*
SAY⁽ⱽ⁾ FACE~s~me *they⁽ᵐ⁾~will~*WALK⁽ⱽ⁾ and~*I~did~make~*REST⁽ⱽ⁾ to~you⁽ᶠˢ⁾
33:15 and~*he~will~*SAY⁽ⱽ⁾ TO~him IF WITHOUT FACE~s~you⁽ᵐˢ⁾ WALK⁽ⱽ⁾~
ing⁽ᵐᵖ⁾ DO.NOT *you⁽ᵐˢ⁾~will~make~*GO.UP⁽ⱽ⁾~us from~THIS **33:16** and~in~
WHAT *he~will~be~*KNOW⁽ⱽ⁾ THEN GIVEN.THAT *I~did~*FIND⁽ⱽ⁾ BEAUTY in~
EYE~s2~you⁽ᵐˢ⁾ I and~PEOPLE~you⁽ᵐˢ⁾ ?~NOT in~>~WALK⁽ⱽ⁾~you⁽ᵐˢ⁾ WITH~us
and~*we~did~be~*BE.DISTINCT⁽ⱽ⁾ I and~PEOPLE~you⁽ᵐˢ⁾ from~ALL the~
PEOPLE WHICH UPON FACE~s the~GROUND **33:17** and~*he~will~*SAY⁽ⱽ⁾
YHWH TO Mosheh ALSO AT the~WORD the~THIS WHICH *you⁽ᵐˢ⁾~did~*much~
SPEAK⁽ⱽ⁾ *I~will~*DO⁽ⱽ⁾ GIVEN.THAT *you⁽ᵐˢ⁾~did~*FIND⁽ⱽ⁾ BEAUTY in~EYE~s2~me
and~*I~will~*KNOW⁽ⱽ⁾*~you*⁽ᵐˢ⁾ in~TITLE **33:18** and~*he~will~*SAY⁽ⱽ⁾ *!⁽ᵐˢ⁾~make~*
SEE⁽ⱽ⁾~me PLEASE AT ARMAMENT~you⁽ᵐˢ⁾ **33:19** and~*he~will~*SAY⁽ⱽ⁾ I *I~will~*
make~CROSS.OVER⁽ⱽ⁾ ALL FUNCTIONAL~me UPON FACE~s~you⁽ᵐˢ⁾ and~*I~*
*did~*CALL.OUT⁽ⱽ⁾ in~TITLE YHWH to~FACE~s~you⁽ᵐˢ⁾ and~*I~did~*
PROVIDE.PROTECTION⁽ⱽ⁾ AT WHICH *I~will~*PROVIDE.PROTECTION⁽ⱽ⁾ and~*I~*
*did~*much~HAVE.COMPASSION⁽ⱽ⁾ AT WHICH *I~will~*much~
HAVE.COMPASSION⁽ⱽ⁾ **33:20** and~*he~will~*SAY⁽ⱽ⁾ NOT *you⁽ᵐˢ⁾~will~*BE.ABLE⁽ⱽ⁾
to~>~SEE⁽ⱽ⁾ AT FACE~s~me GIVEN.THAT NOT *he~will~*SEE⁽ⱽ⁾~me the~
HUMAN and~*he~will~*LIVE⁽ⱽ⁾ **33:21** and~*he~will~*SAY⁽ⱽ⁾ YHWH LOOK AREA
AT~me and~*you⁽ᵐˢ⁾~did~be~*STAND.UP⁽ⱽ⁾ UPON the~BOULDER **33:22** and~
*he~did~*EXIST⁽ⱽ⁾ in~>~CROSS.OVER⁽ⱽ⁾ ARMAMENT~me and~*I~did~*PLACE⁽ⱽ⁾~
you⁽ᵐˢ⁾ in~FISSURE the~BOULDER and~*I~did~*FENCE.AROUND⁽ⱽ⁾ PALM~me
UPON~you⁽ᵐˢ⁾ UNTIL >~CROSS.OVER⁽ⱽ⁾~me **33:23** and~*I~did~make~*
TURN.ASIDE⁽ⱽ⁾ AT PALM~me and~*you⁽ᵐˢ⁾~did~*SEE⁽ⱽ⁾ AT BACK~s~me and~
FACE~s~me NOT *they⁽ᵐ⁾~will~be~*SEE⁽ⱽ⁾

Chapter 34

34:1 and~*he~will~*SAY⁽ⱽ⁾ YHWH TO Mosheh *!⁽ᵐˢ⁾~*SCULPT⁽ⱽ⁾ to~you⁽ᵐˢ⁾ TWO
SLAB~s STONE~s like~FIRST~s and~*I~did~*WRITE⁽ⱽ⁾ UPON the~SLAB~s AT
the~WORD~s WHICH *they~did~*EXIST⁽ⱽ⁾ UPON the~SLAB~s the~FIRST~s
WHICH *you⁽ᵐˢ⁾~did~*CRACK⁽ⱽ⁾ **34:2** and~*!⁽ᵐˢ⁾~*EXIST⁽ⱽ⁾ *be~*PREPARE⁽ⱽ⁾~*ing⁽ᵐˢ⁾*
to~the~MORNING and~*you⁽ᵐˢ⁾~did~*GO.UP⁽ⱽ⁾ in~the~MORNING TO HILL
Sinai and~*you⁽ᵐˢ⁾~did~be~*STAND.UP⁽ⱽ⁾ to~me THERE UPON HEAD the~
HILL **34:3** and~MAN NOT *he~will~*GO.UP⁽ⱽ⁾ WITH~you⁽ᶠˢ⁾ and~ALSO MAN
DO.NOT *he~will~be~*SEE⁽ⱽ⁾ in~ALL the~HILL ALSO the~FLOCKS and~the~
CATTLE DO.NOT *they⁽ᵐ⁾~will~*FEED⁽ⱽ⁾ TO FOREFRONT the~HILL the~
HE **34:4** and~*he~will~*SCULPT⁽ⱽ⁾ TWO SLAB~s STONE~s like~FIRST~s and~*he~*

The Book of Exodus

will~make~DEPART.EARLY^(V) Mosheh in~the~MORNING and~he~will~make~ GO.UP^(V) TO HILL Sinai like~WHICH he~did~much~DIRECT^(V) **YHWH** AT~him and~he~will~TAKE^(V) in~HAND~him TWO SLAB~s STONE~s **34:5** and~he~ will~GO.DOWN^(V) **YHWH** in~CLOUD and~he~will~self~STATION^(V) WITH~him THERE and~he~will~CALL.OUT^(V) in~TITLE **YHWH** **34:6** and~he~will~ CROSS.OVER^(V) **YHWH** UPON FACE~s~him and~he~will~CALL.OUT^(V) **YHWH YHWH** MIGHTY.ONE COMPASSIONATE and~PROTECTIVE SLOW NOSE~s2 and~ABUNDANT KINDNESS and~TRUTH **34:7** PRESERVE^(V)~ing^(ms) KINDNESS to~the~THOUSAND~s LIFT.UP^(V)~ing^(ms) TWISTEDNESS and~OFFENSE and~ FAILURE and~>~much~ACQUIT^(V) NOT he~will~much~ACQUIT^(V) REGISTER^(V)~ ing^(ms) TWISTEDNESS FATHER~s UPON SON~s and~UPON SON~s SON~s UPON THIRD.GENERATION~s and~UPON FOURTH.GENERATION~s **34:8** and~he~will~much~HURRY^(V) Mosheh and~ he~will~BOW.THE.HEAD^(V) LAND~unto and~he~will~self~ BEND.DOWN^(V) **34:9** and~he~will~SAY^(V) IF PLEASE I~did~FIND^(V) BEAUTY in~ EYE~s2~you^(ms) Adonai he~will~WALK^(V) PLEASE Adonai in~INSIDE~us GIVEN.THAT PEOPLE HARD NECK HE and~you^(ms)~will~FORGIVE^(V) to~ TWISTEDNESS~us and~to~FAILURE~us and~you^(ms)~did~INHERIT^(V)~ us **34:10** and~he~will~SAY^(V) LOOK I CUT^(V)~ing^(ms) COVENANT OPPOSITE ALL PEOPLE~you^(ms) I~will~DO^(V) be~PERFORM^(V)~ing^(fp) WHICH NOT they~did~ be~SHAPE^(V) in~ALL the~LAND and~in~ALL the~NATION~s and~he~did~ SEE^(V) ALL the~PEOPLE WHICH YOU^(ms) in~INSIDE~him AT WORK **YHWH** GIVEN.THAT be~FEAR^(V)~ing^(ms) HE WHICH I DO^(V)~ing^(ms) WITH~ you^(fs) **34:11** !^(ms)~SAFEGUARD^(V) to~you^(ms) AT WHICH I much~DIRECT^(V)~ ing^(ms)~you^(ms) the~DAY LOOK~me CAST.OUT^(V)~ing^(ms) from~FACE~s~you^(ms) AT the~Emor~of and~the~Kena'an~of and~the~Hhet~of and~the~Perez~of and~the~Hhiw~of and~the~Yevus~of **34:12** !^(ms)~be~SAFEGUARD^(V) to~ you^(ms) OTHERWISE you^(ms)~will~CUT^(V) COVENANT to~SETTLE^(V)~ing^(ms) the~ LAND WHICH YOU^(ms) he~did~COME^(V) UPON~her OTHERWISE he~will~ EXIST^(V) to~SNARE in~INSIDE~you^(ms) **34:13** GIVEN.THAT AT ALTAR~s~ them^(m) you^(mp)~will~BREAK.DOWN^(V)~must and~AT MONUMENT~s~them^(m) you^(mp)~will~much~CRACK^(V)~must and~AT GROVE~s~him you^(mp)~will~ CUT^(V)~must **34:14** GIVEN.THAT NOT you^(ms)~will~self~BEND.DOWN^(V) to~ MIGHTY.ONE OTHER GIVEN.THAT **YHWH** ZEALOUS TITLE~him MIGHTY.ONE ZEALOUS HE **34:15** OTHERWISE you^(ms)~will~CUT^(V) COVENANT to~ SETTLE^(V)~ing^(ms) the~LAND and~they~did~BE.A.HARLOT^(V) AFTER Elohiym~ them^(m) and~they~did~SACRIFICE^(V) to~Elohiym~them^(m) and~he~did~ CALL.OUT^(V) to~you^(ms) and~you^(ms)~did~EAT^(V) ALTAR~him **34:16** and~ you^(ms)~did~TAKE^(V) from~DAUGHTER~s~him to~SON~s~you^(ms) and~they~ did~BE.A.HARLOT^(V) DAUGHTER~s~him AFTER Elohiym~them^(f) and~they~ did~make~BE.A.HARLOT^(V) AT SON~s~you^(ms) AFTER Elohiym~ them^(f) **34:17** Elohiym CAST.IMAGE NOT you^(ms)~will~DO^(V) to~ you^(fs) **34:18** AT FEAST the~UNLEAVENED.BREAD~s you^(ms)~will~ SAFEGUARD^(V) SEVEN DAY~s you^(ms)~will~EAT^(V) UNLEAVENED.BREAD~s WHICH I~did~much~DIRECT^(V)~you^(ms) to~APPOINTED NEW.MOON the~

Benner's Mechanical Translation of the Torah

GREEN.GRAIN GIVEN.THAT in~NEW.MOON the~GREEN.GRAIN you⁽ᵐˢ⁾~did~ GO.OUT⁽ⱽ⁾ from~Mits'rayim **34:19** ALL BURSTING BOWELS to~me and~ALL LIVESTOCK~you⁽ᵐˢ⁾ you⁽ᵐˢ⁾~will~be~REMEMBER⁽ⱽ⁾ BURSTING OX and~ RAM **34:20** and~BURSTING DONKEY you⁽ᵐˢ⁾~will~RANSOM⁽ⱽ⁾ in~RAM and~IF NOT you⁽ᵐˢ⁾~will~RANSOM⁽ⱽ⁾ and~you⁽ᵐˢ⁾~did~BEHEAD⁽ⱽ⁾~him ALL FIRSTBORN SON~s~you⁽ᵐˢ⁾ you⁽ᵐˢ⁾~will~RANSOM⁽ⱽ⁾ and~NOT they⁽ᵐ⁾~will~ be~SEE⁽ⱽ⁾ FACE~s~me EMPTINESS **34:21** SIX DAY~s you⁽ᵐˢ⁾~will~SERVE⁽ⱽ⁾ and~in~the~DAY the~SEVENTH you⁽ᵐˢ⁾~will~CEASE⁽ⱽ⁾ in~PLOWING and~in~ HARVEST you⁽ᵐˢ⁾~will~CEASE⁽ⱽ⁾ **34:22** and~FEAST WEEK~s you⁽ᵐˢ⁾~will~DO⁽ⱽ⁾ to~you⁽ᵐˢ⁾ FIRST-FRUIT~s HARVEST WHEAT~s and~FEAST the~GATHERING CIRCUIT the~YEAR **34:23** THREE FOOTSTEP~s in~the~YEAR he~will~be~ SEE⁽ⱽ⁾ ALL MEN~you⁽ᵐˢ⁾ AT FACE~s the~LORD **YHWH** Elohiym Yisra'eyl **34:24** GIVEN.THAT I~will~make~POSSESS⁽ⱽ⁾ NATION~s from~ FACE~s~you⁽ᵐˢ⁾ and~I~did~make~WIDEN⁽ⱽ⁾ AT BORDER~you⁽ᵐˢ⁾ and~NOT he~will~CRAVE⁽ⱽ⁾ MAN AT LAND~you⁽ᵐˢ⁾ in~>~GO.UP⁽ⱽ⁾~you⁽ᵐˢ⁾ to~>~be~ SEE⁽ⱽ⁾ AT FACE~s **YHWH** Elohiym~you⁽ᵐˢ⁾ THREE FOOTSTEP~s in~the~ YEAR **34:25** NOT you⁽ᵐˢ⁾~will~SLAY⁽ⱽ⁾ UPON LEAVENED.BREAD BLOOD SACRIFICE~me and~NOT he~will~STAY.THE.NIGHT⁽ⱽ⁾ to~the~MORNING SACRIFICE FEAST the~Pesahh **34:26** SUMMIT FIRST-FRUIT~s GROUND~ you⁽ᵐˢ⁾ you⁽ᵐˢ⁾~will~make~COME⁽ⱽ⁾ HOUSE **YHWH** Elohiym~you⁽ᵐˢ⁾ NOT you⁽ᵐˢ⁾~will~much~BOIL⁽ⱽ⁾ MALE.KID in~the~FAT MOTHER~him **34:27** and~ he~will~SAY⁽ⱽ⁾ **YHWH** TO Mosheh !⁽ᵐˢ⁾~WRITE⁽ⱽ⁾ to~you⁽ᵐˢ⁾ AT the~WORD~s the~THESE GIVEN.THAT UPON MOUTH the~WORD~s the~THESE I~did~ CUT⁽ⱽ⁾ AT~you⁽ᵐˢ⁾ COVENANT and~AT Yisra'eyl **34:28** and~he~will~EXIST⁽ⱽ⁾ THERE WITH **YHWH** FOUR~s DAY and~FOUR~s NIGHT BREAD NOT he~did~ EAT⁽ⱽ⁾ and~WATER~s2 NOT he~did~GULP⁽ⱽ⁾ and~he~will~WRITE⁽ⱽ⁾ UPON the~SLAB~s AT WORD~s the~COVENANT TEN the~WORD~s **34:29** and~he~ will~EXIST⁽ⱽ⁾ in~>~GO.DOWN⁽ⱽ⁾ Mosheh from~HILL Sinai and~TWO SLAB~s the~EVIDENCE in~HAND Mosheh in~>~GO.DOWN⁽ⱽ⁾~him FROM the~HILL and~Mosheh NOT he~did~KNOW⁽ⱽ⁾ GIVEN.THAT he~did~HAVE.HORNS⁽ⱽ⁾ SKIN FACE~s~him in~>~much~SPEAK⁽ⱽ⁾~him AT~him **34:30** and~he~will~ SEE⁽ⱽ⁾ Aharon and~ALL SON~s Yisra'eyl AT Mosheh and~LOOK he~did~ HAVE.HORNS⁽ⱽ⁾ SKIN FACE~s~him and~they⁽ᵐ⁾~will~FEAR⁽ⱽ⁾ from~>~ DRAW.NEAR⁽ⱽ⁾ TO~him **34:31** and~he~will~CALL.OUT⁽ⱽ⁾ TO~them⁽ᵐ⁾ Mosheh and~they⁽ᵐ⁾~will~TURN.BACK⁽ⱽ⁾ TO~him Aharon and~ALL the~CAPTAIN~s in~ the~COMPANY and~he~will~much~SPEAK⁽ⱽ⁾ Mosheh TO~ them⁽ᵐ⁾ **34:32** and~AFTER SO they~did~be~DRAW.NEAR⁽ⱽ⁾ ALL SON~s Yisra'eyl and~he~will~much~DIRECT⁽ⱽ⁾~them⁽ᵐ⁾ AT ALL WHICH he~did~ much~SPEAK⁽ⱽ⁾ **YHWH** AT~him in~HILL Sinai **34:33** and~he~will~much~ FINISH⁽ⱽ⁾ Mosheh >~much~SPEAK⁽ⱽ⁾ AT~them⁽ᵐ⁾ and~he~will~GIVE⁽ⱽ⁾ UPON FACE~s~him HOOD **34:34** and~in~>~COME⁽ⱽ⁾ Mosheh to~FACE~s **YHWH** to~ >~much~SPEAK⁽ⱽ⁾ AT~him he~will~make~TURN.ASIDE⁽ⱽ⁾ AT the~HOOD UNTIL >~GO.OUT⁽ⱽ⁾~him and~he~will~GO.OUT⁽ⱽ⁾ and~he~did~much~ SPEAK⁽ⱽ⁾ TO SON~s Yisra'eyl AT WHICH he~will~be~much~ DIRECT⁽ⱽ⁾ **34:35** and~they~did~SEE⁽ⱽ⁾ SON~s Yisra'eyl AT FACE~s Mosheh

GIVEN.THAT *he~did~*HAVE.HORNS^(V) SKIN FACE~s Mosheh and~*he~did~ make~*TURN.BACK^(V) Mosheh AT the~HOOD UPON FACE~s~him UNTIL >~ COME^(V)~him to~>~*much~*SPEAK^(V) AT~him

Chapter 35

35:1 and~*he~will~*ASSEMBLE^(V) Mosheh AT ALL COMPANY SON~s Yisra'eyl and~*he~will~*SAY^(V) TO~them^(m) THESE the~WORD~s WHICH *he~did~much~* DIRECT^(V) **YHWH** to~>~DO^(V) AT~them^(m) **35:2** SIX DAY~s *she~will~be~*DO^(V) BUSINESS and~*in~the~*DAY the~SEVENTH *he~will~*EXIST^(V) to~you^(mp) SPECIAL CEASING REST.PERIOD to~**YHWH** ALL the~DO^(V)~*ing*^(ms) in~him BUSINESS *he~will~be~make~*DIE^(V) **35:3** NOT *you*^(mp)*~will~much~*BURN^(V) FIRE in~ALL SETTLING~s~you^(mp) in~DAY the~CEASING **35:4** and~*he~will~* SAY^(V) Mosheh TO ALL COMPANY SON~s Yisra'eyl to~>~SAY^(V) THIS the~ WORD WHICH *he~did~much~*DIRECT^(V) **YHWH** to~>~SAY^(V) **35:5** !^(mp)~TAKE^(V) from~AT~you^(mp) OFFERING to~**YHWH** ALL WILLING HEART~him *he~will~ make~*COME^(V)~her AT OFFERING **YHWH** GOLD and~SILVER and~ COPPER **35:6** and~BLUE and~PURPLE and~KERMES SCARLET and~LINEN and~SHE-GOAT~s **35:7** and~SKIN~s BUCK~s *be~much~*BE.RED^(V)~*ing*^(mp) and~SKIN~s DEER~s and~TREE~s ACACIA~s **35:8** and~OIL to~the~LUMINARY and~in~SWEET.SPICE~s to~OIL the~OINTMENT and~to~INCENSE.SMOKE the~AROMATIC.SPICE~s **35:9** and~STONE~s ONYX and~STONE~s INSTALLATION~s to~the~EPHOD and~to~the~BREASTPLATE **35:10** and~ALL SKILLED.ONE HEART in~you^(mp) *they*^(m)*~will~*COME^(V) and~*they*^(m)*~will~*DO^(V) AT ALL WHICH *he~did~much~*DIRECT^(V) **YHWH** **35:11** AT the~DWELLING AT TENT~him and~AT ROOF.COVERING~him AT HOOK~s~him and~AT BOARD~s~him AT WOOD.BAR~s~him AT PILLAR~s~him and~AT FOOTING~s~ him **35:12** AT the~BOX and~AT STRAND~s~him AT the~LID and~AT TENT.CURTAIN the~SCREEN **35:13** AT the~TABLE and~AT STRAND~s~him and~AT ALL UTENSIL~s~him and~AT BREAD the~FACE~s **35:14** and~AT LAMPSTAND the~LUMINARY and~AT UTENSIL~s~her and~AT LAMP~s~her and~AT OIL the~LUMINARY **35:15** and~AT ALTAR the~INCENSE.SMOKE and~AT STRAND~s~him and~AT OIL the~OINTMENT and~AT INCENSE.SMOKE the~AROMATIC.SPICE~s and~AT SCREEN the~OPENING to~ OPENING the~DWELLING **35:16** AT ALTAR the~ASCENSION.OFFERING and~ AT GRATE the~COPPER WHICH to~him AT STRAND~s~him and~AT ALL UTENSIL~s~him AT the~CAULDRON and~AT BASE~him **35:17** AT SLING~s the~COURTYARD AT PILLAR~s~him and~AT FOOTING~s~her and~AT SCREEN GATE the~COURTYARD **35:18** AT TENT.PEG~s the~DWELLING and~AT TENT.PEG~s the~COURTYARD and~AT STRING~s~them^(m) **35:19** AT GARMENT~s the~BRAIDED.WORK to~>~*much~*MINISTER^(V) in~the~SPECIAL AT GARMENT~s the~SPECIAL to~Aharon the~ADMINISTRATOR and~AT GARMENT~s SON~s~him to~>~*much~*ADORN^(V) **35:20** and~*they*^(m)*~will~*

GO.OUT⁽ᵛ⁾ ALL COMPANY SON~s Yisra'eyl from~to~FACE~s
Mosheh **35:21** and~*they*⁽ᵐ⁾~will~COME⁽ᵛ⁾ ALL MAN WHICH *he~did~*
LIFT.UP⁽ᵛ⁾~him HEART~him and~ALL WHICH *she~did~*OFFER.WILLINGLY⁽ᵛ⁾
WIND~him AT~him they~did~make~COME⁽ᵛ⁾ AT OFFERING **YHWH** to~
BUSINESS TENT APPOINTED and~to~ALL SERVICE~him and~to~GARMENT~s
the~SPECIAL **35:22** and~*they*⁽ᵐ⁾~will~COME⁽ᵛ⁾ the~MAN~s UPON the~
WOMAN~s ALL WILLING HEART they~did~make~COME⁽ᵛ⁾ NOSE.RING and~
ORNAMENTAL.RING and~RING and~ARM.BAND ALL UTENSIL GOLD and~ALL
MAN WHICH *he~did~make~*WAVE⁽ᵛ⁾ WAVING GOLD to~**YHWH 35:23** and~
ALL MAN WHICH *he~did~be~*FIND⁽ᵛ⁾ AT~him BLUE and~PURPLE and~
KERMES SCARLET and~LINEN and~SHE-GOAT~s and~SKIN~s BUCK~s *be~
much~*BE.RED⁽ᵛ⁾~*ing*⁽ᵐᵖ⁾ and~SKIN~s DEER~s they~did~make~
COME⁽ᵛ⁾ **35:24** ALL *make~*RAISE.UP⁽ᵛ⁾~*ing*⁽ᵐˢ⁾ OFFERING SILVER and~COPPER
they~did~make~COME⁽ᵛ⁾ AT OFFERING **YHWH** and~ALL WHICH *he~did~be~*
FIND⁽ᵛ⁾ AT~him TREE~s ACACIA~s to~ALL BUSINESS the~SERVICE they~did~
make~COME⁽ᵛ⁾ **35:25** and~ALL WOMAN SKILLED.ONE HEART in~HAND~s~
her they~did~SPIN⁽ᵛ⁾ and~*they*⁽ᵐ⁾~will~make~COME⁽ᵛ⁾ YARN AT the~BLUE
and~AT the~PURPLE AT KERMES the~SCARLET and~AT the~
LINEN **35:26** and~ALL the~WOMAN~s WHICH *he~did~*LIFT.UP⁽ᵛ⁾ HEART~
them⁽ᶠ⁾ AT~them⁽ᶠ⁾ in~SKILL they~did~SPIN⁽ᵛ⁾ AT the~SHE-GOAT~s
35:27 and~the~CAPTAIN~s they~did~make~COME⁽ᵛ⁾ AT STONE~s the~ONYX
and~AT STONE~s the~INSTALLATION~s to~the~EPHOD and~to~the~
BREASTPLATE **35:28** and~AT the~SWEET.SPICE and~AT the~OIL to~the~
LUMINARY and~to~OIL the~OINTMENT and~to~INCENSE.SMOKE the~
AROMATIC.SPICE~s **35:29** ALL MAN and~WOMAN WHICH *he~did~*
OFFER.WILLINGLY⁽ᵛ⁾ HEART~them⁽ᵐ⁾ AT~them⁽ᵐ⁾ to~>~*make~*COME⁽ᵛ⁾ to~
ALL the~BUSINESS WHICH *he~did~much~*DIRECT⁽ᵛ⁾ **YHWH** to~>~DO⁽ᵛ⁾ in~
HAND Mosheh they~did~make~COME⁽ᵛ⁾ SON~s Yisra'eyl
FREEWILL.OFFERING to~**YHWH 35:30** and~*he~will~*SAY⁽ᵛ⁾ Mosheh TO
SON~s Yisra'eyl !⁽ᵐᵖ⁾~SEE⁽ᵛ⁾ *he~did~*CALL.OUT⁽ᵛ⁾ **YHWH** in~TITLE Betsaleyl
SON Uriy SON Hhur to~BRANCH Yehudah **35:31** and~*he~will~much~*FILL⁽ᵛ⁾
AT~him WIND Elohiym in~SKILL in~INTELLIGENCE and~in~DISCERNMENT
and~in~ALL BUSINESS **35:32** and~to~>~THINK⁽ᵛ⁾ INVENTION~s to~>~DO⁽ᵛ⁾
in~the~GOLD and~in~the~SILVER and~in~the~COPPER **35:33** and~in~the~
ENGRAVING STONE to~>~*much~*FILL⁽ᵛ⁾ and~in~the~ENGRAVING TREE to~>~
DO⁽ᵛ⁾ in~ALL BUSINESS INVENTION **35:34** and~to~>~*make~*THROW⁽ᵛ⁾ *he~
did~*GIVE⁽ᵛ⁾ in~HEART~him HE and~Ahaliyav SON Ahhiysamahh to~BRANCH
Dan **35:35** *he~did~much~*FILL⁽ᵛ⁾ AT~them⁽ᵐ⁾ SKILL HEART to~>~DO⁽ᵛ⁾ ALL
BUSINESS ENGRAVER and~THINK⁽ᵛ⁾~*ing*⁽ᵐˢ⁾ and~EMBROIDER⁽ᵛ⁾~*ing*⁽ᵐˢ⁾ in~
the~BLUE and~in~the~PURPLE in~KERMES the~SCARLET and~in~the~LINEN
and~BRAID⁽ᵛ⁾~*ing*⁽ᵐˢ⁾ DO⁽ᵛ⁾~*ing*⁽ᵐᵖ⁾ ALL BUSINESS and~THINK⁽ᵛ⁾~*ing*⁽ᵐᵖ⁾
INVENTION~s

Chapter 36

36:1 and~*he~did~*DO⁽ᵛ⁾ Betsaleyl and~Ahaliyav and~ALL MAN SKILLED.ONE HEART WHICH *he~did~*GIVE⁽ᵛ⁾ YHWH SKILL and~INTELLIGENCE in~THEY⁽ᵐ⁾ to~>~KNOW⁽ᵛ⁾ to~>~DO⁽ᵛ⁾ AT ALL BUSINESS SERVICE the~SPECIAL to~ALL WHICH *he~did~much~*DIRECT⁽ᵛ⁾ YHWH **36:2** and~*he~will~*CALL.OUT⁽ᵛ⁾ Mosheh TO Betsaleyl and~TO Ahaliyav and~TO ALL MAN SKILLED.ONE HEART WHICH *he~did~*GIVE⁽ᵛ⁾ YHWH SKILL in~HEART~him ALL WHICH *he~did~*LIFT.UP⁽ᵛ⁾~him HEART~him to~>~COME.NEAR⁽ᵛ⁾ TO the~BUSINESS to~>~DO⁽ᵛ⁾ AT~her **36:3** and~*they*⁽ᵐ⁾~*will~*TAKE⁽ᵛ⁾ from~to~FACE~s Mosheh AT ALL the~OFFERING WHICH *they~did~make~*COME⁽ᵛ⁾ SON~s Yisra'eyl to~BUSINESS SERVICE the~SPECIAL to~>~DO⁽ᵛ⁾ AT~her and~THEY⁽ᵐ⁾ *they~did~make~*COME⁽ᵛ⁾ TO~him YET.AGAIN FREEWILL.OFFERING in~the~MORNING in~the~MORNING **36:4** and~*they*⁽ᵐ⁾~*will~*COME⁽ᵛ⁾ ALL the~SKILLED.ONE~s the~DO⁽ᵛ⁾~*ing*⁽ᵐᵖ⁾ AT ALL BUSINESS the~SPECIAL MAN MAN from~BUSINESS~him WHICH THEY⁽ᵐ⁾ DO⁽ᵛ⁾~*ing*⁽ᵐᵖ⁾ **36:5** and~*they*⁽ᵐ⁾~*will~*SAY⁽ᵛ⁾ TO Mosheh to~>~SAY⁽ᵛ⁾ *make~*INCREASE.IN.NUMBER⁽ᵛ⁾~*ing*⁽ᵐᵖ⁾ the~PEOPLE to~>~*make~*COME⁽ᵛ⁾ from~SUFFICIENT the~SERVICE to~the~BUSINESS WHICH *he~did~much~*DIRECT⁽ᵛ⁾ YHWH to~>~DO⁽ᵛ⁾ AT~her **36:6** and~*he~will~much~*DIRECT⁽ᵛ⁾ Mosheh and~*they*⁽ᵐ⁾~*will~make~*CROSS.OVER⁽ᵛ⁾ VOICE in~the~CAMP to~>~SAY⁽ᵛ⁾ MAN and~WOMAN DO.NOT *they*⁽ᵐ⁾~*will~*DO⁽ᵛ⁾ YET.AGAIN BUSINESS to~OFFERING the~SPECIAL and~*he~will~be~*RESTRICT⁽ᵛ⁾ the~PEOPLE from~>~*make~*COME⁽ᵛ⁾ **36:7** and~the~BUSINESS *she~did~*EXIST⁽ᵛ⁾ SUFFICIENT~them⁽ᵐ⁾ to~ALL the~BUSINESS to~>~DO⁽ᵛ⁾ AT~her and~>~*make~*LEAVE.BEHIND⁽ᵛ⁾ **36:8** and~*they*⁽ᵐ⁾~*will~*DO⁽ᵛ⁾ ALL SKILLED.ONE HEART in~DO⁽ᵛ⁾~*ing*⁽ᵐᵖ⁾ the~BUSINESS AT the~DWELLING TEN CURTAIN~s LINEN *be~make~*TWIST.TOGETHER⁽ᵛ⁾~*ing*⁽ᵐˢ⁾ and~BLUE and~PURPLE and~KERMES SCARLET KERUV~s WORK THINK⁽ᵛ⁾~*ing*⁽ᵐˢ⁾ *he~did~*DO⁽ᵛ⁾ AT~them⁽ᵐ⁾ **36:9** LENGTH the~CURTAIN the~UNIT EIGHT and~TEN~s in~the~AMMAH and~WIDTH FOUR in~the~AMMAH the~CURTAIN the~UNIT MEASUREMENT UNIT to~ALL the~CURTAIN~s **36:10** and~*he~will~much~*COUPLE⁽ᵛ⁾ AT FIVE the~CURTAIN~s UNIT TO UNIT and~FIVE CURTAIN~s *he~did~much~*COUPLE⁽ᵛ⁾ UNIT TO UNIT **36:11** and~*he~will~*DO⁽ᵛ⁾ LOOP~s BLUE UPON LIP the~CURTAIN the~UNIT from~EXTREMITY in~the~JOINT SO *he~did~*DO⁽ᵛ⁾ in~LIP the~CURTAIN the~OUTER in~the~JOINT the~SECOND **36:12** FIVE~s LOOP~s *he~did~*DO⁽ᵛ⁾ in~the~CURTAIN the~UNIT and~FIVE~s LOOP~s *he~did~*DO⁽ᵛ⁾ in~EXTREMITY the~CURTAIN WHICH in~the~JOINT the~SECOND *make~*RECEIVE⁽ᵛ⁾~*ing*⁽ᶠᵖ⁾ the~LOOP~s UNIT TO UNIT **36:13** and~*he~will~*DO⁽ᵛ⁾ FIVE~s HOOK~s GOLD and~*he~will~much~*COUPLE⁽ᵛ⁾ AT the~CURTAIN~s UNIT TO UNIT in~the~HOOK~s and~*he~will~*EXIST⁽ᵛ⁾ the~DWELLING UNIT **36:14** and~*he~will~*DO⁽ᵛ⁾ CURTAIN~s SHE-GOAT~s to~TENT UPON the~DWELLING ONE TEN CURTAIN~s *he~did~*DO⁽ᵛ⁾ AT~them⁽ᵐ⁾ **36:15** LENGTH the~CURTAIN the~UNIT THREE~s in~the~AMMAH and~FOUR AMMAH~s WIDTH the~CURTAIN the~UNIT

MEASUREMENT UNIT to~ONE TEN CURTAIN~s **36:16** and~he~will~much~
COUPLE$^{(V)}$ AT FIVE the~CURTAIN~s to~STRAND and~AT SIX the~CURTAIN~s
to~STRAND **36:17** and~he~will~DO$^{(V)}$ LOOP~s FIVE~s UPON LIP the~
CURTAIN the~OUTER in~the~JOINT and~FIVE~s LOOP~s he~did~DO$^{(V)}$ UPON
LIP the~CURTAIN the~COUPLING the~SECOND **36:18** and~he~will~DO$^{(V)}$
HOOK~s COPPER FIVE~s to~>~much~COUPLE$^{(V)}$ AT the~TENT to~>~EXIST$^{(V)}$
UNIT **36:19** and~he~will~DO$^{(V)}$ ROOF.COVERING to~the~TENT SKIN~s
BUCK~s be~much~BE.RED$^{(V)}$~ing$^{(mp)}$ and~ROOF.COVERING SKIN~s DEER~s
from~to~UPWARD~unto **36:20** and~he~will~DO$^{(V)}$ AT the~BOARD~s to~
the~DWELLING TREE~s ACACIA~s STAND$^{(V)}$~ing$^{(mp)}$ **36:21** TEN AMMAH~s
LENGTH the~BOARD and~AMMAH and~HALF the~AMMAH WIDTH the~
BOARD the~UNIT **36:22** TWO HAND~s to~the~BOARD the~UNIT be~much~
JOINED.TOGETHER$^{(V)}$~ing$^{(fp)}$ UNIT TO UNIT SO he~did~DO$^{(V)}$ to~ALL BOARD~s
the~DWELLING **36:23** and~he~will~DO$^{(V)}$ AT the~BOARD~s to~the~
DWELLING TEN~s BOARD~s to~EDGE SOUTH SOUTHWARD~
unto **36:24** and~FOUR~s FOOTING~s SILVER he~did~DO$^{(V)}$ UNDER TEN~s
the~BOARD~s TWO FOOTING~s UNDER the~BOARD the~UNIT to~TWO
HAND~s~him and~TWO FOOTING~s UNDER the~BOARD the~UNIT to~TWO
HAND~s~him **36:25** and~to~RIB the~DWELLING the~SECOND to~EDGE
NORTH he~did~DO$^{(V)}$ TEN~s BOARD~s **36:26** and~FOUR~s FOOTING~s~
them$^{(m)}$ SILVER TWO FOOTING~s UNDER the~BOARD the~UNIT and~TWO
FOOTING~s UNDER the~BOARD the~UNIT **36:27** and~to~FLANK~s2 the~
DWELLING SEA~unto he~did~DO$^{(V)}$ SIX BOARD~s **36:28** and~TWO BOARD~s
he~did~DO$^{(V)}$ to~CORNER.POST~s the~DWELLING in~the~FLANK~
s2 **36:29** and~they~did~EXIST$^{(V)}$ BE.DOUBLE$^{(V)}$~ing$^{(mp)}$ from~to~BENEATH
and~TOGETHER they$^{(m)}$~will~EXIST$^{(V)}$ WHOLE TO HEAD~him TO the~RING
the~UNIT SO he~did~DO$^{(V)}$ to~TWO~them$^{(m)}$ to~TWO the~
BUTTRESS~s **36:30** and~they~did~EXIST$^{(V)}$ EIGHT BOARD~s and~
FOOTING~s~them$^{(m)}$ SILVER SIX TEN FOOTING~s TWO FOOTING~s TWO
FOOTING~s UNDER the~BOARD the~UNIT **36:31** and~he~will~DO$^{(V)}$
WOOD.BAR~s TREE~s ACACIA~s FIVE to~BOARD~s RIB the~DWELLING the~
UNIT **36:32** and~FIVE WOOD.BAR~s to~BOARD~s RIB the~DWELLING the~
SECOND and~FIVE WOOD.BAR~s to~BOARD~s the~DWELLING to~the~
FLANK~s2 SEA~unto **36:33** and~he~will~DO$^{(V)}$ AT the~WOOD.BAR the~
MIDDLEMOST to~>~FLEE.AWAY$^{(V)}$ in~MIDST the~BOARD~s FROM the~
EXTREMITY TO the~EXTREMITY **36:34** and~AT the~BOARD~s he~did~much~
OVERLAY$^{(V)}$ GOLD and~AT RING~s~them$^{(m)}$ he~did~DO$^{(V)}$ GOLD HOUSE~s to~
the~WOOD.BAR~s and~he~will~much~OVERLAY$^{(V)}$ AT the~WOOD.BAR~s
GOLD **36:35** and~he~will~DO$^{(V)}$ AT the~TENT.CURTAIN BLUE and~PURPLE
and~KERMES SCARLET and~LINEN be~make~TWIST.TOGETHER$^{(V)}$~ing$^{(ms)}$
WORK THINK$^{(V)}$~ing$^{(ms)}$ he~did~DO$^{(V)}$ AT~her KERUV~s **36:36** and~he~will~
DO$^{(V)}$ to~her FOUR PILLAR~s ACACIA~s and~he~will~much~OVERLAY$^{(V)}$~
them$^{(m)}$ GOLD and~PEG~s~them$^{(m)}$ GOLD and~he~will~POUR.DOWN$^{(V)}$ to~
them$^{(m)}$ FOUR FOOTING~s SILVER **36:37** and~he~will~DO$^{(V)}$ SCREEN to~
OPENING the~TENT BLUE and~PURPLE and~KERMES SCARLET and~LINEN

The Book of Exodus

*be~make~*TWIST.TOGETHER^(V)~*ing*^(ms) WORK EMBROIDER^(V)~*ing*^(ms)
36:38 and~AT PILLAR~s~him FIVE and~AT and~PEG~s~them^(m) and~*he~did~ much~*OVERLAY^(V) HEAD~s~them^(m) and~BINDER~s~them^(m) GOLD and~ FOOTING~s~them^(m) FIVE COPPER

Chapter 37

37:1 and~*he~will~*DO^(V) Betsaleyl AT the~BOX TREE~s ACACIA~s AMMAH~s2 and~HALF LENGTH~him and~AMMAH and~HALF WIDTH~him and~AMMAH and~HALF HEIGHT~him **37:2** and~*he~will~much~*OVERLAY^(V)~him GOLD CLEAN from~HOUSE and~from~OUTSIDE and~*he~will~*DO^(V) to~him MOLDING GOLD ALL.AROUND **37:3** and~*he~will~*POUR.DOWN^(V) to~him FOUR RING~s GOLD UPON FOUR FOOTSTEP~s~him and~TWO RING~s UPON RIB~him the~UNIT and~TWO RING~s UPON RIB~him the~ SECOND **37:4** and~*he~will~*DO^(V) STRAND~s TREE~s ACACIA~s and~*he~will~ much~*OVERLAY^(V) AT~them^(m) GOLD **37:5** and~*he~will~make~*COME^(V) AT the~STRAND~s in~the~RING~s UPON RIB~s the~BOX to~>~LIFT.UP^(V) AT the~BOX **37:6** and~*he~will~*DO^(V) LID GOLD CLEAN AMMAH~s2 and~HALF LENGTH~her and~AMMAH and~HALF WIDTH~her **37:7** and~*he~will~*DO^(V) TWO KERUV~s GOLD BEATEN.WORK *he~did~*DO^(V) AT~them^(m) from~TWO EXTREMITY~s the~LID **37:8** KERUV UNIT from~EXTREMITY from~THIS and~ KERUV UNIT from~EXTREMITY from~THIS FROM the~LID *he~did~*DO^(V) AT the~KERUV~s from~TWO EXTREMITY~s~him **37:9** and~*they*^(m)~*will~*EXIST^(V) the~KERUV~s SPREAD.OUT^(V)~*ing*^(mp) WING~s2 to~UPWARD~unto FENCE.AROUND^(V)~*ing*^(mp) in~WING~s~them^(m) UPON the~LID and~FACE~s~ them^(m) MAN TO BROTHER~him TO the~LID *they~did~*EXIST^(V) FACE~s the~ KERUV~s **37:10** and~*he~will~*DO^(V) AT the~TABLE TREE~s ACACIA~s AMMAH~s2 LENGTH~him and~AMMAH WIDTH~him and~AMMAH and~ HALF HEIGHT~him **37:11** and~*he~will~much~*OVERLAY^(V) AT~him GOLD CLEAN and~*he~will~*DO^(V) to~him MOLDING GOLD ALL.AROUND **37:12** and~ *he~will~*DO^(V) to~him RIM HAND.SPAN ALL.AROUND and~*he~will~*DO^(V) MOLDING GOLD to~RIM~him ALL.AROUND **37:13** and~*he~will~* POUR.DOWN^(V) to~him FOUR RING~s GOLD and~*he~will~*GIVE^(V) AT the~ RING~s UPON FOUR the~EDGE~s WHICH to~FOUR FOOT~s2~him **37:14** to~ ALONGSIDE the~RIM *they~did~*EXIST^(V) the~RING~s HOUSE~s to~the~ STRAND~s to~>~LIFT.UP^(V) AT the~TABLE **37:15** and~*he~will~*DO^(V) AT the~ STRAND~s TREE~s ACACIA~s and~*he~will~much~*OVERLAY^(V) AT~them^(m) GOLD to~>~LIFT.UP^(V) AT the~TABLE **37:16** and~*he~will~*DO^(V) AT the~ UTENSIL~s WHICH UPON the~TABLE AT PLATTER~s~him and~AT PALM~s~ him and~AT SACRIFICIAL.BOWL~s~him and~AT the~JUG~s WHICH *he~will~ be~make~*POUR^(V) in~them^(f) GOLD CLEAN **37:17** and~*he~will~*DO^(V) AT the~ LAMPSTAND GOLD CLEAN BEATEN.WORK *he~did~*DO^(V) AT the~LAMPSTAND MIDSECTION~her and~STALK~her BOWL~s~her KNOB~s~her and~BUD~s~

her FROM~her *they~did*~EXIST⁽ᵛ⁾ **37:18** and~SIX STALK~s GO.OUT⁽ᵛ⁾~*ing*⁽ᵐᵖ⁾ from~SIDE~s~her THREE STALK~s LAMPSTAND from~SIDE~her the~UNIT and~THREE STALK~s LAMPSTAND from~SIDE~her the~ SECOND **37:19** THREE BOWL~s *be~much*~BE.ALMOND.SHAPED⁽ᵛ⁾~*ing*⁽ᵐᵖ⁾ in~ the~STALK the~UNIT KNOB and~BUD and~THREE BOWL~s *be~much*~ BE.ALMOND.SHAPED⁽ᵛ⁾~*ing*⁽ᵐᵖ⁾ in~STALK UNIT KNOB and~BUD SO to~SIX the~STALK~s the~GO.OUT⁽ᵛ⁾~*ing*⁽ᵐᵖ⁾ FROM the~LAMPSTAND **37:20** and~in~ the~LAMPSTAND FOUR BOWL~s *be~much*~BE.ALMOND.SHAPED⁽ᵛ⁾~*ing*⁽ᵐᵖ⁾ KNOB~s~her and~BUD~s~her **37:21** and~KNOB UNDER TWO the~STALK~s FROM~her and~KNOB UNDER TWO the~STALK~s FROM~her and~KNOB UNDER TWO the~STALK~s FROM~her to~SIX the~STALK~s the~GO.OUT⁽ᵛ⁾~ *ing*⁽ᵐᵖ⁾ FROM~her **37:22** KNOB~s~them⁽ᵐ⁾ and~STALK~s~them⁽ᵐ⁾ FROM~her *they~did*~EXIST⁽ᵛ⁾ ALL~her BEATEN.WORK UNIT GOLD CLEAN **37:23** and~*he~ will*~DO⁽ᵛ⁾ AT LAMP~s~her SEVEN and~TONG~s~her and~FIRE.PAN~s~her GOLD CLEAN **37:24** KIKAR GOLD CLEAN *he~did*~DO⁽ᵛ⁾ AT~her and~AT ALL UTENSIL~s~her **37:25** and~*he~will*~DO⁽ᵛ⁾ AT ALTAR the~INCENSE.SMOKE TREE~s ACACIA~s AMMAH LENGTH~him and~AMMAH WIDTH~him BE.SQUARE⁽ᵛ⁾~*ed*⁽ᵐˢ⁾ and~AMMAH~s2 HEIGHT~him FROM~him *they~did*~ EXIST⁽ᵛ⁾ HORN~s~him **37:26** and~*he~will*~*much*~OVERLAY⁽ᵛ⁾ AT~him GOLD CLEAN AT ROOF~him and~AT WALL~s~him ALL.AROUND and~AT HORN~s~ him and~*he~will*~DO⁽ᵛ⁾ to~him MOLDING GOLD ALL.AROUND **37:27** and~ TWO RING~s GOLD *he~did*~DO⁽ᵛ⁾ to~him from~UNDER to~MOLDING~him UPON TWO RIB~s~him UPON TWO SIDE~s~him to~HOUSE~s to~STRAND~s to~>~LIFT.UP⁽ᵛ⁾ AT~him in~them⁽ᵐ⁾ **37:28** and~*he~will*~DO⁽ᵛ⁾ AT the~ STRAND~s TREE~s ACACIA~s and~*he~will*~*much*~OVERLAY⁽ᵛ⁾ AT~them⁽ᵐ⁾ GOLD **37:29** and~*he~will*~DO⁽ᵛ⁾ AT OIL the~OINTMENT SPECIAL and~AT INCENSE.SMOKE the~AROMATIC.SPICE~s CLEAN WORK COMPOUND⁽ᵛ⁾~ *ing*⁽ᵐˢ⁾

Chapter 38

38:1 and~*he~will*~DO⁽ᵛ⁾ AT ALTAR the~ASCENSION.OFFERING TREE~s ACACIA~s FIVE AMMAH~s LENGTH~him and~FIVE AMMAH~s WIDTH~him BE.SQUARE⁽ᵛ⁾~*ed*⁽ᵐˢ⁾ and~THREE AMMAH~s HEIGHT~him **38:2** and~*he~will*~ DO⁽ᵛ⁾ HORN~s~him UPON FOUR CORNER~s~him FROM~him *they~did*~ EXIST⁽ᵛ⁾ HORN~s~him and~*he~will*~*much*~OVERLAY⁽ᵛ⁾ AT~him COPPER **38:3** and~*he~will*~DO⁽ᵛ⁾ AT ALL UTENSIL~s the~ALTAR AT the~ POT~s and~AT the~SHOVEL~s and~AT the~SPRINKLING.BASIN~s AT the~ FORK~s and~AT the~FIRE.PAN~s ALL UTENSIL~s~him *he~did*~DO⁽ᵛ⁾ COPPER **38:4** and~*he~will*~DO⁽ᵛ⁾ to~the~ALTAR GRATE WORK NETTING COPPER UNDER OUTER.RIM~him from~to~BENEATH UNTIL HALF~ him **38:5** and~*he~will*~POUR.DOWN⁽ᵛ⁾ FOUR RING~s in~FOUR the~ EXTREMITY~s to~GRATE the~COPPER HOUSE~s to~the~

The Book of Exodus

STRAND~s **38:6** and~*he*~*will*~DO$^{(V)}$ AT the~STRAND~s TREE~s ACACIA~s and~*he*~*will*~much~OVERLAY$^{(V)}$ AT~them$^{(m)}$ COPPER **38:7** and~*he*~*will*~ make~COME$^{(V)}$ AT the~STRAND~s in~the~RING~s UPON RIB~s the~ALTAR to~>~LIFT.UP$^{(V)}$ AT~him in~them$^{(m)}$ BORE.OUT$^{(V)}$~*ed*$^{(ms)}$ SLAB~s *he*~*did*~DO$^{(V)}$ AT~him **38:8** and~*he*~*will*~DO$^{(V)}$ AT the~CAULDRON COPPER and~AT BASE~ him COPPER in~REFLECTION~s the~MUSTER$^{(V)}$~*ing*$^{(fp)}$ WHICH *they*~*did*~ MUSTER$^{(V)}$ OPENING TENT APPOINTED **38:9** and~*he*~*will*~DO$^{(V)}$ AT the~ COURTYARD to~EDGE SOUTH SOUTHWARD~unto SLING~s the~COURTYARD LINEN *be*~*make*~TWIST.TOGETHER$^{(V)}$~*ing*$^{(ms)}$ HUNDRED in~the~ AMMAH **38:10** PILLAR~s~them$^{(m)}$ TEN~s and~FOOTING~s~them$^{(m)}$ TEN~s COPPER and~PEG~s the~PILLAR~s and~BINDER~s~them$^{(m)}$ SILVER **38:11** and~to~EDGE NORTH HUNDRED in~the~AMMAH PILLAR~s~ them$^{(m)}$ TEN~s and~FOOTING~s~them$^{(m)}$ TEN~s COPPER and~PEG~s the~ PILLAR~s and~BINDER~s~them$^{(m)}$ SILVER **38:12** and~to~EDGE SEA SLING~s FIVE~s in~the~AMMAH PILLAR~s~them$^{(m)}$ TEN and~FOOTING~s~them$^{(m)}$ TEN and~PEG~s the~PILLAR~s and~BINDER~s~them$^{(m)}$ SILVER **38:13** and~ to~EDGE EAST~unto SUNRISE~unto FIVE~s AMMAH **38:14** SLING~s FIVE TEN AMMAH TO the~SHOULDER.PIECE PILLAR~s~them$^{(m)}$ THREE and~ FOOTING~s~them$^{(m)}$ THREE **38:15** and~to~the~SHOULDER.PIECE the~ SECOND from~THIS and~from~THIS to~GATE the~COURTYARD SLING~s FIVE TEN AMMAH PILLAR~s~them$^{(m)}$ THREE and~FOOTING~s~them$^{(m)}$ THREE **38:16** ALL SLING~s the~COURTYARD ALL.AROUND LINEN *be*~*make*~ TWIST.TOGETHER$^{(V)}$~*ing*$^{(ms)}$ **38:17** and~the~FOOTING~s to~the~PILLAR~s COPPER and~PEG~s the~PILLAR~s and~BINDER~s~them$^{(m)}$ SILVER and~ METAL.PLATING HEAD~s~them$^{(m)}$ SILVER and~THEY$^{(m)}$ *be*~much~ATTACH$^{(V)}$~ *ing*$^{(mp)}$ SILVER ALL PILLAR~s the~COURTYARD **38:18** and~SCREEN GATE the~ COURTYARD WORK EMBROIDER$^{(V)}$~*ing*$^{(ms)}$ BLUE and~PURPLE and~KERMES SCARLET and~LINEN *be*~*make*~TWIST.TOGETHER$^{(V)}$~*ing*$^{(ms)}$ and~TEN~s AMMAH LENGTH and~HEIGHT in~WIDTH FIVE AMMAH~s to~ALONGSIDE SLING~s the~COURTYARD **38:19** and~PILLAR~s~them$^{(m)}$ FOUR and~ FOOTING~s~them$^{(m)}$ FOUR COPPER and~PEG~s~them$^{(m)}$ SILVER and~ METAL.PLATING HEAD~s~them$^{(m)}$ and~BINDER~s~them$^{(m)}$ SILVER **38:20** and~ALL the~TENT.PEG~s to~the~DWELLING and~to~ COURTYARD ALL.AROUND COPPER **38:21** THESE REGISTER$^{(V)}$~*ed*$^{(mp)}$ the~ DWELLING DWELLING the~EVIDENCE WHICH *he*~*did*~*be*~much~REGISTER$^{(V)}$ UPON MOUTH Mosheh SERVICE the~Lewi~s in~HAND Iytamar SON Aharon the~ADMINISTRATOR **38:22** and~Betsaleyl SON Uriy SON Hhur to~BRANCH Yehudah *he*~*did*~DO$^{(V)}$ AT ALL WHICH *he*~*did*~much~DIRECT$^{(V)}$ **YHWH** AT Mosheh **38:23** and~AT~him Ahaliyav SON Ahhiysamahh to~BRANCH Dan ENGRAVER and~THINK$^{(V)}$~*ing*$^{(ms)}$ and~EMBROIDER$^{(V)}$~*ing*$^{(ms)}$ in~the~BLUE and~in~the~PURPLE and~in~the~KERMES the~SCARLET and~in~the~ LINEN **38:24** ALL the~GOLD the~DO$^{(V)}$~*ed*$^{(ms)}$ to~the~BUSINESS in~ALL BUSINESS the~SPECIAL and~*he*~*will*~EXIST$^{(V)}$ GOLD the~WAVING NINE and~ TEN~s KIKAR and~SEVEN HUNDRED~s and~THREE~s SHEQEL in~SHEQEL the~SPECIAL **38:25** and~SILVER REGISTER$^{(V)}$~*ed*$^{(mp)}$ the~COMPANY

HUNDRED KIKAR and~THOUSAND and~SEVEN HUNDRED~s and~FIVE and~
SEVEN~s SHEQEL in~SHEQEL the~SPECIAL **38:26** BEQA to~the~SKULL
ONE.HALF the~SHEQEL in~SHEQEL the~SPECIAL to~ALL the~CROSS.OVER$^{(V)}$~
ing$^{(ms)}$ UPON the~REGISTER$^{(V)}$~*ed*$^{(mp)}$ from~SON TEN~s YEAR and~UPWARD~
unto to~SIX HUNDRED~s THOUSAND and~THREE THOUSAND~s and~FIVE
HUNDRED~s and~FIVE~s **38:27** and~*he~will*~EXIST$^{(V)}$ HUNDRED KIKAR the~
SILVER to~>~POUR.DOWN$^{(V)}$ AT FOOTING~s the~SPECIAL and~AT
FOOTING~s the~TENT.CURTAIN HUNDRED FOOTING~s to~HUNDRED the~
KIKAR KIKAR to~the~FOOTING **38:28** and~AT the~THOUSAND and~SEVEN
the~HUNDRED~s and~FIVE and~SEVEN~s *he~did*~DO$^{(V)}$ and~PEG~s to~the~
PILLAR~s and~*he~did~much*~OVERLAY$^{(V)}$ HEAD~s~them$^{(m)}$ and~*he~did~
much*~ATTACH$^{(V)}$ AT~them$^{(m)}$ **38:29** and~COPPER the~WAVING SEVEN~s
KIKAR and~THOUSAND~s2 and~FOUR HUNDRED~s SHEQEL **38:30** and~*he~
will*~DO$^{(V)}$ in~her AT FOOTING~s OPENING TENT APPOINTED and~AT ALTAR
the~COPPER and~AT GRATE the~COPPER WHICH to~him and~AT ALL
UTENSIL~s the~ALTAR **38:31** and~AT FOOTING~s the~COURTYARD
ALL.AROUND and~AT FOOTING~s GATE the~COURTYARD and~AT ALL
TENT.PEG~s the~DWELLING and~AT ALL TENT.PEG~s the~COURTYARD
ALL.AROUND

Chapter 39

39:1 and~FROM the~BLUE and~the~PURPLE and~KERMES the~SCARLET
they~did~DO$^{(V)}$ GARMENT~s BRAIDED.WORK to~>~*much*~MINISTER$^{(V)}$ in~
the~SPECIAL and~*they*$^{(m)}$~*will*~DO$^{(V)}$ AT GARMENT~s the~SPECIAL WHICH
to~Aharon like~WHICH *he~did~much*~DIRECT$^{(V)}$ **YHWH** AT
Mosheh **39:2** and~*he~will*~DO$^{(V)}$ AT the~EPHOD GOLD BLUE and~PURPLE
and~KERMES SCARLET and~LINEN *be~make*~TWIST.TOGETHER$^{(V)}$~
ing$^{(ms)}$ **39:3** and~*they*$^{(m)}$~*will*~HAMMER$^{(V)}$ AT WIRE~s the~GOLD and~*he~
did*~SLICE.OFF$^{(V)}$ CORD~s to~>~DO$^{(V)}$ in~MIDST the~BLUE and~in~MIDST
the~PURPLE and~in~MIDST KERMES the~SCARLET and~in~MIDST the~
LINEN WORK THINK$^{(V)}$~*ing*$^{(ms)}$ **39:4** SHOULDER.PIECE~s *they~did*~DO$^{(V)}$ to~
him COUPLE$^{(V)}$~*ing*$^{(fp)}$ UPON TWO EXTREMITY~s~him COUPLE$^{(V)}$~
ed$^{(ms)}$ **39:5** and~DECORATIVE.BAND EPHOD~him WHICH UPON~him FROM~
him HE like~WORK~him GOLD BLUE and~PURPLE and~KERMES SCARLET
and~LINEN *be~make*~TWIST.TOGETHER$^{(V)}$~*ing*$^{(ms)}$ like~WHICH *he~did~
much*~DIRECT$^{(V)}$ **YHWH** AT Mosheh **39:6** and~*they*$^{(m)}$~*will*~DO$^{(V)}$ AT STONE~s
the~ONYX *be~make*~GO.AROUND$^{(V)}$~*ing*$^{(fp)}$ PLAIT~s GOLD *be~much*~
OPEN$^{(V)}$~*ing*$^{(fp)}$ OPEN$^{(V)}$~*ed*$^{(mp)}$ SEAL UPON TITLE~s SON~s Yisra'eyl **39:7** and~
he~will~PLACE$^{(V)}$ AT~them$^{(m)}$ UPON SHOULDER.PIECE~s the~EPHOD
STONE~s REMEMBRANCE to~SON~s Yisra'eyl like~WHICH *he~did~much*~
DIRECT$^{(V)}$ **YHWH** AT Mosheh **39:8** and~*he~will*~DO$^{(V)}$ AT the~BREASTPLATE
WORK THINK$^{(V)}$~*ing*$^{(ms)}$ like~WORK EPHOD GOLD BLUE and~PURPLE and~

KERMES SCARLET and~LINEN be~make~TWIST.TOGETHER$^{(V)}$~ing$^{(ms)}$ **39:9** BE.SQUARE$^{(V)}$~ed$^{(ms)}$ he~did~EXIST$^{(V)}$ DOUBLE.OVER$^{(V)}$~ed$^{(ms)}$ they~did~DO$^{(V)}$ AT the~BREASTPLATE FINGER.SPAN LENGTH~him and~FINGER.SPAN WIDTH~him DOUBLE.OVER$^{(V)}$~ed$^{(ms)}$ **39:10** and~they$^{(m)}$~will~much~FILL$^{(V)}$ in~him FOUR ROW~s STONE ROW CARNELIAN OLIVINE and~EMERALD the~ROW the~UNIT **39:11** and~the~ROW the~SECOND TURQUOISE LAPIS.LAZULI and~FLINT **39:12** and~the~ROW the~THIRD OPAL AGATE and~AMETHYST **39:13** and~the~ROW the~FOURTH TOPAZ ONYX and~JASPER be~make~GO.AROUND$^{(V)}$~ing$^{(fp)}$ PLAIT~s GOLD in~SETTING~s~them$^{(m)}$ **39:14** and~the~STONE~s UPON TITLE~s SON~s Yisra'eyl THEY$^{(f)}$ TWO TEN UPON TITLE~s~them$^{(m)}$ OPEN$^{(V)}$~ed$^{(mp)}$ SEAL MAN UPON TITLE~him to~TWO TEN STAFF **39:15** and~they$^{(m)}$~will~DO$^{(V)}$ UPON the~BREASTPLATE CHAIN~s EDGING WORK THICK.WOVEN GOLD CLEAN **39:16** and~they$^{(m)}$~will~DO$^{(V)}$ TWO PLAIT~s GOLD and~TWO RING~s GOLD and~they$^{(m)}$~will~GIVE$^{(V)}$ AT TWO the~RING~s UPON TWO EXTREMITY~s the~BREASTPLATE **39:17** and~they$^{(m)}$~will~GIVE$^{(V)}$ TWO the~THICK.WOVEN~s the~GOLD UPON TWO the~RING~s UPON EXTREMITY~s the~BREASTPLATE **39:18** and~AT TWO EXTREMITY~s TWO the~THICK.WOVEN~s they~did~GIVE$^{(V)}$ UPON TWO the~PLAIT~s and~they$^{(m)}$~will~GIVE$^{(V)}$~them$^{(m)}$ UPON SHOULDER.PIECE~s the~EPHOD TO FOREFRONT FACE~s~him **39:19** and~they$^{(m)}$~will~DO$^{(V)}$ TWO RING~s GOLD and~they$^{(m)}$~will~PLACE$^{(V)}$ UPON TWO EXTREMITY~s the~BREASTPLATE UPON LIP~him WHICH TO Ever the~EPHOD HOUSE~unto **39:20** and~they$^{(m)}$~will~DO$^{(V)}$ TWO RING~s GOLD and~they$^{(m)}$~will~GIVE$^{(V)}$~them$^{(m)}$ UPON TWO SHOULDER.PIECE~s the~EPHOD from~to~BENEATH from~FOREFRONT FACE~s~him to~ALONGSIDE JOINT~him from~UPWARD to~DECORATIVE.BAND the~EPHOD **39:21** and~they$^{(m)}$~will~TIE.ON$^{(V)}$ AT the~BREASTPLATE RING~s~him TO RING~s the~EPHOD in~CORD BLUE to~>~EXIST$^{(V)}$ UPON DECORATIVE.BAND the~EPHOD and~NOT he~will~be~LOOSEN$^{(V)}$ the~BREASTPLATE from~UPON the~EPHOD like~WHICH he~did~much~DIRECT$^{(V)}$ **YHWH** AT Mosheh **39:22** and~he~will~DO$^{(V)}$ AT CLOAK the~EPHOD WORK BRAID$^{(V)}$~ing$^{(ms)}$ ENTIRELY BLUE **39:23** and~MOUTH the~CLOAK in~MIDST~him like~MOUTH COLLAR LIP to~MOUTH~him ALL.AROUND NOT he~will~be~TEAR$^{(V)}$ **39:24** and~they$^{(m)}$~will~DO$^{(V)}$ UPON HEM~s the~CLOAK POMEGRANATE~s BLUE and~PURPLE and~KERMES SCARLET be~make~TWIST.TOGETHER$^{(V)}$~ing$^{(ms)}$ **39:25** and~they$^{(m)}$~will~DO$^{(V)}$ BELL~s GOLD CLEAN and~they$^{(m)}$~will~GIVE$^{(V)}$ AT the~BELL~s in~MIDST the~POMEGRANATE~s UPON HEM~s the~CLOAK ALL.AROUND in~MIDST the~POMEGRANATE~s **39:26** BELL and~POMEGRANATE BELL and~POMEGRANATE UPON HEM~s the~CLOAK ALL.AROUND to~>~much~MINISTER$^{(V)}$ like~WHICH he~did~much~DIRECT$^{(V)}$ **YHWH** AT Mosheh **39:27** and~they$^{(m)}$~will~DO$^{(V)}$ AT the~TUNIC~s LINEN WORK BRAID$^{(V)}$~ing$^{(ms)}$ to~Aharon and~to~SON~s~him **39:28** and~AT the~TURBAN LINEN and~AT BONNET~s the~HEADDRESS LINEN and~AT UNDERGARMENT~s the~STRAND LINEN be~make~TWIST.TOGETHER$^{(V)}$~

ing(ms) **39:29** and~AT the~SASH LINEN *be~make*~TWIST.TOGETHER(V)~*ing*(ms) and~BLUE and~PURPLE and~KERMES SCARLET WORK EMBROIDER(V)~*ing*(ms) like~WHICH *he~did~much*~DIRECT(V) **YHWH** AT Mosheh **39:30** and~*they*(m)~*will*~DO(V) AT BLOSSOM DEDICATION the~SPECIAL GOLD CLEAN and~ *they*(m)~*will*~WRITE(V) UPON~him THING.WRITTEN OPEN(V)~*ed*(mp) SEAL SPECIAL to~**YHWH** **39:31** and~*they*(m)~*will*~GIVE(V) UPON~him CORD BLUE to~>~GIVE(V) UPON the~TURBAN from~to~UPWARD~unto like~WHICH *he~did~much*~DIRECT(V) **YHWH** AT Mosheh **39:32** and~*she~will*~FINISH(V) ALL SERVICE DWELLING TENT APPOINTED and~*they*(m)~*will*~DO(V) SON~s Yisra'eyl like~ALL WHICH *he~did~much*~DIRECT(V) **YHWH** AT Mosheh SO *they~did*~DO(V) **39:33** and~*they*(m)~*will~make*~COME(V) AT the~DWELLING TO Mosheh AT the~TENT and~AT ALL UTENSIL~s~him HOOK~s~him BOARD~s~him WOOD.BAR~s~him and~PILLAR~s~him and~FOOTING~s~him **39:34** and~AT ROOF.COVERING SKIN~s the~BUCK~s the~*be~much*~BE.RED(V)~*ing*(mp) and~ AT ROOF.COVERING SKIN~s the~DEER~s and~AT TENT.CURTAIN the~ SCREEN **39:35** AT BOX the~EVIDENCE and~AT STRAND~s~him and~AT the~ LID **39:36** AT the~TABLE AT ALL UTENSIL~s~him and~AT BREAD the~ FACE~s **39:37** AT the~LAMPSTAND the~CLEAN AT LAMP~s~her LAMP~s the~RANK and~AT ALL UTENSIL~s~her and~AT OIL the~ LUMINARY **39:38** and~AT ALTAR the~GOLD and~AT OIL the~OINTMENT and~AT INCENSE.SMOKE the~AROMATIC.SPICE~s and~AT SCREEN OPENING the~TENT **39:39** AT ALTAR the~COPPER and~AT GRATE the~COPPER WHICH to~him AT STRAND~s~him and~AT ALL UTENSIL~s~him AT the~CAULDRON and~AT BASE~him **39:40** AT SLING~s the~COURTYARD AT PILLAR~s~her and~AT FOOTING~s~her and~AT the~SCREEN to~GATE the~COURTYARD AT STRING~s~him and~TENT.PEG~s~her and~AT ALL UTENSIL~s SERVICE the~ DWELLING to~TENT APPOINTED **39:41** AT GARMENT~s the~BRAIDED.WORK to~>~*much*~MINISTER(V) in~the~SPECIAL AT GARMENT~s the~SPECIAL to~ Aharon the~ADMINISTRATOR and~AT GARMENT~s SON~s~him to~>~*much*~ ADORN(V) **39:42** like~ALL WHICH *he~did~much*~DIRECT(V) **YHWH** AT Mosheh SO *they~did*~DO(V) SON~s Yisra'eyl AT ALL the~SERVICE **39:43** and~*he~will*~ SEE(V) Mosheh AT ALL the~BUSINESS and~LOOK *they~did*~DO(V) AT~her like~ WHICH *he~did~much*~DIRECT(V) **YHWH** SO *they~did*~DO(V) and~*he~will~ much*~KNEEL(V) AT~*them*(m) Mosheh

Chapter 40

40:1 and~*he~will~much*~SPEAK(V) **YHWH** TO Mosheh to~>~SAY(V) **40:2** in~ DAY the~NEW.MOON the~FIRST in~UNIT to~the~NEW.MOON *you*(ms)~*will*~ *make*~RISE(V) AT DWELLING TENT APPOINTED **40:3** and~*you*(ms)~*did*~ PLACE(V) THERE AT BOX the~EVIDENCE and~*you*(ms)~*did*~FENCE.AROUND(V) UPON the~BOX AT the~TENT.CURTAIN **40:4** and~*you*(ms)~*did~make*~ COME(V) AT the~TABLE and~*you*(ms)~*did*~ARRANGE(V) AT ARRANGEMENT~

The Book of Exodus

him and~*you*$^{(ms)}$~*did*~*make*~COME$^{(V)}$ AT the~LAMPSTAND and~*you*$^{(ms)}$~*did*~*make*~GO.UP$^{(V)}$ AT LAMP~s~her **40:5** and~*you*$^{(ms)}$~*did*~GIVE$^{(V)}$~& AT ALTAR the~GOLD to~INCENSE.SMOKE to~FACE~s BOX the~EVIDENCE and~*you*$^{(ms)}$~*did*~PLACE$^{(V)}$ AT SCREEN the~OPENING to~the~DWELLING **40:6** and~*you*$^{(ms)}$~*did*~GIVE$^{(V)}$~& AT ALTAR the~ASCENSION.OFFERING to~FACE~s OPENING DWELLING TENT APPOINTED **40:7** and~*you*$^{(ms)}$~*did*~GIVE$^{(V)}$ AT the~CAULDRON BETWEEN TENT APPOINTED and~BETWEEN the~ALTAR and~*you*$^{(ms)}$~*did*~GIVE$^{(V)}$ THERE WATER~s2 **40:8** and~*you*$^{(ms)}$~*did*~PLACE$^{(V)}$ AT the~COURTYARD ALL.AROUND and~*you*$^{(ms)}$~*did*~GIVE$^{(V)}$ AT SCREEN GATE the~COURTYARD **40:9** and~*you*$^{(ms)}$~*did*~TAKE$^{(V)}$ AT OIL the~OINTMENT and~*you*$^{(ms)}$~*did*~SMEAR$^{(V)}$ AT the~DWELLING and~AT ALL WHICH in~him and~*you*$^{(ms)}$~*did*~*much*~SET.APART$^{(V)}$ AT~him and~AT ALL UTENSIL~s~him and~*he*~*did*~EXIST$^{(V)}$ SPECIAL **40:10** and~*you*$^{(ms)}$~*did*~SMEAR$^{(V)}$ AT ALTAR the~ASCENSION.OFFERING and~AT ALL UTENSIL~s~him and~*you*$^{(ms)}$~*did*~*much*~SET.APART$^{(V)}$ AT the~ALTAR and~*he*~*did*~EXIST$^{(V)}$ the~ALTAR SPECIAL SPECIAL~s **40:11** and~*you*$^{(ms)}$~*did*~SMEAR$^{(V)}$ AT the~CAULDRON and~AT BASE~him and~*you*$^{(ms)}$~*did*~*much*~SET.APART$^{(V)}$ AT~him **40:12** and~*you*$^{(ms)}$~*did*~*make*~COME.NEAR$^{(V)}$ AT Aharon and~AT SON~s~him TO OPENING TENT APPOINTED and~*you*$^{(ms)}$~*did*~BATHE$^{(V)}$ AT~them$^{(m)}$ in~the~WATER~s2 **40:13** and~*you*$^{(ms)}$~*did*~*make*~WEAR$^{(V)}$ AT Aharon AT GARMENT~s the~SPECIAL and~*you*$^{(ms)}$~*did*~SMEAR$^{(V)}$ AT~him and~*you*$^{(ms)}$~*did*~*much*~SET.APART$^{(V)}$ AT~him and~*he*~*did*~*much*~ADORN$^{(V)}$ to~me **40:14** and~AT SON~s~him *you*$^{(ms)}$~*will*~*make*~COME.NEAR$^{(V)}$ and~*you*$^{(ms)}$~*did*~*make*~WEAR$^{(V)}$ AT~them$^{(m)}$ TUNIC~s **40:15** and~*you*$^{(ms)}$~*did*~SMEAR$^{(V)}$ AT~them$^{(m)}$ like~WHICH *you*$^{(ms)}$~*did*~SMEAR$^{(V)}$ AT FATHER~them$^{(m)}$ and~*they*~*did*~*much*~ADORN$^{(V)}$ to~me and~*she*~*did*~EXIST$^{(V)}$ to~>~EXIST$^{(V)}$ to~them$^{(m)}$ >~SMEAR$^{(V)}$~them$^{(m)}$ to~ADMINISTRATION DISTANT to~GENERATION~s~them$^{(m)}$ **40:16** and~*he*~*will*~DO$^{(V)}$ Mosheh like~ALL WHICH *he*~*did*~*much*~DIRECT$^{(V)}$ YHWH AT~him SO *he*~*did*~DO$^{(V)}$ **40:17** and~*he*~*will*~EXIST$^{(V)}$ in~the~NEW.MOON the~FIRST in~the~YEAR the~SECOND in~UNIT to~the~NEW.MOON *he*~*did*~*be*~*make*~RISE$^{(V)}$ the~DWELLING **40:18** and~*he*~*will*~*make*~RISE$^{(V)}$ Mosheh AT the~DWELLING and~*he*~*will*~GIVE$^{(V)}$ AT FOOTING~s~him and~*he*~*will*~PLACE$^{(V)}$ AT BOARD~s~him and~*he*~*will*~GIVE$^{(V)}$ AT WOOD.BAR~s~him and~*he*~*will*~*make*~RISE$^{(V)}$ AT PILLAR~s~him **40:19** and~*he*~*will*~SPREAD.OUT$^{(V)}$ AT the~TENT UPON the~DWELLING and~*he*~*will*~PLACE$^{(V)}$ AT ROOF.COVERING the~TENT UPON~him from~to~UPWARD~unto like~WHICH *he*~*did*~*much*~DIRECT$^{(V)}$ YHWH AT Mosheh **40:20** and~*he*~*will*~TAKE$^{(V)}$ and~*he*~*will*~GIVE$^{(V)}$ AT the~EVIDENCE TO the~BOX and~*he*~*will*~PLACE$^{(V)}$ AT the~STRAND~s UPON the~BOX and~*he*~*will*~GIVE$^{(V)}$ AT the~LID UPON the~BOX from~to~UPWARD~unto **40:21** and~*he*~*will*~*make*~COME$^{(V)}$ AT the~BOX TO the~DWELLING and~*he*~*will*~PLACE$^{(V)}$ AT TENT.CURTAIN the~SCREEN and~*he*~*will*~FENCE.AROUND$^{(V)}$ UPON BOX the~EVIDENCE like~WHICH *he*~*did*~*much*~DIRECT$^{(V)}$ YHWH AT Mosheh **40:22** and~*he*~*will*~GIVE$^{(V)}$ AT the~TABLE in~TENT APPOINTED UPON MIDSECTION the~DWELLING NORTH~unto from~

OUTSIDE to~the~TENT.CURTAIN **40:23** and~*he~will*~ARRANGE⁽ᵛ⁾ UPON~him ARRANGEMENT BREAD to~FACE~s **YHWH** like~WHICH *he~did~much*~DIRECT⁽ᵛ⁾ **YHWH** AT Mosheh **40:24** and~*he~will*~PLACE⁽ᵛ⁾ AT the~LAMPSTAND in~TENT APPOINTED IN.FRONT the~TABLE UPON MIDSECTION the~DWELLING SOUTH~unto **40:25** and~*he~will~make*~GO.UP⁽ᵛ⁾ the~LAMP~s to~FACE~s **YHWH** like~WHICH *he~did~much*~DIRECT⁽ᵛ⁾ **YHWH** AT Mosheh **40:26** and~*he~will*~PLACE⁽ᵛ⁾ AT ALTAR the~GOLD in~TENT APPOINTED to~FACE~s the~TENT.CURTAIN **40:27** and~*he~will~make*~BURN.INCENSE⁽ᵛ⁾ UPON~him INCENSE.SMOKE AROMATIC.SPICE~s like~WHICH *he~did~much*~DIRECT⁽ᵛ⁾ **YHWH** AT Mosheh **40:28** and~*he~will*~PLACE⁽ᵛ⁾ AT SCREEN the~OPENING to~the~DWELLING **40:29** and~AT ALTAR the~ASCENSION.OFFERING *he~did*~PLACE⁽ᵛ⁾ OPENING DWELLING TENT APPOINTED and~*he~will~make*~GO.UP⁽ᵛ⁾ UPON~him AT the~ASCENSION.OFFERING and~AT the~DEPOSIT like~WHICH *he~did~much*~DIRECT⁽ᵛ⁾ **YHWH** AT Mosheh **40:30** and~*he~will*~PLACE⁽ᵛ⁾ AT the~CAULDRON BETWEEN TENT APPOINTED and~BETWEEN the~ALTAR and~*he~will*~GIVE⁽ᵛ⁾ THERE~unto WATER~s2 to~>~BATHE⁽ᵛ⁾ **40:31** and~*they~did*~BATHE⁽ᵛ⁾ FROM~him Mosheh and~Aharon and~SON~s~him AT HAND~s2~them⁽ᵐ⁾ and~AT FOOT~s2~them⁽ᵐ⁾ **40:32** in~>~COME⁽ᵛ⁾~them⁽ᵐ⁾ TO TENT APPOINTED and~in~>~COME.NEAR⁽ᵛ⁾~them⁽ᵐ⁾ TO the~ALTAR they⁽ᵐ⁾~will~BATHE⁽ᵛ⁾ like~WHICH *he~did~much*~DIRECT⁽ᵛ⁾ **YHWH** AT Mosheh **40:33** and~*he~will~make*~RISE⁽ᵛ⁾ AT the~COURTYARD ALL.AROUND to~the~DWELLING and~to~the~ALTAR and~*he~will*~GIVE⁽ᵛ⁾ AT SCREEN GATE the~COURTYARD and~*he~will~much*~FINISH⁽ᵛ⁾ Mosheh AT the~BUSINESS **40:34** and~*he~will~much*~COVER.OVER⁽ᵛ⁾ the~CLOUD AT TENT APPOINTED and~ARMAMENT **YHWH** *he~did*~FILL⁽ᵛ⁾ AT the~DWELLING **40:35** and~NOT *he~did*~BE.ABLE⁽ᵛ⁾ Mosheh to~>~COME⁽ᵛ⁾ TO TENT APPOINTED GIVEN.THAT *he~did*~DWELL⁽ᵛ⁾ UPON~him the~CLOUD and~ARMAMENT **YHWH** *he~did*~FILL⁽ᵛ⁾ AT the~DWELLING **40:36** and~in~>~be~GO.UP⁽ᵛ⁾ the~CLOUD from~UPON the~DWELLING they⁽ᵐ⁾~will~JOURNEY⁽ᵛ⁾ SON~s Yisra'eyl in~ALL JOURNEY~s~them⁽ᵐ⁾ **40:37** and~IF NOT *he~will~be*~GO.UP⁽ᵛ⁾ the~CLOUD and~NOT they⁽ᵐ⁾~will~JOURNEY⁽ᵛ⁾ UNTIL DAY >~be~GO.UP⁽ᵛ⁾~him **40:38** GIVEN.THAT CLOUD **YHWH** UPON the~DWELLING DAYTIME and~FIRE *she~will*~EXIST⁽ᵛ⁾ NIGHT in~him to~EYE~s2 ALL HOUSE Yisra'eyl in~ALL JOURNEY~s~them⁽ᵐ⁾

The Book of Exodus

Benner's Mechanical Translation of the Torah

The Book of Leviticus

Chapter 1

1:1 and~*he~will*~CALL.OUT⁽ᵛ⁾ TO Mosheh and~*he~will*~*much*~SPEAK⁽ᵛ⁾ **YHWH** TO~him from~TENT APPOINTED to~>~SAY⁽ᵛ⁾ **1:2** !⁽ᵐˢ⁾~*much*~SPEAK⁽ᵛ⁾ TO SON~s Yisra'eyl and~*you*⁽ᵐˢ⁾~*did*~SAY⁽ᵛ⁾ TO~them⁽ᵐ⁾ HUMAN GIVEN.THAT *he~will~make*~COME.NEAR⁽ᵛ⁾ from~you⁽ᵐᵖ⁾ DONATION to~**YHWH** FROM the~BEAST FROM the~CATTLE and~FROM the~FLOCKS *you*⁽ᵐᵖ⁾~*will~make*~COME.NEAR⁽ᵛ⁾ AT DONATION~you⁽ᵐᵖ⁾ **1:3** IF ASCENSION.OFFERING DONATION~him FROM the~CATTLE MALE WHOLE *he~will~make*~COME.NEAR⁽ᵛ⁾~him TO OPENING TENT APPOINTED *he~will~make*~COME.NEAR⁽ᵛ⁾ AT~him to~SELF-WILL~him to~FACE~s **YHWH** **1:4** and~*he~did*~SUPPORT⁽ᵛ⁾ HAND~him UPON HEAD the~ASCENSION.OFFERING and~*he~did~be*~ACCEPT⁽ᵛ⁾ to~him to~>~*much*~COVER⁽ᵛ⁾ UPON~him **1:5** and~*he~did*~SLAY⁽ᵛ⁾ AT SON the~CATTLE to~FACE~s **YHWH** and~*they~did~make*~COME.NEAR⁽ᵛ⁾ SON~s Aharon the~ADMINISTRATOR~s AT the~BLOOD and~*they~did*~SPRINKLE⁽ᵛ⁾ AT the~BLOOD UPON the~ALTAR ALL.AROUND WHICH OPENING TENT APPOINTED **1:6** and~*he~did~make*~STRIP.OFF⁽ᵛ⁾ AT the~ASCENSION.OFFERING and~*he~did*~*much*~DIVIDE.INTO.PIECES⁽ᵛ⁾ AT~her to~PIECE~s~her **1:7** and~*they~did*~GIVE⁽ᵛ⁾ SON~s Aharon the~ADMINISTRATOR FIRE UPON the~ALTAR and~*they~did*~ARRANGE⁽ᵛ⁾ TREE~s UPON the~FIRE **1:8** and~*they~did*~ARRANGE⁽ᵛ⁾ SON~s Aharon the~ADMINISTRATOR~s AT the~PIECE~s AT the~HEAD and~AT the~SUET UPON the~TREE~s WHICH UPON the~FIRE WHICH UPON the~ALTAR **1:9** and~INSIDE~him and~LEG~s~him *he~will*~BATHE⁽ᵛ⁾ in~the~WATER~s2 and~*he~did~make*~BURN.INCENSE⁽ᵛ⁾ the~ADMINISTRATOR AT the~ALL the~ALTAR~unto ASCENSION.OFFERING FIRE.OFFERING AROMA SWEET to~**YHWH** **1:10** and~IF FROM the~FLOCKS DONATION~him FROM the~SHEEP~s OR FROM the~SHE-GOAT~s to~ASCENSION.OFFERING MALE WHOLE *he~will~make*~COME.NEAR⁽ᵛ⁾~him **1:11** and~*he~did*~SLAY⁽ᵛ⁾ AT~him UPON MIDSECTION the~ALTAR NORTH~unto to~FACE~s **YHWH** and~*they~did*~SPRINKLE⁽ᵛ⁾ SON~s Aharon the~ADMINISTRATOR~s AT BLOOD~him UPON the~ALTAR ALL.AROUND **1:12** and~*he~did*~*much*~DIVIDE.INTO.PIECES⁽ᵛ⁾ AT~him to~PIECE~s~him and~AT HEAD~him and~AT SUET~him and~*he~did*~ARRANGE⁽ᵛ⁾ the~ADMINISTRATOR AT~them⁽ᵐ⁾ UPON the~TREE~s WHICH UPON the~FIRE WHICH UPON the~ALTAR **1:13** and~the~INSIDE and~the~LEG~s2 *he~will*~BATHE⁽ᵛ⁾ in~the~WATER~s2 and~*he~did~make*~COME.NEAR⁽ᵛ⁾ the~ADMINISTRATOR AT the~ALL and~*he~did~make*~BURN.INCENSE⁽ᵛ⁾ the~ALTAR~unto ASCENSION.OFFERING HE FIRE.OFFERING AROMA SWEET to~**YHWH** **1:14** and~IF FROM the~FLYER

The Book of Leviticus

ASCENSION.OFFERING DONATION~him to~**YHWH** and~*he~did~make~*COME.NEAR^(v) FROM the~TURTLEDOVE~s OR FROM SON~s the~DOVE AT DONATION~him **1:15** and~*he~did~make~*COME.NEAR^(v)~him the~ADMINISTRATOR TO the~ALTAR and~*he~did~*SNAP.OFF^(v) AT HEAD~him and~*he~did~make~*BURN.INCENSE^(v) the~ALTAR~unto and~*he~did~be~*DRAIN^(v) BLOOD~him UPON WALL the~ALTAR **1:16** and~*he~did~make~*TURN.ASIDE^(v) AT CROP~him in~PLUMAGE~her and~*he~did~make~*THROW.OUT^(v) AT~her BESIDE the~ALTAR EAST~unto TO AREA the~FATNESS **1:17** and~*he~did~much~*SPLIT.IN.TWO^(v) AT~him in~WING~s~him NOT *he~will~make~*SEPARATE^(v) and~*he~did~make~*BURN.INCENSE^(v) AT~him the~ADMINISTRATOR the~ALTAR~unto UPON the~TREE~s WHICH UPON the~FIRE ASCENSION.OFFERING HE FIRE.OFFERING AROMA SWEET to~**YHWH**

Chapter 2

2:1 and~SOUL GIVEN.THAT *she~will~make~*COME.NEAR^(v) DONATION DEPOSIT to~**YHWH** FLOUR *he~will~*EXIST^(v) DONATION~him and~*he~did~*POUR.DOWN^(v) UPON~her OIL and~*he~did~*GIVE^(v) UPON~her FRANKINCENSE **2:2** and~*he~did~make~*COME^(v)~her TO SON~s Aharon the~ADMINISTRATOR~s and~*he~did~*GRASP^(v) from~THERE FILLING HANDFUL~him from~FLOUR~her and~from~OIL UPON ALL to~FRANKINCENSE~her and~*he~did~make~*BURN.INCENSE^(v) the~ADMINISTRATOR AT MEMORIAL~her the~ALTAR~unto FIRE.OFFERING AROMA SWEET to~**YHWH 2:3** and~the~*be~*LEAVE.BEHIND^(v)~*ing*^(fs) FROM the~DEPOSIT to~Aharon and~to~SON~s~him SPECIAL SPECIAL~s from~FIRE.OFFERING~s **YHWH 2:4** and~GIVEN.THAT *you*^(ms)~*will~make~*COME.NEAR^(v) DONATION DEPOSIT BAKED OVEN FLOUR PIERCED.BREAD~s UNLEAVENED.BREAD~s MIX^(v)~*ed*^(fp) in~the~OIL and~THIN.BREAD~s UNLEAVENED.BREAD~s SMEAR^(v)~*ed*^(mp) in~the~OIL **2:5** and~IF DEPOSIT UPON the~PAN DONATION~*you*^(ms) FLOUR MIX^(v)~*ed*^(fs) in~the~OIL UNLEAVENED.BREAD *she~will~*EXIST^(v) **2:6** >~CRUMBLE^(v) AT~her FRAGMENT~s and~*you*^(ms)~*did~*POUR.DOWN^(v) UPON~her OIL DEPOSIT SHE **2:7** and~IF DEPOSIT BOILING.POT DONATION~*you*^(ms) FLOUR in~the~OIL *she~will~be~*DO^(v) **2:8** and~*you*^(ms)~*did~make~*COME^(v) AT the~DEPOSIT WHICH *he~will~be~*DO^(v) from~THESE to~**YHWH** and~*he~did~make~*COME.NEAR^(v)~her TO the~ADMINISTRATOR and~*he~did~make~*DRAW.NEAR^(v)~her TO the~ALTAR **2:9** and~*he~did~make~*RAISE.UP^(v) the~ADMINISTRATOR FROM the~DEPOSIT AT MEMORIAL~her and~*he~did~make~*BURN.INCENSE^(v) the~ALTAR~unto FIRE.OFFERING AROMA SWEET to~**YHWH 2:10** and~the~*be~*LEAVE.BEHIND^(v)~*ing*^(fs) FROM the~DEPOSIT to~Aharon and~to~SON~s~him SPECIAL SPECIAL~s from~FIRE.OFFERING~s **YHWH 2:11** ALL the~DEPOSIT WHICH *you*^(mp)~*will~make~*COME.NEAR^(v) to~

YHWH NOT *you*⁽ᵐˢ⁾~will~DO⁽ⱽ⁾ LEAVENED.BREAD GIVEN.THAT ALL LEAVEN and~ALL HONEY NOT *you*⁽ᵐᵖ⁾~will~make~BURN.INCENSE⁽ⱽ⁾ FROM~him FIRE.OFFERING to~**YHWH**   **2:12** DONATION SUMMIT *you*⁽ᵐᵖ⁾~will~make~ COME.NEAR⁽ⱽ⁾ AT~them⁽ᵐ⁾ to~**YHWH** and~TO the~ALTAR NOT *they*⁽ᵐ⁾~will~ GO.UP⁽ⱽ⁾ to~AROMA SWEET   **2:13** and~ALL DONATION DEPOSIT~*you*⁽ᵐˢ⁾ in~ the~SALT *you*⁽ᵐˢ⁾~will~SEASON⁽ⱽ⁾ and~NOT *you*⁽ᵐˢ⁾~will~make~CEASE⁽ⱽ⁾ SALT COVENANT Elohiym~*you*⁽ᵐˢ⁾ from~UPON DEPOSIT~*you*⁽ᵐˢ⁾ UPON ALL DONATION~*you*⁽ᵐˢ⁾ *you*⁽ᵐˢ⁾~will~make~COME.NEAR⁽ⱽ⁾ SALT   **2:14** and~IF *you*⁽ᵐˢ⁾~will~make~COME.NEAR⁽ⱽ⁾ DEPOSIT FIRST-FRUIT~s to~**YHWH** GREEN.GRAIN DRY⁽ⱽ⁾~*ed*⁽ᵐˢ⁾ in~the~FIRE BEATEN.GRAIN PLANTATION *you*⁽ᵐˢ⁾~will~make~COME.NEAR⁽ⱽ⁾ AT DEPOSIT FIRST-FRUIT~s~ *you*⁽ᵐˢ⁾   **2:15** and~*you*⁽ᵐˢ⁾~did~GIVE⁽ⱽ⁾ UPON~her OIL and~*you*⁽ᵐˢ⁾~did~ PLACE⁽ⱽ⁾ UPON~her FRANKINCENSE DEPOSIT SHE   **2:16** and~*he*~did~make~ BURN.INCENSE⁽ⱽ⁾ the~ADMINISTRATOR AT MEMORIAL~her from~ BEATEN.GRAIN~her and~from~OIL UPON ALL to~FRANKINCENSE~her FIRE.OFFERING to~**YHWH**

Chapter 3

3:1 and~IF SACRIFICE OFFERING.OF.RESTITUTION~s DONATION~him IF FROM the~CATTLE HE *make*~COME.NEAR⁽ⱽ⁾~*ing*⁽ᵐˢ⁾ IF MALE IF FEMALE WHOLE *he*~will~make~COME.NEAR⁽ⱽ⁾~him to~FACE~s **YHWH**   **3:2** and~*he*~ did~SUPPORT⁽ⱽ⁾ HAND~him UPON HEAD DONATION~him and~*he*~did~ SLAY⁽ⱽ⁾~him OPENING TENT APPOINTED and~*they*~did~SPRINKLE⁽ⱽ⁾ SON~s Aharon the~ADMINISTRATOR~s AT the~BLOOD UPON the~ALTAR ALL.AROUND   **3:3** and~*he*~did~make~COME.NEAR⁽ⱽ⁾ from~SACRIFICE the~ OFFERING.OF.RESTITUTION~s FIRE.OFFERING to~**YHWH** AT the~FAT the~ *much*~COVER.OVER⁽ⱽ⁾~*ing*⁽ᵐˢ⁾ AT the~INSIDE and~AT ALL the~FAT WHICH UPON the~INSIDE   **3:4** and~AT TWO the~KIDNEY~s and~AT the~FAT WHICH UPON~them⁽ᶠ⁾ WHICH UPON the~HIP~s and~AT the~LOBE UPON the~HEAVY UPON the~KIDNEY~s *he*~will~make~TURN.ASIDE⁽ⱽ⁾~her   **3:5** and~*they*~did~ *make*~BURN.INCENSE⁽ⱽ⁾ AT~him SON~s Aharon the~ALTAR~unto UPON the~ ASCENSION.OFFERING WHICH UPON the~TREE~s WHICH UPON the~FIRE FIRE.OFFERING AROMA SWEET to~**YHWH**   **3:6** and~IF FROM the~FLOCKS DONATION~him to~SACRIFICE OFFERING.OF.RESTITUTION~s to~**YHWH** MALE OR FEMALE WHOLE *he*~will~make~COME.NEAR⁽ⱽ⁾~him   **3:7** IF SHEEP HE *make*~COME.NEAR⁽ⱽ⁾~*ing*⁽ᵐˢ⁾ AT DONATION~him and~*he*~did~make~ COME.NEAR⁽ⱽ⁾ AT~him to~FACE~s **YHWH**   **3:8** and~*he*~did~SUPPORT⁽ⱽ⁾ AT HAND~him UPON HEAD DONATION~him and~*he*~did~SLAY⁽ⱽ⁾ AT~him to~ FACE~s TENT APPOINTED and~*they*~did~SPRINKLE⁽ⱽ⁾ SON~s Aharon AT BLOOD~him UPON the~ALTAR ALL.AROUND   **3:9** and~*he*~did~make~ COME.NEAR⁽ⱽ⁾ from~SACRIFICE the~OFFERING.OF.RESTITUTION~s FIRE.OFFERING to~**YHWH** FAT~him the~RUMP WHOLE to~ALONGSIDE the~

SPINE *he~will~make*~TURN.ASIDE⁽ⱽ⁾~her and~AT the~FAT the~*much*~COVER.OVER⁽ⱽ⁾~*ing*⁽ᵐˢ⁾ AT the~INSIDE and~AT ALL the~FAT WHICH UPON the~INSIDE **3:10** and~AT TWO the~KIDNEY~s and~AT the~FAT WHICH UPON~them⁽ᶠ⁾ WHICH UPON the~HIP~s and~AT the~LOBE UPON the~HEAVY UPON the~KIDNEY~s *he~will~make*~TURN.ASIDE⁽ⱽ⁾~her **3:11** and~*he~did~make*~BURN.INCENSE⁽ⱽ⁾~him the~ADMINISTRATOR the~ALTAR~unto BREAD FIRE.OFFERING to~**YHWH** **3:12** and~IF SHE-GOAT DONATION~him and~*he~did~make*~COME.NEAR⁽ⱽ⁾~him to~FACE~s **YHWH** **3:13** and~*he~did*~SUPPORT⁽ⱽ⁾ AT HAND~him UPON HEAD~him and~*he~did*~SLAY⁽ⱽ⁾ AT~him to~FACE~s TENT APPOINTED and~*they~did*~SPRINKLE⁽ⱽ⁾ SON~s Aharon AT BLOOD~him UPON the~ALTAR ALL.AROUND **3:14** and~*he~did~make*~COME.NEAR⁽ⱽ⁾ FROM~him DONATION~him FIRE.OFFERING to~**YHWH** AT the~FAT the~*much*~COVER.OVER⁽ⱽ⁾~*ing*⁽ᵐˢ⁾ AT the~INSIDE and~AT ALL the~FAT WHICH UPON the~INSIDE **3:15** and~AT TWO the~KIDNEY~s and~AT the~FAT WHICH UPON~them⁽ᶠ⁾ WHICH UPON the~HIP~s and~AT the~LOBE UPON the~HEAVY UPON the~KIDNEY~s *he~will~make*~TURN.ASIDE⁽ⱽ⁾~her **3:16** and~*he~did~make*~BURN.INCENSE⁽ⱽ⁾~them⁽ᵐ⁾ the~ADMINISTRATOR the~ALTAR~unto BREAD FIRE.OFFERING to~AROMA SWEET ALL FAT to~**YHWH** **3:17** CUSTOM DISTANT to~GENERATION~s~you⁽ᵐᵖ⁾ in~ALL SETTLING~s~you⁽ᵐᵖ⁾ ALL FAT and~ALL BLOOD NOT *you*⁽ᵐᵖ⁾~*will*~EAT⁽ⱽ⁾

Chapter 4

4:1 and~*he~will~much*~SPEAK⁽ⱽ⁾ **YHWH** TO Mosheh to~>~SAY⁽ⱽ⁾ **4:2** *!*⁽ᵐˢ⁾~*much*~SPEAK⁽ⱽ⁾ TO SON~s Yisra'eyl to~>~SAY⁽ⱽ⁾ SOUL GIVEN.THAT *she~will~*FAIL⁽ⱽ⁾ in~ERROR from~ALL DIRECTIVE~s **YHWH** WHICH NOT *they*⁽ᶠ⁾~*will~be~*DO⁽ⱽ⁾ and~*he~did~*DO⁽ⱽ⁾ from~UNIT from~THEY⁽ᶠ⁾ **4:3** IF the~ADMINISTRATOR the~SMEARED *he~will~*FAIL⁽ⱽ⁾ to~GUILTINESS the~PEOPLE and~*he~did~make~*COME.NEAR⁽ⱽ⁾ UPON FAILURE~him WHICH *he~did~*FAIL⁽ⱽ⁾ BULL SON CATTLE WHOLE to~**YHWH** to~FAILURE **4:4** and~*he~did~make~*COME⁽ⱽ⁾ AT the~BULL TO OPENING TENT APPOINTED to~FACE~s **YHWH** and~*he~did~*SUPPORT⁽ⱽ⁾ AT HAND~him UPON HEAD the~BULL and~*he~did~*SLAY⁽ⱽ⁾ AT the~BULL to~FACE~s **YHWH** **4:5** and~*he~did~*TAKE⁽ⱽ⁾ the~ADMINISTRATOR the~SMEARED from~BLOOD the~BULL and~*he~did~make~*COME⁽ⱽ⁾ AT~him TO TENT APPOINTED **4:6** and~*he~did~*DIP⁽ⱽ⁾ the~ADMINISTRATOR AT FINGER~him in~the~BLOOD and~*he~did~make~*SPATTER⁽ⱽ⁾ FROM the~BLOOD SEVEN FOOTSTEP~s to~FACE~s **YHWH** AT FACE~s TENT.CURTAIN the~SPECIAL **4:7** and~*he~did~*GIVE⁽ⱽ⁾ the~ADMINISTRATOR FROM the~BLOOD UPON HORN~s ALTAR INCENSE.SMOKE the~AROMATIC.SPICE~s to~FACE~s **YHWH** WHICH in~TENT APPOINTED and~AT ALL BLOOD the~BULL *he~will~*POUR.OUT⁽ⱽ⁾ TO BOTTOM.BASE ALTAR the~ASCENSION.OFFERING WHICH OPENING TENT

APPOINTED   **4:8** and~AT ALL FAT BULL the~FAILURE *he~will~make~* RAISE.UP[(V)] FROM~him AT the~FAT the~*much~*COVER.OVER[(V)]~*ing*[(ms)] UPON the~INSIDE and~AT ALL the~FAT WHICH UPON the~INSIDE   **4:9** and~AT TWO the~KIDNEY~s and~AT the~FAT WHICH UPON~them[(f)] WHICH UPON the~HIP~s and~AT the~LOBE UPON the~HEAVY UPON the~KIDNEY~s *he~ will~make~*TURN.ASIDE[(V)]~her   **4:10** like~WHICH *they*[(m)]~*will~make~* RAISE.UP[(V)] from~OX SACRIFICE the~OFFERING.OF.RESTITUTION~s and~*he~ did~make~*BURN.INCENSE[(V)]~them[(m)] the~ADMINISTRATOR UPON ALTAR the~ASCENSION.OFFERING   **4:11** and~AT SKIN the~BULL and~AT ALL FLESH~him UPON HEAD~him and~UPON LEG~s~him and~INSIDE~him and~ DUNG~him   **4:12** and~*he~did~make~*GO.OUT[(V)] AT ALL the~BULL TO from~ OUTSIDE to~the~CAMP TO AREA CLEAN TO POUR.OUT[(V)]~*ing*[(ms)] the~ FATNESS and~*he~did~*CREMATE[(V)] AT~him UPON TREE~s in~the~FIRE UPON POUR.OUT[(V)]~*ing*[(ms)] the~FATNESS *he~will~be~*CREMATE[(V)]   **4:13** and~IF ALL COMPANY Yisra'eyl *they*[(m)]~*will~*GO.ASTRAY[(V)] and~*he~did~be~* BE.OUT.OF.SIGHT[(V)] WORD from~EYE~s2 the~ASSEMBLY and~*they~did~* DO[(V)] UNIT from~ALL DIRECTIVE~s **YHWH** WHICH NOT *they*[(f)]~*will~be~*DO[(V)] and~*they~did~*BE.GUILTY[(V)]   **4:14** and~*she~did~be~*KNOW[(V)] the~FAILURE WHICH *they~did~*FAIL[(V)] UPON~her and~*they~did~make~*COME.NEAR[(V)] the~ASSEMBLY BULL SON CATTLE to~FAILURE and~*they~did~make~*COME[(V)] AT~him to~FACE~s TENT APPOINTED   **4:15** and~*they~did~*SUPPORT[(V)] BEARD~s the~COMPANY AT HAND~s2~them[(m)] UPON HEAD the~BULL to~ FACE~s **YHWH** and~*he~did~*SLAY[(V)] AT the~BULL to~FACE~s **YHWH**   **4:16** and~*he~did~make~*COME[(V)] the~ADMINISTRATOR the~ SMEARED from~BLOOD the~BULL TO TENT APPOINTED   **4:17** and~*he~did~* DIP[(V)] the~ADMINISTRATOR FINGER~him FROM the~BLOOD and~*he~did~ make~*SPATTER[(V)] SEVEN FOOTSTEP~s to~FACE~s **YHWH** AT FACE~s the~ TENT.CURTAIN   **4:18** and~FROM the~BLOOD *he~will~*GIVE[(V)] UPON HORN~s the~ALTAR WHICH to~FACE~s **YHWH** WHICH in~TENT APPOINTED and~AT ALL the~BLOOD *he~will~*POUR.OUT[(V)] TO BOTTOM.BASE ALTAR the~ ASCENSION.OFFERING WHICH OPENING TENT APPOINTED   **4:19** and~AT ALL FAT~him *he~will~make~*RAISE.UP[(V)] FROM~him and~*he~did~make~* BURN.INCENSE[(V)] the~ALTAR~unto   **4:20** and~*he~did~*DO[(V)] to~the~BULL like~WHICH *he~did~*DO[(V)] to~BULL the~FAILURE SO *he~will~*DO[(V)] to~him and~*he~did~much~*COVER[(V)] UPON~them[(m)] the~ADMINISTRATOR and~*he~ did~be~*FORGIVE[(V)] to~them[(m)]   **4:21** and~*he~did~make~*GO.OUT[(V)] AT the~ BULL TO from~OUTSIDE to~the~CAMP and~*he~did~*CREMATE[(V)] AT~him like~WHICH *he~did~*CREMATE[(V)] AT the~BULL the~FIRST FAILURE the~ ASSEMBLY HE   **4:22** WHICH CAPTAIN *he~will~*FAIL[(V)] and~*he~did~*DO[(V)] UNIT from~ALL DIRECTIVE~s **YHWH** Elohiym~him WHICH NOT *they*[(f)]~*will~be~* DO[(V)] in~ERROR and~*he~did~*BE.GUILTY[(V)]   **4:23** OR *he~did~be~make~* KNOW[(V)] TO~him FAILURE~him WHICH *he~did~*FAIL[(V)] in~her and~*he~did~ make~*COME[(V)] AT DONATION~him HAIRY.GOAT SHE-GOAT~s MALE WHOLE   **4:24** and~*he~did~*SUPPORT[(V)] HAND~him UPON HEAD the~ HAIRY.GOAT and~*he~did~*SLAY[(V)] AT~him in~AREA WHICH *he~will~*SLAY[(V)]

The Book of Leviticus

AT the~ASCENSION.OFFERING to~FACE~s **YHWH** FAILURE HE **4:25** and~*he~did*~TAKE⁽ᵛ⁾ the~ADMINISTRATOR from~BLOOD the~FAILURE in~FINGER~him and~*he~did*~GIVE⁽ᵛ⁾ UPON HORN~s ALTAR the~ASCENSION.OFFERING and~AT BLOOD~him *he~will*~POUR.OUT⁽ᵛ⁾ TO BOTTOM.BASE ALTAR the~ASCENSION.OFFERING **4:26** and~AT ALL FAT~him *he~did~make*~BURN.INCENSE⁽ᵛ⁾ the~ALTAR~unto like~FAT SACRIFICE the~OFFERING.OF.RESTITUTION~s and~*he~did~much*~COVER⁽ᵛ⁾ UPON~him the~ADMINISTRATOR from~FAILURE~him and~*he~did~be*~FORGIVE⁽ᵛ⁾ to~him **4:27** and~IF SOUL UNIT *she~will*~FAIL⁽ᵛ⁾ in~ERROR from~PEOPLE the~LAND in~>~DO⁽ᵛ⁾~her UNIT from~DIRECTIVE~s **YHWH** WHICH NOT *they*⁽ᶠ⁾~*will~be*~DO⁽ᵛ⁾ and~*he~did*~BE.GUILTY⁽ᵛ⁾ **4:28** OR *he~did~be~make*~KNOW⁽ᵛ⁾ TO~him FAILURE~him WHICH *he~did*~FAIL⁽ᵛ⁾ and~*he~did~make*~COME⁽ᵛ⁾ DONATION~him HAIRY.GOAT SHE-GOAT~s WHOLE FEMALE UPON FAILURE~him WHICH *he~did*~FAIL⁽ᵛ⁾ **4:29** and~*he~did*~SUPPORT⁽ᵛ⁾ AT HAND~him UPON HEAD the~FAILURE and~*he~did*~SLAY⁽ᵛ⁾ AT the~FAILURE in~AREA the~ASCENSION.OFFERING **4:30** and~*he~did*~TAKE⁽ᵛ⁾ the~ADMINISTRATOR from~BLOOD~her in~FINGER~him and~*he~did*~GIVE⁽ᵛ⁾ UPON HORN~s ALTAR the~ASCENSION.OFFERING and~AT ALL BLOOD~her *he~will*~POUR.OUT⁽ᵛ⁾ TO BOTTOM.BASE the~ALTAR **4:31** and~AT ALL FAT~her *he~will~make*~TURN.ASIDE⁽ᵛ⁾ like~WHICH *he~did~be~make*~TURN.ASIDE⁽ᵛ⁾ FAT from~UPON SACRIFICE the~OFFERING.OF.RESTITUTION~s and~*he~did~make*~BURN.INCENSE⁽ᵛ⁾ the~ADMINISTRATOR the~ALTAR~unto to~AROMA SWEET to~**YHWH** and~*he~did~much*~COVER⁽ᵛ⁾ UPON~him the~ADMINISTRATOR and~*he~did~be*~FORGIVE⁽ᵛ⁾ to~him **4:32** and~IF SHEEP *he~will~make*~COME⁽ᵛ⁾ DONATION~him to~FAILURE FEMALE WHOLE *he~will~make*~COME⁽ᵛ⁾~her **4:33** and~*he~did*~SUPPORT⁽ᵛ⁾ AT HAND~him UPON HEAD the~FAILURE and~*he~did*~SLAY⁽ᵛ⁾ AT~her to~FAILURE in~AREA WHICH *he~will*~SLAY⁽ᵛ⁾ AT the~ASCENSION.OFFERING **4:34** and~*he~did*~TAKE⁽ᵛ⁾ the~ADMINISTRATOR from~BLOOD the~FAILURE in~FINGER~him and~*he~did*~GIVE⁽ᵛ⁾ UPON HORN~s ALTAR the~ASCENSION.OFFERING and~AT ALL BLOOD~her *he~will*~POUR.OUT⁽ᵛ⁾ TO BOTTOM.BASE the~ALTAR **4:35** and~AT ALL FAT~her *he~will~make*~TURN.ASIDE⁽ᵛ⁾ like~WHICH *he~will~be~make*~TURN.ASIDE⁽ᵛ⁾ FAT the~SHEEP from~SACRIFICE the~OFFERING.OF.RESTITUTION~s and~*he~did~make*~BURN.INCENSE⁽ᵛ⁾ the~ADMINISTRATOR AT~them⁽ᵐ⁾ the~ALTAR~unto UPON FIRE.OFFERING~s **YHWH** and~*he~did~much*~COVER⁽ᵛ⁾ UPON~him the~ADMINISTRATOR UPON FAILURE~him WHICH *he~did*~FAIL⁽ᵛ⁾ and~*he~did~be*~FORGIVE⁽ᵛ⁾ to~him

Chapter 5

5:1 and~SOUL GIVEN.THAT *she~will*~FAIL⁽ᵛ⁾ and~*she~did*~HEAR⁽ᵛ⁾ VOICE OATH and~HE WITNESS OR *he~did*~SEE⁽ᵛ⁾ OR *he~did*~KNOW⁽ᵛ⁾ IF NOT *he~will~make*~BE.FACE.TO.FACE⁽ᵛ⁾ and~*he~did*~LIFT.UP⁽ᵛ⁾ TWISTEDNESS~

him **5:2** OR SOUL WHICH *she~will*~TOUCH⁽ᵛ⁾ in~ALL WORD DIRTY OR in~ CARCASS LIVING DIRTY OR in~CARCASS BEAST DIRTY OR in~CARCASS SWARMER DIRTY and~*he~did~be*~BE.OUT.OF.SIGHT⁽ᵛ⁾ FROM~him and~HE DIRTY and~*he~did*~BE.GUILTY⁽ᵛ⁾ **5:3** OR GIVEN.THAT *he~will*~TOUCH⁽ᵛ⁾ in~ DIRTY HUMAN to~ALL DIRTY~him WHICH *he~will*~BE.DIRTY⁽ᵛ⁾ in~her and~ *he~did~be*~BE.OUT.OF.SIGHT⁽ᵛ⁾ FROM~him and~HE *he~did*~KNOW⁽ᵛ⁾ and~ *he~did*~BE.GUILTY⁽ᵛ⁾ **5:4** OR SOUL GIVEN.THAT *she~will~be*~SWEAR⁽ᵛ⁾ to~ >~*much*~UTTER⁽ᵛ⁾ in~LIP~s2 to~>~*make*~BE.DYSFUNCTIONAL⁽ᵛ⁾ OR to~>~ *make*~DO.WELL⁽ᵛ⁾ to~ALL WHICH *he~will~much*~UTTER⁽ᵛ⁾ the~HUMAN in~ SWEARING and~*he~did~be*~BE.OUT.OF.SIGHT⁽ᵛ⁾ FROM~him and~HE *he~ did*~KNOW⁽ᵛ⁾ and~*he~did*~BE.GUILTY⁽ᵛ⁾ to~UNIT from~THESE **5:5** and~*he~ did*~EXIST⁽ᵛ⁾ GIVEN.THAT *he~will*~BE.GUILTY⁽ᵛ⁾ to~UNIT from~THESE and~ *he~did~self*~THROW.THE.HAND⁽ᵛ⁾ WHICH *he~did*~FAIL⁽ᵛ⁾ UPON~ her **5:6** and~*he~did~make*~COME⁽ᵛ⁾ AT GUILT~him to~**YHWH** UPON FAILURE~him WHICH *he~did*~FAIL⁽ᵛ⁾ FEMALE FROM the~FLOCKS SHEEP OR HAIRY.GOAT SHE-GOAT~s to~FAILURE and~*he~did~much*~COVER⁽ᵛ⁾ UPON~ him the~ADMINISTRATOR from~FAILURE~him **5:7** and~IF NOT *she~will*~ *make*~TOUCH⁽ᵛ⁾ HAND~him SUFFICIENT RAM and~*he~did~make*~COME⁽ᵛ⁾ AT GUILT~him WHICH *he~did*~FAIL⁽ᵛ⁾ TWO TURTLEDOVE~s OR TWO SON~s DOVE to~**YHWH** UNIT to~FAILURE and~UNIT to~ ASCENSION.OFFERING **5:8** and~*he~did~make*~COME⁽ᵛ⁾ AT~them⁽ᵐ⁾ TO the~ ADMINISTRATOR and~*he~did~make*~COME.NEAR⁽ᵛ⁾ AT WHICH to~the~ FAILURE FIRST and~*he~did*~SNAP.OFF⁽ᵛ⁾ AT HEAD~him from~FOREFRONT NECK~him and~NOT *he~will~make*~SEPARATE⁽ᵛ⁾ **5:9** and~*he~did~make*~ SPATTER⁽ᵛ⁾ from~BLOOD the~FAILURE UPON WALL the~ALTAR and~the~*be*~ REMAIN⁽ᵛ⁾~*ing*⁽ᵐˢ⁾ in~the~BLOOD *he~will~be*~DRAIN⁽ᵛ⁾ TO BOTTOM.BASE the~ALTAR FAILURE HE **5:10** and~AT the~SECOND *he~will*~DO⁽ᵛ⁾ ASCENSION.OFFERING like~the~DECISION and~*he~did~much*~COVER⁽ᵛ⁾ UPON~him the~ADMINISTRATOR from~FAILURE~him WHICH *he~did*~FAIL⁽ᵛ⁾ and~*he~did~be*~FORGIVE⁽ᵛ⁾ to~him **5:11** and~IF NOT *she~will~make*~ OVERTAKE⁽ᵛ⁾ HAND~him to~TWO TURTLEDOVE~s OR to~TWO SON~s DOVE and~*he~did~make*~COME⁽ᵛ⁾ AT DONATION~him WHICH *he~did*~FAIL⁽ᵛ⁾ TENTH the~EYPHAH FLOUR to~FAILURE NOT *he~will*~PLACE⁽ᵛ⁾ UPON~her OIL and~NOT *he~will*~GIVE⁽ᵛ⁾ UPON~her FRANKINCENSE GIVEN.THAT FAILURE SHE **5:12** and~*he~did~make*~COME⁽ᵛ⁾~her TO the~ ADMINISTRATOR and~*he~did*~GRASP⁽ᵛ⁾ the~ADMINISTRATOR FROM~her FILLING HANDFUL~him AT MEMORIAL~her and~*he~did~make*~ BURN.INCENSE⁽ᵛ⁾ the~ALTAR~unto UPON FIRE.OFFERING~s **YHWH** FAILURE SHE **5:13** and~*he~did~much*~COVER⁽ᵛ⁾ UPON~him the~ADMINISTRATOR UPON FAILURE~him WHICH *he~did*~FAIL⁽ᵛ⁾ from~UNIT from~THESE and~*he~ did~be*~FORGIVE⁽ᵛ⁾ to~him and~*she~did*~EXIST⁽ᵛ⁾ to~the~ADMINISTRATOR like~the~DEPOSIT **5:14** and~*he~will~much*~SPEAK⁽ᵛ⁾ **YHWH** TO Mosheh to~ >~SAY⁽ᵛ⁾ **5:15** SOUL GIVEN.THAT *she~will*~TRANSGRESS⁽ᵛ⁾ TRANSGRESSION and~FAILURE in~ERROR from~SPECIAL~s **YHWH** and~*he~did~make*~COME⁽ᵛ⁾ AT GUILT~him to~**YHWH** BUCK WHOLE FROM the~FLOCKS in~

The Book of Leviticus

ARRANGEMENT~you[ms] SILVER SHEQEL~s in~SHEQEL the~SPECIAL to~ GUILT **5:16** and~AT WHICH *he~did*~FAIL[V] FROM the~SPECIAL *he~will*~ much~MAKE.RESTITUTION[V] and~AT FIFTH~him *he~will~make*~ADD[V] UPON~him and~*he~did*~GIVE[V] AT~him to~the~ADMINISTRATOR and~the~ ADMINISTRATOR *he~will~much*~COVER[V] UPON~him in~BUCK the~GUILT and~*he~did~be*~FORGIVE[V] to~him **5:17** and~IF SOUL GIVEN.THAT *she~ will*~FAIL[V] and~*she~did*~DO[V] UNIT from~ALL DIRECTIVE~s **YHWH** WHICH NOT *they[f]~will~be*~DO[V] and~NOT *he~did*~KNOW[V] and~*he~did*~ BE.GUILTY[V] and~*he~did*~LIFT.UP[V] TWISTEDNESS~him **5:18** and~*he~did*~ *make*~COME[V] BUCK WHOLE FROM the~FLOCKS in~ARRANGEMENT~you[ms] to~GUILT TO the~ADMINISTRATOR and~*he~did~much*~COVER[V] UPON~him the~ADMINISTRATOR UPON ERROR~him WHICH *he~did*~ERR[V] and~HE NOT *he~did*~KNOW[V] and~*he~did~be*~FORGIVE[V] to~him **5:19** GUILT HE >~ BE.GUILTY[V] *he~did*~BE.GUILTY[V] to~**YHWH** **5:20 (6:1)** and~*he~will~much*~ SPEAK[V] **YHWH** TO Mosheh to~>~SAY[V] **5:21 (6:2)** SOUL GIVEN.THAT *she~ will*~FAIL[V] and~*she~did*~TRANSGRESS[V] TRANSGRESSION in~**YHWH** and~ *he~did~much*~DENY[V] in~the~NEIGHBOR~him in~DEPOSITED OR in~ SECURITY.DEPOSIT HAND OR in~PLUCKING OR *he~did*~OPPRESS[V] AT NEIGHBOR~him **5:22 (6:3)** OR *he~did*~FIND[V] LOST.THING and~*he~did*~ much~DENY[V] in~her and~*he~did~be*~SWEAR[V] UPON FALSE UPON UNIT from~ALL WHICH *he~will*~DO[V] the~HUMAN to~>~FAIL[V] in~ them[f] **5:23 (6:4)** and~*he~did*~EXIST[V] GIVEN.THAT *he~will*~FAIL[V] and~*he~ did*~BE.GUILTY[V] and~*he~did~make*~TURN.BACK[V] AT the~PLUCKED WHICH *he~did*~PLUCK.AWAY[V] OR AT the~OPPRESSION WHICH *he~did*~OPPRESS[V] OR AT the~DEPOSITED WHICH *he~did~be~make*~REGISTER[V] AT~him OR AT the~LOST.THING WHICH *he~did*~FIND[V] **5:24 (6:5)** OR from~ALL WHICH *he~will~be*~SWEAR[V] UPON~him to~the~FALSE and~*he~did~much*~ MAKE.RESTITUTION[V] AT~him in~HEAD~him and~FIFTH~s~him *he~will~ make*~ADD[V] UPON~him to~the~WHICH HE to~him *he~will*~GIVE[V]~him in~ DAY GUILTINESS~him **5:25 (6:6)** and~AT GUILT~him *he~will~make*~COME[V] to~**YHWH** BUCK WHOLE FROM the~FLOCKS in~ARRANGEMENT~you[ms] to~ GUILT TO the~ADMINISTRATOR **5:26 (6:7)** and~*he~did~much*~COVER[V] UPON~him the~ADMINISTRATOR to~FACE~s **YHWH** and~*he~did~be*~ FORGIVE[V] to~him UPON UNIT from~ALL WHICH *he~will*~DO[V] to~ GUILTINESS in~her

---

Chapter 6

6:1 (6:8) and~*he~will~much*~SPEAK[V] **YHWH** TO Mosheh to~>~ SAY[V] **6:2 (6:9)** ![ms]~much~DIRECT[V] AT Aharon and~AT SON~s~him to~>~ SAY[V] THIS TEACHING the~ASCENSION.OFFERING SHE the~ ASCENSION.OFFERING UPON SMOLDERING.FIRE UPON the~ALTAR ALL the~ NIGHT UNTIL the~MORNING and~FIRE the~ALTAR *she~will~be~make*~

SMOLDER[(v)] in~him **6:3 (6:10)** and~*he~did*~WEAR[(v)] the~ADMINISTRATOR LONG.GARMENT~him STRAND and~UNDERGARMENT~s STRAND *he~will*~WEAR[(v)] UPON FLESH~him and~*he~did~make*~RAISE.UP[(v)] AT the~FATNESS WHICH *she~will*~EAT[(v)] the~FIRE AT the~ASCENSION.OFFERING UPON the~ALTAR and~*he~did*~PLACE[(v)]~him BESIDE the~ALTAR **6:4 (6:11)** and~*he~did*~STRIP.OFF[(v)] AT GARMENT~s~him and~*he~did*~WEAR[(v)] GARMENT~s OTHER~s and~*he~did~make*~GO.OUT[(v)] AT the~FATNESS TO from~OUTSIDE to~the~CAMP TO AREA CLEAN **6:5 (6:12)** and~the~FIRE UPON the~ALTAR *she~will~be~make*~SMOLDER[(v)] in~him NOT *she~will*~QUENCH[(v)] and~*he~did~much*~BURN[(v)] UPON~her the~ADMINISTRATOR TREE~s in~the~MORNING in~the~MORNING and~*he~did*~ARRANGE[(v)] UPON~her the~ASCENSION.OFFERING and~*he~did~make*~BURN.INCENSE[(v)] UPON~her FAT~s the~OFFERING.OF.RESTITUTION~s **6:6 (6:13)** FIRE CONTINUALLY *she~will~be~make*~SMOLDER[(v)] UPON the~ALTAR NOT *she~will*~QUENCH[(v)] **6:7 (6:14)** and~THIS TEACHING the~DEPOSIT *![(ms)]~make*~COME.NEAR[(v)] AT~her SON~s Aharon to~FACE~s **YHWH** TO FACE~s the~ALTAR **6:8 (6:15)** and~*he~did~make*~RAISE.UP[(v)] FROM~him in~HANDFUL~him from~FLOUR the~DEPOSIT and~from~OIL and~AT ALL the~FRANKINCENSE WHICH UPON the~DEPOSIT and~*he~did~make*~BURN.INCENSE[(v)] the~ALTAR AROMA SWEET MEMORIAL~her to~**YHWH** **6:9 (6:16)** and~the~*be*~LEAVE.BEHIND[(v)]~*ing*[(fs)] FROM~her *they*[(m)]~*will*~EAT[(v)] Aharon and~SON~s~him UNLEAVENED.BREAD~s *she~will~be*~EAT[(v)] in~AREA UNIQUE in~COURTYARD TENT APPOINTED *they*[(m)]~*will*~EAT[(v)]~her **6:10 (6:17)** NOT *she~will~be*~BAKE[(v)] LEAVENED.BREAD DISTRIBUTION~them[(m)] *I~did*~GIVE[(v)] AT~her from~FIRE.OFFERING~s~me SPECIAL SPECIAL~s SHE like~the~FAILURE and~like~GUILT **6:11 (6:18)** ALL MALE in~SON~s Aharon *he~will*~EAT[(v)]~her CUSTOM DISTANT to~GENERATION~s~you[(mp)] from~FIRE.OFFERING~s **YHWH** ALL WHICH *he~will*~TOUCH[(v)] in~them[(m)] *he~will*~SET.APART[(v)] **6:12 (6:19)** and~*he~will~much*~SPEAK[(v)] **YHWH** TO Mosheh to~>~SAY[(v)] **6:13 (6:20)** THIS DONATION Aharon and~SON~s~him WHICH *they*[(m)]~*will~make*~COME.NEAR[(v)] to~**YHWH** in~DAY >~*be*~SMEAR[(v)] AT~him TENTH the~EYPHAH FLOUR DEPOSIT CONTINUALLY ONE.HALF~her in~the~MORNING and~ONE.HALF~her in~the~EVENING **6:14 (6:21)** UPON PAN in~the~OIL *she~will~be*~DO[(v)] *be~make*~FRY[(v)]~*ing*[(fs)] you[(ms)]~*will~make*~COME[(v)]~her COOKED~s DEPOSIT FRAGMENT~s you[(ms)]~*will~make*~COME.NEAR[(v)] AROMA SWEET to~**YHWH** **6:15 (6:22)** and~the~ADMINISTRATOR the~SMEARED UNDER~him from~SON~s~him *he~will*~DO[(v)] AT~her CUSTOM DISTANT to~**YHWH** ENTIRELY *she~will~be~make*~BURN.INCENSE[(v)] **6:16 (6:23)** and~ALL DEPOSIT ADMINISTRATOR ENTIRELY *she~will*~EXIST[(v)] NOT *she~will~be*~EAT[(v)] **6:17 (6:24)** and~*he~will~much*~SPEAK[(v)] **YHWH** TO Mosheh to~>~SAY[(v)] **6:18 (6:25)** *![(ms)]~much*~SPEAK[(v)] TO Aharon and~TO SON~s~him to~>~SAY[(v)] THIS TEACHING the~FAILURE in~AREA WHICH you[(ms)]~*will*~SLAY[(v)] the~ASCENSION.OFFERING you[(ms)]~*will*~SLAY[(v)] the~FAILURE to~FACE~s **YHWH** SPECIAL SPECIAL~s SHE **6:19 (6:26)** the~ADMINISTRATOR the~

much~FAIL⁽ᵛ⁾~ing⁽ᵐˢ⁾ AT~her he~will~EAT⁽ᵛ⁾~her in~AREA UNIQUE she~will~be~EAT⁽ᵛ⁾ in~COURTYARD TENT APPOINTED   **6:20 (6:27)** ALL WHICH he~will~TOUCH⁽ᵛ⁾ in~FLESH~her he~will~SET.APART⁽ᵛ⁾ and~WHICH he~will~SPATTER⁽ᵛ⁾ from~BLOOD~her UPON the~GARMENT WHICH he~will~SPATTER⁽ᵛ⁾ UPON~her you⁽ᵐᵖ⁾~will~much~WASH⁽ᵛ⁾ in~AREA UNIQUE   **6:21 (6:28)** and~UTENSIL CLAY WHICH she~will~be~much~BOIL⁽ᵛ⁾ in~him he~will~be~CRACK⁽ᵛ⁾ and~IF in~UTENSIL COPPER she~did~be~much~BOIL⁽ᵛ⁾ and~he~did~be~much~SCOUR⁽ᵛ⁾ and~he~did~be~much~FLUSH⁽ᵛ⁾ in~the~WATER~s2   **6:22 (6:29)** ALL MALE in~the~ADMINISTRATOR~s he~will~EAT⁽ᵛ⁾ AT~her SPECIAL SPECIAL~s SHE   **6:23 (6:30)** and~ALL FAILURE WHICH he~will~be~make~COME⁽ᵛ⁾ from~BLOOD~her TO TENT APPOINTED to~>~much~COVER⁽ᵛ⁾ in~the~SPECIAL NOT she~will~be~EAT⁽ᵛ⁾ in~the~FIRE you⁽ᵐˢ⁾~will~CREMATE⁽ᵛ⁾

Chapter 7

7:1 and~THIS TEACHING the~GUILT SPECIAL SPECIAL~s HE   **7:2** in~AREA WHICH he~will~SLAY⁽ᵛ⁾~him AT the~ASCENSION.OFFERING he~will~SLAY⁽ᵛ⁾~him AT the~GUILT and~AT BLOOD~him he~will~SPRINKLE⁽ᵛ⁾ UPON the~ALTAR ALL.AROUND   **7:3** and~AT ALL FAT~him he~will~make~COME.NEAR⁽ᵛ⁾ FROM~him AT the~RUMP and~AT the~FAT the~much~COVER.OVER⁽ᵛ⁾~ing⁽ᵐˢ⁾ AT the~INSIDE   **7:4** and~AT TWO the~KIDNEY~s and~AT the~FAT WHICH UPON~them⁽ᶠ⁾ WHICH UPON the~HIP~s and~AT the~LOBE UPON the~HEAVY UPON the~KIDNEY~s he~will~make~TURN.ASIDE⁽ᵛ⁾~her   **7:5** and~he~did~make~BURN.INCENSE⁽ᵛ⁾ AT~them⁽ᵐ⁾ the~ADMINISTRATOR the~ALTAR~unto FIRE.OFFERING to~**YHWH** GUILT HE   **7:6** ALL MALE in~the~ADMINISTRATOR~s he~will~EAT⁽ᵛ⁾~him in~AREA UNIQUE he~will~be~EAT⁽ᵛ⁾ SPECIAL SPECIAL~s HE   **7:7** like~the~FAILURE like~GUILT TEACHING UNIT to~them⁽ᵐ⁾ the~ADMINISTRATOR WHICH he~will~much~COVER⁽ᵛ⁾ in~him to~him he~will~EXIST⁽ᵛ⁾   **7:8** and~the~ADMINISTRATOR the~make~COME.NEAR⁽ᵛ⁾~ing⁽ᵐˢ⁾ AT ASCENSION.OFFERING MAN SKIN the~ASCENSION.OFFERING WHICH he~did~make~COME.NEAR⁽ᵛ⁾ to~the~ADMINISTRATOR to~him he~will~EXIST⁽ᵛ⁾   **7:9** and~ALL DEPOSIT WHICH she~will~be~BAKE⁽ᵛ⁾ in~the~OVEN and~ALL he~did~be~DO⁽ᵛ⁾ in~the~BOILING.POT and~UPON PAN to~the~ADMINISTRATOR the~make~COME.NEAR⁽ᵛ⁾~ing⁽ᵐˢ⁾ AT~her to~him she~will~EXIST⁽ᵛ⁾   **7:10** and~ALL DEPOSIT MIX⁽ᵛ⁾~ed⁽ᶠˢ⁾ in~the~OIL and~DRIED.OUT to~ALL SON~s Aharon she~will~EXIST⁽ᵛ⁾ MAN like~BROTHER~him   **7:11** and~THIS TEACHING SACRIFICE the~OFFERING.OF.RESTITUTION~s WHICH he~will~make~COME.NEAR⁽ᵛ⁾ to~**YHWH**   **7:12** IF UPON THANKS he~will~make~COME.NEAR⁽ᵛ⁾~him and~he~did~make~COME.NEAR⁽ᵛ⁾ UPON SACRIFICE the~THANKS PIERCED.BREAD~s UNLEAVENED.BREAD~s MIX⁽ᵛ⁾~ed⁽ᶠᵖ⁾ in~the~OIL and~THIN.BREAD~s UNLEAVENED.BREAD~s SMEAR⁽ᵛ⁾~ed⁽ᵐᵖ⁾ in~the~OIL and~FLOUR *be~make~*FRY$^{(V)}$~*ing*$^{(fs)}$ PIERCED.BREAD~s MIX$^{(V)}$~*ed*$^{(fp)}$ in~the~ OIL   **7:13** UPON PIERCED.BREAD~s BREAD LEAVENED.BREAD *he~will~make~*COME.NEAR$^{(V)}$ DONATION~him UPON SACRIFICE THANKS OFFERING.OF.RESTITUTION~s~him   **7:14** and~*he~did~make~*COME.NEAR$^{(V)}$ FROM~him UNIT from~ALL DONATION OFFERING to~**YHWH** to~the~ADMINISTRATOR the~SPRINKLE$^{(V)}$~*ing*$^{(ms)}$ AT BLOOD the~OFFERING.OF.RESTITUTION~s to~him *he~will~*EXIST$^{(V)}$ **7:15** and~FLESH SACRIFICE THANKS OFFERING.OF.RESTITUTION~s~him in~DAY DONATION~him *he~will~be~*EAT$^{(V)}$ NOT *he~will~make~*REST$^{(V)}$ FROM~him UNTIL MORNING   **7:16** and~IF VOW OR FREEWILL.OFFERING SACRIFICE DONATION~him in~DAY >~*make~*COME.NEAR$^{(V)}$~him AT SACRIFICE~him *he~will~be~*EAT$^{(V)}$ and~from~MORROW and~the~*be~*LEAVE.BEHIND$^{(V)}$~*ing*$^{(ms)}$ FROM~him *he~will~be~*EAT$^{(V)}$ **7:17** and~the~*be~*LEAVE.BEHIND$^{(V)}$~*ing*$^{(ms)}$ from~FLESH the~SACRIFICE in~the~DAY the~THIRD in~the~FIRE *he~will~be~*CREMATE$^{(V)}$ **7:18** and~IF the~>~*be~*EAT$^{(V)}$ *he~will~be~*EAT$^{(V)}$ from~FLESH SACRIFICE OFFERING.OF.RESTITUTION~s~him in~the~DAY the~THIRD NOT *he~will~be~*ACCEPT$^{(V)}$ the~*make~*COME.NEAR$^{(V)}$~*ing*$^{(ms)}$ AT~him NOT *he~will~be~*THINK$^{(V)}$ to~him FOUL *he~will~*EXIST$^{(V)}$ and~the~SOUL the~EAT$^{(V)}$~*ing*$^{(fs)}$ FROM~him TWISTEDNESS~her *she~will~*LIFT.UP$^{(V)}$ **7:19** and~the~FLESH WHICH *he~will~*TOUCH$^{(V)}$ in~ALL DIRTY NOT *he~will~be~*EAT$^{(V)}$ in~the~FIRE *he~will~be~*CREMATE$^{(V)}$ and~the~FLESH ALL CLEAN *he~will~*EAT$^{(V)}$ FLESH   **7:20** and~the~SOUL WHICH *she~will~*EAT$^{(V)}$ FLESH from~SACRIFICE the~OFFERING.OF.RESTITUTION~s WHICH to~**YHWH** and~DIRTY~him UPON~him and~*she~did~be~*CUT$^{(V)}$ the~SOUL the~SHE from~PEOPLE~s~her   **7:21** and~SOUL GIVEN.THAT *she~will~*TOUCH$^{(V)}$ in~ALL DIRTY in~DIRTY HUMAN OR in~BEAST DIRTY OR in~ALL FILTHY DIRTY and~*he~did~*EAT$^{(V)}$ from~FLESH SACRIFICE the~OFFERING.OF.RESTITUTION~s WHICH to~**YHWH** and~*she~did~be~*CUT$^{(V)}$ the~SOUL the~SHE from~PEOPLE~s~her   **7:22** and~*he~will~much~*SPEAK$^{(V)}$ **YHWH** TO Mosheh to~>~SAY$^{(V)}$ **7:23** !$^{(ms)}$~*much~*SPEAK$^{(V)}$ TO SON~s Yisra'eyl to~>~SAY$^{(V)}$ ALL FAT OX and~SHEEP and~SHE-GOAT NOT *you*$^{(mp)}$~*will~*EAT$^{(V)}$ **7:24** and~FAT CARCASS and~FAT TORN *he~will~be~*DO$^{(V)}$ to~ALL BUSINESS and~>~EAT$^{(V)}$ NOT *you*$^{(mp)}$~*will~*EAT$^{(V)}$~him   **7:25** GIVEN.THAT ALL EAT$^{(V)}$~*ing*$^{(ms)}$ FAT FROM the~BEAST WHICH *he~will~make~*COME.NEAR$^{(V)}$ FROM~her FIRE.OFFERING to~**YHWH** and~*she~did~be~*CUT$^{(V)}$ the~SOUL the~EAT$^{(V)}$~*ing*$^{(fs)}$ from~PEOPLE~s~her   **7:26** and~ALL BLOOD NOT *you*$^{(mp)}$~*will~*EAT$^{(V)}$ in~ALL SETTLING~s~*you*$^{(mp)}$ to~the~FLYER and~to~the~BEAST   **7:27** ALL SOUL WHICH *she~will~*EAT$^{(V)}$ ALL BLOOD and~*she~did~be~*CUT$^{(V)}$ the~SOUL the~SHE from~PEOPLE~s~her   **7:28** and~*he~will~much~*SPEAK$^{(V)}$ **YHWH** TO Mosheh to~>~SAY$^{(V)}$ **7:29** !$^{(ms)}$~*much~*SPEAK$^{(V)}$ TO SON~s Yisra'eyl to~>~SAY$^{(V)}$ the~*make~*COME.NEAR$^{(V)}$~*ing*$^{(ms)}$ AT SACRIFICE OFFERING.OF.RESTITUTION~s~him to~**YHWH** *he~will~make~*COME$^{(V)}$ AT DONATION~him to~**YHWH** from~SACRIFICE OFFERING.OF.RESTITUTION~s~him   **7:30** HAND~s2~him *they*$^{(f)}$~*will~make~*COME$^{(V)}$ AT FIRE.OFFERING~s **YHWH** AT the~FAT UPON the~CHEST *he~will~make~*COME$^{(V)}$~him AT the~CHEST to~>~*make~*WAVE$^{(V)}$ AT~

him WAVING to~FACE~s **YHWH** **7:31** and~*he~did~make*~BURN.INCENSE[(V)] the~ADMINISTRATOR AT the~FAT the~ALTAR~unto and~*he~did*~EXIST[(V)] the~CHEST to~Aharon and~to~SON~s~him **7:32** and~AT THIGH the~RIGHT.HAND *you*[(mp)]*~will~*GIVE[(V)] OFFERING to~the~ADMINISTRATOR from~SACRIFICE~s OFFERING.OF.RESTITUTION~s*~you*[(mp)] **7:33** the~*make*~COME.NEAR[(V)]~*ing*[(ms)] AT BLOOD the~OFFERING.OF.RESTITUTION~s and~AT the~FAT from~SON~s Aharon to~him *she~will~*EXIST[(V)] THIGH the~RIGHT.HAND to~SHARE **7:34** GIVEN.THAT AT CHEST the~WAVING and~AT THIGH the~OFFERING *I~did~*TAKE[(V)] from~AT SON~s Yisra'eyl from~SACRIFICE~s OFFERING.OF.RESTITUTION~s~them[(m)] and~*I~will~*GIVE[(V)] AT~them[(m)] to~Aharon the~ADMINISTRATOR and~to~SON~s~him to~CUSTOM DISTANT from~AT SON~s Yisra'eyl **7:35** THIS OINTMENT Aharon and~OINTMENT SON~s~him from~FIRE.OFFERING~s **YHWH** in~DAY *he~did~make*~COME.NEAR[(V)] AT~them[(m)] to~>~*much*~ADORN[(V)] to~**YHWH** **7:36** WHICH *he~did~much*~DIRECT[(V)] **YHWH** to~>~GIVE[(V)] to~them[(m)] in~DAY >~SMEAR[(V)]~him AT~them[(m)] from~AT SON~s Yisra'eyl CUSTOM DISTANT to~GENERATION~s~them[(m)] **7:37** THIS the~TEACHING to~the~ASCENSION.OFFERING to~the~DEPOSIT and~to~the~FAILURE and~to~the~GUILT and~to~the~SETTING~s and~to~SACRIFICE the~OFFERING.OF.RESTITUTION~s **7:38** WHICH *he~did~much*~DIRECT[(V)] **YHWH** AT Mosheh in~HILL Sinai in~DAY >~*much*~DIRECT[(V)]~him AT SON~s Yisra'eyl to~>~*make*~COME.NEAR[(V)] AT DONATION~s~them[(m)] to~**YHWH** in~WILDERNESS Sinai

Chapter 8

8:1 and~*he~will~much*~SPEAK[(V)] **YHWH** TO Mosheh to~>~SAY[(V)] **8:2** *I*[(ms)]~TAKE[(V)] AT Aharon and~AT SON~s~him AT~him and~AT the~GARMENT~s and~AT OIL the~OINTMENT and~AT BULL the~FAILURE and~AT TWO the~BUCK~s and~AT WICKER.BASKET the~UNLEAVENED.BREAD~s **8:3** and~AT ALL the~COMPANY *I*[(mp)]~*make*~ASSEMBLE[(V)] TO OPENING TENT APPOINTED **8:4** and~*he~will~*DO[(V)] Mosheh like~WHICH *he~did~much~*DIRECT[(V)] **YHWH** AT~him and~*she~will~*ASSEMBLE[(V)] the~COMPANY TO OPENING TENT APPOINTED **8:5** and~*he~will~*SAY[(V)] Mosheh TO the~COMPANY THIS the~WORD WHICH *he~did~much~*DIRECT[(V)] **YHWH** to~>~DO[(V)] **8:6** and~*he~will~make*~COME.NEAR[(V)] Mosheh AT Aharon and~AT SON~s~him and~*he~will~*BATHE[(V)] AT~them[(m)] in~the~WATER~s2 **8:7** and~*he~will~*GIVE[(V)] UPON~him AT the~TUNIC and~*he~will~*GIRD.UP[(V)] AT~him in~SASH and~*he~will~make*~WEAR[(V)] AT~him AT the~CLOAK and~*he~will~*GIVE[(V)] UPON~him AT the~EPHOD and~*he~will~*GIRD.UP[(V)] AT~him in~DECORATIVE.BAND the~EPHOD and~*he~will~*GIRD[(V)] to~him in~him **8:8** and~*he~will~*PLACE[(V)] UPON~him AT the~BREASTPLATE and~*he~will~*GIVE[(V)] TO the~BREASTPLATE AT the~Uriym and~AT the~

Tumiym   **8:9** and~*he*~*will*~PLACE[(v)] AT the~TURBAN UPON HEAD~him and~*he*~*will*~PLACE[(v)] UPON the~TURBAN TO FOREFRONT FACE~s~him AT BLOSSOM the~GOLD DEDICATION the~SPECIAL like~WHICH *he*~*did*~*much*~DIRECT[(v)] **YHWH** AT Mosheh   **8:10** and~*he*~*will*~TAKE[(v)] Mosheh AT OIL the~OINTMENT and~*he*~*will*~SMEAR[(v)] AT the~DWELLING and~AT ALL WHICH in~him and~*he*~*will*~*much*~SET.APART[(v)] AT~them[(m)]   **8:11** and~*he*~*will*~*make*~SPATTER[(v)] FROM~him UPON the~ALTAR SEVEN FOOTSTEP~s and~*he*~*will*~SMEAR[(v)] AT the~ALTAR and~AT ALL UTENSIL~s~him and~AT the~CAULDRON and~AT BASE~him to~>~*much*~SET.APART[(v)]~them[(m)]   **8:12** and~*he*~*will*~POUR.DOWN[(v)] from~OIL the~OINTMENT UPON HEAD Aharon and~*he*~*will*~SMEAR[(v)] AT~him to~>~*much*~SET.APART[(v)]~him   **8:13** and~*he*~*will*~*make*~COME.NEAR[(v)] Mosheh AT SON~s Aharon and~*he*~*will*~*make*~WEAR[(v)]~them[(m)] TUNIC~s and~*he*~*will*~GIRD.UP[(v)] AT~them[(m)] SASH and~*he*~*will*~SADDLE[(v)] to~them[(m)] HEADDRESS~s like~WHICH *he*~*did*~*much*~DIRECT[(v)] **YHWH** AT Mosheh   **8:14** and~*he*~*will*~*make*~DRAW.NEAR[(v)] AT BULL the~FAILURE and~*he*~*will*~SUPPORT[(v)] Aharon and~SON~s~him AT HAND~s2~them[(m)] UPON HEAD BULL the~FAILURE   **8:15** and~*he*~*will*~SLAY[(v)] and~*he*~*will*~TAKE[(v)] Mosheh AT the~BLOOD and~*he*~*will*~GIVE[(v)] UPON HORN~s the~ALTAR ALL.AROUND in~FINGER~him and~*he*~*will*~*much*~FAIL[(v)] AT the~ALTAR and~AT the~BLOOD *he*~*did*~POUR.DOWN[(v)] TO BOTTOM.BASE the~ALTAR and~*he*~*will*~*much*~SET.APART[(v)]~him to~>~*much*~COVER[(v)] UPON~him   **8:16** and~*he*~*will*~TAKE[(v)] AT ALL the~FAT WHICH UPON the~INSIDE and~AT LOBE the~HEAVY and~AT TWO the~KIDNEY~s and~AT FAT~them[(f)] and~*he*~*will*~*make*~BURN.INCENSE[(v)] Mosheh the~ALTAR~unto   **8:17** and~AT the~BULL and~AT SKIN~him and~AT FLESH~him and~AT DUNG~him *he*~*did*~CREMATE[(v)] in~the~FIRE from~OUTSIDE to~the~CAMP like~WHICH *he*~*did*~*much*~DIRECT[(v)] **YHWH** AT Mosheh   **8:18** and~*he*~*will*~*make*~COME.NEAR[(v)] AT BUCK the~ASCENSION.OFFERING and~*they*[(m)]~*will*~SUPPORT[(v)] Aharon and~SON~s~him AT HAND~s2~them[(m)] UPON HEAD the~BUCK   **8:19** and~*he*~*will*~SLAY[(v)] and~*he*~*will*~SPRINKLE[(v)] Mosheh AT the~BLOOD UPON the~ALTAR ALL.AROUND   **8:20** and~AT the~BUCK *he*~*did*~*much*~DIVIDE.INTO.PIECES[(v)] to~PIECE~s~him and~*he*~*will*~*make*~BURN.INCENSE[(v)] Mosheh AT the~HEAD and~AT the~PIECE~s and~AT the~SUET   **8:21** and~AT the~INSIDE and~AT the~LEG~s2 *he*~*did*~BATHE[(v)] in~the~WATER~s2 and~*he*~*will*~*make*~BURN.INCENSE[(v)] Mosheh AT ALL the~BUCK the~ALTAR~unto ASCENSION.OFFERING HE to~AROMA SWEET FIRE.OFFERING HE to~**YHWH** like~WHICH *he*~*did*~*much*~DIRECT[(v)] **YHWH** AT Mosheh   **8:22** and~*he*~*will*~*make*~COME.NEAR[(v)] AT the~BUCK the~SECOND BUCK the~INSTALLATION~s and~*they*[(m)]~*will*~SUPPORT[(v)] Aharon and~SON~s~him AT HAND~s2~them[(m)] UPON HEAD the~BUCK   **8:23** and~*he*~*will*~SLAY[(v)] and~*he*~*will*~TAKE[(v)] Mosheh from~BLOOD~him and~*he*~*will*~GIVE[(v)] UPON TIP EAR Aharon the~RIGHT and~UPON THUMB HAND~him the~RIGHT and~UPON THUMB FOOT~him the~RIGHT   **8:24** and~*he*~*will*~*make*~COME.NEAR[(v)] AT SON~s Aharon and~*he*~*will*~GIVE[(v)] Mosheh FROM the~BLOOD UPON TIP EAR~them[(m)]

The Book of Leviticus

the~RIGHT and~UPON THUMB HAND~them[(m)] the~RIGHT and~UPON THUMB FOOT~them[(m)] the~RIGHT and~*he*~*will*~SPRINKLE[(V)] Mosheh AT the~BLOOD UPON the~ALTAR ALL.AROUND **8:25** and~*he*~*will*~TAKE[(V)] AT the~FAT and~AT the~RUMP and~AT ALL the~FAT WHICH UPON the~INSIDE and~AT LOBE the~HEAVY and~AT TWO the~KIDNEY~s and~AT FAT~them[(f)] and~AT THIGH the~RIGHT.HAND **8:26** and~from~WICKER.BASKET the~UNLEAVENED.BREAD~s WHICH to~FACE~s **YHWH** *he*~*did*~TAKE[(V)] PIERCED.BREAD UNLEAVENED.BREAD UNIT and~PIERCED.BREAD BREAD OIL UNIT and~THIN.BREAD UNIT and~*he*~*will*~PLACE[(V)] UPON the~FAT~s and~UPON THIGH the~RIGHT.HAND **8:27** and~*he*~*will*~GIVE[(V)] AT the~ALL UPON PALM~s2 Aharon and~UPON PALM~s2 SON~s~him and~*he*~*will*~*make*~WAVE[(V)] AT~them[(m)] WAVING to~FACE~s **YHWH** **8:28** and~*he*~*will*~TAKE[(V)] Mosheh AT~them[(m)] from~UPON PALM~s2~them[(m)] and~*he*~*will*~*make*~BURN.INCENSE[(V)] the~ALTAR~unto UPON the~ASCENSION.OFFERING INSTALLATION~s THEY[(m)] to~AROMA SWEET FIRE.OFFERING HE to~**YHWH** **8:29** and~*he*~*will*~TAKE[(V)] Mosheh AT the~CHEST and~*he*~*will*~*make*~WAVE[(V)]~him WAVING to~FACE~s **YHWH** from~BUCK the~INSTALLATION~s to~Mosheh *he*~*did*~EXIST[(V)] to~SHARE like~WHICH *he*~*did*~much~DIRECT[(V)] **YHWH** AT Mosheh **8:30** and~*he*~*will*~TAKE[(V)] Mosheh from~OIL the~OINTMENT and~FROM the~BLOOD WHICH UPON the~ALTAR and~*he*~*will*~*make*~SPATTER[(V)] UPON Aharon UPON GARMENT~s~him and~UPON SON~s~him and~UPON GARMENT~s SON~s~him AT~him and~*he*~*will*~much~SET.APART[(V)] AT Aharon AT GARMENT~s~him and~AT SON~s~him and~AT GARMENT~s SON~s~him AT~him **8:31** and~*he*~*will*~SAY[(V)] Mosheh TO Aharon and~TO SON~s~him ![(mp)]~much~BOIL[(V)] AT the~FLESH OPENING TENT APPOINTED and~THERE *you*[(mp)]~*will*~EAT[(V)] AT~him and~AT the~BREAD WHICH in~WICKER.BASKET the~INSTALLATION~s like~WHICH *I*~*did*~much~DIRECT[(V)] to~>~SAY[(V)] Aharon and~SON~s~him *they*[(m)]~*will*~EAT[(V)]~him **8:32** and~the~*be*~LEAVE.BEHIND[(V)]~*ing*[(ms)] in~the~FLESH and~in~the~BREAD in~the~FIRE *you*[(mp)]~*will*~CREMATE[(V)] **8:33** and~from~OPENING TENT APPOINTED NOT *you*[(mp)]~*will*~GO.OUT[(V)] SEVEN DAY~s UNTIL DAY >~FILL[(V)] DAY~s INSTALLATION~s~*you*[(mp)] GIVEN.THAT SEVEN DAY~s *he*~*will*~much~FILL[(V)] AT HAND~*you*[(mp)] **8:34** like~WHICH *he*~*did*~DO[(V)] in~the~DAY the~THIS *he*~*did*~much~DIRECT[(V)] **YHWH** to~>~DO[(V)] to~>~much~COVER[(V)] UPON~*you*[(mp)] **8:35** and~OPENING TENT APPOINTED *you*[(mp)]~*will*~SETTLE[(V)] DAYTIME and~NIGHT SEVEN DAY~s and~*you*[(mp)]~*did*~SAFEGUARD[(V)] AT CHARGE **YHWH** and~NOT *you*[(mp)]~*will*~DIE[(V)] GIVEN.THAT SO *I*~*did*~*be*~much~DIRECT[(V)] **8:36** and~*he*~*will*~DO[(V)] Aharon and~SON~s~him AT ALL the~WORD~s WHICH *he*~*did*~much~DIRECT[(V)] **YHWH** in~HAND Mosheh

Chapter 9

9:1 and~*he~will*~EXIST^(v) in~the~DAY the~EIGHTH *he~did*~CALL.OUT^(v) Mosheh to~Aharon and~to~SON~s~him and~to~BEARD~s Yisra'eyl **9:2** and~*he~will*~SAY^(v) TO Aharon *!^(ms)*~TAKE^(v) to~you^(ms) BULLOCK SON CATTLE to~FAILURE and~BUCK to~ASCENSION.OFFERING WHOLE~s and~*!^(ms)*~*make*~COME.NEAR^(v) to~FACE~s **YHWH** **9:3** and~TO SON~s Yisra'eyl *you^(ms)~will~much*~SPEAK^(v) to~>~SAY^(v) *!^(mp)*~TAKE^(v) HAIRY.GOAT SHE-GOAT~s to~FAILURE and~BULLOCK and~SHEEP SON~s YEAR WHOLE~s to~ASCENSION.OFFERING **9:4** and~OX and~BUCK to~ OFFERING.OF.RESTITUTION~s to~>~SACRIFICE^(v) to~FACE~s **YHWH** and~ DEPOSIT MIX^(v)~*ed^(fs)* in~the~OIL GIVEN.THAT the~DAY **YHWH** *he~did~be~* SEE^(v) TO~you^(mp) **9:5** and~*they^(m)~will*~TAKE^(v) AT WHICH *he~did~much~* DIRECT^(v) Mosheh TO FACE~s TENT APPOINTED and~*they^(m)~will~* COME.NEAR^(v) ALL the~COMPANY and~*they^(m)~will*~STAND^(v) to~FACE~s **YHWH** **9:6** and~*he~will*~SAY^(v) Mosheh THIS the~WORD WHICH *he~did~ much*~DIRECT^(v) **YHWH** *you^(mp)~will*~DO^(v) and~*he~will~be*~SEE^(v) TO~you^(mp) ARMAMENT **YHWH** **9:7** and~*he~will*~SAY^(v) Mosheh TO Aharon *!^(ms)*~ COME.NEAR^(v) TO the~ALTAR and~*!^(ms)*~DO^(v) AT FAILURE~you^(ms) and~AT ASCENSION.OFFERING~you^(ms) and~*!^(ms)~much*~COVER^(v) in~UNTIL~you^(ms) and~in~UNTIL the~PEOPLE and~*!^(ms)*~DO^(v) AT DONATION the~PEOPLE and~ *!^(ms)~much*~COVER^(v) in~UNTIL~them^(m) like~WHICH *he~did~much*~DIRECT^(v) **YHWH** **9:8** and~*he~will*~COME.NEAR^(v) Aharon TO the~ALTAR and~*he~ will*~SLAY^(v) AT BULLOCK the~FAILURE WHICH to~him **9:9** and~*they^(m)~will~ make*~COME.NEAR^(v) SON~s Aharon AT the~BLOOD TO~him and~*he~will~* DIP^(v) FINGER~him in~the~BLOOD and~*he~will*~GIVE^(v) UPON HORN~s the~ ALTAR and~AT the~BLOOD *he~did*~POUR.DOWN^(v) TO BOTTOM.BASE the~ ALTAR **9:10** and~AT the~FAT and~AT the~KIDNEY~s and~AT the~LOBE FROM the~HEAVY FROM the~FAILURE *he~did~make*~BURN.INCENSE^(v) the~ ALTAR~unto like~WHICH *he~did~much*~DIRECT^(v) **YHWH** AT Mosheh **9:11** and~AT the~FLESH and~AT the~SKIN *he~did*~CREMATE^(v) in~ the~FIRE from~OUTSIDE to~the~CAMP **9:12** and~*he~will*~SLAY^(v) AT the~ ASCENSION.OFFERING and~*they^(m)~will~make*~FIND^(v) SON~s Aharon TO~ him AT the~BLOOD and~*he~will*~SPRINKLE^(v)~him UPON the~ALTAR ALL.AROUND **9:13** and~AT the~ASCENSION.OFFERING *they~did~make~* FIND^(v) TO~him to~PIECE~s~her and~AT the~HEAD and~*he~will~make~* BURN.INCENSE^(v) UPON the~ALTAR **9:14** and~*he~will*~BATHE^(v) AT the~ INSIDE and~AT the~LEG~s2 and~*he~will~make*~BURN.INCENSE^(v) UPON the~ASCENSION.OFFERING the~ALTAR~unto **9:15** and~*he~will~make*~ COME.NEAR^(v) AT DONATION the~PEOPLE and~*he~will*~TAKE^(v) AT HAIRY.GOAT the~FAILURE WHICH to~the~PEOPLE and~*he~will*~SLAY^(v)~him and~*he~will~much*~FAIL^(v)~him like~the~FIRST **9:16** and~*he~will~make~* COME.NEAR^(v) AT the~ASCENSION.OFFERING and~*he~will*~DO^(v)~her like~ the~DECISION **9:17** and~*he~will~make*~COME.NEAR^(v) AT the~DEPOSIT and~*he*~*will*~*much*~FILL^(V) PALM~him FROM~her and~*he*~*will*~*make*~BURN.INCENSE^(V) UPON the~ALTAR from~to~STRAND ASCENSION.OFFERING the~MORNING **9:18** and~*he*~*will*~SLAY^(V) AT the~OX and~AT the~BUCK SACRIFICE the~OFFERING.OF.RESTITUTION~s WHICH to~the~PEOPLE and~*they*^(m)~*will*~*make*~FIND^(V) SON~s Aharon AT the~BLOOD TO~him and~*he*~*will*~SPRINKLE^(V)~him UPON the~ALTAR ALL.AROUND **9:19** and~AT the~FAT~s FROM the~OX and~FROM the~BUCK the~RUMP and~the~*much*~COVER.OVER^(V)~*ing*^(ms) and~the~KIDNEY~s and~LOBE the~HEAVY **9:20** and~*they*^(m)~*will*~PLACE^(V) AT the~FAT~s UPON the~CHEST and~*he*~*will*~*make*~BURN.INCENSE^(V) the~FAT~s the~ALTAR~unto **9:21** and~AT the~CHEST and~AT THIGH the~RIGHT.HAND *he*~*did*~*make*~WAVE^(V) Aharon WAVING to~FACE~s **YHWH** like~WHICH *he*~*did*~*much*~DIRECT^(V) Mosheh **9:22** and~*he*~*will*~LIFT.UP^(V) Aharon AT HAND~him TO the~PEOPLE and~*he*~*will*~*much*~KNEEL^(V)~them^(m) and~*he*~*will*~GO.DOWN^(V) from~>~DO^(V) the~FAILURE and~the~ASCENSION.OFFERING and~the~OFFERING.OF.RESTITUTION~s **9:23** and~*he*~*will*~COME^(V) Mosheh and~Aharon TO TENT APPOINTED and~*they*^(m)~*will*~GO.OUT^(V) and~*they*^(m)~*will*~*much*~KNEEL^(V) AT the~PEOPLE and~*he*~*will*~*be*~SEE^(V) ARMAMENT **YHWH** TO ALL the~PEOPLE **9:24** and~*she*~*will*~GO.OUT^(V) FIRE from~to~FACE~s **YHWH** and~*she*~*will*~EAT^(V) UPON the~ALTAR AT the~ASCENSION.OFFERING and~AT the~FAT~s and~*he*~*will*~SEE^(V) ALL the~PEOPLE and~*they*^(m)~*will*~SHOUT.ALOUD^(V) and~*they*^(m)~*will*~FALL^(V) UPON FACE~s~them^(m)

Chapter 10

10:1 and~*they*^(m)~*will*~TAKE^(V) SON~s Aharon Nadav and~Aviyhu MAN FIRE.PAN~him and~*they*^(m)~*will*~GIVE^(V) in~them^(f) FIRE and~*they*^(m)~*will*~PLACE^(V) UPON~her INCENSE.SMOKE and~*they*^(m)~*will*~*make*~COME.NEAR^(V) to~FACE~s **YHWH** FIRE BE.STRANGE^(V)~*ing*^(fs) WHICH NOT *he*~*did*~*much*~DIRECT^(V) AT~them^(m) **10:2** and~*she*~*will*~GO.OUT^(V) FIRE from~to~FACE~s **YHWH** and~*she*~*will*~EAT^(V) AT~them^(m) and~*they*^(m)~*will*~DIE^(V) to~FACE~s **YHWH** **10:3** and~*he*~*will*~SAY^(V) Mosheh TO Aharon HE WHICH *he*~*did*~*much*~SPEAK^(V) **YHWH** to~>~SAY^(V) in~NEAR~s~me *I*~*will*~*be*~SET.APART^(V) and~UPON FACE~s ALL the~PEOPLE *I*~*will*~*be*~BE.HEAVY^(V) and~*he*~*will*~BE.SILENT^(V) Aharon **10:4** and~*he*~*will*~CALL.OUT^(V) Mosheh TO Miysha'eyl and~TO El'tsaphan SON~s Uziy'eyl UNCLE Aharon and~*he*~*will*~SAY^(V) TO~them^(m) *!*^(mp)~COME.NEAR^(V) *!*^(mp)~LIFT.UP^(V) AT BROTHER~s~you^(mp) from~AT FACE~s the~SPECIAL TO from~OUTSIDE to~the~CAMP **10:5** and~*they*^(m)~*will*~COME.NEAR^(V) and~*they*^(m)~*will*~LIFT.UP^(V)~them^(m) in~TUNIC~s~them^(m) TO from~OUTSIDE to~the~CAMP like~WHICH *he*~*did*~*much*~SPEAK^(V) Mosheh **10:6** and~*he*~*will*~SAY^(V) Mosheh TO Aharon and~to~Elazar and~to~Iytamar SON~s~him HEAD~s~you^(mp) DO.NOT you^(mp)~*will*~LOOSE^(V) and~GARMENT~s~you^(mp) NOT you^(mp)~*will*~RIP^(V) and~NOT you^(mp)~*will*~DIE^(V)

and~UPON ALL the~COMPANY he~will~SNAP⁽ᵛ⁾ and~BROTHER~s~you⁽ᵐᵖ⁾ ALL HOUSE Yisra'eyl they⁽ᵐ⁾~will~WEEP⁽ᵛ⁾ AT the~CREMATING WHICH he~did~CREMATE⁽ᵛ⁾ **YHWH** **10:7** and~from~OPENING TENT APPOINTED NOT you⁽ᵐᵖ⁾~will~GO.OUT⁽ᵛ⁾ OTHERWISE you⁽ᵐᵖ⁾~will~DIE⁽ᵛ⁾ GIVEN.THAT OIL OINTMENT **YHWH** UPON~you⁽ᵐᵖ⁾ and~they⁽ᵐ⁾~will~DO⁽ᵛ⁾ like~WORD Mosheh **10:8** and~he~will~much~SPEAK⁽ᵛ⁾ **YHWH** TO Aharon to~>~SAY⁽ᵛ⁾ **10:9** WINE and~LIQUOR DO.NOT you⁽ᵐˢ⁾~will~GULP⁽ᵛ⁾ YOU⁽ᵐˢ⁾ and~SON~s~you⁽ᵐˢ⁾ AT~you⁽ᶠˢ⁾ in~>~COME⁽ᵛ⁾~you⁽ᵐᵖ⁾ TO TENT APPOINTED and~NOT you⁽ᵐᵖ⁾~will~DIE⁽ᵛ⁾ CUSTOM DISTANT to~GENERATION~s~you⁽ᵐᵖ⁾ **10:10** and~to~>~make~SEPARATE⁽ᵛ⁾ BETWEEN the~SPECIAL and~BETWEEN the~ORDINARY and~BETWEEN the~DIRTY and~BETWEEN the~CLEAN **10:11** and~to~>~make~THROW⁽ᵛ⁾ AT SON~s Yisra'eyl AT ALL the~CUSTOM~s WHICH he~did~much~SPEAK⁽ᵛ⁾ **YHWH** TO~them⁽ᵐ⁾ in~HAND Mosheh **10:12** and~he~will~much~SPEAK⁽ᵛ⁾ Mosheh TO Aharon and~TO Elazar and~TO Iytamar SON~s~him the~be~LEAVE.BEHIND⁽ᵛ⁾~ing⁽ᵐᵖ⁾ !⁽ᵐᵖ⁾~TAKE⁽ᵛ⁾ AT the~DEPOSIT the~be~LEAVE.BEHIND⁽ᵛ⁾~ing⁽ᶠˢ⁾ from~FIRE.OFFERING~s **YHWH** and~!⁽ᵐᵖ⁾~EAT⁽ᵛ⁾~him~& UNLEAVENED.BREAD~s BESIDE the~ALTAR GIVEN.THAT SPECIAL SPECIAL~s SHE **10:13** and~you⁽ᵐᵖ⁾~did~EAT⁽ᵛ⁾ AT~her in~AREA UNIQUE GIVEN.THAT CUSTOM~you⁽ᵐˢ⁾ and~CUSTOM SON~s~you⁽ᵐˢ⁾ SHE from~FIRE.OFFERING~s **YHWH** GIVEN.THAT SO I~did~be~much~DIRECT⁽ᵛ⁾ **10:14** and~AT CHEST the~WAVING and~AT THIGH the~OFFERING you⁽ᵐᵖ⁾~will~EAT⁽ᵛ⁾ in~AREA CLEAN YOU⁽ᵐˢ⁾ and~SON~s~you⁽ᵐˢ⁾ and~DAUGHTER~s~you⁽ᵐˢ⁾ AT~you⁽ᶠˢ⁾ GIVEN.THAT CUSTOM~you⁽ᵐˢ⁾ and~CUSTOM SON~s~you⁽ᵐˢ⁾ they~did~be~GIVE⁽ᵛ⁾ from~SACRIFICE~s OFFERING.OF.RESTITUTION~s SON~s Yisra'eyl **10:15** THIGH the~OFFERING and~CHEST the~WAVING UPON FIRE.OFFERING~s the~FAT~s they⁽ᵐ⁾~will~make~COME⁽ᵛ⁾ to~>~make~WAVE⁽ᵛ⁾ WAVING to~FACE~s **YHWH** and~he~did~EXIST⁽ᵛ⁾ to~you⁽ᵐˢ⁾ and~to~SON~s~you⁽ᵐˢ⁾ AT~you⁽ᵐˢ⁾ to~CUSTOM DISTANT like~WHICH he~did~much~DIRECT⁽ᵛ⁾ **YHWH** **10:16** and~AT HAIRY.GOAT the~FAILURE >~SEEK⁽ᵛ⁾ he~did~SEEK⁽ᵛ⁾ Mosheh and~LOOK he~did~be~much~CREMATE⁽ᵛ⁾ and~he~will~SNAP⁽ᵛ⁾ UPON Elazar and~UPON Iytamar SON~s Aharon the~be~LEAVE.BEHIND⁽ᵛ⁾~ing⁽ᵐᵖ⁾ to~>~SAY⁽ᵛ⁾ **10:17** WHY NOT you⁽ᵐᵖ⁾~did~EAT⁽ᵛ⁾ AT the~FAILURE in~AREA the~SPECIAL GIVEN.THAT SPECIAL SPECIAL~s SHE and~AT~her he~did~GIVE⁽ᵛ⁾ to~you⁽ᵐᵖ⁾ to~>~LIFT.UP⁽ᵛ⁾ AT TWISTEDNESS the~COMPANY to~>~much~COVER⁽ᵛ⁾ UPON~them⁽ᵐ⁾ to~FACE~s **YHWH** **10:18** THOUGH NOT he~did~be~make~COME⁽ᵛ⁾ AT BLOOD~her TO the~SPECIAL FACE~s unto >~EAT⁽ᵛ⁾ you⁽ᵐᵖ⁾~will~EAT⁽ᵛ⁾ AT~her in~the~SPECIAL like~WHICH I~did~much~DIRECT⁽ᵛ⁾ **10:19** and~he~will~much~SPEAK⁽ᵛ⁾ Aharon TO Mosheh THOUGH the~DAY they~did~make~COME.NEAR⁽ᵛ⁾ AT FAILURE~them⁽ᵐ⁾ and~AT ASCENSION.OFFERING~them⁽ᵐ⁾ to~FACE~s **YHWH** and~they⁽ᶠ⁾~will~CALL.OUT⁽ᵛ⁾ AT~me like~THESE and~I~did~EAT⁽ᵛ⁾ FAILURE the~DAY he~will~DO.WELL⁽ᵛ⁾ in~EYE~s2 **YHWH** **10:20** and~he~will~HEAR⁽ᵛ⁾ Mosheh and~he~will~DO.WELL⁽ᵛ⁾ in~EYE~s2~him

Chapter 11

11:1 and~*he*~*will*~*much*~SPEAK^(V) **YHWH** TO Mosheh and~TO Aharon to~>~SAY^(V) TO~them^(m)   **11:2** *I*^(mp)~*much*~SPEAK^(V) TO SON~s Yisra'eyl to~>~SAY^(V) THIS the~LIVING WHICH *you*^(mp)~*will*~EAT^(V) from~ALL the~BEAST WHICH UPON the~LAND   **11:3** ALL *make*~CLEAVE^(V)~*ing*^(fs) HOOF and~SPLIT.IN.TWO^(V)~*ing*^(fs) SPLITTING HOOF~s *make*~GO.UP^(V)~*ing*^(fs) CUD in~the~BEAST AT~her *you*^(mp)~*will*~EAT^(V)   **11:4** SURELY AT THIS NOT *you*^(mp)~*will*~EAT^(V) from~*make*~GO.UP^(V)~*ing*^(mp) the~CUD and~from~*make*~CLEAVE^(V)~*ing*^(mp) the~HOOF AT the~CAMEL GIVEN.THAT *make*~GO.UP^(V)~*ing*^(fs) CUD HE and~HOOF WITHOUT~him *make*~CLEAVE^(V)~*ing*^(ms) DIRTY HE to~you^(mp)   **11:5** and~AT the~RABBIT GIVEN.THAT *make*~GO.UP^(V)~*ing*^(fs) CUD HE and~HOOF NOT *he*~*will*~*make*~CLEAVE^(V) DIRTY HE to~you^(mp)   **11:6** and~AT the~HARE GIVEN.THAT *make*~GO.UP^(V)~*ing*^(fs) CUD SHE and~HOOF NOT *she*~*did*~*make*~CLEAVE^(V) DIRTY SHE to~you^(mp)   **11:7** and~AT the~SWINE GIVEN.THAT *make*~CLEAVE^(V)~*ing*^(ms) HOOF HE and~SPLIT.IN.TWO^(V)~*ing*^(ms) SPLITTING HOOF and~HE CUD NOT *he*~*will*~*be*~CHEW^(V) DIRTY HE to~you^(mp)   **11:8** from~FLESH~them^(m) NOT *you*^(mp)~*will*~EAT^(V) and~in~CARCASS~them^(m) NOT *you*^(mp)~*will*~TOUCH^(V) DIRTY~s THEY^(m) to~you^(mp)   **11:9** AT THIS *you*^(mp)~*will*~EAT^(V) from~ALL WHICH in~the~WATER~s2 ALL WHICH to~him FIN and~SCALES in~the~WATER~s2 in~the~SEA~s and~in~the~WADI~s AT~them^(m) *you*^(mp)~*will*~EAT^(V)   **11:10** and~ALL WHICH WITHOUT to~him FIN and~SCALES in~the~SEA~s and~in~the~WADI~s from~ALL SWARMER the~WATER~s2 and~from~ALL SOUL the~LIVING WHICH in~the~WATER~s2 FILTHY THEY^(m) to~you^(mp)   **11:11** and~FILTHY *they*^(m)~*will*~EXIST^(V) to~you^(mp) from~FLESH~them^(m) NOT *you*^(mp)~*will*~EAT^(V) and~AT CARCASS~them^(m) *you*^(mp)~*will*~*much*~DETEST^(V)   **11:12** ALL WHICH WITHOUT to~him FIN and~SCALES in~the~WATER~s2 FILTHY HE to~you^(mp)   **11:13** and~AT THESE *you*^(mp)~*will*~*much*~DETEST^(V) FROM the~FLYER NOT *they*^(m)~*will*~*be*~EAT^(V) FILTHY THEY^(m) AT the~EAGLE and~AT the~BEARDED.VULTURE and~AT the~OSPREY   **11:14** and~AT the~VULTURE and~AT the~HAWK to~KIND~her   **11:15** AT ALL RAVEN to~KIND~him   **11:16** and~AT DAUGHTER the~OWL and~AT the~NIGHTHAWK and~AT the~SEAGULL and~AT the~FALCON to~KIND~him   **11:17** and~AT the~LITTLE.OWL and~AT the~CORMORANT and~AT the~EARED.OWL   **11:18** and~AT the~IBIS and~AT the~PELICAN and~AT the~GIER-EAGLE   **11:19** and~AT the~STORK the~HERON to~KIND~her and~AT the~GROUSE and~AT the~BAT   **11:20** ALL SWARMER the~FLYER the~WALK^(V)~*ing*^(ms) UPON FOUR FILTHY HE to~you^(mp)   **11:21** SURELY AT THIS *you*^(mp)~*will*~EAT^(V) from~ALL SWARMER the~FLYER the~WALK^(V)~*ing*^(ms) UPON FOUR WHICH NOT LEG~s2 from~UPWARD to~FOOT~s2~him to~>~*much*~LEAP^(V) in~them^(f) UPON the~LAND   **11:22** AT THESE from~them^(m) *you*^(mp)~*will*~EAT^(V) AT the~SWARMING.LOCUST to~KIND~him and~AT the~LOCUST to~KIND~him and~AT the~LEAPING.LOCUST to~KIND~him and~AT the~GRASSHOPPER to~KIND~him   **11:23** and~ALL SWARMER the~FLYER WHICH to~him FOUR FOOT~s2 FILTHY HE to~you$^{(mp)}$ **11:24** and~to~THESE you$^{(mp)}$~will~self~BE.DIRTY$^{(V)}$ ALL the~TOUCH$^{(V)}$~*ing*$^{(ms)}$ in~CARCASS~them$^{(m)}$ he~will~BE.DIRTY$^{(V)}$ UNTIL the~EVENING   **11:25** and~ALL the~LIFT.UP$^{(V)}$~*ing*$^{(ms)}$ from~CARCASS~them$^{(m)}$ he~will~WASH$^{(V)}$ GARMENT~s~him and~he~did~BE.DIRTY$^{(V)}$ UNTIL the~EVENING   **11:26** to~ALL the~BEAST WHICH SHE make~CLEAVE$^{(V)}$~*ing*$^{(fs)}$ HOOF and~SPLITTING WITHOUT~her SPLIT.IN.TWO$^{(V)}$~*ing*$^{(fs)}$ and~CUD WITHOUT~her make~GO.UP$^{(V)}$~*ing*$^{(fs)}$ DIRTY~s THEY$^{(m)}$ to~you$^{(mp)}$ ALL the~TOUCH$^{(V)}$~*ing*$^{(ms)}$ in~them$^{(m)}$ he~will~BE.DIRTY$^{(V)}$ **11:27** and~ALL WALK$^{(V)}$~*ing*$^{(ms)}$ UPON PALM~s2~him in~ALL the~LIVING the~WALK$^{(V)}$~*ing*$^{(fs)}$ UPON FOUR DIRTY~s THEY$^{(m)}$ to~you$^{(mp)}$ ALL the~TOUCH$^{(V)}$~*ing*$^{(ms)}$ in~CARCASS~them$^{(m)}$ he~will~BE.DIRTY$^{(V)}$ UNTIL the~EVENING   **11:28** and~the~LIFT.UP$^{(V)}$~*ing*$^{(ms)}$ AT CARCASS~them$^{(m)}$ he~will~WASH$^{(V)}$ GARMENT~s~him and~he~did~BE.DIRTY$^{(V)}$ UNTIL the~EVENING DIRTY~s THEY$^{(m)}$ to~you$^{(mp)}$ **11:29** and~THIS to~you$^{(mp)}$ the~DIRTY in~the~SWARMER the~SWARM$^{(V)}$~*ing*$^{(ms)}$ UPON the~LAND the~WEASEL and~the~MOUSE and~the~TORTOISE to~KIND~him   **11:30** and~the~FERRET and~the~CHAMELEON and~the~LIZARD and~the~SNAIL and~the~IBIS   **11:31** THESE the~DIRTY~s to~you$^{(mp)}$ in~ALL the~SWARMER ALL the~TOUCH$^{(V)}$~*ing*$^{(ms)}$ in~them$^{(m)}$ in~DEATH~them$^{(m)}$ he~will~BE.DIRTY$^{(V)}$ UNTIL the~EVENING   **11:32** and~ALL WHICH he~will~FALL$^{(V)}$ UPON~him from~them$^{(m)}$ in~DEATH~them$^{(m)}$ he~will~BE.DIRTY$^{(V)}$ from~ALL UTENSIL TREE OR GARMENT OR SKIN OR SACK ALL UTENSIL WHICH he~will~be~DO$^{(V)}$ BUSINESS in~them$^{(m)}$ in~the~WATER~s2 he~will~be~make~COME$^{(V)}$ and~he~did~BE.DIRTY$^{(V)}$ UNTIL the~EVENING and~he~did~BE.CLEAN$^{(V)}$ **11:33** and~ALL UTENSIL CLAY WHICH he~will~FALL$^{(V)}$ from~them$^{(m)}$ TO MIDST~him ALL WHICH in~MIDST~him he~will~BE.DIRTY$^{(V)}$ and~AT~him you$^{(mp)}$~will~CRACK$^{(V)}$ **11:34** from~ALL the~FOODSTUFF WHICH he~will~be~EAT$^{(V)}$ WHICH he~will~COME$^{(V)}$ UPON~him WATER~s2 he~will~BE.DIRTY$^{(V)}$ and~ALL DRINKING WHICH he~will~be~GULP$^{(V)}$ in~ALL UTENSIL he~will~BE.DIRTY$^{(V)}$ **11:35** and~ALL WHICH he~will~FALL$^{(V)}$ from~CARCASS~them$^{(m)}$ UPON~him he~will~BE.DIRTY$^{(V)}$ OVEN and~EARTHENWARE~s2 he~will~be~much~BREAK.DOWN$^{(V)}$ DIRTY~s THEY$^{(m)}$ and~DIRTY~s they$^{(m)}$~will~EXIST$^{(V)}$ to~you$^{(mp)}$ **11:36** SURELY from~the~EYE and~CISTERN COLLECTION WATER~s2 he~will~EXIST$^{(V)}$ CLEAN and~TOUCH$^{(V)}$~*ing*$^{(ms)}$ in~CARCASS~them$^{(m)}$ he~will~BE.DIRTY$^{(V)}$ **11:37** and~GIVEN.THAT he~will~FALL$^{(V)}$ from~CARCASS~them$^{(m)}$ UPON ALL SEED SOWN WHICH he~will~be~SOW$^{(V)}$ CLEAN HE   **11:38** and~GIVEN.THAT he~GIVE$^{(V)}$~*ed*$^{(ms)}$ WATER~s2 UPON SEED and~he~did~FALL$^{(V)}$ from~CARCASS~them$^{(m)}$ UPON~him DIRTY HE to~you$^{(mp)}$ **11:39** and~GIVEN.THAT he~will~DIE$^{(V)}$ FROM the~BEAST WHICH SHE to~you$^{(mp)}$ to~FOOD the~TOUCH$^{(V)}$~*ing*$^{(ms)}$ in~CARCASS~her he~will~BE.DIRTY$^{(V)}$ UNTIL the~EVENING   **11:40** and~the~EAT$^{(V)}$~*ing*$^{(ms)}$ from~CARCASS~her he~will~WASH$^{(V)}$ GARMENT~s~him and~he~did~BE.DIRTY$^{(V)}$ UNTIL the~EVENING and~the~LIFT.UP$^{(V)}$~*ing*$^{(ms)}$ AT CARCASS~her he~will~WASH$^{(V)}$ GARMENT~s~him and~he~did~BE.DIRTY$^{(V)}$ UNTIL the~

The Book of Leviticus

EVENING **11:41** and~ALL the~SWARMER the~SWARM⁽ᵛ⁾~*ing*⁽ᵐˢ⁾ UPON the~LAND FILTHY HE NOT *he~will~be*~EAT⁽ᵛ⁾ **11:42** ALL WALK⁽ᵛ⁾~*ing*⁽ᵐˢ⁾ UPON BELLY and~ALL WALK⁽ᵛ⁾~*ing*⁽ᵐˢ⁾ UPON FOUR UNTIL ALL *make*~INCREASE⁽ᵛ⁾~*ing*⁽ᵐˢ⁾ FOOT~s2 to~ALL the~SWARMER the~SWARM⁽ᵛ⁾~*ing*⁽ᵐˢ⁾ UPON the~LAND NOT *you*⁽ᵐᵖ⁾~*will*~EAT⁽ᵛ⁾~them⁽ᵐ⁾ GIVEN.THAT FILTHY THEY⁽ᵐ⁾ **11:43** DO.NOT *you*⁽ᵐᵖ⁾~*will*~*much*~DETEST⁽ᵛ⁾ AT SOUL~s~you⁽ᵐᵖ⁾ in~ALL the~SWARMER the~SWARM⁽ᵛ⁾~*ing*⁽ᵐˢ⁾ and~NOT *you*⁽ᵐᵖ⁾~*will*~*make*~*self*~BE.DIRTY⁽ᵛ⁾ in~them⁽ᵐ⁾ and~*you*⁽ᵐᵖ⁾~*did*~*be*~BE.DIRTY⁽ᵛ⁾ in~them⁽ᵐ⁾ **11:44** GIVEN.THAT I **YHWH** Elohiym~you⁽ᵐᵖ⁾ and~*you*⁽ᵐᵖ⁾~*did*~*self*~SET.APART⁽ᵛ⁾ and~*you*⁽ᵐᵖ⁾~*did*~EXIST⁽ᵛ⁾ UNIQUE~s GIVEN.THAT UNIQUE I and~NOT *you*⁽ᵐᵖ⁾~*will*~*much*~BE.DIRTY⁽ᵛ⁾ AT SOUL~s~you⁽ᵐᵖ⁾ in~ALL the~SWARMER the~TREAD⁽ᵛ⁾~*ing*⁽ᵐˢ⁾ UPON the~LAND **11:45** GIVEN.THAT I **YHWH** the~*make*~GO.UP⁽ᵛ⁾~*ing*⁽ᵐˢ⁾ AT~you⁽ᵐᵖ⁾ from~LAND Mits'rayim to~>~EXIST⁽ᵛ⁾ to~you⁽ᵐᵖ⁾ to~Elohiym and~*you*⁽ᵐᵖ⁾~*did*~EXIST⁽ᵛ⁾ UNIQUE~s GIVEN.THAT UNIQUE I **11:46** THIS TEACHING the~BEAST and~the~FLYER and~ALL SOUL the~LIVING the~TREAD⁽ᵛ⁾~*ing*⁽ᶠˢ⁾ in~the~WATER~s2 and~to~ALL SOUL the~SWARM⁽ᵛ⁾~*ing*⁽ᶠˢ⁾ UPON the~LAND **11:47** to~>~*make*~SEPARATE⁽ᵛ⁾ BETWEEN the~DIRTY and~BETWEEN the~CLEAN and~BETWEEN the~LIVING the~*be*~EAT⁽ᵛ⁾~*ing*⁽ᶠˢ⁾ and~BETWEEN the~LIVING WHICH NOT *she*~*will*~*be*~EAT⁽ᵛ⁾

Chapter 12

12:1 and~*he*~*will*~*much*~SPEAK⁽ᵛ⁾ **YHWH** TO Mosheh to~>~SAY⁽ᵛ⁾ **12:2** !⁽ᵐˢ⁾~*much*~SPEAK⁽ᵛ⁾ TO SON~s Yisra'eyl to~>~SAY⁽ᵛ⁾ WOMAN GIVEN.THAT *she*~*will*~*make*~SOW⁽ᵛ⁾ and~*she*~*did*~BRING.FORTH⁽ᵛ⁾ MALE and~*she*~*did*~BE.DIRTY⁽ᵛ⁾ SEVEN DAY~s like~DAY~s REMOVAL >~ILL⁽ᵛ⁾~her *she*~*will*~BE.DIRTY⁽ᵛ⁾ **12:3** and~in~the~DAY the~EIGHTH *he*~*will*~*be*~SNIP.OFF⁽ᵛ⁾ FLESH FORESKIN~him **12:4** and~THREE~s DAY and~THREE DAY~s *she*~*will*~SETTLE⁽ᵛ⁾ in~BLOOD~s CLEAN in~ALL SPECIAL NOT *she*~*will*~TOUCH⁽ᵛ⁾ and~TO the~SANCTUARY NOT *she*~*will*~COME⁽ᵛ⁾ UNTIL >~FILL⁽ᵛ⁾ DAY~s CLEAN~her **12:5** and~IF FEMALE *she*~*will*~BRING.FORTH⁽ᵛ⁾ and~*she*~*did*~BE.DIRTY⁽ᵛ⁾ WEEK~s2 like~REMOVAL~her and~SIX~s DAY and~SIX DAY~s *she*~*will*~SETTLE⁽ᵛ⁾ UPON BLOOD~s CLEAN **12:6** and~in~>~FILL⁽ᵛ⁾ DAY~s CLEAN~her to~SON OR to~DAUGHTER *she*~*will*~*make*~COME⁽ᵛ⁾ SHEEP SON YEAR~him to~ASCENSION.OFFERING and~SON DOVE OR TURTLEDOVE to~FAILURE TO OPENING TENT APPOINTED TO the~ADMINISTRATOR **12:7** and~*he*~*did*~*make*~COME.NEAR⁽ᵛ⁾~him to~FACE~s **YHWH** and~*he*~*did*~*much*~COVER⁽ᵛ⁾ UPON~her and~*she*~*did*~BE.CLEAN⁽ᵛ⁾ from~FOUNTAIN BLOOD~s~her THIS TEACHING the~BRING.FORTH⁽ᵛ⁾~*ing*⁽ᶠˢ⁾ to~the~MALE OR to~the~FEMALE **12:8** and~IF NOT *she*~*will*~FIND⁽ᵛ⁾ HAND~her SUFFICIENT RAM and~*she*~*did*~TAKE⁽ᵛ⁾ TWO TURTLEDOVE~s OR TWO SON~s DOVE UNIT to~ASCENSION.OFFERING and~UNIT to~FAILURE and~*he~did~much*~COVER⁽ⱽ⁾ UPON~her the~ADMINISTRATOR and~*she~did*~BE.CLEAN⁽ⱽ⁾

Chapter 13

13:1 and~*he~will~much*~SPEAK⁽ⱽ⁾ **YHWH** TO Mosheh and~TO Aharon to~>~SAY⁽ⱽ⁾   **13:2** HUMAN GIVEN.THAT *he~will*~EXIST⁽ⱽ⁾ in~SKIN FLESH~him >~LIFT.UP⁽ⱽ⁾ OR SCAB OR BRIGHT.SPOT and~*he~did*~EXIST⁽ⱽ⁾ in~SKIN FLESH~him to~TOUCH INFECTION and~*he~did~be~make*~COME⁽ⱽ⁾ TO Aharon the~ADMINISTRATOR OR TO UNIT from~SON~s~him the~ADMINISTRATOR~s   **13:3** and~*he~did*~SEE⁽ⱽ⁾ the~ADMINISTRATOR AT the~TOUCH in~SKIN the~FLESH and~HAIR in~the~TOUCH *he~did*~OVERTURN⁽ⱽ⁾ WHITE and~APPEARANCE the~TOUCH SUNKEN from~SKIN FLESH~him TOUCH INFECTION HE and~*he~did*~SEE⁽ⱽ⁾~him the~ADMINISTRATOR and~*he~did~much*~BE.DIRTY⁽ⱽ⁾ AT~him   **13:4** and~IF BRIGHT.SPOT WHITE SHE in~SKIN FLESH~him and~SUNKEN WITHOUT APPEARANCE~her FROM the~SKIN and~HAIR NOT *he~did*~OVERTURN⁽ⱽ⁾ WHITE and~*he~did~make*~SHUT⁽ⱽ⁾ the~ADMINISTRATOR AT the~TOUCH SEVEN DAY~s   **13:5** and~*he~did*~SEE⁽ⱽ⁾~him the~ADMINISTRATOR in~the~DAY the~SEVENTH and~LOOK the~TOUCH *he~did*~STAND⁽ⱽ⁾ in~EYE~s2~him NOT *he~did*~SPREAD.ACROSS⁽ⱽ⁾ the~TOUCH in~the~SKIN and~*he~did~make*~SHUT⁽ⱽ⁾~him the~ADMINISTRATOR SEVEN DAY~s SECOND   **13:6** and~*he~did*~SEE⁽ⱽ⁾ the~ADMINISTRATOR AT~him in~the~DAY the~SEVENTH SECOND and~LOOK DIMNESS the~TOUCH and~NOT *he~did*~SPREAD.ACROSS⁽ⱽ⁾ the~TOUCH in~the~SKIN and~*he~did~much*~BE.CLEAN⁽ⱽ⁾~him the~ADMINISTRATOR SCAB SHE and~*he~did~much*~WASH⁽ⱽ⁾ GARMENT~s~him and~*he~did*~BE.CLEAN⁽ⱽ⁾   **13:7** and~IF >~SPREAD.ACROSS⁽ⱽ⁾ *she~will*~SEIZE.HOLD⁽ⱽ⁾ the~SCAB in~the~SKIN AFTER >~*be*~SEE⁽ⱽ⁾~him TO the~ADMINISTRATOR to~CLEAN~him and~*he~did~be*~SEE⁽ⱽ⁾ SECOND TO the~ADMINISTRATOR   **13:8** and~*he~did*~SEE⁽ⱽ⁾ the~ADMINISTRATOR and~LOOK *she~did*~SPREAD.ACROSS⁽ⱽ⁾ the~SCAB in~the~SKIN and~*he~did~much*~BE.DIRTY⁽ⱽ⁾~him the~ADMINISTRATOR INFECTION SHE   **13:9** TOUCH INFECTION GIVEN.THAT *she~will*~EXIST⁽ⱽ⁾ in~HUMAN and~*he~did~be~make*~COME⁽ⱽ⁾ TO the~ADMINISTRATOR   **13:10** and~*he~did*~SEE⁽ⱽ⁾ the~ADMINISTRATOR and~LOOK >~LIFT.UP⁽ⱽ⁾ WHITE in~the~SKIN and~SHE *she~did*~OVERTURN⁽ⱽ⁾ HAIR WHITE and~REVIVING FLESH LIVING in~the~ELEVATION   **13:11** INFECTION *be*~SLEEP⁽ⱽ⁾~*ing*⁽ᶠˢ⁾ SHE in~SKIN FLESH~him and~*he~did~much*~BE.DIRTY⁽ⱽ⁾~him the~ADMINISTRATOR NOT *he~will~make*~SHUT⁽ⱽ⁾~him GIVEN.THAT DIRTY HE   **13:12** and~IF >~BURST.OUT⁽ⱽ⁾ *she~will*~BURST.OUT⁽ⱽ⁾ the~INFECTION in~the~SKIN and~*she~did~much*~COVER.OVER⁽ⱽ⁾ the~INFECTION AT ALL SKIN the~TOUCH from~HEAD~him and~UNTIL FOOT~s2~him to~ALL APPEARANCE EYE~s2 the~ADMINISTRATOR   **13:13** and~*he~did*~SEE⁽ⱽ⁾ the~ADMINISTRATOR and~

The Book of Leviticus

LOOK *she~did~much*~COVER.OVER^(V) the~INFECTION AT ALL FLESH~him and~*he~did~much*~BE.CLEAN^(V) AT the~TOUCH ALL~him *he~did~* OVERTURN^(V) WHITE CLEAN HE **13:14** and~in~DAY >~*be*~SEE^(V) in~him FLESH LIVING *he~will*~BE.DIRTY^(V) **13:15** and~*he~did*~SEE^(V) the~ ADMINISTRATOR AT the~FLESH the~LIVING and~*he~did~much*~BE.DIRTY^(V)~ him the~FLESH the~LIVING DIRTY HE INFECTION HE **13:16** OR GIVEN.THAT *he~will*~TURN.BACK^(V) the~FLESH the~LIVING and~*he~did~be*~OVERTURN^(V) to~Lavan and~*he~did*~COME^(V) TO the~ADMINISTRATOR **13:17** and~*he~ did*~SEE^(V)~him the~ADMINISTRATOR and~LOOK *he~did~be*~OVERTURN^(V) the~TOUCH to~WHITE and~*he~did~much*~BE.CLEAN^(V) the~ ADMINISTRATOR AT the~TOUCH CLEAN HE **13:18** and~FLESH GIVEN.THAT *he~will*~EXIST^(V) in~him in~SKIN~him BOILS and~*he~did~be*~ HEAL^(V) **13:19** and~*he~did*~EXIST^(V) in~AREA the~BOILS >~LIFT.UP^(V) WHITE OR BRIGHT.SPOT WHITE REDDISH and~*he~did~be*~SEE^(V) TO the~ ADMINISTRATOR **13:20** and~*he~did*~SEE^(V) the~ADMINISTRATOR and~ LOOK APPEARANCE~her LOW FROM the~SKIN and~HAIR~her *he~did*~ OVERTURN^(V) WHITE and~*he~did~much*~BE.DIRTY^(V)~him the~ ADMINISTRATOR TOUCH INFECTION SHE in~the~BOILS *she~will*~ BURST.OUT^(V) **13:21** and~IF *he~will*~SEE^(V)~her the~ADMINISTRATOR and~ LOOK WITHOUT in~her HAIR WHITE and~LOW WITHOUT~her FROM the~ SKIN and~SHE DIMNESS and~*he~did~make*~SHUT^(V)~him the~ ADMINISTRATOR SEVEN DAY~s **13:22** and~IF >~SPREAD.ACROSS^(V) *she~ will*~SEIZE.HOLD^(V) in~the~SKIN and~*he~did~much*~BE.DIRTY^(V) the~ ADMINISTRATOR AT~him TOUCH SHE **13:23** and~IF UNDER~s~her *she~ will*~STAND^(V) the~BRIGHT.SPOT NOT *she~did*~SPREAD.ACROSS^(V) SEARING the~BOILS SHE and~*he~did~much*~BE.CLEAN^(V)~him the~ ADMINISTRATOR **13:24** OR FLESH GIVEN.THAT *he~will*~EXIST^(V) in~SKIN~ him SINGE.SCAR FIRE and~*she~did*~EXIST^(V) REVIVING the~SINGE.SCAR BRIGHT.SPOT WHITE REDDISH OR WHITE **13:25** and~*he~did*~SEE^(V) AT~her the~ADMINISTRATOR and~LOOK *he~did~be*~OVERTURN^(V) HAIR WHITE in~ the~BRIGHT.SPOT and~APPEARANCE~her SUNKEN FROM the~SKIN INFECTION SHE in~the~SINGE.SCAR *she~will*~BURST.OUT^(V) and~*he~did~ much*~BE.DIRTY^(V) AT~him the~ADMINISTRATOR TOUCH INFECTION SHE **13:26** and~IF *he~will*~SEE^(V)~her the~ADMINISTRATOR and~LOOK WITHOUT in~the~BRIGHT.SPOT HAIR WHITE and~LOW WITHOUT~her FROM the~SKIN and~SHE DIMNESS and~*he~did~make*~SHUT^(V)~him the~ ADMINISTRATOR SEVEN DAY~s **13:27** and~*he~did*~SEE^(V)~him the~ ADMINISTRATOR in~the~DAY the~SEVENTH IF >~SPREAD.ACROSS^(V) *she~ will*~SEIZE.HOLD^(V) in~the~SKIN and~*he~did~much*~BE.DIRTY^(V) the~ ADMINISTRATOR AT~him TOUCH INFECTION SHE **13:28** and~IF UNDER~s~ her *she~will*~STAND^(V) the~BRIGHT.SPOT NOT *she~did*~SPREAD.ACROSS^(V) in~the~SKIN and~SHE DIMNESS >~LIFT.UP^(V) the~SINGE.SCAR SHE and~*he~ did~much*~BE.CLEAN^(V)~him the~ADMINISTRATOR GIVEN.THAT SEARING the~SINGE.SCAR SHE **13:29** and~MAN OR WOMAN GIVEN.THAT *he~will*~ EXIST^(V) in~him TOUCH in~HEAD OR in~BEARD **13:30** and~*he~did*~SEE^(V)

the~ADMINISTRATOR AT the~TOUCH and~LOOK APPEARANCE~him SUNKEN FROM the~SKIN and~in~him HAIR YELLOW SCRAWNY and~*he~did~much~*BE.DIRTY⁽ⱽ⁾ AT~him the~ADMINISTRATOR ERUPTION HE INFECTION the~HEAD OR the~BEARD HE **13:31** and~GIVEN.THAT *he~will~*SEE⁽ⱽ⁾ the~ADMINISTRATOR AT TOUCH the~ERUPTION and~LOOK WITHOUT APPEARANCE~him SUNKEN FROM the~SKIN and~HAIR COAL WITHOUT in~him and~*he~did~make~*SHUT⁽ⱽ⁾ the~ADMINISTRATOR AT TOUCH the~ERUPTION SEVEN DAY~s **13:32** and~*he~did~*SEE⁽ⱽ⁾ the~ADMINISTRATOR AT the~TOUCH in~the~DAY the~SEVENTH and~LOOK NOT *he~did~*SPREAD.ACROSS⁽ⱽ⁾ the~ERUPTION and~NOT *he~did~*EXIST⁽ⱽ⁾ in~him HAIR YELLOW and~APPEARANCE the~ERUPTION WITHOUT SUNKEN FROM the~SKIN **13:33** and~*he~did~self~*SHAVE⁽ⱽ⁾ and~AT the~ERUPTION NOT *he~will~much~*SHAVE⁽ⱽ⁾ and~*he~did~make~*SHUT⁽ⱽ⁾ the~ADMINISTRATOR AT the~ERUPTION SEVEN DAY~s SECOND **13:34** and~*he~did~*SEE⁽ⱽ⁾ the~ADMINISTRATOR AT the~ERUPTION in~the~DAY the~SEVENTH and~LOOK NOT *he~did~*SPREAD.ACROSS⁽ⱽ⁾ the~ERUPTION in~the~SKIN and~APPEARANCE~him WITHOUT~him SUNKEN FROM the~SKIN and~*he~did~much~*BE.CLEAN⁽ⱽ⁾ AT~him the~ADMINISTRATOR and~*he~did~much~*WASH⁽ⱽ⁾ GARMENT~s~him and~*he~did~*BE.CLEAN⁽ⱽ⁾ **13:35** and~IF >~SPREAD.ACROSS⁽ⱽ⁾ *he~will~*SPREAD.ACROSS⁽ⱽ⁾ the~ERUPTION in~the~SKIN AFTER CLEAN~him **13:36** and~*he~did~*SEE⁽ⱽ⁾~him the~ADMINISTRATOR and~LOOK *he~did~*SPREAD.ACROSS⁽ⱽ⁾ the~ERUPTION in~the~SKIN NOT *he~will~much~*INVESTIGATE⁽ⱽ⁾ the~ADMINISTRATOR to~the~HAIR the~YELLOW DIRTY HE **13:37** and~IF in~EYE~s2~him *he~did~*STAND⁽ⱽ⁾ the~ERUPTION and~HAIR COAL *he~did~*SPRING.UP⁽ⱽ⁾ in~him *he~did~be~*HEAL⁽ⱽ⁾ the~ERUPTION CLEAN HE and~*he~did~much~*BE.CLEAN⁽ⱽ⁾~him the~ADMINISTRATOR **13:38** and~MAN OR WOMAN GIVEN.THAT *he~will~*EXIST⁽ⱽ⁾ in~SKIN FLESH~them⁽ᵐ⁾ BRIGHT.SPOT~s BRIGHT.SPOT~s WHITE~s **13:39** and~*he~did~*SEE⁽ⱽ⁾ the~ADMINISTRATOR and~LOOK in~SKIN FLESH~them⁽ᵐ⁾ BRIGHT.SPOT~s DIMNESS~s WHITE~s RASH HE *he~did~*BURST.OUT⁽ⱽ⁾ in~the~SKIN CLEAN HE **13:40** and~MAN GIVEN.THAT *he~will~be~*HAIR.FELL.OUT⁽ⱽ⁾ HEAD~him BALD HE CLEAN HE **13:41** and~IF from~EDGE FACE~s~him *he~will~be~*HAIR.FELL.OUT⁽ⱽ⁾ HEAD~him BARE.SPOT HE CLEAN HE **13:42** and~GIVEN.THAT *he~will~*EXIST⁽ⱽ⁾ in~the~BALD.SPOT OR in~the~BARE.SPOT TOUCH WHITE REDDISH INFECTION BURST.OUT⁽ⱽ⁾~*ing*⁽ᶠˢ⁾ SHE in~BALD.SPOT~him OR in~BARE.SPOT~him **13:43** and~*he~did~*SEE⁽ⱽ⁾ AT~him the~ADMINISTRATOR and~LOOK >~LIFT.UP⁽ⱽ⁾ the~TOUCH WHITE REDDISH in~BALD.SPOT~him OR in~BARE.SPOT~him like~APPEARANCE INFECTION SKIN FLESH **13:44** MAN INFECT⁽ⱽ⁾~*ed*⁽ᵐˢ⁾ HE DIRTY HE *he~did~*BE.DIRTY⁽ⱽ⁾ *he~will~much~*BE.DIRTY⁽ⱽ⁾~him the~ADMINISTRATOR in~HEAD~him TOUCH~him **13:45** and~the~INFECT⁽ⱽ⁾~*ed*⁽ᵐˢ⁾ WHICH in~him the~TOUCH GARMENT~s~him *they*⁽ᵐ⁾~*will~*EXIST⁽ⱽ⁾ RIP⁽ⱽ⁾~*ed*⁽ᵐᵖ⁾ and~HEAD~him *he~will~*EXIST⁽ⱽ⁾ LOOSE⁽ⱽ⁾~*ed*⁽ᵐˢ⁾ and~UPON UPPER.LIP *he~will~*ENWRAP⁽ⱽ⁾ and~*he~did~*BE.DIRTY⁽ⱽ⁾ DIRTY *he~will~*CALL.OUT⁽ⱽ⁾ **13:46** ALL DAY~s WHICH the~TOUCH in~him *he~will~*

The Book of Leviticus

BE.DIRTY⁽ⱽ⁾ DIRTY HE ALONE *he~will*~SETTLE⁽ⱽ⁾ from~OUTSIDE to~the~CAMP SETTLING~him **13:47** and~the~GARMENT GIVEN.THAT *he~will*~EXIST⁽ⱽ⁾ in~him TOUCH INFECTION in~GARMENT WOOL OR in~GARMENT FLAX~s **13:48** OR in~WARP OR in~MIXTURE to~the~FLAX~s and~to~the~WOOL OR in~SKIN OR in~ALL BUSINESS SKIN **13:49** and~*he~did*~EXIST⁽ⱽ⁾ the~TOUCH GREENISH OR REDDISH in~the~GARMENT OR in~the~SKIN OR in~the~WARP OR in~the~MIXTURE OR in~ALL UTENSIL SKIN TOUCH INFECTION HE and~*he~did*~*be~make*~SEE⁽ⱽ⁾ AT the~ADMINISTRATOR **13:50** and~*he~did*~SEE⁽ⱽ⁾ the~ADMINISTRATOR AT the~TOUCH and~*he~did*~*make*~SHUT⁽ⱽ⁾ AT the~TOUCH SEVEN DAY~s **13:51** and~*he~did*~SEE⁽ⱽ⁾ AT the~TOUCH in~the~DAY the~SEVENTH GIVEN.THAT *he~did*~SPREAD.ACROSS⁽ⱽ⁾ the~TOUCH in~the~GARMENT OR in~the~WARP OR in~the~MIXTURE OR in~the~SKIN to~ALL WHICH *he~will*~*be*~DO⁽ⱽ⁾ the~SKIN to~BUSINESS INFECTION *make*~IRRITATE⁽ⱽ⁾~*ing*⁽ᶠˢ⁾ the~TOUCH DIRTY HE **13:52** and~*he~did*~CREMATE⁽ⱽ⁾ AT the~GARMENT OR AT the~WARP OR AT the~MIXTURE in~the~WOOL OR in~the~FLAX~s OR AT ALL UTENSIL the~SKIN WHICH *he~will*~EXIST⁽ⱽ⁾ in~him the~TOUCH GIVEN.THAT INFECTION *make*~IRRITATE⁽ⱽ⁾~*ing*⁽ᶠˢ⁾ SHE in~the~FIRE *you*⁽ᵐˢ⁾~*will*~CREMATE⁽ⱽ⁾ **13:53** and~IF *he~will*~SEE⁽ⱽ⁾ the~ADMINISTRATOR and~LOOK NOT *he~did*~SPREAD.ACROSS⁽ⱽ⁾ the~TOUCH in~the~GARMENT OR in~the~WARP OR in~the~MIXTURE OR in~ALL UTENSIL SKIN **13:54** and~*he~did*~*much*~DIRECT⁽ⱽ⁾ the~ADMINISTRATOR and~*they~did*~*much*~WASH⁽ⱽ⁾ AT WHICH in~him the~TOUCH and~*he~did*~*make*~SHUT⁽ⱽ⁾~him SEVEN DAY~s SECOND **13:55** and~*he~did*~SEE⁽ⱽ⁾ the~ADMINISTRATOR AFTER >~*self*~WASH⁽ⱽ⁾ AT the~TOUCH and~LOOK NOT *he~did*~OVERTURN⁽ⱽ⁾ the~TOUCH AT EYE~him and~the~TOUCH NOT *he~did*~SPREAD.ACROSS⁽ⱽ⁾ DIRTY HE in~the~FIRE *you*⁽ᵐᵖ⁾~*will*~CREMATE⁽ⱽ⁾~him PIT SHE in~BALD.SPOT~him OR in~BARE.SPOT~him **13:56** and~IF *he~did*~SEE⁽ⱽ⁾ the~ADMINISTRATOR and~LOOK DIMNESS the~TOUCH AFTER >~*self*~WASH⁽ⱽ⁾ AT~him and~*he~did*~TEAR⁽ⱽ⁾ AT~him FROM the~GARMENT OR FROM the~SKIN OR FROM the~WARP OR FROM the~MIXTURE **13:57** and~IF *she~will*~*be*~SEE⁽ⱽ⁾ YET.AGAIN in~the~GARMENT OR in~the~WARP OR in~the~MIXTURE OR in~ALL UTENSIL SKIN BURST.OUT⁽ⱽ⁾~*ing*⁽ᶠˢ⁾ SHE in~the~FIRE *you*⁽ᵐᵖ⁾~*will*~CREMATE⁽ⱽ⁾~him AT WHICH in~him the~TOUCH **13:58** and~the~GARMENT OR the~WARP OR the~MIXTURE OR ALL UTENSIL the~SKIN WHICH *you*⁽ᵐᵖ⁾~*will*~*much*~WASH⁽ⱽ⁾ and~*he~did*~TURN.ASIDE⁽ⱽ⁾ from~*them*⁽ᵐ⁾ the~TOUCH and~*he~did*~*be*~*much*~WASH⁽ⱽ⁾ SECOND and~*he~did*~BE.CLEAN⁽ⱽ⁾ **13:59** THIS TEACHING TOUCH INFECTION GARMENT the~WOOL OR the~FLAX~s OR the~WARP OR the~MIXTURE OR ALL UTENSIL SKIN to~>~*much*~BE.CLEAN⁽ⱽ⁾~him OR to~>~*much*~BE.DIRTY⁽ⱽ⁾~him

Chapter 14

14:1 and~*he*~*will*~*much*~SPEAK[(V)] **YHWH** TO Mosheh to~>~SAY[(V)] **14:2** THIS *she*~*will*~EXIST[(V)] TEACHING *the*~*be*~*much*~INFECT[(V)]~*ing*[(ms)] in~DAY CLEAN~him and~*he*~*did*~*be*~*make*~COME[(V)] TO *the*~ADMINISTRATOR **14:3** and~*he*~*will*~GO.OUT[(V)] *the*~ADMINISTRATOR TO from~OUTSIDE to~*the*~CAMP and~*he*~*did*~SEE[(V)] *the*~ADMINISTRATOR and~LOOK *he*~*did*~*be*~HEAL[(V)] TOUCH *the*~INFECTION FROM *the*~INFECT[(V)]~*ed*[(ms)] **14:4** and~*he*~*did*~*much*~DIRECT[(V)] *the*~ADMINISTRATOR and~*he*~*did*~TAKE[(V)] to~*the*~*make*~BE.CLEAN[(V)]~*ing*[(ms)] TWO BIRD~s LIVING~s CLEAN~s and~TREE CEDAR and~SCARLET KERMES and~HYSSOP **14:5** and~*he*~*did*~*much*~DIRECT[(V)] *the*~ADMINISTRATOR and~*he*~*did*~SLAY[(V)] AT *the*~BIRD *the*~UNIT TO UTENSIL CLAY UPON WATER~s2 LIVING~s **14:6** AT *the*~BIRD *the*~LIVING *he*~*will*~TAKE[(V)] AT~her and~AT TREE *the*~CEDAR and~AT SCARLET *the*~KERMES and~AT *the*~HYSSOP and~*he*~*did*~DIP[(V)] AT~them[(m)] and~AT *the*~BIRD *the*~LIVING in~BLOOD *the*~BIRD *the*~SLAY[(V)]~*ed*[(fs)] UPON *the*~WATER~s2 *the*~LIVING~s **14:7** and~*he*~*did*~*make*~SPATTER[(V)] UPON to~*the*~*make*~BE.CLEAN[(V)]~*ing*[(ms)] FROM *the*~INFECTION SEVEN FOOTSTEP~s and~*he*~*did*~*much*~BE.CLEAN[(V)]~him and~*he*~*did*~*much*~SEND[(V)] AT *the*~BIRD *the*~LIVING UPON FACE~s *the*~FIELD **14:8** and~*he*~*did*~*much*~WASH[(V)] to~*the*~*make*~BE.CLEAN[(V)]~*ing*[(ms)] AT GARMENT~s~him and~*he*~*did*~*much*~SHAVE[(V)] AT ALL HAIR~him and~*he*~*did*~BATHE[(V)] in~*the*~WATER~s2 and~*he*~*did*~BE.CLEAN[(V)] and~AFTER *he*~*will*~COME[(V)] TO *the*~CAMP and~*he*~*did*~SETTLE[(V)] from~OUTSIDE to~TENT~him SEVEN DAY~s **14:9** and~*he*~*did*~EXIST[(V)] in~*the*~DAY *the*~SEVENTH *he*~*will*~*much*~SHAVE[(V)] AT ALL HAIR~him AT HEAD~him and~AT BEARD~him and~AT ARCH~s EYE~s2~him and~AT ALL HAIR~him *he*~*will*~*much*~SHAVE[(V)] and~*he*~*did*~*much*~WASH[(V)] AT GARMENT~s~him and~*he*~*did*~BATHE[(V)] AT FLESH~him in~*the*~WATER~s2 and~*he*~*did*~BE.CLEAN[(V)] **14:10** and~in~*the*~DAY *the*~EIGHTH *he*~*will*~TAKE[(V)] TWO SHEEP~s WHOLE~s and~SHEEP UNIT DAUGHTER YEAR~her WHOLE and~THREE ONE.TENTH~s FLOUR DEPOSIT MIX[(V)]~*ed*[(fs)] in~*the*~OIL and~LOG UNIT OIL **14:11** and~*he*~*did*~*make*~STAND[(V)] *the*~ADMINISTRATOR *the*~*much*~BE.CLEAN[(V)]~*ing*[(ms)] AT *the*~MAN to~*the*~*make*~BE.CLEAN[(V)]~*ing*[(ms)] and~AT~them[(m)] to~FACE~s **YHWH** OPENING TENT APPOINTED **14:12** and~*he*~*did*~TAKE[(V)] *the*~ADMINISTRATOR AT *the*~SHEEP *the*~UNIT and~*he*~*did*~*make*~COME.NEAR[(V)] AT~him to~GUILT and~AT LOG *the*~OIL and~*he*~*did*~WAVE[(V)] AT~them[(m)] WAVING to~FACE~s **YHWH 14:13** and~*he*~*did*~SLAY[(V)] AT *the*~SHEEP in~AREA WHICH *he*~*will*~SLAY[(V)] AT *the*~FAILURE and~AT *the*~ASCENSION.OFFERING in~AREA *the*~SPECIAL GIVEN.THAT like~*the*~FAILURE *the*~GUILT HE to~*the*~ADMINISTRATOR SPECIAL SPECIAL~s HE **14:14** and~*he*~*did*~TAKE[(V)] *the*~ADMINISTRATOR from~BLOOD *the*~GUILT and~*he*~*did*~GIVE[(V)] *the*~ADMINISTRATOR UPON TIP EAR to~*the*~*make*~BE.CLEAN[(V)]~*ing*[(ms)] *the*~RIGHT and~UPON THUMB HAND~him *the*~RIGHT and~UPON THUMB FOOT~

The Book of Leviticus

him the~RIGHT   **14:15** and~*he~did*~TAKE^(V) the~ADMINISTRATOR from~LOG the~OIL and~*he~did*~POUR.DOWN^(V) UPON PALM the~ADMINISTRATOR the~LEFT.HAND   **14:16** and~*he~did*~DIP^(V) the~ADMINISTRATOR AT FINGER~him the~RIGHT FROM the~OIL WHICH UPON PALM~him the~LEFT.HAND and~*he~did*~*make*~SPATTER^(V) FROM the~OIL in~FINGER~him SEVEN FOOTSTEP~s to~FACE~s **YHWH**   **14:17** and~from~REMAINDER the~OIL WHICH UPON PALM~him *he~will*~GIVE^(V) the~ADMINISTRATOR UPON TIP EAR to~the~*make*~BE.CLEAN^(V)~*ing*^(ms) the~RIGHT and~UPON THUMB HAND~him the~RIGHT and~UPON THUMB FOOT~him the~RIGHT UPON BLOOD the~GUILT   **14:18** and~the~*be*~LEAVE.BEHIND^(V)~*ing*^(ms) in~the~OIL WHICH UPON PALM the~ADMINISTRATOR *he~will*~GIVE^(V) UPON HEAD to~the~*make*~BE.CLEAN^(V)~*ing*^(ms) and~*he~did*~much~COVER^(V) UPON~him the~ADMINISTRATOR to~FACE~s **YHWH**   **14:19** and~*he~did*~DO^(V) the~ADMINISTRATOR AT the~FAILURE and~*he~did*~much~COVER^(V) UPON to~the~*make*~BE.CLEAN^(V)~*ing*^(ms) from~DIRTY~s~him and~AFTER *he~will*~SLAY^(V) AT the~ASCENSION.OFFERING   **14:20** and~*he~did*~*make*~GO.UP^(V) the~ADMINISTRATOR AT the~ASCENSION.OFFERING and~AT the~DEPOSIT the~ALTAR~unto and~*he~did*~much~COVER^(V) UPON~him the~ADMINISTRATOR and~*he~did*~BE.CLEAN^(V)   **14:21** and~IF HELPLESS HE and~WITHOUT HAND~him *make*~OVERTAKE^(V)~*ing*^(fs) and~*he~did*~TAKE^(V) SHEEP UNIT GUILT to~WAVING to~>~much~COVER^(V) UPON~him and~ONE.TENTH FLOUR UNIT MIX^(V)~*ed*^(ms) in~the~OIL to~DEPOSIT and~LOG OIL   **14:22** and~TWO TURTLEDOVE~s OR TWO SON~s DOVE WHICH *she~will~make*~OVERTAKE^(V) HAND~him and~*he~did*~EXIST^(V) UNIT FAILURE and~the~UNIT ASCENSION.OFFERING   **14:23** and~*he~did*~*make*~COME^(V) AT~them^(m) in~the~DAY the~EIGHTH to~CLEAN~him TO the~ADMINISTRATOR TO OPENING TENT APPOINTED to~FACE~s **YHWH**   **14:24** and~*he~did*~TAKE^(V) the~ADMINISTRATOR AT SHEEP the~GUILT and~AT LOG the~OIL and~*he~did*~WAVE^(V) AT~them^(m) the~ADMINISTRATOR WAVING to~FACE~s **YHWH**   **14:25** and~*he~did*~SLAY^(V) AT SHEEP the~GUILT and~*he~did*~TAKE^(V) the~ADMINISTRATOR from~BLOOD the~GUILT and~*he~did*~GIVE^(V) UPON TIP EAR to~the~*make*~BE.CLEAN^(V)~*ing*^(ms) the~RIGHT and~UPON THUMB HAND~him the~RIGHT and~UPON THUMB FOOT~him the~RIGHT   **14:26** and~FROM the~OIL *he~will*~POUR.DOWN^(V) the~ADMINISTRATOR UPON PALM the~ADMINISTRATOR the~LEFT.HAND   **14:27** and~*he~did*~*make*~SPATTER^(V) the~ADMINISTRATOR in~FINGER~him the~RIGHT FROM the~OIL WHICH UPON PALM~him the~LEFT.HAND SEVEN FOOTSTEP~s to~FACE~s **YHWH**   **14:28** and~*he~did*~GIVE^(V) the~ADMINISTRATOR FROM the~OIL WHICH UPON PALM~him UPON TIP EAR to~the~*make*~BE.CLEAN^(V)~*ing*^(ms) the~RIGHT and~UPON THUMB HAND~him the~RIGHT and~UPON THUMB FOOT~him the~RIGHT UPON AREA BLOOD the~GUILT   **14:29** and~the~*be*~LEAVE.BEHIND^(V)~*ing*^(ms) FROM the~OIL WHICH UPON PALM the~ADMINISTRATOR *he~will*~GIVE^(V) UPON HEAD to~the~*make*~BE.CLEAN^(V)~*ing*^(ms) to~>~much~COVER^(V) UPON~him to~FACE~s **YHWH**   **14:30** and~*he~did*~DO^(V) AT the~UNIT FROM the~

TURTLEDOVE~s OR FROM SON~s the~DOVE from~WHICH *she~will~make~*
OVERTAKE⁽ⱽ⁾ HAND~him   **14:31** AT WHICH *she~will~make~*OVERTAKE⁽ⱽ⁾
HAND~him AT the~UNIT FAILURE and~AT the~UNIT ASCENSION.OFFERING
UPON the~DEPOSIT and~*he~did~much~*COVER⁽ⱽ⁾ the~ADMINISTRATOR
UPON to~the~*make~*BE.CLEAN⁽ⱽ⁾*~ing*⁽ᵐˢ⁾ to~FACE~s **YHWH**   **14:32** THIS
TEACHING WHICH in~him TOUCH INFECTION WHICH NOT *she~will~make~*
OVERTAKE⁽ⱽ⁾ HAND~him in~CLEANSING~him   **14:33** and~*he~will~much~*
SPEAK⁽ⱽ⁾ **YHWH** TO Mosheh and~TO Aharon to~>~SAY⁽ⱽ⁾   **14:34** GIVEN.THAT
you⁽ᵐᵖ⁾*~will~*COME⁽ⱽ⁾ TO LAND Kena'an WHICH I GIVE⁽ⱽ⁾*~ing*⁽ᵐˢ⁾ to~*you*⁽ᵐᵖ⁾
to~HOLDINGS and~*I~did~*GIVE⁽ⱽ⁾ TOUCH INFECTION in~HOUSE LAND
HOLDINGS~*you*⁽ᵐᵖ⁾   **14:35** and~*he~did~*COME⁽ⱽ⁾ WHICH to~him the~HOUSE
and~*he~did~make~*BE.FACE.TO.FACE⁽ⱽ⁾ to~the~ADMINISTRATOR to~>~
SAY⁽ⱽ⁾ like~TOUCH *he~did~be~*SEE⁽ⱽ⁾ to~me in~the~HOUSE   **14:36** and~*he~*
*did~much~*DIRECT⁽ⱽ⁾ the~ADMINISTRATOR and~*they~did~much~*TURN⁽ⱽ⁾ AT
the~HOUSE in~BEFORE *he~will~*COME⁽ⱽ⁾ the~ADMINISTRATOR to~>~SEE⁽ⱽ⁾
AT the~TOUCH and~NOT *he~will~*BE.DIRTY⁽ⱽ⁾ ALL WHICH in~the~HOUSE
and~AFTER SO *he~will~*COME⁽ⱽ⁾ the~ADMINISTRATOR to~>~SEE⁽ⱽ⁾ AT the~
HOUSE   **14:37** and~*he~did~*SEE⁽ⱽ⁾ AT the~TOUCH and~LOOK the~TOUCH in~
WALL~s the~HOUSE SPOT~s GREENISH~s OR REDDISH~s and~
APPEARANCE~s~them⁽ᶠ⁾ LOW FROM the~WALL   **14:38** and~*he~will~*
GO.OUT⁽ⱽ⁾ the~ADMINISTRATOR FROM the~HOUSE TO OPENING the~
HOUSE and~*he~did~make~*SHUT⁽ⱽ⁾ AT the~HOUSE SEVEN
DAY~s   **14:39** and~*he~did~*TURN.BACK⁽ⱽ⁾ the~ADMINISTRATOR in~the~DAY
the~SEVENTH and~*he~did~*SEE⁽ⱽ⁾ and~LOOK *he~did~*SPREAD.ACROSS⁽ⱽ⁾ the~
TOUCH in~WALL~s the~HOUSE   **14:40** and~*he~did~much~*DIRECT⁽ⱽ⁾ the~
ADMINISTRATOR and~*they~did~much~*EXTRACT⁽ⱽ⁾ AT the~STONE~s WHICH
in~them⁽ᶠ⁾ the~TOUCH and~*they~did~make~*THROW.OUT⁽ⱽ⁾ AT~them⁽ᶠ⁾ TO
from~OUTSIDE to~the~CITY TO AREA DIRTY   **14:41** and~AT the~HOUSE *he~*
*will~make~*SCRAPE.OFF⁽ⱽ⁾ from~HOUSE ALL.AROUND and~*they~did~*
POUR.OUT⁽ⱽ⁾ AT the~DIRT WHICH *they~did~make~*SCRAPE.OFF⁽ⱽ⁾ TO from~
OUTSIDE to~the~CITY TO AREA DIRTY   **14:42** and~*they~did~*TAKE⁽ⱽ⁾
STONE~s OTHER~s and~*they~did~make~*COME⁽ⱽ⁾ TO UNDER the~STONE~s
and~DIRT OTHER *he~will~*TAKE⁽ⱽ⁾ and~*he~did~*PLASTER⁽ⱽ⁾ AT the~
HOUSE   **14:43** and~IF *he~will~*TURN.BACK⁽ⱽ⁾ the~TOUCH and~*he~did~*
BURST.OUT⁽ⱽ⁾ in~the~HOUSE AFTER *he~did~much~*EXTRACT⁽ⱽ⁾ AT the~
STONE~s and~AFTER >~*make~*SCRAPE.OFF⁽ⱽ⁾ AT the~HOUSE and~AFTER >~
*be~*PLASTER⁽ⱽ⁾   **14:44** and~*he~did~*COME⁽ⱽ⁾ the~ADMINISTRATOR and~*he~*
*did~*SEE⁽ⱽ⁾ and~LOOK *he~did~*SPREAD.ACROSS⁽ⱽ⁾ the~TOUCH in~the~HOUSE
INFECTION *make~*IRRITATE⁽ⱽ⁾*~ing*⁽ᶠˢ⁾ SHE in~the~HOUSE DIRTY
HE   **14:45** and~*he~did~*BREAK.DOWN⁽ⱽ⁾ AT the~HOUSE AT STONE~s~him
and~AT TREE~s~him and~AT ALL DIRT the~HOUSE and~*he~did~make~*
GO.OUT⁽ⱽ⁾ TO from~OUTSIDE to~the~CITY TO AREA DIRTY   **14:46** and~the~
COME⁽ⱽ⁾*~ing*⁽ᵐˢ⁾ TO the~HOUSE ALL DAY~s *he~did~make~*SHUT⁽ⱽ⁾ AT~him
*he~will~*BE.DIRTY⁽ⱽ⁾ UNTIL the~EVENING   **14:47** and~the~LIE.DOWN⁽ⱽ⁾*~*
ing⁽ᵐˢ⁾ in~the~HOUSE *he~will~*WASH⁽ⱽ⁾ AT GARMENT~s~him and~the~

The Book of Leviticus

EAT⁽ᵛ⁾~*ing*⁽ᵐˢ⁾ in~the~HOUSE *he~will*~WASH⁽ᵛ⁾ AT GARMENT~s~him **14:48** and~IF *!*⁽ᵐˢ⁾~COME⁽ᵛ⁾ *he~will*~COME⁽ᵛ⁾ the~ADMINISTRATOR and~*he~did*~SEE⁽ᵛ⁾ and~LOOK NOT *he~did*~SPREAD.ACROSS⁽ᵛ⁾ the~TOUCH in~the~HOUSE AFTER >~*be*~PLASTER⁽ᵛ⁾ AT the~HOUSE and~*he~did~much*~BE.CLEAN⁽ᵛ⁾ the~ADMINISTRATOR AT the~HOUSE GIVEN.THAT *he~did~be*~HEAL⁽ᵛ⁾ the~TOUCH **14:49** and~*he~did*~TAKE⁽ᵛ⁾ to~>~*much*~FAIL⁽ᵛ⁾ AT the~HOUSE TWO BIRD~s and~TREE CEDAR and~SCARLET KERMES and~HYSSOP **14:50** and~*he~did*~SLAY⁽ᵛ⁾ AT the~BIRD the~UNIT TO UTENSIL CLAY UPON WATER~s2 LIVING~s **14:51** and~*he~did*~TAKE⁽ᵛ⁾ AT TREE the~CEDAR and~AT the~HYSSOP and~AT SCARLET the~KERMES and~AT the~BIRD the~LIVING and~*he~did*~DIP⁽ᵛ⁾ AT~them⁽ᵐ⁾ in~BLOOD the~BIRD the~SLAY⁽ᵛ⁾~*ed*⁽ᶠˢ⁾ and~in~the~WATER~s2 the~LIVING~s and~*he~did~make*~SPATTER⁽ᵛ⁾ TO the~HOUSE SEVEN FOOTSTEP~s **14:52** and~*he~did~much*~FAIL⁽ᵛ⁾ AT the~HOUSE in~BLOOD the~BIRD and~in~the~WATER~s2 the~LIVING~s and~in~the~BIRD the~LIVING and~in~TREE the~CEDAR and~in~the~HYSSOP and~in~SCARLET the~KERMES **14:53** and~*he~did~much*~SEND⁽ᵛ⁾ AT the~BIRD the~LIVING TO from~OUTSIDE to~the~CITY TO FACE~s the~FIELD and~*he~did~much*~COVER⁽ᵛ⁾ UPON the~HOUSE and~*he~did*~BE.CLEAN⁽ᵛ⁾ **14:54** THIS the~TEACHING to~ALL TOUCH the~INFECTION and~to~the~ERUPTION **14:55** and~to~INFECTION the~GARMENT and~to~the~HOUSE **14:56** and~to~the~ELEVATION and~to~the~SCAB and~to~the~BRIGHT.SPOT **14:57** to~>~*make*~THROW⁽ᵛ⁾ in~DAY the~DIRTY and~in~DAY the~CLEAN THIS TEACHING the~INFECTION

Chapter 15

15:1 and~*he~will~much*~SPEAK⁽ᵛ⁾ **YHWH** TO Mosheh and~TO Aharon to~>~SAY⁽ᵛ⁾ **15:2** *!*⁽ᵐᵖ⁾~*much*~SPEAK⁽ᵛ⁾ TO SON~s Yisra'eyl and~*you*⁽ᵐᵖ⁾~*did*~SAY⁽ᵛ⁾ TO~them⁽ᵐ⁾ MAN MAN GIVEN.THAT *he~will*~EXIST⁽ᵛ⁾ ISSUE⁽ᵛ⁾~*ing*⁽ᵐˢ⁾ from~FLESH~him DISCHARGE~him DIRTY HE **15:3** and~THIS *she~will*~EXIST⁽ᵛ⁾ DIRTY~him in~DISCHARGE~him *he~did*~FLOW.OUT⁽ᵛ⁾ FLESH~him AT DISCHARGE~him OR *he~did~make*~SEAL⁽ᵛ⁾ FLESH~him from~DISCHARGE~him DIRTY~him SHE **15:4** ALL the~LYING.PLACE WHICH *he~will*~LIE.DOWN⁽ᵛ⁾ UPON~him the~ISSUE⁽ᵛ⁾~*ing*⁽ᵐˢ⁾ *he~will*~BE.DIRTY⁽ᵛ⁾ and~ALL the~UTENSIL WHICH *he~will*~SETTLE⁽ᵛ⁾ UPON~him *he~will*~BE.DIRTY⁽ᵛ⁾ **15:5** and~MAN WHICH *he~will*~TOUCH⁽ᵛ⁾ in~LYING.PLACE~him *he~will*~WASH⁽ᵛ⁾ GARMENT~s~him and~*he~did*~BATHE⁽ᵛ⁾ in~the~WATER~s2 and~*he~did*~BE.DIRTY⁽ᵛ⁾ UNTIL the~EVENING **15:6** and~the~SETTLE⁽ᵛ⁾~*ing*⁽ᵐˢ⁾ UPON the~UTENSIL WHICH *he~will*~SETTLE⁽ᵛ⁾ UPON~him the~ISSUE⁽ᵛ⁾~*ing*⁽ᵐˢ⁾ *he~will*~WASH⁽ᵛ⁾ GARMENT~s~him and~*he~did*~BATHE⁽ᵛ⁾ in~the~WATER~s2 and~*he~did*~BE.DIRTY⁽ᵛ⁾ UNTIL the~EVENING **15:7** and~the~TOUCH⁽ᵛ⁾~*ing*⁽ᵐˢ⁾ in~FLESH the~ISSUE⁽ᵛ⁾~*ing*⁽ᵐˢ⁾ *he~will*~WASH⁽ᵛ⁾ GARMENT~s~him and~*he~did*~BATHE⁽ᵛ⁾ in~the~WATER~s2 and~*he~did*~

BE.DIRTY⁽ᵛ⁾ UNTIL the~EVENING   **15:8** and~GIVEN.THAT >~SPIT⁽ᵛ⁾ the~ ISSUE⁽ᵛ⁾~*ing⁽ᵐˢ⁾* in~the~CLEAN and~*he~did~much*~WASH⁽ᵛ⁾ GARMENT~s~him and~*he~did*~BATHE⁽ᵛ⁾ in~the~WATER~s2 and~*he~did*~BE.DIRTY⁽ᵛ⁾ UNTIL the~EVENING   **15:9** and~ALL the~SADDLE WHICH *he~will*~RIDE⁽ᵛ⁾ UPON~ him the~ISSUE⁽ᵛ⁾~*ing⁽ᵐˢ⁾ he~will*~BE.DIRTY⁽ᵛ⁾   **15:10** and~ALL the~TOUCH⁽ᵛ⁾~ *ing⁽ᵐˢ⁾* in~ALL WHICH *he~will*~EXIST⁽ᵛ⁾ UNDER~s~him *he~will*~BE.DIRTY⁽ᵛ⁾ UNTIL the~EVENING and~the~LIFT.UP⁽ᵛ⁾~*ing⁽ᵐˢ⁾* AT~them⁽ᵐ⁾ *he~will*~WASH⁽ᵛ⁾ GARMENT~s~him and~*he~did*~BATHE⁽ᵛ⁾ in~the~WATER~s2 and~*he~did*~ BE.DIRTY⁽ᵛ⁾ UNTIL the~EVENING   **15:11** and~ALL WHICH *he~will*~TOUCH⁽ᵛ⁾ in~him the~ISSUE⁽ᵛ⁾~*ing⁽ᵐˢ⁾* and~HAND~s2~him NOT *he~did*~FLUSH⁽ᵛ⁾ in~ the~WATER~s2 and~*he~did~much*~WASH⁽ᵛ⁾ GARMENT~s~him and~*he~did*~ BATHE⁽ᵛ⁾ in~the~WATER~s2 and~*he~did*~BE.DIRTY⁽ᵛ⁾ UNTIL the~ EVENING   **15:12** and~UTENSIL CLAY WHICH *he~will*~TOUCH⁽ᵛ⁾ in~him the~ ISSUE⁽ᵛ⁾~*ing⁽ᵐˢ⁾ he~will~be*~CRACK⁽ᵛ⁾ and~ALL UTENSIL TREE *he~will~be*~ FLUSH⁽ᵛ⁾ in~the~WATER~s2   **15:13** and~GIVEN.THAT *he~will*~BE.CLEAN⁽ᵛ⁾ the~ISSUE⁽ᵛ⁾~*ing⁽ᵐˢ⁾* from~DISCHARGE~him and~*he~did*~COUNT⁽ᵛ⁾ to~him SEVEN DAY~s to~CLEAN~him and~*he~did~much*~WASH⁽ᵛ⁾ GARMENT~s~him and~*he~did*~BATHE⁽ᵛ⁾ FLESH~him in~WATER~s2 LIVING~s and~*he~did*~ BE.CLEAN⁽ᵛ⁾   **15:14** and~in~the~DAY the~EIGHTH *he~will*~TAKE⁽ᵛ⁾ to~him TWO TURTLEDOVE~s OR TWO SON~s DOVE and~*he~did*~COME⁽ᵛ⁾ to~FACE~s **YHWH** TO OPENING TENT APPOINTED and~*he~did*~GIVE⁽ᵛ⁾~them⁽ᵐ⁾ TO the~ ADMINISTRATOR   **15:15** and~*he~did*~DO⁽ᵛ⁾ AT~them⁽ᵐ⁾ the~ ADMINISTRATOR UNIT FAILURE and~the~UNIT ASCENSION.OFFERING and~ *he~did~much*~COVER⁽ᵛ⁾ UPON~him the~ADMINISTRATOR to~FACE~s **YHWH** from~DISCHARGE~him   **15:16** and~MAN GIVEN.THAT *she~will*~GO.OUT⁽ᵛ⁾ FROM~him LYING.DOWN SEED and~*he~did*~BATHE⁽ᵛ⁾ in~the~WATER~s2 AT ALL FLESH~him and~*he~did*~BE.DIRTY⁽ᵛ⁾ UNTIL the~EVENING   **15:17** and~ ALL GARMENT and~ALL SKIN WHICH *he~will*~EXIST⁽ᵛ⁾ UPON~him LYING.DOWN SEED and~*he~did~be~much*~WASH⁽ᵛ⁾ in~the~WATER~s2 and~ *he~did*~BE.DIRTY⁽ᵛ⁾ UNTIL the~EVENING   **15:18** and~WOMAN WHICH *he~ will*~LIE.DOWN⁽ᵛ⁾ MAN AT~her LYING.DOWN SEED and~*they~did*~BATHE⁽ᵛ⁾ in~the~WATER~s2 and~*they~did*~BE.DIRTY⁽ᵛ⁾ UNTIL the~ EVENING   **15:19** and~WOMAN GIVEN.THAT *she~will*~EXIST⁽ᵛ⁾ ISSUE⁽ᵛ⁾~*ing⁽ᶠˢ⁾* BLOOD *he~will*~EXIST⁽ᵛ⁾ DISCHARGE~her in~FLESH~her SEVEN DAY~s *she~ will*~EXIST⁽ᵛ⁾ in~REMOVAL~her and~ALL the~TOUCH⁽ᵛ⁾~*ing⁽ᵐˢ⁾* in~her *he~ will*~BE.DIRTY⁽ᵛ⁾ UNTIL the~EVENING   **15:20** and~ALL WHICH *she~will*~ LIE.DOWN⁽ᵛ⁾ UPON~him in~REMOVAL~her *he~will*~BE.DIRTY⁽ᵛ⁾ and~ALL WHICH *she~will*~SETTLE⁽ᵛ⁾ UPON~him *he~will*~BE.DIRTY⁽ᵛ⁾   **15:21** and~ALL the~TOUCH⁽ᵛ⁾~*ing⁽ᵐˢ⁾* in~LYING.PLACE~her *he~will*~WASH⁽ᵛ⁾ GARMENT~s~ him and~*he~did*~BATHE⁽ᵛ⁾ in~the~WATER~s2 and~*he~did*~BE.DIRTY⁽ᵛ⁾ UNTIL the~EVENING   **15:22** and~ALL the~TOUCH⁽ᵛ⁾~*ing⁽ᵐˢ⁾* in~ALL UTENSIL WHICH *she~will*~SETTLE⁽ᵛ⁾ UPON~him *he~will*~WASH⁽ᵛ⁾ GARMENT~s~him and~*he~ did*~BATHE⁽ᵛ⁾ in~the~WATER~s2 and~*he~did*~BE.DIRTY⁽ᵛ⁾ UNTIL the~ EVENING   **15:23** and~IF UPON the~LYING.PLACE HE OR UPON the~UTENSIL WHICH SHE SETTLE⁽ᵛ⁾~*ing⁽ᶠˢ⁾* UPON~him in~>~TOUCH⁽ᵛ⁾~him in~him *he~will*~

BE.DIRTY⁽ᵛ⁾ UNTIL the~EVENING   **15:24** and~IF >~LIE.DOWN⁽ᵛ⁾ *he~will~* LIE.DOWN⁽ᵛ⁾ MAN AT~her and~*she~will~*EXIST⁽ᵛ⁾ REMOVAL~her UPON~him and~*he~did~*BE.DIRTY⁽ᵛ⁾ SEVEN DAY~s and~ALL the~LYING.PLACE WHICH *he~will~*LIE.DOWN⁽ᵛ⁾ UPON~him *he~will~*BE.DIRTY⁽ᵛ⁾   **15:25** and~WOMAN GIVEN.THAT *he~will~*ISSUE⁽ᵛ⁾ DISCHARGE BLOOD~her DAY~s ABUNDANT~s in~NOT APPOINTED.TIME REMOVAL~her OR GIVEN.THAT *she~will~*ISSUE⁽ᵛ⁾ UPON REMOVAL~her ALL DAY~s DISCHARGE DIRTY~her like~DAY~s REMOVAL~her *she~will~*EXIST⁽ᵛ⁾ DIRTY SHE   **15:26** ALL the~LYING.PLACE WHICH *she~will~*LIE.DOWN⁽ᵛ⁾ UPON~him ALL DAY~s DISCHARGE~her like~LYING.PLACE REMOVAL~her *he~will~*EXIST⁽ᵛ⁾ to~her and~ALL the~UTENSIL WHICH *she~will~*SETTLE⁽ᵛ⁾ UPON~him DIRTY *he~will~*EXIST⁽ᵛ⁾ like~DIRTY REMOVAL~her   **15:27** and~ALL the~TOUCH⁽ᵛ⁾~*ing*⁽ᵐˢ⁾ in~them⁽ᵐ⁾ *he~will~* BE.DIRTY⁽ᵛ⁾ and~*he~did~much~*WASH⁽ᵛ⁾ GARMENT~s~him and~*he~did~* BATHE⁽ᵛ⁾ in~the~WATER~s2 and~*he~did~*BE.DIRTY⁽ᵛ⁾ UNTIL the~ EVENING   **15:28** and~IF *she~did~*BE.CLEAN⁽ᵛ⁾ from~DISCHARGE~her and~ *she~did~*COUNT⁽ᵛ⁾ to~her SEVEN DAY~s and~AFTER *she~will~* BE.CLEAN⁽ᵛ⁾   **15:29** and~in~the~DAY the~EIGHTH *she~will~*TAKE⁽ᵛ⁾ to~her TWO TURTLEDOVE~s OR TWO SON~s DOVE and~*she~did~make~*COME⁽ᵛ⁾ AT~them⁽ᵐ⁾ TO the~ADMINISTRATOR TO OPENING TENT APPOINTED   **15:30** and~*he~did~*DO⁽ᵛ⁾ the~ADMINISTRATOR AT the~UNIT FAILURE and~AT the~UNIT ASCENSION.OFFERING and~*he~did~much~* COVER⁽ᵛ⁾ UPON~her the~ADMINISTRATOR to~FACE~s **YHWH** from~ DISCHARGE DIRTY~her   **15:31** and~*you*⁽ᵐᵖ⁾~*did~make~*DEDICATE⁽ᵛ⁾ AT SON~s Yisra'eyl from~DIRTY~them⁽ᵐ⁾ and~NOT *they*⁽ᵐ⁾~*will~*DIE⁽ᵛ⁾ in~DIRTY~ them⁽ᵐ⁾ in~>~BE.DIRTY⁽ᵛ⁾~them⁽ᵐ⁾ AT DWELLING~me WHICH in~MIDST~ them⁽ᵐ⁾   **15:32** THIS TEACHING the~ISSUE⁽ᵛ⁾~*ing*⁽ᵐˢ⁾ and~WHICH *she~will~* GO.OUT⁽ᵛ⁾ FROM~him LYING.DOWN SEED to~DIRTY~her in~her   **15:33** and~ the~ILLNESS in~REMOVAL~her and~the~ISSUE⁽ᵛ⁾~*ing*⁽ᵐˢ⁾ AT DISCHARGE~him to~the~MALE and~to~the~FEMALE and~to~MAN WHICH *he~will~* LIE.DOWN⁽ᵛ⁾ WITH DIRTY

Chapter 16

16:1 and~*he~will~much~*SPEAK⁽ᵛ⁾ **YHWH** TO Mosheh AFTER DEATH TWO SON~s Aharon in~>~COME.NEAR⁽ᵛ⁾~them⁽ᵐ⁾ to~FACE~s **YHWH** and~*they*⁽ᵐ⁾~ *will~*DIE⁽ᵛ⁾   **16:2** and~*he~will~*SAY⁽ᵛ⁾ **YHWH** TO Mosheh !⁽ᵐˢ⁾*~much~*SPEAK⁽ᵛ⁾ TO Aharon BROTHER~you⁽ᵐˢ⁾ and~DO.NOT *he~will~*COME⁽ᵛ⁾ in~ALL APPOINTED.TIME TO the~SPECIAL from~HOUSE to~the~TENT.CURTAIN TO FACE~s the~LID WHICH UPON the~BOX and~NOT *he~will~*DIE⁽ᵛ⁾ GIVEN.THAT in~CLOUD *I~will~be~*SEE⁽ᵛ⁾ UPON the~LID   **16:3** in~THIS *he~will~*COME⁽ᵛ⁾ Aharon TO the~SPECIAL in~BULL SON CATTLE to~FAILURE and~BUCK to~ ASCENSION.OFFERING   **16:4** TUNIC STRAND SPECIAL *he~will~*WEAR⁽ᵛ⁾ and~ UNDERGARMENT~s STRAND *they*⁽ᵐ⁾~*will~*EXIST⁽ᵛ⁾ UPON FLESH~him and~in~

SASH STRAND *he~will~*GIRD.UP^(V) and~in~TURBAN STRAND *he~will~*WIND.AROUND^(V) GARMENT~s SPECIAL THEY^(m) and~*he~did~*BATHE^(V) in~the~WATER~s2 AT FLESH~him and~*he~did~*WEAR^(V)~them^(m) **16:5** and~from~AT COMPANY SON~s Yisra'eyl *he~will~*TAKE^(V) TWO HAIRY.GOAT~s SHE-GOAT~s to~FAILURE and~BUCK UNIT to~ASCENSION.OFFERING **16:6** and~*he~did~make~*COME.NEAR^(V) Aharon AT BULL the~FAILURE WHICH to~him and~*he~did~much~*COVER^(V) in~UNTIL~him and~in~UNTIL HOUSE~him **16:7** and~*he~did~*TAKE^(V) AT TWO the~HAIRY.GOAT~s and~*he~did~make~*STAND^(V) AT~them^(m) to~FACE~s **YHWH** OPENING TENT APPOINTED **16:8** and~*he~did~*GIVE^(V) Aharon UPON TWO the~HAIRY.GOAT~s LOT~s LOT UNIT to~**YHWH** and~LOT UNIT to~Azazeyl **16:9** and~*he~did~make~*COME.NEAR^(V) Aharon AT the~HAIRY.GOAT WHICH *he~did~*GO.UP^(V) UPON~him the~LOT to~**YHWH** and~*he~did~*DO^(V)~him FAILURE **16:10** and~the~HAIRY.GOAT WHICH *he~did~*GO.UP^(V) UPON~him the~LOT to~Azazeyl *he~will~be~much~*STAND^(V) LIVING to~FACE~s **YHWH** to~>~*much~*COVER^(V) UPON~him to~>~*much~*SEND^(V) AT~him to~Azazeyl the~WILDERNESS~unto **16:11** and~*he~did~make~*COME.NEAR^(V) Aharon AT BULL the~FAILURE WHICH to~him and~*he~did~much~*COVER^(V) in~UNTIL~him and~in~UNTIL HOUSE~him and~*he~did~*SLAY^(V) AT BULL the~FAILURE WHICH to~him **16:12** and~*he~did~*TAKE^(V) FILLING the~FIRE.PAN EMBER~s FIRE from~UPON the~ALTAR from~to~FACE~s **YHWH** and~FILLING CUPPED.HAND~s~him INCENSE.SMOKE AROMATIC.SPICE~s SCRAWNY and~*he~did~make~*COME^(V) from~HOUSE to~the~TENT.CURTAIN **16:13** and~*he~did~*GIVE^(V) AT the~INCENSE.SMOKE UPON the~FIRE to~FACE~s **YHWH** and~*he~did~much~*COVER.OVER^(V) CLOUD the~INCENSE.SMOKE AT the~LID WHICH UPON the~EVIDENCE and~NOT *he~will~*DIE^(V) **16:14** and~*he~did~*TAKE^(V) from~BLOOD the~BULL and~*he~did~make~*SPATTER^(V) in~FINGER~him UPON FACE~s the~LID EAST~unto and~to~FACE~s the~LID *he~will~make~*SPATTER^(V) SEVEN FOOTSTEP~s FROM the~BLOOD in~FINGER~him **16:15** and~*he~did~*SLAY^(V) AT HAIRY.GOAT the~FAILURE WHICH to~the~PEOPLE and~*he~did~make~*COME^(V) AT BLOOD~him TO from~HOUSE to~the~TENT.CURTAIN and~*he~did~*DO^(V) AT BLOOD~him like~WHICH *he~did~*DO^(V) to~BLOOD the~BULL and~*he~did~make~*SPATTER^(V) AT~him UPON the~LID and~to~FACE~s the~LID **16:16** and~*he~did~much~*COVER^(V) UPON the~SPECIAL from~DIRTY~s SON~s Yisra'eyl and~from~OFFENSE~s~them^(m) to~ALL FAILURE~them^(m) and~SO *he~will~*DO^(V) to~TENT APPOINTED the~DWELL^(V)~*ing*^(ms) AT~them^(m) in~MIDST DIRTY~s~them^(m) **16:17** and~ALL HUMAN NOT *he~will~*EXIST^(V) in~TENT APPOINTED in~>~COME^(V)~him to~>~*much~*COVER^(V) in~the~SPECIAL UNTIL >~GO.OUT^(V)~him and~*he~did~much~*COVER^(V) in~UNTIL~him and~in~UNTIL HOUSE~him and~in~UNTIL ALL ASSEMBLY Yisra'eyl **16:18** and~*he~will~*GO.OUT^(V) TO the~ALTAR WHICH to~FACE~s **YHWH** and~*he~did~much~*COVER^(V) UPON~him and~*he~did~*TAKE^(V) from~BLOOD the~BULL and~from~BLOOD the~HAIRY.GOAT and~*he~did~*GIVE^(V) UPON HORN~s the~ALTAR ALL.AROUND **16:19** and~*he~did~make~*

The Book of Leviticus

SPATTER⁽ⱽ⁾ UPON~him FROM the~BLOOD in~FINGER~him SEVEN FOOTSTEP~s and~*he~did~much*~BE.CLEAN⁽ⱽ⁾~him and~*he~did~much*~SET.APART⁽ⱽ⁾~him from~DIRTY~s SON~s Yisra'eyl **16:20** and~*he~did~much*~FINISH⁽ⱽ⁾ from~>~*much*~COVER⁽ⱽ⁾ AT the~SPECIAL and~AT TENT APPOINTED and~AT the~ALTAR and~*he~did~make*~COME.NEAR⁽ⱽ⁾ AT the~HAIRY.GOAT the~LIVING **16:21** and~*he~did*~SUPPORT⁽ⱽ⁾ Aharon AT TWO HAND~him UPON HEAD the~HAIRY.GOAT the~LIVING and~*he~did~self*~THROW.THE.HAND⁽ⱽ⁾ UPON~him AT ALL TWISTEDNESS~s SON~s Yisra'eyl and~AT ALL OFFENSE~s~them⁽ᵐ⁾ to~ALL FAILURE~them⁽ᵐ⁾ and~*he~did*~GIVE⁽ⱽ⁾ AT~them⁽ᵐ⁾ UPON HEAD the~HAIRY.GOAT and~*he~did~much*~SEND⁽ⱽ⁾ in~HAND MAN READY the~WILDERNESS~unto **16:22** and~*he~did*~LIFT.UP⁽ⱽ⁾ the~HAIRY.GOAT UPON~him AT ALL TWISTEDNESS~s~them⁽ᵐ⁾ TO LAND UNINHABITED and~*he~did~much*~SEND⁽ⱽ⁾ AT the~HAIRY.GOAT in~the~WILDERNESS **16:23** and~*he~did*~COME⁽ⱽ⁾ Aharon TO TENT APPOINTED and~*he~did*~STRIP.OFF⁽ⱽ⁾ AT GARMENT~s the~STRAND WHICH *he~did*~WEAR⁽ⱽ⁾ in~>~COME⁽ⱽ⁾~him TO the~SPECIAL and~*he~did~make*~REST⁽ⱽ⁾~them⁽ᵐ⁾ THERE **16:24** and~*he~did*~BATHE⁽ⱽ⁾ AT FLESH~him in~the~WATER~s2 in~AREA UNIQUE and~*he~did*~WEAR⁽ⱽ⁾ AT GARMENT~s~him and~*he~will*~GO.OUT⁽ⱽ⁾ and~*he~did*~DO⁽ⱽ⁾ AT ASCENSION.OFFERING~him and~AT ASCENSION.OFFERING the~PEOPLE and~*he~did~much*~COVER⁽ⱽ⁾ in~UNTIL~him and~in~UNTIL the~PEOPLE **16:25** and~AT FAT the~FAILURE *he~did~make*~BURN.INCENSE⁽ⱽ⁾ the~ALTAR~unto **16:26** and~the~*much*~SEND⁽ⱽ⁾~*ing*⁽ᵐˢ⁾ AT the~HAIRY.GOAT to~Azazeyl *he~will*~WASH⁽ⱽ⁾ GARMENT~s~him and~*he~did*~BATHE⁽ⱽ⁾ AT FLESH~him in~the~WATER~s2 and~AFTER SO *he~will*~COME⁽ⱽ⁾ TO the~CAMP **16:27** and~AT BULL the~FAILURE and~AT HAIRY.GOAT the~FAILURE WHICH *he~did~be~make*~COME⁽ⱽ⁾ AT BLOOD~them⁽ᵐ⁾ to~>~*much*~COVER⁽ⱽ⁾ in~the~SPECIAL *he~will~make*~GO.OUT⁽ⱽ⁾ TO from~OUTSIDE to~the~CAMP and~*they~did*~CREMATE⁽ⱽ⁾ in~the~FIRE AT SKIN~s~them⁽ᵐ⁾ and~AT FLESH~them⁽ᵐ⁾ and~AT DUNG~them⁽ᵐ⁾ **16:28** and~the~CREMATE⁽ⱽ⁾~*ing*⁽ᵐˢ⁾ AT~them⁽ᵐ⁾ *he~will*~WASH⁽ⱽ⁾ GARMENT~s~him and~*he~did*~BATHE⁽ⱽ⁾ AT FLESH~him in~the~WATER~s2 and~AFTER SO *he~will*~COME⁽ⱽ⁾ TO the~CAMP **16:29** and~*she~did*~EXIST⁽ⱽ⁾ to~you⁽ᵐᵖ⁾ to~CUSTOM DISTANT in~the~NEW.MOON the~SEVENTH in~TENTH.ONE to~the~NEW.MOON *you*⁽ᵐᵖ⁾~*will*~AFFLICT⁽ⱽ⁾ AT SOUL~s~you⁽ᵐᵖ⁾ and~ALL BUSINESS NOT *you*⁽ᵐᵖ⁾~*will*~DO⁽ⱽ⁾ the~NATIVE and~the~IMMIGRANT the~IMMIGRATE⁽ⱽ⁾~*ing*⁽ᵐˢ⁾ in~MIDST~you⁽ᵐᵖ⁾ **16:30** GIVEN.THAT in~the~DAY the~THIS *he~will~much*~COVER⁽ⱽ⁾ UPON~you⁽ᵐᵖ⁾ to~>~*much*~BE.CLEAN⁽ⱽ⁾ AT~you⁽ᵐᵖ⁾ from~ALL FAILURE~s~you⁽ᵐᵖ⁾ to~FACE~s **YHWH** *you*⁽ᵐᵖ⁾~*will*~BE.CLEAN⁽ⱽ⁾ **16:31** CEASING REST.PERIOD SHE to~you⁽ᵐᵖ⁾ and~*you*⁽ᵐᵖ⁾~*did~much*~AFFLICT⁽ⱽ⁾ AT SOUL~s~you⁽ᵐᵖ⁾ CUSTOM DISTANT **16:32** and~*he~did~much*~COVER⁽ⱽ⁾ the~ADMINISTRATOR WHICH *he~will*~SMEAR⁽ⱽ⁾ AT~him and~WHICH *he~will~much*~FILL⁽ⱽ⁾ AT HAND~him to~>~*much*~ADORN⁽ⱽ⁾ UNDER FATHER~him and~*he~did*~WEAR⁽ⱽ⁾ AT GARMENT~s the~STRAND GARMENT~s the~SPECIAL **16:33** and~*he~did~much*~COVER⁽ⱽ⁾ AT SANCTUARY the~SPECIAL and~AT TENT APPOINTED and~AT the~ALTAR *he~*

will~much~COVER⁽ᵛ⁾ and~UPON the~ADMINISTRATOR~s and~UPON ALL PEOPLE the~ASSEMBLY *he~will~much*~COVER⁽ᵛ⁾ **16:34** and~*she~did~* EXIST⁽ᵛ⁾ THIS to~you⁽ᵐᵖ⁾ to~CUSTOM DISTANT to~>~*much*~COVER⁽ᵛ⁾ UPON SON~s Yisra'eyl from~ALL FAILURE~them⁽ᵐ⁾ UNIT in~the~YEAR and~*he~will~* DO⁽ᵛ⁾ like~WHICH *he~did~much*~DIRECT⁽ᵛ⁾ **YHWH** AT Mosheh

Chapter 17

17:1 and~*he~will~much*~SPEAK⁽ᵛ⁾ **YHWH** TO Mosheh to~>~SAY⁽ᵛ⁾ **17:2** *I*⁽ᵐˢ⁾~ *much*~SPEAK⁽ᵛ⁾ TO Aharon and~TO SON~s~him and~TO ALL SON~s Yisra'eyl and~*you*⁽ᵐˢ⁾~*did*~SAY⁽ᵛ⁾ TO~them⁽ᵐ⁾ THIS the~WORD WHICH *he~did~much~* DIRECT⁽ᵛ⁾ **YHWH** to~>~SAY⁽ᵛ⁾ **17:3** MAN MAN from~HOUSE Yisra'eyl WHICH *he~will*~SLAY⁽ᵛ⁾ OX OR SHEEP OR SHE-GOAT in~the~CAMP OR WHICH *he~ will~*SLAY⁽ᵛ⁾ from~OUTSIDE to~the~CAMP **17:4** and~TO OPENING TENT APPOINTED NOT *he~did~make*~COME⁽ᵛ⁾~him to~>~*make*~COME.NEAR⁽ᵛ⁾ DONATION to~**YHWH** to~FACE~s DWELLING **YHWH** BLOOD *he~will~be~* THINK⁽ᵛ⁾ to~the~MAN the~HE BLOOD *he~did~*POUR.OUT⁽ᵛ⁾ and~*he~did~be~* CUT⁽ᵛ⁾ the~MAN the~HE from~INSIDE PEOPLE~him **17:5** to~THAT WHICH *they*⁽ᵐ⁾~*will~make*~COME⁽ᵛ⁾ SON~s Yisra'eyl AT SACRIFICE~s~them⁽ᵐ⁾ WHICH THEY⁽ᵐ⁾ SACRIFICE⁽ᵛ⁾~*ing*⁽ᵐᵖ⁾ UPON FACE~s the~FIELD and~*they~did~make*~ COME⁽ᵛ⁾~them⁽ᵐ⁾ to~**YHWH** TO OPENING TENT APPOINTED TO the~ ADMINISTRATOR and~*they~did~*SACRIFICE⁽ᵛ⁾ SACRIFICE~s OFFERING.OF.RESTITUTION~s to~**YHWH** AT~them⁽ᵐ⁾ **17:6** and~*he~did~* SPRINKLE⁽ᵛ⁾ the~ADMINISTRATOR AT the~BLOOD UPON ALTAR **YHWH** OPENING TENT APPOINTED and~*he~did~make*~BURN.INCENSE⁽ᵛ⁾ the~FAT to~AROMA SWEET to~**YHWH** **17:7** and~NOT *they*⁽ᵐ⁾~*will~*SACRIFICE⁽ᵛ⁾ YET.AGAIN AT SACRIFICE~s~them⁽ᵐ⁾ to~the~HAIRY.GOAT~s WHICH THEY⁽ᵐ⁾ BE.A.HARLOT⁽ᵛ⁾~*ing*⁽ᵐᵖ⁾ AFTER~them⁽ᵐ⁾ CUSTOM DISTANT *she~will~*EXIST⁽ᵛ⁾ THIS to~them⁽ᵐ⁾ to~GENERATION~s~them⁽ᵐ⁾ **17:8** and~TO~them⁽ᵐ⁾ *you*⁽ᵐˢ⁾~ *will~*SAY⁽ᵛ⁾ MAN MAN from~HOUSE Yisra'eyl and~FROM the~IMMIGRANT WHICH *he~will~*IMMIGRATE⁽ᵛ⁾ in~MIDST~them⁽ᵐ⁾ WHICH *he~will~*GO.UP⁽ᵛ⁾ ASCENSION.OFFERING OR SACRIFICE **17:9** and~TO OPENING TENT APPOINTED NOT *he~will~make*~COME⁽ᵛ⁾~him to~>~DO⁽ᵛ⁾ AT~him to~**YHWH** and~*he~did~be*~CUT⁽ᵛ⁾ the~MAN the~HE from~PEOPLE~s~him **17:10** and~ MAN MAN from~HOUSE Yisra'eyl and~FROM the~IMMIGRANT the~ IMMIGRATE⁽ᵛ⁾~*ing*⁽ᵐˢ⁾ in~MIDST~them⁽ᵐ⁾ WHICH *he~will~*EAT⁽ᵛ⁾ ALL BLOOD and~*I~did~*GIVE⁽ᵛ⁾ FACE~s~me in~the~SOUL the~EAT⁽ᵛ⁾~*ing*⁽ᶠˢ⁾ AT the~ BLOOD and~*I~did~make*~CUT⁽ᵛ⁾ AT~her from~INSIDE PEOPLE~ her **17:11** GIVEN.THAT SOUL the~FLESH in~the~BLOOD SHE and~I *I~did~* GIVE⁽ᵛ⁾~him to~you⁽ᵐᵖ⁾ UPON the~ALTAR to~>~*much*~COVER⁽ᵛ⁾ UPON SOUL~s~you⁽ᵐᵖ⁾ GIVEN.THAT the~BLOOD HE in~the~SOUL *he~will~much~* COVER⁽ᵛ⁾ **17:12** UPON SO *I~did~*SAY⁽ᵛ⁾ to~SON~s Yisra'eyl ALL SOUL from~ you⁽ᵐᵖ⁾ NOT *you*⁽ᵐˢ⁾~*will~*EAT⁽ᵛ⁾ BLOOD and~the~IMMIGRANT the~

IMMIGRATE⁽ⱽ⁾~*ing*⁽ᵐˢ⁾ in~MIDST~you⁽ᵐᵖ⁾ NOT *he~will*~EAT⁽ⱽ⁾ BLOOD   **17:13** and~MAN MAN from~SON~s Yisra'eyl and~FROM the~ IMMIGRANT the~IMMIGRATE⁽ⱽ⁾~*ing*⁽ᵐˢ⁾ in~MIDST~them⁽ᵐ⁾ WHICH *he~will*~HUNT⁽ⱽ⁾ GAME LIVING OR FLYER WHICH *he~will~be*~EAT⁽ⱽ⁾ and~*he~did*~POUR.OUT⁽ⱽ⁾ AT BLOOD~him and~*he~did~much*~COVER.OVER⁽ⱽ⁾~him in~DIRT   **17:14** GIVEN.THAT SOUL ALL FLESH BLOOD~him in~SOUL~him HE and~*I~will*~SAY⁽ⱽ⁾ to~SON~s Yisra'eyl BLOOD ALL FLESH NOT *you*⁽ᵐᵖ⁾~*will*~EAT⁽ⱽ⁾ GIVEN.THAT SOUL ALL FLESH BLOOD~him SHE ALL EAT⁽ⱽ⁾~*ing*⁽ᵐᵖ⁾~him *he~will~be*~CUT⁽ⱽ⁾   **17:15** and~ALL SOUL WHICH *she~will*~EAT⁽ⱽ⁾ CARCASS and~TORN in~NATIVE and~in~the~IMMIGRANT and~*he~did~much*~WASH⁽ⱽ⁾ GARMENT~s~him and~*he~did*~BATHE⁽ⱽ⁾ in~the~WATER~s2 and~*he~did*~BE.DIRTY⁽ⱽ⁾ UNTIL the~EVENING and~*he~did*~BE.CLEAN⁽ⱽ⁾   **17:16** and~IF NOT *he~will*~WASH⁽ⱽ⁾ and~FLESH~him NOT *he~will*~BATHE⁽ⱽ⁾ and~*he~did*~LIFT.UP⁽ⱽ⁾ TWISTEDNESS~him

Chapter 18

18:1 and~*he~will~much*~SPEAK⁽ⱽ⁾ **YHWH** TO Mosheh to~>~SAY⁽ⱽ⁾   **18:2** !⁽ᵐˢ⁾~*much*~SPEAK⁽ⱽ⁾ TO SON~s Yisra'eyl and~*you*⁽ᵐᵖ⁾~*did*~SAY⁽ⱽ⁾ TO~them⁽ᵐ⁾ I **YHWH** Elohiym~you⁽ᵐᵖ⁾   **18:3** like~WORK LAND Mits'rayim WHICH *you*⁽ᵐᵖ⁾~*did*~SETTLE⁽ⱽ⁾ in~her NOT *you*⁽ᵐᵖ⁾~*will*~DO⁽ⱽ⁾ and~like~WORK LAND Kena'an WHICH I *make*~COME⁽ⱽ⁾~*ing*⁽ᵐˢ⁾ AT~you⁽ᵐᵖ⁾ THERE~unto NOT *you*⁽ᵐᵖ⁾~*will*~DO⁽ⱽ⁾ and~in~CUSTOM~s~them⁽ᵐ⁾ NOT *you*⁽ᵐᵖ⁾~*will*~WALK⁽ⱽ⁾   **18:4** AT DECISION~s~me *you*⁽ᵐᵖ⁾~*will*~DO⁽ⱽ⁾ and~AT CUSTOM~s~me *you*⁽ᵐᵖ⁾~*will*~SAFEGUARD⁽ⱽ⁾ to~>~WALK⁽ⱽ⁾ in~them⁽ᵐ⁾ I **YHWH** Elohiym~you⁽ᵐᵖ⁾   **18:5** and~*you*⁽ᵐᵖ⁾~*did*~SAFEGUARD⁽ⱽ⁾ AT CUSTOM~s~me and~AT DECISION~s~me WHICH *he~will*~DO⁽ⱽ⁾ AT~them⁽ᵐ⁾ the~HUMAN and~*he~did*~LIVE⁽ⱽ⁾ in~them⁽ᵐ⁾ I **YHWH**   **18:6** MAN MAN TO ALL KIN FLESH~him NOT *you*⁽ᵐᵖ⁾~*will*~COME.NEAR⁽ⱽ⁾ to~>~*much*~REMOVE.THE.COVER⁽ⱽ⁾ NAKEDNESS I **YHWH**   **18:7** NAKEDNESS FATHER~you⁽ᵐˢ⁾ and~NAKEDNESS MOTHER~you⁽ᵐˢ⁾ NOT *you*⁽ᵐˢ⁾~*will~much*~REMOVE.THE.COVER⁽ⱽ⁾ MOTHER~you⁽ᵐˢ⁾ SHE NOT *you*⁽ᵐˢ⁾~*will~much*~REMOVE.THE.COVER⁽ⱽ⁾ NAKEDNESS~her   **18:8** NAKEDNESS WOMAN FATHER~you⁽ᵐˢ⁾ NOT *you*⁽ᵐˢ⁾~*will~much*~REMOVE.THE.COVER⁽ⱽ⁾ NAKEDNESS FATHER~you⁽ᵐˢ⁾ SHE   **18:9** NAKEDNESS SISTER~you⁽ᵐˢ⁾ DAUGHTER FATHER~you⁽ᵐˢ⁾ OR DAUGHTER MOTHER~you⁽ᵐˢ⁾ KINDRED HOUSE OR KINDRED OUTSIDE NOT *you*⁽ᵐˢ⁾~*will~much*~REMOVE.THE.COVER⁽ⱽ⁾ NAKEDNESS~them⁽ᶠ⁾   **18:10** NAKEDNESS DAUGHTER SON~you⁽ᵐˢ⁾ OR DAUGHTER DAUGHTER~you⁽ᵐˢ⁾ NOT *you*⁽ᵐˢ⁾~*will~much*~REMOVE.THE.COVER⁽ⱽ⁾ NAKEDNESS~them⁽ᶠ⁾ GIVEN.THAT NAKEDNESS~you⁽ᵐˢ⁾ THEY⁽ᶠ⁾   **18:11** NAKEDNESS DAUGHTER WOMAN FATHER~you⁽ᵐˢ⁾ KINDRED FATHER~you⁽ᵐˢ⁾ SISTER~you⁽ᵐˢ⁾ SHE NOT *you*⁽ᵐˢ⁾~*will~much*~REMOVE.THE.COVER⁽ⱽ⁾ NAKEDNESS~her   **18:12** NAKEDNESS SISTER FATHER~you⁽ᵐˢ⁾ NOT *you*⁽ᵐˢ⁾~*will~much*~REMOVE.THE.COVER⁽ⱽ⁾ KIN

FATHER~you(ms) SHE **18:13** NAKEDNESS SISTER MOTHER~you(ms) NOT *you(ms)~will~much~*REMOVE.THE.COVER(v) GIVEN.THAT KIN MOTHER~you(ms) SHE **18:14** NAKEDNESS BROTHER~of FATHER~you(ms) NOT *you(ms)~will~much~*REMOVE.THE.COVER(v) TO WOMAN~him NOT *you(ms)~will~*COME.NEAR(v) AUNT~you(ms) SHE **18:15** NAKEDNESS DAUGHTER-IN-LAW~you(ms) NOT *you(ms)~will~much~*REMOVE.THE.COVER(v) WOMAN SON~you(ms) SHE NOT *you(ms)~will~much~*REMOVE.THE.COVER(v) NAKEDNESS~her **18:16** NAKEDNESS WOMAN BROTHER~you(ms) NOT *you(ms)~will~much~*REMOVE.THE.COVER(v) NAKEDNESS BROTHER~you(ms) SHE **18:17** NAKEDNESS WOMAN and~DAUGHTER~her NOT *you(ms)~will~much~*REMOVE.THE.COVER(v) AT DAUGHTER SON~her and~AT DAUGHTER DAUGHTER~her NOT *you(ms)~will~*TAKE(v) *to~>~much~*REMOVE.THE.COVER(v) NAKEDNESS~her KIN THEY(f) MISCHIEF SHE **18:18** and~WOMAN TO SISTER~her NOT *you(ms)~will~*TAKE(v) *to~>~*PRESS.IN(v) *to~>~much~*REMOVE.THE.COVER(v) NAKEDNESS~her UPON~her in~LIVING~her **18:19** and~TO WOMAN in~REMOVAL DIRTY~her NOT *you(ms)~will~*COME.NEAR(v) *to~>~much~*REMOVE.THE.COVER(v) NAKEDNESS~her **18:20** and~TO WOMAN NEIGHBOR~you(ms) NOT *you(ms)~will~*GIVE(v) COPULATION~you(ms) to~SEED to~DIRTY~her in~her **18:21** and~SEED~you(ms) NOT *you(ms)~will~*GIVE(v) *to~>~make~*CROSS.OVER(v) to~the~Molekh and~NOT *you(ms)~will~much~*DRILL(v) AT TITLE Elohiym~you(ms) I **YHWH** **18:22** and~AT MALE NOT *you(ms)~will~*LIE.DOWN(v) LYING.PLACE~s WOMAN DISGUSTING SHE **18:23** and~in~ALL BEAST NOT *you(ms)~will~*GIVE(v) COPULATION~you(ms) to~DIRTY~her in~her and~WOMAN NOT *you(ms)~will~*STAND(v) to~FACE~s BEAST *to~>~*BE.SQUARE(v)~her UNNATURAL.MIX HE **18:24** DO.NOT *you(mp)~will~self~*BE.DIRTY(v) in~ALL THESE GIVEN.THAT in~ALL THESE *they~did~be~*BE.DIRTY(v) the~NATION~s WHICH I *much~*SEND(v)~*ing(ms)* from~FACE~s~you(mp) **18:25** and~*she~will~*BE.DIRTY(v) the~LAND and~*I~will~*REGISTER(v) TWISTEDNESS~her UPON~her and~*she~will~much~*VOMIT(v) the~LAND AT SETTLE(v)~*ing(mp)*~her **18:26** and~*you(mp)~did~*SAFEGUARD(v) YOU(mp) AT CUSTOM~s~me and~AT DECISION~s~me and~NOT *you(mp)~will~*DO(v) from~ALL the~DISGUSTING~s the~THESE the~NATIVE and~the~IMMIGRANT the~IMMIGRATE(v)~*ing(ms)* in~MIDST~you(mp) **18:27** GIVEN.THAT AT ALL the~DISGUSTING~s the~THESE *they~did~*DO(v) MAN~s the~LAND WHICH to~FACE~s~you(mp) and~*she~will~*BE.DIRTY(v) the~LAND **18:28** and~NOT *she~will~make~*VOMIT(v) the~LAND AT~you(mp) in~*much~*DIRTY~you(mp) AT~her like~WHICH *she~did~*VOMIT(v) AT the~NATION WHICH to~FACE~s~you(mp) **18:29** GIVEN.THAT ALL WHICH *he~will~*DO(v) from~ALL the~DISGUSTING~s the~THESE and~*they~did~be~*CUT(v) the~SOUL~s the~DO(v)~*ing(fp)* from~INSIDE PEOPLE~them(m) **18:30** and~*you(mp)~did~*SAFEGUARD(v) AT CHARGE~me to~EXCEPT >~DO(v) from~CUSTOM~s the~DISGUSTING~s WHICH *they~did~be~*DO(v) to~FACE~s~you(mp) and~NOT *you(mp)~will~make~self~*BE.DIRTY(v) in~them(m) I **YHWH** Elohiym~you(mp)

Chapter 19

19:1 and~*he*~*will*~*much*~SPEAK⁽ⱽ⁾ **YHWH** TO Mosheh to~>~SAY⁽ⱽ⁾   **19:2** !⁽ᵐˢ⁾~*much*~SPEAK⁽ⱽ⁾ TO ALL COMPANY SON~s Yisra'eyl and~*you*⁽ᵐᵖ⁾~*did*~SAY⁽ⱽ⁾ TO~them⁽ᵐ⁾ UNIQUE~s *you*⁽ᵐᵖ⁾~*will*~EXIST⁽ⱽ⁾ GIVEN.THAT UNIQUE I **YHWH** Elohiym~you⁽ᵐᵖ⁾   **19:3** MAN MOTHER~him and~FATHER~him *you*⁽ᵐᵖ⁾~*will*~FEAR⁽ⱽ⁾ and~AT CEASING~s~me *you*⁽ᵐᵖ⁾~*will*~SAFEGUARD⁽ⱽ⁾ I **YHWH** Elohiym~you⁽ᵐᵖ⁾   **19:4** DO.NOT *you*⁽ᵐᵖ⁾~*will*~TURN⁽ⱽ⁾ TO the~WORTHLESS~s and~Elohiym CAST.IMAGE NOT *you*⁽ᵐᵖ⁾~*will*~DO⁽ⱽ⁾ to~you⁽ᵐᵖ⁾ I **YHWH** Elohiym~you⁽ᵐᵖ⁾   **19:5** and~GIVEN.THAT *you*⁽ᵐˢ⁾~*will*~SACRIFICE⁽ⱽ⁾~him SACRIFICE OFFERING.OF.RESTITUTION~s to~**YHWH** to~SELF-WILL~you⁽ᵐᵖ⁾ *you*⁽ᵐᵖ⁾~*will*~SACRIFICE⁽ⱽ⁾~him   **19:6** in~DAY SACRIFICE~you⁽ᵐᵖ⁾ *he*~*will*~*be*~EAT⁽ⱽ⁾ and~from~MORROW and~the~*be*~LEAVE.BEHIND⁽ⱽ⁾~*ing*⁽ᵐˢ⁾ UNTIL DAY the~THIRD in~the~FIRE *he*~*will*~*be*~CREMATE⁽ⱽ⁾   **19:7** and~IF the~>~*be*~EAT⁽ⱽ⁾ *he*~*will*~*be*~EAT⁽ⱽ⁾ in~the~DAY the~THIRD FOUL HE NOT *he*~*will*~*be*~ACCEPT⁽ⱽ⁾   **19:8** and~EAT⁽ⱽ⁾~*ing*⁽ᵐᵖ⁾~him TWISTEDNESS~him *he*~*will*~LIFT.UP⁽ⱽ⁾ GIVEN.THAT AT SPECIAL **YHWH** *he*~*did*~*much*~DRILL⁽ⱽ⁾ and~*she*~*did*~*be*~CUT⁽ⱽ⁾ the~SOUL the~SHE from~PEOPLE~s~her   **19:9** and~in~>~SEVER⁽ⱽ⁾~you⁽ᵐᵖ⁾ AT HARVEST LAND~you⁽ᵐᵖ⁾ NOT *you*⁽ᵐˢ⁾~*will*~*much*~FINISH⁽ⱽ⁾ EDGE FIELD~you⁽ᵐˢ⁾ to~>~SEVER⁽ⱽ⁾ and~GLEANINGS HARVEST~you⁽ᵐˢ⁾ NOT *you*⁽ᵐˢ⁾~*will*~*much*~PICK.UP⁽ⱽ⁾   **19:10** and~VINEYARD~you⁽ᵐˢ⁾ NOT *you*⁽ᵐˢ⁾~*will*~*much*~ROLL⁽ⱽ⁾ and~FALLEN.GRAPE VINEYARD~you⁽ᵐˢ⁾ NOT *you*⁽ᵐˢ⁾~*will*~*much*~PICK.UP⁽ⱽ⁾ to~AFFLICTION and~to~IMMIGRANT *you*⁽ᵐˢ⁾~*will*~LEAVE⁽ⱽ⁾ AT~them⁽ᵐ⁾ I **YHWH** Elohiym~you⁽ᵐᵖ⁾   **19:11** NOT *you*⁽ᵐˢ⁾~*will*~STEAL⁽ⱽ⁾ and~NOT *you*⁽ᵐᵖ⁾~*will*~*much*~DENY⁽ⱽ⁾ and~NOT *you*⁽ᵐᵖ⁾~*will*~*much*~DEAL.FALSELY⁽ⱽ⁾ MAN in~the~NEIGHBOR~him   **19:12** and~NOT *you*⁽ᵐᵖ⁾~*will*~*be*~SWEAR⁽ⱽ⁾ in~TITLE~me to~the~FALSE and~*you*⁽ᵐˢ⁾~*did*~*much*~DRILL⁽ⱽ⁾ AT TITLE Elohiym~you⁽ᵐˢ⁾ I **YHWH**   **19:13** NOT *you*⁽ᵐˢ⁾~*will*~OPPRESS⁽ⱽ⁾ AT COMPANION~you⁽ᵐˢ⁾ and~NOT *you*⁽ᵐˢ⁾~*will*~PLUCK.AWAY⁽ⱽ⁾ NOT *you*⁽ᵐˢ⁾~*will*~STAY.THE.NIGHT⁽ⱽ⁾ MAKE⁽ⱽ⁾~*ed*⁽ᶠˢ⁾ HIRELING AT~you⁽ᵐˢ⁾ UNTIL MORNING   **19:14** NOT *you*⁽ᵐˢ⁾~*will*~*much*~BELITTLE⁽ⱽ⁾ SILENT and~to~FACE~s BLIND NOT *you*⁽ᵐˢ⁾~*will*~GIVE⁽ⱽ⁾ STUMBLING.BLOCK and~*you*⁽ᵐˢ⁾~*did*~FEAR⁽ⱽ⁾ from~Elohiym~you⁽ᵐˢ⁾ I **YHWH**   **19:15** NOT *you*⁽ᵐᵖ⁾~*will*~DO⁽ⱽ⁾ WICKED in~the~DECISION NOT *you*⁽ᵐˢ⁾~*will*~LIFT.UP⁽ⱽ⁾ FACE~s HELPLESS and~NOT *you*⁽ᵐˢ⁾~*will*~GIVE.HONOR⁽ⱽ⁾ FACE~s GREAT in~STEADFAST *you*⁽ᵐˢ⁾~*will*~DECIDE⁽ⱽ⁾ NEIGHBOR~you⁽ᵐˢ⁾   **19:16** NOT *you*⁽ᵐˢ⁾~*will*~WALK⁽ⱽ⁾ TALEBEARER in~PEOPLE~s~you⁽ᵐˢ⁾ NOT *you*⁽ᵐˢ⁾~*will*~STAND⁽ⱽ⁾ UPON BLOOD COMPANION~you⁽ᵐˢ⁾ I **YHWH**   **19:17** NOT *you*⁽ᵐˢ⁾~*will*~HATE⁽ⱽ⁾ AT BROTHER~you⁽ᵐˢ⁾ in~HEART~you⁽ᵐˢ⁾ >~*make*~REBUKE⁽ⱽ⁾ *you*⁽ᵐˢ⁾~*will*~*make*~REBUKE⁽ⱽ⁾ AT NEIGHBOR~you⁽ᵐˢ⁾ and~NOT *you*⁽ᵐˢ⁾~*will*~LIFT.UP⁽ⱽ⁾ UPON~him FAILURE   **19:18** NOT *you*⁽ᵐˢ⁾~*will*~AVENGE⁽ⱽ⁾ and~NOT *you*⁽ᵐˢ⁾~*will*~KEEP⁽ⱽ⁾ AT SON~s PEOPLE~you⁽ᵐˢ⁾ and~*you*⁽ᵐˢ⁾~*did*~LOVE⁽ⱽ⁾ to~COMPANION~you⁽ᵐˢ⁾ like~THAT.ONE~you⁽ᵐˢ⁾ I **YHWH**   **19:19** AT CUSTOM~s~me *you*⁽ᵐᵖ⁾~*will*~SAFEGUARD⁽ⱽ⁾ BEAST~you⁽ᵐˢ⁾ NOT *you*⁽ᵐˢ⁾~*will*~*make*~BE.SQUARE⁽ⱽ⁾

DIVERSE.KIND~s2 FIELD~you(ms) NOT you(ms)~will~SOW(V) DIVERSE.KIND~s2 and~GARMENT DIVERSE.KIND~s2 LINSEY-WOOLSEY NOT he~will~GO.UP(V) UPON~you(ms) **19:20** and~MAN GIVEN.THAT he~will~LIE.DOWN(V) AT WOMAN LYING.DOWN SEED and~SHE MAID be~CONSORT(V)~ing(fs) to~MAN and~>~be~much~RANSOM(V) NOT she~did~be~RANSOM(V) OR FREEDOM NOT he~did~be~GIVE(V) to~her PUNISHMENT she~will~EXIST(V) NOT they~ will~be~make~DIE(V) GIVEN.THAT NOT she~did~be~much~ FREE(V) **19:21** and~he~did~make~COME(V) AT GUILT~him to~**YHWH** TO OPENING TENT APPOINTED BUCK GUILT **19:22** and~he~did~much~COVER(V) UPON~him the~ADMINISTRATOR in~BUCK the~GUILT to~FACE~s **YHWH** UPON FAILURE~him WHICH he~did~FAIL(V) and~he~did~be~FORGIVE(V) to~ him from~FAILURE~him WHICH he~did~FAIL(V) **19:23** and~GIVEN.THAT you(mp)~will~COME(V) TO the~LAND and~you(mp)~did~PLANT(V) ALL TREE NOURISHMENT and~you(mp)~did~CONSIDERED.UNCIRCUMCISED(V) FORESKIN~him AT PRODUCE~him THREE YEAR~s he~will~EXIST(V) to~you(mp) FORESKIN~s NOT he~will~be~EAT(V) **19:24** and~in~the~YEAR the~FOURTH he~will~EXIST(V) ALL PRODUCE~him SPECIAL SHINING~s to~ **YHWH** **19:25** and~in~the~YEAR the~FIFTH you(mp)~will~EAT(V) AT PRODUCE~him to~>~make~ADD(V) to~you(mp) PRODUCTION~him I **YHWH** Elohiym~you(mp) **19:26** NOT you(mp)~will~EAT(V) UPON the~BLOOD NOT you(mp)~will~much~PREDICT(V) and~NOT you(mp)~will~much~ CONJURE(V) **19:27** NOT you(mp)~will~ENCIRCLE(V) EDGE HEAD~you(mp) and~ NOT you(ms)~will~make~DAMAGE(V) AT EDGE BEARD~you(ms) **19:28** and~ SLICING to~the~SOUL NOT you(mp)~will~GIVE(V) in~FLESH~you(mp) and~ WRITING TATTOO NOT you(mp)~will~GIVE(V) in~you(mp) I **YHWH** **19:29** DO.NOT you(ms)~will~much~DRILL(V) AT DAUGHTER~you(ms) to~>~make~BE.A.HARLOT(V)~her and~NOT she~will~BE.A.HARLOT(V) the~ LAND and~she~did~FILL(V) the~LAND MISCHIEF **19:30** AT CEASING~s~me you(mp)~will~SAFEGUARD(V) and~SANCTUARY~me you(mp)~will~FEAR(V) I **YHWH** **19:31** DO.NOT you(mp)~will~TURN(V) TO the~NECROMANCER~s and~ TO the~KNOWER~s DO.NOT you(mp)~will~much~SEARCH.OUT(V) to~DIRTY~ her in~them(m) I **YHWH** Elohiym~you(mp) **19:32** from~FACE~s GRAY-HEADED you(ms)~will~RISE(V) and~you(ms)~did~GIVE.HONOR FACE~s BEARD and~ you(ms)~did~FEAR(V) from~Elohiym~you(ms) I **YHWH** **19:33** and~GIVEN.THAT he~will~IMMIGRATE(V) AT~you(ms) IMMIGRANT in~LAND~you(mp) NOT you(mp)~will~make~SUPPRESS(V) AT~him **19:34** like~NATIVE from~you(mp) he~will~EXIST(V) to~you(mp) the~IMMIGRANT the~IMMIGRATE(V)~ing(ms) AT~ you(mp) and~you(ms)~did~LOVE(V) to~him like~THAT.ONE~you(ms) GIVEN.THAT IMMIGRANT~s you(mp)~did~EXIST(V) in~LAND Mits'rayim I **YHWH** Elohiym~ you(mp) **19:35** NOT you(mp)~will~DO(V) WICKED in~the~DECISION in~the~ MEASUREMENT in~the~WEIGHT and~in~the~QUANTITY **19:36** BALANCE~ s2 STEADFAST STONE~s STEADFAST EYPHAH STEADFAST and~HIYN STEADFAST he~will~EXIST(V) to~you(mp) I **YHWH** Elohiym~you(mp) WHICH I~ did~make~GO.OUT(V) AT~you(mp) from~LAND Mits'rayim **19:37** and~

The Book of Leviticus

you^(mp)~did~SAFEGUARD^(V) AT ALL CUSTOM~s~me and~AT ALL DECISION~s~me and~you^(mp)~did~DO^(V) AT~them^(m) I **YHWH**

Chapter 20

20:1 and~he~will~much~SPEAK^(V) **YHWH** TO Mosheh to~>~SAY^(V) **20:2** and~TO SON~s Yisra'eyl you^(ms)~will~SAY^(V) MAN MAN from~SON~s Yisra'eyl and~FROM the~IMMIGRANT the~IMMIGRATE^(V)~ing^(ms) in~Yisra'eyl WHICH he~will~GIVE^(V) from~SEED~him to~the~Molekh >~DIE^(V) he~will~be~make~DIE^(V) PEOPLE the~LAND they^(m)~will~KILL.BY.STONING^(V)~him in~the~STONE **20:3** and~I~will~GIVE^(V) AT FACE~s~me in~the~MAN the~HE and~I~did~make~CUT^(V) AT~him from~INSIDE PEOPLE~him GIVEN.THAT from~SEED~him he~did~GIVE^(V) to~the~Molekh to~THAT he~did~BE.DIRTY^(V) AT SANCTUARY~me and~to~>~much~DRILL^(V) AT TITLE SPECIAL~me **20:4** and~IF >~make~BE.OUT.OF.SIGHT^(V) they^(m)~will~make~BE.OUT.OF.SIGHT^(V) PEOPLE the~LAND AT EYE~s2~them^(m) FROM the~MAN the~HE in~>~GIVE^(V)~him from~SEED~him to~the~Molekh to~EXCEPT >~make~DIE^(V) AT~him **20:5** and~I~did~PLACE^(V) I AT FACE~s~me in~the~MAN the~HE and~in~CLAN~him and~I~did~make~CUT^(V) AT~him and~AT ALL the~BE.A.HARLOT^(V)~ing^(mp) AFTER~him to~>~BE.A.HARLOT^(V) AFTER the~Molekh from~INSIDE PEOPLE~them^(m) **20:6** and~the~SOUL WHICH she~will~TURN^(V) TO the~NECROMANCER~s and~TO the~KNOWER~s to~>~BE.A.HARLOT^(V) AFTER~them^(m) and~I~did~GIVE^(V) AT FACE~s~me in~the~SOUL the~SHE and~I~did~make~CUT^(V) AT~him from~INSIDE PEOPLE~him **20:7** and~you^(mp)~did~self~SET.APART^(V) and~you^(mp)~did~EXIST^(V) UNIQUE~s GIVEN.THAT I **YHWH** Elohiym~you^(mp) **20:8** and~you^(mp)~did~SAFEGUARD^(V) AT CUSTOM~s~me and~you^(mp)~did~DO^(V) AT~them^(m) I **YHWH** much~SET.APART^(V)~ing^(ms)~you^(ms) **20:9** GIVEN.THAT MAN MAN WHICH he~will~much~BELITTLE^(V) AT FATHER~him and~AT MOTHER~him >~DIE^(V) he~will~be~make~DIE^(V) FATHER~him and~MOTHER~him he~did~much~BELITTLE^(V) BLOOD~s~him in~him **20:10** and~MAN WHICH he~will~COMMIT.ADULTERY^(V) AT WOMAN MAN WHICH he~will~COMMIT.ADULTERY^(V) AT WOMAN COMPANION~him >~DIE^(V) he~will~be~make~DIE^(V) the~COMMIT.ADULTERY^(V)~ing^(ms) and~the~COMMIT.ADULTERY^(V)~ing^(fs) **20:11** and~MAN WHICH he~will~LIE.DOWN^(V) AT WOMAN FATHER~him NAKEDNESS FATHER~him he~did~much~REMOVE.THE.COVER^(V) >~DIE^(V) they~will~be~make~DIE^(V) TWO~them^(m) BLOOD~s~them^(m) in~them^(m) **20:12** and~MAN WHICH he~will~LIE.DOWN^(V) AT DAUGHTER-IN-LAW~him >~DIE^(V) they~will~be~make~DIE^(V) TWO~them^(m) UNNATURAL.MIX they~did~DO^(V) BLOOD~s~them^(m) in~them^(m) **20:13** and~MAN WHICH he~will~LIE.DOWN^(V) AT MALE LYING.PLACE~s WOMAN DISGUSTING they~did~DO^(V) TWO~them^(m) >~DIE^(V) they~will~be~make~DIE^(V) BLOOD~s~them^(m) in~them^(m) **20:14** and~MAN

WHICH he~will~TAKE⁽ᵛ⁾ AT WOMAN and~AT MOTHER~her MISCHIEF SHE in~
the~FIRE they⁽ᵐ⁾~will~CREMATE⁽ᵛ⁾ AT~him and~AT~them⁽ᶠ⁾ and~NOT she~
will~EXIST⁽ᵛ⁾ MISCHIEF in~MIDST~you⁽ᵐᵖ⁾ **20:15** and~MAN WHICH he~will~
GIVE⁽ᵛ⁾ COPULATION~him in~BEAST >~DIE⁽ᵛ⁾ he~will~be~make~DIE⁽ᵛ⁾ and~
AT the~BEAST they⁽ᵐ⁾~will~KILL⁽ᵛ⁾ **20:16** and~WOMAN WHICH you⁽ᵐˢ⁾~will~
COME.NEAR⁽ᵛ⁾ TO ALL BEAST to~>~BE.SQUARE⁽ᵛ⁾~her AT~her and~you⁽ᵐˢ⁾~
did~KILL⁽ᵛ⁾ AT the~WOMAN and~AT the~BEAST >~DIE⁽ᵛ⁾ they~will~be~
make~DIE⁽ᵛ⁾ BLOOD~s~them⁽ᵐ⁾ in~them⁽ᵐ⁾ **20:17** and~MAN WHICH he~
will~TAKE⁽ᵛ⁾ AT SISTER~him DAUGHTER FATHER~him OR DAUGHTER
MOTHER~him and~he~did~SEE⁽ᵛ⁾ AT NAKEDNESS~her and~SHE you⁽ᵐˢ⁾~will~
SEE⁽ᵛ⁾ AT NAKEDNESS~him KINDNESS HE and~they~did~be~CUT⁽ᵛ⁾ to~EYE~s2
SON~s PEOPLE~them⁽ᵐ⁾ NAKEDNESS SISTER~him he~did~much~
REMOVE.THE.COVER⁽ᵛ⁾ TWISTEDNESS~him he~will~LIFT.UP⁽ᵛ⁾ **20:18** and~
MAN WHICH he~will~LIE.DOWN⁽ᵛ⁾ AT WOMAN ILLNESS and~he~did~much~
REMOVE.THE.COVER⁽ᵛ⁾ AT NAKEDNESS~her AT FOUNTAIN~her he~did~
make~UNCOVER⁽ᵛ⁾ and~SHE she~did~much~REMOVE.THE.COVER⁽ᵛ⁾ AT
FOUNTAIN BLOOD~s~her and~they~did~be~CUT⁽ᵛ⁾ TWO~them⁽ᵐ⁾ from~
INSIDE PEOPLE~them⁽ᵐ⁾ **20:19** and~NAKEDNESS SISTER MOTHER~you⁽ᵐˢ⁾
and~SISTER FATHER~you⁽ᵐˢ⁾ NOT you⁽ᵐˢ⁾~will~much~REMOVE.THE.COVER⁽ᵛ⁾
GIVEN.THAT AT KIN~him he~did~make~UNCOVER⁽ᵛ⁾ TWISTEDNESS~them⁽ᵐ⁾
they⁽ᵐ⁾~will~LIFT.UP⁽ᵛ⁾ **20:20** and~MAN WHICH he~will~LIE.DOWN⁽ᵛ⁾ AT
AUNT~him NAKEDNESS UNCLE~him he~did~much~REMOVE.THE.COVER⁽ᵛ⁾
FAILURE~them⁽ᵐ⁾ they⁽ᵐ⁾~will~LIFT.UP⁽ᵛ⁾ BARREN~s they⁽ᵐ⁾~will~
DIE⁽ᵛ⁾ **20:21** and~MAN WHICH he~will~TAKE⁽ᵛ⁾ AT WOMAN BROTHER~him
REMOVAL SHE NAKEDNESS BROTHER~him he~did~much~
REMOVE.THE.COVER⁽ᵛ⁾ BARREN~s they⁽ᵐ⁾~will~EXIST⁽ᵛ⁾ **20:22** and~you⁽ᵐᵖ⁾~
did~SAFEGUARD⁽ᵛ⁾ AT ALL CUSTOM~s~me and~AT ALL DECISION~s~me and~
you⁽ᵐᵖ⁾~did~DO⁽ᵛ⁾ AT~them⁽ᵐ⁾ and~NOT she~will~make~VOMIT⁽ᵛ⁾ AT~you⁽ᵐᵖ⁾
the~LAND WHICH I make~COME⁽ᵛ⁾~ing⁽ᵐˢ⁾ AT~you⁽ᵐᵖ⁾ THERE~unto to~>~
SETTLE⁽ᵛ⁾ in~her **20:23** and~NOT you⁽ᵐᵖ⁾~will~WALK⁽ᵛ⁾ in~CUSTOM the~
NATION WHICH I much~SEND⁽ᵛ⁾~ing⁽ᵐˢ⁾ from~FACE~s~you⁽ᵐᵖ⁾ GIVEN.THAT
AT ALL THESE they~did~DO⁽ᵛ⁾ and~I~will~LOATHE⁽ᵛ⁾ in~them⁽ᵐ⁾ **20:24** and~
I~will~SAY⁽ᵛ⁾ to~you⁽ᵐᵖ⁾ YOU⁽ᵐᵖ⁾ you⁽ᵐᵖ⁾~will~POSSESS⁽ᵛ⁾ AT GROUND~
them⁽ᵐ⁾ and~I I~will~GIVE⁽ᵛ⁾~her to~you⁽ᵐᵖ⁾ to~the~>~POSSESS⁽ᵛ⁾ AT~her
LAND ISSUE⁽ᵛ⁾~ing⁽ᶠˢ⁾ FAT and~HONEY I **YHWH** Elohiym~you⁽ᵐᵖ⁾ WHICH I~
did~make~SEPARATE⁽ᵛ⁾ AT~you⁽ᵐᵖ⁾ FROM the~PEOPLE~s **20:25** and~
you⁽ᵐᵖ⁾~did~make~SEPARATE⁽ᵛ⁾ BETWEEN the~BEAST the~CLEAN to~the~
DIRTY and~BETWEEN the~FLYER the~DIRTY to~the~CLEAN and~NOT
you⁽ᵐᵖ⁾~will~much~DETEST⁽ᵛ⁾ AT SOUL~s~you⁽ᵐᵖ⁾ in~the~BEAST and~in~the~
FLYER and~in~ALL WHICH she~will~TREAD⁽ᵛ⁾ the~GROUND WHICH I~did~
make~SEPARATE⁽ᵛ⁾ to~you⁽ᵐᵖ⁾ to~>~much~BE.DIRTY⁽ᵛ⁾ **20:26** and~you⁽ᵐᵖ⁾~
did~EXIST⁽ᵛ⁾ to~me UNIQUE~s GIVEN.THAT UNIQUE I **YHWH** and~I~will~
make~SEPARATE⁽ᵛ⁾ AT~you⁽ᵐᵖ⁾ FROM the~PEOPLE~s to~>~EXIST⁽ᵛ⁾ to~
me **20:27** and~MAN OR WOMAN GIVEN.THAT he~will~EXIST⁽ᵛ⁾ in~them⁽ᵐ⁾
NECROMANCER OR KNOWER >~DIE⁽ᵛ⁾ they~will~be~make~DIE⁽ᵛ⁾ in~the~

STONE *they*⁽ᵐ⁾~*will*~KILL.BY.STONING⁽ⱽ⁾ AT~them⁽ᵐ⁾ BLOOD~s~them⁽ᵐ⁾ in~them⁽ᵐ⁾

Chapter 21

21:1 and~*he*~*will*~SAY⁽ⱽ⁾ **YHWH** TO Mosheh *!*⁽ᵐˢ⁾~SAY⁽ⱽ⁾ TO the~ADMINISTRATOR~s SON~s Aharon and~*you*⁽ᵐˢ⁾~*did*~SAY⁽ⱽ⁾ TO~them⁽ᵐ⁾ to~SOUL NOT *he*~*will*~BE.DIRTY⁽ⱽ⁾ in~PEOPLE~s~him **21:2** GIVEN.THAT IF to~KIN~him the~NEAR TO~him to~MOTHER~him and~to~FATHER~him and~to~SON~him and~to~DAUGHTER~him and~to~BROTHER~him **21:3** and~to~SISTER~him the~VIRGIN the~NEAR TO~him WHICH NOT *she*~*did*~EXIST⁽ⱽ⁾ to~MAN to~her *he*~*will*~BE.DIRTY⁽ⱽ⁾ **21:4** NOT *he*~*will*~BE.DIRTY⁽ⱽ⁾ MASTER in~PEOPLE~s~him to~>~*make*~DRILL⁽ⱽ⁾~him **21:5** NOT *he*~*will*~*make*~MAKE.BALD⁽ⱽ⁾~her BALD.SPOT in~HEAD~them⁽ᵐ⁾ and~EDGE BEARD~them⁽ᵐ⁾ NOT *they*⁽ᵐ⁾~*will*~much~SHAVE⁽ⱽ⁾ and~in~FLESH~them⁽ᵐ⁾ NOT *they*⁽ᵐ⁾~*will*~SLICE⁽ⱽ⁾ SLICING **21:6** UNIQUE~s *they*⁽ᵐ⁾~*will*~EXIST⁽ⱽ⁾ to~Elohiym~them⁽ᵐ⁾ and~NOT *they*⁽ᵐ⁾~*will*~much~DRILL⁽ⱽ⁾ TITLE Elohiym~them⁽ᵐ⁾ GIVEN.THAT AT FIRE.OFFERING~s **YHWH** BREAD Elohiym~them⁽ᵐ⁾ THEY⁽ᵐ⁾ *make*~COME.NEAR⁽ⱽ⁾~*ing*⁽ᵐᵖ⁾ and~*they*~*did*~EXIST⁽ⱽ⁾ SPECIAL **21:7** WOMAN BE.A.HARLOT⁽ⱽ⁾~*ing*⁽ᶠˢ⁾ and~DRILLED NOT *they*⁽ᵐ⁾~*will*~TAKE⁽ⱽ⁾ and~WOMAN CAST.OUT⁽ⱽ⁾~*ed*⁽ᶠˢ⁾ from~MAN~her NOT *they*⁽ᵐ⁾~*will*~TAKE⁽ⱽ⁾ GIVEN.THAT UNIQUE HE to~Elohiym~him **21:8** and~*you*⁽ᵐˢ⁾~*did*~much~SET.APART⁽ⱽ⁾~him GIVEN.THAT AT BREAD Elohiym~*you*⁽ᵐˢ⁾ HE *make*~COME.NEAR⁽ⱽ⁾~*ing*⁽ᵐˢ⁾ UNIQUE *he*~*will*~EXIST⁽ⱽ⁾ to~*you*⁽ᶠˢ⁾ GIVEN.THAT UNIQUE I **YHWH** much~SET.APART⁽ⱽ⁾~*ing*⁽ᵐˢ⁾~*you*⁽ᵐˢ⁾ **21:9** and~DAUGHTER MAN ADMINISTRATOR GIVEN.THAT *she*~*will*~*be*~DRILL⁽ⱽ⁾ to~>~BE.A.HARLOT⁽ⱽ⁾ AT FATHER~her SHE much~DRILL⁽ⱽ⁾~*ing*⁽ᶠˢ⁾ in~the~FIRE *you*⁽ᵐˢ⁾~*will*~CREMATE⁽ⱽ⁾ **21:10** and~the~ADMINISTRATOR the~GREAT from~BROTHER~s~him WHICH *he*~*will*~*be*~*make*~POUR.DOWN⁽ⱽ⁾ UPON HEAD~him OIL the~OINTMENT and~*he*~*did*~much~FILL⁽ⱽ⁾ AT HAND~him to~>~WEAR⁽ⱽ⁾ AT the~GARMENT~s AT HEAD~him NOT *he*~*will*~LOOSE⁽ⱽ⁾ and~GARMENT~s~him NOT *he*~*will*~RIP⁽ⱽ⁾ **21:11** and~UPON ALL SOUL~s DIE⁽ⱽ⁾~*ing*⁽ᵐˢ⁾ NOT *he*~*will*~COME⁽ⱽ⁾ to~FATHER~him and~to~MOTHER~him NOT *he*~*will*~BE.DIRTY⁽ⱽ⁾ **21:12** and~FROM the~SANCTUARY NOT *he*~*will*~GO.OUT⁽ⱽ⁾ and~NOT *he*~*will*~much~DRILL⁽ⱽ⁾ AT SANCTUARY Elohiym~him GIVEN.THAT DEDICATION OIL OINTMENT Elohiym~him UPON~him I **YHWH** **21:13** and~HE WOMAN in~VIRGINITY~s~her *he*~*will*~TAKE⁽ⱽ⁾ **21:14** WIDOW and~CAST.OUT⁽ⱽ⁾~*ed*⁽ᶠˢ⁾ and~DRILLED BE.A.HARLOT⁽ⱽ⁾~*ing*⁽ᶠˢ⁾ AT THESE NOT *he*~*will*~TAKE⁽ⱽ⁾ GIVEN.THAT IF VIRGIN from~PEOPLE~s~him *he*~*will*~TAKE⁽ⱽ⁾ WOMAN **21:15** and~NOT *he*~*will*~much~DRILL⁽ⱽ⁾ SEED~him in~PEOPLE~s~him GIVEN.THAT I **YHWH** much~SET.APART⁽ⱽ⁾~*ing*⁽ᵐˢ⁾~him **21:16** and~*he*~*will*~much~SPEAK⁽ⱽ⁾ **YHWH** TO Mosheh to~>~SAY⁽ⱽ⁾ **21:17** *!*⁽ᵐˢ⁾~much~SPEAK⁽ⱽ⁾ TO Aharon to~>~SAY⁽ⱽ⁾ MAN from~SEED~*you*⁽ᵐˢ⁾ to~

GENERATION~s~them⁽ᵐ⁾ WHICH he~will~EXIST⁽ⱽ⁾ in~him BLEMISH NOT he~will~COME.NEAR⁽ⱽ⁾ to~>~make~COME.NEAR⁽ⱽ⁾ BREAD Elohiym~him   **21:18** GIVEN.THAT ALL MAN WHICH in~him BLEMISH NOT he~will~COME.NEAR⁽ⱽ⁾ MAN BLIND OR LAME OR PERFORATE⁽ⱽ⁾~ed⁽ᵐˢ⁾ OR BE.SUPERFLUOUS⁽ⱽ⁾~ed⁽ᵐˢ⁾   **21:19** OR MAN WHICH he~will~EXIST⁽ⱽ⁾ in~him SHATTERING FOOT OR SHATTERING HAND   **21:20** OR HUNCHBACK OR SCRAWNY OR CATARACT in~EYE~him OR IRRITATION OR SKIN.SORE OR CRUMBLED TESTICLES   **21:21** ALL MAN WHICH in~him BLEMISH from~SEED Aharon the~ADMINISTRATOR NOT he~will~DRAW.NEAR⁽ⱽ⁾ to~>~make~COME.NEAR⁽ⱽ⁾ AT FIRE.OFFERING~s **YHWH** BLEMISH in~him AT BREAD Elohiym~him NOT he~will~DRAW.NEAR⁽ⱽ⁾ to~>~make~COME.NEAR⁽ⱽ⁾   **21:22** BREAD Elohiym~him from~SPECIAL~s the~SPECIAL~s and~FROM the~SPECIAL~s he~will~EAT⁽ⱽ⁾   **21:23** SURELY TO the~TENT.CURTAIN NOT he~will~COME⁽ⱽ⁾ and~TO the~ALTAR NOT he~will~DRAW.NEAR⁽ⱽ⁾ GIVEN.THAT BLEMISH in~him and~NOT he~will~much~DRILL⁽ⱽ⁾ AT SANCTUARY~s~me GIVEN.THAT I **YHWH** from~>~much~SET.APART⁽ⱽ⁾~them⁽ᵐ⁾   **21:24** and~he~will~much~SPEAK⁽ⱽ⁾ Mosheh TO Aharon and~TO SON~s~him and~TO ALL SON~s Yisra'eyl

Chapter 22

22:1 and~he~will~much~SPEAK⁽ⱽ⁾ **YHWH** TO Mosheh to~>~SAY⁽ⱽ⁾   **22:2** !⁽ᵐˢ⁾~much~SPEAK⁽ⱽ⁾ TO Aharon and~TO SON~s~him and~they⁽ᵐ⁾~will~be~DEDICATE⁽ⱽ⁾ from~SPECIAL~s SON~s Yisra'eyl and~NOT they⁽ᵐ⁾~will~much~DRILL⁽ⱽ⁾ AT TITLE SPECIAL~me WHICH THEY⁽ᵐ⁾ make~SET.APART⁽ⱽ⁾~ing⁽ᵐᵖ⁾ to~me I **YHWH**   **22:3** !⁽ᵐˢ⁾~SAY⁽ⱽ⁾ TO~them⁽ᵐ⁾ to~GENERATION~s~you⁽ᵐᵖ⁾ ALL MAN WHICH he~will~COME.NEAR⁽ⱽ⁾ from~ALL SEED~you⁽ᵐᵖ⁾ TO the~SPECIAL~s WHICH they⁽ᵐ⁾~will~make~SET.APART⁽ⱽ⁾ SON~s Yisra'eyl to~**YHWH** and~DIRTY~him UPON~him and~she~did~be~CUT⁽ⱽ⁾ the~SOUL the~SHE from~to~FACE~s~me I **YHWH**   **22:4** MAN MAN from~SEED Aharon and~HE INFECT⁽ⱽ⁾~ed⁽ᵐˢ⁾ OR ISSUE⁽ⱽ⁾~ing⁽ᵐˢ⁾ in~the~SPECIAL~s NOT he~will~EAT⁽ⱽ⁾ UNTIL WHICH he~will~BE.CLEAN⁽ⱽ⁾ and~the~TOUCH⁽ⱽ⁾~ing⁽ᵐˢ⁾ in~ALL DIRTY SOUL OR MAN WHICH she~will~GO.OUT⁽ⱽ⁾ FROM~him LYING.DOWN SEED   **22:5** OR MAN WHICH he~will~TOUCH⁽ⱽ⁾ in~ALL SWARMER WHICH he~will~BE.DIRTY⁽ⱽ⁾ to~him OR in~HUMAN WHICH he~will~BE.DIRTY⁽ⱽ⁾ to~him to~ALL DIRTY~him   **22:6** SOUL WHICH she~will~TOUCH⁽ⱽ⁾ in~him and~she~did~BE.DIRTY⁽ⱽ⁾ UNTIL the~EVENING and~NOT he~will~EAT⁽ⱽ⁾ FROM the~SPECIAL~s GIVEN.THAT IF he~did~BATHE⁽ⱽ⁾ FLESH~him in~the~WATER~s2   **22:7** and~he~did~COME⁽ⱽ⁾ the~SUN and~he~did~BE.CLEAN⁽ⱽ⁾ and~AFTER he~will~EAT⁽ⱽ⁾ FROM the~SPECIAL~s GIVEN.THAT BREAD~him HE   **22:8** CARCASS and~TORN NOT he~will~EAT⁽ⱽ⁾ to~DIRTY~her in~her I **YHWH**   **22:9** and~they~did~SAFEGUARD⁽ⱽ⁾ AT CHARGE~me and~NOT they⁽ᵐ⁾~will~LIFT.UP⁽ⱽ⁾ UPON~him FAILURE and~they~did~DIE⁽ⱽ⁾ in~him

The Book of Leviticus

GIVEN.THAT *he~will~much~*DRILL[V]*~*her I **YHWH** from*~>~much~*
SET.APART[V]*~*them[m]   **22:10** and*~*ALL BE.STRANGE[V]*~ing*[ms] NOT *he~will~*
EAT[V] SPECIAL SETTLER ADMINISTRATOR and*~*HIRELING NOT *he~will~*EAT[V]
SPECIAL   **22:11** and*~*ADMINISTRATOR GIVEN.THAT *he~will~*PURCHASE[V]
SOUL MATERIAL SILVER*~*him HE *he~will~*EAT[V] in*~*him and*~*BORN HOUSE*~*
him THEY[m] *they*[m]*~will~*EAT[V] in*~*BREAD*~*him   **22:12** and*~*DAUGHTER
ADMINISTRATOR GIVEN.THAT *she~will~*EXIST[V] to*~*MAN BE.STRANGE[V]*~
ing*[ms] SHE in*~*OFFERING the*~*SPECIAL*~*s NOT *she~will~*EAT[V]   **22:13** and*~*
DAUGHTER ADMINISTRATOR GIVEN.THAT *she~will~*EXIST[V] WIDOW and*~*
CAST.OUT[V]*~ed*[fs] and*~*SEED WITHOUT to*~*her and*~she~did~*TURN.BACK[V]
TO HOUSE FATHER*~*her like*~*YOUNG.AGE*~*s*~*her from*~*BREAD FATHER*~*her
*she~will~*EAT[V] and*~*ALL BE.STRANGE[V]*~ing*[ms] NOT *he~will~*EAT[V] in*~*
him   **22:14** and*~*MAN GIVEN.THAT *he~will~*EAT[V] SPECIAL in*~*ERROR and*~
he~will~*ADD[V] FIVE*~*him UPON*~*him and*~he~did~*GIVE[V] to*~*the*~*
ADMINISTRATOR AT the*~*SPECIAL   **22:15** and*~*NOT *they*[m]*~will~much~*
DRILL[V] AT SPECIAL*~*s SON*~*s Yisra'eyl AT WHICH *they*[m]*~will~make~*
RAISE.UP[V] to*~***YHWH**   **22:16** and*~they~did~make~*LIFT.UP[V] AT*~*them[m]
TWISTEDNESS GUILT in*~>~*EAT[V]*~*them[m] AT SPECIAL*~*s*~*them[m]
GIVEN.THAT I **YHWH** from*~>~much~*SET.APART[V]*~*them[m]   **22:17** and*~*he*~
will~much~*SPEAK[V] **YHWH** TO Mosheh to*~>~*SAY[V]   **22:18** !*(ms)~much~*
SPEAK[V] TO Aharon and*~*TO SON*~*s*~*him and*~*TO ALL SON*~*s Yisra'eyl and*~
you*(ms)*~did~*SAY[V] TO*~*them[m] MAN MAN from*~*HOUSE Yisra'eyl and*~*FROM
the*~*IMMIGRANT in*~*Yisra'eyl WHICH *he~will~make~*COME.NEAR[V]
DONATION*~*him to*~*ALL VOW*~*s*~*them[m] and*~*to*~*ALL FREEWILL.OFFERING*~*
them[m] WHICH *they*[m]*~will~make~*COME.NEAR[V] to*~***YHWH** to*~*
ASCENSION.OFFERING   **22:19** to*~*SELF-WILL*~*you[mp] WHOLE MALE in*~*the*~*
CATTLE in*~*the*~*SHEEP*~*s and*~*in*~*the*~*SHE-GOAT*~*s   **22:20** ALL WHICH in*~*
him BLEMISH NOT *you*[mp]*~will~make~*COME.NEAR[V] GIVEN.THAT NOT to*~*
SELF-WILL *he~will~*EXIST[V] to*~*you[mp]   **22:21** and*~*MAN GIVEN.THAT *he~
will~make~*COME.NEAR[V] SACRIFICE OFFERING.OF.RESTITUTION*~*s to*~*
YHWH to*~>~much~*PERFORM[V] VOW OR to*~*FREEWILL.OFFERING in*~*the*~*
CATTLE OR in*~*the*~*FLOCKS WHOLE *he~will~*EXIST[V] to*~*SELF-WILL ALL
BLEMISH NOT *he~will~*EXIST[V] in*~*him   **22:22** BLINDNESS OR CRACK[V]*~ed*[ms]
OR CUT.SHARPLY[V]*~ed*[ms] OR ULCER OR IRRITATION OR SKIN.SORE NOT
you[mp]*~will~make~*COME.NEAR[V] THESE to*~***YHWH** and*~*FIRE.OFFERING
NOT *you*[mp]*~will~*GIVE[V] from*~*them[m] UPON the*~*ALTAR to*~*
YHWH   **22:23** and*~*OX and*~*RAM BE.SUPERFLUOUS[V]*~ed*[ms] and*~*
DEFORM[V]*~ed*[ms] FREEWILL.OFFERING *you*(ms)*~will~*DO[V] AT*~*him and*~*to*~*
VOW NOT *he~will~be~*ACCEPT[V]   **22:24** and*~*PRESS.FIRMLY[V]*~ed*[ms] and*~*
SMASH[V]*~ed*[ms] and*~*DRAW.AWAY[V]*~ed*[ms] and*~*CUT[V]*~ed*[ms] NOT *you*[mp]*~
will~make~*COME.NEAR[V] to*~***YHWH** and*~*in*~*LAND*~*you[mp] NOT *you*[mp]*~
will~*DO[V]   **22:25** and*~*from*~*HAND SON FOREIGNER NOT *you*[mp]*~will~
make~*COME.NEAR[V] AT BREAD Elohiym*~*you[mp] from*~*ALL THESE
GIVEN.THAT CORRUPTION*~*them[m] in*~*them[m] BLEMISH in*~*them[m] NOT
they[m]*~will~be~*ACCEPT[V] to*~*you[mp]   **22:26** and*~he~will~much~*SPEAK[V]

YHWH TO Mosheh to~>~SAY⁽ᵛ⁾   **22:27** OX OR SHEEP OR SHE-GOAT GIVEN.THAT *he~will~be*~BRING.FORTH⁽ᵛ⁾ and~*he~did*~EXIST⁽ᵛ⁾ SEVEN DAY~s UNDER MOTHER~him and~from~DAY the~EIGHTH and~FURTHER *he~will~be*~ACCEPT⁽ᵛ⁾ to~DONATION FIRE.OFFERING to~**YHWH**   **22:28** and~OX OR RAM AT~him and~AT SON~him NOT *you*⁽ᵐᵖ⁾~*will*~SLAY⁽ᵛ⁾ in~DAY UNIT   **22:29** and~GIVEN.THAT *you*⁽ᵐˢ⁾~*will*~SACRIFICE⁽ᵛ⁾~him SACRIFICE THANKS to~**YHWH** to~SELF-WILL~*you*⁽ᵐᵖ⁾ *you*⁽ᵐˢ⁾~*will*~SACRIFICE⁽ᵛ⁾~him   **22:30** in~the~DAY the~HE *he~will~be*~EAT⁽ᵛ⁾ NOT *you*⁽ᵐᵖ⁾~*will*~make~LEAVE.BEHIND⁽ᵛ⁾ FROM~him UNTIL MORNING I **YHWH**   **22:31** and~*you*⁽ᵐᵖ⁾~*did*~SAFEGUARD⁽ᵛ⁾ DIRECTIVE~s~me and~*you*⁽ᵐᵖ⁾~*did*~DO⁽ᵛ⁾ AT~them⁽ᵐ⁾ I **YHWH**   **22:32** and~NOT *you*⁽ᵐᵖ⁾~*will*~much~DRILL⁽ᵛ⁾ AT TITLE SPECIAL~me and~*I~did~be*~SET.APART⁽ᵛ⁾ in~MIDST SON~s Yisra'eyl I **YHWH** much~SET.APART⁽ᵛ⁾~*ing*⁽ᵐˢ⁾~*you*⁽ᵐˢ⁾   **22:33** the~*make*~GO.OUT⁽ᵛ⁾~*ing*⁽ᵐˢ⁾ AT~*you*⁽ᵐᵖ⁾ from~LAND Mits'rayim to~>~EXIST⁽ᵛ⁾ to~*you*⁽ᵐᵖ⁾ to~Elohiym I **YHWH**

Chapter 23

23:1 and~*he~will*~much~SPEAK⁽ᵛ⁾ **YHWH** TO Mosheh to~>~SAY⁽ᵛ⁾   **23:2** !⁽ᵐˢ⁾~much~SPEAK⁽ᵛ⁾ TO SON~s Yisra'eyl and~*you*⁽ᵐˢ⁾~*did*~SAY⁽ᵛ⁾ TO~them⁽ᵐ⁾ APPOINTED~s **YHWH** WHICH *you*⁽ᵐᵖ⁾~*will*~CALL.OUT⁽ᵛ⁾ AT~them⁽ᵐ⁾ MEETING~s SPECIAL THESE THEY⁽ᵐ⁾ APPOINTED~s   **23:3** SIX DAY~s *she~will~be*~DO⁽ᵛ⁾ BUSINESS and~in~the~DAY the~SEVENTH CEASING REST.PERIOD MEETING SPECIAL ALL BUSINESS NOT *you*⁽ᵐᵖ⁾~*will*~DO⁽ᵛ⁾ CEASING SHE to~**YHWH** in~ALL SETTLING~s~*you*⁽ᵐᵖ⁾   **23:4** THESE APPOINTED~s **YHWH** MEETING~s SPECIAL WHICH *you*⁽ᵐᵖ⁾~*will*~CALL.OUT⁽ᵛ⁾ AT~them⁽ᵐ⁾ in~APPOINTED~them⁽ᵐ⁾   **23:5** in~the~NEW.MOON the~FIRST in~FOUR TEN to~the~NEW.MOON BETWEEN the~EVENING~s2 Pesahh to~**YHWH**   **23:6** and~in~the~FIVE TEN DAY to~the~NEW.MOON the~THIS FEAST the~UNLEAVENED.BREAD~s to~**YHWH** SEVEN DAY~s UNLEAVENED.BREAD~s *you*⁽ᵐᵖ⁾~*will*~EAT⁽ᵛ⁾   **23:7** in~the~DAY the~FIRST MEETING SPECIAL *he~will*~EXIST⁽ᵛ⁾ to~*you*⁽ᵐᵖ⁾ ALL BUSINESS SERVICE NOT *you*⁽ᵐᵖ⁾~*will*~DO⁽ᵛ⁾   **23:8** and~*you*⁽ᵐᵖ⁾~*did*~make~COME.NEAR⁽ᵛ⁾ FIRE.OFFERING to~**YHWH** SEVEN DAY~s in~the~DAY the~SEVENTH MEETING SPECIAL ALL BUSINESS SERVICE NOT *you*⁽ᵐᵖ⁾~*will*~DO⁽ᵛ⁾   **23:9** and~*he~will*~much~SPEAK⁽ᵛ⁾ **YHWH** TO Mosheh to~>~SAY⁽ᵛ⁾   **23:10** !⁽ᵐˢ⁾~much~SPEAK⁽ᵛ⁾ TO SON~s Yisra'eyl and~*you*⁽ᵐˢ⁾~*did*~SAY⁽ᵛ⁾ TO~them⁽ᵐ⁾ GIVEN.THAT *you*⁽ᵐᵖ⁾~*will*~COME⁽ᵛ⁾ TO the~LAND WHICH I GIVE⁽ᵛ⁾~*ing*⁽ᵐˢ⁾ to~*you*⁽ᵐᵖ⁾ and~*you*⁽ᵐᵖ⁾~*did*~SEVER⁽ᵛ⁾ AT HARVEST~her and~*you*⁽ᵐᵖ⁾~*did*~make~COME⁽ᵛ⁾ AT SHEAF SUMMIT HARVEST~*you*⁽ᵐᵖ⁾ TO the~ADMINISTRATOR   **23:11** and~*he~did*~WAVE⁽ᵛ⁾ AT the~SHEAF to~FACE~s **YHWH** to~SELF-WILL~*you*⁽ᵐᵖ⁾ from~MORROW the~CEASING *he~will*~make~WAVE⁽ᵛ⁾~him the~ADMINISTRATOR   **23:12** and~*you*⁽ᵐᵖ⁾~*did*~DO⁽ᵛ⁾ in~DAY >~make~WAVE⁽ᵛ⁾~*you*⁽ᵐᵖ⁾ AT the~SHEAF SHEEP WHOLE SON YEAR~him to~ASCENSION.OFFERING to~**YHWH**   **23:13** and~DEPOSIT~him TWO

The Book of Leviticus

ONE.TENTH~s FLOUR MIX⁽ᵛ⁾~*ed*⁽ᶠˢ⁾ in~the~OIL FIRE.OFFERING to~**YHWH** AROMA SWEET and~POURING~her WINE FOURTH the~HIYN   **23:14** and~ BREAD and~ROASTED.GRAIN and~PLANTATION NOT *you*⁽ᵐᵖ⁾~*will*~EAT⁽ᵛ⁾ UNTIL BONE the~DAY the~THIS UNTIL >~*make*~COME⁽ᵛ⁾~*you*⁽ᵐᵖ⁾ AT DONATION Elohiym~*you*⁽ᵐᵖ⁾ CUSTOM DISTANT to~GENERATION~s~*you*⁽ᵐᵖ⁾ in~ALL SETTLING~s~*you*⁽ᵐᵖ⁾   **23:15** and~*you*⁽ᵐᵖ⁾~*did*~COUNT⁽ᵛ⁾ to~*you*⁽ᵐᵖ⁾ from~MORROW the~CEASING from~DAY >~*make*~COME⁽ᵛ⁾~*you*⁽ᵐᵖ⁾ AT SHEAF the~WAVING SEVEN CEASING~s WHOLE~s *they*⁽ᶠ⁾~*will*~ EXIST⁽ᵛ⁾   **23:16** UNTIL from~MORROW the~CEASING the~SEVENTH *you*⁽ᵐᵖ⁾~ *will*~COUNT⁽ᵛ⁾ FIVE~s DAY and~*you*⁽ᵐᵖ⁾~*did*~*make*~COME.NEAR⁽ᵛ⁾ DEPOSIT NEW to~**YHWH**   **23:17** from~SETTLING~s~*you*⁽ᵐᵖ⁾ *you*⁽ᵐᵖ⁾~*will*~*make*~ COME⁽ᵛ⁾ BREAD WAVING TWO TWO ONE.TENTH~s FLOUR *they*⁽ᶠ⁾~*will*~ EXIST⁽ᵛ⁾ LEAVENED.BREAD *they*⁽ᶠ⁾~*will*~*be*~BAKE⁽ᵛ⁾ FIRST-FRUIT~s to~ **YHWH**   **23:18** and~*you*⁽ᵐᵖ⁾~*did*~*make*~COME.NEAR⁽ᵛ⁾ UPON the~BREAD SEVEN SHEEP~s WHOLE~s SON~s YEAR and~BULL SON CATTLE UNIT and~ BUCK~s TWO *they*⁽ᵐ⁾~*will*~EXIST⁽ᵛ⁾ ASCENSION.OFFERING to~**YHWH** and~ DEPOSIT~them⁽ᵐ⁾ and~POURING~s~them⁽ᵐ⁾ FIRE.OFFERING AROMA SWEET to~**YHWH**   **23:19** and~*you*⁽ᵐᵖ⁾~*did*~DO⁽ᵛ⁾ HAIRY.GOAT SHE-GOAT~s UNIT to~ FAILURE and~TWO SHEEP~s SON~s YEAR to~SACRIFICE OFFERING.OF.RESTITUTION~s   **23:20** and~*he*~*did*~WAVE⁽ᵛ⁾ the~ ADMINISTRATOR AT~them⁽ᵐ⁾ UPON BREAD the~FIRST-FRUIT~s WAVING to~ FACE~s **YHWH** UPON TWO SHEEP~s SPECIAL *they*⁽ᵐ⁾~*will*~EXIST⁽ᵛ⁾ to~**YHWH** to~the~ADMINISTRATOR   **23:21** and~*you*⁽ᵐᵖ⁾~*did*~CALL.OUT⁽ᵛ⁾ in~BONE the~DAY the~THIS MEETING SPECIAL *he*~*will*~EXIST⁽ᵛ⁾ to~*you*⁽ᵐᵖ⁾ ALL BUSINESS SERVICE NOT *you*⁽ᵐᵖ⁾~*will*~DO⁽ᵛ⁾ CUSTOM DISTANT in~ALL SETTLING~s~*you*⁽ᵐᵖ⁾ to~GENERATION~s~*you*⁽ᵐᵖ⁾   **23:22** and~in~>~SEVER⁽ᵛ⁾~ *you*⁽ᵐᵖ⁾ AT HARVEST LAND~*you*⁽ᵐᵖ⁾ NOT *you*⁽ᵐˢ⁾~*will*~*much*~FINISH⁽ᵛ⁾ EDGE FIELD~*you*⁽ᵐˢ⁾ in~>~SEVER⁽ᵛ⁾~*you*⁽ᵐˢ⁾ and~GLEANINGS HARVEST~*you*⁽ᵐˢ⁾ NOT *you*⁽ᵐˢ⁾~*will*~*much*~PICK.UP⁽ᵛ⁾ to~AFFLICTION and~to~IMMIGRANT *you*⁽ᵐˢ⁾~ *will*~LEAVE⁽ᵛ⁾ AT~them⁽ᵐ⁾ I **YHWH** Elohiym~*you*⁽ᵐᵖ⁾   **23:23** and~*he*~*will*~ *much*~SPEAK⁽ᵛ⁾ **YHWH** TO Mosheh to~>~SAY⁽ᵛ⁾   **23:24** !⁽ᵐˢ⁾~*much*~SPEAK⁽ᵛ⁾ TO SON~s Yisra'eyl to~>~SAY⁽ᵛ⁾ in~the~NEW.MOON the~SEVENTH in~UNIT to~the~NEW.MOON *he*~*will*~EXIST⁽ᵛ⁾ to~*you*⁽ᵐᵖ⁾ REST.PERIOD REMEMBRANCE SIGNAL MEETING SPECIAL   **23:25** ALL BUSINESS SERVICE NOT *you*⁽ᵐᵖ⁾~*will*~DO⁽ᵛ⁾ and~*you*⁽ᵐᵖ⁾~*did*~*make*~COME.NEAR⁽ᵛ⁾ FIRE.OFFERING to~**YHWH**   **23:26** and~*he*~*will*~*much*~SPEAK⁽ᵛ⁾ **YHWH** TO Mosheh to~>~SAY⁽ᵛ⁾   **23:27** SURELY in~TENTH.ONE to~the~NEW.MOON the~SEVENTH the~THIS DAY the~ATONEMENT~s HE MEETING SPECIAL *he*~ *will*~EXIST⁽ᵛ⁾ to~*you*⁽ᵐᵖ⁾ and~*you*⁽ᵐᵖ⁾~*did*~*much*~AFFLICT⁽ᵛ⁾ AT SOUL~s~ *you*⁽ᵐᵖ⁾ and~*you*⁽ᵐᵖ⁾~*did*~*make*~COME.NEAR⁽ᵛ⁾ FIRE.OFFERING to~ **YHWH**   **23:28** and~ALL BUSINESS NOT *you*⁽ᵐᵖ⁾~*will*~DO⁽ᵛ⁾ in~BONE the~DAY the~THIS GIVEN.THAT DAY ATONEMENT~s HE to~>~*much*~COVER⁽ᵛ⁾ UPON~ *you*⁽ᵐᵖ⁾ to~FACE~s **YHWH** Elohiym~*you*⁽ᵐᵖ⁾   **23:29** GIVEN.THAT ALL the~ SOUL WHICH NOT *she*~*will*~*be*~*much*~AFFLICT⁽ᵛ⁾ in~BONE the~DAY the~ THIS and~*she*~*did*~*be*~CUT⁽ᵛ⁾ from~PEOPLE~s~her   **23:30** and~ALL the~

SOUL WHICH *you*(ms)~*will*~DO(V) ALL BUSINESS in~BONE the~DAY the~THIS and~*I*~*did*~*make*~PERISH(V) AT the~SOUL the~SHE from~INSIDE PEOPLE~her   **23:31** ALL BUSINESS NOT *you*(mp)~*will*~DO(V) CUSTOM DISTANT to~GENERATION~s~*you*(mp) in~ALL SETTLING~s~*you*(mp)   **23:32** CEASING REST.PERIOD HE to~*you*(mp) and~*you*(mp)~*did*~*much*~AFFLICT(V) AT SOUL~s~*you*(mp) in~NINE to~the~NEW.MOON in~the~EVENING from~EVENING UNTIL EVENING *you*(mp)~*will*~CEASE(V) CEASING~*you*(mp)   **23:33** and~*he*~*will*~*much*~SPEAK(V) **YHWH** TO Mosheh to~>~SAY(V)   **23:34** *!*(ms)~*much*~SPEAK(V) TO SON~s Yisra'eyl to~>~SAY(V) in~the~FIVE TEN DAY to~the~NEW.MOON the~SEVENTH the~THIS FEAST the~BOOTH~s SEVEN DAY~s to~**YHWH**   **23:35** in~the~DAY the~FIRST MEETING SPECIAL ALL BUSINESS SERVICE NOT *you*(mp)~*will*~DO(V)   **23:36** SEVEN DAY~s *you*(mp)~*will*~*make*~COME.NEAR(V) FIRE.OFFERING to~**YHWH** in~the~DAY the~EIGHTH MEETING SPECIAL *he*~*will*~EXIST(V) to~*you*(mp) and~*you*(mp)~*did*~*make*~COME.NEAR(V) FIRE.OFFERING to~**YHWH** CONFERENCE SHE ALL BUSINESS SERVICE NOT *you*(mp)~*will*~DO(V)   **23:37** THESE APPOINTED~s **YHWH** WHICH *you*(mp)~*will*~CALL.OUT(V) AT~them(m) MEETING~s SPECIAL to~>~*make*~COME.NEAR(V) FIRE.OFFERING to~**YHWH** ASCENSION.OFFERING and~DEPOSIT SACRIFICE and~POURING~s WORD DAY in~DAY~him   **23:38** from~to~STRAND CEASING~s **YHWH** and~from~to~STRAND CONTRIBUTION~s~*you*(mp) and~from~to~STRAND ALL VOW~s~*you*(mp) and~from~to~STRAND ALL FREEWILL.OFFERING~*you*(mp) WHICH *you*(mp)~*will*~GIVE(V) to~**YHWH**   **23:39** SURELY in~the~FIVE TEN DAY to~the~NEW.MOON the~SEVENTH in~>~GATHER(V)~*you*(mp) AT PRODUCTION the~LAND *you*(mp)~*will*~HOLD.A.FEAST(V) AT FEAST **YHWH** SEVEN DAY~s in~the~DAY the~FIRST REST.PERIOD and~in~the~DAY the~EIGHTH REST.PERIOD   **23:40** and~*you*(mp)~*did*~TAKE(V) to~*you*(mp) in~the~DAY the~FIRST PRODUCE TREE HONOR PALM~s DATE.PALM~s and~BOUGH TREE THICK.WOVEN and~WILLOW~s WADI and~REJOICING~*you*(mp) to~FACE~s **YHWH** Elohiym~*you*(mp) SEVEN DAY~s   **23:41** and~*you*(mp)~*did*~HOLD.A.FEAST(V) AT~him FEAST to~**YHWH** SEVEN DAY~s in~the~YEAR CUSTOM DISTANT to~GENERATION~s~*you*(mp) in~the~NEW.MOON the~SEVENTH *you*(mp)~*will*~HOLD.A.FEAST(V) AT~him   **23:42** in~the~BOOTH~s *you*(mp)~*will*~SETTLE(V) SEVEN DAY~s ALL the~NATIVE in~Yisra'eyl *they*(m)~*will*~SETTLE(V) in~the~BOOTH~s   **23:43** to~THAT *they*(m)~*will*~KNOW(V) GENERATION~s~*you*(mp) GIVEN.THAT in~the~BOOTH~s *I*~*did*~*be*~*make*~TURN.BACK(V) AT SON~s Yisra'eyl in~>~*make*~GO.OUT(V)~me AT~them(m) from~LAND Mits'rayim I **YHWH** Elohiym~*you*(mp)   **23:44** and~*he*~*will*~*much*~SPEAK(V) Mosheh AT APPOINTED~s **YHWH** TO SON~s Yisra'eyl

Chapter 24

24:1 and~*he~will~*much~SPEAK⁽ᵛ⁾ **YHWH** TO Mosheh to~>~SAY⁽ᵛ⁾ **24:2** *!⁽ᵐˢ⁾~much~*DIRECT⁽ᵛ⁾ AT SON~s Yisra'eyl and~*they⁽ᵐ⁾~will~*TAKE⁽ᵛ⁾ TO~you⁽ᵐˢ⁾ OIL OLIVE REFINED SMASHED to~the~LUMINARY to~>~*make~*GO.UP⁽ᵛ⁾ LAMP CONTINUALLY **24:3** from~OUTSIDE to~TENT.CURTAIN the~EVIDENCE in~TENT APPOINTED *he~will~*ARRANGE⁽ᵛ⁾ AT~him Aharon from~EVENING UNTIL MORNING to~FACE~s **YHWH** CONTINUALLY CUSTOM DISTANT to~GENERATION~s~you⁽ᵐᵖ⁾ **24:4** UPON the~LAMPSTAND the~CLEAN *he~will~*ARRANGE⁽ᵛ⁾ AT the~LAMP~s to~FACE~s **YHWH** CONTINUALLY **24:5** and~*you⁽ᵐˢ⁾~did~*TAKE⁽ᵛ⁾ FLOUR and~*you⁽ᵐˢ⁾~did~*BAKE⁽ᵛ⁾ AT~her TWO TEN PIERCED.BREAD~s TWO ONE.TENTH~s *he~will~*EXIST⁽ᵛ⁾ the~PIERCED.BREAD the~UNIT **24:6** and~*you⁽ᵐˢ⁾~did~*PLACE⁽ᵛ⁾ AT~them⁽ᵐ⁾ TWO from~ARRANGEMENT~s SIX the~IN.LINE UPON the~TABLE the~CLEAN to~FACE~s **YHWH 24:7** and~*you⁽ᵐˢ⁾~did~*GIVE⁽ᵛ⁾ UPON the~IN.LINE FRANKINCENSE REFINED and~*she~did~*EXIST⁽ᵛ⁾ to~the~BREAD to~MEMORIAL FIRE.OFFERING to~**YHWH 24:8** in~DAY the~CEASING in~DAY the~CEASING *he~will~*ARRANGE⁽ᵛ⁾~him to~FACE~s **YHWH** CONTINUALLY from~AT SON~s Yisra'eyl COVENANT DISTANT **24:9** and~*she~did~*EXIST⁽ᵛ⁾ to~Aharon and~to~SON~s~him and~*they~did~*EAT⁽ᵛ⁾~him in~AREA UNIQUE GIVEN.THAT SPECIAL SPECIAL~s HE to~him from~FIRE.OFFERING~s **YHWH** CUSTOM DISTANT **24:10** and~*he~will~*GO.OUT⁽ᵛ⁾ SON WOMAN Yisra'eyl~of and~HE SON MAN Mits'rayim~of in~MIDST SON~s Yisra'eyl and~*they⁽ᵐ⁾~will~*be~STRUGGLE⁽ᵛ⁾ in~the~CAMP SON the~Yisra'eyl~of and~MAN the~Yisra'eyl~of **24:11** and~*he~will~*PIERCE.THROUGH⁽ᵛ⁾ SON the~WOMAN the~Yisra'eyl~of AT the~TITLE and~*he~will~*much~BELITTLE⁽ᵛ⁾ and~*they⁽ᵐ⁾~will~*make~COME⁽ᵛ⁾ AT~him TO Mosheh and~TITLE MOTHER~him Sh'lomiyt DAUGHTER Divriy to~BRANCH Dan **24:12** and~*they⁽ᵐ⁾~will~*make~REST⁽ᵛ⁾~him in~the~CUSTODY to~>~*SPREAD.OUT⁽ᵛ⁾ to~them⁽ᵐ⁾ UPON MOUTH **YHWH 24:13** and~*he~will~*much~SPEAK⁽ᵛ⁾ **YHWH** TO Mosheh to~>~SAY⁽ᵛ⁾ **24:14** *!⁽ᵐᵖ⁾~*make~*GO.OUT⁽ᵛ⁾ AT the~*much~*BELITTLE⁽ᵛ⁾~*ing⁽ᵐˢ⁾ TO from~OUTSIDE to~the~CAMP and~*they~did~*SUPPORT⁽ᵛ⁾ ALL the~HEAR⁽ᵛ⁾~*ing⁽ᵐᵖ⁾ AT HAND~s2~them⁽ᵐ⁾ UPON HEAD~him and~*they~did~*KILL.BY.STONING⁽ᵛ⁾ AT~him ALL the~COMPANY **24:15** and~TO SON~s Yisra'eyl *you⁽ᵐˢ⁾~will~*much~SPEAK⁽ᵛ⁾ to~>~SAY⁽ᵛ⁾ MAN MAN GIVEN.THAT *he~will~*much~*BELITTLE⁽ᵛ⁾ Elohiym~him and~*he~did~*LIFT.UP⁽ᵛ⁾ FAILURE~him **24:16** and~*PIERCE.THROUGH⁽ᵛ⁾~*ing⁽ᵐˢ⁾ TITLE **YHWH** >~DIE⁽ᵛ⁾ *he~will~*be~*make~DIE⁽ᵛ⁾ >~KILL.BY.STONING⁽ᵛ⁾ *they⁽ᵐ⁾~will~*KILL.BY.STONING⁽ᵛ⁾ in~him ALL the~COMPANY like~the~IMMIGRANT like~NATIVE in~>~PIERCE.THROUGH⁽ᵛ⁾~him TITLE *he~will~*be~*make~DIE⁽ᵛ⁾ **24:17** and~MAN GIVEN.THAT *he~will~*make~HIT⁽ᵛ⁾ ALL SOUL HUMAN >~DIE⁽ᵛ⁾ *he~will~*be~*make~DIE⁽ᵛ⁾ **24:18** and~*make~HIT⁽ᵛ⁾~*ing⁽ᵐˢ⁾ SOUL BEAST *he~will~*much~MAKE.RESTITUTION⁽ᵛ⁾~her SOUL UNDER SOUL **24:19** and~MAN GIVEN.THAT *he~will~*GIVE⁽ᵛ⁾ BLEMISH in~the~NEIGHBOR~him like~WHICH *he~did*~DO⁽ᵛ⁾ SO *he~will~be*~DO⁽ᵛ⁾ *to~him*   **24:20** SHATTERING UNDER SHATTERING EYE UNDER EYE TOOTH UNDER TOOTH like~WHICH *he~will~*GIVE⁽ᵛ⁾ BLEMISH in~the~HUMAN SO *he~will~be*~GIVE⁽ᵛ⁾ in~him   **24:21** and~*make*~HIT⁽ᵛ⁾~*ing*⁽ᵐˢ⁾ BEAST *he~will~much*~MAKE.RESTITUTION⁽ᵛ⁾~her and~*make*~HIT⁽ᵛ⁾~*ing*⁽ᵐˢ⁾ HUMAN *he~will~be~make*~DIE⁽ᵛ⁾   **24:22** DECISION UNIT *he~will*~EXIST⁽ᵛ⁾ *to~you*⁽ᵐᵖ⁾ like~the~IMMIGRANT like~NATIVE *he~will~*EXIST⁽ᵛ⁾ GIVEN.THAT I **YHWH** Elohiym~*you*⁽ᵐᵖ⁾   **24:23** and~*he~will~much~*SPEAK⁽ᵛ⁾ Mosheh TO SON~s Yisra'eyl and~*they*⁽ᵐ⁾~*will~make*~GO.OUT⁽ᵛ⁾~him AT the~*much*~BELITTLE⁽ᵛ⁾~*ing*⁽ᵐˢ⁾ TO from~OUTSIDE to~the~CAMP and~*they*⁽ᵐ⁾~*will*~KILL.BY.STONING⁽ᵛ⁾ AT~him STONE and~SON~s Yisra'eyl *they~did~*DO⁽ᵛ⁾ like~WHICH *he~did~much*~DIRECT⁽ᵛ⁾ **YHWH** AT Mosheh

Chapter 25

25:1 and~*he~will~much*~SPEAK⁽ᵛ⁾ **YHWH** TO Mosheh in~HILL Sinai *to~>~*SAY⁽ᵛ⁾   **25:2** *!*⁽ᵐˢ⁾~*much*~SPEAK⁽ᵛ⁾ TO SON~s Yisra'eyl and~*you*⁽ᵐˢ⁾~*did*~SAY⁽ᵛ⁾ TO~*them*⁽ᵐ⁾ GIVEN.THAT *you*⁽ᵐᵖ⁾~*will*~COME⁽ᵛ⁾ TO the~LAND WHICH I GIVE⁽ᵛ⁾~*ing*⁽ᵐˢ⁾ *to~you*⁽ᵐᵖ⁾ and~*she~did*~CEASE⁽ᵛ⁾ the~LAND CEASING to~**YHWH**   **25:3** SIX YEAR~s *you*⁽ᵐˢ⁾~*will*~SOW⁽ᵛ⁾ FIELD~*you*⁽ᵐˢ⁾ and~SIX YEAR~s *you*⁽ᵐˢ⁾~*will*~PLUCK⁽ᵛ⁾ VINEYARD~*you*⁽ᵐˢ⁾ and~*you*⁽ᵐˢ⁾~*did*~GATHER⁽ᵛ⁾ AT PRODUCTION~her   **25:4** and~in~the~YEAR the~SEVENTH CEASING REST.PERIOD *he~will*~EXIST⁽ᵛ⁾ *to~the*~LAND CEASING *to~***YHWH** FIELD~*you*⁽ᵐˢ⁾ NOT *you*⁽ᵐˢ⁾~*will*~SOW⁽ᵛ⁾ and~VINEYARD~*you*⁽ᵐˢ⁾ NOT *you*⁽ᵐˢ⁾~*will*~PLUCK⁽ᵛ⁾   **25:5** AT AFTER.GROWTH HARVEST~*you*⁽ᵐˢ⁾ NOT *you*⁽ᵐˢ⁾~*will*~SEVER⁽ᵛ⁾ and~AT GRAPE~s DEDICATED~*you*⁽ᵐˢ⁾ NOT *you*⁽ᵐˢ⁾~*will*~FENCE.IN⁽ᵛ⁾ YEAR REST.PERIOD *he~will*~EXIST⁽ᵛ⁾ *to~the*~LAND   **25:6** and~*she~did~*EXIST⁽ᵛ⁾ CEASING the~LAND *to~you*⁽ᵐᵖ⁾ *to~*FOOD *to~you*⁽ᵐˢ⁾ and~to~SERVANT~*you*⁽ᵐˢ⁾ and~to~BONDWOMAN~*you*⁽ᵐˢ⁾ and~to~HIRELING~*you*⁽ᵐˢ⁾ and~to~SETTLER~*you*⁽ᵐˢ⁾ the~IMMIGRATE⁽ᵛ⁾~*ing*⁽ᵐᵖ⁾ WITH~*you*⁽ᶠˢ⁾   **25:7** and~to~BEAST~*you*⁽ᵐˢ⁾ and~to~the~LIVING WHICH in~LAND~*you*⁽ᵐˢ⁾ *she~will*~EXIST⁽ᵛ⁾ ALL PRODUCTION~her *to~>~*EAT⁽ᵛ⁾   **25:8** and~*you*⁽ᵐˢ⁾~*did*~COUNT⁽ᵛ⁾ *to~you*⁽ᵐˢ⁾ SEVEN CEASING~s YEAR~s SEVEN YEAR~s SEVEN FOOTSTEP~s and~*they~did*~EXIST⁽ᵛ⁾ *to~you*⁽ᵐˢ⁾ DAY~s SEVEN CEASING~s the~YEAR~s NINE and~FOUR~s YEAR   **25:9** and~*you*⁽ᵐˢ⁾~*did~make*~CROSS.OVER⁽ᵛ⁾ RAM.HORN SIGNAL in~the~NEW.MOON the~SEVENTH in~TENTH.ONE *to~the*~NEW.MOON in~DAY the~ATONEMENT~s *you*⁽ᵐˢ⁾~*will~make*~CROSS.OVER⁽ᵛ⁾ RAM.HORN in~ALL LAND~*you*⁽ᵐᵖ⁾   **25:10** and~*you*⁽ᵐᵖ⁾~*did~much~*SET.APART⁽ᵛ⁾ AT YEAR the~FIVE~s YEAR and~*you*⁽ᵐᵖ⁾~*did~*CALL.OUT⁽ᵛ⁾ FREE.FLOWING in~the~LAND *to~*ALL SETTLE⁽ᵛ⁾~*ing*⁽ᵐᵖ⁾~her JUBILEE SHE *she~will~*EXIST⁽ᵛ⁾ *to~you*⁽ᵐᵖ⁾ and~*you*⁽ᵐᵖ⁾~*did~*TURN.BACK⁽ᵛ⁾ MAN TO HOLDINGS~him and~MAN TO CLAN~him *you*⁽ᵐᵖ⁾~*will*~TURN.BACK⁽ᵛ⁾   **25:11** JUBILEE SHE YEAR the~FIVE~s YEAR *she~will*~EXIST⁽ᵛ⁾ *to~you*⁽ᵐᵖ⁾ NOT *you*⁽ᵐᵖ⁾~*will~*SOW⁽ᵛ⁾ and~NOT *you*⁽ᵐᵖ⁾~*will*~SEVER⁽ᵛ⁾ AT AFTER.GROWTH~her and~NOT *you*⁽ᵐᵖ⁾~

The Book of Leviticus

will~FENCE.IN$^{(V)}$ AT DEDICATED~s~her **25:12** GIVEN.THAT JUBILEE SHE SPECIAL *she*~*will*~EXIST$^{(V)}$ to~you$^{(mp)}$ FROM the~FIELD *you*$^{(mp)}$~*will*~EAT$^{(V)}$ AT PRODUCTION~her **25:13** in~YEAR the~JUBILEE the~THIS *you*$^{(mp)}$~*will*~TURN.BACK$^{(V)}$ MAN TO HOLDINGS~him **25:14** and~GIVEN.THAT *you*$^{(mp)}$~*will*~SELL$^{(V)}$ MERCHANDISE to~the~NEIGHBOR~you$^{(ms)}$ OR >~PURCHASE$^{(V)}$ from~HAND NEIGHBOR~you$^{(ms)}$ DO.NOT *you*$^{(mp)}$~*will*~make~SUPPRESS$^{(V)}$ MAN AT BROTHER~him **25:15** in~NUMBER YEAR~s AFTER the~JUBILEE *you*$^{(ms)}$~*will*~PURCHASE$^{(V)}$ from~AT NEIGHBOR~you$^{(ms)}$ in~NUMBER YEAR~s PRODUCTION~s *he*~*will*~SELL$^{(V)}$ to~you$^{(fs)}$ **25:16** to~MOUTH ABUNDANCE the~YEAR~s *you*$^{(ms)}$~*will*~make~INCREASE$^{(V)}$ ACQUIRED~him and~to~MOUTH >~BE.LESS$^{(V)}$ the~YEAR~s *you*$^{(ms)}$~*will*~make~BE.LESS$^{(V)}$ ACQUIRED~him GIVEN.THAT NUMBER PRODUCTION~s HE SELL$^{(V)}$~*ing*$^{(ms)}$ to~you$^{(fs)}$ **25:17** and~NOT *you*$^{(mp)}$~*will*~make~SUPPRESS$^{(V)}$ MAN AT NEIGHBOR~him and~*you*$^{(ms)}$~*did*~FEAR$^{(V)}$ from~Elohiym~you$^{(ms)}$ GIVEN.THAT I **YHWH** Elohiym~you$^{(mp)}$ **25:18** and~*you*$^{(mp)}$~*did*~DO$^{(V)}$ AT CUSTOM~s~me and~AT DECISION~s~me *you*$^{(mp)}$~*will*~SAFEGUARD$^{(V)}$ and~*you*$^{(mp)}$~*did*~DO$^{(V)}$ AT~them$^{(m)}$ and~*you*$^{(mp)}$~*did*~SETTLE$^{(V)}$ UPON the~LAND to~the~SAFELY **25:19** and~*she*~*did*~GIVE$^{(V)}$ the~LAND PRODUCE~her and~*you*$^{(mp)}$~*did*~EAT$^{(V)}$ to~SATISFACTION and~*you*$^{(mp)}$~*did*~SETTLE$^{(V)}$ to~the~SAFELY UPON~her **25:20** and~GIVEN.THAT *you*$^{(mp)}$~*will*~SAY$^{(V)}$ WHAT *we*~*will*~EAT$^{(V)}$ in~the~YEAR the~SEVENTH THOUGH NOT *we*~*will*~SOW$^{(V)}$ and~NOT *we*~*will*~GATHER$^{(V)}$ AT PRODUCTION~s~him **25:21** and~*I*~*did*~much~DIRECT$^{(V)}$ AT PRESENT~me to~you$^{(mp)}$ in~the~YEAR the~SIXTH and~*she*~*did*~DO$^{(V)}$ AT the~PRODUCTION to~THREE the~YEAR~s **25:22** and~*you*$^{(mp)}$~*did*~SOW$^{(V)}$ AT the~YEAR the~EIGHTH and~*you*$^{(mp)}$~*did*~EAT$^{(V)}$ FROM the~PRODUCTION SLEEPING UNTIL the~YEAR the~NINTH UNTIL *I*$^{(ms)}$~COME$^{(V)}$ PRODUCTION~her *you*$^{(mp)}$~*will*~EAT$^{(V)}$ SLEEPING **25:23** and~the~LAND NOT *she*~*will*~be~SELL$^{(V)}$ to~PERMANENT GIVEN.THAT to~me the~LAND GIVEN.THAT IMMIGRANT~s and~SETTLER~s YOU$^{(mp)}$ BY~me **25:24** and~in~ALL LAND HOLDINGS~you$^{(mp)}$ REDEMPTION *you*$^{(mp)}$~*will*~GIVE$^{(V)}$ to~the~LAND **25:25** GIVEN.THAT *he*~*will*~BE.LOW$^{(V)}$ BROTHER~you$^{(ms)}$ and~*he*~*did*~SELL$^{(V)}$ from~HOLDINGS~him and~*he*~*did*~COME$^{(V)}$ REDEEM$^{(V)}$~*ing*$^{(ms)}$~him the~NEAR TO~him and~*he*~*did*~REDEEM$^{(V)}$ AT MERCHANDISE BROTHER~him **25:26** and~MAN GIVEN.THAT NOT *he*~*will*~EXIST$^{(V)}$ to~him REDEEM$^{(V)}$~*ing*$^{(ms)}$ and~*she*~*did*~make~OVERTAKE$^{(V)}$ HAND~him and~*he*~*did*~FIND$^{(V)}$ like~SUFFICIENT REDEMPTION~him **25:27** and~*he*~*did*~much~THINK$^{(V)}$ AT YEAR~s MERCHANDISE~him and~*he*~*did*~make~TURN.BACK$^{(V)}$ AT the~EXCEED$^{(V)}$~*ing*$^{(ms)}$ to~the~MAN WHICH *he*~*did*~SELL$^{(V)}$ to~him and~*he*~*did*~TURN.BACK$^{(V)}$ to~HOLDINGS~him **25:28** and~IF NOT *she*~*did*~FIND$^{(V)}$ HAND~him SUFFICIENT >~make~TURN.BACK$^{(V)}$ to~him and~*he*~*did*~EXIST$^{(V)}$ MERCHANDISE~him in~HAND the~PURCHASE$^{(V)}$~*ing*$^{(ms)}$ AT~him UNTIL YEAR the~JUBILEE and~*he*~*will*~GO.OUT$^{(V)}$ in~the~JUBILEE and~*he*~*did*~TURN.BACK$^{(V)}$ to~HOLDINGS~him **25:29** and~MAN GIVEN.THAT *he*~*will*~SELL$^{(V)}$ HOUSE SETTLING CITY RAMPART and~*she*~*did*~EXIST$^{(V)}$ REDEMPTION~him UNTIL >~BE.WHOLE$^{(V)}$ YEAR MERCHANDISE~him DAY~s

*she~will~*EXIST[(V)] REDEMPTION~him   **25:30** and~IF NOT *he~will~be~*
REDEEM[(V)] UNTIL >~FILL[(V)] to~him YEAR WHOLE and~*he~did~*RISE[(V)] the~
HOUSE WHICH in~the~CITY WHICH NOT RAMPART to~PERMANENT to~
PURCHASE[(V)]~*ing*[(ms)] AT~him to~GENERATION~s~him NOT *he~will~*
GO.OUT[(V)] in~the~JUBILEE   **25:31** and~HOUSE~s the~COURTYARD~s WHICH
WITHOUT to~them[(m)] RAMPART ALL.AROUND UPON FIELD the~LAND *he~*
*will~be~*THINK[(V)] REDEMPTION *she~will~*EXIST[(V)] to~him and~in~the~
JUBILEE *he~will~*GO.OUT[(V)]   **25:32** and~CITY~s the~Lewi~s HOUSE~s CITY~s
HOLDINGS~them[(m)] REDEMPTION DISTANT *she~will~*EXIST[(V)] to~
Lewi~s   **25:33** and~WHICH *he~will~*REDEEM[(V)] FROM the~Lewi~s and~*he~*
*will~*GO.OUT[(V)] MERCHANDISE HOUSE and~CITY HOLDINGS~him in~the~
JUBILEE GIVEN.THAT HOUSE~s CITY~s the~Lewi~s SHE HOLDINGS~them[(m)]
in~MIDST SON~s Yisra'eyl   **25:34** and~FIELD OPEN.SPACE CITY~s~them[(m)]
NOT *he~will~be~*SELL[(V)] GIVEN.THAT HOLDINGS DISTANT HE to~
them[(m)]   **25:35** and~GIVEN.THAT *he~will~*BE.LOW[(V)] BROTHER~you[(ms)] and~
*she~did~*TOTTER[(V)] HAND~him WITH~you[(fs)] and~*you*[(ms)]~*did~*make~SEIZE[(V)]
in~him IMMIGRANT and~SETTLER and~*he~did~*LIVE[(V)] WITH~
you[(fs)]   **25:36** DO.NOT *you*[(ms)]~*will~*TAKE[(V)] from~AT~him USURY and~
INTEREST and~*you*[(ms)]~*did~*FEAR[(V)] from~Elohiym~you[(ms)] and~LIVING
BROTHER~you[(ms)] WITH~you[(fs)]   **25:37** AT SILVER~you[(ms)] NOT *you*[(ms)]~*will~*
GIVE[(V)] to~him in~USURY and~in~GREAT.NUMBER NOT *you*[(ms)]~*will~*GIVE[(V)]
FOODSTUFF~you[(ms)]   **25:38** I **YHWH** Elohiym~you[(mp)] WHICH *I~did~*make~
GO.OUT[(V)] AT~you[(mp)] from~LAND Mits'rayim to~>~GIVE[(V)] to~you[(mp)] AT
LAND Kena'an to~>~EXIST[(V)] to~you[(mp)] to~Elohiym   **25:39** and~GIVEN.THAT
*he~will~*BE.LOW[(V)] BROTHER~you[(ms)] WITH~you[(fs)] and~*he~did~be~*SELL[(V)]
to~you[(fs)] NOT *you*[(ms)]~*will~*SERVE[(V)] in~him SERVICE SERVANT   **25:40** like~
HIRELING like~SETTLER *he~will~*EXIST[(V)] WITH~you[(fs)] UNTIL YEAR the~
JUBILEE *he~will~*SERVE[(V)] WITH~you[(fs)]   **25:41** and~*he~will~*GO.OUT[(V)] from~
WITH~you[(ms)] HE and~SON~s~him WITH~him and~*he~did~*TURN.BACK[(V)] TO
CLAN~him and~TO HOLDINGS FATHER~s~him *he~will~*
TURN.BACK[(V)]   **25:42** GIVEN.THAT SERVANT~s~me THEY[(m)] WHICH *I~did~*
make~GO.OUT[(V)] AT~them[(m)] from~LAND Mits'rayim NOT *they*[(m)]~*will~be~*
SELL[(V)] MERCHANDISE SERVANT   **25:43** NOT *you*[(ms)]~*will~*RULE[(V)] in~him in~
WHIP and~*you*[(ms)]~*did~*FEAR[(V)] from~Elohiym~you[(ms)]   **25:44** and~SERVANT~
you[(ms)] and~BONDWOMAN~you[(ms)] WHICH *they*[(m)]~*will~*EXIST[(V)] to~you[(fs)]
from~AT the~NATION~s WHICH ALL.AROUND~s~you[(mp)] from~them[(m)]
you[(ms)]~*will~*PURCHASE[(V)] SERVANT and~BONDWOMAN   **25:45** and~ALSO
from~SON~s the~SETTLER~s the~IMMIGRATE[(V)]~*ing*[(mp)] WITH~you[(mp)] from~
them[(m)] *you*[(ms)]~*will~*PURCHASE[(V)] and~CLAN~them[(m)] WHICH WITH~you[(mp)]
WHICH *they~did~*make~BRING.FORTH[(V)] in~LAND~you[(mp)] and~*they~did~*
EXIST[(V)] to~you[(mp)] to~HOLDINGS   **25:46** and~*you*[(mp)]~*will~self~*INHERIT[(V)]
AT~them[(m)] to~SON~s~you[(mp)] AFTER~you[(mp)] to~the~>~POSSESS[(V)]
HOLDINGS to~DISTANT in~them[(m)] *you*[(mp)]~*will~*SERVE[(V)] and~in~
BROTHER~s~you[(mp)] SON~s Yisra'eyl MAN in~BROTHER~him NOT *you*[(ms)]~
*will~*RULE[(V)] in~him in~WHIP   **25:47** and~GIVEN.THAT *she~will~*make~

OVERTAKE⁽ᵛ⁾ HAND IMMIGRANT and~SETTLER WITH~you⁽ᶠˢ⁾ and~*he~did~*
BE.LOW⁽ᵛ⁾ BROTHER~you⁽ᵐˢ⁾ WITH~him and~*he~did~be~*SELL⁽ᵛ⁾ to~
IMMIGRANT SETTLER WITH~you⁽ᶠˢ⁾ OR to~OFFSHOOT CLAN
IMMIGRANT   **25:48** AFTER *he~did~be~*SELL⁽ᵛ⁾ REDEMPTION *she~will~*
EXIST⁽ᵛ⁾ to~him UNIT from~BROTHER~s~him *he~will~*REDEEM⁽ᵛ⁾~
him   **25:49** OR UNCLE~him OR SON UNCLE~him *he~will~*REDEEM⁽ᵛ⁾~him OR
from~REMAINS FLESH~him from~CLAN~him *he~will~*REDEEM⁽ᵛ⁾~him OR
*she~did~make~*OVERTAKE⁽ᵛ⁾ HAND~him and~*he~did~be~*
REDEEM⁽ᵛ⁾   **25:50** and~*he~did~much~*THINK⁽ᵛ⁾ WITH PURCHASE⁽ᵛ⁾~*ing⁽ᵐˢ⁾~*
him from~YEAR >~*be~*SELL⁽ᵛ⁾~him to~him UNTIL YEAR the~JUBILEE and~*he~
did~*EXIST⁽ᵛ⁾ SILVER MERCHANDISE~him in~NUMBER YEAR~s like~DAY~s
HIRELING *he~will~*EXIST⁽ᵛ⁾ WITH~him   **25:51** IF YET.AGAIN ABUNDANT in~
the~YEAR~s to~MOUTH~them⁽ᶠ⁾ *he~will~make~*TURN.BACK⁽ᵛ⁾
REDEMPTION~him from~SILVER ACQUIRED~him   **25:52** and~IF
SMALL.AMOUNT *he~did~be~*REMAIN⁽ᵛ⁾ in~the~YEAR~s UNTIL YEAR the~
JUBILEE and~*he~did~much~*THINK⁽ᵛ⁾ to~him like~MOUTH YEAR~s~him *he~
will~make~*TURN.BACK⁽ᵛ⁾ AT REDEMPTION~him   **25:53** like~HIRELING YEAR
in~YEAR *he~will~*EXIST⁽ᵛ⁾ WITH~him NOT *he~will~*RULE⁽ᵛ⁾~him in~WHIP to~
EYE~s2~you⁽ᵐˢ⁾   **25:54** and~IF NOT *he~will~be~*REDEEM⁽ᵛ⁾ in~THESE and~
*he~will~*GO.OUT⁽ᵛ⁾ in~YEAR the~JUBILEE HE and~SON~s~him WITH~
him   **25:55** GIVEN.THAT to~me SON~s Yisra'eyl SERVANT~s SERVANT~s~me
THEY⁽ᵐ⁾ WHICH *I~did~make~*GO.OUT⁽ᵛ⁾ AT~them⁽ᵐ⁾ from~LAND Mits'rayim I
YHWH Elohiym~you⁽ᵐᵖ⁾

Chapter 26

26:1 NOT *you⁽ᵐᵖ⁾~will~*DO⁽ᵛ⁾ to~you⁽ᵐᵖ⁾ WORTHLESS~s and~SCULPTURE and~
MONUMENT NOT *you⁽ᵐᵖ⁾~will~make~*RISE⁽ᵛ⁾ to~you⁽ᵐᵖ⁾ and~STONE
IMAGERY NOT *you⁽ᵐᵖ⁾~will~*GIVE⁽ᵛ⁾ in~LAND~you⁽ᵐᵖ⁾ to~>~*self~*
BEND.DOWN⁽ᵛ⁾ UPON~her GIVEN.THAT I **YHWH** Elohiym~you⁽ᵐᵖ⁾   **26:2** AT
CEASING~s~me *you⁽ᵐᵖ⁾~will~*SAFEGUARD⁽ᵛ⁾ and~SANCTUARY~me *you⁽ᵐᵖ⁾~
will~*FEAR⁽ᵛ⁾ I **YHWH**   **26:3** IF in~CUSTOM~s~me *you⁽ᵐᵖ⁾~will~*WALK⁽ᵛ⁾ and~
AT DIRECTIVE~s~me *you⁽ᵐᵖ⁾~will~*SAFEGUARD⁽ᵛ⁾ and~*you⁽ᵐᵖ⁾~did~*DO⁽ᵛ⁾ AT~
them⁽ᵐ⁾   **26:4** and~*I~did~*GIVE⁽ᵛ⁾ RAIN.SHOWER~s~you⁽ᵐᵖ⁾ in~
APPOINTED.TIME~them⁽ᵐ⁾ and~*she~did~*GIVE⁽ᵛ⁾ the~LAND PRODUCT~her
and~TREE the~FIELD *he~will~*GIVE⁽ᵛ⁾ PRODUCE~him   **26:5** and~*he~did~
make~*OVERTAKE⁽ᵛ⁾ to~you⁽ᵐᵖ⁾ THRESHING AT VINTAGE and~VINTAGE *he~
will~make~*OVERTAKE⁽ᵛ⁾ AT SEED and~*you⁽ᵐᵖ⁾~did~*EAT⁽ᵛ⁾ BREAD~you⁽ᵐᵖ⁾ to~
SATISFACTION and~*you⁽ᵐᵖ⁾~did~*SETTLE⁽ᵛ⁾ to~the~SAFELY in~LAND~
you⁽ᵐᵖ⁾   **26:6** and~*I~did~*GIVE⁽ᵛ⁾ COMPLETENESS in~the~LAND and~*you⁽ᵐᵖ⁾~
did~*LIE.DOWN⁽ᵛ⁾ and~WITHOUT *make~*TREMBLE⁽ᵛ⁾~*ing⁽ᵐˢ⁾* and~*I~did~
make~*CEASE⁽ᵛ⁾ LIVING DYSFUNCTIONAL FROM the~LAND and~SWORD NOT
*you⁽ᵐˢ⁾~will~*CROSS.OVER⁽ᵛ⁾ in~LAND~you⁽ᵐᵖ⁾   **26:7** and~*you⁽ᵐᵖ⁾~did~*

PURSUE(V) AT ATTACK(V)~ing(mp)~you(mp) and~they~did~FALL(V) to~FACE~s~ you(mp) to~SWORD **26:8** and~they~did~PURSUE(V) from~you(mp) FIVE HUNDRED and~HUNDRED from~you(mp) MYRIAD they(m)~will~PURSUE(V) and~they~did~FALL(V) ATTACK(V)~ing(mp)~you(mp) to~FACE~s~you(mp) to~ SWORD **26:9** and~I~did~TURN(V) TO~you(mp) and~I~did~make~ REPRODUCE(V) AT~you(mp) and~I~did~make~INCREASE(V) AT~you(mp) and~I~ did~make~RISE(V) AT COVENANT~me AT~you(mp) **26:10** and~you(mp)~did~ EAT(V) SLEEPING be~SLEEP(V)~ing(ms) and~SLEEPING from~FACE~s NEW you(mp)~will~make~GO.OUT(V) **26:11** and~I~did~GIVE(V) DWELLING~me in~ MIDST~you(mp) and~NOT she~will~CAST.AWAY(V) SOUL~me AT~ you(mp) **26:12** and~I~did~self~WALK(V) in~MIDST~you(mp) and~I~did~EXIST(V) to~you(mp) to~Elohiym and~YOU(mp) you(mp)~will~EXIST(V) to~me to~ PEOPLE **26:13** I **YHWH** Elohiym~you(mp) WHICH I~did~make~GO.OUT(V) AT~ you(mp) from~LAND Mits'rayim from~>~EXIST(V) to~them(m) SERVANT~s and~ I~will~CRACK(V) POLE~s YOKE~you(mp) and~I~will~make~WALK(V) AT~you(mp) VERTICAL **26:14** and~IF NOT you(mp)~will~HEAR(V) to~me and~NOT you(mp)~ will~DO(V) AT ALL the~DIRECTIVE~s the~THESE **26:15** and~IF in~ CUSTOM~s~me you(mp)~will~REJECT(V) and~IF AT DECISION~s~me she~will~ CAST.AWAY(V) SOUL~you(ms) to~EXCEPT >~DO(V) AT ALL DIRECTIVE~s~me to~ >~make~BREAK(V)~you(mp) AT COVENANT~me **26:16** MOREOVER I I~will~ DO(V) THIS to~you(mp) and~I~did~make~REGISTER(V) UPON~you(mp) DISMAY AT the~CONSUMPTION and~AT the~FEVER much~FINISH(V)~ing(fp) EYE~s2 and~make~SORROW(V)~ing(fp) SOUL and~you(mp)~did~SOW(V) to~the~EMPTY SEED~you(mp) and~they~did~EAT(V)~him ATTACK(V)~ing(mp)~ you(mp) **26:17** and~I~did~GIVE(V) FACE~s~me in~you(mp) and~you(mp)~did~ be~SMITE(V) to~FACE~s ATTACK(V)~ing(mp)~you(mp) and~they~did~RULE(V) in~ you(mp) HATE(V)~ing(mp)~you(mp) and~you(mp)~did~FLEE(V) and~WITHOUT PURSUE(V)~ing(ms) AT~you(mp) **26:18** and~IF UNTIL THESE NOT you(mp)~will~ HEAR(V) to~me and~I~did~ADD(V) to~>~much~CORRECT(V)~her AT~you(mp) SEVEN UPON FAILURE~s~you(mp) **26:19** and~I~did~CRACK(V) AT MAJESTY BOLDNESS~you(mp) and~I~did~GIVE(V) AT SKY~s2~you(mp) like~IRON and~AT LAND~you(mp) like~the~BRASS **26:20** and~he~did~BE.WHOLE(V) to~the~ EMPTY STRENGTH~you(mp) and~NOT she~will~GIVE(V) LAND~you(mp) AT PRODUCT~her and~TREE the~LAND NOT he~will~GIVE(V) PRODUCE~ him **26:21** and~IF you(mp)~will~WALK(V) WITH~me CONTRARY and~NOT you(mp)~will~CONSENT(V) to~>~HEAR(V) to~me and~I~did~ADD(V) UPON~ you(mp) HITTING SEVEN like~FAILURE~s~you(mp) **26:22** and~I~did~make~ SEND(V) in~you(mp) AT LIVING the~FIELD and~she~did~much~BE.CHILDLESS(V) AT~you(mp) and~she~did~make~CUT(V) AT BEAST~you(mp) and~she~did~ make~BE.LESS(V) AT~you(mp) and~they~did~be~DESOLATE(V) ROAD~s **26:23** and~IF in~THESE NOT you(ms)~will~be~CORRECT(V) to~me and~you(mp)~did~WALK(V) WITH~me CONTRARY **26:24** and~I~did~WALK(V) MOREOVER I WITH~you(mp) in~CONTRARY and~I~did~make~HIT(V) AT~ you(mp) ALSO I SEVEN UPON FAILURE~s~you(mp) **26:25** and~I~will~make~ COME(V) UPON~you(mp) SWORD AVENGE(V)~ing(fs) VENGEANCE COVENANT

The Book of Leviticus

and~you$^{(mp)}$~did~be~GATHER$^{(V)}$ TO CITY~s~you$^{(mp)}$ and~I~did~much~SEND$^{(V)}$ EPIDEMIC in~MIDST~you$^{(mp)}$ and~you$^{(mp)}$~did~be~GIVE$^{(V)}$ in~HAND ATTACK$^{(V)}$~ing$^{(ms)}$ 26:26 in~>~CRACK$^{(V)}$~me to~you$^{(mp)}$ BRANCH BREAD and~they~will~BAKE$^{(V)}$ TEN WOMAN~s BREAD~you$^{(mp)}$ in~OVEN UNIT and~they~did~make~TURN.BACK$^{(V)}$ BREAD~you$^{(mp)}$ in~the~WEIGHT and~you$^{(mp)}$~did~EAT$^{(V)}$ and~NOT you$^{(mp)}$~will~BE.SATISFIED$^{(V)}$ 26:27 and~IF in~THIS NOT you$^{(mp)}$~will~HEAR$^{(V)}$ to~me and~you$^{(mp)}$~did~WALK$^{(V)}$ WITH~me in~CONTRARY   26:28 and~I~did~WALK$^{(V)}$ WITH~you$^{(mp)}$ in~FURY CONTRARY and~I~did~much~CORRECT$^{(V)}$ AT~you$^{(mp)}$ MOREOVER I SEVEN UPON FAILURE~s~you$^{(mp)}$ 26:29 and~you$^{(mp)}$~did~EAT$^{(V)}$ FLESH SON~s~you$^{(mp)}$ and~FLESH DAUGHTER~s~you$^{(mp)}$ you$^{(mp)}$~will~EAT$^{(V)}$ 26:30 and~I~did~make~DESTROY$^{(V)}$ AT PLATFORM~s~you$^{(mp)}$ and~I~did~make~CUT$^{(V)}$ AT SUN.IDOL~s~you$^{(mp)}$ and~I~did~GIVE$^{(V)}$ AT CORPSE~s~you$^{(mp)}$ UPON CORPSE~s IDOL~s~you$^{(mp)}$ and~she~did~CAST.AWAY$^{(V)}$ SOUL~me AT~you$^{(mp)}$ 26:31 and~I~did~GIVE$^{(V)}$ AT CITY~s~you$^{(mp)}$ DRIED.OUT and~I~did~make~DESOLATE$^{(V)}$ AT SANCTUARY~s~you$^{(mp)}$ and~NOT I~will~make~SMELL$^{(V)}$ in~AROMA SWEET~you$^{(mp)}$ 26:32 and~I~did~make~DESOLATE$^{(V)}$ I AT the~LAND and~they~did~DESOLATE$^{(V)}$ UPON~her ATTACK$^{(V)}$~ing$^{(mp)}$~you$^{(mp)}$ the~SETTLE$^{(V)}$~ing$^{(mp)}$ in~her   26:33 and~AT~you$^{(mp)}$ I~will~much~DISPERSE$^{(V)}$ in~the~NATION~s and~I~did~make~DRAW.OUT$^{(V)}$ AFTER~you$^{(mp)}$ SWORD and~she~did~EXIST$^{(V)}$ LAND~you$^{(mp)}$ DESOLATE and~CITY~s~you$^{(mp)}$ they$^{(m)}$~will~EXIST$^{(V)}$ DRIED.OUT   26:34 AT.THAT.TIME she~will~ACCEPT$^{(V)}$ the~LAND AT CEASING~s~her ALL DAY~s >~be~make~DESOLATE$^{(V)}$~her and~YOU$^{(mp)}$ in~LAND ATTACK$^{(V)}$~ing$^{(mp)}$~you$^{(mp)}$ AT.THAT.TIME she~will~CEASE$^{(V)}$ the~LAND and~she~did~make~ACCEPT$^{(V)}$ AT CEASING~s~her   26:35 ALL DAY~s >~be~make~DESOLATE$^{(V)}$~her she~will~CEASE$^{(V)}$ AT WHICH NOT she~did~CEASE$^{(V)}$ in~CEASING~s~you$^{(mp)}$ in~>~SETTLE$^{(V)}$~you$^{(mp)}$ UPON~her   26:36 and~the~be~REMAIN$^{(V)}$~ing$^{(mp)}$ in~you$^{(mp)}$ and~I~will~make~COME$^{(V)}$ FAINT in~HEART~them$^{(m)}$ in~LAND~s ATTACK$^{(V)}$~ing$^{(ms)}$~s~them$^{(m)}$ and~he~did~PURSUE$^{(V)}$ AT~them$^{(m)}$ VOICE LEAF be~TWIRL$^{(V)}$~ing$^{(ms)}$ and~they~did~FLEE$^{(V)}$ FLEEING SWORD and~they~did~FALL$^{(V)}$ and~WITHOUT PURSUE$^{(V)}$~ing$^{(ms)}$ 26:37 and~they~did~TOPPLE$^{(V)}$ MAN in~BROTHER~him like~from~FACE~s SWORD and~PURSUE$^{(V)}$~ing$^{(ms)}$ WITHOUT and~NOT she~will~EXIST$^{(V)}$ to~you$^{(mp)}$ HIGH.PLACE to~FACE~s ATTACK$^{(V)}$~ing$^{(mp)}$~you$^{(mp)}$ 26:38 and~you$^{(mp)}$~did~PERISH$^{(V)}$ in~the~NATION~s and~she~did~EAT$^{(V)}$ AT~you$^{(mp)}$ LAND ATTACK$^{(V)}$~ing$^{(mp)}$~you$^{(mp)}$ 26:39 and~the~be~REMAIN$^{(V)}$~ing$^{(mp)}$ in~you$^{(mp)}$ they$^{(m)}$~will~be~ROT$^{(V)}$ in~the~TWISTEDNESS~them$^{(m)}$ in~LAND~s ATTACK$^{(V)}$~ing$^{(mp)}$~you$^{(mp)}$ and~MOREOVER in~the~TWISTEDNESS~s FATHER~s~them$^{(m)}$ AT~them$^{(m)}$ they$^{(m)}$~will~be~ROT$^{(V)}$ 26:40 and~they~did~self~THROW.THE.HAND$^{(V)}$ AT TWISTEDNESS~them$^{(m)}$ and~AT TWISTEDNESS FATHER~s~them$^{(m)}$ in~TRANSGRESSION~them$^{(m)}$ WHICH they~did~TRANSGRESS$^{(V)}$ in~me and~MOREOVER WHICH they~did~WALK$^{(V)}$ WITH~me in~CONTRARY   26:41 MOREOVER I I~will~WALK$^{(V)}$ WITH~them$^{(m)}$ in~CONTRARY and~I~will~make~COME$^{(V)}$ AT~them$^{(m)}$ in~LAND ATTACK$^{(V)}$~ing$^{(ms)}$~s~them$^{(m)}$

OR AT.THAT.TIME he~will~be~LOWER$^{(V)}$ HEART~them$^{(m)}$ the~ UNCIRCUMCISED and~AT.THAT.TIME they$^{(m)}$~will~ACCEPT$^{(V)}$ AT TWISTEDNESS~them$^{(m)}$ **26:42** and~I~did~REMEMBER$^{(V)}$ AT COVENANT~me Ya'aqov and~MOREOVER AT COVENANT~me Yits'hhaq and~MOREOVER AT COVENANT~me Avraham I~will~REMEMBER$^{(V)}$ and~the~LAND I~will~ REMEMBER$^{(V)}$ **26:43** and~the~LAND she~will~be~LEAVE$^{(V)}$ from~them$^{(m)}$ and~she~will~ACCEPT$^{(V)}$ AT CEASING~s her in~>~be~make~DESOLATE$^{(V)}$ from~them$^{(m)}$ and~THEY$^{(m)}$ they$^{(m)}$~will~ACCEPT$^{(V)}$ AT TWISTEDNESS~ them$^{(m)}$ SEEING.AS and~in~SEEING.AS in~DECISION~s~me they~did~ REJECT$^{(V)}$ and~AT CUSTOM~s~me she~did~CAST.AWAY$^{(V)}$ SOUL~ them$^{(m)}$ **26:44** and~MOREOVER ALSO THIS in~>~EXIST$^{(V)}$~them$^{(m)}$ in~LAND ATTACK$^{(V)}$~ing$^{(ms)}$~s~them$^{(m)}$ NOT I~did~REJECT$^{(V)}$~them$^{(m)}$ and~NOT I~did~ CAST.AWAY$^{(V)}$~them$^{(m)}$ to~>~much~FINISH$^{(V)}$~them$^{(m)}$ to~>~make~BREAK$^{(V)}$ COVENANT~me AT~them$^{(m)}$ GIVEN.THAT I **YHWH** Elohiym~ them$^{(m)}$ **26:45** and~I~did~REMEMBER$^{(V)}$ to~them$^{(m)}$ COVENANT FIRST~s WHICH I~did~make~GO.OUT$^{(V)}$ AT~them$^{(m)}$ from~LAND Mits'rayim to~EYE~ s2 the~NATION~s to~>~EXIST$^{(V)}$ to~them$^{(m)}$ to~Elohiym I **YHWH** **26:46** THESE the~CUSTOM~s and~the~DECISION~s and~the~ TEACHING~s WHICH he~did~GIVE$^{(V)}$ **YHWH** BETWEEN~him and~BETWEEN SON~s Yisra'eyl in~HILL Sinai in~HAND Mosheh

Chapter 27

27:1 and~he~will~much~SPEAK$^{(V)}$ **YHWH** TO Mosheh to~>~SAY$^{(V)}$ **27:2** I$^{(ms)}$~ much~SPEAK$^{(V)}$ TO SON~s Yisra'eyl and~you$^{(ms)}$~did~SAY$^{(V)}$ TO~them$^{(m)}$ MAN GIVEN.THAT he~will~make~PERFORM$^{(V)}$ VOW in~ARRANGEMENT~you$^{(ms)}$ SOUL~s to~**YHWH** **27:3** and~he~did~EXIST$^{(V)}$ ARRANGEMENT~you$^{(ms)}$ the~ MALE from~SON TEN~s YEAR and~UNTIL SON SIX~s YEAR and~he~did~ EXIST$^{(V)}$ ARRANGEMENT~you$^{(ms)}$ FIVE~s SHEQEL SILVER in~SHEQEL the~ SPECIAL **27:4** and~IF FEMALE SHE and~he~did~EXIST$^{(V)}$ ARRANGEMENT~ you$^{(ms)}$ THREE~s SHEQEL **27:5** and~IF from~SON FIVE YEAR~s and~UNTIL SON TEN~s YEAR and~he~did~EXIST$^{(V)}$ ARRANGEMENT~you$^{(ms)}$ the~MALE TEN~s SHEQEL~s and~to~the~FEMALE TEN SHEQEL~s **27:6** and~IF from~ SON NEW.MOON and~UNTIL SON FIVE YEAR~s and~he~did~EXIST$^{(V)}$ ARRANGEMENT~you$^{(ms)}$ the~MALE FIVE SHEQEL~s SILVER and~to~the~ FEMALE ARRANGEMENT~you$^{(ms)}$ THREE SHEQEL~s SILVER **27:7** and~IF from~SON SIX~s YEAR and~UPWARD~unto IF MALE and~he~did~EXIST$^{(V)}$ ARRANGEMENT~you$^{(ms)}$ FIVE TEN SHEQEL and~to~the~FEMALE TEN SHEQEL~s **27:8** and~IF he~did~BE.LOW$^{(V)}$ HE from~ARRANGEMENT~you$^{(ms)}$ and~he~did~make~STAND$^{(V)}$~him to~FACE~s the~ADMINISTRATOR and~he~ did~make~ARRANGE$^{(V)}$ AT~him the~ADMINISTRATOR UPON MOUTH WHICH she~will~make~OVERTAKE$^{(V)}$ HAND the~MAKE.A.VOW$^{(V)}$~ing$^{(ms)}$ he~will~ make~ARRANGE$^{(V)}$~him the~ADMINISTRATOR **27:9** and~IF BEAST WHICH

The Book of Leviticus

they$^{(m)}$~will~make~COME.NEAR$^{(V)}$ FROM~her DONATION to~**YHWH** ALL WHICH he~will~GIVE$^{(V)}$ FROM~him to~**YHWH** he~will~EXIST$^{(V)}$ SPECIAL **27:10** NOT he~will~make~PASS.OVER$^{(V)}$~him and~NOT he~will~make~CONVERT$^{(V)}$ AT~him FUNCTIONAL in~DYSFUNCTIONAL OR DYSFUNCTIONAL in~FUNCTIONAL and~IF >~make~CONVERT$^{(V)}$ he~will~make~CONVERT$^{(V)}$ BEAST in~BEAST and~he~did~EXIST$^{(V)}$ HE and~EXCHANGE~him he~will~EXIST$^{(V)}$ SPECIAL **27:11** and~IF ALL BEAST DIRTY WHICH NOT they$^{(m)}$~will~make~COME.NEAR$^{(V)}$ FROM~her DONATION to~**YHWH** and~he~did~make~STAND$^{(V)}$ AT the~BEAST to~FACE~s the~ADMINISTRATOR **27:12** and~he~did~make~ARRANGE$^{(V)}$ the~ADMINISTRATOR AT~her BETWEEN FUNCTIONAL and~BETWEEN DYSFUNCTIONAL like~ARRANGEMENT~you$^{(ms)}$ the~ADMINISTRATOR SO he~will~EXIST$^{(V)}$ **27:13** and~IF >~REDEEM$^{(V)}$ he~will~REDEEM$^{(V)}$~her and~he~will~ADD$^{(V)}$ FIFTH~him UPON ARRANGEMENT~you$^{(ms)}$ **27:14** and~MAN GIVEN.THAT he~will~make~SET.APART$^{(V)}$ AT HOUSE~him SPECIAL to~**YHWH** and~he~did~make~ARRANGE$^{(V)}$~him the~ADMINISTRATOR BETWEEN FUNCTIONAL and~BETWEEN DYSFUNCTIONAL like~WHICH he~will~make~ARRANGE$^{(V)}$ AT~him the~ADMINISTRATOR SO he~will~RISE$^{(V)}$ **27:15** and~IF the~make~SET.APART$^{(V)}$~ing$^{(ms)}$ he~will~REDEEM$^{(V)}$ AT HOUSE~him and~he~will~ADD$^{(V)}$ FIFTH SILVER ARRANGEMENT~you$^{(ms)}$ UPON~him and~he~did~EXIST$^{(V)}$ to~him **27:16** and~IF from~FIELD HOLDINGS~him he~will~make~SET.APART$^{(V)}$ MAN to~**YHWH** and~he~did~EXIST$^{(V)}$ ARRANGEMENT~you$^{(ms)}$ to~MOUTH SEED~him SEED HHOMER BARLEY~s in~the~FIVE~s SHEQEL SILVER **27:17** IF from~YEAR the~JUBILEE he~will~make~SET.APART$^{(V)}$ FIELD~him like~ARRANGEMENT~you$^{(ms)}$ he~will~RISE$^{(V)}$ **27:18** and~IF AFTER the~JUBILEE he~will~make~SET.APART$^{(V)}$ FIELD~him and~he~did~much~THINK$^{(V)}$ to~him the~ADMINISTRATOR AT the~SILVER UPON MOUTH the~YEAR~s the~be~LEAVE.BEHIND$^{(V)}$~ing$^{(fp)}$ UNTIL YEAR the~JUBILEE and~he~did~be~TAKE.AWAY$^{(V)}$ from~ARRANGEMENT~you$^{(ms)}$ **27:19** and~IF >~REDEEM$^{(V)}$ he~will~REDEEM$^{(V)}$ AT the~FIELD the~make~SET.APART$^{(V)}$~ing$^{(ms)}$ AT~him and~he~will~ADD$^{(V)}$ FIVE SILVER ARRANGEMENT~you$^{(ms)}$ UPON~him and~he~did~RISE$^{(V)}$ to~him **27:20** and~IF NOT he~will~REDEEM$^{(V)}$ AT the~FIELD and~IF he~did~SELL$^{(V)}$ AT the~FIELD to~MAN OTHER NOT he~will~be~REDEEM$^{(V)}$ YET.AGAIN **27:21** and~he~did~EXIST$^{(V)}$ the~FIELD in~>~GO.OUT$^{(V)}$~him in~the~JUBILEE SPECIAL to~**YHWH** like~FIELD the~ASSIGNED to~the~ADMINISTRATOR she~will~EXIST$^{(V)}$ HOLDINGS~him **27:22** and~IF AT FIELD ACQUIRED~him WHICH NOT from~FIELD HOLDINGS~him he~will~make~SET.APART$^{(V)}$ to~**YHWH** **27:23** and~he~did~much~THINK$^{(V)}$ to~him the~ADMINISTRATOR AT WORTH the~ARRANGEMENT~you$^{(ms)}$ UNTIL YEAR the~JUBILEE and~he~did~GIVE$^{(V)}$ AT the~ARRANGEMENT~you$^{(ms)}$ in~the~DAY the~HE SPECIAL to~**YHWH** **27:24** in~YEAR the~JUBILEE he~will~TURN.BACK$^{(V)}$ the~FIELD to~the~WHICH he~did~PURCHASE$^{(V)}$~him from~AT~him to~the~WHICH to~him HOLDINGS the~LAND **27:25** and~ALL ARRANGEMENT~you$^{(ms)}$ he~will~EXIST$^{(V)}$ in~SHEQEL the~SPECIAL TEN~s GERAH he~will~EXIST$^{(V)}$ the~SHEQEL **27:26** SURELY FIRSTBORN WHICH he~

will~be~much~BE.FIRSTBORN⁽ᵛ⁾ to~**YHWH** in~BEAST NOT *he~will~make~*SET.APART⁽ᵛ⁾ MAN AT~him IF OX IF RAM to~**YHWH** HE   **27:27** and~IF in~the~BEAST the~DIRTY and~*he~did*~RANSOM⁽ᵛ⁾ in~ARRANGEMENT~you⁽ᵐˢ⁾ and~*he~will*~ADD⁽ᵛ⁾ FIVE~him UPON~him and~IF NOT *he~will~be~*REDEEM⁽ᵛ⁾ and~*he~did~be*~SELL⁽ᵛ⁾ in~ARRANGEMENT~you⁽ᵐˢ⁾   **27:28** SURELY ALL ASSIGNED WHICH *he~will~make*~ASSIGN⁽ᵛ⁾ MAN to~**YHWH** from~ALL WHICH to~him from~HUMAN and~BEAST and~from~FIELD HOLDINGS~him NOT *he~will~be*~SELL⁽ᵛ⁾ and~NOT *he~will~be~*REDEEM⁽ᵛ⁾ ALL ASSIGNED SPECIAL SPECIAL~s HE to~**YHWH**   **27:29** ALL ASSIGNED WHICH *he~will~be~make*~ASSIGN⁽ᵛ⁾ FROM the~HUMAN NOT *he~will~be~*RANSOM⁽ᵛ⁾ >~DIE⁽ᵛ⁾ *he~will~be~make*~DIE⁽ᵛ⁾   **27:30** and~ALL TENTH.PART the~LAND from~SEED the~LAND from~PRODUCE the~TREE to~**YHWH** HE SPECIAL to~**YHWH**   **27:31** and~IF >~REDEEM⁽ᵛ⁾ *he~will~*REDEEM⁽ᵛ⁾ MAN from~TENTH.PART~him FIVE~him *he~will~make*~ADD⁽ᵛ⁾ UPON~him   **27:32** and~ALL TENTH.PART CATTLE and~FLOCKS ALL WHICH *he~will*~CROSS.OVER⁽ᵛ⁾ UNDER the~STAFF the~TENTH *he~will*~EXIST⁽ᵛ⁾ SPECIAL to~**YHWH**   **27:33** NOT *he~will~much*~INVESTIGATE⁽ᵛ⁾ BETWEEN FUNCTIONAL to~the~DYSFUNCTIONAL and~NOT *he~will~make~*CONVERT⁽ᵛ⁾~him and~IF >~*make*~CONVERT⁽ᵛ⁾ *he~will~make*~CONVERT⁽ᵛ⁾~him and~*he~did*~EXIST⁽ᵛ⁾ HE and~EXCHANGE~him *he~will*~EXIST⁽ᵛ⁾ SPECIAL NOT *he~will~be~*REDEEM⁽ᵛ⁾   **27:34** THESE the~DIRECTIVE~s WHICH *he~did~much*~DIRECT⁽ᵛ⁾ **YHWH** AT Mosheh TO SON~s Yisra'eyl in~HILL Sinai

The Book of Leviticus

Benner's Mechanical Translation of the Torah

The Book of Numbers

Chapter 1

1:1 and~*he~will~much*~SPEAK$^{(V)}$ **YHWH** TO Mosheh in~WILDERNESS Sinai in~TENT APPOINTED in~UNIT to~the~NEW.MOON the~SECOND in~the~YEAR the~SECOND to~>~GO.OUT$^{(V)}$~them$^{(m)}$ from~LAND Mits'rayim to~>~SAY$^{(V)}$ **1:2** *l*$^{(mp)}$~LIFT.UP$^{(V)}$ AT HEAD ALL COMPANY SON~s Yisra'eyl to~CLAN~s~them$^{(m)}$ to~HOUSE FATHER~s~them$^{(m)}$ in~NUMBER TITLE~s ALL MALE to~SKULL~them$^{(m)}$ **1:3** from~SON TEN~s YEAR and~UPWARD~unto ALL GO.OUT$^{(V)}$~*ing*$^{(ms)}$ ARMY in~Yisra'eyl *you*$^{(mp)}$~*will*~REGISTER$^{(V)}$ AT~them$^{(m)}$ to~ARMY~s~them$^{(m)}$ YOU$^{(ms)}$ and~Aharon **1:4** and~AT~you$^{(mp)}$ *they*$^{(m)}$~*will*~EXIST$^{(V)}$ MAN MAN to~the~BRANCH MAN HEAD to~HOUSE FATHER~s~him HE **1:5** and~THESE TITLE~s the~MAN~s WHICH *they*$^{(m)}$~*will*~STAND$^{(V)}$ AT~you$^{(mp)}$ to~Re'uven Elitsur SON Shedeyur **1:6** to~Shimon Shelumi'eyl SON Tsurishaddai **1:7** to~Yehudah Nahhshon SON Amiynadav **1:8** to~Yis'sas'khar Nataneyl SON Tso'ar **1:9** to~Zevulun Eli'av SON Hheylon **1:10** to~SON~s Yoseph to~Ephrayim Elishama SON Amihud to~Menasheh Gamli'eyl SON Pedatsur **1:11** to~Binyamin Avidan SON Gidoni **1:12** to~Dan Ahhi'ezer SON Amishaddai **1:13** to~Asher Pagi'eyl SON Akhran **1:14** to~Gad Elyasaph SON De'u'eyl **1:15** to~Naphtali Ahhira SON Eynan **1:16** THESE SELECTED~s the~COMPANY CAPTAIN~s BRANCH FATHER~s~them$^{(m)}$ HEAD~s THOUSAND~s Yisra'eyl THEY$^{(m)}$ **1:17** and~*he~will*~TAKE$^{(V)}$ Mosheh and~Aharon AT the~MAN~s the~THESE WHICH *they~did~be*~PIERCE.THROUGH$^{(V)}$ in~TITLE~s **1:18** and~AT ALL the~COMPANY *they~did~make*~ASSEMBLE$^{(V)}$ in~UNIT to~the~NEW.MOON the~SECOND and~*they*$^{(m)}$~*will~make*~BRING.FORTH$^{(V)}$ UPON CLAN~s~them$^{(m)}$ to~HOUSE FATHER~s~them$^{(m)}$ in~NUMBER TITLE~s from~SON TEN~s YEAR and~UPWARD~unto to~SKULL~them$^{(m)}$ **1:19** like~WHICH *he~did~much~*DIRECT$^{(V)}$ **YHWH** AT Mosheh and~*he~will*~REGISTER$^{(V)}$~them$^{(m)}$ in~WILDERNESS Sinai **1:20** and~*they*$^{(m)}$~*will*~EXIST$^{(V)}$ SON~s Re'uven FIRSTBORN Yisra'eyl BIRTHING~s~them$^{(m)}$ to~CLAN~s~them$^{(m)}$ to~HOUSE FATHER~s~them$^{(m)}$ in~NUMBER TITLE~s to~SKULL~them$^{(m)}$ ALL MALE from~SON TEN~s YEAR and~UPWARD~unto ALL GO.OUT$^{(V)}$~*ing*$^{(ms)}$ ARMY **1:21** REGISTER$^{(V)}$~*ed*$^{(mp)}$~them$^{(m)}$ to~BRANCH Re'uven SIX and~FOUR~s THOUSAND and~FIVE HUNDRED~s **1:22** to~SON~s Shimon BIRTHING~s~them$^{(m)}$ to~CLAN~s~them$^{(m)}$ to~HOUSE FATHER~s~them$^{(m)}$ REGISTER$^{(V)}$~*ed*$^{(mp)}$~him in~NUMBER TITLE~s to~SKULL~them$^{(m)}$ ALL MALE from~SON TEN~s YEAR and~UPWARD~unto ALL GO.OUT$^{(V)}$~*ing*$^{(ms)}$ ARMY **1:23** REGISTER$^{(V)}$~*ed*$^{(mp)}$~them$^{(m)}$ to~BRANCH Shimon NINE and~FIVE~s THOUSAND and~THREE HUNDRED~s **1:24** to~SON~s Gad BIRTHING~s~them$^{(m)}$ to~CLAN~s~them$^{(m)}$ to~HOUSE FATHER~s~them$^{(m)}$ in~

The Book of Numbers

NUMBER TITLE~s from~SON TEN~s YEAR and~UPWARD~unto ALL GO.OUT$^{(V)}$~*ing*$^{(ms)}$ ARMY **1:25** REGISTER$^{(V)}$~*ed*$^{(mp)}$~them$^{(m)}$ to~BRANCH Gad FIVE and~FOUR~s THOUSAND and~SIX HUNDRED~s and~FIVE~s **1:26** to~SON~s Yehudah BIRTHING~s~them$^{(m)}$ to~CLAN~s~them$^{(m)}$ to~HOUSE FATHER~s~them$^{(m)}$ in~NUMBER TITLE~s from~SON TEN~s YEAR and~UPWARD~unto ALL GO.OUT$^{(V)}$~*ing*$^{(ms)}$ ARMY **1:27** REGISTER$^{(V)}$~*ed*$^{(mp)}$~them$^{(m)}$ to~BRANCH Yehudah FOUR and~SEVEN~s THOUSAND and~SIX HUNDRED~s **1:28** to~SON~s Yis'sas'khar BIRTHING~s~them$^{(m)}$ to~CLAN~s~them$^{(m)}$ to~HOUSE FATHER~s~them$^{(m)}$ in~NUMBER TITLE~s from~SON TEN~s YEAR and~UPWARD~unto ALL GO.OUT$^{(V)}$~*ing*$^{(ms)}$ ARMY **1:29** REGISTER$^{(V)}$~*ed*$^{(mp)}$~them$^{(m)}$ to~BRANCH Yis'sas'khar FOUR and~FIVE~s THOUSAND and~FOUR HUNDRED~s **1:30** to~SON~s Zevulun BIRTHING~s~them$^{(m)}$ to~CLAN~s~them$^{(m)}$ to~HOUSE FATHER~s~them$^{(m)}$ in~NUMBER TITLE~s from~SON TEN~s YEAR and~UPWARD~unto ALL GO.OUT$^{(V)}$~*ing*$^{(ms)}$ ARMY **1:31** REGISTER$^{(V)}$~*ed*$^{(mp)}$~them$^{(m)}$ to~BRANCH Zevulun SEVEN and~FIVE~s THOUSAND and~FOUR HUNDRED~s **1:32** to~SON~s Yoseph to~SON~s Ephrayim BIRTHING~s~them$^{(m)}$ to~CLAN~s~them$^{(m)}$ to~HOUSE FATHER~s~them$^{(m)}$ in~NUMBER TITLE~s from~SON TEN~s YEAR and~UPWARD~unto ALL GO.OUT$^{(V)}$~*ing*$^{(ms)}$ ARMY **1:33** REGISTER$^{(V)}$~*ed*$^{(mp)}$~them$^{(m)}$ to~BRANCH Ephrayim FOUR~s THOUSAND and~FIVE HUNDRED~s **1:34** to~SON~s Menasheh BIRTHING~s~them$^{(m)}$ to~CLAN~s~them$^{(m)}$ to~HOUSE FATHER~s~them$^{(m)}$ in~NUMBER TITLE~s from~SON TEN~s YEAR and~UPWARD~unto ALL GO.OUT$^{(V)}$~*ing*$^{(ms)}$ ARMY **1:35** REGISTER$^{(V)}$~*ed*$^{(mp)}$~them$^{(m)}$ to~BRANCH Menasheh TWO and~THREE~s THOUSAND and~HUNDRED~s2 **1:36** to~SON~s Binyamin BIRTHING~s~them$^{(m)}$ to~CLAN~s~them$^{(m)}$ to~HOUSE FATHER~s~them$^{(m)}$ in~NUMBER TITLE~s from~SON TEN~s YEAR and~UPWARD~unto ALL GO.OUT$^{(V)}$~*ing*$^{(ms)}$ ARMY **1:37** REGISTER$^{(V)}$~*ed*$^{(mp)}$~them$^{(m)}$ to~BRANCH Binyamin FIVE and~THREE~s THOUSAND and~FOUR HUNDRED~s **1:38** to~SON~s Dan BIRTHING~s~them$^{(m)}$ to~CLAN~s~them$^{(m)}$ to~HOUSE FATHER~s~them$^{(m)}$ in~NUMBER TITLE~s from~SON TEN~s YEAR and~UPWARD~unto ALL GO.OUT$^{(V)}$~*ing*$^{(ms)}$ ARMY **1:39** REGISTER$^{(V)}$~*ed*$^{(mp)}$~them$^{(m)}$ to~BRANCH Dan TWO and~SIX~s THOUSAND and~SEVEN HUNDRED~s **1:40** to~SON~s Asher BIRTHING~s~them$^{(m)}$ to~CLAN~s~them$^{(m)}$ to~HOUSE FATHER~s~them$^{(m)}$ in~NUMBER TITLE~s from~SON TEN~s YEAR and~UPWARD~unto ALL GO.OUT$^{(V)}$~*ing*$^{(ms)}$ ARMY **1:41** REGISTER$^{(V)}$~*ed*$^{(mp)}$~them$^{(m)}$ to~BRANCH Asher UNIT and~FOUR~s THOUSAND and~FIVE HUNDRED~s **1:42** SON~s Naphtali BIRTHING~s~them$^{(m)}$ to~CLAN~s~them$^{(m)}$ to~HOUSE FATHER~s~them$^{(m)}$ in~NUMBER TITLE~s from~SON TEN~s YEAR and~UPWARD~unto ALL GO.OUT$^{(V)}$~*ing*$^{(ms)}$ ARMY **1:43** REGISTER$^{(V)}$~*ed*$^{(mp)}$~them$^{(m)}$ to~BRANCH Naphtali THREE and~FIVE~s THOUSAND and~FOUR HUNDRED~s **1:44** THESE the~REGISTER$^{(V)}$~*ed*$^{(mp)}$ WHICH *he~did~*REGISTER$^{(V)}$ Mosheh and~Aharon and~CAPTAIN~s Yisra'eyl TWO TEN MAN MAN UNIT to~HOUSE FATHER~s~him *they~did~*EXIST$^{(V)}$ **1:45** and~*they*$^{(m)}$~*will~*EXIST$^{(V)}$ ALL REGISTER$^{(V)}$~*ed*$^{(mp)}$ SON~s Yisra'eyl to~HOUSE FATHER~s~them$^{(m)}$ from~SON TEN~s YEAR and~UPWARD~unto ALL GO.OUT$^{(V)}$~*ing*$^{(ms)}$

ARMY in~Yisra'eyl   **1:46** and~*they*⁽ᵐ⁾*~will~*EXIST⁽ⱽ⁾ ALL the~REGISTER⁽ⱽ⁾~ *ed*⁽ᵐᵖ⁾ SIX HUNDRED~s THOUSAND and~THREE THOUSAND~s and~FIVE HUNDRED~s and~FIVE~s   **1:47** and~the~Lewi~s to~BRANCH FATHER~s~ them⁽ᵐ⁾ NOT *they~did~self~*REGISTER⁽ⱽ⁾ in~MIDST~them⁽ᵐ⁾   **1:48** and~*he~ will~much~*SPEAK⁽ⱽ⁾ **YHWH** TO Mosheh to~>~SAY⁽ⱽ⁾   **1:49** SURELY AT BRANCH Lewi NOT *you*⁽ᵐˢ⁾*~will~*REGISTER⁽ⱽ⁾ and~AT HEAD~them⁽ᵐ⁾ NOT *you*⁽ᵐˢ⁾*~will~*LIFT.UP⁽ⱽ⁾ in~MIDST SON~s Yisra'eyl   **1:50** and~YOU⁽ᵐˢ⁾ *I*⁽ᵐˢ⁾*~ make~*REGISTER⁽ⱽ⁾ AT the~Lewi~s UPON DWELLING the~EVIDENCE and~ UPON ALL UTENSIL~s~him and~UPON ALL WHICH to~him THEY⁽ᵐ⁾ *they*⁽ᵐ⁾*~ will~*LIFT.UP⁽ⱽ⁾ AT the~DWELLING and~AT ALL UTENSIL~s~him and~THEY⁽ᵐ⁾ *they*⁽ᵐ⁾*~will~much~*MINISTER⁽ⱽ⁾*~*him and~ALL.AROUND to~the~DWELLING *they*⁽ᵐ⁾*~will~*CAMP⁽ⱽ⁾   **1:51** and~in~>~JOURNEY⁽ⱽ⁾ the~DWELLING *they*⁽ᵐ⁾*~ will~make~*GO.DOWN⁽ⱽ⁾ AT~him the~Lewi~s and~in~>~CAMP⁽ⱽ⁾ the~ DWELLING *they*⁽ᵐ⁾*~will~make~*RISE⁽ⱽ⁾ AT~him the~Lewi~s and~the~ BE.STRANGE⁽ⱽ⁾*~ing*⁽ᵐˢ⁾ the~INSIDE *he~will~be~make~*DIE⁽ⱽ⁾   **1:52** and~*they~ did~*CAMP⁽ⱽ⁾ SON~s Yisra'eyl MAN UPON CAMP~him and~MAN UPON BANNER~him to~ARMY~s~them⁽ᵐ⁾   **1:53** and~the~Lewi~s *they*⁽ᵐ⁾*~will~* CAMP⁽ⱽ⁾ ALL.AROUND to~DWELLING the~EVIDENCE and~NOT *he~will~* EXIST⁽ⱽ⁾ SPLINTER UPON COMPANY SON~s Yisra'eyl and~*they~did~* SAFEGUARD⁽ⱽ⁾ the~Lewi~s AT CHARGE DWELLING the~EVIDENCE   **1:54** and~ *they*⁽ᵐ⁾*~will~*DO⁽ⱽ⁾ SON~s Yisra'eyl like~ALL WHICH *he~did~much~*DIRECT⁽ⱽ⁾ **YHWH** AT Mosheh SO *they~did~*DO⁽ⱽ⁾

Chapter 2

2:1 and~*he~will~much~*SPEAK⁽ⱽ⁾ **YHWH** TO Mosheh and~TO Aharon to~>~ SAY⁽ⱽ⁾   **2:2** MAN UPON BANNER~him in~SIGN~s to~HOUSE FATHER~s~ them⁽ᵐ⁾ *they*⁽ᵐ⁾*~will~*CAMP⁽ⱽ⁾ SON~s Yisra'eyl from~OPPOSITE ALL.AROUND to~TENT APPOINTED *they*⁽ᵐ⁾*~will~*CAMP⁽ⱽ⁾   **2:3** and~the~CAMP⁽ⱽ⁾*~ing*⁽ᵐᵖ⁾ EAST~unto SUNRISE~unto BANNER CAMP Yehudah to~ARMY~s~them⁽ᵐ⁾ and~CAPTAIN to~SON~s Yehudah Nahhshon SON Amiynadav   **2:4** and~ ARMY~him and~REGISTER⁽ⱽ⁾*~ed*⁽ᵐᵖ⁾*~*them⁽ᵐ⁾ FOUR and~SEVEN~s THOUSAND and~SIX HUNDRED~s   **2:5** and~the~CAMP⁽ⱽ⁾*~ing*⁽ᵐᵖ⁾ UPON~him BRANCH Yis'sas'khar and~CAPTAIN to~SON~s Yis'sas'khar Nataneyl SON Tso'ar   **2:6** and~ARMY~him and~REGISTER⁽ⱽ⁾*~ed*⁽ᵐᵖ⁾*~*him FOUR and~FIVE~s THOUSAND and~FOUR HUNDRED~s   **2:7** BRANCH Zevulun and~CAPTAIN to~ SON~s Zevulun Eli'av SON Hheylon   **2:8** and~ARMY~him and~REGISTER⁽ⱽ⁾~ *ed*⁽ᵐᵖ⁾*~*him SEVEN and~FIVE~s THOUSAND and~FOUR HUNDRED~s   **2:9** ALL the~REGISTER⁽ⱽ⁾*~ed*⁽ᵐᵖ⁾ to~CAMP Yehudah HUNDRED THOUSAND and~ EIGHT~s THOUSAND and~SIX THOUSAND~s and~FOUR HUNDRED~s to~ ARMY~s~them⁽ᵐ⁾ FIRST *they*⁽ᵐ⁾*~will~*JOURNEY⁽ⱽ⁾   **2:10** BANNER CAMP Re'uven SOUTHWARD~unto to~ARMY~s~them⁽ᵐ⁾ and~CAPTAIN to~SON~s Re'uven Elitsur SON Shedeyur   **2:11** and~ARMY~him and~REGISTER⁽ⱽ⁾~

ed^(mp)~him SIX and~FOUR~s THOUSAND and~FIVE HUNDRED~s **2:12** and~ the~CAMP^((V))~*ing*^(mp) UPON~him BRANCH Shimon and~CAPTAIN to~SON~s Shimon Shelumi'eyl SON Tsurishaddai **2:13** and~ARMY~him and~ REGISTER^((V))~*ed*^(mp)~them^((m)) NINE and~FIVE~s THOUSAND and~THREE HUNDRED~s **2:14** and~BRANCH Gad and~CAPTAIN to~SON~s Gad Elyasaph SON Re'u'eyl **2:15** and~ARMY~him and~REGISTER^((V))~*ed*^(mp)~them^((m)) FIVE and~FOUR~s THOUSAND and~SIX HUNDRED~s and~FIVE~s **2:16** ALL the~ REGISTER^((V))~*ed*^(mp) to~CAMP Re'uven HUNDRED THOUSAND and~UNIT and~ FIVE~s THOUSAND and~FOUR HUNDRED~s and~FIVE~s to~ARMY~s~them^((m)) and~SECOND *they*^((m))~*will*~JOURNEY^((V)) **2:17** and~*he~did*~JOURNEY^((V)) TENT APPOINTED CAMP the~Lewi~s in~MIDST the~CAMP~s like~WHICH *they*^((m))~ *will*~CAMP^((V)) SO *they*^((m))~*will*~JOURNEY^((V)) MAN UPON HAND~him to~ BANNER~s~them^((m)) **2:18** BANNER CAMP Ephrayim to~ARMY~s~them^((m)) SEA~unto and~CAPTAIN to~SON~s Ephrayim Elishama SON Amihud **2:19** and~ARMY~him and~REGISTER^((V))~*ed*^(mp)~them^((m)) FOUR~s THOUSAND and~FIVE HUNDRED~s **2:20** and~UPON~him BRANCH Menasheh and~CAPTAIN to~SON~s Menasheh Gamli'eyl SON Pedatsur **2:21** and~ARMY~him and~REGISTER^((V))~*ed*^(mp)~them^((m)) TWO and~ THREE~s THOUSAND and~HUNDRED~s2 **2:22** and~BRANCH Binyamin and~ CAPTAIN to~SON~s Binyamin Avidan SON Gidoni **2:23** and~ARMY~him and~REGISTER^((V))~*ed*^(mp)~them^((m)) FIVE and~THREE~s THOUSAND and~FOUR HUNDRED~s **2:24** ALL the~REGISTER^((V))~*ed*^(mp) to~CAMP Ephrayim HUNDRED THOUSAND and~EIGHT THOUSAND~s and~HUNDRED to~ ARMY~s~them^((m)) and~THIRD~s *they*^((m))~*will*~JOURNEY^((V)) **2:25** BANNER CAMP Dan NORTH~unto to~ARMY~s~them^((m)) and~CAPTAIN to~SON~s Dan Ahhi'ezer SON Amishaddai **2:26** and~ARMY~him and~REGISTER^((V))~*ed*^(mp)~ them^((m)) TWO and~SIX~s THOUSAND and~SEVEN HUNDRED~s **2:27** and~ the~CAMP^((V))~*ing*^(mp) UPON~him BRANCH Asher and~CAPTAIN to~SON~s Asher Pagi'eyl SON Akhran **2:28** and~ARMY~him and~REGISTER^((V))~*ed*^(mp)~ them^((m)) UNIT and~FOUR~s THOUSAND and~FIVE HUNDRED~s **2:29** and~ BRANCH Naphtali and~CAPTAIN to~SON~s Naphtali Ahhira SON Eynan **2:30** and~ARMY~him and~REGISTER^((V))~*ed*^(mp)~them^((m)) THREE and~ FIVE~s THOUSAND and~FOUR HUNDRED~s **2:31** ALL the~REGISTER^((V))~*ed*^(mp) to~CAMP Dan HUNDRED THOUSAND and~SEVEN and~FIVE~s THOUSAND and~SIX HUNDRED~s to~the~LAST *they*^((m))~*will*~JOURNEY^((V)) to~BANNER~s~ them^((m)) **2:32** THESE REGISTER^((V))~*ed*^(mp) SON~s Yisra'eyl to~HOUSE FATHER~s~them^((m)) ALL REGISTER^((V))~*ed*^(mp) the~CAMP~s to~ARMY~s~them^((m)) SIX HUNDRED~s THOUSAND and~THREE THOUSAND~s and~FIVE HUNDRED~s and~FIVE~s **2:33** and~the~Lewi~s NOT *they~did~self~* REGISTER^((V)) in~MIDST SON~s Yisra'eyl like~WHICH *he~did~much~*DIRECT^((V)) **YHWH** AT Mosheh **2:34** and~*they*^((m))~*will*~DO^((V)) SON~s Yisra'eyl like~ALL WHICH *he~did~much~*DIRECT^((V)) **YHWH** AT Mosheh SO *they~did~*CAMP^((V)) to~ BANNER~s~them^((m)) and~SO *they~did~*JOURNEY^((V)) MAN to~CLAN~s~him UPON HOUSE FATHER~s~him

Chapter 3

3:1 and~THESE BIRTHING~s Aharon and~Mosheh in~DAY *he~did~much~* SPEAK$^{(V)}$ **YHWH** AT Mosheh in~HILL Sinai **3:2** and~THESE TITLE~s SON~s Aharon the~FIRSTBORN Nadav and~Aviyhu Elazar and~Iytamar **3:3** THESE TITLE~s SON~s Aharon the~ADMINISTRATOR~s the~SMEAR$^{(V)}$~*ed*$^{(mp)}$ WHICH *he~did~much~*FILL$^{(V)}$ HAND~them$^{(m)}$ to~>~*much~*ADORN$^{(V)}$ **3:4** and~*he~will~*DIE$^{(V)}$ Nadav and~Aviyhu to~FACE~s **YHWH** in~>~*make~*COME.NEAR$^{(V)}$~them$^{(m)}$ FIRE BE.STRANGE$^{(V)}$~*ing*$^{(fs)}$ to~FACE~s **YHWH** in~WILDERNESS Sinai and~SON~s NOT *they~did~*EXIST$^{(V)}$ to~them$^{(m)}$ and~*he~will~much~*ADORN$^{(V)}$ Elazar and~Iytamar UPON FACE~s Aharon FATHER~them$^{(m)}$ **3:5** and~*he~will~much~*SPEAK$^{(V)}$ **YHWH** TO Mosheh to~>~SAY$^{(V)}$ **3:6** !$^{(ms)}$~*make~*COME.NEAR$^{(V)}$ AT BRANCH Lewi and~*you*$^{(ms)}$~*did~make~*STAND$^{(V)}$ AT~him to~FACE~s Aharon the~ADMINISTRATOR and~*they~did~much~*MINISTER$^{(V)}$ AT~him **3:7** and~*they~did~*SAFEGUARD$^{(V)}$ AT CHARGE~him and~AT CHARGE ALL the~COMPANY to~FACE~s TENT APPOINTED to~>~SERVE$^{(V)}$ AT SERVICE the~DWELLING **3:8** and~*they~did~*SAFEGUARD$^{(V)}$ AT ALL UTENSIL~s TENT APPOINTED and~AT CHARGE SON~s Yisra'eyl to~>~SERVE$^{(V)}$ AT SERVICE the~DWELLING **3:9** and~*you*$^{(ms)}$~*did~*GIVE$^{(V)}$~& AT the~Lewi~s to~Aharon and~to~SON~s~him GIVE$^{(V)}$~*ed*$^{(mp)}$ GIVE$^{(V)}$~*ed*$^{(mp)}$ THEY$^{(m)}$ to~him from~AT SON~s Yisra'eyl **3:10** and~AT Aharon and~AT SON~s~him *you*$^{(ms)}$~*will~*REGISTER$^{(V)}$ and~*they~did~*SAFEGUARD$^{(V)}$ AT ADMINISTRATION~them$^{(m)}$ and~the~BE.STRANGE$^{(V)}$~*ing*$^{(ms)}$ the~INSIDE *he~will~be~make~*DIE$^{(V)}$ **3:11** and~*he~will~much~*SPEAK$^{(V)}$ **YHWH** TO Mosheh to~>~SAY$^{(V)}$ **3:12** and~I LOOK *I~did~*TAKE$^{(V)}$ AT the~Lewi~s from~MIDST SON~s Yisra'eyl UNDER ALL FIRSTBORN BURSTING BOWELS from~SON~s Yisra'eyl and~*they~did~*EXIST$^{(V)}$ to~me the~Lewi~s **3:13** GIVEN.THAT to~me ALL FIRSTBORN in~DAY >~*make~*HIT$^{(V)}$~me ALL FIRSTBORN in~LAND Mits'rayim *I~did~make~*SET.APART$^{(V)}$ to~me ALL FIRSTBORN in~Yisra'eyl from~HUMAN UNTIL BEAST to~me *they*$^{(m)}$~*will~*EXIST$^{(V)}$ I **YHWH** **3:14** and~*he~will~much~*SPEAK$^{(V)}$ **YHWH** TO Mosheh in~WILDERNESS Sinai to~>~SAY$^{(V)}$ **3:15** !$^{(ms)}$~REGISTER$^{(V)}$ AT SON~s Lewi to~HOUSE FATHER~s~them$^{(m)}$ to~CLAN~s~them$^{(m)}$ ALL MALE from~SON NEW.MOON and~UPWARD~unto *you*$^{(ms)}$~*will~*REGISTER$^{(V)}$~them$^{(m)}$ **3:16** and~*he~will~*REGISTER$^{(V)}$ AT~them$^{(m)}$ Mosheh UPON MOUTH **YHWH** like~WHICH *he~did~be~much~*DIRECT$^{(V)}$ **3:17** and~*they*$^{(m)}$~*will~*EXIST$^{(V)}$ THESE SON~s Lewi in~TITLE~s~them$^{(m)}$ Gershon and~Qehat and~Merari **3:18** and~THESE TITLE~s SON~s Gershon to~CLAN~s~them$^{(m)}$ Liyvniy and~Shiymiy **3:19** and~SON~s Qehat to~CLAN~s~them$^{(m)}$ Amram and~Yits'har Hhevron and~Uziy'eyl **3:20** and~SON~s Merari to~CLAN~s~them$^{(m)}$ Mahh'liy and~Mushiy THESE THEY$^{(m)}$ CLAN~s the~Lewi to~HOUSE FATHER~s~them$^{(m)}$ **3:21** to~Gershon CLAN the~Liyvniy and~CLAN the~Shiymiy THESE THEY$^{(m)}$ CLAN~s the~Gershon~of **3:22** REGISTER$^{(V)}$~*ed*$^{(mp)}$~them$^{(m)}$ in~NUMBER ALL MALE from~SON NEW.MOON and~UPWARD~unto REGISTER$^{(V)}$~*ed*$^{(mp)}$~them$^{(m)}$ SEVEN THOUSAND~s and~FIVE

The Book of Numbers

HUNDRED~s **3:23** CLAN~s the~Gershon~of AFTER the~DWELLING *they*⁽ᵐ⁾~ *will*~CAMP⁽ⱽ⁾ SEA~unto **3:24** and~CAPTAIN HOUSE FATHER to~the~ Gershon~of Elyasaph SON La'eyl **3:25** and~CHARGE SON~s Gershon in~ TENT APPOINTED the~DWELLING and~the~TENT ROOF.COVERING~him and~SCREEN OPENING TENT APPOINTED **3:26** and~SLING~s the~ COURTYARD and~AT SCREEN OPENING the~COURTYARD WHICH UPON the~ DWELLING and~UPON the~ALTAR ALL.AROUND and~AT STRING~s~him to~ ALL SERVICE~him **3:27** and~to~Qehat CLAN the~Amram~of and~CLAN the~ Yits'har~of and~CLAN the~Hhevron~of and~CLAN the~Uziy'eyl~of THESE THEY⁽ᵐ⁾ CLAN~s the~Qehat~of **3:28** in~NUMBER ALL MALE from~SON NEW.MOON and~UPWARD~unto EIGHT THOUSAND~s and~SIX HUNDRED~s SAFEGUARD⁽ⱽ⁾~*ing*⁽ᵐᵖ⁾ CHARGE the~SPECIAL **3:29** CLAN~s SON~s Qehat *they*⁽ᵐ⁾~*will*~CAMP⁽ⱽ⁾ UPON MIDSECTION the~DWELLING SOUTHWARD~ unto **3:30** and~CAPTAIN HOUSE FATHER to~CLAN~s the~Qehat~of Elitsaphan SON Uziy'eyl **3:31** and~CHARGE~them⁽ᵐ⁾ the~BOX and~the~ TABLE and~the~LAMPSTAND and~the~ALTAR~s and~UTENSIL~s the~ SPECIAL WHICH *they*⁽ᵐ⁾~*will*~much~MINISTER⁽ⱽ⁾ in~them⁽ᵐ⁾ and~the~ SCREEN and~ALL SERVICE~him **3:32** and~CAPTAIN CAPTAIN~s the~Lewi Elazar SON Aharon the~ADMINISTRATOR OVERSIGHT SAFEGUARD⁽ⱽ⁾~*ing*⁽ᵐᵖ⁾ CHARGE the~SPECIAL **3:33** to~Merari CLAN the~Mahh'liy and~CLAN the~ Mushiy THESE THEY⁽ᵐ⁾ CLAN~s Merari **3:34** and~REGISTER⁽ⱽ⁾~*ed*⁽ᵐᵖ⁾~them⁽ᵐ⁾ in~NUMBER ALL MALE from~SON NEW.MOON and~UPWARD~unto SIX THOUSAND~s and~HUNDRED~s2 **3:35** and~CAPTAIN HOUSE FATHER to~ CLAN~s Merari Tsuri'eyl SON Avihha'il UPON MIDSECTION the~DWELLING *they*⁽ᵐ⁾~*will*~CAMP⁽ⱽ⁾ NORTH~unto **3:36** and~OVERSIGHT CHARGE SON~s Merari BOARD~s the~DWELLING and~WOOD.BAR~s~him and~PILLAR~s~ him and~FOOTING~s~him and~ALL UTENSIL~s~him and~ALL SERVICE~ him **3:37** and~PILLAR~s the~COURTYARD ALL.AROUND and~FOOTING~s~ them⁽ᵐ⁾ and~TENT.PEG~s~them⁽ᵐ⁾ and~STRING~s~them⁽ᵐ⁾ **3:38** and~the~ CAMP⁽ⱽ⁾~*ing*⁽ᵐᵖ⁾ to~FACE~s the~DWELLING EAST~unto to~FACE~s TENT APPOINTED SUNRISE~unto Mosheh and~Aharon and~SON~s~him SAFEGUARD⁽ⱽ⁾~*ing*⁽ᵐᵖ⁾ CHARGE the~SANCTUARY to~CHARGE SON~s Yisra'eyl and~the~BE.STRANGE⁽ⱽ⁾~*ing*⁽ᵐˢ⁾ the~INSIDE *he*~*will*~*be*~*make*~ DIE⁽ⱽ⁾ **3:39** ALL REGISTER⁽ⱽ⁾~*ed*⁽ᵐᵖ⁾ the~Lewi~s WHICH *he*~*did*~REGISTER⁽ⱽ⁾ Mosheh and~Aharon UPON MOUTH **YHWH** to~CLAN~s~them⁽ᵐ⁾ ALL MALE from~SON NEW.MOON and~UPWARD~unto TWO and~TEN~s THOUSAND **3:40** and~*he*~*will*~SAY⁽ⱽ⁾ **YHWH** TO Mosheh *!*⁽ᵐˢ⁾~REGISTER⁽ⱽ⁾ ALL FIRSTBORN MALE to~SON~s Yisra'eyl from~SON NEW.MOON and~ UPWARD~unto and~ *!*⁽ᵐˢ⁾~LIFT.UP⁽ⱽ⁾ AT NUMBER TITLE~s~them⁽ᵐ⁾ **3:41** and~ *you*⁽ᵐˢ⁾~*did*~TAKE⁽ⱽ⁾ AT the~Lewi~s to~me I **YHWH** UNDER ALL FIRSTBORN in~SON~s Yisra'eyl and~AT BEAST the~Lewi~s UNDER ALL FIRSTBORN in~ BEAST SON~s Yisra'eyl **3:42** and~*he*~*will*~REGISTER⁽ⱽ⁾ Mosheh like~WHICH *he*~*did*~much~DIRECT⁽ⱽ⁾ **YHWH** AT~him AT ALL FIRSTBORN in~SON~s Yisra'eyl **3:43** and~*he*~*will*~EXIST⁽ⱽ⁾ ALL FIRSTBORN MALE in~NUMBER TITLE~s from~SON NEW.MOON and~UPWARD~unto to~REGISTER⁽ⱽ⁾~*ed*⁽ᵐᵖ⁾~

them⁽ᵐ⁾ TWO and~TEN~s THOUSAND THREE and~SEVEN~s and~HUNDRED~s2   **3:44** and~*he~will*~much~SPEAK⁽ⱽ⁾ **YHWH** TO Mosheh to~>~SAY⁽ⱽ⁾   **3:45** *!*⁽ᵐˢ⁾~TAKE⁽ⱽ⁾ AT the~Lewi~s UNDER ALL FIRSTBORN in~SON~s Yisra'eyl and~AT BEAST the~Lewi~s UNDER BEAST~them⁽ᵐ⁾ and~*they~did*~EXIST⁽ⱽ⁾ to~me the~Lewi~s I **YHWH**   **3:46** and~AT REDEEMED~s the~THREE and~the~SEVEN~s and~the~HUNDRED~s2 the~EXCEED⁽ⱽ⁾~*ing*⁽ᵐᵖ⁾ UPON the~Lewi~s from~FIRSTBORN SON~s Yisra'eyl   **3:47** and~*you*⁽ᵐˢ⁾~*did*~TAKE⁽ⱽ⁾ FIVE FIVE SHEQEL~s to~the~SKULL in~SHEQEL the~SPECIAL *you*⁽ᵐˢ⁾~*will*~TAKE⁽ⱽ⁾ TEN~s GERAH the~SHEQEL   **3:48** and~*you*⁽ᵐˢ⁾~*did*~GIVE⁽ⱽ⁾~& the~SILVER to~Aharon and~to~SON~s~him REDEEMED~s the~EXCEED⁽ⱽ⁾~*ing*⁽ᵐᵖ⁾ in~them⁽ᵐ⁾   **3:49** and~*he~will*~TAKE⁽ⱽ⁾ Mosheh AT SILVER the~RANSOM.PRICE from~AT the~EXCEED⁽ⱽ⁾~*ing*⁽ᵐᵖ⁾ UPON REDEEMED~s the~Lewi~s   **3:50** from~AT FIRSTBORN SON~s Yisra'eyl *he~did*~TAKE⁽ⱽ⁾ AT the~SILVER FIVE and~SIX~s and~THREE HUNDRED~s and~THOUSAND in~SHEQEL the~SPECIAL   **3:51** and~*he~will*~GIVE⁽ⱽ⁾ Mosheh AT SILVER the~REDEEMED~s to~Aharon and~to~SON~s~him UPON MOUTH **YHWH** like~WHICH *he~did*~much~DIRECT⁽ⱽ⁾ **YHWH** AT Mosheh

Chapter 4

4:1 and~*he~will*~much~SPEAK⁽ⱽ⁾ **YHWH** TO Mosheh and~TO Aharon to~>~SAY⁽ⱽ⁾   **4:2** >~LIFT.UP⁽ⱽ⁾ AT HEAD SON~s Qehat from~MIDST SON~s Lewi to~CLAN~s~them⁽ᵐ⁾ to~HOUSE FATHER~s~them⁽ᵐ⁾   **4:3** from~SON THREE~s YEAR and~UPWARD~unto and~UNTIL SON FIVE~s YEAR ALL *he~did*~COME⁽ⱽ⁾ to~the~ARMY to~>~DO⁽ⱽ⁾ BUSINESS in~TENT APPOINTED   **4:4** THIS SERVICE SON~s Qehat in~TENT APPOINTED SPECIAL the~SPECIAL~s   **4:5** and~*he~did*~COME⁽ⱽ⁾ Aharon and~SON~s~him in~>~JOURNEY⁽ⱽ⁾ the~CAMP and~*they~did*~make~GO.DOWN⁽ⱽ⁾ AT TENT.CURTAIN the~SCREEN and~*they*⁽ᵐ⁾~*did*~much~COVER.OVER⁽ⱽ⁾ in~her AT BOX the~EVIDENCE   **4:6** and~*they~did*~GIVE⁽ⱽ⁾ UPON~him OUTER.COVERING SKIN DEER and~*they~did*~SPREAD.OUT⁽ⱽ⁾ GARMENT ENTIRELY BLUE from~to~UPWARD~unto and~*they~did*~PLACE⁽ⱽ⁾ STRAND~s~him   **4:7** and~UPON TABLE the~FACE~s *they*⁽ᵐ⁾~*will*~SPREAD.OUT⁽ⱽ⁾ GARMENT BLUE and~*they~did*~GIVE⁽ⱽ⁾ UPON~him AT the~PLATTER~s and~AT the~PALM~s and~AT the~SACRIFICIAL.BOWL and~AT JUG the~POURING and~BREAD the~CONTINUALLY UPON~him *he~will*~EXIST⁽ⱽ⁾   **4:8** and~*they~did*~SPREAD.OUT⁽ⱽ⁾ UPON~them⁽ᵐ⁾ GARMENT KERMES SCARLET and~*they*⁽ᵐ⁾~*did*~much~COVER.OVER⁽ⱽ⁾ AT~him in~ROOF.COVERING SKIN DEER and~*they~did*~PLACE⁽ⱽ⁾ AT STRAND~s~him   **4:9** and~*they~did*~TAKE⁽ⱽ⁾ GARMENT BLUE and~*they*⁽ᵐ⁾~*did*~much~COVER.OVER⁽ⱽ⁾ AT LAMPSTAND the~LUMINARY and~AT LAMP~s~her and~AT TONG~s~her and~AT FIRE.PAN~s~her and~AT ALL UTENSIL~s OIL~her WHICH *they*⁽ᵐ⁾~*will*~much~MINISTER⁽ⱽ⁾ to~her in~them⁽ᵐ⁾   **4:10** and~*they~did*~GIVE⁽ⱽ⁾ AT~her and~AT ALL UTENSIL~s~her TO ROOF.COVERING SKIN

DEER and~they~did~GIVE[(V)] UPON the~BAR 4:11 and~UPON ALTAR the~ GOLD they[(m)]~will~SPREAD.OUT[(V)] GARMENT BLUE and~they[(m)]~did~much~ COVER.OVER[(V)] AT~him in~ROOF.COVERING SKIN DEER and~they~did~ PLACE[(V)] AT STRAND~s~him 4:12 and~they~did~TAKE[(V)] AT ALL UTENSIL~s the~MINISTRY WHICH they[(m)]~will~much~MINISTER[(V)] in~them[(m)] in~the~ SPECIAL and~they~did~GIVE[(V)] TO GARMENT BLUE and~they[(m)]~did~much~ COVER.OVER[(V)] AT~them[(m)] in~ROOF.COVERING SKIN DEER and~they~did~ GIVE[(V)] UPON the~BAR 4:13 and~they~did~much~MAKE.FAT[(V)] AT the~ ALTAR and~they~did~SPREAD.OUT[(V)] UPON~him GARMENT PURPLE 4:14 and~they~did~GIVE[(V)] UPON~him AT ALL UTENSIL~s~him WHICH they[(m)]~will~much~MINISTER[(V)] UPON~him in~them[(m)] AT the~ FIRE.PAN~s AT the~FORK~s and~AT the~SHOVEL~s and~AT the~ SPRINKLING.BASIN~s ALL UTENSIL~s the~ALTAR and~they~did~ SPREAD.OUT[(V)] UPON~him OUTER.COVERING SKIN DEER and~they~did~ PLACE[(V)] STRAND~s~him 4:15 and~he~did~much~FINISH[(V)] Aharon and~ SON~s~him to~>~much~COVER.OVER[(V)] AT the~SPECIAL and~AT ALL UTENSIL~s the~SPECIAL in~>~JOURNEY[(V)] the~CAMP and~AFTER SO they[(m)]~ will~COME[(V)] SON~s Qehat to~>~LIFT.UP[(V)] and~NOT they[(m)]~will~TOUCH[(V)] TO the~SPECIAL and~they~did~DIE[(V)] THESE LOAD SON~s Qehat in~TENT APPOINTED 4:16 and~OVERSIGHT Elazar SON Aharon the~ADMINISTRATOR OIL the~LUMINARY and~INCENSE.SMOKE the~AROMATIC.SPICE~s and~ DEPOSIT the~CONTINUALLY and~OIL the~OINTMENT OVERSIGHT ALL the~ DWELLING and~ALL WHICH in~him in~SPECIAL and~in~UTENSIL~s~ him 4:17 and~he~will~much~SPEAK[(V)] **YHWH** TO Mosheh and~TO Aharon to~>~SAY[(V)] 4:18 DO.NOT you[(mp)]~will~make~CUT[(V)] AT STAFF CLAN~s the~ Qehat~of from~MIDST the~Lewi~s 4:19 and~THIS ![(mp)]~DO[(V)] to~them[(m)] and~ ![(mp)]~LIVE[(V)] and~NOT they[(m)]~will~DIE[(V)] in~>~DRAW.NEAR[(V)]~them[(m)] AT SPECIAL the~SPECIAL~s Aharon and~SON~s~him they[(m)]~will~COME[(V)] and~they~did~PLACE[(V)] AT~them[(m)] MAN MAN UPON SERVICE~him and~TO LOAD~him 4:20 and~NOT they[(m)]~will~COME[(V)] to~>~SEE[(V)] like~>~much~ SWALLOW[(V)] AT the~SPECIAL and~they~did~DIE[(V)] 4:21 and~he~will~much~ SPEAK[(V)] **YHWH** TO Mosheh to~>~SAY[(V)] 4:22 >~LIFT.UP[(V)] AT HEAD SON~s Gershon ALSO THEY[(m)] to~HOUSE FATHER~s~them[(m)] to~CLAN~s~ them[(m)] 4:23 from~SON THREE~s YEAR and~UPWARD~unto UNTIL SON FIVE~s YEAR you[(ms)]~will~REGISTER[(V)] AT~them[(m)] ALL the~COME[(V)]~ing[(ms)] to~>~MUSTER[(V)] ARMY to~>~SERVE[(V)] SERVICE in~TENT APPOINTED 4:24 THIS SERVICE CLAN~s the~Gershon~of to~>~SERVE[(V)] and~to~LOAD 4:25 and~they~did~LIFT.UP[(V)] AT CURTAIN~s the~DWELLING and~AT TENT APPOINTED ROOF.COVERING~him and~ROOF.COVERING the~ DEER WHICH UPON~him from~to~UPWARD~unto and~AT SCREEN OPENING TENT APPOINTED 4:26 and~AT SLING~s the~COURTYARD and~AT SCREEN OPENING GATE the~COURTYARD WHICH UPON the~DWELLING and~UPON the~ALTAR ALL.AROUND and~AT STRING~s~them[(m)] and~AT ALL UTENSIL~s SERVICE~them[(m)] and~AT ALL WHICH he~will~be~DO[(V)] to~them[(m)] and~ they~did~SERVE[(V)] 4:27 UPON MOUTH Aharon and~SON~s~him she~will~

EXIST⁽ⱽ⁾ ALL SERVICE SON~s the~Gershon~of to~ALL LOAD~them⁽ᵐ⁾ and~to~ ALL SERVICE~them⁽ᵐ⁾ and~*you*⁽ᵐᵖ⁾~*did*~REGISTER⁽ⱽ⁾ UPON~them⁽ᵐ⁾ in~ CHARGE AT ALL LOAD~them⁽ᵐ⁾   **4:28** THIS SERVICE CLAN~s SON~s the~ Gershon~of in~TENT APPOINTED and~CHARGE~them⁽ᵐ⁾ in~HAND Iytamar SON Aharon the~ADMINISTRATOR   **4:29** SON~s Merari to~CLAN~s~them⁽ᵐ⁾ to~HOUSE FATHER~s~them⁽ᵐ⁾ *you*⁽ᵐˢ⁾~*will*~REGISTER⁽ⱽ⁾ AT~ them⁽ᵐ⁾   **4:30** from~SON THREE~s YEAR and~UPWARD~unto and~UNTIL SON FIVE~s YEAR *you*⁽ᵐˢ⁾~*will*~REGISTER⁽ⱽ⁾~them⁽ᵐ⁾ ALL the~COME⁽ⱽ⁾~*ing*⁽ᵐˢ⁾ to~the~ARMY to~>~SERVE⁽ⱽ⁾ AT SERVICE TENT APPOINTED   **4:31** and~THIS CHARGE LOAD~them⁽ᵐ⁾ to~ALL SERVICE~them⁽ᵐ⁾ in~TENT APPOINTED BOARD~s the~DWELLING and~WOOD.BAR~s~him and~PILLAR~s~him and~ FOOTING~s~him   **4:32** and~PILLAR~s the~COURTYARD ALL.AROUND and~ FOOTING~s~them⁽ᵐ⁾ and~TENT.PEG~s~them⁽ᵐ⁾ and~STRING~s~them⁽ᵐ⁾ to~ ALL UTENSIL~them⁽ᵐ⁾ and~to~ALL SERVICE~them⁽ᵐ⁾ and~in~TITLE~s *you*⁽ᵐᵖ⁾~ *will*~REGISTER⁽ⱽ⁾ AT UTENSIL~s CHARGE LOAD~them⁽ᵐ⁾   **4:33** THIS SERVICE CLAN~s SON~s Merari to~ALL SERVICE~them⁽ᵐ⁾ in~TENT APPOINTED in~ HAND Iytamar SON Aharon the~ADMINISTRATOR   **4:34** and~*he*~*will*~ REGISTER⁽ⱽ⁾ Mosheh and~Aharon and~CAPTAIN~s the~COMPANY AT SON~s the~Qehat~of to~CLAN~s~them⁽ᵐ⁾ and~to~HOUSE FATHER~s~ them⁽ᵐ⁾   **4:35** from~SON THREE~s YEAR and~UPWARD~unto and~UNTIL SON FIVE~s YEAR ALL the~COME⁽ⱽ⁾~*ing*⁽ᵐˢ⁾ to~the~ARMY to~the~SERVICE in~TENT APPOINTED   **4:36** and~*they*⁽ᵐ⁾~*will*~EXIST⁽ⱽ⁾ REGISTER⁽ⱽ⁾~*ed*⁽ᵐᵖ⁾~ them⁽ᵐ⁾ to~CLAN~s~them⁽ᵐ⁾ THOUSAND~s2 SEVEN HUNDRED~s and~ FIVE~s   **4:37** THESE REGISTER⁽ⱽ⁾~*ed*⁽ᵐᵖ⁾ CLAN~s the~Qehat~of ALL the~ SERVE⁽ⱽ⁾~*ing*⁽ᵐˢ⁾ in~TENT APPOINTED WHICH *he*~*did*~REGISTER⁽ⱽ⁾ Mosheh and~Aharon UPON MOUTH **YHWH** in~HAND Mosheh   **4:38** and~ REGISTER⁽ⱽ⁾~*ed*⁽ᵐᵖ⁾ SON~s Gershon to~CLAN~s~them⁽ᵐ⁾ and~to~HOUSE FATHER~s~them⁽ᵐ⁾   **4:39** from~SON THREE~s YEAR and~UPWARD~unto and~UNTIL SON FIVE~s YEAR ALL the~COME⁽ⱽ⁾~*ing*⁽ᵐˢ⁾ to~the~ARMY to~the~ SERVICE in~TENT APPOINTED   **4:40** and~*they*⁽ᵐ⁾~*will*~EXIST⁽ⱽ⁾ REGISTER⁽ⱽ⁾~ *ed*⁽ᵐᵖ⁾~them⁽ᵐ⁾ to~CLAN~s~them⁽ᵐ⁾ to~HOUSE FATHER~s~them⁽ᵐ⁾ THOUSAND~s2 and~SIX HUNDRED~s and~THREE~s   **4:41** THESE REGISTER⁽ⱽ⁾~*ed*⁽ᵐᵖ⁾ CLAN~s SON~s Gershon ALL the~SERVE⁽ⱽ⁾~*ing*⁽ᵐˢ⁾ in~TENT APPOINTED WHICH *he*~*did*~REGISTER⁽ⱽ⁾ Mosheh and~Aharon UPON MOUTH **YHWH**   **4:42** and~REGISTER⁽ⱽ⁾~*ed*⁽ᵐᵖ⁾ CLAN~s SON~s Merari to~CLAN~s~ them⁽ᵐ⁾ to~HOUSE FATHER~s~them⁽ᵐ⁾   **4:43** from~SON THREE~s YEAR and~ UPWARD~unto and~UNTIL SON FIVE~s YEAR ALL the~COME⁽ⱽ⁾~*ing*⁽ᵐˢ⁾ to~ the~ARMY to~the~SERVICE in~TENT APPOINTED   **4:44** and~*they*⁽ᵐ⁾~*will*~ EXIST⁽ⱽ⁾ REGISTER⁽ⱽ⁾~*ed*⁽ᵐᵖ⁾~them⁽ᵐ⁾ to~CLAN~s~them⁽ᵐ⁾ THREE THOUSAND~s and~HUNDRED~s2   **4:45** THESE REGISTER⁽ⱽ⁾~*ed*⁽ᵐᵖ⁾ CLAN~s SON~s Merari WHICH *he*~*did*~REGISTER⁽ⱽ⁾ Mosheh and~Aharon UPON MOUTH **YHWH** in~HAND Mosheh   **4:46** ALL the~REGISTER⁽ⱽ⁾~*ed*⁽ᵐᵖ⁾ WHICH *he*~*did*~REGISTER⁽ⱽ⁾ Mosheh and~Aharon and~CAPTAIN~s Yisra'eyl AT the~ Lewi~s to~CLAN~s~them⁽ᵐ⁾ and~to~HOUSE FATHER~s~them⁽ᵐ⁾   **4:47** from~ SON THREE~s YEAR and~UPWARD~unto and~UNTIL SON FIVE~s YEAR ALL the~COME$^{(V)}$~ing$^{(ms)}$ to~>~SERVE$^{(V)}$ SERVICE SERVICE and~SERVICE LOAD in~ TENT APPOINTED   **4:48**   and~*they$^{(m)}$~will*~EXIST$^{(V)}$ REGISTER$^{(V)}$~ed$^{(mp)}$~ them$^{(m)}$ EIGHT THOUSAND~s and~FIVE HUNDRED~s and~ EIGHT~s   **4:49**   UPON MOUTH **YHWH** *he~did*~REGISTER$^{(V)}$ AT~them$^{(m)}$ in~ HAND Mosheh MAN MAN UPON SERVICE~him and~UPON LOAD~him and~ REGISTER$^{(V)}$~ed$^{(mp)}$~him WHICH *he~did~much*~DIRECT$^{(V)}$ **YHWH** AT Mosheh

Chapter 5

5:1   and~*he~will~much*~SPEAK$^{(V)}$ **YHWH** TO Mosheh to~>~SAY$^{(V)}$ **5:2**   *!$^{(ms)}$~ much*~DIRECT$^{(V)}$ AT SON~s Yisra'eyl and~*they$^{(m)}$~will~much*~SEND$^{(V)}$ FROM the~CAMP ALL INFECT$^{(V)}$~ed$^{(ms)}$ and~ALL ISSUE$^{(V)}$~ing$^{(ms)}$ and~ALL DIRTY to~ the~SOUL   **5:3**   from~the~MALE UNTIL FEMALE *you$^{(mp)}$~will~much*~SEND$^{(V)}$ TO from~OUTSIDE to~the~CAMP *you$^{(mp)}$~will~much*~SEND$^{(V)}$~them$^{(m)}$ and~ NOT *they~will*~BE.DIRTY$^{(V)}$ AT CAMP~s~them$^{(m)}$ WHICH I DWELL$^{(V)}$~ing$^{(ms)}$ in~ MIDST~them$^{(m)}$ **5:4**   and~*they$^{(m)}$~will*~DO$^{(V)}$ SO SON~s Yisra'eyl and~*they$^{(m)}$~ will~much*~SEND$^{(V)}$ AT~them$^{(m)}$ TO from~OUTSIDE to~the~CAMP like~ WHICH *he~did~much*~SPEAK$^{(V)}$ **YHWH** TO Mosheh SO *they~did*~DO$^{(V)}$ SON~s Yisra'eyl   **5:5**   and~*he~will~much*~SPEAK$^{(V)}$ **YHWH** TO Mosheh to~>~ SAY$^{(V)}$ **5:6**   *!$^{(ms)}$~much*~SPEAK$^{(V)}$ TO SON~s Yisra'eyl MAN OR WOMAN GIVEN.THAT *they$^{(m)}$~will*~DO$^{(V)}$ from~ALL FAILURE~s the~HUMAN to~>~ TRANSGRESS$^{(V)}$ TRANSGRESSION in~**YHWH** and~*she~did*~BE.GUILTY$^{(V)}$ the~ SOUL the~SHE   **5:7**   and~*they~did~self*~THROW.THE.HAND$^{(V)}$ AT FAILURE~ them$^{(m)}$ WHICH *they~did*~DO$^{(V)}$ and~*he~did~make*~TURN.BACK$^{(V)}$ AT GUILT~ him in~HEAD~him and~FIFTH~him *he~will~make*~ADD$^{(V)}$ UPON~him and~ *he~did*~GIVE$^{(V)}$ to~the~WHICH *he~did*~BE.GUILTY$^{(V)}$ to~him   **5:8**   and~IF WITHOUT to~the~MAN REDEEM$^{(V)}$~ing$^{(ms)}$ to~>~*make*~TURN.BACK$^{(V)}$ the~ GUILT TO~him the~GUILT the~*be~make*~TURN.BACK$^{(V)}$~ing$^{(ms)}$ to~**YHWH** to~ the~ADMINISTRATOR from~to~STRAND BUCK the~ATONEMENT~s WHICH *he~will~much*~COVER$^{(V)}$ in~him UPON~him   **5:9**   and~ALL OFFERING to~ALL SPECIAL~s SON~s Yisra'eyl WHICH *they$^{(m)}$~will~make*~COME.NEAR$^{(V)}$ to~the~ ADMINISTRATOR to~him *he~will*~EXIST$^{(V)}$ **5:10**   and~MAN AT SPECIAL~s~ him to~him *they$^{(m)}$~will*~EXIST$^{(V)}$ MAN WHICH *he~will*~GIVE$^{(V)}$ to~the~ ADMINISTRATOR to~him *he~will*~EXIST$^{(V)}$ **5:11**   and~*he~will~much*~SPEAK$^{(V)}$ **YHWH** TO Mosheh to~>~SAY$^{(V)}$ **5:12**   *!$^{(ms)}$~much*~SPEAK$^{(V)}$ TO SON~s Yisra'eyl and~*you$^{(ms)}$~did*~SAY$^{(V)}$ TO~them$^{(m)}$ MAN MAN GIVEN.THAT *she~ will*~GO.ASIDE$^{(V)}$ WOMAN~him and~*she~did*~TRANSGRESS$^{(V)}$ in~him TRANSGRESSION   **5:13**   and~*he~did*~LIE.DOWN$^{(V)}$ MAN AT~her LYING.DOWN SEED and~*he~did~be*~BE.OUT.OF.SIGHT$^{(V)}$ from~EYE~s2 MAN~her and~*she~ did~be*~HIDE$^{(V)}$ and~SHE *she~did~be*~BE.DIRTY$^{(V)}$ and~WITNESS WITHOUT in~her and~SHE NOT *she~did~be*~SEIZE.HOLD$^{(V)}$ **5:14**   and~*he~did*~ CROSS.OVER$^{(V)}$ UPON~him WIND ZEALOUSNESS and~*he~did~much*~ BE.ZEALOUS$^{(V)}$ AT WOMAN~him and~SHE *she~did~be*~BE.DIRTY$^{(V)}$ OR *he~*

did~CROSS.OVER(V) UPON~him WIND ZEALOUSNESS and~he~did~much~ BE.ZEALOUS(V) AT WOMAN~him and~SHE NOT she~did~be~ BE.DIRTY(V)   **5:15**   and~he~did~make~COME(V) the~MAN AT WOMAN~him TO the~ADMINISTRATOR and~he~did~make~COME(V) AT DONATION~her UPON~her TENTH the~EYPHAH GRAIN.FLOUR BARLEY~s NOT he~will~ POUR.DOWN(V) UPON~him OIL and~NOT he~will~GIVE(V) UPON~him FRANKINCENSE GIVEN.THAT DEPOSIT ZEALOUSNESS~s HE DEPOSIT REMEMBRANCE make~REMEMBER(V)~ing(fs) TWISTEDNESS   **5:16**   and~he~ did~make~COME.NEAR(V) AT~her the~ADMINISTRATOR and~he~did~make~ STAND(V)~her to~FACE~s **YHWH**   **5:17**   and~he~did~TAKE(V) the~ ADMINISTRATOR WATER~s2 UNIQUE~s in~UTENSIL CLAY and~FROM the~ DIRT WHICH he~will~EXIST(V) in~BOTTOM the~DWELLING he~will~TAKE(V) the~ADMINISTRATOR and~he~did~GIVE(V) TO the~WATER~s2   **5:18**   and~ he~did~make~STAND(V) the~ADMINISTRATOR AT the~WOMAN to~FACE~s **YHWH** and~he~did~LOOSE(V) AT HEAD the~WOMAN and~he~did~GIVE(V) UPON PALM~s2~her AT DEPOSIT the~REMEMBRANCE DEPOSIT ZEALOUSNESS~s SHE and~in~HAND the~ADMINISTRATOR they(m)~will~ EXIST(V) WATER~s2 the~BITTER~s the~much~SPIT.UPON(V)~ ing(mp)   **5:19**   and~he~did~make~SWEAR(V) AT~her the~ADMINISTRATOR and~he~did~SAY(V) TO the~WOMAN IF NOT he~did~LIE.DOWN(V) MAN AT~ you(fs) and~IF NOT you(fs)~did~GO.ASIDE(V) DIRTY UNDER MAN~you(fs) I(fs)~ be~ACQUIT(V) from~WATER~s2 the~BITTER~s the~much~SPIT.UPON(V)~ ing(mp) the~THESE   **5:20**   and~YOU(fs) GIVEN.THAT you(fs)~did~GO.ASIDE(V) UNDER MAN~you(fs) and~GIVEN.THAT you(fs)~did~be~BE.DIRTY(V) and~he~ will~GIVE(V) MAN in~you(fs) AT COPULATION~him from~APART.FROM MAN~ you(fs)   **5:21**   and~he~did~make~SWEAR(V) the~ADMINISTRATOR AT the~ WOMAN in~SWEARING the~OATH and~he~did~SAY(V) the~ADMINISTRATOR to~WOMAN he~will~GIVE(V) **YHWH** AT~you(fs) to~OATH and~to~SWEARING in~MIDST PEOPLE~you(fs) in~>~GIVE(V) **YHWH** AT MIDSECTION~you(fs) FALL(V)~ing(fs) and~AT WOMB~you(fs) SWELLING   **5:22**   and~they~did~ COME(V) the~WATER~s2 the~much~SPIT.UPON(V)~ing(mp) the~THESE in~ ABDOMEN~s~you(ms) to~>~make~SWELL(V) WOMB and~to~>~make~FALL(V) MIDSECTION and~she~did~SAY(V) the~WOMAN SO.BE.IT SO.BE.IT   **5:23**   and~he~did~WRITE(V) AT the~OATH~s the~THESE the~ ADMINISTRATOR in~the~SCROLL and~he~did~WIPE.AWAY(V) TO WATER~s2 the~BITTER~s   **5:24**   and~he~did~make~DRINK(V) AT the~WOMAN AT WATER~s2 the~BITTER~s the~much~SPIT.UPON(V)~ing(mp) and~they~did~ COME(V) in~her the~WATER~s2 the~much~SPIT.UPON(V)~ing(mp) to~ BITTER~s   **5:25**   and~he~did~TAKE(V) the~ADMINISTRATOR from~HAND the~ WOMAN AT DEPOSIT the~ZEALOUSNESS~s and~he~did~WAVE(V) AT the~ DEPOSIT to~FACE~s **YHWH** and~he~did~make~COME.NEAR(V) AT~her TO the~ALTAR   **5:26**   and~he~did~GRASP(V) the~ADMINISTRATOR FROM the~ DEPOSIT AT MEMORIAL~her and~he~did~make~BURN.INCENSE(V) the~ ALTAR~unto and~AFTER he~will~make~DRINK(V) AT the~WOMAN AT the~ WATER~s2   **5:27**   and~he~did~make~DRINK(V)~her AT the~WATER~s2 and~

*she~did~*EXIST⁽ⱽ⁾ IF *she~did~be~*BE.DIRTY⁽ⱽ⁾ and~*she~will~*TRANSGRESS⁽ⱽ⁾ TRANSGRESSION in~MAN~her and~*they~did~*COME⁽ⱽ⁾ in~her the~WATER~s2 the~*much~*SPIT.UPON⁽ⱽ⁾*~ing*⁽ᵐᵖ⁾ to~BITTER~s and~*she~did~*SWELL⁽ⱽ⁾ WOMB~her and~*she~did~*FALL⁽ⱽ⁾ MIDSECTION~her and~*she~did~*EXIST⁽ⱽ⁾ the~WOMAN to~OATH in~INSIDE PEOPLE~her **5:28** and~IF NOT *she~did~be~*BE.DIRTY⁽ⱽ⁾ the~WOMAN and~CLEAN SHE and~*she~did~be~*ACQUIT⁽ⱽ⁾ and~*she~did~be~*SOW⁽ⱽ⁾ SEED **5:29** THIS TEACHING the~ZEALOUSNESS~s WHICH *she~will~*GO.ASIDE⁽ⱽ⁾ WOMAN UNDER MAN~her and~*she~did~be~*BE.DIRTY⁽ⱽ⁾ **5:30** OR MAN WHICH *she~will~*CROSS.OVER⁽ⱽ⁾ UPON~him WIND ZEALOUSNESS and~*he~did~much~*BE.ZEALOUS⁽ⱽ⁾ AT WOMAN~him and~*he~did~make~*STAND⁽ⱽ⁾ AT the~WOMAN to~FACE~s **YHWH** and~*he~did~*DO⁽ⱽ⁾ to~her the~ADMINISTRATOR AT ALL the~TEACHING the~THIS **5:31** and~*he~did~be~*ACQUIT⁽ⱽ⁾ the~MAN from~TWISTEDNESS and~the~WOMAN the~SHE *she~will~*LIFT.UP⁽ⱽ⁾ AT TWISTEDNESS~her

---

Chapter 6

6:1 and~*he~will~much~*SPEAK⁽ⱽ⁾ **YHWH** TO Mosheh to~>~SAY⁽ⱽ⁾ **6:2** *!*⁽ᵐˢ⁾*~much~*SPEAK⁽ⱽ⁾ TO SON~s Yisra'eyl and~*you*⁽ᵐˢ⁾*~did~*SAY⁽ⱽ⁾ TO~them⁽ᵐ⁾ MAN OR WOMAN GIVEN.THAT *he~will~make~*PERFORM⁽ⱽ⁾ to~MAKE.A.VOW⁽ⱽ⁾ VOW DEDICATED to~>~*make~*DEDICATE⁽ⱽ⁾ to~**YHWH** **6:3** from~WINE and~LIQUOR *he~will~make~*DEDICATE⁽ⱽ⁾ VINEGAR WINE and~VINEGAR LIQUOR NOT *he~will~*GULP⁽ⱽ⁾ and~ALL JUICE GRAPE~s NOT *he~will~*GULP⁽ⱽ⁾ and~GRAPE~s MOIST~s and~DRY~s NOT *he~will~*EAT⁽ⱽ⁾ **6:4** ALL DAY~s DEDICATION~him from~ALL WHICH *he~will~be~*DO⁽ⱽ⁾ from~GRAPEVINE the~WINE from~KERNEL~s and~UNTIL GRAPE.SKIN NOT *he~will~*EAT⁽ⱽ⁾ **6:5** ALL DAY~s VOW DEDICATION~him RAZOR NOT *he~will~*CROSS.OVER⁽ⱽ⁾ UPON HEAD~him UNTIL >~FILL⁽ⱽ⁾ the~DAY~s WHICH *he~will~make~*DEDICATE⁽ⱽ⁾ to~**YHWH** UNIQUE *he~will~*EXIST⁽ⱽ⁾ >~*much~*MAGNIFY⁽ⱽ⁾ LONG.HAIR HAIR HEAD~him **6:6** ALL DAY~s >~*make~*DEDICATE⁽ⱽ⁾~him to~**YHWH** UPON SOUL DIE⁽ⱽ⁾*~ing*⁽ᵐˢ⁾ NOT *he~will~*COME⁽ⱽ⁾ **6:7** to~FATHER~him and~to~MOTHER~him to~BROTHER~him and~to~SISTER~him NOT *he~will~*BE.DIRTY⁽ⱽ⁾ to~them⁽ᵐ⁾ in~DEATH~them⁽ᵐ⁾ GIVEN.THAT DEDICATION Elohiym~him UPON HEAD~him **6:8** ALL DAY~s DEDICATION~him UNIQUE HE to~**YHWH** **6:9** and~GIVEN.THAT *he~will~*DIE⁽ⱽ⁾ DIE⁽ⱽ⁾*~ing*⁽ᵐˢ⁾ UPON~him in~INSTANT SUDDENLY and~*he~did~much~*BE.DIRTY⁽ⱽ⁾ HEAD DEDICATION~him and~*he~did~much~*SHAVE⁽ⱽ⁾ HEAD~him in~DAY CLEAN~him in~the~DAY the~SEVENTH *he~will~much~*SHAVE⁽ⱽ⁾~him **6:10** and~in~the~DAY the~EIGHTH *he~will~make~*COME⁽ⱽ⁾ TWO TURTLEDOVE~s OR TWO SON~s DOVE TO the~ADMINISTRATOR TO OPENING TENT APPOINTED **6:11** and~*he~did~*DO⁽ⱽ⁾ the~ADMINISTRATOR UNIT to~FAILURE and~UNIT to~ASCENSION.OFFERING and~*he~did~much~*COVER⁽ⱽ⁾ UPON~him from~WHICH *he~did~*FAIL⁽ⱽ⁾ UPON the~SOUL and~*he~did~much~*SET.APART⁽ⱽ⁾ AT

HEAD~him in~the~DAY the~HE **6:12** and~*he~did~make*~DEDICATE$^{(V)}$ to~**YHWH** AT DAY~s DEDICATION~him and~*he~did~make*~COME$^{(V)}$ SHEEP SON YEAR~him to~GUILT and~the~DAY~s the~FIRST~s they$^{(m)}$~*will*~FALL$^{(V)}$ GIVEN.THAT DIRTY DEDICATION~him **6:13** and~THIS TEACHING the~DEDICATED in~DAY >~FILL$^{(V)}$ DAY~s DEDICATION~him *he~will~make*~COME$^{(V)}$ AT~him TO OPENING TENT APPOINTED **6:14** and~*he~did~make*~COME.NEAR$^{(V)}$ AT DONATION~him to~**YHWH** SHEEP SON YEAR~him WHOLE UNIT to~ASCENSION.OFFERING and~SHEEP UNIT DAUGHTER YEAR~her WHOLE to~FAILURE and~BUCK UNIT WHOLE to~OFFERING.OF.RESTITUTION~s **6:15** and~WICKER.BASKET UNLEAVENED.BREAD~s FLOUR PIERCED.BREAD~s MIX$^{(V)}$~*ed*$^{(fp)}$ in~the~OIL and~THIN.BREAD~s UNLEAVENED.BREAD~s SMEAR$^{(V)}$~*ed*$^{(mp)}$ in~the~OIL and~DEPOSIT~them$^{(m)}$ and~POURING~s~them$^{(m)}$ **6:16** and~*he~did~make*~COME.NEAR$^{(V)}$ the~ADMINISTRATOR to~FACE~s **YHWH** and~*he~did*~DO$^{(V)}$ AT FAILURE~him and~AT ASCENSION.OFFERING~him **6:17** and~AT the~BUCK *he~will*~DO$^{(V)}$ SACRIFICE OFFERING.OF.RESTITUTION~s to~**YHWH** UPON WICKER.BASKET the~UNLEAVENED.BREAD~s and~*he~did*~DO$^{(V)}$ the~ADMINISTRATOR AT DEPOSIT~him and~AT POURING~him **6:18** and~*he~did~much*~SHAVE$^{(V)}$ the~DEDICATED OPENING TENT APPOINTED AT HEAD DEDICATION~him and~*he~did*~TAKE$^{(V)}$ AT HAIR HEAD DEDICATION~him and~*he~did*~GIVE$^{(V)}$ UPON the~FIRE WHICH UNDER SACRIFICE the~OFFERING.OF.RESTITUTION~s **6:19** and~*he~did*~TAKE$^{(V)}$ the~ADMINISTRATOR AT the~ARM in~BOILED FROM the~BUCK and~PIERCED.BREAD UNLEAVENED.BREAD UNIT FROM the~WICKER.BASKET and~THIN.BREAD UNLEAVENED.BREAD UNIT and~*he~did*~GIVE$^{(V)}$ UPON PALM~s2 the~DEDICATED AFTER *he~did~self*~SHAVE$^{(V)}$~him AT DEDICATION~him **6:20** and~*he~did*~WAVE$^{(V)}$ AT~them$^{(m)}$ the~ADMINISTRATOR WAVING to~FACE~s **YHWH** SPECIAL HE to~the~ADMINISTRATOR UPON CHEST the~WAVING and~UPON THIGH the~OFFERING and~AFTER *he~will*~GULP$^{(V)}$ the~DEDICATED WINE **6:21** THIS TEACHING the~DEDICATED WHICH *he~will*~MAKE.A.VOW$^{(V)}$ DONATION~him to~**YHWH** UPON DEDICATION~him from~to~STRAND WHICH *she~will~make*~OVERTAKE$^{(V)}$ HAND~him like~MOUTH VOW~him WHICH *he~will*~MAKE.A.VOW$^{(V)}$ SO *he~will*~DO$^{(V)}$ UPON TEACHING DEDICATION~him **6:22** and~*he~will~much*~SPEAK$^{(V)}$ **YHWH** TO Mosheh to~>~SAY$^{(V)}$ **6:23** !$^{(ms)}$~*much*~SPEAK$^{(V)}$ TO Aharon and~TO SON~s~him to~>~SAY$^{(V)}$ IN.THIS.WAY you$^{(mp)}$~*will~much*~KNEEL$^{(V)}$ AT SON~s Yisra'eyl >~SAY$^{(V)}$ to~them$^{(m)}$ **6:24** *he~will~much*~KNEEL$^{(V)}$~you$^{(ms)}$ **YHWH** and~*he~will*~SAFEGUARD$^{(V)}$~you$^{(ms)}$ **6:25** *he~will~make*~LIGHT$^{(V)}$ **YHWH** FACE~s~him TO~you$^{(ms)}$ and~*he~will*~PROVIDE.PROTECTION$^{(V)}$~you$^{(ms)}$ **6:26** *he~will*~LIFT.UP$^{(V)}$ **YHWH** FACE~s~him TO~you$^{(ms)}$ and~*he~will*~PLACE$^{(V)}$ to~you$^{(ms)}$ COMPLETENESS **6:27** and~*they~did*~PLACE$^{(V)}$ AT TITLE~me UPON SON~s Yisra'eyl and~I *I~will~much*~KNEEL$^{(V)}$~them$^{(m)}$

Chapter 7

7:1 and~*he~will*~EXIST$^{(V)}$ in~DAY >~*much*~FINISH$^{(V)}$ Mosheh to~>~*make*~ RISE$^{(V)}$ AT the~DWELLING and~*he~will*~SMEAR$^{(V)}$ AT~him and~*he~will*~ *much*~SET.APART$^{(V)}$ AT~him and~AT ALL UTENSIL~s~him and~AT the~ALTAR and~AT ALL UTENSIL~s~him and~*he~will*~SMEAR$^{(V)}$~them$^{(m)}$ and~*he~will*~ *much*~SET.APART$^{(V)}$ AT~them$^{(m)}$ **7:2** and~*they*$^{(m)}$~*will*~*make*~COME.NEAR$^{(V)}$ CAPTAIN~s Yisra'eyl HEAD~s HOUSE FATHER~s~them$^{(m)}$ THEY$^{(m)}$ CAPTAIN~s the~BRANCH~s THEY$^{(m)}$ the~STAND$^{(V)}$~*ing*$^{(mp)}$ UPON the~REGISTER$^{(V)}$~ *ed*$^{(mp)}$ **7:3** and~*they*$^{(m)}$~*will*~*make*~COME$^{(V)}$ AT DONATION~them$^{(m)}$ to~ FACE~s **YHWH** SIX CART~s COVERED and~TWO TEN CATTLE CART UPON TWO the~CAPTAIN~s and~OX to~UNIT and~*they*$^{(m)}$~*will*~*make*~ COME.NEAR$^{(V)}$ AT~them$^{(m)}$ to~FACE~s the~DWELLING **7:4** and~*he~will*~ SAY$^{(V)}$ **YHWH** TO Mosheh to~>~SAY$^{(V)}$ **7:5** *I*$^{(ms)}$~TAKE$^{(V)}$ from~AT~them$^{(m)}$ and~*they~did*~EXIST$^{(V)}$ to~>~SERVE$^{(V)}$ AT SERVICE TENT APPOINTED and~ *you*$^{(ms)}$~*did*~GIVE$^{(V)}$~& AT~them$^{(m)}$ TO the~Lewi~s MAN like~MOUTH SERVICE~him **7:6** and~*he~will*~TAKE$^{(V)}$ Mosheh AT the~CART~s and~AT the~CATTLE and~*he~will*~GIVE$^{(V)}$ AT~them$^{(m)}$ TO the~Lewi~s **7:7** AT TWO the~CART~s and~AT FOUR the~CATTLE *he~did*~GIVE$^{(V)}$ to~SON~s Gershon like~MOUTH SERVICE~them$^{(m)}$ **7:8** and~AT FOUR the~CART~s and~AT EIGHT the~CATTLE *he~did*~GIVE$^{(V)}$ to~SON~s Merari like~MOUTH SERVICE~ them$^{(m)}$ in~HAND Iytamar SON Aharon the~ADMINISTRATOR **7:9** and~to~ SON~s Qehat NOT *he~did*~GIVE$^{(V)}$ GIVEN.THAT SERVICE the~SPECIAL UPON~ them$^{(m)}$ in~the~SHOULDER.PIECE *they*$^{(m)}$~*will*~LIFT.UP$^{(V)}$ **7:10** and~*they*$^{(m)}$~ *will*~*make*~COME.NEAR$^{(V)}$ the~CAPTAIN~s AT DEVOTION the~ALTAR in~DAY >~*be*~SMEAR$^{(V)}$ AT~him and~*they*$^{(m)}$~*will*~*make*~COME.NEAR$^{(V)}$ the~ CAPTAIN~s AT DONATION~them$^{(m)}$ to~FACE~s the~ALTAR **7:11** and~*he~ will*~SAY$^{(V)}$ **YHWH** TO Mosheh CAPTAIN UNIT to~the~DAY CAPTAIN UNIT to~ the~DAY *they*$^{(m)}$~*will*~*make*~COME.NEAR$^{(V)}$ AT DONATION~them$^{(m)}$ to~the~ DEVOTION the~ALTAR **7:12** and~*he~will*~EXIST$^{(V)}$ the~*make*~ COME.NEAR$^{(V)}$~*ing*$^{(ms)}$ in~the~DAY the~FIRST AT DONATION~him Nahhshon SON Amiynadav to~BRANCH Yehudah **7:13** and~DONATION~him PLATTER SILVER UNIT THREE~s and~HUNDRED WEIGHT~her SPRINKLING.BASIN UNIT SILVER SEVEN~s SHEQEL in~SHEQEL the~SPECIAL TWO~them$^{(m)}$ FULL~s FLOUR MIX$^{(V)}$~*ed*$^{(fs)}$ in~the~OIL to~DEPOSIT **7:14** PALM UNIT TEN GOLD FULL INCENSE.SMOKE **7:15** BULL UNIT SON CATTLE BUCK UNIT SHEEP UNIT SON YEAR~him to~ASCENSION.OFFERING **7:16** HAIRY.GOAT SHE-GOAT~s UNIT to~FAILURE **7:17** and~to~SACRIFICE the~ OFFERING.OF.RESTITUTION~s CATTLE TWO BUCK~s FIVE MALE.GOAT~s FIVE SHEEP~s SON~s YEAR FIVE THIS DONATION Nahhshon SON Amiynadav **7:18** in~the~DAY the~SECOND *he~did*~*make*~COME.NEAR$^{(V)}$ Nataneyl SON Tso'ar CAPTAIN Yis'sas'khar **7:19** *he~did*~*make*~ COME.NEAR$^{(V)}$ AT DONATION~him PLATTER SILVER UNIT THREE~s and~ HUNDRED WEIGHT~her SPRINKLING.BASIN UNIT SILVER SEVEN~s SHEQEL in~SHEQEL the~SPECIAL TWO~them[(m)] FULL~s FLOUR MIX[(V)]~ed[(fs)] in~the~ OIL to~DEPOSIT   **7:20** PALM UNIT TEN GOLD FULL INCENSE.SMOKE   **7:21** BULL UNIT SON CATTLE BUCK UNIT SHEEP UNIT SON YEAR~him to~ASCENSION.OFFERING   **7:22** HAIRY.GOAT SHE-GOAT~s UNIT to~FAILURE   **7:23** and~to~SACRIFICE the~OFFERING.OF.RESTITUTION~s CATTLE TWO BUCK~s FIVE MALE.GOAT~s FIVE SHEEP~s SON~s YEAR FIVE THIS DONATION Nataneyl SON Tso'ar   **7:24** in~the~DAY the~THIRD CAPTAIN to~SON~s Zevulun Eli'av SON Hheylon   **7:25** DONATION~him PLATTER SILVER UNIT THREE~s and~HUNDRED WEIGHT~her SPRINKLING.BASIN UNIT SILVER SEVEN~s SHEQEL in~SHEQEL the~SPECIAL TWO~them[(m)] FULL~s FLOUR MIX[(V)]~ed[(fs)] in~the~OIL to~DEPOSIT   **7:26** PALM UNIT TEN GOLD FULL INCENSE.SMOKE   **7:27** BULL UNIT SON CATTLE BUCK UNIT SHEEP UNIT SON YEAR~him to~ASCENSION.OFFERING   **7:28** HAIRY.GOAT SHE-GOAT~s UNIT to~FAILURE   **7:29** and~to~SACRIFICE the~OFFERING.OF.RESTITUTION~s CATTLE TWO BUCK~s FIVE MALE.GOAT~s FIVE SHEEP~s SON~s YEAR FIVE THIS DONATION Eli'av SON Hheylon   **7:30** in~the~DAY the~FOURTH CAPTAIN to~SON~s Re'uven Elitsur SON Shedeyur   **7:31** DONATION~him PLATTER SILVER UNIT THREE~s and~HUNDRED WEIGHT~her SPRINKLING.BASIN UNIT SILVER SEVEN~s SHEQEL in~SHEQEL the~SPECIAL TWO~them[(m)] FULL~s FLOUR MIX[(V)]~ed[(fs)] in~the~OIL to~DEPOSIT   **7:32** PALM UNIT TEN GOLD FULL INCENSE.SMOKE   **7:33** BULL UNIT SON CATTLE BUCK UNIT SHEEP UNIT SON YEAR~him to~ASCENSION.OFFERING   **7:34** HAIRY.GOAT SHE-GOAT~s UNIT to~FAILURE   **7:35** and~to~SACRIFICE the~OFFERING.OF.RESTITUTION~s CATTLE TWO BUCK~s FIVE MALE.GOAT~s FIVE SHEEP~s SON~s YEAR FIVE THIS DONATION Elitsur SON Shedeyur   **7:36** in~the~DAY the~FIFTH CAPTAIN to~SON~s Shimon Shelumi'eyl SON Tsurishaddai   **7:37** DONATION~him PLATTER SILVER UNIT THREE~s and~HUNDRED WEIGHT~her SPRINKLING.BASIN UNIT SILVER SEVEN~s SHEQEL in~SHEQEL the~SPECIAL TWO~them[(m)] FULL~s FLOUR MIX[(V)]~ed[(fs)] in~the~OIL to~DEPOSIT   **7:38** PALM UNIT TEN GOLD FULL INCENSE.SMOKE   **7:39** BULL UNIT SON CATTLE BUCK UNIT SHEEP UNIT SON YEAR~him to~ASCENSION.OFFERING   **7:40** HAIRY.GOAT SHE-GOAT~s UNIT to~FAILURE   **7:41** and~to~SACRIFICE the~OFFERING.OF.RESTITUTION~s CATTLE TWO BUCK~s FIVE MALE.GOAT~s FIVE SHEEP~s SON~s YEAR FIVE THIS DONATION Shelumi'eyl SON Tsurishaddai   **7:42** in~the~DAY the~SIXTH CAPTAIN to~SON~s Gad Elyasaph SON De'u'eyl   **7:43** DONATION~him PLATTER SILVER UNIT THREE~s and~HUNDRED WEIGHT~her SPRINKLING.BASIN UNIT SILVER SEVEN~s SHEQEL in~SHEQEL the~SPECIAL TWO~them[(m)] FULL~s FLOUR MIX[(V)]~ed[(fs)] in~the~OIL to~DEPOSIT   **7:44** PALM UNIT TEN GOLD FULL INCENSE.SMOKE   **7:45** BULL UNIT SON CATTLE BUCK UNIT SHEEP UNIT SON YEAR~him to~ASCENSION.OFFERING   **7:46** HAIRY.GOAT SHE-GOAT~s UNIT to~FAILURE   **7:47** and~to~SACRIFICE the~OFFERING.OF.RESTITUTION~s CATTLE TWO BUCK~s FIVE MALE.GOAT~s FIVE SHEEP~s SON~s YEAR FIVE THIS

The Book of Numbers

DONATION Elyasaph SON De'u'eyl **7:48** in~the~DAY the~SEVENTH CAPTAIN to~SON~s Ephrayim Elishama SON Amihud **7:49** DONATION~him PLATTER SILVER UNIT THREE~s and~HUNDRED WEIGHT~her SPRINKLING.BASIN UNIT SILVER SEVEN~s SHEQEL in~SHEQEL the~SPECIAL TWO~them$^{(m)}$ FULL~s FLOUR MIX$^{(V)}$~ed$^{(fs)}$ in~the~OIL to~DEPOSIT **7:50** PALM UNIT TEN GOLD FULL INCENSE.SMOKE **7:51** BULL UNIT SON CATTLE BUCK UNIT SHEEP UNIT SON YEAR~him to~ASCENSION.OFFERING **7:52** HAIRY.GOAT SHE-GOAT~s UNIT to~FAILURE **7:53** and~to~SACRIFICE the~OFFERING.OF.RESTITUTION~s CATTLE TWO BUCK~s FIVE MALE.GOAT~s FIVE SHEEP~s SON~s YEAR FIVE THIS DONATION Elishama SON Amihud **7:54** in~the~DAY the~EIGHTH CAPTAIN to~SON~s Menasheh Gamli'eyl SON Pedatsur **7:55** DONATION~him PLATTER SILVER UNIT THREE~s and~HUNDRED WEIGHT~her SPRINKLING.BASIN UNIT SILVER SEVEN~s SHEQEL in~SHEQEL the~SPECIAL TWO~them$^{(m)}$ FULL~s FLOUR MIX$^{(V)}$~ed$^{(fs)}$ in~the~OIL to~DEPOSIT **7:56** PALM UNIT TEN GOLD FULL INCENSE.SMOKE **7:57** BULL UNIT SON CATTLE BUCK UNIT SHEEP UNIT SON YEAR~him to~ASCENSION.OFFERING **7:58** HAIRY.GOAT SHE-GOAT~s UNIT to~FAILURE **7:59** and~to~SACRIFICE the~OFFERING.OF.RESTITUTION~s CATTLE TWO BUCK~s FIVE MALE.GOAT~s FIVE SHEEP~s SON~s YEAR FIVE THIS DONATION Gamli'eyl SON Pedatsur **7:60** in~the~DAY the~NINTH CAPTAIN to~SON~s Binyamin Avidan SON Gidoni **7:61** DONATION~him PLATTER SILVER UNIT THREE~s and~HUNDRED WEIGHT~her SPRINKLING.BASIN UNIT SILVER SEVEN~s SHEQEL in~SHEQEL the~SPECIAL TWO~them$^{(m)}$ FULL~s FLOUR MIX$^{(V)}$~ed$^{(fs)}$ in~the~OIL to~DEPOSIT **7:62** PALM UNIT TEN GOLD FULL INCENSE.SMOKE **7:63** BULL UNIT SON CATTLE BUCK UNIT SHEEP UNIT SON YEAR~him to~ASCENSION.OFFERING **7:64** HAIRY.GOAT SHE-GOAT~s UNIT to~FAILURE **7:65** and~to~SACRIFICE the~OFFERING.OF.RESTITUTION~s CATTLE TWO BUCK~s FIVE MALE.GOAT~s FIVE SHEEP~s SON~s YEAR FIVE THIS DONATION Avidan SON Gidoni **7:66** in~the~DAY the~TENTH CAPTAIN to~SON~s Dan Ahhi'ezer SON Amishaddai **7:67** DONATION~him PLATTER SILVER UNIT THREE~s and~HUNDRED WEIGHT~her SPRINKLING.BASIN UNIT SILVER SEVEN~s SHEQEL in~SHEQEL the~SPECIAL TWO~them$^{(m)}$ FULL~s FLOUR MIX$^{(V)}$~ed$^{(fs)}$ in~the~OIL to~DEPOSIT **7:68** PALM UNIT TEN GOLD FULL INCENSE.SMOKE **7:69** BULL UNIT SON CATTLE BUCK UNIT SHEEP UNIT SON YEAR~him to~ASCENSION.OFFERING **7:70** HAIRY.GOAT SHE-GOAT~s UNIT to~FAILURE **7:71** and~to~SACRIFICE the~OFFERING.OF.RESTITUTION~s CATTLE TWO BUCK~s FIVE MALE.GOAT~s FIVE SHEEP~s SON~s YEAR FIVE THIS DONATION Ahhi'ezer SON Amishaddai **7:72** in~DAY ONE TEN DAY CAPTAIN to~SON~s Asher Pagi'eyl SON Akhran **7:73** DONATION~him PLATTER SILVER UNIT THREE~s and~HUNDRED WEIGHT~her SPRINKLING.BASIN UNIT SILVER SEVEN~s SHEQEL in~SHEQEL the~SPECIAL TWO~them$^{(m)}$ FULL~s FLOUR MIX$^{(V)}$~ed$^{(fs)}$ in~the~OIL to~DEPOSIT **7:74** PALM UNIT TEN GOLD FULL INCENSE.SMOKE **7:75** BULL UNIT SON CATTLE BUCK UNIT SHEEP UNIT SON

YEAR~him to~ASCENSION.OFFERING   **7:76** HAIRY.GOAT SHE-GOAT~s UNIT to~FAILURE   **7:77** and~to~SACRIFICE the~OFFERING.OF.RESTITUTION~s CATTLE TWO BUCK~s FIVE MALE.GOAT~s FIVE SHEEP~s SON~s YEAR FIVE THIS DONATION Pagi'eyl SON Akhran   **7:78** in~DAY TWO TEN DAY CAPTAIN to~SON~s Naphtali Ahhira SON Eynan   **7:79** DONATION~him PLATTER SILVER UNIT THREE~s and~HUNDRED WEIGHT~her SPRINKLING.BASIN UNIT SILVER SEVEN~s SHEQEL in~SHEQEL the~SPECIAL TWO~them$^{(m)}$ FULL~s FLOUR MIX$^{(V)}$~ed$^{(fs)}$ in~the~OIL to~DEPOSIT   **7:80** PALM UNIT TEN GOLD FULL INCENSE.SMOKE   **7:81** BULL UNIT SON CATTLE BUCK UNIT SHEEP UNIT SON YEAR~him to~ASCENSION.OFFERING   **7:82** HAIRY.GOAT SHE-GOAT~s UNIT to~FAILURE   **7:83** and~to~SACRIFICE the~OFFERING.OF.RESTITUTION~s CATTLE TWO BUCK~s FIVE MALE.GOAT~s FIVE SHEEP~s SON~s YEAR FIVE THIS DONATION Ahhira SON Eynan   **7:84** THIS DEVOTION the~ALTAR in~DAY >~*be*~SMEAR$^{(V)}$ AT~him from~AT CAPTAIN~s Yisra'eyl PLATTER~s SILVER TWO TEN SPRINKLING.BASIN~s SILVER TWO TEN PALM~s GOLD TWO TEN   **7:85** THREE~s and~HUNDRED the~PLATTER the~UNIT SILVER and~SEVEN~s the~SPRINKLING.BASIN the~UNIT ALL SILVER the~UTENSIL~s THOUSAND~s2 and~FOUR HUNDRED~s in~SHEQEL the~SPECIAL   **7:86** PALM~s GOLD TWO TEN FULL~s INCENSE.SMOKE TEN TEN the~PALM in~SHEQEL the~SPECIAL ALL GOLD the~PALM~s TEN~s and~HUNDRED   **7:87** ALL the~CATTLE to~the~ASCENSION.OFFERING TWO TEN BULL~s BUCK~s TWO TEN SHEEP~s SON~s YEAR TWO TEN and~DEPOSIT~them$^{(m)}$ and~HAIRY.GOAT~s SHE-GOAT~s TWO TEN to~FAILURE   **7:88** and~ALL CATTLE SACRIFICE the~OFFERING.OF.RESTITUTION~s TEN~s and~FOUR BULL~s BUCK~s SIX~s MALE.GOAT~s SIX~s SHEEP~s SON~s YEAR SIX~s THIS DEVOTION the~ALTAR AFTER >~*be*~SMEAR$^{(V)}$ AT~him   **7:89** and~in~>~COME$^{(V)}$ Mosheh TO TENT APPOINTED to~>~*much*~SPEAK$^{(V)}$ AT~him and~he~will~HEAR$^{(V)}$ AT the~VOICE >~*much*~SPEAK$^{(V)}$ TO~him from~UPON the~LID WHICH UPON BOX the~EVIDENCE from~BETWEEN TWO the~KERUV~s and~he~will~*much*~SPEAK$^{(V)}$ TO~him

---

Chapter 8

8:1 and~*he*~will~*much*~SPEAK$^{(V)}$ **YHWH** TO Mosheh to~>~SAY$^{(V)}$ **8:2** !$^{(ms)}$~*much*~SPEAK$^{(V)}$ TO Aharon and~you$^{(ms)}$~did~SAY$^{(V)}$ TO~him in~>~*make*~GO.UP$^{(V)}$~you$^{(ms)}$ AT the~LAMP~s TO FOREFRONT FACE~s the~LAMPSTAND they$^{(m)}$~will~*make*~LIGHT$^{(V)}$ SEVEN the~LAMP~s   **8:3** and~*he*~will~DO$^{(V)}$ SO Aharon TO FOREFRONT FACE~s the~LAMPSTAND *he*~did~*make*~GO.UP$^{(V)}$ LAMP~s~her like~WHICH *he*~did~*much*~DIRECT$^{(V)}$ **YHWH** AT Mosheh   **8:4** and~THIS WORK the~LAMPSTAND BEATEN.WORK GOLD UNTIL MIDSECTION~her UNTIL BUD~her BEATEN.WORK SHE like~the~APPEARANCE WHICH *he*~did~*make*~SEE$^{(V)}$ **YHWH** AT Mosheh SO *he*~did~DO$^{(V)}$ AT the~LAMPSTAND   **8:5** and~*he*~will~*much*~SPEAK$^{(V)}$ **YHWH** TO

The Book of Numbers

Mosheh to~>~SAY$^{(V)}$ **8:6** !$^{(ms)}$~TAKE$^{(V)}$ AT the~Lewi~s from~MIDST SON~s Yisra'eyl and~you$^{(ms)}$~did~much~BE.CLEAN$^{(V)}$ AT~them$^{(m)}$ **8:7** and~ IN.THIS.WAY you$^{(ms)}$~will~DO$^{(V)}$ to~them$^{(m)}$ to~>~much~BE.CLEAN$^{(V)}$~them$^{(m)}$!$^{(ms)}$~make~SPATTER$^{(V)}$ UPON~them$^{(m)}$ WATER~s2 FAILURE and~they~did~ make~CROSS.OVER$^{(V)}$ RAZOR UPON ALL FLESH~them$^{(m)}$ and~they~did~ much~WASH$^{(V)}$ GARMENT~s~them$^{(m)}$ and~they~did~be~make~ BE.CLEAN$^{(V)}$ **8:8** and~they~did~TAKE$^{(V)}$ BULL SON CATTLE and~DEPOSIT~ him FLOUR MIX$^{(V)}$~ed$^{(fs)}$ in~the~OIL and~BULL SECOND SON CATTLE you$^{(ms)}$~ will~TAKE$^{(V)}$ to~FAILURE **8:9** and~you$^{(ms)}$~did~make~COME.NEAR$^{(V)}$ AT the~ Lewi~s to~FACE~s TENT APPOINTED and~you$^{(ms)}$~did~make~ASSEMBLE$^{(V)}$ AT ALL COMPANY SON~s Yisra'eyl **8:10** and~you$^{(ms)}$~did~make~COME.NEAR$^{(V)}$ AT the~Lewi~s to~FACE~s **YHWH** and~they~did~SUPPORT$^{(V)}$ SON~s Yisra'eyl AT HAND~s2~them$^{(m)}$ UPON the~Lewi~s **8:11** and~he~did~WAVE$^{(V)}$ Aharon AT the~Lewi~s WAVING to~FACE~s **YHWH** from~AT SON~s Yisra'eyl and~ they~did~EXIST$^{(V)}$ to~>~SERVE$^{(V)}$ AT SERVICE **YHWH** **8:12** and~the~Lewi~s they$^{(m)}$~will~SUPPORT$^{(V)}$ AT HAND~s2~them$^{(m)}$ UPON HEAD the~BULL~s and~ !$^{(ms)}$~DO$^{(V)}$ AT the~UNIT FAILURE and~AT the~UNIT ASCENSION.OFFERING to~**YHWH** to~>~much~COVER$^{(V)}$ UPON the~ Lewi~s **8:13** and~you$^{(ms)}$~did~make~STAND$^{(V)}$ AT the~Lewi~s to~FACE~s Aharon and~to~FACE~s SON~s~him and~you$^{(ms)}$~did~make~WAVE$^{(V)}$ AT~ them$^{(m)}$ WAVING to~**YHWH** **8:14** and~you$^{(ms)}$~did~make~SEPARATE$^{(V)}$ AT the~Lewi~s from~MIDST SON~s Yisra'eyl and~they~did~EXIST$^{(V)}$ to~me the~ Lewi~s **8:15** and~AFTER SO they$^{(m)}$~will~COME$^{(V)}$ the~Lewi~s to~>~SERVE$^{(V)}$ AT TENT APPOINTED and~you$^{(ms)}$~did~much~BE.CLEAN$^{(V)}$ AT~them$^{(m)}$ and~ you$^{(ms)}$~did~make~WAVE$^{(V)}$ AT~them$^{(m)}$ WAVING **8:16** GIVEN.THAT GIVE$^{(V)}$~ ed$^{(mp)}$ GIVE$^{(V)}$~ed$^{(mp)}$ THEY$^{(m)}$ to~me from~MIDST SON~s Yisra'eyl UNDER BURSTING ALL BOWELS FIRSTBORN ALL from~SON~s Yisra'eyl I~did~TAKE$^{(V)}$ AT~them$^{(m)}$ to~me **8:17** GIVEN.THAT to~me ALL FIRSTBORN in~SON~s Yisra'eyl in~the~HUMAN and~in~the~BEAST in~DAY >~make~HIT$^{(V)}$~me ALL FIRSTBORN in~LAND Mits'rayim I~did~make~SET.APART$^{(V)}$ AT~them$^{(m)}$ to~ me **8:18** and~I~will~TAKE$^{(V)}$ AT the~Lewi~s UNDER ALL FIRSTBORN in~ SON~s Yisra'eyl **8:19** and~I~will~GIVE$^{(V)}$ AT the~Lewi~s GIVE$^{(V)}$~ed$^{(mp)}$ to~ Aharon and~to~SON~s~him from~MIDST SON~s Yisra'eyl to~>~SERVE$^{(V)}$ AT SERVICE SON~s Yisra'eyl in~TENT APPOINTED and~to~>~much~COVER$^{(V)}$ UPON SON~s Yisra'eyl and~NOT he~will~EXIST$^{(V)}$ in~SON~s Yisra'eyl STRIKING in~>~DRAW.NEAR$^{(V)}$ SON~s Yisra'eyl TO the~SPECIAL **8:20** and~ he~will~DO$^{(V)}$ Mosheh and~Aharon and~ALL COMPANY SON~s Yisra'eyl to~ Lewi~s like~ALL WHICH he~did~much~DIRECT$^{(V)}$ **YHWH** AT Mosheh to~ Lewi~s SO they~did~DO$^{(V)}$ to~them$^{(m)}$ SON~s Yisra'eyl **8:21** and~they$^{(m)}$~he~ will~self~FAIL$^{(V)}$ the~Lewi~s and~they$^{(m)}$~will~much~WASH$^{(V)}$ GARMENT~s~ them$^{(m)}$ and~he~will~make~WAVE$^{(V)}$ Aharon AT~them$^{(m)}$ WAVING to~ FACE~s **YHWH** and~he~will~much~COVER$^{(V)}$ UPON~them$^{(m)}$ Aharon to~>~ much~BE.CLEAN$^{(V)}$~them$^{(m)}$ **8:22** and~AFTER SO they~did~COME$^{(V)}$ the~ Lewi~s to~>~SERVE$^{(V)}$ AT SERVICE~them$^{(m)}$ in~TENT APPOINTED to~FACE~s Aharon and~to~FACE~s SON~s~him like~WHICH he~did~much~DIRECT$^{(V)}$

YHWH AT Mosheh UPON the~Lewi~s SO they~did~DO[V] to~them[m] **8:23** and~he~will~much~SPEAK[V] **YHWH** TO Mosheh to~>~SAY[V] **8:24** THIS WHICH to~Lewi~s from~SON FIVE and~TEN~s YEAR and~UPWARD~unto he~will~COME[V] to~>~MUSTER[V] ARMY in~the~SERVICE TENT APPOINTED **8:25** and~from~SON FIVE~s YEAR he~will~TURN.BACK[V] from~ARMY the~SERVICE and~NOT he~will~SERVE[V] YET.AGAIN **8:26** and~he~did~much~MINISTER[V] AT BROTHER~s~him in~TENT APPOINTED to~>~SAFEGUARD[V] CHARGE and~SERVICE NOT he~will~SERVE[V] like~IN.THIS.WAY you[ms]~will~DO[V] to~Lewi~s in~CUSTODY~s~them[m]

Chapter 9

9:1 and~he~will~much~SPEAK[V] **YHWH** TO Mosheh in~WILDERNESS Sinai in~the~YEAR the~SECOND to~>~GO.OUT[V]~them[m] from~LAND Mits'rayim in~the~NEW.MOON the~FIRST to~>~SAY[V] **9:2** and~they[m]~will~DO[V] SON~s Yisra'eyl AT the~Pesahh in~APPOINTED~him **9:3** in~FOUR TEN DAY in~the~NEW.MOON the~THIS BETWEEN the~EVENING~s2 you[mp]~will~DO[V] AT~him in~APPOINTED~him like~ALL CUSTOM~s~him and~like~ALL DECISION~s~him you[mp]~will~DO[V] AT~him **9:4** and~he~will~much~SPEAK[V] Mosheh TO SON~s Yisra'eyl to~>~DO[V] the~Pesahh **9:5** and~they[m]~will~DO[V] AT the~Pesahh in~the~FIRST in~FOUR TEN DAY to~the~NEW.MOON BETWEEN the~EVENING~s2 in~WILDERNESS Sinai like~ALL WHICH he~did~much~DIRECT[V] **YHWH** AT Mosheh SO they~did~DO[V] SON~s Yisra'eyl **9:6** and~he~will~EXIST[V] MAN~s WHICH they~did~EXIST[V] DIRTY~s to~SOUL HUMAN and~NOT they~did~BE.ABLE[V] to~>~DO[V] the~Pesahh in~the~DAY the~HE and~they[m]~will~COME.NEAR[V] to~FACE~s Mosheh and~to~FACE~s Aharon in~the~DAY the~HE **9:7** and~they[m]~will~SAY[V] the~MAN~s the~THEY[m] TO~him WE DIRTY~s to~SOUL HUMAN to~WHAT we~will~be~TAKE.AWAY[V] to~EXCEPT >~make~COME.NEAR[V] AT DONATION **YHWH** in~APPOINTED~him in~MIDST SON~s Yisra'eyl **9:8** and~he~will~SAY[V] TO~them[m] Mosheh ![mp]~STAND[V] and~I~will~HEAR[V]~& WHAT he~will~much~DIRECT[V] **YHWH** to~you[mp] **9:9** and~he~will~much~SPEAK[V] **YHWH** TO Mosheh to~>~SAY[V] **9:10** ![ms]~much~SPEAK[V] TO SON~s Yisra'eyl to~>~SAY[V] MAN MAN GIVEN.THAT he~will~EXIST[V] DIRTY to~the~SOUL OR in~ROAD DISTANCE to~you[mp] OR to~GENERATION~s~you[mp] and~he~did~DO[V] Pesahh to~**YHWH** **9:11** in~the~NEW.MOON the~SECOND in~FOUR TEN DAY BETWEEN the~EVENING~s2 they[m]~will~DO[V] AT~him UPON UNLEAVENED.BREAD~s and~BITTER.HERBS~s they[m]~will~EAT[V]~him **9:12** NOT they[m]~will~make~REMAIN[V] FROM~him UNTIL MORNING and~BONE NOT they[m]~will~CRACK[V] in~him like~ALL CUSTOM the~Pesahh they[m]~will~DO[V] AT~him **9:13** and~the~MAN WHICH HE CLEAN and~in~ROAD NOT he~did~EXIST[V] and~he~did~TERMINATE[V] to~>~DO[V] the~Pesahh and~she~did~be~CUT[V] the~SOUL the~SHE from~

PEOPLE~s~her GIVEN.THAT DONATION **YHWH** NOT *he~did~make~* COME.NEAR^(V) in~APPOINTED~him FAILURE~him *he~will~*LIFT.UP^(V) the~ MAN the~HE **9:14** and~GIVEN.THAT *he~will~*IMMIGRATE^(V) AT~you^(mp) IMMIGRANT and~*he~did~*DO^(V) Pesahh to~**YHWH** like~CUSTOM the~Pesahh and~like~DECISION~him SO *he~will~*DO^(V) CUSTOM UNIT *he~will~*EXIST^(V) to~you^(mp) and~to~IMMIGRANT and~to~NATIVE the~LAND **9:15** and~in~ DAY >~*make~*RISE^(V) AT the~DWELLING *he~did~much~*COVER.OVER^(V) the~ CLOUD AT the~DWELLING to~TENT the~EVIDENCE and~in~the~EVENING *he~will~*EXIST^(V) UPON the~DWELLING like~APPEARANCE FIRE UNTIL MORNING **9:16** SO *he~will~*EXIST^(V) CONTINUALLY the~CLOUD *he~will~ much~*COVER.OVER^(V)~him and~APPEARANCE FIRE NIGHT **9:17** and~to~ MOUTH to~>~*be~*GO.UP^(V) the~CLOUD from~UPON the~TENT and~AFTER SO *they*^(m)*~will~*JOURNEY^(V) SON~s Yisra'eyl and~in~AREA WHICH *he~will~* DWELL^(V) THERE the~CLOUD THERE *they*^(m)*~will~*CAMP^(V) SON~s Yisra'eyl **9:18** UPON MOUTH **YHWH** *they*^(m)*~will~*JOURNEY^(V) SON~s Yisra'eyl and~UPON MOUTH **YHWH** *they*^(m)*~will~*CAMP^(V) ALL DAY~s WHICH *he~will~*DWELL^(V) the~CLOUD UPON the~DWELLING *they*^(m)*~will~* CAMP^(V) **9:19** and~in~>~*make~*PROLONG^(V) the~CLOUD UPON the~ DWELLING DAY~s ABUNDANT~s and~*they~did~*SAFEGUARD^(V) SON~s Yisra'eyl AT CHARGE **YHWH** and~NOT *they*^(m)*~will~*JOURNEY^(V) **9:20** and~ THERE.IS WHICH *he~will~*EXIST^(V) the~CLOUD DAY~s NUMBER UPON the~ DWELLING UPON MOUTH **YHWH** *they*^(m)*~will~*CAMP^(V) and~UPON MOUTH **YHWH** *they*^(m)*~will~*JOURNEY^(V) **9:21** and~THERE.IS WHICH *he~will~*EXIST^(V) the~CLOUD from~EVENING UNTIL MORNING and~*he~did~be~*GO.UP^(V) the~ CLOUD in~the~MORNING and~*they~did~*JOURNEY^(V) OR DAYTIME and~ NIGHT and~*he~did~be~*GO.UP^(V) the~CLOUD and~*they~did~* JOURNEY^(V) **9:22** OR DAY~s2 OR NEW.MOON OR DAY~s in~>~*make~* PROLONG^(V) the~CLOUD UPON the~DWELLING to~>~DWELL^(V) UPON~him *they*^(m)*~will~*CAMP^(V) SON~s Yisra'eyl and~NOT *they*^(m)*~will~*JOURNEY^(V) and~ in~>~*make~*GO.UP^(V)~him *they*^(m)*~will~*JOURNEY^(V) **9:23** UPON MOUTH **YHWH** *they*^(m)*~will~*CAMP^(V) and~UPON MOUTH **YHWH** *they*^(m)*~will~* JOURNEY^(V) AT CHARGE **YHWH** *they~did~*SAFEGUARD^(V) UPON MOUTH **YHWH** in~HAND Mosheh

Chapter 10

10:1 and~*he~will~much~*SPEAK^(V) **YHWH** TO Mosheh to~>~SAY^(V) **10:2** *!*^(ms)*~* DO^(V) to~you^(ms) TWO STRAIGHT.TRUMPET~s SILVER BEATEN.WORK *you*^(ms)*~ will~*DO^(V) AT~them^(m) and~*they~did~*EXIST^(V) to~you^(ms) to~MEETING the~ COMPANY and~to~JOURNEY AT the~CAMP~s **10:3** and~*they~did~* THRUST^(V) in~them^(f) and~*they~did~be~*APPOINT^(V) TO~you^(ms) ALL the~ COMPANY TO OPENING TENT APPOINTED **10:4** and~IF in~UNIT *they*^(m)*~ will~*THRUST^(V) and~*they~did~be~*APPOINT^(V) TO~you^(ms) the~CAPTAIN~s

HEAD~s THOUSAND~s Yisra'eyl **10:5** and~*you*^(mp)^~*did*~THRUST^(V)^ SIGNAL and~*they*~*did*~JOURNEY^(V)^ the~CAMP~s the~CAMP^(V)^~*ing*^(mp)^ EAST~ unto **10:6** and~*you*^(mp)^~*did*~THRUST^(V)^ SIGNAL SECOND and~*they*~*did*~ JOURNEY^(V)^ the~CAMP~s the~CAMP^(V)^~*ing*^(mp)^ SOUTHWARD~unto SIGNAL *they*^(m)^~*will*~THRUST^(V)^ to~JOURNEY~s~them^(m)^ **10:7** and~>~*make*~ ASSEMBLE^(V)^ AT the~ASSEMBLY *you*^(mp)^~*will*~THRUST^(V)^ and~NOT *you*^(mp)^~ *will*~*make*~SIGNAL^(V)^ **10:8** and~SON~s Aharon the~ADMINISTRATOR~s *they*^(m)^~*will*~THRUST^(V)^ in~the~STRAIGHT.TRUMPET and~*they*~*did*~EXIST^(V)^ to~*you*^(mp)^ to~CUSTOM DISTANT to~GENERATION~s~*you*^(mp)^ **10:9** and~ GIVEN.THAT *you*^(mp)^~*will*~COME^(V)^ BATTLE in~LAND~*you*^(mp)^ UPON the~ NARROW the~PRESS.IN^(V)^~*ing*^(ms)^ AT~*you*^(mp)^ and~*you*^(mp)^~*did*~*make*~ SIGNAL^(V)^ in~the~STRAIGHT.TRUMPET and~*you*^(mp)^~*did*~*be*~REMEMBER^(V)^ to~FACE~s **YHWH** Elohiym~*you*^(mp)^ and~*you*^(mp)^~*did*~*be*~RESCUE^(V)^ from~ ATTACK^(V)^~*ing*^(mp)^~*you*^(mp)^ **10:10** and~in~DAY REJOICING~*you*^(mp)^ and~in~ APPOINTED~s~*you*^(mp)^ and~in~HEAD~s NEW.MOON~s~*you*^(mp)^ and~*you*^(mp)^~ *did*~THRUST^(V)^ in~the~STRAIGHT.TRUMPET UPON ASCENSION.OFFERING~s~ *you*^(mp)^ and~UPON SACRIFICE~s OFFERING.OF.RESTITUTION~s~*you*^(mp)^ and~ *they*~*did*~EXIST^(V)^ to~*you*^(mp)^ to~REMEMBRANCE to~FACE~s Elohiym~*you*^(mp)^ I **YHWH** Elohiym~*you*^(mp)^ **10:11** and~*he*~*will*~EXIST^(V)^ in~the~YEAR the~ SECOND in~the~NEW.MOON the~SECOND in~TEN~s in~the~NEW.MOON *he*~*did*~*be*~GO.UP^(V)^ the~CLOUD from~UPON DWELLING the~ EVIDENCE **10:12** and~*they*^(m)^~*will*~JOURNEY^(V)^ SON~s Yisra'eyl to~ JOURNEY~s~them^(m)^ from~WILDERNESS Sinai and~*he*~*will*~DWELL^(V)^ the~ CLOUD in~WILDERNESS Paran **10:13** and~*they*^(m)^~*will*~JOURNEY^(V)^ in~the~ FIRST UPON MOUTH **YHWH** in~HAND Mosheh **10:14** and~*he*~*will*~ JOURNEY^(V)^ BANNER CAMP SON~s Yehudah in~the~FIRST to~ARMY~s~ them^(m)^ and~UPON ARMY~him Nahhshon SON Amiynadav **10:15** and~ UPON ARMY BRANCH SON~s Yis'sas'khar Nataneyl SON Tso'ar **10:16** and~ UPON ARMY BRANCH SON~s Zevulun Eli'av SON Hheylon **10:17** and~*he*~ *did*~*be*~*make*~GO.DOWN^(V)^ the~DWELLING and~*they*~*did*~JOURNEY^(V)^ SON~s Gershon and~SON~s Merari LIFT.UP^(V)^~*ing*^(mp)^ the~ DWELLING **10:18** and~*he*~*did*~JOURNEY^(V)^ BANNER CAMP Re'uven to~ ARMY~s~them^(m)^ and~UPON ARMY~him Elitsur SON Shedeyur **10:19** and~ UPON ARMY BRANCH SON~s Shimon Shelumi'eyl SON Tsurishaddai **10:20** and~UPON ARMY BRANCH SON~s Gad Elyasaph SON De'u'eyl **10:21** and~*they*~*did*~JOURNEY^(V)^ the~Qehat~s LIFT.UP^(V)^~*ing*^(mp)^ the~SANCTUARY and~*they*~*did*~*make*~RISE^(V)^ AT the~DWELLING UNTIL >~ COME^(V)^~them^(m)^ **10:22** and~*he*~*did*~JOURNEY^(V)^ BANNER CAMP SON~s Ephrayim to~ARMY~s~them^(m)^ and~UPON ARMY~him Elishama SON Amihud **10:23** and~UPON ARMY BRANCH SON~s Menasheh Gamli'eyl SON Pedatsur **10:24** and~UPON ARMY BRANCH SON~s Binyamin Avidan SON Gidoni **10:25** and~*he*~*did*~JOURNEY^(V)^ BANNER CAMP SON~s Dan *much*~ GATHER^(V)^~*ing*^(ms)^ to~ALL the~CAMP~s to~ARMY~s~them^(m)^ and~UPON ARMY~him Ahhi'ezer SON Amishaddai **10:26** and~UPON ARMY BRANCH SON~s Asher Pagi'eyl SON Akhran **10:27** and~UPON ARMY BRANCH SON~s

The Book of Numbers

Naphtali Ahhira SON Eynan   **10:28** THESE JOURNEY~s SON~s Yisra'eyl to~ ARMY~s~them⁽ᵐ⁾ and~they⁽ᵐ⁾~will~JOURNEY⁽ⱽ⁾   **10:29** and~he~will~SAY⁽ⱽ⁾ Mosheh to~Hhovav SON Re'u'eyl the~Mid'yan~of BE.AN.IN-LAW⁽ⱽ⁾~ing⁽ᵐˢ⁾ Mosheh JOURNEY⁽ⱽ⁾~ing⁽ᵐᵖ⁾ WE TO the~AREA WHICH he~did~SAY⁽ⱽ⁾ **YHWH** AT~him I~will~GIVE⁽ⱽ⁾ to~you⁽ᵐᵖ⁾ !⁽ᵐˢ⁾~WALK⁽ⱽ⁾ & AT~us and~we~did~make~ DO.WELL⁽ⱽ⁾ to~you⁽ᶠˢ⁾ GIVEN.THAT **YHWH** he~did~much~SPEAK⁽ⱽ⁾ FUNCTIONAL UPON Yisra'eyl   **10:30** and~he~will~SAY⁽ⱽ⁾ TO~him NOT I~will~ WALK⁽ⱽ⁾ GIVEN.THAT IF TO LAND~me and~TO KINDRED~me I~will~ WALK⁽ⱽ⁾   **10:31** and~he~will~SAY⁽ⱽ⁾ DO.NOT PLEASE you⁽ᵐˢ⁾~will~LEAVE⁽ⱽ⁾ AT~us GIVEN.THAT UPON SO you⁽ᵐˢ⁾~did~KNOW⁽ⱽ⁾ >~CAMP⁽ⱽ⁾~us in~the~ WILDERNESS and~you⁽ᵐˢ⁾~did~EXIST⁽ⱽ⁾ to~us to~EYE~s2   **10:32** and~he~did~ EXIST⁽ⱽ⁾ GIVEN.THAT you⁽ᵐˢ⁾~will~WALK⁽ⱽ⁾ WITH~us and~he~did~EXIST⁽ⱽ⁾ the~FUNCTIONAL the~HE WHICH he~will~make~DO.WELL⁽ⱽ⁾ **YHWH** WITH~ us and~we~did~make~DO.WELL⁽ⱽ⁾ to~you⁽ᶠˢ⁾   **10:33** and~they⁽ᵐ⁾~will~ JOURNEY⁽ⱽ⁾ from~HILL **YHWH** ROAD THREE DAY~s and~BOX COVENANT **YHWH** JOURNEY⁽ⱽ⁾~ing⁽ᵐˢ⁾ to~FACE~s~them⁽ᵐ⁾ ROAD THREE DAY~s to~>~ SCOUT⁽ⱽ⁾ to~them⁽ᵐ⁾ OASIS   **10:34** and~CLOUD **YHWH** UPON~them⁽ᵐ⁾ DAYTIME in~>~JOURNEY⁽ⱽ⁾~them⁽ᵐ⁾ FROM the~CAMP   **10:35** and~he~will~ EXIST⁽ⱽ⁾ in~>~JOURNEY⁽ⱽ⁾ the~BOX and~he~will~SAY⁽ⱽ⁾ Mosheh !⁽ᵐᵖ⁾~RISE⁽ⱽ⁾~ & **YHWH** and~they⁽ᵐ⁾~will~SCATTER.ABROAD⁽ⱽ⁾ ATTACK⁽ⱽ⁾~ing⁽ᵐᵖ⁾~s~you⁽ᵐˢ⁾ and~they⁽ᵐ⁾~will~FLEE⁽ⱽ⁾ much~HATE⁽ⱽ⁾~ing⁽ᵐᵖ⁾~you⁽ᵐˢ⁾ from~FACE~s~ you⁽ᵐˢ⁾   **10:36** and~in~>~REST⁽ⱽ⁾~her he~will~SAY⁽ⱽ⁾ !⁽ᵐˢ⁾~TURN.BACK⁽ⱽ⁾~& **YHWH** MYRIAD~s THOUSAND~s Yisra'eyl

Chapter 11

11:1 and~he~will~EXIST⁽ⱽ⁾ the~PEOPLE like~self~COMPLAIN⁽ⱽ⁾~ing⁽ᵐᵖ⁾ DYSFUNCTIONAL in~EAR~s2 **YHWH** and~he~will~HEAR⁽ⱽ⁾ **YHWH** and~he~ will~FLARE.UP⁽ⱽ⁾ NOSE~him and~she~will~BURN⁽ⱽ⁾ in~them⁽ᵐ⁾ FIRE **YHWH** and~she~will~EAT⁽ⱽ⁾ in~EXTREMITY the~CAMP   **11:2** and~he~will~ CRY.OUT⁽ⱽ⁾ the~PEOPLE TO Mosheh and~he~will~self~PLEAD⁽ⱽ⁾ Mosheh TO **YHWH** and~she~will~DROWN⁽ⱽ⁾ the~FIRE   **11:3** and~he~will~CALL.OUT⁽ⱽ⁾ TITLE the~AREA the~HE Taveyrah GIVEN.THAT she~did~BURN⁽ⱽ⁾ in~them⁽ᵐ⁾ FIRE **YHWH**   **11:4** and~the~MIXED.MULTITUDE WHICH in~INSIDE~him they⁽ᵐ⁾~will~self~YEARN⁽ⱽ⁾ YEARNING and~they⁽ᵐ⁾~will~TURN.BACK⁽ⱽ⁾ and~ they⁽ᵐ⁾~will~WEEP⁽ⱽ⁾ ALSO SON~s Yisra'eyl and~they⁽ᵐ⁾~will~SAY⁽ⱽ⁾ WHO he~ will~make~EAT⁽ⱽ⁾~us FLESH   **11:5** we~did~REMEMBER⁽ⱽ⁾ AT the~FISH WHICH we~will~EAT⁽ⱽ⁾ in~Mits'rayim FREELY AT the~CUCUMBER~s and~AT the~MELON~s and~AT the~HERBAGE and~AT the~ONION~s and~AT the~ GARLIC~s   **11:6** and~NOW SOUL~us DRY WITHOUT ALL EXCEPT TO the~ Mahn EYE~s2~us   **11:7** and~the~Mahn like~SEED CORIANDER HE and~EYE~ him like~EYE the~AMBER   **11:8** they~did~GO⁽ⱽ⁾ the~PEOPLE and~they~did~ PICK.UP⁽ⱽ⁾ and~they~did~GRIND⁽ⱽ⁾ in~the~MILLSTONE~s OR they~did~

GROUND.TO.PIECES⁽ᵛ⁾ in~the~MORTAR.AND.PESTLE and~*they~did~much~* BOIL⁽ᵛ⁾ in~the~SKILLET and~*they~did~*DO⁽ᵛ⁾ AT~him BAKED.BREAD~s and~ *he~did~*EXIST⁽ᵛ⁾ FLAVOR~him like~FLAVOR FRESH the~OIL   **11:9** and~in~>~ GO.DOWN⁽ᵛ⁾ the~DEW UPON the~CAMP NIGHT *he~will~*GO.DOWN⁽ᵛ⁾ the~ Mahn UPON~him   **11:10** and~*he~will~*HEAR⁽ᵛ⁾ Mosheh AT the~PEOPLE WEEP⁽ᵛ⁾~*ing*⁽ᵐˢ⁾ to~CLAN~s~him MAN to~OPENING TENT~him and~*he~will~* FLARE.UP⁽ᵛ⁾ NOSE **YHWH** MANY and~in~EYE~s2 Mosheh DYSFUNCTIONAL   **11:11** and~*he~will~*SAY⁽ᵛ⁾ Mosheh TO **YHWH** to~WHAT *you*⁽ᵐˢ⁾*~did~make~*BE.DYSFUNCTIONAL⁽ᵛ⁾ to~SERVANT~*you*⁽ᵐˢ⁾ and~to~ WHAT NOT *I~did~*FIND⁽ᵛ⁾ BEAUTY in~EYE~s2~*you*⁽ᵐˢ⁾ to~>~PLACE⁽ᵛ⁾ AT LOAD ALL the~PEOPLE the~THIS UPON~me   **11:12** ?~I *I~did~*CONCEIVE⁽ᵛ⁾ AT ALL the~PEOPLE the~THIS IF I *I~did~*BRING.FORTH⁽ᵛ⁾~him GIVEN.THAT *you*⁽ᵐˢ⁾*~ will~*SAY⁽ᵛ⁾ TO~me *I*⁽ᵐˢ⁾*~*LIFT.UP⁽ᵛ⁾~him in~BOSOM~*you*⁽ᵐˢ⁾ like~WHICH *he~ will~*LIFT.UP⁽ᵛ⁾ the~SECURE⁽ᵛ⁾~*ing*⁽ᵐˢ⁾ AT the~SUCKLE⁽ᵛ⁾~*ing*⁽ᵐˢ⁾ UPON the~ GROUND WHICH *you*⁽ᵐˢ⁾*~did~be~*SWEAR⁽ᵛ⁾ to~FATHER~s~him   **11:13** from~ WITHOUT to~me FLESH to~>~GIVE⁽ᵛ⁾ to~ALL the~PEOPLE the~THIS GIVEN.THAT *they*⁽ᵐ⁾*~will~*WEEP⁽ᵛ⁾ UPON~me to~>~SAY⁽ᵛ⁾ *I*⁽ᵐˢ⁾*~*GIVE⁽ᵛ⁾~& to~ us FLESH and~we~will~EAT⁽ᵛ⁾~&   **11:14** NOT *I~will~*BE.ABLE⁽ᵛ⁾ I to~STRAND~ me to~>~LIFT.UP⁽ᵛ⁾ AT ALL the~PEOPLE the~THIS GIVEN.THAT HEAVY FROM~me   **11:15** and~IF like~IN.THIS.WAY YOU⁽ᶠˢ⁾ DO⁽ᵛ⁾~*ing*⁽ᵐˢ⁾ to~me *I*⁽ᵐˢ⁾*~* KILL⁽ᵛ⁾~me PLEASE >~KILL⁽ᵛ⁾ IF *I~did~*FIND⁽ᵛ⁾ BEAUTY in~EYE~s2~*you*⁽ᵐˢ⁾ and~ DO.NOT *I~will~*SEE⁽ᵛ⁾ in~DYSFUNCTIONAL~me   **11:16** and~*he~will~*SAY⁽ᵛ⁾ **YHWH** TO Mosheh ?~*I*⁽ᵐˢ⁾*~*GATHER⁽ᵛ⁾ to~me SEVEN~s MAN from~BEARD~s Yisra'eyl WHICH *you*⁽ᵐˢ⁾*~did~*KNOW⁽ᵛ⁾ GIVEN.THAT THEY⁽ᵐ⁾ BEARD~s the~ PEOPLE and~OFFICER~s~him and~*you*⁽ᵐˢ⁾*~did~*TAKE⁽ᵛ⁾ AT~them⁽ᵐ⁾ TO TENT APPOINTED and~ *I*⁽ᵐᵖ⁾*~self~*STATION⁽ᵛ⁾ THERE WITH~*you*⁽ᶠˢ⁾   **11:17** and~*I~ did~*GO.DOWN⁽ᵛ⁾ and~*I~did~much~*SPEAK⁽ᵛ⁾ WITH~*you*⁽ᵐˢ⁾ THERE and~*I~ did~*SET.ASIDE⁽ᵛ⁾ FROM the~WIND WHICH UPON~*you*⁽ᵐˢ⁾ and~*I~did~*PLACE⁽ᵛ⁾ UPON~them⁽ᵐ⁾ and~*they~did~*LIFT.UP⁽ᵛ⁾ AT~*you*⁽ᵐˢ⁾ in~LOAD the~PEOPLE and~NOT *you*⁽ᵐˢ⁾*~will~*LIFT.UP⁽ᵛ⁾ YOU⁽ᵐˢ⁾ to~STRAND~*you*⁽ᵐˢ⁾   **11:18** and~TO the~PEOPLE *you*⁽ᵐˢ⁾*~will~*SAY⁽ᵛ⁾ *they*⁽ᵐ⁾*~will~self~*SET.APART⁽ᵛ⁾ to~ TOMORROW and~*you*⁽ᵐᵖ⁾*~did~*EAT⁽ᵛ⁾ FLESH GIVEN.THAT *you*⁽ᵐᵖ⁾*~did~* WEEP⁽ᵛ⁾ in~EAR~s2 **YHWH** to~>~SAY⁽ᵛ⁾ WHO *he~will~make~*EAT⁽ᵛ⁾~us FLESH GIVEN.THAT FUNCTIONAL to~us in~Mits'rayim and~*he~did~*GIVE⁽ᵛ⁾ **YHWH** to~*you*⁽ᵐᵖ⁾ FLESH and~*you*⁽ᵐᵖ⁾*~did~*EAT⁽ᵛ⁾   **11:19** NOT DAY UNIT *you*⁽ᵐˢ⁾*~will~* EAT⁽ᵛ⁾~must and~NOT DAY~s2 and~NOT FIVE DAY~s and~NOT TEN DAY~s and~NOT TEN~s DAY   **11:20** UNTIL NEW.MOON DAY~s UNTIL WHICH *he~ will~*GO.OUT⁽ᵛ⁾ from~NOSE~*you*⁽ᵐᵖ⁾ and~*he~did~*EXIST⁽ᵛ⁾ to~*you*⁽ᵐᵖ⁾ to~ VOMIT SEEING.AS GIVEN.THAT *you*⁽ᵐᵖ⁾*~did~*REJECT⁽ᵛ⁾ AT **YHWH** WHICH in~ INSIDE~*you*⁽ᵐᵖ⁾ and~*you*⁽ᵐᵖ⁾*~will~*WEEP⁽ᵛ⁾ to~FACE~s~him to~>~SAY⁽ᵛ⁾ to~ WHAT THIS *we~did~*GO.OUT⁽ᵛ⁾ from~Mits'rayim   **11:21** and~*he~will~*SAY⁽ᵛ⁾ Mosheh SIX HUNDRED~s THOUSAND ON.FOOT the~PEOPLE WHICH I in~ INSIDE~him and~YOU⁽ᵐˢ⁾ *you*⁽ᵐˢ⁾*~did~*SAY⁽ᵛ⁾ FLESH *I~will~*GIVE⁽ᵛ⁾ to~them⁽ᵐ⁾ and~*they~did~*EAT⁽ᵛ⁾ NEW.MOON DAY~s   **11:22** ?~FLOCKS and~CATTLE *he~ will~be~*SLAY⁽ᵛ⁾ to~them⁽ᵐ⁾ and~*he~did~*FIND⁽ᵛ⁾ to~them⁽ᵐ⁾ IF AT ALL FISH~s the~SEA he~will~be~GATHER⁽ᵛ⁾ to~them⁽ᵐ⁾ and~he~did~FIND⁽ᵛ⁾ to~them⁽ᵐ⁾ **11:23** and~he~will~SAY⁽ᵛ⁾ **YHWH** TO Mosheh ?~HAND **YHWH** she~will~SEVER⁽ᵛ⁾ NOW you⁽ᵐˢ⁾~will~SEE⁽ᵛ⁾ he~will~MEET⁽ᵛ⁾~you⁽ᵐˢ⁾ WORD~me IF NOT **11:24** and~he~will~GO.OUT⁽ᵛ⁾ Mosheh and~he~will~much~SPEAK⁽ᵛ⁾ TO the~PEOPLE AT WORD~s **YHWH** and~he~will~GATHER⁽ᵛ⁾ SEVEN~s MAN from~BEARD~s the~PEOPLE and~he~will~make~STAND⁽ᵛ⁾ AT~them⁽ᵐ⁾ ALL.AROUND~s the~TENT **11:25** and~he~will~GO.DOWN⁽ᵛ⁾ **YHWH** in~CLOUD and~he~will~much~SPEAK⁽ᵛ⁾ TO~him and~he~will~make~SET.ASIDE⁽ᵛ⁾ FROM the~WIND WHICH UPON~him and~he~will~GIVE⁽ᵛ⁾ UPON SEVEN~s MAN the~BEARD~s and~he~will~EXIST⁽ᵛ⁾ like~>~REST⁽ᵛ⁾ UPON~them⁽ᵐ⁾ the~WIND and~they⁽ᵐ⁾~will~self~ANNOUNCE⁽ᵛ⁾ and~NOT they~did~ADD⁽ᵛ⁾ **11:26** and~they⁽ᵐ⁾~will~be~REMAIN⁽ᵛ⁾ TWO MAN~s in~the~CAMP TITLE the~UNIT Eldad and~TITLE the~SECOND Meydad and~she~will~REST⁽ᵛ⁾ UPON~them⁽ᵐ⁾ the~WIND and~THEY⁽ᵐ⁾ in~the~WRITE⁽ᵛ⁾~ed⁽ᵐᵖ⁾ and~NOT they~did~GO.OUT⁽ᵛ⁾ the~TENT~unto and~they⁽ᵐ⁾~will~self~ANNOUNCE⁽ᵛ⁾ in~the~CAMP **11:27** and~he~will~RUN⁽ᵛ⁾ the~YOUNG.MAN and~he~will~make~BE.FACE.TO.FACE⁽ᵛ⁾ to~Mosheh and~he~will~SAY⁽ᵛ⁾ Eldad and~Meydad self~ANNOUNCE⁽ᵛ⁾~ing⁽ᵐᵖ⁾ in~the~CAMP **11:28** and~he~will~ANSWER⁽ᵛ⁾ Yehoshu'a SON Nun much~MINISTER⁽ᵛ⁾~ing⁽ᵐˢ⁾ Mosheh from~YOUTH and~he~will~SAY⁽ᵛ⁾ LORD~me Mosheh !⁽ᵐˢ⁾~RESTRICT⁽ᵛ⁾~them⁽ᵐ⁾ **11:29** and~he~will~SAY⁽ᵛ⁾ to~him Mosheh ?~much~BE.ZEALOUS⁽ᵛ⁾~ing⁽ᵐˢ⁾ YOU⁽ᵐˢ⁾ to~me and~WHO he~will~GIVE⁽ᵛ⁾ ALL PEOPLE **YHWH** ANNOUNCER~s GIVEN.THAT he~will~GIVE⁽ᵛ⁾ **YHWH** AT WIND~him UPON~them⁽ᵐ⁾ **11:30** and~he~will~be~GATHER⁽ᵛ⁾ Mosheh TO the~CAMP HE and~BEARD~s Yisra'eyl **11:31** and~WIND he~did~JOURNEY⁽ᵛ⁾ from~AT **YHWH** and~he~will~SWEEP⁽ᵛ⁾ QUAIL~s FROM the~SEA and~he~will~LEAVE.ALONE⁽ᵛ⁾ UPON the~CAMP like~ROAD DAY IN.THIS.WAY and~like~ROAD DAY IN.THIS.WAY ALL.AROUND~s the~CAMP and~like~AMMAH~s2 UPON FACE~s the~LAND **11:32** and~he~will~RISE⁽ᵛ⁾ the~PEOPLE ALL the~DAY the~HE and~ALL the~NIGHT and~ALL DAY the~MORROW and~they⁽ᵐ⁾~will~GATHER⁽ᵛ⁾ AT the~QUAIL the~make~BE.LESS⁽ᵛ⁾~ing⁽ᵐˢ⁾ he~did~GATHER⁽ᵛ⁾ TEN HHOMER~s and~they⁽ᵐ⁾~will~SPREAD⁽ᵛ⁾ to~them⁽ᵐ⁾ >~SPREAD⁽ᵛ⁾ ALL.AROUND~s the~CAMP **11:33** the~FLESH YET.AGAIN~him BETWEEN TOOTH~s~them⁽ᵐ⁾ BEFORE he~will~be~CUT⁽ᵛ⁾ and~NOSE **YHWH** he~did~FLARE.UP⁽ᵛ⁾ in~the~PEOPLE and~he~will~make~HIT⁽ᵛ⁾ **YHWH** in~the~PEOPLE HITTING ABUNDANT MANY **11:34** and~he~will~CALL.OUT⁽ᵛ⁾ AT TITLE the~AREA the~HE Qivrot-Hata'awah GIVEN.THAT THERE they~did~BURY⁽ᵛ⁾ AT the~PEOPLE the~self~YEARN⁽ᵛ⁾~ing⁽ᵐᵖ⁾ **11:35** from~Qivrot-Hata'awah they~did~JOURNEY⁽ᵛ⁾ the~PEOPLE Hhatsarot and~they⁽ᵐ⁾~will~EXIST⁽ᵛ⁾ in~Hhatsarot

Chapter 12

12:1 and~*she*~*will*~*much*~SPEAK⁽ⱽ⁾ Mir'yam and~Aharon in~Mosheh UPON CONCERNING the~WOMAN the~Kush~of WHICH *he*~*did*~TAKE⁽ⱽ⁾ GIVEN.THAT WOMAN Kush~of *he*~*did*~TAKE⁽ⱽ⁾ **12:2** and~*they*⁽ᵐ⁾~*will*~SAY⁽ⱽ⁾ ?~ONLY SURELY in~Mosheh *he*~*did*~*much*~SPEAK⁽ⱽ⁾ **YHWH** ?~NOT ALSO in~ us *he*~*did*~*much*~SPEAK⁽ⱽ⁾ and~*he*~*will*~HEAR⁽ⱽ⁾ **YHWH** **12:3** and~the~MAN Mosheh GENTLE MANY from~ALL the~HUMAN WHICH UPON FACE~s the~GROUND **12:4** and~*he*~*will*~SAY⁽ⱽ⁾ **YHWH** SUDDENLY TO Mosheh and~TO Aharon and~TO Mir'yam *!*⁽ᵐᵖ⁾~GO.OUT⁽ⱽ⁾ THREE~*you*⁽ᵐᵖ⁾ TO TENT APPOINTED and~*they*⁽ᵐ⁾~*will*~GO.OUT⁽ⱽ⁾ THREE~*them*⁽ᵐ⁾ **12:5** and~*he*~*will*~GO.DOWN⁽ⱽ⁾ **YHWH** in~PILLAR CLOUD and~*he*~*will*~STAND⁽ⱽ⁾ OPENING the~TENT and~*he*~*will*~CALL.OUT⁽ⱽ⁾ Aharon and~Mir'yam and~*they*⁽ᵐ⁾~*will*~GO.OUT⁽ⱽ⁾ TWO~*them*⁽ᵐ⁾ **12:6** and~*he*~*will*~SAY⁽ⱽ⁾ *!*⁽ᵐᵖ⁾~HEAR⁽ⱽ⁾ PLEASE WORD~s~me IF *he*~*will*~EXIST⁽ⱽ⁾ ANNOUNCER~*you*⁽ᵐᵖ⁾ **YHWH** in~the~APPEARANCE TO~him *I*~*will*~*self*~KNOW⁽ⱽ⁾ in~the~DREAM *I*~*will*~*much*~SPEAK⁽ⱽ⁾ in~him **12:7** NOT SO SERVANT~me Mosheh in~ALL HOUSE~me *be*~SECURE⁽ⱽ⁾~*ing*⁽ᵐˢ⁾ HE **12:8** MOUTH TO MOUTH *I*~*will*~*much*~SPEAK⁽ⱽ⁾ in~him and~APPEARANCE and~NOT in~RIDDLE~s and~RESEMBLANCE **YHWH** *he*~*will*~*make*~STARE⁽ⱽ⁾ and~WHY NOT *you*⁽ᵐᵖ⁾~*did*~FEAR⁽ⱽ⁾ to~>~*much*~SPEAK⁽ⱽ⁾ in~SERVANT~me in~Mosheh **12:9** and~*he*~*will*~FLARE.UP⁽ⱽ⁾ NOSE **YHWH** in~*them*⁽ᵐ⁾ and~*he*~*will*~WALK⁽ⱽ⁾ **12:10** and~the~CLOUD *he*~*did*~TURN.ASIDE⁽ⱽ⁾ from~UPON the~TENT and~LOOK Mir'yam *be*~*much*~INFECT⁽ⱽ⁾~*ing*⁽ᶠˢ⁾ like~the~SNOW and~*he*~*will*~TURN⁽ⱽ⁾ Aharon TO Mir'yam and~LOOK *be*~*much*~INFECT⁽ⱽ⁾~*ing*⁽ᶠˢ⁾ **12:11** and~*he*~*will*~SAY⁽ⱽ⁾ Aharon TO Mosheh in~me LORD~me DO.NOT PLEASE *you*⁽ᵐˢ⁾~*will*~SET.DOWN⁽ⱽ⁾ UPON~us FAILURE WHICH *we*~*did*~*be*~FOOLISH⁽ⱽ⁾ and~WHICH *we*~*did*~FAIL⁽ⱽ⁾ **12:12** DO.NOT PLEASE *she*~*will*~EXIST⁽ⱽ⁾ like~the~DIE⁽ⱽ⁾~*ing*⁽ᵐˢ⁾ WHICH in~>~GO.OUT⁽ⱽ⁾~him from~BOWELS MOTHER~him and~*he*~*will*~*be*~EAT⁽ⱽ⁾ HALF FLESH~him **12:13** and~*he*~*will*~CRY.OUT⁽ⱽ⁾ Mosheh TO **YHWH** to~>~SAY⁽ⱽ⁾ MIGHTY.ONE PLEASE *!*⁽ᵐˢ⁾~HEAL⁽ⱽ⁾ PLEASE to~her **12:14** and~*he*~*will*~SAY⁽ⱽ⁾ **YHWH** TO Mosheh and~FATHER~her >~SPIT⁽ⱽ⁾ *he*~*did*~SPIT⁽ⱽ⁾ in~FACE~s~her ?~NOT *she*~*will*~*be*~SHAME⁽ⱽ⁾ SEVEN DAY~s *she*~*will*~*be*~SHUT⁽ⱽ⁾ SEVEN DAY~s from~OUTSIDE to~the~CAMP and~AFTER *she*~*will*~*be*~GATHER⁽ⱽ⁾ **12:15** and~*she*~*will*~*be*~SHUT⁽ⱽ⁾ Mir'yam from~OUTSIDE to~the~CAMP SEVEN DAY~s and~the~PEOPLE NOT *he*~*did*~JOURNEY⁽ⱽ⁾ UNTIL >~*be*~GATHER⁽ⱽ⁾ Mir'yam **12:16** and~AFTER *they*~*did*~JOURNEY⁽ⱽ⁾ the~PEOPLE from~Hhatsarot and~*they*⁽ᵐ⁾~*will*~CAMP⁽ⱽ⁾ in~WILDERNESS Paran

Chapter 13

13:1 and~*he*~*will*~*much*~SPEAK[(V)] **YHWH** TO Mosheh to~>~SAY[(V)] **13:2** ![(ms)]~SEND[(V)] to~you[(ms)] MAN~s and~*they*[(mp)]~*will*~SCOUT[(V)] AT LAND Kena'an WHICH I GIVE[(V)]~*ing*[(ms)] to~SON~s Yisra'eyl MAN UNIT MAN UNIT to~BRANCH FATHER~s~him *you*[(mp)]~*will*~SEND[(V)] ALL CAPTAIN in~them[(m)] **13:3** and~*he*~*will*~SEND[(V)] AT~them[(m)] Mosheh from~WILDERNESS Paran UPON MOUTH **YHWH** ALL~them[(m)] MAN~s HEAD~s SON~s Yisra'eyl THEY[(m)] **13:4** and~THESE TITLE~s~them[(m)] to~BRANCH Re'uven Shamu'a SON Zakur **13:5** to~BRANCH Shimon Shaphat SON Hhoriy **13:6** to~BRANCH Yehudah Kaleyv SON Yephunah **13:7** to~BRANCH Yis'sas'khar Yigal SON Yoseph **13:8** to~BRANCH Ephrayim Hosheya SON Nun **13:9** to~BRANCH Binyamin Palti SON Raphu **13:10** to~BRANCH Zevulun Gad'di'eyl SON Sodi **13:11** to~BRANCH Yoseph to~BRANCH Menasheh Gad'diy SON Susiy **13:12** to~BRANCH Dan Ami'eyl SON Gemali **13:13** to~BRANCH Asher Setur SON Mika'eyl **13:14** to~BRANCH Naphtali Nahhbi SON Waphsi **13:15** to~BRANCH Gad Ge'u'eyl SON Makhi **13:16** THESE TITLE~s the~MAN~s WHICH *he*~*did*~SEND[(V)] Mosheh to~>~SCOUT[(V)] AT the~LAND and~*he*~*will*~CALL.OUT[(V)] Mosheh to~Hosheya SON Nun Yehoshu'a **13:17** and~*he*~*will*~SEND[(V)] AT~them[(m)] Mosheh to~>~SCOUT[(V)] AT LAND Kena'an and~*he*~*will*~SAY[(V)] TO~them[(m)] ![(mp)]~GO.UP[(V)] THIS in~the~SOUTH and~*you*[(mp)]~*did*~GO.UP[(V)] AT the~HILL **13:18** and~*you*[(mp)]~*did*~SEE[(V)] AT the~LAND WHAT SHE and~AT the~PEOPLE the~SETTLE[(V)]~*ing*[(ms)] UPON~her ?~FORCEFUL HE ?~FRAIL ?~SMALL.AMOUNT HE IF ABUNDANT **13:19** and~WHAT the~LAND WHICH HE SETTLE[(V)]~*ing*[(ms)] in~her ?~FUNCTIONAL SHE IF DYSFUNCTIONAL and~WHAT the~CITY~s WHICH HE SETTLE[(V)]~*ing*[(ms)] in~them[(f)] ?~in~CAMP~s IF in~FORTIFICATION~s **13:20** and~WHAT the~LAND ?~OIL SHE IF LEAN ?~THERE.IS in~her TREE IF WITHOUT and~*you*[(mp)]~*did*~*self*~SEIZE[(V)] and~*you*[(mp)]~*did*~TAKE[(V)] from~PRODUCE the~LAND and~the~DAY~s FIRST-FRUIT~s GRAPE~s **13:21** and~*they*[(m)]~*will*~GO.UP[(V)] and~*they*[(m)]~*will*~SCOUT[(V)] AT the~LAND from~WILDERNESS Tsin UNTIL Rehhov to~>~COME[(V)] Hhamat **13:22** and~*they*[(m)]~*will*~GO.UP[(V)] in~the~SOUTH and~*he*~*will*~COME[(V)] UNTIL Hhevron and~THERE Ahhiman Sheyshai and~Talmai BORN~s the~Anaq and~Hhevron SEVEN YEAR~s *she*~*did*~*be*~BUILD[(V)] to~FACE~s Tso'an Mits'rayim **13:23** and~*they*[(m)]~*will*~COME[(V)] UNTIL WADI Eshkol and~*they*[(m)]~*will*~CUT[(V)] from~THERE VINE and~CLUSTER GRAPE~s UNIT and~*they*[(m)]~*will*~LIFT.UP[(V)]~him in~the~BRANCH in~TWO and~FROM the~POMEGRANATE~s and~FROM FIG~s **13:24** to~the~AREA the~HE *he*~*did*~CALL.OUT[(V)] WADI Eshkol UPON CONCERNING the~CLUSTER WHICH *they*~*did*~CUT[(V)] from~THERE SON~s Yisra'eyl **13:25** and~*they*[(m)]~*will*~TURN.BACK[(V)] from~>~SCOUT[(V)] the~LAND from~CONCLUSION FOUR~s DAY **13:26** and~*they*[(m)]~*will*~WALK[(V)] and~*they*[(m)]~*will*~COME[(V)] TO Mosheh and~TO Aharon and~TO ALL COMPANY SON~s Yisra'eyl TO WILDERNESS

Paran Qadesh~unto and~they$^{(m)}$~will~make~TURN.BACK$^{(V)}$ AT~them$^{(m)}$ WORD and~AT ALL the~COMPANY and~they$^{(m)}$~will~make~SEE$^{(V)}$~them$^{(m)}$ AT PRODUCE the~LAND   **13:27** and~they$^{(m)}$~will~COUNT$^{(V)}$ to~him and~ they$^{(m)}$~will~SAY$^{(V)}$ we~did~COME$^{(V)}$ TO the~LAND WHICH you$^{(ms)}$~did~ SEND$^{(V)}$~us and~ALSO ISSUE$^{(V)}$~ing$^{(fs)}$ FAT and~HONEY SHE and~THIS PRODUCE~her   **13:28** FAR.END GIVEN.THAT STRONG the~PEOPLE the~ SETTLE$^{(V)}$~ing$^{(ms)}$ in~the~LAND and~the~CITY~s FENCE.IN$^{(V)}$~ed$^{(fp)}$ GREAT~s MANY and~ALSO BOY~s the~Anaq we~did~SEE$^{(V)}$ THERE   **13:29** Amaleq SETTLE$^{(V)}$~ing$^{(ms)}$ in~LAND the~SOUTH and~the~Hhet~of and~the~Yevus~of and~the~Emor~of SETTLE$^{(V)}$~ing$^{(ms)}$ in~the~HILL and~the~Kena'an~of SETTLE$^{(V)}$~ing$^{(ms)}$ UPON the~SEA and~UPON HAND the~Yarden   **13:30** and~ he~will~SILENCE$^{(V)}$ Kaleyv AT the~PEOPLE TO Mosheh and~he~will~SAY$^{(V)}$ >~ GO.UP$^{(V)}$ we~will~GO.UP$^{(V)}$~& and~we~did~POSSESS$^{(V)}$ AT~her GIVEN.THAT >~BE.ABLE$^{(V)}$ we~will~BE.ABLE$^{(V)}$ to~her   **13:31** and~the~MAN~s WHICH they~did~GO.UP$^{(V)}$ WITH~him they~did~SAY$^{(V)}$ NOT we~will~BE.ABLE$^{(V)}$ to~ >~GO.UP$^{(V)}$ TO the~PEOPLE GIVEN.THAT FORCEFUL HE FROM~ us   **13:32** and~they$^{(m)}$~will~make~GO.OUT$^{(V)}$~him SLANDER the~LAND WHICH they~did~SCOUT$^{(V)}$ AT~her TO SON~s Yisra'eyl to~>~SAY$^{(V)}$ the~LAND WHICH >~CROSS.OVER$^{(V)}$~us in~her to~>~SCOUT$^{(V)}$ AT~her LAND EAT$^{(V)}$~ ing$^{(fs)}$ SETTLE$^{(V)}$~ing$^{(mp)}$~her SHE and~ALL the~PEOPLE WHICH we~did~SEE$^{(V)}$ in~MIDST~her MAN~s MEASUREMENT~s   **13:33** and~THERE we~did~SEE$^{(V)}$ AT the~Nephilim~s SON~s Anaq FROM the~Nephilim~s and~we~will~ EXIST$^{(V)}$ in~EYE~s2~us like~GRASSHOPPER~s and~SO we~did~EXIST$^{(V)}$ in~ EYE~s2~them$^{(m)}$

Chapter 14

14:1 and~she~will~LIFT.UP$^{(V)}$ ALL the~COMPANY and~they$^{(m)}$~will~GIVE$^{(V)}$ AT VOICE~them$^{(m)}$ and~they$^{(m)}$~will~WEEP$^{(V)}$ the~PEOPLE in~the~NIGHT the~ HE   **14:2** and~they$^{(m)}$~will~be~MURMUR$^{(V)}$ UPON Mosheh and~UPON Aharon ALL SON~s Yisra'eyl and~they$^{(m)}$~will~SAY$^{(V)}$ TO~them$^{(m)}$ ALL the~ COMPANY WOULD.THAT we~did~DIE$^{(V)}$ in~LAND Mits'rayim OR in~the~ WILDERNESS the~THIS WOULD.THAT we~did~DIE$^{(V)}$ **14:3** and~to~WHAT YHWH make~COME$^{(V)}$~ing$^{(ms)}$ AT~us TO the~LAND the~THIS to~>~FALL$^{(V)}$ in~ the~SWORD WOMAN~s~us and~BABIES~us they$^{(m)}$~will~EXIST$^{(V)}$ to~the~ PLUNDER ?~NOT FUNCTIONAL to~us >~TURN.BACK$^{(V)}$ Mits'rayim~ unto   **14:4** and~they$^{(m)}$~will~SAY$^{(V)}$ MAN TO BROTHER~him we~did~GIVE$^{(V)}$ HEAD and~we~did~TURN.BACK$^{(V)}$ Mits'rayim~unto   **14:5** and~he~will~ FALL$^{(V)}$ Mosheh and~Aharon UPON FACE~s~them$^{(m)}$ to~FACE~s ALL ASSEMBLY COMPANY SON~s Yisra'eyl   **14:6** and~Yehoshu'a SON Nun and~ Kaleyv SON Yephunah FROM the~SCOUT$^{(V)}$~ing$^{(mp)}$ AT the~LAND they~did~ TEAR$^{(V)}$ GARMENT~s~them$^{(m)}$ **14:7** and~they$^{(m)}$~will~SAY$^{(V)}$ TO ALL COMPANY SON~s Yisra'eyl to~>~SAY$^{(V)}$ the~LAND WHICH >~CROSS.OVER$^{(V)}$~

us in~her to~>~SCOUT⁽ⱽ⁾ AT~her FUNCTIONAL the~LAND MANY MANY **14:8** IF he~did~DELIGHT⁽ⱽ⁾ in~us **YHWH** and~he~did~make~COME⁽ⱽ⁾ AT~us TO the~LAND the~THIS and~he~did~GIVE⁽ⱽ⁾~her to~us LAND WHICH SHE ISSUE⁽ⱽ⁾~ing⁽ᶠˢ⁾ FAT and~HONEY **14:9** SURELY in~**YHWH** DO.NOT you⁽ᵐᵖ⁾~will~REBEL⁽ⱽ⁾ and~YOU⁽ᵐᵖ⁾ DO.NOT you⁽ᵐᵖ⁾~will~FEAR⁽ⱽ⁾ AT PEOPLE the~LAND GIVEN.THAT BREAD~us THEY⁽ᵐ⁾ he~did~TURN.ASIDE⁽ⱽ⁾ SHADOW~them⁽ᵐ⁾ from~UPON~them⁽ᵐ⁾ and~**YHWH** AT~us DO.NOT you⁽ᵐᵖ⁾~will~FEAR⁽ⱽ⁾~them⁽ᵐ⁾ **14:10** and~they⁽ᵐ⁾~will~SAY⁽ⱽ⁾ ALL the~COMPANY to~>~KILL.BY.STONING⁽ⱽ⁾ AT~them⁽ᵐ⁾ in~the~STONE~s and~ARMAMENT **YHWH** he~did~be~SEE⁽ⱽ⁾ in~TENT APPOINTED TO ALL SON~s Yisra'eyl **14:11** and~he~will~SAY⁽ⱽ⁾ **YHWH** TO Mosheh UNTIL WHEREVER they⁽ᵐ⁾~will~much~PROVOKE⁽ⱽ⁾~me the~PEOPLE the~THIS and~UNTIL WHEREVER NOT they⁽ᵐ⁾~will~make~SECURE⁽ⱽ⁾ in~me in~ALL the~SIGN~s WHICH I~did~DO⁽ⱽ⁾ in~INSIDE~him **14:12** I~will~make~HIT⁽ⱽ⁾~him in~the~EPIDEMIC and~I~will~make~POSSESS⁽ⱽ⁾~him and~I~will~DO⁽ⱽ⁾~& AT~you⁽ᵐˢ⁾ to~NATION GREAT and~NUMEROUS FROM~him **14:13** and~he~will~SAY⁽ⱽ⁾ Mosheh TO **YHWH** and~they~did~HEAR⁽ⱽ⁾ Mits'rayim GIVEN.THAT you⁽ᵐˢ⁾~did~make~GO.UP⁽ⱽ⁾ in~STRENGTH~you⁽ᵐˢ⁾ AT the~PEOPLE the~THIS from~INSIDE~him **14:14** and~they~did~SAY⁽ⱽ⁾ TO SETTLE⁽ⱽ⁾~ing⁽ᵐˢ⁾ the~LAND the~THIS they~did~HEAR⁽ⱽ⁾ GIVEN.THAT YOU⁽ᵐˢ⁾ **YHWH** in~INSIDE the~PEOPLE the~THIS WHICH EYE in~EYE he~did~be~SEE⁽ⱽ⁾ YOU⁽ᵐˢ⁾ **YHWH** and~CLOUD~you⁽ᵐˢ⁾ STAND⁽ⱽ⁾~ing⁽ᵐˢ⁾ UPON~them⁽ᵐ⁾ and~in~PILLAR CLOUD YOU⁽ᵐˢ⁾ WALK⁽ⱽ⁾~ing⁽ᵐˢ⁾ to~FACE~s~them⁽ᵐ⁾ DAYTIME and~in~PILLAR FIRE NIGHT **14:15** and~you⁽ᵐˢ⁾~did~make~DIE⁽ⱽ⁾ AT the~PEOPLE the~THIS like~MAN UNIT and~they~did~SAY⁽ⱽ⁾ the~NATION~s WHICH they~did~HEAR⁽ⱽ⁾ AT REPORT~you⁽ᵐˢ⁾ to~>~SAY⁽ⱽ⁾ **14:16** from~EXCEPT >~BE.ABLE⁽ⱽ⁾ **YHWH** to~>~make~COME⁽ⱽ⁾ AT the~PEOPLE the~THIS TO the~LAND WHICH he~did~be~SWEAR⁽ⱽ⁾ to~them⁽ᵐ⁾ and~he~will~SLAY⁽ⱽ⁾~them⁽ᵐ⁾ in~the~WILDERNESS **14:17** and~NOW he~will~MAGNIFY⁽ⱽ⁾ PLEASE STRENGTH Adonai like~WHICH you⁽ᵐˢ⁾~did~much~SPEAK⁽ⱽ⁾ to~>~SAY⁽ⱽ⁾ **14:18** **YHWH** SLOW NOSE~s2 and~ABUNDANT KINDNESS LIFT.UP⁽ⱽ⁾~ing⁽ᵐˢ⁾ TWISTEDNESS and~OFFENSE and~>~much~ACQUIT⁽ⱽ⁾ NOT he~will~much~ACQUIT⁽ⱽ⁾ REGISTER⁽ⱽ⁾~ing⁽ᵐˢ⁾ TWISTEDNESS FATHER~s UPON SON~s UPON THIRD.GENERATION~s and~UPON FOURTH.GENERATION~s **14:19** I⁽ᵐˢ⁾~FORGIVE⁽ⱽ⁾ PLEASE to~the~TWISTEDNESS the~PEOPLE the~THIS like~MAGNIFICENCE KINDNESS~you⁽ᵐˢ⁾ and~like~WHICH you⁽ᵐˢ⁾~did~LIFT.UP⁽ⱽ⁾ to~the~PEOPLE the~THIS from~Mits'rayim and~UNTIL TO.THIS.POINT **14:20** and~he~will~SAY⁽ⱽ⁾ **YHWH** I~did~FORGIVE⁽ⱽ⁾ like~WORD~you⁽ᵐˢ⁾ **14:21** and~BUT LIVING I and~he~will~be~FILL⁽ⱽ⁾ ARMAMENT **YHWH** AT ALL the~LAND **14:22** GIVEN.THAT ALL the~MAN~s the~SEE⁽ⱽ⁾~ing⁽ᵐᵖ⁾ AT ARMAMENT~me and~AT SIGN~s~me WHICH I~did~DO⁽ⱽ⁾ in~Mits'rayim and~in~the~WILDERNESS and~they⁽ᵐ⁾~will~much~TEST⁽ⱽ⁾ AT~me THIS TEN FOOTSTEP~s and~NOT they~did~HEAR⁽ⱽ⁾ in~VOICE~me **14:23** IF they⁽ᵐ⁾~will~SEE⁽ⱽ⁾ AT the~LAND WHICH I~did~be~SWEAR⁽ⱽ⁾ to~FATHER~s~them⁽ᵐ⁾ and~ALL much~PROVOKE⁽ⱽ⁾~ing⁽ᵐᵖ⁾~me NOT he~will~SEE⁽ⱽ⁾~

her **14:24** and~SERVANT~me Kaleyv CONSEQUENCE *she~did*~EXIST^(V) WIND OTHER WITH~him and~*he~will~much*~FILL^(V) AFTER~me and~*I~did~make*~COME^(V)~him TO the~LAND WHICH *he~did*~COME^(V) THERE~unto and~SEED~him *he~will~make*~POSSESS^(V)~her **14:25** and~the~Amaleq~of and~the~Kena'an~of SETTLE^(V)~*ed*^(ms) in~the~VALLEY TOMORROW !^(mp)~TURN^(V) and~!^(mp)~JOURNEY^(V) to~you^(mp) the~WILDERNESS ROAD SEA REEDS **14:26** and~*he~will~much*~SPEAK^(V) **YHWH** TO Mosheh and~TO Aharon to~>~SAY^(V) **14:27** UNTIL HOW.LONG to~the~COMPANY the~DYSFUNCTIONAL the~THIS WHICH THEY^(m) *make*~MURMUR^(V)~*ing*^(mp) UPON~me AT MURMURING SON~s Yisra'eyl WHICH THEY^(m) *make*~MURMUR^(V)~*ing*^(mp) UPON~me *I~did*~HEAR^(V) **14:28** !^(ms)~SAY^(V) TO~them^(m) LIVING I DECLARE^(V)~*ed*^(ms) **YHWH** IF NOT like~WHICH *you*^(mp)~*did~much*~SPEAK^(V) in~EAR~s2~me SO *I~will*~DO^(V) to~you^(mp) **14:29** in~the~WILDERNESS the~THIS *they*^(m)~*will*~FALL^(V) CORPSE~s~you^(mp) and~ALL REGISTER^(V)~*ed*^(mp)~you^(mp) to~ALL NUMBER~you^(mp) from~SON TEN~s YEAR and~UPWARD~unto WHICH *you*^(mp)~*did~make*~MURMUR^(V) UPON~me **14:30** IF YOU^(mp) *you*^(mp)~*will*~COME^(V) TO the~LAND WHICH *I~did*~LIFT.UP^(V) AT HAND~me to~>~DWELL^(V) AT~you^(mp) in~her GIVEN.THAT IF Kaleyv SON Yephunah and~Yehoshu'a SON Nun **14:31** and~BABIES~you^(mp) WHICH *you*^(mp)~*did*~SAY^(V) to~the~PLUNDER *he~will*~EXIST^(V) and~*I~did~make*~COME^(V) AT~them^(m) and~*they~did*~KNOW^(V) AT the~LAND WHICH *you*^(mp)~*did*~REJECT^(V) in~her **14:32** and~CORPSE~s~you^(mp) YOU^(mp) *they*^(m)~*will*~FALL^(V) in~the~WILDERNESS the~THIS **14:33** and~SON~s~you^(mp) *they*^(m)~*will*~EXIST^(V) FEED^(V)~*ing*^(mp) in~the~WILDERNESS FOUR~s YEAR and~*they~did*~LIFT.UP^(V) AT WHOREDOM~you^(mp) UNTIL >~BE.WHOLE^(V) CORPSE~s~you^(mp) in~the~WILDERNESS **14:34** in~NUMBER the~DAY~s WHICH *you*^(ms)~*did*~SCOUT^(V) AT the~LAND FOUR~s DAY DAY to~the~YEAR DAY to~the~YEAR *you*^(mp)~*will*~LIFT.UP^(V) AT TWISTEDNESS~s~you^(mp) FOUR~s YEAR and~*you*^(mp)~*did*~KNOW^(V) AT DEFIANCE~me **14:35** I **YHWH** *I~did~much*~SPEAK^(V) IF NOT THIS *I~will*~DO^(V) to~ALL the~COMPANY the~DYSFUNCTIONAL the~THIS the~*be*~APPOINT^(V)~*ing*^(mp) UPON~me in~the~WILDERNESS the~THIS *they*^(m)~*will*~BE.WHOLE^(V) and~THERE *they*^(m)~*will*~DIE^(V) **14:36** and~the~MAN~s WHICH *he~did*~SEND^(V) Mosheh to~>~SCOUT^(V) AT the~LAND and~*they*^(m)~*will*~TURN.BACK^(V) and~*they*^(m)~*will*~*be*~MURMUR^(V) UPON~him AT ALL the~COMPANY to~>~*make*~GO.OUT^(V) SLANDER UPON the~LAND **14:37** and~*they*^(m)~*will*~DIE^(V) the~MAN~s *make*~GOING.OUT~s SLANDER the~LAND DYSFUNCTIONAL in~the~PESTILENCE to~FACE~s **YHWH** **14:38** and~Yehoshu'a SON Nun and~Kaleyv SON Yephunah !^(mp)~LIVE^(V) FROM the~MAN~s the~THEY^(m) the~WALK^(V)~*ing*^(mp) to~>~SCOUT^(V) AT the~LAND **14:39** and~*he~will~much*~SPEAK^(V) Mosheh AT the~WORD~s the~THESE TO ALL SON~s Yisra'eyl and~*they*^(m)~*will~self*~MOURN^(V) the~PEOPLE MANY **14:40** and~*they*^(m)~*will~make*~DEPART.EARLY^(V) in~the~MORNING and~*they*^(m)~*will*~GO.UP^(V) TO HEAD the~HILL to~>~SAY^(V) LOOK~us and~*we*~GO.UP^(V) TO the~AREA WHICH *he~did*~SAY^(V) **YHWH** GIVEN.THAT *we~did*~FAIL^(V) **14:41** and~*he~will*~SAY^(V)

The Book of Numbers

Mosheh to~WHAT THIS YOU⁽ᵐᵖ⁾ CROSS.OVER⁽ᵛ⁾~*ing*⁽ᵐᵖ⁾ AT MOUTH **YHWH** and~SHE NOT *she~will*~PROSPER⁽ᵛ⁾ **14:42** DO.NOT *you*⁽ᵐᵖ⁾~*will*~GO.UP⁽ᵛ⁾ GIVEN.THAT WITHOUT **YHWH** in~INSIDE~you⁽ᵐᵖ⁾ and~NOT *you*⁽ᵐᵖ⁾~*will*~be~ SMITE⁽ᵛ⁾ to~FACE~s ATTACK⁽ᵛ⁾~*ing*⁽ᵐᵖ⁾~*you*⁽ᵐᵖ⁾ **14:43** GIVEN.THAT the~ Amaleq~of and~the~Kena'an~of THERE to~FACE~s~you⁽ᵐᵖ⁾ and~*you*⁽ᵐᵖ⁾~ *did*~FALL⁽ᵛ⁾ in~SWORD GIVEN.THAT UPON SO *you*⁽ᵐᵖ⁾~*did*~TURN.BACK⁽ᵛ⁾ from~AFTER **YHWH** and~NOT *he~will*~EXIST⁽ᵛ⁾ **YHWH** WITH~ you⁽ᵐᵖ⁾ **14:44** and~*they*⁽ᵐ⁾~*will*~make~PRESUME⁽ᵛ⁾ to~>~GO.UP⁽ᵛ⁾ TO HEAD the~HILL and~BOX COVENANT **YHWH** and~Mosheh NOT *they~did*~ MOVE.AWAY⁽ᵛ⁾ from~INSIDE the~CAMP **14:45** and~*he~will*~GO.DOWN⁽ᵛ⁾ the~Amaleq~of and~the~Kena'an~of the~SETTLE⁽ᵛ⁾~*ing*⁽ᵐˢ⁾ in~the~HILL the~ HE and~*they*⁽ᵐ⁾~*will*~make~HIT⁽ᵛ⁾~them⁽ᵐ⁾ and~*they*⁽ᵐ⁾~*will*~make~ SMASH⁽ᵛ⁾~them⁽ᵐ⁾ UNTIL the~Hharmah

Chapter 15

15:1 and~*he~will*~much~SPEAK⁽ᵛ⁾ **YHWH** TO Mosheh to~>~SAY⁽ᵛ⁾ **15:2** !⁽ᵐˢ⁾~ much~SPEAK⁽ᵛ⁾ TO SON~s Yisra'eyl and~*you*⁽ᵐˢ⁾~*did*~SAY⁽ᵛ⁾ TO~them⁽ᵐ⁾ GIVEN.THAT *you*⁽ᵐᵖ⁾~*will*~COME⁽ᵛ⁾ TO LAND SETTLING~s~you⁽ᵐᵖ⁾ WHICH I GIVE⁽ᵛ⁾~*ing*⁽ᵐˢ⁾ to~you⁽ᵐᵖ⁾ **15:3** and~*you*⁽ᵐᵖ⁾~*did*~DO⁽ᵛ⁾ FIRE.OFFERING to~ **YHWH** ASCENSION.OFFERING OR SACRIFICE to~>~much~PERFORM⁽ᵛ⁾ VOW OR in~FREEWILL.OFFERING OR in~APPOINTED~s~you⁽ᵐᵖ⁾ to~>~DO⁽ᵛ⁾ AROMA SWEET to~**YHWH** FROM the~CATTLE OR FROM the~FLOCKS **15:4** and~*he~ did*~make~COME.NEAR⁽ᵛ⁾ the~make~COME.NEAR⁽ᵛ⁾~*ing*⁽ᵐˢ⁾ DONATION~him to~**YHWH** DEPOSIT FLOUR ONE.TENTH MIX⁽ᵛ⁾~*ed*⁽ᵐˢ⁾ in~FOURTH the~HIYN OIL **15:5** and~WINE to~the~POURING FOURTH the~HIYN *you*⁽ᵐˢ⁾~*will*~DO⁽ᵛ⁾ UPON the~ASCENSION.OFFERING OR to~the~SACRIFICE to~the~SHEEP the~ UNIT **15:6** OR to~the~BUCK *you*⁽ᵐˢ⁾~*will*~DO⁽ᵛ⁾ DEPOSIT FLOUR TWO ONE.TENTH~s MIX⁽ᵛ⁾~*ed*⁽ᶠˢ⁾ in~the~OIL THIRD the~HIYN **15:7** and~WINE to~ the~POURING THIRD the~HIYN *you*⁽ᵐˢ⁾~*will*~make~COME.NEAR⁽ᵛ⁾ AROMA SWEET to~**YHWH** **15:8** and~GIVEN.THAT *you*⁽ᵐˢ⁾~*will*~DO⁽ᵛ⁾ SON CATTLE ASCENSION.OFFERING OR SACRIFICE to~>~much~PERFORM⁽ᵛ⁾ VOW OR OFFERING.OF.RESTITUTION~s to~**YHWH** **15:9** and~*he~did*~make~ COME.NEAR⁽ᵛ⁾ UPON SON the~CATTLE DEPOSIT FLOUR THREE ONE.TENTH~s MIX⁽ᵛ⁾~*ed*⁽ᵐˢ⁾ in~the~OIL HALF the~HIYN **15:10** and~WINE *you*⁽ᵐˢ⁾~*will*~ make~COME.NEAR⁽ᵛ⁾ to~the~POURING HALF the~HIYN FIRE.OFFERING AROMA SWEET to~**YHWH** **15:11** like~IN.THIS.WAY *he~will*~be~DO⁽ᵛ⁾ to~ the~OX the~UNIT OR to~the~BUCK the~UNIT OR to~the~RAM in~the~ SHEEP~s OR in~the~SHE-GOAT~s **15:12** like~the~NUMBER WHICH *you*⁽ᵐᵖ⁾~ *will*~DO⁽ᵛ⁾ like~IN.THIS.WAY *you*⁽ᵐᵖ⁾~*will*~DO⁽ᵛ⁾ to~UNIT like~NUMBER~ them⁽ᵐ⁾ **15:13** ALL the~NATIVE *he~will*~DO⁽ᵛ⁾ like~IN.THIS.WAY AT THESE to~>~make~COME.NEAR⁽ᵛ⁾ FIRE.OFFERING AROMA SWEET to~ **YHWH** **15:14** and~GIVEN.THAT *he~will*~IMMIGRATE⁽ᵛ⁾ AT~you⁽ᵐᵖ⁾

IMMIGRANT OR WHICH in~MIDST~you(mp) to~GENERATION~s~you(mp) and~ he~did~DO(V) FIRE.OFFERING AROMA SWEET to~**YHWH** like~WHICH *you(mp)~ will~*DO(V) SO he~will~DO(V)   **15:15** the~ASSEMBLY CUSTOM UNIT to~you(mp) and~to~IMMIGRANT the~IMMIGRATE(V)~*ing(ms)* CUSTOM DISTANT to~ GENERATION~s~you(mp) like~you(mp) like~the~IMMIGRANT he~will~EXIST(V) to~FACE~s **YHWH**   **15:16** TEACHING UNIT and~DECISION UNIT he~will~ EXIST(V) to~you(mp) and~to~IMMIGRANT the~IMMIGRATE(V)~*ing(ms)* AT~ you(mp)   **15:17** and~he~will~much~SPEAK(V) **YHWH** TO Mosheh to~>~ SAY(V)   **15:18** *!(ms)~much~*SPEAK(V) TO SON~s Yisra'eyl and~*you(mp)~did~*SAY(V) TO~them(m) in~>~COME(V)~you(mp) TO the~LAND WHICH I *make*~COME(V)~ *ing(ms)* AT~you(mp) THERE~unto   **15:19** and~he~did~EXIST(V) in~>~EAT(V)~ you(mp) from~BREAD the~LAND *you(mp)~will~make*~RAISE.UP(V) OFFERING to~**YHWH**   **15:20** SUMMIT BREAD.MEAL~s~you(mp) PIERCED.BREAD *you(mp)~ will~make*~RAISE.UP(V) OFFERING like~OFFERING FLOOR SO *you(mp)~will~ make*~RAISE.UP(V) AT~her   **15:21** from~SUMMIT BREAD.MEAL~s~you(mp) *you(mp)~will~*GIVE(V) to~**YHWH** OFFERING to~GENERATION~s~ you(mp)   **15:22** and~GIVEN.THAT *you(ms)~will~*GO.ASTRAY(V) and~NOT *you(mp)~will~*DO(V) AT ALL the~DIRECTIVE~s the~THESE WHICH he~did~ much~SPEAK(V) **YHWH** TO Mosheh   **15:23** AT ALL WHICH he~did~much~ DIRECT(V) **YHWH** TO~you(mp) in~HAND Mosheh FROM the~DAY WHICH he~ did~much~DIRECT(V) **YHWH** and~FURTHER to~GENERATION~s~ you(mp)   **15:24** and~he~did~EXIST(V) IF from~EYE~s2 the~COMPANY she~did~ be~DO(V) to~ERROR and~*they~did~*DO(V) ALL the~COMPANY BULL SON CATTLE UNIT to~ASCENSION.OFFERING to~AROMA SWEET to~**YHWH** and~ DEPOSIT~him and~POURING~him like~the~DECISION and~HAIRY.GOAT SHE-GOAT~s UNIT to~FAILURE   **15:25** and~he~did~much~COVER(V) the~ ADMINISTRATOR UPON ALL COMPANY SON~s Yisra'eyl and~he~did~be~ FORGIVE(V) to~them(m) GIVEN.THAT ERROR SHE and~THEY(m) *they~did~ make*~COME(V) AT DONATION~them(m) FIRE.OFFERING to~**YHWH** and~ FAILURE~them(m) to~FACE~s **YHWH** UPON ERROR~them(m)   **15:26** and~he~ did~be~FORGIVE(V) to~ALL COMPANY SON~s Yisra'eyl and~to~IMMIGRANT the~IMMIGRATE(V)~*ing(ms)* in~MIDST~them(m) GIVEN.THAT to~ALL the~ PEOPLE in~ERROR   **15:27** and~IF SOUL UNIT *she~will~*FAIL(V) in~ERROR and~ *she~did~make*~COME.NEAR(V) SHE-GOAT DAUGHTER YEAR~her to~ FAILURE   **15:28** and~he~did~much~COVER(V) the~ADMINISTRATOR UPON the~SOUL the~ERR(V)~*ing(fs)* in~>~FAIL(V)~& in~ERROR to~FACE~s **YHWH** to~ >~much~COVER(V) UPON~him and~he~did~be~FORGIVE(V) to~ him   **15:29** the~NATIVE in~SON~s Yisra'eyl and~to~IMMIGRANT the~ IMMIGRATE(V)~*ing(ms)* in~MIDST~them(m) TEACHING UNIT he~will~EXIST(V) to~you(mp) to~the~DO(V)~*ing(ms)* in~ERROR   **15:30** and~the~SOUL WHICH *she~will~*DO(V) in~HAND RAISED~*ing(fs)* FROM the~NATIVE and~FROM the~ IMMIGRANT AT **YHWH** HE much~TAUNT(V)~*ing(ms)* and~*she~did~be~*CUT(V) the~SOUL the~SHE from~INSIDE PEOPLE~her   **15:31** GIVEN.THAT WORD **YHWH** he~did~DISDAIN(V) and~AT DIRECTIVE~him he~did~*make*~BREAK(V) >~be~CUT(V) *she~will~be~*CUT(V) the~SOUL the~SHE TWISTEDNESS~her in~

her **15:32** and~*they*⁽ᵐ⁾~*will*~EXIST⁽ⱽ⁾ SON~s Yisra'eyl in~the~WILDERNESS and~*they*⁽ᵐ⁾~*will*~FIND⁽ⱽ⁾ MAN *much*~COLLECT⁽ⱽ⁾~*ing*⁽ᵐˢ⁾ TREE~s in~DAY the~CEASING **15:33** and~*they*⁽ᵐ⁾~*will*~*make*~COME.NEAR⁽ⱽ⁾ AT~him FIND⁽ⱽ⁾~*ing*⁽ᵐᵖ⁾ AT~him *much*~COLLECT⁽ⱽ⁾~*ing*⁽ᵐˢ⁾ TREE~s TO Mosheh and~TO Aharon and~TO ALL the~COMPANY **15:34** and~*they*⁽ᵐ⁾~*will*~*make*~REST⁽ⱽ⁾ AT~him in~the~CUSTODY GIVEN.THAT NOT *he*~*did*~*be*~*much*~SPREAD.OUT⁽ⱽ⁾ WHAT *he*~*will*~*be*~DO⁽ⱽ⁾ to~him **15:35** and~*he*~*will*~SAY⁽ⱽ⁾ **YHWH** TO Mosheh >~DIE⁽ⱽ⁾ *he*~*will*~*be*~*make*~DIE⁽ⱽ⁾ the~MAN >~KILL.BY.STONING⁽ⱽ⁾ AT~him in~the~STONE~s ALL the~COMPANY from~OUTSIDE to~the~CAMP **15:36** and~*they*⁽ᵐ⁾~*will*~*make*~GO.OUT⁽ⱽ⁾ AT~him ALL the~COMPANY TO from~OUTSIDE to~the~CAMP and~*they*⁽ᵐ⁾~*will*~KILL.BY.STONING⁽ⱽ⁾ AT~him in~the~STONE~s and~*he*~*will*~DIE⁽ⱽ⁾ like~WHICH *he*~*did*~*much*~DIRECT⁽ⱽ⁾ **YHWH** AT Mosheh **15:37** and~*he*~*will*~SAY⁽ⱽ⁾ **YHWH** TO Mosheh to~>~SAY⁽ⱽ⁾ **15:38** *!*⁽ᵐˢ⁾~*much*~SPEAK⁽ⱽ⁾ TO SON~s Yisra'eyl and~*you*⁽ᵐˢ⁾~*did*~SAY⁽ⱽ⁾ TO~them⁽ᵐ⁾ and~*they*~*did*~DO⁽ⱽ⁾ to~them⁽ᵐ⁾ FRINGE UPON WING~s GARMENT~s~them⁽ᵐ⁾ to~GENERATION~s~them⁽ᵐ⁾ and~*they*~*did*~GIVE⁽ⱽ⁾ UPON FRINGE the~WING CORD BLUE **15:39** and~*he*~*did*~EXIST⁽ⱽ⁾ to~you⁽ᵐᵖ⁾ to~FRINGE and~*you*⁽ᵐᵖ⁾~*did*~SEE⁽ⱽ⁾ AT~him and~*you*⁽ᵐᵖ⁾~*did*~REMEMBER⁽ⱽ⁾ AT ALL DIRECTIVE~s **YHWH** and~*you*⁽ᵐᵖ⁾~*did*~DO⁽ⱽ⁾ AT~them⁽ᵐ⁾ and~NOT *you*⁽ᵐᵖ⁾~*will*~SCOUT⁽ⱽ⁾ AFTER HEART~*you*⁽ᵐᵖ⁾ and~AFTER EYE~s2~*you*⁽ᵐᵖ⁾ WHICH YOU⁽ᵐᵖ⁾ BE.A.HARLOT⁽ⱽ⁾~*ing*⁽ᵐᵖ⁾ AFTER~them⁽ᵐ⁾ **15:40** to~THAT *you*⁽ᵐᵖ⁾~*will*~REMEMBER⁽ⱽ⁾ and~*you*⁽ᵐᵖ⁾~*did*~DO⁽ⱽ⁾ AT ALL DIRECTIVE~s~me and~*you*⁽ᵐᵖ⁾~*did*~EXIST⁽ⱽ⁾ UNIQUE~s to~Elohiym~*you*⁽ᵐᵖ⁾ **15:41** I **YHWH** Elohiym~*you*⁽ᵐᵖ⁾ WHICH *I*~*did*~*make*~GO.OUT⁽ⱽ⁾ AT~*you*⁽ᵐᵖ⁾ from~LAND Mits'rayim to~>~EXIST⁽ⱽ⁾ to~*you*⁽ᵐᵖ⁾ to~Elohiym I **YHWH** Elohiym~*you*⁽ᵐᵖ⁾

Chapter 16

16:1 and~*he*~*will*~TAKE⁽ⱽ⁾ Qorahh SON Yits'har SON Qehat SON Lewi and~Datan and~Aviram SON~s Eli'av and~On SON Pelet SON~s Re'uven **16:2** and~*they*⁽ᵐ⁾~*will*~RISE⁽ⱽ⁾ to~FACE~s Mosheh and~MAN~s from~SON~s Yisra'eyl FIVE~s and~HUNDRED~s2 CAPTAIN~s WITNESS SELECTED~s APPOINTED MAN~s TITLE **16:3** and~*they*⁽ᵐ⁾~*will*~*be*~ASSEMBLE⁽ⱽ⁾ UPON Mosheh and~UPON Aharon and~*they*⁽ᵐ⁾~*will*~SAY⁽ⱽ⁾ TO~them⁽ᵐ⁾ ABUNDANT to~*you*⁽ᵐᵖ⁾ GIVEN.THAT ALL the~COMPANY ALL~them⁽ᵐ⁾ UNIQUE~s and~in~MIDST~them⁽ᵐ⁾ **YHWH** and~WHY *you*⁽ᵐᵖ⁾~*will*~*self*~LIFT.UP⁽ⱽ⁾ UPON ASSEMBLY **YHWH** **16:4** and~*he*~*will*~HEAR⁽ⱽ⁾ Mosheh and~*he*~*will*~FALL⁽ⱽ⁾ UPON FACE~s~him **16:5** and~*he*~*will*~*much*~SPEAK⁽ⱽ⁾ TO Qorahh and~TO ALL COMPANY~him to~>~SAY⁽ⱽ⁾ MORNING and~*he*~*will*~*make*~KNOW⁽ⱽ⁾ **YHWH** AT WHICH to~him and~AT the~UNIQUE and~*he*~*did*~*make*~COME.NEAR⁽ⱽ⁾ TO~him and~AT WHICH *he*~*will*~CHOOSE⁽ⱽ⁾ in~him *he*~*will*~*make*~COME.NEAR⁽ⱽ⁾ TO~him **16:6** THIS *!*⁽ᵐᵖ⁾~DO⁽ⱽ⁾ *!*⁽ᵐᵖ⁾~TAKE⁽ⱽ⁾ to~*you*⁽ᵐᵖ⁾ FIRE.PAN~s Qorahh and~ALL COMPANY~him **16:7** and~*!*⁽ᵐᵖ⁾~GIVE⁽ⱽ⁾

in~them⁽ᶠ⁾ FIRE and~*they~did*~PLACE⁽ⱽ⁾ UPON~them⁽ᶠ⁾ INCENSE.SMOKE to~FACE~s **YHWH** TOMORROW and~*he~did*~EXIST⁽ⱽ⁾ the~MAN WHICH *he~will*~CHOOSE⁽ⱽ⁾ **YHWH** HE the~UNIQUE ABUNDANT to~you⁽ᵐᵖ⁾ SON~s Lewi **16:8** and~*he~will~*SAY⁽ⱽ⁾ Mosheh TO Qorahh *!⁽ᵐᵖ⁾*~HEAR⁽ⱽ⁾ PLEASE SON~s Lewi **16:9** ?~SMALL.AMOUNT from~you⁽ᵐᵖ⁾ GIVEN.THAT *he~did~make*~SEPARATE⁽ⱽ⁾ Elohiym Yisra'eyl AT~you⁽ᵐᵖ⁾ from~COMPANY Yisra'eyl to~>~*make*~COME.NEAR⁽ⱽ⁾ AT~you⁽ᵐᵖ⁾ TO~him to~>~SERVE⁽ⱽ⁾ AT SERVICE DWELLING **YHWH** and~to~>~STAND⁽ⱽ⁾ to~FACE~s the~COMPANY to~>~much~MINISTER⁽ⱽ⁾~them⁽ᵐ⁾ **16:10** and~*he~will~make*~COME.NEAR⁽ⱽ⁾ AT~you⁽ᵐˢ⁾ and~AT ALL BROTHER~s~you⁽ᵐˢ⁾ SON~s Lewi AT~you⁽ᶠˢ⁾ and~*you⁽ᵐᵖ⁾~did*~much~SEARCH.OUT⁽ⱽ⁾ ALSO ADMINISTRATION **16:11** to~SO YOU⁽ᵐˢ⁾ and~ALL COMPANY~you⁽ᵐˢ⁾ the~*be*~APPOINT⁽ⱽ⁾~*ing⁽ᵐᵖ⁾* UPON **YHWH** and~Aharon WHAT HE GIVEN.THAT *you⁽ᵐᵖ⁾~will~be*~MURMUR⁽ⱽ⁾ UPON~him **16:12** and~*he~will*~SEND⁽ⱽ⁾ Mosheh to~>~CALL.OUT⁽ⱽ⁾ to~Datan and~to~Aviram SON~s Eli'av and~*they⁽ᵐ⁾~will~*SAY⁽ⱽ⁾ NOT *we~will~*GO.UP⁽ⱽ⁾~& **16:13** ?~SMALL.AMOUNT GIVEN.THAT *you⁽ᵐˢ⁾~did~make*~GO.UP⁽ⱽ⁾~us from~LAND ISSUE⁽ⱽ⁾~*ing⁽ᶠˢ⁾* FAT and~HONEY to~>~*make*~DIE⁽ⱽ⁾~us in~the~WILDERNESS GIVEN.THAT *you⁽ᵐˢ⁾~will~self~*TURN.ASIDE⁽ⱽ⁾ UPON~us ALSO >~*self*~TURN.ASIDE⁽ⱽ⁾ **16:14** MOREOVER NOT TO LAND ISSUE⁽ⱽ⁾~*ing⁽ᶠˢ⁾* FAT and~HONEY *you⁽ᵐˢ⁾~did~make*~COME⁽ⱽ⁾~us and~*you⁽ᵐˢ⁾~will*~GIVE⁽ⱽ⁾ to~us INHERITANCE FIELD and~VINEYARD ?~EYE~s2 the~MAN~s the~THEY⁽ᵐ⁾ *you⁽ᵐˢ⁾~will*~much~PICK.OUT⁽ⱽ⁾ NOT *we~will~*GO.UP⁽ⱽ⁾~& **16:15** and~*he~will*~FLARE.UP⁽ⱽ⁾ to~Mosheh MANY and~*he~will~*SAY⁽ⱽ⁾ TO **YHWH** DO.NOT *you⁽ᵐˢ⁾~will~*TURN⁽ⱽ⁾ TO DEPOSIT~them⁽ᵐ⁾ NOT DONKEY UNIT from~them⁽ᵐ⁾ *I~did*~LIFT.UP⁽ⱽ⁾ and~NOT *I~did~make~*BE.DYSFUNCTIONAL⁽ⱽ⁾ AT UNIT from~them⁽ᵐ⁾ **16:16** and~*he~will~*SAY⁽ⱽ⁾ Mosheh TO Qorahh YOU⁽ᵐˢ⁾ and~ALL COMPANY~you⁽ᵐˢ⁾ *!⁽ᵐᵖ⁾*~EXIST⁽ⱽ⁾ to~FACE~s **YHWH** YOU⁽ᵐˢ⁾ and~THEY⁽ᵐ⁾ and~Aharon TOMORROW **16:17** and~*!⁽ᵐᵖ⁾*~TAKE⁽ⱽ⁾ MAN FIRE.PAN~him and~*you⁽ᵐᵖ⁾~did*~GIVE⁽ⱽ⁾ UPON~them⁽ᵐ⁾ INCENSE.SMOKE and~*you⁽ᵐᵖ⁾~did~make*~COME.NEAR⁽ⱽ⁾ to~FACE~s **YHWH** MAN FIRE.PAN~him FIVE~s and~HUNDRED~s2 FIRE.PAN~s and~YOU⁽ᵐˢ⁾ and~Aharon MAN FIRE.PAN~him **16:18** and~*they⁽ᵐ⁾~will~*TAKE⁽ⱽ⁾ MAN FIRE.PAN~him and~*they⁽ᵐ⁾~will~*GIVE⁽ⱽ⁾ UPON~them⁽ᵐ⁾ FIRE and~*they⁽ᵐ⁾~will~*PLACE⁽ⱽ⁾ UPON~them⁽ᵐ⁾ INCENSE.SMOKE and~*they⁽ᵐ⁾~will~*STAND⁽ⱽ⁾ OPENING TENT APPOINTED and~Mosheh and~Aharon **16:19** and~*he~will~*ASSEMBLE⁽ⱽ⁾ UPON~them⁽ᵐ⁾ Qorahh AT ALL the~COMPANY TO OPENING TENT APPOINTED and~*he~will~be*~SEE⁽ⱽ⁾ ARMAMENT **YHWH** TO ALL the~COMPANY **16:20** and~*he~will~*much~SPEAK⁽ⱽ⁾ **YHWH** TO Mosheh and~TO Aharon to~>~SAY⁽ⱽ⁾ **16:21** *!⁽ᵐᵖ⁾~be*~SEPARATE⁽ⱽ⁾ from~MIDST the~COMPANY the~THIS and~*I~will~*much~FINISH⁽ⱽ⁾ AT~them⁽ᵐ⁾ like~MOMENT **16:22** and~*they⁽ᵐ⁾~will~*FALL⁽ⱽ⁾ UPON FACE~s~them⁽ᵐ⁾ and~*they⁽ᵐ⁾~will~*SAY⁽ⱽ⁾ MIGHTY.ONE Elohiym the~WIND~s to~ALL FLESH the~MAN UNIT *he~will~*FAIL⁽ⱽ⁾ and~UPON ALL the~COMPANY *you⁽ᵐˢ⁾~will~*SNAP⁽ⱽ⁾ **16:23** and~*he~will*~much~SPEAK⁽ⱽ⁾ **YHWH** TO Mosheh to~>~SAY⁽ⱽ⁾ **16:24** *!⁽ᵐˢ⁾*~much~SPEAK⁽ⱽ⁾ TO the~COMPANY to~>~SAY⁽ⱽ⁾ *!⁽ᵐᵖ⁾~be*~GO.UP⁽ⱽ⁾ from~ALL.AROUND to~DWELLING Qorahh Datan and~

Aviram **16:25** and~*he~will*~RISE$^{(V)}$ Mosheh and~*he~will*~WALK$^{(V)}$ TO Datan and~Aviram and~*they$^{(m)}$~will*~WALK$^{(V)}$ AFTER~him BEARD~s Yisra'eyl **16:26** and~*he~will*~*much*~SPEAK$^{(V)}$ TO the~COMPANY to~>~SAY$^{(V)}$ *!$^{(mp)}$*~TURN.ASIDE$^{(V)}$ PLEASE from~UPON TENT~s the~MAN~s the~LOST~s the~THESE and~DO.NOT *you$^{(mp)}$~will*~TOUCH$^{(V)}$ in~ALL WHICH to~them$^{(m)}$ OTHERWISE *you$^{(mp)}$~will*~ADD$^{(V)}$ in~ALL FAILURE~them$^{(m)}$ **16:27** and~*they$^{(m)}$~will*~*be*~GO.UP$^{(V)}$ from~UPON DWELLING Qorahh Datan and~Aviram from~ALL.AROUND and~Datan and~Aviram *they~did*~GO.OUT$^{(V)}$ *be*~STAND.UP$^{(V)}$~*ing$^{(mp)}$* OPENING TENT~s~them$^{(m)}$ and~WOMAN~s~them$^{(m)}$ and~SON~s~them$^{(m)}$ and~BABIES~them$^{(m)}$ **16:28** and~*he~will*~SAY$^{(V)}$ Mosheh in~THIS *you$^{(mp)}$~will*~KNOW$^{(V)}$~*must* GIVEN.THAT **YHWH** *he~did*~SEND$^{(V)}$~me to~>~DO$^{(V)}$ AT ALL the~WORK~s the~THESE GIVEN.THAT NOT from~HEART~me **16:29** IF like~DEATH ALL the~HUMAN *they$^{(m)}$~will*~DIE$^{(V)}$~*must* THESE and~OVERSIGHT ALL the~HUMAN *he~will*~*be*~REGISTER$^{(V)}$ UPON~them$^{(m)}$ NOT **YHWH** *he~did*~SEND$^{(V)}$~me **16:30** and~IF SHAPE *he~will*~SHAPE$^{(V)}$ **YHWH** and~*she~did*~PART$^{(V)}$ the~GROUND AT MOUTH~her and~*she~did*~SWALLOW$^{(V)}$ AT~them$^{(m)}$ and~AT ALL WHICH to~them$^{(m)}$ and~*they~will*~GO.DOWN$^{(V)}$ LIVING~s UNDERWORLD~unto and~*you$^{(mp)}$~did*~KNOW$^{(V)}$ GIVEN.THAT *they~did*~*much*~PROVOKE$^{(V)}$ the~MAN~s the~THESE AT **YHWH** **16:31** and~*he~will*~EXIST$^{(V)}$ like~>~*much*~FINISH$^{(V)}$~him to~>~*much*~SPEAK$^{(V)}$ AT ALL the~WORD~s the~THESE and~*she~will*~*be*~CLEAVE.OPEN$^{(V)}$ the~GROUND WHICH UNDER~s~them$^{(m)}$ **16:32** and~*she~will*~OPEN$^{(V)}$ the~LAND AT MOUTH~her and~*she~will*~SWALLOW$^{(V)}$ AT~them$^{(m)}$ and~AT HOUSE~s~them$^{(m)}$ and~AT ALL the~HUMAN WHICH to~Qorahh and~AT ALL the~GOODS **16:33** and~*they$^{(m)}$~will*~GO.DOWN$^{(V)}$ THEY$^{(m)}$ and~ALL WHICH to~them$^{(m)}$ LIVING~s UNDERWORLD~unto and~*she~will*~*much*~COVER.OVER$^{(V)}$ UPON~them$^{(m)}$ the~LAND and~*they$^{(m)}$~will*~PERISH$^{(V)}$ from~MIDST the~ASSEMBLY **16:34** and~ALL Yisra'eyl WHICH ALL.AROUND~s~them$^{(m)}$ *they~did*~FLEE$^{(V)}$ to~VOICE~them$^{(m)}$ GIVEN.THAT *they~did*~SAY$^{(V)}$ OTHERWISE *she~will*~SWALLOW$^{(V)}$~us the~LAND **16:35** and~FIRE *she~did*~GO.OUT$^{(V)}$ from~AT **YHWH** and~*she~will*~EAT$^{(V)}$ AT the~FIVE~s and~HUNDRED~s2 MAN *make*~COME.NEAR$^{(V)}$~*ing$^{(mp)}$* the~INCENSE.SMOKE

Chapter 17

17:1 (16:36) and~*he~will*~*much*~SPEAK$^{(V)}$ **YHWH** TO Mosheh to~>~SAY$^{(V)}$ **17:2 (16:37)** *!$^{(ms)}$*~SAY$^{(V)}$ TO Elazar SON Aharon the~ADMINISTRATOR and~*he~will*~*make*~RAISE.UP$^{(V)}$ AT the~FIRE.PAN~s from~BETWEEN the~CREMATING and~AT the~FIRE *!$^{(ms)}$*~DISPERSE$^{(V)}$ FURTHER GIVEN.THAT *they~did*~SET.APART$^{(V)}$ **17:3 (16:38)** AT FIRE.PAN~s the~FAILURE~s the~THESE in~SOUL~s~them$^{(m)}$ and~*they~did*~DO$^{(V)}$ AT~them$^{(m)}$ FLAT WIRE~s METAL.PLATING to~the~ALTAR GIVEN.THAT *they~did*~*make*~

COME.NEAR⁽ᵛ⁾~them⁽ᵐ⁾ to~FACE~s **YHWH** and~*they⁽ᵐ⁾~will*~SET.APART⁽ᵛ⁾ and~*they⁽ᵐ⁾~will*~EXIST⁽ᵛ⁾ to~SIGN to~SON~s Yisra'eyl   **17:4 (16:39)** and~*he~ will*~TAKE⁽ᵛ⁾ Elazar the~ADMINISTRATOR AT FIRE.PAN~s the~COPPER WHICH *they~did~make*~COME.NEAR⁽ᵛ⁾ the~CREMATE⁽ᵛ⁾~*ing*⁽ᵐᵖ⁾ and~*they⁽ᵐ⁾~will*~ HAMMER⁽ᵛ⁾~them⁽ᵐ⁾ METAL.PLATING to~the~ ALTAR   **17:5 (16:40)** REMEMBRANCE to~SON~s Yisra'eyl to~THAT WHICH NOT *he~will*~COME.NEAR⁽ᵛ⁾ MAN BE.STRANGE⁽ᵛ⁾~*ing*⁽ᵐˢ⁾ WHICH NOT from~ SEED Aharon HE to~>~*make*~BURN.INCENSE⁽ᵛ⁾ INCENSE.SMOKE to~FACE~s **YHWH** and~NOT *he~will*~EXIST⁽ᵛ⁾ like~Qorahh and~like~COMPANY~him like~WHICH *he~did~much~*SPEAK⁽ᵛ⁾ **YHWH** in~HAND Mosheh to~ him   **17:6 (16:41)** and~*they⁽ᵐ⁾~will~be*~MURMUR⁽ᵛ⁾ ALL COMPANY SON~s Yisra'eyl from~MORROW UPON Mosheh and~UPON Aharon to~>~SAY⁽ᵛ⁾ YOU⁽ᵐᵖ⁾ *you⁽ᵐᵖ⁾~did~make*~DIE⁽ᵛ⁾ AT PEOPLE **YHWH**   **17:7 (16:42)** and~*he~ will*~EXIST⁽ᵛ⁾ in~>~*be*~ASSEMBLE⁽ᵛ⁾ the~COMPANY UPON Mosheh and~ UPON Aharon and~*they⁽ᵐ⁾~will*~TURN⁽ᵛ⁾ TO TENT APPOINTED and~LOOK *he~ did~much~*COVER.OVER⁽ᵛ⁾~him the~CLOUD and~*he~will~be*~SEE⁽ᵛ⁾ ARMAMENT **YHWH**   **17:8 (16:43)** and~*he~will*~COME⁽ᵛ⁾ Mosheh and~ Aharon TO FACE~s TENT APPOINTED   **17:9 (16:44)** and~*he~will~much~* SPEAK⁽ᵛ⁾ **YHWH** TO Mosheh to~>~SAY⁽ᵛ⁾   **17:10 (16:45)** !⁽ᵐᵖ⁾~*be~*LIFT⁽ᵛ⁾ from~MIDST the~COMPANY the~THIS and~*I~will~much~*FINISH⁽ᵛ⁾ AT~ them⁽ᵐ⁾ like~MOMENT and~*they⁽ᵐ⁾~will*~FALL⁽ᵛ⁾ UPON FACE~s~ them⁽ᵐ⁾   **17:11 (16:46)** and~*he~will*~SAY⁽ᵛ⁾ Mosheh TO Aharon !⁽ᵐˢ⁾~TAKE⁽ᵛ⁾ AT the~FIRE.PAN and~ !⁽ᵐˢ⁾~GIVE⁽ᵛ⁾ UPON~her FIRE from~UPON the~ALTAR and~ !⁽ᵐˢ⁾~PLACE⁽ᵛ⁾ INCENSE.SMOKE and~WALK⁽ᵛ⁾~*ing*⁽ᵐˢ⁾ QUICKLY TO the~ COMPANY and~ !⁽ᵐˢ⁾~*much*~COVER⁽ᵛ⁾ UPON~them⁽ᵐ⁾ GIVEN.THAT *he~did~* GO.OUT⁽ᵛ⁾ the~SPLINTER from~to~FACE~s **YHWH** *he~did~make*~DRILL⁽ᵛ⁾ the~STRIKING   **17:12 (16:47)** and~*he~will*~TAKE⁽ᵛ⁾ Aharon like~WHICH *he~ did~much~*SPEAK⁽ᵛ⁾ Mosheh and~*he~will*~RUN⁽ᵛ⁾ TO MIDST the~ASSEMBLY and~LOOK *he~did~make*~DRILL⁽ᵛ⁾ the~STRIKING in~the~PEOPLE and~*he~ will*~GIVE⁽ᵛ⁾ AT the~INCENSE.SMOKE and~*he~will~much*~COVER⁽ᵛ⁾ UPON the~PEOPLE   **17:13 (16:48)** and~*he~will*~STAND⁽ᵛ⁾ BETWEEN the~DIE⁽ᵛ⁾~ *ing*⁽ᵐᵖ⁾ and~BETWEEN the~LIVING~s and~*she~will~be*~STOP⁽ᵛ⁾ the~ PESTILENCE   **17:14 (16:49)** and~*they⁽ᵐ⁾~will*~EXIST⁽ᵛ⁾ the~DIE⁽ᵛ⁾~*ing*⁽ᵐᵖ⁾ in~ the~PESTILENCE FOUR TEN THOUSAND and~SEVEN HUNDRED~s from~to~ STRAND the~DIE⁽ᵛ⁾~*ing*⁽ᵐᵖ⁾ UPON WORD Qorahh   **17:15 (16:50)** and~*he~ will*~TURN.BACK⁽ᵛ⁾ Aharon TO Mosheh TO OPENING TENT APPOINTED and~ the~PESTILENCE *she~did~be*~STOP⁽ᵛ⁾   **17:16 (17:1)** and~*he~will~much~* SPEAK⁽ᵛ⁾ **YHWH** TO Mosheh to~>~SAY⁽ᵛ⁾   **17:17 (17:2)** !⁽ᵐˢ⁾~*much*~SPEAK⁽ᵛ⁾ TO SON~s Yisra'eyl and~ !⁽ᵐˢ⁾~TAKE⁽ᵛ⁾ from~AT~them⁽ᵐ⁾ BRANCH BRANCH to~ HOUSE FATHER from~AT ALL CAPTAIN~s~them⁽ᵐ⁾ to~HOUSE FATHER~s~ them⁽ᵐ⁾ TWO TEN BRANCH MAN AT TITLE~him *you⁽ᵐˢ⁾~will*~WRITE⁽ᵛ⁾ UPON BRANCH~him   **17:18 (17:3)** and~AT TITLE Aharon *you⁽ᵐˢ⁾~will*~WRITE⁽ᵛ⁾ UPON BRANCH Lewi GIVEN.THAT BRANCH UNIT to~HEAD HOUSE FATHER~s~them⁽ᵐ⁾   **17:19 (17:4)** and~*you⁽ᵐˢ⁾~did~make*~REST⁽ᵛ⁾~them⁽ᵐ⁾ in~ TENT APPOINTED to~FACE~s the~EVIDENCE WHICH *I~will~be*~APPOINT⁽ᵛ⁾

to~you(mp) THERE~unto **17:20 (17:5)** and~*he*~*did*~EXIST(V) the~MAN WHICH *I*~*will*~CHOOSE(V) in~him BRANCH~him *he*~*will*~BURST.OUT(V) and~*I*~*did*~make~SUBSIDE(V) from~UPON~me AT MURMURING SON~s Yisra'eyl WHICH THEY(m) *make*~MURMUR(V)~*ing*(mp) UPON~you(mp) **17:21 (17:6)** and~*he*~*will*~much~SPEAK(V) Mosheh TO SON~s Yisra'eyl and~*they*(m)~*will*~GIVE(V) TO~him ALL CAPTAIN~s~them(m) BRANCH to~CAPTAIN UNIT BRANCH to~CAPTAIN UNIT to~HOUSE FATHER~s~them(m) TWO TEN BRANCH and~BRANCH Aharon in~MIDST BRANCH~them(m) **17:22 (17:7)** and~*he*~*will*~*make*~REST(V) Mosheh AT the~BRANCH~s to~FACE~s **YHWH** in~TENT the~EVIDENCE **17:23 (17:8)** and~*he*~*will*~EXIST(V) from~MORROW and~*he*~*will*~COME(V) Mosheh TO TENT the~EVIDENCE and~LOOK *he*~*did*~BURST.OUT(V) BRANCH Aharon to~HOUSE Lewi and~*he*~*will*~*make*~GO.OUT(V) BUD and~*he*~*will*~*be*~BLOOM(V) BLOSSOM and~*he*~*will*~YIELD(V) ALMOND **17:24 (17:9)** and~*he*~*will*~*make*~GO.OUT(V) Mosheh AT ALL the~BRANCH~s from~to~FACE~s **YHWH** TO ALL SON~s Yisra'eyl and~*they*(m)~*will*~SEE(V) and~*they*(m)~*will*~TAKE(V) MAN BRANCH~him **17:25 (17:10)** and~*he*~*will*~SAY(V) **YHWH** TO Mosheh *!*(ms)~*make*~TURN.BACK(V) AT BRANCH Aharon to~FACE~s the~EVIDENCE to~CHARGE to~SIGN to~SON~s REBELLIOUS and~*she*~*will*~much~FINISH(V) MURMURING~s~them(m) from~UPON~me and~NOT *they*(m)~*will*~DIE(V) **17:26 (17:11)** and~*he*~*will*~DO(V) Mosheh like~WHICH *he*~*did*~much~DIRECT(V) **YHWH** AT~him SO *he*~*did*~DO(V) **17:27 (17:12)** and~*they*(m)~*will*~SAY(V) SON~s Yisra'eyl TO Mosheh to~>~SAY(V) THOUGH we~*did*~EXPIRE(V) we~*did*~PERISH(V) ALL~us we~*did*~PERISH(V) **17:28 (17:13)** ALL the~INSIDE the~INSIDE TO DWELLING **YHWH** *he*~*will*~DIE(V) ?~IF we~*did*~BE.WHOLE(V) to~>~EXPIRE(V)

Chapter 18

18:1 and~*he*~*will*~SAY(V) **YHWH** TO Aharon YOU(ms) and~SON~s~you(ms) and~HOUSE FATHER~you(ms) AT~you(fs) *you*(mp)~*will*~LIFT.UP(V) AT TWISTEDNESS the~SANCTUARY and~YOU(ms) and~SON~s~you(ms) AT~you(fs) *you*(mp)~*will*~LIFT.UP(V) AT TWISTEDNESS ADMINISTRATION~you(mp) **18:2** and~ALSO AT BROTHER~s~you(ms) BRANCH Lewi STAFF FATHER~you(ms) *!*(ms)~*make*~COME.NEAR(V) AT~you(fs) and~*they*(m)~*will*~*be*~JOIN(V) UPON~you(ms) and~*they*(m)~*will*~much~MINISTER(V)~you(ms) and~YOU(ms) and~SON~s~you(ms) AT~you(fs) to~FACE~s TENT the~EVIDENCE **18:3** and~*they*~*did*~SAFEGUARD(V) CHARGE~you(ms) and~CHARGE ALL the~TENT SURELY TO UTENSIL~s the~SPECIAL and~TO the~ALTAR NOT *they*(m)~*will*~COME.NEAR(V) and~NOT *they*(m)~*will*~DIE(V) ALSO THEY(m) ALSO YOU(mp) **18:4** and~*they*~*did*~*be*~JOIN(V) UPON~you(ms) and~*they*~*did*~SAFEGUARD(V) AT CHARGE TENT APPOINTED to~ALL SERVICE the~TENT and~BE.STRANGE(V)~*ing*(ms) NOT *he*~*will*~COME.NEAR(V) TO~you(mp) **18:5** and~*you*(mp)~*did*~SAFEGUARD(V) AT CHARGE the~SPECIAL and~AT CHARGE the~ALTAR and~NOT *he*~*will*~EXIST(V)

Benner's Mechanical Translation of the Torah

YET.AGAIN SPLINTER UPON SON~s Yisra'eyl **18:6** and~I LOOK *I~did*~TAKE^(V) AT BROTHER~s~you^(mp) the~Lewi~s from~MIDST SON~s Yisra'eyl to~you^(mp) CONTRIBUTION GIVE^(V)~*ed*^(mp) to~**YHWH** to~>~SERVE^(V) AT SERVICE TENT APPOINTED **18:7** and~YOU^(ms) and~SON~s~you^(ms) AT~you^(ms) *you*^(ms)~*will*~SAFEGUARD^(V) AT ADMINISTRATION~you^(mp) to~ALL WORD the~ALTAR and~to~from~HOUSE to~the~TENT.CURTAIN and~*you*^(mp)~*will*~SERVE^(V) SERVICE CONTRIBUTION *I~will*~GIVE^(V) AT ADMINISTRATION~you^(mp) and~the~BE.STRANGE^(V)~*ing*^(ms) the~INSIDE *he~will~be~make*~DIE^(V) **18:8** and~*he~will~much*~SPEAK^(V) **YHWH** TO Aharon and~I LOOK *I~did*~GIVE^(V) to~you^(ms) AT CHARGE OFFERING~s~me to~ALL SPECIAL~s SON~s Yisra'eyl to~you^(ms) *I~did*~GIVE^(V)~them^(m) to~>~SMEAR^(V) and~to~SON~s~you^(ms) to~CUSTOM DISTANT **18:9** THIS *he~will*~EXIST^(V) to~you^(ms) from~SPECIAL the~SPECIAL~s FROM the~FIRE ALL DONATION~them^(m) to~ALL DEPOSIT~them^(m) and~to~ALL FAILURE~them^(m) and~to~ALL GUILT~them^(m) WHICH *they*^(m)~*will~make*~TURN.BACK^(V) to~me SPECIAL SPECIAL~s to~you^(ms) HE and~to~SON~s~you^(ms) **18:10** in~SPECIAL the~SPECIAL~s *you*^(ms)~*will*~EAT^(V)~him ALL MALE *he~will*~EAT^(V) AT~him SPECIAL *he~will*~EXIST^(V) to~you^(fs) **18:11** and~THIS to~you^(ms) OFFERING GIFT~them^(m) to~ALL WAVING~s SON~s Yisra'eyl to~you^(ms) *I~did*~GIVE^(V)~them^(m) and~to~SON~s~you^(ms) and~to~DAUGHTER~s~you^(ms) AT~you^(ms) to~CUSTOM DISTANT ALL CLEAN in~HOUSE~you^(ms) *he~will*~EAT^(V) AT~him **18:12** ALL FAT FRESH.OIL and~ALL FAT FRESH.WINE and~CEREAL SUMMIT~them^(m) WHICH *they*^(m)~*will*~GIVE^(V) to~**YHWH** to~you^(ms) *I~did*~GIVE^(V)~them^(m) **18:13** FIRST-FRUIT~s ALL WHICH in~LAND~them^(m) WHICH *they*^(m)~*will~make*~COME^(V) to~**YHWH** to~you^(ms) *he~will*~EXIST^(V) ALL CLEAN in~HOUSE~you^(ms) *he~will*~EAT^(V)~him **18:14** ALL ASSIGNED in~Yisra'eyl to~you^(ms) *he~will*~EXIST^(V) **18:15** ALL BURSTING BOWELS to~ALL FLESH WHICH *they*^(m)~*will~make*~COME.NEAR^(V) to~**YHWH** in~the~HUMAN and~in~the~BEAST *he~will*~EXIST^(V) to~you^(fs) SURELY >~RANSOM^(V) *you*^(ms)~*will*~RANSOM^(V) AT FIRSTBORN the~HUMAN and~AT FIRSTBORN the~BEAST the~DIRTY *you*^(ms)~*will*~RANSOM^(V) **18:16** and~RANSOM^(V)~*ed*^(ms)~him from~SON NEW.MOON *you*^(ms)~*will*~RANSOM^(V) in~ARRANGEMENT~you^(ms) SILVER FIVE SHEQEL~s in~SHEQEL the~SPECIAL TEN~s GERAH HE **18:17** SURELY FIRSTBORN OX OR FIRSTBORN SHEEP OR FIRSTBORN SHE-GOAT NOT *you*^(ms)~*will*~RANSOM^(V) SPECIAL THEY^(m) AT BLOOD~them^(m) *you*^(ms)~*will*~SPRINKLE^(V) UPON the~ALTAR and~AT FAT~them^(m) *you*^(ms)~*will~make*~BURN.INCENSE^(V) FIRE.OFFERING to~AROMA SWEET to~**YHWH** **18:18** and~FLESH~them^(m) *he~will*~EXIST^(V) to~you^(fs) like~the~CHEST the~WAVING and~like~THIGH the~RIGHT.HAND to~you^(ms) *he~will*~EXIST^(V) **18:19** ALL OFFERING~s the~SPECIAL~s WHICH *they*^(m)~*will~make*~RAISE.UP^(V) SON~s Yisra'eyl to~**YHWH** *I~did*~GIVE^(V) to~you^(ms) and~to~SON~s~you^(ms) and~to~DAUGHTER~s~you^(ms) AT~you^(ms) to~CUSTOM DISTANT COVENANT SALT DISTANT SHE to~FACE~s **YHWH** to~you^(ms) and~to~SEED~you^(ms) AT~you^(fs) **18:20** and~*he~will*~SAY^(V) **YHWH** TO Aharon in~LAND~them^(m) NOT *you*^(ms)~*will*~INHERIT^(V) and~DISTRIBUTION NOT *he~will*~EXIST^(V) to~you^(ms) in~MIDST~them^(m) I

DISTRIBUTION~you$^{(ms)}$ and~INHERITANCE~you$^{(ms)}$ in~MIDST SON~s Yisra'eyl **18:21** and~to~SON~s Lewi LOOK *I~did*~GIVE$^{(V)}$ ALL TENTH.PART in~Yisra'eyl to~INHERITANCE FOR SERVICE~them$^{(m)}$ WHICH THEY$^{(m)}$ SERVE$^{(V)}$~ing$^{(mp)}$ AT SERVICE TENT APPOINTED **18:22** and~NOT *they*$^{(m)}$~*will*~COME.NEAR$^{(V)}$ YET.AGAIN SON~s Yisra'eyl TO TENT APPOINTED to~>~LIFT.UP$^{(V)}$ FAILURE to~>~DIE$^{(V)}$ **18:23** and~he~did~SERVE$^{(V)}$ the~Lewi HE AT SERVICE TENT APPOINTED and~THEY$^{(m)}$ *they*$^{(m)}$~*will*~LIFT.UP$^{(V)}$ TWISTEDNESS~them$^{(m)}$ CUSTOM DISTANT to~GENERATION~s~you$^{(mp)}$ and~in~MIDST SON~s Yisra'eyl NOT *they*$^{(m)}$~*will*~INHERIT$^{(V)}$ INHERITANCE **18:24** GIVEN.THAT AT TENTH.PART SON~s Yisra'eyl WHICH *they*$^{(m)}$~*will*~*make*~RAISE.UP$^{(V)}$ to~**YHWH** OFFERING *I~did*~GIVE$^{(V)}$ to~Lewi~s to~INHERITANCE UPON SO *I~did*~SAY$^{(V)}$ to~them$^{(m)}$ in~MIDST SON~s Yisra'eyl NOT *they*$^{(m)}$~*will*~INHERIT$^{(V)}$ INHERITANCE **18:25** and~he~will~much~SPEAK$^{(V)}$ **YHWH** TO Mosheh to~>~SAY$^{(V)}$ **18:26** and~TO the~Lewi~s *you*$^{(ms)}$~*will*~much~SPEAK$^{(V)}$ and~*you*$^{(ms)}$~*did*~SAY$^{(V)}$ TO~them$^{(m)}$ GIVEN.THAT *you*$^{(mp)}$~*will*~TAKE$^{(V)}$ from~AT SON~s Yisra'eyl AT the~TENTH.PART WHICH *I~did*~GIVE$^{(V)}$ to~you$^{(mp)}$ from~AT~them$^{(m)}$ in~INHERITANCE~you$^{(mp)}$ and~*you*$^{(mp)}$~*did*~*make*~RAISE.UP$^{(V)}$ FROM~him OFFERING **YHWH** TENTH.PART FROM the~TENTH.PART **18:27** and~he~did~be~THINK$^{(V)}$ to~you$^{(mp)}$ OFFERING~you$^{(mp)}$ like~CEREAL FROM the~FLOOR and~like~the~FULL FROM the~WINE.TROUGH **18:28** SO *you*$^{(mp)}$~*will*~*make*~RAISE.UP$^{(V)}$ ALSO YOU$^{(mp)}$ OFFERING **YHWH** from~ALL from~TENTH.PART~s~you$^{(mp)}$ WHICH *you*$^{(mp)}$~*will*~TAKE$^{(V)}$ from~AT SON~s Yisra'eyl and~*you*$^{(mp)}$~*did*~GIVE$^{(V)}$ FROM~him AT OFFERING **YHWH** to~Aharon the~ADMINISTRATOR **18:29** from~ALL CONTRIBUTION~s~you$^{(mp)}$ *you*$^{(mp)}$~*will*~*make*~RAISE.UP$^{(V)}$ AT ALL OFFERING **YHWH** from~ALL FAT~him AT SANCTUARY~him FROM~him **18:30** and~*you*$^{(ms)}$~*did*~SAY$^{(V)}$ TO~them$^{(m)}$ in~>~*make*~RAISE.UP$^{(V)}$~you$^{(mp)}$ AT FAT~him FROM~him and~he~did~be~THINK$^{(V)}$ to~Lewi~s like~PRODUCTION FLOOR and~like~PRODUCTION WINE.TROUGH **18:31** and~*you*$^{(mp)}$~*did*~EAT$^{(V)}$ AT~him in~ALL AREA YOU$^{(mp)}$ and~HOUSE~you$^{(mp)}$ GIVEN.THAT WAGE HE to~you$^{(mp)}$ FOR SERVICE~you$^{(mp)}$ in~TENT APPOINTED **18:32** and~NOT *you*$^{(mp)}$~*will*~LIFT.UP$^{(V)}$ UPON~him FAILURE in~>~*make*~RAISE.UP$^{(V)}$~you$^{(mp)}$ AT FAT~him FROM~him and~AT SPECIAL~s SON~s Yisra'eyl NOT *you*$^{(mp)}$~*will*~much~DRILL$^{(V)}$ and~NOT *you*$^{(mp)}$~*will*~DIE$^{(V)}$

Chapter 19

19:1 and~he~will~much~SPEAK$^{(V)}$ **YHWH** TO Mosheh and~TO Aharon to~>~SAY$^{(V)}$ **19:2** THIS CUSTOM the~TEACHING WHICH he~did~much~DIRECT$^{(V)}$ **YHWH** to~>~SAY$^{(V)}$ *!*$^{(ms)}$~much~SPEAK$^{(V)}$ TO SON~s Yisra'eyl and~*they*$^{(m)}$~*will*~TAKE$^{(V)}$ TO~you$^{(ms)}$ COW RED WHOLE WHICH WITHOUT in~her BLEMISH WHICH NOT he~did~GO.UP$^{(V)}$ UPON~her YOKE **19:3** and~*you*$^{(mp)}$~*did*~GIVE$^{(V)}$ AT~her TO Elazar the~ADMINISTRATOR and~he~did~*make*~

GO.OUT$^{(V)}$ AT~her TO from~OUTSIDE to~the~CAMP and~*he~did*~SLAY$^{(V)}$ AT~her to~FACE~s~him **19:4** and~*he~did*~TAKE$^{(V)}$ Elazar the~ADMINISTRATOR from~BLOOD~her in~FINGER~him and~*he~did*~make~SPATTER$^{(V)}$ TO IN.FRONT FACE~s TENT APPOINTED from~BLOOD~her SEVEN FOOTSTEP~s **19:5** and~*he~did*~CREMATE$^{(V)}$ AT the~COW to~EYE~s2~him AT SKIN~her and~AT FLESH~her and~AT BLOOD~her UPON DUNG~her *he~will*~CREMATE$^{(V)}$ **19:6** and~*he~did*~TAKE$^{(V)}$ the~ADMINISTRATOR TREE CEDAR and~HYSSOP and~SCARLET KERMES and~*he~did~make~*THROW.OUT$^{(V)}$ TO MIDST CREMATING the~COW **19:7** and~*he~did~much~*WASH$^{(V)}$ GARMENT~s~him the~ADMINISTRATOR and~*he~did*~BATHE$^{(V)}$ FLESH~him in~the~WATER~s2 and~AFTER *he~will*~COME$^{(V)}$ TO the~CAMP and~*he~did*~BE.DIRTY$^{(V)}$ the~ADMINISTRATOR UNTIL the~EVENING **19:8** and~the~CREMATE$^{(V)}$~*ing*$^{(ms)}$ AT~her *he~will*~WASH$^{(V)}$ GARMENT~s~him in~the~WATER~s2 and~*he~did*~BATHE$^{(V)}$ FLESH~him in~the~WATER~s2 and~*he~did*~BE.DIRTY$^{(V)}$ UNTIL the~EVENING **19:9** and~*he~did*~GATHER$^{(V)}$ MAN CLEAN AT ASH the~COW and~*he~did~make*~REST$^{(V)}$ from~OUTSIDE to~the~CAMP in~AREA CLEAN and~*she~did*~EXIST$^{(V)}$ to~the~COMPANY SON~s Yisra'eyl to~CHARGE to~WATER~s2 REMOVAL FAILURE SHE **19:10** and~*he~did~much*~WASH$^{(V)}$ the~GATHER$^{(V)}$~*ing*$^{(ms)}$ AT ASH the~COW AT GARMENT~s~him and~*he~did*~BE.DIRTY$^{(V)}$ UNTIL the~EVENING and~*she~did*~EXIST$^{(V)}$ to~SON~s Yisra'eyl and~to~IMMIGRANT the~IMMIGRATE$^{(V)}$~*ing*$^{(ms)}$ in~MIDST~them$^{(m)}$ to~CUSTOM DISTANT **19:11** the~TOUCH$^{(V)}$~*ing*$^{(ms)}$ in~DIE$^{(V)}$~*ing*$^{(ms)}$ to~ALL SOUL HUMAN and~*he~did*~BE.DIRTY$^{(V)}$ SEVEN DAY~s **19:12** HE *he~will~self*~FAIL$^{(V)}$ in~him in~the~DAY the~THIRD and~in~the~DAY the~SEVENTH *he~will*~BE.CLEAN$^{(V)}$ and~IF NOT *he~will~self*~FAIL$^{(V)}$ in~the~DAY the~THIRD and~in~the~DAY the~SEVENTH NOT *he~will*~BE.CLEAN$^{(V)}$ **19:13** ALL the~TOUCH$^{(V)}$~*ing*$^{(ms)}$ in~DIE$^{(V)}$~*ing*$^{(ms)}$ in~SOUL the~HUMAN WHICH *he~will*~DIE$^{(V)}$ and~NOT *he~will~self*~FAIL$^{(V)}$ AT DWELLING **YHWH** *he~did~much*~BE.DIRTY$^{(V)}$ and~*she~did~be*~CUT$^{(V)}$ the~SOUL the~SHE from~Yisra'eyl GIVEN.THAT WATER~s2 REMOVAL NOT SPRINKLE$^{(V)}$~*ed*$^{(ms)}$ UPON~him DIRTY *he~will*~EXIST$^{(V)}$ YET.AGAIN DIRTY~him in~him **19:14** THIS the~TEACHING HUMAN GIVEN.THAT *he~will*~DIE$^{(V)}$ in~TENT ALL the~COME$^{(V)}$~*ing*$^{(ms)}$ TO the~TENT and~ALL WHICH in~the~TENT *he~will*~BE.DIRTY$^{(V)}$ SEVEN DAY~s **19:15** and~ALL UTENSIL OPEN$^{(V)}$~*ed*$^{(ms)}$ WHICH WITHOUT BRACELET CORD UPON~him DIRTY HE **19:16** and~ALL WHICH *he~will*~TOUCH$^{(V)}$ UPON FACE~s the~FIELD in~DRILLED SWORD OR in~DIE$^{(V)}$~*ing*$^{(ms)}$ OR in~BONE HUMAN OR in~GRAVE *he~will*~BE.DIRTY$^{(V)}$ SEVEN DAY~s **19:17** and~*they~did*~TAKE$^{(V)}$ to~the~DIRTY from~DIRT CREMATING the~FAILURE and~*he~did*~GIVE$^{(V)}$ UPON~him WATER~s2 LIVING~s TO UTENSIL **19:18** and~*he~did*~TAKE$^{(V)}$ HYSSOP and~*he~did*~DIP$^{(V)}$ in~the~WATER~s2 MAN CLEAN and~*he~did~make*~SPATTER$^{(V)}$ UPON the~TENT and~UPON ALL the~UTENSIL~s and~UPON the~SOUL~s WHICH *they~did*~EXIST$^{(V)}$ THERE and~UPON the~TOUCH$^{(V)}$~*ing*$^{(ms)}$ in~the~BONE OR in~DRILLED OR in~the~DIE$^{(V)}$~*ing*$^{(ms)}$ OR in~the~GRAVE **19:19** and~*he~did~make*~SPATTER$^{(V)}$ the~CLEAN UPON the~DIRTY in~the~DAY the~THIRD and~

The Book of Numbers

in~the~DAY the~SEVENTH and~*he~did~much~*FAIL⁽ⱽ⁾~him in~the~DAY the~ SEVENTH and~*he~did~much~*WASH⁽ⱽ⁾ GARMENT~s~him and~*he~did~* BATHE⁽ⱽ⁾ in~the~WATER~s2 and~*he~did~*BE.CLEAN⁽ⱽ⁾ in~the~ EVENING **19:20** and~MAN WHICH *he~will~*BE.DIRTY⁽ⱽ⁾ and~NOT *he~will~* *self~*FAIL⁽ⱽ⁾ and~*she~did~be~*CUT⁽ⱽ⁾ the~SOUL the~SHE from~MIDST the~ ASSEMBLY GIVEN.THAT AT SANCTUARY **YHWH** *he~did~much~*BE.DIRTY⁽ⱽ⁾ WATER~s2 REMOVAL NOT SPRINKLE⁽ⱽ⁾~*ed*⁽ᵐˢ⁾ UPON~him DIRTY HE **19:21** and~*she~did~*EXIST⁽ⱽ⁾ to~them⁽ᵐ⁾ to~CUSTOM DISTANT and~ *make~*SPATTER⁽ⱽ⁾~*ing*⁽ᵐˢ⁾ WATER~s2 the~REMOVAL *he~will~*WASH⁽ⱽ⁾ GARMENT~s~him and~the~TOUCH⁽ⱽ⁾~*ing*⁽ᵐˢ⁾ in~WATER~s2 the~REMOVAL *he~will~*BE.DIRTY⁽ⱽ⁾ UNTIL the~EVENING **19:22** and~ALL WHICH *he~will~* TOUCH⁽ⱽ⁾ in~him the~DIRTY *he~will~*BE.DIRTY⁽ⱽ⁾ and~the~SOUL the~ TOUCH⁽ⱽ⁾~*ing*⁽ᶠˢ⁾ *she~will~*BE.DIRTY⁽ⱽ⁾ UNTIL the~EVENING

Chapter 20

20:1 and~*they*⁽ᵐ⁾~*will~*COME⁽ⱽ⁾ SON~s Yisra'eyl ALL the~COMPANY WILDERNESS Tsin in~the~NEW.MOON the~FIRST and~*he~will~*SETTLE⁽ⱽ⁾ the~PEOPLE in~Qadesh and~*she~will~*DIE⁽ⱽ⁾ THERE Mir'yam and~*she~will~* *be~*BURY⁽ⱽ⁾ THERE **20:2** and~NOT *he~did~*EXIST⁽ⱽ⁾ WATER~s2 to~the~ COMPANY and~*they*⁽ᵐ⁾~*will~be~*ASSEMBLE⁽ⱽ⁾ UPON Mosheh and~UPON Aharon **20:3** and~*he~will~*DISPUTE⁽ⱽ⁾ the~PEOPLE WITH Mosheh and~ *they*⁽ᵐ⁾~*will~*SAY⁽ⱽ⁾ to~>~SAY⁽ⱽ⁾ and~WOULD.THAT *we~did~*EXPIRE⁽ⱽ⁾ in~ EXPIRE⁽ⱽ⁾ BROTHER~s~us to~FACE~s **YHWH** **20:4** and~to~WHAT *you*⁽ᵐᵖ⁾~ *did~make~*COME⁽ⱽ⁾ AT ASSEMBLY **YHWH** TO the~WILDERNESS the~THIS to~ >~DIE⁽ⱽ⁾ THERE WE and~CATTLE~us **20:5** and~to~WHAT *you*⁽ᵐᵖ⁾~*did~make~* GO.UP⁽ⱽ⁾~us from~Mits'rayim to~>~*make~*COME⁽ⱽ⁾ AT~us TO the~AREA the~ DYSFUNCTIONAL the~THIS NOT AREA SEED and~FIG and~GRAPEVINE and~ POMEGRANATE and~WATER~s2 WITHOUT to~>~GULP⁽ⱽ⁾ **20:6** and~*he~* *will~*COME⁽ⱽ⁾ Mosheh and~Aharon from~FACE~s the~ASSEMBLY TO OPENING TENT APPOINTED and~*they*⁽ᵐ⁾~*will~*FALL⁽ⱽ⁾ UPON FACE~s~them⁽ᵐ⁾ and~*he~will~be~*SEE⁽ⱽ⁾ ARMAMENT **YHWH** TO~them⁽ᵐ⁾ **20:7** and~*he~will~* *much~*SPEAK⁽ⱽ⁾ **YHWH** TO Mosheh to~>~SAY⁽ⱽ⁾ **20:8** !⁽ᵐˢ⁾~TAKE⁽ⱽ⁾ AT the~ BRANCH and~ !⁽ᵐˢ⁾~*make~*ASSEMBLE⁽ⱽ⁾ AT the~COMPANY YOU⁽ᵐˢ⁾ and~ Aharon BROTHER~you⁽ᵐˢ⁾ and~*you*⁽ᵐᵖ⁾~*did~much~*SPEAK⁽ⱽ⁾ TO the~CLIFF to~ EYE~s2~them⁽ᵐ⁾ and~*he~did~*GIVE⁽ⱽ⁾ WATER~s2~him and~*you*⁽ᵐˢ⁾~*did~* *make~*GO.OUT⁽ⱽ⁾ to~them⁽ᵐ⁾ WATER~s2 FROM the~CLIFF and~*you*⁽ᵐˢ⁾~*did~* *make~*DRINK⁽ⱽ⁾ AT the~COMPANY and~AT CATTLE~them⁽ᵐ⁾ **20:9** and~*he~* *will~*TAKE⁽ⱽ⁾ Mosheh AT the~BRANCH from~to~FACE~s **YHWH** like~WHICH *he~did~much~*DIRECT⁽ⱽ⁾~him **20:10** and~*they*⁽ᵐ⁾~*will~make~*ASSEMBLE⁽ⱽ⁾ Mosheh and~Aharon AT the~ASSEMBLY TO FACE~s the~CLIFF and~*he~will~* SAY⁽ⱽ⁾ to~them⁽ᵐ⁾ !⁽ᵐᵖ⁾~HEAR⁽ⱽ⁾ PLEASE the~DISOBEY⁽ⱽ⁾~*ing*⁽ᵐᵖ⁾ ?~FROM the~ CLIFF the~THIS *we~will~make~*GO.OUT⁽ⱽ⁾ to~you⁽ᵐᵖ⁾ WATER~s2 **20:11** and~

he~will~make~RAISE.UP⁽ᵛ⁾ Mosheh AT HAND~him and~*he~will~make*~HIT⁽ᵛ⁾ AT the~CLIFF in~BRANCH~him FOOTSTEP~s2 and~*they⁽ᵐ⁾~will*~GO.OUT⁽ᵛ⁾ WATER~s2 ABUNDANT~s and~*she~will*~GULP⁽ᵛ⁾ the~COMPANY and~ CATTLE~them⁽ᵐ⁾ **20:12** and~*he~will*~SAY⁽ᵛ⁾ **YHWH** TO Mosheh and~TO Aharon SEEING.AS NOT *you⁽ᵐᵖ⁾~did~make*~SECURE⁽ᵛ⁾ in~me to~>~*make*~ SET.APART⁽ᵛ⁾~me to~EYE~s2 SON~s Yisra'eyl to~SO NOT *you⁽ᵐᵖ⁾~will~make*~ COME⁽ᵛ⁾ AT the~ASSEMBLY the~THIS TO the~LAND WHICH *I~did*~GIVE⁽ᵛ⁾ to~ them⁽ᵐ⁾ **20:13** THEY⁽ᵐ⁾ WATER~s2 Meriyvah WHICH *they~did*~DISPUTE⁽ᵛ⁾ SON~s Yisra'eyl AT **YHWH** and~*he~will~be*~SET.APART⁽ᵛ⁾ in~ them⁽ᵐ⁾ **20:14** and~*he~will*~SEND⁽ᵛ⁾ Mosheh MESSENGER~s from~Qadesh TO KING Edom IN.THIS.WAY *he~did~*SAY⁽ᵛ⁾ BROTHER~you⁽ᵐˢ⁾ Yisra'eyl YOU⁽ᵐˢ⁾ *you⁽ᵐˢ⁾~did*~KNOW⁽ᵛ⁾ AT ALL the~TROUBLE WHICH *she~did*~FIND⁽ᵛ⁾~ us **20:15** and~*they⁽ᵐ⁾~will*~GO.DOWN⁽ᵛ⁾ FATHER~s~us Mits'rayim~unto and~*we~will*~SETTLE⁽ᵛ⁾ in~Mits'rayim DAY~s ABUNDANT~s and~*they⁽ᵐ⁾~ will~make*~BE.DYSFUNCTIONAL⁽ᵛ⁾ to~us Mits'rayim and~to~FATHER~s~ us **20:16** and~*we~will*~CRY.OUT⁽ᵛ⁾ TO **YHWH** and~*he~will*~HEAR⁽ᵛ⁾ VOICE~ us and~*he~will*~SEND⁽ᵛ⁾ MESSENGER and~*he~will~make*~GO.OUT⁽ᵛ⁾~us from~Mits'rayim and~LOOK WE in~Qadesh CITY EXTREMITY BORDER~ you⁽ᵐˢ⁾ **20:17** *we~will*~CROSS.OVER⁽ᵛ⁾~& PLEASE in~LAND~you⁽ᵐˢ⁾ NOT *we~ will*~CROSS.OVER⁽ᵛ⁾ in~FIELD and~in~VINEYARD and~NOT *we~will*~GULP⁽ᵛ⁾ WATER~s2 WELL ROAD the~KING *we~will*~WALK⁽ᵛ⁾ NOT *we~will*~EXTEND⁽ᵛ⁾ RIGHT.HAND and~LEFT.HAND UNTIL WHICH *we~will*~CROSS.OVER⁽ᵛ⁾ BORDER~you⁽ᵐˢ⁾ **20:18** and~*he~will*~SAY⁽ᵛ⁾ TO~him Edom NOT *you⁽ᵐˢ⁾~will*~ CROSS.OVER⁽ᵛ⁾ in~me OTHERWISE in~the~SWORD *I~will*~GO.OUT⁽ᵛ⁾ to~>~ MEET⁽ᵛ⁾~you⁽ᵐˢ⁾ **20:19** and~*they⁽ᵐ⁾~will*~SAY⁽ᵛ⁾ TO~him SON~s Yisra'eyl in~ the~HIGHWAY *we~will*~GO.UP⁽ᵛ⁾~& and~IF WATER~s2~you⁽ᵐˢ⁾ *we~will*~ GULP⁽ᵛ⁾ I and~LIVESTOCK~s~me and~*I~did*~GIVE⁽ᵛ⁾ VALUE~them⁽ᵐ⁾ ONLY WITHOUT WORD in~FOOT~s~me *I~will*~CROSS.OVER⁽ᵛ⁾~& **20:20** and~*he~ will*~SAY⁽ᵛ⁾ NOT *you⁽ᵐˢ⁾~will*~CROSS.OVER⁽ᵛ⁾ and~*he~will*~GO.OUT⁽ᵛ⁾ Edom to~>~MEET⁽ᵛ⁾~him in~PEOPLE HEAVY and~in~HAND FORCEFUL **20:21** and~ *he~will~much*~REFUSE⁽ᵛ⁾ Edom >~GIVE⁽ᵛ⁾ AT Yisra'eyl *!⁽ᵐˢ⁾*~CROSS.OVER⁽ᵛ⁾ in~ BORDER~him and~*he~will*~EXTEND⁽ᵛ⁾ Yisra'eyl from~UPON~ him **20:22** and~*they⁽ᵐ⁾~will*~JOURNEY⁽ᵛ⁾ from~Qadesh and~*they⁽ᵐ⁾~will*~ COME⁽ᵛ⁾ SON~s Yisra'eyl ALL the~COMPANY Hor the~HILL **20:23** and~*he~ will*~SAY⁽ᵛ⁾ **YHWH** TO Mosheh and~TO Aharon in~Hor the~HILL UPON BORDER LAND Edom to~>~SAY⁽ᵛ⁾ **20:24** *he~will~be*~GATHER⁽ᵛ⁾ Aharon TO PEOPLE~s~him GIVEN.THAT NOT *he~will*~COME⁽ᵛ⁾ TO the~LAND WHICH *I~ did*~GIVE⁽ᵛ⁾ to~SON~s Yisra'eyl UPON WHICH *you⁽ᵐˢ⁾~did*~DISOBEY⁽ᵛ⁾ AT MOUTH~me to~WATER~s2 Meriyvah **20:25** *!⁽ᵐˢ⁾*~TAKE⁽ᵛ⁾ AT Aharon and~AT Elazar SON~him and~*!⁽ᵐˢ⁾~make*~GO.UP⁽ᵛ⁾ AT~them⁽ᵐ⁾ Hor the~ HILL **20:26** and~*!⁽ᵐˢ⁾~make*~STRIP.OFF⁽ᵛ⁾ AT Aharon AT GARMENT~s~him and~*you⁽ᵐˢ⁾~did~make*~WEAR⁽ᵛ⁾~them⁽ᵐ⁾ AT Elazar SON~him and~Aharon *he~will~be*~GATHER⁽ᵛ⁾ and~*he~did*~DIE⁽ᵛ⁾ THERE **20:27** and~*he~will*~DO⁽ᵛ⁾ Mosheh like~WHICH *he~did~much*~DIRECT⁽ᵛ⁾ **YHWH** and~*they⁽ᵐ⁾~will*~ GO.UP⁽ᵛ⁾ TO Hor the~HILL to~EYE~s2 ALL the~COMPANY **20:28** and~*he~*

The Book of Numbers

*will~make~*STRIP.OFF[(V)] Mosheh AT Aharon AT GARMENT~s~him and~*he~will~make~*WEAR[(V)] AT~them[(m)] AT Elazar SON~him and~*he~will~*DIE[(V)] Aharon THERE in~HEAD the~HILL and~*he~will~*GO.DOWN[(V)] Mosheh and~ Elazar FROM the~HILL **20:29** and~*they*[(m)]~*will~*SEE[(V)] ALL the~COMPANY GIVEN.THAT *he~did~*EXPIRE[(V)] Aharon and~*they*[(m)]~*will~*WEEP[(V)] AT Aharon THREE~s DAY ALL HOUSE Yisra'eyl

Chapter 21

21:1 and~*he~will~*HEAR[(V)] the~Kena'an~of KING Arad SETTLE[(V)]~*ing*[(ms)] the~ SOUTH GIVEN.THAT *he~did~*COME[(V)] Yisra'eyl ROAD the~Atariym and~*he~ will~be~*FIGHT[(V)] in~Yisra'eyl and~*he~will~*CAPTURE[(V)] FROM~him CAPTIVE **21:2** and~*he~will~*MAKE.A.VOW[(V)] Yisra'eyl VOW to~**YHWH** and~ *he~will~*SAY[(V)] IF >~*GIVE*[(V)] *you*[(ms)]~*will~*GIVE[(V)] AT the~PEOPLE the~THIS in~ HAND~me and~*I~did~make~*ASSIGN[(V)] AT CITY~s~them[(m)] **21:3** and~*he~ will~*HEAR[(V)] **YHWH** in~VOICE Yisra'eyl and~*he~will~*GIVE[(V)] AT the~Kena'an~ of and~*he~will~make~*ASSIGN[(V)] AT~them[(m)] and~AT CITY~s~them[(m)] and~ *he~will~*CALL.OUT[(V)] TITLE the~AREA Hharmah **21:4** and~*they*[(m)]~*will~* JOURNEY[(V)] from~Hor the~HILL ROAD SEA REEDS to~>~GO.AROUND[(V)] AT LAND Edom and~*she~will~*SEVER[(V)] SOUL the~PEOPLE in~the~ ROAD **21:5** and~*he~will~much~*SPEAK[(V)] the~PEOPLE in~Elohiym and~in~ Mosheh to~WHAT *you*[(mp)]~*did~make~*GO.UP[(V)]~us from~Mits'rayim to~>~ DIE[(V)] in~the~WILDERNESS GIVEN.THAT WITHOUT BREAD and~WITHOUT WATER~s2 and~SOUL~us *he~did~*LOATHE[(V)] in~the~BREAD the~ LIGHTWEIGHT **21:6** and~*he~will~much~*SEND[(V)] **YHWH** in~the~PEOPLE AT the~SERPENT~s the~VENOMOUS~s and~*they*[(m)]~*will~*BITE[(V)] AT the~PEOPLE and~*he~will~*DIE[(V)] PEOPLE ABUNDANT from~Yisra'eyl **21:7** and~*he~will~* COME[(V)] the~PEOPLE TO Mosheh and~*they*[(m)]~*will~*SAY[(V)] we~*did~*FAIL[(V)] GIVEN.THAT we~*did~much~*SPEAK[(V)] in~**YHWH** and~in~*you*[(fs)] *!*[(ms)]~*self~* PLEAD[(V)] TO **YHWH** and~*he~will~make~*TURN.ASIDE[(V)] from~UPON~us AT the~SERPENT and~*he~will~self~*PLEAD[(V)] Mosheh in~UNTIL the~ PEOPLE **21:8** and~*he~will~*SAY[(V)] **YHWH** TO Mosheh *!*[(ms)~*DO*[(V)] to~*you*[(ms)] VENOMOUS and~ *!*[(ms)~*PLACE*[(V)] AT~him UPON STANDARD and~*he~did~* EXIST[(V)] ALL the~BITE[(V)]~*ed*[(ms)] and~*he~did~*SEE[(V)] AT~him and~*he~will~* LIVE[(V)] **21:9** and~*he~will~*DO[(V)] Mosheh SERPENT COPPER and~*he~will~* PLACE[(V)]~him UPON the~STANDARD and~*he~did~*EXIST[(V)] IF *he~did~*BITE[(V)] the~SERPENT AT MAN and~*he~did~make~*STARE[(V)] TO SERPENT the~ COPPER and~*he~will~*LIVE[(V)] **21:10** and~*they*[(m)]~*will~*JOURNEY[(V)] SON~s Yisra'eyl and~*they*[(m)]~*will~*CAMP[(V)] in~Ovot **21:11** and~*they*[(m)]~*will~* JOURNEY[(V)] from~Ovot and~*they*[(m)]~*will~*CAMP[(V)] in~Iyey-Ha'a'variym in~ the~WILDERNESS WHICH UPON FACE~s Mo'av from~SUNRISE the~ SUN **21:12** from~THERE *they~did~*JOURNEY[(V)] and~*they*[(m)]~*will~*CAMP[(V)] in~ WADI Zered **21:13** from~THERE *they~did~*JOURNEY[(V)] and~*they*[(m)]~*will~*

CAMP[(v)] from~OTHER.SIDE Arnon WHICH in~the~WILDERNESS the~
GO.OUT[(v)]~*ing*[(ms)] from~BORDER the~Emor~of GIVEN.THAT Arnon BORDER
Mo'av BETWEEN Mo'av and~BETWEEN the~Emor~of   **21:14** UPON SO *he~
will~be*~SAY[(v)] in~SCROLL BATTLE~s **YHWH** AT and~Waheyv in~Suphah and~
AT the~WADI~s Arnon   **21:15** and~BANKS the~WADI~s WHICH *he~did~*
EXTEND[(v)] to~>~SETTLE[(v)] Ar and~*he~did~be*~LEAN[(v)] to~BORDER
Mo'av   **21:16** and~from~THERE B'er~unto SHE the~WELL WHICH *he~did~*
SAY[(v)] **YHWH** to~Mosheh *!*[(ms)]*~*GATHER[(v)] AT the~PEOPLE and~*l~will~*
GIVE[(v)]~& to~them[(m)] WATER~s2   **21:17** AT.THAT.TIME *he~will~*SING[(v)]
Yisra'eyl AT the~SONG the~THIS *!*[(mp)]*~*GO.UP[(v)] WELL *!*[(mp)]*~*ANSWER[(v)] to~
her   **21:18** WELL *they~did~*DIG.OUT[(v)]~her NOBLE~s *they~did~*DIG[(v)]~her
WILLING~s the~PEOPLE in~*much*~INSCRIBE[(v)]~*ing*[(ms)] in~STAVE~s~them[(m)]
and~from~WILDERNESS Matanah   **21:19** and~from~Matanah Nahhali'eyl
and~from~Nahhali'eyl Bamot   **21:20** and~from~Bamot the~STEEP.VALLEY
WHICH in~FIELD Mo'av HEAD the~Pisgah and~*she~did~be*~LOOK.DOWN[(v)]
UPON FACE~s the~DESOLATE.WILDERNESS   **21:21** and~*he~will~*SEND[(v)]
Yisra'eyl MESSENGER~s TO Sihhon KING the~Emor~of to~>~SAY[(v)]   **21:22** *l~
will~*CROSS.OVER[(v)]~& in~LAND~you[(ms)] NOT *we~will~*EXTEND[(v)] in~FIELD
and~in~VINEYARD NOT *we~will~*GULP[(v)] WATER~s2 WELL in~ROAD the~
KING *we~will~*WALK[(v)] UNTIL WHICH *we~will~*CROSS.OVER[(v)] BORDER~
you[(ms)]   **21:23** and~NOT *he~did~*GIVE[(v)] Sihhon AT Yisra'eyl *!*[(ms)]*~*
CROSS.OVER[(v)] in~BORDER~him and~*he~will~*GATHER[(v)] Sihhon AT ALL
PEOPLE~him and~*he~will~*GO.OUT[(v)] to~>~MEET[(v)] Yisra'eyl the~
WILDERNESS~unto and~*he~will~*COME[(v)] Yahats~unto and~*he~will~be*~
FIGHT[(v)] in~Yisra'eyl   **21:24** and~*he~will~*make~HIT[(v)]~him Yisra'eyl to~
MOUTH SWORD and~*he~will~*POSSESS[(v)] AT LAND~him from~Arnon UNTIL
Yaboq UNTIL SON~s Amon GIVEN.THAT STRONG BORDER SON~s
Amon   **21:25** and~*he~will~*TAKE[(v)] Yisra'eyl AT ALL the~CITY~s the~THESE
and~*he~will~*SETTLE[(v)] Yisra'eyl in~ALL CITY~s the~Emor~of in~Hheshbon
and~in~ALL DAUGHTER~s~her   **21:26** GIVEN.THAT Hheshbon CITY Sihhon
KING the~Emor~of SHE and~HE *he~did~be*~FIGHT[(v)] in~KING Mo'av the~
FIRST and~*he~will~*TAKE[(v)] AT ALL LAND~him from~HAND~him UNTIL
Arnon   **21:27** UPON SO *they*[(m)]*~will~*SAY[(v)] the~REGULATE[(v)]~*ing*[(mp)] *!*[(mp)]*~*
COME[(v)] Hheshbon *she~will~be*~BUILD[(v)] and~*she~will~self*~PREPARE[(v)] CITY
Sihhon   **21:28** GIVEN.THAT FIRE *she~did~*GO.OUT[(v)] from~Hheshbon
GLIMMERING from~METROPOLIS Sihhon *!*[(ms)]*~*EAT[(v)] Ar Mo'av MASTER~s
PLATFORM~s Arnon   **21:29** OH to~you[(ms)] Mo'av *you*[(ms)]*~did~*PERISH[(v)]
PEOPLE Kemosh *he~did~*GIVE[(v)] SON~s~him ESCAPED~s and~DAUGHTER~s~
him in~the~CAPTIVITY to~KING Emor~of Sihhon   **21:30** and~*we~will~*
THROW[(v)]~them[(m)] *he~did~*PERISH[(v)] Hheshbon UNTIL Dibon and~*we~will~*
make~DESOLATE[(v)] UNTIL Nophahh WHICH UNTIL Meydva   **21:31** and~*he~
will~*SETTLE[(v)] Yisra'eyl in~LAND the~Emor~of   **21:32** and~*he~will~*SEND[(v)]
Mosheh to~>~*much*~TREAD.ABOUT[(v)] AT Yazeyr and~*they*[(m)]*~will~*TRAP[(v)]
DAUGHTER~s~her and~*he~will~*POSSESS[(v)] AT the~Emor~of WHICH
THERE   **21:33** and~*they*[(m)]*~will~*TURN[(v)] and~*they*[(m)]*~will~*GO.UP[(v)] ROAD

the~Bashan and~*he~will*~GO.OUT$^{(V)}$ Og KING the~Bashan to~>~MEET$^{(V)}$~them$^{(m)}$ HE and~ALL PEOPLE~him to~the~BATTLE Ed're'i **21:34** and~*he~will*~SAY$^{(V)}$ **YHWH** TO Mosheh DO.NOT *you$^{(ms)}$~will*~FEAR$^{(V)}$ AT~him GIVEN.THAT in~HAND~you$^{(ms)}$ *I~did*~GIVE$^{(V)}$ AT~him and~AT ALL PEOPLE~him and~AT LAND~him and~*you$^{(ms)}$~did*~DO$^{(V)}$ to~him like~WHICH *you$^{(ms)}$~did*~DO$^{(V)}$ to~Sihhon KING the~Emor~of WHICH SETTLE$^{(V)}$~*ing$^{(ms)}$* in~Hheshbon **21:35** and~*they$^{(m)}$~will*~make~HIT$^{(V)}$ AT~him and~AT SON~s~him and~AT ALL PEOPLE~him UNTIL EXCEPT *he~did~make*~REMAIN$^{(V)}$ to~him SURVIVOR and~*they$^{(m)}$~will*~POSSESS$^{(V)}$ AT LAND~him

Chapter 22

22:1 and~*they$^{(m)}$~will*~JOURNEY$^{(V)}$ SON~s Yisra'eyl and~*they$^{(m)}$~will*~CAMP$^{(V)}$ in~DESERT~s Mo'av from~OTHER.SIDE to~Yarden Ye'rey'hho **22:2** and~*he~will*~SEE$^{(V)}$ Balaq SON Tsipor AT ALL WHICH *he~did*~DO$^{(V)}$ Yisra'eyl to~the~Emor~of **22:3** and~*he~will*~IMMIGRATE$^{(V)}$ Mo'av from~FACE~s the~PEOPLE MANY GIVEN.THAT ABUNDANT HE and~*he~will*~LOATHE$^{(V)}$ Mo'av from~FACE~s SON~s Yisra'eyl **22:4** and~*he~will*~SAY$^{(V)}$ Mo'av TO BEARD~s Mid'yan NOW *they$^{(m)}$~will*~much~LICK$^{(V)}$ the~ASSEMBLY AT ALL ALL.AROUND~s~us like~>~LICK$^{(V)}$ the~OX AT GREEN the~FIELD and~Balaq SON Tsipor KING to~Mo'av in~the~APPOINTED.TIME the~SHE **22:5** and~*he~will*~SEND$^{(V)}$ MESSENGER~s TO Bilam SON Be'or Petor~unto WHICH UPON the~RIVER LAND SON~s PEOPLE~him to~>~CALL.OUT$^{(V)}$ to~him to~>~SAY$^{(V)}$ LOOK PEOPLE *he~did*~GO.OUT$^{(V)}$ from~Mits'rayim LOOK *he~did~much*~COVER.OVER$^{(V)}$ AT EYE the~LAND and~HE SETTLE$^{(V)}$~*ing$^{(ms)}$* from~FOREFRONT~me **22:6** and~NOW *!$^{(ms)}$*~WALK$^{(V)}$~& PLEASE *!$^{(ms)}$*~SPIT.UPON$^{(V)}$~& to~me AT the~PEOPLE the~THIS GIVEN.THAT NUMEROUS HE FROM~me POSSIBLY *I~will*~BE.ABLE$^{(V)}$ *we~will~make*~HIT$^{(V)}$ in~him and~*I~will~much*~CAST.OUT$^{(V)}$~him FROM the~LAND GIVEN.THAT *I~did*~KNOW$^{(V)}$ AT WHICH *you$^{(ms)}$~will~much*~KNEEL$^{(V)}$ be~much~KNEEL$^{(V)}$~*ing$^{(ms)}$* and~WHICH *you$^{(ms)}$~will*~SPIT.UPON$^{(V)}$ *he~will~be~make*~SPIT.UPON$^{(V)}$ **22:7** and~*they$^{(m)}$~will*~WALK$^{(V)}$ BEARD~s Mo'av and~BEARD~s Mid'yan and~DIVINATION~s in~HAND~them$^{(m)}$ and~*they$^{(m)}$~will*~COME$^{(V)}$ TO Bilam and~*they$^{(m)}$~will~much*~SPEAK$^{(V)}$ TO~him WORD~s Balaq **22:8** and~*he~will*~SAY$^{(V)}$ TO~them$^{(m)}$ *!$^{(mp)}$*~STAY.THE.NIGHT$^{(V)}$ HERE the~NIGHT and~*I~did~make*~TURN.BACK$^{(V)}$ AT~you$^{(mp)}$ WORD like~WHICH *he~will~much*~SPEAK$^{(V)}$ **YHWH** TO~me and~*they$^{(m)}$~will*~SETTLE$^{(V)}$ NOBLE~s Mo'av WITH Bilam **22:9** and~*he~will*~COME$^{(V)}$ Elohiym TO Bilam and~*he~will*~SAY$^{(V)}$ WHO the~MAN~s the~THESE WITH~you$^{(fs)}$ **22:10** and~*he~will*~SAY$^{(V)}$ Bilam TO the~Elohiym Balaq SON Tsipor KING Mo'av *he~did*~SEND$^{(V)}$ TO~me **22:11** LOOK the~PEOPLE the~GO.OUT$^{(V)}$~*ing$^{(ms)}$* from~Mits'rayim and~*he~will~much*~COVER.OVER$^{(V)}$ AT EYE the~LAND NOW *!$^{(ms)}$*~WALK$^{(V)}$~& *!$^{(ms)}$*~HOLLOW.OUT$^{(V)}$~& to~me AT~him POSSIBLY *I~will*~BE.ABLE$^{(V)}$ to~>~be~

Benner's Mechanical Translation of the Torah

FIGHT^(v) in~him and~I~did~much~CAST.OUT^(v)~him **22:12** and~he~will~SAY^(v) Elohiym TO Bilam NOT you^(ms)~will~WALK^(v) WITH~them^(m) NOT you^(ms)~will~SPIT.UPON^(v) AT the~PEOPLE GIVEN.THAT KNEEL^(v)~ed^(ms) HE **22:13** and~he~will~RISE^(v) Bilam in~the~MORNING and~he~will~SAY^(v) TO NOBLE~s Balaq !^(mp)~WALK^(v) TO LAND~you^(mp) GIVEN.THAT he~did~much~REFUSE^(v) **YHWH** to~>~GIVE^(v)~me to~>~WALK^(v) WITH~you^(mp) **22:14** and~they^(m)~will~RISE^(v) NOBLE~s Mo'av and~they^(m)~will~COME^(v) TO Balaq and~they^(m)~will~SAY^(v) he~did~much~REFUSE^(v) Bilam >~WALK^(v) WITH~us **22:15** and~he~will~make~ADD^(v) YET.AGAIN Balaq >~SEND^(v) NOBLE~s ABUNDANT~s and~be~BE.HEAVY^(v)~ing^(mp) from~THESE **22:16** and~they^(m)~will~COME^(v) TO Bilam and~they^(m)~will~SAY^(v) to~him IN.THIS.WAY he~did~SAY^(v) Balaq SON Tsipor DO.NOT PLEASE you^(ms)~will~be~WITHHOLD^(v) from~>~WALK^(v) TO~me **22:17** GIVEN.THAT >~much~BE.HEAVY^(v) I~will~much~BE.HEAVY^(v)~you^(ms) MANY and~ALL WHICH you^(ms)~will~SAY^(v) TO~me I~will~DO^(v) and~!^(ms)~WALK^(v)~& PLEASE !^(ms)~HOLLOW.OUT^(v)~& to~me AT the~PEOPLE the~THIS **22:18** and~he~will~ANSWER^(v) Bilam and~he~will~SAY^(v) TO SERVANT~s Balaq IF he~will~GIVE^(v) to~me Balaq FILLING HOUSE~him SILVER and~GOLD NOT I~will~BE.ABLE^(v) to~the~>~CROSS.OVER^(v) AT MOUTH **YHWH** Elohiym~me to~>~DO^(v) SMALL OR GREAT **22:19** and~NOW !^(mp)~SETTLE^(v) PLEASE in~THIS ALSO YOU^(mp) the~NIGHT and~I~will~KNOW^(v)~& WHAT ADD^(v)~ing^(ms) **YHWH** !^(ms)~much~SPEAK^(v) WITH~me **22:20** and~he~will~COME^(v) Elohiym TO Bilam NIGHT and~he~will~SAY^(v) to~him IF to~>~CALL.OUT^(v) to~you^(ms) they~did~COME^(v) the~MAN~s !^(ms)~RISE^(v) !^(ms)~WALK^(v) AT~them^(m) and~SURELY AT the~WORD WHICH I~will~much~SPEAK^(v) TO~you^(ms) AT~him you^(ms)~will~DO^(v) **22:21** and~he~will~RISE^(v) Bilam in~the~MORNING and~he~will~SADDLE^(v) AT SHE-DONKEY~him and~he~will~WALK^(v) WITH NOBLE~s Mo'av **22:22** and~he~will~FLARE.UP^(v) NOSE Elohiym GIVEN.THAT WALK^(v)~ing^(ms) HE and~he~will~self~STATION^(v) MESSENGER **YHWH** in~the~ROAD to~OPPONENT to~him and~HE RIDE^(v)~ing^(ms) UPON SHE-DONKEY~him and~TWO YOUNG.MAN~s^(ms)~him WITH~him **22:23** and~she~will~SEE^(v) the~SHE-DONKEY AT MESSENGER **YHWH** be~STAND.UP^(v)~ing^(ms) in~the~ROAD and~SWORD~him PULL.OUT^(v)~ed^(fs) in~HAND~him and~she~will~EXTEND^(v) the~SHE-DONKEY FROM the~ROAD and~she~will~WALK^(v) in~the~FIELD and~he~will~make~HIT^(v) Bilam AT the~SHE-DONKEY to~>~make~EXTEND^(v)~her the~ROAD **22:24** and~he~will~STAND^(v) MESSENGER **YHWH** in~NARROW.WAY the~VINEYARD~s FENCE from~THIS and~FENCE from~THIS **22:25** and~she~will~SEE^(v) the~SHE-DONKEY AT MESSENGER **YHWH** and~she~will~SQUEEZE^(v) TO the~WALL and~she~will~SQUEEZE^(v) AT FOOT Bilam TO the~WALL and~he~will~make~ADD^(v) to~>~make~HIT^(v)~her **22:26** and~he~will~make~ADD^(v) MESSENGER **YHWH** >~CROSS.OVER^(v) and~he~will~STAND^(v) in~AREA NARROW WHICH WITHOUT ROAD to~>~EXTEND^(v) RIGHT.HAND and~LEFT.HAND **22:27** and~she~will~SEE^(v) the~SHE-DONKEY AT MESSENGER **YHWH** and~she~will~STRETCH.OUT^(v) UNDER Bilam and~he~will~FLARE.UP^(v) NOSE Bilam and~he~will~make~HIT^(v) AT the~SHE-DONKEY in~the~ROD **22:28** and~he~will~OPEN$^{(V)}$ **YHWH** AT MOUTH the~SHE-DONKEY and~she~will~SAY$^{(V)}$ to~Bilam WHAT I~did~DO$^{(V)}$ to~you$^{(ms)}$ GIVEN.THAT you$^{(ms)}$~did~make~HIT$^{(V)}$~me THIS THREE FOOT~s **22:29** and~he~will~SAY$^{(V)}$ Bilam to~the~SHE-DONKEY GIVEN.THAT you$^{(fs)}$~did~self~WORK.OVER$^{(V)}$ in~me WOULD.THAT THERE.IS SWORD in~HAND~me GIVEN.THAT NOW I~did~KILL$^{(V)}$~you$^{(fs)}$ **22:30** and~she~will~SAY$^{(V)}$ the~SHE-DONKEY TO Bilam ?~NOT I SHE-DONKEY~you$^{(ms)}$ WHICH you$^{(ms)}$~did~RIDE$^{(V)}$ UPON~me from~YET.AGAIN~you$^{(ms)}$ UNTIL the~DAY the~THIS ?~>~make~BENEFIT$^{(V)}$ I~did~make~BENEFIT$^{(V)}$ to~>~DO$^{(V)}$ to~you$^{(ms)}$ IN.THIS.WAY and~he~will~SAY$^{(V)}$ NOT **22:31** and~he~will~much~REMOVE.THE.COVER$^{(V)}$ **YHWH** AT EYE~s2 Bilam and~he~will~SEE$^{(V)}$ AT MESSENGER **YHWH** be~STAND.UP$^{(V)}$~ing$^{(ms)}$ in~the~ROAD and~SWORD~him PULL.OUT$^{(V)}$~ed$^{(fs)}$ in~HAND~him and~he~will~BOW.THE.HEAD$^{(V)}$ and~he~will~self~BEND.DOWN$^{(V)}$ to~NOSE~s~him **22:32** and~he~will~SAY$^{(V)}$ TO~him MESSENGER **YHWH** UPON WHAT you$^{(ms)}$~did~make~HIT$^{(V)}$ AT SHE-DONKEY~you$^{(ms)}$ THIS THREE FOOT~s LOOK I I~did~GO.OUT$^{(V)}$ to~OPPONENT GIVEN.THAT he~did~HAND.OVER$^{(V)}$ the~ROAD to~BE.FACE.TO.FACE$^{(V)}$~me **22:33** and~she~will~SEE$^{(V)}$~me the~SHE-DONKEY and~she~will~EXTEND$^{(V)}$ to~FACE~s~me THIS THREE FOOT~s POSSIBLY she~did~EXTEND$^{(V)}$ from~FACE~s~me GIVEN.THAT NOW ALSO AT~you$^{(ms)}$ I~did~KILL$^{(V)}$ and~SIGN~her I~did~make~LIVE$^{(V)}$ **22:34** and~he~will~SAY$^{(V)}$ Bilam TO MESSENGER **YHWH** I~did~FAIL$^{(V)}$ GIVEN.THAT NOT I~did~KNOW$^{(V)}$ GIVEN.THAT YOU$^{(ms)}$ be~STAND.UP$^{(V)}$~ing$^{(ms)}$ to~>~MEET$^{(V)}$~me in~the~ROAD and~NOW IF DYSFUNCTIONAL in~EYE~s2~you$^{(ms)}$ I~will~TURN.BACK$^{(V)}$~& to~me **22:35** and~he~will~SAY$^{(V)}$ MESSENGER **YHWH** TO Bilam !$^{(ms)}$~WALK$^{(V)}$ WITH the~MAN~s and~FAR.END AT the~WORD WHICH I~will~much~SPEAK$^{(V)}$ TO~you$^{(ms)}$ AT~him you$^{(ms)}$~will~much~SPEAK$^{(V)}$ and~he~will~WALK$^{(V)}$ Bilam WITH NOBLE~s Balaq **22:36** and~he~will~HEAR$^{(V)}$ Balaq GIVEN.THAT he~did~COME$^{(V)}$ Bilam and~he~will~GO.OUT$^{(V)}$ to~>~MEET$^{(V)}$~him TO CITY Mo'av WHICH UPON BORDER Arnon WHICH in~EXTREMITY the~BORDER **22:37** and~he~will~SAY$^{(V)}$ Balaq TO Bilam ?~NOT >~SEND$^{(V)}$ I~did~SEND$^{(V)}$ TO~you$^{(ms)}$ to~>~CALL.OUT$^{(V)}$ to~you$^{(fs)}$ to~WHAT NOT you$^{(ms)}$~did~WALK$^{(V)}$ TO~me ?~INDEED NOT I~will~BE.ABLE$^{(V)}$ >~much~BE.HEAVY$^{(V)}$~you$^{(ms)}$ **22:38** and~he~will~SAY$^{(V)}$ Bilam TO Balaq LOOK I~did~COME$^{(V)}$ TO~you$^{(ms)}$ NOW ?~>~BE.ABLE$^{(V)}$ I~will~BE.ABLE$^{(V)}$!$^{(ms)}$~much~SPEAK$^{(V)}$ ANYTHING the~WORD WHICH he~will~PLACE$^{(V)}$ Elohiym in~MOUTH~me AT~him I~will~much~SPEAK$^{(V)}$ **22:39** and~he~will~WALK$^{(V)}$ Bilam WITH Balaq and~they$^{(m)}$~will~COME$^{(V)}$ METROPOLIS Hhutsot **22:40** and~he~will~SACRIFICE$^{(V)}$ Balaq CATTLE and~FLOCKS and~he~will~much~SEND$^{(V)}$ to~Bilam and~to~the~NOBLE~s WHICH AT~him **22:41** and~he~will~EXIST$^{(V)}$ in~the~MORNING and~he~will~TAKE$^{(V)}$ Balaq AT Bilam and~he~will~make~GO.UP$^{(V)}$~him PLATFORM~s Ba'al and~he~will~SEE$^{(V)}$ from~THERE EXTREMITY the~PEOPLE

Chapter 23

23:1 and~he~will~SAY⁽ⱽ⁾ Bilam TO Balaq !⁽ᵐˢ⁾~BUILD⁽ⱽ⁾ to~me in~THIS SEVEN ALTAR~s and~!⁽ᵐˢ⁾~make~PREPARE⁽ⱽ⁾ to~me in~THIS SEVEN BULL~s and~ SEVEN BUCK~s **23:2** and~he~will~DO⁽ⱽ⁾ Balaq like~WHICH he~did~much~ SPEAK⁽ⱽ⁾ Bilam and~he~will~make~GO.UP⁽ⱽ⁾ Balaq and~Bilam BULL and~ BUCK in~the~ALTAR **23:3** and~he~will~SAY⁽ⱽ⁾ Bilam to~Balaq !⁽ᵐˢ⁾~self~ STAND.UP⁽ⱽ⁾ UPON ASCENSION.OFFERING~you⁽ᵐˢ⁾ and~I~will~WALK⁽ⱽ⁾~& POSSIBLY he~will~be~MEET⁽ⱽ⁾ **YHWH** to~>~MEET⁽ⱽ⁾~me and~WORD WHAT he~will~make~SEE⁽ⱽ⁾~me and~I~did~make~BE.FACE.TO.FACE⁽ⱽ⁾ to~you⁽ᶠˢ⁾ and~he~will~WALK⁽ⱽ⁾ BARE.PLACE **23:4** and~he~will~MEET⁽ⱽ⁾ Elohiym TO Bilam and~he~will~SAY⁽ⱽ⁾ TO~him AT SEVEN the~ALTAR~s I~did~ARRANGE⁽ⱽ⁾ and~I~will~make~GO.UP⁽ⱽ⁾ BULL and~BUCK in~the~ALTAR **23:5** and~he~ will~PLACE⁽ⱽ⁾ **YHWH** WORD in~MOUTH Bilam and~he~will~SAY⁽ⱽ⁾ !⁽ᵐˢ⁾~ TURN.BACK⁽ⱽ⁾ TO Balaq and~IN.THIS.WAY you⁽ᵐˢ⁾~will~much~ SPEAK⁽ⱽ⁾ **23:6** and~he~will~TURN.BACK⁽ⱽ⁾ TO~him and~LOOK be~ STAND.UP⁽ⱽ⁾~ing⁽ᵐˢ⁾ UPON ASCENSION.OFFERING~him HE and~ALL NOBLE~s Mo'av **23:7** and~he~will~LIFT.UP⁽ⱽ⁾ PARABLE~him and~he~will~SAY⁽ⱽ⁾ FROM Aram he~will~make~GUIDE⁽ⱽ⁾~me Balaq KING Mo'av from~HILL~s EAST !⁽ᵐˢ⁾~WALK⁽ⱽ⁾~& !⁽ᵐˢ⁾~SPIT.UPON⁽ⱽ⁾~& to~me Ya'aqov and~!⁽ᵐˢ⁾~ WALK⁽ⱽ⁾~& !⁽ᵐˢ⁾~ENRAGE⁽ⱽ⁾~& Yisra'eyl **23:8** WHAT I~will~HOLLOW.OUT⁽ⱽ⁾ NOT he~did~HOLLOW.OUT⁽ⱽ⁾~her MIGHTY.ONE and~WHAT I~will~ ENRAGE⁽ⱽ⁾ NOT he~did~ENRAGE⁽ⱽ⁾ **YHWH** **23:9** GIVEN.THAT from~HEAD BOULDER~s I~will~SEE⁽ⱽ⁾~him and~from~KNOLL~s I~will~LOOK.UPON⁽ⱽ⁾~him THOUGH PEOPLE to~ALONE he~will~DWELL⁽ⱽ⁾ and~in~the~NATION~s NOT he~will~self~THINK⁽ⱽ⁾ **23:10** WHO he~did~RECKON⁽ⱽ⁾ DIRT Ya'aqov and~ NUMBER AT FOURTH.PART Yisra'eyl she~will~DIE⁽ⱽ⁾ SOUL~me DEATH STRAIGHT~s and~she~will~EXIST⁽ⱽ⁾ END~me like~THAT.ONE~ him **23:11** and~he~will~SAY⁽ⱽ⁾ Balaq TO Bilam WHAT you⁽ᵐˢ⁾~did~DO⁽ⱽ⁾ to~ me to~>~HOLLOW.OUT⁽ⱽ⁾ ATTACK⁽ⱽ⁾~ing⁽ᵐˢ⁾~s~me I~did~TAKE⁽ⱽ⁾~you⁽ᵐˢ⁾ and~LOOK you⁽ᵐˢ⁾~did~much~KNEEL⁽ⱽ⁾ >~much~KNEEL⁽ⱽ⁾ **23:12** and~he~ will~ANSWER⁽ⱽ⁾ and~he~will~SAY⁽ⱽ⁾ ?~NOT AT WHICH he~will~PLACE⁽ⱽ⁾ **YHWH** in~MOUTH~me AT~him I~will~SAFEGUARD⁽ⱽ⁾ to~>~much~ SPEAK⁽ⱽ⁾ **23:13** and~he~will~SAY⁽ⱽ⁾ TO~him Balaq to~you⁽ᵐˢ⁾ PLEASE AT~me TO AREA OTHER WHICH you⁽ᵐˢ⁾~will~SEE⁽ⱽ⁾~him from~THERE FAR.END EXTREMITY~him you⁽ᵐˢ⁾~will~SEE⁽ⱽ⁾ and~ALL~him NOT you⁽ᵐˢ⁾~will~SEE⁽ⱽ⁾ and~!⁽ᵐˢ⁾~HOLLOW.OUT⁽ⱽ⁾~him to~me from~THERE **23:14** and~they⁽ᵐ⁾~ will~TAKE⁽ⱽ⁾~him FIELD Tsophim TO HEAD the~Pisgah and~he~will~BUILD⁽ⱽ⁾ SEVEN ALTAR~s and~he~will~make~GO.UP⁽ⱽ⁾ BULL and~BUCK in~the~ ALTAR **23:15** and~he~will~SAY⁽ⱽ⁾ TO Balaq !⁽ᵐˢ⁾~self~STAND.UP⁽ⱽ⁾ IN.THIS.WAY UPON ASCENSION.OFFERING~you⁽ᵐˢ⁾ and~I I~will~be~MEET⁽ⱽ⁾ IN.THIS.WAY **23:16** and~he~will~MEET⁽ⱽ⁾ **YHWH** TO Bilam and~he~will~ PLACE⁽ⱽ⁾ WORD in~MOUTH~him and~he~will~SAY⁽ⱽ⁾ !⁽ᵐˢ⁾~TURN.BACK⁽ⱽ⁾ TO Balaq and~IN.THIS.WAY you⁽ᵐˢ⁾~will~much~SPEAK⁽ⱽ⁾ **23:17** and~he~will~

The Book of Numbers

COME⁽ᵛ⁾ TO~him and~LOOK~him *be*~STAND.UP⁽ᵛ⁾~*ing*⁽ᵐˢ⁾ UPON ASCENSION.OFFERING~him and~NOBLE~s Mo'av AT~him and~*he*~*will*~SAY⁽ᵛ⁾ to~him Balaq WHAT *he*~*did*~*much*~SPEAK⁽ᵛ⁾ **YHWH** **23:18** and~*he*~*will*~LIFT.UP⁽ᵛ⁾ PARABLE~him and~*he*~*will*~SAY⁽ᵛ⁾ *!*⁽ᵐˢ⁾~RISE⁽ᵛ⁾ Balaq and~*!*⁽ᵐˢ⁾~HEAR⁽ᵛ⁾ *!*⁽ᵐˢ⁾~*make*~WEIGH.OUT⁽ᵛ⁾~& UNTIL~me SON~him Tsipor **23:19** NOT MAN MIGHTY.ONE and~*he*~*will*~*much*~LIE⁽ᵛ⁾ and~SON HUMAN and~*he*~*will*~*self*~COMFORT⁽ᵛ⁾ ?~HE *he*~*did*~SAY⁽ᵛ⁾ and~NOT *he*~*will*~DO⁽ᵛ⁾ and~*he*~*did*~*much*~SPEAK⁽ᵛ⁾ and~NOT *he*~*will*~*make*~RISE⁽ᵛ⁾~her **23:20** LOOK >~*much*~KNEEL⁽ᵛ⁾ *I*~*did*~TAKE⁽ᵛ⁾ and~*he*~*did*~*much*~KNEEL⁽ᵛ⁾ and~NOT *I*~*will*~*make*~TURN.BACK⁽ᵛ⁾~her **23:21** NOT *he*~*did*~*make*~STARE⁽ᵛ⁾ BARRENNESS in~Ya'aqov and~NOT *he*~*did*~SEE⁽ᵛ⁾ LABOR in~Yisra'eyl **YHWH** Elohiym~him WITH~him and~the~SIGNAL KING in~him **23:22** MIGHTY.ONE *make*~GO.OUT⁽ᵛ⁾~*ing*⁽ᵐˢ⁾~them⁽ᵐ⁾ from~Mits'rayim like~BULK~s RHINOCEROS to~him **23:23** GIVEN.THAT NOT PREDICTION in~Ya'aqov and~NOT DIVINATION in~Yisra'eyl like~the~APPOINTED.TIME *he*~*will*~*be*~SAY⁽ᵛ⁾ to~Ya'aqov and~to~Yisra'eyl WHAT *he*~*did*~MAKE⁽ᵛ⁾ MIGHTY.ONE **23:24** THOUGH PEOPLE like~LIONESS *he*~*will*~RISE⁽ᵛ⁾ and~like~LION *he*~*will*~*self*~LIFT.UP⁽ᵛ⁾ NOT *he*~*will*~LIE.DOWN⁽ᵛ⁾ UNTIL *he*~*will*~EAT⁽ᵛ⁾ PREY and~BLOOD DRILLED~s *he*~*will*~GULP⁽ᵛ⁾ **23:25** and~*he*~*will*~SAY⁽ᵛ⁾ Balaq TO Bilam ALSO >~HOLLOW.OUT⁽ᵛ⁾ NOT *you*⁽ᵐᵖ⁾~*will*~HOLLOW.OUT⁽ᵛ⁾~him ALSO >~*much*~KNEEL⁽ᵛ⁾ NOT *you*⁽ᵐˢ⁾~*will*~*much*~KNEEL⁽ᵛ⁾~him **23:26** and~*he*~*will*~ANSWER⁽ᵛ⁾ Bilam and~*he*~*will*~SAY⁽ᵛ⁾ TO Balaq ?~NOT *I*~*did*~*much*~SPEAK⁽ᵛ⁾ TO~*you*⁽ᵐˢ⁾ to~>~SAY⁽ᵛ⁾ ALL WHICH *he*~*will*~*much*~SPEAK⁽ᵛ⁾ **YHWH** AT~him *I*~*will*~DO⁽ᵛ⁾ **23:27** and~*he*~*will*~SAY⁽ᵛ⁾ Balaq TO Bilam *!*⁽ᵐˢ⁾~WALK⁽ᵛ⁾~& PLEASE *I*~*will*~TAKE⁽ᵛ⁾~*you*⁽ᵐˢ⁾ TO AREA OTHER POSSIBLY *he*~*will*~BE.STRAIGHT⁽ᵛ⁾ in~EYE~s2 the~Elohiym and~*you*⁽ᵐˢ⁾~*did*~HOLLOW.OUT⁽ᵛ⁾~him to~me from~THERE **23:28** and~*he*~*will*~TAKE⁽ᵛ⁾ Balaq AT Bilam HEAD the~Pe'or the~*be*~LOOK.DOWN⁽ᵛ⁾~*ing*⁽ᵐˢ⁾ UPON FACE~s the~DESOLATE.WILDERNESS **23:29** and~*he*~*will*~SAY⁽ᵛ⁾ Bilam TO Balaq *!*⁽ᵐˢ⁾~BUILD⁽ᵛ⁾ to~me in~THIS SEVEN ALTAR~s and~*!*⁽ᵐˢ⁾~*make*~PREPARE⁽ᵛ⁾ to~me in~THIS SEVEN BULL~s and~SEVEN BUCK~s **23:30** and~*he*~*will*~DO⁽ᵛ⁾ Balaq like~WHICH *he*~*did*~SAY⁽ᵛ⁾ Bilam and~*he*~*will*~*make*~GO.UP⁽ᵛ⁾ BULL and~BUCK in~the~ALTAR

Chapter 24

24:1 and~*he*~*will*~SEE⁽ᵛ⁾ Bilam GIVEN.THAT FUNCTIONAL in~EYE~s2 **YHWH** to~>~*much*~KNEEL⁽ᵛ⁾ AT Yisra'eyl and~NOT *he*~*did*~WALK⁽ᵛ⁾ like~FOOTSTEP in~FOOTSTEP to~>~MEET⁽ᵛ⁾ PREDICTION~s and~*he*~*will*~SET.DOWN⁽ᵛ⁾ TO the~WILDERNESS FACE~s~him **24:2** and~*he*~*will*~LIFT.UP⁽ᵛ⁾ Bilam AT EYE~s2~him and~*he*~*will*~SEE⁽ᵛ⁾ AT Yisra'eyl DWELL⁽ᵛ⁾~*ing*⁽ᵐˢ⁾ to~STAFF~s~him and~*she*~*will*~EXIST⁽ᵛ⁾ UPON~him WIND Elohiym **24:3** and~*he*~*will*~LIFT.UP⁽ᵛ⁾ PARABLE~him and~*he*~*will*~SAY⁽ᵛ⁾ DECLARE⁽ᵛ⁾~*ed*⁽ᵐˢ⁾ Bilam SON~

him Be'or and~DECLARE⁽ᵛ⁾~ed⁽ᵐˢ⁾ the~WARRIOR WIDE.OPEN⁽ᵛ⁾ the~
EYE **24:4** DECLARE⁽ᵛ⁾~ed⁽ᵐˢ⁾ HEAR⁽ᵛ⁾~ing⁽ᵐˢ⁾ STATEMENT~s MIGHTY.ONE
WHICH VISION Shaddai *he~will*~PERCEIVE⁽ᵛ⁾ FALL⁽ᵛ⁾~ing⁽ᵐˢ⁾ and~
REMOVE.THE.COVER⁽ᵛ⁾~ed⁽ᵐˢ⁾ EYE~s2 **24:5** WHAT FUNCTIONAL~him TENT~
you⁽ᵐˢ⁾ Ya'aqov DWELLING~s~you⁽ᵐˢ⁾ Yisra'eyl **24:6** like~WADI~s *they~did*~
be~EXTEND⁽ᵛ⁾ like~GARDEN~s UPON RIVER like~ALOE~s *he~did*~PLANT⁽ᵛ⁾
YHWH like~CEDAR~s UPON WATER~s2 **24:7** *he~will*~FLOW⁽ᵛ⁾ WATER~s2
from~BUCKET~s~him and~SEED~him in~WATER~s2 ABUNDANT~s and~*he~
will*~RAISE.UP⁽ᵛ⁾ from~Agag KING~him and~*she~will~self*~LIFT.UP⁽ᵛ⁾
EMPIRE~him **24:8** MIGHTY.ONE *make*~GO.OUT⁽ᵛ⁾~ing⁽ᵐˢ⁾~him from~
Mits'rayim like~BULK~s RHINOCEROS to~him *he~will*~EAT⁽ᵛ⁾ NATION~s
NARROW~s~him and~BONE~s~them⁽ᵐ⁾ *he~will~much*~GNAW⁽ᵛ⁾ and~
ARROW~s *he~will*~STRIKE.THROUGH⁽ᵛ⁾ **24:9** *he~did*~STOOP⁽ᵛ⁾ *he~did*~
LIE.DOWN⁽ᵛ⁾ like~LION and~like~LIONESS WHO *he~will~make*~RISE⁽ᵛ⁾~him
much~KNEEL⁽ᵛ⁾~ing⁽ᵐᵖ⁾~you⁽ᵐˢ⁾ KNEEL⁽ᵛ⁾~ed⁽ᵐˢ⁾ and~SPIT.UPON⁽ᵛ⁾~ing⁽ᵐᵖ⁾~
you⁽ᵐˢ⁾ SPIT.UPON⁽ᵛ⁾~ed⁽ᵐˢ⁾ **24:10** and~*he~will*~FLARE.UP⁽ᵛ⁾ NOSE Balaq TO
Bilam and~*he~will*~CLASP⁽ᵛ⁾ AT PALM~s2~him and~*he~will*~SAY⁽ᵛ⁾ Balaq TO
Bilam to~>~HOLLOW.OUT⁽ᵛ⁾ ATTACK⁽ᵛ⁾~ing⁽ᵐˢ⁾~s~me *I~did*~CALL.OUT⁽ᵛ⁾~
you⁽ᵐˢ⁾ and~LOOK *you*⁽ᵐˢ⁾~*did~much*~KNEEL⁽ᵛ⁾ >~*much*~KNEEL⁽ᵛ⁾ THIS THREE
FOOTSTEP~s **24:11** and~NOW *!*⁽ᵐˢ⁾~FLEE.AWAY⁽ᵛ⁾ to~you⁽ᵐˢ⁾ TO AREA~
you⁽ᵐˢ⁾ *I~did*~SAY⁽ᵛ⁾ *!*⁽ᵐˢ⁾~*much*~BE.HEAVY⁽ᵛ⁾ *I~will~much*~BE.HEAVY⁽ᵛ⁾~
you⁽ᵐˢ⁾ and~LOOK *he~did*~WITHHOLD⁽ᵛ⁾~you⁽ᵐˢ⁾ **YHWH** from~
ARMAMENT **24:12** and~*he~will*~SAY⁽ᵛ⁾ Bilam TO Balaq ?~NOT ALSO TO
MESSENGER~s~you⁽ᵐˢ⁾ WHICH *you*⁽ᵐˢ⁾~*did*~SEND⁽ᵛ⁾ TO~me *I~did~much*~
SPEAK⁽ᵛ⁾ to~>~SAY⁽ᵛ⁾ **24:13** IF *he~will*~GIVE⁽ᵛ⁾ to~me Balaq FILLING HOUSE~
him SILVER and~GOLD NOT *I~will*~BE.ABLE⁽ᵛ⁾ to~the~>~CROSS.OVER⁽ᵛ⁾ AT
MOUTH **YHWH** to~>~DO⁽ᵛ⁾ FUNCTIONAL OR DYSFUNCTIONAL from~HEART~
me WHICH *he~will~much*~SPEAK⁽ᵛ⁾ **YHWH** AT~him *I~will~much*~
SPEAK⁽ᵛ⁾ **24:14** and~NOW LOOK~me WALK⁽ᵛ⁾~ing⁽ᵐˢ⁾ to~PEOPLE~me *!*⁽ᵐˢ⁾~
WALK⁽ᵛ⁾~& *I~will*~GIVE.ADVICE⁽ᵛ⁾~you⁽ᵐˢ⁾ WHICH *he~will*~DO⁽ᵛ⁾ the~PEOPLE
the~THIS to~PEOPLE~you⁽ᵐˢ⁾ in~END the~DAY~s **24:15** and~*he~will*~
LIFT.UP⁽ᵛ⁾ PARABLE~him and~*he~will*~SAY⁽ᵛ⁾ DECLARE⁽ᵛ⁾~ed⁽ᵐˢ⁾ Bilam SON~
him Be'or and~DECLARE⁽ᵛ⁾~ed⁽ᵐˢ⁾ the~WARRIOR WIDE.OPEN⁽ᵛ⁾ the~
EYE **24:16** DECLARE⁽ᵛ⁾~ed⁽ᵐˢ⁾ HEAR⁽ᵛ⁾~ing⁽ᵐˢ⁾ STATEMENT~s MIGHTY.ONE
and~KNOW⁽ᵛ⁾~ing⁽ᵐˢ⁾ DISCERNMENT Elyon VISION Shaddai *he~will*~
PERCEIVE⁽ᵛ⁾ FALL⁽ᵛ⁾~ing⁽ᵐˢ⁾ and~REMOVE.THE.COVER⁽ᵛ⁾~ed⁽ᵐˢ⁾ EYE~
s2 **24:17** *I~will*~SEE⁽ᵛ⁾~him and~NOT NOW *I~will*~LOOK.UPON⁽ᵛ⁾~him and~
NOT NEAR *he~did*~TAKE.STEPS⁽ᵛ⁾ STAR from~Ya'aqov and~*he~did*~RISE⁽ᵛ⁾
STAFF from~Yisra'eyl and~*he~did*~STRIKE.THROUGH⁽ᵛ⁾ EDGE~s Mo'av and~
he~did~much~TOSS.OUT⁽ᵛ⁾ ALL SON~s Shet **24:18** and~*he~did*~EXIST⁽ᵛ⁾
Edom PROPERTY and~*he~did*~EXIST⁽ᵛ⁾ PROPERTY Se'iyr ATTACK⁽ᵛ⁾~ing⁽ᵐˢ⁾~s~
him and~Yisra'eyl DO⁽ᵛ⁾~ing⁽ᵐˢ⁾ FORCE **24:19** and~*he~will*~GO.DOWN⁽ᵛ⁾
from~Ya'aqov and~*he~did~make*~PERISH⁽ᵛ⁾ SURVIVOR from~
CITY **24:20** and~*he~will*~SEE⁽ᵛ⁾ AT Amaleq and~*he~will*~LIFT.UP⁽ᵛ⁾
PARABLE~him and~*he~will*~SAY⁽ᵛ⁾ SUMMIT NATION~s Amaleq and~END~

him UNTIL PERISH⁽ⱽ⁾~ing⁽ᵐˢ⁾ **24:21** and~he~will~SEE⁽ⱽ⁾ AT the~Qayin~of and~he~will~LIFT.UP⁽ⱽ⁾ PARABLE~him and~he~will~SAY⁽ⱽ⁾ CONSISTENCY SETTLING~you⁽ᵐˢ⁾ and~!⁽ᵐˢ⁾~PLACE⁽ⱽ⁾ in~the~CLIFF NEST~you⁽ᵐˢ⁾ **24:22** GIVEN.THAT IF he~will~EXIST⁽ⱽ⁾ to~>~much~BURN⁽ⱽ⁾ Qayin UNTIL WHAT Ashur she~will~CAPTURE⁽ⱽ⁾~you⁽ᵐˢ⁾ **24:23** and~he~will~LIFT.UP⁽ⱽ⁾ PARABLE~him and~he~will~SAY⁽ⱽ⁾ OH WHO he~will~LIVE⁽ⱽ⁾ >~PLACE⁽ⱽ⁾~him MIGHTY.ONE **24:24** and~NOMAD~s from~HAND Kit~s and~they~did~much~AFFLICT⁽ⱽ⁾ Ashur and~they~did~much~AFFLICT⁽ⱽ⁾ Ever and~ALSO HE UNTIL PERISH⁽ⱽ⁾~ing⁽ᵐˢ⁾ **24:25** and~he~will~RISE⁽ⱽ⁾ Bilam and~he~will~WALK⁽ⱽ⁾ and~he~will~TURN.BACK⁽ⱽ⁾ to~AREA~him and~ALSO Balaq he~did~WALK⁽ⱽ⁾ to~ROAD~him

Chapter 25

25:1 and~he~will~SETTLE⁽ⱽ⁾ Yisra'eyl in~Shitiym and~he~will~make~DRILL⁽ⱽ⁾ the~PEOPLE to~>~BE.A.HARLOT⁽ⱽ⁾ TO DAUGHTER~s Mo'av **25:2** and~they⁽ᶠ⁾~will~CALL.OUT⁽ⱽ⁾ to~the~PEOPLE to~SACRIFICE~s Elohiym~them⁽ᶠ⁾ and~he~will~EAT⁽ⱽ⁾ the~PEOPLE and~they⁽ᵐ⁾~will~self~BEND.DOWN⁽ⱽ⁾ to~Elohiym~them⁽ᶠ⁾ **25:3** and~he~will~be~FASTEN⁽ⱽ⁾ Yisra'eyl to~Ba'al-Pe'or and~he~will~FLARE.UP⁽ⱽ⁾ NOSE **YHWH** in~Yisra'eyl **25:4** and~he~will~SAY⁽ⱽ⁾ **YHWH** TO Mosheh !⁽ᵐˢ⁾~TAKE⁽ⱽ⁾ AT ALL HEAD~s the~PEOPLE and~!⁽ᵐˢ⁾~make~DISLOCATE⁽ⱽ⁾ AT~them⁽ᵐ⁾ to~**YHWH** OPPOSITE the~SUN and~he~will~TURN.BACK⁽ⱽ⁾ FLAMING.WRATH NOSE **YHWH** from~Yisra'eyl **25:5** and~he~will~SAY⁽ⱽ⁾ Mosheh TO DECIDE⁽ⱽ⁾~ing⁽ᵐᵖ⁾ Yisra'eyl !⁽ᵐᵖ⁾~KILL⁽ⱽ⁾ MAN MAN~s~him the~be~FASTEN⁽ⱽ⁾~ing⁽ᵐᵖ⁾ to~Ba'al-Pe'or **25:6** and~LOOK MAN from~SON~s Yisra'eyl he~did~COME⁽ⱽ⁾ and~he~will~make~COME.NEAR⁽ⱽ⁾ TO BROTHER~s~him AT the~Mid'yan~of to~EYE~s2 Mosheh and~to~EYE~s ALL COMPANY SON~s Yisra'eyl and~THEY⁽ᵐ⁾ WEEP⁽ⱽ⁾~ing⁽ᵐᵖ⁾ OPENING TENT APPOINTED **25:7** and~he~will~SEE⁽ⱽ⁾ Piynhhas SON Elazar SON Aharon the~ADMINISTRATOR and~he~will~RISE⁽ⱽ⁾ from~MIDST the~COMPANY and~he~will~TAKE⁽ⱽ⁾ SPEAR in~HAND~him **25:8** and~he~will~COME⁽ⱽ⁾ AFTER MAN Yisra'eyl TO the~HUT and~he~will~PIERCE⁽ⱽ⁾ AT TWO~them⁽ᵐ⁾ AT MAN Yisra'eyl and~AT the~WOMAN TO STOMACH~her and~she~will~be~STOP⁽ⱽ⁾ the~PESTILENCE from~UPON SON~s Yisra'eyl **25:9** and~they⁽ᵐ⁾~will~EXIST⁽ⱽ⁾ the~DIE⁽ⱽ⁾~ing⁽ᵐᵖ⁾ in~the~PESTILENCE FOUR and~TEN~s THOUSAND **25:10** and~he~will~much~SPEAK⁽ⱽ⁾ **YHWH** TO Mosheh to~>~SAY⁽ⱽ⁾ **25:11** Piynhhas SON Elazar SON Aharon the~ADMINISTRATOR he~did~make~TURN.BACK⁽ⱽ⁾ AT FURY~me from~UPON SON~s Yisra'eyl in~>~much~BE.ZEALOUS⁽ⱽ⁾~him AT ZEALOUSNESS~me in~MIDST~them⁽ᵐ⁾ and~NOT I~did~much~much~FINISH⁽ⱽ⁾ AT SON~s Yisra'eyl in~ZEALOUSNESS~me **25:12** to~SO !⁽ᵐˢ⁾~SAY⁽ⱽ⁾ LOOK~me GIVE⁽ⱽ⁾~ing⁽ᵐˢ⁾ to~him AT COVENANT~me COMPLETENESS **25:13** and~she~did~EXIST⁽ⱽ⁾ to~him and~to~SEED~him AFTER~him COVENANT ADMINISTRATION DISTANT UNDER

WHICH he~did~much~BE.ZEALOUS⁽ⱽ⁾ to~Elohiym~him and~he~will~much~ COVER⁽ⱽ⁾ UPON SON~s Yisra'eyl **25:14** and~TITLE MAN Yisra'eyl the~*be~ make*~HIT⁽ⱽ⁾~*ing*⁽ᵐˢ⁾ WHICH he~did~be~make~HIT⁽ⱽ⁾ AT the~Mid'yan~of Zimri SON Salu CAPTAIN HOUSE FATHER to~Shimon~of **25:15** and~TITLE the~WOMAN the~*be~make*~HIT⁽ⱽ⁾~*ing*⁽ᶠˢ⁾ the~Mid'yan~of Kazbi DAUGHTER Tsur HEAD TRIBE~s HOUSE FATHER in~Mid'yan HE **25:16** and~*he~will~ much*~SPEAK⁽ⱽ⁾ **YHWH** TO Mosheh to~>~SAY⁽ⱽ⁾ **25:17** >~PRESS.IN⁽ⱽ⁾ AT the~ Mid'yan~s and~*you*⁽ᵐᵖ⁾~*did~make*~HIT⁽ⱽ⁾ AT~them⁽ᵐ⁾ **25:18** GIVEN.THAT PRESS.IN⁽ⱽ⁾~*ing*⁽ᵐᵖ⁾ THEY⁽ᵐ⁾ to~you⁽ᵐᵖ⁾ in~CRAFTINESS~s~them⁽ᵐ⁾ WHICH *they~did~much*~BE.CRAFTY⁽ⱽ⁾ to~you⁽ᵐᵖ⁾ UPON WORD Pe'or and~UPON WORD Kazbi DAUGHTER CAPTAIN Mid'yan SISTER~them⁽ᵐ⁾ the~*be~make~* HIT⁽ⱽ⁾~*ing*⁽ᶠˢ⁾ in~DAY the~PESTILENCE UPON WORD Pe'or **25:19** and~*he~ will*~EXIST⁽ⱽ⁾ AFTER the~PESTILENCE

Chapter 26

26:1 and~*he~will*~SAY⁽ⱽ⁾ **YHWH** TO Mosheh and~TO Elazar SON Aharon the~ ADMINISTRATOR to~>~SAY⁽ⱽ⁾ **26:2** !⁽ᵐᵖ⁾~LIFT.UP⁽ⱽ⁾ AT HEAD ALL COMPANY SON~s Yisra'eyl from~SON TEN~s YEAR and~UPWARD~unto to~HOUSE FATHER~s~them⁽ᵐ⁾ ALL GO.OUT⁽ⱽ⁾~*ing*⁽ᵐˢ⁾ ARMY in~Yisra'eyl **26:3** and~*he~ will~much*~SPEAK⁽ⱽ⁾ Mosheh and~Elazar the~ADMINISTRATOR AT~them⁽ᵐ⁾ in~DESERT~s Mo'av UPON Yarden Ye'rey'hho to~>~SAY⁽ⱽ⁾ **26:4** from~SON TEN~s YEAR and~UPWARD~unto like~WHICH he~did~much~DIRECT⁽ⱽ⁾ **YHWH** AT Mosheh and~SON~s Yisra'eyl the~GO.OUT⁽ⱽ⁾~*ing*⁽ᵐᵖ⁾ from~LAND Mits'rayim **26:5** Re'uven FIRSTBORN Yisra'eyl SON~s Re'uven Hhanokh CLAN the~Hhanokh~of to~Palu CLAN the~Palu~of **26:6** to~Hhetsron CLAN the~Hhetsron~of to~Karmi CLAN the~Karmi **26:7** THESE CLAN~s the~ Re'uven~of and~*they*⁽ᵐ⁾~*will*~EXIST⁽ⱽ⁾ REGISTER⁽ⱽ⁾~*ed*⁽ᵐᵖ⁾~them⁽ᵐ⁾ THREE and~FOUR~s THOUSAND and~SEVEN HUNDRED~s and~THREE~s **26:8** and~ SON~s Palu Eli'av **26:9** and~SON~s Eli'av Nemu'eyl and~Datan and~Aviram HE Datan and~Aviram CALL.OUT⁽ⱽ⁾~*ed*⁽ᵐᵖ⁾ the~COMPANY WHICH *they~did~ make*~STRUGGLE⁽ⱽ⁾ UPON Mosheh and~UPON Aharon in~the~COMPANY Qorahh in~>~*make*~STRUGGLE⁽ⱽ⁾~them⁽ᵐ⁾ UPON **YHWH** **26:10** and~*she~ will*~OPEN⁽ⱽ⁾ the~LAND AT MOUTH~her and~*she~will*~SWALLOW⁽ⱽ⁾ AT~ them⁽ᵐ⁾ and~AT Qorahh in~DEATH the~COMPANY in~>~EAT⁽ⱽ⁾ the~FIRE AT FIVE~s and~HUNDRED~s2 MAN and~*they*⁽ᵐ⁾~*will*~EXIST⁽ⱽ⁾ to~ STANDARD **26:11** and~SON~s Qorahh NOT *they~did*~DIE⁽ⱽ⁾ **26:12** SON~s Shimon to~CLAN~s~them⁽ᵐ⁾ to~Nemu'eyl CLAN the~Nemu'eyl~of to~Yamin CLAN the~Yamin~of to~Yakhin CLAN the~Yakhin~of **26:13** to~Zerahh CLAN the~Zerahh~of to~Sha'ul CLAN the~Sha'ul~of **26:14** THESE CLAN~s the~ Shimon~of TWO and~TEN~s THOUSAND and~HUNDRED~s2 **26:15** SON~s Gad to~CLAN~s~them⁽ᵐ⁾ to~Tsaphon CLAN the~Tsaphon~of to~Hhagi CLAN the~Hhagi to~Shuni CLAN the~Shuni~of **26:16** to~Azni CLAN the~Azni~of

The Book of Numbers

to~Eyriy CLAN the~Eyriy **26:17** to~Arwad CLAN the~Arwad~of to~Areliy CLAN the~Areliy **26:18** THESE CLAN~s SON~s Gad to~REGISTER$^{(V)}$~ed$^{(mp)}$~them$^{(m)}$ FOUR~s THOUSAND and~FIVE HUNDRED~s **26:19** SON~s Yehudah Eyr and~Onan and~*he~will~*DIE$^{(V)}$ Eyr and~Onan in~LAND Kena'an **26:20** and~*they$^{(m)}$~will~*EXIST$^{(V)}$ SON~s Yehudah to~CLAN~s~them$^{(m)}$ to~Sheylah CLAN the~Sheylah~of to~Perets CLAN the~Perets~of to~Zerahh CLAN the~Zerahh~of **26:21** and~*they$^{(m)}$~will~*EXIST$^{(V)}$ SON~s Perets to~Hhetsron CLAN the~Hhetsron~of to~Hhamul CLAN the~Hhamul~of **26:22** THESE CLAN~s Yehudah to~REGISTER$^{(V)}$~ed$^{(mp)}$~them$^{(m)}$ SIX and~SEVEN~s THOUSAND and~FIVE HUNDRED~s **26:23** SON~s Yis'sas'khar to~CLAN~s~them$^{(m)}$ Tola CLAN the~Tola~of to~Pu'a CLAN the~Pun~of **26:24** to~Yashuv CLAN the~Yashuv~of to~Shimron CLAN the~Shimron~of **26:25** THESE CLAN~s Yis'sas'khar to~REGISTER$^{(V)}$~ed$^{(mp)}$~them$^{(m)}$ FOUR and~SIX~s THOUSAND and~THREE HUNDRED~s **26:26** SON~s Zevulun to~CLAN~s~them$^{(m)}$ to~Sered CLAN the~Sered~of to~Elyon CLAN the~Eylon~of to~Yahh'le'el CLAN the~Yahh'le'el **26:27** THESE CLAN~s the~Zevulun~of to~REGISTER$^{(V)}$~ed$^{(mp)}$~them$^{(m)}$ SIX~s THOUSAND and~FIVE HUNDRED~s **26:28** SON~s Yoseph to~CLAN~s~them$^{(m)}$ Menasheh and~Ephrayim **26:29** SON~s Menasheh to~Makhir CLAN the~Makhir~of and~Makhir *he~did~make~*BRING.FORTH$^{(V)}$ AT Gil'ad to~Gil'ad CLAN the~Gil'ad~of **26:30** THESE SON~s Gil'ad I'ezer CLAN the~I'ezer~of to~Hheleq CLAN the~Hheleq~of **26:31** and~Asri'eyl CLAN the~Asri'eyl~of and~Shekhem CLAN the~Shekhem~of **26:32** and~Shemida CLAN the~Shemida~of and~Hheypher CLAN the~Hheypher~of **26:33** and~Tselaph'hhad SON Hheypher NOT *they~did~*EXIST$^{(V)}$ to~him SON~s GIVEN.THAT IF DAUGHTER~s and~TITLE DAUGHTER~s Tselaph'hhad Mahhlah and~No'ah Hhaglah Milkah and~Tirtsah **26:34** THESE CLAN~s Menasheh and~REGISTER$^{(V)}$~ed$^{(mp)}$~them$^{(m)}$ TWO and~FIVE~s THOUSAND and~SEVEN HUNDRED~s **26:35** THESE SON~s Ephrayim to~CLAN~s~them$^{(m)}$ to~Shutelahh CLAN the~Shutelahh to~Bekher CLAN the~Bekher~of to~Tahhan CLAN the~Tahhan~of **26:36** and~THESE SON~s Shutelahh to~Eyran CLAN the~Eyran~of **26:37** THESE CLAN~s SON~s Ephrayim to~REGISTER$^{(V)}$~ed$^{(mp)}$~them$^{(m)}$ TWO and~THREE~s THOUSAND and~FIVE HUNDRED~s THESE SON~s Yoseph to~CLAN~s~them$^{(m)}$ **26:38** SON~s Binyamin to~CLAN~s~them$^{(m)}$ to~Bela CLAN the~Bela~of to~Ashbeyl CLAN the~Ashbeyl~of to~Ahhiram CLAN the~Ahhiram~of **26:39** to~Sheshupham CLAN the~Sheshupham~of to~Hhupham CLAN the~Hhupham~of **26:40** and~*they$^{(m)}$~will~*EXIST$^{(V)}$ SON~s Bela Ard and~Na'aman CLAN the~Ard~of to~Na'aman CLAN the~Na'amah~of **26:41** THESE SON~s Binyamin to~CLAN~s~them$^{(m)}$ and~REGISTER$^{(V)}$~ed$^{(mp)}$~them$^{(m)}$ FIVE and~FOUR~s THOUSAND and~SIX HUNDRED~s **26:42** THESE SON~s Dan to~CLAN~s~them$^{(m)}$ to~Shuhham CLAN the~Shuhham~of THESE CLAN~s Dan to~CLAN~s~them$^{(m)}$ **26:43** ALL CLAN~s the~Shuhham~of to~REGISTER$^{(V)}$~ed$^{(mp)}$~them$^{(m)}$ FOUR and~SIX~s THOUSAND and~FOUR HUNDRED~s **26:44** SON~s Asher to~CLAN~s~them$^{(m)}$ to~Yimnah CLAN the~Yimnah to~Yishwiy CLAN the~Yishwiy to~

Beri'ah CLAN the~Beri'ah~of **26:45** to~SON~s Beri'ah to~Hhever CLAN the~Hhever~of to~Malki'el CLAN the~Malki'el~of **26:46** and~TITLE DAUGHTER Asher Serahh **26:47** THESE CLAN~s SON~s Asher to~REGISTER$^{(V)}$~ed$^{(mp)}$~them$^{(m)}$ THREE and~FIVE~s THOUSAND and~FOUR HUNDRED~s **26:48** SON~s Naphtali to~CLAN~s~them$^{(m)}$ to~Yahhtse'el CLAN the~Yahhtse'el~of to~Guni CLAN the~Guni **26:49** to~Yetser CLAN the~Yetser~of to~Shalem CLAN the~Shalem~of **26:50** THESE CLAN~s Naphtali to~CLAN~s~them$^{(m)}$ and~REGISTER$^{(V)}$~ed$^{(mp)}$~them$^{(m)}$ FIVE and~FOUR~s THOUSAND and~FOUR HUNDRED~s **26:51** THESE REGISTER$^{(V)}$~ed$^{(mp)}$ SON~s Yisra'eyl SIX HUNDRED~s THOUSAND and~THOUSAND SEVEN HUNDRED~s and~THREE~s **26:52** and~*he*~*will*~*much*~SPEAK$^{(V)}$ **YHWH** TO Mosheh to~>~SAY$^{(V)}$ **26:53** to~THESE *she*~*will*~*be*~DISTRIBUTE$^{(V)}$ the~LAND in~INHERITANCE in~NUMBER TITLE~s **26:54** to~ABUNDANT *you*$^{(ms)}$~*will*~*make*~INCREASE$^{(V)}$ INHERITANCE~him and~to~the~SMALL.AMOUNT *you*$^{(ms)}$~*will*~*make*~BE.LESS$^{(V)}$ INHERITANCE~him MAN to~MOUTH REGISTER$^{(V)}$~ed$^{(mp)}$~him *he*~GIVE$^{(V)}$~ed$^{(ms)}$ INHERITANCE~him **26:55** SURELY in~LOT *he*~*will*~*be*~DISTRIBUTE$^{(V)}$ AT the~LAND to~TITLE~s BRANCH FATHER~s~them$^{(m)}$ *they*$^{(m)}$~*will*~INHERIT$^{(V)}$ **26:56** UPON MOUTH the~LOT *she*~*will*~*be*~DISTRIBUTE$^{(V)}$ INHERITANCE~him BETWEEN ABUNDANT to~SMALL.AMOUNT **26:57** and~THESE REGISTER$^{(V)}$~ed$^{(mp)}$ the~Lewi to~CLAN~s~them$^{(m)}$ to~Gershon CLAN the~Gershon~of to~Qehat CLAN the~Qehat~of to~Merari CLAN the~Merari **26:58** THESE CLAN~s Lewi CLAN the~Liyvniy CLAN the~Hhevron~of CLAN the~Mahh'liy CLAN the~Mushiy CLAN the~Qorahh~of and~Qehat *he*~*did*~*make*~BRING.FORTH$^{(V)}$ AT Amram **26:59** and~TITLE WOMAN Amram Yokheved DAUGHTER Lewi WHICH *she*~*did*~BRING.FORTH$^{(V)}$ AT~her to~Lewi in~Mits'rayim and~*she*~*will*~BRING.FORTH$^{(V)}$ to~Amram AT Aharon and~AT Mosheh and~AT Mir'yam SISTER~them$^{(m)}$ **26:60** and~*he*~*will*~*be*~BRING.FORTH$^{(V)}$ to~Aharon AT Nadav and~AT Aviyhu AT Elazar and~AT Iytamar **26:61** and~*he*~*will*~DIE$^{(V)}$ Nadav and~Aviyhu in~>~*make*~COME.NEAR$^{(V)}$~them$^{(m)}$ FIRE BE.STRANGE$^{(V)}$~ing$^{(fs)}$ to~FACE~s **YHWH** **26:62** and~*they*$^{(m)}$~*will*~EXIST$^{(V)}$ REGISTER$^{(V)}$~ed$^{(mp)}$~them$^{(m)}$ THREE and~TEN~s THOUSAND ALL MALE from~SON NEW.MOON and~UPWARD~unto GIVEN.THAT NOT *they*~*did*~*self*~REGISTER$^{(V)}$ in~MIDST SON~s Yisra'eyl GIVEN.THAT NOT *he*~*did*~*be*~GIVE$^{(V)}$ to~them$^{(m)}$ INHERITANCE in~MIDST SON~s Yisra'eyl **26:63** THESE REGISTER$^{(V)}$~ed$^{(mp)}$ Mosheh and~Elazar the~ADMINISTRATOR WHICH *they*~*did*~REGISTER$^{(V)}$ AT SON~s Yisra'eyl in~DESERT~s Mo'av UPON Yarden Ye'rey'hho **26:64** and~in~THESE NOT *he*~*did*~EXIST$^{(V)}$ MAN from~REGISTER$^{(V)}$~ed$^{(mp)}$ Mosheh and~Aharon the~ADMINISTRATOR WHICH *they*~*did*~REGISTER$^{(V)}$ AT SON~s Yisra'eyl in~WILDERNESS Sinai **26:65** GIVEN.THAT *he*~*did*~SAY$^{(V)}$ **YHWH** to~them$^{(m)}$ >~DIE$^{(V)}$ *they*$^{(m)}$~*will*~DIE$^{(V)}$ in~the~WILDERNESS and~NOT *he*~*did*~*be*~LEAVE.BEHIND$^{(V)}$ from~them$^{(m)}$ MAN GIVEN.THAT IF Kaleyv SON Yephunah and~Yehoshu'a SON Nun

Chapter 27

27:1 and~*they*^(f)~*will*~COME.NEAR^(V) DAUGHTER~s Tselaph'hhad SON Hheypher SON Gil'ad SON Makhir SON Menasheh to~CLAN~s Menasheh SON Yoseph and~THESE TITLE~s DAUGHTER~s~him Mahhlah No'ah and~Hhaglah and~Milkah and~Tirtsah **27:2** and~*they*^(f)~*will*~STAND^(V) to~FACE~s Mosheh and~to~FACE~s Elazar the~ADMINISTRATOR and~to~FACE~s the~CAPTAIN~s and~ALL the~COMPANY OPENING TENT APPOINTED to~>~SAY^(V) **27:3** FATHER~us *he*~*did*~DIE^(V) in~the~WILDERNESS and~HE NOT *he*~*did*~EXIST^(V) in~MIDST the~COMPANY the~*be*~APPOINT^(V)~*ing*^(mp) UPON YHWH in~the~COMPANY Qorahh GIVEN.THAT in~FAILURE~him *he*~*did*~DIE^(V) and~SON~s NOT *they*~*did*~EXIST^(V) to~him **27:4** to~WHAT *he*~*will*~*be*~TAKE.AWAY^(V) TITLE FATHER~us from~MIDST CLAN~him GIVEN.THAT WITHOUT to~him SON !^(ms)~GIVE^(V)~& to~us HOLDINGS in~MIDST BROTHER~s FATHER~us **27:5** and~*he*~*will*~*make*~COME.NEAR^(V) Mosheh AT DECISION~them^(f) to~FACE~s **YHWH** **27:6** and~*he*~*will*~SAY^(V) **YHWH** TO Mosheh to~>~SAY^(V) **27:7** SO DAUGHTER~s Tselaph'hhad SPEAK^(V)~*ing*^(fp) >~GIVE^(V) *you*^(ms)~*will*~GIVE^(V) to~them^(m) HOLDINGS INHERITANCE in~MIDST BROTHER~s FATHER~them^(m) and~*you*^(ms)~*did*~*make*~CROSS.OVER^(V) AT INHERITANCE FATHER~them^(f) to~them^(f) **27:8** and~TO SON~s Yisra'eyl *you*^(ms)~*will*~much~SPEAK^(V) to~>~SAY^(V) MAN GIVEN.THAT *he*~*will*~DIE^(V) and~SON WITHOUT to~him and~*you*^(mp)~*did*~*make*~CROSS.OVER^(V) AT INHERITANCE~him to~DAUGHTER~him **27:9** and~IF WITHOUT to~him DAUGHTER and~*you*^(mp)~*did*~GIVE^(V) AT INHERITANCE~him to~BROTHER~s~him **27:10** and~IF WITHOUT to~him BROTHER~s and~*you*^(mp)~*did*~GIVE^(V) AT INHERITANCE~him to~BROTHER~s FATHER~him **27:11** and~IF WITHOUT BROTHER~s to~FATHER~him and~*you*^(mp)~*did*~GIVE^(V) AT INHERITANCE~him to~KIN~him the~NEAR TO~him from~CLAN~him and~*he*~*did*~POSSESS^(V) AT~her and~*she*~*did*~EXIST^(V) to~SON~s Yisra'eyl to~CUSTOM DECISION like~WHICH *he*~*did*~much~DIRECT^(V) **YHWH** AT Mosheh **27:12** and~*he*~*will*~SAY^(V) **YHWH** TO Mosheh !^(ms)~GO.UP^(V) TO HILL the~Ever~s the~THIS and~!^(ms)~SEE^(V) AT the~LAND WHICH *I*~*did*~GIVE^(V) to~SON~s Yisra'eyl **27:13** and~*you*^(ms)~*did*~SEE^(V) AT~her and~*you*^(ms)~*did*~*be*~GATHER^(V) TO PEOPLE~s~*you*^(ms) ALSO YOU^(ms) like~WHICH *he*~*did*~*be*~GATHER^(V) Aharon BROTHER~you^(ms) **27:14** like~WHICH *you*^(ms)~*did*~DISOBEY^(V) MOUTH~me in~WILDERNESS Tsin in~CONTENTION the~COMPANY to~>~*make*~SET.APART^(V)~me in~the~WATER~s2 to~EYE~s2~them^(m) THEY^(m) WATER~s2 Meriyvah Qadesh WILDERNESS Tsin **27:15** and~*he*~*will*~much~SPEAK^(V) Mosheh TO **YHWH** to~>~SAY^(V) **27:16** *he*~*will*~REGISTER^(V) **YHWH** Elohiym the~WIND~s to~ALL FLESH MAN UPON the~COMPANY **27:17** WHICH *he*~*will*~GO.OUT^(V) to~FACE~s~them^(m) and~WHICH *he*~*will*~COME.IN^(V) to~FACE~s~them^(m) and~WHICH *he*~*will*~*make*~GO.OUT^(V)~them^(m) and~WHICH *he*~*will*~*make*~COME^(V)~them^(m) and~NOT *she*~*will*~EXIST^(V) COMPANY **YHWH** like~the~FLOCKS WHICH WITHOUT to~

them⁽ᵐ⁾ FEED⁽ⱽ⁾~ing⁽ᵐˢ⁾ **27:18** and~he~will~SAY⁽ⱽ⁾ **YHWH** TO Mosheh !⁽ᵐˢ⁾~ TAKE⁽ⱽ⁾ to~you⁽ᵐˢ⁾ AT Yehoshu'a SON Nun MAN WHICH WIND in~him and~ you⁽ᵐˢ⁾~did~SUPPORT⁽ⱽ⁾ AT HAND~you⁽ᵐˢ⁾ UPON~him **27:19** and~you⁽ᵐˢ⁾~ did~make~STAND⁽ⱽ⁾ AT~him to~FACE~s Elazar the~ADMINISTRATOR and~ to~FACE~s ALL the~COMPANY and~you⁽ᵐˢ⁾~did~much~DIRECT⁽ⱽ⁾ AT~him to~ EYE~s2~them⁽ᵐ⁾ **27:20** and~you⁽ᵐˢ⁾~did~GIVE⁽ⱽ⁾~& from~SPLENDOR~you⁽ᵐˢ⁾ UPON~him to~THAT they⁽ᵐ⁾~will~HEAR⁽ⱽ⁾ ALL COMPANY SON~s Yisra'eyl **27:21** and~to~FACE~s Elazar the~ADMINISTRATOR he~will~ STAND⁽ⱽ⁾ and~he~did~INQUIRE⁽ⱽ⁾ to~him in~DECISION the~Uriym to~FACE~s **YHWH** UPON MOUTH~him they⁽ᵐ⁾~will~GO.OUT⁽ⱽ⁾ and~UPON MOUTH~him they⁽ᵐ⁾~will~COME⁽ⱽ⁾ HE and~ALL SON~s Yisra'eyl AT~him and~ALL the~ COMPANY **27:22** and~he~will~DO⁽ⱽ⁾ Mosheh like~WHICH he~did~much~ DIRECT⁽ⱽ⁾ **YHWH** AT~him and~he~will~TAKE⁽ⱽ⁾ AT Yehoshu'a and~he~will~ make~STAND⁽ⱽ⁾~him to~FACE~s Elazar the~ADMINISTRATOR and~to~ FACE~s ALL the~COMPANY **27:23** and~he~will~SUPPORT⁽ⱽ⁾ AT HAND~s2~ him UPON~him and~he~will~much~DIRECT⁽ⱽ⁾~him like~WHICH he~did~ much~SPEAK⁽ⱽ⁾ **YHWH** in~HAND Mosheh

Chapter 28

28:1 and~he~will~much~SPEAK⁽ⱽ⁾ **YHWH** TO Mosheh to~>~SAY⁽ⱽ⁾ **28:2** !⁽ᵐˢ⁾~ much~DIRECT⁽ⱽ⁾ AT SON~s Yisra'eyl and~you⁽ᵐˢ⁾~did~SAY⁽ⱽ⁾ TO~them⁽ᵐ⁾ AT DONATION~me BREAD~me to~FIRE.OFFERING~s~me AROMA SWEET~me you⁽ᵐᵖ⁾~will~SAFEGUARD⁽ⱽ⁾ to~>~make~COME.NEAR⁽ⱽ⁾ to~me in~ APPOINTED~him **28:3** and~you⁽ᵐˢ⁾~did~SAY⁽ⱽ⁾ to~them⁽ᵐ⁾ THIS the~ FIRE.OFFERING WHICH you⁽ᵐᵖ⁾~will~make~COME.NEAR⁽ⱽ⁾ to~**YHWH** SHEEP~s SON~s YEAR WHOLE~s TWO to~the~DAY ASCENSION.OFFERING CONTINUALLY **28:4** AT the~SHEEP UNIT you⁽ᵐˢ⁾~will~DO⁽ⱽ⁾ in~the~ MORNING and~AT the~SHEEP the~SECOND you⁽ᵐˢ⁾~will~DO⁽ⱽ⁾ BETWEEN the~EVENING~s2 **28:5** and~TENTH the~EYPHAH FLOUR to~DEPOSIT MIX⁽ⱽ⁾~ ed⁽ᶠˢ⁾ in~OIL SMASHED FOURTH the~HIYN **28:6** ASCENSION.OFFERING CONTINUALLY the~DO⁽ⱽ⁾~ed⁽ᶠˢ⁾ in~HILL Sinai to~AROMA SWEET FIRE.OFFERING to~**YHWH** **28:7** and~POURING~him FOURTH the~HIYN to~ the~SHEEP the~UNIT in~the~SPECIAL !⁽ᵐˢ⁾~make~POUR⁽ⱽ⁾ POURING LIQUOR to~**YHWH** **28:8** and~AT the~SHEEP the~SECOND you⁽ᵐˢ⁾~will~DO⁽ⱽ⁾ BETWEEN the~EVENING~s2 like~DEPOSIT the~MORNING and~like~ POURING~him you⁽ᵐˢ⁾~will~DO⁽ⱽ⁾ FIRE.OFFERING AROMA SWEET to~ **YHWH** **28:9** and~in~DAY the~CEASING TWO SHEEP~s SON~s YEAR WHOLE~s and~TWO ONE.TENTH~s FLOUR DEPOSIT MIX⁽ⱽ⁾~ed⁽ᶠˢ⁾ in~the~OIL and~POURING~him **28:10** ASCENSION.OFFERING CEASING in~CEASING~ him UPON ASCENSION.OFFERING the~CONTINUALLY and~POURING~ her **28:11** and~in~HEAD~s NEW.MOON~s~you⁽ᵐᵖ⁾ you⁽ᵐᵖ⁾~will~make~ COME.NEAR⁽ⱽ⁾ ASCENSION.OFFERING to~**YHWH** BULL~s SON~s CATTLE TWO

The Book of Numbers

and~BUCK UNIT SHEEP~s SON~s YEAR SEVEN WHOLE~s **28:12** and~THREE ONE.TENTH~s FLOUR DEPOSIT MIX$^{(V)}$~*ed$^{(fs)}$* in~the~OIL to~the~BULL the~UNIT and~TWO ONE.TENTH~s FLOUR DEPOSIT MIX$^{(V)}$~*ed$^{(fs)}$* in~the~OIL to~the~BUCK the~UNIT **28:13** and~ONE.TENTH ONE.TENTH FLOUR DEPOSIT MIX$^{(V)}$~*ed$^{(fs)}$* in~the~OIL to~the~SHEEP the~UNIT ASCENSION.OFFERING AROMA SWEET FIRE.OFFERING to~**YHWH** **28:14** and~POURING~s~them$^{(m)}$ HALF the~HIYN *he~will*~EXIST$^{(V)}$ to~the~BULL and~THIRD the~HIYN to~the~BUCK and~FOURTH the~HIYN to~the~SHEEP WINE THIS ASCENSION.OFFERING NEW.MOON in~NEW.MOON~him to~NEW.MOON~s the~YEAR **28:15** and~HAIRY.GOAT SHE-GOAT~s UNIT to~FAILURE to~**YHWH** UPON ASCENSION.OFFERING the~CONTINUALLY *he~will~be*~DO$^{(V)}$ and~POURING~him **28:16** and~in~the~NEW.MOON the~FIRST in~FOUR TEN DAY to~the~NEW.MOON Pesahh to~**YHWH** **28:17** and~in~the~FIVE TEN DAY to~the~NEW.MOON the~THIS FEAST SEVEN DAY~s UNLEAVENED.BREAD~s *he~will~be*~EAT$^{(V)}$ **28:18** in~the~DAY the~FIRST MEETING SPECIAL ALL BUSINESS SERVICE NOT *you$^{(mp)}$~will*~DO$^{(V)}$ **28:19** and~*you$^{(mp)}$~did~make*~COME.NEAR$^{(V)}$ FIRE.OFFERING ASCENSION.OFFERING to~**YHWH** BULL~s SON~s CATTLE TWO and~BUCK UNIT and~SEVEN SHEEP~s SON~s YEAR WHOLE~s *they$^{(m)}$~will*~EXIST$^{(V)}$ to~you$^{(mp)}$ **28:20** and~DEPOSIT~them$^{(m)}$ FLOUR MIX$^{(V)}$~*ed$^{(fs)}$* in~the~OIL THREE ONE.TENTH~s to~the~BULL and~TWO ONE.TENTH~s to~the~BUCK *you$^{(mp)}$~will*~DO$^{(V)}$ **28:21** ONE.TENTH ONE.TENTH *you$^{(ms)}$~will*~DO$^{(V)}$ to~the~SHEEP the~UNIT to~SEVEN the~SHEEP~s **28:22** and~HAIRY.GOAT FAILURE UNIT to~>~*much*~COVER$^{(V)}$ UPON~you$^{(mp)}$ **28:23** from~to~STRAND ASCENSION.OFFERING the~MORNING WHICH to~ASCENSION.OFFERING the~CONTINUALLY *you$^{(mp)}$~will*~DO$^{(V)}$ AT THESE **28:24** like~THESE *you$^{(mp)}$~will*~DO$^{(V)}$ to~the~DAY SEVEN DAY~s BREAD FIRE.OFFERING AROMA SWEET to~**YHWH** UPON ASCENSION.OFFERING the~CONTINUALLY *he~will~be*~DO$^{(V)}$ and~POURING~him **28:25** and~in~the~DAY the~SEVENTH MEETING SPECIAL *he~will*~EXIST$^{(V)}$ to~you$^{(mp)}$ ALL BUSINESS SERVICE NOT *you$^{(mp)}$~will*~DO$^{(V)}$ **28:26** and~in~DAY the~FIRST-FRUIT~s in~>~*make*~COME.NEAR$^{(V)}$~you$^{(mp)}$ DEPOSIT NEW to~**YHWH** in~WEEK~s~you$^{(mp)}$ MEETING SPECIAL *he~will*~EXIST$^{(V)}$ to~you$^{(mp)}$ ALL BUSINESS SERVICE NOT *you$^{(mp)}$~will*~DO$^{(V)}$ **28:27** and~*you$^{(mp)}$~did~make*~COME.NEAR$^{(V)}$ ASCENSION.OFFERING to~AROMA SWEET to~**YHWH** BULL~s SON~s CATTLE TWO BUCK UNIT SEVEN SHEEP~s SON~s YEAR **28:28** and~DEPOSIT~them$^{(m)}$ FLOUR MIX$^{(V)}$~*ed$^{(fs)}$* in~the~OIL THREE ONE.TENTH~s to~the~BULL the~UNIT TWO ONE.TENTH~s to~the~BUCK the~UNIT **28:29** ONE.TENTH ONE.TENTH to~the~SHEEP the~UNIT to~SEVEN the~SHEEP~s **28:30** HAIRY.GOAT SHE-GOAT~s UNIT to~>~*much*~COVER$^{(V)}$ UPON~you$^{(mp)}$ **28:31** from~to~STRAND ASCENSION.OFFERING the~CONTINUALLY and~DEPOSIT~him *you$^{(mp)}$~will*~DO$^{(V)}$ WHOLE~s *they$^{(m)}$~will*~EXIST$^{(V)}$ to~you$^{(mp)}$ and~POURING~s~them$^{(m)}$

Chapter 29

29:1 and~in~the~NEW.MOON the~SEVENTH in~UNIT to~the~NEW.MOON MEETING SPECIAL *he~will*~EXIST$^{(V)}$ to~you$^{(mp)}$ ALL BUSINESS SERVICE NOT you$^{(mp)}$~will~DO$^{(V)}$ DAY SIGNAL *he~will*~EXIST$^{(V)}$ to~you$^{(mp)}$ **29:2** and~you$^{(mp)}$~did~DO$^{(V)}$ ASCENSION.OFFERING to~AROMA SWEET to~**YHWH** BULL SON CATTLE UNIT BUCK UNIT SHEEP~s SON~s YEAR SEVEN WHOLE~s **29:3** and~DEPOSIT~them$^{(m)}$ FLOUR MIX$^{(V)}$~*ed$^{(fs)}$* in~the~OIL THREE ONE.TENTH~s to~the~BULL TWO ONE.TENTH~s to~the~BUCK **29:4** and~ONE.TENTH UNIT to~the~SHEEP the~UNIT to~SEVEN the~SHEEP~s **29:5** and~HAIRY.GOAT SHE-GOAT~s UNIT FAILURE to~>~*much*~COVER$^{(V)}$ UPON~you$^{(mp)}$ **29:6** from~to~STRAND ASCENSION.OFFERING the~NEW.MOON and~DEPOSIT~her and~ASCENSION.OFFERING the~CONTINUALLY and~DEPOSIT~her and~POURING~s~them$^{(m)}$ like~DECISION~them$^{(m)}$ to~AROMA SWEET FIRE.OFFERING to~**YHWH** **29:7** and~in~TENTH.ONE to~the~NEW.MOON the~SEVENTH the~THIS MEETING SPECIAL *he~will*~EXIST$^{(V)}$ to~you$^{(mp)}$ and~*you$^{(mp)}$~did~much*~AFFLICT$^{(V)}$ AT SOUL~s~you$^{(mp)}$ ALL BUSINESS NOT you$^{(mp)}$~will~DO$^{(V)}$ **29:8** and~you$^{(mp)}$~did~make~COME.NEAR$^{(V)}$ ASCENSION.OFFERING to~**YHWH** AROMA SWEET BULL SON CATTLE UNIT BUCK UNIT SHEEP~s SON~s YEAR SEVEN WHOLE~s *they$^{(m)}$~will*~EXIST$^{(V)}$ to~you$^{(mp)}$ **29:9** and~DEPOSIT~them$^{(m)}$ FLOUR MIX$^{(V)}$~*ed$^{(fs)}$* in~the~OIL THREE ONE.TENTH~s to~the~BULL TWO ONE.TENTH~s to~the~BUCK the~UNIT **29:10** ONE.TENTH ONE.TENTH to~the~SHEEP the~UNIT to~SEVEN the~SHEEP~s **29:11** HAIRY.GOAT SHE-GOAT~s UNIT FAILURE from~to~STRAND FAILURE the~ATONEMENT~s and~ASCENSION.OFFERING the~CONTINUALLY and~DEPOSIT~her and~POURING~s~them$^{(m)}$ **29:12** and~in~the~FIVE TEN DAY to~the~NEW.MOON the~SEVENTH MEETING SPECIAL *he~will*~EXIST$^{(V)}$ to~you$^{(mp)}$ ALL BUSINESS SERVICE NOT you$^{(mp)}$~will~DO$^{(V)}$ and~you$^{(mp)}$~did~HOLD.A.FEAST$^{(V)}$ FEAST to~**YHWH** SEVEN DAY~s **29:13** and~you$^{(mp)}$~did~make~COME.NEAR$^{(V)}$ ASCENSION.OFFERING FIRE.OFFERING AROMA SWEET to~**YHWH** BULL~s SON~s CATTLE THREE TEN BUCK~s TWO SHEEP~s SON~s YEAR FOUR TEN WHOLE~s *they$^{(m)}$~will*~EXIST$^{(V)}$ **29:14** and~DEPOSIT~them$^{(m)}$ FLOUR MIX$^{(V)}$~*ed$^{(fs)}$* in~the~OIL THREE ONE.TENTH~s to~the~BULL the~UNIT to~THREE TEN BULL~s TWO ONE.TENTH~s to~the~BUCK the~UNIT to~TWO the~BUCK~s **29:15** and~ONE.TENTH ONE.TENTH to~the~SHEEP the~UNIT to~FOUR TEN SHEEP~s **29:16** and~HAIRY.GOAT SHE-GOAT~s UNIT FAILURE from~to~STRAND ASCENSION.OFFERING the~CONTINUALLY DEPOSIT~her and~POURING~her **29:17** and~in~the~DAY the~SECOND BULL~s SON~s CATTLE TWO TEN BUCK~s TWO SHEEP~s SON~s YEAR FOUR TEN WHOLE~s **29:18** and~DEPOSIT~them$^{(m)}$ and~POURING~s~them$^{(m)}$ to~the~BULL~s to~the~BUCK~s and~to~the~SHEEP~s in~NUMBER~them$^{(m)}$ like~the~DECISION **29:19** and~HAIRY.GOAT SHE-GOAT~s UNIT FAILURE from~to~STRAND ASCENSION.OFFERING the~CONTINUALLY and~DEPOSIT~her and~POURING~s~them$^{(m)}$ **29:20** and~in~the~DAY the~THIRD

The Book of Numbers

BULL~s ONE TEN BUCK~s TWO SHEEP~s SON~s YEAR FOUR TEN WHOLE~s **29:21** and~DEPOSIT~them$^{(m)}$ and~POURING~s~them$^{(m)}$ to~the~BULL~s to~the~BUCK~s and~to~the~SHEEP~s in~NUMBER~them$^{(m)}$ like~the~DECISION **29:22** and~HAIRY.GOAT FAILURE UNIT from~to~STRAND ASCENSION.OFFERING the~CONTINUALLY and~DEPOSIT~her and~POURING~her **29:23** and~in~the~DAY the~FOURTH BULL~s TEN BUCK~s TWO SHEEP~s SON~s YEAR FOUR TEN WHOLE~s **29:24** DEPOSIT~them$^{(m)}$ and~POURING~s~them$^{(m)}$ to~the~BULL~s to~the~BUCK~s and~to~the~SHEEP~s in~NUMBER~them$^{(m)}$ like~the~DECISION **29:25** and~HAIRY.GOAT SHE-GOAT~s UNIT FAILURE from~to~STRAND ASCENSION.OFFERING the~CONTINUALLY DEPOSIT~her and~POURING~her **29:26** and~in~the~DAY the~FIFTH BULL~s NINE BUCK~s TWO SHEEP~s SON~s YEAR FOUR TEN WHOLE~s **29:27** and~DEPOSIT~them$^{(m)}$ and~POURING~s~them$^{(m)}$ to~the~BULL~s to~the~BUCK~s and~to~the~SHEEP~s in~NUMBER~them$^{(m)}$ like~the~DECISION **29:28** and~HAIRY.GOAT FAILURE UNIT from~to~STRAND ASCENSION.OFFERING the~CONTINUALLY and~DEPOSIT~her and~POURING~her **29:29** and~in~the~DAY the~SIXTH BULL~s EIGHT BUCK~s TWO SHEEP~s SON~s YEAR FOUR TEN WHOLE~s **29:30** and~DEPOSIT~them$^{(m)}$ and~POURING~s~them$^{(m)}$ to~the~BULL~s to~the~BUCK~s and~to~the~SHEEP~s in~NUMBER~them$^{(m)}$ like~the~DECISION **29:31** and~HAIRY.GOAT FAILURE UNIT from~to~STRAND ASCENSION.OFFERING the~CONTINUALLY DEPOSIT~her and~POURING~s~her **29:32** and~in~the~DAY the~SEVENTH BULL~s SEVEN BUCK~s TWO SHEEP~s SON~s YEAR FOUR TEN WHOLE~s **29:33** and~DEPOSIT~them$^{(m)}$ and~POURING~them$^{(m)}$ to~the~BULL~s to~the~BUCK~s and~to~the~SHEEP~s in~NUMBER~them$^{(m)}$ like~DECISION~them$^{(m)}$ **29:34** and~HAIRY.GOAT FAILURE UNIT from~to~STRAND ASCENSION.OFFERING the~CONTINUALLY DEPOSIT~her and~POURING~her **29:35** in~the~DAY the~EIGHTH CONFERENCE *she*~*will*~EXIST$^{(V)}$ to~you$^{(mp)}$ ALL BUSINESS SERVICE NOT *you*$^{(mp)}$~*will*~DO$^{(V)}$ **29:36** and~*you*$^{(mp)}$~*did*~*make*~COME.NEAR$^{(V)}$ ASCENSION.OFFERING FIRE.OFFERING AROMA SWEET to~**YHWH** BULL UNIT BUCK UNIT SHEEP~s SON~s YEAR SEVEN WHOLE~s **29:37** DEPOSIT~them$^{(m)}$ and~POURING~s~them$^{(m)}$ to~the~BULL to~the~BUCK and~to~the~SHEEP~s in~NUMBER~them$^{(m)}$ like~the~DECISION **29:38** and~HAIRY.GOAT FAILURE UNIT from~to~STRAND ASCENSION.OFFERING the~CONTINUALLY and~DEPOSIT~her and~POURING~her **29:39** THESE *you*$^{(mp)}$~*will*~DO$^{(V)}$ to~**YHWH** in~APPOINTED~s~you$^{(mp)}$ to~STRAND from~VOW~s~you$^{(mp)}$ and~FREEWILL.OFFERING~s~you$^{(mp)}$ to~ASCENSION.OFFERING~s~you$^{(mp)}$ and~to~DEPOSIT~s~you$^{(mp)}$ and~to~POURING~s~you$^{(mp)}$ and~to~OFFERING.OF.RESTITUTION~s~you$^{(mp)}$

Chapter 30

30:1 (29:40) and~*he~will*~SAY⁽ᵛ⁾ Mosheh TO SON~s Yisra'eyl like~ALL WHICH *he~did~much*~DIRECT⁽ᵛ⁾ **YHWH** AT Mosheh   **30:2 (30:1)** and~*he~will~much*~SPEAK⁽ᵛ⁾ Mosheh TO HEAD~s the~BRANCH to~SON~s Yisra'eyl to~>~SAY⁽ᵛ⁾ THIS the~WORD WHICH *he~did~much*~DIRECT⁽ᵛ⁾ **YHWH**   **30:3 (30:2)** MAN GIVEN.THAT *he~will*~MAKE.A.VOW⁽ᵛ⁾ VOW to~**YHWH** OR >~*be*~SWEAR⁽ᵛ⁾ SWEARING to~>~TIE.UP⁽ᵛ⁾ BOND UPON SOUL~him NOT *he~will~make*~DRILL⁽ᵛ⁾ WORD~him like~ALL the~GO.OUT⁽ᵛ⁾~*ing*⁽ᵐˢ⁾ from~MOUTH~him *he~will*~DO⁽ᵛ⁾   **30:4 (30:3)** and~WOMAN GIVEN.THAT *you*⁽ᵐˢ⁾~*will*~MAKE.A.VOW⁽ᵛ⁾ VOW to~**YHWH** and~*she~did*~TIE.UP⁽ᵛ⁾ BOND in~HOUSE FATHER~her in~YOUNG.AGE~her   **30:5 (30:4)** and~*he~did*~HEAR⁽ᵛ⁾ FATHER~her AT VOW~her and~BOND~her WHICH *she~did*~TIE.UP⁽ᵛ⁾ UPON SOUL~her and~*he~did~make*~KEEP.SILENT⁽ᵛ⁾ to~her FATHER~her and~*they~did*~RISE⁽ᵛ⁾ ALL VOW~s~her and~ALL BOND WHICH *she~did*~TIE.UP⁽ᵛ⁾ UPON SOUL~her *he~will*~RISE⁽ᵛ⁾   **30:6 (30:5)** and~IF *he~did~make*~FORBID⁽ᵛ⁾ FATHER~her AT~her in~DAY >~HEAR⁽ᵛ⁾~him ALL VOW~s~her and~BOND~s~her WHICH *she~did*~TIE.UP⁽ᵛ⁾ UPON SOUL~her NOT *he~will*~RISE⁽ᵛ⁾ and~**YHWH** *he~will*~FORGIVE⁽ᵛ⁾ to~her GIVEN.THAT *he~did~make*~FORBID⁽ᵛ⁾ FATHER~her AT~her   **30:7 (30:6)** and~IF >~EXIST⁽ᵛ⁾ *she~will*~EXIST⁽ᵛ⁾ to~MAN and~VOW~s~her UPON~her OR UTTERANCE LIP~s2~her WHICH *she~did*~TIE.UP⁽ᵛ⁾ UPON SOUL~her   **30:8 (30:7)** and~*he~did*~HEAR⁽ᵛ⁾ MAN~her in~DAY >~HEAR⁽ᵛ⁾~him and~*he~did~make*~KEEP.SILENT⁽ᵛ⁾ to~her and~*they~did*~RISE⁽ᵛ⁾ VOW~s~her and~BOND~her WHICH *she~did*~TIE.UP⁽ᵛ⁾ UPON SOUL~her *they*⁽ᵐ⁾~*will*~RISE⁽ᵛ⁾   **30:9 (30:8)** and~IF in~DAY >~HEAR⁽ᵛ⁾ MAN~her *he~will~make*~FORBID⁽ᵛ⁾ SIGN~her and~*he~did~make*~BREAK⁽ᵛ⁾ AT VOW~her WHICH UPON~her and~AT UTTERANCE LIP~s2~her WHICH *she~did*~TIE.UP⁽ᵛ⁾ UPON SOUL~her and~**YHWH** *he~will*~FORGIVE⁽ᵛ⁾ to~her   **30:10 (30:9)** and~VOW WIDOW and~CAST.OUT⁽ᵛ⁾~*ed*⁽ᶠˢ⁾ ALL WHICH *she~did*~TIE.UP⁽ᵛ⁾ UPON SOUL~her *he~will*~RISE⁽ᵛ⁾ UPON~her   **30:11 (30:10)** and~IF HOUSE MAN~her *she~did*~MAKE.A.VOW⁽ᵛ⁾ OR *she~did*~TIE.UP⁽ᵛ⁾ BOND UPON SOUL~her in~SWEARING   **30:12 (30:11)** and~*he~did*~HEAR⁽ᵛ⁾ MAN~her and~*he~did~make*~KEEP.SILENT⁽ᵛ⁾ to~her NOT *he~did~make*~FORBID⁽ᵛ⁾ AT~her and~*they~did*~RISE⁽ᵛ⁾ ALL VOW~s~her and~ALL BOND WHICH *she~did*~TIE.UP⁽ᵛ⁾ UPON SOUL~her *he~will*~RISE⁽ᵛ⁾   **30:13 (30:12)** and~IF >~*make*~BREAK⁽ᵛ⁾ *he~will~make*~BREAK⁽ᵛ⁾ AT~them⁽ᵐ⁾ MAN~her in~DAY >~HEAR⁽ᵛ⁾~him ALL GOING.OUT LIP~s2~her to~VOW~s~her and~to~BOND SOUL~her NOT *he~will*~RISE⁽ᵛ⁾ MAN~her *he~did~make*~BREAK⁽ᵛ⁾~them⁽ᵐ⁾ and~**YHWH** *he~will*~FORGIVE⁽ᵛ⁾ to~her   **30:14 (30:13)** ALL VOW and~ALL SWEARING BOND to~>~*much*~AFFLICT⁽ᵛ⁾ SOUL MAN~her *he~will~make*~RISE⁽ᵛ⁾~him and~MAN~her *he~will~make*~BREAK⁽ᵛ⁾~him   **30:15 (30:14)** and~IF >~*make*~KEEP.SILENT⁽ᵛ⁾ *he~will~make*~KEEP.SILENT⁽ᵛ⁾ to~her MAN~her from~DAY TO DAY and~*he~did~make*~RISE⁽ᵛ⁾ AT ALL VOW~s~her OR AT ALL BOND~s~her WHICH UPON~her *he~did~make*~RISE⁽ᵛ⁾ AT~them⁽ᵐ⁾ GIVEN.THAT *he~did~*

The Book of Numbers

make~KEEP.SILENT⁽ᵛ⁾ to~her in~DAY >~HEAR⁽ᵛ⁾~him **30:16 (30:15)** and~IF >~make~BREAK⁽ᵛ⁾ he~will~make~BREAK⁽ᵛ⁾ AT~them⁽ᵐ⁾ AFTER >~HEAR⁽ᵛ⁾~him and~he~did~LIFT.UP⁽ᵛ⁾ AT TWISTEDNESS~her **30:17 (30:16)** THESE the~CUSTOM~s WHICH he~did~much~DIRECT⁽ᵛ⁾ **YHWH** AT Mosheh BETWEEN MAN to~WOMAN~him BETWEEN FATHER to~DAUGHTER~him in~YOUNG.AGE~her HOUSE FATHER~her

Chapter 31

31:1 and~he~will~much~SPEAK⁽ᵛ⁾ **YHWH** TO Mosheh to~>~SAY⁽ᵛ⁾ **31:2** !⁽ᵐˢ⁾~AVENGE⁽ᵛ⁾ VENGEANCE SON~s Yisra'eyl from~AT the~Mid'yan~s AFTER you⁽ᵐˢ⁾~will~be~GATHER⁽ᵛ⁾ TO PEOPLE~s~you⁽ᵐˢ⁾ **31:3** and~he~will~much~SPEAK⁽ᵛ⁾ Mosheh TO the~PEOPLE to~>~SAY⁽ᵛ⁾ !⁽ᵐᵖ⁾~be~EXTRACT⁽ᵛ⁾ from~AT~you⁽ᵐᵖ⁾ MAN~s to~the~ARMY and~they⁽ᵐ⁾~will~EXIST⁽ᵛ⁾ UPON Mid'yan to~>~GIVE⁽ᵛ⁾ VENGEANCE YHWH in~Mid'yan **31:4** THOUSAND to~the~BRANCH THOUSAND to~the~BRANCH to~ALL BRANCH Yisra'eyl you⁽ᵐᵖ⁾~will~SEND⁽ᵛ⁾ to~the~ARMY **31:5** and~they⁽ᵐ⁾~will~be~COMMIT⁽ᵛ⁾ from~THOUSAND~s Yisra'eyl THOUSAND to~the~BRANCH TWO TEN THOUSAND EXTRACT⁽ᵛ⁾~ed⁽ᵐᵖ⁾ ARMY **31:6** and~he~will~SEND⁽ᵛ⁾ AT~them⁽ᵐ⁾ Mosheh THOUSAND to~the~BRANCH to~the~ARMY AT~them⁽ᵐ⁾ and~AT Piynhhas SON Elazar the~ADMINISTRATOR to~the~ARMY and~UTENSIL~s the~SPECIAL and~STRAIGHT.TRUMPET~s the~SIGNAL in~HAND~him **31:7** and~they⁽ᵐ⁾~will~MUSTER⁽ᵛ⁾ UPON Mid'yan like~WHICH he~did~much~DIRECT⁽ᵛ⁾ **YHWH** AT Mosheh and~they⁽ᵐ⁾~will~KILL⁽ᵛ⁾ ALL MALE **31:8** and~AT KING~s Mid'yan they~did~KILL⁽ᵛ⁾ UPON DRILLED~s~them⁽ᵐ⁾ AT Ewi and~AT Reqem and~AT Tsur and~AT Hhur and~AT Reva FIVE KING~s Mid'yan and~AT Bilam SON Be'or they~did~KILL⁽ᵛ⁾ in~SWORD **31:9** and~they⁽ᵐ⁾~will~CAPTURE⁽ᵛ⁾ SON~s Yisra'eyl AT WOMAN~s Mid'yan and~AT BABIES~them⁽ᵐ⁾ and~AT ALL BEAST~them⁽ᵐ⁾ and~AT ALL LIVESTOCK~them⁽ᵐ⁾ and~AT ALL FORCE~them⁽ᵐ⁾ they~did~PLUNDER⁽ᵛ⁾ **31:10** and~AT ALL CITY~s~them⁽ᵐ⁾ in~SETTLING~them⁽ᵐ⁾ and~AT ALL ROW.OF.TENTS~s~them⁽ᵐ⁾ they~did~CREMATE⁽ᵛ⁾ in~the~FIRE **31:11** and~they⁽ᵐ⁾~will~TAKE⁽ᵛ⁾ AT ALL the~SPOIL and~AT ALL the~BOOTY in~the~HUMAN and~in~the~BEAST **31:12** and~they⁽ᵐ⁾~will~make~COME⁽ᵛ⁾ TO Mosheh and~TO Elazar the~ADMINISTRATOR and~TO COMPANY SON~s Yisra'eyl AT the~CAPTIVE and~AT the~BOOTY and~AT the~SPOIL TO the~CAMP TO DESERT~s Mo'av WHICH UPON Yarden Ye'rey'hho **31:13** and~they⁽ᵐ⁾~will~GO.OUT⁽ᵛ⁾ Mosheh and~Elazar the~ADMINISTRATOR and~ALL CAPTAIN~s the~COMPANY to~>~MEET⁽ᵛ⁾~them⁽ᵐ⁾ TO from~OUTSIDE to~the~CAMP **31:14** and~he~will~SNAP⁽ᵛ⁾ Mosheh UPON REGISTER⁽ᵛ⁾~ed⁽ᵐᵖ⁾ the~FORCE NOBLE~s the~THOUSAND~s and~NOBLE~s the~HUNDRED~s the~COME⁽ᵛ⁾~ing⁽ᵐᵖ⁾ from~ARMY the~BATTLE **31:15** and~he~will~SAY⁽ᵛ⁾ TO~them⁽ᵐ⁾ Mosheh ?~you⁽ᵐᵖ⁾~>~did~LIVE⁽ᵛ⁾ ALL FEMALE **31:16** THOUGH THEY⁽ᶠ⁾ they~did~EXIST⁽ᵛ⁾ to~SON~s

Yisra'eyl in~WORD Bilam to~>~COMMIT$^{(v)}$ TRANSGRESSION in~**YHWH** UPON WORD Pe'or and~*she~will*~EXIST$^{(v)}$ the~PESTILENCE in~the~COMPANY **YHWH**   **31:17** and~NOW *!$^{(mp)}$*~KILL$^{(v)}$ ALL MALE in~the~BABIES and~ALL WOMAN KNOW$^{(v)}$~*ing$^{(fs)}$* MAN to~LYING.PLACE MALE *!$^{(mp)}$*~KILL$^{(v)}$ **31:18** and~ALL the~BABIES in~the~WOMAN~s WHICH NOT *they~did*~KNOW$^{(v)}$ LYING.PLACE MALE *!$^{(mp)}$~make*~LIVE$^{(v)}$ to~you$^{(mp)}$ **31:19** and~YOU$^{(mp)}$ *!$^{(mp)}$*~CAMP$^{(v)}$ from~OUTSIDE to~the~CAMP SEVEN DAY~s ALL KILL$^{(v)}$~*ing$^{(ms)}$* SOUL and~ALL TOUCH$^{(v)}$~*ing$^{(ms)}$* in~DRILLED you$^{(mp)}$~*will~self*~FAIL$^{(v)}$ in~the~DAY the~THIRD and~in~the~DAY the~SEVENTH YOU$^{(mp)}$ and~CAPTIVE~you$^{(mp)}$ **31:20** and~ALL GARMENT and~ALL UTENSIL SKIN and~ALL WORK SHE-GOAT~s and~ALL UTENSIL TREE *you$^{(mp)}$~will~self*~FAIL$^{(v)}$ **31:21** and~*he~will*~SAY$^{(v)}$ Elazar the~ADMINISTRATOR TO MAN~s the~ARMY the~COME$^{(v)}$~*ing$^{(mp)}$* to~the~BATTLE THIS CUSTOM the~TEACHING WHICH *he~did~much*~DIRECT$^{(v)}$ **YHWH** AT Mosheh   **31:22** SURELY AT the~GOLD and~AT the~SILVER AT the~COPPER AT the~IRON AT the~TIN and~AT the~LEAD   **31:23** ALL WORD WHICH *he~will*~COME$^{(v)}$ in~the~FIRE *you$^{(ms)}$~will~make*~CROSS.OVER$^{(v)}$ in~the~FIRE and~*he~did*~BE.CLEAN$^{(v)}$ SURELY in~WATER~s2 REMOVAL *he~will~self*~FAIL$^{(v)}$ and~ALL WHICH NOT *he~will*~COME$^{(v)}$ in~the~FIRE *you$^{(ms)}$~will~make*~CROSS.OVER$^{(v)}$ in~the~WATER~s2   **31:24** and~*you$^{(mp)}$~did~much*~WASH$^{(v)}$ GARMENT~s~you$^{(mp)}$ in~the~DAY the~SEVENTH and~CLEAN~them$^{(m)}$ and~AFTER *you$^{(mp)}$~will*~COME$^{(v)}$ TO the~CAMP   **31:25** and~*he~will*~SAY$^{(v)}$ **YHWH** TO Mosheh to~>~SAY$^{(v)}$ **31:26** *!$^{(ms)}$*~LIFT.UP$^{(v)}$ AT HEAD BOOTY the~CAPTIVE in~the~HUMAN and~in~the~BEAST YOU$^{(ms)}$ and~Elazar the~ADMINISTRATOR and~HEAD~s FATHER~s the~COMPANY   **31:27** and~*you$^{(ms)}$~did*~DIVIDE$^{(v)}$ AT the~BOOTY BETWEEN SEIZE.HOLD$^{(v)}$~*ing$^{(mp)}$* the~BATTLE the~GO.OUT$^{(v)}$~*ing$^{(mp)}$* to~the~ARMY and~BETWEEN ALL the~COMPANY   **31:28** and~*you$^{(ms)}$~did~make*~RAISE.UP$^{(v)}$ TRIBUTE to~**YHWH** from~AT MAN~s the~BATTLE the~GO.OUT$^{(v)}$~*ing$^{(mp)}$* to~the~ARMY UNIT SOUL from~FIVE the~HUNDRED~s FROM the~HUMAN and~FROM the~CATTLE and~FROM the~DONKEY~s and~FROM the~FLOCKS   **31:29** from~ONE.HALF~them$^{(m)}$ *you$^{(mp)}$~will*~TAKE$^{(v)}$ and~*you$^{(ms)}$~did*~GIVE$^{(v)}$~& to~Elazar the~ADMINISTRATOR OFFERING **YHWH**   **31:30** and~from~ONE.HALF SON~s Yisra'eyl *you$^{(ms)}$~will*~TAKE$^{(v)}$ UNIT TAKE.HOLD$^{(v)}$~*ed$^{(ms)}$* FROM the~FIVE~s FROM the~HUMAN FROM the~CATTLE FROM the~DONKEY~s and~FROM the~FLOCKS from~ALL the~BEAST and~*you$^{(ms)}$~did*~GIVE$^{(v)}$~& AT~them$^{(m)}$ to~Lewi~s SAFEGUARD$^{(v)}$~*ing$^{(mp)}$* CHARGE DWELLING **YHWH**   **31:31** and~*he~will*~DO$^{(v)}$ Mosheh and~Elazar the~ADMINISTRATOR like~WHICH *he~did~much*~DIRECT$^{(v)}$ **YHWH** AT Mosheh   **31:32** and~*he~will*~EXIST$^{(v)}$ the~BOOTY REMAINDER the~PLUNDER WHICH *they~did*~PLUNDER$^{(v)}$ PEOPLE the~ARMY FLOCKS SIX HUNDRED~s THOUSAND and~SEVEN~s THOUSAND and~FIVE THOUSAND~s   **31:33** and~CATTLE TWO and~SEVEN~s THOUSAND   **31:34** and~DONKEY~s UNIT and~SIX~s THOUSAND   **31:35** and~SOUL HUMAN FROM the~WOMAN~s WHICH NOT *they~did*~KNOW$^{(v)}$ LYING.PLACE MALE ALL SOUL TWO and~THREE~s

THOUSAND **31:36** and~*she~will*~EXIST⁽ⱽ⁾ the~HALF.THE.SPOILS DISTRIBUTION the~GO.OUT⁽ⱽ⁾~*ing*⁽ᵐᵖ⁾ in~the~ARMY NUMBER the~FLOCKS THREE HUNDRED~s THOUSAND and~THREE~s THOUSAND and~SEVEN THOUSAND~s and~FIVE HUNDRED~s **31:37** and~*he~will*~EXIST⁽ⱽ⁾ the~TRIBUTE to~**YHWH** FROM the~FLOCKS SIX HUNDRED~s FIVE and~SEVEN~s **31:38** and~the~CATTLE SIX and~THREE~s THOUSAND and~TRIBUTE~them⁽ᵐ⁾ to~**YHWH** TWO and~SEVEN~s **31:39** and~DONKEY~s THREE~s THOUSAND and~FIVE HUNDRED~s and~TRIBUTE~them⁽ᵐ⁾ to~**YHWH** UNIT and~SIX~s **31:40** and~SOUL HUMAN SIX TEN THOUSAND and~TRIBUTE~them⁽ᵐ⁾ to~**YHWH** TWO and~THREE~s SOUL **31:41** and~*he~will*~GIVE⁽ⱽ⁾ Mosheh AT TRIBUTE OFFERING **YHWH** to~Elazar the~ADMINISTRATOR like~WHICH *he~did~much*~DIRECT⁽ⱽ⁾ **YHWH** AT Mosheh **31:42** and~from~ONE.HALF SON~s Yisra'eyl WHICH *he~did*~DIVIDE⁽ⱽ⁾ Mosheh FROM the~MAN~s the~MUSTER⁽ⱽ⁾~*ing*⁽ᵐᵖ⁾ **31:43** and~*she~will*~EXIST⁽ⱽ⁾ HALF.THE.SPOILS the~COMPANY FROM the~FLOCKS THREE HUNDRED~s THOUSAND and~THREE~s THOUSAND SEVEN THOUSAND~s and~FIVE HUNDRED~s **31:44** and~CATTLE SIX and~THREE~s THOUSAND **31:45** and~DONKEY~s THREE~s THOUSAND and~FIVE HUNDRED~s **31:46** and~SOUL HUMAN SIX TEN THOUSAND **31:47** and~*he~will*~TAKE⁽ⱽ⁾ Mosheh from~ONE.HALF SON~s Yisra'eyl AT the~TAKE.HOLD⁽ⱽ⁾~*ed*⁽ᵐˢ⁾ UNIT FROM the~FIVE~s FROM the~HUMAN and~FROM the~BEAST and~*he~will*~GIVE⁽ⱽ⁾ AT~them⁽ᵐ⁾ to~Lewi~s SAFEGUARD⁽ⱽ⁾~*ing*⁽ᵐᵖ⁾ CHARGE DWELLING **YHWH** like~WHICH *he~did~much*~DIRECT⁽ⱽ⁾ **YHWH** AT Mosheh **31:48** and~*they*⁽ᵐ⁾*~will*~COME.NEAR⁽ⱽ⁾ TO Mosheh the~REGISTER⁽ⱽ⁾~*ed*⁽ᵐᵖ⁾ WHICH to~THOUSAND~s the~ARMY NOBLE~s the~THOUSAND~s and~NOBLE~s the~HUNDRED~s **31:49** and~*they*⁽ᵐ⁾*~will*~SAY⁽ⱽ⁾ TO Mosheh SERVANT~s~you⁽ᵐˢ⁾ *they~did*~LIFT.UP⁽ⱽ⁾ AT HEAD MAN~s the~BATTLE WHICH in~HAND~us and~NOT *he~did~be*~REGISTER⁽ⱽ⁾ FROM~us MAN **31:50** and~*we~will~make*~COME.NEAR⁽ⱽ⁾ AT DONATION **YHWH** MAN WHICH *he~did*~FIND⁽ⱽ⁾ UTENSIL GOLD ARMLET and~BRACELET RING EARRING and~ARM.BAND to~>~*much*~COVER⁽ⱽ⁾ UPON SOUL~s~us to~FACE~s **YHWH** **31:51** and~*he~will*~TAKE⁽ⱽ⁾ Mosheh and~Elazar the~ADMINISTRATOR AT the~GOLD from~AT~them⁽ᵐ⁾ ALL UTENSIL WORK **31:52** and~*he~will*~EXIST⁽ⱽ⁾ ALL GOLD the~OFFERING WHICH *they~did~make*~RAISE.UP⁽ⱽ⁾ to~**YHWH** SIX TEN THOUSAND SEVEN HUNDRED~s and~FIVE~s SHEQEL from~AT NOBLE~s the~THOUSAND~s and~from~AT NOBLE~s the~HUNDRED~s **31:53** MAN~s the~ARMY *they~did*~PLUNDER⁽ⱽ⁾ MAN to~him **31:54** and~*he~will*~TAKE⁽ⱽ⁾ Mosheh and~Elazar the~ADMINISTRATOR AT the~GOLD from~AT NOBLE~s the~THOUSAND~s and~the~HUNDRED~s and~*they*⁽ᵐ⁾*~will~make*~COME⁽ⱽ⁾ AT~him TO TENT APPOINTED REMEMBRANCE to~SON~s Yisra'eyl to~FACE~s **YHWH**

Chapter 32

32:1 and~LIVESTOCK ABUNDANT *he~did*~EXIST$^{(V)}$ to~SON~s Re'uven and~to~SON~s Gad NUMEROUS MANY and~*they*$^{(m)}$~*will*~SEE$^{(V)}$ AT LAND Yazeyr and~AT LAND Gil'ad and~LOOK the~AREA AREA LIVESTOCK **32:2** and~*they*$^{(m)}$~*will*~COME$^{(V)}$ SON~s Gad and~SON~s Re'uven and~*they*$^{(m)}$~*will*~SAY$^{(V)}$ TO Mosheh and~TO Elazar the~ADMINISTRATOR and~TO CAPTAIN~s the~COMPANY to~>~SAY$^{(V)}$ **32:3** Atarot and~Dibon and~Yazeyr and~Nimrah and~Hheshbon and~Elaley and~Sevam and~Nevo and~Be'on **32:4** the~LAND WHICH *he~did*~*make*~HIT$^{(V)}$ **YHWH** to~FACE~s COMPANY Yisra'eyl LAND LIVESTOCK SHE and~to~SERVANT~s~you$^{(ms)}$ LIVESTOCK **32:5** and~*they*$^{(m)}$~*will*~SAY$^{(V)}$ IF *we~did*~FIND$^{(V)}$ BEAUTY in~EYE~s2~you$^{(ms)}$ *he*~GIVE$^{(V)}$~*ed*$^{(ms)}$ AT the~LAND the~THIS to~SERVANT~s~you$^{(ms)}$ to~HOLDINGS DO.NOT *you*$^{(ms)}$~*will*~*make*~CROSS.OVER$^{(V)}$~us AT the~Yarden **32:6** and~*he~will*~SAY$^{(V)}$ Mosheh to~SON~s Gad and~to~SON~s Re'uven ?~BROTHER~s~you$^{(mp)}$ *they*$^{(m)}$~*will*~COME$^{(V)}$ to~the~BATTLE and~YOU$^{(mp)}$ *you*$^{(mp)}$~*will*~SETTLE$^{(V)}$ HERE **32:7** and~to~WHAT *you*$^{(mp)}$~*will*~FORBID$^{(V)}$~must AT HEART SON~s Yisra'eyl from~>~CROSS.OVER$^{(V)}$ TO the~LAND WHICH *he~did*~GIVE$^{(V)}$ to~them$^{(m)}$ **YHWH** **32:8** IN.THIS.WAY *they~did*~DO$^{(V)}$ FATHER~s~you$^{(mp)}$ in~>~*much*~SEND$^{(V)}$~me AT~them$^{(m)}$ from~Qadesh Barneya to~>~SEE$^{(V)}$ AT the~LAND **32:9** and~*they*$^{(m)}$~*will*~GO.UP$^{(V)}$ UNTIL WADI Eshkol and~*they*$^{(m)}$~*will*~SEE$^{(V)}$ AT the~LAND and~*they*$^{(m)}$~*will*~FORBID$^{(V)}$ AT HEART SON~s Yisra'eyl to~EXCEPT >~COME$^{(V)}$ TO the~LAND WHICH *he~did*~GIVE$^{(V)}$ to~them$^{(m)}$ **YHWH** **32:10** and~*he~will*~FLARE.UP$^{(V)}$ NOSE **YHWH** in~the~DAY the~HE and~*he~will~be*~SWEAR$^{(V)}$ to~>~SAY$^{(V)}$ **32:11** IF *they*$^{(m)}$~*will*~SEE$^{(V)}$ the~MAN~s the~GO.UP$^{(V)}$~*ing*$^{(ms)}$ from~Mits'rayim from~SON TEN~s YEAR and~UPWARD~unto AT the~GROUND WHICH *I~did~be*~SWEAR$^{(V)}$ to~Avraham to~Yits'hhaq and~to~Ya'aqov GIVEN.THAT NOT *!*$^{(mp)}$~FILL$^{(V)}$ AFTER~me **32:12** EXCEPT Kaleyv SON Yephunah the~Qenaz~of and~Yehoshu'a SON Nun GIVEN.THAT *!*$^{(mp)}$~FILL$^{(V)}$ AFTER **YHWH** **32:13** and~*he~will*~FLARE.UP$^{(V)}$ NOSE **YHWH** in~Yisra'eyl and~*he~will*~*make*~STAGGER$^{(V)}$~them$^{(m)}$ in~the~WILDERNESS FOUR~s YEAR UNTIL >~BE.WHOLE$^{(V)}$ ALL the~GENERATION the~DO$^{(V)}$~*ing*$^{(ms)}$ the~DYSFUNCTIONAL in~EYE~s2 **YHWH** **32:14** and~LOOK *you*$^{(mp)}$~*did*~RISE$^{(V)}$ UNDER FATHER~s~you$^{(mp)}$ GREAT.AMOUNT MAN~s FAILURE~s to~>~CONSUME$^{(V)}$ YET.AGAIN UPON FLAMING.WRATH NOSE **YHWH** TO Yisra'eyl **32:15** GIVEN.THAT *you*$^{(mp)}$~*will*~TURN.BACK$^{(V)}$~must from~AFTER~him and~*he~will*~ADD$^{(V)}$ YET.AGAIN to~>~*make*~REST$^{(V)}$~him in~the~WILDERNESS and~*you*$^{(mp)}$~*did*~*much*~DAMAGE$^{(V)}$ to~ALL the~PEOPLE the~THIS **32:16** and~*they*$^{(m)}$~*will*~DRAW.NEAR$^{(V)}$ TO~him and~*they*$^{(m)}$~*will*~SAY$^{(V)}$ FENCE~s FLOCKS *we~will*~BUILD$^{(V)}$ to~LIVESTOCK~us HERE and~CITY~s to~BABIES~us **32:17** and~WE *we~will~be*~EXTRACT$^{(V)}$ MAKE.HASTE$^{(V)}$~*ed*$^{(mp)}$ to~FACE~s SON~s Yisra'eyl UNTIL WHICH IF *we~did*~*make*~COME$^{(V)}$~them$^{(m)}$ TO AREA~them$^{(m)}$ and~*he~did*~SETTLE$^{(V)}$ BABIES~us in~CITY~s the~

The Book of Numbers

FORTIFICATION from~FACE~s SETTLE^(V)~*ing*^(mp) the~LAND **32:18** NOT *we~will*~TURN.BACK^(V) TO HOUSE~s~us UNTIL >~*self*~INHERIT^(V) SON~s Yisra'eyl MAN INHERITANCE~him **32:19** GIVEN.THAT NOT *we~will*~INHERIT^(V) AT~them^(m) from~OTHER.SIDE to~Yarden and~FURTHER GIVEN.THAT *she~did*~COME^(V) INHERITANCE~us TO~us from~OTHER.SIDE the~Yarden SUNRISE~unto **32:20** and~*he~will*~SAY^(V) TO~them^(m) Mosheh IF *you*^(ms)~*will*~DO^(V)~must AT the~WORD the~THIS IF *you*^(ms)~*will*~be~EXTRACT^(V) to~FACE~s YHWH to~the~BATTLE **32:21** and~*he~did*~CROSS.OVER^(V) to~you^(mp) ALL EXTRACT^(V)~*ed*^(ms) AT the~Yarden to~FACE~s YHWH UNTIL *he~did~make*~POSSESS^(V)~him AT ATTACK^(V)~*ing*^(ms)~s~him from~FACE~s~him **32:22** and~*she~did~be*~SUBDUE^(V) the~LAND to~FACE~s YHWH and~AFTER *you*^(mp)~*will*~TURN.BACK^(V) and~*you*^(mp)~*did*~EXIST^(V) INNOCENCE~s from~**YHWH** and~from~Yisra'eyl and~*she~did*~EXIST^(V) the~LAND the~THIS to~you^(mp) to~HOLDINGS to~FACE~s YHWH **32:23** and~IF NOT *you*^(ms)~*will*~DO^(V)~must SO LOOK *you*^(mp)~*did*~FAIL^(V) to~**YHWH** and~*!*^(mp)~KNOW^(V) FAILURE~you^(mp) WHICH *she~will*~FIND^(V) AT~you^(mp) **32:24** *!*^(mp)~BUILD^(V) to~you^(mp) CITY~s to~BABIES~you^(mp) and~FENCE~s to~FLOCKS~you^(mp) and~the~GO.OUT^(V)~*ing*^(ms) from~MOUTH~you^(mp) *you*^(mp)~*will*~DO^(V) **32:25** and~*he~will*~SAY^(V) SON~s Gad and~SON~s Re'uven TO Mosheh to~>~SAY^(V) SERVANT~s~you^(ms) *they*^(m)~*will*~DO^(V) like~WHICH LORD~me *much*~DIRECT^(V)~*ing*^(ms) **32:26** BABIES~us WOMAN~s~us LIVESTOCK~us and~ALL BEAST~us *they*^(m)~*will*~EXIST^(V) THERE in~CITY~s the~Gil'ad **32:27** and~SERVANT~s~you^(ms) *they*^(m)~*will*~CROSS.OVER^(V) ALL EXTRACT^(V)~*ed*^(ms) ARMY to~FACE~s YHWH to~the~BATTLE like~WHICH LORD~me SPEAK^(V)~*ing*^(ms) **32:28** and~*he~will~much*~DIRECT^(V) to~them^(m) Mosheh AT Elazar the~ADMINISTRATOR and~AT Yehoshu'a SON Nun and~AT HEAD~s FATHER~s the~BRANCH to~SON~s Yisra'eyl **32:29** and~*he~will*~SAY^(V) Mosheh TO~them^(m) IF *they*^(m)~*will*~CROSS.OVER^(V) SON~s Gad and~SON~s Re'uven AT~you^(mp) AT the~Yarden ALL EXTRACT^(V)~*ed*^(ms) to~the~BATTLE to~FACE~s YHWH and~*she~did~be*~SUBDUE^(V) the~LAND to~FACE~s~you^(mp) and~*you*^(mp)~*did*~GIVE^(V) to~them^(m) AT LAND the~Gil'ad to~HOLDINGS **32:30** and~IF NOT *they*^(m)~*will*~CROSS.OVER^(V) EXTRACT^(V)~*ed*^(mp) AT~you^(mp) and~*they~did~be*~TAKE.HOLD^(V) in~MIDST~you^(mp) in~LAND Kena'an **32:31** and~*they*^(m)~*will*~ANSWER^(V) SON~s Gad and~SON~s Re'uven to~>~SAY^(V) AT WHICH *he~did~much*~SPEAK^(V) YHWH TO SERVANT~s~you^(ms) SO *we~will*~DO^(V) **32:32** WE *we~will*~CROSS.OVER^(V) EXTRACT^(V)~*ed*^(mp) to~FACE~s YHWH LAND Kena'an and~AT~us HOLDINGS INHERITANCE~us from~OTHER.SIDE to~Yarden **32:33** and~*he~will*~GIVE^(V) to~them^(m) Mosheh to~SON~s Gad and~to~SON~s Re'uven and~to~the~HALF STAFF Menasheh SON Yoseph AT KINGDOM Sihhon KING the~Emor~of and~AT KINGDOM Og KING the~Bashan the~LAND to~CITY~s~her in~BORDER~s CITY~s the~LAND ALL.AROUND **32:34** and~*they*^(m)~*will*~BUILD^(V) SON~s Gad AT Dibon and~AT *Atarot* and~AT Aro'eyr **32:35** and~AT At'rot-Shophan and~AT Yazeyr and~Yagbahah **32:36** and~AT Beyt-Nimrah and~AT Beyt-Haran CITY~s FORTIFICATION and~FENCE~s FLOCKS **32:37** and~SON~s Re'uven *they~did*~

BUILD⁽ᵛ⁾ AT Hheshbon and~AT Elaley and~AT Qiryatayim **32:38** and~AT Nevo and~AT Ba'al-Me'on *be~make*~GO.AROUND⁽ᵛ⁾~*ing⁽ᶠᵖ⁾* TITLE and~AT Sevam and~*they⁽ᵐ⁾~will*~CALL.OUT⁽ᵛ⁾ in~TITLE~s AT TITLE~s the~CITY~s WHICH *they~did*~BUILD⁽ᵛ⁾ **32:39** and~*they⁽ᵐ⁾~will*~WALK⁽ᵛ⁾ SON~s Makhir SON Menasheh Gil'ad~unto and~*they⁽ᵐ⁾~will*~TRAP⁽ᵛ⁾~her and~POSSESS⁽ᵛ⁾~*ing⁽ᵐˢ⁾* AT the~Emor~of WHICH in~her **32:40** and~*he~will*~GIVE⁽ᵛ⁾ Mosheh AT the~Gil'ad to~Makhir SON Menasheh and~*he~will*~SETTLE⁽ᵛ⁾ in~her **32:41** and~Ya'ir SON Menasheh *he~did*~WALK⁽ᵛ⁾ and~*he~will*~TRAP⁽ᵛ⁾ AT TOWN~s~them⁽ᵐ⁾ and~*he~will*~CALL.OUT⁽ᵛ⁾ AT~them⁽ᶠ⁾ Hhawot Ya'ir **32:42** and~Novahh *he~did*~WALK⁽ᵛ⁾ and~*he~will*~TRAP⁽ᵛ⁾ AT Qenat and~AT DAUGHTER~s~her and~*he~will*~CALL.OUT⁽ᵛ⁾ to~her Novahh in~TITLE~him

Chapter 33

33:1 THESE JOURNEY~s SON~s Yisra'eyl WHICH *they~did*~GO.OUT⁽ᵛ⁾ from~LAND Mits'rayim to~ARMY~s~them⁽ᵐ⁾ in~HAND Mosheh and~Aharon **33:2** and~*he~will*~WRITE⁽ᵛ⁾ Mosheh AT GOING.OUT~s~them⁽ᵐ⁾ to~JOURNEY~s~them⁽ᵐ⁾ UPON MOUTH **YHWH** and~THESE JOURNEY~s~them⁽ᵐ⁾ to~GOING.OUT~s~them⁽ᵐ⁾ **33:3** and~*they⁽ᵐ⁾~will*~JOURNEY⁽ᵛ⁾ from~Ra'meses in~the~NEW.MOON the~FIRST in~the~FIVE TEN DAY to~the~NEW.MOON the~FIRST from~MORROW the~Pesahh *they~did*~GO.OUT⁽ᵛ⁾ SON~s Yisra'eyl in~HAND RAISED~*ing⁽ᶠˢ⁾* to~EYE~s2 ALL Mits'rayim **33:4** and~Mits'rayim *much*~BURY⁽ᵛ⁾~*ing⁽ᵐᵖ⁾* AT WHICH *he~did*~*make*~HIT⁽ᵛ⁾ **YHWH** in~them⁽ᵐ⁾ ALL FIRSTBORN and~in~Elohiym~them⁽ᵐ⁾ *he~did*~DO⁽ᵛ⁾ **YHWH** JUDGMENT~s **33:5** and~*they⁽ᵐ⁾~will*~JOURNEY⁽ᵛ⁾ SON~s Yisra'eyl from~Ra'meses and~*they⁽ᵐ⁾~will*~CAMP⁽ᵛ⁾ in~Suk'kot **33:6** and~*they⁽ᵐ⁾~will*~JOURNEY⁽ᵛ⁾ from~Suk'kot and~*they⁽ᵐ⁾~will*~CAMP⁽ᵛ⁾ in~Eytam WHICH in~EXTREMITY the~WILDERNESS **33:7** and~*they⁽ᵐ⁾~will*~JOURNEY⁽ᵛ⁾ from~Eytam and~*he~will*~TURN.BACK⁽ᵛ⁾ UPON Piy-Hahhiyrot WHICH UPON FACE~s Ba'al-Tsephon and~*they⁽ᵐ⁾~will*~CAMP⁽ᵛ⁾ to~FACE~s Migdol **33:8** and~*they⁽ᵐ⁾~will*~JOURNEY⁽ᵛ⁾ from~FACE~s the~Hhirot and~*they⁽ᵐ⁾~will*~CROSS.OVER⁽ᵛ⁾ in~MIDST the~SEA the~WILDERNESS~unto and~*they⁽ᵐ⁾~will*~WALK⁽ᵛ⁾ ROAD THREE DAY~s in~WILDERNESS Eytam and~*they⁽ᵐ⁾~will*~CAMP⁽ᵛ⁾ in~Marah **33:9** and~*they⁽ᵐ⁾~will*~JOURNEY⁽ᵛ⁾ from~Marah and~*they⁽ᵐ⁾~will*~COME⁽ᵛ⁾ Eyliym~unto and~in~Eyliym TWO TEN EYE~s WATER~s2 and~SEVEN~s DATE.PALM~s and~*they⁽ᵐ⁾~will*~CAMP⁽ᵛ⁾ THERE **33:10** and~*they⁽ᵐ⁾~will*~JOURNEY⁽ᵛ⁾ from~Eyliym and~*they⁽ᵐ⁾~will*~CAMP⁽ᵛ⁾ UPON SEA REEDS **33:11** and~*they⁽ᵐ⁾~will*~JOURNEY⁽ᵛ⁾ from~SEA REEDS and~*they⁽ᵐ⁾~will*~CAMP⁽ᵛ⁾ in~WILDERNESS Sin **33:12** and~*they⁽ᵐ⁾~will*~JOURNEY⁽ᵛ⁾ from~WILDERNESS Sin and~*they⁽ᵐ⁾~will*~CAMP⁽ᵛ⁾ in~Daphqah **33:13** and~*they⁽ᵐ⁾~will*~JOURNEY⁽ᵛ⁾ from~Daphqah and~*they⁽ᵐ⁾~will*~CAMP⁽ᵛ⁾ in~Alush **33:14** and~*they⁽ᵐ⁾~will*~JOURNEY⁽ᵛ⁾ from~Alush and~

The Book of Numbers

they$^{(m)}$~will~CAMP$^{(V)}$ in~Rephiydiym and~NOT he~did~EXIST$^{(V)}$ THERE WATER~s2 to~the~PEOPLE to~>~GULP$^{(V)}$ **33:15** and~they$^{(m)}$~will~JOURNEY$^{(V)}$ from~Rephiydiym and~they$^{(m)}$~will~CAMP$^{(V)}$ in~WILDERNESS Sinai **33:16** and~they$^{(m)}$~will~JOURNEY$^{(V)}$ from~WILDERNESS Sinai and~they$^{(m)}$~will~CAMP$^{(V)}$ in~Qivrot-Hata'awah **33:17** and~they$^{(m)}$~will~JOURNEY$^{(V)}$ from~Qivrot-Hata'awah and~they$^{(m)}$~will~CAMP$^{(V)}$ in~Hhatsarot **33:18** and~they$^{(m)}$~will~JOURNEY$^{(V)}$ from~Hhatsarot and~they$^{(m)}$~will~CAMP$^{(V)}$ in~Ritmah **33:19** and~they$^{(m)}$~will~JOURNEY$^{(V)}$ from~Ritmah and~they$^{(m)}$~will~CAMP$^{(V)}$ in~Rimon-Perets **33:20** and~they$^{(m)}$~will~JOURNEY$^{(V)}$ from~Rimon-Perets and~they$^{(m)}$~will~CAMP$^{(V)}$ in~Livnah **33:21** and~they$^{(m)}$~will~JOURNEY$^{(V)}$ from~Livnah and~they$^{(m)}$~will~CAMP$^{(V)}$ in~Risah **33:22** and~they$^{(m)}$~will~JOURNEY$^{(V)}$ from~Risah and~they$^{(m)}$~will~CAMP$^{(V)}$ in~Qe'hey'latah **33:23** and~they$^{(m)}$~will~JOURNEY$^{(V)}$ from~Qe'hey'latah and~they$^{(m)}$~will~CAMP$^{(V)}$ in~HILL Shapher **33:24** and~they$^{(m)}$~will~JOURNEY$^{(V)}$ from~HILL Shapher and~they$^{(m)}$~will~CAMP$^{(V)}$ in~Hharadah **33:25** and~they$^{(m)}$~will~JOURNEY$^{(V)}$ from~Hharadah and~they$^{(m)}$~will~CAMP$^{(V)}$ in~Maqheylot **33:26** and~they$^{(m)}$~will~JOURNEY$^{(V)}$ from~Maqheylot and~they$^{(m)}$~will~CAMP$^{(V)}$ in~Tahhat **33:27** and~they$^{(m)}$~will~JOURNEY$^{(V)}$ from~Tahhat and~they$^{(m)}$~will~CAMP$^{(V)}$ in~Terahh **33:28** and~they$^{(m)}$~will~JOURNEY$^{(V)}$ from~Terahh and~they$^{(m)}$~will~CAMP$^{(V)}$ in~Mitqah **33:29** and~they$^{(m)}$~will~JOURNEY$^{(V)}$ from~Mitqah and~they$^{(m)}$~will~CAMP$^{(V)}$ in~Hhashmonah **33:30** and~they$^{(m)}$~will~JOURNEY$^{(V)}$ from~Hhashmonah and~they$^{(m)}$~will~CAMP$^{(V)}$ in~Moseyrot **33:31** and~they$^{(m)}$~will~JOURNEY$^{(V)}$ from~Moseyrot and~they$^{(m)}$~will~CAMP$^{(V)}$ in~B'ney-Ya'aqan **33:32** and~they$^{(m)}$~will~JOURNEY$^{(V)}$ from~B'ney-Ya'aqan and~they$^{(m)}$~will~CAMP$^{(V)}$ in~Hhor-Hagidgad **33:33** and~they$^{(m)}$~will~JOURNEY$^{(V)}$ from~Hhor-Hagidgad and~they$^{(m)}$~will~CAMP$^{(V)}$ in~Yatvatah **33:34** and~they$^{(m)}$~will~JOURNEY$^{(V)}$ from~Yatvatah and~they$^{(m)}$~will~CAMP$^{(V)}$ in~Evronah **33:35** and~they$^{(m)}$~will~JOURNEY$^{(V)}$ from~Evronah and~they$^{(m)}$~will~CAMP$^{(V)}$ in~Etsi'on-Gaver **33:36** and~they$^{(m)}$~will~JOURNEY$^{(V)}$ from~Etsi'on-Gaver and~they$^{(m)}$~will~CAMP$^{(V)}$ in~WILDERNESS Tsin SHE Qadesh **33:37** and~they$^{(m)}$~will~JOURNEY$^{(V)}$ from~Qadesh and~they$^{(m)}$~will~CAMP$^{(V)}$ in~Hor the~HILL in~EXTREMITY LAND Edom **33:38** and~he~will~make~GO.UP$^{(V)}$ Aharon the~ADMINISTRATOR TO Hor the~HILL UPON MOUTH **YHWH** and~he~will~DIE$^{(V)}$ THERE in~YEAR the~FOUR~s to~>~GO.OUT$^{(V)}$ SON~s Yisra'eyl from~LAND Mits'rayim in~the~NEW.MOON the~FIFTH in~UNIT to~the~NEW.MOON **33:39** and~Aharon SON THREE and~TEN~s and~HUNDRED YEAR in~DEATH~him in~Hor the~HILL **33:40** and~he~will~HEAR$^{(V)}$ the~Kena'an~of KING Arad and~HE SETTLE$^{(V)}$~ing$^{(ms)}$ in~the~SOUTH in~LAND Kena'an in~>~COME$^{(V)}$ SON~s Yisra'eyl **33:41** and~they$^{(m)}$~will~JOURNEY$^{(V)}$ from~Hor the~HILL and~they$^{(m)}$~will~CAMP$^{(V)}$ in~Tsalmonah **33:42** and~they$^{(m)}$~will~JOURNEY$^{(V)}$ from~Tsalmonah and~they$^{(m)}$~will~CAMP$^{(V)}$ in~Punon **33:43** and~they$^{(m)}$~will~JOURNEY$^{(V)}$ from~Punon and~they$^{(m)}$~will~CAMP$^{(V)}$ in~Ovot **33:44** and~they$^{(m)}$~will~JOURNEY$^{(V)}$ from~Ovot and~they$^{(m)}$~will~CAMP$^{(V)}$ in~Iyey-Ha'a'variym in~

BORDER Mo'av   **33:45** and~*they*(m)~*will*~JOURNEY(V) from~Iy'yim and~*they*(m)~*will*~CAMP(V) in~Dibon-Gad   **33:46** and~*they*(m)~*will*~JOURNEY(V) from~Dibon-Gad and~*they*(m)~*will*~CAMP(V) in~Almon-Divlatayim   **33:47** and~*they*(m)~*will*~JOURNEY(V) from~Almon-Divlatayim and~*they*(m)~*will*~CAMP(V) in~HILL~s the~Ever~s to~FACE~s Nevo   **33:48** and~*they*(m)~*will*~JOURNEY(V) from~HILL~s the~Ever~s and~*they*(m)~*will*~CAMP(V) in~DESERT~s Mo'av UPON Yarden Ye'rey'hho   **33:49** and~*they*(m)~*will*~CAMP(V) UPON the~Yarden from~Beyt-Hayishmot UNTIL Aveyl-Hashit'tim in~DESERT~s Mo'av   **33:50** and~*he*~*will*~*much*~SPEAK(V) **YHWH** TO Mosheh in~DESERT~s Mo'av UPON Yarden Ye'rey'hho to~>~SAY(V)   **33:51** !(ms)~*much*~SPEAK(V) TO SON~s Yisra'eyl and~*you*(ms)~*did*~SAY(V) TO~them(m) GIVEN.THAT YOU(mp) CROSS.OVER(V)~*ing*(mp) AT the~Yarden TO LAND Kena'an   **33:52** and~*you*(mp)~*did*~*make*~POSSESS(V) AT ALL SETTLE(V)~*ing*(mp) the~LAND from~FACE~s~*you*(mp) and~*you*(mp)~*did*~*much*~PERISH(V) AT ALL IMAGERY~them(m) and~AT ALL IMAGE~s CAST.IMAGE~s~them(m) *you*(ms)~*will*~*much*~PERISH(V) and~AT ALL PLATFORM~s~them(m) *you*(mp)~*will*~*make*~DESTROY(V)   **33:53** and~*you*(mp)~*did*~*make*~POSSESS(V) AT the~LAND and~*you*(mp)~*did*~SETTLE(V) in~her GIVEN.THAT to~*you*(mp) *I*~*did*~GIVE(V) AT the~LAND to~the~>~POSSESS(V) AT~her   **33:54** and~*you*(mp)~*will*~*self*~INHERIT(V) AT the~LAND in~LOT to~CLAN~s~*you*(mp) to~ABUNDANT *you*(mp)~*will*~*make*~INCREASE(V) AT INHERITANCE~him and~to~the~SMALL.AMOUNT *you*(ms)~*will*~*make*~BE.LESS(V) AT INHERITANCE~him TO WHICH *he*~*will*~GO.OUT(V) to~him THERE~unto the~LOT to~him *he*~*will*~EXIST(V) to~BRANCH FATHER~s~*you*(mp) *you*(mp)~*will*~*self*~INHERIT(V)   **33:55** and~IF NOT *you*(mp)~*will*~*make*~POSSESS(V) AT SETTLE(V)~*ing*(mp) the~LAND from~FACE~s~*you*(mp) and~*he*~*did*~EXIST(V) WHICH *you*(mp)~*will*~*make*~LEAVE.BEHIND(V) from~them(m) to~STICKERBUSH~s in~EYE~s2~*you*(mp) and~to~PRICKLY.THORN~s in~SIDE~s~*you*(mp) and~*they*~*did*~PRESS.IN(V) AT~*you*(mp) UPON the~LAND WHICH YOU(mp) SETTLE(V)~*ing*(mp) in~her   **33:56** and~*he*~*did*~EXIST(V) like~WHICH *I*~*did*~*much*~RESEMBLE(V) to~>~DO(V) to~them(m) *I*~*will*~DO(V) to~*you*(mp)

Chapter 34

34:1 and~*he*~*will*~*much*~SPEAK(V) **YHWH** TO Mosheh to~>~SAY(V)   **34:2** !(ms)~*much*~DIRECT(V) AT SON~s Yisra'eyl and~*you*(ms)~*did*~SAY(V) TO~them(m) GIVEN.THAT YOU(mp) COME(V)~*ing*(mp) TO the~LAND Kena'an THIS the~LAND WHICH *she*~*will*~FALL(V) to~*you*(mp) in~INHERITANCE LAND Kena'an to~BORDER~s~her   **34:3** and~*he*~*did*~EXIST(V) to~*you*(mp) EDGE SOUTH from~WILDERNESS Tsin UPON HAND~s2 Edom and~*he*~*did*~EXIST(V) to~*you*(mp) BORDER SOUTH from~EXTREMITY SEA the~SALT EAST~unto   **34:4** and~*he*~*did*~*be*~GO.AROUND(V) to~*you*(mp) the~BORDER from~SOUTH to~ASCENT Aqrabiym and~*he*~*did*~CROSS.OVER(V) Tsin~unto and~*he*~*did*~EXIST(V)

GOINGS~s~him from~SOUTH to~Qadesh Barneya and~*he~will*~GO.OUT$^{(V)}$ Hhatsar-Adar and~*he~did*~CROSS.OVER$^{(V)}$ Atsmon~unto **34:5** and~*he~did~* be~GO.AROUND$^{(V)}$ the~BORDER from~Atsmon WADI~unto Mits'rayim and~ *they~did*~EXIST$^{(V)}$ GOINGS~s~him the~SEA~unto **34:6** and~BORDER SEA and~*he~did*~EXIST$^{(V)}$ to~you$^{(mp)}$ the~SEA the~GREAT and~BORDER THIS *he~ will*~EXIST$^{(V)}$ to~you$^{(mp)}$ BORDER SEA **34:7** and~THIS *he~will*~EXIST$^{(V)}$ to~ you$^{(mp)}$ BORDER NORTH FROM the~SEA the~GREAT *you$^{(mp)}$~will~much~ POINT*$^{(V)}$ to~you$^{(mp)}$ Hor the~HILL **34:8** from~Hor the~HILL *you$^{(mp)}$~will~ much~POINT*$^{(V)}$ to~>~COME$^{(V)}$ Hhamat and~*they~did*~EXIST$^{(V)}$ GOINGS~s the~BORDER Tsedad~unto **34:9** and~*he~will*~GO.OUT$^{(V)}$ the~BORDER Ziphron~unto and~*they~did*~EXIST$^{(V)}$ GOINGS~s~him Hhatsar-Eynan THIS *he~will*~EXIST$^{(V)}$ to~you$^{(mp)}$ BORDER NORTH **34:10** and~*you$^{(mp)}$~did~self~* POINT.OUT$^{(V)}$ to~you$^{(mp)}$ to~BORDER EAST~unto from~Hhatsar-Eynan Shepham~unto **34:11** and~*he~did*~GO.DOWN$^{(V)}$ the~BORDER from~ Shepham the~Rivlah from~EAST to~Ayin and~*he~did*~GO.DOWN$^{(V)}$ the~ BORDER and~*he~did*~WIPE.AWAY$^{(V)}$ UPON SHOULDER.PIECE SEA Kineret EAST~unto **34:12** and~*he~did*~GO.DOWN$^{(V)}$ the~BORDER the~Yarden~unto and~*they~did*~EXIST$^{(V)}$ GOINGS~s~him SEA the~SALT THIS *she~will*~EXIST$^{(V)}$ to~you$^{(mp)}$ the~LAND to~BORDER~s~her ALL.AROUND **34:13** and~*he~will~ much~*DIRECT$^{(V)}$ Mosheh AT SON~s Yisra'eyl to~>~SAY$^{(V)}$ THIS the~LAND WHICH *you$^{(mp)}$~will~self~*INHERIT$^{(V)}$ AT~her in~LOT WHICH *he~did~much~* DIRECT$^{(V)}$ YHWH to~>~GIVE$^{(V)}$ to~NINE the~BRANCH and~HALF the~ BRANCH **34:14** GIVEN.THAT *they~will*~TAKE$^{(V)}$ BRANCH SON~s the~ Re'uven~of to~HOUSE FATHER~s~them$^{(m)}$ and~BRANCH SON~s the~Gad~of to~HOUSE FATHER~s~them$^{(m)}$ and~HALF BRANCH Menasheh *they~will*~ TAKE$^{(V)}$ INHERITANCE~them$^{(m)}$ **34:15** TWO the~BRANCH and~HALF the~ BRANCH *they~will*~TAKE$^{(V)}$ INHERITANCE~them$^{(m)}$ from~OTHER.SIDE to~ Yarden Ye'rey'hho EAST~unto SUNRISE~unto **34:16** and~*he~will~much~* SPEAK$^{(V)}$ YHWH TO Mosheh to~>~SAY$^{(V)}$ **34:17** THESE TITLE~s the~MAN~s WHICH *they$^{(m)}$~will*~INHERIT$^{(V)}$ to~you$^{(mp)}$ AT the~LAND Elazar the~ ADMINISTRATOR and~Yehoshu'a SON Nun **34:18** and~CAPTAIN UNIT CAPTAIN UNIT from~BRANCH *you$^{(mp)}$~will*~TAKE$^{(V)}$ to~>~INHERIT$^{(V)}$ AT the~ LAND **34:19** and~THESE TITLE~s the~MAN~s to~BRANCH Yehudah Kaleyv SON Yephunah **34:20** and~to~BRANCH SON~s Shimon Shemu'eyl SON Amihud **34:21** to~BRANCH Binyamin Elidad SON Kislon **34:22** and~to~ BRANCH SON~s Dan CAPTAIN Buqi SON Yagli **34:23** to~SON~s Yoseph to~ BRANCH SON~s Menasheh CAPTAIN Hhani'eyl SON Ephod **34:24** and~to~ BRANCH SON~s Ephrayim CAPTAIN Qemu'el SON Shaphtan **34:25** and~to~ BRANCH SON~s Zevulun CAPTAIN Elitsaphan SON Parnakh **34:26** and~to~ BRANCH SON~s Yis'sas'khar CAPTAIN Palti'eyl SON Azan **34:27** and~to~ BRANCH SON~s Asher CAPTAIN Ahhihud SON Shelomiy **34:28** and~to~ BRANCH SON~s Naphtali CAPTAIN Pedah'eyl SON Amihud **34:29** THESE WHICH *he~did~much~*DIRECT$^{(V)}$ YHWH to~INHERITANCE AT SON~s Yisra'eyl in~LAND Kena'an

Chapter 35

35:1 and~*he~will~much*~SPEAK(V) **YHWH** TO Mosheh in~DESERT~s Mo'av UPON Yarden Ye'rey'hho to~>~SAY(V) **35:2** !(ms)~*much*~DIRECT(V) AT SON~s Yisra'eyl and~*they~did*~GIVE(V) to~Lewi~s from~INHERITANCE HOLDINGS~them(m) CITY~s to~the~>~SETTLE(V) and~OPEN.SPACE to~CITY~s ALL.AROUND~s~them(m) *you(mp)~will*~GIVE(V) to~Lewi~s **35:3** and~*they~did*~EXIST(V) the~CITY~s to~them(m) to~the~>~SETTLE(V) and~OPEN.SPACE~s~them(m) *they(m)~will*~EXIST(V) to~BEAST~them(m) and~to~GOODS~them(m) and~to~ALL LIVING~them(m) **35:4** and~OPEN.SPACE~s the~CITY~s WHICH *you(mp)~will*~GIVE(V) to~Lewi~s from~WALL the~CITY and~OUTSIDE~unto THOUSAND AMMAH ALL.AROUND **35:5** and~*you(mp)~did*~MEASURE(V) from~OUTSIDE to~the~CITY AT EDGE EAST~unto THOUSAND~s2 in~the~AMMAH and~AT EDGE SOUTH THOUSAND~s2 in~the~AMMAH and~AT EDGE SEA THOUSAND~s2 in~the~AMMAH and~AT EDGE NORTH THOUSAND~s2 in~the~AMMAH and~the~CITY in~the~MIDST THIS *he~will*~EXIST(V) to~them(m) OPEN.SPACE~s the~CITY~s **35:6** and~AT the~CITY~s WHICH *you(mp)~will*~GIVE(V) to~Lewi~s AT SIX CITY~s the~ASYLUM WHICH *you(mp)~will*~GIVE(V) >~FLEE(V) THERE~unto the~MURDER(V)~*ing*(ms) and~UPON~them(m) *you(mp)~will*~GIVE(V) FOUR~s and~TWO CITY **35:7** ALL the~CITY~s WHICH *you(mp)~will*~GIVE(V) to~Lewi~s FOUR~s and~EIGHT CITY AT~them(f) and~AT OPEN.SPACE~s~them(f) **35:8** and~the~CITY~s WHICH *you(mp)~will*~GIVE(V) from~HOLDINGS SON~s Yisra'eyl from~AT the~ABUNDANT *you(mp)~will~make*~INCREASE(V) and~from~AT ?~SMALL.AMOUNT *you(mp)~will~make*~BE.LESS(V) MAN like~MOUTH INHERITANCE~him WHICH *they(m)~will*~INHERIT(V) *he~will*~GIVE(V) from~CITY~s~him to~Lewi~s **35:9** and~*he~will~much*~SPEAK(V) **YHWH** TO Mosheh to~>~SAY(V) **35:10** !(ms)~*much*~SPEAK(V) TO SON~s Yisra'eyl and~*you(ms)~did*~SAY(V) TO~them(m) GIVEN.THAT YOU(mp) CROSS.OVER(V)~*ing*(mp) AT the~Yarden LAND~unto Kena'an **35:11** and~*you(mp)~did~make*~COME.NEAR(V) to~you(mp) CITY~s CITY~s ASYLUM *they(f)~will*~EXIST(V) to~you(mp) and~*he~did*~FLEE(V) THERE~unto MURDER(V)~*ing*(ms) *make*~HIT(V)~*ing*(ms) SOUL in~ERROR **35:12** and~*they~did*~EXIST(V) to~you(mp) the~CITY~s to~ASYLUM from~REDEEM(V)~*ing*(ms) and~NOT *he~will*~DIE(V) the~MURDER(V)~*ing*(ms) UNTIL >~STAND(V)~him to~FACE~s the~COMPANY to~the~DECISION **35:13** and~the~CITY~s WHICH *you(mp)~will*~GIVE(V) SIX CITY~s ASYLUM *they(f)~will*~EXIST(V) to~you(mp) **35:14** AT THREE the~CITY~s *you(mp)~will*~GIVE(V) from~OTHER.SIDE to~Yarden and~AT THREE the~CITY~s *you(mp)~will*~GIVE(V) in~LAND Kena'an CITY~s ASYLUM *they(f)~will*~EXIST(V) **35:15** to~SON~s Yisra'eyl and~to~IMMIGRANT and~to~the~SETTLER in~MIDST~them(m) *they(f)~will*~EXIST(V) SIX the~CITY~s the~THESE to~ASYLUM to~>~FLEE(V) THERE~unto ALL *make*~HIT(V)~*ing*(ms) SOUL in~ERROR **35:16** and~IF in~UTENSIL IRON *he~did~make*~HIT(V)~him and~*he~will*~DIE(V) MURDER(V)~*ing*(ms) HE >~DIE(V) *he~will~be~make*~DIE(V) the~

MURDER⁽ⱽ⁾~ing⁽ᵐˢ⁾ **35:17** and~IF in~STONE HAND WHICH he~will~DIE⁽ⱽ⁾ in~her he~did~make~HIT⁽ⱽ⁾~him and~he~will~DIE⁽ⱽ⁾ MURDER⁽ⱽ⁾~ing⁽ᵐˢ⁾ HE >~DIE⁽ⱽ⁾ he~will~be~make~DIE⁽ⱽ⁾ the~MURDER⁽ⱽ⁾~ing⁽ᵐˢ⁾ **35:18** OR in~UTENSIL TREE HAND WHICH he~will~DIE⁽ⱽ⁾ in~him he~did~make~HIT⁽ⱽ⁾~him and~he~will~DIE⁽ⱽ⁾ MURDER⁽ⱽ⁾~ing⁽ᵐˢ⁾ HE >~DIE⁽ⱽ⁾ he~will~be~make~DIE⁽ⱽ⁾ the~MURDER⁽ⱽ⁾~ing⁽ᵐˢ⁾ **35:19** REDEEM⁽ⱽ⁾~ing⁽ᵐˢ⁾ the~BLOOD HE he~will~make~DIE⁽ⱽ⁾ AT the~MURDER⁽ⱽ⁾~ing⁽ᵐˢ⁾ in~>~REACH⁽ⱽ⁾~him in~him HE he~will~make~DIE⁽ⱽ⁾~him **35:20** and~IF in~HATE he~will~PUSH.AWAY⁽ⱽ⁾~him OR he~did~make~THROW.OUT⁽ⱽ⁾ UPON~him in~AMBUSH and~he~will~DIE⁽ⱽ⁾ **35:21** OR in~HOSTILITY he~did~make~HIT⁽ⱽ⁾~him in~HAND~him and~he~will~DIE⁽ⱽ⁾ >~DIE⁽ⱽ⁾ he~will~be~make~DIE⁽ⱽ⁾ make~HIT⁽ⱽ⁾~ing⁽ᵐˢ⁾ MURDER⁽ⱽ⁾~ing⁽ᵐˢ⁾ HE REDEEM⁽ⱽ⁾~ing⁽ᵐˢ⁾ the~BLOOD he~will~make~DIE⁽ⱽ⁾ AT the~MURDER⁽ⱽ⁾~ing⁽ᵐˢ⁾ in~>~REACH⁽ⱽ⁾~him in~him **35:22** and~IF in~INSTANT in~NOT HOSTILITY he~did~PUSH.AWAY⁽ⱽ⁾~him OR he~did~make~THROW.OUT⁽ⱽ⁾ UPON~him ALL UTENSIL in~NOT AMBUSH **35:23** OR in~ALL STONE WHICH he~will~DIE⁽ⱽ⁾ in~her in~NOT >~SEE⁽ⱽ⁾ and~he~will~make~FALL⁽ⱽ⁾ UPON~him and~he~will~DIE⁽ⱽ⁾ and~HE NOT ATTACK⁽ⱽ⁾~ing⁽ᵐˢ⁾ to~him and~NOT much~SEARCH.OUT⁽ⱽ⁾~ing⁽ᵐˢ⁾ DYSFUNCTIONAL~him **35:24** and~they~did~DECIDE⁽ⱽ⁾ the~COMPANY BETWEEN make~HIT⁽ⱽ⁾~ing⁽ᵐˢ⁾ and~BETWEEN REDEEM⁽ⱽ⁾~ing⁽ᵐˢ⁾ the~BLOOD UPON the~DECISION~s the~THESE **35:25** and~they~did~make~DELIVER⁽ⱽ⁾ the~COMPANY AT the~MURDER⁽ⱽ⁾~ing⁽ᵐˢ⁾ from~HAND REDEEM⁽ⱽ⁾~ing⁽ᵐˢ⁾ the~BLOOD and~they~did~make~TURN.BACK⁽ⱽ⁾ AT~him the~COMPANY TO CITY ASYLUM~him WHICH he~did~FLEE⁽ⱽ⁾ THERE~unto and~he~did~SETTLE⁽ⱽ⁾ in~her UNTIL DEATH the~ADMINISTRATOR the~GREAT WHICH he~did~SMEAR⁽ⱽ⁾ AT~him in~OIL the~SPECIAL **35:26** and~IF >~GO.OUT⁽ⱽ⁾ he~will~GO.OUT⁽ⱽ⁾ the~MURDER⁽ⱽ⁾~ing⁽ᵐˢ⁾ AT BORDER CITY ASYLUM~him WHICH he~will~FLEE⁽ⱽ⁾ THERE~unto **35:27** and~he~did~FIND⁽ⱽ⁾ AT~him REDEEM⁽ⱽ⁾~ing⁽ᵐˢ⁾ the~BLOOD from~OUTSIDE to~BORDER CITY ASYLUM~him and~he~did~MURDER⁽ⱽ⁾ REDEEM⁽ⱽ⁾~ing⁽ᵐˢ⁾ the~BLOOD AT the~MURDER⁽ⱽ⁾~ing⁽ᵐˢ⁾ WITHOUT to~him BLOOD **35:28** GIVEN.THAT in~CITY ASYLUM~him he~will~SETTLE⁽ⱽ⁾ UNTIL DEATH the~ADMINISTRATOR the~GREAT and~AFTER DEATH the~ADMINISTRATOR the~GREAT he~will~TURN.BACK⁽ⱽ⁾ the~MURDER⁽ⱽ⁾~ing⁽ᵐˢ⁾ TO LAND HOLDINGS~him **35:29** and~they~did~EXIST⁽ⱽ⁾ THESE to~you⁽ᵐᵖ⁾ to~CUSTOM DECISION to~GENERATION~s~you⁽ᵐᵖ⁾ in~ALL SETTLING~s~you⁽ᵐᵖ⁾ **35:30** ALL make~HIT⁽ⱽ⁾~ing⁽ᵐˢ⁾ SOUL to~MOUTH WITNESS~s he~will~MURDER⁽ⱽ⁾ AT the~MURDER⁽ⱽ⁾~ing⁽ᵐˢ⁾ and~WITNESS UNIT NOT he~will~ANSWER⁽ⱽ⁾ in~SOUL to~>~DIE⁽ⱽ⁾ **35:31** and~NOT you⁽ᵐᵖ⁾~will~TAKE⁽ⱽ⁾ COVERING to~SOUL MURDER⁽ⱽ⁾~ing⁽ᵐˢ⁾ WHICH HE LOST to~>~DIE⁽ⱽ⁾ GIVEN.THAT >~DIE⁽ⱽ⁾ he~will~be~make~DIE⁽ⱽ⁾ **35:32** and~NOT you⁽ᵐᵖ⁾~will~TAKE⁽ⱽ⁾ COVERING to~>~FLEE⁽ⱽ⁾ TO CITY ASYLUM~him to~>~TURN.BACK⁽ⱽ⁾ to~>~SETTLE⁽ⱽ⁾ in~the~LAND UNTIL DEATH the~ADMINISTRATOR **35:33** and~NOT you⁽ᵐᵖ⁾~will~make~BE.FILTHY⁽ⱽ⁾ AT the~LAND WHICH YOU⁽ᵐᵖ⁾ in~her GIVEN.THAT the~BLOOD HE he~will~make~BE.FILTHY⁽ⱽ⁾ AT the~LAND and~to~the~LAND NOT he~will~be~much~

COVER⁽ᵛ⁾ to~the~BLOOD WHICH POUR.OUT⁽ᵛ⁾~ed⁽ᵐˢ⁾ in~her GIVEN.THAT IF in~BLOOD POUR.OUT⁽ᵛ⁾~ing⁽ᵐˢ⁾~him **35:34** and~NOT you⁽ᵐˢ⁾~will~much~BE.DIRTY⁽ᵛ⁾ AT the~LAND WHICH YOU⁽ᵐᵖ⁾ SETTLE⁽ᵛ⁾~ing⁽ᵐᵖ⁾ in~her WHICH I DWELL⁽ᵛ⁾~ing⁽ᵐˢ⁾ in~MIDST~her GIVEN.THAT I **YHWH** DWELL⁽ᵛ⁾~ing⁽ᵐˢ⁾ in~MIDST SON~s Yisra'eyl

Chapter 36

36:1 and~*they*⁽ᵐ⁾~*will*~COME.NEAR⁽ᵛ⁾ HEAD~s the~FATHER~s to~CLAN SON~s Gil'ad SON Makhir SON Menasheh from~CLAN~s SON~s Yoseph and~*they*⁽ᵐ⁾~*will*~much~SPEAK⁽ᵛ⁾ to~FACE~s Mosheh and~to~FACE~s the~CAPTAIN~s HEAD~s FATHER~s to~SON~s Yisra'eyl **36:2** and~*they*⁽ᵐ⁾~*will*~SAY⁽ᵛ⁾ AT LORD~me *he*~*did*~much~DIRECT⁽ᵛ⁾ **YHWH** to~>~GIVE⁽ᵛ⁾ AT the~LAND in~INHERITANCE in~LOT to~SON~s Yisra'eyl and~LORD~me *he*~*did*~be~much~DIRECT⁽ᵛ⁾ in~**YHWH** to~>~GIVE⁽ᵛ⁾ AT INHERITANCE Tselaph'hhad BROTHER~us to~DAUGHTER~s~him **36:3** and~*they*~*did*~EXIST⁽ᵛ⁾ to~UNIT from~SON~s STAFF~s SON~s Yisra'eyl to~WOMAN~s and~*she*~*did*~be~TAKE.AWAY⁽ᵛ⁾ INHERITANCE from~INHERITANCE FATHER~s~us and~*he*~*did*~ADD⁽ᵛ⁾ UPON INHERITANCE the~BRANCH WHICH *they*⁽ᶠ⁾~*will*~EXIST⁽ᵛ⁾ to~them⁽ᵐ⁾ and~from~LOT INHERITANCE~us *he*~*will*~be~TAKE.AWAY⁽ᵛ⁾ **36:4** and~IF *he*~*will*~EXIST⁽ᵛ⁾ the~JUBILEE to~SON~s Yisra'eyl and~*she*~*did*~be~ADD⁽ᵛ⁾ INHERITANCE UPON INHERITANCE the~BRANCH WHICH *they*⁽ᶠ⁾~*will*~EXIST⁽ᵛ⁾ to~them⁽ᵐ⁾ and~from~INHERITANCE BRANCH FATHER~s~us *he*~*will*~be~TAKE.AWAY⁽ᵛ⁾ INHERITANCE **36:5** and~*he*~*will*~much~DIRECT⁽ᵛ⁾ Mosheh AT SON~s Yisra'eyl UPON MOUTH **YHWH** to~>~SAY⁽ᵛ⁾ SO BRANCH SON~s Yoseph SPEAK⁽ᵛ⁾~*ing*⁽ᵐᵖ⁾ **36:6** THIS the~WORD WHICH *he*~*did*~much~DIRECT⁽ᵛ⁾ **YHWH** to~DAUGHTER~s Tselaph'hhad to~>~SAY⁽ᵛ⁾ to~the~FUNCTIONAL in~EYE~s2~them⁽ᵐ⁾ *they*⁽ᶠ⁾~*will*~EXIST⁽ᵛ⁾ to~WOMAN~s SURELY to~CLAN BRANCH FATHER~them⁽ᵐ⁾ *they*⁽ᶠ⁾~*will*~EXIST⁽ᵛ⁾ to~WOMAN~s **36:7** and~NOT *she*~*will*~GO.AROUND⁽ᵛ⁾ INHERITANCE to~SON~s Yisra'eyl from~BRANCH TO BRANCH GIVEN.THAT MAN in~INHERITANCE BRANCH FATHER~s~him *they*⁽ᵐ⁾~*will*~ADHERE⁽ᵛ⁾ SON~s Yisra'eyl **36:8** and~ALL DAUGHTER POSSESS⁽ᵛ⁾~*ing*⁽ᶠˢ⁾ INHERITANCE from~BRANCH~s SON~s Yisra'eyl to~UNIT from~CLAN BRANCH FATHER~her *she*~*will*~EXIST⁽ᵛ⁾ to~WOMAN to~THAT *they*⁽ᵐ⁾~*will*~POSSESS⁽ᵛ⁾ SON~s Yisra'eyl MAN INHERITANCE FATHER~s~him **36:9** and~NOT *she*~*will*~GO.AROUND⁽ᵛ⁾ INHERITANCE from~BRANCH to~BRANCH OTHER GIVEN.THAT MAN in~INHERITANCE~him *they*⁽ᵐ⁾~*will*~ADHERE⁽ᵛ⁾ BRANCH SON~s Yisra'eyl **36:10** like~WHICH *he*~*did*~much~DIRECT⁽ᵛ⁾ **YHWH** AT Mosheh SO *they*~*did*~DO⁽ᵛ⁾ DAUGHTER~s Tselaph'hhad **36:11** and~*they*⁽ᶠ⁾~*will*~EXIST⁽ᵛ⁾ Mahhlah Tirtsah and~Hhaglah and~Milkah and~No'ah DAUGHTER~s Tselaph'hhad to~SON~s UNCLE~s~them⁽ᶠ⁾ to~WOMAN~s **36:12** from~CLAN~s SON~s Menasheh SON Yoseph *they*~*did*~EXIST⁽ᵛ⁾ to~WOMAN~s and~*she*~*will*~EXIST[(V)] INHERITANCE UPON BRANCH CLAN FATHER~them[(f)] **36:13** THESE the~DIRECTIVE~s and~the~DECISION~s WHICH *he~did*~*much*~DIRECT[(V)] **YHWH** in~HAND Mosheh TO SON~s Yisra'eyl in~DESERT~s Mo'av UPON Yarden Ye'rey'hho

Benner's Mechanical Translation of the Torah

The Book of Deuteronomy

Chapter 1

1:1 THESE the~WORD~s WHICH *he~did~much*~SPEAK$^{(V)}$ Mosheh TO ALL Yisra'eyl in~OTHER.SIDE the~Yarden in~the~WILDERNESS in~the~DESERT FOREFRONT REEDS BETWEEN Paran and~BETWEEN Tophel and~Lavan and~ Hhatsarot and~Di-Zahav   **1:2** UNIT TEN DAY from~Hhorev ROAD HILL Se'iyr UNTIL Qadesh Barneya   **1:3** and~*he~will*~EXIST$^{(V)}$ in~FOUR~s YEAR in~ONE TEN NEW.MOON in~UNIT to~the~NEW.MOON *he~did~much*~SPEAK$^{(V)}$ Mosheh TO SON~s Yisra'eyl like~ALL WHICH *he~did~much*~DIRECT$^{(V)}$ **YHWH** AT~him TO~them$^{(m)}$ **1:4** AFTER >~*make*~HIT$^{(V)}$~him AT Sihhon KING the~ Emor~of WHICH SETTLE$^{(V)}$~*ing*$^{(ms)}$ in~Hheshbon and~AT Og KING the~Bashan WHICH SETTLE$^{(V)}$~*ing*$^{(ms)}$ in~Ashterot in~Ed're'i   **1:5** in~OTHER.SIDE the~ Yarden in~LAND Mo'av *he~did~make*~TAKE.UPON$^{(V)}$ Mosheh *he~did~much*~ EXPLAIN$^{(V)}$ AT the~TEACHING the~THIS to~>~SAY$^{(V)}$ **1:6 YHWH** Elohiym~us *he~did~much*~SPEAK$^{(V)}$ TO~us in~Hhorev to~>~SAY$^{(V)}$ ABUNDANT to~you$^{(mp)}$ >~SETTLE$^{(V)}$ in~the~HILL the~THIS   **1:7** *!*$^{(mp)}$~TURN$^{(V)}$ and~ *!*$^{(mp)}$~JOURNEY$^{(V)}$ to~you$^{(mp)}$ and~ *!*$^{(mp)}$~COME$^{(V)}$ HILL the~Emor~of and~TO ALL DWELLER~s~ him in~the~DESERT in~the~HILL and~in~the~LOWLAND and~in~the~SOUTH and~in~SHORE the~SEA LAND the~Kena'an~of and~the~Levanon UNTIL the~RIVER the~GREAT RIVER Perat   **1:8** *!*$^{(ms)}$~SEE$^{(V)}$ *I~did*~GIVE$^{(V)}$ to~FACE~s~ you$^{(mp)}$ AT the~LAND *!*$^{(mp)}$~COME$^{(V)}$ and~ *!*$^{(mp)}$~POSSESS$^{(V)}$ AT the~LAND WHICH *he~did~be*~SWEAR$^{(V)}$ **YHWH** to~FATHER~s~you$^{(mp)}$ to~Avraham to~ Yits'hhaq and~to~Ya'aqov to~>~GIVE$^{(V)}$ to~them$^{(m)}$ and~to~SEED~them$^{(m)}$ AFTER~them$^{(m)}$ **1:9** and~*I~will*~SAY$^{(V)}$ TO~you$^{(mp)}$ in~the~APPOINTED.TIME the~SHE to~>~SAY$^{(V)}$ NOT *I~will*~BE.ABLE$^{(V)}$ to~STRAND~me >~LIFT.UP$^{(V)}$ AT~ you$^{(mp)}$ **1:10 YHWH** Elohiym~you$^{(mp)}$ *he~did~make*~INCREASE$^{(V)}$ AT~you$^{(mp)}$ and~LOOK~you$^{(mp)}$ the~DAY like~STAR~s the~SKY~s2 to~ ABUNDANCE   **1:11 YHWH** Elohiym FATHER~s~you$^{(mp)}$ *he~will~make*~ADD$^{(V)}$ UPON~you$^{(mp)}$ like~you$^{(mp)}$ THOUSAND FOOTSTEP~s and~*he~will~much*~ KNEEL$^{(V)}$ AT~you$^{(mp)}$ like~WHICH *he~did~much*~SPEAK$^{(V)}$ to~ you$^{(mp)}$ **1:12** HOW *I~will*~LIFT.UP$^{(V)}$ to~STRAND~me HEAVY.BURDEN~you$^{(mp)}$ and~LOAD~you$^{(mp)}$ and~DISPUTE~you$^{(mp)}$ **1:13** *!*$^{(mp)}$~PROVIDE$^{(V)}$ to~you$^{(mp)}$ MAN~s SKILLED.ONE~s and~*be*~UNDERSTAND$^{(V)}$~*ing*$^{(mp)}$ and~KNOW$^{(V)}$~ *ed*$^{(mp)}$ to~STAFF~s~you$^{(mp)}$ and~*I~will*~PLACE$^{(V)}$~them$^{(m)}$ in~HEAD~s~ you$^{(mp)}$ **1:14** and~*you*$^{(mp)}$~*will*~ANSWER$^{(V)}$ AT~me and~*you*$^{(mp)}$~*will*~SAY$^{(V)}$ FUNCTIONAL the~WORD WHICH *you*$^{(ms)}$~*did~much*~SPEAK$^{(V)}$ to~>~ DO$^{(V)}$ **1:15** and~*I~will*~TAKE$^{(V)}$ AT HEAD~s STAFF~s~you$^{(mp)}$ MAN~s SKILLED.ONE~s and~KNOW$^{(V)}$~*ed*$^{(mp)}$ and~*I~will*~GIVE$^{(V)}$ AT~them$^{(m)}$ HEAD~s UPON~you$^{(mp)}$ NOBLE~s THOUSAND~s and~NOBLE~s HUNDRED~s and~ NOBLE~s FIVE~s and~NOBLE~s TEN~s and~OFFICER~s to~STAFF~s~you$^{(mp)}$

1:16 and~I~will~much~DIRECT⁽ⱽ⁾ AT DECIDE⁽ⱽ⁾~ing⁽ᵐᵖ⁾~you⁽ᵐᵖ⁾ in~the~ APPOINTED.TIME the~SHE to~>~SAY⁽ⱽ⁾ >~HEAR⁽ⱽ⁾ BETWEEN BROTHER~s~ you⁽ᵐᵖ⁾ and~*you*⁽ᵐᵖ⁾~*did*~DECIDE⁽ⱽ⁾ STEADFAST BETWEEN MAN and~ BETWEEN BROTHER~him and~BETWEEN IMMIGRANT~him **1:17** NOT *you*⁽ᵐᵖ⁾~*will*~*make*~RECOGNIZE⁽ⱽ⁾ FACE~s in~the~DECISION like~the~SMALL like~the~GREAT *you*⁽ᵐᵖ⁾~*will*~HEAR⁽ⱽ⁾~must NOT *you*⁽ᵐᵖ⁾~*will*~BE.AFRAID⁽ⱽ⁾ from~FACE~s MAN GIVEN.THAT the~DECISION to~Elohiym HE and~the~ WORD WHICH *he~will*~BE.HARD⁽ⱽ⁾ from~you⁽ᵐᵖ⁾ *you*⁽ᵐᵖ⁾~*will*~ COME.NEAR⁽ⱽ⁾~must TO~me and~I~*did*~HEAR⁽ⱽ⁾~him **1:18** and~I~will~ much~DIRECT⁽ⱽ⁾ AT~you⁽ᵐᵖ⁾ in~the~APPOINTED.TIME the~SHE AT ALL the~ WORD~s WHICH *you*⁽ᵐˢ⁾~*will*~DO⁽ⱽ⁾~must **1:19** and~we~will~JOURNEY⁽ⱽ⁾ from~Hhorev and~*we~did*~WALK⁽ⱽ⁾ AT ALL the~WILDERNESS the~GREAT and~the~*be*~FEAR⁽ⱽ⁾~*ing*⁽ᵐˢ⁾ the~HE WHICH *you*⁽ᵐᵖ⁾~*did*~SEE⁽ⱽ⁾ ROAD HILL the~Emor~of like~WHICH *he~did*~much~DIRECT⁽ⱽ⁾ **YHWH** Elohiym~us AT~us and~*we~will*~COME⁽ⱽ⁾ UNTIL Qadesh Barneya **1:20** and~I~will~SAY⁽ⱽ⁾ TO~ you⁽ᵐᵖ⁾ *you*⁽ᵐᵖ⁾~*did*~COME⁽ⱽ⁾ UNTIL HILL the~Emor~of WHICH **YHWH** Elohiym~us GIVE⁽ⱽ⁾~*ing*⁽ᵐˢ⁾ to~us **1:21** !⁽ᵐˢ⁾~SEE⁽ⱽ⁾ *he~did*~GIVE⁽ⱽ⁾ **YHWH** Elohiym~you⁽ᵐˢ⁾ to~FACE~s~you⁽ᵐˢ⁾ AT the~LAND !⁽ᵐˢ⁾~GO.UP⁽ⱽ⁾ !⁽ᵐˢ⁾~ POSSESS⁽ⱽ⁾ like~WHICH *he~did*~much~SPEAK⁽ⱽ⁾ **YHWH** Elohiym FATHER~s~ you⁽ᵐˢ⁾ to~you⁽ᶠˢ⁾ DO.NOT *you*⁽ᵐˢ⁾~*will*~FEAR⁽ⱽ⁾ and~DO.NOT *you*⁽ᵐˢ⁾~*will*~ BE.SHATTERED⁽ⱽ⁾ **1:22** and~*you*⁽ᵐᵖ⁾~*will*~COME.NEAR⁽ⱽ⁾~must TO~me ALL~ you⁽ᵐᵖ⁾ and~*you*⁽ᵐᵖ⁾~*will*~SAY⁽ⱽ⁾ we~will~SEND⁽ⱽ⁾~& MAN~s to~FACE~s~us and~*they*⁽ᵐ⁾~*will*~DIG.OUT⁽ⱽ⁾ to~us AT the~LAND and~*they*⁽ᵐ⁾~*will*~ TURN.BACK⁽ⱽ⁾ AT~us WORD AT the~ROAD WHICH we~will~GO.UP⁽ⱽ⁾~& in~ her and~AT the~CITY~s WHICH we~will~COME⁽ⱽ⁾ TO~them⁽ᶠ⁾ **1:23** and~he~ will~DO.WELL⁽ⱽ⁾ in~EYE~s2~me the~WORD and~I~will~TAKE⁽ⱽ⁾ from~you⁽ᵐᵖ⁾ TWO TEN MAN~s MAN UNIT to~the~STAFF **1:24** and~*they*⁽ᵐ⁾~*will*~TURN⁽ⱽ⁾ and~*they*⁽ᵐ⁾~*will*~GO.UP⁽ⱽ⁾ the~HILL~unto and~*they*⁽ᵐ⁾~*will*~COME⁽ⱽ⁾ UNTIL WADI Eshkol and~*they*⁽ᵐ⁾~*will*~much~TREAD.ABOUT⁽ⱽ⁾ AT~her **1:25** and~ *they*⁽ᵐ⁾~*will*~TAKE⁽ⱽ⁾ in~HAND~them⁽ᵐ⁾ from~PRODUCE the~LAND and~ *they*⁽ᵐ⁾~*will*~*make*~GO.DOWN⁽ⱽ⁾ TO~us and~*they*⁽ᵐ⁾~*will*~*make*~ TURN.BACK⁽ⱽ⁾ AT~us WORD and~*they*⁽ᵐ⁾~*will*~SAY⁽ⱽ⁾ FUNCTIONAL the~LAND WHICH **YHWH** Elohiym~us GIVE⁽ⱽ⁾~*ing*⁽ᵐˢ⁾ to~us **1:26** and~NOT *you*⁽ᵐᵖ⁾~*did*~ CONSENT⁽ⱽ⁾ to~>~GO.UP⁽ⱽ⁾ and~*you*⁽ᵐᵖ⁾~*will*~*make*~DISOBEY⁽ⱽ⁾ AT MOUTH **YHWH** Elohiym~you⁽ᵐᵖ⁾ **1:27** and~*you*⁽ᵐᵖ⁾~*will*~*be*~WHISPER⁽ⱽ⁾ in~TENT~s~ you⁽ᵐᵖ⁾ and~*you*⁽ᵐᵖ⁾~*will*~SAY⁽ⱽ⁾ in~HATE **YHWH** AT~us *he~did*~*make*~ GO.OUT⁽ⱽ⁾~us from~LAND Mits'rayim to~>~GIVE⁽ⱽ⁾ AT~us in~HAND the~ Emor~of to~>~*make*~DESTROY⁽ⱽ⁾~us **1:28** WHEREVER WE GO.UP⁽ⱽ⁾~*ing*⁽ᵐᵖ⁾ BROTHER~s~us *they~did*~*make*~MELT.AWAY⁽ⱽ⁾ AT HEART~us to~>~SAY⁽ⱽ⁾ PEOPLE GREAT and~RAISE.UP⁽ⱽ⁾~*ing*⁽ᵐˢ⁾ FROM~us CITY~s GREAT~s and~ FENCE.IN⁽ⱽ⁾~*ed*⁽ᶠᵖ⁾ in~the~SKY~s2 and~ALSO SON~s Anaq~s *we~did*~SEE⁽ⱽ⁾ THERE **1:29** and~I~will~SAY⁽ⱽ⁾ TO~you⁽ᵐᵖ⁾ NOT *you*⁽ᵐᵖ⁾~*will*~ BE.TERRIFIED⁽ⱽ⁾~must and~NOT *you*⁽ᵐᵖ⁾~*will*~FEAR⁽ⱽ⁾~must from~ them⁽ᵐ⁾ **1:30 YHWH** Elohiym~you⁽ᵐᵖ⁾ the~WALK⁽ⱽ⁾~*ing*⁽ᵐˢ⁾ to~FACE~s~ you⁽ᵐᵖ⁾ HE *will~be*~FIGHT⁽ⱽ⁾ to~you⁽ᵐᵖ⁾ like~ALL WHICH *he~did*~DO⁽ⱽ⁾ AT~

you⁽ᵐᵖ⁾ in~Mits'rayim to~EYE~s2~you⁽ᵐᵖ⁾   **1:31** and~in~the~WILDERNESS WHICH *you*⁽ᵐˢ⁾*~did*~SEE⁽ⱽ⁾ WHICH *he~did*~LIFT.UP⁽ⱽ⁾~*you*⁽ᵐˢ⁾ **YHWH** Elohiym~*you*⁽ᵐˢ⁾ like~WHICH *he~will*~LIFT.UP⁽ⱽ⁾ MAN AT SON~him in~ALL the~ROAD WHICH *you*⁽ᵐᵖ⁾*~did*~WALK⁽ⱽ⁾ UNTIL in~>~COME⁽ⱽ⁾~*you*⁽ᵐᵖ⁾ UNTIL the~AREA the~THIS   **1:32** and~in~the~WORD the~THIS WITHOUT~*you*⁽ᵐᵖ⁾ *make*~SECURE⁽ⱽ⁾~*ing*⁽ᵐᵖ⁾ in~**YHWH** Elohiym~*you*⁽ᵐᵖ⁾   **1:33** the~WALK⁽ⱽ⁾~*ing*⁽ᵐˢ⁾ to~FACE~s~*you*⁽ᵐᵖ⁾ in~the~ROAD to~>~SCOUT⁽ⱽ⁾ to~*you*⁽ᵐᵖ⁾ AREA to~>~CAMP⁽ⱽ⁾~*you*⁽ᵐˢ⁾ in~the~FIRE NIGHT to~>~*make*~SEE⁽ⱽ⁾~*you*⁽ᵐᵖ⁾ in~the~ROAD WHICH *you*⁽ᵐᵖ⁾*~will*~WALK⁽ⱽ⁾ in~her and~in~CLOUD DAYTIME   **1:34** and~*he~will*~HEAR⁽ⱽ⁾ **YHWH** AT VOICE WORD~s~*you*⁽ᵐᵖ⁾ and~*he~will*~SNAP⁽ⱽ⁾ and~*he~will~be*~SWEAR⁽ⱽ⁾ to~>~SAY⁽ⱽ⁾   **1:35** IF *he~will*~SEE⁽ⱽ⁾ MAN in~MAN~s the~THESE the~GENERATION the~DYSFUNCTIONAL the~THIS AT the~LAND the~FUNCTIONAL WHICH *I~did~be*~SWEAR⁽ⱽ⁾ to~>~GIVE⁽ⱽ⁾ to~FATHER~s~*you*⁽ᵐᵖ⁾   **1:36** WITH.THE.EXCEPTION~of Kaleyv SON Yephunah HE *he~will*~SEE⁽ⱽ⁾~her and~to~him *I~will*~GIVE⁽ⱽ⁾ AT the~LAND WHICH *he~did*~TAKE.STEPS⁽ⱽ⁾ in~her and~to~SON~s~him SEEING.AS WHICH *he~did~much*~FILL⁽ⱽ⁾ AFTER **YHWH**   **1:37** ALSO in~me *he~did~self*~SNORT⁽ⱽ⁾ **YHWH** in~ON.ACCOUNT.OF~*you*⁽ᵐᵖ⁾ to~>~SAY⁽ⱽ⁾ ALSO YOU⁽ᵐˢ⁾ NOT *you*⁽ᵐˢ⁾*~will*~COME⁽ⱽ⁾ THERE   **1:38** Yehoshu'a SON Nun the~STAND⁽ⱽ⁾~*ing*⁽ᵐˢ⁾ to~FACE~s~*you*⁽ᵐˢ⁾ HE *he~will*~COME⁽ⱽ⁾ THERE~unto AT~him *!*⁽ᵐˢ⁾*~much*~SEIZE⁽ⱽ⁾ GIVEN.THAT HE *he~will~make*~INHERIT⁽ⱽ⁾~her AT Yisra'eyl   **1:39** and~BABIES~*you*⁽ᵐᵖ⁾ WHICH *you*⁽ᵐᵖ⁾*~did*~SAY⁽ⱽ⁾ to~the~PLUNDER *he~will*~EXIST⁽ⱽ⁾ and~SON~s~*you*⁽ᵐᵖ⁾ WHICH NOT *they~did*~KNOW⁽ⱽ⁾ the~DAY FUNCTIONAL and~DYSFUNCTIONAL THEY⁽ᵐ⁾ *they*⁽ᵐ⁾*~will*~COME⁽ⱽ⁾ THERE~unto and~to~them⁽ᵐ⁾ *I~will*~GIVE⁽ⱽ⁾~her and~THEY⁽ᵐ⁾ *they*⁽ᵐ⁾*~will*~POSSESS⁽ⱽ⁾~her   **1:40** and~YOU⁽ᵐᵖ⁾ *!*⁽ᵐᵖ⁾*~*TURN⁽ⱽ⁾ to~*you*⁽ᵐᵖ⁾ and~ *!*⁽ᵐᵖ⁾*~*JOURNEY⁽ⱽ⁾ the~WILDERNESS~unto ROAD SEA REEDS   **1:41** and~*you*⁽ᵐᵖ⁾*~will*~ANSWER⁽ⱽ⁾ and~*you*⁽ᵐᵖ⁾*~will*~SAY⁽ⱽ⁾ TO~me *we~did*~FAIL⁽ⱽ⁾ to~**YHWH** WE *we~will*~GO.UP⁽ⱽ⁾~& and~*we~did~be*~FIGHT⁽ⱽ⁾ like~ALL WHICH *he~did~much*~DIRECT⁽ⱽ⁾~us **YHWH** Elohiym~us and~*you*⁽ᵐᵖ⁾*~will*~GIRD.UP⁽ⱽ⁾ MAN AT UTENSIL~s BATTLE~him and~*you*⁽ᵐᵖ⁾*~will~make*~SUFFICIENT⁽ⱽ⁾ to~>~GO.UP⁽ⱽ⁾ the~HILL~unto   **1:42** and~*he~will*~SAY⁽ⱽ⁾ **YHWH** TO~me *!*⁽ᵐˢ⁾*~*SAY⁽ⱽ⁾ to~them⁽ᵐ⁾ NOT *you*⁽ᵐᵖ⁾*~will*~GO.UP⁽ⱽ⁾ and~NOT *you*⁽ᵐᵖ⁾*~will~be*~FIGHT⁽ⱽ⁾ GIVEN.THAT WITHOUT~me in~INSIDE~*you*⁽ᵐᵖ⁾ and~NOT *you*⁽ᵐᵖ⁾*~will~be*~SMITE⁽ⱽ⁾ to~FACE~s ATTACK⁽ⱽ⁾~*ing*⁽ᵐᵖ⁾~*you*⁽ᵐᵖ⁾   **1:43** and~*I~will~much*~SPEAK⁽ⱽ⁾ TO~*you*⁽ᵐᵖ⁾ and~NOT *you*⁽ᵐᵖ⁾*~did*~HEAR⁽ⱽ⁾ and~*you*⁽ᵐᵖ⁾*~will~make*~DISOBEY⁽ⱽ⁾ AT MOUTH **YHWH** and~*you*⁽ᵐᵖ⁾*~will~make*~SIMMER⁽ⱽ⁾ and~*you*⁽ᵐᵖ⁾*~will*~GO.UP⁽ⱽ⁾ the~HILL~unto   **1:44** and~*he~will*~GO.OUT⁽ⱽ⁾ the~Emor~of the~SETTLE⁽ⱽ⁾~*ing*⁽ᵐˢ⁾ in~the~HILL the~HE to~>~MEET⁽ⱽ⁾~them⁽ᵐ⁾ and~*they*⁽ᵐ⁾*~will*~PURSUE⁽ⱽ⁾ AT~*you*⁽ᵐᵖ⁾ like~WHICH *they*⁽ᶠ⁾*~will~be*~DO⁽ⱽ⁾ the~BEE~s and~*they*⁽ᵐ⁾*~will~make*~SMASH⁽ⱽ⁾ AT~*you*⁽ᵐᵖ⁾ in~Se'iyr UNTIL Hharmah   **1:45** and~*you*⁽ᵐᵖ⁾*~will*~TURN.BACK⁽ⱽ⁾ and~*you*⁽ᵐᵖ⁾*~will*~WEEP⁽ⱽ⁾ to~FACE~s **YHWH** and~NOT *he~did*~HEAR⁽ⱽ⁾ **YHWH** in~VOICE~*you*⁽ᵐᵖ⁾ and~NOT *he~did~make*~WEIGH.OUT⁽ⱽ⁾ TO~*you*⁽ᵐᵖ⁾   **1:46** and~*you*⁽ᵐᵖ⁾*~will*~

SETTLE⁽ᵛ⁾ in~Qadesh DAY~s ABUNDANT~s like~the~DAY~s WHICH you⁽ᵐᵖ⁾~did~SETTLE⁽ᵛ⁾

Chapter 2

2:1 and~*we~will*~TURN⁽ᵛ⁾ and~*we~will*~JOURNEY⁽ᵛ⁾ the~WILDERNESS~unto ROAD SEA REEDS like~WHICH *he~did~much*~SPEAK⁽ᵛ⁾ **YHWH** TO~me and~*we~will*~GO.AROUND⁽ᵛ⁾ AT HILL Se'iyr DAY~s ABUNDANT~s **2:2** and~*he~will*~SAY⁽ᵛ⁾ **YHWH** TO~me to~>~SAY⁽ᵛ⁾ **2:3** ABUNDANT to~you⁽ᵐᵖ⁾ >~GO.AROUND⁽ᵛ⁾ AT the~HILL the~THIS *!*⁽ᵐᵖ⁾~TURN⁽ᵛ⁾ to~you⁽ᵐᵖ⁾ NORTH~unto **2:4** and~AT the~PEOPLE *!*⁽ᵐˢ⁾~*much*~DIRECT⁽ᵛ⁾ to~>~SAY⁽ᵛ⁾ YOU⁽ᵐᵖ⁾ CROSS.OVER⁽ᵛ⁾~*ing*⁽ᵐᵖ⁾ in~BORDER BROTHER~s~you⁽ᵐᵖ⁾ SON~s Esaw the~SETTLE⁽ᵛ⁾~*ing*⁽ᵐᵖ⁾ in~Se'iyr and~*they*⁽ᵐ⁾~*will*~FEAR⁽ᵛ⁾ from~you⁽ᵐᵖ⁾ and~you⁽ᵐᵖ⁾~*will*~be~SAFEGUARD⁽ᵛ⁾ MANY **2:5** DO.NOT you⁽ᵐᵖ⁾~*will*~*self*~MEDDLE⁽ᵛ⁾ in~them⁽ᵐ⁾ GIVEN.THAT NOT *I~will*~GIVE⁽ᵛ⁾ to~you⁽ᵐᵖ⁾ from~LAND~them⁽ᵐ⁾ UNTIL STEP PALM FOOT GIVEN.THAT HERITAGE to~Esaw *I~did*~GIVE⁽ᵛ⁾ AT HILL Se'iyr **2:6** FOODSTUFF you⁽ᵐᵖ⁾~*will*~EXCHANGE⁽ᵛ⁾ from~AT~them⁽ᵐ⁾ in~SILVER and~*you*⁽ᵐᵖ⁾~*did*~EAT⁽ᵛ⁾ and~ALSO WATER~s2 you⁽ᵐᵖ⁾~*will*~DIG⁽ᵛ⁾ from~AT~them⁽ᵐ⁾ in~SILVER and~*you*⁽ᵐᵖ⁾~*did*~GULP⁽ᵛ⁾ **2:7** GIVEN.THAT **YHWH** Elohiym~you⁽ᵐˢ⁾ *he~did~much*~KNEEL⁽ᵛ⁾~you⁽ᵐˢ⁾ in~ALL WORK HAND~you⁽ᵐˢ⁾ *he~did*~KNOW⁽ᵛ⁾ >~WALK⁽ᵛ⁾~you⁽ᵐˢ⁾ AT the~WILDERNESS the~GREAT the~THIS THIS FOUR~s YEAR **YHWH** Elohiym~you⁽ᵐˢ⁾ WITH~you⁽ᶠˢ⁾ NOT *you*⁽ᵐˢ⁾~*did*~DIMINISH⁽ᵛ⁾ WORD **2:8** and~*we~will*~CROSS.OVER⁽ᵛ⁾ from~AT BROTHER~s~us SON~s Esaw the~SETTLE⁽ᵛ⁾~*ing*⁽ᵐᵖ⁾ in~Se'iyr from~ROAD the~DESERT from~Eylot and~from~Etsi'on-Gaver and~*we~will*~TURN⁽ᵛ⁾ and~*we~will*~CROSS.OVER⁽ᵛ⁾ ROAD WILDERNESS Mo'av **2:9** and~*he~will*~SAY⁽ᵛ⁾ **YHWH** TO~me DO.NOT *you*⁽ᵐˢ⁾~*will*~SMACK⁽ᵛ⁾ AT Mo'av and~DO.NOT *you*⁽ᵐˢ⁾~*will*~*self*~MEDDLE⁽ᵛ⁾ in~them⁽ᵐ⁾ BATTLE GIVEN.THAT NOT *I~will*~GIVE⁽ᵛ⁾ to~you⁽ᵐˢ⁾ from~LAND~him HERITAGE GIVEN.THAT to~SON~s Lot *I~did*~GIVE⁽ᵛ⁾ AT Ar HERITAGE **2:10** the~Eym~s to~FACE~s *they~did*~SETTLE⁽ᵛ⁾ in~her PEOPLE GREAT and~ABUNDANT and~RAISE.UP⁽ᵛ⁾~*ing*⁽ᵐˢ⁾ like~the~Anaq~s **2:11** Rapha~s *they*⁽ᵐ⁾~*will*~be~THINK⁽ᵛ⁾ MOREOVER THEY⁽ᵐ⁾ like~the~Anaq~s and~the~Mo'av~s *they*⁽ᵐ⁾~*will*~CALL.OUT⁽ᵛ⁾ to~them⁽ᵐ⁾ Eym~s **2:12** and~in~Se'iyr *they~did*~SETTLE⁽ᵛ⁾ the~Hhor~s to~FACE~s and~SON~s Esaw *they*⁽ᵐ⁾~*will*~POSSESS⁽ᵛ⁾~them⁽ᵐ⁾ and~*they*⁽ᵐ⁾~*will*~*make*~DESTROY⁽ᵛ⁾~them⁽ᵐ⁾ from~FACE~s~them⁽ᵐ⁾ and~*they*⁽ᵐ⁾~*will*~SETTLE⁽ᵛ⁾ UNDER~them⁽ᵐ⁾ like~WHICH *he~did*~DO⁽ᵛ⁾ Yisra'eyl to~LAND HERITAGE~him WHICH *he~did*~GIVE⁽ᵛ⁾ **YHWH** to~them⁽ᵐ⁾ **2:13** NOW *!*⁽ᵐᵖ⁾~RISE⁽ᵛ⁾ and~*!*⁽ᵐᵖ⁾~CROSS.OVER⁽ᵛ⁾ to~you⁽ᵐᵖ⁾ AT WADI Zered and~*we~will*~CROSS.OVER⁽ᵛ⁾ AT WADI Zered **2:14** and~the~DAY~s WHICH *we~did*~WALK⁽ᵛ⁾ from~Qadesh Barneya UNTIL WHICH >~CROSS.OVER⁽ᵛ⁾~us AT WADI Zered THREE~s and~EIGHT YEAR UNTIL >~BE.WHOLE⁽ᵛ⁾ ALL the~GENERATION MAN~s the~

BATTLE from~INSIDE the~CAMP like~WHICH *he~did~be*~SWEAR[(v)] **YHWH** to~them[(m)]   **2:15** and~ALSO HAND **YHWH** *she~did*~EXIST[(v)] in~them[(m)] to~>~CONFUSE[(v)]~them[(m)] from~INSIDE the~CAMP UNTIL >~*be*~BE.WHOLE[(v)]~them[(m)]   **2:16** and~*he~will*~EXIST[(v)] like~WHICH *they~did*~BE.WHOLE[(v)] ALL MAN~s the~BATTLE to~>~DIE[(v)] from~INSIDE the~PEOPLE   **2:17** and~*he~will~much*~SPEAK[(v)] **YHWH** TO~me to~>~SAY[(v)]   **2:18** YOU[(ms)] CROSS.OVER[(v)]~*ing*[(ms)] the~DAY AT BORDER Mo'av AT Ar   **2:19** and~*you*[(ms)]~*did*~COME.NEAR[(v)] FOREFRONT SON~s Amon DO.NOT *you*[(ms)]~*will*~SMACK[(v)]~them[(m)] and~DO.NOT *you*[(ms)]~*will~self*~MEDDLE[(v)] in~them[(m)] GIVEN.THAT NOT *I~will*~GIVE[(v)] from~LAND SON~s Amon to~you[(ms)] HERITAGE GIVEN.THAT to~SON~s Lot *I~did*~GIVE[(v)]~her HERITAGE   **2:20** LAND Rapha~s *she~will~be*~THINK[(v)] MOREOVER SHE Rapha~s *they~did*~SETTLE[(v)] in~her to~FACE~s and~the~Amon~s *they*[(m)]~*will*~CALL.OUT[(v)] to~them[(m)] Zamzum~s   **2:21** PEOPLE GREAT and~ABUNDANT and~RAISE.UP[(v)]~*ing*[(ms)] like~the~Anaq~s and~*he~will*~make~DESTROY[(v)]~them[(m)] **YHWH** from~FACE~s~them[(m)] and~*they*[(m)]~*will*~POSSESS[(v)]~them[(m)] and~*they*[(m)]~*will*~SETTLE[(v)] UNDER~them[(m)]   **2:22** like~WHICH *he~did*~DO[(v)] to~SON~s Esaw the~SETTLE[(v)]~*ing*[(mp)] in~Se'iyr WHICH *he~did*~make~DESTROY[(v)] AT the~Hhor~of from~FACE~s~them[(m)] and~*they*[(m)]~*will*~POSSESS[(v)]~them[(m)] and~*they*[(m)]~*will*~SETTLE[(v)] UNDER~them[(m)] UNTIL the~DAY the~THIS   **2:23** and~the~Awi~s the~SETTLE[(v)]~*ing*[(mp)] in~Hhatsariym UNTIL Ghaza Kaphtor~s the~GO.OUT[(v)]~*ing*[(mp)] from~Kaphtor *they~did*~make~DESTROY[(v)]~them[(m)] and~*they*[(m)]~*will*~SETTLE[(v)] UNDER~them[(m)]   **2:24** *!*[(mp)]~RISE[(v)] *!*[(ms)]~JOURNEY[(v)] and~ *!*[(mp)]~CROSS.OVER[(v)] AT WADI Arnon *!*[(ms)]~SEE[(v)] *I~did*~GIVE[(v)] in~HAND~you[(ms)] AT Sihhon KING Hheshbon the~Emor~of and~AT LAND~him *!*[(ms)]~make~DRILL[(v)] *!*[(ms)]~POSSESS[(v)] and~ *!*[(ms)]~*self*~MEDDLE[(v)] in~him BATTLE   **2:25** the~DAY the~THIS *I~will*~make~DRILL[(v)] >~GIVE[(v)] AWE~you[(ms)] and~FEARFULNESS~you[(ms)] UPON FACE~s the~PEOPLE~s UNDER ALL the~SKY~s2 WHICH *they*[(m)]~*will*~HEAR[(v)]~must REPORT~you[(ms)] and~*they~did*~SHAKE[(v)] and~*they~did*~TWIST[(v)] from~FACE~s~you[(ms)]   **2:26** and~*I~will*~SEND[(v)] MESSENGER~s from~WILDERNESS Qedeymot TO Sihhon KING Hheshbon WORD~s COMPLETENESS to~>~SAY[(v)]   **2:27** *I~will*~CROSS.OVER[(v)]~& in~LAND~you[(ms)] in~the~ROAD in~the~ROAD *I~will*~WALK[(v)] NOT *I~will*~TURN.ASIDE[(v)] RIGHT.HAND and~LEFT.HAND   **2:28** FOODSTUFF in~SILVER *you*[(ms)]~*will*~make~EXCHANGE[(v)]~me and~*I~did*~EAT[(v)] and~WATER~s2 in~SILVER *you*[(ms)]~*will*~GIVE[(v)] to~me and~*I~did*~GULP[(v)] ONLY *I~will*~CROSS.OVER[(v)]~& in~FOOT~s~me   **2:29** like~WHICH *they~did*~DO[(v)] to~me SON~s Esaw the~SETTLE[(v)]~*ing*[(mp)] in~Se'iyr and~the~Mo'av~s the~SETTLE[(v)]~*ing*[(mp)] in~Ar UNTIL WHICH *I~will*~CROSS.OVER[(v)] AT the~Yarden TO the~LAND WHICH **YHWH** Elohiym~us GIVE[(v)]~*ing*[(ms)] to~us   **2:30** and~NOT *he~did*~CONSENT[(v)] Sihhon KING Hheshbon >~make~CROSS.OVER[(v)]~us in~him GIVEN.THAT *he~did*~make~BE.HARD[(v)] **YHWH** Elohiym~you[(ms)] AT WIND~him and~*he~did~much*~BE.STRONG[(v)] AT HEART~him to~THAT >~GIVE[(v)]~him in~HAND~you[(ms)] like~the~DAY the~THIS   **2:31** and~*he~will*~SAY[(v)] **YHWH** TO~me

The Book of Deuteronomy

!$^{(ms)}$~SEE$^{(V)}$ I~did~make~DRILL$^{(V)}$ >~GIVE$^{(V)}$ to~FACE~s~you$^{(ms)}$ AT Sihhon and~ AT LAND~him !$^{(ms)}$~make~DRILL$^{(V)}$!$^{(ms)}$~POSSESS$^{(V)}$ to~the~>~POSSESS$^{(V)}$ AT LAND~him **2:32** and~he~will~GO.OUT$^{(V)}$ Sihhon to~>~MEET$^{(V)}$~us HE and~ ALL PEOPLE~him to~the~BATTLE Yahats~unto **2:33** and~he~will~GIVE$^{(V)}$~ him **YHWH** Elohiym~us to~FACE~s~us and~we~will~make~HIT$^{(V)}$ AT~him and~AT SON~him and~AT ALL PEOPLE~him **2:34** and~we~will~TRAP$^{(V)}$ AT ALL CITY~s~him in~the~APPOINTED.TIME the~SHE and~we~will~make~ PERFORATE$^{(V)}$ AT ALL CITY MORTAL.MAN~s and~the~WOMAN~s and~the~ BABIES NOT we~did~make~REMAIN$^{(V)}$ SURVIVOR **2:35** ONLY the~BEAST we~did~PLUNDER$^{(V)}$ to~us and~SPOIL the~CITY~s WHICH we~did~ TRAP$^{(V)}$ **2:36** from~Aro'eyr WHICH UPON LIP WADI Arnon and~the~CITY WHICH in~WADI and~UNTIL the~Gil'ad NOT she~did~EXIST$^{(V)}$ METROPOLIS WHICH she~did~LIFT.HIGH$^{(V)}$ FROM~us AT the~ALL he~did~GIVE$^{(V)}$ **YHWH** Elohiym~us to~FACE~s~us **2:37** ONLY TO LAND SON~s Amon NOT you$^{(ms)}$~ did~COME.NEAR$^{(V)}$ ALL HAND WADI Yaboq and~CITY~s the~HILL and~ALL WHICH he~did~much~DIRECT$^{(V)}$ **YHWH** Elohiym~us

Chapter 3

3:1 and~we~will~TURN$^{(V)}$ and~we~will~GO.UP$^{(V)}$ ROAD the~Bashan and~he~ will~GO.OUT$^{(V)}$ Og KING the~Bashan to~>~MEET$^{(V)}$~us HE and~ALL PEOPLE~ him to~the~BATTLE Ed're'i **3:2** and~he~will~SAY$^{(V)}$ **YHWH** TO~me DO.NOT you$^{(ms)}$~will~FEAR$^{(V)}$ AT~him GIVEN.THAT in~HAND~you$^{(ms)}$ I~did~GIVE$^{(V)}$ AT~ him and~AT ALL PEOPLE~him and~AT LAND~him and~you$^{(ms)}$~did~DO$^{(V)}$ to~ him like~WHICH you$^{(ms)}$~did~DO$^{(V)}$ to~Sihhon KING the~Emor~of WHICH SETTLE$^{(V)}$~ing$^{(ms)}$ in~Hheshbon **3:3** and~he~will~GIVE$^{(V)}$ **YHWH** Elohiym~us in~HAND~us ALSO AT Og KING the~Bashan and~AT ALL PEOPLE~him and~ we~will~make~HIT$^{(V)}$~him UNTIL EXCEPT he~did~make~REMAIN$^{(V)}$ to~him SURVIVOR **3:4** and~we~will~TRAP$^{(V)}$ AT ALL CITY~s~him in~the~ APPOINTED.TIME the~SHE NOT she~did~EXIST$^{(V)}$ METROPOLIS WHICH NOT we~did~TAKE$^{(V)}$ from~AT~them$^{(m)}$ SIX~s CITY ALL REGION Argov KINGDOM Og in~Bashan **3:5** ALL THESE CITY~s FENCE.IN$^{(V)}$~ed$^{(fp)}$ RAMPART HIGH~her DOOR~s and~WOOD.BAR to~STRAND from~CITY~s the~VILLAGE >~make~ INCREASE$^{(V)}$ MANY **3:6** and~we~will~make~PERFORATE$^{(V)}$ AT~them$^{(m)}$ like~ WHICH we~did~DO$^{(V)}$ to~Sihhon KING Hheshbon >~make~PERFORATE$^{(V)}$ ALL CITY MORTAL.MAN~s the~WOMAN~s and~the~BABIES **3:7** and~ALL the~ BEAST and~SPOIL the~CITY~s we~did~PLUNDER$^{(V)}$ to~us **3:8** and~we~will~ TAKE$^{(V)}$ in~the~APPOINTED.TIME the~SHE AT the~LAND from~HAND TWO KING~s the~Emor~of WHICH in~OTHER.SIDE the~Yarden from~WADI Arnon UNTIL HILL Hhermon **3:9** Tsidon~s they$^{(m)}$~will~CALL.OUT$^{(V)}$ to~Hhermon Siryon and~the~Emor~of they$^{(m)}$~will~CALL.OUT$^{(V)}$ to~him Senir **3:10** ALL CITY~s the~PLAIN and~ALL the~Gil'ad and~ALL the~Bashan UNTIL Salkah and~Ed're'i CITY~s KINGDOM Og in~Bashan **3:11** GIVEN.THAT ONLY Og

KING the~Bashan *he~did~be*~REMAIN^(V) from~REMAINDER the~Rapha~s LOOK MATTRESS~him MATTRESS IRON ?~NOT SHE in~Ravah SON~s Amon NINE AMMAH~s LENGTH~her and~FOUR AMMAH~s WIDTH~her in~ AMMAH MAN   **3:12** and~AT the~LAND the~THIS *we~did*~POSSESS^(V) in~ the~APPOINTED.TIME the~SHE from~Aro'eyr WHICH UPON WADI Arnon and~HALF HILL the~Gil'ad and~CITY~s~him *I~did*~GIVE^(V) to~the~Re'uven~of and~to~the~Gad~of   **3:13** and~REMAINDER the~Gil'ad and~ALL the~ Bashan KINGDOM Og *I~did*~GIVE^(V) to~the~HALF STAFF the~Menasheh ALL REGION the~Argov to~ALL the~Bashan the~HE *he~will~be*~CALL.OUT^(V) LAND Rapha~s   **3:14** Ya'ir SON Menasheh *he~did*~TAKE^(V) AT ALL REGION Argov UNTIL BORDER the~Geshur~of and~the~Ma'akhah~of and~*he~will~* CALL.OUT^(V) AT~them^(m) UPON TITLE~him AT the~Bashan Hhawot Ya'ir UNTIL the~DAY the~THIS   **3:15** and~to~Makhir *I~did*~GIVE^(V) AT the~ Gil'ad   **3:16** and~to~the~Re'uven~of and~to~the~Gad~of *I~did*~GIVE^(V) FROM the~Gil'ad and~UNTIL WADI Arnon MIDST the~WADI and~BORDER and~UNTIL Yaboq the~WADI BORDER SON~s Amon   **3:17** and~the~DESERT and~the~Yarden and~BORDER from~Kineret and~UNTIL SEA the~DESERT SEA the~SALT UNDER RAVINE~s the~Pisgah SUNRISE~unto   **3:18** and~*I~ will~much~*DIRECT^(V) AT~you^(mp) in~the~APPOINTED.TIME the~SHE to~>~ SAY^(V) **YHWH** Elohiym~you^(mp) *he~did*~GIVE^(V) to~you^(mp) AT the~LAND the~ THIS to~>~POSSESS^(V)~her EXTRACT^(V)~*ed*^(mp) *you*^(mp)~*will*~CROSS.OVER^(V) to~ FACE~s BROTHER~s~you^(mp) SON~s Yisra'eyl ALL SON~s FORCE   **3:19** ONLY WOMAN~s~you^(mp) and~BABIES~you^(mp) and~LIVESTOCK~you^(mp) *I~did~* KNOW^(V) GIVEN.THAT LIVESTOCK ABUNDANT to~you^(mp) *they*^(m)~*will~* SETTLE^(V) in~CITY~s~you^(mp) WHICH *I~did*~GIVE^(V) to~you^(mp)   **3:20** UNTIL WHICH *he~will~make*~REST^(V) **YHWH** to~BROTHER~s~you^(mp) like~you^(mp) and~*they~did*~POSSESS^(V) ALSO THEY^(m) AT the~LAND WHICH **YHWH** Elohiym~you^(mp) GIVE^(V)~*ing*^(ms) to~them^(m) in~OTHER.SIDE the~Yarden and~ *you*^(mp)~*did*~TURN.BACK^(V) MAN to~HERITAGE~him WHICH *I~did*~GIVE^(V) to~ you^(mp)   **3:21** and~AT Yehoshu'a *I~did~much~*DIRECT^(V) in~the~ APPOINTED.TIME the~SHE to~>~SAY^(V) EYE~s2~you^(ms) the~SEE^(V)~*ing*^(fp) AT ALL WHICH *he~did*~DO^(V) **YHWH** Elohiym~you^(mp) to~TWO the~KING~s the~ THESE SO *he~will*~DO^(V) **YHWH** to~ALL the~KINGDOM~s WHICH YOU^(ms) CROSS.OVER^(V)~*ing*^(ms) THERE~unto   **3:22** NOT *you*^(mp)~*will*~FEAR^(V)~them^(m) GIVEN.THAT **YHWH** Elohiym~you^(mp) HE *be*~FIGHT^(V)~*ing*^(ms) to~ you^(mp)   **3:23** and~*I~will~make~self*~PROVIDE.PROTECTION^(V) TO **YHWH** in~ the~APPOINTED.TIME the~SHE to~>~SAY^(V)   **3:24** Adonai **YHWH** YOU^(ms) *you*^(ms)~*did~make~*DRILL^(V) to~>~*make~*SEE^(V) AT SERVANT~you^(ms) AT MAGNIFICENCE~you^(ms) and~AT HAND~you^(ms) the~FORCEFUL WHICH WHO MIGHTY.ONE in~the~SKY~s2 and~in~the~LAND WHICH *he~will*~DO^(V) like~ WORK~s~you^(ms) and~like~BRAVERY~s~you^(ms)   **3:25** *I~will*~CROSS.OVER^(V)~ & PLEASE and~*I~will*~SEE^(V) AT the~LAND the~FUNCTIONAL WHICH in~ OTHER.SIDE the~Yarden the~HILL the~FUNCTIONAL the~THIS and~the~ Levanon   **3:26** and~*he~will~self*~CROSS.OVER^(V) **YHWH** in~me to~THAT~ you^(mp) and~NOT *he~did*~HEAR^(V) TO~me and~*he~will*~SAY^(V) **YHWH** TO~me

ABUNDANT to~you⁽ᶠˢ⁾ DO.NOT *you⁽ᵐˢ⁾~will~make~*ADD⁽ⱽ⁾ *!⁽ᵐˢ⁾~much~*SPEAK⁽ⱽ⁾ TO~me YET.AGAIN in~the~WORD the~THIS **3:27** *!⁽ᵐˢ⁾~*GO.UP⁽ⱽ⁾ HEAD the~Pisgah and~ *!⁽ᵐˢ⁾~*LIFT.UP⁽ⱽ⁾ EYE~s2~you⁽ᵐˢ⁾ SEA~unto and~NORTH~unto and~SOUTHWARD~unto and~SUNRISE~unto and~ *!⁽ᵐˢ⁾~*SEE⁽ⱽ⁾ in~EYE~s2~you⁽ᵐˢ⁾ GIVEN.THAT NOT *you⁽ᵐˢ⁾~will~*CROSS.OVER⁽ⱽ⁾ AT the~Yarden the~THIS **3:28** and~ *!⁽ᵐˢ⁾~much~*DIRECT⁽ⱽ⁾ AT Yehoshu'a and~ *!⁽ᵐˢ⁾~much~*SEIZE⁽ⱽ⁾~him and~ *!⁽ᵐˢ⁾~much~*BE.STRONG⁽ⱽ⁾~him GIVEN.THAT HE *he~will~*CROSS.OVER⁽ⱽ⁾ to~FACE~s the~PEOPLE the~THIS and~HE *he~will~make~*INHERIT⁽ⱽ⁾ AT~them⁽ᵐ⁾ AT the~LAND WHICH *you⁽ᵐˢ⁾~will~*SEE⁽ⱽ⁾ **3:29** and~*we~will~*SETTLE⁽ⱽ⁾ in~the~STEEP.VALLEY FOREFRONT Beyt-Pe'or

Chapter 4

4:1 and~NOW Yisra'eyl *!⁽ᵐˢ⁾~*HEAR⁽ⱽ⁾ TO the~CUSTOM~s and~TO the~DECISION~s WHICH I *much~*LEARN⁽ⱽ⁾*~ing⁽ᵐˢ⁾* AT~you⁽ᵐᵖ⁾ to~>~DO⁽ⱽ⁾ to~THAT *you⁽ᵐᵖ⁾~will~*LIVE⁽ⱽ⁾ and~*you⁽ᵐᵖ⁾~did~*COME⁽ⱽ⁾ and~*you⁽ᵐᵖ⁾~did~*POSSESS⁽ⱽ⁾ AT the~LAND WHICH **YHWH** Elohiym FATHER~s~you⁽ᵐᵖ⁾ GIVE⁽ⱽ⁾*~ing⁽ᵐˢ⁾* to~you⁽ᵐᵖ⁾ **4:2** NOT *you⁽ᵐᵖ⁾~will~make~*ADD⁽ⱽ⁾ UPON the~WORD WHICH I *much~*DIRECT⁽ⱽ⁾*~ing⁽ᵐˢ⁾* AT~you⁽ᵐᵖ⁾ and~NOT *you⁽ᵐᵖ⁾~will~*TAKE.AWAY⁽ⱽ⁾ FROM~him to~>~SAFEGUARD⁽ⱽ⁾ AT DIRECTIVE~s **YHWH** Elohiym~you⁽ᵐᵖ⁾ WHICH I *much~*DIRECT⁽ⱽ⁾*~ing⁽ᵐˢ⁾* AT~you⁽ᵐᵖ⁾ **4:3** EYE~s2~you⁽ᵐᵖ⁾ the~SEE⁽ⱽ⁾*~ing⁽ᶠᵖ⁾* AT WHICH *he~did~*DO⁽ⱽ⁾ **YHWH** in~Ba'al-Pe'or GIVEN.THAT ALL the~MAN WHICH *he~did~*WALK⁽ⱽ⁾ AFTER Ba'al-Pe'or *he~did~make~*DESTROY⁽ⱽ⁾~him **YHWH** Elohiym~you⁽ᵐˢ⁾ from~INSIDE~you⁽ᵐˢ⁾ **4:4** and~YOU⁽ᵐᵖ⁾ the~FASTENER~s in~**YHWH** Elohiym~you⁽ᵐᵖ⁾ LIVING~s ALL~you⁽ᵐᵖ⁾ the~DAY **4:5** *!⁽ᵐˢ⁾~*SEE⁽ⱽ⁾ *I~did~much~*LEARN⁽ⱽ⁾ AT~you⁽ᵐᵖ⁾ CUSTOM~s and~DECISION~s like~WHICH *he~did~much~*DIRECT⁽ⱽ⁾*~*me **YHWH** Elohiym~me to~>~DO⁽ⱽ⁾ SO in~INSIDE the~LAND WHICH YOU⁽ᵐᵖ⁾ COME⁽ⱽ⁾*~ing⁽ᵐᵖ⁾* THERE~unto to~>~POSSESS⁽ⱽ⁾~her **4:6** and~*you⁽ᵐᵖ⁾~did~*SAFEGUARD⁽ⱽ⁾ and~*you⁽ᵐᵖ⁾~did~*DO⁽ⱽ⁾ GIVEN.THAT SHE SKILL~you⁽ᵐᵖ⁾ and~UNDERSTANDING~you⁽ᵐᵖ⁾ to~EYE~s2 the~PEOPLE~s WHICH *they⁽ᵐ⁾~will~*HEAR⁽ⱽ⁾~must AT ALL the~CUSTOM~s the~THESE and~*they~did~*SAY⁽ⱽ⁾ ONLY PEOPLE SKILLED.ONE and~*be~*UNDERSTAND⁽ⱽ⁾*~ing⁽ᵐˢ⁾* the~NATION the~GREAT the~THIS **4:7** GIVEN.THAT WHO NATION GREAT WHICH to~him Elohiym NEAR~s TO~him like~**YHWH** Elohiym~us in~ALL >~CALL.OUT⁽ⱽ⁾~us TO~him **4:8** and~WHO NATION GREAT WHICH to~him CUSTOM~s and~DECISION~s STEADFAST.ONE~s like~ALL the~TEACHING the~THIS WHICH I GIVE⁽ⱽ⁾*~ing⁽ᵐˢ⁾* to~FACE~s~you⁽ᵐᵖ⁾ the~DAY **4:9** ONLY *!⁽ᵐˢ⁾~be~*SAFEGUARD⁽ⱽ⁾ to~you⁽ᵐˢ⁾ and~>~SAFEGUARD⁽ⱽ⁾ SOUL~you⁽ᵐˢ⁾ MANY OTHERWISE *you⁽ᵐˢ⁾~will~*FORGET⁽ⱽ⁾ AT the~WORD~s WHICH *they~did~*SEE⁽ⱽ⁾ EYE~s2~you⁽ᵐˢ⁾ and~OTHERWISE *they⁽ᵐ⁾~will~*TURN.ASIDE⁽ⱽ⁾ from~HEART~you⁽ᵐˢ⁾ ALL DAY~s LIVING~s~you⁽ᵐˢ⁾ and~*you⁽ᵐᵖ⁾~did~make~*KNOW⁽ⱽ⁾~them⁽ᵐ⁾ to~SON~s you⁽ᵐˢ⁾ and~to~SON~s SON~s~you⁽ᵐˢ⁾ **4:10** DAY WHICH *you*⁽ᵐˢ⁾*~did~*STAND⁽ⱽ⁾ to~FACE~s **YHWH** Elohiym~you⁽ᵐˢ⁾ in~Hhorev in~>~SAY⁽ⱽ⁾ **YHWH** TO~me *!*⁽ᵐᵖ⁾*~make~*ASSEMBLE⁽ⱽ⁾ to~me AT the~PEOPLE and~*I~will~make~*HEAR⁽ⱽ⁾~them⁽ᵐ⁾ AT WORD~s~me WHICH *they*⁽ᵐ⁾*~will~*LEARN⁽ⱽ⁾~must to~>~FEAR⁽ⱽ⁾ AT~me ALL the~DAY~s WHICH THEY⁽ᵐ⁾ LIVING~s UPON the~GROUND and~AT SON~s~them⁽ᵐ⁾ *they*⁽ᵐ⁾*~will~much~*LEARN⁽ⱽ⁾~must **4:11** and~*you*⁽ᵐᵖ⁾*~will~*COME.NEAR⁽ⱽ⁾~must and~*you*⁽ᵐᵖ⁾*~will~*STAND⁽ⱽ⁾~must UNDER the~HILL and~the~HILL BURN⁽ⱽ⁾~*ing*⁽ᵐˢ⁾ in~the~FIRE UNTIL HEART the~SKY~s2 DARKNESS CLOUD and~THICK.DARKNESS **4:12** and~*he~will~much~*SPEAK⁽ⱽ⁾ **YHWH** TO~you⁽ᵐᵖ⁾ from~MIDST the~FIRE VOICE WORD~s YOU⁽ᵐᵖ⁾ HEAR⁽ⱽ⁾~*ing*⁽ᵐᵖ⁾ and~RESEMBLANCE WITHOUT~you⁽ᵐᵖ⁾ SEE⁽ⱽ⁾~*ing*⁽ᵐᵖ⁾ WITH.THE.EXCEPTION~of VOICE **4:13** and~*he~will~make~*BE.FACE.TO.FACE⁽ⱽ⁾ to~you⁽ᵐᵖ⁾ AT COVENANT~him WHICH *he~did~much~*DIRECT⁽ⱽ⁾ AT~you⁽ᵐᵖ⁾ to~>~DO⁽ⱽ⁾ TEN the~WORD~s and~*he~will~*WRITE⁽ⱽ⁾~them⁽ᵐ⁾ UPON TWO SLAB~s STONE~s **4:14** and~AT~me *he~did~much~*DIRECT⁽ⱽ⁾ **YHWH** in~the~APPOINTED.TIME the~SHE to~>~*much~*LEARN⁽ⱽ⁾ AT~you⁽ᵐᵖ⁾ CUSTOM~s and~DECISION~s to~>~DO⁽ⱽ⁾~you⁽ᵐᵖ⁾ AT~them⁽ᵐ⁾ in~the~LAND WHICH YOU⁽ᵐᵖ⁾ CROSS.OVER⁽ⱽ⁾~*ing*⁽ᵐᵖ⁾ THERE~unto to~>~POSSESS⁽ⱽ⁾~her **4:15** and~*you*⁽ᵐᵖ⁾*~will~be~*SAFEGUARD⁽ⱽ⁾ MANY to~SOUL~s~you⁽ᵐᵖ⁾ GIVEN.THAT NOT *you*⁽ᵐᵖ⁾*~did~*SEE⁽ⱽ⁾ ALL RESEMBLANCE in~DAY *he~did~much~*SPEAK⁽ⱽ⁾ **YHWH** TO~you⁽ᵐᵖ⁾ in~Hhorev from~MIDST the~FIRE **4:16** OTHERWISE *you*⁽ᵐᵖ⁾*~will~make~*DAMAGE⁽ⱽ⁾~must and~*you*⁽ᵐᵖ⁾*~did~*DO⁽ⱽ⁾ to~you⁽ᵐᵖ⁾ SCULPTURE RESEMBLANCE ALL FIGURE PATTERN MALE OR FEMALE **4:17** PATTERN ALL BEAST WHICH in~the~LAND PATTERN ALL BIRD WING WHICH *she~will~*FLY⁽ⱽ⁾ in~the~SKY~s2 **4:18** PATTERN ALL TREAD⁽ⱽ⁾~*ing*⁽ᵐˢ⁾ in~GROUND PATTERN ALL FISH WHICH in~the~WATER~s2 from~UNDER to~the~LAND **4:19** and~OTHERWISE *you*⁽ᵐˢ⁾*~will~*LIFT.UP⁽ⱽ⁾ EYE~s2~you⁽ᵐˢ⁾ the~SKY~s2~unto and~*you*⁽ᵐˢ⁾*~did~*SEE⁽ⱽ⁾ AT the~SUN and~AT the~MOON and~AT the~STAR~s ALL ARMY the~SKY~s2 and~*you*⁽ᵐˢ⁾*~did~be~*DRIVE.OUT⁽ⱽ⁾ and~*you*⁽ᵐˢ⁾*~did~self~*BEND.DOWN⁽ⱽ⁾ to~them⁽ᵐ⁾ and~*you*⁽ᵐˢ⁾*~did~*SERVE⁽ⱽ⁾~them⁽ᵐ⁾ WHICH *he~did~*DISTRIBUTE⁽ⱽ⁾ **YHWH** Elohiym~you⁽ᵐˢ⁾ AT~them⁽ᵐ⁾ to~ALL the~PEOPLE~s UNDER ALL the~SKY~s2 **4:20** and~AT~you⁽ᵐᵖ⁾ *he~did~*TAKE⁽ⱽ⁾ **YHWH** and~*he~will~make~*GO.OUT⁽ⱽ⁾ AT~you⁽ᵐᵖ⁾ from~CRUCIBLE the~IRON from~Mits'rayim to~>~EXIST⁽ⱽ⁾ to~him to~PEOPLE INHERITANCE like~the~DAY the~THIS **4:21** and~**YHWH** *he~did~self~*SNORT⁽ⱽ⁾ in~me UPON WORD~s~you⁽ᵐᵖ⁾ and~*he~will~be~*SWEAR⁽ⱽ⁾ to~EXCEPT >~CROSS.OVER⁽ⱽ⁾~me AT the~Yarden and~to~EXCEPT >~COME⁽ⱽ⁾ TO the~LAND the~FUNCTIONAL WHICH **YHWH** Elohiym~you⁽ᵐˢ⁾ GIVE⁽ⱽ⁾~*ing*⁽ᵐˢ⁾ to~you⁽ᵐˢ⁾ INHERITANCE **4:22** GIVEN.THAT I DIE⁽ⱽ⁾~*ing*⁽ᵐˢ⁾ in~the~LAND the~THIS WITHOUT~me CROSS.OVER⁽ⱽ⁾~*ing*⁽ᵐˢ⁾ AT the~Yarden and~YOU⁽ᵐᵖ⁾ CROSS.OVER⁽ⱽ⁾~*ing*⁽ᵐᵖ⁾ and~*you*⁽ᵐᵖ⁾*~did~*POSSESS⁽ⱽ⁾ AT the~LAND the~FUNCTIONAL the~THIS **4:23** *!*⁽ᵐᵖ⁾*~be~*SAFEGUARD⁽ⱽ⁾ to~you⁽ᵐᵖ⁾ OTHERWISE *you*⁽ᵐᵖ⁾*~will~*FORGET⁽ⱽ⁾ AT COVENANT **YHWH** Elohiym~you⁽ᵐᵖ⁾ WHICH *he~did~*CUT⁽ⱽ⁾ WITH~you⁽ᵐᵖ⁾ and~*you*⁽ᵐᵖ⁾*~did~*DO⁽ⱽ⁾ to~you⁽ᵐᵖ⁾ SCULPTURE RESEMBLANCE ALL WHICH *he~did~much~*DIRECT⁽ⱽ⁾~

you*(ms)* **YHWH** Elohiym~you*(ms)* **4:24** GIVEN.THAT **YHWH** Elohiym~you*(ms)* FIRE EAT*(V)*~ing*(fs)* HE MIGHTY.ONE ZEALOUS **4:25** GIVEN.THAT *you(ms)~will~ make*~BRING.FORTH*(V)* SON~s and~SON~s SON~s and~*you(mp)~did~be*~ SLEEP*(V)* in~the~LAND and~*you(mp)~did~make*~DAMAGE*(V)* and~*you(mp)~did*~ DO*(V)* SCULPTURE RESEMBLANCE ALL and~*you(mp)~did*~DO*(V)* the~ DYSFUNCTIONAL in~EYE~s2 **YHWH** Elohiym~you*(ms)* to~>~*make*~ BE.ANGRY*(V)*~him **4:26** *I~did~make*~WRAP.AROUND*(V)* in~you*(mp)* the~DAY AT the~SKY~s2 and~AT the~LAND GIVEN.THAT >~PERISH*(V)* *you(ms)~will*~ PERISH*(V)*~must QUICKLY from~UPON the~LAND WHICH YOU*(mp)* CROSS.OVER*(V)*~ing*(mp)* AT the~Yarden THERE~unto to~>~POSSESS*(V)*~her NOT *you(mp)~will~make*~PROLONG*(V)*~must DAY~s UPON~her GIVEN.THAT >~*be*~DESTROY*(V)* *you(mp)~will~be*~DESTROY*(V)*~must **4:27** and~*he~did~ make*~SCATTER.ABROAD*(V)* **YHWH** AT~you*(mp)* in~the~PEOPLE~s and~ *you(mp)~did~be*~REMAIN*(V)* MORTAL.MAN~s NUMBER in~the~NATION~s WHICH *he~will~much*~DRIVE*(V)* **YHWH** AT~you*(mp)* THERE~unto **4:28** and~ *you(mp)~will*~SERVE*(V)* THERE Elohiym WORK HAND~s2 HUMAN TREE and~ STONE WHICH NOT *they(m)~will*~SEE*(V)*~must and~NOT *they(m)~will*~HEAR*(V)*~ must and~NOT *he~will*~EAT*(V)*~must and~NOT *he~will~make*~SMELL*(V)*~ must **4:29** and~*you(mp)~did~much*~SEARCH.OUT*(V)* from~THERE AT **YHWH** Elohiym~you*(ms)* and~*you(ms)~did*~FIND*(V)* GIVEN.THAT *you(ms)~will*~SEEK*(V)*~ him in~ALL HEART~you*(ms)* and~in~ALL SOUL~you*(ms)* **4:30** in~the~NARROW to~you*(ms)* and~*they~did*~FIND*(V)*~you*(ms)* ALL the~WORD~s the~THESE in~ END the~DAY~s and~*you(ms)~did*~TURN.BACK*(V)* UNTIL **YHWH** Elohiym~ you*(ms)* and~*you(ms)~did*~HEAR*(V)* in~VOICE~him **4:31** GIVEN.THAT MIGHTY.ONE COMPASSIONATE **YHWH** Elohiym~you*(ms)* NOT *he~will~make*~ SINK.DOWN*(V)*~you*(ms)* and~NOT *he~will~make*~DAMAGE*(V)*~you*(ms)* and~ NOT *he~will*~FORGET*(V)* AT COVENANT FATHER~s~you*(ms)* WHICH *he~did~ be*~SWEAR*(V)* to~them*(m)* **4:32** GIVEN.THAT *!(ms)*~INQUIRE*(V)* PLEASE to~ DAY~s FIRST~s WHICH *they~did*~EXIST*(V)* to~FACE~s~you*(ms)* to~FROM the~ DAY WHICH *he~did*~SHAPE*(V)* Elohiym HUMAN UPON the~LAND and~to~ EXTREMITY the~SKY~s2 and~UNTIL EXTREMITY the~SKY~s2 ?~*he~did~be*~ EXIST*(V)* like~the~WORD the~GREAT the~THIS OR ?~*he~did~be*~HEAR*(V)* like~ THAT.ONE~him **4:33** ?~*he~did*~HEAR*(V)* PEOPLE VOICE Elohiym >~*much*~ SPEAK*(V)*~ing*(ms)* from~MIDST the~FIRE like~WHICH *you(ms)~did*~HEAR*(V)* YOU*(ms)* and~*he~will*~LIVE*(V)* **4:34** OR ?~*he~did~much*~TEST*(V)* Elohiym to~>~ COME*(V)* to~>~TAKE*(V)* to~him NATION from~INSIDE NATION in~TRIAL~s in~ SIGN~s and~in~WONDER~s and~in~BATTLE and~in~HAND FORCEFUL and~ in~ARM EXTEND*(V)*~ed*(fs)* and~in~FEARING~s GREAT~s like~ALL WHICH *he~ did*~DO*(V)* to~you*(mp)* **YHWH** Elohiym~you*(mp)* in~Mits'rayim to~EYE~s2~ you*(ms)* **4:35** YOU*(ms)* *you(ms)~did~be~make*~SEE*(V)* to~>~KNOW*(V)* GIVEN.THAT **YHWH** HE the~Elohiym WITHOUT YET.AGAIN from~to~ STRAND~him **4:36** FROM the~SKY~s2 *he~did~make*~HEAR*(V)*~you*(ms)* AT VOICE~him to~>~*much*~CORRECT*(V)*~you*(ms)* and~UPON the~LAND *he~did~ make*~SEE*(V)*~you*(ms)* AT FIRE~him the~GREAT and~WORD~s~him *you(ms)~ did*~HEAR*(V)* from~MIDST the~FIRE **4:37** and~UNDER GIVEN.THAT *he~did*~

LOVE$^{(v)}$ AT FATHER~s~you$^{(ms)}$ and~*he~will*~CHOOSE$^{(v)}$ in~SEED~him AFTER~ him and~*he~will~make*~GO.OUT$^{(v)}$~you$^{(ms)}$ in~FACE~s~him in~STRENGTH~ him the~GREAT from~Mits'rayim   **4:38** to~>~*make*~POSSESS$^{(v)}$ NATION~s GREAT~s and~NUMEROUS~s FROM~you$^{(ms)}$ from~FACE~s~you$^{(ms)}$ to~>~ *make*~COME$^{(v)}$~you$^{(ms)}$ to~>~GIVE$^{(v)}$ to~you$^{(ms)}$ AT LAND~them$^{(m)}$ INHERITANCE like~the~DAY the~THIS   **4:39** and~*you$^{(ms)}$~did*~KNOW$^{(v)}$ the~ DAY and~*you$^{(ms)}$~did~make*~TURN.BACK$^{(v)}$ TO HEART~you$^{(ms)}$ GIVEN.THAT YHWH HE the~Elohiym in~the~SKY~s2 from~UPWARD and~UPON the~ LAND from~UNDER WITHOUT YET.AGAIN   **4:40** and~*you$^{(ms)}$~did*~ SAFEGUARD$^{(v)}$ AT CUSTOM~s~him and~AT DIRECTIVE~s~him WHICH I much~DIRECT$^{(v)}$~*ing$^{(ms)}$*~you$^{(ms)}$ the~DAY WHICH *he~will*~DO.WELL$^{(v)}$ to~ you$^{(ms)}$ and~to~SON~s~you$^{(ms)}$ AFTER~you$^{(ms)}$ and~to~THAT *you$^{(ms)}$~will*~ *make*~PROLONG$^{(v)}$ DAY~s UPON the~GROUND WHICH **YHWH** Elohiym~ you$^{(ms)}$ GIVE$^{(v)}$~*ing$^{(ms)}$* to~you$^{(ms)}$ ALL the~DAY~s   **4:41** AT.THAT.TIME *he~ will~make*~SEPARATE$^{(v)}$ Mosheh THREE CITY~s in~OTHER.SIDE the~Yarden SUNRISE~unto SUN   **4:42** >~FLEE$^{(v)}$ THERE~unto MURDER$^{(v)}$~*ing$^{(ms)}$* WHICH *he~will*~MURDER$^{(v)}$ AT COMPANION~him in~UNAWARE DISCERNMENT and~HE NOT HATE$^{(v)}$~*ing$^{(ms)}$* to~him from~YESTERDAY THREE.DAYS.AGO and~*he~did*~FLEE$^{(v)}$ TO UNIT FROM the~CITY~s the~THESE and~*he~will*~ LIVE$^{(v)}$ **4:43** AT Betser in~the~WILDERNESS in~LAND the~PLAIN to~the~ Re'uven~of and~AT Ramot in~Gil'ad to~the~Gad~of and~AT Golan in~ Bashan to~the~Menasheh~of   **4:44** and~THIS the~TEACHING WHICH *he~ did*~PLACE$^{(v)}$ Mosheh to~FACE~s SON~s Yisra'eyl   **4:45** THESE the~ WITNESS~s and~the~CUSTOM~s and~the~DECISION~s WHICH *he~did*~ much~SPEAK$^{(v)}$ Mosheh TO SON~s Yisra'eyl in~>~GO.OUT$^{(v)}$~them$^{(m)}$ from~ Mits'rayim   **4:46** in~OTHER.SIDE the~Yarden in~the~STEEP.VALLEY FOREFRONT Beyt-Pe'or in~LAND Sihhon KING the~Emor~of WHICH SETTLE$^{(v)}$~*ing$^{(ms)}$* in~Hheshbon WHICH *he~did~make*~HIT$^{(v)}$ Mosheh and~ SON~s Yisra'eyl in~>~GO.OUT$^{(v)}$~them$^{(m)}$ from~Mits'rayim   **4:47** and~ *they$^{(m)}$~will*~POSSESS$^{(v)}$ AT LAND~him and~AT LAND Og KING the~Bashan TWO KING~s the~Emor~of WHICH in~OTHER.SIDE the~Yarden SUNRISE SUN **4:48** from~Aro'eyr WHICH UPON LIP WADI Arnon and~UNTIL HILL Si'on HE Hhermon   **4:49** and~ALL the~DESERT OTHER.SIDE the~Yarden SUNRISE~ unto and~UNTIL SEA the~DESERT UNDER RAVINE~s the~Pisgah

Chapter 5

5:1 and~*he~will*~CALL.OUT$^{(v)}$ Mosheh TO ALL Yisra'eyl and~*he~will*~SAY$^{(v)}$ TO~them$^{(m)}$!$^{(ms)}$~HEAR$^{(v)}$ Yisra'eyl AT the~CUSTOM~s and~AT the~ DECISION~s WHICH I SPEAK$^{(v)}$~*ing$^{(ms)}$* in~EAR~s2~you$^{(mp)}$ the~DAY and~ *you$^{(mp)}$~did*~LEARN$^{(v)}$ AT~them$^{(m)}$ and~*you$^{(mp)}$~did*~SAFEGUARD$^{(v)}$ to~>~ DO$^{(v)}$~them$^{(m)}$ **5:2 YHWH** Elohiym~us *he~did*~CUT$^{(v)}$ WITH~us COVENANT in~Hhorev   **5:3** NOT AT FATHER~s~us *he~did*~CUT$^{(v)}$ **YHWH** AT the~

The Book of Deuteronomy

COVENANT the~THIS GIVEN.THAT AT~us WE THESE HERE the~DAY ALL~us LIVING~s **5:4** FACE~s in~FACE~s *he~did~much*~SPEAK$^{(V)}$ **YHWH** WITH~you$^{(mp)}$ in~the~HILL from~MIDST the~FIRE **5:5** I STAND$^{(V)}$~*ing*$^{(ms)}$ BETWEEN **YHWH** and~BETWEEN~you$^{(mp)}$ in~the~APPOINTED.TIME the~SHE to~>~*make*~BE.FACE.TO.FACE$^{(V)}$ to~you$^{(mp)}$ AT WORD **YHWH** GIVEN.THAT *you*$^{(mp)}$~*did*~FEAR$^{(V)}$ from~FACE~s the~FIRE and~NOT *you*$^{(mp)}$~*did*~*make*~GO.UP$^{(V)}$ in~the~HILL to~>~SAY$^{(V)}$ **5:6** I **YHWH** Elohiym~you$^{(ms)}$ WHICH *I*~*did*~*make*~GO.OUT$^{(V)}$~you$^{(ms)}$ from~LAND Mits'rayim from~HOUSE SERVANT~s **5:7** NOT *he*~*will*~EXIST$^{(V)}$ to~you$^{(ms)}$ Elohiym OTHER~s UPON FACE~s~me **5:8** NOT *you*$^{(ms)}$~*will*~DO$^{(V)}$ to~you$^{(ms)}$ SCULPTURE ALL RESEMBLANCE WHICH in~the~SKY~s2 from~UPWARD and~WHICH in~the~LAND from~UNDER and~WHICH in~the~WATER~s2 from~UNDER to~the~LAND **5:9** NOT *you*$^{(ms)}$~*will*~*self*~BEND.DOWN$^{(V)}$ to~them$^{(m)}$ and~NOT *you*$^{(ms)}$~*will*~*be*~*make*~SERVE$^{(V)}$~them$^{(m)}$ GIVEN.THAT I **YHWH** Elohiym~you$^{(ms)}$ MIGHTY.ONE ZEALOUS REGISTER$^{(V)}$~*ing*$^{(ms)}$ TWISTEDNESS FATHER~s UPON SON~s and~UPON THIRD.GENERATION~s and~UPON FOURTH.GENERATION~s to~HATE$^{(V)}$~*ing*$^{(mp)}$~me **5:10** and~DO$^{(V)}$~*ing*$^{(ms)}$ KINDNESS to~the~THOUSAND~s to~LOVE$^{(V)}$~*ing*$^{(mp)}$~me and~to~SAFEGUARD$^{(V)}$~*ing*$^{(mp)}$ DIRECTIVE~s~him **5:11** NOT *you*$^{(ms)}$~*will*~LIFT.UP$^{(V)}$ AT TITLE **YHWH** Elohiym~you$^{(ms)}$ to~the~FALSENESS GIVEN.THAT NOT *he*~*will*~*much*~ACQUIT$^{(V)}$ **YHWH** AT WHICH *he*~*will*~LIFT.UP$^{(V)}$ AT TITLE~him to~the~FALSENESS **5:12** >~SAFEGUARD$^{(V)}$ AT DAY the~CEASING to~>~*much*~SET.APART$^{(V)}$~him like~WHICH *he*~*did*~*much*~DIRECT$^{(V)}$~you$^{(ms)}$ **YHWH** Elohiym~you$^{(ms)}$ **5:13** SIX DAY~s *you*$^{(ms)}$~*will*~SERVE$^{(V)}$ and~*you*$^{(ms)}$~*did*~DO$^{(V)}$ ALL BUSINESS~you$^{(ms)}$ **5:14** and~DAY the~SEVENTH CEASING to~**YHWH** Elohiym~you$^{(ms)}$ NOT *you*$^{(ms)}$~*will*~DO$^{(V)}$ ALL BUSINESS YOU$^{(ms)}$ and~SON~you$^{(ms)}$ and~DAUGHTER~you$^{(ms)}$ and~SERVANT~you$^{(ms)}$ and~BONDWOMAN~you$^{(ms)}$ and~OX~you$^{(ms)}$ and~DONKEY~you$^{(ms)}$ and~ALL BEAST~you$^{(ms)}$ and~IMMIGRANT~you$^{(ms)}$ WHICH in~GATE~s~you$^{(ms)}$ to~THAT *he*~*will*~REST$^{(V)}$ SERVANT~you$^{(ms)}$ and~BONDWOMAN~you$^{(ms)}$ like~THAT.ONE~you$^{(ms)}$ **5:15** and~*you*$^{(ms)}$~*did*~REMEMBER$^{(V)}$ GIVEN.THAT SERVANT *you*$^{(ms)}$~*did*~EXIST$^{(V)}$ in~LAND Mits'rayim and~*he*~*will*~*make*~GO.OUT$^{(V)}$~you$^{(ms)}$ **YHWH** Elohiym~you$^{(ms)}$ from~THERE in~HAND FORCEFUL and~in~ARM EXTEND$^{(V)}$~*ed*$^{(fs)}$ UPON SO *he*~*did*~*much*~DIRECT$^{(V)}$~you$^{(ms)}$ **YHWH** Elohiym~you$^{(ms)}$ to~>~DO$^{(V)}$ AT DAY the~CEASING **5:16** !$^{(ms)}$~*much*~BE.HEAVY$^{(V)}$ AT FATHER~you$^{(ms)}$ and~AT MOTHER~you$^{(ms)}$ like~WHICH *he*~*did*~*much*~DIRECT$^{(V)}$~you$^{(ms)}$ **YHWH** Elohiym~you$^{(ms)}$ to~THAT *they*$^{(m)}$~*will*~*make*~PROLONG$^{(V)}$~must DAY~s~you$^{(ms)}$ and~to~THAT *he*~*will*~DO.WELL$^{(V)}$ to~you$^{(fs)}$ UPON the~GROUND WHICH **YHWH** Elohiym~you$^{(ms)}$ GIVE$^{(V)}$~*ing*$^{(ms)}$ to~you$^{(fs)}$ **5:17** NOT *you*$^{(ms)}$~*will*~MURDER$^{(V)}$ **5:18** and~NOT *you*$^{(ms)}$~*will*~COMMIT.ADULTERY$^{(V)}$ **5:19** and~NOT *you*$^{(ms)}$~*will*~STEAL$^{(V)}$ **5:20** and~NOT *you*$^{(ms)}$~*will*~AFFLICT$^{(V)}$ in~COMPANION~you$^{(ms)}$ WITNESS FALSENESS **5:21** and~NOT *you*$^{(ms)}$~*will*~CRAVE$^{(V)}$ WOMAN COMPANION~you$^{(ms)}$ and~NOT *you*$^{(ms)}$~*will*~*self*~YEARN$^{(V)}$ HOUSE COMPANION~you$^{(ms)}$ FIELD~him and~SERVANT~him and~BONDWOMAN~him OX~him and~

DONKEY~him and~ALL WHICH to~COMPANION~you(ms) **5:22** AT the~ WORD~s the~THESE *he~did~much~*SPEAK(V) **YHWH** TO ALL ASSEMBLY~ you(mp) in~the~HILL from~MIDST the~FIRE the~CLOUD and~the~ THICK.DARKNESS VOICE GREAT and~NOT *he~did~*ADD(V) and~*he~will~* WRITE(V)~them(m) UPON TWO SLAB~s STONE~s and~*he~will~*GIVE(V)~them(m) TO~me **5:23** and~*he~will~*EXIST(V) like~>~HEAR(V)~you(mp) AT the~VOICE from~MIDST the~DARKNESS and~the~HILL BURN(V)~*ing*(ms) in~the~FIRE and~*you*(mp)~*will~*COME.NEAR(V)~must TO~me ALL HEAD~s STAFF~s~you(mp) and~BEARD~s~you(mp) **5:24** and~*you*(mp)~*will~*SAY(V) THOUGH *he~did~ make~*SEE(V)~us **YHWH** Elohiym~us AT ARMAMENT~him and~AT MAGNIFICENCE~him and~AT VOICE~him *we~did~*HEAR(V) from~MIDST the~ FIRE the~DAY the~THIS *we~did~*SEE(V) GIVEN.THAT *he~will~much~*SPEAK(V) Elohiym AT the~HUMAN and~*he~will~*LIVE(V) **5:25** and~NOW to~WHAT *we~will~*DIE(V) GIVEN.THAT *she~will~*EAT(V)~us the~FIRE the~GREAT the~ THIS IF ADD(V)~*ing*(mp) WE to~>~HEAR(V) AT VOICE **YHWH** Elohiym~us YET.AGAIN and~*we~did~*DIE(V) **5:26** GIVEN.THAT WHO ALL FLESH WHICH *he~did~*HEAR(V) VOICE Elohiym LIVING~s >~*much~*SPEAK(V)~*ing*(ms) from~ MIDST the~FIRE like~THAT.ONE~us and~*he~will~*LIVE(V) **5:27** !(ms)~ COME.NEAR(V) YOU(ms) and~!(ms)~HEAR(V) AT ALL WHICH *he~will~*SAY(V) **YHWH** Elohiym~us and~YOU(fs) *you*(ms)~*will~much~*SPEAK(V) TO~us AT ALL WHICH *he~will~much~*SPEAK(V) **YHWH** Elohiym~us TO~you(ms) and~*we~did~* HEAR(V) and~*we~did~*DO(V) **5:28** and~*he~will~*HEAR(V) **YHWH** AT VOICE WORD~s~you(mp) in~>~*much~*SPEAK(V)~you(mp) TO~me and~*he~will~*SAY(V) **YHWH** TO~me *I~did~*HEAR(V) AT VOICE WORD~s the~PEOPLE the~THIS WHICH *they~did~much~*SPEAK(V) TO~you(ms) *they~did~make~*DO.WELL(V) ALL WHICH *they~did~much~*SPEAK(V) **5:29** WHO *he~will~*GIVE(V) and~*he~did~* EXIST(V) HEART~them(m) THIS to~them(m) to~>~FEAR(V) AT~me and~to~>~ SAFEGUARD(V) AT ALL DIRECTIVE~s~me ALL the~DAY~s to~THAT *he~will~* DO.WELL(V) to~them(m) and~to~SON~s~them(m) to~DISTANT **5:30** !(ms)~ WALK(V) !(ms)~SAY(V) to~them(m) !(mp)~TURN.BACK(V) to~you(mp) to~TENT~s~ you(mp) **5:31** and~YOU(ms) HERE >~STAND(V) BY~me and~*I~will~much~* SPEAK(V) TO~you(ms) AT ALL the~DIRECTIVE and~the~CUSTOM~s and~the~ DECISION~s WHICH *you*(ms)~*will~much~*LEARN(V)~them(m) and~*they~did~* DO(V) in~the~LAND WHICH I GIVE(V)~*ing*(ms) to~them(m) to~>~POSSESS(V)~ her **5:32** and~*you*(mp)~*did~*SAFEGUARD(V) to~>~DO(V) like~WHICH *he~did~ much~*DIRECT(V) **YHWH** Elohiym~you(mp) AT~you(mp) NOT *you*(mp)~*will~* TURN.ASIDE(V) RIGHT.HAND and~LEFT.HAND **5:33** in~ALL the~ROAD WHICH *he~did~much~*DIRECT(V) **YHWH** Elohiym~you(mp) AT~you(mp) *you*(mp)~*will~* WALK(V) to~THAT *you*(mp)~*will~*LIVE(V)~must and~*he~did~*DO.WELL(V) to~ you(mp) and~*you*(mp)~*did~make~*PROLONG(V) DAY~s in~the~LAND WHICH *you*(mp)~*will~*POSSESS(V)

Chapter 6

6:1 and~THIS the~DIRECTIVE the~CUSTOM~s and~the~DECISION~s WHICH *he~did~much*~DIRECT^(V) **YHWH** Elohiym~you^(mp) to~>~*much*~LEARN^(V) AT~ you^(mp) to~>~*DO*^(V) in~the~LAND WHICH YOU^(mp) CROSS.OVER^(V)~*ing*^(mp) THERE~unto to~>~POSSESS^(V)~her **6:2** to~THAT *you*^(ms)~*will*~FEAR^(V) AT **YHWH** Elohiym~you^(ms) to~>~SAFEGUARD^(V) AT ALL CUSTOM~s~him and~ DIRECTIVE~s~him WHICH I *much*~DIRECT^(V)~*ing*^(ms)~you^(ms) YOU^(ms) and~ SON~you^(ms) and~SON SON~you^(ms) ALL DAY~s LIVING~s~you^(ms) and~to~ THAT *they*^(m)~*will*~*make*~PROLONG^(V)~must DAY~s~you^(ms) **6:3** and~*you*^(ms)~ *did*~HEAR^(V) Yisra'eyl and~*you*^(ms)~*did*~SAFEGUARD^(V) to~>~DO^(V) WHICH *he*~ *will*~DO.WELL^(V) to~you^(ms) and~WHICH *you*^(mp)~*will*~INCREASE^(V)~must MANY like~WHICH *he~did~much*~SPEAK^(V) **YHWH** Elohiym FATHER~s~you^(ms) to~you^(fs) LAND ISSUE^(V)~*ing*^(fs) FAT and~HONEY **6:4** *!*^(ms)~HEAR^(V) Yisra'eyl **YHWH** Elohiym~us **YHWH** UNIT **6:5** and~*you*^(ms)~*did*~LOVE^(V) AT **YHWH** Elohiym~you^(ms) in~ALL HEART~you^(ms) and~in~ALL SOUL~you^(ms) and~in~ALL MANY~you^(ms) **6:6** and~*they~did*~EXIST^(V) the~WORD~s the~THESE WHICH I *much*~DIRECT^(V)~*ing*^(ms)~you^(ms) the~DAY UPON HEART~you^(ms) **6:7** and~ *you*^(ms)~*did~much*~WHET^(V)~them^(m) to~SON~s~you^(ms) and~*you*^(ms)~*did*~ *much*~SPEAK^(V) in~them^(m) in~>~SETTLE^(V)~you^(ms) in~HOUSE~you^(ms) and~ in~>~WALK^(V)~you^(ms) in~the~ROAD and~in~>~LIE.DOWN^(V)~you^(ms) and~in~ >~RISE^(V)~you^(ms) **6:8** and~*you*^(ms)~*did*~TIE^(V)~them^(m) to~SIGN UPON HAND~ you^(ms) and~*they~did*~EXIST^(V) to~MARKER~s BETWEEN EYE~s2~ you^(ms) **6:9** and~*you*^(ms)~*did*~WRITE^(V)~them^(m) UPON DOORPOST~s HOUSE~ you^(ms) and~in~GATE~s~you^(ms) **6:10** and~*he~did*~EXIST^(V) GIVEN.THAT *he~ will~make*~COME^(V)~you^(ms) **YHWH** Elohiym~you^(ms) TO the~LAND WHICH *he~did~be*~SWEAR^(V) to~FATHER~s~you^(ms) to~Avraham to~Yits'hhaq and~ to~Ya'aqov to~>~GIVE^(V) to~you^(fs) CITY~s GREAT~s and~FUNCTIONAL~s WHICH NOT *you*^(ms)~*did*~BUILD^(V) **6:11** and~HOUSE~s FULL~s ALL FUNCTIONAL WHICH NOT *you*^(ms)~*did~much*~FILL^(V) and~CISTERN~s HEW^(V)~ *ed*^(mp) WHICH NOT *you*^(ms)~*did*~HEW^(V) VINEYARD~s and~OLIVE~s WHICH NOT *you*^(ms)~*did*~PLANT^(V) and~*you*^(ms)~*did*~EAT^(V) and~*you*^(ms)~*did*~ BE.SATISFIED^(V) **6:12** *!*^(ms)~*be*~SAFEGUARD^(V) to~you^(ms) OTHERWISE *you*^(ms)~ *will*~FORGET^(V) AT **YHWH** WHICH *he~did~make*~GO.OUT^(V)~you^(ms) from~ LAND Mits'rayim from~HOUSE SERVANT~s **6:13** AT **YHWH** Elohiym~you^(ms) *you*^(ms)~*will*~FEAR^(V) and~AT~him *you*^(ms)~*will*~SERVE^(V) and~in~TITLE~him *you*^(ms)~*will~be*~SWEAR^(V) **6:14** NOT *you*^(mp)~*will*~WALK^(V)~must AFTER Elohiym OTHER~s from~Elohiym the~PEOPLE~s WHICH ALL.AROUND~s~ you^(mp) **6:15** GIVEN.THAT MIGHTY.ONE ZEALOUS **YHWH** Elohiym~you^(ms) in~ INSIDE~you^(ms) OTHERWISE *he~will*~FLARE.UP^(V) NOSE **YHWH** Elohiym~ you^(ms) in~you^(fs) and~*he~did~make*~DESTROY^(V)~you^(ms) from~UPON FACE~s the~GROUND **6:16** NOT *you*^(mp)~*will*~TEST^(V) AT **YHWH** Elohiym~you^(mp) like~WHICH *you*^(mp)~*did~much*~TEST^(V) in~Mas'sah **6:17** >~SAFEGUARD^(V) *you*^(mp)~*will*~SAFEGUARD^(V)~must AT DIRECTIVE~s **YHWH** Elohiym~you^(mp)

and~WITNESS~s~him and~CUSTOM~s~him WHICH *he~did~much~* DIRECT^(V)~you^(ms)   **6:18** and~*you^(ms)~did~*DO^(V) the~STRAIGHT and~the~ FUNCTIONAL in~EYE~s2 **YHWH** to~THAT *he~will~*DO.WELL^(V) to~you^(fs) and~ *you^(ms)~did~*COME^(V) and~*you^(ms)~did~*POSSESS^(V) AT the~LAND the~ FUNCTIONAL WHICH *he~did~be~*SWEAR^(V) **YHWH** to~FATHER~s~ you^(ms)   **6:19** to~>~PUSH.AWAY^(V) AT ALL ATTACK^(V)~*ing^(mp)*~s~you^(ms) from~ FACE~s~you^(ms) like~WHICH *he~did~much~*SPEAK^(V)
YHWH   **6:20** GIVEN.THAT *he~will~*INQUIRE^(V)~you^(ms) SON~you^(ms) TOMORROW to~>~SAY^(V) WHAT the~WITNESS~s and~the~CUSTOM~s and~ the~DECISION~s WHICH *he~did~much~*DIRECT^(V) **YHWH** Elohiym~us AT~ you^(mp)   **6:21** and~*you^(ms)~did~*SAY^(V) to~SON~you^(ms) SERVANT~s *we~did~* EXIST^(V) to~Paroh in~Mits'rayim and~*he~did~make~*GO.OUT^(V)~us **YHWH** from~Mits'rayim in~HAND FORCEFUL   **6:22** and~*he~will~*GIVE^(V) **YHWH** SIGN~s and~WONDER~s GREAT~s and~DYSFUNCTIONAL~s in~Mits'rayim in~ Paroh and~in~ALL HOUSE~him to~EYE~s2~us   **6:23** and~AT~us *he~did~ make~*GO.OUT^(V) from~THERE to~THAT >~*make~*COME^(V) AT~us to~>~ GIVE^(V) to~us AT the~LAND WHICH *he~did~be~*SWEAR^(V) to~FATHER~s~ us   **6:24** and~*he~will~much~*DIRECT^(V)~us **YHWH** to~>~DO^(V) AT ALL the~ CUSTOM~s the~THESE to~>~FEAR^(V) AT **YHWH** Elohiym~us to~FUNCTIONAL to~us ALL the~DAY~s to~>~*much~*LIVE^(V)~us like~the~DAY the~ THIS   **6:25** and~STEADFASTNESS *she~will~*EXIST^(V) to~us GIVEN.THAT *we~ will~*SAFEGUARD^(V) to~>~DO^(V) AT ALL the~DIRECTIVE the~THIS to~FACE~s **YHWH** Elohiym~us like~WHICH *he~did~much~*DIRECT^(V)~us

Chapter 7

7:1 GIVEN.THAT *he~will~make~*COME^(V)~you^(ms) **YHWH** Elohiym~you^(ms) TO the~LAND WHICH YOU^(ms) *he~did~*COME^(V) THERE~unto to~>~POSSESS^(V)~ her and~*he~did~*CAST.OFF^(V) NATION~s ABUNDANT~s from~FACE~s~you^(ms) the~Hhet~of and~the~Girgash~of and~the~Emor~of and~the~Kena'an~of and~the~Perez~of and~the~Hhiw~of and~the~Yevus~of SEVEN NATION~s ABUNDANT~s and~NUMEROUS~s FROM~you^(ms)   **7:2** and~*he~did~*GIVE^(V)~ them^(m) **YHWH** Elohiym~you^(ms) to~FACE~s~you^(ms) and~*you^(ms)~did~make~* HIT^(V)~them^(m) >~*make~*PERFORATE^(V) *you^(ms)~will~make~*PERFORATE^(V) AT~ them^(m) NOT *you^(ms)~will~*CUT^(V) to~them^(m) COVENANT and~NOT *you^(ms)~ will~*PROVIDE.PROTECTION^(V)~them^(m)   **7:3** and~NOT *you^(ms)~will~self~* BE.AN.IN-LAW^(V) in~them^(m) DAUGHTER~you^(ms) NOT *you^(ms)~will~*GIVE^(V) to~ SON~him and~DAUGHTER~him NOT *you^(ms)~will~*TAKE^(V) to~SON~ you^(ms)   **7:4** GIVEN.THAT *he~will~make~*TURN.ASIDE^(V) AT SON~you^(ms) from~AFTER~me and~*they~did~*SERVE^(V) Elohiym OTHER~s and~*he~did~* FLARE.UP^(V) NOSE **YHWH** in~you^(mp) and~*he~did~make~*DESTROY^(V)~you^(ms) QUICKLY   **7:5** GIVEN.THAT IF IN.THIS.WAY *you^(mp)~will~*DO^(V) to~them^(m) ALTAR~s~them^(m) *you^(mp)~will~*BREAK.DOWN^(V) and~MONUMENT~s~them^(m)

The Book of Deuteronomy

you(mp)~*will*~*much*~CRACK(V) and~GROVE~them(m) *you*(mp)~*will*~*much*~CUT.DOWN(V)~must and~SCULPTURE~s~them(m) *you*(mp)~*will*~CREMATE(V)~must in~the~FIRE **7:6** GIVEN.THAT PEOPLE UNIQUE YOU(ms) to~**YHWH** Elohiym~you(ms) in~you(ms) *he*~*did*~CHOOSE(V) **YHWH** Elohiym~you(ms) to~>~EXIST(V) to~him to~PEOPLE JEWEL from~ALL the~PEOPLE~s WHICH UPON FACE~s the~GROUND **7:7** NOT from~>~INCREASE.IN.NUMBER(V)~you(mp) from~ALL the~PEOPLE~s *he*~*did*~ATTACH(V) **YHWH** in~you(mp) and~*he*~*will*~CHOOSE(V) in~you(mp) GIVEN.THAT YOU(mp) the~SMALL.AMOUNT from~ALL the~PEOPLE~s **7:8** GIVEN.THAT from~AFFECTION **YHWH** AT~you(mp) and~>~SAFEGUARD(V)~him AT the~SWEARING WHICH *he*~*did*~*be*~SWEAR(V) to~FATHER~s~you(mp) *he*~*did*~*make*~GO.OUT(V) **YHWH** AT~you(mp) in~HAND FORCEFUL and~*he*~*will*~RANSOM(V)~you(ms) from~HOUSE SERVANT~s from~HAND Paroh KING Mits'rayim **7:9** and~*you*(ms)~*did*~KNOW(V) GIVEN.THAT **YHWH** Elohiym~you(ms) HE the~Elohiym the~MIGHTY.ONE the~*be*~SECURE(V)~*ing*(ms) SAFEGUARD(V)~*ing*(ms) the~COVENANT and~the~KINDNESS to~LOVE(V)~*ing*(mp)~him and~to~SAFEGUARD(V)~*ing*(mp) DIRECTIVE~s~him to~THOUSAND GENERATION **7:10** and~*much*~MAKE.RESTITUTION(V)~*ing*(ms) to~HATE(V)~*ing*(mp)~him TO FACE~s~him to~>~*make*~PERISH(V)~him NOT *he*~*will*~*much*~DELAY(V) to~HATE(V)~*ing*(ms)~him TO FACE~s~him *he*~*will*~*much*~MAKE.RESTITUTION(V) to~him **7:11** and~*you*(ms)~*did*~SAFEGUARD(V) AT the~DIRECTIVE and~AT the~CUSTOM~s and~AT the~DECISION~s WHICH I *much*~DIRECT(V)~*ing*(ms)~you(ms) the~DAY to~>~DO(V)~them(m) **7:12** and~*he*~*did*~EXIST(V) CONSEQUENCE *you*(mp)~*will*~HEAR(V)~must AT the~DECISION~s the~THESE and~*you*(mp)~*did*~SAFEGUARD(V) and~*you*(mp)~*did*~DO(V) AT~them(m) and~*he*~*did*~SAFEGUARD(V) **YHWH** Elohiym~you(ms) to~you(ms) AT the~COVENANT and~AT the~KINDNESS WHICH *he*~*did*~*be*~SWEAR(V) to~FATHER~s~you(ms) **7:13** and~*he*~*did*~LOVE(V)~you(ms) and~*he*~*did*~*much*~KNEEL(V)~you(ms) and~*he*~*did*~*make*~INCREASE(V)~you(ms) and~*he*~*did*~*much*~KNEEL(V) PRODUCE WOMB~you(ms) and~PRODUCE GROUND~you(ms) CEREAL~you(ms) and~FRESH.WINE~you(ms) and~FRESH.OIL~you(ms) BIRTH BOVINE~s~you(ms) and~YOUNG.SHEEP~s FLOCKS~you(ms) UPON the~GROUND WHICH *he*~*did*~*be*~SWEAR(V) to~FATHER~s~you(ms) to~>~GIVE(V) to~you(fs) **7:14** KNEEL(V)~*ed*(ms) *you*(ms)~*will*~EXIST(V) from~ALL the~PEOPLE~s NOT *he*~*will*~EXIST(V) in~you(ms) STERILE and~STERILE and~in~BEAST~you(ms) **7:15** and~*he*~*did*~*make*~TURN.ASIDE(V) **YHWH** FROM~you(ms) ALL INFIRMITY and~ALL DISEASE~s Mits'rayim the~DYSFUNCTIONAL~s WHICH *you*(ms)~*did*~KNOW(V) NOT *he*~*will*~PLACE(V)~them(m) in~you(fs) and~*he*~*did*~GIVE(V)~them(m) in~ALL HATE(V)~*ing*(mp)~you(ms) **7:16** and~*you*(ms)~*did*~EAT(V) AT ALL the~PEOPLE~s WHICH **YHWH** Elohiym~you(ms) GIVE(V)~*ing*(ms) to~you(fs) NOT *you*(ms)~*will*~SPARE(V) EYE~you(ms) UPON~them(m) and~NOT *you*(ms)~*will*~SERVE(V) AT Elohiym~them(m) GIVEN.THAT SNARE HE to~you(fs) **7:17** GIVEN.THAT *you*(ms)~*will*~SAY(V) in~HEART~you(ms) ABUNDANT~s the~NATION~s the~THESE FROM~me HOW *I*~*will*~BE.ABLE(V) to~>~*make*~POSSESS(V)~them(m) **7:18** NOT *you*(ms)~*will*~FEAR(V) from~them(m) >~REMEMBER(V) *you*(ms)~*will*~REMEMBER(V) AT WHICH *he*~*did*~DO(V) **YHWH**

Elohiym~you(ms) to~Paroh and~to~ALL Mits'rayim **7:19** the~TRIAL~s the~ GREAT~s WHICH they~did~SEE(V) EYE~s2~you(ms) and~the~SIGN~s and~the~ WONDER~s and~the~HAND the~FORCEFUL and~the~ARM the~EXTEND(V)~ ed(fs) WHICH he~did~make~GO.OUT(V)~you(ms) **YHWH** Elohiym~you(ms) SO he~will~DO(V) **YHWH** Elohiym~you(ms) to~ALL the~PEOPLE~s WHICH YOU(ms) FEAR(V)~ing(ms) from~FACE~s~them(m) **7:20** and~ALSO AT the~HORNET he~ will~much~SEND(V) **YHWH** Elohiym~you(ms) in~them(m) UNTIL >~PERISH(V) the~be~REMAIN(V)~ing(mp) and~the~be~HIDE(V)~ing(mp) from~FACE~s~ you(ms) **7:21** NOT you(ms)~will~BE.TERRIFIED(V) from~FACE~s~them(m) GIVEN.THAT **YHWH** Elohiym~you(ms) in~INSIDE~you(ms) MIGHTY.ONE GREAT and~be~FEAR(V)~ing(ms) **7:22** and~he~did~CAST.OFF(V) **YHWH** Elohiym~ you(ms) AT the~NATION~s the~THESE from~FACE~s~you(ms) SMALL.AMOUNT SMALL.AMOUNT NOT you(ms)~will~BE.ABLE(V) >~much~FINISH(V)~them(m) QUICKLY OTHERWISE she~will~INCREASE(V) UPON~you(ms) LIVING the~FIELD **7:23** and~he~did~GIVE(V)~them(m) **YHWH** Elohiym~you(ms) to~FACE~s~you(ms) and~he~did~ROAR(V)~them(m) TUMULT GREAT UNTIL >~be~DESTROY(V)~ them(m) **7:24** and~he~did~GIVE(V) KING~s~them(m) in~HAND~you(ms) and~ you(ms)~did~make~PERISH(V) AT TITLE~them(m) from~UNDER the~SKY~s2 NOT he~will~self~STATION(V) MAN in~FACE~s~you(ms) UNTIL >~make~ DESTROY(V)~you(ms) AT~them(m) **7:25** SCULPTURE~s Elohiym~them(m) you(mp)~will~CREMATE(V)~must in~the~FIRE NOT you(ms)~will~CRAVE(V) SILVER and~GOLD UPON~them(m) and~you(ms)~did~TAKE(V) to~you(fs) OTHERWISE you(ms)~will~be~SNARE(V) in~him GIVEN.THAT DISGUSTING **YHWH** Elohiym~you(ms) HE **7:26** and~NOT you(ms)~will~make~COME(V) DISGUSTING TO HOUSE~you(ms) and~you(ms)~did~EXIST(V) ASSIGNED like~ THAT.ONE~him >~much~DETEST(V) you(mp)~will~much~DETEST(V)~him and~ >~much~ABHOR(V) you(ms)~will~much~ABHOR(V)~him GIVEN.THAT ASSIGNED HE

Chapter 8

8:1 ALL the~DIRECTIVE WHICH I much~DIRECT(V)~ing(ms)~you(ms) the~DAY you(mp)~will~SAFEGUARD(V)~must to~>~DO(V) to~THAT you(mp)~will~LIVE(V)~ must and~you(mp)~did~make~INCREASE(V) and~you(mp)~did~COME(V) and~ you(mp)~did~POSSESS(V) AT the~LAND WHICH he~did~be~SWEAR(V) **YHWH** to~FATHER~s~you(mp) **8:2** and~you(ms)~did~REMEMBER(V) AT ALL the~ROAD WHICH he~did~make~WALK(V)~you(ms) **YHWH** Elohiym~you(ms) THIS FOUR~s YEAR in~the~WILDERNESS to~THAT >~much~AFFLICT(V)~you(ms) to~>~much~ TEST(V)~you(ms) to~>~KNOW(V) AT WHICH in~HEART~you(ms) ?~you(ms)~will~ SAFEGUARD(V) DIRECTIVE~s~him IF NOT **8:3** and~he~will~much~AFFLICT(V)~ you(ms) and~he~will~make~BE.HUNGRY(V)~you(ms) and~he~will~make~ EAT(V)~you(ms) AT the~Mahn WHICH NOT you(ms)~did~KNOW(V) and~NOT they~did~KNOW(V)~must FATHER~s~you(ms) to~THAT >~make~KNOW(V)~

The Book of Deuteronomy

you⁽ᵐˢ⁾ GIVEN.THAT NOT UPON the~BREAD to~STRAND~him he~will~LIVE⁽ⱽ⁾ the~HUMAN GIVEN.THAT UPON ALL GOING.OUT MOUTH **YHWH** he~will~LIVE⁽ⱽ⁾ the~HUMAN **8:4** APPAREL~you⁽ᵐˢ⁾ NOT *she~did*~WEAR.OUT⁽ⱽ⁾ from~UPON~you⁽ᵐˢ⁾ and~FOOT~you⁽ᵐˢ⁾ NOT *she~did*~SWELL.UP⁽ⱽ⁾ THIS FOUR~s YEAR **8:5** and~*you⁽ᵐˢ⁾~did*~KNOW⁽ⱽ⁾ WITH HEART~you⁽ᵐˢ⁾ GIVEN.THAT like~WHICH *he~will~much*~CORRECT⁽ⱽ⁾ MAN AT SON~him **YHWH** Elohiym~you⁽ᵐˢ⁾ *much*~CORRECT⁽ⱽ⁾~*ing*⁽ᵐˢ⁾~you⁽ᵐˢ⁾ **8:6** and~*you⁽ᵐˢ⁾~did*~SAFEGUARD⁽ⱽ⁾ AT DIRECTIVE~s **YHWH** Elohiym~you⁽ᵐˢ⁾ to~>~WALK⁽ⱽ⁾ in~ROAD~s~him and~to~>~FEAR⁽ⱽ⁾ AT~him **8:7** GIVEN.THAT **YHWH** Elohiym~you⁽ᵐˢ⁾ *make*~COME⁽ⱽ⁾~*ing*⁽ᵐˢ⁾~you⁽ᵐˢ⁾ TO LAND FUNCTIONAL LAND WADI~s WATER~s2 EYE~s and~DEEP.WATER~s GO.OUT⁽ⱽ⁾~*ing*⁽ᵐᵖ⁾ in~the~LEVEL.VALLEY and~in~the~HILL **8:8** LAND WHEAT and~BARLEY and~GRAPEVINE and~FIG and~POMEGRANATE LAND OLIVE OIL and~HONEY **8:9** LAND WHICH NOT in~POVERTY you⁽ᵐˢ⁾~will~EAT⁽ⱽ⁾ in~her BREAD NOT you⁽ᵐˢ⁾~will~DIMINISH⁽ⱽ⁾ ALL in~her LAND WHICH STONE~s~her IRON and~from~HILL~s~her you⁽ᵐˢ⁾~will~HEW⁽ⱽ⁾ COPPER **8:10** and~*you⁽ᵐˢ⁾~did*~EAT⁽ⱽ⁾ and~*you⁽ᵐˢ⁾~did*~BE.SATISFIED⁽ⱽ⁾ and~*you⁽ᵐˢ⁾~did~much*~KNEEL⁽ⱽ⁾ AT **YHWH** Elohiym~you⁽ᵐˢ⁾ UPON the~LAND the~FUNCTIONAL WHICH *he~did*~GIVE⁽ⱽ⁾ to~you⁽ᶠˢ⁾ **8:11** !⁽ᵐˢ⁾~be~SAFEGUARD⁽ⱽ⁾ to~you⁽ᵐˢ⁾ OTHERWISE you⁽ᵐˢ⁾~will~FORGET⁽ⱽ⁾ AT **YHWH** Elohiym~you⁽ᵐˢ⁾ to~EXCEPT >~SAFEGUARD⁽ⱽ⁾ DIRECTIVE~s~him and~DECISION~s~him and~CUSTOM~s~him WHICH I *much*~DIRECT⁽ⱽ⁾~*ing*⁽ᵐˢ⁾~you⁽ᵐˢ⁾ the~DAY **8:12** OTHERWISE and~*you⁽ᵐˢ⁾~will*~EAT⁽ⱽ⁾ and~*you⁽ᵐˢ⁾~did*~BE.SATISFIED⁽ⱽ⁾ and~HOUSE~s FUNCTIONAL~s you⁽ᵐˢ⁾~will~BUILD⁽ⱽ⁾ and~*you⁽ᵐˢ⁾~did*~SETTLE⁽ⱽ⁾ **8:13** and~CATTLE~you⁽ᵐˢ⁾ and~FLOCKS~you⁽ᵐˢ⁾ *they*⁽ᵐ⁾~will~INCREASE⁽ⱽ⁾~must and~SILVER and~GOLD he~will~INCREASE⁽ⱽ⁾ to~you⁽ᶠˢ⁾ and~ALL WHICH to~you⁽ᵐˢ⁾ he~will~INCREASE⁽ⱽ⁾ **8:14** and~*he~did*~RAISE.UP⁽ⱽ⁾ HEART~you⁽ᵐˢ⁾ and~*you⁽ᵐˢ⁾~did*~FORGET⁽ⱽ⁾ AT **YHWH** Elohiym~you⁽ᵐˢ⁾ the~*make*~GO.OUT⁽ⱽ⁾~*ing*⁽ᵐˢ⁾~you⁽ᵐˢ⁾ from~LAND Mits'rayim from~HOUSE SERVANT~s **8:15** ?~*make*~WALK⁽ⱽ⁾~*ing*⁽ᵐˢ⁾~you⁽ᵐˢ⁾ in~the~WILDERNESS the~GREAT and~?~be~FEAR⁽ⱽ⁾~*ing*⁽ᵐˢ⁾ SERPENT VENOMOUS and~SCORPION and~THIRSTY.LAND WHICH WITHOUT WATER~s2 ?~*make*~GO.OUT⁽ⱽ⁾~*ing*⁽ᵐˢ⁾ to~you⁽ᵐˢ⁾ WATER~s2 from~BOULDER the~QUARTZ **8:16** the~*make*~EAT⁽ⱽ⁾~*ing*⁽ᵐˢ⁾~you⁽ᵐˢ⁾ Mahn in~the~WILDERNESS WHICH NOT they~*did*~KNOW⁽ⱽ⁾~must FATHER~s~you⁽ᵐˢ⁾ to~THAT >~*much*~AFFLICT⁽ⱽ⁾~you⁽ᵐˢ⁾ and~to~THAT >~*much*~TEST⁽ⱽ⁾~you⁽ᵐˢ⁾ to~>~DO.WELL⁽ⱽ⁾~you⁽ᵐˢ⁾ in~END~you⁽ᵐˢ⁾ **8:17** and~*you⁽ᵐˢ⁾~did*~SAY⁽ⱽ⁾ in~HEART~you⁽ᵐˢ⁾ STRENGTH~me and~BRAWN HAND~me *he~did*~DO⁽ⱽ⁾ to~me AT the~FORCE the~THIS **8:18** and~*you⁽ᵐˢ⁾~did*~REMEMBER⁽ⱽ⁾ AT **YHWH** Elohiym~you⁽ᵐˢ⁾ GIVEN.THAT HE the~GIVE⁽ⱽ⁾~*ing*⁽ᵐˢ⁾ to~you⁽ᵐˢ⁾ STRENGTH to~>~DO⁽ⱽ⁾ FORCE to~THAT >~*make*~RISE⁽ⱽ⁾ AT COVENANT~him WHICH *he~did~be*~SWEAR⁽ⱽ⁾ to~FATHER~s~you⁽ᵐˢ⁾ like~the~DAY the~THIS **8:19** and~*he~did*~EXIST⁽ⱽ⁾ IF >~FORGET⁽ⱽ⁾ you⁽ᵐˢ⁾~will~FORGET⁽ⱽ⁾ AT **YHWH** Elohiym~you⁽ᵐˢ⁾ and~*you⁽ᵐˢ⁾~did*~WALK⁽ⱽ⁾ AFTER Elohiym OTHER~s and~*you⁽ᵐˢ⁾~did*~SERVE⁽ⱽ⁾~them⁽ᵐ⁾ and~*you⁽ᵐˢ⁾~did~self*~BEND.DOWN⁽ⱽ⁾ to~them⁽ᵐ⁾ I~*did~make*~WRAP.AROUND⁽ⱽ⁾ in~you⁽ᵐᵖ⁾ the~

DAY GIVEN.THAT >~PERISH⁽ⱽ⁾ you⁽ᵐˢ⁾~will~PERISH⁽ⱽ⁾~must 8:20 like~the~ NATION~s WHICH **YHWH** make~PERISH⁽ⱽ⁾~ing⁽ᵐˢ⁾ from~FACE~s~you⁽ᵐᵖ⁾ SO you⁽ᵐᵖ⁾~will~PERISH⁽ⱽ⁾~must CONSEQUENCE NOT you⁽ᵐᵖ⁾~will~HEAR⁽ⱽ⁾~must in~VOICE **YHWH** Elohiym~you⁽ᵐᵖ⁾

Chapter 9

9:1 !⁽ᵐˢ⁾~HEAR⁽ⱽ⁾ Yisra'eyl YOU⁽ᵐˢ⁾ CROSS.OVER⁽ⱽ⁾~ing⁽ᵐˢ⁾ the~DAY AT the~ Yarden to~>~COME⁽ⱽ⁾ to~the~>~POSSESS⁽ⱽ⁾ NATION~s GREAT~s and~ NUMEROUS~s FROM~you⁽ᵐˢ⁾ CITY~s GREAT~s and~FENCE.IN⁽ⱽ⁾~ed⁽ᶠᵖ⁾ in~the~ SKY~s2 **9:2** PEOPLE GREAT and~RAISE.UP⁽ⱽ⁾~ing⁽ᵐˢ⁾ SON~s Anaq~s WHICH YOU⁽ᵐˢ⁾ you⁽ᵐˢ⁾~did~KNOW⁽ⱽ⁾ and~YOU⁽ᵐˢ⁾ you⁽ᵐˢ⁾~did~HEAR⁽ⱽ⁾ WHO he~ will~self~STATION⁽ⱽ⁾ to~FACE~s SON~s Anaq **9:3** and~you⁽ᵐˢ⁾~did~KNOW⁽ⱽ⁾ the~DAY GIVEN.THAT **YHWH** Elohiym~you⁽ᵐˢ⁾ HE the~CROSS.OVER⁽ⱽ⁾~ing⁽ᵐˢ⁾ to~FACE~s~you⁽ᵐˢ⁾ FIRE EAT⁽ⱽ⁾~ing⁽ᶠˢ⁾ HE he~will~make~DESTROY⁽ⱽ⁾~them⁽ᵐ⁾ and~HE he~will~make~LOWER⁽ⱽ⁾~them⁽ᵐ⁾ to~FACE~s~you⁽ᵐˢ⁾ and~you⁽ᵐˢ⁾~ did~make~POSSESS⁽ⱽ⁾~them⁽ᵐ⁾ and~you⁽ᵐˢ⁾~did~make~PERISH⁽ⱽ⁾~them⁽ᵐ⁾ QUICKLY like~WHICH he~did~much~SPEAK⁽ⱽ⁾ **YHWH** to~you⁽ᶠˢ⁾ **9:4** DO.NOT you⁽ᵐˢ⁾~will~SAY⁽ⱽ⁾ in~HEART~you⁽ᵐˢ⁾ in~>~PUSH.AWAY⁽ⱽ⁾ **YHWH** Elohiym~ you⁽ᵐˢ⁾ AT~them⁽ᵐ⁾ from~to~FACE~s~you⁽ᵐˢ⁾ to~>~SAY⁽ⱽ⁾ in~ STEADFASTNESS~me he~did~make~COME⁽ⱽ⁾~me **YHWH** to~the~>~ POSSESS⁽ⱽ⁾ AT the~LAND the~THIS and~in~WAYWARDNESS the~NATION~s the~THESE **YHWH** make~POSSESS⁽ⱽ⁾~ing⁽ᵐˢ⁾~them⁽ᵐ⁾ from~FACE~s~ you⁽ᵐˢ⁾ **9:5** NOT in~STEADFASTNESS~you⁽ᵐˢ⁾ and~in~STRAIGHTNESS HEART~you⁽ᵐˢ⁾ YOU⁽ᵐˢ⁾ he~did~COME⁽ⱽ⁾ to~the~>~POSSESS⁽ⱽ⁾ AT LAND~ them⁽ᵐ⁾ GIVEN.THAT in~WAYWARDNESS the~NATION~s the~THESE **YHWH** Elohiym~you⁽ᵐˢ⁾ make~POSSESS⁽ⱽ⁾~ing⁽ᵐˢ⁾~them⁽ᵐ⁾ from~FACE~s~you⁽ᵐˢ⁾ and~to~THAT >~make~RISE⁽ⱽ⁾ AT the~WORD WHICH he~did~be~SWEAR⁽ⱽ⁾ **YHWH** to~FATHER~s~you⁽ᵐˢ⁾ to~Avraham to~Yits'hhaq and~to~ Ya'aqov **9:6** and~you⁽ᵐˢ⁾~did~KNOW⁽ⱽ⁾ GIVEN.THAT NOT in~ STEADFASTNESS~you⁽ᵐˢ⁾ **YHWH** Elohiym~you⁽ᵐˢ⁾ GIVE⁽ⱽ⁾~ing⁽ᵐˢ⁾ to~you⁽ᵐˢ⁾ AT the~LAND the~FUNCTIONAL the~THIS to~>~POSSESS⁽ⱽ⁾~her GIVEN.THAT PEOPLE HARD NECK YOU⁽ᵐˢ⁾ **9:7** !⁽ᵐˢ⁾~REMEMBER⁽ⱽ⁾ DO.NOT you⁽ᵐˢ⁾~will~ FORGET⁽ⱽ⁾ AT WHICH you⁽ᵐˢ⁾~did~make~SNAP⁽ⱽ⁾ AT **YHWH** Elohiym~you⁽ᵐˢ⁾ in~the~WILDERNESS to~FROM the~DAY WHICH you⁽ᵐˢ⁾~did~GO.OUT⁽ⱽ⁾ from~LAND Mits'rayim UNTIL in~>~COME⁽ⱽ⁾~you⁽ᵐᵖ⁾ UNTIL the~AREA the~ THIS make~DISOBEY⁽ⱽ⁾~ing⁽ᵐᵖ⁾ you⁽ᵐᵖ⁾~did~EXIST⁽ⱽ⁾ WITH **YHWH** **9:8** and~ in~Hhorev you⁽ᵐᵖ⁾~did~make~SNAP⁽ⱽ⁾ AT **YHWH** and~he~will~self~SNORT⁽ⱽ⁾ **YHWH** in~you⁽ᵐᵖ⁾ to~>~make~DESTROY⁽ⱽ⁾ AT~you⁽ᵐᵖ⁾ **9:9** in~>~GO.UP⁽ⱽ⁾~ me the~HILL~unto to~>~TAKE⁽ⱽ⁾ SLAB~s the~STONE~s SLAB~s the~ COVENANT WHICH he~did~CUT⁽ⱽ⁾ **YHWH** WITH~you⁽ᵐᵖ⁾ and~I~will~SETTLE⁽ⱽ⁾ in~the~HILL FOUR~s DAY and~FOUR~s NIGHT BREAD NOT I~did~EAT⁽ⱽ⁾ and~ WATER~s2 NOT I~did~GULP⁽ⱽ⁾ **9:10** and~he~will~GIVE⁽ⱽ⁾ **YHWH** TO~me AT

The Book of Deuteronomy

TWO SLAB~s the~STONE~s WRITE$^{(V)}$~ed$^{(mp)}$ in~FINGER Elohiym and~UPON~them$^{(m)}$ like~ALL the~WORD~s WHICH he~did~much~SPEAK$^{(V)}$ **YHWH** WITH~you$^{(mp)}$ in~the~HILL from~MIDST the~FIRE in~DAY the~ASSEMBLY **9:11** and~he~will~EXIST$^{(V)}$ from~CONCLUSION FOUR~s DAY and~FOUR~s NIGHT he~did~GIVE$^{(V)}$ **YHWH** TO~me AT TWO SLAB~s the~STONE~s SLAB~s the~COVENANT **9:12** and~he~will~SAY$^{(V)}$ **YHWH** TO~me !$^{(ms)}$~RISE$^{(V)}$!$^{(ms)}$~GO.DOWN$^{(V)}$ QUICKLY from~THIS GIVEN.THAT he~did~much~DAMAGE$^{(V)}$ PEOPLE~you$^{(ms)}$ WHICH you$^{(ms)}$~did~make~GO.OUT$^{(V)}$ from~Mits'rayim they~did~TURN.ASIDE$^{(V)}$ QUICKLY FROM the~ROAD WHICH I~did~much~DIRECT$^{(V)}$~them$^{(m)}$ they~did~DO$^{(V)}$ to~them$^{(m)}$ CAST.IMAGE **9:13** and~he~will~SAY$^{(V)}$ **YHWH** TO~me to~>~SAY$^{(V)}$ I~did~SEE$^{(V)}$ AT the~PEOPLE the~THIS and~LOOK PEOPLE HARD NECK HE **9:14** !$^{(ms)}$~make~SINK.DOWN$^{(V)}$ FROM~me and~I~will~make~DESTROY$^{(V)}$~them$^{(m)}$ and~I~will~WIPE.AWAY$^{(V)}$ AT TITLE~them$^{(m)}$ from~UNDER the~SKY~s2 and~I~will~DO$^{(V)}$~& AT~you$^{(ms)}$ to~NATION NUMEROUS and~ABUNDANT FROM~him **9:15** and~I~did~TURN$^{(V)}$ and~I~will~GO.DOWN$^{(V)}$ FROM the~HILL and~the~HILL BURN$^{(V)}$~ing$^{(ms)}$ in~the~FIRE and~TWO SLAB~s the~COVENANT UPON TWO HAND~s2~me **9:16** and~I~will~SEE$^{(V)}$ and~LOOK you$^{(mp)}$~did~FAIL$^{(V)}$ to~**YHWH** Elohiym~you$^{(mp)}$ you$^{(mp)}$~did~DO$^{(V)}$ to~you$^{(mp)}$ BULLOCK CAST.IMAGE you$^{(mp)}$~did~TURN.ASIDE$^{(V)}$ QUICKLY FROM the~ROAD WHICH he~did~much~DIRECT$^{(V)}$ **YHWH** AT~you$^{(mp)}$ **9:17** and~I~will~SEIZE.HOLD$^{(V)}$ in~TWO the~SLAB~s and~I~will~make~THROW.OUT$^{(V)}$~them$^{(m)}$ from~UPON TWO HAND~s2~me and~I~will~CRACK$^{(V)}$~them$^{(m)}$ to~EYE~s2~you$^{(mp)}$ **9:18** and~I~will~self~FALL$^{(V)}$ to~FACE~s **YHWH** like~the~FIRST FOUR~s DAY and~FOUR~s NIGHT BREAD NOT I~did~EAT$^{(V)}$ and~WATER~s2 NOT I~did~GULP$^{(V)}$ UPON ALL FAILURE~you$^{(mp)}$ WHICH you$^{(mp)}$~did~FAIL$^{(V)}$ to~>~DO$^{(V)}$ the~DYSFUNCTIONAL in~EYE~s2 **YHWH** to~>~make~BE.ANGRY$^{(V)}$~him **9:19** GIVEN.THAT I~did~BE.AFRAID$^{(V)}$ from~FACE~s the~NOSE and~the~FURY WHICH he~did~SNAP$^{(V)}$ **YHWH** UPON~you$^{(mp)}$ to~>~make~DESTROY$^{(V)}$ AT~you$^{(mp)}$ and~he~will~HEAR$^{(V)}$ **YHWH** TO~me ALSO in~the~FOOTSTEP the~SHE **9:20** and~in~Aharon he~did~self~SNORT$^{(V)}$ **YHWH** MANY to~>~make~DESTROY$^{(V)}$~him and~I~will~make~self~PLEAD$^{(V)}$ ALSO in~UNTIL Aharon in~the~APPOINTED.TIME the~SHE **9:21** and~AT FAILURE~you$^{(mp)}$ WHICH you$^{(mp)}$~did~DO$^{(V)}$ AT the~BULLOCK I~did~TAKE$^{(V)}$ and~I~will~CREMATE$^{(V)}$ AT~him in~the~FIRE and~I~will~SMASH$^{(V)}$ AT~him >~GRIND$^{(V)}$ >~make~DO.WELL$^{(V)}$ UNTIL WHICH he~did~BEAT.SMALL$^{(V)}$ to~DIRT and~I~will~THROW.OUT$^{(V)}$ AT DIRT~him TO the~WADI the~GO.DOWN$^{(V)}$~ing$^{(ms)}$ FROM the~HILL **9:22** and~in~Taveyrah and~in~Mas'sah and~in~Qivrot-Hata'awah make~SNAP$^{(V)}$~ing$^{(mp)}$ you$^{(mp)}$~did~EXIST$^{(V)}$ AT **YHWH** **9:23** and~in~>~SEND$^{(V)}$ **YHWH** AT~you$^{(mp)}$ from~Qadesh Barneya to~>~SAY$^{(V)}$!$^{(mp)}$~GO.UP$^{(V)}$ and~!$^{(mp)}$~POSSESS$^{(V)}$ AT the~LAND WHICH I~did~GIVE$^{(V)}$ to~you$^{(mp)}$ and~you$^{(mp)}$~will~make~DISOBEY$^{(V)}$ AT MOUTH **YHWH** Elohiym~you$^{(mp)}$ and~NOT you$^{(mp)}$~did~make~SECURE$^{(V)}$ to~him and~NOT you$^{(mp)}$~did~HEAR$^{(V)}$ in~VOICE~him **9:24** make~DISOBEY$^{(V)}$~ing$^{(mp)}$ you$^{(mp)}$~did~EXIST$^{(V)}$ WITH **YHWH** from~DAY I~did~KNOW$^{(V)}$ AT~

you(mp)   **9:25** and~I~will~self~FALL(V) to~FACE~s **YHWH** AT FOUR~s the~DAY and~AT FOUR~s the~NIGHT WHICH I~did~self~FALL(V) GIVEN.THAT *he~did~* SAY(V) **YHWH** to~>~*make~*DESTROY(V) AT~you(mp)   **9:26** and~I~will~make~ self~PLEAD(V) TO **YHWH** and~I~will~SAY(V) Adonai **YHWH** DO.NOT you(ms)~ will~DAMAGE(V) PEOPLE~you(ms) and~INHERITANCE~you(ms) WHICH you(ms)~ did~RANSOM(V) in~GREAT~you(ms) WHICH you(ms)~did~make~GO.OUT(V) from~Mits'rayim in~HAND FORCEFUL   **9:27** !(ms)~REMEMBER(V) to~ SERVANT~s~you(ms) to~Avraham to~Yits'hhaq and~to~Ya'aqov DO.NOT you(ms)~will~TURN(V) TO STUBBORNNESS the~PEOPLE the~THIS and~TO LOST~him and~TO FAILURE~him   **9:28** OTHERWISE *they(m)~will~*SAY(V) the~ LAND WHICH you(ms)~did~make~GO.OUT(V)~us from~THERE from~ UNAWARE >~BE.ABLE(V) **YHWH** to~>~*make~*COME(V)~them(m) TO the~LAND WHICH *he~did~much~*SPEAK(V) to~them(m) and~from~HATE~him AT~them(m) *he~did~make~*GO.OUT(V)~them(m) to~>~*make~*DIE(V)~them(m) in~the~ WILDERNESS   **9:29** and~THEY(m) PEOPLE~you(ms) and~INHERITANCE~you(ms) WHICH you(ms)~did~make~GO.OUT(V) in~STRENGTH~you(ms) the~GREAT and~ in~ARM~you(ms) the~EXTEND(V)~ed(fs)

Chapter 10

10:1 in~the~APPOINTED.TIME the~SHE *he~did~*SAY(V) **YHWH** TO~me !(ms)~ SCULPT(V) to~you(ms) TWO SLAB~s STONE~s like~FIRST~s and~!(ms)~GO.UP(V) TO~me the~HILL~unto and~you(ms)~did~DO(V) to~you(ms) BOX TREE   **10:2** and~I~will~WRITE(V) UPON the~SLAB~s AT the~WORD~s WHICH *they~did~*EXIST(V) UPON the~SLAB~s the~FIRST~s WHICH you(ms)~did~ CRACK(V) and~you(mp)~did~PLACE(V)~them(m) in~the~BOX   **10:3** and~I~will~ DO(V) BOX TREE~s ACACIA~s and~I~will~SCULPT(V) TWO SLAB~s STONE~s like~FIRST~s and~I~will~make~GO.UP(V) the~HILL~unto and~TWO the~ SLAB~s in~HAND~me   **10:4** and~*he~will~*WRITE(V) UPON the~SLAB~s like~ the~THING.WRITTEN the~FIRST AT TEN the~WORD~s WHICH *he~did~much~* SPEAK(V) **YHWH** TO~you(mp) in~the~HILL from~MIDST the~FIRE in~DAY the~ ASSEMBLY and~*he~will~*GIVE(V)~them(m) **YHWH** TO~me   **10:5** and~I~did~ TURN(V) and~I~will~GO.DOWN(V) FROM the~HILL and~I~will~PLACE(V) AT the~SLAB~s in~the~BOX WHICH I~did~DO(V) and~*they(m)~will~*EXIST(V) THERE like~WHICH *he~did~much~*DIRECT(V)~me **YHWH**   **10:6** and~SON~s Yisra'eyl *they~did~*JOURNEY(V) from~WELL~s B'ney-Ya'aqan Moseyrah THERE *he~did~* DIE(V) Aharon and~*he~will~be~*BURY(V) THERE and~*he~will~much~*ADORN(V) Elazar SON~him UNDER~him   **10:7** from~THERE *they~did~*JOURNEY(V) the~ Gudgodah and~FROM the~Gudgodah Yatvatah LAND WADI~s WATER~ s2   **10:8** in~the~APPOINTED.TIME the~SHE *he~did~make~*SEPARATE(V) **YHWH** AT STAFF the~Lewi to~>~LIFT.UP(V) AT BOX COVENANT **YHWH** to~>~ STAND(V) to~FACE~s **YHWH** to~>~*much~*MINISTER(V)~him and~to~>~*much~* KNEEL(V) in~TITLE~him UNTIL the~DAY the~THIS   **10:9** UPON SO NOT *he~*

did~EXIST^(V) to~Lewi DISTRIBUTION and~INHERITANCE WITH BROTHER~s~him **YHWH** HE INHERITANCE~him like~WHICH *he~did~much*~SPEAK^(V) **YHWH** Elohiym~you^(ms) to~him   **10:10** and~I *I~did*~STAND^(V) in~the~HILL like~the~DAY~s the~FIRST~s FOUR~s DAY and~FOUR~s NIGHT and~*he~will*~HEAR^(V) **YHWH** TO~me ALSO in~the~FOOTSTEP the~SHE NOT *he~did*~CONSENT^(V) **YHWH** >~*make*~DAMAGE^(V)~you^(ms)   **10:11** and~*he~will*~SAY^(V) **YHWH** TO~me *!^(ms)~*RISE^(V) *!^(ms)~*WALK^(V) to~JOURNEY to~FACE~s the~PEOPLE and~*they^(m)~will*~COME^(V) and~*they^(m)~will*~POSSESS^(V) AT the~LAND WHICH *I~did~be*~SWEAR^(V) to~FATHER~s~them^(m) to~>~GIVE^(V) to~them^(m)   **10:12** and~NOW Yisra'eyl WHAT **YHWH** Elohiym~you^(ms) INQUIRE^(V)~*ing^(ms)* from~WITH~you^(ms) GIVEN.THAT IF to~>~FEAR^(V) AT **YHWH** Elohiym~you^(ms) to~>~WALK^(V) in~ALL ROAD~s~him and~to~>~LOVE^(V) AT~him and~to~>~SERVE^(V) AT **YHWH** Elohiym~you^(ms) in~ALL HEART~you^(ms) and~in~ALL SOUL~you^(ms)   **10:13** to~>~SAFEGUARD^(V) AT DIRECTIVE~s **YHWH** and~AT CUSTOM~s~him WHICH I *much*~DIRECT^(V)~*ing^(ms)*~you^(ms) the~DAY to~FUNCTIONAL to~you^(fs)   **10:14** THOUGH to~**YHWH** Elohiym~you^(ms) the~SKY~s2 and~SKY~s2 the~SKY~s2 the~LAND and~ALL WHICH in~her   **10:15** ONLY in~FATHER~s~you^(ms) *he~did*~ATTACH^(V) **YHWH** to~>~LOVE^(V) AT~them^(m) and~*he~will*~CHOOSE^(V) in~SEED~them^(m) AFTER~them^(m) in~you^(mp) from~ALL the~PEOPLE~s like~the~DAY the~THIS   **10:16** and~*you^(mp)~did*~SNIP.OFF^(V) AT FORESKIN HEART~you^(mp) and~NECK~you^(mp) NOT *you^(mp)~will~make*~BE.HARD^(V) YET.AGAIN   **10:17** GIVEN.THAT **YHWH** Elohiym~you^(mp) HE Elohiym the~Elohiym and~LORD~s the~LORD~s the~MIGHTY.ONE the~GREAT the~COURAGEOUS and~the~*be*~FEAR^(V)~*ing^(ms)* WHICH NOT *he~will*~LIFT.UP^(V) FACE~s and~NOT *he~will*~TAKE^(V) BRIBE   **10:18** DO^(V)~*ing^(ms)* DECISION ORPHAN and~WIDOW and~LOVE^(V)~*ing^(ms)* IMMIGRANT to~>~GIVE^(V) to~him BREAD and~APPAREL   **10:19** and~*you^(mp)~did*~LOVE^(V) AT the~IMMIGRANT GIVEN.THAT IMMIGRANT~s *you^(mp)~did*~EXIST^(V) in~LAND Mits'rayim   **10:20** AT **YHWH** Elohiym~you^(ms) *you^(ms)~will*~FEAR^(V) AT~him *you^(ms)~will*~SERVE^(V) and~in~him *you^(ms)~will*~ADHERE^(V) and~in~TITLE~him *you^(ms)~will~be*~SWEAR^(V)   **10:21** HE ADORATION~you^(ms) and~HE Elohiym~you^(ms) WHICH *he~did*~DO^(V) AT~you^(ms) AT the~GREAT~s and~AT the~*be*~FEAR^(V)~*ing^(fp)* the~THESE WHICH *they~did*~SEE^(V) EYE~s2~you^(ms)   **10:22** in~SEVEN~s SOUL *they~will*~GO.DOWN^(V) FATHER~s~you^(ms) Mits'rayim~unto and~NOW *he~did*~PLACE^(V)~you^(ms) **YHWH** Elohiym~you^(ms) like~STAR~s the~SKY~s2 to~ABUNDANCE

Chapter 11

11:1 and~*you^(ms)~did*~LOVE^(V) AT **YHWH** Elohiym~you^(ms) and~*you^(ms)~did*~SAFEGUARD^(V) CHARGE~him and~CUSTOM~s~him and~DECISION~s~him and~DIRECTIVE~s~him ALL the~DAY~s   **11:2** and~*you^(mp)~did*~KNOW^(V) the~

DAY GIVEN.THAT NOT AT SON~s~you$^{(mp)}$ WHICH NOT they~did~KNOW$^{(V)}$ and~WHICH NOT they~did~SEE$^{(V)}$ AT DISCIPLINE YHWH Elohiym~you$^{(mp)}$ AT MAGNIFICENCE~him AT HAND~him the~FORCEFUL and~ARM~him the~EXTEND$^{(V)}$~ed$^{(fs)}$ 11:3 and~AT SIGN~s~him and~AT WORK~s~him WHICH he~did~DO$^{(V)}$ in~MIDST Mits'rayim to~Paroh KING Mits'rayim and~to~ALL LAND~him   11:4 and~WHICH he~did~DO$^{(V)}$ to~FORCE Mits'rayim to~HORSE~s~him and~to~VEHICLE~him WHICH he~did~make~FLOAT$^{(V)}$ AT WATER~s2 SEA REEDS UPON FACE~s~them$^{(m)}$ in~>~PURSUE$^{(V)}$~them$^{(m)}$ AFTER~you$^{(mp)}$ and~he~will~much~PERISH$^{(V)}$~them$^{(m)}$ YHWH UNTIL the~DAY the~THIS   11:5 and~WHICH he~did~DO$^{(V)}$ to~you$^{(mp)}$ in~the~WILDERNESS UNTIL in~>~COME$^{(V)}$~you$^{(mp)}$ UNTIL the~AREA the~THIS   11:6 and~WHICH he~did~DO$^{(V)}$ to~Datan and~to~Aviram SON~s Eli'av SON Re'uven WHICH she~did~PART$^{(V)}$ the~LAND AT MOUTH~her and~she~will~SWALLOW$^{(V)}$~them$^{(m)}$ and~AT HOUSE~s~them$^{(m)}$ and~AT TENT~s~them$^{(m)}$ and~AT ALL the~SUBSTANCE WHICH in~FOOT~s~them$^{(m)}$ in~INSIDE ALL Yisra'eyl   11:7 GIVEN.THAT EYE~s2~you$^{(mp)}$ the~SEE$^{(V)}$~ing$^{(fp)}$ AT ALL WORK YHWH the~GREAT WHICH he~did~DO$^{(V)}$ 11:8 and~you$^{(mp)}$~did~SAFEGUARD$^{(V)}$ AT ALL the~DIRECTIVE WHICH I much~DIRECT$^{(V)}$~ing$^{(ms)}$~you$^{(ms)}$ the~DAY to~THAT you$^{(mp)}$~will~SEIZE$^{(V)}$ and~you$^{(mp)}$~did~COME$^{(V)}$ and~you$^{(mp)}$~did~POSSESS$^{(V)}$ AT the~LAND WHICH YOU$^{(mp)}$ CROSS.OVER$^{(V)}$~ing$^{(mp)}$ THERE~unto to~>~POSSESS$^{(V)}$~her   11:9 and~to~THAT you$^{(mp)}$~will~make~PROLONG$^{(V)}$ DAY~s UPON the~GROUND WHICH he~did~be~SWEAR$^{(V)}$ YHWH to~FATHER~s~you$^{(mp)}$ to~>~GIVE$^{(V)}$ to~them$^{(m)}$ and~to~SEED~them$^{(m)}$ LAND ISSUE$^{(V)}$~ing$^{(fs)}$ FAT and~HONEY   11:10 GIVEN.THAT the~LAND WHICH YOU$^{(ms)}$ he~did~COME$^{(V)}$ THERE~unto to~>~POSSESS$^{(V)}$~her NOT like~LAND Mits'rayim SHE WHICH you$^{(mp)}$~did~GO.OUT$^{(V)}$ from~THERE WHICH you$^{(ms)}$~will~SOW$^{(V)}$ AT SEED~you$^{(ms)}$ and~you$^{(ms)}$~did~make~DRINK$^{(V)}$ in~FOOT~you$^{(ms)}$ like~GARDEN the~GREEN   11:11 and~the~LAND WHICH YOU$^{(mp)}$ CROSS.OVER$^{(V)}$~ing$^{(mp)}$ THERE~unto to~>~POSSESS$^{(V)}$~her LAND HILL~s and~LEVEL.VALLEY~s to~PRECIPITATION the~SKY~s2 you$^{(ms)}$~will~GULP$^{(V)}$ WATER~s2   11:12 LAND WHICH YHWH Elohiym~you$^{(ms)}$ SEEK$^{(V)}$~ing$^{(ms)}$ AT~her CONTINUALLY EYE~s2 YHWH Elohiym~you$^{(ms)}$ in~her from~SUMMIT the~YEAR and~UNTIL END YEAR   11:13 and~he~did~EXIST$^{(V)}$ IF >~HEAR$^{(V)}$ you$^{(mp)}$~will~HEAR$^{(V)}$ TO DIRECTIVE~s~me WHICH I much~DIRECT$^{(V)}$~ing$^{(ms)}$ AT~you$^{(mp)}$ the~DAY to~>~LOVE$^{(V)}$ AT YHWH Elohiym~you$^{(mp)}$ and~to~>~SERVE$^{(V)}$~him in~ALL HEART~you$^{(mp)}$ and~in~ALL SOUL~you$^{(ms)}$ 11:14 and~I~did~GIVE$^{(V)}$ PRECIPITATION LAND~you$^{(mp)}$ in~APPOINTED.TIME~him FIRST.RAIN and~LATE.RAIN and~you$^{(ms)}$~did~GATHER$^{(V)}$ CEREAL~you$^{(ms)}$ and~FRESH.WINE~you$^{(ms)}$ and~FRESH.OIL~you$^{(ms)}$ 11:15 and~I~did~GIVE$^{(V)}$ HERB in~FIELD~you$^{(ms)}$ to~BEAST~you$^{(ms)}$ and~you$^{(ms)}$~did~EAT$^{(V)}$ and~you$^{(ms)}$~did~BE.SATISFIED$^{(V)}$ 11:16 I$^{(mp)}$~be~SAFEGUARD$^{(V)}$ to~you$^{(mp)}$ OTHERWISE he~will~SPREAD.WIDE$^{(V)}$ HEART~you$^{(mp)}$ and~you$^{(mp)}$~did~TURN.ASIDE$^{(V)}$ and~you$^{(mp)}$~will~SERVE$^{(V)}$ Elohiym OTHER~s and~you$^{(mp)}$~did~self~BEND.DOWN$^{(V)}$ to~them$^{(m)}$ 11:17 and~he~did~FLARE.UP$^{(V)}$ NOSE YHWH in~you$^{(mp)}$ and~he~did~STOP$^{(V)}$ AT the~SKY~s2 and~NOT he~will~EXIST$^{(V)}$

The Book of Deuteronomy

PRECIPITATION and~the~GROUND NOT *she~will*~GIVE[(V)] AT PRODUCT~her and~*you*[(mp)]~*did*~PERISH[(V)] QUICKLY from~UPON the~LAND the~ FUNCTIONAL WHICH **YHWH** GIVE[(V)]~*ing*[(ms)] to~you[(mp)]   **11:18** and~*you*[(mp)]~*did*~PLACE[(V)] AT WORD~s~me THESE UPON HEART~you[(mp)] and~UPON SOUL~you[(ms)] and~*you*[(mp)]~*did*~TIE[(V)] AT~them[(m)] to~SIGN UPON HAND~you[(mp)] and~*they*[*did*]~EXIST[(V)] to~MARKER~s BETWEEN EYE~s2~you[(mp)]   **11:19** and~*you*[(mp)]~*did*~*much*~LEARN[(V)] AT~them[(m)] AT SON~s~you[(mp)] to~>~*much*~SPEAK[(V)] in~them[(m)] in~>~SETTLE[(V)]~you[(ms)] in~HOUSE~you[(ms)] and~in~>~WALK[(V)]~you[(ms)] in~the~ROAD and~in~>~LIE.DOWN[(V)]~you[(ms)] and~in~>~RISE[(V)]~you[(ms)]   **11:20** and~*you*[(ms)]~*did*~WRITE[(V)]~them[(m)] UPON DOORPOST~s HOUSE~you[(ms)] and~in~GATE~s~you[(ms)]   **11:21** to~THAT *they*[(m)]~*will*~INCREASE[(V)] DAY~s~you[(mp)] and~DAY~s SON~s~you[(mp)] UPON the~GROUND WHICH *he~did~be*~SWEAR[(V)] **YHWH** to~FATHER~s~you[(mp)] to~>~GIVE[(V)] to~them[(m)] like~DAY~s the~SKY~s2 UPON the~ LAND   **11:22** GIVEN.THAT IF >~SAFEGUARD[(V)] *you*[(mp)]~*will*~SAFEGUARD[(V)] must AT ALL the~DIRECTIVE the~THIS WHICH I *much*~DIRECT[(V)]~*ing*[(ms)] AT~you[(mp)] to~>~DO[(V)]~her to~>~LOVE[(V)] AT **YHWH** Elohiym~you[(mp)] to~>~WALK[(V)] in~ALL ROAD~s~him and~to~>~ADHERE[(V)] in~him   **11:23** and~*he~did~make*~POSSESS[(V)] **YHWH** AT ALL the~NATION~s the~THESE from~to~FACE~s~you[(mp)] and~*you*[(mp)]~*did*~POSSESS[(V)] NATION~s GREAT~s and~NUMEROUS~s from~you[(mp)]   **11:24** ALL the~AREA WHICH *you*[(ms)]~*will*~TAKE.STEPS[(V)] PALM FOOT~you[(mp)] in~him to~you[(mp)] *he~will*~EXIST[(V)] FROM the~WILDERNESS and~the~Levanon FROM the~RIVER RIVER Perat and~UNTIL the~SEA the~LAST *he~will*~EXIST[(V)] BORDER~you[(mp)]   **11:25** NOT *he~will~self*~STATION[(V)] MAN in~FACE~s~you[(mp)] AWE~you[(mp)] and~FEARING~you[(mp)] *he~will*~GIVE[(V)] **YHWH** Elohiym~you[(mp)] UPON FACE~s ALL the~LAND WHICH *you*[(mp)]~*will*~TAKE.STEPS[(V)] in~her like~WHICH *he~did~much*~SPEAK[(V)] to~you[(mp)]   **11:26** ![(ms)]~SEE[(V)] I GIVE[(V)]~*ing*[(ms)] to~FACE~s~you[(mp)] the~DAY PRESENT and~ANNOYANCE   **11:27** AT the~PRESENT WHICH *you*[(mp)]~*will*~HEAR[(V)] TO DIRECTIVE~s **YHWH** Elohiym~you[(mp)] WHICH I *much*~DIRECT[(V)]~*ing*[(ms)] AT~you[(mp)] the~DAY   **11:28** and~the~ANNOYANCE IF NOT *you*[(mp)]~*will*~HEAR[(V)] TO DIRECTIVE~s **YHWH** Elohiym~you[(mp)] and~*you*[(mp)]~*did*~TURN.ASIDE[(V)] FROM the~ROAD WHICH I *much*~DIRECT[(V)]~*ing*[(ms)] AT~you[(mp)] the~DAY to~>~WALK[(V)] AFTER Elohiym OTHER~s WHICH NOT *you*[(mp)]~*did*~KNOW[(V)]   **11:29** and~*he~did*~EXIST[(V)] GIVEN.THAT *he~will~make*~COME[(V)]~you[(ms)] **YHWH** Elohiym~you[(ms)] TO the~LAND WHICH YOU[(ms)] *he~did*~COME[(V)] THERE~unto to~>~POSSESS[(V)]~her and~*you*[(ms)]~*did*~GIVE[(V)]~& AT the~PRESENT UPON HILL Gerizim and~AT the~ANNOYANCE UPON HILL Eyval   **11:30** ?~NOT THEY[(m)] in~OTHER.SIDE the~Yarden AFTER ROAD ENTRANCE the~SUN in~LAND the~Kena'an~of the~SETTLE[(V)]~*ing*[(ms)] in~the~DESERT FOREFRONT the~Gilgal BESIDE GREAT.TREE~s Moreh   **11:31** GIVEN.THAT YOU[(mp)] CROSS.OVER[(V)]~*ing*[(mp)] AT the~Yarden to~>~COME[(V)] to~the~>~POSSESS[(V)] AT the~LAND WHICH **YHWH** Elohiym~you[(mp)] GIVE[(V)]~*ing*[(ms)] to~you[(mp)] and~*you*[(mp)]~*did*~POSSESS[(V)] AT~her and~*you*[(mp)]~*did*~SETTLE[(V)] in~her   **11:32** and~*you*[(mp)]~*did*~SAFEGUARD[(V)] to~>~DO[(V)] AT

ALL the~CUSTOM~s and~AT the~DECISION~s WHICH I GIVE⁽ⱽ⁾~ing⁽ᵐˢ⁾ to~ FACE~s~you⁽ᵐᵖ⁾ the~DAY

Chapter 12

12:1 THESE the~CUSTOM~s and~the~DECISION~s WHICH *you⁽ᵐᵖ⁾~will*~ SAFEGUARD⁽ⱽ⁾~must to~>~DO⁽ⱽ⁾ in~the~LAND WHICH *he~did*~GIVE⁽ⱽ⁾ **YHWH** Elohiym FATHER~s~you⁽ᵐˢ⁾ to~you⁽ᵐˢ⁾ to~>~POSSESS⁽ⱽ⁾~her ALL the~DAY~s WHICH YOU⁽ᵐᵖ⁾ LIVING~s UPON the~GROUND **12:2** >~*much*~PERISH⁽ⱽ⁾ *you⁽ᵐˢ⁾~will~much*~PERISH⁽ⱽ⁾~must AT ALL the~AREA~s WHICH *they~did*~ SERVE⁽ⱽ⁾ THERE the~NATION~s WHICH YOU⁽ᵐᵖ⁾ POSSESS⁽ⱽ⁾~*ing⁽ᵐᵖ⁾* AT~ them⁽ᵐ⁾ AT Elohiym~them⁽ᵐ⁾ UPON the~HILL~s the~RAISE.UP⁽ⱽ⁾~*ing⁽ᵐᵖ⁾* and~ UPON the~KNOLL~s and~UNDER ALL TREE FLOURISHING **12:3** and~*you⁽ᵐᵖ⁾~ did~much*~BREAK.DOWN⁽ⱽ⁾ AT ALTAR~s~them⁽ᵐ⁾ and~*you⁽ᵐᵖ⁾~did~much*~ CRACK⁽ⱽ⁾ AT MONUMENT~s~them⁽ᵐ⁾ and~GROVE~s~them⁽ᵐ⁾ *you⁽ᵐᵖ⁾~will*~ CREMATE⁽ⱽ⁾~must in~the~FIRE and~SCULPTURE~s Elohiym~them⁽ᵐ⁾ *you⁽ᵐᵖ⁾~ will~much*~CUT.DOWN⁽ⱽ⁾~must and~*you⁽ᵐᵖ⁾~did~much*~PERISH⁽ⱽ⁾ AT TITLE~ them⁽ᵐ⁾ FROM the~AREA the~HE **12:4** NOT *you⁽ᵐˢ⁾~will*~DO⁽ⱽ⁾~must SO to~ **YHWH** Elohiym~you⁽ᵐᵖ⁾ **12:5** GIVEN.THAT IF TO the~AREA WHICH *he~will*~ CHOOSE⁽ⱽ⁾ **YHWH** Elohiym~you⁽ᵐᵖ⁾ from~ALL STAFF~s~you⁽ᵐᵖ⁾ to~>~PLACE⁽ⱽ⁾ AT TITLE~him THERE to~>~DWELL⁽ⱽ⁾~him *you⁽ᵐᵖ⁾~will*~SEEK⁽ⱽ⁾ and~*you⁽ᵐˢ⁾~ did*~COME⁽ⱽ⁾ THERE~unto **12:6** and~*you⁽ᵐᵖ⁾~did~make*~COME⁽ⱽ⁾ THERE~ unto ASCENSION.OFFERING~s~you⁽ᵐᵖ⁾ and~SACRIFICE~s~you⁽ᵐᵖ⁾ and~AT from~TENTH.PART~s~you⁽ᵐᵖ⁾ and~AT OFFERING HAND~you⁽ᵐᵖ⁾ and~ VOW~s~you⁽ᵐᵖ⁾ and~FREEWILL.OFFERING~s~you⁽ᵐᵖ⁾ and~FIRSTBORN~s CATTLE~you⁽ᵐᵖ⁾ and~FLOCKS~you⁽ᵐᵖ⁾ **12:7** and~*you⁽ᵐᵖ⁾~did*~EAT⁽ⱽ⁾ THERE to~FACE~s **YHWH** Elohiym~you⁽ᵐᵖ⁾ and~REJOICING~you⁽ᵐᵖ⁾ in~ALL SENDING HAND~you⁽ᵐᵖ⁾ YOU⁽ᵐᵖ⁾ and~HOUSE~s~you⁽ᵐᵖ⁾ WHICH *he~did~much*~ KNEEL⁽ⱽ⁾~you⁽ᵐˢ⁾ **YHWH** Elohiym~you⁽ᵐˢ⁾ **12:8** NOT *you⁽ᵐˢ⁾~will*~DO⁽ⱽ⁾~must like~ALL WHICH WE DO⁽ⱽ⁾~*ing⁽ᵐᵖ⁾* HERE the~DAY MAN ALL the~STRAIGHT in~EYE~s2~him **12:9** GIVEN.THAT NOT *you⁽ᵐᵖ⁾~did*~COME⁽ⱽ⁾ UNTIL NOW TO the~OASIS and~TO the~INHERITANCE WHICH **YHWH** Elohiym~you⁽ᵐˢ⁾ GIVE⁽ⱽ⁾~*ing⁽ᵐˢ⁾* to~you⁽ᶠˢ⁾ **12:10** and~*you⁽ᵐᵖ⁾~did*~CROSS.OVER⁽ⱽ⁾ AT the~ Yarden and~*you⁽ᵐᵖ⁾~did*~SETTLE⁽ⱽ⁾ in~the~LAND WHICH **YHWH** Elohiym~ you⁽ᵐᵖ⁾ *make*~INHERIT⁽ⱽ⁾~*ing⁽ᵐˢ⁾* AT~you⁽ᵐᵖ⁾ and~*he~did~make*~REST⁽ⱽ⁾ to~ you⁽ᵐᵖ⁾ from~ALL ATTACK⁽ⱽ⁾~*ing⁽ᵐᵖ⁾*~you⁽ᵐᵖ⁾ from~ALL.AROUND and~*you⁽ᵐᵖ⁾~ did*~SETTLE⁽ⱽ⁾ SAFELY **12:11** and~*he~did*~EXIST⁽ⱽ⁾ the~AREA WHICH *he~will*~ CHOOSE⁽ⱽ⁾ **YHWH** Elohiym~you⁽ᵐᵖ⁾ in~him to~>~DWELL⁽ⱽ⁾ TITLE~him THERE THERE~unto *you⁽ᵐᵖ⁾~will~make*~COME⁽ⱽ⁾ AT ALL WHICH I *much*~DIRECT⁽ⱽ⁾~ *ing⁽ᵐˢ⁾* AT~you⁽ᵐᵖ⁾ ASCENSION.OFFERING~s~you⁽ᵐᵖ⁾ and~SACRIFICE~s~you⁽ᵐᵖ⁾ from~TENTH.PART~s~you⁽ᵐᵖ⁾ and~OFFERING HAND~you⁽ᵐᵖ⁾ and~ALL CHOSEN VOW~s~you⁽ᵐᵖ⁾ WHICH *you⁽ᵐᵖ⁾~will*~MAKE.A.VOW⁽ⱽ⁾ to~ **YHWH** **12:12** and~REJOICING~you⁽ᵐᵖ⁾ to~FACE~s **YHWH** Elohiym~you⁽ᵐᵖ⁾

YOU(mp) and~SON~s~you(mp) and~DAUGHTER~s~you(mp) and~SERVANT~s~you(mp) and~BONDWOMAN~s~you(mp) and~the~Lewi WHICH in~GATE~s~you(mp) GIVEN.THAT WITHOUT to~him DISTRIBUTION and~INHERITANCE AT~you(mp) **12:13** !(ms)~be~SAFEGUARD(V) to~you(ms) OTHERWISE you(ms)~will~make~GO.UP(V) ASCENSION.OFFERING~s~you(ms) in~ALL AREA WHICH you(ms)~will~SEE(V) **12:14** GIVEN.THAT IF in~the~AREA WHICH he~will~CHOOSE(V) **YHWH** in~UNIT STAFF~s~you(ms) THERE you(ms)~will~make~GO.UP(V) ASCENSION.OFFERING~s~you(ms) and~THERE you(ms)~will~DO(V) ALL WHICH I much~DIRECT(V)~ing(ms)~you(ms) **12:15** ONLY in~ALL DESIRE SOUL~you(ms) you(ms)~will~SACRIFICE(V) and~you(ms)~did~EAT(V) FLESH like~PRESENT **YHWH** Elohiym~you(ms) WHICH he~did~GIVE(V) to~you(ms) in~ALL GATE~s~you(ms) the~DIRTY and~the~CLEAN he~will~EAT(V)~him like~the~GAZELLE and~like~BUCK **12:16** ONLY the~BLOOD NOT you(mp)~will~EAT(V) UPON the~LAND you(ms)~will~POUR.OUT(V)~him like~the~WATER~s2 **12:17** NOT you(ms)~will~BE.ABLE(V) to~>~EAT(V) in~GATE~s~you(ms) TENTH.PART CEREAL~you(ms) and~FRESH.WINE~you(ms) and~FRESH.OIL~you(ms) and~FIRSTBORN~s CATTLE~you(ms) and~FLOCKS~you(ms) and~ALL VOW~s~you(ms) WHICH you(ms)~will~MAKE.A.VOW(V) and~FREEWILL.OFFERING~you(ms) and~OFFERING HAND~you(ms) **12:18** GIVEN.THAT IF to~FACE~s **YHWH** Elohiym~you(ms) you(ms)~will~EAT(V)~him in~the~AREA WHICH he~will~CHOOSE(V) **YHWH** Elohiym~you(ms) in~him YOU(ms) and~SON~you(ms) and~DAUGHTER~you(ms) and~SERVANT~you(ms) and~BONDWOMAN~you(ms) and~the~Lewi WHICH in~GATE~s~you(ms) and~you(ms)~did~REJOICE(V) to~FACE~s **YHWH** Elohiym~you(ms) in~ALL SENDING HAND~you(ms) **12:19** !(ms)~be~SAFEGUARD(V) to~you(ms) OTHERWISE you(ms)~will~LEAVE(V) AT the~Lewi ALL DAY~s~you(ms) UPON GROUND~you(ms) **12:20** GIVEN.THAT he~will~make~WIDEN(V) **YHWH** Elohiym~you(ms) AT BORDER~you(ms) like~WHICH he~did~much~SPEAK(V) to~you(fs) and~you(ms)~did~SAY(V) I~will~EAT(V)~& FLESH GIVEN.THAT she~will~much~YEARN(V) SOUL~you(ms) to~>~EAT(V) FLESH in~ALL DESIRE SOUL~you(ms) you(ms)~will~EAT(V) FLESH **12:21** GIVEN.THAT he~will~BE.FAR(V) FROM~you(ms) the~AREA WHICH he~will~CHOOSE(V) **YHWH** Elohiym~you(ms) to~>~PLACE(V) TITLE~him THERE and~you(ms)~did~SACRIFICE(V) from~CATTLE~you(ms) and~from~FLOCKS~you(ms) WHICH he~did~GIVE(V) **YHWH** to~you(ms) like~WHICH I~did~much~DIRECT(V)~you(ms) and~you(ms)~did~EAT(V) in~GATE~s~you(ms) in~ALL DESIRE SOUL~you(ms) **12:22** SURELY like~WHICH he~will~be~EAT(V) AT the~GAZELLE and~AT the~BUCK SO you(ms)~will~EAT(V)~him the~DIRTY and~the~CLEAN TOGETHER he~will~EAT(V)~him **12:23** ONLY !(ms)~SEIZE(V) to~EXCEPT >~EAT(V) the~BLOOD GIVEN.THAT the~BLOOD HE the~SOUL and~NOT you(ms)~will~EAT(V) the~SOUL WITH the~FLESH **12:24** NOT you(ms)~will~EAT(V)~him UPON the~LAND you(ms)~will~POUR.OUT(V)~him like~the~WATER~s2 **12:25** NOT you(ms)~will~EAT(V)~him to~THAT he~will~DO.WELL(V) to~you(ms) and~to~SON~s~you(ms) AFTER~you(ms) GIVEN.THAT you(ms)~will~DO(V) the~STRAIGHT in~EYE~s2 **YHWH** **12:26** ONLY SPECIAL~s~you(ms) WHICH they(m)~will~EXIST(V) to~you(ms) and~VOW~s~you(ms) you(ms)~will~LIFT.UP(V) and~*you*(ms)~*did*~COME(V) TO the~AREA WHICH *he*~*will*~CHOOSE(V) YHWH   **12:27** and~*you*(ms)~*did*~DO(V) ASCENSION.OFFERING~s~*you*(ms) the~FLESH and~the~BLOOD UPON ALTAR YHWH Elohiym~*you*(ms) and~BLOOD SACRIFICE~s~*you*(ms) *he*~*will*~*be*~POUR.OUT(V) UPON ALTAR YHWH Elohiym~*you*(ms) and~the~FLESH *you*(ms)~*will*~EAT(V)   **12:28** >~SAFEGUARD(V) and~*you*(ms)~*did*~HEAR(V) AT ALL the~WORD~s the~THESE WHICH I *much*~DIRECT(V)~*ing*(ms)~*you*(ms) to~THAT *he*~*will*~DO.WELL(V) to~*you*(ms) and~to~SON~s~*you*(ms) AFTER~*you*(ms) UNTIL DISTANT GIVEN.THAT *you*(ms)~*will*~DO(V) the~FUNCTIONAL and~the~STRAIGHT in~EYE~s2 YHWH Elohiym~*you*(ms)   **12:29** GIVEN.THAT *he*~*will*~*make*~CUT(V) YHWH Elohiym~*you*(ms) AT the~NATION~s WHICH YOU(ms) *he*~*did*~COME(V) THERE~unto to~the~>~POSSESS(V) AT~them(m) from~FACE~s~*you*(ms) and~*you*(ms)~*did*~POSSESS(V) AT~them(m) and~*you*(ms)~*did*~SETTLE(V) in~LAND~them(m)   **12:30** !(ms)~*be*~SAFEGUARD(V) to~*you*(ms) OTHERWISE *you*(ms)~*will*~*be*~ENSNARE(V) AFTER~them(m) AFTER >~*be*~DESTROY(V)~them(m) from~FACE~s~*you*(ms) and~OTHERWISE *you*(ms)~*will*~SEEK(V) to~Elohiym~them(m) to~>~SAY(V) HOW *they*(m)~*will*~SERVE(V) the~NATION~s the~THESE AT Elohiym~them(m) and~*I*~*will*~DO(V)~& SO ALSO I   **12:31** NOT *you*(ms)~*will*~DO(V) SO to~YHWH Elohiym~*you*(ms) GIVEN.THAT ALL DISGUSTING YHWH WHICH *he*~*did*~HATE(V) *they*~*did*~DO(V) to~Elohiym~them(m) GIVEN.THAT ALSO AT SON~s~them(m) and~AT DAUGHTER~s~them(m) *they*(m)~*will*~CREMATE(V) in~the~FIRE to~Elohiym~them(m)

Chapter 13

13:1 (12:32) AT ALL the~WORD WHICH I *much*~DIRECT(V)~*ing*(ms) AT~*you*(mp) AT~him *you*(mp)~*will*~SAFEGUARD(V) to~>~DO(V) NOT *you*(ms)~*will*~*make*~ADD(V) UPON~him and~NOT *you*(ms)~*will*~TAKE.AWAY(V) FROM~him   **13:2 (13:1)** GIVEN.THAT *he*~*will*~RISE(V) in~INSIDE~*you*(ms) ANNOUNCER OR DREAM(V)~*ing*(ms) DREAM and~*he*~*did*~GIVE(V) TO~*you*(ms) SIGN OR WONDER   **13:3 (13:2)** and~*he*~*did*~COME(V) the~SIGN and~the~WONDER WHICH *he*~*did*~*much*~SPEAK(V) TO~*you*(ms) to~>~SAY(V) *we*~*will*~WALK(V)~& AFTER Elohiym OTHER~s WHICH NOT *you*(ms)~*did*~KNOW(V)~them(m) and~*we*~*will*~*be*~*make*~SERVE(V)~them(m)   **13:4 (13:3)** NOT *you*(ms)~*will*~HEAR(V) TO WORD~s the~ANNOUNCER the~HE OR TO DREAM(V)~*ing*(ms) the~DREAM the~HE GIVEN.THAT *much*~TEST(V)~*ing*(ms) YHWH Elohiym~*you*(mp) AT~*you*(mp) to~>~KNOW(V) ?~THERE.IS~*you*(mp) LOVE(V)~*ing*(mp) AT YHWH Elohiym~*you*(mp) in~ALL HEART~*you*(mp) and~in~ALL SOUL~*you*(ms)   **13:5 (13:4)** AFTER YHWH Elohiym~*you*(mp) *you*(mp)~*will*~WALK(V) and~AT~him *you*(mp)~*will*~FEAR(V) and~AT DIRECTIVE~s~him *you*(mp)~*will*~SAFEGUARD(V) and~in~VOICE~him *you*(mp)~*will*~HEAR(V) and~AT~him *you*(mp)~*will*~SERVE(V) and~in~him *you*(mp)~*will*~ADHERE(V)~must   **13:6 (13:5)** and~the~ANNOUNCER the~HE OR DREAM(V)~*ing*(ms) the~

The Book of Deuteronomy

DREAM the~HE *he~will~be~make~*DIE⁽ⱽ⁾ GIVEN.THAT *he~did~much~*SPEAK⁽ⱽ⁾ TURNING.ASIDE UPON **YHWH** Elohiym~you⁽ᵐᵖ⁾ the~*make~*GO.OUT⁽ⱽ⁾~*ing*⁽ᵐˢ⁾ AT~you⁽ᵐᵖ⁾ from~LAND Mits'rayim and~the~RANSOM⁽ⱽ⁾~*ing*⁽ᵐˢ⁾~you⁽ᵐˢ⁾ from~HOUSE SERVANT~s to~>~*make~*DRIVE.OUT⁽ⱽ⁾~you⁽ᵐˢ⁾ FROM the~ROAD WHICH *he~did~much~*DIRECT⁽ⱽ⁾~you⁽ᵐˢ⁾ **YHWH** Elohiym~you⁽ᵐˢ⁾ to~>~WALK⁽ⱽ⁾ in~her and~*you*⁽ᵐˢ⁾*~did~much~*BURN⁽ⱽ⁾ the~DYSFUNCTIONAL from~INSIDE~you⁽ᵐˢ⁾ **13:7 (13:6)** GIVEN.THAT *he~will~make~*PERSUADE⁽ⱽ⁾~you⁽ᵐˢ⁾ BROTHER~you⁽ᵐˢ⁾ SON MOTHER~you⁽ᵐˢ⁾ OR SON~you⁽ᵐˢ⁾ OR DAUGHTER~you⁽ᵐˢ⁾ OR WOMAN BOSOM~you⁽ᵐˢ⁾ OR COMPANION~you⁽ᵐˢ⁾ WHICH like~SOUL~you⁽ᵐˢ⁾ in~the~HIDING to~>~SAY⁽ⱽ⁾ *we~will~*WALK⁽ⱽ⁾~& and~*we~will~*SERVE⁽ⱽ⁾~& Elohiym OTHER~s WHICH NOT *you*⁽ᵐˢ⁾*~did~*KNOW⁽ⱽ⁾ YOU⁽ᵐˢ⁾ and~FATHER~s~you⁽ᵐˢ⁾ **13:8 (13:7)** from~Elohiym the~PEOPLE~s WHICH ALL.AROUND~s~you⁽ᵐᵖ⁾ the~NEAR~s TO~you⁽ᵐˢ⁾ OR the~DISTANCE~s FROM~you⁽ᵐˢ⁾ from~EXTREMITY the~LAND and~UNTIL EXTREMITY the~LAND **13:9 (13:8)** NOT *you*⁽ᵐˢ⁾*~will~*CONSENT⁽ⱽ⁾ to~him and~NOT *you*⁽ᵐˢ⁾*~will~*HEAR⁽ⱽ⁾ TO~him and~NOT *she~will~*SPARE⁽ⱽ⁾ EYE~you⁽ᵐˢ⁾ UPON~him and~NOT *you*⁽ᵐˢ⁾*~will~*SHOW.PITY⁽ⱽ⁾ and~NOT *you*⁽ᵐˢ⁾*~will~much~*COVER.OVER⁽ⱽ⁾ UPON~him **13:10 (13:9)** GIVEN.THAT >~KILL⁽ⱽ⁾ *you*⁽ᵐˢ⁾*~will~*KILL⁽ⱽ⁾~him HAND~you⁽ᵐˢ⁾ *she~will~*EXIST⁽ⱽ⁾ in~him in~the~FIRST to~>~*make~*DIE⁽ⱽ⁾~him and~HAND ALL the~PEOPLE in~the~LAST **13:11 (13:10)** and~*you*⁽ᵐˢ⁾*~did~*STONE⁽ⱽ⁾~him in~the~STONE~s and~*he~did~*DIE⁽ⱽ⁾ GIVEN.THAT *he~did~much~*SEARCH.OUT⁽ⱽ⁾ to~>~*make~*DRIVE.OUT⁽ⱽ⁾~you⁽ᵐˢ⁾ from~UPON **YHWH** Elohiym~you⁽ᵐˢ⁾ the~*make~*GO.OUT⁽ⱽ⁾~*ing*⁽ᵐˢ⁾~you⁽ᵐˢ⁾ from~LAND Mits'rayim from~HOUSE SERVANT~s **13:12 (13:11)** and~ALL Yisra'eyl *they*⁽ᵐ⁾*~will~*HEAR⁽ⱽ⁾ and~*they*⁽ᵐ⁾*~will~*FEAR⁽ⱽ⁾~must and~NOT *they*⁽ᵐ⁾*~will~make~*ADD⁽ⱽ⁾ to~>~DO⁽ⱽ⁾ like~the~WORD the~DYSFUNCTIONAL the~THIS in~INSIDE~you⁽ᵐˢ⁾ **13:13 (13:12)** GIVEN.THAT *you*⁽ᵐˢ⁾*~will~*HEAR⁽ⱽ⁾ in~UNIT CITY~s~you⁽ᵐˢ⁾ WHICH **YHWH** Elohiym~you⁽ᵐˢ⁾ GIVE⁽ⱽ⁾~*ing*⁽ᵐˢ⁾ to~you⁽ᵐˢ⁾ to~>~SETTLE⁽ⱽ⁾ THERE to~>~SAY⁽ⱽ⁾ **13:14 (13:13)** *they~did~*GO.OUT⁽ⱽ⁾ MAN~s SON~s Beli'ya'al from~INSIDE~you⁽ᵐˢ⁾ and~*they*⁽ᵐ⁾*~will~make~*DRIVE.OUT⁽ⱽ⁾ AT SETTLE⁽ⱽ⁾~*ing*⁽ᵐᵖ⁾ CITY~them⁽ᵐ⁾ to~>~SAY⁽ⱽ⁾ *we~will~*WALK⁽ⱽ⁾~& and~*we~will~*SERVE⁽ⱽ⁾~& Elohiym OTHER~s WHICH NOT *you*⁽ᵐᵖ⁾*~did~*KNOW⁽ⱽ⁾ **13:15 (13:14)** and~*you*⁽ᵐˢ⁾*~did~*SEEK⁽ⱽ⁾ and~*you*⁽ᵐˢ⁾*~did~*EXAMINE⁽ⱽ⁾ and~*you*⁽ᵐˢ⁾*~did~*INQUIRE⁽ⱽ⁾ >~*make~*DO.WELL⁽ⱽ⁾ and~LOOK TRUTH *be~*PREPARE⁽ⱽ⁾~*ing*⁽ᵐˢ⁾ the~WORD *she~did~be~*DO⁽ⱽ⁾ the~DISGUSTING the~THIS in~INSIDE~you⁽ᵐˢ⁾ **13:16 (13:15)** >~*make~*HIT⁽ⱽ⁾ *you*⁽ᵐˢ⁾*~will~make~*HIT⁽ⱽ⁾ AT SETTLE⁽ⱽ⁾~*ing*⁽ᵐᵖ⁾ the~CITY the~HE to~MOUTH SWORD >~*make~*PERFORATE⁽ⱽ⁾ AT~her and~AT ALL WHICH in~her and~AT BEAST~her to~MOUTH SWORD **13:17 (13:16)** and~AT ALL SPOIL~her *you*⁽ᵐˢ⁾*~will~*GATHER.TOGETHER⁽ⱽ⁾ TO MIDST STREET~unto and~*you*⁽ᵐˢ⁾*~did~*CREMATE⁽ⱽ⁾ in~the~FIRE AT the~CITY and~AT ALL SPOIL~her ENTIRELY to~**YHWH** Elohiym~you⁽ᵐˢ⁾ and~*she~did~*EXIST⁽ⱽ⁾ RUIN DISTANT NOT *she~will~be~*BUILD⁽ⱽ⁾ YET.AGAIN **13:18 (13:17)** and~NOT *he~will~*ADHERE⁽ⱽ⁾ in~HAND~you⁽ᵐˢ⁾ ANYTHING FROM the~PERFORATED to~THAT *he~will~*

TURN.BACK^(V) **YHWH** from~FLAMING.WRATH NOSE~him and~*he~did~* GIVE^(V) to~you^(ms) BOWELS~s and~*he~did~much~*HAVE.COMPASSION^(V)~ you^(ms) and~*he~did~make~*INCREASE^(V)~you^(ms) like~WHICH *he~did~be~* SWEAR^(V) to~FATHER~s~you^(ms) **13:19 (13:18)** GIVEN.THAT *you*^(ms)~*will~* HEAR^(V) in~VOICE **YHWH** Elohiym~you^(ms) to~>~SAFEGUARD^(V) AT ALL DIRECTIVE~s~him WHICH I *much~*DIRECT^(V)~*ing*^(ms)~you^(ms) the~DAY to~>~ DO^(V) the~STRAIGHT in~EYE~s2 **YHWH** Elohiym~you^(ms)

Chapter 14

14:1 SON~s YOU^(mp) to~**YHWH** Elohiym~you^(mp) NOT *you*^(mp)~*will~self~* BAND.TOGETHER^(V) and~NOT *you*^(mp)~*will~*PLACE^(V) BALD.SPOT BETWEEN EYE~s2~you^(mp) to~the~DIE^(V)~*ing*^(ms) **14:2** GIVEN.THAT PEOPLE UNIQUE YOU^(ms) to~**YHWH** Elohiym~you^(ms) and~in~you^(ms) *he~did~*CHOOSE^(V) **YHWH** to~>~EXIST^(V) to~him to~PEOPLE JEWEL from~ALL the~PEOPLE~s WHICH UPON FACE~s the~GROUND **14:3** NOT *you*^(ms)~*will~*EAT^(V) ALL DISGUSTING **14:4** THIS the~BEAST WHICH *you*^(mp)~*will~*EAT^(V) OX RAM SHEEP~s and~RAM SHE-GOAT~s **14:5** BUCK and~GAZELLE and~ROEBUCK and~WILD.GOAT and~ANTELOPE and~ORYX and~MOUNTAIN-SHEEP **14:6** and~ALL BEAST *make~*CLEAVE^(V)~*ing*^(fs) HOOF and~ SPLIT.IN.TWO^(V)~*ing*^(fs) SPLITTING TWO HOOF~s *make~*GO.UP^(V)~*ing*^(fs) CUD in~the~BEAST AT~her *you*^(mp)~*will~*EAT^(V) **14:7** SURELY AT THIS NOT *you*^(mp)~*will~*EAT^(V) from~*make~*GO.UP^(V)~*ing*^(mp) the~CUD and~from~*make~* CLEAVE^(V)~*ing*^(mp) the~HOOF the~SPLIT.IN.TWO^(V)~*ed*^(fs) AT the~CAMEL and~ AT the~HARE and~AT the~RABBIT GIVEN.THAT *make~*GO.UP^(V)~*ing*^(fs) CUD THEY^(m) and~HOOF NOT *they~did~make~*CLEAVE^(V) DIRTY~s THEY^(m) to~ you^(mp) **14:8** and~AT the~SWINE GIVEN.THAT *make~*CLEAVE^(V)~*ing*^(ms) HOOF HE and~NOT CUD DIRTY HE to~you^(mp) from~FLESH~them^(m) NOT *you*^(mp)~ *will~*EAT^(V) and~in~CARCASS~them^(m) NOT *you*^(mp)~*will~*TOUCH^(V) **14:9** AT THIS *you*^(mp)~*will~*EAT^(V) from~ALL WHICH in~the~WATER~s2 ALL WHICH to~ him FIN and~SCALES *you*^(mp)~*will~*EAT^(V) **14:10** and~ALL WHICH WITHOUT to~him FIN and~SCALES NOT *you*^(mp)~*will~*EAT^(V) DIRTY HE to~ you^(mp) **14:11** ALL BIRD CLEAN *you*^(mp)~*will~*EAT^(V) **14:12** and~THIS WHICH NOT *you*^(mp)~*will~*EAT^(V) from~them^(m) the~EAGLE and~the~ BEARDED.VULTURE and~the~OSPREY **14:13** and~the~KITE and~AT the~ HAWK and~the~VULTURE to~KIND~her **14:14** and~AT ALL RAVEN to~ KIND~him **14:15** and~AT DAUGHTER the~OWL and~AT the~NIGHTHAWK and~AT the~SEAGULL and~AT the~FALCON to~KIND~him **14:16** AT the~ LITTLE.OWL and~AT the~EARED.OWL and~the~IBIS **14:17** and~the~ PELICAN and~AT the~GIER-EAGLE and~AT the~CORMORANT **14:18** and~ the~STORK and~the~HERON to~KIND~her and~the~GROUSE and~the~ BAT **14:19** and~ALL SWARMER the~FLYER DIRTY HE to~you^(mp) NOT *they*^(m)~ *will~be~*EAT^(V) **14:20** ALL FLYER CLEAN *you*^(mp)~*will~*EAT^(V) **14:21** NOT

The Book of Deuteronomy

you⁽ᵐᵖ⁾~will~EAT⁽ⱽ⁾ ALL CARCASS to~the~IMMIGRANT WHICH in~GATE~s~*you*⁽ᵐˢ⁾ *you*⁽ᵐˢ⁾~will~GIVE⁽ⱽ⁾~her and~*he*~*did*~EAT⁽ⱽ⁾~her OR >~SELL⁽ⱽ⁾ to~FOREIGNER GIVEN.THAT PEOPLE UNIQUE YOU⁽ᵐˢ⁾ to~YHWH Elohiym~*you*⁽ᵐˢ⁾ NOT *you*⁽ᵐˢ⁾~will~much~BOIL⁽ⱽ⁾ MALE.KID in~the~FAT MOTHER~him **14:22** >~much~GIVE.A.TENTH⁽ⱽ⁾ *you*⁽ᵐˢ⁾~will~GIVE.A.TENTH⁽ⱽ⁾ AT ALL PRODUCTION SEED~*you*⁽ᵐˢ⁾ the~GO.OUT⁽ⱽ⁾~*ing*⁽ᵐˢ⁾ the~FIELD YEAR YEAR **14:23** and~*you*⁽ᵐˢ⁾~*did*~EAT⁽ⱽ⁾ to~FACE~s YHWH Elohiym~*you*⁽ᵐˢ⁾ in~the~AREA WHICH *he*~will~CHOOSE⁽ⱽ⁾ to~>~DWELL⁽ⱽ⁾ TITLE~him THERE TENTH.PART CEREAL~*you*⁽ᵐˢ⁾ FRESH.WINE~*you*⁽ᵐˢ⁾ and~FRESH.OIL~*you*⁽ᵐˢ⁾ and~FIRSTBORN~s CATTLE~*you*⁽ᵐˢ⁾ and~FLOCKS~*you*⁽ᵐˢ⁾ to~THAT *you*⁽ᵐˢ⁾~will~LEARN⁽ⱽ⁾ to~>~FEAR⁽ⱽ⁾ AT YHWH Elohiym~*you*⁽ᵐˢ⁾ ALL the~DAY~s **14:24** and~GIVEN.THAT *he*~will~INCREASE⁽ⱽ⁾ FROM~*you*⁽ᵐˢ⁾ the~ROAD GIVEN.THAT NOT *you*⁽ᵐˢ⁾~will~BE.ABLE⁽ⱽ⁾ >~LIFT.UP⁽ⱽ⁾~him GIVEN.THAT *he*~will~BE.FAR⁽ⱽ⁾ FROM~*you*⁽ᵐˢ⁾ the~AREA WHICH *he*~will~CHOOSE⁽ⱽ⁾ YHWH Elohiym~*you*⁽ᵐˢ⁾ to~>~PLACE⁽ⱽ⁾ TITLE~him THERE GIVEN.THAT *he*~will~much~KNEEL⁽ⱽ⁾~*you*⁽ᵐˢ⁾ YHWH Elohiym~*you*⁽ᵐˢ⁾ **14:25** and~*you*⁽ᵐˢ⁾~*did*~GIVE⁽ⱽ⁾~& in~SILVER and~*you*⁽ᵐˢ⁾~*did*~SMACK⁽ⱽ⁾ the~SILVER in~HAND~*you*⁽ᵐˢ⁾ and~*you*⁽ᵐˢ⁾~*did*~WALK⁽ⱽ⁾ TO the~AREA WHICH *he*~will~CHOOSE⁽ⱽ⁾ YHWH Elohiym~*you*⁽ᵐˢ⁾ in~him **14:26** and~*you*⁽ᵐˢ⁾~*did*~GIVE⁽ⱽ⁾~& the~SILVER in~ALL WHICH *she*~will~much~YEARN⁽ⱽ⁾ SOUL~*you*⁽ᵐˢ⁾ in~the~CATTLE and~in~the~FLOCKS and~in~the~WINE and~in~the~LIQUOR and~in~ALL WHICH *she*~will~INQUIRE⁽ⱽ⁾~*you*⁽ᵐˢ⁾ SOUL~*you*⁽ᵐˢ⁾ and~*you*⁽ᵐˢ⁾~*did*~EAT⁽ⱽ⁾ THERE to~FACE~s YHWH Elohiym~*you*⁽ᵐˢ⁾ and~*you*⁽ᵐˢ⁾~*did*~REJOICE⁽ⱽ⁾ YOU⁽ᵐˢ⁾ and~HOUSE~*you*⁽ᵐˢ⁾ **14:27** and~the~Lewi WHICH in~GATE~s~*you*⁽ᵐˢ⁾ NOT *you*⁽ᵐˢ⁾~will~LEAVE⁽ⱽ⁾~him GIVEN.THAT WITHOUT to~him DISTRIBUTION and~INHERITANCE WITH~*you*⁽ᶠˢ⁾ **14:28** from~EXTREMITY THREE YEAR~s *you*⁽ᵐˢ⁾~will~make~GO.OUT⁽ⱽ⁾ AT ALL TENTH.PART PRODUCTION~*you*⁽ᵐˢ⁾ in~the~YEAR the~SHE and~*you*⁽ᵐˢ⁾~*did*~make~REST⁽ⱽ⁾ in~GATE~s~*you*⁽ᵐˢ⁾ **14:29** and~*he*~*did*~COME⁽ⱽ⁾ the~Lewi GIVEN.THAT WITHOUT to~him DISTRIBUTION and~INHERITANCE WITH~*you*⁽ᶠˢ⁾ and~the~IMMIGRANT and~the~ORPHAN and~the~WIDOW WHICH in~GATE~s~*you*⁽ᵐˢ⁾ and~*they*~*did*~EAT⁽ⱽ⁾ and~*they*~*did*~BE.SATISFIED⁽ⱽ⁾ to~THAT *he*~will~much~KNEEL⁽ⱽ⁾~*you*⁽ᵐˢ⁾ YHWH Elohiym~*you*⁽ᵐˢ⁾ in~ALL WORK HAND~*you*⁽ᵐˢ⁾ WHICH *you*⁽ᵐˢ⁾~will~DO⁽ⱽ⁾

Chapter 15

15:1 from~CONCLUSION SEVEN YEAR~s *you*⁽ᵐˢ⁾~will~DO⁽ⱽ⁾ RELEASE **15:2** and~THIS WORD the~RELEASE >~RELEASE⁽ⱽ⁾ ALL MASTER LOAN HAND~him WHICH *he*~will~make~OVERLOOK⁽ⱽ⁾ in~COMPANION~him NOT *he*~will~PUSH⁽ⱽ⁾ AT COMPANION~him and~AT BROTHER~him GIVEN.THAT *he*~*did*~CALL.OUT⁽ⱽ⁾ RELEASE to~YHWH **15:3** AT the~FOREIGNER *you*⁽ᵐˢ⁾~will~PUSH⁽ⱽ⁾ and~WHICH *he*~will~EXIST⁽ⱽ⁾ to~*you*⁽ᵐˢ⁾ AT

BROTHER~you[(ms)] *you[(ms)]~will~make*~RELEASE[(V)] HAND~you[(ms)]   **15:4** FAR.END GIVEN.THAT NOT *he~will*~EXIST[(V)] in~you[(ms)] NEEDY GIVEN.THAT >~*much*~KNEEL[(V)] *he~will~much*~KNEEL[(V)]~you[(ms)] **YHWH** in~the~LAND WHICH **YHWH** Elohiym~you[(ms)] GIVE[(V)]~*ing[(ms)]* to~you[(ms)] INHERITANCE to~>~POSSESS[(V)]~her   **15:5** ONLY IF >~HEAR[(V)] *you[(ms)]~will*~HEAR[(V)] in~VOICE **YHWH** Elohiym~you[(ms)] to~>~SAFEGUARD[(V)] to~>~DO[(V)] AT ALL the~DIRECTIVE the~THIS WHICH I *much*~DIRECT[(V)]~*ing[(ms)]*~you[(ms)] the~DAY   **15:6** GIVEN.THAT **YHWH** Elohiym~you[(ms)] *he~did~much*~KNEEL[(V)]~you[(ms)] like~WHICH *he~did~much*~SPEAK[(V)] to~you[(fs)] and~*you[(ms)]~did~make*~MAKE.A.PLEDGE[(V)] NATION~s ABUNDANT~s and~YOU[(ms)] NOT *you[(ms)]~will*~MAKE.A.PLEDGE[(V)] and~*you[(ms)]~did*~REGULATE[(V)] in~NATION~s ABUNDANT~s and~in~you[(ms)] NOT *they[(m)]~will*~REGULATE[(V)]   **15:7** GIVEN.THAT *he~will*~EXIST[(V)] in~you[(ms)] NEEDY from~UNIT BROTHER~s~you[(ms)] in~UNIT GATE~s~you[(ms)] in~LAND~you[(ms)] WHICH **YHWH** Elohiym~you[(ms)] GIVE[(V)]~*ing[(ms)]* to~you[(fs)] NOT *you[(ms)]~will~much*~BE.STRONG[(V)] AT HEART~you[(ms)] and~NOT *you[(ms)]~will*~CLOSE[(V)] AT HAND~you[(ms)] from~to~BROTHER~you[(ms)] the~NEEDY   **15:8** GIVEN.THAT >~OPEN[(V)] *she~will*~OPEN[(V)] AT HAND~you[(ms)] to~him and~>~*make*~MAKE.A.PLEDGE[(V)] *you[(ms)]~will~make*~MAKE.A.PLEDGE[(V)]~him SUFFICIENT LACKING~him WHICH *he~will*~DIMINISH[(V)] to~him   **15:9** ![(ms)]~be~SAFEGUARD[(V)] to~you[(ms)] OTHERWISE *he~will*~EXIST[(V)] WORD WITH HEART~you[(ms)] UNAWARE + *he~will*~Gain[(V)] to~>~SAY[(V)] *she~did*~COME.NEAR[(V)] YEAR the~SEVEN YEAR the~RELEASE and~*she~did*~BE.DYSFUNCTIONAL[(V)] EYE~you[(ms)] in~BROTHER~you[(ms)] the~NEEDY and~NOT *you[(ms)]~will*~GIVE[(V)] to~him and~*he~did*~CALL.OUT[(V)] UPON~you[(ms)] TO **YHWH** and~*he~did*~EXIST[(V)] in~you[(ms)] FAILURE   **15:10** >~GIVE[(V)] *you[(ms)]~will*~GIVE[(V)] to~him and~NOT *he~will*~BE.DYSFUNCTIONAL[(V)] HEART~you[(ms)] in~>~GIVE[(V)]~you[(ms)] to~him GIVEN.THAT in~ON.ACCOUNT.OF the~WORD the~THIS *he~will~much*~KNEEL[(V)]~you[(ms)] **YHWH** Elohiym~you[(ms)] in~ALL WORK~you[(ms)] and~in~ALL SENDING HAND~you[(ms)]   **15:11** GIVEN.THAT NOT *he~will*~TERMINATE[(V)] NEEDY from~INSIDE the~LAND UPON SO I *much*~DIRECT[(V)]~*ing[(ms)]*~you[(ms)] to~>~SAY[(V)] >~OPEN[(V)] *she~will*~OPEN[(V)] AT HAND~you[(ms)] to~BROTHER~you[(ms)] to~AFFLICTION~you[(ms)] and~to~NEEDY~you[(ms)] in~LAND~you[(ms)]   **15:12** GIVEN.THAT *he~will~be*~SELL[(V)] to~you[(ms)] BROTHER~you[(ms)] the~Ever~of OR the~Ever~of and~*he~did*~SERVE[(V)]~you[(ms)] SIX YEAR~s and~in~the~YEAR the~SEVENTH *you[(ms)]~will~much*~SEND[(V)]~him FREE from~WITH~you[(ms)]   **15:13** and~GIVEN.THAT *you[(ms)]~will~much*~SEND[(V)]~him FREE from~WITH~you[(ms)] NOT *you[(ms)]~will~much*~SEND[(V)]~him EMPTINESS   **15:14** >~*make*~ENCOMPASS[(V)] *you[(ms)]~will~make*~ENCOMPASS[(V)] to~him from~FLOCKS~you[(ms)] and~from~FLOOR~you[(ms)] and~from~WINE.TROUGH~you[(ms)] WHICH *he~did~much*~KNEEL[(V)]~you[(ms)] **YHWH** Elohiym~you[(ms)] *you[(ms)]~will*~GIVE[(V)] to~him   **15:15** and~*you[(ms)]~did*~REMEMBER[(V)] GIVEN.THAT SERVANT *you[(ms)]~did*~EXIST[(V)] in~LAND Mits'rayim and~*he~will*~RANSOM[(V)]~you[(ms)] **YHWH** Elohiym~you[(ms)] UPON SO I *much*~DIRECT[(V)]~*ing[(ms)]*~you[(ms)] AT the~WORD the~THIS the~

DAY **15:16** and~*he*~*did*~EXIST⁽ᵛ⁾ GIVEN.THAT *he*~*will*~SAY⁽ᵛ⁾ TO~you⁽ᵐˢ⁾ NOT *I*~*will*~GO.OUT⁽ᵛ⁾ from~WITH~you⁽ᵐˢ⁾ GIVEN.THAT *he*~*did*~LOVE⁽ᵛ⁾~you⁽ᵐˢ⁾ and~AT HOUSE~you⁽ᵐˢ⁾ GIVEN.THAT FUNCTIONAL to~him WITH~you⁽ᶠˢ⁾ **15:17** and~*you*⁽ᵐˢ⁾~*did*~TAKE⁽ᵛ⁾ AT the~AWL and~*you*⁽ᵐˢ⁾~*did*~GIVE⁽ᵛ⁾~& in~EAR~him and~in~the~DOOR and~*he*~*did*~EXIST⁽ᵛ⁾ to~you⁽ᵐˢ⁾ SERVANT DISTANT and~MOREOVER to~the~BONDWOMAN~you⁽ᵐˢ⁾ *you*⁽ᵐˢ⁾~*will*~DO⁽ᵛ⁾ SO **15:18** NOT *he*~*will*~BE.HARD⁽ᵛ⁾ in~EYE~you⁽ᵐˢ⁾ in~>~much~SEND⁽ᵛ⁾ AT~him FREE from~WITH~you⁽ᵐˢ⁾ GIVEN.THAT DOUBLE WAGE HIRELING *he*~*did*~SERVE⁽ᵛ⁾~you⁽ᵐˢ⁾ SIX YEAR~s and~*he*~*did*~much~KNEEL⁽ᵛ⁾~you⁽ᵐˢ⁾ **YHWH** Elohiym~you⁽ᵐˢ⁾ in~ALL WHICH *you*⁽ᵐˢ⁾~*will*~DO⁽ᵛ⁾ **15:19** ALL the~FIRSTBORN WHICH *he*~*will*~*be*~BRING.FORTH⁽ᵛ⁾ in~CATTLE~you⁽ᵐˢ⁾ and~in~FLOCKS~you⁽ᵐˢ⁾ the~MALE *you*⁽ᵐˢ⁾~*will*~make~SET.APART⁽ᵛ⁾ to~**YHWH** Elohiym~you⁽ᵐˢ⁾ NOT *you*⁽ᵐˢ⁾~*will*~SERVE⁽ᵛ⁾ in~FIRSTBORN OX~s you⁽ᵐˢ⁾ and~NOT *you*⁽ᵐˢ⁾~*will*~SHEAR⁽ᵛ⁾ FIRSTBORN FLOCKS~you⁽ᵐˢ⁾ **15:20** to~FACE~s **YHWH** Elohiym~you⁽ᵐˢ⁾ *you*⁽ᵐˢ⁾~*will*~EAT⁽ᵛ⁾~him YEAR in~YEAR in~the~AREA WHICH *he*~*will*~CHOOSE⁽ᵛ⁾ **YHWH** YOU⁽ᵐˢ⁾ and~HOUSE~you⁽ᵐˢ⁾ **15:21** and~GIVEN.THAT *he*~*will*~EXIST⁽ᵛ⁾ in~him BLEMISH LAME OR BLIND ALL BLEMISH DYSFUNCTIONAL NOT *you*⁽ᵐˢ⁾~*will*~SACRIFICE⁽ᵛ⁾~him to~**YHWH** Elohiym~you⁽ᵐˢ⁾ **15:22** in~GATE~s~you⁽ᵐˢ⁾ *you*⁽ᵐˢ⁾~*will*~EAT⁽ᵛ⁾~him the~DIRTY and~the~CLEAN TOGETHER like~the~GAZELLE and~like~BUCK **15:23** ONLY AT BLOOD~him NOT *you*⁽ᵐˢ⁾~*will*~EAT⁽ᵛ⁾ UPON the~LAND *you*⁽ᵐˢ⁾~*will*~POUR.OUT⁽ᵛ⁾~him like~the~WATER~s2

Chapter 16

16:1 >~SAFEGUARD⁽ᵛ⁾ AT NEW.MOON the~GREEN.GRAIN and~*you*⁽ᵐˢ⁾~*did*~DO⁽ᵛ⁾ Pesahh to~**YHWH** Elohiym~you⁽ᵐˢ⁾ GIVEN.THAT in~NEW.MOON the~GREEN.GRAIN *he*~*did*~make~GO.OUT⁽ᵛ⁾~you⁽ᵐˢ⁾ **YHWH** Elohiym~you⁽ᵐˢ⁾ from~Mits'rayim NIGHT **16:2** and~*you*⁽ᵐˢ⁾~*did*~SACRIFICE⁽ᵛ⁾ Pesahh to~**YHWH** Elohiym~you⁽ᵐˢ⁾ FLOCKS and~CATTLE in~the~AREA WHICH *he*~*will*~CHOOSE⁽ᵛ⁾ **YHWH** to~>~DWELL⁽ᵛ⁾ TITLE~him THERE **16:3** NOT *you*⁽ᵐˢ⁾~*will*~EAT⁽ᵛ⁾ UPON~him LEAVENED.BREAD SEVEN DAY~s *you*⁽ᵐˢ⁾~*will*~EAT⁽ᵛ⁾ UPON~him UNLEAVENED.BREAD~s BREAD AFFLICTION GIVEN.THAT in~HASTE *you*⁽ᵐˢ⁾~*did*~GO.OUT⁽ᵛ⁾ from~LAND Mits'rayim to~THAT *you*⁽ᵐˢ⁾~*will*~REMEMBER⁽ᵛ⁾ AT DAY >~GO.OUT⁽ᵛ⁾~you⁽ᵐˢ⁾ from~LAND Mits'rayim ALL DAY~s LIVING~s~you⁽ᵐˢ⁾ **16:4** and~NOT *he*~*will*~*be*~SEE⁽ᵛ⁾ to~you⁽ᵐˢ⁾ LEAVEN in~ALL BORDER~you⁽ᵐˢ⁾ SEVEN DAY~s and~NOT *he*~*will*~STAY.THE.NIGHT⁽ᵛ⁾ FROM the~FLESH WHICH *you*⁽ᵐˢ⁾~*will*~SACRIFICE⁽ᵛ⁾ in~the~EVENING in~the~DAY the~FIRST to~the~MORNING **16:5** NOT *you*⁽ᵐˢ⁾~*will*~BE.ABLE⁽ᵛ⁾ to~>~SACRIFICE⁽ᵛ⁾ AT the~Pesahh in~UNIT GATE~s~you⁽ᵐˢ⁾ WHICH **YHWH** Elohiym~you⁽ᵐˢ⁾ GIVE⁽ᵛ⁾~*ing*⁽ᵐˢ⁾ to~you⁽ᶠˢ⁾ **16:6** GIVEN.THAT IF TO the~AREA WHICH *he*~*will*~CHOOSE⁽ᵛ⁾ **YHWH** Elohiym~you⁽ᵐˢ⁾ to~>~DWELL⁽ᵛ⁾ TITLE~him THERE *you*⁽ᵐˢ⁾~*will*~SACRIFICE⁽ᵛ⁾ AT the~Pesahh in~the~

EVENING like~>~COME^(V) the~SUN APPOINTED >~GO.OUT^(V)~you^(ms) from~
Mits'rayim   **16:7** and~*you^(ms)~did~much*~BOIL^(V) and~*you^(ms)~did*~EAT^(V) in~
the~AREA WHICH *he~will*~CHOOSE^(V) **YHWH** Elohiym~you^(ms) in~him and~
you^(ms)~did~TURN^(V) in~the~MORNING and~*you^(ms)~did*~WALK^(V) to~TENT~
you^(ms)   **16:8** SIX DAY~s *you^(ms)~will*~EAT^(V) UNLEAVENED.BREAD~s and~in~
the~DAY the~SEVENTH CONFERENCE to~**YHWH** Elohiym~you^(ms) NOT
you^(ms)~will~DO^(V) BUSINESS   **16:9** SEVEN WEEK~s *you^(ms)~will*~COUNT^(V) to~
you^(fs) from~>~*make*~DRILL^(V) SICKLE in~the~GRAIN.STALK *you^(ms)~will*~
make~DRILL^(V) to~>~COUNT^(V) SEVEN WEEK~s   **16:10** and~*you^(ms)~did*~DO^(V)
FEAST WEEK~s to~**YHWH** Elohiym~you^(ms) PROPORTION
FREEWILL.OFFERING HAND~you^(ms) WHICH *you^(ms)~will*~GIVE^(V) like~WHICH
he~will~much~KNEEL^(V)~you^(ms) **YHWH** Elohiym~you^(ms)   **16:11** and~*you^(ms)~
did*~REJOICE^(V) to~FACE~s **YHWH** Elohiym~you^(ms) YOU^(ms) and~SON~you^(ms)
and~DAUGHTER~you^(ms) and~SERVANT~you^(ms) and~BONDWOMAN~you^(ms)
and~the~Lewi WHICH in~GATE~s~you^(ms) and~the~IMMIGRANT and~the~
ORPHAN and~the~WIDOW WHICH in~INSIDE~you^(ms) in~the~AREA WHICH
he~will~CHOOSE^(V) **YHWH** Elohiym~you^(ms) to~>~DWELL^(V) TITLE~him
THERE   **16:12** and~*you^(ms)~did*~REMEMBER^(V) GIVEN.THAT SERVANT *you^(ms)~
did*~EXIST^(V) in~Mits'rayim and~*you^(ms)~did*~SAFEGUARD^(V) and~*you^(ms)~did*~
DO^(V) AT the~CUSTOM~s the~THESE   **16:13** FEAST the~BOOTH~s *you^(ms)~
will*~DO^(V) to~you^(ms) SEVEN DAY~s in~>~GATHER^(V)~you^(ms) from~FLOOR~
you^(ms) and~from~WINE.TROUGH~you^(ms)   **16:14** and~*you^(ms)~did*~REJOICE^(V)
in~FEAST~you^(ms) YOU^(ms) and~SON~you^(ms) and~DAUGHTER~you^(ms) and~
SERVANT~you^(ms) and~BONDWOMAN~you^(ms) and~the~Lewi and~the~
IMMIGRANT and~the~ORPHAN and~the~WIDOW WHICH in~GATE~s~
you^(ms)   **16:15** SEVEN DAY~s *you^(ms)~will*~HOLD.A.FEAST^(V) to~**YHWH**
Elohiym~you^(ms) in~the~AREA WHICH *he~will*~CHOOSE^(V) **YHWH**
GIVEN.THAT *he~will~much*~KNEEL^(V)~you^(ms) **YHWH** Elohiym~you^(ms) in~ALL
PRODUCTION~you^(ms) and~in~ALL WORK HAND~s2~you^(ms) and~*you^(ms)~did*~
EXIST^(V) SURELY REJOICING   **16:16** THREE FOOTSTEP~s in~the~YEAR *he~will~
be*~SEE^(V) ALL MEN~you^(ms) AT FACE~s **YHWH** Elohiym~you^(ms) in~the~AREA
WHICH *he~will*~CHOOSE^(V) in~FEAST the~UNLEAVENED.BREAD~s and~in~
FEAST the~WEEK~s and~in~FEAST the~BOOTH~s and~NOT *he~will~be*~
SEE^(V) AT FACE~s **YHWH** EMPTINESS   **16:17** MAN like~CONTRIBUTION
HAND~him like~PRESENT **YHWH** Elohiym~you^(ms) WHICH *he~did*~GIVE^(V) to~
you^(fs)   **16:18** DECIDE^(V)~*ing*^(mp) and~OFFICER~s *you^(ms)~will*~GIVE^(V) to~
you^(ms) in~ALL GATE~s~you^(ms) WHICH **YHWH** Elohiym~you^(ms) GIVE^(V)~*ing*^(ms)
to~you^(ms) to~STAFF~s~you^(ms) and~*they~did*~DECIDE^(V) AT the~PEOPLE
DECISION STEADFAST   **16:19** NOT *you^(ms)~will*~*make*~EXTEND^(V) DECISION
NOT *you^(ms)~will*~*make*~RECOGNIZE^(V) FACE~s and~NOT *you^(ms)~will*~TAKE^(V)
BRIBE GIVEN.THAT the~BRIBE *he~will~much*~BLIND^(V) EYE~s2
SKILLED.ONE~s and~*he~will~much*~TWIST.BACKWARDS^(V) WORD~s
STEADFAST.ONE~s   **16:20** STEADFAST STEADFAST *you^(ms)~will*~PURSUE^(V)
to~THAT *you^(ms)~will*~LIVE^(V) and~*you^(ms)~did*~POSSESS^(V) AT the~LAND
WHICH **YHWH** Elohiym~you^(ms) GIVE^(V)~*ing*^(ms) to~you^(fs)   **16:21** NOT *you^(ms)~*

will~PLANT⁽ⱽ⁾ to~you⁽ᵐˢ⁾ GROVE ALL TREE BESIDE ALTAR **YHWH** Elohiym~you⁽ᵐˢ⁾ WHICH *you*⁽ᵐˢ⁾~*will*~DO⁽ⱽ⁾ to~you⁽ᶠˢ⁾   **16:22** and~NOT *you*⁽ᵐˢ⁾~*will*~*make*~RISE⁽ⱽ⁾ to~you⁽ᵐˢ⁾ MONUMENT WHICH *he*~*did*~HATE⁽ⱽ⁾ **YHWH** Elohiym~you⁽ᵐˢ⁾

Chapter 17

17:1 NOT *you*⁽ᵐˢ⁾~*will*~SACRIFICE⁽ⱽ⁾ to~**YHWH** Elohiym~you⁽ᵐˢ⁾ OX and~RAM WHICH *he*~*will*~EXIST⁽ⱽ⁾ in~him BLEMISH ALL WORD DYSFUNCTIONAL GIVEN.THAT DISGUSTING **YHWH** Elohiym~you⁽ᵐˢ⁾ HE   **17:2** GIVEN.THAT *he*~*will*~*be*~FIND⁽ⱽ⁾ in~INSIDE~you⁽ᵐˢ⁾ in~UNIT GATE~s~you⁽ᵐˢ⁾ WHICH **YHWH** Elohiym~you⁽ᵐˢ⁾ GIVE⁽ⱽ⁾~*ing*⁽ᵐˢ⁾ to~you⁽ᶠˢ⁾ MAN OR WOMAN WHICH *he*~*will*~DO⁽ⱽ⁾ AT the~DYSFUNCTIONAL in~EYE~s2 **YHWH** Elohiym~you⁽ᵐˢ⁾ to~the~>~CROSS.OVER⁽ⱽ⁾ COVENANT~him   **17:3** and~*he*~*will*~WALK⁽ⱽ⁾ and~*he*~*will*~SERVE⁽ⱽ⁾ Elohiym OTHER~s and~*he*~*will*~*self*~BEND.DOWN⁽ⱽ⁾ to~them⁽ᵐ⁾ and~to~the~SUN OR to~the~MOON OR to~ALL ARMY the~SKY~s2 WHICH NOT *I*~*did*~*much*~DIRECT⁽ⱽ⁾   **17:4** and~*he*~*did*~*be*~*make*~BE.FACE.TO.FACE⁽ⱽ⁾ to~you⁽ᵐˢ⁾ and~*you*⁽ᵐˢ⁾~*did*~HEAR⁽ⱽ⁾ and~*you*⁽ᵐˢ⁾~*did*~SEEK⁽ⱽ⁾ >~*make*~DO.WELL⁽ⱽ⁾ and~LOOK TRUTH *be*~PREPARE⁽ⱽ⁾~*ing*⁽ᵐˢ⁾ the~WORD *she*~*did*~*be*~DO⁽ⱽ⁾ the~DISGUSTING the~THIS in~Yisra'eyl   **17:5** and~*you*⁽ᵐˢ⁾~*did*~*make*~GO.OUT⁽ⱽ⁾ AT the~MAN the~HE OR AT the~WOMAN the~SHE WHICH *they*~*did*~DO⁽ⱽ⁾ AT the~WORD the~DYSFUNCTIONAL the~THIS TO GATE~s~you⁽ᵐˢ⁾ AT the~MAN OR AT the~WOMAN and~*you*⁽ᵐˢ⁾~*did*~STONE⁽ⱽ⁾~them⁽ᵐ⁾ in~the~STONE~s and~*they*~*did*~DIE⁽ⱽ⁾   **17:6** UPON MOUTH TWO WITNESS~s OR THREE WITNESS~s *he*~*will*~*be*~*make*~DIE⁽ⱽ⁾ the~DIE⁽ⱽ⁾~*ing*⁽ᵐˢ⁾ NOT *he*~*will*~*be*~*make*~DIE⁽ⱽ⁾ UPON MOUTH WITNESS UNIT   **17:7** HAND the~WITNESS~s *she*~*will*~EXIST⁽ⱽ⁾ in~him in~the~FIRST to~>~*make*~DIE⁽ⱽ⁾~him and~HAND ALL the~PEOPLE in~the~LAST and~*you*⁽ᵐˢ⁾~*did*~*much*~BURN⁽ⱽ⁾ the~DYSFUNCTIONAL from~INSIDE~you⁽ᵐˢ⁾   **17:8** GIVEN.THAT *he*~*will*~*be*~PERFORM⁽ⱽ⁾ FROM~you⁽ᵐˢ⁾ WORD to~the~DECISION BETWEEN BLOOD to~BLOOD BETWEEN PLEA to~PLEA and~BETWEEN TOUCH to~the~TOUCH WORD~s DISPUTE~s in~GATE~s~you⁽ᵐˢ⁾ and~*you*⁽ᵐˢ⁾~*did*~RISE⁽ⱽ⁾ and~*you*⁽ᵐˢ⁾~*did*~GO.UP⁽ⱽ⁾ TO the~AREA WHICH *he*~*will*~CHOOSE⁽ⱽ⁾ **YHWH** Elohiym~you⁽ᵐˢ⁾ in~him   **17:9** and~*you*⁽ᵐˢ⁾~*did*~COME⁽ⱽ⁾ TO the~ADMINISTRATOR~s the~Lewi~s and~TO the~DECIDE⁽ⱽ⁾~*ing*⁽ᵐˢ⁾ WHICH *he*~*will*~EXIST⁽ⱽ⁾ in~the~DAY~s the~THEY⁽ᵐ⁾ and~*you*⁽ᵐˢ⁾~*did*~SEEK⁽ⱽ⁾ and~*they*~*did*~*make*~BE.FACE.TO.FACE⁽ⱽ⁾ to~you⁽ᵐˢ⁾ AT WORD the~DECISION   **17:10** and~*you*⁽ᵐˢ⁾~*did*~DO⁽ⱽ⁾ UPON MOUTH the~WORD WHICH *they*⁽ᵐ⁾~*will*~*make*~BE.FACE.TO.FACE⁽ⱽ⁾ to~you⁽ᵐˢ⁾ FROM the~AREA the~HE WHICH *he*~*will*~CHOOSE⁽ⱽ⁾ **YHWH** and~*you*⁽ᵐˢ⁾~*did*~SAFEGUARD⁽ⱽ⁾ to~>~DO⁽ⱽ⁾ like~ALL WHICH *they*⁽ᵐ⁾~*will*~*make*~THROW⁽ⱽ⁾~you⁽ᵐˢ⁾   **17:11** UPON MOUTH the~TEACHING WHICH *they*⁽ᵐ⁾~*will*~*make*~THROW⁽ⱽ⁾~you⁽ᵐˢ⁾ and~UPON the~DECISION WHICH *they*⁽ᵐ⁾~*will*~SAY⁽ⱽ⁾ to~you⁽ᵐˢ⁾ *you*⁽ᵐˢ⁾~*will*~DO⁽ⱽ⁾

NOT you[ms]~will~TURN.ASIDE[V] FROM the~WORD WHICH they[m]~will~ make~BE.FACE.TO.FACE[V] to~you[ms] RIGHT.HAND and~ LEFT.HAND **17:12** and~the~MAN WHICH he~will~DO[V] in~ARROGANCE to~ EXCEPT >~HEAR[V] TO the~ADMINISTRATOR the~STAND[V]~ing[ms] to~>~ much~MINISTER[V] THERE AT **YHWH** Elohiym~you[ms] OR TO the~DECIDE[V]~ ing[ms] and~he~did~DIE[V] the~MAN the~HE and~you[ms]~did~much~BURN[V] the~DYSFUNCTIONAL from~Yisra'eyl **17:13** and~ALL the~PEOPLE they[m]~ will~HEAR[V] and~they[m]~will~FEAR[V] and~NOT he~will~make~SIMMER[V]~ must YET.AGAIN **17:14** GIVEN.THAT you[ms]~will~COME[V] TO the~LAND WHICH **YHWH** Elohiym~you[ms] GIVE[V]~ing[ms] to~you[fs] and~you[ms]~did~ POSSESS[V]~her and~you[ms]~did~SETTLE[V]~& in~her and~you[ms]~did~SAY[V] I~will~PLACE[V]~& UPON~me KING like~ALL the~NATION~s WHICH ALL.AROUND~s~me **17:15** >~PLACE[V] you[ms]~will~PLACE[V] UPON~you[ms] KING WHICH he~will~CHOOSE[V] **YHWH** Elohiym~you[ms] in~him from~INSIDE BROTHER~s~you[ms] you[ms]~will~PLACE[V] UPON~you[ms] KING NOT you[ms]~ will~BE.ABLE[V] to~>~GIVE[V] UPON~you[ms] MAN FOREIGN WHICH NOT BROTHER~you[ms] HE **17:16** ONLY NOT he~will~make~INCREASE[V] to~him HORSE~s and~NOT he~will~make~TURN.BACK[V] AT the~PEOPLE Mits'rayim~unto to~THAT the~>~INCREASE[V] HORSE and~**YHWH** he~did~ SAY[V] to~you[mp] NOT you[mp]~will~make~ADD[V]~must to~>~TURN.BACK[V] in~the~ROAD the~THIS YET.AGAIN **17:17** and~NOT he~will~make~ INCREASE[V] to~him WOMAN~s and~NOT he~will~TURN.ASIDE[V] HEART~him and~SILVER and~GOLD NOT he~will~make~INCREASE[V] to~him MANY **17:18** and~he~did~EXIST[V] like~>~SETTLE[V]~him UPON SEAT KINGDOM~him and~he~did~WRITE[V] to~him AT DOUBLE the~TEACHING the~THIS UPON SCROLL from~to~FACE~s the~ADMINISTRATOR~s the~ Lewi~s **17:19** and~she~did~EXIST[V] WITH~him and~he~did~CALL.OUT[V] in~ him ALL DAY~s LIVING~s~him to~THAT he~will~LEARN[V] to~>~FEAR[V] AT **YHWH** Elohiym~him to~>~SAFEGUARD[V] AT ALL WORD~s the~TEACHING the~THIS and~AT the~CUSTOM~s the~THESE to~>~DO[V]~ them[m] **17:20** to~EXCEPT >~RAISE.UP[V] HEART~him from~BROTHER~s~him and~to~EXCEPT >~TURN.ASIDE[V] FROM the~DIRECTIVE RIGHT.HAND and~ LEFT.HAND to~THAT he~will~make~PROLONG[V] DAY~s UPON KINGDOM~ him HE and~SON~s~him in~INSIDE Yisra'eyl

Chapter 18

18:1 NOT he~will~EXIST[V] to~the~ADMINISTRATOR~s the~Lewi~s ALL STAFF Lewi DISTRIBUTION and~INHERITANCE WITH Yisra'eyl FIRE.OFFERING~s **YHWH** and~INHERITANCE~him he~will~EAT[V]~must **18:2** and~ INHERITANCE NOT he~will~EXIST[V] to~him in~INSIDE BROTHER~s~him **YHWH** HE INHERITANCE~him like~WHICH he~did~much~SPEAK[V] to~ him **18:3** and~THIS he~will~EXIST[V] DECISION the~ADMINISTRATOR~s from~AT the~PEOPLE from~AT SACRIFICE$^{(V)}$~ing$^{(mp)}$ the~SACRIFICE IF OX IF RAM and~he~did~GIVE$^{(V)}$ to~the~ADMINISTRATOR the~ARM and~the~JAW~s2 and~the~STOMACH   **18:4** SUMMIT CEREAL~you$^{(ms)}$ FRESH.WINE~you$^{(ms)}$ and~FRESH.OIL~you$^{(ms)}$ and~SUMMIT FLEECE FLOCKS~you$^{(ms)}$ you$^{(ms)}$~will~GIVE$^{(V)}$ to~him   **18:5** GIVEN.THAT in~him he~did~CHOOSE$^{(V)}$ **YHWH** Elohiym~you$^{(ms)}$ from~ALL STAFF~s~you$^{(ms)}$ to~>~STAND$^{(V)}$ to~>~much~MINISTER$^{(V)}$ in~TITLE **YHWH** HE and~SON~s~him ALL the~DAY~s   **18:6** and~GIVEN.THAT he~will~COME$^{(V)}$ the~Lewi from~UNIT GATE~s~you$^{(ms)}$ from~ALL Yisra'eyl WHICH HE he~did~IMMIGRATE$^{(V)}$ THERE and~he~did~COME$^{(V)}$ in~ALL DESIRE SOUL~him TO the~AREA WHICH he~will~CHOOSE$^{(V)}$ **YHWH**   **18:7** and~he~did~much~MINISTER$^{(V)}$ in~TITLE **YHWH** Elohiym~him like~ALL BROTHER~s~him the~Lewi~s the~STAND$^{(V)}$~ing$^{(mp)}$ THERE to~FACE~s **YHWH**   **18:8** DISTRIBUTION like~DISTRIBUTION they$^{(m)}$~will~EAT$^{(V)}$ to~STRAND MERCHANDISE~s~him UPON the~FATHER~s   **18:9** GIVEN.THAT YOU$^{(ms)}$ he~did~COME$^{(V)}$ TO the~LAND WHICH **YHWH** Elohiym~you$^{(ms)}$ GIVE$^{(V)}$~ing$^{(ms)}$ to~you$^{(fs)}$ NOT you$^{(ms)}$~will~LEARN$^{(V)}$ to~>~DO$^{(V)}$ like~DISGUSTING~s the~NATION~s the~THEY$^{(m)}$ **18:10** NOT he~will~be~FIND$^{(V)}$ in~you$^{(ms)}$ make~CROSS.OVER$^{(V)}$~ing$^{(ms)}$ SON~him and~DAUGHTER~him in~the~FIRE DIVINE$^{(V)}$~ing$^{(ms)}$ DIVINATION~s much~CONJURE$^{(V)}$~ing$^{(ms)}$ and~much~PREDICT$^{(V)}$~ing$^{(ms)}$ and~much~DO.SORCERY$^{(V)}$~ing$^{(ms)}$ **18:11** and~COUPLE$^{(V)}$~ing$^{(ms)}$ COUPLE and~INQUIRE$^{(V)}$~ing$^{(ms)}$ NECROMANCER and~KNOWER and~SEEK$^{(V)}$~ing$^{(ms)}$ TO the~DIE$^{(V)}$~ing$^{(mp)}$ **18:12** GIVEN.THAT DISGUSTING **YHWH** ALL DO$^{(V)}$~ing$^{(ms)}$ THESE and~in~ON.ACCOUNT.OF the~DISGUSTING~s the~THESE **YHWH** Elohiym~you$^{(ms)}$ make~POSSESS$^{(V)}$~ing$^{(ms)}$ AT~them$^{(m)}$ from~FACE~s~you$^{(ms)}$ **18:13** WHOLE you$^{(ms)}$~will~EXIST$^{(V)}$ WITH **YHWH** Elohiym~you$^{(ms)}$ **18:14** GIVEN.THAT the~NATION~s the~THESE WHICH YOU$^{(ms)}$ POSSESS$^{(V)}$~ing$^{(ms)}$ AT~them$^{(m)}$ TO much~CONJURE$^{(V)}$~ing$^{(mp)}$ and~TO DIVINE$^{(V)}$~ing$^{(mp)}$ they$^{(m)}$~will~HEAR$^{(V)}$ and~YOU$^{(ms)}$ NOT SO he~did~GIVE$^{(V)}$ to~you$^{(ms)}$ **YHWH** Elohiym~you$^{(ms)}$ **18:15** ANNOUNCER from~INSIDE~you$^{(ms)}$ from~BROTHER~s~you$^{(ms)}$ like~THAT.ONE~me he~will~make~RISE$^{(V)}$ to~you$^{(ms)}$ **YHWH** Elohiym~you$^{(ms)}$ TO~him you$^{(mp)}$~will~HEAR$^{(V)}$~must   **18:16** like~ALL WHICH you$^{(ms)}$~did~INQUIRE$^{(V)}$ from~WITH **YHWH** Elohiym~you$^{(ms)}$ in~Hhorev in~DAY the~ASSEMBLY to~>~SAY$^{(V)}$ NOT ADD$^{(V)}$~ing$^{(ms)}$ to~>~HEAR$^{(V)}$ AT VOICE **YHWH** Elohiym~me and~AT the~FIRE the~GREAT the~THIS NOT I~will~SEE$^{(V)}$ YET.AGAIN and~NOT I~will~DIE$^{(V)}$ **18:17** and~he~will~SAY$^{(V)}$ **YHWH** TO~me they~did~make~DO.WELL$^{(V)}$ WHICH they~did~much~SPEAK$^{(V)}$ **18:18** ANNOUNCER I~will~make~RISE$^{(V)}$ to~them$^{(m)}$ from~INSIDE BROTHER~s~them$^{(m)}$ like~THAT.ONE~you$^{(ms)}$ and~I~did~GIVE$^{(V)}$ WORD~s~me in~MOUTH~him and~he~did~much~SPEAK$^{(V)}$ TO~them$^{(m)}$ AT ALL WHICH I~will~much~DIRECT$^{(V)}$~him   **18:19** and~he~did~EXIST$^{(V)}$ the~MAN WHICH NOT he~will~HEAR$^{(V)}$ TO WORD~s~me WHICH he~will~much~SPEAK$^{(V)}$ in~TITLE~me I I~will~SEEK$^{(V)}$ from~WITH~him   **18:20** SURELY the~ANNOUNCER WHICH he~will~make~SIMMER$^{(V)}$ to~>~much~SPEAK$^{(V)}$ WORD in~TITLE~me AT WHICH NOT I~did~much~DIRECT$^{(V)}$~him to~>~much~SPEAK$^{(V)}$ and~WHICH he~will~much~SPEAK$^{(V)}$ in~

TITLE Elohiym OTHER~s and~*he~did*~DIE(V) the~ANNOUNCER the~
HE   **18:21** and~GIVEN.THAT *you*(ms)~*will*~SAY(V) in~HEART~*you*(ms) HOW *we will*~KNOW(V) AT the~WORD WHICH NOT *he~did~much*~SPEAK(V)~him
YHWH   **18:22** WHICH *he~will~much*~SPEAK(V) the~ANNOUNCER in~TITLE
YHWH and~NOT *he~will*~EXIST(V) the~WORD and~NOT *he~will*~COME(V) HE the~WORD WHICH NOT *he~did~much*~SPEAK(V)~him **YHWH** in~ARROGANCE *he~did~much*~SPEAK(V)~him the~ANNOUNCER NOT *you*(ms)~*will*~BE.AFRAID(V) FROM~him

Chapter 19

19:1 GIVEN.THAT *he~will~make*~CUT(V) **YHWH** Elohiym~*you*(ms) AT the~NATION~s WHICH **YHWH** Elohiym~*you*(ms) GIVE(V)~*ing*(ms) to~*you*(ms) AT LAND~them(m) and~*you*(ms)~*did*~POSSESS(V)~them(m) and~*you*(ms)~*did*~SETTLE(V) in~CITY~s~them(m) and~in~HOUSE~s~them(m)   **19:2** THREE CITY~s *you*(ms)~*will~make*~SEPARATE(V) to~*you*(fs) in~MIDST LAND~*you*(ms) WHICH **YHWH** Elohiym~*you*(ms) GIVE(V)~*ing*(ms) to~*you*(ms) to~>~POSSESS(V)~her   **19:3** *you*(ms)~*will~make*~PREPARE(V) to~*you*(ms) the~ROAD and~*you*(ms)~*did~much*~BE.THREEFOLD(V) AT BORDER LAND~*you*(ms) WHICH *he~will~make*~INHERIT(V)~*you*(ms) **YHWH** Elohiym~*you*(ms) and~*he~did*~EXIST(V) to~>~FLEE(V) THERE~unto ALL MURDER(V)~*ing*(ms)   **19:4** and~THIS WORD the~MURDER(V)~*ing*(ms) WHICH *he~will*~FLEE(V) THERE~unto and~*he~will*~LIVE(V) WHICH *he~will~make*~HIT(V) AT COMPANION~him in~UNAWARE DISCERNMENT and~HE NOT HATE(V)~*ing*(ms) to~him from~YESTERDAY THREE.DAYS.AGO   **19:5** and~WHICH *he~will*~COME(V) AT COMPANION~him in~the~FOREST to~>~CARVE(V) TREE~s and~*she~did~be*~DRIVE.OUT(V) HAND~him in~the~AX to~>~CUT(V) the~TREE and~*he~did*~CAST.OFF(V) the~IRON FROM the~TREE and~*he~did*~FIND(V) AT COMPANION~him and~*he~did*~DIE(V) HE *he~will*~FLEE(V) TO UNIT the~CITY~s the~THESE and~*he~will*~LIVE(V)   **19:6** OTHERWISE *he~will*~PURSUE(V) REDEEM(V)~*ing*(ms) the~BLOOD AFTER the~MURDER(V)~*ing*(ms) GIVEN.THAT *he~will*~HEAT(V) HEART~him and~*he~did~make*~OVERTAKE(V)~him GIVEN.THAT *he~will*~INCREASE(V) the~ROAD and~*he~did~make*~HIT(V)~him SOUL and~to~him WITHOUT DECISION DEATH GIVEN.THAT NOT HATE(V)~*ing*(ms) HE to~him from~YESTERDAY THREE.DAYS.AGO   **19:7** UPON SO I *much*~DIRECT(V)~*ing*(ms)~*you*(ms) to~>~SAY(V) THREE CITY~s *you*(ms)~*will~make*~SEPARATE(V) to~*you*(fs)   **19:8** and~IF *he~will~make*~WIDEN(V) **YHWH** Elohiym~*you*(ms) AT BORDER~*you*(ms) like~WHICH *he~did~be*~SWEAR(V) to~FATHER~s~*you*(ms) and~*he~did*~GIVE(V) to~*you*(ms) AT ALL the~LAND WHICH *he~did~much*~SPEAK(V) to~>~GIVE(V) to~FATHER~s~*you*(ms)   **19:9** GIVEN.THAT *you*(ms)~*will*~SAFEGUARD(V) AT ALL the~DIRECTIVE the~THIS to~>~DO(V)~her WHICH I *much*~DIRECT(V)~*ing*(ms)~*you*(ms) the~DAY to~>~LOVE(V) AT **YHWH** Elohiym~*you*(ms) and~to~>~WALK(V) in~ROAD~s~him ALL the~DAY~s and~*you*(ms)~*did*~ADD(V) to~*you*(ms)

The Book of Deuteronomy

YET.AGAIN THREE CITY~s UPON the~THREE the~THESE **19:10** and~NOT *he~will~be~*POUR.OUT⁽ᵛ⁾ BLOOD INNOCENT in~INSIDE LAND~you⁽ᵐˢ⁾ WHICH **YHWH** Elohiym~you⁽ᵐˢ⁾ GIVE⁽ᵛ⁾~*ing*⁽ᵐˢ⁾ to~you⁽ᵐˢ⁾ INHERITANCE and~*he~did~*EXIST⁽ᵛ⁾ UPON~you⁽ᵐˢ⁾ BLOOD~s **19:11** and~GIVEN.THAT *he~will~*EXIST⁽ᵛ⁾ MAN HATE⁽ᵛ⁾~*ing*⁽ᵐˢ⁾ to~COMPANION~him and~*he~did~*AMBUSH⁽ᵛ⁾ to~him and~*he~did~*RISE⁽ᵛ⁾ UPON~him and~*he~did~*make~HIT⁽ᵛ⁾~him SOUL and~*he~did~*DIE⁽ᵛ⁾ and~*he~did~*FLEE⁽ᵛ⁾ TO UNIT the~CITY~s the~THESE **19:12** and~*they~did~*SEND⁽ᵛ⁾ BEARD~s CITY~him and~*they~did~*TAKE⁽ᵛ⁾ AT~him from~THERE and~*they~did~*GIVE⁽ᵛ⁾ AT~him in~HAND REDEEM⁽ᵛ⁾~*ing*⁽ᵐˢ⁾ the~BLOOD and~*he~did~*DIE⁽ᵛ⁾ **19:13** NOT *she~will~*SPARE⁽ᵛ⁾ EYE~you⁽ᵐˢ⁾ UPON~him and~*you*⁽ᵐˢ⁾*~did~*much~BURN⁽ᵛ⁾ BLOOD the~INNOCENT from~Yisra'eyl and~*he~did~*DO.WELL⁽ᵛ⁾ to~you⁽ᶠˢ⁾ **19:14** NOT *you*⁽ᵐˢ⁾*~will~*make~OVERTAKE⁽ᵛ⁾ BORDER COMPANION~you⁽ᵐˢ⁾ WHICH *they~did~*BOUND⁽ᵛ⁾ FIRST~s in~INHERITANCE~you⁽ᵐˢ⁾ WHICH *you*⁽ᵐˢ⁾*~will~*INHERIT⁽ᵛ⁾ in~the~LAND WHICH **YHWH** Elohiym~you⁽ᵐˢ⁾ GIVE⁽ᵛ⁾~*ing*⁽ᵐˢ⁾ to~you⁽ᵐˢ⁾ to~>~POSSESS⁽ᵛ⁾~her **19:15** NOT *he~will~*RISE⁽ᵛ⁾ WITNESS UNIT in~MAN to~ALL TWISTEDNESS and~to~ALL FAILURE in~ALL FAILURE WHICH *he~will~*FAIL⁽ᵛ⁾ UPON MOUTH TWO WITNESS~s OR UPON MOUTH THREE WITNESS~s *he~will~*RISE⁽ᵛ⁾ WORD **19:16** GIVEN.THAT *he~will~*RISE⁽ᵛ⁾ WITNESS VIOLENCE in~MAN to~>~ANSWER⁽ᵛ⁾ in~him TURNING.ASIDE **19:17** and~*they~did~*STAND⁽ᵛ⁾ TWO the~MAN~s WHICH to~them⁽ᵐ⁾ the~DISPUTE to~FACE~s **YHWH** to~FACE~s the~ADMINISTRATOR~s and~the~DECIDE⁽ᵛ⁾~*ing*⁽ᵐᵖ⁾ WHICH *they*⁽ᵐ⁾*~will~*EXIST⁽ᵛ⁾ in~the~DAY~s the~THEY⁽ᵐ⁾ **19:18** and~*they~did~*SEEK⁽ᵛ⁾ the~DECIDE⁽ᵛ⁾~*ing*⁽ᵐᵖ⁾ >~make~DO.WELL⁽ᵛ⁾ and~LOOK WITNESS FALSE the~WITNESS FALSE *he~did~*AFFLICT⁽ᵛ⁾ in~BROTHER~him **19:19** and~*you*⁽ᵐᵖ⁾*~did~*DO⁽ᵛ⁾ to~him like~WHICH *he~did~*PLOT⁽ᵛ⁾ to~>~DO⁽ᵛ⁾ to~BROTHER~him and~*you*⁽ᵐˢ⁾*~did~*much~BURN⁽ᵛ⁾ the~DYSFUNCTIONAL from~INSIDE~you⁽ᵐˢ⁾ **19:20** and~the~*be~*REMAIN⁽ᵛ⁾~*ing*⁽ᵐᵖ⁾ *they*⁽ᵐ⁾*~will~*HEAR⁽ᵛ⁾ and~*they*⁽ᵐ⁾*~will~*FEAR⁽ᵛ⁾ and~NOT *they*⁽ᵐ⁾*~will~*make~ADD⁽ᵛ⁾ to~>~DO⁽ᵛ⁾ YET.AGAIN like~the~WORD the~DYSFUNCTIONAL the~THIS in~INSIDE~you⁽ᵐˢ⁾ **19:21** and~NOT *she~will~*SPARE⁽ᵛ⁾ EYE~you⁽ᵐˢ⁾ SOUL in~SOUL EYE in~EYE TOOTH in~TOOTH HAND in~HAND FOOT in~FOOT

Chapter 20

20:1 GIVEN.THAT *you*⁽ᵐˢ⁾*~will~*GO.OUT⁽ᵛ⁾ to~the~BATTLE UPON ATTACK⁽ᵛ⁾~*ing*⁽ᵐᵖ⁾*~*s~you⁽ᵐˢ⁾ and~*you*⁽ᵐˢ⁾*~did~*SEE⁽ᵛ⁾ HORSE and~VEHICLE PEOPLE ABUNDANT FROM~you⁽ᵐˢ⁾ NOT *you*⁽ᵐˢ⁾*~will~*FEAR⁽ᵛ⁾ from~them⁽ᵐ⁾ GIVEN.THAT **YHWH** Elohiym~you⁽ᵐˢ⁾ WITH~you⁽ᶠˢ⁾ *make~*GO.UP⁽ᵛ⁾~*ing*⁽ᵐˢ⁾~you⁽ᵐˢ⁾ from~LAND Mits'rayim **20:2** and~*he~did~*EXIST⁽ᵛ⁾ like~>~COME.NEAR⁽ᵛ⁾~you⁽ᵐᵖ⁾ TO the~BATTLE and~*he~did~be~*DRAW.NEAR⁽ᵛ⁾ the~ADMINISTRATOR and~*he~did~*much~SPEAK⁽ᵛ⁾ TO the~PEOPLE **20:3** and~

*he~did~*SAY(v) TO~them(m) *l(ms)~*HEAR(v) Yisra'eyl YOU(mp) INSIDE~s the~DAY to~the~BATTLE UPON ATTACK(v)~*ing(mp)~*you(mp) DO.NOT *he~will~*BE.SOFT(v) HEART~you(mp) DO.NOT *you(mp)~will~*FEAR(v) and~DO.NOT *you(mp)~will~* HASTEN(v) and~DO.NOT *you(mp)~will~*BE.TERRIFIED(v) from~FACE~s~ them(m) **20:4** GIVEN.THAT **YHWH** Elohiym~you(mp) the~WALK(v)~*ing(ms)* WITH~you(mp) to~>~*be~*FIGHT(v) to~you(mp) WITH ATTACK(v)~*ing(mp)~*you(mp) to~>~*make~*RESCUE(v) AT~you(mp) **20:5** and~*they~did~much~*SPEAK(v) the~ OFFICER~s TO the~PEOPLE to~>~SAY(v) WHO the~MAN WHICH *he~did~* BUILD(v) HOUSE NEW and~NOT *he~did~*DEVOTE(v)~him *he~will~*WALK(v) and~*he~will~*TURN.BACK(v) to~HOUSE~him OTHERWISE *he~will~*DIE(v) in~ the~BATTLE and~MAN OTHER *he~will~*DEVOTE(v)~him **20:6** and~WHO the~ MAN WHICH *he~did~*PLANT(v) VINEYARD and~NOT *he~did~much~*DRILL(v)~ him *he~will~*WALK(v) and~*he~will~*TURN.BACK(v) to~HOUSE~him OTHERWISE *he~will~*DIE(v) in~the~BATTLE and~MAN OTHER *he~will~much~* DRILL(v)~him **20:7** and~WHO the~MAN WHICH *he~did~much~*BETROTH(v) WOMAN and~NOT *he~did~*TAKE(v)~her *he~will~*WALK(v) and~*he~will~* TURN.BACK(v) to~HOUSE~him OTHERWISE *he~will~*DIE(v) in~the~BATTLE and~MAN OTHER *he~will~*TAKE(v)~her **20:8** and~*they~did~*ADD(v) the~ OFFICER~s to~>~*much~*SPEAK(v) TO the~PEOPLE and~*they~did~*SAY(v) WHO the~MAN the~FEAR(v)~*ing(ms)* and~TENDER the~HEART *he~will~*WALK(v) and~*he~will~*TURN.BACK(v) to~HOUSE~him and~NOT *he~will~be~* MELT.AWAY(v) AT HEART BROTHER~s~him like~HEART~him **20:9** and~*he~ did~*EXIST(v) like~>~*much~*FINISH(v) the~OFFICER~s to~>~*much~*SPEAK(v) TO the~PEOPLE and~*they~did~*REGISTER(v) NOBLE~s ARMY~s in~HEAD the~ PEOPLE **20:10** GIVEN.THAT *you(ms)~will~*COME.NEAR(v) TO CITY to~>~*be~* FIGHT(v) UPON~her and~*you(ms)~did~*CALL.OUT(v) TO~her to~ COMPLETENESS **20:11** and~*he~did~*EXIST(v) IF COMPLETENESS *you(ms)~will~* AFFLICT(v)~you(ms) and~*she~did~*OPEN(v) to~you(fs) and~*he~did~*EXIST(v) ALL the~PEOPLE the~*be~*FIND(v)~*ing(ms)* in~her *they(m)~will~*EXIST(v) to~you(ms) to~the~TASK.WORK and~*they~did~*SERVE(v)~you(ms) **20:12** and~IF NOT *she~ will~make~*MAKE.RESTITUTION(v) WITH~you(fs) and~*she~did~*DO(v) WITH~ you(ms) BATTLE and~*you(ms)~did~*SMACK(v) UPON~her **20:13** and~*he~did~* GIVE(v)~her **YHWH** Elohiym~you(ms) in~HAND~you(ms) and~*you(ms)~did~* *make~*HIT(v) AT ALL MEN~her to~MOUTH SWORD **20:14** ONLY the~ WOMAN~s and~the~BABIES and~the~BEAST and~ALL WHICH *he~will~* EXIST(v) in~the~CITY ALL SPOIL~her *you(ms)~will~*PLUNDER(v) to~you(fs) and~ *you(ms)~did~*EAT(v) AT SPOIL ATTACK(v)~*ing(mp)~*s~you(ms) WHICH *he~did~* GIVE(v) **YHWH** Elohiym~you(ms) to~you(fs) **20:15** SO *you(ms)~will~*DO(v) to~ALL the~CITY~s the~DISTANCE FROM~you(ms) MANY WHICH NOT from~CITY~s the~NATION~s the~THESE THEY(f) **20:16** ONLY from~CITY~s the~PEOPLE~s the~THESE WHICH **YHWH** Elohiym~you(ms) GIVE(v)~*ing(ms)* to~you(ms) INHERITANCE NOT *you(ms)~will~much~*LIVE(v) ALL
BREATH **20:17** GIVEN.THAT >~*make~*PERFORATE(v) *you(ms)~will~make~* PERFORATE(v)~them(m) the~Hhet~of and~the~Emor~of the~Kena'an~of and~the~Perez~of the~Hhiw~of and~the~Yevus~of like~WHICH *he~did~*

much~DIRECT⁽ⱽ⁾~you⁽ᵐˢ⁾ **YHWH** Elohiym~you⁽ᵐˢ⁾ **20:18** to~THAT WHICH NOT they⁽ᵐ⁾~will~much~LEARN⁽ⱽ⁾ AT~you⁽ᵐᵖ⁾ to~>~DO⁽ⱽ⁾ like~ALL DISGUSTING~s~them⁽ᵐ⁾ WHICH they~did~DO⁽ⱽ⁾ to~Elohiym~them⁽ᵐ⁾ and~ you⁽ᵐᵖ⁾~did~FAIL⁽ⱽ⁾ to~**YHWH** Elohiym~you⁽ᵐᵖ⁾ **20:19** GIVEN.THAT you⁽ᵐˢ⁾~ will~FENCE.IN⁽ⱽ⁾ TO CITY DAY~s ABUNDANT~s to~>~be~FIGHT⁽ⱽ⁾ UPON~her to~>~SEIZE.HOLD⁽ⱽ⁾~her NOT you⁽ᵐˢ⁾~will~make~DAMAGE⁽ⱽ⁾ AT TREE~her to~>~DRIVE.OUT⁽ⱽ⁾ UPON~him AX GIVEN.THAT FROM~him you⁽ᵐˢ⁾~will~ EAT⁽ⱽ⁾ and~AT~him NOT you⁽ᵐˢ⁾~will~CUT⁽ⱽ⁾ GIVEN.THAT the~HUMAN TREE the~FIELD to~>~COME⁽ⱽ⁾ from~FACE~s~you⁽ᵐˢ⁾ in~the~SMACKED **20:20** ONLY TREE WHICH you⁽ᵐˢ⁾~will~KNOW⁽ⱽ⁾ GIVEN.THAT NOT TREE NOURISHMENT HE AT~him you⁽ᵐˢ⁾~will~make~DAMAGE⁽ⱽ⁾ and~you⁽ᵐˢ⁾~will~ CUT⁽ⱽ⁾ and~you⁽ᵐˢ⁾~did~BUILD⁽ⱽ⁾ SMACKED UPON the~CITY WHICH SHE DO⁽ⱽ⁾~ing⁽ᶠˢ⁾ WITH~you⁽ᵐˢ⁾ BATTLE UNTIL >~GO.DOWN⁽ⱽ⁾~her

Chapter 21

21:1 GIVEN.THAT he~will~be~FIND⁽ⱽ⁾ DRILLED in~GROUND WHICH **YHWH** Elohiym~you⁽ᵐˢ⁾ GIVE⁽ⱽ⁾~ing⁽ᵐˢ⁾ to~you⁽ᵐˢ⁾ to~>~POSSESS⁽ⱽ⁾~her FALL⁽ⱽ⁾~ ing⁽ᵐˢ⁾ in~the~FIELD NOT he~did~be~KNOW⁽ⱽ⁾ WHO he~did~make~HIT⁽ⱽ⁾~ him **21:2** and~they~did~GO.OUT⁽ⱽ⁾ BEARD~s~you⁽ᵐˢ⁾ and~DECIDE⁽ⱽ⁾~ ing⁽ᵐᵖ⁾~you⁽ᵐˢ⁾ and~they~did~MEASURE⁽ⱽ⁾ TO the~CITY~s WHICH ALL.AROUND~s the~DRILLED **21:3** and~he~did~EXIST⁽ⱽ⁾ the~CITY the~NEAR TO the~DRILLED and~they~did~TAKE⁽ⱽ⁾ BEARD~s the~CITY the~SHE HEIFER CATTLE WHICH NOT SERVE⁽ⱽ⁾~ed⁽ᵐˢ⁾ in~her WHICH NOT she~did~DRAW⁽ⱽ⁾ in~YOKE **21:4** and~they~did~make~GO.DOWN⁽ⱽ⁾ BEARD~s the~CITY the~ SHE AT the~HEIFER TO WADI CONSISTENCY WHICH NOT he~will~be~ SERVE⁽ⱽ⁾ in~him and~NOT he~will~be~SOW⁽ⱽ⁾ and~they~did~BEHEAD⁽ⱽ⁾ THERE AT the~HEIFER in~the~WADI **21:5** and~they~did~be~DRAW.NEAR⁽ⱽ⁾ the~ADMINISTRATOR~s SON~s Lewi GIVEN.THAT in~them⁽ᵐ⁾ he~did~ CHOOSE⁽ⱽ⁾ **YHWH** Elohiym~you⁽ᵐˢ⁾ to~>~much~MINISTER⁽ⱽ⁾~him and~to~>~ much~KNEEL⁽ⱽ⁾ in~TITLE **YHWH** and~UPON MOUTH~them⁽ᵐ⁾ he~will~EXIST⁽ⱽ⁾ ALL DISPUTE and~ALL TOUCH **21:6** and~ALL BEARD~s the~CITY the~SHE the~NEAR~s TO the~DRILLED they⁽ᵐ⁾~will~BATHE⁽ⱽ⁾ AT HAND~s2~them⁽ᵐ⁾ UPON the~HEIFER the~BEHEAD⁽ⱽ⁾~ed⁽ᶠˢ⁾ in~the~WADI **21:7** and~they~did~ ANSWER⁽ⱽ⁾ and~they~did~SAY⁽ⱽ⁾ HAND~s2~us NOT she~did~POUR.OUT⁽ⱽ⁾ AT the~BLOOD the~THIS and~EYE~s2~us NOT they~did~SEE⁽ⱽ⁾ **21:8** l⁽ᵐˢ⁾~ much~COVER⁽ⱽ⁾ to~PEOPLE~you⁽ᵐˢ⁾ Yisra'eyl WHICH you⁽ᵐˢ⁾~did~RANSOM⁽ⱽ⁾ **YHWH** and~DO.NOT you⁽ᵐˢ⁾~will~GIVE⁽ⱽ⁾ BLOOD INNOCENT in~INSIDE PEOPLE~you⁽ᵐˢ⁾ Yisra'eyl and~he~did~self~COVER⁽ⱽ⁾ to~them⁽ᵐ⁾ the~ BLOOD **21:9** and~YOU⁽ᵐˢ⁾ you⁽ᵐˢ⁾~will~much~BURN⁽ⱽ⁾ the~BLOOD the~ INNOCENT from~INSIDE~you⁽ᵐˢ⁾ GIVEN.THAT you⁽ᵐˢ⁾~will~DO⁽ⱽ⁾ the~ STRAIGHT in~EYE~s2 **YHWH** **21:10** GIVEN.THAT you⁽ᵐˢ⁾~will~GO.OUT⁽ⱽ⁾ to~ the~BATTLE UPON ATTACK⁽ⱽ⁾~ing⁽ᵐᵖ⁾~s~you⁽ᵐˢ⁾ and~he~did~GIVE⁽ⱽ⁾~him

YHWH Elohiym~you$^{(ms)}$ in~HAND~you$^{(ms)}$ and~*you$^{(ms)}$~did*~CAPTURE$^{(V)}$ CAPTIVE~him **21:11** and~*you$^{(ms)}$~did*~SEE$^{(V)}$ in~the~CAPTIVE WOMAN BEAUTIFUL FORM and~*you$^{(ms)}$~did*~ATTACH$^{(V)}$ in~her and~*you$^{(ms)}$~did*~TAKE$^{(V)}$ to~you$^{(ms)}$ to~WOMAN **21:12** and~*you$^{(ms)}$~did*~make~COME$^{(V)}$~her TO MIDST HOUSE~you$^{(ms)}$ and~*she~did~much*~SHAVE$^{(V)}$ AT HEAD~her and~*she~did*~DO$^{(V)}$ AT POINT~s~her **21:13** and~*she~did~make*~TURN.ASIDE$^{(V)}$ AT APPAREL CAPTIVE~her from~UPON~her and~*she~did*~SETTLE$^{(V)}$ in~HOUSE~you$^{(ms)}$ and~*she~did*~WEEP$^{(V)}$ AT FATHER~her and~AT MOTHER~her MOON DAY~s and~AFTER SO *you$^{(ms)}$~will*~COME$^{(V)}$ TO~her and~*you$^{(ms)}$~did*~MARRY$^{(V)}$~her and~*she~did*~EXIST$^{(V)}$ to~you$^{(ms)}$ to~WOMAN **21:14** and~*he~did*~EXIST$^{(V)}$ IF NOT *you$^{(ms)}$~did*~DELIGHT$^{(V)}$ in~her and~*you$^{(ms)}$~did*~SEND$^{(V)}$~her to~SOUL~her and~>~SELL$^{(V)}$ NOT *you$^{(mp)}$~will*~SELL$^{(V)}$~her in~SILVER NOT *you$^{(ms)}$~will~self*~BUNDLE$^{(V)}$ in~her UNDER WHICH *you$^{(ms)}$~did~much*~AFFLICT$^{(V)}$~her **21:15** GIVEN.THAT *they$^{(f)}$~will*~EXIST$^{(V)}$ to~MAN TWO WOMAN~s the~UNIT LOVE$^{(V)}$~*ed$^{(fs)}$* and~the~UNIT HATE$^{(V)}$~*ed$^{(fs)}$* and~*they$^{(m)}$~will*~BRING.FORTH$^{(V)}$ to~him SON~s the~LOVE$^{(V)}$~*ed$^{(fs)}$* and~the~HATE$^{(V)}$~*ed$^{(fs)}$* and~*he~did*~EXIST$^{(V)}$ the~SON the~FIRSTBORN to~the~HATED **21:16** and~*he~did*~EXIST$^{(V)}$ in~DAY >~*make*~INHERIT$^{(V)}$~him AT SON~s~him AT WHICH *he~will*~EXIST$^{(V)}$ to~him NOT *he~will*~BE.ABLE$^{(V)}$ to~>~*much*~BE.FIRSTBORN$^{(V)}$ AT SON the~LOVE$^{(V)}$~*ed$^{(fs)}$* UPON FACE~s SON the~HATE$^{(V)}$~*ed$^{(fs)}$* the~FIRSTBORN **21:17** GIVEN.THAT AT the~FIRSTBORN SON the~HATE$^{(V)}$~*ed$^{(fs)}$* *he~will~make*~RECOGNIZE$^{(V)}$ to~>~GIVE$^{(V)}$ to~him MOUTH TWO in~ALL WHICH *he~will~be*~FIND$^{(V)}$ to~him GIVEN.THAT HE SUMMIT VIGOR~him to~him DECISION the~BIRTHRIGHT **21:18** GIVEN.THAT *he~will*~EXIST$^{(V)}$ to~MAN SON BE.STUBBORN$^{(V)}$~*ing$^{(ms)}$* and~DISOBEY$^{(V)}$~*ing$^{(ms)}$* WITHOUT~him HEAR$^{(V)}$~*ing$^{(ms)}$* in~VOICE FATHER~him and~in~VOICE MOTHER~him and~*they~did~much*~CORRECT$^{(V)}$ AT~him and~NOT *he~will*~HEAR$^{(V)}$ TO~them$^{(m)}$ **21:19** and~*they~will*~SEIZE.HOLD$^{(V)}$ in~him FATHER~him and~MOTHER~him and~*!$^{(mp)}$~make*~GO.OUT$^{(V)}$ AT~him TO BEARD~s CITY~him and~TO GATE AREA~him **21:20** and~*they~did*~SAY$^{(V)}$ TO BEARD~s CITY~him SON~us THIS BE.STUBBORN$^{(V)}$~*ing$^{(ms)}$* and~DISOBEY$^{(V)}$~*ing$^{(ms)}$* WITHOUT~him HEAR$^{(V)}$~*ing$^{(ms)}$* in~VOICE~us GLUTTON$^{(V)}$~*ing$^{(ms)}$* and~IMBIBE$^{(V)}$~*ing$^{(ms)}$* **21:21** and~*they~did*~KILL.BY.STONING$^{(V)}$~him ALL MAN~s CITY~him in~the~STONE~s and~*he~did*~DIE$^{(V)}$ and~*you$^{(ms)}$~did~much*~BURN$^{(V)}$ the~DYSFUNCTIONAL from~INSIDE~you$^{(ms)}$ and~ALL Yisra'eyl *they$^{(m)}$~will*~HEAR$^{(V)}$ and~*they$^{(m)}$~will*~FEAR$^{(V)}$ **21:22** and~GIVEN.THAT *he~will*~EXIST$^{(V)}$ in~MAN FAILURE DECISION DEATH and~*he~did~be~make*~DIE$^{(V)}$ and~*you$^{(ms)}$~did*~HANG$^{(V)}$ AT~him UPON TREE **21:23** NOT *you$^{(ms)}$~will*~STAY.THE.NIGHT$^{(V)}$ CARCASS~him UPON the~TREE GIVEN.THAT >~BURY$^{(V)}$ *you$^{(ms)}$~will*~BURY$^{(V)}$~him in~the~DAY the~HE GIVEN.THAT ANNOYANCE Elohiym HANG$^{(V)}$~*ed$^{(ms)}$* and~NOT *you$^{(ms)}$~will~much*~BE.DIRTY$^{(V)}$ AT GROUND~you$^{(ms)}$ WHICH **YHWH** Elohiym~you$^{(ms)}$ GIVE$^{(V)}$~*ing$^{(ms)}$* to~you$^{(ms)}$ INHERITANCE

Chapter 22

22:1 NOT *you*⁽ᵐˢ⁾~*will*~SEE⁽ⱽ⁾ AT OX BROTHER~*you*⁽ᵐˢ⁾ OR AT RAM~him *be*~DRIVE.OUT⁽ⱽ⁾~*ing*⁽ᵐᵖ⁾ and~*you*⁽ᵐˢ⁾~*did*~*self*~BE.OUT.OF.SIGHT⁽ⱽ⁾ from~them⁽ᵐ⁾ *!*⁽ᵐˢ⁾~*make*~TURN.BACK⁽ⱽ⁾ *you*⁽ᵐˢ⁾~*will*~*make*~TURN.BACK⁽ⱽ⁾~them⁽ᵐ⁾ to~BROTHER~*you*⁽ᵐˢ⁾ **22:2** and~IF NOT NEAR BROTHER~*you*⁽ᵐˢ⁾ TO~*you*⁽ᵐˢ⁾ and~NOT *you*⁽ᵐˢ⁾~*did*~KNOW⁽ⱽ⁾~him and~*you*⁽ᵐˢ⁾~*did*~GATHER⁽ⱽ⁾~him TO MIDST HOUSE~*you*⁽ᵐˢ⁾ and~*he*~*did*~EXIST⁽ⱽ⁾ WITH~*you*⁽ᵐˢ⁾ UNTIL >~SEEK⁽ⱽ⁾ BROTHER~*you*⁽ᵐˢ⁾ AT~him and~*you*⁽ᵐˢ⁾~*did*~*make*~TURN.BACK⁽ⱽ⁾~him to~him **22:3** and~SO *you*⁽ᵐˢ⁾~*will*~DO⁽ⱽ⁾ to~DONKEY~him and~SO *you*⁽ᵐˢ⁾~*will*~DO⁽ⱽ⁾ to~APPAREL~him and~SO *you*⁽ᵐˢ⁾~*will*~DO⁽ⱽ⁾ to~ALL LOST.THING BROTHER~*you*⁽ᵐˢ⁾ WHICH *she*~*will*~PERISH⁽ⱽ⁾ FROM~him and~*you*⁽ᵐˢ⁾~*did*~FIND⁽ⱽ⁾ NOT *you*⁽ᵐˢ⁾~*will*~BE.ABLE⁽ⱽ⁾ to~>~*self*~BE.OUT.OF.SIGHT⁽ⱽ⁾ **22:4** NOT *you*⁽ᵐˢ⁾~*will*~SEE⁽ⱽ⁾ AT DONKEY BROTHER~*you*⁽ᵐˢ⁾ OR OX~him FALL⁽ⱽ⁾~*ing*⁽ᵐᵖ⁾ in~the~ROAD and~*you*⁽ᵐˢ⁾~*did*~*self*~BE.OUT.OF.SIGHT⁽ⱽ⁾ from~them⁽ᵐ⁾ *!*⁽ᵐˢ⁾~*make*~RISE⁽ⱽ⁾ *you*⁽ᵐˢ⁾~*will*~*make*~RISE⁽ⱽ⁾ WITH~him **22:5** NOT *he*~*will*~EXIST⁽ⱽ⁾ UTENSIL WARRIOR UPON WOMAN and~NOT *he*~*will*~WEAR⁽ⱽ⁾ WARRIOR APPAREL WOMAN GIVEN.THAT DISGUSTING **YHWH** Elohiym~*you*⁽ᵐˢ⁾ ALL DO⁽ⱽ⁾~*ing*⁽ᵐˢ⁾ THESE **22:6** GIVEN.THAT *he*~*will*~*be*~MEET⁽ⱽ⁾ NEST BIRD to~FACE~s~*you*⁽ᵐˢ⁾ in~the~ROAD in~ALL TREE OR UPON the~LAND CHICK~s OR EGG~s and~the~MOTHER STRETCH.OUT⁽ⱽ⁾~*ing*⁽ᶠˢ⁾ UPON the~CHICK~s OR UPON the~EGG~s NOT *you*⁽ᵐˢ⁾~*will*~TAKE⁽ⱽ⁾ the~MOTHER UPON the~SON~s **22:7** >~*much*~SEND⁽ⱽ⁾ *you*⁽ᵐˢ⁾~*will*~*much*~SEND⁽ⱽ⁾ AT the~MOTHER and~AT the~SON~s *you*⁽ᵐˢ⁾~*will*~TAKE⁽ⱽ⁾ to~*you*⁽ᶠˢ⁾ to~THAT *he*~*will*~DO.WELL⁽ⱽ⁾ to~*you*⁽ᶠˢ⁾ and~*you*⁽ᵐˢ⁾~*did*~*make*~PROLONG⁽ⱽ⁾ DAY~s **22:8** GIVEN.THAT *you*⁽ᵐˢ⁾~*will*~BUILD⁽ⱽ⁾ HOUSE NEW and~*you*⁽ᵐˢ⁾~*did*~DO⁽ⱽ⁾ PARAPET to~ROOF~*you*⁽ᵐˢ⁾ and~NOT *you*⁽ᵐˢ⁾~*will*~PLACE⁽ⱽ⁾ BLOOD~s in~HOUSE~*you*⁽ᵐˢ⁾ GIVEN.THAT *he*~*will*~FALL⁽ⱽ⁾ the~FALL⁽ⱽ⁾~*ing*⁽ᵐˢ⁾ FROM~him **22:9** NOT *you*⁽ᵐˢ⁾~*will*~SOW⁽ⱽ⁾ VINEYARD~*you*⁽ᵐˢ⁾ DIVERSE.KIND~s2 OTHERWISE *she*~*will*~SET.APART⁽ⱽ⁾ the~RIPE.FRUIT the~SEED WHICH *you*⁽ᵐˢ⁾~*will*~SOW⁽ⱽ⁾ and~PRODUCTION the~VINEYARD **22:10** NOT *you*⁽ᵐˢ⁾~*will*~SCRATCH⁽ⱽ⁾ in~OX and~in~the~DONKEY TOGETHER **22:11** NOT *you*⁽ᵐˢ⁾~*will*~WEAR⁽ⱽ⁾ LINSEY-WOOLSEY WOOL and~FLAX~s TOGETHER **22:12** TASSEL~s *you*⁽ᵐˢ⁾~*will*~DO⁽ⱽ⁾ to~*you*⁽ᶠˢ⁾ UPON FOUR WING~s RAIMENT~*you*⁽ᵐˢ⁾ WHICH *you*⁽ᵐˢ⁾~*will*~*much*~COVER.OVER⁽ⱽ⁾ in~her **22:13** GIVEN.THAT *he*~*will*~TAKE⁽ⱽ⁾ MAN WOMAN and~*he*~*did*~COME⁽ⱽ⁾ TO~her and~*he*~*did*~HATE⁽ⱽ⁾~her **22:14** and~*he*~*did*~PLACE⁽ⱽ⁾ to~her WORKINGS~s WORD~s and~*he*~*did*~*make*~GO.OUT⁽ⱽ⁾ UPON~her TITLE DYSFUNCTIONAL and~*he*~*did*~SAY⁽ⱽ⁾ AT the~WOMAN the~THIS *I*~*did*~TAKE⁽ⱽ⁾ and~*I*~*will*~COME.NEAR⁽ⱽ⁾ TO~her and~NOT *I*~*did*~FIND⁽ⱽ⁾ to~her VIRGINITY~s **22:15** and~*he*~*did*~TAKE⁽ⱽ⁾ FATHER~of the~YOUNG.MAN and~MOTHER~her and~ *!*⁽ᵐᵖ⁾~*make*~GO.OUT⁽ⱽ⁾ AT VIRGINITY~s the~YOUNG.MAN TO BEARD~s the~CITY the~GATE~unto **22:16** and~*he*~*did*~SAY⁽ⱽ⁾ FATHER~of the~YOUNG.MAN TO the~BEARD~s AT DAUGHTER~me *I*~*did*~GIVE⁽ⱽ⁾ to~

the~MAN the~THIS to~WOMAN and~*he*~*will*~HATE⁽ⱽ⁾~her **22:17** and~
LOOK HE *he*~*did*~PLACE⁽ⱽ⁾ WORKINGS~s WORD~s to~>~SAY⁽ⱽ⁾ NOT *I*~*did*~
FIND⁽ⱽ⁾ to~DAUGHTER~you⁽ᵐˢ⁾ VIRGINITY~s and~THESE VIRGINITY~s
DAUGHTER~me and~*they*~*did*~SPREAD.OUT⁽ⱽ⁾ the~APPAREL to~FACE~s
BEARD~s the~CITY **22:18** and~*they*~*did*~TAKE⁽ⱽ⁾ BEARD~s the~CITY the~SHE
AT the~MAN and~*they*~*did*~much~CORRECT⁽ⱽ⁾ AT~him **22:19** and~*they*~
did~FINE⁽ⱽ⁾ AT~him HUNDRED SILVER and~*they*~*did*~GIVE⁽ⱽ⁾ to~the~
FATHER~of the~YOUNG.WOMAN GIVEN.THAT *he*~*did*~*make*~GO.OUT⁽ⱽ⁾
TITLE DYSFUNCTIONAL UPON VIRGIN Yisra'eyl and~to~him *she*~*will*~EXIST⁽ⱽ⁾
to~WOMAN NOT *he*~*will*~BE.ABLE⁽ⱽ⁾ to~>~much~SEND⁽ⱽ⁾~her ALL DAY~s~
him **22:20** and~IF TRUTH *he*~*did*~EXIST⁽ⱽ⁾ the~WORD the~THIS NOT *they*~
did~*be*~FIND⁽ⱽ⁾ VIRGIN~s to~YOUNG.MAN **22:21** and~*!⁽ᵐᵖ⁾*~*make*~
GO.OUT⁽ⱽ⁾ AT the~YOUNG.MAN TO OPENING HOUSE FATHER~her and~
they~*did*~STONE⁽ⱽ⁾~her MAN~s CITY~her in~the~STONE~s and~*she*~*did*~
DIE⁽ⱽ⁾ GIVEN.THAT *she*~*did*~DO⁽ⱽ⁾ FOLLY in~Yisra'eyl to~>~BE.A.HARLOT⁽ⱽ⁾
HOUSE FATHER~her and~*you*⁽ᵐˢ⁾~*did*~much~BURN⁽ⱽ⁾ the~DYSFUNCTIONAL
from~INSIDE~you⁽ᵐˢ⁾ **22:22** GIVEN.THAT *he*~*will*~*be*~FIND⁽ⱽ⁾ MAN
LIE.DOWN⁽ⱽ⁾~*ing*⁽ᵐˢ⁾ WITH WOMAN MARRY⁽ⱽ⁾~*ed*⁽ᶠˢ⁾ MASTER and~*they*~*did*~
DIE⁽ⱽ⁾ ALSO TWO~them⁽ᵐ⁾ the~MAN the~LIE.DOWN⁽ⱽ⁾~*ing*⁽ᵐˢ⁾ WITH the~
WOMAN and~the~WOMAN and~*you*⁽ᵐˢ⁾~*did*~much~BURN⁽ⱽ⁾ the~
DYSFUNCTIONAL from~Yisra'eyl **22:23** GIVEN.THAT *he*~*will*~EXIST⁽ⱽ⁾
YOUNG.MAN VIRGIN *be*~much~BETROTH⁽ⱽ⁾~*ing*⁽ᶠˢ⁾ to~MAN and~*he*~*did*~
FIND⁽ⱽ⁾~her MAN in~the~CITY and~*he*~*did*~LIE.DOWN⁽ⱽ⁾ WITH~
her **22:24** and~*you*⁽ᵐᵖ⁾~*did*~*make*~GO.OUT⁽ⱽ⁾ AT TWO~them⁽ᵐ⁾ TO GATE
the~CITY the~SHE and~*you*⁽ᵐᵖ⁾~*did*~STONE⁽ⱽ⁾ AT~them⁽ᵐ⁾ in~the~STONE~s
and~*they*~*did*~DIE⁽ⱽ⁾ AT the~YOUNG.MAN UPON WORD WHICH NOT *she*~
did~CRY.OUT⁽ⱽ⁾ in~the~CITY and~AT the~MAN UPON WORD WHICH *he*~*did*~
much~AFFLICT⁽ⱽ⁾ AT WOMAN COMPANION~him and~*you*⁽ᵐˢ⁾~*did*~much~
BURN⁽ⱽ⁾ the~DYSFUNCTIONAL from~INSIDE~you⁽ᵐˢ⁾ **22:25** and~IF in~the~
FIELD *he*~*will*~FIND⁽ⱽ⁾ the~MAN AT the~YOUNG.MAN the~*be*~much~
BETROTH⁽ⱽ⁾~*ing*⁽ᶠˢ⁾ and~*he*~*did*~*make*~SEIZE⁽ⱽ⁾ in~her the~MAN and~*he*~*did*~
LIE.DOWN⁽ⱽ⁾ WITH~her and~*he*~*did*~DIE⁽ⱽ⁾ the~MAN WHICH *he*~*did*~
LIE.DOWN⁽ⱽ⁾ WITH~her to~STRAND~him **22:26** and~to~YOUNG.MAN NOT
you⁽ᵐˢ⁾~*will*~DO⁽ⱽ⁾ WORD WITHOUT to~YOUNG.MAN FAILURE DEATH
GIVEN.THAT like~WHICH *he*~*will*~RISE⁽ⱽ⁾ MAN UPON COMPANION~him and~
he~*did*~MURDER⁽ⱽ⁾~him SOUL SO the~WORD the~THIS **22:27** GIVEN.THAT
in~the~FIELD *he*~*did*~FIND⁽ⱽ⁾~her *she*~*did*~CRY.OUT⁽ⱽ⁾ the~YOUNG.MAN
the~*be*~much~BETROTH⁽ⱽ⁾~*ing*⁽ᶠˢ⁾ and~WITHOUT *make*~RESCUE⁽ⱽ⁾~*ing*⁽ᵐˢ⁾
to~her **22:28** GIVEN.THAT *he*~*will*~FIND⁽ⱽ⁾ MAN YOUNG.MAN VIRGIN
WHICH NOT *she*~*did*~*be*~much~BETROTH⁽ⱽ⁾ and~*he*~*will*~SEIZE.HOLD⁽ⱽ⁾~her
and~*he*~*did*~LIE.DOWN⁽ⱽ⁾ WITH~her and~*they*~*did*~*be*~FIND⁽ⱽ⁾ **22:29** and~
he~*did*~GIVE⁽ⱽ⁾ the~MAN the~LIE.DOWN⁽ⱽ⁾~*ing*⁽ᶠˢ⁾ WITH~her to~the~
FATHER~of the~YOUNG.MAN FIVE~s SILVER and~to~him *she*~*will*~EXIST⁽ⱽ⁾
to~WOMAN UNDER WHICH *he*~*did*~much~AFFLICT⁽ⱽ⁾~her NOT *he*~*will*~
BE.ABLE⁽ⱽ⁾ >~much~SEND⁽ⱽ⁾~her ALL DAY~s~him

Chapter 23

23:1 (22:30) NOT *he~will*~TAKE^(V) MAN AT WOMAN FATHER~him and~NOT *he~will~much*~REMOVE.THE.COVER^(V) WING FATHER~him **23:2 (23:1)** NOT *he~will*~COME^(V) WOUND^(V)~*ed*^(ms) BROKEN and~CUT^(V)~*ed*^(ms) PENIS in~ASSEMBLY **YHWH** **23:3 (23:2)** NOT *he~will*~COME^(V) BASTARD in~ASSEMBLY **YHWH** ALSO GENERATION TENTH NOT *he~will*~COME^(V) to~him in~ASSEMBLY **YHWH** **23:4 (23:3)** NOT *he~will*~COME^(V) Amon~of and~Mo'av~of in~ASSEMBLY **YHWH** ALSO GENERATION TENTH NOT *he~will*~COME^(V) to~them^(m) in~ASSEMBLY **YHWH** UNTIL DISTANT **23:5 (23:4)** UPON WORD WHICH NOT *they~did~much*~FACE.TOWARD^(V) AT~you^(mp) in~the~BREAD and~in~the~WATER~s2 in~the~ROAD in~>~GO.OUT^(V)~you^(mp) from~Mits'rayim and~WHICH *he~did*~HIRE^(V) UPON~you^(ms) AT Bilam SON Be'or from~Petor Aram-Nahara'im to~>~*much*~BELITTLE^(V)~you^(ms) **23:6 (23:5)** and~NOT *he~did*~CONSENT^(V) **YHWH** Elohiym~you^(ms) to~>~HEAR^(V) TO Bilam and~*he~will*~OVERTURN^(V) **YHWH** Elohiym~you^(ms) to~you^(ms) AT the~ANNOYANCE to~PRESENT GIVEN.THAT *he~did*~LOVE^(V)~you^(ms) **YHWH** Elohiym~you^(ms) **23:7 (23:6)** NOT *you^(ms)~will*~SEEK^(V) COMPLETENESS~them^(m) and~FUNCTIONAL~them^(m) ALL DAY~s~you^(ms) to~DISTANT **23:8 (23:7)** NOT *you^(ms)~will~much*~ABHOR^(V) Edom~of GIVEN.THAT BROTHER~you^(ms) HE NOT *you^(ms)~will~much*~ABHOR^(V) Mits'rayim~of GIVEN.THAT IMMIGRANT *you^(ms)~did*~EXIST^(V) in~LAND~him **23:9 (23:8)** SON~s WHICH *they^(m)~will~be*~BRING.FORTH^(V) to~them^(m) GENERATION THIRD *he~will*~COME^(V) to~them^(m) in~ASSEMBLY **YHWH** **23:10 (23:9)** GIVEN.THAT *she~will*~GO.OUT^(V) CAMP UPON ATTACK^(V)~*ing*^(mp)~s~you^(ms) and~*you^(ms)~will~be*~SAFEGUARD^(V) from~ALL WORD DYSFUNCTIONAL **23:11 (23:10)** GIVEN.THAT *he~will*~EXIST^(V) in~you^(ms) MAN WHICH NOT *he~will*~EXIST^(V) CLEAN from~EVENT NIGHT and~*he~will*~GO.OUT^(V) TO from~OUTSIDE to~the~CAMP NOT *he~will*~COME^(V) TO MIDST the~CAMP **23:12 (23:11)** and~*he~did*~EXIST^(V) to~>~TURN^(V) EVENING *he~will*~BATHE^(V) in~the~WATER~s2 and~like~>~COME^(V) the~SUN *he~will*~COME^(V) TO MIDST the~CAMP **23:13 (23:12)** and~HAND *she~will*~EXIST^(V) to~you^(ms) from~OUTSIDE to~the~CAMP and~*you^(ms)~did*~GO.OUT^(V) THERE~unto OUTSIDE **23:14 (23:13)** and~TENT.PEG *she~will*~EXIST^(V) to~you^(ms) UPON TOOLS~you^(ms) and~*he~did*~EXIST^(V) in~>~SETTLE^(V)~you^(ms) OUTSIDE and~*you^(ms)~did*~DIG.OUT^(V)~& in~her and~*you^(ms)~did*~TURN.BACK^(V) and~*you^(ms)~did*~COVER.OVER^(V) AT >~GO.OUT^(V)~you^(ms) **23:15 (23:14)** GIVEN.THAT **YHWH** Elohiym~you^(ms) *self*~WALK^(V)~*ing*^(ms) in~INSIDE CAMP~you^(ms) to~>~*make*~DELIVER^(V)~you^(ms) and~to~>~GIVE^(V) ATTACK^(V)~*ing*^(mp)~s~you^(ms) to~FACE~s~you^(ms) and~*he~did*~EXIST^(V) CAMP~s~you^(ms) UNIQUE and~NOT *he~will*~SEE^(V) in~you^(ms) NAKEDNESS WORD and~*he~did*~TURN.BACK^(V) from~AFTER~you^(ms) **23:16 (23:15)** NOT *you^(ms)~will~make*~SHUT^(V) SERVANT TO LORD~s~him WHICH *he~will~be*~DELIVER^(V) TO~you^(ms) from~WITH LORD~s~him **23:17 (23:16)** WITH~you^(ms)

he~will~SETTLE^(V) in~INSIDE~*you*^(ms) in~the~AREA WHICH *he~will*~CHOOSE^(V) in~UNIT GATE~s~*you*^(ms) in~the~FUNCTIONAL to~him NOT *you*^(ms)~*will*~*make*~SUPPRESS^(V)~him   **23:18 (23:17)** NOT *she~will*~EXIST^(V) PROSTITUTE from~DAUGHTER~s Yisra'eyl and~NOT *he~will*~EXIST^(V) PROSTITUTE from~SON~s Yisra'eyl   **23:19 (23:18)** NOT *you*^(ms)~*will*~*make*~COME^(V) WAGES BE.A.HARLOT^(V)~*ing*^(fs) and~PRICE DOG HOUSE **YHWH** Elohiym~*you*^(ms) to~ALL VOW GIVEN.THAT DISGUSTING **YHWH** Elohiym~*you*^(ms) ALSO TWO~them^(m)   **23:20 (23:19)** NOT *you*^(ms)~*will*~*make*~BITE^(V) to~BROTHER~*you*^(ms) USURY SILVER USURY FOODSTUFF USURY ALL WORD WHICH *he~will*~BITE^(V)   **23:21 (23:20)** to~the~FOREIGNER *you*^(ms)~*will*~*make*~BITE^(V) and~to~BROTHER~*you*^(ms) NOT *you*^(ms)~*will*~*make*~BITE^(V) to~THAT *he~will*~much~KNEEL^(V)~*you*^(ms) **YHWH** Elohiym~*you*^(ms) in~ALL SENDING HAND~*you*^(ms) UPON the~LAND WHICH YOU^(ms) COME^(V)~*ing*^(ms) THERE~unto to~>~POSSESS^(V)~her   **23:22 (23:21)** GIVEN.THAT *you*^(ms)~*will*~MAKE.A.VOW^(V) VOW to~**YHWH** Elohiym~*you*^(ms) NOT *you*^(ms)~*will*~much~DELAY^(V) to~>~MAKE.RESTITUTION^(V)~him GIVEN.THAT >~SEEK^(V) *he~will*~SEEK^(V)~him **YHWH** Elohiym~*you*^(ms) from~WITH~*you*^(ms) and~*he~did*~EXIST^(V) in~*you*^(ms) FAILURE   **23:23 (23:22)** and~GIVEN.THAT *you*^(ms)~*will*~TERMINATE^(V) to~MAKE.A.VOW^(V) NOT *he~will*~EXIST^(V) in~*you*^(ms) FAILURE   **23:24 (23:23)** GOING.OUT LIP~s2~*you*^(ms) *you*^(ms)~*will*~SAFEGUARD^(V) and~*you*^(ms)~*did*~DO^(V) like~WHICH *you*^(ms)~*did*~MAKE.A.VOW^(V) to~**YHWH** Elohiym~*you*^(ms) FREEWILL.OFFERING WHICH *you*^(ms)~*did*~much~SPEAK^(V) in~MOUTH~*you*^(ms)   **23:25 (23:24)** GIVEN.THAT *you*^(ms)~*will*~COME^(V) in~VINEYARD COMPANION~*you*^(ms) and~*you*^(ms)~*did*~EAT^(V) GRAPE~s like~SOUL~*you*^(ms) PLENTY~*you*^(ms) and~TO UTENSIL~*you*^(ms) NOT *you*^(ms)~*will*~GIVE^(V)   **23:26 (23:25)** GIVEN.THAT *you*^(ms)~*will*~COME^(V) in~GRAIN.STALK COMPANION~*you*^(ms) and~*you*^(ms)~*did*~CROP.OFF^(V) HEAD.OF.WHEAT in~HAND~*you*^(ms) and~SICKLE NOT *you*^(ms)~*will*~*make*~WAVE^(V) UPON GRAIN.STALK COMPANION~*you*^(ms)

Chapter 24

24:1 GIVEN.THAT *he~will*~TAKE^(V) MAN WOMAN and~*he~did*~MARRY^(V)~her and~*he~did*~EXIST^(V) IF NOT *she~will*~FIND^(V) BEAUTY in~EYE~s2~him GIVEN.THAT *he~did*~FIND^(V) in~her NAKEDNESS WORD and~*he~did*~WRITE^(V) to~her SCROLL DIVORCE and~*he~did*~GIVE^(V) in~HAND~her and~*he~did*~much~SEND^(V)~her from~HOUSE~him   **24:2** and~*she~did*~GO.OUT^(V) from~HOUSE~him and~*she~did*~WALK^(V) and~*she~did*~EXIST^(V) to~MAN OTHER   **24:3** and~*he~did*~HATE^(V)~her the~MAN the~LAST and~*he~did*~WRITE^(V) to~her SCROLL DIVORCE and~*he~did*~GIVE^(V) in~HAND~her and~*he~did*~much~SEND^(V)~her from~HOUSE~him OR GIVEN.THAT *he~will*~DIE^(V) the~MAN the~LAST WHICH *he~did*~TAKE^(V)~her to~him to~WOMAN   **24:4** NOT *he~will*~BE.ABLE^(V) MASTER~her the~FIRST WHICH *he~*

The Book of Deuteronomy

*did~much~*SEND^(V)~her to~>~TURN.BACK^(V) to~>~TAKE^(V)~her to~>~EXIST^(V) to~him to~WOMAN AFTER WHICH *she~did~be~make~*BE.DIRTY^(V) GIVEN.THAT DISGUSTING SHE to~FACE~s **YHWH** and~NOT *you^(ms)~will~ make~*FAIL^(V) AT the~LAND WHICH **YHWH** Elohiym~you^(ms) GIVE^(V)~*ing*^(ms) to~ you^(ms) INHERITANCE **24:5** GIVEN.THAT *he~will~*TAKE^(V) MAN WOMAN NEW NOT *he~will~*GO.OUT^(V) in~the~ARMY and~NOT *he~will~*CROSS.OVER^(V) UPON~him to~ALL WORD INNOCENT *he~will~*EXIST^(V) to~HOUSE~him YEAR UNIT and~*he~did~*REJOICE^(V) AT WOMAN~him WHICH *he~did~* TAKE^(V) **24:6** NOT *he~will~*TAKE.AS.A.PLEDGE^(V) MILLSTONE~s and~VEHICLE GIVEN.THAT SOUL HE TAKE.AS.A.PLEDGE^(V)~*ing*^(ms) **24:7** GIVEN.THAT *he~ will~be~*FIND^(V) MAN STEAL^(V)~*ing*^(ms) SOUL from~BROTHER~s~him from~ SON~s Yisra'eyl and~*he~did~self~*BUNDLE^(V) in~him and~*he~did~*SELL^(V)~him and~*he~did~*DIE^(V) the~THIEF the~HE and~*you^(ms)~did~much~*BURN^(V) the~ DYSFUNCTIONAL from~INSIDE~you^(ms) **24:8** *!^(ms)~be~*SAFEGUARD^(V) in~ TOUCH the~INFECTION to~>~SAFEGUARD^(V) MANY and~to~>~DO^(V) like~ALL WHICH *they^(m)~will~make~*THROW^(V) AT~you^(mp) the~ADMINISTRATOR~s the~Lewi~s like~WHICH *I~did~much~*DIRECT^(V)~them^(m) *you^(mp)~will~* SAFEGUARD^(V) to~>~DO^(V) **24:9** >~REMEMBER^(V) AT WHICH *he~did~*DO^(V) **YHWH** Elohiym~you^(ms) to~Mir'yam in~the~ROAD in~>~GO.OUT^(V)~you^(mp) from~Mits'rayim **24:10** GIVEN.THAT *you^(ms)~will~make~*OVERLOOK^(V) in~ COMPANION~you^(ms) LOAN ANYTHING NOT *you^(ms)~will~*COME^(V) TO HOUSE~him to~the~>~MAKE.A.PLEDGE^(V) >~MAKE.A.PLEDGE^(V) **24:11** in~ the~OUTSIDE *you^(ms)~will~*STAND^(V) and~the~MAN WHICH YOU^(ms) OVERLOOK^(V)~*ing*^(ms) in~him *he~will~make~*GO.OUT^(V) TO~you^(ms) AT the~ PLEDGE the~OUTSIDE~unto **24:12** and~IF MAN AFFLICTION HE NOT *you^(ms)~will~*LIE.DOWN^(V) in~the~PLEDGE~him **24:13** *!^(ms)~make~* TURN.BACK^(V) *you^(ms)~will~*TURN.BACK^(V) to~him AT the~PLEDGE like~>~ COME^(V) the~SUN and~*he~did~*LIE.DOWN^(V) in~OUTER.GARMENT~him and~ *he~did~much~*KNEEL^(V)~you^(ms) and~to~you^(ms) *she~will~*EXIST^(V) STEADFASTNESS to~FACE~s **YHWH** Elohiym~you^(ms) **24:14** NOT *you^(ms)~will~* OPPRESS^(V) HIRELING AFFLICTION and~NEEDY from~BROTHER~s~you^(ms) OR from~IMMIGRANT~you^(ms) WHICH in~LAND~you^(ms) in~GATE~s~ you^(ms) **24:15** in~DAY~him *you^(ms)~will~*GIVE^(V) WAGE~him and~NOT *she~ will~*COME^(V) UPON~him the~SUN GIVEN.THAT AFFLICTION HE and~TO~him HE LIFT.UP^(V)~*ing*^(ms) AT SOUL~him and~NOT *he~will~*CALL.OUT^(V) UPON~ you^(ms) TO **YHWH** and~*he~did~*EXIST^(V) in~you^(ms) FAILURE **24:16** NOT *they~ will~be~make~*DIE^(V) FATHER~s UPON SON~s and~SON~s NOT *they~will~be~ make~*DIE^(V) UPON FATHER~s MAN in~FAILURE~him *they~will~be~make~* DIE^(V) **24:17** NOT *you^(ms)~will~make~*EXTEND^(V) DECISION IMMIGRANT ORPHAN and~NOT *you^(ms)~will~*TAKE.AS.A.PLEDGE^(V) GARMENT WIDOW **24:18** and~*you^(ms)~did~*REMEMBER^(V) GIVEN.THAT SERVANT *you^(ms)~did~*EXIST^(V) in~Mits'rayim and~*he~will~*RANSOM^(V)~you^(ms) **YHWH** Elohiym~you^(ms) from~THERE UPON SO I *much~*DIRECT^(V)~*ing*^(ms)~you^(ms) to~ >~DO^(V) AT the~WORD the~THIS **24:19** GIVEN.THAT *you^(ms)~will~*SEVER^(V) HARVEST~you^(ms) in~FIELD~you^(ms) and~*you^(ms)~did~*FORGET^(V) SHEAF in~

the~FIELD NOT *you*⁽ᵐˢ⁾~*will*~TURN.BACK⁽ⱽ⁾ to~>~TAKE⁽ⱽ⁾~him to~the~ IMMIGRANT to~the~ORPHAN and~to~the~WIDOW *he~will*~EXIST⁽ⱽ⁾ to~ THAT *he~will~much*~KNEEL⁽ⱽ⁾~*you*⁽ᵐˢ⁾ **YHWH** Elohiym~*you*⁽ᵐˢ⁾ in~ALL WORK HAND~s2~*you*⁽ᵐˢ⁾ **24:20** GIVEN.THAT *you*⁽ᵐˢ⁾~*will*~KNOCK⁽ⱽ⁾ OLIVE~*you*⁽ᵐˢ⁾ NOT *you*⁽ᵐˢ⁾~*will~much*~DECORATE⁽ⱽ⁾ AFTER~*you*⁽ᵐˢ⁾ to~the~IMMIGRANT to~the~ORPHAN and~to~the~WIDOW *he~will*~EXIST⁽ⱽ⁾ **24:21** GIVEN.THAT *you*⁽ᵐˢ⁾~*will*~FENCE.IN⁽ⱽ⁾ VINEYARD~*you*⁽ᵐˢ⁾ NOT *you*⁽ᵐˢ⁾~*will~much*~ROLL⁽ⱽ⁾ AFTER~*you*⁽ᵐˢ⁾ to~the~IMMIGRANT to~the~ORPHAN and~to~the~WIDOW *he~will*~EXIST⁽ⱽ⁾ **24:22** and~*you*⁽ᵐˢ⁾~*did*~REMEMBER⁽ⱽ⁾ GIVEN.THAT SERVANT *you*⁽ᵐˢ⁾~*did*~EXIST⁽ⱽ⁾ in~LAND Mits'rayim UPON SO I *much*~DIRECT⁽ⱽ⁾~*ing*⁽ᵐˢ⁾~*you*⁽ᵐˢ⁾ to~>~DO⁽ⱽ⁾ AT the~WORD the~THIS

Chapter 25

25:1 GIVEN.THAT *he~will*~EXIST⁽ⱽ⁾ DISPUTE BETWEEN MAN~s and~*they~did~be*~DRAW.NEAR⁽ⱽ⁾ TO the~DECISION and~*they~did*~DECIDE⁽ⱽ⁾~them⁽ᵐ⁾ and~*they~did~much*~BE.STEADFAST⁽ⱽ⁾ AT the~STEADFAST.ONE and~*they~did*~make~DEPART⁽ⱽ⁾ AT the~LOST **25:2** and~*he~did*~EXIST⁽ⱽ⁾ IF SON >~*make*~HIT⁽ⱽ⁾ the~LOST and~*he~did~make*~FALL⁽ⱽ⁾~him the~DECIDE⁽ⱽ⁾~*ing*⁽ᵐˢ⁾ and~*he~did~make*~HIT⁽ⱽ⁾~him to~FACE~s~him like~SUFFICIENT WAYWARDNESS~him in~NUMBER **25:3** FOUR~s *he~will~make*~HIT⁽ⱽ⁾~him NOT *he~will~make*~ADD⁽ⱽ⁾ OTHERWISE *he~will~make*~ADD⁽ⱽ⁾ to~>~*make*~HIT⁽ⱽ⁾~him UPON THESE HITTING ABUNDANT and~*he~did~be*~DRY⁽ⱽ⁾ BROTHER~*you*⁽ᵐˢ⁾ to~EYE~s2~*you*⁽ᵐˢ⁾ **25:4** NOT *you*⁽ᵐˢ⁾~*will*~MUZZLE⁽ⱽ⁾ OX in~>~THRESH⁽ⱽ⁾ **25:5** GIVEN.THAT *they*⁽ᵐ⁾~*will*~SETTLE⁽ⱽ⁾ BROTHER~s TOGETHER and~*he~did*~DIE⁽ⱽ⁾ UNIT from~them⁽ᵐ⁾ and~SON WITHOUT to~him NOT *she~will*~EXIST⁽ⱽ⁾ WOMAN the~DIE⁽ⱽ⁾~*ing*⁽ᵐˢ⁾ the~OUTSIDE~unto to~MAN BE.STRANGE⁽ⱽ⁾~*ing*⁽ᵐˢ⁾ BROTHER-IN-LAW~her *he~will*~COME⁽ⱽ⁾ UPON~her and~*he~did*~TAKE⁽ⱽ⁾~her to~him to~WOMAN and~*he~did~much*~DO.THE.MARRIAGE.DUTY⁽ⱽ⁾~her **25:6** and~*he~did*~EXIST⁽ⱽ⁾ the~FIRSTBORN WHICH *she~will*~BRING.FORTH⁽ⱽ⁾ *he~will*~RISE⁽ⱽ⁾ UPON TITLE BROTHER~him the~DIE⁽ⱽ⁾~*ing*⁽ᵐˢ⁾ and~NOT *he~will~be*~WIPE.AWAY⁽ⱽ⁾ TITLE~him from~Yisra'eyl **25:7** and~IF NOT *he~will*~DELIGHT⁽ⱽ⁾ the~MAN to~>~TAKE⁽ⱽ⁾ AT SISTER-in-law~him and~*she~did*~GO.UP⁽ⱽ⁾ SISTER-in-law~him the~GATE~unto TO the~BEARD~s and~*she~did*~SAY⁽ⱽ⁾ *he~did~much*~REFUSE⁽ⱽ⁾ >~*much*~DO.THE.MARRIAGE.DUTY⁽ⱽ⁾~me to~>~*make*~RISE⁽ⱽ⁾ to~BROTHER~him TITLE in~Yisra'eyl NOT *he~did*~CONSENT⁽ⱽ⁾ >~*much*~DO.THE.MARRIAGE.DUTY⁽ⱽ⁾~me **25:8** and~*they~did*~CALL.OUT⁽ⱽ⁾ to~him BEARD~s CITY~him and~*they~did~much*~SPEAK⁽ⱽ⁾ TO~him and~*he~did*~STAND⁽ⱽ⁾ and~*he~did*~SAY⁽ⱽ⁾ NOT *I~did*~DELIGHT⁽ⱽ⁾ to~>~TAKE⁽ⱽ⁾~her **25:9** and~*she~did~be*~DRAW.NEAR⁽ⱽ⁾ SISTER-in-law~him TO~him to~EYE~s2 the~BEARD~s and~*she~did*~EXTRACT⁽ⱽ⁾ SANDAL~him from~UPON FOOT~him and~*she~did*~SPIT⁽ⱽ⁾ in~FACE~s~him and~*she~did*~ANSWER⁽ⱽ⁾

The Book of Deuteronomy

and~she~did~SAY⁽ⱽ⁾ like~IN.THIS.WAY he~will~be~DO⁽ⱽ⁾ to~the~MAN WHICH NOT he~will~BUILD⁽ⱽ⁾ AT HOUSE BROTHER~him **25:10** and~he~did~ be~CALL.OUT⁽ⱽ⁾ TITLE~him in~Yisra'eyl HOUSE EXTRACT⁽ⱽ⁾~ed⁽ᵐˢ⁾ the~ SANDAL **25:11** GIVEN.THAT they⁽ᵐ⁾~will~be~STRUGGLE⁽ⱽ⁾ MAN~s TOGETHER MAN and~BROTHER~him and~she~did~COME.NEAR⁽ⱽ⁾ WOMAN the~UNIT to~>~make~DELIVER⁽ⱽ⁾ AT MAN~her from~HAND make~HIT⁽ⱽ⁾~ ing⁽ᵐˢ⁾~him and~she~did~SEND⁽ⱽ⁾ HAND~her and~she~did~make~SEIZE⁽ⱽ⁾ in~the~GENITALS~s~him **25:12** and~you⁽ᵐˢ⁾~did~SLICE.OFF⁽ⱽ⁾ AT PALM~her NOT she~will~SPARE⁽ⱽ⁾ EYE~you⁽ᵐˢ⁾ **25:13** NOT he~will~EXIST⁽ⱽ⁾ to~you⁽ᵐˢ⁾ in~BAG~you⁽ᵐˢ⁾ STONE and~STONE GREAT and~SMALL **25:14** NOT he~will~ EXIST⁽ⱽ⁾ to~you⁽ᵐˢ⁾ in~HOUSE~you⁽ᵐˢ⁾ EYPHAH and~EYPHAH GREAT and~ SMALL **25:15** STONE COMPLETENESS and~STEADFAST he~will~EXIST⁽ⱽ⁾ to~ you⁽ᶠˢ⁾ EYPHAH COMPLETENESS and~STEADFAST he~will~EXIST⁽ⱽ⁾ to~you⁽ᶠˢ⁾ to~THAT they⁽ᵐ⁾~will~make~PROLONG⁽ⱽ⁾ DAY~s~you⁽ᵐˢ⁾ UPON the~GROUND WHICH **YHWH** Elohiym~you⁽ᵐˢ⁾ GIVE⁽ⱽ⁾~ing⁽ᵐˢ⁾ to~you⁽ᶠˢ⁾ **25:16** GIVEN.THAT DISGUSTING **YHWH** Elohiym~you⁽ᵐˢ⁾ ALL DO⁽ⱽ⁾~ing⁽ᵐˢ⁾ THESE ALL DO⁽ⱽ⁾~ ing⁽ᵐˢ⁾ WICKED **25:17** >~REMEMBER⁽ⱽ⁾ AT WHICH he~did~DO⁽ⱽ⁾ to~you⁽ᵐˢ⁾ Amaleq in~the~ROAD in~>~GO.OUT⁽ⱽ⁾~you⁽ᵐᵖ⁾ from~ Mits'rayim **25:18** WHICH he~did~MEET⁽ⱽ⁾~you⁽ᵐˢ⁾ in~the~ROAD and~he~ will~much~ATTACK.THE.REAR⁽ⱽ⁾ in~you⁽ᵐˢ⁾ ALL the~be~SHATTER⁽ⱽ⁾~ing⁽ᵐᵖ⁾ AFTER~you⁽ᵐˢ⁾ and~YOU⁽ᵐˢ⁾ TIRED and~WEARY and~NOT he~did~FEAR⁽ⱽ⁾ Elohiym **25:19** and~he~did~EXIST⁽ⱽ⁾ in~>~make~REST⁽ⱽ⁾ **YHWH** Elohiym~ you⁽ᵐˢ⁾ to~you⁽ᵐˢ⁾ from~ALL ATTACK⁽ⱽ⁾~ing⁽ᵐᵖ⁾~s~you⁽ᵐˢ⁾ from~ALL.AROUND in~the~LAND WHICH **YHWH** Elohiym~you⁽ᵐˢ⁾ GIVE⁽ⱽ⁾~ing⁽ᵐˢ⁾ to~you⁽ᵐˢ⁾ INHERITANCE to~>~POSSESS⁽ⱽ⁾~her you⁽ᵐˢ⁾~will~WIPE.AWAY⁽ⱽ⁾ AT MEMORY Amaleq from~UNDER the~SKY~s2 NOT you⁽ᵐˢ⁾~will~FORGET⁽ⱽ⁾

Chapter 26

26:1 and~he~did~EXIST⁽ⱽ⁾ GIVEN.THAT you⁽ᵐˢ⁾~will~COME⁽ⱽ⁾ TO the~LAND WHICH **YHWH** Elohiym~you⁽ᵐˢ⁾ GIVE⁽ⱽ⁾~ing⁽ᵐˢ⁾ to~you⁽ᵐˢ⁾ INHERITANCE and~ you⁽ᵐˢ⁾~did~POSSESS⁽ⱽ⁾~her and~you⁽ᵐˢ⁾~did~SETTLE⁽ⱽ⁾ in~her **26:2** and~ you⁽ᵐˢ⁾~did~TAKE⁽ⱽ⁾ from~SUMMIT ALL PRODUCE the~GROUND WHICH you⁽ᵐˢ⁾~will~make~COME⁽ⱽ⁾ from~LAND~you⁽ᵐˢ⁾ WHICH **YHWH** Elohiym~ you⁽ᵐˢ⁾ GIVE⁽ⱽ⁾~ing⁽ᵐˢ⁾ to~you⁽ᶠˢ⁾ and~you⁽ᵐˢ⁾~did~PLACE⁽ⱽ⁾ in~the~REED-BASKET and~you⁽ᵐˢ⁾~did~WALK⁽ⱽ⁾ TO the~AREA WHICH he~will~CHOOSE⁽ⱽ⁾ **YHWH** Elohiym~you⁽ᵐˢ⁾ to~>~DWELL⁽ⱽ⁾ TITLE~him THERE **26:3** and~you⁽ᵐˢ⁾~ did~COME⁽ⱽ⁾ TO the~ADMINISTRATOR WHICH he~will~EXIST⁽ⱽ⁾ in~the~ DAY~s the~THEY⁽ᵐ⁾ and~you⁽ᵐˢ⁾~did~SAY⁽ⱽ⁾ TO~him I~did~make~ BE.FACE.TO.FACE⁽ⱽ⁾ the~DAY to~**YHWH** Elohiym~you⁽ᵐˢ⁾ GIVEN.THAT I~did~ COME⁽ⱽ⁾ TO the~LAND WHICH he~did~be~SWEAR⁽ⱽ⁾ **YHWH** to~FATHER~s~us to~>~GIVE⁽ⱽ⁾ to~us **26:4** and~he~did~TAKE⁽ⱽ⁾ the~ADMINISTRATOR the~ REED-BASKET from~HAND~you⁽ᵐˢ⁾ and~he~did~make~REST⁽ⱽ⁾~him to~

FACE~s ALTAR **YHWH** Elohiym~you⁽ᵐˢ⁾   **26:5** and~*you⁽ᵐˢ⁾~did*~ANSWER⁽ᵛ⁾ and~*you⁽ᵐˢ⁾~did*~SAY⁽ᵛ⁾ to~FACE~s **YHWH** Elohiym~you⁽ᵐˢ⁾ Aram~of PERISH⁽ᵛ⁾~*ing*⁽ᵐˢ⁾ FATHER~me and~*he~will*~GO.DOWN⁽ᵛ⁾ Mits'rayim~unto and~*he~will*~IMMIGRATE⁽ᵛ⁾ THERE in~MORTAL.MAN~s SMALL.AMOUNT and~*he~will*~EXIST⁽ᵛ⁾ THERE to~NATION GREAT NUMEROUS and~ ABUNDANT   **26:6** and~*they⁽ᵐ⁾~will~make*~BE.DYSFUNCTIONAL⁽ᵛ⁾ AT~us the~ Mits'rayim~s and~*they⁽ᵐ⁾~will~much*~AFFLICT⁽ᵛ⁾~us and~*they⁽ᵐ⁾~will*~GIVE⁽ᵛ⁾ UPON~us SERVICE HARD   **26:7** and~*we~will*~CRY.OUT⁽ᵛ⁾ TO **YHWH** Elohiym FATHER~s~us and~*he~will*~HEAR⁽ᵛ⁾ **YHWH** AT VOICE~us and~*he~will*~SEE⁽ᵛ⁾ AT AFFLICTION~us and~AT LABOR~us and~AT SQUEEZING~us   **26:8** and~ *he~will~make*~GO.OUT⁽ᵛ⁾~us **YHWH** from~Mits'rayim in~HAND FORCEFUL and~in~ARM EXTEND⁽ᵛ⁾~*ed*⁽ᶠˢ⁾ and~in~FEARING GREAT and~in~SIGN~s and~ in~WONDER~s   **26:9** and~*he~will~make*~COME⁽ᵛ⁾~us TO the~AREA the~ THIS and~*he~will*~GIVE⁽ᵛ⁾ to~us AT the~LAND the~THIS LAND ISSUE⁽ᵛ⁾~*ing*⁽ᶠˢ⁾ FAT and~HONEY   **26:10** and~NOW LOOK *I~did~make*~COME⁽ᵛ⁾ AT SUMMIT PRODUCE the~GROUND WHICH *you⁽ᵐˢ⁾~did*~GIVE⁽ᵛ⁾ to~me **YHWH** and~ *you⁽ᵐˢ⁾~did~make*~REST⁽ᵛ⁾~him to~FACE~s **YHWH** Elohiym~you⁽ᵐˢ⁾ and~ *you⁽ᵐˢ⁾~did~self*~BEND.DOWN⁽ᵛ⁾ to~FACE~s **YHWH** Elohiym~ you⁽ᵐˢ⁾   **26:11** and~*you⁽ᵐˢ⁾~did*~REJOICE⁽ᵛ⁾ in~ALL the~FUNCTIONAL WHICH *he~did*~GIVE⁽ᵛ⁾ to~you⁽ᵐˢ⁾ **YHWH** Elohiym~you⁽ᵐˢ⁾ and~to~HOUSE~you⁽ᵐˢ⁾ YOU⁽ᵐˢ⁾ and~the~Lewi and~the~IMMIGRANT WHICH in~INSIDE~ you⁽ᵐˢ⁾   **26:12** GIVEN.THAT *you⁽ᵐˢ⁾~will~much*~FINISH⁽ᵛ⁾ to~>~*make*~ GIVE.A.TENTH⁽ᵛ⁾ AT ALL TENTH.PART PRODUCTION~you⁽ᵐˢ⁾ in~the~YEAR the~THIRD YEAR the~TENTH.PART and~*you⁽ᵐˢ⁾~did*~GIVE⁽ᵛ⁾~& to~Lewi to~ the~IMMIGRANT to~the~ORPHAN and~to~the~WIDOW and~*they~did*~ EAT⁽ᵛ⁾ in~GATE~s~you⁽ᵐˢ⁾ and~*they~did*~BE.SATISFIED⁽ᵛ⁾   **26:13** and~*you⁽ᵐˢ⁾~ did~SAY*⁽ᵛ⁾ to~FACE~s **YHWH** Elohiym~you⁽ᵐˢ⁾ *I~did~much*~BURN⁽ᵛ⁾ the~ SPECIAL FROM the~HOUSE and~ALSO *I~did*~GIVE⁽ᵛ⁾~him to~Lewi and~to~ IMMIGRANT to~the~ORPHAN and~to~the~WIDOW like~ALL DIRECTIVE~s~ you⁽ᵐˢ⁾ WHICH *you⁽ᵐˢ⁾~did~much*~DIRECT⁽ᵛ⁾~me NOT *I~did*~CROSS.OVER⁽ᵛ⁾ from~DIRECTIVE~s~you⁽ᵐˢ⁾ and~NOT *I~did*~FORGET⁽ᵛ⁾   **26:14** NOT *I~did*~ EAT⁽ᵛ⁾ in~BARRENNESS~me FROM~him and~NOT *I~did~much*~BURN⁽ᵛ⁾ FROM~him in~DIRTY and~NOT *I~did*~GIVE⁽ᵛ⁾ FROM~him to~DIE⁽ᵛ⁾~*ing*⁽ᵐˢ⁾ *I~ did*~HEAR⁽ᵛ⁾ in~VOICE **YHWH** Elohiym~me *I~did*~DO⁽ᵛ⁾ like~ALL WHICH *you⁽ᵐˢ⁾~did~much*~DIRECT⁽ᵛ⁾~me   **26:15** !⁽ᵐˢ⁾~*make*~LOOK.DOWN⁽ᵛ⁾~& from~HABITATION SPECIAL~you⁽ᵐˢ⁾ FROM the~SKY~s2 and~!⁽ᵐˢ⁾~*much*~ KNEEL⁽ᵛ⁾ AT PEOPLE~you⁽ᵐˢ⁾ AT Yisra'eyl and~AT the~GROUND WHICH *you⁽ᵐˢ⁾~did*~GIVE⁽ᵛ⁾ to~us like~WHICH *you⁽ᵐˢ⁾~did~be*~SWEAR⁽ᵛ⁾ to~ FATHER~s~us LAND ISSUE⁽ᵛ⁾~*ing*⁽ᶠˢ⁾ FAT and~HONEY   **26:16** the~DAY the~ THIS **YHWH** Elohiym~you⁽ᵐˢ⁾ *much*~DIRECT⁽ᵛ⁾~*ing*⁽ᵐˢ⁾~you⁽ᵐˢ⁾ to~>~DO⁽ᵛ⁾ AT the~CUSTOM~s the~THESE and~AT the~DECISION~s and~*you⁽ᵐˢ⁾~did*~ SAFEGUARD⁽ᵛ⁾ and~*you⁽ᵐˢ⁾~did*~DO⁽ᵛ⁾ AT~them⁽ᵐ⁾ in~ALL HEART~you⁽ᵐˢ⁾ and~in~ALL SOUL~you⁽ᵐˢ⁾   **26:17** AT **YHWH** *you⁽ᵐˢ⁾~did~make*~SAY⁽ᵛ⁾ the~ DAY to~>~EXIST⁽ᵛ⁾ to~you⁽ᵐˢ⁾ to~Elohiym and~to~>~WALK⁽ᵛ⁾ in~ROAD~s~ him and~to~>~SAFEGUARD⁽ᵛ⁾ CUSTOM~s~him and~DIRECTIVE~s~him and~

The Book of Deuteronomy

DECISION~s~him and~to~>~HEAR$^{(V)}$ in~VOICE~him **26:18** and~**YHWH** *he~did~make*~SAY$^{(V)}$~you$^{(ms)}$ the~DAY to~>~EXIST$^{(V)}$ to~him to~PEOPLE JEWEL like~WHICH *he~did~much*~SPEAK$^{(V)}$ to~you$^{(fs)}$ and~to~>~SAFEGUARD$^{(V)}$ ALL DIRECTIVE~s~him **26:19** and~to~>~GIVE$^{(V)}$~you$^{(ms)}$ UPPER UPON ALL the~NATION~s WHICH *he~did*~DO$^{(V)}$ to~ADORATION and~to~Shem and~to~DECORATION and~to~>~GIVE$^{(V)}$~you$^{(ms)}$ PEOPLE UNIQUE to~**YHWH** Elohiym~you$^{(ms)}$ like~WHICH *he~did~much*~SPEAK$^{(V)}$

Chapter 27

27:1 and~*he~will~much*~DIRECT$^{(V)}$ Mosheh and~BEARD~s Yisra'eyl AT the~PEOPLE to~>~SAY$^{(V)}$ >~SAFEGUARD$^{(V)}$ AT ALL the~DIRECTIVE WHICH I *much~DIRECT$^{(V)}$~ing$^{(ms)}$* AT~you$^{(mp)}$ the~DAY **27:2** and~*he~did*~EXIST$^{(V)}$ in~the~DAY WHICH you$^{(mp)}$~*will*~CROSS.OVER$^{(V)}$ AT the~Yarden TO the~LAND WHICH **YHWH** Elohiym~you$^{(ms)}$ GIVE$^{(V)}$~*ing$^{(ms)}$* to~you$^{(fs)}$ and~*you$^{(ms)}$~did~make*~RISE$^{(V)}$ to~you$^{(ms)}$ STONE~s GREAT~s and~*you$^{(ms)}$~did*~DAUB$^{(V)}$ AT~them$^{(m)}$ in~the~LIME **27:3** and~*you$^{(ms)}$~did*~WRITE$^{(V)}$ UPON~them$^{(f)}$ AT ALL WORD~s the~TEACHING the~THIS in~>~CROSS.OVER$^{(V)}$~you$^{(ms)}$ to~THAT WHICH you$^{(ms)}$~*will*~COME$^{(V)}$ TO the~LAND WHICH **YHWH** Elohiym~you$^{(ms)}$ GIVE$^{(V)}$~*ing$^{(ms)}$* to~you$^{(ms)}$ LAND ISSUE$^{(V)}$~*ing$^{(fs)}$* FAT and~HONEY like~WHICH *he~did~much*~SPEAK$^{(V)}$ **YHWH** Elohiym FATHER~s~you$^{(ms)}$ to~you$^{(fs)}$ **27:4** and~*he~did*~EXIST$^{(V)}$ in~>~CROSS.OVER$^{(V)}$~you$^{(mp)}$ AT the~Yarden you$^{(mp)}$~*will~make*~RISE$^{(V)}$ AT the~STONE~s the~THESE WHICH I *much*~DIRECT$^{(V)}$~*ing$^{(ms)}$* AT~you$^{(mp)}$ the~DAY in~HILL Eyval and~*you$^{(ms)}$~did*~DAUB$^{(V)}$ AT~them$^{(m)}$ in~the~LIME **27:5** and~*you$^{(ms)}$~did*~BUILD$^{(V)}$ THERE ALTAR to~**YHWH** Elohiym~you$^{(ms)}$ ALTAR STONE~s NOT *you$^{(ms)}$~will~make*~WAVE$^{(V)}$ UPON~them$^{(m)}$ IRON **27:6** STONE~s COMPLETENESS~s *you$^{(ms)}$~will*~BUILD$^{(V)}$ AT ALTAR **YHWH** Elohiym~you$^{(ms)}$ and~*you$^{(ms)}$~did~make*~GO.UP$^{(V)}$ UPON~him ASCENSION.OFFERING to~**YHWH** Elohiym~you$^{(ms)}$ **27:7** and~*you$^{(ms)}$~did*~SACRIFICE$^{(V)}$ OFFERING.OF.RESTITUTION~s and~*you$^{(ms)}$~did*~EAT$^{(V)}$ THERE and~*you$^{(ms)}$~did*~REJOICE$^{(V)}$ to~FACE~s **YHWH** Elohiym~you$^{(ms)}$ **27:8** and~*you$^{(ms)}$~did*~WRITE$^{(V)}$ UPON the~STONE~s AT ALL WORD~s the~TEACHING the~THIS >~*much*~EXPLAIN$^{(V)}$ >~*make*~DO.WELL$^{(V)}$ **27:9** and~*he~will~much*~SPEAK$^{(V)}$ Mosheh and~the~ADMINISTRATOR~s the~Lewi~s TO ALL Yisra'eyl to~>~SAY$^{(V)}$!$^{(ms)}$~*make*~TAKE.HEED$^{(V)}$ and~!$^{(ms)}$~HEAR$^{(V)}$ Yisra'eyl the~DAY the~THIS *you$^{(ms)}$~did~be*~EXIST$^{(V)}$ to~PEOPLE to~**YHWH** Elohiym~you$^{(ms)}$ **27:10** and~*you$^{(ms)}$~did*~HEAR$^{(V)}$ in~VOICE **YHWH** Elohiym~you$^{(ms)}$ and~*you$^{(ms)}$~did*~DO$^{(V)}$ AT DIRECTIVE~s~him and~AT CUSTOM~s~him WHICH I *much*~DIRECT$^{(V)}$~*ing$^{(ms)}$*~you$^{(ms)}$ the~DAY **27:11** and~*he~will~much*~DIRECT$^{(V)}$ Mosheh AT the~PEOPLE in~the~DAY the~HE to~>~SAY$^{(V)}$ **27:12** THESE *they$^{(m)}$~will*~STAND$^{(V)}$ to~>~*much*~KNEEL$^{(V)}$ AT the~PEOPLE UPON HILL Gerizim in~>~CROSS.OVER$^{(V)}$~you$^{(mp)}$ AT the~Yarden Shimon and~Lewi and~Yehudah and~Yis'sas'khar and~Yoseph and~

360

Binyamin **27:13** and~THESE *they*⁽ᵐ⁾~*will*~STAND⁽ⱽ⁾ UPON the~ANNOYANCE in~HILL Eyval Re'uven Gad and~Asher and~Zevulun Dan and~
Naphtali **27:14** and~*they~did*~ANSWER⁽ⱽ⁾ the~Lewi~s and~*they~did*~SAY⁽ⱽ⁾ TO ALL MAN Yisra'eyl VOICE RAISE.UP⁽ⱽ⁾~*ing*⁽ᵐˢ⁾ **27:15** SPIT.UPON⁽ⱽ⁾~*ed*⁽ᵐˢ⁾ the~MAN WHICH *he~will*~DO⁽ⱽ⁾ SCULPTURE and~CAST.IMAGE DISGUSTING **YHWH** WORK HAND~s2 ENGRAVER and~*he~did*~PLACE⁽ⱽ⁾ in~the~HIDING and~*they~did*~ANSWER⁽ⱽ⁾ ALL the~PEOPLE and~*they~did*~SAY⁽ⱽ⁾ SO.BE.IT **27:16** SPIT.UPON⁽ⱽ⁾~*ed*⁽ᵐˢ⁾ *make*~DRY⁽ⱽ⁾~*ing*⁽ᵐˢ⁾ FATHER~him and~MOTHER~him and~*he~did*~SAY⁽ⱽ⁾ ALL the~PEOPLE SO.BE.IT **27:17** SPIT.UPON⁽ⱽ⁾~*ed*⁽ᵐˢ⁾ *make*~OVERTAKE⁽ⱽ⁾~*ing*⁽ᵐˢ⁾ BORDER COMPANION~him and~*he~did*~SAY⁽ⱽ⁾ ALL the~PEOPLE SO.BE.IT **27:18** SPIT.UPON⁽ⱽ⁾~*ed*⁽ᵐˢ⁾ *make*~GO.ASTRAY⁽ⱽ⁾~*ing*⁽ᵐˢ⁾ BLIND in~the~ROAD and~*he~did*~SAY⁽ⱽ⁾ ALL the~PEOPLE SO.BE.IT **27:19** SPIT.UPON⁽ⱽ⁾~*ed*⁽ᵐˢ⁾ *make*~EXTEND⁽ⱽ⁾~*ing*⁽ᵐˢ⁾ DECISION IMMIGRANT ORPHAN and~WIDOW and~*he~did*~SAY⁽ⱽ⁾ ALL the~PEOPLE SO.BE.IT **27:20** SPIT.UPON⁽ⱽ⁾~*ed*⁽ᵐˢ⁾ LIE.DOWN⁽ⱽ⁾~*ing*⁽ᵐˢ⁾ WITH WOMAN FATHER~him GIVEN.THAT *he~did*~*much*~REMOVE.THE.COVER⁽ⱽ⁾ WING FATHER~him and~*he~did*~SAY⁽ⱽ⁾ ALL the~PEOPLE SO.BE.IT **27:21** SPIT.UPON⁽ⱽ⁾~*ed*⁽ᵐˢ⁾ LIE.DOWN⁽ⱽ⁾~*ing*⁽ᵐˢ⁾ WITH ALL BEAST and~*he~did*~SAY⁽ⱽ⁾ ALL the~PEOPLE SO.BE.IT **27:22** SPIT.UPON⁽ⱽ⁾~*ed*⁽ᵐˢ⁾ LIE.DOWN⁽ⱽ⁾~*ing*⁽ᵐˢ⁾ WITH SISTER~him DAUGHTER FATHER~him OR DAUGHTER MOTHER~him and~*he~did*~SAY⁽ⱽ⁾ ALL the~PEOPLE SO.BE.IT **27:23** SPIT.UPON⁽ⱽ⁾~*ed*⁽ᵐˢ⁾ LIE.DOWN⁽ⱽ⁾~*ing*⁽ᵐˢ⁾ WITH BE.AN.IN-LAW⁽ⱽ⁾~*ing*⁽ᶠˢ⁾~him and~*he~did*~SAY⁽ⱽ⁾ ALL the~PEOPLE SO.BE.IT **27:24** SPIT.UPON⁽ⱽ⁾~*ed*⁽ᵐˢ⁾ *make*~HIT⁽ⱽ⁾~*ing*⁽ᵐˢ⁾ COMPANION~him in~the~HIDING and~*he~did*~SAY⁽ⱽ⁾ ALL the~PEOPLE SO.BE.IT **27:25** SPIT.UPON⁽ⱽ⁾~*ed*⁽ᵐˢ⁾ TAKE⁽ⱽ⁾~*ing*⁽ᵐˢ⁾ BRIBE to~>~*make*~HIT⁽ⱽ⁾ SOUL BLOOD INNOCENT and~*he~did*~SAY⁽ⱽ⁾ ALL the~PEOPLE SO.BE.IT **27:26** SPIT.UPON⁽ⱽ⁾~*ed*⁽ᵐˢ⁾ WHICH NOT *he~will*~*make*~RISE⁽ⱽ⁾ AT WORD~s the~TEACHING the~THIS to~>~DO⁽ⱽ⁾ AT~them⁽ᵐ⁾ and~*he~did*~SAY⁽ⱽ⁾ ALL the~PEOPLE SO.BE.IT

Chapter 28

28:1 and~*he~did*~EXIST⁽ⱽ⁾ IF >~HEAR⁽ⱽ⁾ *you*⁽ᵐˢ⁾~*will*~HEAR⁽ⱽ⁾ in~VOICE **YHWH** Elohiym~*you*⁽ᵐˢ⁾ to~>~SAFEGUARD⁽ⱽ⁾ to~>~DO⁽ⱽ⁾ AT ALL DIRECTIVE~s~him WHICH I *much*~DIRECT⁽ⱽ⁾~*ing*⁽ᵐˢ⁾~*you*⁽ᵐˢ⁾ the~DAY and~*he~did*~GIVE⁽ⱽ⁾~*you*⁽ᵐˢ⁾ **YHWH** Elohiym~*you*⁽ᵐˢ⁾ UPPER UPON ALL NATION~s the~LAND **28:2** and~*they~did*~COME⁽ⱽ⁾ UPON~*you*⁽ᵐˢ⁾ ALL the~PRESENT~s the~THESE and~*they~did*~*make*~OVERTAKE⁽ⱽ⁾~*you*⁽ᵐˢ⁾ GIVEN.THAT *you*⁽ᵐˢ⁾~*will*~HEAR⁽ⱽ⁾ in~VOICE **YHWH** Elohiym~*you*⁽ᵐˢ⁾ **28:3** KNEEL⁽ⱽ⁾~*ed*⁽ᵐˢ⁾ YOU⁽ᵐˢ⁾ in~the~CITY and~KNEEL⁽ⱽ⁾~*ed*⁽ᵐˢ⁾ YOU⁽ᵐˢ⁾ in~the~FIELD **28:4** KNEEL⁽ⱽ⁾~*ed*⁽ᵐˢ⁾ PRODUCE WOMB~*you*⁽ᵐˢ⁾ and~PRODUCE GROUND~*you*⁽ᵐˢ⁾ and~PRODUCE

The Book of Deuteronomy

BEAST~you^(ms) BIRTH BOVINE~s~you^(ms) and~YOUNG.SHEEP~s FLOCKS~you^(ms) **28:5** KNEEL^(V)~ed^(ms) REED-BASKET~you^(ms) and~KNEADING.BOWL~you^(ms) **28:6** KNEEL^(V)~ed^(ms) YOU^(ms) in~>~COME^(V)~you^(ms) and~KNEEL^(V)~ed^(ms) YOU^(ms) in~>~GO.OUT^(V)~you^(ms) **28:7** he~will~GIVE^(V) **YHWH** AT ATTACK^(V)~ing^(mp)~s~you^(ms) the~RISE^(V)~ing^(mp) UPON~you^(ms) be~SMITE^(V)~ing^(mp) to~FACE~s~you^(ms) in~ROAD UNIT they^(m)~will~GO.OUT^(V) TO~you^(ms) and~in~SEVEN ROAD~s they^(m)~will~FLEE^(V) to~FACE~s~you^(ms) **28:8** he~will~much~DIRECT^(V) **YHWH** AT~you^(ms) AT the~PRESENT in~BARN~s~you^(ms) and~in~ALL SENDING HAND~you^(ms) and~he~did~much~KNEEL^(V)~you^(ms) in~the~LAND WHICH **YHWH** Elohiym~you^(ms) GIVE^(V)~ing^(ms) to~you^(fs) **28:9** he~will~make~RISE^(V)~you^(ms) **YHWH** to~him to~PEOPLE UNIQUE like~WHICH he~did~be~SWEAR^(V) to~you^(fs) GIVEN.THAT you^(ms)~will~SAFEGUARD^(V) AT DIRECTIVE~s **YHWH** Elohiym~you^(ms) and~you^(ms)~did~WALK^(V) in~ROAD~s~him **28:10** and~they~did~SEE^(V) ALL PEOPLE~s the~LAND GIVEN.THAT TITLE **YHWH** he~did~be~MEET^(V) UPON~you^(ms) and~they~did~FEAR^(V) FROM~you^(ms) **28:11** and~he~did~make~LEAVE.BEHIND^(V)~you^(ms) **YHWH** to~FUNCTIONAL in~PRODUCE WOMB~you^(ms) and~in~PRODUCE BEAST~you^(ms) and~in~PRODUCE GROUND~you^(ms) UPON the~GROUND WHICH he~did~be~SWEAR^(V) **YHWH** to~FATHER~s~you^(ms) to~>~GIVE^(V) to~you^(fs) **28:12** he~will~OPEN^(V) **YHWH** to~you^(ms) AT SUPPLY.HOUSE~him the~FUNCTIONAL AT the~SKY~s2 to~>~GIVE^(V) PRECIPITATION LAND~you^(ms) in~APPOINTED.TIME~him and~to~>~much~KNEEL^(V) AT ALL WORK HAND~you^(ms) and~you^(ms)~did~make~JOIN^(V) NATION~s ABUNDANT~s and~YOU^(ms) NOT you^(ms)~will~JOIN^(V) **28:13** and~he~did~GIVE^(V)~you^(ms) **YHWH** to~HEAD and~NOT to~TAIL and~you^(ms)~did~EXIST^(V) ONLY to~UPWARD~unto and~NOT you^(ms)~will~EXIST^(V) to~the~BENEATH GIVEN.THAT you^(ms)~will~HEAR^(V) TO DIRECTIVE~s **YHWH** Elohiym~you^(ms) WHICH I much~DIRECT^(V)~ing^(ms)~you^(ms) the~DAY to~>~SAFEGUARD^(V) and~to~>~DO^(V) **28:14** and~NOT you^(ms)~will~TURN.ASIDE^(V) from~ALL the~WORD~s WHICH I much~DIRECT^(V)~ing^(ms) AT~you^(mp) the~DAY RIGHT.HAND and~LEFT.HAND to~>~WALK^(V) AFTER Elohiym OTHER~s to~>~SERVE^(V)~them^(m) **28:15** and~he~did~EXIST^(V) IF NOT you^(ms)~will~HEAR^(V) in~VOICE **YHWH** Elohiym~you^(ms) to~>~SAFEGUARD^(V) to~>~DO^(V) AT ALL DIRECTIVE~s~him and~CUSTOM~s~him WHICH I much~DIRECT^(V)~ing^(ms)~you^(ms) the~DAY and~they~did~COME^(V) UPON~you^(ms) ALL the~ANNOYANCE~s the~THESE and~they~did~make~OVERTAKE^(V)~you^(ms) **28:16** SPIT.UPON^(V)~ed^(ms) YOU^(ms) in~the~CITY and~SPIT.UPON^(V)~ed^(ms) YOU^(ms) in~the~FIELD **28:17** SPIT.UPON^(V)~ed^(ms) REED-BASKET~you^(ms) and~KNEADING.BOWL~you^(ms) **28:18** SPIT.UPON^(V)~ed^(ms) PRODUCE WOMB~you^(ms) and~PRODUCE GROUND~you^(ms) BIRTH BOVINE~s~you^(ms) and~YOUNG.SHEEP~s FLOCKS~you^(ms) **28:19** SPIT.UPON^(V)~ed^(ms) YOU^(ms) in~>~COME^(V)~you^(ms) and~SPIT.UPON^(V)~ed^(ms) YOU^(ms) in~>~GO.OUT^(V)~you^(ms) **28:20** he~will~much~SEND^(V) **YHWH** in~you^(ms) AT the~SPITTING AT the~TUMULT and~AT the~REPROOF in~ALL SENDING HAND~you^(ms) WHICH you^(ms)~will~DO^(V) UNTIL >~be~DESTROY^(V)~you^(ms) and~UNTIL >~PERISH^(V)~you^(ms) QUICKLY from~

Benner's Mechanical Translation of the Torah

FACE~s DYSFUNCTIONAL WORKS~s~you(ms) WHICH *you*(ms)~*did*~LEAVE(V)~ me **28:21** *he~will~make*~ADHERE(V) **YHWH** in~you(ms) AT the~EPIDEMIC UNTIL >~*much*~FINISH(V)~him AT~you(ms) from~UPON the~GROUND WHICH YOU(ms) *he~did*~COME(V) THERE~unto to~>~POSSESS(V)~her **28:22** *he~will~make*~HIT(V)~you(ms) **YHWH** in~the~CONSUMPTION and~in~the~FEVER and~ in~the~INFLAMMATION and~in~the~BURNING.FLAME and~in~the~SWORD and~in~the~BLASTING and~in~the~MILDEW and~*they~did*~PURSUE(V)~ you(ms) UNTIL >~PERISH(V)~you(ms) **28:23** and~*they~did*~EXIST(V) SKY~s2~ you(ms) WHICH UPON HEAD~you(ms) COPPER and~the~LAND WHICH UNDER~s~you(ms) IRON **28:24** *he~will*~GIVE(V) **YHWH** AT PRECIPITATION LAND~you(ms) DUST and~DIRT FROM the~SKY~s2 *he~will*~GO.DOWN(V) UPON~you(ms) UNTIL >~*be*~DESTROY(V)~you(ms) **28:25** *he~will*~GIVE(V)~ you(ms) **YHWH** *be*~SMITE(V)~*ing*(ms) to~FACE~s ATTACK(V)~*ing*(mp)~s~you(ms) in~ ROAD UNIT *you*(ms)~*will*~GO.OUT(V) TO~him and~in~SEVEN ROAD~s *you*(ms)~ *will*~FLEE(V) to~FACE~s~him and~*you*(ms)~*did*~EXIST(V) to~AGITATION to~ALL KINGDOM~s the~LAND **28:26** and~*she~did*~EXIST(V) CARCASS~you(ms) to~ NOURISHMENT to~ALL FLYER the~SKY~s2 and~to~BEAST the~LAND and~ WITHOUT *make*~TREMBLE(V)~*ing*(ms) **28:27** *he~will~make*~HIT(V)~you(ms) **YHWH** in~BOILS Mits'rayim and~in~the~TUMOR~s and~in~the~IRRITATION and~in~the~ITCH WHICH NOT *you*(ms)~*will*~BE.ABLE(V) to~>~*make*~ HEAL(V) **28:28** *he~will~make*~HIT(V)~you(ms) **YHWH** in~MADNESS and~in~ BLINDNESS and~in~ASTONISHMENT HEART **28:29** and~*you*(ms)~*did*~EXIST(V) *much*~GROPE(V)~*ing*(ms) in~the~GLISTENING~s2 like~WHICH *he~will~much*~ GROPE(V) the~BLIND in~the~THICK.GLOOMINESS and~NOT *you*(ms)~*will*~ *make*~PROSPER(V) AT ROAD~s~you(ms) and~*you*(ms)~*did*~EXIST(V) SURELY OPPRESS(V)~*ed*(ms) and~PLUCK.AWAY(V)~*ed*(ms) ALL the~DAY~s and~WITHOUT *make*~RESCUE(V)~*ing*(ms) **28:30** WOMAN *you*(ms)~*will~much*~BETROTH(V) and~MAN OTHER *he~will*~COPULATE(V)~her HOUSE *you*(ms)~*will*~BUILD(V) and~NOT *you*(ms)~*will*~SETTLE(V) in~him VINEYARD *you*(ms)~*will*~PLANT(V) and~NOT *you*(ms)~*will~much*~DRILL(V)~him **28:31** OX~you(ms) BUTCHER(V)~ *ed*(ms) to~EYE~s2~you(ms) and~NOT *you*(ms)~*will*~EAT(V) FROM~him DONKEY~ you(ms) PLUCK.AWAY(V)~*ed*(ms) from~to~FACE~s~you(ms) and~NOT *he~will*~ TURN.BACK(V) to~you(fs) FLOCKS~you(ms) GIVE(V)~*ed*(fp) to~ATTACK(V)~ *ing*(mp)~s~you(ms) and~WITHOUT to~you(ms) *make*~RESCUE(V)~ *ing*(ms) **28:32** SON~s~you(ms) and~DAUGHTER~s~you(ms) GIVE(V)~*ed*(mp) to~ PEOPLE OTHER and~EYE~s2~you(ms) SEE(V)~*ing*(fp) and~CONSUMING~s TO~ them(m) ALL the~DAY and~WITHOUT to~MIGHTY.ONE HAND~ you(ms) **28:33** PRODUCE GROUND~you(ms) and~ALL TOIL~you(ms) *he~will*~ EAT(V) PEOPLE WHICH NOT *you*(ms)~*did*~KNOW(V) and~*you*(ms)~*did*~EXIST(V) ONLY OPPRESS(V)~*ed*(ms) and~CRUSH(V)~*ed*(ms) ALL the~DAY~s **28:34** and~ *you*(ms)~*did*~EXIST(V) *be~much*~RAVE(V)~*ing*(ms) from~APPEARANCE EYE~s2~ you(ms) WHICH *you*(ms)~*will*~SEE(V) **28:35** *he~will~make*~HIT(V)~you(ms) **YHWH** in~BOILS DYSFUNCTIONAL UPON the~KNEE~s2 and~UPON the~THIGH~s2 WHICH NOT *you*(ms)~*will*~BE.ABLE(V) to~>~*make*~HEAL(V) from~PALM FOOT~ you(ms) and~UNTIL TOP.OF.THE.HEAD~you(ms) **28:36** *he~will~make*~WALK(V)

The Book of Deuteronomy

YHWH AT~you⁽ᵐˢ⁾ and~AT KING~you⁽ᵐˢ⁾ WHICH *you*⁽ᵐˢ⁾~*will*~*make*~RISE⁽ⱽ⁾ UPON~you⁽ᵐˢ⁾ TO NATION WHICH NOT *you*⁽ᵐˢ⁾~*did*~KNOW⁽ⱽ⁾ YOU⁽ᵐˢ⁾ and~ FATHER~s~you⁽ᵐˢ⁾ and~*you*⁽ᵐˢ⁾~*did*~SERVE⁽ⱽ⁾ THERE Elohiym OTHER~s TREE and~STONE **28:37** and~*you*⁽ᵐˢ⁾~*did*~EXIST⁽ⱽ⁾ to~DESOLATE to~PARABLE and~to~PIERCING in~ALL the~PEOPLE~s WHICH *he*~*will*~*much*~DRIVE⁽ⱽ⁾~ you⁽ᵐˢ⁾ YHWH THERE~unto **28:38** SEED ABUNDANT *you*⁽ᵐˢ⁾~*will*~*make*~ GO.OUT⁽ⱽ⁾ the~FIELD and~SMALL.AMOUNT *you*⁽ᵐˢ⁾~*will*~GATHER⁽ⱽ⁾ GIVEN.THAT *he*~*will*~DEVOUR⁽ⱽ⁾~him the~ SWARMING.LOCUST **28:39** VINEYARD~s *you*⁽ᵐˢ⁾~*will*~PLANT⁽ⱽ⁾ and~*you*⁽ᵐˢ⁾~ *did*~SERVE⁽ⱽ⁾ and~WINE NOT *you*⁽ᵐˢ⁾~*will*~GULP⁽ⱽ⁾ and~NOT *you*⁽ᵐˢ⁾~*will*~ GATHER.FOOD⁽ⱽ⁾ GIVEN.THAT *you*⁽ᵐˢ⁾~*will*~EAT⁽ⱽ⁾~him the~ KERMES **28:40** OLIVE~s *they*⁽ᵐ⁾~*will*~EXIST⁽ⱽ⁾ to~you⁽ᵐˢ⁾ in~ALL BORDER~ you⁽ᵐˢ⁾ and~OIL NOT *you*⁽ᵐˢ⁾~*will*~POUR.DOWN⁽ⱽ⁾ GIVEN.THAT *he*~*will*~ CAST.OFF⁽ⱽ⁾ OLIVE~you⁽ᵐˢ⁾ **28:41** SON~s and~DAUGHTER~s *you*⁽ᵐˢ⁾~*will*~ *make*~BRING.FORTH⁽ⱽ⁾ and~NOT *they*⁽ᵐ⁾~*will*~EXIST⁽ⱽ⁾ to~you⁽ᶠˢ⁾ GIVEN.THAT *they*⁽ᵐ⁾~*will*~WALK⁽ⱽ⁾ in~the~CAPTIVE **28:42** ALL TREE~you⁽ᵐˢ⁾ and~ PRODUCE GROUND~you⁽ᵐˢ⁾ *he*~*will*~*much*~POSSESS⁽ⱽ⁾ the~ WHIRRING.LOCUST **28:43** the~IMMIGRANT WHICH in~INSIDE~you⁽ᵐˢ⁾ *he*~ *will*~GO.UP⁽ⱽ⁾ UPON~you⁽ᵐˢ⁾ UPWARD~unto UPWARD~unto and~YOU⁽ᵐˢ⁾ *you*⁽ᵐˢ⁾~*will*~GO.DOWN⁽ⱽ⁾ BENEATH BENEATH **28:44** HE *he*~*will*~*make*~ JOIN⁽ⱽ⁾~you⁽ᵐˢ⁾ and~YOU⁽ᵐˢ⁾ NOT *you*⁽ᵐᵖ⁾~*will*~*make*~JOIN⁽ⱽ⁾~him HE *he*~*will*~ EXIST⁽ⱽ⁾ to~HEAD and~YOU⁽ᵐˢ⁾ *you*⁽ᵐˢ⁾~*will*~EXIST⁽ⱽ⁾ to~TAIL **28:45** and~ *they*~*did*~COME⁽ⱽ⁾ UPON~you⁽ᵐˢ⁾ ALL the~ANNOYANCE~s the~THESE and~ *they*~*did*~PURSUE⁽ⱽ⁾~you⁽ᵐˢ⁾ and~*they*~*did*~*make*~OVERTAKE⁽ⱽ⁾~you⁽ᵐˢ⁾ UNTIL >~*be*~DESTROY⁽ⱽ⁾~you⁽ᵐˢ⁾ GIVEN.THAT NOT *you*⁽ᵐˢ⁾~*did*~HEAR⁽ⱽ⁾ in~ VOICE YHWH Elohiym~you⁽ᵐˢ⁾ to~>~SAFEGUARD⁽ⱽ⁾ DIRECTIVE~s~him and~ CUSTOM~s~him WHICH *he*~*did*~*much*~DIRECT⁽ⱽ⁾~you⁽ᵐˢ⁾ **28:46** and~*they*~ *did*~EXIST⁽ⱽ⁾ in~you⁽ᵐˢ⁾ to~SIGN and~to~WONDER and~in~SEED~you⁽ᵐˢ⁾ UNTIL DISTANT **28:47** UNDER WHICH NOT *you*⁽ᵐˢ⁾~*did*~SERVE⁽ⱽ⁾ AT YHWH Elohiym~you⁽ᵐˢ⁾ in~REJOICING and~in~FUNCTIONAL HEART from~ ABUNDANCE ALL **28:48** and~*you*⁽ᵐˢ⁾~*did*~SERVE⁽ⱽ⁾ AT ATTACK⁽ⱽ⁾~*ing*⁽ᵐᵖ⁾~s~ you⁽ᵐˢ⁾ WHICH *he*~*will*~*much*~SEND⁽ⱽ⁾~him YHWH in~you⁽ᶠˢ⁾ in~HUNGER and~in~THIRST and~in~NAKED and~in~WANTING ALL and~*he*~*did*~GIVE⁽ⱽ⁾ YOKE IRON UPON BACK.OF.THE.NECK~you⁽ᵐˢ⁾ UNTIL *he*~*did*~*make*~ DESTROY⁽ⱽ⁾~him AT~you⁽ᶠˢ⁾ **28:49** *he*~*will*~LIFT.UP⁽ⱽ⁾ YHWH UPON~you⁽ᵐˢ⁾ NATION from~DISTANCE from~EXTREMITY the~LAND like~WHICH *he*~*will*~ DIVE⁽ⱽ⁾ the~EAGLE NATION WHICH NOT *you*⁽ᵐˢ⁾~*will*~HEAR⁽ⱽ⁾ TONGUE~ him **28:50** NATION STRONG FACE~s WHICH NOT *he*~*will*~LIFT.UP⁽ⱽ⁾ FACE~s to~BEARD and~YOUNG.MAN NOT *he*~*will*~ PROVIDE.PROTECTION⁽ⱽ⁾ **28:51** and~*he*~*did*~EAT⁽ⱽ⁾ PRODUCE BEAST~you⁽ᵐˢ⁾ and~PRODUCE GROUND~you⁽ᵐˢ⁾ UNTIL >~*be*~DESTROY⁽ⱽ⁾~you⁽ᵐˢ⁾ WHICH NOT *he*~*will*~*make*~REMAIN⁽ⱽ⁾ to~you⁽ᵐˢ⁾ CEREAL FRESH.WINE and~ FRESH.OIL BIRTH BOVINE~s~you⁽ᵐˢ⁾ and~YOUNG.SHEEP~s FLOCKS~you⁽ᵐˢ⁾ UNTIL >~*make*~PERISH⁽ⱽ⁾~him AT~you⁽ᶠˢ⁾ **28:52** and~*he*~*did*~*make*~ PRESS.IN⁽ⱽ⁾ to~you⁽ᵐˢ⁾ in~ALL GATE~s~you⁽ᵐˢ⁾ UNTIL >~GO.DOWN⁽ⱽ⁾

RAMPART~s~you⁽ᵐˢ⁾ the~HIGH~s and~the~FENCE.IN⁽ⱽ⁾~ed⁽ᶠᵖ⁾ WHICH YOU⁽ᵐˢ⁾ CLING⁽ⱽ⁾~ing⁽ᵐˢ⁾ in~them⁽ᶠ⁾ in~ALL LAND~you⁽ᵐˢ⁾ and~he~did~make~ PRESS.IN⁽ⱽ⁾ to~you⁽ᵐˢ⁾ in~ALL GATE~s~you⁽ᵐˢ⁾ in~ALL LAND~you⁽ᵐˢ⁾ WHICH he~did~GIVE⁽ⱽ⁾ **YHWH** Elohiym~you⁽ᵐˢ⁾ to~you⁽ᶠˢ⁾   **28:53** and~you⁽ᵐˢ⁾~did~ EAT⁽ⱽ⁾ PRODUCE WOMB~you⁽ᵐˢ⁾ FLESH SON~s~you⁽ᵐˢ⁾ and~DAUGHTER~s~ you⁽ᵐˢ⁾ WHICH he~did~GIVE⁽ⱽ⁾ to~you⁽ᵐˢ⁾ **YHWH** Elohiym~you⁽ᵐˢ⁾ in~ SMACKED and~in~STRESS WHICH he~will~make~HARASS⁽ⱽ⁾ to~you⁽ᵐˢ⁾ ATTACK⁽ⱽ⁾~ing⁽ᵐˢ⁾~you⁽ᵐˢ⁾   **28:54** the~MAN the~TENDER in~you⁽ᵐˢ⁾ and~the~ SOFT MANY she~will~BE.DYSFUNCTIONAL⁽ⱽ⁾ EYE~him in~BROTHER~him and~in~WOMAN BOSOM~him and~in~REMAINDER SON~s~him WHICH he~ will~make~LEAVE.BEHIND⁽ⱽ⁾   **28:55** >~GIVE⁽ⱽ⁾ to~UNIT from~them⁽ᵐ⁾ from~ FLESH SON~s~him WHICH he~will~EAT⁽ⱽ⁾ from~UNAWARE he~did~make~ REMAIN⁽ⱽ⁾ to~him ALL in~SMACKED and~in~STRESS WHICH he~will~make~ HARASS⁽ⱽ⁾ to~you⁽ᵐˢ⁾ ATTACK⁽ⱽ⁾~ing⁽ᵐˢ⁾~you⁽ᵐˢ⁾ in~ALL GATE~s~ you⁽ᵐˢ⁾   **28:56** the~TENDER in~you⁽ᵐˢ⁾ and~the~SOFT WHICH NOT she~did~ much~TEST⁽ⱽ⁾ PALM FOOT~her >~make~LEAVE.IN.PLACE⁽ⱽ⁾ UPON the~LAND from~>~self~SOFT⁽ⱽ⁾ and~from~TENDERNESS she~will~ BE.DYSFUNCTIONAL⁽ⱽ⁾ EYE~her in~MAN BOSOM~her and~in~SON~her and~ in~DAUGHTER~her   **28:57** and~in~INFANT~her the~GO.OUT⁽ⱽ⁾~ing⁽ᶠᵖ⁾ from~ BETWEEN FOOT~s~her and~in~SON~s~her WHICH she~will~BRING.FORTH⁽ⱽ⁾ GIVEN.THAT you⁽ᵐˢ⁾~will~EAT⁽ⱽ⁾~them⁽ᵐ⁾ in~WANTING ALL in~the~HIDING in~SMACKED and~in~STRESS WHICH he~will~make~HARASS⁽ⱽ⁾ to~you⁽ᵐˢ⁾ ATTACK⁽ⱽ⁾~ing⁽ᵐˢ⁾~you⁽ᵐˢ⁾ in~GATE~s~you⁽ᵐˢ⁾   **28:58** IF NOT you⁽ᵐˢ⁾~will~ SAFEGUARD⁽ⱽ⁾ to~>~DO⁽ⱽ⁾ AT ALL WORD~s the~TEACHING the~THIS the~ WRITE⁽ⱽ⁾~ed⁽ᵐᵖ⁾ in~the~SCROLL the~THIS to~>~FEAR⁽ⱽ⁾ AT the~TITLE the~ be~BE.HEAVY⁽ⱽ⁾~ing⁽ᵐˢ⁾ and~the~be~FEAR⁽ⱽ⁾~ing⁽ᵐˢ⁾ the~THIS AT **YHWH** Elohiym~you⁽ᵐˢ⁾   **28:59** and~he~did~make~PERFORM⁽ⱽ⁾ **YHWH** AT HITTING~s~you⁽ᵐˢ⁾ and~AT HITTING~s SEED~you⁽ᵐˢ⁾ HITTING~s GREAT~s and~be~SECURE⁽ⱽ⁾~ing⁽ᶠᵖ⁾ and~INFIRMITY~s DYSFUNCTIONAL~s and~be~ SECURE⁽ⱽ⁾~ing⁽ᵐᵖ⁾   **28:60** and~he~did~make~TURN.BACK⁽ⱽ⁾ in~you⁽ᵐˢ⁾ AT ALL DISEASE Mits'rayim WHICH you⁽ᵐˢ⁾~did~BE.AFRAID⁽ⱽ⁾ from~FACE~s~them⁽ᵐ⁾ and~they~did~ADHERE⁽ⱽ⁾ in~you⁽ᶠˢ⁾   **28:61** ALSO ALL INFIRMITY and~ALL HITTING WHICH NOT WRITE⁽ⱽ⁾~ed⁽ᵐˢ⁾ in~SCROLL the~TEACHING the~THIS he~will~make~GO.UP⁽ⱽ⁾~them⁽ᵐ⁾ **YHWH** UPON~you⁽ᵐˢ⁾ UNTIL >~be~ DESTROY⁽ⱽ⁾~you⁽ᵐˢ⁾   **28:62** and~you⁽ᵐᵖ⁾~did~be~REMAIN⁽ⱽ⁾ in~ MORTAL.MAN~s SMALL.AMOUNT UNDER WHICH you⁽ᵐᵖ⁾~did~EXIST⁽ⱽ⁾ like~ STAR~s the~SKY~s2 to~ABUNDANCE GIVEN.THAT NOT you⁽ᵐˢ⁾~did~HEAR⁽ⱽ⁾ in~VOICE **YHWH** Elohiym~you⁽ᵐˢ⁾   **28:63** and~he~did~EXIST⁽ⱽ⁾ like~WHICH he~did~SKIP.WITH.JOY⁽ⱽ⁾ **YHWH** UPON~you⁽ᵐᵖ⁾ to~>~make~DO.WELL⁽ⱽ⁾ AT~ you⁽ᵐᵖ⁾ and~to~>~make~INCREASE⁽ⱽ⁾ AT~you⁽ᵐᵖ⁾ SO he~will~ SKIP.WITH.JOY⁽ⱽ⁾ **YHWH** UPON~you⁽ᵐᵖ⁾ to~>~make~PERISH⁽ⱽ⁾ AT~you⁽ᵐᵖ⁾ and~to~>~make~DESTROY⁽ⱽ⁾ AT~you⁽ᵐᵖ⁾ and~you⁽ᵐᵖ⁾~did~be~TEAR.AWAY⁽ⱽ⁾ from~UPON the~GROUND WHICH YOU⁽ᵐˢ⁾ he~did~COME⁽ⱽ⁾ THERE~unto to~ >~POSSESS⁽ⱽ⁾~her   **28:64** and~he~did~make~SCATTER.ABROAD⁽ⱽ⁾~you⁽ᵐˢ⁾ **YHWH** in~ALL the~PEOPLE~s from~EXTREMITY the~LAND and~UNTIL

EXTREMITY the~LAND and~*you*(ms)~*did*~SERVE(V) THERE Elohiym OTHER~s WHICH NOT *you*(ms)~*did*~KNOW(V) YOU(ms) and~FATHER~s~you(ms) TREE and~ STONE **28:65** and~in~the~NATION~s the~THEY(m) NOT *you*(ms)~*will*~*make*~ REPOSE(V) and~NOT *he*~*will*~EXIST(V) OASIS to~PALM FOOT~you(ms) and~*he*~ *did*~GIVE(V) **YHWH** to~you(ms) THERE HEART SHAKING and~FAILING EYE~s2 and~BROODING SOUL **28:66** and~*they*~*did*~EXIST(V) LIVING~s~you(ms) HANG(V)~*ed*(mp) to~you(ms) from~OPPOSITE and~*you*(ms)~*did*~SHAKE.IN.AWE(V) NIGHT and~DAYTIME and~NOT *you*(ms)~*will*~*make*~SECURE(V) in~LIVING~s~ you(ms) **28:67** in~the~MORNING *you*(ms)~*will*~SAY(V) WHO *he*~*will*~GIVE(V) EVENING and~in~the~EVENING *you*(ms)~*will*~SAY(V) WHO *he*~*will*~GIVE(V) MORNING from~AWE HEART~you(ms) WHICH *you*(ms)~*will*~SHAKE.IN.AWE(V) and~from~APPEARANCE EYE~s2~you(ms) WHICH *you*(ms)~*will*~ SEE(V) **28:68** and~*he*~*did*~*make*~TURN.BACK(V)~you(ms) **YHWH** Mits'rayim in~the~SHIP~s in~the~ROAD WHICH *I*~*did*~SAY(V) to~you(ms) NOT *you*(ms)~ *will*~*make*~ADD(V) YET.AGAIN to~>~SEE(V)~her and~*you*(mp)~*did*~*self*~SELL(V) THERE to~ATTACK(V)~*ing*(mp)~s~you(ms) to~the~SERVANT~s and~to~MAID~s and~WITHOUT PURCHASE(V)~*ing*(ms) **28:69 (29:1)** THESE WORD~s the~ COVENANT WHICH *he*~*did*~*much*~DIRECT(V) **YHWH** AT Mosheh to~>~CUT(V) AT SON~s Yisra'eyl in~LAND Mo'av from~to~STRAND the~COVENANT WHICH *he*~*did*~CUT(V) AT~them(m) in~Hhorev

Chapter 29

29:1 (29:2) and~*he*~*will*~CALL.OUT(V) Mosheh TO ALL Yisra'eyl and~*he*~*will*~ SAY(V) TO~them(m) YOU(mp) *you*(mp)~*did*~SEE(V) AT ALL WHICH *he*~*did*~DO(V) **YHWH** to~EYE~s2~you(mp) in~LAND Mits'rayim to~Paroh and~to~ALL SERVANT~s~him and~to~ALL LAND~him **29:2 (29:3)** the~TRIAL~s the~ GREAT~s WHICH *they*~*did*~SEE(V) EYE~s2~you(ms) the~SIGN~s and~the~ WONDER~s the~GREAT~s the~THEY(m) **29:3 (29:4)** and~NOT *he*~*did*~GIVE(V) **YHWH** to~you(mp) HEART to~>~KNOW(V) and~EYE~s2 to~>~SEE(V) and~EAR~s to~>~HEAR(V) UNTIL the~DAY the~THIS **29:4 (29:5)** and~*I*~*will*~*make*~ WALK(V) AT~you(mp) FOUR~s YEAR in~the~WILDERNESS NOT *they*~*did*~ WEAR.OUT(V) OUTER.GARMENT~s~you(mp) from~UPON~you(mp) and~ SANDAL~s~you(ms) NOT *she*~*did*~WEAR.OUT(V) from~UPON FOOT~ you(ms) **29:5 (29:6)** BREAD NOT *you*(mp)~*did*~EAT(V) and~WINE and~LIQUOR NOT *you*(mp)~*did*~GULP(V) to~THAT *you*(mp)~*will*~KNOW(V) GIVEN.THAT I **YHWH** Elohiym~you(mp) **29:6 (29:7)** and~*you*(mp)~*will*~COME(V) TO the~AREA the~THIS and~*he*~*will*~GO.OUT(V) Sihhon KING Hheshbon and~Og KING the~ Bashan to~>~MEET(V)~us to~the~BATTLE and~*we*~*will*~*make*~ HIT(V) **29:7 (29:8)** and~*we*~*will*~TAKE(V) AT LAND~them(m) and~*we*~*will*~ GIVE(V) to~INHERITANCE to~the~Re'uven~of and~to~the~Gad~of and~to~ the~HALF STAFF the~Menasheh~of **29:8 (29:9)** and~*you*(mp)~*did*~ SAFEGUARD(V) AT WORD~s the~COVENANT the~THIS and~*you*(mp)~*did*~DO(V)

AT~them⁽ᵐ⁾ to~THAT you⁽ᵐᵖ⁾~will~make~CALCULATE⁽ᵛ⁾ AT ALL WHICH you⁽ᵐˢ⁾~will~DO⁽ᵛ⁾~must **29:9 (29:10)** YOU⁽ᵐᵖ⁾ be~STAND.UP⁽ᵛ⁾~ing⁽ᵐᵖ⁾ the~ DAY ALL~you⁽ᵐᵖ⁾ to~FACE~s **YHWH** Elohiym~you⁽ᵐᵖ⁾ HEAD~s~you⁽ᵐᵖ⁾ STAFF~s~you⁽ᵐᵖ⁾ BEARD~s~you⁽ᵐᵖ⁾ and~OFFICER~s~you⁽ᵐᵖ⁾ ALL MAN Yisra'eyl **29:10 (29:11)** BABIES~you⁽ᵐᵖ⁾ WOMAN~s~you⁽ᵐᵖ⁾ and~ IMMIGRANT~you⁽ᵐˢ⁾ WHICH in~INSIDE CAMP~s~you⁽ᵐˢ⁾ from~CARVE⁽ᵛ⁾~ ing⁽ᵐˢ⁾ TREE~s~you⁽ᵐˢ⁾ UNTIL DRAW.WATER⁽ᵛ⁾~ing⁽ᵐˢ⁾ WATER~s2~ you⁽ᵐˢ⁾ **29:11 (29:12)** to~>~CROSS.OVER⁽ᵛ⁾~you⁽ᵐˢ⁾ in~COVENANT **YHWH** Elohiym~you⁽ᵐˢ⁾ and~in~OATH~him WHICH **YHWH** Elohiym~you⁽ᵐˢ⁾ CUT⁽ᵛ⁾~ ing⁽ᵐˢ⁾ WITH~you⁽ᵐˢ⁾ the~DAY **29:12 (29:13)** to~THAT >~*make*~RISE⁽ᵛ⁾ AT~ you⁽ᵐˢ⁾ the~DAY to~him to~PEOPLE and~HE he~will~EXIST⁽ᵛ⁾ to~you⁽ᵐˢ⁾ to~ Elohiym like~WHICH he~did~much~SPEAK⁽ᵛ⁾ to~you⁽ᶠˢ⁾ and~like~WHICH he~ did~be~SWEAR⁽ᵛ⁾ to~FATHER~s~you⁽ᵐˢ⁾ to~Avraham to~Yits'hhaq and~to~ Ya'aqov **29:13 (29:14)** and~NOT AT~you⁽ᵐᵖ⁾ to~STRAND~you⁽ᵐᵖ⁾ I CUT⁽ᵛ⁾~ ing⁽ᵐˢ⁾ AT the~COVENANT the~THIS and~AT the~OATH the~ THIS **29:14 (29:15)** GIVEN.THAT AT WHICH THERE.IS~him HERE WITH~us STAND⁽ᵛ⁾~ing⁽ᵐˢ⁾ the~DAY to~FACE~s **YHWH** Elohiym~us and~AT WHICH WITHOUT~him HERE WITH~us the~DAY **29:15 (29:16)** GIVEN.THAT YOU⁽ᵐᵖ⁾ you⁽ᵐᵖ⁾~did~KNOW⁽ᵛ⁾ AT WHICH we~did~SETTLE⁽ᵛ⁾ in~LAND Mits'rayim and~ AT WHICH >~CROSS.OVER⁽ᵛ⁾~us in~INSIDE the~NATION~s WHICH you⁽ᵐᵖ⁾~ did~CROSS.OVER⁽ᵛ⁾ **29:16 (29:17)** and~you⁽ᵐᵖ⁾~will~SEE⁽ᵛ⁾ AT FILTHINESS~s~ them⁽ᵐ⁾ and~AT IDOL~s~them⁽ᵐ⁾ TREE and~STONE SILVER and~GOLD WHICH WITH~them⁽ᵐ⁾ **29:17 (29:18)** OTHERWISE THERE.IS in~you⁽ᵐᵖ⁾ MAN OR WOMAN OR CLAN OR STAFF WHICH HEART~him TURN⁽ᵛ⁾~ing⁽ᵐˢ⁾ the~DAY from~WITH **YHWH** Elohiym~us to~>~WALK⁽ᵛ⁾ to~>~SERVE⁽ᵛ⁾ AT Elohiym the~NATION~s the~THEY⁽ᵐ⁾ OTHERWISE THERE.IS in~you⁽ᵐᵖ⁾ ROOT REPRODUCE⁽ᵛ⁾~ing⁽ᵐˢ⁾ VENOM and~HEMLOCK **29:18 (29:19)** and~*he~did*~ EXIST⁽ᵛ⁾ in~>~HEAR⁽ᵛ⁾~him AT WORD~s the~OATH the~THIS and~*he~did*~ self~KNEEL⁽ᵛ⁾ in~HEART~him to~>~SAY⁽ᵛ⁾ COMPLETENESS he~will~EXIST⁽ᵛ⁾ to~me GIVEN.THAT in~IMAGINATION HEART~me I~will~WALK⁽ᵛ⁾ to~THAT >~ CONSUME⁽ᵛ⁾ the~WATERED AT the~THIRST **29:19 (29:20)** NOT he~will~ CONSENT⁽ᵛ⁾ **YHWH** >~FORGIVE⁽ᵛ⁾ to~him GIVEN.THAT AT.THAT.TIME he~ will~SMOKE⁽ᵛ⁾ NOSE **YHWH** and~ZEALOUSNESS~him in~the~MAN the~HE and~*she~did*~STRETCH.OUT⁽ᵛ⁾ in~him ALL the~OATH the~WRITE⁽ᵛ⁾~ed⁽ᶠˢ⁾ in~ the~SCROLL the~THIS and~*he~did*~WIPE.AWAY⁽ᵛ⁾ **YHWH** AT TITLE~him from~UNDER the~SKY~s2 **29:20 (29:21)** and~*he~did~make*~SEPARATE⁽ᵛ⁾~ him **YHWH** to~DYSFUNCTIONAL from~ALL STAFF~s Yisra'eyl like~ALL OATH~s the~COVENANT the~WRITE⁽ᵛ⁾~ed⁽ᶠˢ⁾ in~SCROLL the~TEACHING the~ THIS **29:21 (29:22)** and~*he~did*~SAY⁽ᵛ⁾ the~GENERATION the~LAST SON~s~ you⁽ᵐᵖ⁾ WHICH they⁽ᵐ⁾~will~RISE⁽ᵛ⁾ from~AFTER~you⁽ᵐᵖ⁾ and~the~ FOREIGNER WHICH he~will~COME⁽ᵛ⁾ from~LAND DISTANCE and~they~did~ SEE⁽ᵛ⁾ AT HITTING~s the~LAND the~SHE and~AT SICK~s~her WHICH he~did~ much~BE.SICK⁽ᵛ⁾ **YHWH** in~her **29:22 (29:23)** BRIMSTONE and~SALT CREMATING ALL LAND~her NOT she~will~be~SOW⁽ᵛ⁾ and~NOT you⁽ᵐˢ⁾~will~ SPRING.UP⁽ᵛ⁾ and~NOT he~will~GO.UP⁽ᵛ⁾ in~her ALL HERB like~

The Book of Deuteronomy

OVERTHROWING Sedom and~Ghamorah Admah and~Tseviim WHICH *he~did*~OVERTURN^(V) **YHWH** in~NOSE~him and~in~FURY~him   **29:23 (29:24)** and~*they~did*~SAY^(V) ALL the~NATION~s UPON WHAT *he~did*~DO^(V) **YHWH** like~IN.THIS.WAY to~the~LAND the~THIS WHAT FLAMING the~NOSE the~GREAT the~THIS   **29:24 (29:25)** and~*they~did*~SAY^(V) UPON WHICH *they~did*~LEAVE^(V) AT COVENANT **YHWH** Elohiym FATHER~s~them^(m) WHICH *he~did*~CUT^(V) WITH~them^(m) in~>~*make*~GO.OUT^(V)~him AT~them^(m) from~LAND Mits'rayim   **29:25 (29:26)** and~*they*^(m)~*will*~WALK^(V) and~*they*^(m)~*will*~SERVE^(V) Elohiym OTHER~s and~*they*^(m)~*will~self*~BEND.DOWN^(V) to~them^(m) Elohiym WHICH NOT *they~did*~KNOW^(V)~them^(m) and~NOT *he~did*~DISTRIBUTE^(V) to~them^(m)   **29:26 (29:27)** and~*he~will*~FLARE.UP^(V) NOSE **YHWH** in~the~LAND the~SHE to~>~*make*~COME^(V) UPON~her AT ALL the~ANNOYANCE the~WRITE^(V)~*ed*^(fs) in~the~SCROLL the~THIS   **29:27 (29:28)** and~*he~will*~ROOT.OUT^(V)~them^(m) **YHWH** from~UPON GROUND~them^(m) in~NOSE and~in~FURY and~in~SPLINTER GREAT and~*he~will*~*make*~THROW.OUT^(V)~them^(m) TO LAND OTHER like~the~DAY the~THIS   **29:28 (29:29)** the~*be*~HIDE^(V)~*ing*^(fp) to~**YHWH** Elohiym~us and~the~*be*~REMOVE.THE.COVER^(V)~*ing*^(fp) to~us and~to~SON~s~us UNTIL DISTANT to~>~DO^(V) AT ALL WORD~s the~TEACHING the~THIS

Chapter 30

30:1 and~*he~did*~EXIST^(V) GIVEN.THAT *they*^(m)~*will*~COME^(V) UPON~you^(ms) ALL the~WORD~s the~THESE the~PRESENT and~the~ANNOYANCE WHICH *I~did*~GIVE^(V) to~FACE~s~you^(ms) and~*you*^(ms)~*did*~*make*~TURN.BACK^(V) TO HEART~you^(ms) in~ALL the~NATION~s WHICH *he~did*~*make*~DRIVE.OUT^(V)~you^(ms) **YHWH** Elohiym~you^(ms) THERE~unto   **30:2** and~*you*^(ms)~*did*~TURN.BACK^(V) UNTIL **YHWH** Elohiym~you^(ms) and~*you*^(ms)~*did*~HEAR^(V) in~VOICE~him like~ALL WHICH I *much*~DIRECT^(V)~*ing*^(ms)~you^(ms) the~DAY YOU^(ms) and~SON~s~you^(ms) in~ALL HEART~you^(ms) and~in~ALL SOUL~you^(ms)   **30:3** and~*he~did*~TURN.BACK^(V) **YHWH** Elohiym~you^(ms) AT CAPTIVITY~you^(ms) and~*he~did*~*much*~HAVE.COMPASSION^(V)~you^(ms) and~*he~did*~TURN.BACK^(V) and~*he~did*~*much*~GATHER.TOGETHER^(V)~you^(ms) from~ALL the~PEOPLE~s WHICH *he~did*~*make*~SCATTER.ABROAD^(V)~you^(ms) **YHWH** Elohiym~you^(ms) THERE~unto   **30:4** IF *he~will*~EXIST^(V) *be*~DRIVE.OUT^(V)~*ing*^(ms)~you^(ms) in~EXTREMITY the~SKY~s2 from~THERE *he~will*~*much*~GATHER.TOGETHER^(V)~you^(ms) **YHWH** Elohiym~you^(ms) and~from~THERE *he~will*~TAKE^(V)~you^(ms)   **30:5** and~*he~did*~*make*~COME^(V)~you^(ms) **YHWH** Elohiym~you^(ms) TO the~LAND WHICH *they~did*~POSSESS^(V) FATHER~s~you^(ms) and~*you*^(ms)~*did*~POSSESS^(V)~her and~*he~did*~*make*~DO.WELL^(V)~you^(ms) and~*he~did*~*make*~INCREASE^(V)~you^(ms) from~FATHER~s~you^(ms)   **30:6** and~*he~did*~SNIP.OFF^(V) **YHWH** Elohiym~you^(ms) AT

HEART~you(ms) and~AT HEART SEED~you(ms) to~>~LOVE(V) AT **YHWH** Elohiym~you(ms) in~ALL HEART~you(ms) and~in~ALL SOUL~you(ms) to~THAT LIVING~s~you(ms)   **30:7** and~*he~did*~GIVE(V) **YHWH** Elohiym~you(ms) AT ALL the~OATH~s the~THESE UPON ATTACK(V)~*ing(mp)*~s~you(ms) and~UPON HATE(V)~*ing(mp)*~you(ms) WHICH *they~did*~PURSUE(V)~you(ms)   **30:8** and~ YOU(ms) *you(ms)~will*~TURN.BACK(V) and~*you(ms)~did*~HEAR(V) in~VOICE **YHWH** and~*you(ms)~did*~DO(V) AT ALL DIRECTIVE~s~him WHICH I *much*~DIRECT(V)~ *ing(ms)*~you(ms) the~DAY   **30:9** and~*he~did~make*~LEAVE.BEHIND(V)~you(ms) **YHWH** Elohiym~you(ms) in~ALL WORK HAND~you(ms) in~PRODUCE WOMB~ you(ms) and~in~PRODUCE BEAST~you(ms) and~in~PRODUCE GROUND~you(ms) to~FUNCTIONAL GIVEN.THAT *he~will*~TURN.BACK(V) **YHWH** >~ SKIP.WITH.JOY(V) UPON~you(ms) to~FUNCTIONAL like~WHICH *he~did*~ SKIP.WITH.JOY(V) UPON FATHER~s~you(ms)   **30:10** GIVEN.THAT *you(ms)~will*~ HEAR(V) in~VOICE **YHWH** Elohiym~you(ms) to~>~SAFEGUARD(V) DIRECTIVE~s~ him and~CUSTOM~s~him the~WRITE(V)~*ed(fs)* in~SCROLL the~TEACHING the~THIS GIVEN.THAT *you(ms)~will*~TURN.BACK(V) TO **YHWH** Elohiym~you(ms) in~ALL HEART~you(ms) and~in~ALL SOUL~you(ms)   **30:11** GIVEN.THAT the~ DIRECTIVE the~THIS WHICH I *much*~DIRECT(V)~*ing(ms)*~you(ms) the~DAY NOT *be*~PERFORM(V)~*ing(fs)* SHE FROM~you(ms) and~NOT DISTANCE SHE   **30:12** NOT in~the~SKY~s2 SHE to~>~SAY(V) WHO *he~will*~GO.UP(V) to~ us the~SKY~s2 unto and~*he~will*~TAKE(V)~her to~us and~*he~will~make*~ HEAR(V)~us AT~her and~*we~will*~DO(V)~her   **30:13** and~NOT from~ OTHER.SIDE to~the~SEA SHE to~>~SAY(V) WHO *he~will*~CROSS.OVER(V) to~us TO OTHER.SIDE the~SEA and~*he~will*~TAKE(V)~her to~us and~*he~will*~ make~HEAR(V)~us AT~her and~*we~will*~DO(V)~her   **30:14** GIVEN.THAT NEAR TO~you(ms) the~WORD MANY in~MOUTH~you(ms) and~in~HEART~you(ms) to~ >~DO(V)~him   **30:15** !*(ms)*~SEE(V) *I~did*~GIVE(V) to~FACE~s~you(ms) the~DAY AT the~LIVING~s and~AT the~FUNCTIONAL and~AT the~DEATH and~AT the~ DYSFUNCTIONAL   **30:16** WHICH I *much*~DIRECT(V)~*ing(ms)*~you(ms) the~DAY to~>~LOVE(V) AT **YHWH** Elohiym~you(ms) to~>~WALK(V) in~ROAD~s~him and~ to~>~SAFEGUARD(V) DIRECTIVE~s~him and~CUSTOM~s~him and~ DECISION~s~him and~*you(ms)~did*~LIVE(V) and~*you(ms)~did*~INCREASE(V) and~ *he~did~much*~KNEEL(V)~you(ms) **YHWH** Elohiym~you(ms) in~the~LAND WHICH YOU(ms) COME(V)~*ing(ms)* THERE~unto to~>~POSSESS(V)~her   **30:17** and~IF *he~will*~TURN(V) HEART~you(ms) and~NOT *you(ms)~will*~HEAR(V) and~*you(ms)~ did~be*~DRIVE.OUT(V) and~*you(ms)~did~self*~BEND.DOWN(V) to~Elohiym OTHER~s and~*you(ms)~did*~SERVE(V)~them(m)   **30:18** *I~did~make*~ BE.FACE.TO.FACE(V) to~you(mp) the~DAY GIVEN.THAT >~PERISH(V) *you(ms)~ will*~PERISH(V)~must NOT *you(mp)~will~make*~PROLONG(V)~must DAY~s UPON the~GROUND WHICH YOU(ms) CROSS.OVER(V)~*ing(ms)* AT the~Yarden to~>~COME(V) THERE~unto to~>~POSSESS(V)~her   **30:19** *I~did~make*~ WRAP.AROUND(V) in~you(mp) the~DAY AT the~SKY~s2 and~AT the~LAND the~LIVING~s and~the~DEATH *I~did*~GIVE(V) to~FACE~s~you(ms) the~ PRESENT and~the~ANNOYANCE and~*you(ms)~did*~CHOOSE(V) in~LIVING~s to~THAT *you(ms)~will*~LIVE(V) YOU(ms) and~SEED~you(ms)   **30:20** to~>~LOVE(V)

AT **YHWH** Elohiym~you$^{(ms)}$ to~>~HEAR$^{(V)}$ in~VOICE~him and~to~>~ADHERE$^{(V)}$ in~him GIVEN.THAT HE LIVING~s~you$^{(ms)}$ and~LENGTH DAY~s~you$^{(ms)}$ to~>~SETTLE$^{(V)}$ UPON the~GROUND WHICH *he~did~be*~SWEAR$^{(V)}$ **YHWH** to~FATHER~s~you$^{(ms)}$ to~Avraham to~Yits'hhaq and~to~Ya'aqov to~>~GIVE$^{(V)}$ to~them$^{(m)}$

Chapter 31

31:1 and~*he~will*~WALK$^{(V)}$ Mosheh and~*he~will~much*~SPEAK$^{(V)}$ AT the~WORD~s the~THESE TO ALL Yisra'eyl **31:2** and~*he~will*~SAY$^{(V)}$ TO~them$^{(m)}$ SON HUNDRED and~TEN~s YEAR I the~DAY NOT *I~will*~BE.ABLE$^{(V)}$ YET.AGAIN to~>~GO.OUT$^{(V)}$ and~to~>~COME$^{(V)}$ and~**YHWH** *he~did*~SAY$^{(V)}$ TO~me NOT *you$^{(ms)}$~will*~CROSS.OVER$^{(V)}$ AT the~Yarden the~THIS **31:3 YHWH** Elohiym~you$^{(ms)}$ HE CROSS.OVER$^{(V)}$~*ing$^{(ms)}$* to~FACE~s~you$^{(ms)}$ HE *he~will~make*~DESTROY$^{(V)}$ AT the~NATION~s the~THESE from~to~FACE~s~you$^{(ms)}$ and~*you$^{(ms)}$~did*~POSSESS$^{(V)}$~them$^{(m)}$ Yehoshu'a HE CROSS.OVER$^{(V)}$~*ing$^{(ms)}$* to~FACE~s~you$^{(ms)}$ like~WHICH *he~did~much*~SPEAK$^{(V)}$ **YHWH** **31:4** and~*he~did*~DO$^{(V)}$ **YHWH** to~them$^{(m)}$ like~WHICH *he~did*~DO$^{(V)}$ to~Sihhon and~to~Og KING~s the~Emor~of and~to~LAND~them$^{(m)}$ WHICH *he~did~make*~DESTROY$^{(V)}$ AT~them$^{(m)}$ **31:5** and~*he~did*~GIVE$^{(V)}$~them$^{(m)}$ **YHWH** to~FACE~s~you$^{(mp)}$ and~*you$^{(mp)}$~did*~DO$^{(V)}$ to~them$^{(m)}$ like~ALL the~DIRECTIVE WHICH *I~did~much*~DIRECT$^{(V)}$ AT~you$^{(mp)}$ **31:6** *!$^{(mp)}$*~SEIZE$^{(V)}$ and~*!$^{(mp)}$*~BE.STRONG$^{(V)}$ DO.NOT *you$^{(mp)}$~will*~FEAR$^{(V)}$ and~DO.NOT *you$^{(mp)}$~will*~BE.TERRIFIED$^{(V)}$ from~FACE~s~them$^{(m)}$ GIVEN.THAT **YHWH** Elohiym~you$^{(ms)}$ HE the~WALK$^{(V)}$~*ing$^{(ms)}$* WITH~you$^{(fs)}$ NOT *he~will~make*~SINK.DOWN$^{(V)}$~you$^{(ms)}$ and~NOT *he~will*~LEAVE$^{(V)}$~you$^{(ms)}$ **31:7** and~*he~will*~CALL.OUT$^{(V)}$ Mosheh to~Yehoshu'a and~*he~will*~SAY$^{(V)}$ TO~him to~EYE~s2 ALL Yisra'eyl *!$^{(ms)}$*~SEIZE$^{(V)}$ and~*!$^{(ms)}$*~BE.STRONG$^{(V)}$ GIVEN.THAT YOU$^{(ms)}$ *you$^{(ms)}$~will*~COME$^{(V)}$ AT the~PEOPLE the~THIS TO the~LAND WHICH *he~did~be*~SWEAR$^{(V)}$ **YHWH** to~FATHER~s~them$^{(m)}$ to~>~GIVE$^{(V)}$ to~them$^{(m)}$ and~YOU$^{(ms)}$ *you$^{(ms)}$~will~make*~INHERIT$^{(V)}$~her AT~them$^{(m)}$ **31:8** and~**YHWH** HE the~WALK$^{(V)}$~*ing$^{(ms)}$* to~FACE~s~you$^{(ms)}$ HE *he~will*~EXIST$^{(V)}$ WITH~you$^{(fs)}$ NOT *he~will~make*~SINK.DOWN$^{(V)}$~you$^{(ms)}$ and~NOT *he~will*~LEAVE$^{(V)}$~you$^{(ms)}$ NOT *you$^{(ms)}$~will*~FEAR$^{(V)}$ and~NOT *you$^{(ms)}$~will*~BE.SHATTERED$^{(V)}$ **31:9** and~*he~will*~WRITE$^{(V)}$ Mosheh AT the~TEACHING the~THIS and~*he~will*~GIVE$^{(V)}$~her TO the~ADMINISTRATOR~s SON~s Lewi the~LIFT.UP$^{(V)}$~*ing$^{(mp)}$* AT BOX COVENANT **YHWH** and~TO ALL BEARD~s Yisra'eyl **31:10** and~*he~will~much*~DIRECT$^{(V)}$ Mosheh AT~them$^{(m)}$ to~>~SAY$^{(V)}$ from~CONCLUSION SEVEN YEAR~s in~APPOINTED YEAR the~RELEASE in~FEAST the~BOOTH~s **31:11** >~COME$^{(V)}$ ALL Yisra'eyl to~>~*be*~SEE$^{(V)}$ AT FACE~s **YHWH** Elohiym~you$^{(ms)}$ in~the~AREA WHICH *he~will*~CHOOSE$^{(V)}$ *she~will*~CALL.OUT$^{(V)}$ AT the~TEACHING the~THIS OPPOSITE ALL Yisra'eyl in~EAR~s2~them$^{(m)}$ **31:12** *!$^{(mp)}$~make*~ASSEMBLE$^{(V)}$ AT the~PEOPLE the~MAN~s and~the~WOMAN~s and~the~BABIES and~IMMIGRANT~you(ms) WHICH in~GATE~s~you(ms) to~THAT they(m)~will~HEAR(v) and~to~THAT they(m)~will~much~LEARN(v) and~they~did~FEAR(v) AT **YHWH** Elohiym~you(mp) and~they~did~SAFEGUARD(v) to~>~DO(v) AT ALL WORD~s the~TEACHING the~THIS   **31:13** and~SON~s~them(m) WHICH NOT they~did~KNOW(v) they(m)~will~HEAR(v) and~they~did~LEARN(v) to~>~FEAR(v) AT **YHWH** Elohiym~you(mp) ALL the~DAY~s WHICH YOU(mp) LIVING~s UPON the~GROUND WHICH YOU(mp) CROSS.OVER(v)~ing(mp) AT the~Yarden THERE~unto to~>~POSSESS(v)~her   **31:14** and~he~will~SAY(v) **YHWH** TO Mosheh THOUGH they~did~COME.NEAR(v) DAY~s~you(ms) to~>~DIE(v) MEETING AT Yehoshu'a and~ !(mp)~self~STATION(v) in~TENT APPOINTED and~I~will~much~DIRECT(v)~him and~he~will~WALK(v) Mosheh and~Yehoshu'a and~they(m)~will~be~make~STAND.UP(v) in~TENT APPOINTED   **31:15** and~he~will~be~SEE(v) **YHWH** in~the~TENT in~PILLAR CLOUD and~he~will~STAND(v) PILLAR the~CLOUD UPON OPENING the~TENT   **31:16** and~he~will~SAY(v) **YHWH** TO Mosheh LOOK~you(ms) LIE.DOWN(v)~ing(ms) WITH FATHER~s~you(ms) and~he~did~RISE(v) the~PEOPLE the~THIS and~he~did~BE.A.HARLOT(v) AFTER Elohiym FOREIGNER the~LAND WHICH HE he~did~COME(v) THERE~unto in~INSIDE~him and~he~did~LEAVE(v)~me and~he~did~make~BREAK(v) AT COVENANT~me WHICH I~did~CUT(v) AT~him   **31:17** and~he~did~FLARE.UP(v) NOSE~me in~him in~the~DAY the~HE and~I~did~LEAVE(v)~them(m) and~I~did~make~HIDE(v) FACE~s~me from~them(m) and~he~did~EXIST(v) to~>~EAT(v) and~they~did~FIND(v)~him DYSFUNCTIONAL~s ABUNDANT and~PERSECUTION and~he~did~SAY(v) in~the~DAY the~HE ?~NOT UPON GIVEN.THAT WITHOUT Elohiym~me in~INSIDE~me they~did~FIND(v)~me the~DYSFUNCTIONAL~s the~THESE   **31:18** and~I >~make~HIDE(v) I~will~make~HIDE(v) FACE~s~me in~the~DAY the~HE UPON ALL the~DYSFUNCTIONAL WHICH he~did~DO(v) GIVEN.THAT he~did~TURN(v) TO Elohiym OTHER~s   **31:19** and~NOW !(mp)~WRITE(v) to~you(mp) AT the~SONG the~THIS and~ !(ms)~much~LEARN(v)~her AT SON~s Yisra'eyl !(ms)~PLACE(v)~her in~MOUTH~them(m) to~THAT she~will~EXIST(v) to~me the~SONG the~THIS to~WITNESS in~SON~s Yisra'eyl   **31:20** GIVEN.THAT I~will~make~COME(v)~him TO the~GROUND WHICH I~did~be~SWEAR(v) to~FATHER~s~him ISSUE(v)~ing(fs) FAT and~HONEY and~he~did~EAT(v) and~he~did~BE.SATISFIED(v) and~he~did~MAKE.FAT(v) and~he~did~TURN(v) TO Elohiym OTHER~s and~they~did~SERVE(v)~them(m) and~they~did~much~PROVOKE(v)~me and~he~did~make~BREAK(v) AT COVENANT~me   **31:21** and~he~did~EXIST(v) GIVEN.THAT they(f)~will~FIND(v) AT~him DYSFUNCTIONAL~s ABUNDANT and~PERSECUTION and~she~did~ANSWER(v) the~SONG the~THIS to~FACE~s~him to~WITNESS GIVEN.THAT NOT she~will~be~FORGET(v) from~MOUTH SEED~him GIVEN.THAT I~did~KNOW(v) AT THOUGHT~him WHICH HE DO(v)~ing(ms) the~DAY in~BEFORE I~will~make~COME(v)~him TO the~LAND WHICH I~did~be~SWEAR(v)   **31:22** and~he~will~WRITE(v) Mosheh AT the~SONG the~THIS in~the~DAY the~HE and~he~will~much~LEARN(v)~her AT SON~s Yisra'eyl   **31:23** and~he~will~much~DIRECT(v)

The Book of Deuteronomy

AT Yehoshu'a SON Nun and~*he*~*will*~SAY[(V)] *!*[(ms)]~SEIZE[(V)] and~*!*[(ms)]~
BE.STRONG[(V)] GIVEN.THAT YOU[(ms)] *you*[(ms)]~*will*~*make*~COME[(V)] AT SON~s
Yisra'eyl TO the~LAND WHICH *I~did~be*~SWEAR[(V)] to~them[(m)] and~*I I~will*~
EXIST[(V)] WITH~*you*[(fs)]   **31:24** and~*he*~*will*~EXIST[(V)] like~>~*much*~FINISH[(V)]
Mosheh to~>~WRITE[(V)] AT WORD~s the~TEACHING the~THIS UPON SCROLL
UNTIL >~*be*~BE.WHOLE[(V)]~them[(m)]   **31:25** and~*he*~*will*~*much*~DIRECT[(V)]
Mosheh AT the~Lewi~s LIFT.UP[(V)]~*ing*[(mp)] BOX COVENANT **YHWH** to~>~
SAY[(V)]   **31:26** >~TAKE[(V)] AT SCROLL the~TEACHING the~THIS and~*you*[(mp)]~
did~PLACE[(V)] AT~him from~SIDE BOX COVENANT **YHWH** Elohiym~*you*[(mp)]
and~*he*~*did*~EXIST[(V)] THERE in~*you*[(ms)] to~WITNESS   **31:27** GIVEN.THAT I *I*~
did~KNOW[(V)] AT REBELLIOUS~*you*[(ms)] and~AT NECK~*you*[(ms)] the~HARD
THOUGH in~YET.AGAIN~me LIVING WITH~*you*[(mp)] the~DAY *make*~
DISOBEY[(V)]~*ing*[(mp)] *you*[(mp)]~*did*~EXIST[(V)] WITH **YHWH** and~MOREOVER
GIVEN.THAT AFTER DEATH~me   **31:28** *!*[(mp)]~*make*~ASSEMBLE[(V)] TO~me AT
ALL BEARD~s STAFF~s[(mp)] and~OFFICER~s[(mp)] and~*I~will~much*~
SPEAK[(V)] in~EAR~s2~them[(m)] AT the~WORD~s the~THESE and~*I~will~make*~
WITNESS~& in~them[(m)] AT the~SKY~s2 and~AT the~
LAND   **31:29** GIVEN.THAT *I~did*~KNOW[(V)] AFTER DEATH~me GIVEN.THAT >~
make~DAMAGE[(V)] *you*[(mp)]~*will*~*make*~DAMAGE[(V)]~must and~*you*[(mp)]~*did*~
TURN.ASIDE[(V)] FROM the~ROAD WHICH *I~did~much*~DIRECT[(V)] AT~*you*[(mp)]
and~*you*[(fs)]~*did*~CALL.OUT[(V)] AT~*you*[(mp)] the~DYSFUNCTIONAL in~END the~
DAY~s GIVEN.THAT *you*[(mp)]~*will*~DO[(V)] AT the~DYSFUNCTIONAL in~EYE~s2
YHWH to~>~*make*~BE.ANGRY[(V)]~him in~WORK HAND~s2~
you[(mp)]   **31:30** and~*he*~*will*~*much*~SPEAK[(V)] Mosheh in~EAR~s2 ALL
ASSEMBLY Yisra'eyl AT WORD~s the~SONG the~THIS UNTIL >~*be*~
BE.WHOLE[(V)]~them[(m)]

Chapter 32

32:1 *!*[(mp)]~*make*~WEIGH.OUT[(V)] the~SKY~s2 and~*I~will~much*~SPEAK[(V)]~&
and~*she*~*will*~HEAR[(V)] the~LAND STATEMENT~s MOUTH~me   **32:2** *he*~*will*~
DROP[(V)] like~the~PRECIPITATION LEARNING~me *she*~*will*~FLOW[(V)] like~the~
DEW SPEECH~me like~RAINDROP~s UPON GRASS and~like~SHOWERS~s
UPON HERB   **32:3** GIVEN.THAT TITLE **YHWH** *I~will*~CALL.OUT[(V)] *!*[(mp)]~
PROVIDE[(V)] MAGNIFICENCE to~Elohiym~us   **32:4** the~BOULDER WHOLE
DEED~him GIVEN.THAT ALL ROAD~s~him DECISION MIGHTY.ONE SECURE
and~WITHOUT WICKED STEADFAST.ONE and~STRAIGHT HE   **32:5** *he*~*did*~
much~DAMAGE[(V)] to~him NOT SON~s~him BLEMISH~them[(m)] GENERATION
CROOKED and~TWISTED   **32:6** ?~to~**YHWH** *you*[(mp)]~*will*~YIELD[(V)] THIS
PEOPLE FOOL and~NOT SKILLED.ONE ?~NOT HE FATHER~*you*[(ms)] *he*~*did*~
PURCHASE[(V)]~*you*[(ms)] HE *he*~*did*~DO[(V)]~*you*[(ms)] and~*he*~*will*~*much*~
PREPARE[(V)]~*you*[(ms)]   **32:7** *!*[(ms)]~REMEMBER[(V)] DAY~s DISTANT *!*[(mp)]~
UNDERSTAND[(V)] YEAR~s GENERATION and~GENERATION *!*[(ms)]~INQUIRE[(V)]

FATHER~you(ms) and~he~will~make~BE.FACE.TO.FACE(V)~you(ms) BEARD~s~ you(ms) and~they(m)~will~SAY(V) to~you(fs) **32:8** in~>~make~INHERIT(V) Elyon NATION~s in~>~make~DIVIDE.APART(V)~him SON~s HUMAN he~will~make~ STAND.UP(V) BORDER~s PEOPLE~s to~NUMBER SON~s Yisra'eyl **32:9** GIVEN.THAT DISTRIBUTION **YHWH** PEOPLE~him Ya'aqov REGION INHERITANCE~him **32:10** he~will~FIND(V)~him in~LAND WILDERNESS and~ in~CONFUSION HOWLING DESOLATE.WILDERNESS he~will~much~ GO.AROUND(V)~him he~will~much~UNDERSTAND(V)~him he~will~ PRESERVE(V)~him like~DEEP.BLACK EYE~him **32:11** like~EAGLE he~will~ make~STIR.UP(V) NEST~him UPON YOUNG.PIGEON~s~him he~will~much~ FLUTTER(V) he~will~SPREAD.OUT(V) WING~s~him he~will~TAKE(V)~him he~ will~LIFT.UP(V)~him UPON FEATHER~him **32:12 YHWH** ALONE he~will~ make~GUIDE(V)~him and~WITHOUT WITH~him MIGHTY.ONE FOREIGNER **32:13** they(m)~will~make~RIDE(V) UPON PLATFORM~s LAND and~he~will~EAT(V) BOUNTY~s FIELD and~they(m)~will~make~SUCKLE(V) HONEY from~CLIFF and~OIL from~QUARTZ BOULDER **32:14** CHEESE CATTLE and~FAT FLOCKS WITH FAT DEPRESSION~s and~BUCK~s SON~s Bashan and~ MALE.GOAT~s WITH FAT KIDNEY~s WHEAT and~BLOOD GRAPE you(ms)~will~ GULP(V) SLIME **32:15** and~he~will~GROW.FAT(V) Yeshurun and~he~will~ KICK(V) you(fs)~did~GROW.FAT(V) you(ms)~did~BE.THICK(V) you(ms)~did~ COVER.OVER(V) and~he~will~LEAVE.ALONE(V) POWER he~did~DO(V)~him and~he~will~much~FADE(V) BOULDER RELIEF~him **32:16** they(m)~will~ make~BE.ZEALOUS(V)~him in~BE.STRANGE(V)~s in~DISGUSTING~s he~will~ make~BE.ANGRY(V)~him **32:17** they(m)~will~SACRIFICE(V) to~the~BREAST~s NOT POWER Elohiym NOT they~did~KNOW(V)~them(m) NEW~s from~NEAR they~did~COME(V) NOT they~did~STORM(V)~them(m) FATHER~s~ you(mp) **32:18** BOULDER he~did~BRING.FORTH(V)~you(ms) you(ms)~will~ BE.UNMINDFUL(V) and~you(ms)~will~FORGET(V) MIGHTY.ONE much~TWIST(V)~ ing(ms)~you(ms) **32:19** and~he~will~SEE(V) **YHWH** and~he~will~PROVOKE(V) from~ANGER SON~s~him and~DAUGHTER~s~him **32:20** and~he~will~ SAY(V) I~will~make~HIDE(V)~& FACE~s~me from~them(m) I~will~SEE(V) WHAT END~them(m) GIVEN.THAT GENERATION UPSIDE.DOWN~s THEY(m) SON~s NOT SECURE in~them(m) **32:21** THEY(m) they~did~much~BE.ZEALOUS(V)~me in~NOT MIGHTY.ONE they~did~much~BE.ANGRY(V)~me in~VANITY~s~ them(m) and~I I~will~make~BE.ZEALOUS(V)~them(m) in~NOT PEOPLE in~ NATION FOOL I~will~make~BE.ANGRY(V)~them(m) **32:22** GIVEN.THAT FIRE she~did~KINDLE(V) in~NOSE~me and~she~will~SMOLDER(V) UNTIL UNDERWORLD LOWER.PART and~she~will~EAT(V) LAND and~PRODUCT~her and~she~will~much~BLAZE(V) FOUNDATION~s HILL~s **32:23** I~will~make~ CONSUME(V) UPON~him DYSFUNCTIONAL~s ARROW~me I~will~much~ FINISH(V) in~them(m) **32:24** EXHAUSTED~s HUNGER and~FIGHT(V)~ed(mp) SPARK and~DESTRUCTION HARSH and~TOOTH BEAST~s I~will~much~ SEND(V) in~them(m) WITH FURY CRAWL(V)~ing(mp) DIRT **32:25** from~OUTSIDE she~will~be~BE.CHILDLESS(V) SWORD and~from~CHAMBER~s TERROR ALSO CHOOSE(V)~ed(ms) ALSO VIRGIN SUCKLE(V)~ing(ms) WITH MAN GRAY-

The Book of Deuteronomy

HEADED **32:26** *I~did*~SAY$^{(V)}$ *I~will~make*~BLOW.AWAY$^{(V)}$~them$^{(m)}$ *I~will~make*~CEASE$^{(V)}$~& from~MAN MEMORY~them$^{(m)}$ **32:27** UNLESS ANGER ATTACK$^{(V)}$~*ing*$^{(ms)}$ *I~will*~IMMIGRATE$^{(V)}$ OTHERWISE *they*$^{(m)}$~*will~much*~RECOGNIZE$^{(V)}$ NARROW~s~them$^{(m)}$ OTHERWISE *they*$^{(m)}$~*will*~SAY$^{(V)}$ HAND~s2~us RAISED~*ing*$^{(fs)}$ and~NOT **YHWH** *he~did*~MAKE$^{(V)}$ ALL THIS **32:28** GIVEN.THAT NATION PERISH$^{(V)}$~*ing*$^{(ms)}$ COUNSEL~s THEY$^{(m)}$ and~WITHOUT in~them$^{(m)}$ INTELLIGENCE **32:29** WOULD.THAT *they~did*~BE.SKILLED$^{(V)}$ *they*$^{(m)}$~*will~make*~CALCULATE$^{(V)}$ THIS *they*$^{(m)}$~*will*~UNDERSTAND$^{(V)}$~must to~END~them$^{(m)}$ **32:30** HOW *he~will*~PURSUE$^{(V)}$ UNIT THOUSAND and~TWO *they*$^{(m)}$~*will~make*~FLEE$^{(V)}$ MYRIAD IF NOT GIVEN.THAT BOULDER~them$^{(m)}$ *he~did*~SELL$^{(V)}$~them$^{(m)}$ and~**YHWH** *he~did~make*~SHUT$^{(V)}$~them$^{(m)}$ **32:31** GIVEN.THAT NOT like~BOULDER~us BOULDER~them$^{(m)}$ and~ATTACK$^{(V)}$~*ing*$^{(mp)}$~us JUDGE~s **32:32** GIVEN.THAT from~GRAPEVINE Sedom GRAPEVINE~them$^{(m)}$ and~from~CROPLAND Ghamorah GRAPE~s~him GRAPE~s VENOM CLUSTER~s GALL~s to~them$^{(m)}$ **32:33** FURY CROCODILE~s WINE~them$^{(m)}$ and~VENOM ASP~s CRUEL **32:34** ?~NOT HE STORE$^{(V)}$~*ed*$^{(ms)}$ BY~me SEAL$^{(V)}$~*ed*$^{(ms)}$ in~SUPPLY.HOUSE~s~me **32:35** to~me VENGEANCE and~RECOMPENSE to~APPOINTED.TIME *she~will*~TOTTER$^{(V)}$ FOOT~them$^{(m)}$ GIVEN.THAT NEAR DAY CALAMITY~them$^{(m)}$ and~*he~did*~MAKE.HASTE$^{(V)}$ PREPARED~s to~them$^{(m)}$ **32:36** GIVEN.THAT *he~will*~MODERATE$^{(V)}$ **YHWH** PEOPLE~him and~UPON SERVANT~s~him *he~will~self*~COMFORT$^{(V)}$ GIVEN.THAT *he~will*~SEE$^{(V)}$ GIVEN.THAT *she~did*~WAVER$^{(V)}$ HAND and~FAR.END STOP$^{(V)}$~*ed*$^{(ms)}$ and~LEAVE$^{(V)}$~*ed*$^{(ms)}$ **32:37** and~*he~did*~SAY$^{(V)}$ WHERE Elohiym~him BOULDER *they~did*~TAKE.REFUGE$^{(V)}$ in~him **32:38** WHICH FAT SACRIFICE~s~them$^{(m)}$ *they*$^{(m)}$~*will*~EAT$^{(V)}$ *they*$^{(m)}$~*will*~GULP$^{(V)}$ WINE POURED.OUT~you$^{(mp)}$ *they*$^{(m)}$~*will*~RISE$^{(V)}$ and~*they*$^{(m)}$~*will*~HELP$^{(V)}$~you$^{(mp)}$ *he~will*~EXIST$^{(V)}$ UPON~you$^{(mp)}$ HIDING **32:39** *!*$^{(mp)}$~SEE$^{(V)}$ NOW GIVEN.THAT I I HE and~WITHOUT Elohiym BY~me I *I~will~make*~DIE$^{(V)}$ and~*I~will~much*~LIVE$^{(V)}$ *I~did*~STRIKE.THROUGH$^{(V)}$ and~I *I~will*~HEAL$^{(V)}$ and~WITHOUT from~HAND~me *!*$^{(ms)}$~*make*~DELIVER$^{(V)}$ **32:40** GIVEN.THAT *I~will*~LIFT.UP$^{(V)}$ TO SKY~s2 HAND~me and~*I~did*~SAY$^{(V)}$ LIVING I to~DISTANT **32:41** IF *I~did*~WHET$^{(V)}$ FLASH SWORD~me and~*she~will*~TAKE.HOLD$^{(V)}$ in~DECISION HAND~me *I~will~make*~TURN.BACK$^{(V)}$ VENGEANCE to~NARROW~s~me and~to~*much*~HATE$^{(V)}$~*ing*$^{(mp)}$~me *I~will~much*~MAKE.RESTITUTION$^{(V)}$ **32:42** *I~will~make*~BE.DRUNK$^{(V)}$ ARROW~me from~BLOOD and~SWORD~me *she~will*~EAT$^{(V)}$ FLESH from~BLOOD DRILLED and~CAPTIVE from~HEAD LONG.HAIR~s ATTACK$^{(V)}$~*ing*$^{(ms)}$ **32:43** *!*$^{(mp)}$~*make*~SHOUT.ALOUD$^{(V)}$ NATION~s PEOPLE~him GIVEN.THAT BLOOD SERVANT~s~him *he~will*~RISE$^{(V)}$ and~VENGEANCE *he~will~make*~TURN.BACK$^{(V)}$ to~NARROW~s~him and~*he~did~much*~COVER$^{(V)}$ GROUND~him PEOPLE~him **32:44** and~*he~will*~COME$^{(V)}$ Mosheh and~*he~will~much*~SPEAK$^{(V)}$ AT ALL WORD~s the~SONG the~THIS in~EAR~s2 the~PEOPLE HE and~Hosheya SON Nun **32:45** and~*he~will~much*~FINISH$^{(V)}$ Mosheh to~>~*much*~SPEAK$^{(V)}$ AT ALL the~WORD~s the~THESE TO ALL Yisra'eyl **32:46** and~*he~will*~SAY$^{(V)}$ TO~them$^{(m)}$ *!*$^{(mp)}$~PLACE$^{(V)}$ HEART~

you⁽ᵐᵖ⁾ to~ALL the~WORD~s WHICH I *make*~WRAP.AROUND⁽ⱽ⁾~*ing*⁽ᵐˢ⁾ in~ you⁽ᵐᵖ⁾ the~DAY WHICH *you*⁽ᵐˢ⁾~*will*~much~DIRECT⁽ⱽ⁾~them⁽ᵐ⁾ AT SON~s~ you⁽ᵐᵖ⁾ to~>~SAFEGUARD⁽ⱽ⁾ to~>~DO⁽ⱽ⁾ AT ALL WORD~s the~TEACHING the~ THIS **32:47** GIVEN.THAT NOT WORD EMPTY HE from~you⁽ᵐᵖ⁾ GIVEN.THAT HE LIVING~s~you⁽ᵐᵖ⁾ and~in~the~WORD the~THIS *you*⁽ᵐᵖ⁾~*will*~make~ PROLONG⁽ⱽ⁾ DAY~s UPON the~GROUND WHICH YOU⁽ᵐᵖ⁾ CROSS.OVER⁽ⱽ⁾~ *ing*⁽ᵐᵖ⁾ AT the~Yarden THERE~unto to~>~POSSESS⁽ⱽ⁾~her **32:48** and~*he*~ *will*~much~SPEAK⁽ⱽ⁾ **YHWH** TO Mosheh in~BONE the~DAY the~THIS to~>~ SAY⁽ⱽ⁾ **32:49** *!*⁽ᵐˢ⁾~GO.UP⁽ⱽ⁾ TO HILL the~Ever~s the~THIS HILL Nevo WHICH in~LAND Mo'av WHICH UPON FACE~s Ye'rey'hho and~ *!*⁽ᵐˢ⁾~SEE⁽ⱽ⁾ AT LAND Kena'an WHICH I GIVE⁽ⱽ⁾~*ing*⁽ᵐˢ⁾ to~SON~s Yisra'eyl to~ HOLDINGS **32:50** and~*!*⁽ᵐˢ⁾~DIE⁽ⱽ⁾ in~the~HILL WHICH YOU⁽ᵐˢ⁾ GO.UP⁽ⱽ⁾~ *ing*⁽ᵐˢ⁾ THERE~unto and~ *!*⁽ᵐˢ⁾~be~GATHER⁽ⱽ⁾ TO PEOPLE~s~you⁽ᵐˢ⁾ like~ WHICH *he*~*did*~DIE⁽ⱽ⁾ Aharon BROTHER~you⁽ᵐˢ⁾ in~Hor the~HILL and~*he*~ *will*~be~GATHER⁽ⱽ⁾ TO PEOPLE~s~him **32:51** UPON WHICH *you*⁽ᵐᵖ⁾~*did*~ TRANSGRESS⁽ⱽ⁾ in~me in~MIDST SON~s Yisra'eyl in~WATER~s2 Meriyvah Qadesh WILDERNESS Tsin UPON WHICH NOT *you*⁽ᵐᵖ⁾~*did*~much~ SET.APART⁽ⱽ⁾ SIGN~me in~MIDST SON~s Yisra'eyl **32:52** GIVEN.THAT from~ OPPOSITE *you*⁽ᵐˢ⁾~*will*~SEE⁽ⱽ⁾ AT the~LAND and~THERE~unto NOT *you*⁽ᵐˢ⁾~ *will*~COME⁽ⱽ⁾ TO the~LAND WHICH I GIVE⁽ⱽ⁾~*ing*⁽ᵐˢ⁾ to~SON~s Yisra'eyl

Chapter 33

33:1 and~THIS the~PRESENT WHICH *he*~*did*~much~KNEEL⁽ⱽ⁾ Mosheh MAN the~Elohiym AT SON~s Yisra'eyl to~FACE~s DEATH~him **33:2** and~*he*~*will*~ SAY⁽ⱽ⁾ **YHWH** from~Sinai *he*~*did*~COME⁽ⱽ⁾ and~*he*~*did*~COME.UP⁽ⱽ⁾ from~ Se'iyr to~them⁽ᵐ⁾ *he*~*did*~make~BE.BRIGHT⁽ⱽ⁾ from~HILL Paran and~*he*~*did*~ ARRIVE⁽ⱽ⁾ from~MYRIAD~s SPECIAL from~RIGHT.HAND~him Eyshdat to~ them⁽ᵐ⁾ **33:3** MOREOVER CHERISH⁽ⱽ⁾~*ing*⁽ᵐˢ⁾ PEOPLE~s ALL UNIQUE~s~him in~HAND~you⁽ᵐˢ⁾ and~THEY⁽ᵐ⁾ *they*~*did*~be~much~SIT.DOWN⁽ⱽ⁾ to~FOOT~ you⁽ᵐˢ⁾ *he*~*will*~LIFT.UP⁽ⱽ⁾ WORD~s~you⁽ᵐˢ⁾ **33:4** TEACHING *he*~*did*~much~ DIRECT⁽ⱽ⁾ to~us Mosheh POSSESSION ASSEMBLY Ya'aqov **33:5** and~*he*~*will*~ EXIST⁽ⱽ⁾ in~Yeshurun KING in~>~self~GATHER⁽ⱽ⁾ HEAD~s PEOPLE TOGETHER STAFF~s Yisra'eyl **33:6** *he*~*will*~LIVE⁽ⱽ⁾ Re'uven and~DO.NOT *he*~*will*~DIE⁽ⱽ⁾ and~*he*~*will*~EXIST⁽ⱽ⁾ MORTAL.MAN~s~him NUMBER **33:7** and~THIS to~ Yehudah and~*he*~*will*~SAY⁽ⱽ⁾ *!*⁽ᵐˢ⁾~HEAR⁽ⱽ⁾ **YHWH** VOICE Yehudah and~TO PEOPLE~him *you*⁽ᵐˢ⁾~*will*~make~COME⁽ⱽ⁾~him HAND~s2~him ABUNDANT to~him and~HELP from~NARROW~s~him *you*⁽ᵐˢ⁾~*will*~EXIST⁽ⱽ⁾ **33:8** and~ to~Lewi *he*~*did*~SAY⁽ⱽ⁾ Tumiym~you⁽ᵐˢ⁾ and~Uriym~you⁽ᵐˢ⁾ to~MAN KIND.ONE~you⁽ᵐˢ⁾ WHICH *you*⁽ᵐˢ⁾~*did*~much~TEST⁽ⱽ⁾~him in~Mas'sah *you*⁽ᵐˢ⁾~*will*~DISPUTE⁽ⱽ⁾~him UPON WATER~s2 Meriyvah **33:9** the~SAY⁽ⱽ⁾~ *ing*⁽ᵐˢ⁾ to~FATHER~him and~to~MOTHER~him NOT *I*~*did*~SEE⁽ⱽ⁾~him and~AT BROTHER~s~him NOT *he*~*did*~make~RECOGNIZE⁽ⱽ⁾ and~AT SON~him NOT

The Book of Deuteronomy

he~did~KNOW$^{(V)}$ GIVEN.THAT they~did~SAFEGUARD$^{(V)}$ SPEECH~you$^{(ms)}$ and~COVENANT~you$^{(ms)}$ they$^{(m)}$~will~PRESERVE$^{(V)}$ **33:10** they$^{(m)}$~will~make~THROW$^{(V)}$ DECISION~s~you$^{(ms)}$ to~Ya'aqov and~TEACHING~you$^{(ms)}$ to~Yisra'eyl they$^{(m)}$~will~PLACE$^{(V)}$ INCENSE.SMOKE in~NOSE~you$^{(ms)}$ and~ENTIRELY UPON ALTAR~you$^{(ms)}$ **33:11** >~much~KNEEL$^{(V)}$ **YHWH** FORCE~him and~DEED HAND~s2~him you$^{(ms)}$~will~ACCEPT$^{(V)}$!$^{(ms)}$~STRIKE.THROUGH$^{(V)}$ WAIST~s2 RISE$^{(V)}$~ing$^{(mp)}$~him and~much~HATE$^{(V)}$~ing$^{(mp)}$~him FROM they$^{(m)}$~will~RISE$^{(V)}$~must **33:12** to~Binyamin he~did~SAY$^{(V)}$ CHERISHED **YHWH** he~will~DWELL$^{(V)}$ to~the~SAFELY UPON~him BLANKET$^{(V)}$~ing$^{(ms)}$ UPON~him ALL the~DAY and~BETWEEN SHOULDER.PIECE~s~him he~did~DWELL$^{(V)}$ **33:13** and~to~Yoseph he~did~SAY$^{(V)}$ be~much~KNEEL$^{(V)}$~ing$^{(fs)}$ **YHWH** LAND~him from~PRECIOUS SKY~s2 from~DEW and~from~DEEP.WATER STRETCH.OUT$^{(V)}$~ing$^{(fs)}$ UNDER **33:14** and~from~PRECIOUS PRODUCTION~s SUN and~from~PRECIOUS BROUGHT.OUT MOON~s **33:15** and~from~HEAD the~HILL~s EAST and~from~PRECIOUS KNOLL~s DISTANT **33:16** and~from~PRECIOUS LAND and~FILLING~her and~SELF-WILL DWELL$^{(V)}$~ing$^{(ms)}$~me THORN.BUSH she~will~COME$^{(V)}$~& to~HEAD Yoseph and~to~TOP.OF.THE.HEAD DEDICATED BROTHER~s~him **33:17** FIRSTBORN OX~him HONOR to~him and~HORN~s RHINOCEROS HORN~s~him in~them$^{(m)}$ PEOPLE~s he~will~much~GORE$^{(V)}$ TOGETHER FAR.END~s LAND and~THEY$^{(m)}$ MYRIAD~s Ephrayim and~THEY$^{(m)}$ THOUSAND~s Menasheh **33:18** and~to~Zevulun he~did~SAY$^{(V)}$!$^{(ms)}$~REJOICE$^{(V)}$ Zevulun in~>~GO.OUT$^{(V)}$~you$^{(ms)}$ and~Yis'sas'khar in~TENT~s~you$^{(ms)}$ **33:19** PEOPLE~s HILL they$^{(m)}$~will~CALL.OUT$^{(V)}$ THERE they$^{(m)}$~will~SACRIFICE$^{(V)}$ SACRIFICE~s STEADFAST GIVEN.THAT ABOUNDING SEA~s they$^{(m)}$~will~SUCKLE$^{(V)}$ and~BOARDED.UP$^{(V)}$~ing$^{(mp)}$ SUBMERGE$^{(V)}$~ed$^{(mp)}$ SAND **33:20** and~to~Gad he~did~SAY$^{(V)}$ KNEEL$^{(V)}$~ed$^{(ms)}$ make~WIDEN$^{(V)}$~ing$^{(ms)}$ Gad like~LIONESS he~did~DWELL$^{(V)}$ and~he~did~TEAR.INTO.PIECES$^{(V)}$ ARM MOREOVER TOP.OF.THE.HEAD **33:21** and~he~will~SEE$^{(V)}$ SUMMIT to~him GIVEN.THAT THERE PARCEL much~INSCRIBE$^{(V)}$~ing$^{(ms)}$ BOARDED.UP$^{(V)}$~ed$^{(ms)}$ and~he~will~ARRIVE$^{(V)}$ HEAD~s PEOPLE STEADFASTNESS **YHWH** he~did~DO$^{(V)}$ and~DECISION~s~him WITH Yisra'eyl **33:22** and~to~Dan he~did~SAY$^{(V)}$ Dan WHELP LION he~will~much~JUMP$^{(V)}$ FROM the~Bashan **33:23** and~to~Naphtali he~did~SAY$^{(V)}$ Naphtali PLENTY SELF-WILL and~FULL PRESENT **YHWH** SEA and~SOUTHERN !$^{(ms)}$~POSSESS$^{(V)}$~& **33:24** and~to~Asher he~did~SAY$^{(V)}$ KNEEL$^{(V)}$~ed$^{(ms)}$ from~SON~s Asher he~will~EXIST$^{(V)}$ ACCEPT$^{(V)}$~ed$^{(ms)}$ BROTHER~s~him and~DIP$^{(V)}$~ing$^{(ms)}$ in~the~OIL FOOT~him **33:25** IRON and~COPPER SANDAL~s~you$^{(ms)}$ and~like~DAY~s~you$^{(ms)}$ TOUGHNESS~you$^{(ms)}$ **33:26** WITHOUT like~MIGHTY.ONE Yeshurun RIDE$^{(V)}$~ing$^{(ms)}$ SKY~s2 in~HELP~you$^{(ms)}$ and~in~PRIDE~him DUST.CLOUD~s **33:27** HABITATION Elohiym EAST and~from~UNDER ARM~s DISTANT and~he~will~much~CAST.OUT$^{(V)}$ from~FACE~s~you$^{(ms)}$ ATTACK$^{(V)}$~ing$^{(ms)}$ and~he~will~SAY$^{(V)}$!$^{(ms)}$~make~DESTROY$^{(V)}$ **33:28** and~he~will~DWELL$^{(V)}$ Yisra'eyl SAFELY ALONE EYE Ya'aqov TO LAND CEREAL and~FRESH.WINE MOREOVER SKY~s2~him they$^{(m)}$~will~DROP$^{(V)}$

DEW **33:29** HAPPY~you*(ms)* Yisra'eyl WHO like~THAT.ONE~you*(ms)* PEOPLE *he~did~be*~RESCUE*(V)* in~**YHWH** SHIELD HELP~you*(ms)* and~WHICH SWORD PRIDE~you*(ms)* and~*they(m)~will~be*~DENY*(V)* ATTACK*(V)*~*ing(mp)*~s~you*(ms)* to~you*(fs)* and~YOU*(ms)* UPON PLATFORM~s~them*(m)* *you(ms)~will*~TAKE.STEPS*(V)*

Chapter 34

34:1 and~*he~will~make*~GO.UP*(V)* Mosheh from~DESERT~s Mo'av TO HILL Nevo HEAD the~Pisgah WHICH UPON FACE~s Ye'rey'hho and~*he~will~make*~SEE*(V)*~him **YHWH** AT ALL the~LAND AT the~Gil'ad UNTIL Dan **34:2** and~AT ALL Naphtali and~AT LAND Ephrayim and~Menasheh and~AT ALL LAND Yehudah UNTIL the~SEA the~LAST **34:3** and~AT the~SOUTH and~AT the~ROUNDNESS LEVEL.VALLEY Ye'rey'hho CITY the~DATE.PALM~s UNTIL Tso'ar **34:4** and~*he~will*~SAY*(V)* **YHWH** TO~him THIS the~LAND WHICH *I~did~be*~SWEAR*(V)* to~Avraham to~Yits'hhaq and~to~Ya'aqov to~>~SAY*(V)* to~SEED~you*(ms)* *I~will*~GIVE*(V)*~her *I~did~make*~SEE*(V)*~you*(ms)* in~EYE~s2~you*(ms)* and~THERE~unto NOT *you(ms)~will*~CROSS.OVER*(V)* **34:5** and~*he~will*~DIE*(V)* THERE Mosheh SERVANT **YHWH** in~LAND Mo'av UPON MOUTH **YHWH** **34:6** and~*he~will*~BURY*(V)* AT~him in~the~STEEP.VALLEY in~LAND Mo'av FOREFRONT Beyt-Pe'or and~NOT *he~did*~KNOW*(V)* MAN AT BURIAL.PLACE~him UNTIL the~DAY the~THIS **34:7** and~Mosheh SON HUNDRED and~TEN~s YEAR in~DEATH~him NOT *she~did*~DIM*(V)* EYE~him and~NOT *he~did*~FLEE*(V)* MOIST~her **34:8** and~*they(m)~will*~WEEP*(V)* SON~s Yisra'eyl AT Mosheh in~DESERT~s Mo'av THREE~s DAY and~*they(m)~will*~BE.WHOLE*(V)* DAY~s WEEPING MOURNING Mosheh **34:9** and~Yehoshu'a SON Nun *he~did*~FILL*(V)* WIND SKILL GIVEN.THAT *he~did*~SUPPORT*(V)* Mosheh AT HAND~s2~him UPON~him and~*they(m)~will*~HEAR*(V)* TO~him SON~s Yisra'eyl and~*they(m)~will*~DO*(V)* like~WHICH *he~did~much*~DIRECT*(V)* **YHWH** AT Mosheh **34:10** and~NOT *he~did*~RISE*(V)* ANNOUNCER YET.AGAIN in~Yisra'eyl like~Mosheh WHICH *he~did*~KNOW*(V)*~him **YHWH** FACE~s TO FACE~s **34:11** to~ALL the~SIGN~s and~the~WONDER~s WHICH *he~did*~SEND*(V)*~him **YHWH** to~>~DO*(V)* in~LAND Mits'rayim to~Paroh and~to~ALL SERVANT~s~him and~to~ALL LAND~him **34:12** and~to~ALL the~HAND the~FORCEFUL and~to~ALL the~FEARING the~GREAT WHICH *he~did*~DO*(V)* Mosheh to~EYE~s2 ALL Yisra'eyl

The Book of Deuteronomy

Dictionary

Prefixes and Suffixes

?~: The interrogative 'Hey,' which converts the sentence into a question.
~&: Paragogic 'Hey,' which is added to the ordinary forms of words, to express additional emphasis, or some change in the sense.
~+~: This symbol is placed between the two words of a compound word or name.
~her: Third person feminine singular pronoun (her) also used as a possessive pronoun ("of her" or "hers").
~him: Third person masculine singular pronoun (him) also used as a possessive pronoun ("of him" or "his").
~me: First person common singular pronoun (me), also used as a possessive pronoun ("of me" or "my") .
~must: Paragogic 'Nun,' which emphasizes the intensity of action of the verb. *Alternate Translations:* shall; cannot (when attached to a verb that is preceded by a negative participle)
~of: Identifies the noun as singular possessive.
~s: Identifies the noun as a plural. When attached to the name of a person it identifies the name as plural possessive.
~s2: Identifies the noun as a dual plural.
~them[f]: person feminine plural pronoun (them) also used as a possessive pronoun ("of them" or "their").
~them[m]: Third person masculine plural pronoun (them) also used as a possessive pronoun ("of them" or "their").
~unto: Directional 'Hey,' which implies movement toward the location identified in the word this suffix is attached to. *Alternate Translations:* into; upon
~us: First person common plural pronoun (we), also used as a possessive pronoun ("of us" or "our"). In some instances, this suffix is used as the third person, masculine, singular possessive pronoun ("of him" or "his").
~you[fp]: Second person feminine plural pronoun (you), also used as a possessive pronoun ("of you" or "your").
~you[fs]: Second person feminine singular pronoun (you), alsoused as a possessive pronoun ("of you" or "your").
~you[mp]: Second person masculine plural pronoun (you), also used as a possessive pronoun ("of you" or "your").
~you[ms]: Second person masculine singular pronoun (you), also used as a possessive pronoun ("of you" or "your").

Dictionary

and~: The conjunction meaning "and." Often used as the 'V*av*' consecutive when prefixed to a verb and will usually reverse the tense of the verb. *Alternate Translations:* as; but; or; so; that; then; when.

from~: A preposition meaning "from." *Alternate Translations:* above; at; by; in; kinds; more than; of; on; out of; rather than; some of; to; including; because of.

in~: A preposition meaning "in" or "with." *Alternate Translations:* among; at; by; on; over; to; with; excuse me (when suffixed with "me~").

like~: A preposition meaning "like." *Alternate Translations:* about; as; same; when.

the~: The definite article meaning "the."

to~: A preposition meaning "to" or "for." *Alternate Translations:* about; as; at; belong to; by; for; has; have; so; with; within.

which~: A preposition meaning "which" or "who."

Conjugations

***!*(fp)~**: Identifies (the verb as a feminine plural imperative.
***!*(fs)~**: Identifies the verb as a feminine singular imperative.
***!*(mp)~**: Identifies the verb as a masculine plural imperative.
***!*(ms)~**: Identifies the verb as a masculine singular imperative.
~ed(fp): Feminine plural verb passive participle denoting an action (such as "baked").
~ed(fs): Feminine singular verb passive participle denoting an action (such as "baked").
~ed(mp): Masculine plural verb passive participle denoting an action (such as "baked").
~ed(ms): Masculine singular verb passive participle denoting an action (such as "baked").
~ing(fp): Feminine plural verb participle denoting an action (such as "baking") or one of action (such as a "baking ones," or "bakers").
~ing(fs): Feminine singular verb participle denoting an action (such as "baking") or one of action (such as a "baking one," or "baker").
~ing(mp): Masculine plural verb participle denoting an action (such as "baking") or one of action (such as a "baking ones," or "bakers").
~ing(ms): Masculine singular verb participle denoting an action (such as "baking") or one of action (such as a "baking one," or "baker").
>~: Identifies the verb form as infinitive.
be~ : Identifies the voice of the verb as passive.
did~: Identifies the tense of the verb as perfect. The perfect tense is a completed action and in most cases is related to the English past tense. *Alternate Translations:* had (when the subject of the verb precedes the verb).
he~: Identifies the subject of the verb as third person masculine singular. *Alternate Translations:* any; it; one; that.
I~: Identifies the subject of the verb as first person common singular.
make~: Identifies the mood of the verb as causative. *Alternate Translations:* cause; give; let; take.
much~: Identifies the the mood of the verb as intensive. *Alternate Translations:* many, completely.
self~: Identifies the voice of the verb as reflexive. *Alternate Translations:* act.
she~: Identifies the subject of the verb as third person feminine singular.
they(f)~: Identifies the subject of the verb as third person feminine plural.
they(m)~: Identifies the subject of the verb as third person masculine plural.
they~: Identifies the subject of the verb as third person common plural.
we~: Identifies the subject of the verb as first person common plural.

Dictionary

will~: Identifies the tense of the verb as imperfect. The imperfect tense is an incomplete action and is closely related to the English present and future tenses. *Alternate Translations:* do.

you$^{(fp)}$~ Identifies the subject of the verb as second person feminine plural.

you$^{(fs)}$~ Identifies the subject of the verb as second person feminine singular.

you$^{(mp)}$~ Identifies the subject of the verb as second person masculine plural.

you$^{(ms)}$~ Identifies the subject of the verb as second person masculine singular.

Hebrew Names

Adah: ADORNMENT *Strong's:* #5711
Adbe'el: MIST + in~MIGHTY.ONE *Strong's:* #0110
Admah: GROUND *Strong's:* #0126, #0128
Adonai: LORD~s~me *Strong's:* #0136
Adulam: WITNESS + and~SHEPHERD.STAFF *Strong's:* #5725, #5726
Agag: I~will~OVERTOP *Strong's:* #0090
Ahalivamah: TENT~of + PLATFORM *Strong's:* #0173
Ahaliyav: TENT~of + FATHER *Strong's:* #0171
Aharon: LIGHT.BRINGER *Strong's:* #0175
Ahhi'ezer: BROTHER~me + HELP *Strong's:* #0295
Ahhihud: BROTHER~me + SPLENDOR *Strong's:* #0282
Ahhiman: BROTHER~me + SHARE *Strong's:* #0289
Ahhira: BROTHER~me + DYSFUNCTIONAL *Strong's:* #0299
Ahhiram: BROTHER~me + RAISED *Strong's:* #0297, #0298
Ahhiysamahh: BROTHER~me + he~did~SUPPORT(V) *Strong's:* #0294
Ahhuzat: HOLDINGS *Strong's:* #0276
Akad: DELICATE *Strong's:* #0390
Akhbor: MOUSE *Strong's:* #5907
Akhran: DISTURBED.ONE *Strong's:* #5918
Almodad: MIGHTY.ONE + MEASURING *Strong's:* #0486
Almon-Divlatayim: OUT.OF.SIGHT + CAKE~s2 *Strong's:* #5963

Alon-Bakhut: GREAT.TREE + WEEPING *Strong's:* #0439
Alush: I~will~KNEAD(V) *Strong's:* #0442
Alwah: WICKEDNESS *Strong's:* #5933
Alwan: LOFT *Strong's:* #5935
Amaleq: PEOPLE + GATHERED.UP *Strong's:* #6002, #6003
Ami'eyl: PEOPLE~of + MIGHTY.ONE *Strong's:* #5988
Amihud: PEOPLE~of + SPLENDOR *Strong's:* #5989
Amishaddai: PEOPLE~of + BREAST~s~me *Strong's:* #5996
Amiynadav: PEOPLE~me + OFFERED.WILLINGLY *Strong's:* #5992
Amon: TRIBAL *Strong's:* #5983, #5984, #5985
Amram: PEOPLE + RAISED *Strong's:* #6019
Amraphel: SAYER~+~FALL *Strong's:* #0569
Anah: ANSWERED *Strong's:* #6034
Anam: AFFLICTION + WATER~s2 *Strong's:* #6047
Anaq: NECK.BAND *Strong's:* #6061, #6062
Aner: YOUNG.BOY *Strong's:* #6063
Aqabariym: SHARP.SIGHTED *Strong's:* #4610
Aqan: SHARP.SIGHTED *Strong's:* #6130
Ar: ENEMY *Strong's:* #6144
Arad: WILD.DONKEY *Strong's:* #6166
Aram: PALACE *Strong's:* #0758
Aram-Nahara'im: PALACE + RIVER~s2 *Strong's:* #0763
Aran: I~will~SHOUT.ALOUD(V) *Strong's:* #0765

Dictionary

Araq: GNAWED *Strong's:* #6208
Ararat: HIGH.LAND *Strong's:* #0780
Ard: I~will~GO.DOWN⁽ⱽ⁾ *Strong's:* #0714
Areliy: LION + MIGHTY.ONE~me *Strong's:* #0692
Argov: I~will~CLOD *Strong's:* #0709
Arnon: I~will~SHOUT.ALOUD⁽ⱽ⁾ *Strong's:* #0769
Arodiy: ROAMING~me *Strong's:* #0722
Aro'eyr: UNPROTECTED *Strong's:* #6177
Arpakhshad: I~will~DECLINE + BREAST *Strong's:* #0775
Arwad: ROAMING *Strong's:* #0719, #0721
Aryokh: LION.LIKE *Strong's:* #0746
Ashbeyl: I~will~EXCHANGE⁽ⱽ⁾ *Strong's:* #0788
Asher: HAPPY *Strong's:* #0836
Ashkanaz: FIRE + SPRINKLED *Strong's:* #0813
Ashterot: YOUNG.SHEEP~s *Strong's:* #6252
Ashterot-Qar'nayim: YOUNG.SHEEP~s + HORN~s2 *Strong's:* #6255
Ashur: HAPPY *Strong's:* #0804
Asiyr: PRISONER *Strong's:* #0617
Asnat: BELONGING.TO.NAT *Strong's:* #0621
Asri'eyl: HAPPY⁽ⱽ⁾~me + MIGHTY.ONE *Strong's:* #0844, #0845
Atariym: SITE~s *Strong's:* #0871
Atarot: WREATH~s *Strong's:* #5852
Atsmon: ABUNDANT.ONE *Strong's:* #6111
At'rot-Shophan: WREATH~s RABBIT *Strong's:* #5855
Aveyl-Hashit'tim: MOURNING + the~ACACIA~s2 *Strong's:* #0063
Aveyl-Mitsrayim: MOURNING + STRAIT~s2 *Strong's:* #0067

Avida: FATHER~me + he~did~KNOW⁽ⱽ⁾ *Strong's:* #0028
Avidan: FATHER~me + MODERATOR *Strong's:* #0027
Avihha'il: FATHER~me + FORCE *Strong's:* #0032
Aviram: FATHER~me + RAISED *Strong's:* #0048
Aviyasaph: FATHER~me + he~did~GATHER⁽ⱽ⁾ *Strong's:* #0023
Aviyhu: FATHER~me + HE *Strong's:* #0030
Aviyma'el: FATHER~me + from~MIGHTY.ONE *Strong's:* #0039
Aviymelekh: FATHER~me + KING *Strong's:* #0040
Avraham: FATHER + LIFTED *Strong's:* #0085
Avram: FATHER + RAISED *Strong's:* #0087
Awi: TWIST *Strong's:* #5757, #5761
Awit: RUINED.HEAP~s *Strong's:* #5762
Ay: RUINED.HEAP *Strong's:* #5857
Ayah: HAWK *Strong's:* #0345
Ayin: EYE *Strong's:* #5871
Azan: STRONG.ONE *Strong's:* #5821
Azazeyl: STRONG + >~WAVER⁽ⱽ⁾ *Strong's:* #5799
Azni: EAR~me *Strong's:* #0241, #0244
Ba'al: MASTER *Strong's:* #1168
Ba'al-Hhanan: MASTER + BEAUTY *Strong's:* #1177
Ba'al-Me'on: MASTER + HABITATION *Strong's:* #1186
Ba'al-Pe'or: MASTER + OPENED.WIDE *Strong's:* #1187
Ba'al-Tsephon: MASTER + NORTH *Strong's:* #1189
Balaq: he~did~LAY.WASTE⁽ⱽ⁾ *Strong's:* #1111

Bamot: PLATFORM~s *Strong's:* #1120
Barneya: GRAIN + RATTLE *Strong's:* #6947
Bashan: SHAME *Strong's:* #1316
Basmat: FRAGRANCE *Strong's:* #1315
Bavel: MIXED.UP *Strong's:* #0894
Bedad: ALONE *Strong's:* #0911
Be'eri: WELL~me *Strong's:* #0882
Be'er-Lahhiy-Ro'iy: WELL + to~LIVING + SEE(V)+ing(ms)~me *Strong's:* #0883
Bekher: YOUNG.CAMEL *Strong's:* #1071
Bela: SWALLOWED *Strong's:* #1106
Beli'ya'al: UNAWARE + he~will~Gain(V) *Strong's:* #1100
Ben-Amiy: SON + PEOPLE~me *Strong's:* #1151
Ben-Oni: SON + VIGOR~me *Strong's:* #1126
Be'on: in~COHABITATION *Strong's:* #1194
Be'or: IGNITING *Strong's:* #1160
B'er: WELL *Strong's:* #0876
Bera: in~DYSFUNCTIONAL *Strong's:* #1298
Bered: HAILSTONES *Strong's:* #1260
Beri'ah: in~COMPANION *Strong's:* #1283
B'er-Sheva: WELL + SEVEN *Strong's:* #0884
Betsaleyl: in~SHADOW + MIGHTY.ONE *Strong's:* #1212
Betser: PRECIOUS.METAL *Strong's:* #1221
Betu'el: HOUSE~them(m) + MIGHTY.ONE *Strong's:* #1328
Beyt-El: HOUSE + MIGHTY.ONE *Strong's:* #1008
Beyt-Haran: HOUSE + HILL.COUNTRY *Strong's:* #1028
Beyt-Hayishmot: HOUSE + THERE.IS + DEATH *Strong's:* #1020
Beyt-Lehhem: HOUSE + BREAD *Strong's:* #1035
Beyt-Nimrah: HOUSE + LEOPARD *Strong's:* #1039
Beyt-Pe'or: HOUSE + OPENED.WIDE *Strong's:* #1047
Bilam: NONE + PEOPLE *Strong's:* #1109
Bilhah: DISMAY *Strong's:* #1090
Bilhan: DISMAY~them(f) *Strong's:* #1092
Binyamin: SON + RIGHT.HAND *Strong's:* #1144
Birsha: in~LOST *Strong's:* #1306
B'ney-Ya'aqan: SON~s2 + he~will~BE.SHARP.SIGHTED(V) *Strong's:* #1142
Botsrah: SHEEP.PEN *Strong's:* #1224
Buqi: VACANT *Strong's:* #1231
Buz: DESPISED *Strong's:* #0938
Dameseq: BLOOD + SACK *Strong's:* #1834
Dan: MODERATOR *Strong's:* #1835
Daphqah: she~did~BEAT.OUT(V) *Strong's:* #1850
Datan: LAWFUL *Strong's:* #1885
Dedan: LOW.COUNTRY *Strong's:* #1719
De'u'eyl: they~did~KNOW(V) + MIGHTY.ONE *Strong's:* #1845
Devorah: BEE *Strong's:* #1683
Dibon: BROODING *Strong's:* #1769
Dibon-Gad: PLEA + GIFT.OFFERING *Strong's:* #1769
Dinah: PLEA *Strong's:* #1783
Dinhavah: PLEA + GIFT.OFFERING *Strong's:* #1838
Diqlah: PALM.GROVE *Strong's:* #1853
Dishan: THRESHER *Strong's:* #1789
Dishon: ANTELOPE *Strong's:* #1787
Divriy: WORD~me *Strong's:* #1704
Di-Zahav: SUFFICIENT + GOLD *Strong's:* #1774

Dictionary

Dodan: LOW.COUNTRY *Strong's:* #1721
Dotan: LAWFUL *Strong's:* #1886
Dumah: SILENCED *Strong's:* #1746
Eden: PLEASURE *Strong's:* #5731
Edom: RED *Strong's:* #0123, #0130
Ed're'i: ENERGY~me *Strong's:* #0154
Ehyeh: I~will~EXIST⁽ⱽ⁾ *Strong's:* #1961
Elaley: MIGHTY.ONE + >~GO.UP⁽ⱽ⁾ *Strong's:* #0500
Elam: ANCIENT *Strong's:* #5867
Elasar: MIGHTY.ONE + NOBLE *Strong's:* #0495
Elazar: MIGHTY.ONE + he~did~HELP⁽ⱽ⁾ *Strong's:* #0499
El-Beyt-El: MIGHTY.ONE + HOUSE + MIGHTY.ONE *Strong's:* #0416
Elda'ah: MIGHTY.ONE + he~did~KNOW⁽ⱽ⁾ *Strong's:* #0420
Eldad: MIGHTY.ONE + TEAT *Strong's:* #0419
El-Elohey-Yisra'eyl: MIGHTY.ONE + POWER~s + he~will~TURN.ASIDE⁽ⱽ⁾ + MIGHTY.ONE *Strong's:* #0415
Eli'av: MIGHTY.ONE + FATHER *Strong's:* #0446
Elidad: MIGHTY.ONE~me + TEAT *Strong's:* #0449
Eli'ezer: MIGHTY.ONE~me + he~did~HELP⁽ⱽ⁾ *Strong's:* #0461
Eliphaz: MIGHTY.ONE~me + PURE.GOLD *Strong's:* #0464
Elishah: MIGHTY.ONE~me + EQUATED *Strong's:* #0473
Elishama: MIGHTY.ONE~me + he~did~HEAR⁽ⱽ⁾ *Strong's:* #0476
Elitsaphan: MIGHTY.ONE~me + he~did~CONCEAL⁽ⱽ⁾ *Strong's:* #0469
Elitsur: MIGHTY.ONE~me + BOULDER *Strong's:* #0468
Eliysheva: MIGHTY.ONE~me + he~did~SWEAR⁽ⱽ⁾ *Strong's:* #0472
Elohiym: POWER~s *Strong's:* #0430
Elqanah: MIGHTY.ONE + he~did~PURCHASE⁽ⱽ⁾ *Strong's:* #0511
El-Ra'iy: MIGHTY.ONE + he~did~SEE⁽ⱽ⁾~me *Strong's:* #0410 & #7200
El'tsaphan: MIGHTY.ONE + he~did~CONCEAL⁽ⱽ⁾ *Strong's:* #0469
Elyasaph: MIGHTY.ONE + he~did~ADD⁽ⱽ⁾ *Strong's:* #0460
Elyon: UPPER *Strong's:* #5945
Emor: SAYER *Strong's:* #0567
Enosh: MAN *Strong's:* #0583
Epher: DIRT *Strong's:* #6081
Ephod: EPHOD *Strong's:* #0641
Ephrat: I~will~INTERPRET⁽ⱽ⁾ *Strong's:* #0672
Ephrayim: ASH~s2 *Strong's:* #0669
Ephron: POWDERY *Strong's:* #6085
Erekh: SLOW *Strong's:* #0751
Esaw: DOING *Strong's:* #6215
Eseq: STRIFE *Strong's:* #6230
Eshban: I~will~GROW *Strong's:* #0790
Eshkol: CLUSTER *Strong's:* #0812
Etsbon: WORKING *Strong's:* #0675
Etsi'on-Gaver: ABUNDANT.ONE *Strong's:* #6100
Ever: OTHER.SIDE *Strong's:* #5677, #5680, #5681, #5682
Evronah: CROSSING.ONE *Strong's:* #5684
Ewi: YEARN~me *Strong's:* #0189
Eyhhiy: BROTHER~me *Strong's:* #0278
Eylah: OAK *Strong's:* #0425
Eyliym: BUCK~s *Strong's:* #0362
Eylon: GREAT.TREE *Strong's:* #0356
Eylot: DOE~s *Strong's:* #0359
Eyl-Paran: BUCK + DECORATED *Strong's:* #0364
Eym: TERROR *Strong's:* #0368

Eynan: HAVING.AN.EYE *Strong's:* #5851
Eynayim: EYE~s2 *Strong's:* #5879
Eyn-Mishpat: EYE + DECISION *Strong's:* #5880
Eyphah: MURKINESS *Strong's:* #5891
Eyr: ENEMY *Strong's:* #6147
Eyran: BARE.ONE *Strong's:* #6197
Eyriy: BARE.SKIN~me *Strong's:* #6179, #6180
Eyshdat: FIRE + LAW *Strong's:* #0799+#1881
Eytam: PLOWSHARE~them$^{(m)}$ *Strong's:* #0864
Eytser: he~did~STORE.UP$^{(V)}$ *Strong's:* #0687
Eyval: ROUND.STONE *Strong's:* #5858
Gad: FORTUNE *Strong's:* #1410
Gad'di'eyl: FORTUNE~me + MIGHTY.ONE *Strong's:* #1427
Gad'diy: FORTUNE~me *Strong's:* #1426
Gahham: BURNT *Strong's:* #1514
Galeyd: MOUND + WITNESS *Strong's:* #1567
Gamli'eyl: CAMEL~me + MIGHTY.ONE *Strong's:* #1583
Gatam: BURNT.VALLEY *Strong's:* #1609
Gemali: CAMEL~me *Strong's:* #1582
Gera: SEED.OF.GRAIN *Strong's:* #1617
Gerar: CHEWED *Strong's:* #1642
Gerizim: CUTTING~s *Strong's:* #1630
Gershom: EVICTED *Strong's:* #1647
Gershon: EVICTED *Strong's:* #1648
Geshur: CLINGING *Strong's:* #1650, #1651
Getar: AGITATED *Strong's:* #1666
Ge'u'eyl: !$^{(ms)}$~RISE.UP$^{(V)}$ + MIGHTY.ONE *Strong's:* #1345

Ghamorah: SUBMERSION *Strong's:* #6017
Ghaza: SHE-GOAT *Strong's:* #5804
Gidoni: HEWN.ONE~me *Strong's:* #1441
Gil'ad: DANCING.AROUND + WITNESS *Strong's:* #1568
Gilgal: ROLLING.THING *Strong's:* #1537
Girgash: IMMIGRANT + CLAYEY.SOIL *Strong's:* #1622
Giyhhon: BURSTING.FORTH *Strong's:* #1521
Golan: BURNT.OFFERING~them$^{(f)}$ *Strong's:* #1474
Gomer: CONCLUDED *Strong's:* #1586
Goren-Ha'atad: FLOOR + the~BRAMBLE.THORN *Strong's:* #0329, #1637
Goshen: DRAWING.NEAR *Strong's:* #1657
Goyim: NATION~s *Strong's:* #1471
Gudgodah: FORTUNES *Strong's:* #1412
Guni: DEFENDER~me *Strong's:* #1476
Hadad: the~TEAT *Strong's:* #1908
Hadar: HONOR *Strong's:* #1924
Hadoram: HONOR~them$^{(m)}$ *Strong's:* #1913
Hagar: the~IMMIGRANT *Strong's:* #1904
Ham: ROARING *Strong's:* #1990
Haran: HILL.COUNTRY *Strong's:* #2039
Hevel: VANITY *Strong's:* #1893
Heymam: CONFUSED *Strong's:* #1967
Hhadad: he~did~SHARP$^{(V)}$ *Strong's:* #2316
Hhagi: FEAST~me *Strong's:* #2291
Hhaglah: PARTRIDGE *Strong's:* #2295

Dictionary

Hham: FATHER-IN-LAW *Strong's:* #2526
Hhamat: SKIN.BAG *Strong's:* #2574, #2575, #2577
Hhamor: DONKEY *Strong's:* #2544
Hhamul: PITIED *Strong's:* #2538, #2539
Hhani'eyl: BEAUTY~of + MIGHTY.ONE *Strong's:* #2592
Hhanokh: DEVOTED *Strong's:* #2585
Hharadah: TREMBLING *Strong's:* #2732
Hharan: FLAMING.WRATH *Strong's:* #2771
Hharmah: ASSIGNED *Strong's:* #2767
Hhashmonah: WEALTHY *Strong's:* #2832
Hhatsar-Adar: COURTYARD + he~did~BE.EMINENT$^{(V)}$ *Strong's:* #2692
Hhatsar-Eynan: COURTYARD + HAVING.AN.EYE *Strong's:* #2704
Hhatsariym: COURTYARD~s *Strong's:* #2699
Hhatsarmawet: COURTYARD + DEATH *Strong's:* #2700
Hhatsarot: COURTYARD~s *Strong's:* #2698
Hhats'tson-Tamar: DIVIDING + DATE.PALM *Strong's:* #2688
Hhawah: TOWN *Strong's:* #2332
Hhawilah: TWIST.AROUND *Strong's:* #2341
Hhawot: TOWN~s *Strong's:* #2334
Hhazo: LOOK.INTO~him *Strong's:* #2375
Hheleq: DISTRIBUTION *Strong's:* #2507, #2516
Hhemdan: DESIRED *Strong's:* #2533
Hhermon: PERFORATED.ONE *Strong's:* #2768
Hheshbon: REASON *Strong's:* #2809
Hhet: TREMBLING.IN.FEAR *Strong's:* #2845, #2850
Hhetsron: SURROUNDED.BY.A.WALL *Strong's:* #2696
Hhever: COUPLE *Strong's:* #2268
Hhevron: ASSOCIATION *Strong's:* #2275, #2276
Hheylon: WINDOW *Strong's:* #2497
Hheypher: DUG.OUT.WELL *Strong's:* #2660
Hhideqel: RAPID *Strong's:* #2313
Hhirot: CISTERN~s *Strong's:* #6367
Hhiw: TOWN *Strong's:* #2340
Hhiyrah: NOBILITY *Strong's:* #2437
Hhor: PALE *Strong's:* #2752
Hhorev: PARCHING.HEAT *Strong's:* #2722
Hhor-Hagidgad: PARCHING.HEAT *Strong's:* #2735
Hhoriy: PALENESS *Strong's:* #2753
Hhovah: WITHDRAWING *Strong's:* #2327
Hhovav: CHERISH$^{(V)}$~ing$^{(ms)}$ *Strong's:* #2246
Hhul: SAND *Strong's:* #2343
Hhupham: SHORE~them$^{(m)}$ *Strong's:* #2349
Hhupim: SHORE~s *Strong's:* #2650
Hhur: PALE *Strong's:* #2354
Hhush: HASTY *Strong's:* #2366
Hhusham: HASTILY *Strong's:* #2367
Hhutsot: OUTSIDE~s *Strong's:* #7155
Hor: HILL *Strong's:* #2023
Hosheya: !$^{(ms)}$~make~RESCUE$^{(V)}$ *Strong's:* #1954
I'ezer: ISLAND + HELP *Strong's:* #0372, #0373
Irad: FLEET *Strong's:* #5897
Iyey-Ha'a'variym: PILE.OF.RUINS~s + the~OTHER.SIDE~s *Strong's:* #5863
Iyram: CITY~them$^{(m)}$ *Strong's:* #5902
Iytamar: ISLAND + DATE.PALM *Strong's:* #0385

Iy'yim: PILE.OF.RUINS~s *Strong's:* #5864
Kalahh: FULL.AGE *Strong's:* #3625
Kaleyv: DOG *Strong's:* #3612
Kalneh: FORTRESS.OF.ANU *Strong's:* #3641
Kaphtor: KNOB *Strong's:* #3731, #3732
Karmi: VINEYARD~me *Strong's:* #3756
Kasluhh: FORTIFIED *Strong's:* #3695
Kazbi: LIE~me *Strong's:* #3579
Kedarla'omer: FIGHTING + to~the~SHEAF *Strong's:* #3540
Kemosh: SUBDUER *Strong's:* #3645
Kena'an: LOWERED *Strong's:* #3667, #3669
Keran: LYRE *Strong's:* #3763
Kesed: INCREASING *Strong's:* #3777, #3778
Keziv: LIE *Strong's:* #3580
Kineret: HARP *Strong's:* #3672
Kislon: CONFIDENT.ONE *Strong's:* #3692
Kit: BRUISER *Strong's:* #3794
Kush: BLACKISH *Strong's:* #3568, #3569, #3571
La'eyl: to~MIGHTY.ONE *Strong's:* #3815
Lamekh: DESPAIRING *Strong's:* #3929
Lavan: WHITE *Strong's:* #3837
Le'ah: IMPATIENT *Strong's:* #3812
Lehav: GLIMMER *Strong's:* #3853
Lesha: CRACK.OPEN *Strong's:* #3962
Letush: SHARPENED *Strong's:* #3912
Le'um: COMMUNITY *Strong's:* #3817
Levanon: WHITE.ONE *Strong's:* #3844
Lewi: JOINING~me *Strong's:* #3878, #3881
Livnah: BRICK *Strong's:* #3841
Liyvniy: to~SON~my *Strong's:* #3845
Lot: TIGHTLY.WRAPPED *Strong's:* #3876
Lotan: WRAPPER *Strong's:* #3877
Lud: NATIVITY *Strong's:* #3865, #3866
Luz: HAZEL *Strong's:* #3870
Ma'akhah: FIRMLY.PRESSED *Strong's:* #4601
Madai: LONG.GARMENT~s~me *Strong's:* #4074
Magdi'eyl: PRECIOUS + MIGHTY.ONE *Strong's:* #4025
Magog: ROOFING *Strong's:* #4031
Mahalalel: SHINE + MIGHTY.ONE *Strong's:* #4111
Mahhalat: SICKENED *Strong's:* #4257, #4258
Mahhanayim: CAMP~s2 *Strong's:* #4266
Mahhlah: SICKNESS *Strong's:* #4244
Mahh'liy: SICKNESS~me *Strong's:* #4249
Mahn: SHARE *Strong's:* #4478
Makhi: BEING.LOW *Strong's:* #4352
Makhir: PRICE *Strong's:* #4353
Makhpelah: DOUBLED *Strong's:* #4375
Malki'el: KING~me + MIGHTY.ONE *Strong's:* #4439
Malkiy-Tsedeq: KING~me + STEADFAST *Strong's:* #4442
Mamre: FLAPPING.WING *Strong's:* #4471
Manahhat: OASIS *Strong's:* #4506
Maqheylot: GRASSLAND~s *Strong's:* #4722
Marah: BITTER *Strong's:* #4785
Masa: LOAD *Strong's:* #4854
Mash: DRAWN.OUT *Strong's:* #4851
Masreyqah: CHOICE.VINEYARD *Strong's:* #4957
Mas'sah: TRIAL *Strong's:* #4532
Matanah: CONTRIBUTION *Strong's:* #4980

Dictionary

Matreyd: CONTINUOUS *Strong's:* #4308
Medan: DISCORD *Strong's:* #4091
Meheytaveyl: FAVORED + MIGHTY.ONE *Strong's:* #4105
Mehhuya'el: BATTERING.RAM + MIGHTY.ONE *Strong's:* #4232
Menasheh: CAUSING.TO.OVERLOOK *Strong's:* #4519
Merari: BITTERNESS~me *Strong's:* #4847
Meriyvah: CONTENTION *Strong's:* #4809
Mesha: TUMULTUOUS *Strong's:* #4852
Meshek: ACQUIRING *Strong's:* #4902
Metusha'el: DEATH~him + he~did~ENQUIRE(V) *Strong's:* #4967
Metushelahh: DEATH~him + he~did~SEND(V) *Strong's:* #4968
Meydad: THROWING *Strong's:* #4312
Meydva: WATER + TOUGHNESS *Strong's:* #4311
Mey-Zahav: WATER~s2 + GOLD *Strong's:* #4314
Mid'yan: QUARREL *Strong's:* #4080
Migdal-Eyder: TOWER + DROVE *Strong's:* #4029
Migdol: TOWER *Strong's:* #4024
Mika'eyl: WHO + like~MIGHTY.ONE *Strong's:* #4317
Milkah: QUEEN *Strong's:* #4435
Mir'yam: BITTER + SEA *Strong's:* #4813
Mishma: HEARING *Strong's:* #4927
Mitqah: SWEETNESS *Strong's:* #4989
Mitspah: WATCHTOWER *Strong's:* #4708, #4709
Mits'rayim: STRAIT~s2 *Strong's:* #4713, #4714

Mivsam: SPICE.PLACE *Strong's:* #4017
Mivtsar: FORTIFICATION *Strong's:* #4014
Miysha'eyl: WHO + he~did~ENQUIRE(V) *Strong's:* #4332
Miz'zah: EXHAUSTED *Strong's:* #4199
Mo'av: THAT.ONE + FATHER *Strong's:* #4124
Molekh: REIGN(V)~ing(ms) *Strong's:* #4432
Moreh: THROW(V)~ing(ms) *Strong's:* #4176
Moriyah: THROW(V)~ing(ms)~me + EXISTING *Strong's:* #4179
Moseyrah: STRAP~s *Strong's:* #4149
Moseyrot: STRAP~s *Strong's:* #4149
Mosheh: PLUCKED.OUT *Strong's:* #4872
Mupim: SNAKE~s *Strong's:* #4649
Mushiy: MOVING~me *Strong's:* #4187
Na'amah: DELIGHTFUL *Strong's:* #5279
Na'aman: PLEASANTNESS *Strong's:* #5283
Nadav: he~did~OFFER.WILLINGLY(V) *Strong's:* #5070
Nahhali'eyl: WADI~of + MIGHTY.ONE *Strong's:* #5160
Nahhat: QUIETNESS *Strong's:* #5184
Nahhbi: WITHDRAWN *Strong's:* #5147
Nahhor: SNORTING *Strong's:* #5152
Nahhshon: PREDICTOR *Strong's:* #5177
Naphish: DEEP.BREATH *Strong's:* #5305
Naphtali: WRESTLING~me *Strong's:* #5321
Naphtuhh: DOORWAY *Strong's:* #5320

Nataneyl: >~GIVE(V) + MIGHTY.ONE *Strong's:* #5417
Nemu'eyl: SEA + MIGHTY.ONE *Strong's:* #5241
Nepheg: SPROUT.UP *Strong's:* #5298
Nephilim: make~FALL(V)~ing(mp) *Strong's:* #5303
Nevayot: FLOURISHED~s *Strong's:* #5032
Nevo: FLOURISHED~him *Strong's:* #5015
Nimrah: LEOPARD *Strong's:* #5247
Nimrod: REBELLING *Strong's:* #5248
Ninweh: ABODE.OF.NINUS *Strong's:* #5210
No'ah: STAGGERING *Strong's:* #5270
No'ahh: REST *Strong's:* #5146
Nod: NODDING *Strong's:* #5113
Nophahh: EXHALE(V)~ing(ms) *Strong's:* #5302
Novahh: BARK(V)~ing(ms) *Strong's:* #5025
Nun: CONTINUE *Strong's:* #5126
Og: BAKED.BREAD *Strong's:* #5747
Ohad: UNITED *Strong's:* #0161
Omar: MATTER *Strong's:* #0201
On: VIGOR *Strong's:* #0204
Onam: COMPLAINER *Strong's:* #0208
Onan: COMPLAINER *Strong's:* #0209
Ophir: REDUCED.TO.ASHES *Strong's:* #0211
Ovot: NECROMANCER~s *Strong's:* #0088
Padan: SUET *Strong's:* #6307
Padan-Aram: SUET + PALACE *Strong's:* #6307
Pagi'eyl: ENCOUNTER~of + MIGHTY.ONE *Strong's:* #6295
Palti: ESCAPING~me *Strong's:* #6406
Palti'eyl: ESCAPING~me + MIGHTY.ONE *Strong's:* #6409

Palu: PERFORMING *Strong's:* #6396
Paran: DECORATED *Strong's:* #6290
Parnakh: FRAGILE *Strong's:* #6535
Paroh: GREAT.HOUSE *Strong's:* #6547
Patros: SOUTHERN.REGION *Strong's:* #6624, #6625
Pa'u: SCREAMING *Strong's:* #6464
Pedah'eyl: RANSOMED + MIGHTY.ONE *Strong's:* #6300
Pedatsur: RANSOMED + BOULDER *Strong's:* #6301
Peleg: TRIBUTARY *Strong's:* #6389
Peleshet: WALLOWER *Strong's:* #6429, #6430
Pelet: SWIFTNESS *Strong's:* #6431
Peni'el: FACE~s + MIGHTY.ONE *Strong's:* #6439
Pe'or: OPENED.WIDE *Strong's:* #1187, #6465
Perat: FRUITFULNESS *Strong's:* #6578
Perets: BREACH *Strong's:* #6557
Perez: PEASANT *Strong's:* #6522
Pesahh: HOPPING *Strong's:* #6453
Petor: INTERPRETING *Strong's:* #6604
Pikhol: MOUTH + ALL *Strong's:* #6369
Pildash: FLAME.OF.FIRE *Strong's:* #6394
Pinon: AROUND.THE.CORNER *Strong's:* #6373
Pisgah: CLEFT *Strong's:* #6449
Pishon: SCATTERED *Strong's:* #6376
Pitom: CITY.OF.JUSTICE *Strong's:* #6619
Piy-Hahhiyrot: MOUTH + the~CISTERN~s *Strong's:* #6367
Piynhhas: MOUTH + SERPENT *Strong's:* #6372
Potee-Phera: BELONGING~of + LONG.HAIR *Strong's:* #6319
Potiphar: BELONGING~of + BULL *Strong's:* #6318

Dictionary

Pu'a: BLOWN *Strong's:* #6312
Pu'ah: SPLENDID *Strong's:* #6326
Pun: DISTRACTED *Strong's:* #6325
Punon: DISTRACTED.ONE *Strong's:* #6325
Put: BELONGING *Strong's:* #6316
Putiy'eyl: BELONGING~of + MIGHTY.ONE *Strong's:* #6317
Qadesh: PROSTITUTE *Strong's:* #6946
Qadmon: EASTERN *Strong's:* #6935
Qayin: SPEARHEAD *Strong's:* #7014, #7017, #8423
Qedar: GRAY *Strong's:* #6938
Qedeymot: PAST.TIME~s *Strong's:* #6932
Qedmah: PAST.TIME *Strong's:* #6929
Qehat: ALLIED *Strong's:* #6955
Qe'hey'latah: ASSEMBLY~her *Strong's:* #6954
Qemu'el: !$^{(ms)}$~RISE$^{(V)}$ + MIGHTY.ONE *Strong's:* #7055
Qenat: PURCHASED *Strong's:* #7079
Qenaz: STALKER *Strong's:* #7073, #7074
Qeturah: BURN.INCENSE$^{(V)}$~ed$^{(fs)}$ *Strong's:* #6989
Qeynan: NESTING *Strong's:* #7018
Qiryat-Arba: WALL + FOUR *Strong's:* #7153
Qiryatayim: METROPOLIS~s2 *Strong's:* #7156
Qivrot-Hata'awah: GRAVE~s + the~YEARNING *Strong's:* #6914
Qorahh: BALDING *Strong's:* #7141
Rahhel: EWE *Strong's:* #7354
Ramah: MANE.OF.A.HORSE *Strong's:* #7484
Ra'meses: CHILD.OF.THE.SUN *Strong's:* #7486
Ramot: CORAL~s *Strong's:* #7216
Rapha: DEAD *Strong's:* #7497
Raphu: HEAL$^{(V)}$~ed$^{(ms)}$ *Strong's:* #7505

Ravah: ABUNDANT *Strong's:* #7237
Rehhov: STREET *Strong's:* #7340
Rehhovot: STREET~s *Strong's:* #7344
Rehhovot-Ghir: STREET~s + CITY *Strong's:* #7344, #5892
Rephiydiym: PILLAR.BASE *Strong's:* #7508
Reqem: EMBROIDERY *Strong's:* #7552
Resen: HALTER *Strong's:* #7449
Re'u: COMPANION *Strong's:* #7466
Re'u'eyl: COMPANION + MIGHTY.ONE *Strong's:* #7467
Re'umah: ELEVATED *Strong's:* #7208
Re'uven: !$^{(ms)}$~SEE$^{(V)}$ + SON *Strong's:* #7205
Reva: QUARTER *Strong's:* #7254
Rimon-Perets: OVERTHROWN *Strong's:* #7428
Riphat: SPOKEN *Strong's:* #7384
Risah: OVERTHROWN *Strong's:* #7446
Ritmah: JUNIPER *Strong's:* #7575
Rivlah: FRUITFUL *Strong's:* #7247
Rivqah: FATTENING *Strong's:* #7259
Rosh: HEAD *Strong's:* #7220
Salkah: MIGRATION *Strong's:* #5548
Salu: COMPARE$^{(V)}$~ed$^{(ms)}$ *Strong's:* #5543
Samlah: APPAREL *Strong's:* #8072
Sarah: NOBLEWOMAN *Strong's:* #8297
Sarai: RULER~s~me *Strong's:* #8283
Savtah: GO.ABOUT *Strong's:* #5454
Savtekha: BEATING *Strong's:* #5455
Sedom: SCORCHING *Strong's:* #5467
Se'iyr: HAIRY.GOAT *Strong's:* #8165
Senir: SNOW.MOUNTAIN *Strong's:* #8149
Sephar: SCROLL *Strong's:* #5611
Serahh: OVERHANG *Strong's:* #8294

Sered: BRAIDED.WORK *Strong's:* #5624
Serug: TWIG *Strong's:* #8286
Setur: HIDE$^{(V)}$~ed$^{(ms)}$ *Strong's:* #5639
Seva: DRUNKARD *Strong's:* #5434
Sevam: BALSAM *Strong's:* #7643
Shaddai: BREAST~s~me *Strong's:* #7706
Shalem: OFFERING.OF.RESTITUTION *Strong's:* #8004
Sham'mah: DESOLATE *Strong's:* #8048
Shamu'a: HEAR$^{(V)}$~ed$^{(ms)}$ *Strong's:* #8051
Shaphat: he~did~DECIDE$^{(V)}$ *Strong's:* #8202
Shapher: BRIGHT *Strong's:* #8234
Shaphtan: JUDICIAL *Strong's:* #8204
Sha'ul: ENQUIRE$^{(V)}$~ed$^{(ms)}$ *Strong's:* #7586
Shaweh: EQUAL *Strong's:* #7740
Shaweh-Qiryatayim: EQUAL~s + WALL~s *Strong's:* #7741
Shedeyur: BREAST~s + LIGHT$^{(V)}$ *Strong's:* #7707
Shekhem: SHOULDER *Strong's:* #7927, #7928
Shelahh: PROJECTILE *Strong's:* #7974
Sheleph: PULLED.OUT *Strong's:* #8026
Shelomiy: COMPLETENESS~me *Strong's:* #8015
Shelumi'eyl: COMPLETENESS~of + MIGHTY.ONE *Strong's:* #8017
Shem: TITLE *Strong's:* #8035
Shemever: TITLE + LONG.WINGED *Strong's:* #8038
Shemida: TITLE~me + OPINION *Strong's:* #8061, #8062
Shemu'eyl: TITLE~him + MIGHTY.ONE *Strong's:* #8050
Shepham: SCRAPED.BARE *Strong's:* #8221
Shepho: BARE.PLACE *Strong's:* #8195
Sheshupham: ADDER *Strong's:* #7781, 8197
Shet: BUTTOCKS *Strong's:* #8352
Sheva: SEVEN *Strong's:* #7614
Sheylah: REQUEST *Strong's:* #7956
Sheyshai: LINEN~s~me *Strong's:* #8344
Shilem: RECOMPENSE *Strong's:* #8006
Shimon: HEARER *Strong's:* #8095
Shimron: GUARD *Strong's:* #8110
Shinar: COUNTRY.OF.TWO.RIVERS *Strong's:* #8152
Shinav: TOOTH + FATHER *Strong's:* #8134
Shiphrah: BRIGHTNESS *Strong's:* #8236
Shitiym: ACACIA~s *Strong's:* #7851
Shivah: SEVENFOLD *Strong's:* #7656
Shiymiy: REPORT~me *Strong's:* #8096
Sh'lomiyt: OFFERING.OF.RESTITUTION~of *Strong's:* #8019
Shoval: UPPER.LEG *Strong's:* #7732
Shu'a: SHOUTING.OUT *Strong's:* #7770
Shu'ahh: SINKING *Strong's:* #7744
Shuhham: PIT.DIGGER *Strong's:* #7748, #7749
Shuni: FORTUNATE~of *Strong's:* #7764
Shur: ROCK.WALL *Strong's:* #7793
Shutelahh: SET.DOWN$^{(V)}$~ed$^{(ms)}$ + MOIST *Strong's:* #7803, #8364
Sidim: FIELD~s *Strong's:* #7708
Sihhon: MEDITATING.ONE *Strong's:* #5511
Sin: SHARP.THORN *Strong's:* #5513
Sinai: SHARP.THORN~s~me *Strong's:* #5514
Si'on: HIGH.ONE *Strong's:* #7865
Siryon: HARNESS *Strong's:* #8303

Dictionary

Sitnah: OPPOSITION *Strong's:* #7856
Sitriy: PROTECTION~me *Strong's:* #5644
Sodi: CONFIDENCE~me *Strong's:* #5476
Suk'kot: BOOTH~s *Strong's:* #5523
Suphah: WHIRLWIND *Strong's:* #5492
Susiy: HORSE~s *Strong's:* #5485
Tahhan: CAMPSITE *Strong's:* #8465, #8470
Tahhash: DEER *Strong's:* #8477
Tahhat: UNDER *Strong's:* #8480
Talmai: FURROW~s~me *Strong's:* #8526
Tamar: DATE.PALM *Strong's:* #8559
Tarshish: TOPAZ *Strong's:* #8659
Taveyrah: KINDLED *Strong's:* #8404
Terahh: STATIONED *Strong's:* #8646
Tevahh: SLAUGHTERING *Strong's:* #2875
Teyma: DESERT.REGION *Strong's:* #8485
Teyman: SOUTHWARD *Strong's:* #8487, #8489
Tidal: YOKE.BREAKER *Strong's:* #8413
Timna: WITHHOLDING *Strong's:* #8555
Timnat: SOUTHWARD *Strong's:* #8553
Tiras: DESIRABLE *Strong's:* #8494
Tirtsah: you$^{(ms)}$~will~ACCEPT$^{(V)}$ *Strong's:* #8656
Togarmah: you$^{(ms)}$~will~GNAW$^{(V)}$~her *Strong's:* #8425
Tola: KERMES *Strong's:* #8439
Tophel: UNSEASONED *Strong's:* #8603
Tsalmonah: IMAGING *Strong's:* #6758
Tsaphnat-Paneyahh: TREASURY + GLORIOUS.REST *Strong's:* #6847
Tsaphon: NORTH *Strong's:* #6827
Tsedad: MOUNTAINSIDE *Strong's:* #6657
Tselaph'hhad: SHADOW + AWE *Strong's:* #6765
Tsemar: WOOL *Strong's:* #6786
Tsepho: WATCHMAN~him *Strong's:* #6825
Tseviim: GAZELLE~s *Strong's:* #6636
Tsidon: HUNTING *Strong's:* #6721
Tsilah: SHADOW *Strong's:* #6741
Tsin: FLOCKS *Strong's:* #6790
Tsiphyon: WATCHER *Strong's:* #6837
Tsipor: BIRD *Strong's:* #6834
Tsiporah: BIRD *Strong's:* #6855
Tsiv'on: SPLASHED *Strong's:* #6649
Tso'an: REMOVED *Strong's:* #6814
Tso'ar: TINY *Strong's:* #6820, #6686
Tsohhar: REDDISH.GRAY *Strong's:* #6714
Tsophim: KEEP.WATCH$^{(V)}$~ed$^{(mp)}$ *Strong's:* #6839
Tsur: BOULDER *Strong's:* #6701
Tsuri'eyl: BOULDER~me + MIGHTY.ONE *Strong's:* #6700
Tsurishaddai: BOULDER~me + BREAST~s~me *Strong's:* #6701
Tumiym: FULL.STRENGTH~s *Strong's:* #8550
Tuval: you$^{(ms)}$~will~BRING$^{(V)}$ *Strong's:* #8422
Tuval-Qayin: you$^{(ms)}$~will~BRING$^{(V)}$ + SPEARHEAD *Strong's:* #8423
Ur: LIGHT *Strong's:* #0218
Uriy: LIGHT~me *Strong's:* #0221
Uriym: LIGHT~s *Strong's:* #0224
Uts: PLAN *Strong's:* #5780
Uval: ROUNDED *Strong's:* #5745
Uzal: I~will~BE.LAVISH$^{(V)}$~ed$^{(ms)}$ *Strong's:* #0187
Uziy'eyl: BOLDNESS~me + MIGHTY.ONE *Strong's:* #5816
Waheyv: and~GIFT.OFFERING *Strong's:* #2052

Waphsi: and~WRIST~me *Strong's:* #2058
Ya'aqov: he~will~RESTRAIN^(V) *Strong's:* #3290
Yaboq: he~will~EMPTY.OUT^(V) *Strong's:* #2999
Yagbahah: he~will~BE.HIGH^(V)~her *Strong's:* #3011
Yagli: he~will~REMOVE.THE.COVER^(V) *Strong's:* #3020
Yah: EXISTING *Strong's:* #3050
Yahats: STAMPED.DOWN *Strong's:* #3096
Yahh'le'el: he~will~STAY^(V) + MIGHTY.ONE *Strong's:* #3177, #3178
Yahhtse'el: he~will~DIVIDE^(V) + MIGHTY.ONE *Strong's:* #3183
Ya'ir: he~will~make~LIGHT^(V) *Strong's:* #2971
Yakhin: he~will~PREPARE^(V) *Strong's:* #3199
Yalam: he~will~BE.OUT.OF.SIGHT^(V) *Strong's:* #3281
Yamin: RIGHT.HAND *Strong's:* #3226
Yaphet: WONDER *Strong's:* #3315
Yaq'shan: SNARER *Strong's:* #3370
Yaqtan: he~will~BE.SMALL^(V) *Strong's:* #3355
Yarden: DESCENDER *Strong's:* #3383
Yared: he~will~GO.DOWN^(V) *Strong's:* #3382
Yashuv: he~will~TURN.BACK^(V) *Strong's:* #3437
Yatvatah: WELLNESS~her *Strong's:* #3193
Yaval: WATERCOURSE *Strong's:* #2989
Yawan: MIRE *Strong's:* #3120
Yazeyr: he~will~HELP^(V) *Strong's:* #3270

Yegar-Sa'haduta: AFRAID + RECORD *Strong's:* #3026
Yehoshu'a: EXISTING + he~will~RESCUE^(V) *Strong's:* #3091
Yehudah: THANKSGIVING *Strong's:* #3063
Yehudit: THANKSGIVING *Strong's:* #3067
Ye'ish: he~will~MAKE.HASTE^(V) *Strong's:* #3274
Yemu'el: DAY + MIGHTY.ONE *Strong's:* #3223
Yephunah: he~will~be~TURN^(V) *Strong's:* #3312
Yerahh: MOON *Strong's:* #3392
Ye'rey'hho: MOON~him *Strong's:* #3405
Yeshurun: STRAIGHT.ONE *Strong's:* #3484
Yeter: REMAINDER *Strong's:* #3500
Yetet: NAIL *Strong's:* #3509
Yetser: THOUGHT *Strong's:* #3337
Yetur: he~will~ROW^(V) *Strong's:* #3195
Yevus: he~will~TRAMPLE.DOWN^(V) *Strong's:* #2982, #2983
YHWH: he~will~BE^(V) *Strong's:* #3068
YHWH-Nisiy: he~will~BE^(V) + STANDARD~me *Strong's:* #3071
YHWH-Yireh: he~will~BE^(V) + he~will~SEE^(V) *Strong's:* #3070
Yidlap: he~will~DRIP^(V) *Strong's:* #3044
Yigal: he~will~REDEEM^(V) *Strong's:* #3008
Yimnah: he~will~RECKON^(V) *Strong's:* #3232
Yish'baq: he~will~BE.LET.ALONE^(V) *Strong's:* #3435
Yishma'el: he~will~HEAR^(V) + MIGHTY.ONE *Strong's:* #3458
Yishwah: he~will~EQUATE^(V) *Strong's:* #3438

Dictionary

Yishwiy: he~will~EQUATE⁽ⱽ⁾~me *Strong's:* #3440, #3441
Yiskah: he~will~LOOK.FORTH *Strong's:* #3252
Yisra'eyl: he~will~TURN.ASIDE⁽ⱽ⁾ + MIGHTY.ONE *Strong's:* #3478
Yis'sas'khar: THERE.IS + WAGE *Strong's:* #3485
Yitran: RESERVER *Strong's:* #3506
Yitro: REMAINDER~him *Strong's:* #3503
Yits'har: he~will~PRESS.OUT.OIL⁽ⱽ⁾ *Strong's:* #3324
Yits'hhaq: he~will~LAUGH⁽ⱽ⁾ *Strong's:* #3327
Yokheved: EXISTING + HEAVY *Strong's:* #3115
Yoseph: ADD⁽ⱽ⁾~ing⁽ᵐˢ⁾ *Strong's:* #3130
Yov: HOWLING *Strong's:* #3102
Yovav: HOWL⁽ⱽ⁾~ing⁽ᵐˢ⁾ *Strong's:* #3103
Yuval: CREEK *Strong's:* #3106
Za'awan: TROUBLED *Strong's:* #2190
Zakur: REMEMBER⁽ⱽ⁾~ed⁽ᵐˢ⁾ *Strong's:* #2139
Zamzum: MISCHIEVOUS *Strong's:* #2157
Zerahh: RISING.SUN *Strong's:* #2226, #2227
Zered: EXUBERANT *Strong's:* #2218
Zevulun: RESIDENT *Strong's:* #2074
Zikh'riy: MEMORY~me *Strong's:* #2147
Zilpah: TRICKLING *Strong's:* #2153
Zimran: MUSICIAN *Strong's:* #2175
Zimri: SINGER~me *Strong's:* #2174
Ziphron: FRAGRANT.ONE *Strong's:* #2202
Zuz: ENTRYWAY *Strong's:* #2104

Benner's Mechanical Translation of the Torah

Lexicon Cross References

The numbers following each word from this translation is the corresponding number in *Benner's Lexicon of Biblical Hebrew*.

ABDOMEN: 2091
ABHOR: 4658
ABIDE: 2250
ABODE: 2251
ABOUNDING: 4475
ABUNDANCE: 3807
ABUNDANT: 3783
ACACIA: 4261
ACCEPT: 4063
ACCUMULATE: 3980
ACQUIRED: 3653
ACQUISITION: 2176
ACQUIT: 2369
ADD: 2635
ADDER: 4461
ADHERE: 379
ADMINISTRATION: 1683
ADMINISTRATOR: 1684
ADORATION: 890
ADORN: 1682
ADVANCE: 2992
AFFECTION: 866
AFFLICT: 4728
AFFLICTION: 4729
AFTER: 1388
AFTER.GROWTH: 3051
AGATE: 4160
AGE: 1695
AGITATION: 1008
AGONY: 1198
AGREE: 145
AH: 13
ALL: 1657
ALL.AROUND: 2447
ALMOND: 4454
ALOE: 898
ALONE: 159
ALONGSIDE: 2841
ALSO: 583
ALTAR: 221
AMBER: 4946
AMBUSH: 3355

AMBUSH: 3795
AMETHYST: 1207
AMMAH: 62
AMPLIFY: 687
ANGER: 2896
ANNOUNCE: 153
ANNOUNCER: 154
ANNOYANCE: 3622
ANSWER: 2872
ANTELOPE: 852
ANYTHING: 2056
APART.FROM: 4947
APPAREL: 2582
APPEARANCE: 3779
APPOINT: 2739
APPOINTED: 2740
APPOINTED.TIME: 2983
APPROACH: 87
ARCH: 459
AREA: 3636
ARM: 1051
ARM.BAND: 1671
ARM.FOR.BATTLE: 2168
ARMAMENT: 1578
ARMLET: 3460
ARMY: 3333
AROMA: 3920
AROMATIC.SPICE: 2569
ARRANGE: 841
ARRANGEMENT: 842
ARRIVE: 144
ARROGANCE: 945
ARROW: 1348
ASCENSION.OFFERING: 2797
ASCENT: 2794
ASH: 3197
ASP: 3306
ASSEMBLE: 3623
ASSEMBLY: 3624
ASSIGN: 1417
ASSIGNED: 1418

ASTONISHMENT: 4630
ASYLUM: 1873
AT: 143
AT.THAT.TIME: 26
AT.THIS.POINT: 902
ATONEMENT: 1346
ATTACH: 1427
ATTACK: 5
ATTACK.THE.REAR: 1002
AUNT: 695
AVENGE: 3643
AWAKE: 3691
AWE: 362
AWL: 4079
AX: 648
BABIES: 1508
BACK: 1387
BACK.OF.THE.NECK: 3493
BACKWARD: 1392
BAG: 1725
BAKE: 95
BAKED: 96
BAKED.BREAD: 2728
BALANCE: 995
BALD: 3738
BALD.SPOT: 3739
BALM: 3486
BAND: 492
BAND.TOGETHER: 491
BANKS: 4222
BANNER: 576
BANQUET: 4572
BAR: 2019
BARE.PLACE: 4460
BARE.SPOT: 472
BARLEY: 4757
BARN: 2571
BARREN: 2959
BARRENNESS: 22
BARTER: 2969
BASE: 1675
BASIN: 2619

397

Lexicon Cross References

BASTARD: 1055
BAT: 4987
BATHE: 3935
BATTLE: 1282
BE: 881
BE.A.HARLOT: 996
BE.ABLE: 1659
BE.ABUNDANT: 2935
BE.AFRAID: 642
BE.ALMOND.SHAPED: 4453
BE.AMAZED: 1104
BE.AN.IN-LAW: 1455
BE.ANGRY: 2895
BE.ASHAMED: 435
BE.BITTER: 2115
BE.BOLD: 2747
BE.BRIGHT: 3155
BE.CHILDLESS: 4277
BE.CLEAN: 1517
BE.CRAFTY: 1665
BE.DELIGHTFUL: 2843
BE.DIRTY: 1493
BE.DISTINCT: 3097
BE.DOUBLE: 4626
BE.DRUNK: 4545
BE.DYSFUNCTIONAL: 4140
BE.EMINENT: 807
BE.FACE.TO.FACE: 2217
BE.FAR: 3975
BE.FILTHY: 1305
BE.FIRSTBORN: 209
BE.FRUITFUL: 3203
BE.GUILTY: 4365
BE.HARD: 3755
BE.HEAVY: 1575
BE.HUNGRY: 4148
BE.IMPATIENT: 1834
BE.IN.MISERY: 1571
BE.LESS: 3597
BE.LOW: 2027
BE.NUMB: 3000
BE.OLD: 1691
BE.OUT.OF.SIGHT: 2821
BE.OVERSHADOWED: 3398
BE.RED: 744
BE.RICH: 133
BE.SAD: 1012
BE.SATISFIED: 2456
BE.SHATTERED: 1448

BE.SICK: 1192
BE.SILENT: 741
BE.SKILLED: 1250
BE.SMALL: 3604
BE.SOFT: 3959
BE.SOUR: 1263
BE.SQUARE: 3826
BE.STEADFAST: 3362
BE.STRAIGHT: 4525
BE.STRANGE: 1037
BE.STRONG: 2095
BE.STUBBORN: 2660
BE.SUPERFLUOUS: 2695
BE.TERRIFIED: 4071
BE.THICK: 4702
BE.THREEFOLD: 4345
BE.UNMINDFUL: 4227
BE.WARM: 1244
BE.WHOLE: 4624
BE.ZEALOUS: 3656
BEARD: 1692
BEARDED.VULTURE: 3244
BEAST: 304
BEAT: 2865
BEAT.OUT: 794
BEAT.SMALL: 800
BEATEN.GRAIN: 655
BEATEN.WORK: 3758
BEAUTIFUL: 1560
BEAUTY: 1289
BED: 2275
BEE: 828
BEFORE: 1526
BEHEAD: 2976
BELITTLE: 3620
BELL: 2867
BELLY: 537
BEND.DOWN: 4235
BEND.THE.KNEE: 411
BENEATH: 2278
BENEFIT: 2528
BEQA: 3174
BESIDE: 3402
BEST: 1469
BETROTH: 4115
BETWEEN: 324
BIND: 3574
BIND.UP: 1902
BINDER: 1429
BIRD: 3263

BIRD.OF.PREY: 2759
BIRTH: 4537
BIRTHED: 1832
BIRTHING: 1833
BIRTHRIGHT: 213
BITE: 2414
BITTER: 2112
BITTER.HERBS: 2120
BLACK: 1242
BLANKET: 1328
BLAST: 795
BLASTING: 796
BLAZE: 1866
BLAZING: 1867
BLEMISH: 2055
BLIND: 4747
BLIND: 4748
BLINDNESS: 4749
BLOOD: 740
BLOOM: 3466
BLOSSOM: 3467
BLOW: 2417
BLOW.AWAY: 3028
BLUE: 1629
BOARD: 3747
BOARDED.UP: 2643
BODY: 518
BOIL: 974
BOILED: 975
BOILING.POT: 4245
BOILS: 4233
BOLDNESS: 2748
BOND: 2665
BONDWOMAN: 60
BONE: 2936
BONNET: 3199
BOOTH: 2513
BOOTY: 1971
BORDER: 566
BORE.OUT: 2192
BORE.THROUGH: 4078
BORN: 1831
BOSOM: 1065
BOTTOM: 5010
BOTTOM.BASE: 2478
BOUGH: 2344
BOULDER: 3499
BOUND: 564
BOUND.SHEAF: 1904
BOUND.UP: 3577

BOUNDARY: 568
BOUNTY: 2195
BOVINE: 57
BOW: 3749
BOW.THE.HEAD: 3559
BOWELS: 1285
BOWL: 476
BOX: 110
BOY: 1827
BRACELET: 2024
BRAID: 3840
BRAIDED.WORK: 2685
BRAMBLE: 3688
BRANCH: 2017
BRASS: 1443
BRAVERY: 422
BRAWN: 2939
BREACH: 3250
BREAD: 1280
BREAD.MEAL: 2975
BREAK: 3195
BREAK.DOWN: 2429
BREAK.OUT: 3249
BREAST: 4218
BREASTPLATE: 1426
BREATH: 4380
BREATHE.DEEPLY: 3278
BRIBE: 1126
BRICK: 328
BRIDE.PRICE: 2134
BRIGHT: 4478
BRIGHT.SPOT: 396
BRIMSTONE: 3217
BRING.FORTH: 1826
BROKEN: 720
BROODING: 677
BROTHER: 28
BROTHER-IN-LAW: 307
BROUGHT.OUT: 662
BUCK: 49
BUCKET: 734
BUD: 3234
BUDDING: 4950
BUILD: 318
BUILD.UP: 2544
BULK: 2911
BULL: 3193
BULLOCK: 581
BULRUSH: 588
BUNCH: 493

BUNDLE: 2860
BURDEN: 295
BURIAL.PLACE: 3554
BURN: 352
BURN.BLACK: 1274
BURN.INCENSE: 3608
BURNING: 354
BURNING.FLAME: 1379
BURST.OUT: 3233
BURSTING: 3224
BURY: 3552
BUSINESS: 1876
BUT: 1840
BUTCHER: 222
BUTTRESS: 3703
BY: 2852
CALAMITY: 12
CALCULATE: 1667
CALL.OUT: 3719
CAMEL: 590
CAMP: 1298
CAMP: 1299
CAPTAIN: 2323
CAPTIVE: 4168
CAPTIVITY: 4167
CAPTURE: 4166
CARAVAN: 3914
CARCASS: 289
CARNELIAN: 748
CARRY: 293
CART: 577
CARTILAGE: 652
CARVE: 1359
CASSIA: 3701
CAST.AWAY: 612
CAST.DOWN: 4017
CAST.IMAGE: 3480
CAST.OFF: 4315
CAST.OUT: 661
CATARACT: 255
CATTLE: 3209
CAULDRON: 1767
CAVE: 1756
CEASE: 4200
CEASING: 4201
CEDAR: 3903
CENTER: 1349
CEREAL: 684
CHAIN: 4503
CHAMBER: 1114

CHAMELEON: 1612
CHANGE: 4410
CHARGE: 2611
CHARIOT: 3943
CHEESE: 1246
CHERISH: 1058
CHERISHED: 696
CHEST: 1138
CHESTNUT: 4768
CHEW: 629
CHICK: 3235
CHIEF: 58
CHILD: 1825
CHIMNEY: 3799
CHOICE.FRUIT: 2396
CHOICE.VINE: 2699
CHOOSE: 203
CHOSEN: 207
CINNAMON: 3665
CIRCUIT: 3671
CIRCUMCISION: 2050
CISTERN: 392
CITY: 4752
CLAN: 3058
CLASP: 2646
CLAY: 4068
CLEAN: 1519
CLEANLINESS: 1520
CLEANSING: 1518
CLEAVE: 3242
CLEAVE.OPEN: 3173
CLIFF: 2562
CLING: 3019
CLOAK: 2802
CLOSE: 3680
CLOTHING: 444
CLOUD: 4727
CLUSTER: 4280
COAL: 4542
COAT: 2704
COHABITATION: 2874
COLD: 3715
COLLAR: 1395
COLLECT: 3751
COLLECTION: 3578
COLT: 4754
COME: 149
COME.NEAR: 3816
COME.TO.AN.END: 3150
COME.UP: 3924

Lexicon Cross References

COMFORT: 2270
COMMIT: 2682
COMMIT.ADULTERY: 102
COMMUNITY: 1912
COMPANION: 4027
COMPANY: 2732
COMPASSIONATE: 1287
COMPEL: 105
COMPLAIN: 86
COMPLETENESS: 4337
COMPLETION: 1625
COMPOUND: 3586
CONCEAL: 3463
CONCEIVE: 922
CONCERNING: 10
CONCLUSION: 3681
CONCUBINE: 4995
CONFERENCE: 2943
CONFIDENCE: 2475
CONFIDENT: 1729
CONFUSE: 905
CONFUSION: 4586
CONJURE: 2870
CONSENT: 178
CONSEQUENCE: 2772
CONSIDERED.UNCIRCUMCI
   SED: 4762
CONSISTENCY: 4643
CONSORT: 1224
CONSUME: 2631
CONSUMING: 1654
CONSUMPTION: 4251
CONTENTION: 3811
CONTINUALLY: 1996
CONTRARY: 3717
CONTRIBUTION: 4651
CONVERT: 2137
COOKED: 97
COPPER: 1442
COPULATE: 4316
COPULATION: 4206
CORD: 4619
CORIANDER: 490
CORMORANT: 4333
CORNER: 3146
CORNER.POST: 3704
CORPSE: 3007
CORRECT: 2676
CORRUPTION: 4255
COUCH: 3439

COUNSEL: 2918
COUNT: 2648
COUPLE: 1076
COUPLE: 1077
COUPLING: 1082
COURAGEOUS: 424
COURTYARD: 1367
COVENANT: 401
COVER: 1341
COVER.OVER: 1719
COVERED: 3326
COVERING: 1345
COW: 3194
CRACK: 3265
CRAFTINESS: 1666
CRAFTSMAN: 1235
CRASH: 4153
CRAVE: 1255
CRAVING: 1737
CRAWL: 1201
CREMATE: 4053
CREMATING: 4055
CROCODILE: 4639
CROOKED: 4744
CROP: 3782
CROP.OFF: 3607
CROPLAND: 4220
CROSS.OVER: 425
CROSSING: 428
CRUCIBLE: 1764
CRUEL: 1608
CRUMBLE: 3294
CRUMBLED: 2147
CRUSH: 4058
CRY: 3384
CRY.OUT: 3383
CUCUMBER: 3753
CUD: 621
CUP: 1723
CUPPED.HAND: 1336
CURDLE: 3669
CURTAIN: 4039
CUSTODY: 2610
CUSTOM: 1373
CUT: 3694
CUT.DOWN: 504
CUT.IN.TWO: 235
CUT.OFF: 2053
CUT.PIECE: 236
CUT.SHARPLY: 1226

DAMAGE: 4253
DAMAGING: 4256
DANCE: 1199
DARK: 4240
DARKEN: 4239
DARKNESS: 4243
DASH.TO.PIECES: 4075
DATE.PALM: 2157
DAUB: 2479
DAUGHTER: 310
DAUGHTER-IN-LAW: 1633
DAWN: 4540
DAY: 1551
DAYTIME: 1552
DEAL.DECEITFULLY: 4609
DEAL.FALSELY: 4553
DEATH: 2180
DECEIT: 3986
DECEIVE: 2402
DECIDE: 3060
DECISION: 3063
DECLARE: 1128
DECLARE: 2305
DECORATE: 3198
DECORATION: 3201
DECORATIVE.BAND: 4178
DEDICATE: 2253
DEDICATED: 2255
DEDICATION: 2254
DEEP.BLACK: 124
DEEP.WATER: 910
DEER: 4600
DEFEAT: 1220
DEFIANCE: 2191
DEFORM: 1872
DELAY: 1382
DELICACY: 1505
DELIGHT: 1339
DELIVER: 3415
DELIVER.UP: 603
DENY: 1615
DEPART: 4442
DEPART.EARLY: 4281
DEPOSIT: 2265
DEPOSIT: 2266
DEPOSITED: 3184
DEPRESSION: 1753
DEPTH: 3414
DERISION: 4399
DESERT: 4760

DESIRE: 18
DESOLATE: 4362
DESOLATE: 4363
DESOLATE.WILDERNESS: 4373
DESPISE: 190
DESTROY: 4382
DESTRUCTION: 3600
DETEST: 3712
DEVOTE: 1171
DEVOTION: 1173
DEVOUR: 2554
DEW: 1484
DIE: 2179
DIG: 1762
DIG.OUT: 1747
DIM: 1596
DIMINISH: 1321
DIMNESS: 1597
DIP: 284
DIRECT: 3370
DIRECTIVE: 3371
DIRT: 3220
DIRTY: 1494
DISCERNMENT: 784
DISCHARGE: 935
DISCIPLINE: 2678
DISDAIN: 187
DISEASE: 704
DISGRACE: 1420
DISGUSTING: 4659
DISLOCATE: 3667
DISMAY: 264
DISOBEY: 2135
DISPERSE: 1033
DISPUTE: 3809
DISPUTE: 3810
DISSOLVE: 1987
DISTANCE: 3978
DISTANT: 2824
DISTRESS: 2924
DISTRESSING.PAIN: 2925
DISTRIBUTE: 1952
DISTRIBUTION: 1953
DISTURB: 2769
DIVE: 699
DIVERSE.KIND: 1649
DIVIDE: 1354
DIVIDE.APART: 3226
DIVIDE.INTO.PIECES: 4594

DIVIDED.PART: 533
DIVINATION: 2587
DIVINE: 2586
DIVORCE: 3696
DO: 2893
DO.NOT: 1802
DO.SORCERY: 4471
DO.THE.MARRIAGE.DUTY: 306
DO.WELL: 1468
DOE: 50
DOG: 1662
DONATION: 3821
DONKEY: 1270
DOOR: 729
DOORPOST: 955
DOUBLE: 4413
DOUBLE.OVER: 3102
DOUGH: 341
DOVE: 1554
DOWRY: 937
DRAIN: 2102
DRAW: 2173
DRAW.AWAY: 2430
DRAW.NEAR: 669
DRAW.OUT: 4094
DRAW.UP: 732
DRAW.WATER: 4164
DREAD: 1446
DREAM: 1204
DREAM: 1206
DRIED.OUT: 1406
DRILL: 1185
DRILLED: 1186
DRINK: 4490
DRINKING: 4492
DRIVE: 2201
DRIVE.OUT: 2237
DROP: 665
DROP.DOWN: 2426
DROVE: 839
DROWN: 4259
DRY: 440
DRY: 3626
DRY.GROUND: 441
DRY.LAND: 442
DRY.OUT: 439
DRY.UP: 1404
DULL.RED: 1170
DUNG: 3285

DUST: 374
DUST.CLOUD: 4258
DWELL: 2539
DWELLER: 2540
DWELLING: 2541
DYSFUNCTIONAL: 4139
EAGLE: 2422
EAR: 994
EAR.OF.GRAIN: 302
EARED.OWL: 2419
EARRING: 579
EARTHENWARE: 1769
EAST: 764
EAST.WIND: 765
EASTWARD: 766
EAT: 1639
EDGE: 2997
EDGING: 565
EGG: 370
EIGHT: 4387
EIGHTH: 4389
ELEVATION: 2440
EMBER: 1200
EMBRACE: 1074
EMBROIDER: 4103
EMERALD: 414
EMINENT: 809
EMPIRE: 1887
EMPTINESS: 4102
EMPTY: 4101
ENCIRCLE: 3673
ENCOMPASS: 2889
ENCOUNTER: 3008
END: 1384
ENDOW: 936
ENGRAVE: 1236
ENGRAVER: 1231
ENGRAVING: 1234
ENGRAVING.TOOL: 1221
ENRAGE: 1010
ENSNARE: 3764
ENTANGLED: 245
ENTIRELY: 1634
ENTRANCE: 150
ENTWINE: 4618
ENVELOP: 2761
ENWRAP: 2754
EPHOD: 3012
EPIDEMIC: 826
ERR: 4209

Lexicon Cross References

ERROR: 4210
ERUPTION: 2431
ESCAPED: 3120
ESTIMATE: 1716
EUNUCH: 2694
EVENING: 4759
EVENT: 3724
EVIDENCE: 2733
EWE: 3934
EXAMINE: 1776
EXCEED: 2481
EXCEPT: 282
EXCHANGE: 297
EXCHANGE: 2140
EXHALE: 3047
EXHAUSTED: 2000
EXIST: 882
EXPERIENCED: 1172
EXPIRE: 606
EXPLAIN: 389
EXPOSE: 2639
EXTEND: 2277
EXTRACT: 1214
EXTREME.OLD.AGE: 1693
EXTREMITY: 3687
EYE: 2882
EYPHAH: 98
FACE: 3144
FACE.TOWARD: 763
FADE: 287
FAIL: 1152
FAILING: 1631
FAILURE: 1153
FAINT: 1837
FAINT: 3969
FALCON: 2345
FALL: 3104
FALL.UPON: 4466
FALLEN.GRAPE: 3238
FALSE: 4554
FALSENESS: 4228
FAMILY.IDOL: 4041
FAMINE: 4150
FAR.BE.IT: 1188
FAR.END: 3151
FASTEN: 2021
FASTENER: 380
FAT: 1821
FATHER: 1
FATHER-IN-LAW: 1237

FATNESS: 855
FEAR: 1562
FEARFUL: 1563
FEARFULNESS: 1564
FEARING: 1565
FEAST: 1088
FEATHER: 387
FED.FAT: 400
FEED: 4031
FEEDING.PLACE: 4036
FEEL: 2167
FEMALE: 3544
FEMALE.OWNER: 419
FENCE: 823
FENCE.AROUND: 2511
FENCE.IN: 3513
FERRET: 2365
FEVER: 3569
FEW: 3444
FIELD: 2474
FIFTH: 2172
FIFTH.PART: 2171
FIG: 85
FIGHT: 1279
FIGURE: 2581
FILL: 2038
FILLING: 2043
FILTHINESS: 3714
FILTHY: 3713
FIN: 4983
FIND: 2101
FINE: 2891
FINGER: 366
FINGER.SPAN: 1026
FINISH: 1653
FIRE: 116
FIRE.OFFERING: 122
FIRE.PAN: 1445
FIRST: 4121
FIRST.FRUIT: 216
FIRST.RAIN: 1567
FIRST.TIME: 1184
FIRSTBORN: 212
FIRSTBORN.FEMALE: 211
FISH: 683
FISSURE: 1796
FIST: 660
FIVE: 2170
FLAKE.OFF: 4960
FLAMING: 1377

FLAMING.WRATH: 1378
FLANK: 3968
FLARE.UP: 1396
FLASH: 413
FLAT: 4107
FLAVOR: 1504
FLAX: 3292
FLEE: 2328
FLEE.AWAY: 3212
FLEECE: 519
FLEEING: 2330
FLESH: 3509
FLINT: 903
FLOAT: 1021
FLOCKS: 3429
FLOOD: 270
FLOOR: 653
FLOUR: 2550
FLOURISHING: 4040
FLOW: 978
FLOW.OUT: 4110
FLUSH: 4484
FLUTTER: 1347
FLY: 2908
FLYER: 2909
FOLLOWING: 4496
FOLLY: 292
FOOD: 1640
FOODSTUFF: 1644
FOOL: 291
FOOLISH: 1812
FOOT: 3861
FOOTING: 776
FOOTSTEP: 2866
FOR: 1209
FORBID: 2190
FORCE: 1176
FORCEFUL: 1146
FOREFRONT: 2049
FOREHEAD: 2105
FOREIGN: 1793
FOREIGNER: 1791
FORESKIN: 4764
FOREST: 4750
FORGET: 1621
FORGIVE: 2558
FORK: 977
FORM: 4678
FORTIFICATION: 3518
FORTUNE: 489

FOUL: 3002
FOUNDATION: 2477
FOUNDED: 2476
FOUNTAIN: 1766
FOUR: 3830
FOURTH: 3831
FOURTH.GENERATION: 3828
FOURTH.PART: 3829
FRAGMENT: 3293
FRAIL: 4048
FRANKINCENSE: 330
FRAUD: 3987
FREE: 3273
FREE: 3274
FREE.FLOWING: 805
FREEDOM: 3276
FREELY: 1293
FREEWILL.OFFERING: 2234
FRESH: 1982
FRESH.OIL: 3496
FRESH.WINE: 4131
FRIEND: 4028
FRINGE: 3468
FROG: 5007
FROM: 2074
FRUIT.PRESS: 761
FRY: 3825
FULL: 2039
FUNCTIONAL: 1467
FURNACE: 346
FURTHER: 901
FURY: 1238
Gain: 2798
GALBANUM: 1822
GALL: 2119
GAME: 3360
GARDEN: 593
GARLIC: 4370
GARMENT: 3016
GATE: 4550
GATHER: 2623
GATHER.FOOD: 630
GATHER.TOGETHER: 3550
GATHERING: 2625
GAZELLE: 3330
GENERATION: 818
GENITALS: 438
GENTLE: 2876
GERAH: 622

GIER-EAGLE: 1286
GIFT: 4650
GIRD: 3011
GIRD.UP: 1095
GIRL: 1828
GIVE: 4649
GIVE.A.TENTH: 2899
GIVE.ADVICE: 2922
GIVE.HONOR: 812
GIVE.MILK: 555
GIVEN.THAT: 1624
GLEANINGS: 1973
GLIMMERING: 1819
GLISTENING: 3495
GLUTTON: 967
GNAT: 1676
GNAW: 651
GO: 4266
GO.AROUND: 2446
GO.ASIDE: 2500
GO.ASTRAY: 4213
GO.DOWN: 3888
GO.OUT: 3321
GO.RIGHT: 2068
GO.UP: 2792
GOBLET: 598
GOING.OUT: 3322
GOINGS: 3325
GOLD: 931
GOODS: 3982
GOPHER: 3218
GORE: 2205
GORER: 2206
GOVERNOR: 4329
GRAIN: 381
GRAIN.FLOUR: 3645
GRAIN.SACK: 4593
GRAIN.SEEDS: 298
GRAIN.STALK: 3633
GRAPE: 2199
GRAPE.SKIN: 943
GRAPEVINE: 1746
GRAPPLE: 373
GRASP: 1148
GRASP: 3648
GRASS: 848
GRASSHOPPER: 479
GRATE: 1587
GRAVE: 3553
GRAYHEADED: 2454

GREAT: 501
GREAT.AMOUNT: 3786
GREAT.NUMBER: 3784
GREAT.TREE: 52
GREEN: 4097
GREEN.GRAIN: 2
GREENISH: 4100
GRIEF: 2139
GRIND: 1309
GROANING: 2367
GROPE: 2163
GROUND: 746
GROUND.TO.PIECES: 724
GROUSE: 727
GROVE: 4510
GROW.DARK: 4758
GROW.FAT: 4385
GUIDE: 2261
GUILT: 4366
GUILTINESS: 4367
GULP: 4570
GUST: 2413
GUZZLE: 587
HABITATION: 2875
HAILSTONES: 3891
HAIR: 4755
HAIR.FELL.OUT: 2148
HAIRY.GOAT: 4756
HALF: 1351
HALF.THE.SPOILS: 1355
HAMMER: 4105
HAND: 1542
HAND.OVER: 3954
HAND.SPAN: 3043
HANDFUL: 3649
HANG: 4612
HAPPINESS: 4513
HAPPY: 4508
HAPPY: 4509
HARASS: 3391
HARD: 3756
HARDSHIP: 2929
HARE: 4943
HARM: 2592
HARP: 2400
HARSH: 2121
HARVEST: 3710
HASTE: 1335
HASTEN: 1334
HATE: 2595

Lexicon Cross References

HATE: 2596
HATED: 2597
HAVE.COMPASSION: 1284
HAVE.HORNS: 4013
HAWK: 17
HAZEL: 1850
HE: 859
HE-GOAT: 4698
HEAD: 4117
HEAD.OF.WHEAT: 2030
HEADDRESS: 478
HEADREST: 4124
HEAL: 4042
HEAP: 2221
HEAR: 4391
HEART: 1813
HEAT: 1249
HEAVINESS: 1577
HEAVY: 1576
HEAVY.BURDEN: 1525
HEEL: 2771
HEIFER: 582
HEIGHT: 3635
HEIR: 2314
HELP: 2751
HELP: 2752
HELPLESS: 728
HEM: 4298
HEMLOCK: 1938
HERB: 2897
HERBAGE: 2556
HERE: 3029
HERITAGE: 4130
HERON: 101
HEW: 1361
HEWN.STONE: 520
HHOMER: 1272
HIDE: 2707
HIDING: 2708
HIGH: 465
HIGH.PLACE: 3637
HIGHWAY: 2546
HILL: 919
HIP: 1730
HIRE: 2532
HIRELING: 2534
HIT: 2295
HITTING: 2297
HIYN: 917
HOARFROST: 1343

HOLD.A.FEAST: 1089
HOLD.A.GRUDGE: 2502
HOLD.BACK: 3169
HOLD.UP: 2742
HOLDINGS: 1136
HOLLOW.OUT: 3540
HONEY: 681
HONOR: 813
HOOD: 2489
HOOF: 3245
HOOK: 3742
HOP: 3152
HORDE: 3815
HORN: 4014
HORNET: 4147
HORSE: 2616
HORSEMAN: 3243
HOSTILITY: 7
HOT: 1241
HOUSE: 450
HOW: 38
HOW.LONG: 2178
HOWLING: 1895
HUMAN: 745
HUNCHBACK: 474
HUNDRED: 1986
HUNGER: 4149
HUNT: 3357
HUNTER: 3358
HURL: 1477
HURRY: 2131
HUT: 3539
HYSSOP: 928
I: 77
IBIS: 4381
ICE: 3736
IDOL: 548
IF: 64
ILL: 702
ILLNESS: 703
ILLUMINATE: 1031
IMAGE: 3420
IMAGERY: 3469
IMAGINATION: 4507
IMBIBE: 2449
IMITATE: 4654
IMMIGRANT: 636
IMMIGRATE: 635
IMMIGRATION: 639
IN.FRONT: 1620

IN.LAW: 1456
IN.LINE: 845
IN.THIS.WAY: 1600
INCENSE.SMOKE: 3609
INCREASE: 3804
INCREASE.IN.NUMBER: 3792
INDEED: 75
INFANT: 4302
INFECT: 4145
INFECTION: 4146
INFIRMITY: 1194
INFLAME: 1950
INFLAMMATION: 1951
INHERIT: 2267
INHERITANCE: 2269
INNOCENCE: 2361
INNOCENT: 2359
INQUIRE: 4292
INSCRIBE: 1370
INSIDE: 3818
INSTALLATION: 2044
INSTANT: 3308
INTELLIGENCE: 322
INTERCEDE: 4696
INTEREST: 3787
INTERPRET: 3256
INTERPRETATION: 3258
INVADE: 496
INVENTION: 4179
INVESTIGATE: 3190
IRON: 4948
IRRITATE: 2127
IRRITATION: 645
ISLAND: 84
ISSUE: 934
ITCH: 4069
JAR: 1589
JASPER: 4467
JAW: 1852
JEWEL: 2467
JOIN: 1841
JOINED.TOGETHER: 4343
JOINT: 1080
JOURNEY: 2335
JOURNEY: 2334
JUBILEE: 275
JUDGE: 3082
JUDGMENT: 3061
JUG: 1710

JUICE: 4500
JUMP: 1005
KEEP: 3523
KEEP.BACK: 2519
KEEP.SECRET: 1118
KEEP.SILENT: 1431
KEEP.WATCH: 3449
KERMES: 1931
KERNEL: 1228
KERUV: 1422
KICK: 351
KIDNEY: 1627
KIKAR: 1781
KILL: 3844
KILL.BY.STONING: 3864
KIN: 4517
KIND: 2075
KIND.ONE: 1319
KINDLE: 3568
KINDNESS: 1318
KINDRED: 1830
KING: 1884
KINGDOM: 1888
KISS: 2420
KITE: 3775
KNEAD: 1979
KNEADING.BOWL: 2667
KNEE: 409
KNEEL: 408
KNIFE: 1642
KNOB: 4967
KNOCK: 1066
KNOLL: 477
KNOW: 787
KNOWER: 790
LABOR: 2833
LACE: 2693
LACKING: 1326
LADDER: 2551
LAME: 3153
LAMENT: 2640
LAMENTING: 2641
LAMP: 2375
LAMPSTAND: 2384
LAND: 4060
LAPIS.LAZULI: 2651
LAST: 1389
LAST.NIGHT: 2164
LATE: 3091
LATE.RAIN: 1977

LAUDANUM: 1862
LAUGH: 1374
LAUGHTER: 1375
LAY.IN.WAIT: 3353
LEAD: 3222
LEAD: 2302
LEADER: 3403
LEAF: 2793
LEAN: 3907
LEAN: 4449
LEAP: 2433
LEAPING.LOCUST: 4962
LEARN: 1920
LEARNING: 1969
LEAVE: 941
LEAVE.ALONE: 1532
LEAVE.BEHIND: 4683
LEAVE.IN.PLACE: 3350
LEAVEN: 2666
LEAVENED.BREAD: 1264
LEFT.HAND: 4981
LEG: 1785
LENGTH: 3965
LENTIL: 856
LEVEL.VALLEY: 3176
LICK: 1853
LID: 1344
LIE: 1604
LIE.DOWN: 4204
LIEUTENANT: 4347
LIFT: 3989
LIFT.HIGH: 481
LIFT.UP: 2318
LIGHT: 111
LIGHT: 112
LIGHTWEIGHT: 3619
LIKENESS: 755
LIME: 2480
LIMP: 3367
LINE: 1068
LINEN: 4557
LINGER: 1998
LINSEY-WOOLSEY: 5016
LINTEL: 4458
LION: 3896
LIONESS: 1817
LIP: 2620
LIQUOR: 4546
LITTLE.ONE: 3442
LITTLE.OWL: 1724

LIVE: 1162
LIVELY: 1163
LIVESTOCK: 3661
LIVING: 1160
LIZARD: 1865
LO: 858
LOAD: 2088
LOAD: 2320
LOAN: 2404
LOATHE: 3596
LOBE: 4690
LOCUST: 2563
LOG: 1823
LOIN.WRAP: 1097
LOINS: 1215
LONG.GARMENT: 1988
LONG.HAIR: 3247
LOOK: 914
LOOK.DOWN: 4455
LOOK.UPON: 4520
LOOK.WITH.RESPECT: 4433
LOOP: 1892
LOOSE: 3246
LOOSEN: 957
LORD: 777
LOST: 4443
LOST.THING: 161
LOT: 650
LOUD.NOISE: 4142
LOVE: 864
LOW: 3132
LOWER: 1698
LOWER.PART: 4598
LOWLAND: 3133
LUMINARY: 114
LYING.DOWN: 4205
LYING.PLACE: 4207
MADNESS: 4217
MAGGOT: 4003
MAGICIAN: 1223
MAGNIFICENCE: 502
MAGNIFIED: 499
MAGNIFY: 498
MAID: 3057
MAJESTY: 455
MAKE: 2834
MAKE.A.PLEDGE: 2724
MAKE.A.VOW: 2241
MAKE.BALD: 3737

Lexicon Cross References

MAKE.BRICKS: 326
MAKE.FAT: 854
MAKE.HASTE: 4769
MAKE.RESTITUTION: 4335
MAKINGS: 2835
MALE: 1771
MALE.GOAT: 4774
MALE.KID: 4709
MAN: 2411
MANDRAKES: 698
MANY: 11
MARCH: 3456
MARKER: 1483
MARRY: 2804
MARSH.GRASS: 31
MARVEL: 4628
MASTER: 2805
MATERIAL: 3655
MATTRESS: 2974
MATURE: 4623
MEASURE: 1992
MEASURE: 4530
MEASURED.AMOUNT: 1707
MEASUREMENT: 1989
MEAT: 1001
MEDDLE: 634
MEDITATE: 2495
MEET: 3723
MEETING: 3727
MELON: 3025
MELT.AWAY: 2080
MEMORIAL: 1774
MEMORY: 1772
MEN: 1773
MERCHANDISE: 1789
MESSENGER: 1874
METAL.PLATING: 1019
METROPOLIS: 3725
MIDDLEMOST: 4606
MIDSECTION: 3967
MIDST: 4604
MIGHTY.ONE: 39
MILDEW: 4099
MILLSTONE: 3915
MIMIC: 1945
MINISTER: 4555
MINISTRY: 4556
MISCHIEF: 982
MISERY: 1573

MIST: 8
MISTAKE: 4208
MIX: 252
MIX: 2085
MIXED.MULTITUDE: 2629
MIXTURE: 3813
MODERATE: 778
MOIST: 1851
MOLD: 3503
MOLDING: 1025
MOMENT: 3853
MONUMENT: 3340
MOON: 3919
MOREOVER: 94
MORNING: 3211
MORROW: 1386
MORTAL.MAN: 2177
MORTAR: 1271
MORTAR.AND.PESTLE: 725
MOTHER: 59
MOUND: 539
MOUNT: 921
MOUNTAIN.SHEEP: 2390
MOURN: 256
MOURNING: 257
MOUSE: 4989
MOUTH: 3027
MOVE.AWAY: 2166
MULTITUDE: 904
MURDER: 4076
MURMUR: 4010
MURMURING: 4012
MUSIC: 2397
MUSTER: 3332
MUTE: 1905
MUZZLE: 1453
MYRIAD: 3793
MYRRH: 2138
NAKED: 2957
NAKEDNESS: 2967
NARROW: 3483
NARROW.WAY: 4448
NATAPH: 1511
NATION: 517
NATIVE: 3927
NEAR: 3820
NECK: 2977
NECKLACE: 3824
NECROMANCER: 3
NEEDY: 238

NEIGHBOR: 2839
NEST: 3652
NET: 4183
NETTING: 4112
NEVERTHELESS: 258
NEW: 1116
NEW.MOON: 1117
NIGHT: 1898
NIGHT.WATCH: 2613
NIGHTHAWK: 1262
NINE: 4428
NINTH: 4429
NOBLEMAN: 2655
NOD: 2228
NOMAD: 3387
NORTH: 3447
NOSE: 93
NOSE.RING: 1149
NOT: 1808
NOURISHMENT: 1641
NOW: 2985
NUDE: 2956
NUMBER: 2653
NUMEROUS: 2938
OAK: 41
OASIS: 2264
OATH: 44
OBEDIENCE: 3580
OFFENSE: 3291
OFFER.WILLINGLY: 2233
OFFERING: 4001
OFFERING.OF.RESTITUTION: 4336
OFFICER: 4271
OFFSHOOT: 4741
OH: 20
OIL: 4386
OINTMENT: 2011
OINTMENT.MIXTURE: 3590
OLD.AGE: 1694
OLIVE: 1056
OLIVINE: 3059
OMER: 2864
ON.ACCOUNT.OF: 545
ON.FOOT: 3863
ONE: 140
ONE.HALF: 1350
ONE.TENTH: 2903
ONION: 973

Benner's Mechanical Translation of the Torah

ONLY: 4090	PARCHING.HEAT: 1407	PLATTER: 1797
ONYCHA: 4249	PART: 3158	PLEA: 779
ONYX: 4368	PARTNER: 4030	PLEAD: 3081
OPAL: 4378	PASS.OVER: 1208	PLEASANT: 1257
OPEN: 3300	PASTE: 1268	PLEASE: 2186
OPEN.SPACE: 664	PASTURE: 2187	PLEASURE: 2483
OPEN.UP: 3185	PATH: 3913	PLEDGE: 2725
OPENING: 3301	PATTERN: 321	PLENTY: 2457
OPPONENT: 2504	PAYMENT: 2537	PLOT: 984
OPPOSITE: 2218	PEDESTAL: 1679	PLOWING: 1233
OPPRESS: 127	PEEL: 980	PLUCK: 2388
OPPRESSION: 132	PEG: 927	PLUCK.AWAY: 527
OR: 19	PELICAN: 3533	PLUCK.OUT: 2165
ORDINARY: 1174	PENIS: 3080	PLUCK.UP: 4738
ORNAMENT: 509	PEOPLE: 2838	PLUCKED: 529
ORNAMENTAL.RING: 989	PERCEIVE: 1137	PLUCKING: 528
ORPHAN: 4634	PERFORATE: 1415	PLUMAGE: 2358
ORYX: 4576	PERFORATED: 1416	PLUNDER: 183
OSPREY: 2760	PERFORM: 3093	PLUNDER: 185
OTHER: 1383	PERFORMANCE: 3094	POINT: 3264
OTHER.SIDE: 426	PERISH: 160	POINT: 4577
OTHERWISE: 3139	PERMANENT: 2184	POINT.OUT: 25
OUTCRY: 4436	PERSECUTION: 3484	POLE: 2020
OUTER: 3684	PERSUADE: 2703	POMEGRANATE: 3988
OUTER.COVERING: 1722	PESTILENCE: 2215	POOL: 585
OUTER.GARMENT: 2561	PICK.OUT: 1795	POPLAR: 331
OUTER.RIM: 4969	PICK.UP: 1972	POSSESS: 4127
OUTSIDE: 1356	PIECE: 4595	POSSESSION: 4129
OVEN: 2383	PIERCE: 3735	POSSIBLY: 1839
OVERCOME: 417	PIERCE.THROUGH: 3542	POST: 3342
OVERHANG: 2687	PIERCED.BREAD: 1175	POSTERITY: 2299
OVERHANG: 2688	PIERCING: 4406	POT: 2681
OVERLAY: 1017	PILE: 4004	POUCH: 3489
OVERLOOK: 2406	PILE.UP: 3347	POUR: 3478
OVERSEER: 3180	PILLAR: 2851	POUR.DOWN: 3474
OVERSIGHT: 3182	PISTACHIO: 232	POUR.OUT: 3078
OVERTAKE: 2466	PIT: 3299	POURED.OUT: 3482
OVERTHROWING: 3070	PIT: 4237	POURING: 3479
OVERTURN: 3068	PITCH: 1016	POVERTY: 2531
OVERTURNING: 3069	PITCH.TENT: 897	POWER: 45
OWL: 2880	PITY: 1303	PRECIOUS: 508
OWNER: 420	PLACE: 2572	PRECIPITATE: 1528
OX: 4521	PLACE.OF.LODGING: 1925	PRECIPITATION: 1529
PACK: 1506	PLACE.TO.BURN: 3611	PREDICT: 1439
PALENESS: 1400	PLAIN: 4529	PREDICTION: 1441
PALM: 1740	PLAIT: 4198	PREGNANCY: 924
PAN: 1087	PLANT: 2283	PREGNANT: 923
PARABLE: 4310	PLANTATION: 4972	PREPARE: 1687
PARAPET: 2948	PLASTER: 1478	PREPARED: 2990
PARCEL: 1954	PLATFORM: 305	PRESENT: 410

Lexicon Cross References

PRESERVE: 3524
PRESS: 2497
PRESS.FIRMLY: 2766
PRESS.HARD: 3527
PRESS.IN: 3488
PRESUME: 2914
PREY: 3521
PRICE: 1788
PRICKLY.THORN: 2591
PRIDE: 457
PRISON: 2669
PRISONER: 2663
PRODUCE: 3206
PRODUCT: 274
PRODUCTION: 151
PROFIT: 196
PROLONG: 3960
PROPERTY: 4128
PROPORTION: 2078
PROSPER: 3416
PROSTITUTE: 1120
PROSTITUTION: 991
PROTECTIVE: 1296
PROVENDER: 2630
PROVIDE: 868
PROVIDE.FOOD: 1937
PROVIDE.PROTECTION: 1294
PROVISIONS: 3359
PROVOKE: 2351
PULL.OUT: 4342
PULVERIZE: 4257
PUNISHMENT: 3192
PURCHASE: 3660
PURPLE: 3843
PURSUE: 3870
PUSH: 708
PUSH: 2210
PUSH.AWAY: 792
PUSTULE: 348
QESHIYTAH: 3766
QUAIL: 2552
QUARTER: 3827
QUARTZ: 4958
QUENCH: 1574
QUICKLY: 2132
QUIVER: 4608
RABBIT: 4474
RAFTER: 3730
RAIMENT: 1712

RAIN.SHOWER: 4375
RAINDROP: 2716
RAISE.UP: 3997
RAM: 2488
RAM.HORN: 4481
RAMPART: 1248
RANK: 844
RANSOM: 3009
RANSOM: 3013
RANSOM.PRICE: 3010
RASH: 376
RAVE: 4216
RAVEN: 4761
RAVINE: 4223
RAW: 2185
RAZOR: 2952
REACH: 3003
READY: 2984
REBEL: 2143
REBELLIOUS: 2113
REBUKE: 1613
RECEIVE: 3555
RECKLESS: 3055
RECKON: 2064
RECOGNIZE: 1790
RECOMPENSE: 4338
RED: 747
REDDISH: 749
REDEEM: 551
REDEEMED: 3014
REDEMPTION: 552
REED.BASKET: 1500
REED.PIPE: 486
REEDS: 2633
REFINE: 3032
REFINED: 959
REFLECTION: 3776
REFUSE: 2062
REFUSING: 2063
REGISTER: 3179
REGULATE: 4309
REGULATION: 4314
REIGN: 1883
REJECT: 2081
REJOICE: 2579
REJOICING: 2580
RELEASE: 4383
RELEASE: 4384
RELIEF: 4440
REMAIN: 4515

REMAINDER: 4684
REMAINS: 4516
REMEMBER: 1770
REMEMBRANCE: 1775
REMNANT: 4518
REMOVAL: 2232
REMOVE.THE.COVER: 553
REPLACEMENT: 1212
REPORT: 4392
REPOSE: 3852
REPRODUCE: 3205
REPROOF: 616
REPROVE: 614
RESCUE: 4437
RESEMBLANCE: 2067
RESEMBLE: 754
RESIDE: 938
RESPITE: 3918
REST: 2262
REST.PERIOD: 4203
RESTRAIN: 2770
RESTRICT: 1646
REVIVING: 1164
RHINOCEROS: 3994
RIB: 3411
RICH: 134
RICHES: 135
RIDDLE: 1110
RIDE: 3938
RIGHT: 2070
RIGHT.HAND: 2069
RIM: 2525
RING: 359
RIP: 3241
RIPE.FRUIT: 2040
RIPEN: 2281
RISE: 3634
RISE.UP: 510
RIVER: 2378
ROAD: 3922
ROAM: 3886
ROAR: 909
ROAST: 3412
ROASTED.GRAIN: 3617
ROBE: 808
ROCK.WALL: 4522
ROD: 3616
ROEBUCK: 1273
ROLL: 543
ROOF: 488

Benner's Mechanical Translation of the Torah

ROOF.COVERING: 1720
ROOT: 4087
ROOT.OUT: 2432
ROT: 2108
ROUNDNESS: 1780
ROW: 1521
ROW.OF.TENTS: 1522
RUDDY: 750
RUIN: 4607
RULE: 3885
RUMP: 42
RUN: 4065
SACK: 2654
SACRIFICE: 218
SACRIFICE: 219
SACRIFICIAL.BOWL: 2360
SADDLE: 1085
SADDLE: 3942
SADDLEBAG: 3313
SAFEGUARD: 2605
SAFEGUARDING: 2612
SAFELY: 3020
SALT: 1857
SANCTUARY: 1124
SAND: 1196
SANDAL: 2810
SASH: 233
SATISFACTION: 2460
SAY: 2031
SCAB: 3050
SCALES: 1715
SCARLET: 4404
SCATTER: 3162
SCATTER.ABROAD: 3159
SCORPION: 4992
SCOUR: 2150
SCOUT: 4679
SCRAPE.OFF: 3686
SCRATCH: 1230
SCRAWNY: 799
SCREEN: 2507
SCROLL: 2649
SCULPT: 2567
SCULPTURE: 2568
SE'AH: 2439
SEA: 1547
SEAGULL: 4250
SEAL: 4635
SEAL: 4636
SEARCH: 1337

SEARCH.OUT: 3177
SEARCHING: 1461
SEARING: 3529
SEASON: 1856
SEAT: 1718
SECOND: 4412
SECRET: 1861
SECURE: 65
SECURE: 71
SECURITY.DEPOSIT: 2573
SEE: 3778
SEED: 1044
SEEING: 3186
SEEING.AS: 2879
SEEK: 833
SEIZE: 1145
SEIZE.HOLD: 4665
SELECTED: 3720
SELF-WILL: 4064
SELL: 1786
SEND: 4320
SEND.OFF: 4324
SENDING: 4323
SEPARATE: 167
SERPENT: 1440
SERVANT: 2719
SERVE: 2718
SERVICE: 2723
SET.APART: 1119
SET.ASIDE: 3401
SET.DOWN: 4573
SETTING: 2045
SETTLE: 4173
SETTLER: 4175
SETTLING: 4174
SEVEN: 4188
SEVENTH: 4192
SEVENTH.TIME: 4191
SEVER: 3708
SEW.TOGETHER: 4666
SHA'AR: 4551
SHADOW: 3395
SHAKE: 3855
SHAKE.IN.AWE: 361
SHAKE.OFF: 2437
SHAKING: 3856
SHAKING.IN.FEAR: 3873
SHAME: 1917
SHAPE: 394
SHAPE: 393

SHARE: 2057
SHARP.STONE: 3485
SHARPEN: 1531
SHATTER: 4303
SHATTERING: 3266
SHAVE: 571
SHE: 860
SHE-DONKEY: 4642
SHE-GOAT: 4715
SHEAF: 2863
SHEAR: 521
SHEEP: 1726
SHEET: 4106
SHEQEL: 4354
SHIELD: 595
SHINE: 891
SHINING: 896
SHIP: 92
SHOOT: 2346
SHORE: 1331
SHORT: 1586
SHORTNESS: 3711
SHOULDER: 4282
SHOULDER.PIECE: 1751
SHOUT.ALOUD: 4005
SHOVEL: 1556
SHOW.PITY: 1302
SHOWERS: 3794
SHRUB: 2516
SHUT: 2521
SHUT.UP: 2706
SICK: 1191
SICKLE: 4963
SICKNESS: 1193
SIDE: 3351
SIGH: 2258
SIGHTLESSNESS: 2524
SIGN: 146
SIGNAL: 4141
SIGNAL: 4143
SILENCE: 918
SILENT: 1432
SILVER: 1738
SIMMER: 947
SINEW: 497
SING: 4531
SINGE.SCAR: 1602
SINGEING: 1601
SINK: 358
SINK.DOWN: 4047

Lexicon Cross References

SISTER: 29
SISTER-IN-LAW: 308
SIT.DOWN: 4603
SIX: 4564
SIXTH: 4565
SKILL: 1252
SKILLED.ONE: 1251
SKILLET: 3196
SKIN: 2965
SKIN.BAG: 1239
SKIN.SORE: 1940
SKIP.WITH.JOY: 2615
SKULL: 542
SKY: 4369
SLAB: 1855
SLANDER: 672
SLAUGHTERING: 223
SLAY: 4246
SLEEP: 4416
SLEEPING: 4417
SLICE: 2689
SLICE.OFF: 3685
SLICING: 2690
SLICK: 1958
SLIME: 1269
SLING: 3630
SLIP.AWAY: 1870
SLOW: 3961
SMACK: 3498
SMACKED: 3501
SMALL: 3605
SMALL.AMOUNT: 3598
SMASH: 1799
SMASHED: 1800
SMEAR: 2009
SMEARED: 2012
SMELL: 3916
SMITE: 2213
SMOKE: 2981
SMOKE: 2982
SMOLDER: 3560
SMOLDERING.FIRE: 3562
SMOOTH: 1959
SNAIL: 2025
SNAP: 3705
SNAP.OFF: 1978
SNARE: 3760
SNARE: 3761
SNIP.OFF: 2048
SNOOZE: 4409

SNORT: 99
SNOW: 4319
SO: 1677
SO.BE.IT: 67
SOFT: 2884
SOFT: 2885
SOFTLY: 34
SOLITARY: 1109
SON: 309
SONG: 4532
SOOT: 3041
SORROW: 679
SORROW: 1540
SOUL: 3279
SOUTH: 2216
SOUTHERN: 832
SOUTHWARD: 2071
SOW: 1043
SOWN: 1045
SPARE: 1314
SPARK: 4473
SPATTER: 2252
SPEAK: 824
SPEAR: 2016
SPECIAL: 1123
SPECKLED: 3564
SPEECH: 2033
SPELT: 1736
SPICE: 2294
SPICE.MIXTURE: 3589
SPIN: 1473
SPINE: 2920
SPIT: 4096
SPIT.UPON: 4108
SPITTING: 4109
SPLENDOR: 878
SPLINTER: 3706
SPLIT: 3109
SPLIT.IN.TWO: 4424
SPLITTING: 4425
SPOIL: 4289
SPOT: 1487
SPOT: 5017
SPOTTED: 3892
SPREAD: 1480
SPREAD.ACROSS: 3271
SPREAD.OUT: 3284
SPREAD.WIDE: 3295
SPRING: 2883
SPRING.UP: 2014

SPRINKLE: 1048
SPRINKLING.BASIN: 1049
SPROUT: 847
SQUEEZE: 1963
SQUEEZING: 1964
STACK: 853
STAFF: 177
STAGGER: 2436
STAIR.STEP: 2780
STALK: 1686
STAND: 2848
STAND.UP: 3338
STANDARD: 2315
STAR: 1588
STARE: 2197
STATEMENT: 2032
STATION: 3336
STAVE: 4451
STAY.THE.NIGHT: 1924
STEADFAST: 3363
STEADFAST.ONE: 3365
STEADFASTNESS: 3364
STEAL: 599
STEEP.VALLEY: 458
STEP: 3923
STERILE: 4739
STEW: 949
STICKERBUSH: 2506
STINK: 431
STIR: 263
STIR.UP: 2964
STOMACH: 3537
STONE: 3628
STONE: 314
STONE.STOOL: 315
STOOL: 1709
STOOP: 1784
STOP: 2941
STORE: 1674
STOREHOUSE: 2530
STORK: 1320
STORM: 2713
STRAIGHT: 4526
STRAIGHT.TRUMPET: 4961
STRAIGHTNESS: 4527
STRAND: 157
STRAW: 311
STREAM: 1561
STREET: 3972
STRENGTH: 1611

STRESS: 3393
STRETCH.OUT: 3832
STRIKE.THROUGH: 2006
STRIKING: 2214
STRING: 4528
STRIP: 981
STRIP.OFF: 3289
STRIPED: 3575
STRIPED.BRUISE: 1081
STRIVE: 2898
STRONG: 2744
STRUGGLE: 2354
STUBBLE: 3748
STUBBORNNESS: 3750
STUMBLING.BLOCK: 4308
SUBDUE: 344
SUBMERGE: 1495
SUBSIDE: 4274
SUBSTANCE: 3640
SUBTLE: 4767
SUBTLETY: 4766
SUCKLE: 2371
SUDDENLY: 3309
SUET: 3026
SUFFICIENT: 714
SUFFICIENT: 915
SUM: 1708
SUMMER: 3693
SUMMIT: 4119
SUN: 4401
SUN.IDOL: 1243
SUNKEN: 2858
SUNRISE: 3926
SUPPLY.HOUSE: 3492
SUPPORT: 2576
SUPPRESS: 2249
SURE: 68
SURELY: 1681
SURVIVOR: 2686
SUSTAIN: 1656
SWALLOW: 279
SWARM: 4084
SWARMER: 4085
SWARMING.LOCUST: 3806
SWEAR: 4194
SWEARING: 4195
SWEAT: 1006
SWEEP: 525
SWEET: 2290
SWEET.SPICE: 2575

SWELL: 3334
SWELL.UP: 340
SWELLING: 3335
SWINE: 1054
SWORD: 1405
TABLE: 4325
TAIL: 1003
TAKE: 1968
TAKE.A.FIFTH: 2169
TAKE.AS.A.PLEDGE: 1067
TAKE.AWAY: 656
TAKE.HEED: 2538
TAKE.HOLD: 1135
TAKE.REFUGE: 1312
TAKE.STEPS: 3921
TAKE.UPON: 48
TALEBEARER: 3947
TALK: 2029
TAMARISK: 4291
TAMBOURINE: 4661
TASK.WORK: 2077
TASSEL: 500
TASTE.SWEET: 4668
TASTY.FOOD: 2485
TATTOO: 3666
TAUNT: 505
TEACHING: 1568
TEAR: 3743
TEAR.AWAY: 2332
TEAR.INTO.PIECES: 3520
TEAR.OFF: 3253
TEN: 2900
TENDER: 3958
TENDERNESS: 3966
TENT: 899
TENT.CURTAIN: 3240
TENT.PEG: 4583
TENTH: 2904
TENTH.ONE: 2902
TENTH.PART: 2901
TERMINATE: 738
TERROR: 1549
TEST: 2326
TESTICLES: 4275
THANKS: 1543
THAT: 2868
THAT.ONE: 1999
THEFT: 601
THEN: 3030
THERE: 4359

THERE.IS: 1570
THESE: 887
THEY(f): 862
THEY(m): 861
THICK: 4699
THICK.DARKNESS: 4993
THICK.GLOOMINESS: 3088
THICK.SMOKE: 3613
THICK.WOVEN: 4700
THIEF: 600
THIGH: 4494
THIGH.MUSCLE: 2407
THIN: 4089
THIN.BREAD: 4093
THING.WRITTEN: 4695
THINK: 4177
THIRD: 4351
THIRD.GENERATION: 4350
THIRST: 3423
THIRST: 3424
THIRSTY.LAND: 3425
THIS: 950
THIS.ONE: 1847
THISTLE: 804
THORN.BUSH: 2598
THOUGH: 912
THOUGHT: 3504
THOUSAND: 56
THREAD: 1156
THREE: 4349
THREE.DAYS.AGO: 4352
THRESH: 846
THRESHING: 851
THROW: 1566
THROW.DOWN: 3996
THROW.OUT: 4332
THROW.THE.HAND: 1546
THRUST: 4673
THUMB: 317
TIE: 3769
TIE.ON: 3772
TIE.UP: 2661
TIME: 2066
TIME.OF.WEEPING: 243
TIN: 169
TIP: 2298
TIRED: 2913
TITLE: 4358
TO: 40
TO.THIS.POINT: 913

Lexicon Cross References

TOGETHER: 1108
TOIL: 609
TOKEN: 2972
TOMORROW: 1385
TONG: 1970
TONGUE: 1985
TOOLS: 993
TOOTH: 4402
TOP.OF.THE.HEAD: 3558
TOPAZ: 4114
TOPPLE: 4304
TORCH: 1941
TORN: 3522
TORTOISE: 3327
TOSS: 2223
TOSS.OUT: 1763
TOTTER: 2018
TOUCH: 2212
TOUCH: 2211
TOUGHNESS: 678
TOWER: 503
TOWN: 1127
TRADE: 3928
TRANCE: 772
TRANQUILITY: 4297
TRANSGRESS: 2807
TRANSGRESSION: 2808
TRAP: 1965
TRAPPINGS: 2734
TREAD: 4021
TREAD.ABOUT: 3860
TREADER: 4022
TREASURE: 1496
TREE: 2917
TREMBLE: 1410
TREMBLING: 1411
TREMBLING.IN.FEAR: 1444
TRIAL: 2327
TRIBE: 63
TRIBUTE: 1714
TROUBLE: 1835
TROUGH: 3953
TRUTH: 69
TUMOR: 2915
TUMULT: 911
TUNIC: 1801
TURBAN: 3455
TURN: 3143
TURN.ASIDE: 2672
TURN.AWAY: 2671

TURN.BACK: 4169
TURNING.ASIDE: 2674
TURQUOISE: 3077
TURTLEDOVE: 4680
TWIG: 3849
TWILIGHT: 2820
TWIN: 4627
TWIRL: 2240
TWIST: 1195
TWIST: 4772
TWIST.BACKWARDS: 2564
TWIST.TOGETHER: 4538
TWISTED: 4620
TWISTEDNESS: 4714
TWO: 4411
ULCER: 273
UNAWARE: 249
UNCIRCUMCISED: 4763
UNCLE: 693
UNCOVER: 2960
UNDER: 4596
UNDERGARMENT: 1697
UNDERSTAND: 323
UNDERSTANDING: 325
UNDERWORLD: 4295
UNFILLED: 181
UNINHABITED: 534
UNIQUE: 1122
UNIT: 1103
UNITE: 1107
UNLEAVENED.BREAD: 2094
UNLESS: 1807
UNNATURAL.MIX: 254
UNTIL: 2731
UPHOLD: 2589
UPON: 2776
UPPER: 2784
UPPER.LIP: 2621
UPRISING: 2322
UPSIDE.DOWN: 3073
UPWARD: 2779
USURY: 2415
UTENSIL: 1626
UTTER: 228
UTTERANCE: 229
VALIANT: 388
VALLEY: 2855
VALUE: 1787
VANITY: 262

VEHICLE: 3939
VEIL: 3440
VENGEANCE: 3644
VENOM: 4122
VENOMOUS: 4054
VERTICAL: 3639
VESSEL: 4579
VIGOR: 89
VILLAGE: 3231
VINE: 2395
VINEGAR: 1267
VINEYARD: 1782
VINTAGE: 3516
VIOLENCE: 1261
VIRGIN: 176
VIRGINITY: 175
VISION: 1139
VOICE: 3627
VOMIT: 1030
VOMIT: 3534
VOW: 2242
VULTURE: 700
WADI: 2268
WAFER: 3462
WAGE: 2533
WAGES: 4644
WAIST: 4646
WALK: 1877
WALL: 3734
WANDER: 4655
WANTING: 1324
WARP: 4568
WARRIOR: 418
WASH: 343
WATCH.OVER: 198
WATER: 1997
WATERED: 3898
WATERING.TROUGH: 4495
WAVE: 2340
WAVER: 968
WAVING: 2343
WAYWARDNESS: 4444
WE: 78
WEAKEN: 1218
WEAR: 443
WEAR.OUT: 266
WEARY: 608
WEASEL: 1203
WEAVE: 4196
WEEK: 4189

WEEP: 242
WEEPINGS: 244
WEIGH: 4353
WEIGH.OUT: 992
WEIGHT: 4355
WELL: 390
WHAT: 2058
WHEAT: 2282
WHEEL: 3142
WHELP: 637
WHERE: 35
WHEREIN: 952
WHEREVER: 76
WHET: 4405
WHICH: 4511
WHIP: 3239
WHIRRING.LOCUST: 966
WHISPER: 3867
WHITE: 327
WHO: 2059
WHOLE: 4625
WHOREDOM: 997
WHY: 786
WICKED: 4721
WICKER.BASKET: 2542
WIDE: 3971
WIDE.OPEN: 4638
WIDEN: 3970
WIDOW: 1908
WIDOWHOOD: 1909
WIDTH: 3973
WILD.ASS: 3204
WILD.GOAT: 106
WILDERNESS: 831
WILLING: 2235
WILLOW: 3814
WIND: 3917
WIND.AROUND: 3452
WINDOW: 1180
WINE: 1555
WINE.TROUGH: 3541
WING: 1701
WINTER: 1225
WIPE.AWAY: 2004
WIRE: 3033
WITH: 2842
WITH.THE.EXCEPTION: 970
WITHDRAW: 1059
WITHER: 3428
WITHHOLD: 2076

WITHOUT: 90
WITNESS: 2730
WOLF: 929
WOMAN: 2412
WOMB: 231
WONDER: 3298
WOOD.BAR: 3213
WOOL: 2155
WORD: 825
WORK: 2894
WORK.OVER: 2786
WORKINGS: 2789
WORKS: 2787
WORTH: 1713
WORTHLESS: 1804
WOULD.THAT: 1838
WOUND: 3167
WOUND: 3168
WOVEN.BASKET: 1498
WOVEN.MATERIAL: 4199
WRAP: 2828
WRAP.AROUND: 2736
WRATH: 427
WRESTLING: 4621
WRIST: 3147
WRITE: 4692
WRITING: 4694
YARN: 1474
YEAR: 4403
YEARN: 15
YEARNING: 16
YELL: 1015
YELL.OUT: 1014
YELLOW: 933
YEMIM: 1548
YESTERDAY: 2051
YET.AGAIN: 2737
YIELD: 589
YOKE: 2796
YOU (fp): 82
YOU (fs): 81
YOU (mp): 80
YOU (ms): 79
YOUNG.AGE: 2815
YOUNG.MAIDEN: 2823
YOUNG.MAN: 2813
YOUNG.PIGEON: 530
YOUNG.SHEEP: 4994
YOUNG.WOMAN: 2814
YOUTH: 206

YOUTHFULNESS: 3443
ZEALOUS: 3657
ZEALOUSNESS: 3658

www.ingramcontent.com/pod-product-compliance
Lightning Source LLC
Chambersburg PA
CBHW060104170426
43198CB00010B/759